Looking Forward to Sunday Morning

LOOKING FORWARD *to* SUNDAY MORNING

Reflections on the Church Year

Carl C. Fickenscher II

Artwork by John Hrehov

CONCORDIA PUBLISHING HOUSE · SAINT LOUIS

Published by Concordia Publishing House
3558 S. Jefferson Ave., St. Louis, MO 63118-3968
1-800-325-3040 · cph.org

Artwork by John Hrehov

Manufactured in China/064630/340386

---

1 2 3 4 5 6 7 8 9 10 34 33 32 31 30 29 28 27 26 25

To Claire and to our kids, Rachel, Daniel, and Gabriel . . .
. . . and the faithful, confessional Lutherans they've chosen
and brought to the font.

Contents

Acknowledgments

Back in 2014, Jeff Schwarz, a good friend on the Commission on Theology and Church Relations (CTCR) of The Lutheran Church–Missouri Synod (LCMS—more initials yet to come), leaned over to me at a break and asked, "You use the three-year lectionary, right?" Yep. "We'd like to do a weekly show on the propers coming up each Sunday. Would you be interested?" Jeff was the producer of the daily radio program *Issues, Etc.*, which I'd been a guest on many times. Let me think about it schedule-wise, but, sure, I'd love to do it. And from January 2015 through January three years later, we did an hour interview each week with Rev. Todd Wilken discussing the Scripture readings and other propers folks would be hearing in church that Sunday. Most often it was live from the first-rate studio *Issues* helped build on the campus of Concordia Theological Seminary, Fort Wayne, Indiana (with technical support from John Elmer of the CTSFW staff). But sometimes it was on the phone from First Lutheran in Boston or Immanuel Lutheran in Orange, California, or a guest room in Lakeway, Texas, or streamed from places like the Lutheran Theological Seminary in Tshwane, Pretoria, South Africa.

"What would you like to call the show?" We kicked around a few ideas, but (I think) the best one I suggested was *Looking Forward to Sunday Morning.* It stuck. Thanks, Jeff! Thanks, Todd! Thanks, John! It was a pleasure!

Some time during the run, Dr. Ken Schurb, a buddy from way back and a man of diverse titles including mission exec of the LCMS Central Illinois District (CID, if you want to initialize that one), was subbing for Todd on *Issues* and said to me off mike, "You know you have a book here." I'm not sure I did know at the time, Ken, so thanks for the idea!

It couldn't have happened, though, without the permission and enthusiasm of my real employer and boss, CTSFW and president Dr. Lawrence Rast. The seminary and its leadership have always understood that God has given us unique opportunities to serve the Church at large. It's part of what makes our calls to the seminary so invigorating. In this case, Dr. Rast first okayed the weekly program. But the book couldn't have happened without two sabbaticals to get it started and then a delightful arrangement called modified service, in which I now teach full time at the sem winter and spring quarters and am free to write in the summer and fall. Both of these were championed by our provost, Dr. Charles Gieschen. And where better than the Fort Wayne Seminary to pick up tips of expertise on anything related to worship? We've got the likes of Dr. Paul Grime, the driving force for the whole *Lutheran Service Book* (yes, *LSB*) project. Thanks, CTSFW! Thanks, Larry! Thanks, Chuck! Thanks, Paul! I love serving there with you and the entire gang!

A huge encouragement to do this book was the response of listeners to the *Issues, Etc.* version. I can't tell you how many times I've gotten into conversations with new friends somewhere on the road who say they enjoyed the program. The biggest grin was on a Sunday when my family and I were traveling, visiting a new church, and after service a gent who'd been sitting a couple of pews in front turned around and asked if I was Dr. Fickenscher. The show *is* radio, and I don't sing on the air. I guess he could hear enough to guess. Truth is, when you're alone in a studio booth and Jeff and Todd are on the other end of the internet 360 miles away, you wonder if anyone is listening. Apparently so. Perhaps those who find value in what they hear will be blessed by what they read. Thanks, people—especially, as Todd often says, "our beloved on-demand listeners."

It goes without saying—but mustn't—that thanks are due everyone at Concordia Publishing House, especially Scot Kinnaman, senior editor for periodicals and consumer book development, who advanced this project and even did a substantial portion of the copyediting. Thanks, CPH! You're our publisher!

And a partner from the very beginning of putting this in print has been John Hrehov, head of the of art and design department at Purdue University Fort Wayne. (Locally, we call it PFW.) The art you'll see leading off each devotion-study has for years been an appreciated feature in the Sunday bulletins at St. Paul's Lutheran Church, Fort Wayne. When we decided to do the book, it was a natural to ask Professor Hrehov to share his work. Thanks, John!

Of course, next to the Lord Himself, I thank above all my wife, Claire. Not only is she the dearest wife God could have given me, the ideal pastor's wife, and beloved on our seminary campus and in our congregations, but she's a very insightful Bible student. She's been preparing for Sundays by reading the lessons long before I started speaking or writing this, which made her the perfect person to fine tune parts of the manuscript on which I had the most questions. Thanks, Sweetheart!

For all of you I've acknowledged, for others I should have, and for this book . . .

To God be the glory!

Introduction

Every pastor looks forward to Sunday morning—constantly. While carrying out all the other pastoral duties—hospital visits, "well visits," outreach visits, teaching confirmation classes, teaching Thursday morning Bible studies, attending meetings, attending meetings, planning, administration, continuing education, devotional reading and prayer—the pastor always knows Sunday's comin'. There's a certain healthy level of stress with that, but it's truly exciting; he wants to be the most faithful proclaimer of the saving Gospel, Jesus Christ and Him crucified, that he can be for the precious souls entrusted to him. He's always looking forward to Sunday morning.

The rest of God's dear people may not have quite the same laser focus on Sunday as they go about preparing meals and doing laundry, meeting report deadlines or meeting bosses' expectations or meeting bottom lines, putting babies to bed or putting wet wipes to babies' bottoms, getting into college, going to college, paying for college, being a kid, raising kids, running kids here and there, lying awake thinking, laying away for retirement. But Sunday morning is precisely where God equips us for all that, and looking forward to Sunday brings Him into the midst of all our Monday through Saturday busyness. It also makes the precious ninety minutes in God's house so much more than that.

This book is intended to help both pastors and laypeople do this very thing—prepare for and look forward with delight to God coming to us on Sunday morning.

Read This First: How to Use This Book

I'm glad you're reading this page now, because then you'll know not simply to turn to page 1 next. This book begins wherever you are today—that is, wherever you find yourself in the church year. I won't be offended if you don't read it cover to cover. I'd much rather you read it page 126 to page 129, or 356 to 359, or 534 to 537. Just read four pages this week—the four pages that help you look forward to whichever Sunday morning is coming for you next.

For example, if you just received this book for Christmas and you're actually putting your presents to use that very afternoon, find the page for the First Sunday after Christmas in whichever year this happens to be. (It could be Year A, Year B, or Year C, but we'll get to that in a minute.) Read that one devotion-study, just those four pages, to look forward to the Sunday that's actually coming next. Next week, you'll read another devotion-study.

But let's say that as you're reading this today, it's July. Now you're in the part of the church year called the Sundays after Pentecost. Again, it might be Year A, B, or C, but once we explain that, you'll check the date this coming Sunday will occur and you'll turn to the devotion-study for the seven-day range within which it falls—like July 10–16 or July 17–23. You'll start there. And next week, you'll read the next four pages. It won't take you long to get the hang of this, and if after you read this introduction you're still confused, ask your pastor.

Don't worry about anything you've missed by starting in the middle. If you stick with it, you'll get to the end of the book, and the very next Sunday will take you—at long last—to page 1. In the weeks, months, up to three years ahead, you'll read everything you skipped. Of course, if you do miss a week or two or three of reading—and you will—you'll be fine simply going on from wherever you resume. Nearly all of the devotion-studies stand on their own. Back fill only if time allows and inclination moves you. Besides, there will always be three years from now.

Notice we call each four pages a "devotion-study." We needed a hyphenated term, because each one is both. They're intended to be devotional. That is, ideally, you'll sit or lie in a comfortable place and read thoughtfully, prayerfully. Reading God's Word is our time to commune with Him, because He truly speaks to us in Holy Scripture, and the words He speaks to us become the basis for our speaking back to Him in prayer. We ask for what He promises, and we thank Him for what He reminds us He's done. I'd particularly encourage you to consider using these readings as family devotions. Pray the **Collect** together. Pass the Bible around to share the readings. And, as you'll see, each study invites you to sing the coming Sunday's **Hymn of the Day**. For young families: Mom and Dad, it might be wise to read the full devotion together, just the two of you, one night and then pick out just a brief portion to read with the kids tomorrow.

Again, though, each week's reading is also intended to be a study. You'll need your Bible open and your hymnal, *Lutheran Service Book*, within reach. (If you don't have the latter, by the way, don't wait till next Christmas to acquire one. Borrow one from church until your order from Concordia Publishing House can arrive promptly. We'll in fact put the hymnal to use already a few pages from now.) The studies are designed to take you deeply into each Scripture lesson and other propers of the week. They can't be exhaustive commentaries on each text, but they're intended to reflect good scholarship.

For pastors, that means they're intended to be helpful both for teaching and preaching. Many of you are perhaps already offering weekly Bible classes looking at the lessons for each Sunday. I've found those to be very well received. These studies may help you with that. As to preaching, I always stress to my lay students and listeners that these studies are never intended to tell them what their pastor will preach that coming Sunday. You gentlemen, pastors, will immediately recognize what I mean. When we preach, we generally base our sermons on a single text. Our exegetical task is to discover the point of those select verses, and then, homiletically, we apply that point to our hearers' lives. On the other hand, the studies in this book seek to identify a unifying theme, a single point, of all the week's propers *in total*—one theme for all the propers combined. That, obviously, is going to be broader than the THEME you formulate for your sermon on just one of the lessons. (Former hom students of mine or readers of *Concordia Pulpit Resources*, the preaching journal that I edit, thank you for noticing my use of SMALL CAPS when mentioning the technical, homiletical, sermon THEME.) So the direction you go with your sermon will certainly, usually, be different from the theme I give for the Sunday (even though I do give it in SMALL CAPS).

Still, my intention is to be helpful to pastors for preaching. We do surely offer particular exegetical observations on the various readings of the day; I hope you'll find those on your chosen text insightful. Further, the connections we note among the propers are sometimes valuable clues to the exegesis of the individual texts; the lectionary, after all, is designed to let Scripture interpret Scripture. Very often this is significant, especially if you're preaching on the **Old Testament Reading**; its Christological intent may become clear in light of the **Holy Gospel**. Even beyond this benefit to exegesis, pointing out connections among the propers can often enrich the sermon for our hearers. What's more, there is the possibility of occasionally preaching a true multiple text sermon (one that gives equal attention to two or more of the readings); in such a case, the theme I've offered for the combined propers *might* be close to the THEME you'd choose for your sermon.

Most important for preaching, though, these studies I hope describe the context in which your people hear your sermon. The sermon, we understand, doesn't really begin with "Grace, mercy, and peace . . ." It begins with everything our hearers bring with them to the moment. Much of that is their Monday through Saturday. The devotional applications of these studies are intended to explore that life as they know it. But some of what our hearers bring to the sermon is what they've picked up just in the preceding twenty or twenty-five minutes. At least by the first appointed proper, the **Introit,** (and often before) worshipers can pick up hints as to where the sermon might go. Perhaps they're also asking themselves questions: "What does that mean?" "Why would God do that?" "What's that got to do with anything else we're talking about this morning?" As preachers, we want to anticipate those questions and answer them if possible. Otherwise, that *unanswered* question, rather than anything in your sermon, may wind up being one worshiper's takeaway from the service.

Meanwhile, for all of you who look forward to sitting in the pew on Sunday morning, the study aspect of these devotion-studies should be helpful too. There's enough material in the weekly propers to keep us busy literally for seven days. In Luther's time, services were offered every day, twice or more on Sundays, and in one service (Sunday morning), the **Holy Gospel** was preached, in another (Sunday evening), the **Epistle**.

We always get more out of an event if we've put something into it ahead. We've all shown up for a school class after forgetting (or simply choosing not) to do the reading assignment. But maybe we've also had the rich experience of vacationing at a historic site or a city in the news after doing a little research on it first. The service on Sunday morning packs countless loaded phrases, vivid images, and fertile implications into a very short time. We can process more of them if we reflect beforehand and come with a sense of what to expect. You'll have those questions; you'll listen for answers. We'll feel we have some "skin in the game"; we'll probably put more into the worship time mentally and spiritually if we've invested a bit in advance.

I'll emphasize, as before, that these devotion-studies are never intended to suggest what your pastor will—or should—preach. He's not wrong if he takes a totally different tack. As we explained, he's usually working with a single text, not trying to synthesize all the propers. He'll go into depth where that one text directs him, and he may or may not even touch on the others. Far more critically, he's thinking of *you*—specifically—and how a text speaks to the needs of his beloved flock. This book can't do that. There's even the perfectly legitimate reality that equally faithful interpreters of Scripture will come to differing conclusions about what this or that verse of God's Word means. Faithful Lutheran pastors all agree on the big picture—Christ and His cross with all their ramifications, all exposited in the Lutheran Confessions. But on individual passages, there may be permissible differences . . . and your pastor is the one called by God to be the interpreter and proclaimer of Holy Scripture in your congregation.

But studying ahead will help you more fully appreciate your pastor's preaching—and the service as a whole. While he's limited to (I still tell my students) perhaps fifteen to twenty minutes, you can listen and nod and make connections in your own mind to background material he doesn't have time to address. For example, as you listen to a sermon on the **Holy Gospel**, you'll smile to yourself when it occurs to you how the **Old Testament Reading** prefigures it. As you discover how all the pieces fit together, as you see again and again the unity of the sacred writings, your faith will be deepened to help you understand that all these connections can't be coincidence! They must come from one divine Author, Creator, Savior! You'll also appreciate more fully the genius of liturgical worship. The whole Church—for millennia!—has put so much more thought into what we do each Sunday than could any one pastor designing a single Sunday service or a six-week series of sermons. It's with excellent and historic reasons that we Lutherans worship as we do!

A Three-Year Lectionary? . . . and How It Works

Yes, what we look forward to this coming Sunday morning really does come down to us through millennia.

Dating back to the last centuries before Christ, the Jews in their synagogues used what we call a "lectionary"—that is, a schedule calling for certain readings ("lections" or lessons) from the Bible on certain days. Prior to the writing of the New Testament, readings for each Sabbath came from the Torah, or Law (the first five books of the Old Testament, the Pentateuch, written by Moses), the Prophets (such as the books of Isaiah, Jeremiah, and Ezekiel), and the Psalms. When Jesus went to the synagogue in Nazareth one Sabbath (Lk 4:16–30), He knew that the reading of the Prophets that day would be from Isaiah 61. Thus, He came prepared to preach a sermon on that text.

The early Christians followed this practice of a lectionary, incorporating, obviously, the New Testament writings, from the Gospels (Matthew, Mark, Luke, and John) and the Epistles (letters by Paul, like Romans and Galatians, and by other apostles, like 1 and 2 Peter), along with readings from the Old Testament. As a church year gradually developed, the lectionary naturally manifested it—especially during the months of the year that commemorate the great events in the life of Christ: His birth, His death and resurrection, His ascension back to heaven, and His sending of the Holy Spirit. During this half of the church year—Christmas (which also includes the seasons of Advent and Epiphany) and Easter (extending from Lent through Easter to Ascension and Pentecost)—the lectionary readings declare the events and themes of Jesus' earthly ministry.

By the seventh and eighth centuries, a one-year schedule of readings was fairly firm and widely followed. That included readings for the remaining months of the year, what we call the Time of the Church or the Sundays after Pentecost. Rather than highlight the highlight events in Jesus' life, these Sundays consider His teachings on issues Christians face as we await His return. Thus, over a one-year period, the chief events and teachings of Christ and His Word would be covered—and then repeated each subsequent year. The Lutheran reformers of the sixteenth century generally kept this lectionary, making some modifications.

Of course, a lectionary of once-a-week readings cannot cover all the words of Scripture. Another word for a reading or lection, in fact, is *pericope* (pronounced pe-RIC-o-pee), from a Greek word that means "cutting around." With time expectations on our worship services, we have to cut things. (Thus, the lectionary is also called a pericopal system.) Of the roughly 31,000 verses in the Bible, our current one-year lectionary selects just over 2,700 verses, or 8.7 percent. (Of the New Testament, the much shorter of the two and with two readings per week, 23.1 percent is incorporated. Just 3.7 percent of the much longer Old Testament is read.)

So in the early 1960s, one directive from the Roman Catholic Second Vatican Council (Vatican II) was to devise a three-year lectionary—three years worth of Bible readings instead of the traditional one. In short order, Protestants and Lutherans developed three-year lectionaries of their own, heavily based on the Vatican II design, but with appropriate editing, not drawing from the Apocrypha read by Roman Catholics. Largely because of the attraction of hearing that much more of the Bible, three-year lectionaries are now used by a very substantial majority of congregations, including in the LCMS. The three-year lectionary this book studies is from *LSB* (2006), a gentle revision of what appeared in its predecessor hymnal, *Lutheran Worship* (1982).

Turn to *LSB* pages xiv–xix to see how the three-year lectionary works.

Each of the three years is designated as either Series A or "Year A" (pp xiv–xv), Series B or "Year B" (pp xvi–xvii), or Series C or "Year C" (pp xviii–xix). (The one-year lectionary is shown on pp xx–xxi, and festivals, which are the same for all three years and both lectionaries, follow on pp xxii–xxiii.) Which year are you in now? Well, for an historical benchmark, it happens that 2017, the five hundredth anniversary of the Reformation, was a Year A. That meant that 2018 was a Year B and 2019 was a Year C. (Actually, the church year begins with Advent 1 in late November or early December of the preceding calendar year, so that Year A of the Reformation anniversary in fact began on November 27, 2016, but you get the idea.) Then the cycle repeats: 2020 was A, 2021 was B, and 2022 was C. Which means that 2023, 2026, 2029, 2032, and so on are basically Year A. Likewise, 2024, 2027, 2030, 2033, and all that follow in turn are Year B. And 2025, 2028, 2031, 2034, and so on are Year C. Still not sure? Ask Pastor. He's the ultimate go-to for all such questions.

Now back to *LSB* pages xiv–xix. See how the left column of each page gives the day of the church year? Then look at the far right-hand column: Holy Gospel. The design for each Sunday or festival begins with the **Holy Gospel**. Scan the

Gospel readings on these pages. Notice that for Year A, the Gospels are primarily from the book of Matthew, for Year B, they are from Mark, and for Year C, they are from Luke, with John woven into all three, slightly more in Year B because of Mark's shorter length. Check a few of your Sunday bulletins and see which book of the Bible the Gospels are coming from. You've got it.

The **Old Testament Reading** (the second column) is selected to reflect some relationship to the Gospel lesson. It might declare a prophecy that is then fulfilled in the Gospel lesson. (If you'd like, look up the Old Testament and Gospel readings for Advent 4, Year A.) Or the Old Testament Reading might be a narrative, a story, that illustrates a teaching in the Gospel lesson (for example, with Year A Proper 19). Or the Old Testament Reading may simply teach the same doctrine as the Gospel lesson (say, Epiphany 7, Year A).

A very wholesome exception in this second column is that during the Easter season, the **First Reading** is taken not from the Old Testament but from the book of Acts. Seeing the risen Christ at Easter was the impetus that drove the apostles forth into their missionary endeavors, as Acts relates.

The **Epistle** (third column) is chosen different ways in different seasons of the church year. During Advent, Christmas season, Lent, and major festivals such as the days of Epiphany, Transfiguration, Easter, Ascension, Pentecost, and Trinity Sunday, the Epistle, as expected, reflects the theme set by the Gospel lesson. However, during the Epiphany *season*, Easter *season*, and the Sundays after Pentecost, the Epistles instead spend consecutive Sundays in a particular letter. This lets us get the flow of that book. See, for instance, how the Epistles for Epiphany 2–8, Year A, read continuously through Paul's first letter to the Corinthians. Since these readings follow the order of the book they're taken from, they can't be expected to make the same points as the Gospels for those days. With high frequency, nevertheless, close examination of these Epistles will discover *some* elements that can embellish the theme of the day.

There's one more vocab word we've been using but should be sure we understand: *propers*. Properly speaking (sorry!), the propers are all the elements of the worship service that change from week to week. (The elements that don't change or have just a couple of options shown in the hymnal are called the "ordinaries.") The hymns we sing on a given Sunday, some particular prayers, and, as we've seen, these Scripture lessons are propers. But there are a few other propers to recognize, because they are also assigned to accompany the lectionary readings on specific Sundays.

The first of these other propers, as named earlier, is the **Introit** (from a Latin word meaning "entrance," referring to the pastor going to the altar). The Introit is usually selected verses from the Psalms, and it begins and ends with an identical passage called the antiphon. The Introit—especially the antiphon—is intended to introduce the overall theme of the day. Except during Holy Week (the days of Christ's Passion and death), the Introit includes the Gloria Patri ("Glory be to the Father and to the Son and to the Holy Spirit . . .") as a reminder that the God of the Old Testament psalms is the one and only true God, the Holy Trinity.

Soon after comes a prayer called the **Collect** of the Day. In ancient worship, the congregation would kneel for silent prayer, after which the pastor would vocalize a prayer intended to "collect" in a quite general way the petitions on the hearts of all the people. Very early in the Church's history, prayers for this purpose were written down—according to a definite, specific form—and came to be used widely. Those early prayers are among our appointed Collects yet today. For the three-year lectionary, though, many new Collects have been composed so that they address the themes of the additional Sundays.

As the hymnal of Old Testament Israel, the Psalms have always had an honored place in Christian worship. Not only does the Introit draw from the Psalter, but the propers also appoint a full **Psalm**. The Psalm usually amplifies the message of the Old Testament Reading, and since that reading is selected according to the day's Gospel lesson, the Psalm is also usually on point to the overall Sunday theme. Congregations that do not routinely use the Psalm when celebrating Holy Communion may nonetheless use it in the Matins service (*LSB*, p 221).

Instead of the full psalm, many congregations place another proper called the **Gradual** after the Old Testament Reading. Originally chanted as the pastor moved into position for the next reading (*gradus* means "step"), the Gradual is also frequently verses from the Psalms. In the three-year lectionary, a particular Gradual is used for an entire season (all four Sundays of Advent, for example) or for part (four to seven weeks) of the lengthy season that includes the Sundays after Pentecost. Thus, the Gradual suggests a theme not for a Sunday but for the season.

The **Verse** is easily overlooked. It's brief. It often quotes words that will be repeated moments later in the Gospel. But rather than being "predundant," on many Sundays the Verse may be the most explicit articulation of the service's theme. Notice that we stand for it in anticipation of the Gospel. And very significant is the fact that, except during Lent, it's framed in Alleluias. *Alleluia* is derived from the Hebrew meaning "Praise Yahweh (the Lord)" (Ps 104:35; 105:45; 106:1, 48; and many, many more). Why is that so important? Because praising the Lord is never to be simply an outburst that our emotions generate; legitimate praise of the Lord is always in response to the great and gracious things He has done. The last proper to mention here is a uniquely Lutheran contribution to the worship tradition: the **Hymn of the Day**. Lutherans of the sixteenth and seventeenth centuries (and since!) wrote numerous hymns that became part of the weekly Sunday rhythm. Many of these sang the stories and teachings of the Gospel lessons and came to be associated with the Sundays when those lessons were read. The Hymns of the Day give a fine sample of the hymnal and help keep the Lutheran Church "the singing church."

For so much more on the history, theology, and practice of liturgical, lectionary worship, you might find the following interesting:

Paul J. Grime, ed., *Lutheran Service Book: Companion to the Services* (St. Louis: Concordia Publishing House, 2022); especially pages 181–262 by D. Richard Stuckwisch Jr. and pages 470–544 by Grime.

Luther D. Reed, *The Lutheran Liturgy: A Study of the Common Liturgy of the Lutheran Church in America*, rev. ed. (Philadelphia: Fortress Press, 1960), 288–300, 450–64.

James L. Brauer, "The Church Year," in *Lutheran Worship: History and Practice*, ed. Fred L. Precht (St. Louis: Concordia Publishing House, 1993), 146–74.

Paul J. Grime and Dean W. Nadasdy, eds., *Preaching Is Worship: The Sermon in Context* (St. Louis: Concordia Publishing House, 2011).

One Final (Introductory) Word

As we've already acknowledged, this book came out of three years of radio programs on *Issues, Etc.* Not only was it a delight to study each week's propers in preparation for the interviews, but it was truly pleasant to speak live (or on demand!) to interested tuners-in and downloaders. That is always reinforced as I travel here and there for professional engagements or family vacations and someone says, "I recognize your voice." Actually talking with people (even when, I suppose, I'm mostly limited to talking *to* them) is so much more fun than writing. So I've tried, as best I could, to carry on a chat with you in this book. My English teachers, professors, and dissertation advisers all advised—no, required—that I write in third person, which is to say, impersonally. And they were right—for their genres. Radio and this book are different genres. As we look forward to Sunday morning—me at St. Paul's Lutheran, Fort Wayne, Indiana, or Immanuel Lutheran, Orange, California, and you wherever that might be—I pray that this book helps us look forward to Sunday morning *together*. Because that, the unity in Christ Jesus shared through centuries and around the world, is the great virtue of liturgy, lectionary, and all those things proper.

Rev. Dr. Carl C. Fickenscher II

YEAR A

First Sunday in Advent Year A

READINGS

Isaiah 2:1–5
Psalm 122 (antiphon: v 6)
Romans 13:(8–10) 11–14
Matthew 21:1–11
or Matthew 24:36–44

HYMN OF THE DAY

LSB 332 "Savior of the Nations, Come"

We'll begin where a new church year begins: the First Sunday in Advent—although I assume if you acquired this book in, say, midsummer of Year B, you actually began reading maybe a year and a half ago somewhere around page 412. In fact, if today happens to be midsummer in Year B, I suggest you skip ahead and start there (and maybe even consult the Introduction to see what "Year B" means). This book will be best read week by week, according to whichever pages of the church calendar you're living. And this page will still be here waiting for you when Advent 1, Year A, comes around again.

So assuming it's the week of Advent 1, read and pray with me, or perhaps with family, the **Gradual** for this season of Advent:

> *Rejoice greatly, O daughter of Zion. Shout aloud, O daughter of Jerusalem. Behold, your king is coming to you; righteous and having salvation. Blessed is he who comes in the name of the Lord. From the house of the Lord we bless you. (Zech 9:9; Ps 118:26, alt)*

Those Old Testament verses set the theme for the entire season of Advent. (That, by the way, is always the function of the Gradual—to express the unifying idea for the particular *season* of the church year.) We'll hear this same Gradual all four Sundays of Advent.

We'll even hear some of those words already again this week in the **Introit** (whose function is to begin to suggest the theme for this *specific Sunday*). Again from Zechariah 9 and Psalm 118, the Introit:

Behold, your king is coming to you; righteous and having salvation.

Save us, we pray, O LORD! O LORD, we pray, give us success! Blessed is he who comes in the name of the LORD! We bless you from the house of the LORD. The LORD is God, and He has made His light to shine upon us. Bind the festal sacrifice with cords, up to the horns of the altar! You are my God, and I will give thanks to You; You are my God; I will extol You.

Glory be to the Father and to the Son and to the Holy Spirit; as it was in the beginning, is now, and will be forever. Amen.

Behold, your king is coming to you; righteous and having salvation. (Ps 118:25–28; antiphon: Zech 9:9b, alt)

Finally, to begin, pray also the **Collect** for this Sunday:

Stir up Your power, O Lord, and come, that by Your protection we may be rescued from the threatening perils of our sins and saved by Your mighty deliverance; for You live and reign with the Father and the Holy Spirit, one God, now and forever. Amen.

The season of Advent, of course, is all about the coming of Christ. (*Advent* means "coming.") That's quite obvious to us who know how to read properly even the secular signs we pass on the way to church in late November and early December. Christmas is coming! But the Advent coming of Christ isn't just a time of year. It's always! The six (count 'em) references to coming already appearing in the propers above (with lots more to see in the readings) don't refer exclusively or even mostly to Christmas. Advent celebrates a threefold coming of Christ: in His birth at Bethlehem, certainly, but also at the end of time and every day to us in the meantime in the Means of Grace, His Word and Sacraments.

Already in the Introit, the Collect, and the Gradual, we notice several key elements about this "always coming" of Christ that will recur throughout the other propers.

We notice that He comes to His own chosen *place*: "We bless you from the house of the LORD" (Introit). We notice that He makes "His *light* to shine upon us" (Introit). Had He not, we'd always be in the dark about who He is and how He's disposed toward us; we'd always imagine Him as overpowering and demanding that we placate Him.

Instead, why does He come each time? He is "righteous and having salvation" (Gradual and Introit). "Save us, we pray" (Introit). "That . . . we may be . . . saved" (Collect). Christ comes to *save* us!

All of which means we can't help but notice that Christ's coming is *stirring*, thrilling! I'm not as troubled as some Christians might be about the hoopla the world brings to Christmas. It can be distracting, no doubt, but it also reminds us that when Christ comes to save us, it's exciting! We'll come to church this First Sunday in Advent with—admit it!—a little greater anticipation than on, say, the Sixteenth Sunday after Pentecost. We know why they've decked the malls. And those who don't know, well, we've got an opportunity to capitalize, to let them know what all the hubbub's really about. Three of the four Sundays in Advent will raise a thrilling prayer that God would "*stir up*" something (Collect). "Rejoice greatly. . . . Shout aloud" (Gradual)!

The liturgical **Verse** for the Sunday captures this: "Alleluia. Lift up your heads, O gates! And be lifted up, O ancient doors, that the King of glory may come in. Alleluia" (Ps 24:7). Recognize those words? It's probably because of two marvelous Advent hymns: the classic "Lift Up Your Heads, Ye Mighty Gates" (*LSB* 340/341) and a twenty-first–century new classic by Stephen Starke, "Lift Up Your Heads, You Everlasting Doors" (*LSB* 339). When Christ comes, we can't help but look up! It's stirring! You can't take Advent sitting down!

Let's see how the lessons of the day pick up and develop these elements.

Look up the **Old Testament Reading**, Isaiah 2:1–5, in your Bible. This is a "word" Isaiah "saw" (2:1)! We don't usually think of seeing a word (other than on a printed page like this that's full of them). Isaiah isn't talking about a written word he saw; he's describing a spectacular vision of what we call the messianic age, the end times that would begin with Christ's first coming and then continue through history, past His return at the end of the world, and on into eternity. God's word to Isaiah was so real, he could see all that! (The Hebrew language understands this concept well. The word דָּבָר, *dabar*, can be equally well translated "the word" or "the thing.")

Can you picture the word Isaiah saw? Nations, all nations, streaming up a mountain to the house of the Lord (2:2). Israel always envisioned the temple as "up"—sitting as it did atop Mount Zion in the citadel of Jerusalem. Why are the nations going up to the temple? Because that's the *place* where God's Word teaches us (2:3). And with otherworldly results: instead of war, we learn peace (2:4). The Lord has turned His *light* on us to see Him as He really is, loving and forgiving (recall the Introit). Therefore, even amid the wars that will continue until earth's end, Christians love and forgive; we "walk in the light of the LORD" (2:5).

See, what Christ started by coming to earth the first time (which Isaiah also foresaw and which we'll see further in Old Testament Readings the next three Sundays) isn't on hold until He comes again on the Last Day—when, of course, all wars will cease. What Christ started is also happening right now as He comes to us in His Word and Sacrament. And remember (this is crucial!), this coming happens in the *place* the Lord decides to come. Read Psalm 122 and see how David places the peace we learn in Christ. He was glad when they said, "Let us go to the house of the LORD!" (122:1). In 122:4, he even says "go up." The house of the Lord is still the place He chooses to come to us. Christ is omnipresent, He's everywhere, sure, but the place He promises to forgive our sins and give us everlasting salvation is, above all, where His people gather on the First Sunday of Advent and every other week: His Church.

St. Paul picks up several of these same elements in the **Epistle**, Romans 13:(8–10) 11–14. The hour has come "to wake from sleep" (13:11)! Lift up your heads! Stirring events are happening! Walk in the light, "properly as in the daytime." There's no time for the "works of darkness," the things people try to get away with under the cover of night—"orgies and drunkenness," "sexual immorality and sensuality," "quarreling and jealousy" (13:12–13). Rather, "let us put on the armor of light" (13:12) and be seen loving the neighbor (13:9–10). The obvious reason is that Christ is coming soon, and all things will be exposed.

That's the focus of one of the two **Holy Gospels** for this day, Matthew 24:36–44, which describes the Parousia, or final advent, of Christ. "As were the days of Noah, so will be the coming of the Son of Man." And we know what happened! "The flood came and swept them all away" (24:37, 39). That's a vital warning even for Christians, and it reminds of the close connection between Advent 1 and the final Sundays of the church year with their emphasis on Judgment Day.

Significantly, though, St. Paul in the Epistle gives a different reason for walking not in darkness but in the light, a reason more in keeping with the overall tone of Advent 1: Yes, Christ is coming, coming soon, but He is coming to save; the countdown to His coming at the end of the world means "*salvation* is nearer to us now than when we first believed" (Rom 13:11).

All this taken together explains why the historic **Holy Gospel** for the First Sunday in Advent, Matthew 21:1–11, is so very appropriate—even if we recognize it as not Christmas but Palm Sunday. Everything Zechariah, David, Isaiah, and Paul see coming is because Jesus came not just to Bethlehem but also to Jerusalem. Jesus rides the donkey down the Mount of Olives and then up the steep slope of the temple mount, a whole multitude streaming with Him. The city is all astir! The scene is electric! Matthew knows Jesus is fulfilling Zechariah's prophecy that we heard in both the Gradual and Introit: "Your King is coming!" The crowd quotes the words of Psalm 118 we heard in the Introit, "*Save us,* we pray, O LORD!"; they just quote it in the way we better recognize: one Hebrew word, "Hosanna!"

Yes, He comes to save. And He comes to *the place* He has appointed to save—not only the manger, but also the cross. It's by dying five days later, there in Jerusalem, that our King saves us. And now, having died and risen, He continues to save us each time we gather in the place He comes in preaching and His Supper. We'll be in the right place to begin Advent this Sunday morning.

**SINCE OUR KING
IS ALWAYS COMING TO SAVE US,
LET US UP AND GO UP,
WALKING IN THE LIGHT,
TO THE PLACE HE COMES.**

Close your preparation for Advent 1 by singing the **Hymn of the Day**, "Savior of the Nations, Come" (*LSB* 332), and notice its history: St. Ambrose (fourth century), with the German version by Martin Luther.

Second Sunday in Advent Year A

READINGS

Isaiah 11:1–10

Psalm 72:1–7 (antiphon: v 18)

Romans 15:4–13

Matthew 3:1–12

HYMN OF THE DAY

LSB 344 "On Jordan's Bank the Baptist's Cry"

Rejoice greatly, O daughter of Zion. Shout aloud, O daughter of Jerusalem. Behold, your king is coming to you." Our **Gradual** (see last week) set that tone for the entire season of Advent.

This Sunday and next, the second and third in Advent, we'll hear about the coming of Christ largely through the voice of John the Baptist. John, we know, was a different bird; the locusts and wild honey he ate are a pretty good indication. And we know that from John we'll hear lots of shouting aloud, "O daughter of Jerusalem." But will we hear any rejoicing?

We probably picture John, and rightly so, as a fiery preacher of repentance. He doesn't pull any punches; he calls sin for what it is, sin, whether the ones on the other end of the punch are plain folks of Judea or the high and mighty Pharisees and Sadducees of Jerusalem—or us! "You brood of vipers! . . . Every tree therefore that does not bear good fruit is cut down and thrown into the fire" (Mt 3:7, 10). Shouting! Scary shouting!

So is there any cause for rejoicing from John the Baptist this Second Sunday in Advent? Let's begin our preparation for this coming Sunday morning by singing the **Hymn of the Day**, "On Jordan's Bank the Baptist's Cry" (*LSB* 344). You won't hear me, but you know I'll be singing quite loudly too. It's one of my favorites.

What did you notice? You've sure got John's loud and ringing voice "announc[ing] that the Lord is nigh." But when we awake and hearken, what do we hear? "Glad tidings from the King of kings!" (st 1). There's going to be a call that every life be cleansed from sin, that we "Make straight the way for God within," all right (st 2). But John's big message is "glad tidings." Christ is coming to save.

By the way, another excellent hymn you might sing this week or next begins like this: "When all the world was cursed by Moses' condemnation, Saint John the Baptist came *with words of consolation*" (*LSB* 346). Rejoice greatly, O daughter of Zion!

This will be an important understanding to carry throughout our listening this Sunday, because our propers are going to use words like "judge" and "judgment" and "justice" that also can be scary. Heard properly, though, for us as Christians, those words, too, will be consoling, reasons for rejoicing.

The first of the appointed propers most of us will hear Sunday morning is the **Introit**:

> *In the wilderness prepare the way of the LORD; make straight in the desert a highway for our God.*
>
> *Seek the LORD and His strength; seek His presence continually! Remember the wondrous works that He has done, His miracles, and the judgments He uttered, O offspring of Abraham, His servant, children of Jacob, His chosen ones! He is the LORD our God; His judgments are in all the earth. He remembers His covenant forever, the word that He commanded, for a thousand generations.*
>
> *Glory be to the Father and to the Son and to the Holy Spirit; as it was in the beginning, is now, and will be forever. Amen.*
>
> *In the wilderness prepare the way of the LORD; make straight in the desert a highway for our God. (Ps 105:4–8; antiphon: Is 40:3b)*

The antiphon has a very "John the Baptist" ring to it, and that's no coincidence. Isaiah 40, from which it's taken, includes this clear prophecy of the ministry of John. Matthew will quote it about John in our Gospel lesson later, and it will give us the Old Testament Reading for this Sunday next year, Year B. This is that familiar message of John: "prepare the way of the LORD" is a call to repent, to remove any obstacles, sin, or distractions to receiving the Messiah.

Notice also the first reference to judgment: "His judgments are in all the earth." Those not prepared when Christ comes cannot hope to escape punishment. There will be nowhere to hide, because the judgment will indeed be for "all the earth." That, of course, is why John came—so that Christ's coming would be announced and known so all could be prepared. There is more to say, though, about judgment, because it is a two-edged sword—including not just the edge that we fear! Remember, John brings glad tidings!

Pray now the **Collect** for this Sunday:

> *Stir up our hearts, O Lord, to make ready the way of Your only-begotten Son, that by His coming we may be enabled to serve You with pure minds; through the same Jesus Christ, our Lord, who lives and reigns with You and the Holy Spirit, one God, now and forever. Amen.*

This is the second of three "stir up" collects in Advent. (The final one will occur on Advent 4.) Last week, we prayed that God would stir up, or use, His mighty power on our behalf. This time, we pray that He would stir up our hearts. That's tremendously significant for this week's propers in connection with John's call to prepare, repent. "Prepare" is spoken to us again and again this Sunday as an imperative, a command, something we are to do. But this collect recognizes the truth and prays for help. The truth is, we cannot properly prepare ourselves; we can't clear the way. The command is given to us, but if we're to do it, we must be given the power from outside. Excellent—and very Lutheran!—theology, eh? Repentance, good works, and, especially, faith are all things that happen in us, but they must all be worked in us by God Himself. And so we pray, "O Lord, *You* please stir up our hearts so that we can make ready the way of Christ. By *His coming* enable us to serve You!" A prayer not just for Advent but for all seasons!

The call to repent is repeated in the **Verse**: "Alleluia. Prepare the way of the Lord, make His paths straight; all flesh shall see the salvation of God. Alleluia" (Lk 3:4b, 6, but actually a citation of, again, Is 40:3, 5). Here's an important advance, however: Remember that judgment would be in all the earth. What does all flesh see this time? Salvation! Yes, there's more to judgment than punishment.

At this point, we've introduced all the major elements of this week's propers, so let's offer our Theme for the week and see how the Scripture readings develop it further:

Through John the Baptist, God Calls Us to Prepare for Christ's Coming to Judge in Righteousness for All Nations.

Our **Old Testament Reading** is Isaiah 11:1–10. Read it in your Bible, and then we'll talk. Notice that, like last week, we have a vivid picture of the Messianic Age, another vision that Isaiah saw. God's people universally recognized the Messiah as being the "Son of David," so the reference to "a shoot from the stump of Jesse," David's father, is unmistakably Christ. Unfortunately, by Isaiah's day—and progressively worse so thereafter—the mighty kingdom of David was reduced to a stump. Israel was destroyed by Assyria; Judah would go into captivity in Babylon, and even her return would never reestablish real kingship. But the Messiah would! His kingdom, in fact, would transform creation, bringing in an age in which predators like wolves and leopards and bears and lions would get along just fine with lambs and goats and cows. Even little children could be playmates with cobras (11:6–8). All this, we realize, will be realized in heaven. But the vision is also picturesque of what has already happened: Christ's death and resurrection has reconciled God and man so that there exists even now peace on earth—for now, in hiddenness.

The Messiah, the shoot from Jesse, will also judge (11:3–4). But we're starting to recognize the comfort in that. He will judge the poor, the meek, "with righteousness" (11:4). That is, He won't judge the way the world would, slanted in favor of those who appear to deserve it—the powerful, rich, seemingly holy ("what His eyes see," 11:3). He'll judge in favor of those who realize their helplessness and cling to Him for righteousness, the righteousness that comes from faith in the "shoot from the stump of Jesse," while those who oppress them, the wicked, will be killed. For all who are in Christ, judgment is consoling.

This is why in our **Psalm**, Solomon (or a psalmist writing *for* Solomon) can ask God for "justice." He, too, wishes to judge the poor with righteousness, and under that kind of judgment the righteous may actually "flourish" (Ps 72:1–7). Christ is coming, our theme has said, to judge in righteousness.

To judge in righteousness *for all nations*, Paul wants to emphasize once again in the **Epistle**, Romans 15:4–13. Isaiah had ended our earlier reading with a mention that "the root of Jesse" would "stand as a signal for *the peoples*—of Him shall *the nations* inquire" (Is 11:10). Now Paul paraphrases that verse in Romans (15:12). As in the Introit and Isaiah 40 (quoted in the Verse), the Old Testament makes not infrequent declarations that the Messiah of Israel will be for "the nations," the Gentiles too. But in the ministry of Paul, that exploded upon the planet. Paul says that "Christ became a servant to the circumcised," Israel, *both* to confirm the promises He made to "the patriarchs" (Abraham, Isaac, and Jacob, for their descendants, Israel) *and* "that the Gentiles might glorify God for His mercy" (15:8–9). See how many times Paul speaks of the Gentiles in 15:8–12. What becomes obvious is that Gentiles are the "we," the "our," and the "you" for whom "the encouragement of the Scriptures" and "hope" are intended (15:4–7, 13). The judgments in all the earth bring *us* hope, bring us *hope*!

Of course, our theme and all the preceding propers are predicated on the **Holy Gospel**, the account of John's ministry, Matthew 3:1–12. All the elements our theme has summarized arise from God's call to us through John the Baptist. This strange man calls us to repent, to prepare the way of the Lord. His wilderness setting (and his wilderness lifestyle) underscore that nothing—no trappings of comfort, no pleasures or conveniences—are to draw our attention away from Jesus' coming. "The kingdom of heaven is at hand!" (3:2). Heaven Himself has come down to earth! Nothing could be more urgent—or even second-most urgent. Receiving God's Christ when He comes is *all* there is!

The crowds get it. Confessing their sins, they are baptized. Not so the religious leaders. They come as hypocrites—either to pass their own judgment or out of curiosity or because this is the place to be seen. John sees through that (judges not as eyes see) and lowers the boom! When Christ comes, He brings judgment—even unquenchable fire.

But that's not the judgment He really came to bring. The kingdom of heaven didn't come to earth to destroy it; that could have been done from outside. The Kingdom left heaven, became part of His earth, to gather the wheat, the poor, into His barn, into His kingdom. He would do that by Himself being cut down *on* a tree and Himself being cast away as chaff. But then He would send His Holy Spirit, whose Baptism would stir up our hearts and prepare us for His return.

Those are the glad tidings John brings!

Third Sunday in Advent Year A

READINGS

Isaiah 35:1–10
Psalm 146 (antiphon: v 5)
James 5:7–11
Matthew 11:2–15

HYMN OF THE DAY

LSB 345 "Hark! A Thrilling Voice Is Sounding"

Let's pretend it's not Monday or Tuesday or Thursday or whatever day you're reading this *before* the Third Sunday in Advent. Let's pretend you've just settled into your favorite pew and the prelude for Advent 3 is nearing coda. This week, let's look forward to Sunday morning as if it's already Sunday. You follow? We'll walk through the steps that'll happen during the Divine Service this Sunday as if they're happening right now. Okay?

It's almost Christmas. It looks like it outside. It looks like it here in the sanctuary too. We've reached the third candle on the Advent wreath, and you've come to know that the pink one—we call it rose—is for today (although you do remember once thinking the acolyte must have goofed; the oddball candle has to go last, if not first, right?). And you remember that the rose candle hints at the theme of Advent 3. Maybe you even remember, or maybe the bulletin tells you, that this Sunday has traditionally been called Gaudete. (Bonus points if you remember that *Gaudete* is Latin for "Rejoice.") That's right, the rose candle reminds us that the Third Sunday in Advent is about joy.

A familiar Advent opening hymn (there are so many!), the Invocation, Versicles, and Confession and Absolution, and it's time for the first appointed proper, the **Introit**:

Rejoice in the Lord always; again I will say, Rejoice.

I will hope continually and will praise You yet more and more. My mouth will tell of Your righteous acts, of Your deeds of salvation all the day, for their number is past my knowledge. With the mighty deeds of the

Lord God I will come; I will remind them of Your righteousness, Yours alone. O God, from my youth You have taught me, and I still proclaim Your wondrous deeds. So even to old age and gray hairs, O God, do not forsake me, until I proclaim Your might to another generation, Your power to all those to come.

Glory be to the Father and to the Son and to the Holy Spirit; as it was in the beginning, is now, and will be forever. Amen.

Rejoice in the Lord always; again I will say, Rejoice. (Ps 71:14–18; antiphon: Phil 4:4)

Ah, Gaudete! Rejoice! Always! You recognize the antiphon from Paul's glorious exhortation in Philippians. It began the Epistle lesson this Sunday last year (Year C).

The psalm portion of the Introit goes on to tell why we can always rejoice: "My mouth will tell of Your righteous acts, of Your deeds of salvation all the day, for their number is past my knowledge." The righteous acts, the things God does to save us, are more than we can count! Your mind wanders off for a moment in a wholesome direction: "Let's see: (1) He died for me; (2) He lets me sit here in church, where I'm receiving forgiveness and life—and a break from all those pre-Christmas hurry-ups; (3) He's given me people who love me, lots of them right here; (4) . . ."

Oh, what did I miss? ". . . even to old age and gray hairs, O God, do not forsake me." Fill in your own age-appropriate reaction to that one. Me, I'm appreciating it more and more.

You're settled in for rose Sunday, "Joy Sunday."

Kyrie, Hymn of Praise: "The Lord be with you." "And also with you." "Let us pray."

Lord Jesus Christ, we implore You to hear our prayers and to lighten the darkness of our hearts by Your gracious visitation; for You live and reign with the Father and the Holy Spirit, one God, now and forever. Amen.

Hmm. That's not a "stir up" **Collect** like we get so often in Advent. Sounds fairly generic, except, of course, for "Your gracious visitation." That's Advent, Christ coming. Light/darkness fits almost any time. I wonder if there's any particular thing the light is supposed to help us see that we'd be dark about otherwise. I'm listening for joy.

"If you brought your Bibles this morning"—I always used to say that in my parishes, hint, hint—"please turn with me to our **Old Testament Reading**, Isaiah 35:1–10."

"The wilderness and the dry land shall be glad; the desert shall *rejoice* and blossom like the crocus; it shall blossom abundantly and *rejoice* with *joy* and singing" (35:1–2). There's our Gaudete! You can almost see the rose (candle!) of Sharon blooming, what with all those crocuses and cedars of Lebanon and majesty of Carmel and reeds and rushes flourishing in the desert, the streams and springs and pools of water!

And that's not even the best part of the vision Isaiah's seeing. "Weak hands," "feeble knees," "an anxious heart" all strengthened (35:3–4). "Then the eyes of the blind shall be opened, and the ears of the deaf unstopped; then shall the lame man leap like a deer, and the tongue of the mute sing for *joy*" (35:5–6). There's reason for rejoicing! Just like the last two Sundays' Old Testament Readings, also from Isaiah, it's the Messianic Age. We don't see all this until heaven, but when Christ came and reconciled the world to God on the cross, this became the present reality. No matter what our eyes are seeing right now—the corruption we, Adam, and Eve brought on the landscape and on human well-being—the ravages of sin have been healed. "And the ransomed of the LORD shall . . . come to Zion with singing; everlasting *joy* shall be upon their heads; they shall obtain gladness and *joy*, and sorrow and sighing shall flee away" (35:10). "This is the Word of the Lord." "Thanks be to God!" Yes, indeed!

It's just as the **Gradual** has been exhorting all through the season: "Rejoice greatly, O daughter of Zion. Shout aloud, O daughter of Jerusalem. Behold, your king is coming to you; righteous and having salvation."

Or maybe your congregation will choose to use the **Psalm** in place of the Gradual. You'll speak or chant responsively Psalm 146. Plenty of praising the Lord going on there, even if we never use the *joy* word. But there's also kind of a downer: The Lord "executes justice for the oppressed, . . . gives food to the hungry. The LORD sets the prisoners free; the LORD opens the eyes of the blind. The LORD lifts up those who are bowed down; . . . The LORD watches over the sojourners; He upholds the widow and the fatherless" (146:7–9). All good news; God is making wrong right. But who wants to think about oppression and hunger and orphanage today? It's rose Sunday. "Rejoice in the Lord always!"

"The **Epistle** for this Third Sunday in Advent is James chapter 5, verses 7 to 11."

Wait a minute! *The Lutheran Study Bible* (which I just might bring to church this Sunday, thank you) heads that section "Patience in Suffering." Where's the rose in that? "Be patient, therefore, brothers, until the coming of the Lord. See how the farmer waits for the precious fruit of the earth, being patient about it, until it receives the early and the late rains" (5:7). But what if it doesn't rain? "As an example of suffering and patience, brothers, take the prophets who spoke in the name of the Lord" (5:10). Yeah, and a lot of them got killed. "Rejoice in the Lord *always*"? In suffering?

And it gets worse. "The **Holy Gospel** according to St. Matthew, the eleventh chapter, beginning at the second verse. 'Now when John heard in prison . . .' "

The bloom is definitely off the rose!

So what gives here? Look at the story, Matthew 11:2–15. John the Baptist is in prison, and you know this isn't going to end well. He's there because Herodias, "King" Herod's "wife," can't stand the truth about her adultery with her real husband's brother, and before long, she and her daughter will have the Baptist's head. From prison, John sends his disciples to ask Jesus if He really is the one to come, the promised Christ. John has already told the world that Jesus *is* the

Lamb of God, who takes away the sin of the world (Jn 1:29), but he asks. Why? Martin Luther and C. F. W. Walther suggest that John was confident of the answer but was sending his disciples to Jesus so that *their* faith would be reassured. Maybe. But I picture a guy rotting in the dungeon for doing precisely what he thinks God wants him to do and feeling the way I would. "Almighty God, did I miss the boat? I know what I said about this Jesus, and I was pretty sure I got that from You. But if I've really been doing what You want, why am I in here?"

I'm guessing we've all felt that way. In fact, it's very possible that Gaudete Sunday lost you already at "Rejoice in the Lord always!" That's easy for Paul to say, maybe? And when the psalmist told us that the Lord's deeds of salvation are more than we can count, your mind might have wandered off instead to count all kinds of things that don't feel so joyful at all. Like the stress and depression that's so common at Christmas. Like those gray hairs and the effects of aging that are no joke for many of us or many of our loved ones. Like the dark places that the Collect's "darkness of our hearts" finds us all too often. So where's the Gaudete, the rose, the joy, in all that?

Jesus answers by citing the very signs of the Messiah that Isaiah gave us in the Old Testament Reading—people who are blind, deaf, or lame are healed—plus an additional sign from later in Isaiah (good news preached to the poor, Is 61:1). And then, very significantly, Jesus adds, "And blessed is the one who is not offended by Me" (Mt 11:6). That last line is key. True, Jesus did many things John could see as evidence that He was the Messiah. But we're always tempted to trust only in those things we see—and that fit our expectations of what God should do. It's natural—though wrong and sinful—to expect that when we're faithful to God He'll bless us in ways that are immediate and tangible and visible. And the most visible, tangible evidence John had right now was that he was in prison and likely to be murdered. It's easy to be offended with Christ when God chooses to work *that* way, easy to give up on *any* idea of joy in the Lord when our circumstances seem to count up on the deficit side.

The fact is, Paul wrote our antiphon to the Philippians from—guess where?—prison! And the fact is, what Jesus was indeed coming to do, to take away the sins of the world by going to the cross, does give us every one of those joys the Gaudete propers have been suggesting, even when we don't see them. Christ *is* with us—in youth, in old age, in our darkest moments. He *is* strong for us when we are weak. We *will be vindicated* against those who oppress, even imprison, us. We may have to wait patiently and suffer, but we *will see* the Messianic Age in its fullness.

THE COMING OF THE ONE WHO IS TO COME DOES INDEED GIVE US REASON TO REJOICE— WHEN WE SEE THOSE REASONS *AND* WHEN WE DON'T.

"Let us now join in singing together our sermon hymn, the **Hymn of the Day**, 'Hark! A Thrilling Voice Is Sounding.' "

You're ready to sit back and hear a sermon on joy.

Fourth Sunday in Advent Year A

READINGS

Isaiah 7:10–17

Psalm 24 (antiphon: v 7)

Romans 1:1–7

Matthew 1:18–25

HYMN OF THE DAY

LSB 357 "O Come, O Come, Emmanuel"

It's been true all through Advent, but looking forward to Sunday morning this week, the Fourth (and final) Sunday in Advent, really means looking forward to Christmas. This week, our propers focus on the imminent arrival of the immanent God, Immanuel, God with us. It's an opportunity to prepare our hearts that we don't want to miss!

The **Hymn of the Day** for this Sunday, "O Come, O Come, Emmanuel" (*LSB* 357), not only picks up that key theme idea but also comes with a wonderful tool for our devotional preparation. Turn to the hymn in *Lutheran Service Book*. As you may know, it's a hymnic rendering of the historic "Great O Antiphons," which date back to perhaps the sixth century. See how the hymnal shows the days on which each is to be used. A delightful enhancement to your daily devotions could be to sing stanzas 1 and 2 and speak the "O Wisdom" antiphon on December 17, sing stanza 3 and speak "O Adonai" (Hebrew for "Lord") on December 18, and so on, concluding on December 23 by singing again stanza 1 and speaking "O Emmanuel." We'll intersperse these into our devotion-study here too.

Let's get started. Sing, maybe with family, stanzas 1 and 2 and then pray together the first O Antiphon, "O Wisdom."

Okay. Now very important in this Sunday's proclamation of Immanuel, God coming to be with us, is the remarkable *way* He chooses to come. Our first appointed proper, the **Introit**, raises this issue:

> *Oh that You would rend the heavens and come down, that the mountains might quake at Your presence.*

I wait for the Lord, *my soul waits, and in His word I hope; my soul waits for the Lord more than watchmen for the morning, more than watchmen for the morning. O Israel, hope in the* Lord*! For with the* Lord *there is steadfast love, and with Him is plentiful redemption. And He will redeem Israel from all his iniquities.*

Glory be to the Father and to the Son and to the Holy Spirit; as it was in the beginning, is now, and will be forever. Amen.

Oh that You would rend the heavens and come down, that the mountains might quake at Your presence. (Ps 130:5–8; antiphon: Is 64:1)

The antiphon (Is 64:1) will be the opening verse of the Old Testament Reading for Advent 1, Year B, next year. It's obviously a prayer for Advent, that the Lord would come down to His people. But notice the way Isaiah asks the Lord to come: powerfully, dramatically, shaking the mountains, reminiscent of what He did when He gave the Ten Commandments at Mount Sinai (Ex 19:16–20). Turns out that later, in Isaiah 64, the prophet rethinks his request for God to unleash His power. (More on that next year.) The psalmody, in fact, takes the tack to which Isaiah will eventually come around: "I wait for the Lord, my soul waits, and in His word I hope" (Ps 130:5). There's no less eagerness for the Lord to come; the longing is intense, like those who just can't wait for the sun to come up. But instead of looking for a power display, we wait, hoping simply in the Lord's Word, trusting His promise to come whenever and however He judges best. As we'll witness later today in our Gospel reading, He won't really come in an earthquake at all. Quite the opposite.

Sing now stanza 3 of *LSB* 357 and then pray the second O Antiphon, "O Adonai."

The way the Lord chooses to come must serve the purpose of His coming. An indication of that purpose is found in the **Collect** for this Sunday, the last of three "stir up" collects for Advent. Pray it with me:

Stir up Your power, O Lord, and come and help us by Your might, that the sins which weigh us down may be quickly lifted by Your grace and mercy; for You live and reign with the Father and the Holy Spirit, one God, now and forever. Amen.

Our prayer is that the Lord would come so "that the sins which weigh us down may be quickly lifted." How can that happen? By God quaking the mountains and blowing away all opposition? No! If God had come as Isaiah initially asked, we ourselves could only have been part of that opposition to be shattered. That's what sin makes us! Our prayer is that the Lord would lift our sin off our shoulders—and that could only happen if God came in a very different way. Certainly, His way of coming will be powerful ("Stir up Your power"); His help will be "by [His] might." But God's might, His power, will be veiled, hidden, so that we are shielded and it is turned against not us but against our real enemy. This we'll see yet more explicitly in the Gospel reading ahead.

Now sing stanza 4 of *LSB* 357 and pray the third O Antiphon, "O Root of Jesse."

It may be at the **Old Testament Reading** for Advent 4 that our sweetest imaginations really start to race toward Christmas. "Behold, the virgin shall conceive and bear a son, and shall call His name Immanuel" (Is 7:14). "O come! O come, Immanuel!" We all know the prophecy of the virgin birth; it used to make every Sunday School Christmas program. Do, though, look back at your Bible and read also the verses preceding our lesson (Is 7:1–9 as well as 10–17). The history here is crucial to understanding the prophecy.

Here's the situation: It's the 730s BC. Since the death of Solomon two centuries earlier, God's people have been divided into the Southern Kingdom, known as Judah, ruled by heirs of David and Solomon, and the Northern Kingdom, called simply Israel. For many of these years, they've already been at war, but now Israel has allied itself with Syria, a pagan country farther north, to attack Judah. Judah's king, the very wicked Ahaz, is terrified. So, despite Ahaz's unworthiness, the Lord sends Isaiah with just the news he needs: Yahweh will deliver you; the plans of Israel and Syria will be thwarted.

Then our reading: Through Isaiah, the Lord offers Ahaz a sign to confirm His message. The Lord even lets Ahaz pick the sign, any sign: "deep as Sheol or high as heaven" (7:11). Ahaz, unfortunately, declines God's gracious offer: "I will not put the Lord to the test" (7:12). Sounds pious (we *aren't* to test the Lord), but in reality, he didn't want God's help. He'd already decided to ask Assyria—the *really* big, bad power—to attack Israel and Syria for him. Ahaz wanted that unbridled show of might rather than whatever means of saving God would have in mind. (Read in 2 Kings 20:1–11 how different when, not many years later, Ahaz's son, very *good* King Hezekiah, *does* take the Lord up on His invitation to choose a sign. It's high as heaven, an astronomical miracle!)

So about that sign. If Ahaz ("O house of David") didn't want one he could see, God would instead give a sign no one would see until seven centuries later. Rather than a human father, the virgin's son would be the very Son of God, God Himself, coming to live on earth with us! The Hebrew *Immanu-el* gives us that English word *immanent*, which means "existing or operating within." And *el* is short for *Elohim*, Hebrew for "God." God existing, operating, within His creation as one of us. (By the way, don't be bothered by the different spellings "Immanuel" and "Emmanuel"; they mean the same. Ancient Hebrew had no vowels, so they're just best guesses added later.)

The grace and eternal genius of God! Ahaz insists on doing things his own way: relying on earthly might. God gives a sign of *His* way to save: the virgin birth—a mighty miracle, but not picked up on any seismograph—and it's blessed us ever since.

Sing stanza 5 of *LSB* 357 and pray the fourth antiphon, "O Key of David."

The key verse of the **Psalm** we addressed as the Verse of Advent 1 (Ps 24:7). This time, two additional notes: First, the immense irony that "the earth is the LORD's and the fullness thereof" (24:1), and yet He becomes a single fertilized cell inside Mary. Second, that only those may "ascend the hill of the LORD" who are clean and pure (24:3–4). We are clean, pure, only when sins are forgiven. That, as we've observed and will see again, is the purpose of Christ coming the way He did.

Now sing stanza 6 of *LSB* 357, along with the fifth O Antiphon, "O Dayspring."

Romans 1:1–7 may seem a surprising choice as the **Epistle** for Advent 4. It's the beginning of Paul's inspired treatise on justification, but by no means is it a cool academic prologue. Instead, it teaches us that the substance of Advent 4 is the essential basis of our forgiveness by God's grace that we receive through faith. Notice the implications of the virgin birth: Being born of Mary, Jesus is "descended from David according to the flesh" (1:3), a real human being who can take our place. But having no human father, He is also the Son of God (1:4)—and, crucially, not tainted with original sin, which is passed on by human fathers. Paul's point is that everything he's now going to write to the Romans, how we poor sinners are justified, right, with God, what we Lutherans call "the article on which the Church stands or falls," is dependent on Jesus being both God and sinless man—possible only by the virgin birth.

Sing now stanza 7 of *LSB* 357 and pray the sixth antiphon, "O King of Nations."

"Now the birth of Jesus Christ took place in this way." The **Holy Gospel** for Advent 4, Matthew 1:18–25, is as close as we can come to Christmas without being there. This part of the story is almost as familiar as Luke 2. Imagine the shock and hurt Joseph feels when Mary's pregnancy becomes known—though I've always appreciated my own mother's observation that quite marvelously Joseph *could* have believed his beloved: "You *are* the one-in-millions who's the fulfillment of Isaiah 7:14!" It took the angel in a dream to connect those very dots. (This, by the way, is the first of ten Old Testament prophecy fulfillments Matthew identifies.)

Besides setting straight for Joseph the once-in-all-history facts, the angel brings home to us the reason for it all—the very point Paul made in Romans, what we prayed for in the Collect, what Psalm 24 said we needed to ascended the Lord's hill: "You shall call His name Jesus, for He will save His people from their sins." "Jesus," "Yeshua," "Joshua": "Yahweh saves"—specifically, from our sins. That couldn't happen by God coming on strong like another quaking Sinai. It had to be God's way, an invisible miracle of the Holy Spirit worked in the womb of gentle Mary. By the virgin birth, God could come to be with us, to share our lives, to die for all human sin. And by that death and resurrection, we are reconciled to God so that He can be with us and we with Him forever.

THE PROPHECY FOR WHICH GOD'S PEOPLE WAITED IN HOPE IS NOW FULFILLED—THAT IN COMING HIS WAY, THE VIRGIN BIRTH, GOD IS WITH US!

Close with, again, stanza 1 of *LSB* 357 and the final O Antiphon, "O Emmanuel"—and count the days to Christmas!

The Nativity of Our Lord Years A, B, C

READINGS

Christmas Eve
Isaiah 7:10–14
Psalm 110:1–4
(antiphon: v 2a)
1 John 4:7–16
Matthew 1:18–25

Christmas Midnight
Isaiah 9:2–7
Psalm 96
(antiphon: v 2)
Titus 2:11–14
Luke 2:1–14 (15–20)

Christmas Dawn
Isaiah 62:10–12
Psalm 98
(antiphon: v 2)
Titus 3:4–7
Luke 2:(1–14) 15–20

Christmas Day
Isaiah 52:7–10
Psalm 2
(antiphon: v 7)
Hebrews 1:1–6 (7–12)
John 1:1–14 (15–18)

HYMNS OF THE DAY

LSB 359 "Lo, How a Rose E'er Blooming"

LSB 358 "From Heaven Above to Earth I Come"

LSB 375 "Come, Your Hearts and Voices Raising"

LSB 382 "We Praise You, Jesus, at Your Birth"

"But . . .
Mary treasured up all these things, pondering them in her heart." (Lk 2:19)

Merry Christmas! Or perhaps a merry last day or two looking forward to Christmas!

The last days before Christmas, and even Christmas Eve and Christmas Day themselves, are, quite unfortunately, not always the easiest days to stop and *ponder*. Frankly, if you're reading this on one of the last days before Christmas, I'm delighted and surprised. We all understand; we're so busy with last-minute baking and buying, racing and wrapping, that deep, contemplative thought just has to wait till after the bowl games. Even when we do plop down in the pew on Christmas Eve, it's hard to focus, hard to slow the mind down to listen, to reflect.

We've heard it all before. It's unlikely the Christmas texts are going to raise a news flash that grabs our attention. And yet, we know this is one of the biggies. Christ, the Savior, is born! We want our worship—hearing and receiving the Word of Bethlehem—to be what our Christmas is all about. We don't want Christmas to go by without savoring these eternal moments.

Well, it can be that passages of Scripture that are indeed quite familiar will be just what we need. The better, really, to ponder. Passages we know well already, that don't require processing lots of new information, can be right where our minds and hearts can dwell, treasure, consider more deeply. Christmas services are occasions to listen with eyes closed, to picture, and let the words themselves take us along. And there *is* so much more to discover. Let us suggest that

The Incarnation of Our God at Christmas Gives Us Enough to Ponder Not Only for Two Days or for a Short Season, but Also for Eternity.

Rather than our usual "looking forward to Sunday" approach, let's work with this idea that for this day of the year, less information but more contemplation is the goal. I'll just invite you to read—slowly, thoughtfully, aloud if you're several together—prayers and passages you've heard before. And then at church on Christmas Eve, Christmas morning, hear which of all these treasures the pastor opens up for you.

First, an explanation that *may be* more information. For the Nativity of Our Lord, the three-year lectionary doesn't offer different sets of propers for Years A, B, and C. Instead, for all three years, it gives the same four sets of full propers: a set for Christmas Eve, another for Christmas Midnight, a third for Christmas Dawn, and a fourth for Christmas Day. (See how they appear on the first page here.) In practice, most pastors mix and match. That is, at your Christmas Eve service, you may very well hear the Old Testament Reading for Christmas Midnight (Is 9:2–7), the Epistle for Christmas Day (from Hebrews 1), and the expanded Gospel lesson for Christmas Dawn (Lk 2:1–20).

For that reason, we're considering all four services together under the one rather broad theme introduced above, and we're only studying the Christmas propers in our discussions of Year A. (In Years B and C, you might want to turn back here and review what we've said.) This also means we're selecting just a few of the propers to address. Others you'll surely want to ponder on your own.

Let's begin with prayer, the **Collect for Christmas Eve**:

O God, You make us glad with the yearly remembrance of the birth of Your only-begotten Son, Jesus Christ. Grant that as we joyfully receive Him as our Redeemer, we may with sure confidence behold Him when He comes to be our Judge; through the same Jesus Christ, our Lord, who lives and reigns with You and the Holy Spirit, one God, now and forever. Amen.

The gladness of this yearly remembrance! Ponder the joy that Jesus' coming as Redeemer will hold for us when He comes again on the Last Day!

Read as our first lesson the **Holy Gospel for Christmas Day**, John 1:1–18.

"In the beginning was the Word, and the Word was with God, and the Word was God. . . . And the Word became flesh and dwelt among us, and we have seen His glory, glory as of the only Son from the Father, full of grace and truth" (1:1, 14). The beginning. Before there was a world, a universe, the first Scotch pine, the first man and woman, there was God. And His very Person—Second Person—was active to create all this, simply by speaking. The Word. The Creator of all things, the Creator of all flesh. And now He becomes flesh. One of us. God does not change. Ponder how He becomes a human being and never ceases to be God.

"We have seen His glory." So tiny, helpless, on a bed of straw. Glory? The glory of God Almighty? Mary, Joseph, the shepherds seeing the glory of God? Who built and moved mountains? Who turned on every star? There, in that manger?

Let us pray. The **Collect for Christmas Midnight**:

O God, You make this most holy night to shine with the brightness of the true Light. Grant that as we have known the mysteries of that Light on earth we may also come to the fullness of His joys in heaven; through the same Jesus Christ, Your Son, our Lord, who lives and reigns with You and the Holy Spirit, one God, now and forever. Amen.

Lights are always most beautiful in the darkness. At midday, we take the light for granted or look for shade. At night, we thrill to spot Orion's Belt and the Dippers. This time of year we darken the living room to admire the candles on the wreath and the thousand points of light on the tree. Ponder: What would we *not* know if not for the true Light? What was our darkness? Whom do we know who still lives in it?

But one holy night, the Light came: the **Old Testament Reading for Christmas Midnight**, Isaiah 9:2–7. Read and ponder.

"The people who walked in darkness have seen a great light; those who dwelt in a land of deep darkness, on them has light shined" (9:2). In this light, see what we *do* see: "For to us a child is born, to us a son is given; and the government shall be upon His shoulder, and His name shall be called Wonderful Counselor, Mighty God, Everlasting Father, Prince of Peace" (9:6).

See that? God is a child. But God is mighty. And God is for us. It's all clear now in the Light of Bethlehem. Ponder each of those magnificent names: When do you need a Wonderful Counselor? How good is it that the Mighty God is one of us?—and how amazing? Christ as Everlasting *Father*?

Dwell especially on this one: He is our Prince of Peace, the one who has put us at peace with God. Ponder how He did that: We by our sin were enemies of God. We had started the war, and we were hell-bent on continuing it. So committed to our wicked cause—ourselves—that we would kill Him for it. But ponder how He could turn that evil to good. Peace with God. Together again. If we are reconciled to the Source of Every Good, ponder what we have!

Pray the **Collect for Christmas Dawn**:

Most merciful God, You gave Your eternal Word to become incarnate of the pure Virgin. Grant Your people grace to put away fleshly lusts, that they may be ready for Your visitation; through Jesus Christ, our Lord, who lives and reigns with You and the Holy Spirit, one God, now and forever. Amen.

Christmas Dawn (that sounds early!) may be an occasion when we're reminded how fleshly we still are. Mom and Dad want to stay in bed. Kids may be thinking a bit materialistically. Each others' feelings may not be a high priority. There may even be an exchange of words that has nothing to do with peace on earth, goodwill toward men.

For a time like that, read two of the Christmas **Epistles**, both from one letter of St. Paul: Titus 2:11–14 and Titus 3:4–7.

Remember, we prayed for "grace to put away fleshly lusts"—and "the grace of God *has* appeared, bringing salvation for all people, training us to renounce ungodliness and worldly passions, and to live self-controlled, upright, and godly lives" (2:11–12). Ponder what that life looks like. Once we're finished saying all the "Merry Christmases" to friends and strangers, how will we love friends and strangers? And ponder who it is Paul is calling to live the godly life. It's not the old you. It's the you who's been "saved . . . by the washing of regeneration and renewal of the Holy Spirit" (3:5). The made-new-in-Baptism you. Ponder what the new you looks like.

Finally, pray the **Collect for Christmas Day**:

Almighty God, grant that the birth of Your only-begotten Son in the flesh may set us free from the bondage of sin; through Jesus Christ, Your Son, our Lord, who lives and reigns with You and the Holy Spirit, one God, now and forever. Amen.

The birth of the only Son of God. God has taken on human flesh. Just how He could do that we'll ponder for all eternity. But for now, let the miracle of the Incarnation invite you to ponder four last thoughts during this Christmas season and beyond.

First, without the incarnation of the Son of God, we could never be free from the bondage of sin. God had to become man in order to fulfill the demands the Law makes upon mankind, and yet the Savior had to be God for His sacrifice on the cross to be sufficient for all humanity. Ponder how much this means to each of us for eternity.

Second, each time you come to the altar during these holy days and throughout the year, ponder that you are receiving the Gift of Christmas.

Third, ponder that in seeing the Son of God incarnate, we are seeing what we were created to be: perfect in love, perfect in holiness—what we are being remade to be.

Fourth, ponder that the Son of God incarnate is how even in heaven we will see God. Even in heaven we can't expect to see God the Father. The one who was laid in the manger is the fullness of God that we will not only see but also hold and be held by. The fullness of God before us in the flesh—that we will certainly ponder for all eternity.

Now, the best for last. Read (if possible, aloud with loved ones) the **Holy Gospel for Christmas Midnight and Christmas Dawn**: Luke 2:1–20. May I even suggest you get out the old family Bible (or your smartphone or tablet) and read the King James Version. With Mary, treasure these things, and ponder them in your heart.

First Sunday after Christmas Year A

READINGS

Isaiah 63:7–14

Psalm 111 (antiphon: v 9a, b)

Galatians 4:4–7

Matthew 2:13–23

HYMN OF THE DAY

LSB 389 "Let All Together Praise Our God"

To us a child is born, to us a son is given; and the government shall be upon His shoulder. And His name shall be called Wonderful Counselor, Mighty God, Everlasting Father, Prince of Peace. Sing to the Lord a new song, for He has done marvelous things! (Is 9:6; Ps 98:1a)

The **Gradual** reminds us that when we come to church this Sunday, it will still be very much the season of Christmas. So will the hymns we'll no doubt sing. "Let all together praise our God," the **Hymn of the Day** shouts! "Today He opens heav'n again to give us His own Son." See? The First Sunday after Christmas is still "today" when it comes to our Christian celebration of Christmas! And the **Psalm** echoes, "Praise the LORD! . . . He sent redemption to His people" (Ps 111:1, 9a).

Perhaps, though, the Christmas rush has subsided sufficiently, maybe already by Christmas afternoon, that you've had a chance to relax a bit and think more about what the birth of Christ means for us. That's the goal of having Twelve Days of Christmas, including these Sundays.

The **Collect** for this First Sunday after Christmas includes a phrase that I think is an excellent cue for our further consideration of the (real!) true meaning of Christmas. Let's pray:

O God, our Maker and Redeemer, You wonderfully created us and in the incarnation of Your Son yet more wondrously restored our human nature. Grant that we may ever be alive in Him who made Himself to be like us; through Jesus Christ, our Lord, who lives and reigns with You and the Holy Spirit, one God, now and forever. Amen.

The phrase I'm focusing on is "made Himself to be like us." That, of course, is what the Son of God did when He took on human flesh. He identified with us. He put Himself in our place. As we go through the propers for this Sunday, we'll discover how consistently that idea is affirmed. More important—very important in the case of the Introit and the Gospel!—will be the comfort that offers us in the midst of this life's suffering.

If you were to hear the **Introit** cold this Sunday, you might well wonder if you were really in a Christmas service after all:

When Israel was a child, I loved him, and out of Egypt I called My son.

Thus says the Lord: "A voice is heard in Ramah, lamentation and bitter weeping. Rachel is weeping for her children; she refuses to be comforted for her children, because they are no more." Thus says the Lord: "Keep your voice from weeping, and your eyes from tears, for there is a reward for your work, declares the Lord, and they shall come back from the land of the enemy. There is hope for your future, declares the Lord, and your children shall come back to their own country."

Glory be to the Father and to the Son and to the Holy Spirit; as it was in the beginning, is now, and will be forever. Amen.

When Israel was a child, I loved him, and out of Egypt I called My son. (Jer 31:15–17; antiphon: Hos 11:1)

Perhaps you already recognize these passages and see the Christmas connection; Matthew will quote both Hosea 11 and Jeremiah 31 in our Gospel reading. But one step at a time.

The antiphon, in its original context, had a simple meaning. The Old Testament prophet Hosea has been rehearsing the long story of Yahweh's faithfulness despite Israel's adulteries. A foundational chapter in that story, of course, was God bringing Israel out of slavery in Egypt. It was early in the relationship; Israel is well characterized as "a child," and God graciously calls him "My son."

Then, "A voice is heard in Ramah. . . . Rachel is weeping for her children." Here Jeremiah is actually seeing God's people being deported to captivity in Babylon (see Jer 40:1). He uses as an illustration Rachel, one of the mothers of the original children of Israel (the beloved wife of Jacob, the mother of Joseph and Benjamin, already thirteen centuries before Jeremiah's time; Gen 29:1–30:24; 35:16–20). It's as if she is mourning her children being dragged off in chains. An unspeakable tragedy, as a mother who has lost a child might best understand.

Where's the Christmas? How does either Hosea or Jeremiah suggest that the Son of

God "made Himself to be like us," identified with us? It's coming.

The **Old Testament Reading** has a more explicit reference to the Lord identifying with us, putting Himself in our place. See if you can spot it: Isaiah 63:7–14.

Did you see it? This is another recounting of God's faithfulness ("steadfast love," 63:7) and His people's straying ("but they rebelled," 63:10). The Lord has been down this road with Israel again and again. But He keeps seeing them as His. "He became [aaagain!] their Savior"—and *"In all their affliction He was afflicted"* (63:9). There it is! The Lord so closely identifies with Israel that when they hurt, He hurts. And so He remembers His saving acts of old and comes to their rescue one more time (63:11–14).

This is how God has loved His people from eternity. This is the God who planned Christmas. Now you know what's coming!

Read the **Epistle**, Galatians 4:4–7.

Now it's Christmas! Just at the moment God determined best! Looking back, we can see some of what made that holy night in Bethlehem "the fullness of time." Caesar's census that moved the world and moved an otherwise anonymous young couple to the place the Christ had to be born (Mic 5:2). The pax Romana, the peace that the Roman Empire established, that would soon allow the Gospel to spread more quickly—along its excellent road system—than possible ever before in history. And surely there are as many invisible, spiritual factors of timing as there are precious souls won for eternity. God only knows how it was the fullness of time so that *you* would be saved.

God's Son, "born of woman, born under the law, to redeem those who were under the law, so that we might receive adoption as sons" (4:4–5). "Made Himself to be like us!" This is where God—and Christmas—has been headed from the beginning.

The eternal God, who made Mary, took her flesh. The God of Mount Sinai, who gave the Ten Commandments—all ten designed according to who and what He is (perfect love)—put Himself in a position where He would be condemned by His own Law. That is, He put Himself in our position, made Himself like us. And He did it to buy us back from our breaking of His Law.

The result? He's made us like Him! Sons! Which includes daughters. We are all sons of God as Christ is. "And because you are sons, God has sent the Spirit of His Son into our hearts, crying, 'Abba! Father!' " (4:6). We get to call the heavenly Father "Daddy." Might seem irreverent for us to say, but St. Paul didn't think so; that's what "Abba" means. Nor did Jesus; in His most desperate hour, that's what He called His Father too (Mk 14:36). We are all sons of God as Jesus is.

"And if a son, then an heir through God" (4:7). What's His is ours. What belongs to the Son now belongs to all the children. The unconditional love of the Father that the Son has received even infinitely before Day 1, each of us has. The rule over creation that is Christ's (Col 1:16), that was given to our first parents and was forfeited, is ours. The unending bliss of heaven that has always been the Son's now is shared by every son and daughter of God. The real true meaning of Christmas quite rightly includes gifts!

"Gift *exchange*," really. Because all that we have from the Son also means He received what we had to give. When the Son of God made Himself like us, He knew what He was also getting. We see that vividly in our **Holy Gospel**. Read Matthew 2:13–23.

"When *they* had departed . . ." We've skipped ahead, obviously. The wise men (we'll see them again for Epiphany) have come and gone, not disclosing to Herod where the Christ Child was to be found. And he's furious! A madman, he executed his favorite wife over a foolish jealousy, and as he neared death, he tried to murder all the nobles of the Jews so that weeping over them would fill the void when no one mourned for him. Any potential rival, even a baby "King of the Jews" (Mt 2:2), has to die!

Joseph, as solid and reliable as a husband and father could be, is warned in a dream, and he doesn't waste a minute. Good thing! Herod's soldiers could ride horseback from Jerusalem to Bethlehem in *minutes*!

Here, then, is why the Introit antiphon for this day quotes Hosea. The Holy Family will flee to Egypt and remain there until Herod is dead. So God will call His Son—not Israel this time, but Jesus—out of Egypt. See what we've discovered by now, though. Matthew takes Hosea's words to be a "type" (or a prefiguring) of Jesus. Why does that work? Because in a very real sense, Israel is Christ and Christ is Israel. The Son exchanged what was His for what was Israel's and what was Israel's for what was His. We see the blessing in this exchange.

But what about Jeremiah's prophecy, Rachel weeping? Herod's soldiers do arrive, and, just to be sure, Herod has them kill all baby boys in the area two and under (based on the wise men's report of their star's appearing, Mt 2:7). So now real mothers are weeping for their children who are no more. No mother wants that in exchange for anything!

When the Son makes Himself like us, we receive what's His. But that's because He takes what's ours. Ours is death. We might think it's innocent death, as when a child dies. But the fact is, every one of us from the moment of conception is sinful (Ps 51:5). We all deserve to die, and whether at two or ninety-two, we all will. That's what's ours.

And that's what Jesus took as He made Himself like us. He is all those children. The Father delivered His Son this time—but only so He wouldn't suffer quick, though tragic, death. Instead, He would suffer the prolonged agony of all human anguish for thirty-three years and then the tortures of eternal hell as He died on the cross so that every little boy and his mother and father and sisters could have what the Son has: suffering, but also the joy of the Father every day as we live now and then in new life that never ends. So the Introit concludes, "Keep your voice from weeping. . . . There is hope for your future, . . . and your children shall come back."

**God's Son
Made Himself to Be like Us
So That He Became
as the Children We Were
and We Become as the Son He Is.**

"He undertakes a great exchange, puts on our human frame, and in return gives us His realm, His glory, and His name, His glory, and His name" (*LSB* 389:4).

Holy Innocents and New Year Years A, B, C

READINGS

Holy Innocents
Jeremiah 31:15–17
Psalm 54 (antiphon: v 4)
Revelation 14:1–5
Matthew 2:13–18

New Year's Eve	New Year's Day
Isaiah 30:(8–14) 15–17	Numbers 6:22–27
Psalm 90:1–12 (antiphon: v 17)	Psalm 8 (antiphon: v 9)
Romans 8:31b–39	Galatians 3:23–29
Luke 12:35–40	Luke 2:21

HYMNS OF THE DAY

LSB 764 "When Aimless Violence Takes Those We Love"
LSB 899 "Across the Sky the Shades of Night"
LSB 900 "Jesus! Name of Wondrous Love"
LSB 896 "Now Greet the Swiftly Changing Year"

Many—perhaps most—of our churches have some sort of special observance of what for the moment we'll broadly call New Year. Commonly, it's a New Year's Eve evening service—either to end the year right or to begin the night's festivities in a wholesome way. A few congregations go head-to-head with the Rose Parade on New Year's morning. And some years, of course, New Year's Day or Eve falls on a Sunday, and congregations choose to use the propers for these days in lieu of the Christmas 1 appointments.

But there's really no universal or even standard way congregations handle this. There are full propers for New Year's Eve, which are often used for the evening service, certainly, but are sometimes also used on New Year's Day or a concurring Sunday, whether that's December 31 or January 1. There's also a full set of propers for New Year's Day, which is likewise used any of these days and times. And for our devotion-study here, we'll even add a closing note for blending in Holy Innocents, actually on the church calendar for December 28, as part of this mix. Finally, it will go almost without saying here, but surely will be evident in the sanctuary, that we are still very much in the season of Christmas. Many congregations will use this occasion to sing more favorite Christmas hymns.

We'll begin our looking forward with the propers for New Year's Eve, which are directed toward the last day on the Western secular calendar, the end of a year. Then we'll consider the propers for New Year's Day, which observe the eighth day in the young life of our Lord.

New Year's Eve, finding sacred significance in the secular day, marks the passing of time. The **Collect for New Year's Eve** summarizes this well:

Eternal God, we commit to Your mercy and forgiveness the year now ending and commend to Your blessing and love the times yet to come. In the new year, abide among us with Your Holy Spirit that we may always trust in the saving name of our Lord Jesus Christ, who lives and reigns with You and the Holy Spirit, one God, now and forever. Amen.

A year of God's grace is coming to an end, and the year to come is in His hands. The Lord Jesus has been our Savior in the past, extending to us God's mercy and forgiveness, and we trust Him for the same in the new year. So much ahead is uncertain, but we can always trust Jesus' saving name because the day He died on the cross can never be stricken from history. *That is certain!*

A sampling of key words from among the other propers for this day:

From the **Introit**: "Our help is in the name of the Lord, who made heaven and earth. . . . Oh sing to the LORD a new song, for He has done marvelous things! His right hand and His holy arm have worked salvation for Him. . . . He has remembered His steadfast love and faithfulness" (Ps 124:8; 98:1, 3a). Our help is in the Lord's strong arm, and it is steadfast, reliable. Notice, by the way, that Psalm 98, the "new song," is used extensively in the Christmas propers.

From the **Old Testament Reading**: "Inscribe it in a book, that it may be for the time to come as a witness forever. . . . Thus said the Lord GOD, the Holy One of Israel, 'In returning and rest you shall be saved; in quietness and in trust shall be your strength'" (Is 30:8, 15). The Lord is our strength for all time.

From the **Epistle**: "For I am *sure* that neither death nor life, nor angels nor rulers, nor things present nor things to come, nor powers, nor height nor depth, nor anything else in all creation, will be able to separate us from the love of God in Christ Jesus our Lord" (Rom 8:38–39). Whatever else may be, God's love in Christ Jesus is sure.

From the **Holy Gospel**: "You also must be ready, for the Son of Man is coming at an hour you do not expect" (Lk 12:40). We don't even know that there *will be* a new year!

But the word of the Lord most associated with New Year's Eve and the passing of time may well be the **Psalm** (which also is the basis for the **Gradual**). Read all of Psalm 90. You'll recognize it: "LORD, You have been our dwelling place in all generations. Before the mountains were brought forth, or ever You had formed the earth and the world, from everlasting to everlasting You are God. . . . For a thousand years in Your sight are but as yesterday when it is past, or as a watch in the night. . . . The years of our life are seventy, or even by reason of strength eighty; yet their span is but toil and trouble; they are soon gone, and we fly away. . . . So teach us to number our days that we may get a heart of wisdom" (Ps 90:1–2, 4, 10, 12).

If those words do sound familiar, it may well be because they are so beautifully paraphrased by hymnwriter Isaac Watts, and for our THEME for New Year's Eve we can do no better than to borrow from him (*LSB* 733):

OUR GOD, OUR HELP IN AGES PAST, IS OUR CERTAIN HELP AND STRENGTH FOR THE UNCERTAIN YEARS TO COME.

The celebration appointed for January 1 actually gives no explicit recognition to New Year's Day. Rather, it's observed as the Circumcision and Name of Jesus. The occasioning event is recorded immediately after Christ's beloved birth narrative as the lectionary's briefest **Holy Gospel**, Luke 2:21: "And at the end of eight days, when He was circumcised, He was called Jesus, the name given by the angel before He was conceived in the womb."

The two foci of the festival, Jesus' circumcision and His naming, are integrally related in a way that may not be obvious.

Circumcision, first, was the sign, very personal to every Israelite male, of God's Old Testament covenant. God had initiated this covenant with Abraham (Gen 17:9–14) and commanded it be marked for all baby boys on their eighth day (seventh by our counting; hence the celebration one week after Christmas). The covenant gave the blessings of being God's people; circumcision was the Old Testament sacrament. For their part, recipients of the covenant were obligated to keep God's ceremonial and civil law. (*All* people are obligated to keep His moral law!)

Therefore, several of the propers for this day refer to the Law. The **Introit** includes this: "I said, 'Behold, I have come; in the scroll of the book it is written of me: I desire to do Your will, O my God; Your law is within my heart'" (Ps 40:7–8). And the **Gradual**:

> *This is the covenant that I will make with the house of Israel after those days, declares the Lord: I will put My laws into their minds, and write them on their hearts. I will be their God, and they shall be My people. I will remember their sins and their lawless deeds no more. (Heb 8:10; 10:17)*

But already these are actually references to a *new* covenant. (Hebrews is quoting Jer 31:33–34, where the preceding 31:31 makes this clear.) In this new covenant, the Law is written on the heart, not on tablets of stone or cut into the body. That is, under the new covenant, "I *desire* to do [God's] will," rather than obeying His commands by coercion.

This Paul explains in the **Epistle**. Read Galatians 3:23–29. Formerly, "we were held captive under the law" (3:23). The law was "our guardian" (3:24). But "we are no longer under a guardian, . . . for as many of you as were baptized into Christ have put on Christ" (3:25, 27). That, not circumcision, is how we are now "Abraham's offspring" (3:29). In other words, circumcision and the entire Old Testament ceremonial (and civil) law were pointing to the coming of Christ.

Now at *His* circumcision, Jesus puts Himself under that (His own-given) law. Mary and Joseph do for Jesus what the law requires, and that is a must, because, to be our Savior, Jesus must fulfill in our place all the demands of the Law (and here we capitalize intentionally, because we don't mean just the ceremonial and civil law of Israel).

And there's yet more to it.

At His circumcision, Jesus is also given His name. That was customary, as a pastor may ask parents or sponsors at a Baptism today, "How is this child to be named?" For Jesus, though, the name meant much more.

The name of God is always significant. "O Lord, our Lord, how majestic is Your name in all the earth!" our **Psalm** exclaims (Ps 8:1, 9). See how the entire psalm exalts God's name; God's "name" stands for God Himself, so His name is seen as majestic when His magnificent works are recounted.

Look up also the **Old Testament Reading**, Numbers 6:22–27. At every Divine Service, we hear the very familiar Aaronic Benediction, but notice what follows: When Aaron (or your pastor) speaks these words, "So shall they put My name upon the people of Israel, and I will bless them" (6:27). When God's Word is spoken, it—and He!—does what it says. God blesses us, above all with peace (the Hebrew *shalom*), the condition of complete well-being that accrues when and only when God and man are at peace, reconciled. And all those blessings the benediction gives us because God's "name" is put upon us (6:27). Having God's name is having God Himself and all His blessings!

All this is understood on Jesus' eighth day. Remember that the name we speak as "Jesus" (*Yeshua* in Hebrew, often rendered as "Joshua") means "Yahweh saves." As the angel told Joseph, "You shall call His name Jesus, for He will save His people from their sins" (Mt 1:21, also the **Verse** for this day).

And it's here that the circumcision and naming of Jesus are conjoined. Consider carefully the **Collect for New Year's Day**:

Lord God, You made Your beloved Son, our Savior, subject to the Law and caused Him to shed His blood on our behalf. Grant us the true circumcision of the Spirit that our hearts may be made pure from all sins; through Jesus Christ, our Lord, who lives and reigns with You and the Holy Spirit, one God, now and forever. Amen.

What happens at a circumcision? Those few drops of blood are the first hint of what Jesus will do to save us from our sins.

The First Shedding of Jesus' Blood Is a Tiny Anticipation of the Shedding of Blood by Which He Will Live Up to His Name.

Do we see how Holy Innocents might be observed with this day? Read again what we've written about Matthew 2:13–18 in the previous chapter, Christmas 1. The boys of Bethlehem die, but Jesus is not really spared. He will die soon enough to save also them. Think about children killed by abortion. Then pray the **Collect for Holy Innocents**:

Almighty God, the martyred innocents of Bethlehem showed forth Your praise not by speaking but by dying. Put to death in us all that is in conflict with Your will that our lives may bear witness to the faith we profess with our lips; through Jesus Christ, our Lord, who lives and reigns with You and the Holy Spirit, one God, now and forever. Amen.

Second Sunday after Christmas Years A, B, C

READINGS

1 Kings 3:4–15
Psalm 119:97–104
(antiphon: v 99)
Ephesians 1:3–14
Luke 2:40–52

HYMN OF THE DAY

LSB 410 "Within the Father's House"

"The Word became flesh and dwelt among us, and we have seen His glory, glory as of the only Son from the Father, full of grace and truth." (Jn 1:14)

"Alleluia. The child grew and became strong, filled with wisdom. And the favor of God was upon Him. Alleluia" (Lk 2:40).

The antiphon to the **Introit** continues to announce Christmas. But the **Verse** for Christmas 2 tells us we're progressing. Jesus isn't a baby anymore; He's growing. By the end of our service today, He'll be twelve years old. (Many years, unfortunately, don't have two Sundays between December 25 and Epiphany, January 6—that is, when Christmas falls on a Sunday, Monday, or Tuesday. Hence only one set of propers for A, B, and C years. When we do have two, so much the better! More Christmas!)

Besides just setting the scene, the Introit antiphon and the Verse are two of the most likely places to find indications of the Sunday's theme. That's very much the case this week. Two key elements stand out in these two propers, and, sure enough, they'll turn out to be recurrent throughout all the propers of the day. The key elements we see already here are the Word and wisdom. So this week, let me guide our looking forward to Sunday morning by offering my THEME right up front:

IN THE WORD IS WISDOM.

Jesus, we know, is the Word who became flesh. But there's always a double entendre when we speak of Christ that way, because He's also the entire content of the written, inscripturated, Word. And our Gospel lesson today is the twelve-year-old Jesus in the temple discussing the Scriptures with the teachers, ending this way: "And Jesus increased in wisdom and in stature and in favor with God and man" (Lk 2:52). So we have the Word Incarnate—plenty of wisdom in Him. But we also have the Word of Holy Scripture, which imparts wisdom. There's wisdom in it too. In the Word is wisdom.

Let's explore that idea, beginning with the full Introit:

The Word became flesh and dwelt among us, and we have seen His glory, glory as of the only Son from the Father, full of grace and truth.

Praise the LORD! For it is good to sing praises to our God; for it is pleasant, and a song of praise is fitting. Great is our Lord, and abundant in power; His understanding is beyond measure. But the LORD takes pleasure in those who fear Him, in those who hope in His steadfast love. Praise the LORD, O Jerusalem! Praise your God, O Zion!

Glory be to the Father and to the Son and to the Holy Spirit; as it was in the beginning, is now, and will be forever. Amen.

The Word became flesh and dwelt among us, and we have seen His glory, glory as of the only Son from the Father, full of grace and truth. (Ps 147:1, 5, 11–12; antiphon: Jn 1:14)

John 1:14 we heard as the climactic moment in the Gospel lesson for Christmas Day, and we discussed the passage briefly then. Christ as the Word reminds us that the eternal Son of God is the one by whom the Father acts in His creation. God created the universe by speaking (Gen 1:3; Heb 11:3); John attributes that to the Son (Jn 1:3). Throughout the Old Testament, God's appearances to speak to His people are almost certainly the Son, often identified as "the angel of the LORD" (e.g., Gen 16:7–13; Ex 3:1–4; Judg 13:3, 15–22). And when the fullness of time comes for God to enter into His world, it is the Son who becomes incarnate. Thus every word Jesus speaks is the Word of God. Likewise, everything He *did*, His atoning death, even His fleshly living and breathing, reveals who God is, so that's the Word of God too (1 Jn 1:1–3).

It takes more than human wisdom to understand this. The Introit tells us that "His understanding is beyond measure." But we are wise *enough* when we fear and trust the Word: "His understanding is beyond measure. But the LORD takes pleasure in those who fear Him, in those who hope in His steadfast love."

The **Collect** for this Sunday also connects the Word with wisdom:

Almighty God, You have poured into our hearts the true Light of Your incarnate Word. Grant that this Light may shine forth in our lives; through the same Jesus Christ, Your Son, our Lord, who lives and reigns with You and the Holy Spirit, one God, now and forever. Amen.

Here wisdom is seen in the true Light. The Light, of course, is again the incarnate Word. The Son of God appearing in the flesh enables us to see God as the loving Redeemer He is; He turns on the light, so to speak. Seeing God rightly is true wisdom.

One last time, we hear the **Gradual** for the Christmas season:

> *To us a child is born, to us a son is given; and the government shall be upon His shoulder. And His name shall be called Wonderful Counselor, Mighty God, Everlasting Father, Prince of Peace. Sing to the Lord a new song, for He has done marvelous things! (Is 9:6; Ps 98:1a)*

This Sunday, we might especially appreciate our Child as Wonderful Counselor. How confusing are the news stories, the fake news, the scientific theories, the scientific "facts," the freeways, the bus routes, the boy-meets-girl thrills, the boy-loses-girl depressions, the whys of lost loved ones, the medical diagnoses, the medical bills, the job offers, the rejection e-mails, the advice of friends, the appointment schedules, the unscheduleds? Imagine facing all these thinking, "I'm my only final source of wisdom"! Imagine the false counselors I might follow! Many of us know! We've followed lots of them. And all those who don't know the Wonderful Counselor really do have only their own wisdom to explain their world.

It is a marvelous thing God has done, ordering all things for our good! It is a marvelous thing Christ has done, enlightening us to see that! *Marvelous.* We often use this word simply to mean "really great!" or "real good!" But *marvelous* is a wisdom word. We *marvel* that God's wisdom really is able to make sense out of all our mess!

Now the lessons for the day. Read the **Old Testament Reading**, 1 Kings 3:4–15.

Solomon receives quite the Christmas gift: you name it (though, often overlooked, is that God *doesn't* promise He'll *give* Solomon anything he might ask). Solomon realizes that there's so much more out there to understand than he does: "I am but a little child. I do not know . . ." (3:7). So he—wisely—asks for wisdom. And not for his own glory, but so that he can care for God's people (3:9). Not only does God delight to give Solomon the wisdom for which he is still famous three millennia later, but He also tacks on lots more (3:12–14).

What was Solomon's wisdom? He himself tells us: "The fear of the Lord is the beginning of wisdom" (Prov 9:10). And Solomon knows who that Lord is. He knows very well that he is occupying the throne of his father, David, only until the fulfillment of the house of David, the true Solomon (*Shalom*), comes (2 Sam 7:11b–17; see also Gen 49:10, where it may read "until Shiloh comes," another form of the Hebrew *shalom*). In *that* Son of David is wisdom.

The **Psalm** for the Second Sunday after Christmas now directs us to wisdom in the Word of Scripture. Read Psalm 119:97–104. Psalm 119 is one of the "Torah Psalms." The Hebrew *torah* is usually translated "law," but don't misunderstand. The Torah, often also equated with the Pentateuch, the first five books of the Old Testament, is the very foundation for what we call Gospel. "Oh," the psalmist says, "how I love Your law [*torah,* also "commandments," "testimonies," "precepts," "rules," and "words"]!" Quite emphatically, he loves to study the Bible! Why? It makes him "wiser than [his] enemies," to "understand more than the aged" (119:98, 100). Experience is an excellent teacher, but not as insightful as Holy Scripture. "I [even] have more understanding than all my teachers" (119:99). Do you see a boy in the temple?

The **Epistle** raises another challenge that will always exceed our wisdom: election and predestination. Read Ephesians 1:3–14. No, we're not going to explain it here or anytime else in this life—why some are predestined for salvation and others are not. We might not understand it in heaven either. It's way above our "wisdom grade." Yet, "in all wisdom and insight," God is "making known to us the mystery of His will." That is, He's giving us whatever wisdom, insight into "His purpose," we need. And His purpose *"He set forth in Christ"* (1:8–9). No, we won't understand predestination, but count the number of times in these verses God says it is "in" or "through" Christ. I count eleven. If predestination, however it works, is in Christ and the "redemption through His blood" shed on the cross (1:7), then we can be sure it is also "in love" (1:4–5). Believing that, we are wise!

Finally, it was the **Holy Gospel** that got us here. It begins and ends with wisdom, and everywhere in between is the Word—incarnate and inscripturated. Read Luke 2:40–52.

Such a great story! And it's the only mention of Jesus' years from infancy until He begins His ministry. Passover, we remember, was the commemoration of God delivering His people from slavery in Egypt (Exodus 12), more than 1,400 years before the birth of Christ but commanded by God to be observed every year. When Jesus' parents discover He has stayed behind, they—in panic, no doubt—look, no doubt, in all the places you'd expect to find a twelve-year-old boy. Why should the temple be the last place?

Jesus' wisdom and understanding with the teachers (that's right, Ps 119:99) is amazing, astonishing (2:47, 48). He is, after all, the Word of God. He is the Son in His Father's house, thoroughly at home in the family business (compare translations of 2:49).

But notice, He not only answers questions wisely (2:47) but also asks and listens. His questions might have been Socratic teaching, leading toward answers He already knew. And most certainly the divine Son is all knowing. But remember that during His state of humiliation, Christ used His divine powers only when doing so served His saving mission, never for His own convenience. Remember, too, the closing verse: "Jesus *increased* in wisdom" (2:52). Jesus learned! His mission, His cross, became clearer to Him. Most likely, His questions really were to gain further understanding. What He surely knew—perhaps from the Torah Psalms!—was that the Scriptures were the place to gain wisdom. These same Scriptures we have for our study. In them is wisdom—because they speak of Him in whom is all wisdom.

Close by singing the **Hymn of the Day**, "Within the Father's House" (*LSB* 410), noting especially stanzas 2, 3, and 5.

The Epiphany of Our Lord Years A, B, C

READINGS

Isaiah 60:1–6
Psalm 72:1–11 (12–15) (antiphon: v 18)
Ephesians 3:1–12
Matthew 2:1–12

HYMN OF THE DAY

LSB 395 "O Morning Star, How Fair and Bright"

The Epiphany of Our Lord is a rich occasion, which—like the Second Sunday of Christmas, the dual New Year's possibilities (New Year's Eve and New Year's Day, the Circumcision and Name of Jesus), Holy Innocents, and even the various sets of propers for Christmas—may not always receive its due. Surely that's not for lack of interest. Every pastor and every congregation would love to hear every year the story of the star, the wise men, and the toddler Jesus with gold, frankincense, and myrrh. As throughout the Christmas season, it's a matter of the vagaries of the calendar—and an overabundance of wonderful material.

The Day of Epiphany is January 6, the day after the twelfth day of Christmas. That much is set. And some congregations do have an annual Epiphany service on that day, regardless of the day of the week on which it falls. However, for those six out of seven years when January 6 is not a Sunday, most congregations have to make a choice. Will they use the propers for the Epiphany of Our Lord on either the Sunday before the 6th (omitting Christmas 2 or even Christmas 1) or the Sunday after? Or will they skip Epiphany altogether and proceed on to the propers for the First Sunday after the Epiphany? The latter is a not-to-be-missed festival in itself: the Baptism of Our Lord. Decisions, decisions!

My observation is that most congregations now choose to celebrate the Baptism and omit the Epiphany. My own practice as a parish pastor was always to use the Epiphany propers on the Sunday closest after January 6, but then to observe the Baptism of Our Lord on the following Sunday, actually the Second Sunday after the Epiphany. It was a way of maximizing the Christmas season since, of course, the wise men are still part of the full nativity narrative of Christ—still a Sunday for Christmas hymns along with Epiphany ones. I would then choose one of the later Sundays of the Epiphany season to omit, getting back on track at latest by Transfiguration. One way or another, it seems Epiphany should be celebrated every year.

The coming of the wise men to worship little Jesus is well named Epiphany. The word *epiphany* comes from the Greek ἐπιφαίνω (*epiphaino*), "to show forth," "to appear," with its root, φαίνω, meaning "to shine," "to bring to light," and the prefix ἐπι, "upon." Thus an epiphany refers very literally to "a shining upon," a manifestation, something that can be observed, or a revealing, making known. Epiphany is all about revealing Jesus.

The **Introit** introduces us to this idea and begins to suggest what is being shown forth about the Christ:

I will cause Your name to be remembered in all generations; therefore nations will praise You forever and ever.

Your throne, O God, is forever and ever. The scepter of Your kingdom is a scepter of uprightness; You have loved righteousness and hated wickedness. Therefore God, Your God, has anointed You with the oil of gladness beyond Your companions; Your robes are all fragrant with myrrh and aloes and cassia.

Glory be to the Father and to the Son and to the Holy Spirit; as it was in the beginning, is now, and will be forever. Amen.

I will cause Your name to be remembered in all generations; therefore nations will praise You forever and ever. (Ps 45:6–8a; antiphon: Ps 45:17)

"I will cause Your name to be remembered"—to shine forth, be known, revealed. Psalm 45 was probably a celebration of the marriage of Solomon. It clearly looks toward the Messiah, of whom Solomon is a type.

Specifically, Solomon prefigures Christ as King of God's people: "Your throne, O God, is forever and ever. The scepter of Your kingdom is a scepter of uprightness. . . . Therefore God, Your God, has anointed You." Anointing with oil designated a man to be king (or priest). The Hebrew that gives us our word *Messiah* and the Greek that we render as *Christ* both mean "anointed one."

And while Solomon and Christ were kings of Israel, "*nations* will praise You forever and ever." The "nations" were seen by Israel as enemies, Gentiles, not the people of God. St. Paul will elaborate in our Epistle what a revelation—even shocking—it would be that the Messiah would be the King also of the Gentiles.

Oh, and while we're still on the Introit for Epiphany, don't overlook that the Messiah's "robes are all fragrant with myrrh."

The **Collect** for Epiphany begins to picture the story we'll hear in the Holy Gospel as it amplifies the revelation we just saw in the Introit:

> *O God, by the leading of a star You made known Your only-begotten Son to the Gentiles. Lead us, who know You by faith, to enjoy in heaven the fullness of Your divine presence; through the same Jesus Christ, our Lord, who lives and reigns with You and the Holy Spirit, one God, now and forever. Amen.*

We know we'll hear about the star. And it will be Gentile wise men who follow it.

The better we know that story of the wise men, the more our ears will perk up as we hear the Old Testament Reading and the Psalm.

Read Isaiah 60:1–6. Where did you see magi and Bethlehem? Light . . . nations . . . kings . . . camels . . . gold and frankincense! (And remember, we've already smelled the myrrh.) Won't it be exciting to sit down in heaven with Isaiah and ask, "Was it like God giving you movie previews of Jesus?" Between 7:14; 9:6; 52:13–53:12, et cetera, et cetera, et cetera, it seems he got to see at least all the highlights. "No," he'll tell us, "I had to ask Micah *where* He was going to be born." (It is likely, by the way, that the two eighth-century prophets did compare notes. See Is 2:1–4; Micah 4:1–3; and Micah 5:2.)

Some of what we read in Isaiah's vision and in Psalm 72 may actually be as formative in our imagination of the wise men as is the actual account in Matthew. Read the psalm and, again, picture. As with our Introit, Psalm 72 honors the king of Israel, Solomon. He will "have dominion from sea to sea, and from the River to the ends of the earth!" (72:8)—that is, well beyond the borders of Israel. The king of Israel will be king of all nations. In fact, "the kings of Tarshish and of the coastlands render him tribute; may the kings of Sheba and Seba bring gifts!"—even the "gold of Sheba" (there's that gold again, 72:15). "May all kings fall down before him" (72:10–11). A vivid type of the Christ.

Be aware, though, that visions of prophets and psalmists *aren't* really movie clips, especially not clips of documentaries or movie newsreels. They're images that communicate a message without intending to convey every detail. To wit, these two Old Testament passages have formed in many people's (and artists') minds the assumption that the wise men who brought gifts to the Messiah were kings. Almost surely not—certainly Matthew's account suggests otherwise—and Isaiah and the psalmist didn't mean to suggest that they were. Through the centuries, kings of many nations have indeed worshiped the messianic King—but probably not that day in Bethlehem.

So the propers have shined a light for us to see the Christ as King and as King of all peoples. In case that strikes us as Captain Obvious, St. Paul in the **Epistle** declares what an epiphany—what an eye-opener!—that truly was! Read Ephesians 3:1–12.

Paul reminds that his ministry is "on behalf of you Gentiles" (3:1). That's familiar enough to us now. But see that four times in our reading he speaks of a "mystery" (3:3, 4, 6, 9). And the mystery is specifically "that the Gentiles are fellow heirs, members of the same body, and partakers of the promise in Christ Jesus through the gospel" (3:6). We probably do take that for granted now, but it "was not made known to the sons of men in other generations" (3:5). It was "hidden for ages in God" (3:9). Most of God's faithful people simply had no idea that salvation was also intended for the Gentiles, that the Christ was their King too. This was a radical concept, an entirely new world view. Only now, in "the manifold wisdom of God" (3:10), was it time for that to be made known, time for the epiphany. For any of us Christians who are not of Jewish descent, this is nothing less than heaven and deliverance from hell!

The Old Testament anticipates. St. Paul fully unpacks. But the actual epiphany was in the Epiphany, the event recorded in the **Holy Gospel**. Read Matthew 2:1–12.

We really don't know much about the wise men—their names (though tradition has given them names), where they were from (just "the east"), when they came (surely not on Christmas Day, since they came not to a manger scene but to a "house," 2:11), even how many there were (three is just the number of different gifts). The term *magi* (μάγοι) refers to a class of advisers to the royalty of Babylon and Persia (but who were not themselves kings) who studied the stars. And that, of course, is what set them in motion. God created a unique "shining upon" to catch their eye (quite possibly after their reading of Num 24:17, which the Jews' exile to Babylon centuries earlier supplied them).

When the magi arrived in Jerusalem, in the days of Herod, the illegitimate "king of the Jews" (actually not Jewish by lineage at all, but Idumaean), they asked, "Where is He who has been born king of the Jews?" Here is the very point of the story, for these Gentiles had "come to worship Him" (2:2). Their coming in itself could have been meaningless; they might have presumed to worship a king who cared nothing for them. But the stars of this showing forth are not the wise men. The star is the "star," because it was placed in the sky by God Himself. God causing the star to shine was God announcing over the whole earth that the child born in Bethlehem was King not just of the Jews but of all.

There was the ultimate epiphany of this day: that the King, the King of all nations, was *this little boy*. This Jesus is the King. And there's much more to discover about Him.

The Coming of the Wise Men Is Just the Beginning of the Epiphany, the Revealing, of Our Lord.

Over the coming Sundays, the season of Epiphany, much more will be revealed about this Jesus—until the time for Him to begin His final trek to the cross. There everything revealed about Him will be fulfilled. Until then, the **Gradual** anticipates further reasons we'll see to extol this Jesus:

> *Praise the Lord, all nations! Extol Him, all peoples! For great is His steadfast love toward us, and the faithfulness of the Lord endures forever. Ascribe to the Lord the glory due His name; bring an offering, and come into His courts! (Ps 117:1–2a; Ps 96:8)*

The Baptism of Our Lord Year A

READINGS

Isaiah 42:1–9
Psalm 29 (antiphon: v 3)
Romans 6:1–11
Matthew 3:13–17

HYMN OF THE DAY

LSB 406, 407 "To Jordan Came the Christ, Our Lord"

The season of Epiphany began with a great epiphany indeed: God's special star shining upon the toddler Jesus, so that Gentile wise men traversed afar and worshiped Him as also their King. That event sets the direction for the whole season, because each Sunday will include new or amplified revelations, showings forth, of Jesus and His glory.

The **Gradual** for the season of Epiphany:

> *Praise the Lord, all nations! Extol Him, all peoples! For great is His steadfast love toward us, and the faithfulness of the Lord endures forever. Ascribe to the Lord the glory due His name; bring an offering, and come into His courts! (Ps 117:1–2a; 96:8)*

The First Sunday after the Epiphany is dedicated to the Baptism of Our Lord, the remembrance of Jesus' Baptism by John the Baptist in the Jordan River. It will manifest Jesus' glory in a very special such revelation.

The propers for this day are nearly the same for Years A, B, and C; only the Old Testament Reading and Holy Gospel vary year to year. The overlaps are likely a concession that congregations may not observe the Baptism every year; when January 6 falls late in a week, near Sunday—say, on a Friday or Saturday—they may choose to use the propers for the Day of Epiphany on that Sunday instead. Choosing either one over the other is unfortunate. See in the last chapter my discussion of finding plenty of room for both festivals every year.

What is common to all three years, whether retold by Matthew, Mark, or Luke, is Jesus coming to the Jordan to be baptized by John, giving the clearest trinitarian appearance in the Bible. Immediately after the Baptism, the Holy Spirit descends upon Jesus in the form of a dove and God the Father speaks from heaven, proclaiming Jesus to be His beloved Son with whom He is well pleased. Thus the **Verse** for all three years: "Alleluia. You are My beloved Son; with You I am well pleased. Alleluia" (Mk 1:11b).

Because so many of the propers are the same for all three years of the lectionary, we'll look for our themes in those propers that do vary. But first, we'll consider the elements that won't change.

The **Introit** for the Baptism of Our Lord is unchanging among the three years:

> *Behold My servant, whom I uphold, My chosen, in whom My soul delights.*
>
> *I will tell of the decree: The Lord said to me, "You are My Son; today I have begotten You. Ask of Me, and I will make the nations Your heritage, and the ends of the earth Your possession. You shall break them with a rod of iron and dash them in pieces like a potter's vessel." Now therefore, O kings, be wise; be warned, O rulers of the earth. Serve the Lord with fear, and rejoice with trembling, for His wrath is quickly kindled. Blessèd are all who take refuge in Him.*
>
> *Glory be to the Father and to the Son and to the Holy Spirit; as it was in the beginning, is now, and will be forever. Amen.*
>
> *Behold My servant, whom I uphold, My chosen, in whom My soul delights. (Ps 2:7–11, 12c; antiphon: Is 42:1a)*

The obvious connection to Jesus' Baptism is the psalm declaring, "You are My Son" and Isaiah adding that the Lord's "soul delights" in Him. More subtly, that the antiphon comes from the first "Servant Song" in Isaiah is an Old Testament indication of the Trinity, that Yahweh has a Servant who is also Himself Yahweh. Verse 1b, not quoted in the antiphon, even adds mention of the Spirit. (A side point of interest: including the Gloria Patri ["Glory be to the Father and to the Son and to the Holy Spirit . . ."] in every introit is a confession that the God of the Old Testament psalms is the same triune God seen so transparently in the New Testament.)

As is so often the case on festival days, the **Collect** prays explicitly about the event of the celebration and asks God to apply it to our lives:

> *Father in heaven, at the Baptism of Jesus in the Jordan River You proclaimed Him Your beloved Son and anointed Him with the Holy Spirit. Make all who are baptized in His name faithful in their calling as Your children and inheritors with Him of everlasting life; through the same Jesus Christ, our Lord, who lives and reigns with You and the Holy Spirit, one God, now and forever. Amen.*

Notice that the address and acknowledgment (the first sentence of the prayer) identify all three persons of the Trinity. Then notice that the Baptism of Jesus is intimately joined to our own Baptism: "At the Baptism of Jesus . . . make all who are baptized in His name." It is by our Baptism that we become God's "children and inheritors with [Jesus] of everlasting life."

The ear-catching connection of the **Psalm** to the narrative of Jesus' Baptism is "the voice." Read Psalm 29, with special attention to verse 3. God's voice *booms*—specifically, "over the waters." The threefold "ascribe to the LORD" (29:1–2a) may be a reference to the three persons of the Trinity. (Compare, for example, Is 6:3: "Holy, holy, holy.") In any case, the Father's booming voice over the Jordan River certainly ascribes to His Son glory and strength: "I am well pleased" with Him!

Finally, the **Epistle** for the Baptism of Our Lord is also the same for Years A, B, and C. Read Romans 6:1–11.

St. Paul writes explicitly about our Baptism, but the Baptism of Jesus is certainly assumed to be foundational. The assumption is that by our Baptism, we are united with Jesus. In other words, what we go through in our Baptism, He went through in His. By Baptism, we die with Jesus (6:3). By Baptism, we are raised with Jesus (6:5). By Baptism, therefore, we also live with—and in and like—Jesus (6:4, 8).

While this Epistle corroborates well with the Gospel readings for all three years, one element is particularly germane to the emphasis that Year A's Holy Gospel will bring out. Paul's actual argument in this lesson is that we Christians are to live a new kind of life—a righteous and holy life. "Are we to continue in sin that grace may abound? By no means!" (6:1). No way! If we've died with Christ in our Baptism, it means that "our old self was crucified with Him in order that the body of sin might be brought to nothing, so that we would no longer be enslaved to sin" (6:6). By our Baptism, we share in Christ's righteousness. Our lives should no longer be lives of sin but should be lived righteously, abounding in good works. Jesus will explain in our Gospel lesson how His Baptism would work this.

Now the **Old Testament Reading** for this day is unique to Year A. Read Isaiah 42:1–9.

As we observed earlier, this lesson is the first of four Servant Songs in Isaiah: "Behold My servant" (42:1; see the other three in 49:1–13; 50:4–11; 52:13–53:12). In each of these, a "servant of the LORD" is described or speaks, and over the four songs His identity becomes progressively more clear as none other than the Messiah, Yahweh Himself, Jesus Christ.

In this first song, the Servant is pictured as gentle, caring for the weak, saving: "He will not cry aloud or lift up His voice, or make it heard in the street; a bruised reed He will not break, and a faintly burning wick He will not quench." He will "open the eyes that are blind, . . . bring out the prisoners from the dungeon, from the prison those who sit in darkness" (42:2–3a, 7). All this He will accomplish when "He will bring forth justice to the nations. . . . [He will] faithfully bring forth justice. . . . [He] has established justice in the earth" (42:1c, 3c, 4b). Back in our devotion-study for Advent 2, we saw that "justice" is not a terrifying word when the Lord is bringing justice to those who realize they are like a "bruised reed" or a "faintly burning wick" or like "prisoners"—helpless and in need of a gentle stroke. On the contrary, for the helpless who cling to Him in faith, God's justice is to save them. This is His righteous judgment. And this is the mission of Yahweh's Servant: "I am the LORD; I have called you in righteousness" (42:6). The Messiah is righteous to deliver God's righteousness.

See how Matthew's account of the Baptism of Jesus brings this to focus: our **Holy Gospel**, Matthew 3:13–17.

While the event of Jesus' Baptism—the Baptism itself, the appearance of the Holy Spirit, and the voice of the Father—are common to all three synoptic Gospels (Matthew, Mark, and Luke, the Gospels that, unlike John, "see together" much of the same material), Matthew alone gives us the dialogue between Jesus and John. This is telling. John tries to prevent Jesus from being baptized because he (John) is sinful, while Jesus is not. Jesus has nothing to repent; John knows that he needs Jesus' forgiveness! But Jesus replies, "Let it be so now, for thus it is fitting for us to fulfill all righteousness" (3:15).

Christ's entire mission—going all the way back to our fall in the Garden of Eden—was to fulfill what mankind had failed to do and thus separated ourselves from God. To do that, He had to put Himself in our place ("born of woman, born under the law, to redeem those who were under the law," Gal 4:4–5). If we were sinful, Jesus had to assume the position. He could not, as John had thought, remain in His sinlessness above the fray. Not if He was to save us.

So now Jesus goes forth to fulfill all righteousness for us, to keep the Law perfectly in our place. His next stop (which we'll hear about on the First Sunday in Lent) will be in the wilderness, where He will resist temptations as we failed to do. Finally, He will fulfill all righteousness by taking upon Himself the righteous punishment for all sin. On the cross, the heavenly Father will pour out His wrath on His own Son.

Ironically, that is entirely consistent with the Father's words this day: "My beloved Son, with whom I am well pleased." For from all eternity, the Father has been loving, has been pleased with, the Son—and the Holy Spirit has been declaring that love to the world. That's the nature of the Holy Trinity. But on this day, the Father was expressing His pleasure specifically with the Son taking on, at His Baptism, the place of sinful man—to redeem sinful man finally by going to that horrific cross. The voice and the dove reveal that the Father and the Spirit fully endorse this! Thus this day,

JESUS' BAPTISM IS AN EPIPHANY OF HIS FULFILLING ALL RIGHTEOUSNESS ON BEHALF OF THE HOLY TRINITY.

To conclude, sing the **Hymn of the Day**, *LSB* 406 or 407. Appreciate the way Luther interweaves the story of Jesus' Baptism with the meaning of our Baptism.

Second Sunday after the Epiphany Year A

READINGS

Isaiah 49:1–7
Psalm 40:1–11 (antiphon: v 3)
1 Corinthians 1:1–9
John 1:29–42a

HYMN OF THE DAY

LSB 402 "The Only Son from Heaven"

The word *epiphany*, we remember, means "a shining upon," "a showing forth," "a revealing," and so far this Epiphany season, we've seen Jesus revealed by some remarkable events—a star leading the wise men to come bearing gifts and Jesus' Baptism in the Jordan River with the Father and the Holy Spirit giving their dramatic endorsements. Much of what we learn about Jesus is shown forth in events, things He does.

However, this particular year, Year A in the three-year lectionary, each of our remaining Epiphany Sundays will reveal Jesus by what He *says*, or *what's said about Him*. The Holy Gospels for Epiphany Year B, which are primarily from Mark, will shine upon Jesus almost exclusively by reporting His actions. But Matthew's Gospel shows a special interest in the preaching of Jesus. So this year, as all but one of our Gospel lessons come from Matthew, Jesus' ongoing epiphanies will be mostly through words, either His or, this week, from His devoted forerunner. (Luke in Year C, by the way, will offer a balanced mix of words and actions.) This week's Gospel reading happens to be the one which, this year, is not from Matthew, but John certainly leads into this focus on words that we'll see in the coming Sundays.

The emphasis on words is evident from the very first, well, words of the **Introit**:

> *Let the words of my mouth and the meditation of my heart be acceptable in Your sight, O Lord, my rock and my redeemer.*
>
> *The heavens declare the glory of God, and the sky above proclaims His*

handiwork. Day to day pours out speech, and night to night reveals knowledge. There is no speech, nor are there words, whose voice is not heard. Their measuring line goes out through all the earth, and their words to the end of the world. In them He has set a tent for the sun.

Glory be to the Father and to the Son and to the Holy Spirit; as it was in the beginning, is now, and will be forever. Amen.

Let the words of my mouth and the meditation of my heart be acceptable in Your sight, O Lord, my rock and my redeemer. (Ps 19:1–4a, b; antiphon: Ps 19:14)

More than a few pastors have begun every sermon by praying the antiphon, Psalm 19:14. Not only is it a most appropriate petition for our preaching, but it meaningfully frames the rest of the Introit in between.

The portion of Psalm 19 in between talks about proclamation of another sort, actually without words. All creation ("the heavens," "the sky"), the psalmist David says, shouts out that there is a God who made all this. The ordered marvels of the universe "declare," "proclaim," God's "handiwork." David goes so far as to call this "speech," even "words." These "words" are heard "to the end of the world." It's true—no matter where on planet Earth one lives, no matter what else one hears, whether Christian or unbeliever, everyone hears this "voice." Though some try to deny it, creation shouts that there is a God.

But this voice is not really speaking words, and that's important. The witness of the universe—what we call general revelation—can indeed bring anyone to believe that there is a god, but it reveals only that He is mighty and mighty smart. It cannot reveal how He feels about us. And to know there's One out there powerful enough and smart enough to create a universe but not know whether He's pleased or angry with me is actually a terrifying thought. My best guess, based only on general revelation, is that I have to get myself in good with Him, earn His pleasure. That's the way things naturally work in our world.

To know instead that the Creator God loves me and is gracious to me—that requires real words, special revelation. It requires that He tell me. David understands this, and his mouth gives us words that are "acceptable in [God's] sight." What do the words of his mouth reveal? The Lord is "my rock and my redeemer." Those are the words we need to hear! Those are the words our propers will beautifully elaborate.

The **Collect** reiterates God's power over His universe, but it also prays that He use His power *for* us:

Almighty and everlasting God, who governs all things in heaven and on earth, mercifully hear the prayers of Your people and grant us Your peace through all our days; through Jesus Christ, Your Son, our Lord, who lives and reigns with You and the Holy Spirit, one God, now and forever. Amen.

God who created all things in heaven and on earth does govern them. But our prayer is that He would grant us His "peace." That's asking that He quiet our terror of His mighty power, that He assure us He is not angry with us, that He would embrace us as our loving God. We cannot earn that, because our sin puts us in mortal conflict with God. So will our prayer be answered? The way the Church's collects are written expresses our faith that if our prayer is to be answered, it will always be "through Jesus Christ, [God's] Son, our Lord." Do we have in Jesus the one who has earned us a hearing from God, who has reconciled us to God by taking away our sin? That's the word we need to hear!

"Listen to Me," our **Old Testament Reading** begins. If You're speaking, Lord, we're listening. We need to hear a word from You! So we read Isaiah 49:1–7.

This is the second Servant Song of Isaiah. (Review last week's devotion-study if you'd like to refresh your memory on the four Servant Songs.) These passages are among the most revealing introductions of the Messiah in the entire Old Testament. Though Isaiah is writing (and it's seven centuries before Jesus' birth), it's actually Christ speaking; He's revealing Himself by His own words. "He [the LORD] made My mouth like a sharp sword," Christ says (49:2).

The servant Messiah reveals that He will be "deeply despised, abhorred" by His own nation (49:7). It will seem as if "I have labored in vain" (49:4). But as it will turn out, "It is too light a thing" that He should only "raise up the tribes of Jacob" (Israel). He will also be "a light for the nations, that My salvation may reach to the end of the earth" (49:6). We recognize that as a major theme throughout Epiphany, beginning with the star inviting Gentile wise men to come and worship Jesus. Christ is the Savior of the whole world. We certainly need to hear that word!

Even when Christ isn't doing the actual talking, it's still very much His Word when we hear from inspired writers of Scripture—or from fellow believers sharing Scripture. Read the **Psalm** of the day, Psalm 40:1–11.

Again it's David who says of the Lord, "He put a new song *in my mouth*" (40:3). God has had "mercy . . . ; Your steadfast love and Your faithfulness will ever preserve me!" (40:11). The Lord "drew me up from the pit of destruction, out of the miry bog, and set my feet upon a rock, making my steps secure" (40:2). I experienced this salvation, David says, and "I have not concealed Your steadfast love and Your faithfulness from the great congregation" (40:10b). Of course not! It's Epiphany, revealing, showing forth!

Just as it's Epiphany for each of us. Say aloud *for yourself* the "I" just as David said it: "*I* will proclaim and tell of . . . the LORD's wondrous deeds and thoughts toward us . . . *I* have told the glad news of deliverance in the great congregation; behold, *I* have not restrained my lips, as You know, O LORD. *I* have not hidden Your deliverance within my heart; *I* have spoken of Your faithfulness and Your salvation" (40:5, 9–10). All the world needs to hear these words!

And few have ever said them as powerfully and succinctly as John the Baptist in our **Holy Gospel**, John 1:29–42a.

This one departure from the Year A Epiphany Gospels in Matthew is well worth the digression. It follows naturally after last Sunday's Baptism of Our Lord, as John cites that event: "I saw the Spirit descend from heaven like a dove, and it remained on Him" (1:32). It comfortably precedes next week's Holy Gospel, when Jesus returns to Galilee and begins His public ministry there. And it is among the most revealing moments of the entire Epiphany.

"Behold, the Lamb of God, who takes away the sin of the world!" (1:29). A complete sermon in itself!

John's original hearers knew graphically the Old Testament sacrificial system. Every morning and every evening, a lamb was sacrificed in the temple. Every day, unnumbered lambs were sacrificed as special offerings. And every Passover, every Jewish family sacrificed a lamb—thousands of them in total. Bleating. Bloody. The sacrifices were God's sign that the sins of the people would be atoned. But they went on for centuries, always reminding that sin remained, always teaching that yet another sacrifice was needed. Nevertheless, the faithful knew that one day one sacrifice would end them all, would be enough. And now John points to Jesus and says, "This One is the sacrifice that finishes it, that will pay for every sin ever committed—not only for the tribes of Jacob (that's too light a thing) but also for the nations, to the end of the earth."

John's one sentence said that Jesus would die the death of the whole world's sin. He would go as a lamb led to the slaughter. And for the sins of the world, it could be no ordinary death. Not only bloody but blighted, stripped bare even of his Father's concern. This was the word we all needed to hear.

This is the word that answered our prayer in the Collect: Yes, the almighty God has granted us His peace, reconciliation with Him, because Jesus' death on the cross has taken away our sins. This is the word that says the Lord is our Rock and our Redeemer; Jesus' cross has redeemed us. This is the word David couldn't conceal but had to proclaim and tell and speak; Jesus' suffering and death are the Lord's wondrous deeds that delivered us from the pit, the miry bog. David's words. Isaiah's words. John's words.

And Just What Do the Words of His Mouth Reveal? The Lamb of God, Who Takes Away the Sin of the World!

We leave to St. Paul in the **Epistle** the last word, only because he is so emphatic in giving us the One to whom John pointed as the Last Word. Read 1 Corinthians 1:1–9. Paul is beginning a letter that will cover a wide breadth of crucial doctrinal and churchly issues (and which we'll follow each of the next seven Sundays). He barely hints at them here. But he does want the Corinthians to be "enriched . . . in all speech" (1:5) as they wait for a final "revealing" (1:7). Speech (words!) about? Revealing whom? Read again and see that *in every verse*, all nine, Paul is explicit about "Christ Jesus," "our Lord Jesus Christ," "Christ," "Jesus Christ our Lord," or "Him." Jesus is the Last Word of revelation.

May He be our last word too.

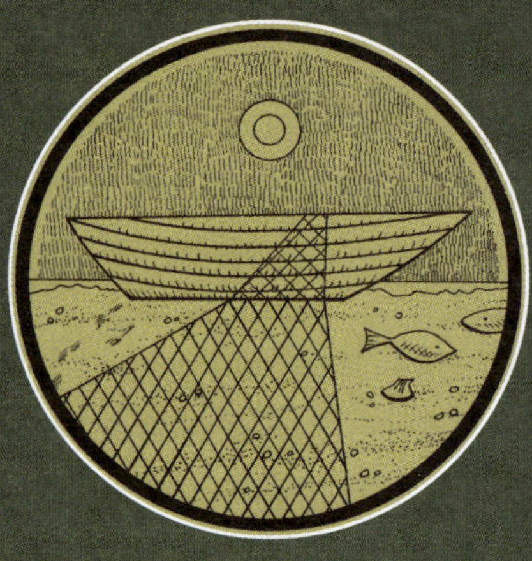

Third Sunday after the Epiphany Year A

READINGS

Isaiah 9:1–4
Psalm 27:1–9 (10–14)
(antiphon: v 1)
1 Corinthians 1:10–18
Matthew 4:12–25

HYMN OF THE DAY

LSB 839 "O Christ, Our True and Only Light"

In the introduction to this volume, I explained the process by which I look forward to Sunday morning—whether in my years as an every-Sunday preacher or for my radio programs on *Issues, Etc.* or in writing these devotion-studies. In short, my goal is always to discover what all the propers have in common, the unifying idea, which I then try to express in one summary sentence, my THEME. This week, let's walk through that process with the propers for an actual Sunday, the Third Sunday after the Epiphany. We'll look at each element, see which words or phrases or concepts are most prominent, and then try to formulate them into a sentence that summarizes the Big Idea.

We begin by collecting what we already know about the season and anything special about the day. In this case, we know we are in the season of Epiphany—shining upon, revealing, Jesus. And from our earlier preview of the whole season in Year A, which draws primarily from Matthew's Gospel, we know that most of the revealing will be not by Jesus' works (as next year in Mark) but by words, preaching, by Him or about Him. In fact, the lectionary shows us that next week we'll begin five straight Sundays hearing Jesus' Sermon on the Mount. So as we look at this week's propers, we'll be alert to these cues.

Although we might read the propers starting with the Holy Gospel or even the Verse (we'll do that another week), most often I read them more nearly in the order they'll be heard in worship. That anticipates the Sunday-in-the-pew experience. This means we begin by reading the **Introit**:

I will tell of Your name to my brothers; in the midst of the congregation I will praise You.

All the ends of the earth shall remember and turn to the LORD, and all the families of the nations shall worship before You. For kingship belongs to the LORD, and He rules over the nations. All the prosperous of the earth eat and worship; before Him shall bow all who go down to the dust, even the one who could not keep himself alive. Posterity shall serve Him; it shall be told of the Lord to the coming generation; they shall come and proclaim His righteousness to a people yet unborn, that He has done it.

Glory be to the Father and to the Son and to the Holy Spirit; as it was in the beginning, is now, and will be forever. Amen.

I will tell of Your name to my brothers; in the midst of the congregation I will praise You. (Ps 22:27–31; anti phon: Ps 22:22)

You'll usually want to read these propers simply devotionally—just letting God's Word speak to you. But for this exercise, go back and look more analytically. What's the source of this Introit? Maybe you recall Psalm 22 as the one Jesus quoted from the cross: "My God, My God, why have You forsaken Me?" (Ps 22:1; Mt 27:46). So although David is writing, we can truly hear Jesus speaking.

Now which words, phrases, or ideas stood out to you? Remembering what we've said about these Epiphany Sundays revealing Jesus by words or speaking, I marked the phrases "I will tell" and "they shall come and proclaim." I also noted "kingship" and "the LORD . . . rules over the nations" as a significant point being made. Finally, I was touched by the contrast between "the prosperous" and "all who go down to the dust, even the one who could not keep himself alive." But both prosperous and destitute, apparently, will be among those who "proclaim [the Lord's] righteousness to a people yet unborn." At this point, we'll just hold all these thoughts and see if they show up again in the other propers.

Next, read the **Collect**. Even though we're being analytical this week, don't forget that it's a prayer you're really praying:

Almighty and everlasting God, mercifully look upon our infirmities and stretch forth the hand of Your majesty to heal and defend us; through Jesus Christ, Your Son, our Lord, who lives and reigns with You and the Holy Spirit, one God, now and forever. Amen.

After saying a real "Amen," I put on my studious cap again and notice two striking elements: first, "our infirmities," and, second, "the hand of [God's] majesty" stretching out to us in those infirmities. Infirmities can be the many pains, illnesses, weaknesses, failures, attacks—all because of sin—that we go through. Here we certainly don't want just to analyze academically; this is our life. And the coupling of majesty with gentle reaching out is remarkable—and wonderfully comforting! Not everyone who's got it goin' on cares about me in my needs. All right then, back to analyzing. Notice that "majesty" does second the mention of "kingship" in the Introit, and "infirmities" matches the down-and-outers in the Introit who could not even keep themselves alive. Once we see an idea repeat, it bears watching for our THEME.

This might be a good time to revisit the **Gradual**, which, of course, we've heard in previous weeks because it's the same throughout the season. It does express the theme for the whole season, but that also means it's more general, rather than tied just to this particular of the Epiphany Sundays.

Praise the LORD, all nations! Extol Him, all peoples! For great is His steadfast love toward us, and the faithfulness of the LORD endures forever. Ascribe to the LORD the glory due His name; bring an offering, and come into His courts! (Ps 117:1–2a; 96:8)

In connection to what we've found so far in the propers, "His courts" recalls kingship, and we see everyone ("all nations," "all peoples") getting into the act of revealing by speaking or proclamation.

The final thematic clue before looking at the readings—and it's a big one!—is the **Verse**. Most Sundays, like this one, the Verse is drawn from the Holy Gospel, and very often it gives the main point of the reading. This week's Verse: "Alleluia. From that time Jesus began to preach, saying, 'Repent, for the kingdom of heaven is at hand.' Alleluia" (Mt 4:17). Preaching and kingdom! There's an excellent chance we're on the right track toward our THEME.

The **Old Testament Reading** is always chosen to reflect the Holy Gospel in some way. Sometimes it's a prophecy that's fulfilled in the Gospel reading, sometimes simply a parallel story, and so on. So the Old Testament Reading, too, is very important to the theme of the day. Read Isaiah 9:1–4.

Most of these verses were heard at Christmas (9:2–7), but the familiar "to us a child is born . . ." is deleted, and see what's added in verse 1: Zebulun and Naphtali were two tribes of Israel that drew the short straws when the Promised Land was parceled out (Josh 18:10; 19:10, 32). Their lands were on the northern fringe of Israel, near the Sea of Galilee, so they were often invaded, and pagan neighbors were a constant temptation to idolatry. They easily succumbed to that spiritual darkness; they were in "gloom" and "anguish," and even other Israelites viewed them with "contempt" (9:1–2; also 1 Ki 9:11–13). These were the down-and-outers of the tribes of Israel. But these down-and-outers will see "a great light"; "the rod of his oppressor" God would break (Is 9:2, 4). That would happen when a powerful king would again rule over Israel and drive out the invaders.

Got the connection? Those in the dust who couldn't keep themselves alive (Introit) and those like us who suffer infirmities (Collect) will "rejoice" (9:3) in the new kingdom (Introit, Collect, Gradual, Verse).

The **Psalm** is often picturesque on some aspect of the day's theme. Read Psalm 27. Every psalm of David, Israel's greatest king, brings to mind the kingdom. But see how even David finds himself down and out: evildoers assail him (27:2); an army camps against him (27:3); he even imagines his father and mother forsaking him (27:10). Unlikely, one thinks, that David would proclaim the Lord's kingdom at a time like that. Yet, "I will offer . . . sacrifices with shouts of joy; I will sing and make melody to the Lord" (27:6). David knows "He will hide me in His shelter in the day of trouble" (27:5).

As we explained in our book's introduction, this is a time of year when the **Epistle** follows the progression of a particular Bible book (these weeks, 1 Corinthians) rather than being chosen for its connection with the Gospel reading. Nevertheless, let's read 1 Corinthians 1:10–18 and see if any of the thematic elements we've discovered so far appear. Usually some do.

Sure enough. St. Paul has quite a different issue in mind: divisions in the Corinthian Church. But that discussion raises a point highly germane to this Sunday's other propers. The Corinthians are not to become attached to a particular preacher—Paul or Apollos or Peter (Cephas)—because the preacher himself matters nothing. Preaching (very relevant to our Epiphany revelation!) is about Christ and His cross, not the person preaching (1:17–18). In fact, the preacher may be the most unlikely choice. Paul, we know from his life story, was just as down-and-out a candidate to preach Christ as those we've met in the Introit, the Collect, the Old Testament Reading, and the Psalm. Apparently, too, he was no eloquent orator (1:17). And what does he preach? The most unlikely message: the folly of a cross (1:18).

Which brings us to the **Holy Gospel**, Matthew 4:12–25. If we've followed the right leads, they should all come together here.

First, obviously, we see the fulfillment of Isaiah 9. Jesus comes to the down-and-outers of Galilee (4:12–16). Second, it is precisely the epiphany we're expecting. Jesus' revelation is by speaking; He begins to preach (4:17a). Finally, His message is proclamation of the kingdom (4:17b). Jesus is the Kingdom of heaven. Christ, the Kingdom, is what David prefigured; it's what the oft-invaded land of Zebulun and Naphtali needed. When we struggle in all our infirmities, we need to know that we are in the Kingdom, not forgotten or out.

And see where this goes. Jesus begins to choose His disciples (4:18–22), and they're just like Paul—the least likely to proclaim the kingdom. But *Jesus* will *make them* fishers of men, catching the same souls He will—those with diseases and afflictions, those oppressed by demons, those with epilepsy or paralysis (4:23–25). The least likely for a King, who will catch them in the least likely way: that cross.

So how about this for our Theme?

Even the Least Likely
Will Not Only
Hear the Kingdom Proclaimed
but Will Proclaim It Themselves.

Close by singing "O Christ, Our True and Only Light." What connections do you see here (Is 9:1–4; Mt 4:12–16)?

Fourth Sunday after the Epiphany Year A

READINGS

Micah 6:1–8
Psalm 15 (antiphon: Psalm 16:1)
1 Corinthians 1:18–31
Matthew 5:1–12

HYMN OF THE DAY

LSB 842 "Son of God, Eternal Savior"

In recent weeks, we've heard Jesus revealed—that is, "epiphanied"—through words about Him and by Him. This Sunday, and for the four that follow, that continues with perhaps the most famous sermon ever—so famous that we capitalize it: Jesus' Sermon on the Mount.

The Sermon on the Mount does indeed reveal so much about who Jesus is and why He came. Unfortunately, the sermon, and especially the first portion, the Beatitudes, our Gospel reading for this week, is often badly misinterpreted. When that happens, it actually manifests a different Jesus than the one who really came to be our Savior. Misunderstanding the Sermon on the Mount can make Jesus appear to be a new Lawgiver, rather than the source of all blessing.

The Beatitudes are so well known (they're even in our own lectionary again on All Saints' Day) that you'd think their meaning would be crystal clear to all. "Blessed are the poor in spirit, for theirs is the kingdom of heaven. Blessed are those who mourn, for they shall be comforted. Blessed are the meek, . . . the merciful, . . . the peacemakers . . ." (Mt 5:3–5a, 7a, 9a). Wonderful words of comfort—or a bar set so high I could only stress or despair trying to jump over it. Do I get to be blessed if I make peace with others? if I mourn? What if I'm not meek? Or does Christ fix things so I don't have to have mercy? What is Jesus saying to us—and about Himself?

One of the great benefits of the lectionary is that it lets us hear a difficult teaching like the Beatitudes in the context of various related selections from Scripture. All the propers read together help us correctly interpret each. That's certainly true this week. Beginning with the

Introit, we'll get valuable clues to understand the Beatitudes by the time we hear from Jesus in Matthew's Gospel:

> *For the LORD knows the way of the righteous, but the way of the wicked will perish.*
>
> *Blessèd is the man who walks not in the counsel of the wicked, nor stands in the way of sinners, nor sits in the seat of scoffers; but his delight is in the law of the LORD, and on His law he meditates day and night. He is like a tree planted by streams of water that yields its fruit in its season, and its leaf does not wither. In all that he does, he prospers. The wicked are not so, but are like chaff that the wind drives away. Therefore the wicked will not stand in the judgment, nor sinners in the congregation of the righteous.*
>
> *Glory be to the Father and to the Son and to the Holy Spirit; as it was in the beginning, is now, and will be forever. Amen.*
>
> *For the LORD knows the way of the righteous, but the way of the wicked will perish. (Ps 1:1–5; antiphon: Ps 1:6)*

The entire psalter begins with the same English word (and cognate Hebrew word) that will begin each beatitude: "blessèd" (אַשְׁרֵי, Ps 1:1). What a difference between the blessèd "righteous" and the "wicked"! Picture the scene and the progression: the wicked might first just "walk" around the fringes of evil, but soon enough they "stand" amongst "sinners" and, finally, plop right down to "sit" in the inner circle of "scoffers." On the other hand, the blessèd delight to gather around and meditate on "the law of the LORD," the Torah or teachings of God's Holy Book. And contrast the results: the blessèd righteous man is planted like a tree, standing firm, stable, solid, immovable, while the wicked one is—wwhhoo!—blown away like chaff in the wind. He won't stand. He will perish. The question is, Is one counted as righteous and will therefore stand as blessed because he meditates like he should and doesn't hang out where he shouldn't? That will be the question with the Beatitudes too.

The **Collect** begins to suggest the answer:

> *Almighty God, You know we live in the midst of so many dangers that in our frailty we cannot stand upright. Grant strength and protection to support us in all dangers and carry us through all temptations; through Jesus Christ, Your Son, our Lord, who lives and reigns with You and the Holy Spirit, one God, now and forever. Amen.*

So much for avoiding bad company! We live right "in the midst of so many dangers." And just as the psalmist says, when we're surrounded by evil, "in our frailty we cannot stand upright." Our prayer, then, is that almighty God would "support us" and enable us to stand.

The **Old Testament Reading** actually tightens the screws a bit. Read Micah 6:1–8. It's a courtroom scene. God is bringing the charges, and we, with Judah, are the defendants. Notice the venue, by the way: the mountains. We'll be going to one again shortly, you know.

God's case against us is open and shut (6:3–5). God has done every good thing to save His people—brought them out of slavery in Egypt, given them faithful leaders, turned Balaam's curse into a blessing (Numbers 22–24), to cite just a few. Yet Judah in Micah's day was, as usual, walking, then standing, in the way of their sinful neighbors, sitting in the seat of Baal-worshiping scoffers (see 6:16). The verdict: Guilty!

Is Judah's answer "try harder" to turn its condemnation into blessing? Won't work. Nothing it might offer (6:6–7) will satisfy. Instead, "What does the Lord require of you but to do justice, and to love kindness, and to walk humbly with your God?" (6:8). Oh. Be just and caring toward the disadvantaged; be kind to everyone; trust in God, not ourselves, above all things. And that God *requires*! That's what it takes to be blessed? Gulp.

All right then, Lord, "Who *shall* dwell on Your holy hill?" (Almost back to the mountain again.) Read this Sunday's **Psalm**, Psalm 15, and see if it offers any help.

"Who shall dwell on Your holy hill? He who walks blamelessly" (15:1b–2a). Blamelessly! Micah has already shown us we're guilty, and now David adds quite the list of "he does and does nots." Speaks truth, does not slander, does no evil to his neighbor, lots more. "He who does these things shall never be moved" (15:5), will stand firm. But who does all that? Who can stand on the mountain among the blessed?

We've pointed out that during the Epiphany season (as also during the Easter and Pentecost seasons, except for the festivals themselves), the **Epistles** read consecutively through epistle books rather than being chosen to amplify the Holy Gospel. But as we've also said, the Epistle usually still contributes to our understanding of the Sunday. This week, that's especially true. Read the third installment in our seven weeks in 1 Corinthians: 1 Corinthians 1:18–31.

This lesson is another of those few so significant that it occurs twice in the lectionary (also Lent 3, Year B). The cross of Jesus Christ. Christ crucified. That message is the power of God! This is what it's *all* about! This word of the cross is how God saves.

But it makes no sense. It seems like folly. Christ dying seems to be the ultimate defeat. "Jews demand signs"—like the miracles Jesus performed, which they still didn't believe. "Greeks seek wisdom"; what could be less wise than trusting a dead man to rescue? And we want assurances we can see in good health, successful kids, and cars, homes, and washing machines never needing repair.

Here, though, is our real folly: following "the wisdom of the world" (1:20) that says our blessings have to be earned. Paul says, "It is written, 'Let the one who boasts, boast in the Lord'" (1:31). He's answering our very natural and very sinful inclination to believe that what we have is ours to boast about. If I am blessed, it must be because I myself have cleared the high bar, that I've delighted in the law of the Lord, walked humbly enough with my God, somehow earned the right to stand atop the holy hill. That's folly! But it's precisely the reason the cross seems foolish. When I can stand on my own, it's quite foolish of God to die over me.

So, our Epistle lesson teaches us, when we talk blessing, it can't be me; it's all Christ crucified.

Well then, "Blessed are the poor in spirit, for theirs is the kingdom of heaven." Read the **Holy Gospel**, Matthew 5:1–12.

Now we are on the mountain. And Jesus sits down. The rabbi, the teacher, would always sit; his students would stand. And eager students of the Torah, the teachings of God, gather 'round Him. Then, opening His mouth, He taught them: "Blessed."

The false or faithful interpretation of the Sermon on the Mount hinges on how we are blessed. All nine beatitudes (*beatitude* comes from the Latin for "blessed") express a condition of the blessed person and then a particular blessing. Very often that condition ("poor in spirit," "mourn," "meek," "hunger and thirst for righteousness," or the rest) is held up as the primary focus. Such a sermon is about becoming poor in spirit or merciful or pure in heart. But if that's what Jesus means by His Beatitudes, then He is indeed revealing Himself to be that new Lawgiver, raising the bar even higher than all those passages that already found us guilty. Some epiphany! And who really does ever measure up? None of us, as our preceding propers have made painfully obvious.

But, in fact, the Beatitudes reveal Jesus as the one who can lay claim to standing atop God's holy hill. Go back through each one and give your own examples of how Jesus is the perfect peacemaker, the one persecuted for righteousness' sake, and so on. And while you're at it, go back, too, to the Introit and the Old Testament Reading and the Psalm and see Jesus as the one who does what the Lord requires in each.

But now we are baptized into Christ. And that means that what He is, we are. We have died the death of that foolish cross, and by its power we are each forgiven for every one of our frailties, every sin that prevents us from standing upright. So the true focus in each beatitude is not on the condition of the blessed person, her or his own meekness or purity of heart. What Christ is, we are. God says we who are baptized into Christ *are* poor in spirit and *do* hunger and thirst for righteousness. Already. So the focus in each beatitude is on the word "blessed." We *are* blessed! With all those nine blessings!

One last step, though. Because we are in Christ and are blessed, we now truly desire to do—and in fact do, though imperfectly—all those things the Lord requires. Go back once more through the Beatitudes and each other proper and think of ways you do or would desire to do every one of those things the righteous do. You see,

WE DO STAND ON THE HOLY MOUNTAIN IN OUR GUILT AND WEAKNESS AND MEEKNESS AND POVERTY, BLESSED IN THE POWER OF THE CROSS—EVEN TO DO WHAT THE LORD REQUIRES.

Close by singing the **Hymn of the Day**, "Son of God, Eternal Savior" (*LSB* 842).

Fifth Sunday after the Epiphany Year A

READINGS

Isaiah 58:3–9a
Psalm 112:1–9 (antiphon: v 4)
1 Corinthians 2:1–12 (13–16)
Matthew 5:13–20

HYMN OF THE DAY

LSB 578 "Thy Strong Word"

The "epiphanies" of Jesus, His being revealed, continue this week with the second installment of the Sermon on the Mount in our Gospel reading. Last week, the Beatitudes told us a great deal about Jesus because they really are first of all about Him. Now this week, we get a twist. Jesus is going to be preaching, but, Jesus will tell us, the real epiphany will be through us. That is, when people see His followers, you and me, they should be able to see Jesus shined upon, shown forth, revealed. We will be the epiphanies of Jesus to the world.

Here's the way Jesus puts that in the sermon, as it's quoted in the **Verse** for this week: "Alleluia. Let your light shine before others, so that they may see your good works and give glory to your Father who is in heaven. Alleluia" (Mt 5:16b).

Let's begin with prayer, using the **Collect** for this Fifth Sunday after the Epiphany:

> *O Lord, keep Your family the Church continually in the true faith that, relying on the hope of Your heavenly grace, we may ever be defended by Your mighty power; through Jesus Christ, Your Son, our Lord, who lives and reigns with You and the Holy Spirit, one God, now and forever. Amen.*

A most appropriate prayer any week of the year! Nothing is more important for Christians than that God keep us in faith until we reach eternal joy in heaven. This week, though, especially consider the phrase "Your family the Church." The Church, God's visible family on earth, is how the world sees Him. Think how proud a parent is when a child's Christian witness at school or with friends reflects the faith and love shared at home by Mom and Dad. God's people living as His sons and daughters, as brothers and sisters, are the light by which others glorify the Father.

The **Introit** begins with the same word we appreciated so much last week, "blessèd." But last week, we were being declared blessed by God. This week, we are blessing Him:

Blessèd are You, O Lord; teach me Your statutes!

How can a young man keep his way pure? By guarding it according to Your word. With my whole heart I seek You; let me not wander from Your commandments! I have stored up Your word in my heart, that I might not sin against You. Blessèd are You, O Lord; teach me Your statutes! With my lips I declare all the just decrees of Your mouth. In the way of Your testimonies I delight as much as in all riches. I will meditate on Your precepts and fix my eyes on Your ways. I will delight in Your statutes; I will not forget Your word.

Glory be to the Father and to the Son and to the Holy Spirit; as it was in the beginning, is now, and will be forever. Amen.

Blessèd are You, O Lord; teach me Your statutes! (Ps 119:9–16; antiphon: Ps 119:12)

When we bless God, it's always because of what He's done. We bless Him in Psalm 119 for giving us His precious "statutes" (also called "word," "commandments," "just decrees," "testimonies," and "ways"). Recall our previous discussions about this and other "Torah Psalms." Words like "commandments" that sound so thoroughly Law to our Lutheran Law-Gospel ears actually mean all of God's holy teachings, which are both Law and Gospel—with Gospel winning out. So the psalmist is thankful for these words. In fact, the new man in him loves to do even the commandments of the Law. He realizes that God's Law does not restrict his "fun" or limit what he'd really like to do. On the contrary, God is laying out what's truly most joyful.

The Introit is a beautiful picture of one poring over the sacred texts—and savoring it! YouTube the song "If I Were a Rich Man" from *Fiddler on the Roof* and hear Tevye (tragically, not a believer in the Fulfiller of the Old Testament!) dream of discussing "the Holy Books" seven hours every day. "That would be the sweetest thing of all."

A chief reason that the new person, the believer, also in us, loves to obey God's commands is that they let the world see God. "How can a young man keep his way pure?" The question could be restated: What does a life of light look like? What are the good works we want others to see so that they will glorify our Father? The answer, then, is found in all those instructions of Scripture.

The **Old Testament Reading**, Isaiah 58:3–9a, gives some practical examples.

Last week, in the Old Testament Reading from Micah, God brought a complaint against His people. This week, God's people are complaining against Him. They're fasting—quite piously, they claim, complete with bowing down, sackcloth, and ashes (58:5)—but God isn't giving them any credit (58:3a). The complaint lasts only half a verse, however, because already in verse 3b, God responds. Their "fast" is actually self-serving (58:3b–4). Instead, here's the fast God chooses: "to loose the bonds of wickedness, . . . to let the oppressed go free, . . . to share your bread with the hungry and bring the homeless poor into your house; when you see the naked, to cover him" (58:6–7).

The result? "Then shall your light break forth like the dawn" (58:8). Caring for the oppressed, the hungry, the homeless, the naked—these are real-life opportunities for our lights to shine before others, good works the world can see, leading them to know God. These days, the Christian Church is often reviled in media and public opinion as being unloving, judgmental, bigoted, sexist. Caring for the needy with real and tangible acts of mercy is the best way Christians can dispel that slander. When the Church is seen providing for people's physical needs, it will evince the love we have in Christ.

We see more examples in the **Psalm**. Read Psalm 112:1–9. Once again, the Christian life is how "light dawns in the darkness" (112:4a). In a world of evil, of darkness—particularly darkness about how loving God and His Church are—we are light when we are "gracious, merciful, and righteous" (112:4b). Specifically, the shining light is one "who deals generously and lends; who conducts his affairs with justice. . . . He has distributed freely; he has given to the poor" (112:5, 9). The sinner in each of us sees these as duties, even heavy burdens. But the believer in us trusts that because of Christ, we are "blessed"; "wealth and riches" and "righteousness . . . forever" are constantly being provided for us in God's perfect measure. Therefore, the new person in us "greatly delights" to do all this (112:1–3). We know that being light to others is great joy.

The **Epistle** lesson continues our reading through 1 Corinthians, building on last week and giving us what I consider *the* paradigm for all Christian preaching. As you read 1 Corinthians 2:1–16, take your best guess as to the verse I find essential for every sermon.

Which verse did you mark? Verse 2: "For I decided to know nothing among you except Jesus Christ and Him crucified." For the whole eighteen months Paul was in Corinth on his second missionary journey, he says, that was it. All he preached. Nothing but that. That doesn't mean Paul simply kept repeating himself like a broken record. It means that Jesus dying on the cross is the point of every text, is the solution to every life problem, for now and for eternity. (The diversity of topics Paul addresses in 1 Corinthians—skim it quickly—gives just a sample of how many issues the cross addresses.) How can this be? How can the cross be the answer to *everything*? It's because Jesus' death on the cross took away the sin separating us from God. That was the whole problem, every problem. If we're separated from God, we receive no good thing. But when sin is removed, no longer between us and God, we're reconciled. And when we're back together with God, we have everything that He knows is truly good for us. There's simply no limit to the ways that applies. (Which is why the cross is to be the point of every sermon every week, and yet every sermon is to be different.)

Now, of course, that's all too simplistic for the world. The "wisdom of men" (2:5) or the "wisdom of this age" (2:6) seeks to solve its problems any way but the cross. (Paul said last week the cross is "folly to those who are perishing.") But this is God's wisdom (2:6–7).

And here's where we become epiphanies of Christ. Paul will let his light shine before others by preaching Christ and Him crucified. The cross, not "lofty speech" or our own wisdom (2:1), should also be our testimony. What's more, our lives of obedience to God's commandments, of caring for the hungry and homeless, of dealing generously and lending—those lights we shine—are always because we know we've been reconciled to God by the cross of Christ, meaning that we have all of God's good blessings. So the lights we shine by our loving obedience are lights that reveal Christ as the one who in God's wisdom went to the cross.

Our key verse for the week, as we said, comes from the **Holy Gospel**. Read the full lesson, Matthew 5:13–20.

Jesus gives two other illustrations of our theme concept (5:13–14). A little salt makes the entire steak or casserole taste better. A city on a hill gives all the surrounding villagers a sense of something higher and more noble. So it is with Christians in the world.

The chief illustration begins, though, when Jesus tells us, "You are the light of the world" (5:14a). What makes this so remarkable is that twice in John's Gospel Jesus says, "*I* am the light of the world" (Jn 8:12; 9:5). Jesus says we are what He is. Here, of course, is the epiphany. When our lights shine, Jesus is shining. That's because Jesus is the one who has done everything that the psalmist and Isaiah and Jesus Himself would call light: "Do not think that I have come to abolish the Law or the Prophets; I have not come to abolish them but to fulfill them" (5:17). Jesus is the perfect "young man" who did "keep his way pure" (Introit). He did fulfill the fast God prescribes by freeing the oppressed and feeding the hungry (Old Testament Reading). He is the blessed man who "deals generously" and "conducts his affairs with justice" (Psalm). And, above all, He is the one who, according to the "hidden wisdom of God, which God decreed before the ages," became the "crucified . . . Lord of glory" (Epistle).

Now, because we are baptized into Him, our righteousness, too, "exceeds that of the scribes and Pharisees" (5:20). Therefore,

Let Your Light Shine before Others So That They May See the Wisdom of Jesus' Cross Revealed.

When you sing the **Hymn of the Day**, "Thy Strong Word," Sunday, enjoy how fully it reiterates the major elements of the day's theme: light imagery throughout, God's wisdom shining from the cross (st 4), and the prayer that God would give *us* lips and tongues and throats and mouths to shine the light for others (st 5).

Sixth Sunday after the Epiphany Year A

READINGS

Deuteronomy 30:15–20
Psalm 119:1–8 (antiphon: v 1)
1 Corinthians 3:1–9
Matthew 5:21–37

HYMN OF THE DAY

LSB 394 "Songs of Thankfulness and Praise"

Our Holy Gospel for the Sixth Sunday after the Epiphany will continue revealing Jesus through His preaching in the third of five cuttings from the Sermon on the Mount. This Gospel lesson, though, as we'll see, has virtually *no Gospel.* It's all Law. Very, very stern Law. What, then, will our propers this week reveal about Jesus? Well, to see an epiphany of our gracious Savior is going to require a very close look—and some patience.

Already, our **Collect** for this Sunday will have us on our knees, begging for mercy:

> *O Lord, graciously hear the prayers of Your people that we who justly suffer the consequence of our sin may be mercifully delivered by Your goodness to the glory of Your name; through Jesus Christ, Your Son, our Lord, who lives and reigns with You and the Holy Spirit, one God, now and forever. Amen.*

"We who justly suffer the consequence of our sin." Yes, we do. The consequences of our sin are just. We do deserve to suffer for it. We do sin against God in thought, word, and deed. By the time we pray this Collect in the service Sunday, we'll already have confessed that. If we didn't mean it, Jesus will soon enough drive it home in the Gospel lesson. And whether we realize it or not, we do indeed suffer those well-deserved consequences. We get sick. We lose jobs. We fail tests. Our evenings at home aren't always harmonious. We sometimes sleep fitfully—or can't fall asleep at all. Fires burn. Hurricanes blow. Someday we'll each die. Not, in most cases, because of any particular sin I've committed that's comin' back to bite me, but because, ever since Adam, Eve, and I sinned, the whole world system has been messed up, filled with sinful people with sinful motivations. Even nature itself is out of kilter. We suffer. And we deserve it. "Lord, graciously hear the prayers of Your people that we . . . may be mercifully delivered by Your goodness . . . ; through Jesus Christ."

The **Old Testament Reading** was a warning of these consequences—which too often then and now has gone unheeded. Read Deuteronomy 30:15–20.

Deuteronomy means "second law," and it is Moses' reiteration of the Ten Commandments and final instructions before the second generation of Israelites could enter the Promised Land. Their parents have now all died in the wilderness because they refused God's gift, so it should be obvious that sin has deadly results. The choice should be a no-brainer: "life and good, death and evil" (30:15), "life and death, blessing and curse" (30:19). "If you obey . . . you shall live and multiply, and the Lord your God will bless you in the land that you are entering. . . . But if your heart turns away, . . . you shall surely perish. . . . Therefore choose life" (30:16, 17, 18, 19). Easy choice, right?

But every single day, we choose death—every time we sin. *Thousands of times every day* in the United States and Canada, mothers and fathers choose death for their own unborn children (though we pray that in the lifespan of this volume that will cease!). And every one of us chooses death whenever we break even the least of those Ten Commandments. Just a little coveting, just a little bit jealous? "You shall surely perish!" We justly suffer the consequence of our sin.

Again this week, the **Psalm** is a stanza of Psalm 119, this week the first (Ps 119:1–8). The psalmist makes a point that Jesus will heighten in the Gospel reading: "You [Lord] have commanded Your precepts to be kept *diligently*" (119:4). No half-hearted, do-the-best-you-can commandments. And how do we like these? "Blessed are those whose way is blameless, . . . who also do no wrong" (119:1, 3). Who among us would that be? We remember from recent devotion-studies what underlies these "Torah Psalms," but—thank the Lord!—we'll get to that. For now, the Law of the Lord really is that binding. We must be blameless. We must do *no* wrong. Lord, may we be mercifully delivered by Your goodness, through Jesus Christ.

The **Epistle** doesn't even soften the blow by being poetic. St. Paul looks us right in the eye and says, "you"! Read 1 Corinthians 3:1–9.

"I, brothers, could not address you as spiritual people, but as people of the flesh" (3:1). We've seen what a dysfunctional church Paul was dealing with in Corinth, especially on the matter of divisions and rivalries. "You are still of the flesh. For while there is jealousy and strife among you, are you not of the flesh and behaving only in a human way?" (3:3). When a person "cheers for" Paul over Apollos, it's really himself he's cheering for. We USC or Ohio State or Alabama fans are usually out to one-up the guy who roots for UCLA or Michigan or Auburn or Clemson or LSU. In weightier matters, like our life as the Church, Paul says that by such behavior we are not "spiritual people" but "merely human" (3:1, 4)—that is, just the old sinful nature procreated at the moment of conception, before the Holy Spirit created faith in Jesus in our hearts. Not good.

How often do we see behavior just like this in our churches? "I follow Senior Pastor Smith." "I follow Associate Pastor Jones." "I follow organist L." "I follow choir director M." "I follow largest contributor $." "I follow matriarch W." "We're confessional." "We're missional." "We're realistic." "We trust the Lord." Never heard that? Come on. Be real. "I," Paul would say, "cannot address you as spiritual people." We justly suffer the consequence of our sin.

But no one convicts us with the impact of our Lord Himself. Read the **Holy Gospel**, Matthew 5:21–37.

If you could find any clear Gospel in these verses, write and let me know. The Sermon on the Mount is a magnificent Law-and-Gospel sermon, with the rich grace of God in Christ certainly predominating. (Remember how blessed we are being in Christ in the Beatitudes! And last week, Jesus declared us the lights of the world.) More Gospel is coming later in the sermon. But not this week. It's all Law.

Four times in these verses, Jesus uses the formula "But I say to you" (5:22, 28, 32, 34). Jesus' hearers found this remarkable. Unlike even the most learned rabbis, Jesus was speaking on His own authority (see 7:28–29). On His authority, Jesus gives the definitive interpretation of each of His Old Testament texts. He adds nothing to the old laws; He, after all, is the one who gave them in the first place, and quite perfectly then. But He does explain them with clarity that shows just how demanding God's Law has always really been.

We know the Fifth Commandment condemns suicide skyjackings and school shootings. But Jesus says to us that unrighteous anger and unkind words condemn us to hell and require reconciliation (5:21–26). Extramarital affairs and sex before marriage—sinful, of course. But the thought counts too, Jesus says (5:27–30). How many among us have divorced for reasons other than the other party breaking the marriage bond? And how many of us have said nothing as our churches have allowed this to become commonplace—or have even attacked pastors who've said no to divorce (5:31–32)? Lying under oath, yes, that's always been wrong. But Jesus says that every word a Christian speaks should be absolutely truthful—yes when the situation calls for yes and no when it calls for no—so that we're always trustworthy without any oath.

This is the Gospel of the Lord.

Who's still standing? Lord, mercifully deliver us by Your goodness, for Your own name's sake!

It's time for an epiphany of Christ Jesus as our Savior! The **Introit** for this Sunday:

The L*ORD* *has made known His salvation; He has revealed His righteousness in the sight of the nations.*

Let the sea roar, and all that fills it; the world and those who dwell in it!

Let the rivers clap their hands; let the hills sing for joy together before the Lord, *for He comes to judge the earth. He will judge the world with righteousness, and the peoples with equity.*

Glory be to the Father and to the Son and to the Holy Spirit; as it was in the beginning, is now, and will be forever. Amen.

The Lord *has made known His salvation; He has revealed His righteousness in the sight of the nations. (Ps 98:7–9; antiphon: Ps 98:2)*

"The Lord has made known . . . ; He has revealed." That's epiphany language. What has He made known? "His salvation." That's what we've been waiting for. And parallel to "His salvation"? "His righteousness."

Psalm 98 is the basis for the Christmas hymn "Joy to the World," so it's got to be Good News. We see the world—the sea and rivers and hills and all the creatures that live in them—rejoicing, clapping hands. But they're clapping because the Lord "comes to judge the earth." Where's the salvation?

"Judge" strikes us as another Law word, but we wrote once before about how judgment can be Gospel. In this case, "He will judge the world with righteousness," and, remember, in this psalm, "righteousness" is parallel to "salvation." Hebrew poetry often uses parallelism to express synonymous ideas (say it once one way; say the same thing again another way). So we, too, have reason to rejoice that the Lord will judge the world in righteousness. It means He's going to save us. And it's for the reason you know, even if it's not expressed in today's Gospel reading.

It is expressed in the **Verse**. The Verse this week is, quite significantly, not drawn from the Gospel lesson or from any of the other propers, as it usually is. It's instead Ephesians 5:2: "Alleluia. Walk in love, as Christ loved us and gave Himself up for us, a fragrant offering and sacrifice to God. Alleluia." There's the reason that when the Lord comes to judge, He won't condemn us. There's the answer to our prayer:

> Lord, we do justly suffer the consequence of our sin, but mercifully deliver us by Your goodness.

It *is* through Jesus Christ, who loved us and gave Himself as the sacrifice for us.

This Sunday morning, we'll see Jesus revealed as one who can preach the Law with the best of 'em. No, as *the* One who preaches the Law better than any of "them." But we'll also see Him as the Savior, who sacrificed Himself on the cross for all our sins His preaching reveals. So now we can also pray,

O Lord, We Thank You
That We Who Justly Suffer
the Consequences of Our Sin
Are Mercifully Delivered
by Your Righteous Judgment,
Which Is Your Goodness
through Jesus Christ,
Who Loved Us
and Gave Himself for Us.

It's taken this long to get here, but now at last we do have reason to sing the **Hymn of the Day**, "Songs of Thankfulness and Praise" (*LSB* 394).

Seventh Sunday after the Epiphany Year A

READINGS

Leviticus 19:1–2, 9–18
Psalm 119:33–40
(antiphon: v 35)
1 Corinthians 3:10–23
Matthew 5:38–48

HYMN OF THE DAY

LSB 820 "My Soul, Now Praise Your Maker" or

LSB 834 "O God, O Lord of Heaven and Earth"

You're probably well aware—and perhaps have already been reminded this year—that the season of Epiphany varies in length quite substantially. That's because Epiphany is always assigned the number of Sundays to "fill in" between Epiphany Day, January 6, and Ash Wednesday, which, of course, is earlier or later depending on the date of Easter. (See the helpful, though yet a bit IQ-testing, explanation of the moving date of Easter in *Lutheran Service Book*, p xxiii.) With a very early Easter in March, Epiphany can have as few as three Sundays, plus Transfiguration. When Easter falls in late April, there can be as many as eight, plus. So if you're reading this devotion-study for the Seventh Sunday after the Epiphany, chances are it's one of those years in which Easter is fairly late.

If you're still with us, we'll hear Jesus continue that tough section in the Sermon on the Mount in which He recalls an Old Testament passage ("You have heard that it was said, . . .") and then clarifies just how demanding it really is: "But I say to you . . ." They're kinder, gentler commands He gives us this week, but they're still commands, Law. As we'll see, kinder, gentler actually makes them more difficult for us. And Jesus concludes with this: "You therefore must be perfect, as your heavenly Father is perfect" (Mt 5:48). What does that say to us who aren't perfect?

The Gospel in the Gospel lesson will be easier to see once we've picked up its trail in the other propers—like the **Introit**, from one of the great psalms of praise:

> *Bless the* Lord*, O my soul, and forget not all His benefits, who forgives all*

your iniquity, who heals all your diseases.

The Lord is merciful and gracious, slow to anger and abounding in steadfast love. He will not always chide, nor will He keep His anger forever. He does not deal with us according to our sins, nor repay us according to our iniquities. For as high as the heavens are above the earth, so great is His steadfast love toward those who fear Him.

Glory be to the Father and to the Son and to the Holy Spirit; as it was in the beginning, is now, and will be forever. Amen.

Bless the Lord, O my soul, and forget not all His benefits, who forgives all your iniquity, who heals all your diseases. (Ps 103:8–11; antiphon: Ps 103:2–3)

Psalm 103 is so instructive when we think of how we bless (could also be translated "praise") God. We often feel (and we choose that word intentionally!) that God is praised by our excitement; praise is happening if *I* feel it! But praise of God, blessing God, actually happens when His people recall what *He* has done—sometimes with high emotion, certainly, but just as well when His works are recounted in simple speaking or reading or praying, even singing in a minor key. See how David praises God: "Bless the Lord, O my soul, and forget not all His benefits"—above all, His forgiving all our iniquity.

Simply believing and receiving God's forgiveness is praise. It's saying, even if it's just in our hearts, that He is gracious, loving, good. It's not about us. Declaring that *He* heals, *He* is merciful, *He* does not chide, *He* ceases His anger, that's praising God. Step outside tonight, look at the distance of the stars, the immensity of the sky, and consider: "As high as the heavens are above the earth, so great is His steadfast love toward those who fear Him." Whether that brings a deep awe into your heart, or just a "Hmm. That's pretty neat," that's praise. And everything God does for us comes from, again, His most praiseworthy act: not dealing with us "according to our sins," nor repaying us "according to our iniquities."

Not included in the Introit, but memorable, is verse 1 of Psalm 103: "Bless the Lord, O my soul, and all that is within me, bless His holy name!" "God's name is certainly holy in itself," but as we pray in the First Petition of the Lord's Prayer, in Psalm 103 we bless it as holy also. In fact, that Gospel to be found in our propers this week is very much about participating in His holiness also.

As you pray the **Collect** for this week, both today and on Sunday, fill in your personal particulars:

O God, the strength of all who put their trust in You, mercifully grant that by Your power we may be defended against all adversity; through Jesus Christ, Your Son, our Lord, who lives and reigns with You and the Holy Spirit, one God, now and forever. Amen.

What adversities are you facing this week? The Church is praying with you, but each of us is asking God to defend us against unique assaults of the devil—some illness, some threat to the harmony of our family, some opposition to our faith. For Jesus' sake, our heavenly Father hears each of those countless prayers individually. None is overlooked or lost or confused.

In keeping with the week's other propers, don't miss the reminder in the Collect that all things we accomplish, if in any way we are to fulfill those demanding commands Christ speaks, will be "by Your power," O God.

This Sunday's **Psalm** is yet another stanza of Psalm 119. (There will be others. There are, after all, twenty-two of them.) By now, we should be getting a pretty good handle on what it means: Psalm 119:33–40.

We know how deeply the psalmist loves the Lord's *torah*, "law" (and all the other words he uses for it). The new man in him knows that every word of God's instruction is not only for his good but also truly a "delight" to study, "keep," and "observe" (that is, live). The new man is even able to say, "Teach me, O Lord, the way of Your statutes; and I *will keep it* to the end" (119:33). He must be perfect, as his heavenly Father is perfect.

Most of us probably don't open to Leviticus to pass a spare moment, but this week's **Old Testament Reading** actually appears in whole or in part three times in the lectionary. Read Leviticus 19:1–2, 9–18.

These verses, in their three appearances (also during the Pentecost seasons in Year A, Proper 25, and Year C, Proper 10), are the only words from Leviticus in the lectionary—and we understand why. Most of Leviticus is ceremonial law given to Israel that is not binding on the Church today. In fact, though, Israel carrying out these laws of God was intended to be an acting-out by which others could see God's holiness. As one regulation after another is piled up (burnt offerings and grain offerings and peace offerings, rules about which animals could be eaten and which couldn't, tests for leprosy, meticulous procedures for priests, and on and on), we do well to picture Jesus Christ carrying out every command of God to the *n*th degree. And He obeyed every command in our stead!

Already in the Old Testament, Israel's obedience to the holiness code in Leviticus was to be the way pagan nations would see Yahweh. It was Old Testament "evangelism." Obeying God's laws, which called people to "love your neighbor as yourself" (19:18), Israel would look conspicuously different from all other nations, who lived immorally and brutishly. Thus, seeing Israel's holiness would draw foreigners to Yahweh. (Consider Deuteronomy 4:5–8.)

Therefore God said to Israel, "You shall be holy, for I the Lord your God am holy" (19:2). What follows are Yahweh's heartfelt concerns for the poor, the sojourner, the oppressed, the hired worker, those who are deaf or blind, and for all, that none would be robbed or deceived or cheated or slandered. And the refrain, the reason for doing good, is always, "I am the Lord [Yahweh]" (19:10, 12, 14, 16, 18). "You shall be holy, for I am holy. You must be holy—perfectly holy!—because that will show the world My holiness."

The **Epistle**, 1 Corinthians 3:10–23, illustrates holy living with the example of a construction project. Some building materials won't pass the test of fire: wood, hay, straw. These are teachings that are false, contrary to God's Word, or thoughts, words, and deeds that are sinful, not loving to our neighbor or to the Lord. Other materials, gold, silver, precious stones, will last. These are true teachings and other good works of believers, which will be remembered even after the Last Day. What gives anything permanence, though, is the foundation on which it's built, Jesus Christ (3:11). Faith in Him even enables us to survive, though we ourselves have built with some shoddy materials. "You are Christ's," Paul says (3:23).

One more reference to the Epistle still to come.

The **Holy Gospel**, we've said, ends with Jesus' demand, "You therefore must be perfect, as your heavenly Father is perfect." And how hard is that? Read Matthew 5:38–48.

Christ's commands in this portion of the Sermon on the Mount are indeed as kind and gentle as could be. But that's what makes them so difficult to obey. Not only are we to give to those who beg, much as Leviticus exhorted holiness to the poor and the alien. But now we're even to love our enemies and go the extra mile to accommodate the one who is evil. For God loves them too—gives them the same sunny day and rain for their crops He gives us (5:45). It's not good enough to love only those who love you. Being perfect means loving *all* your neighbors.

You must be perfectly holy, Jesus tells us. You shall be holy, the Lord says in Leviticus. The new man will be holy in keeping God's way, writes the psalmist. Oh, and Paul back in the Epistle adds this: "Do you not know that you are God's temple and that God's Spirit dwells in you? . . . God's temple is holy, and you are that temple" (1 Cor 3:16, 17). God's temple is—and you are—holy!

Jesus' words in verse 48 are generally translated as we've been offering them here, and quite understandably, because the Greek form of the verb *to be* (ἔσεσθε) fits the imperatival usage (like "Be perfect" or, of course, "You must be perfect"). But the very same Greek form can also be second person plural future indicative: "You shall be" or "You will be." "You will be perfect." The grammar can go either way.

There's no question, however, that when, as David sang in the Introit, God forgives our iniquities for the sake of Jesus' death on the cross, we share in His holy name. When we are baptized into Christ's death, we are the new man of the psalm who *will* keep God's way, because Christ did for us. When Jesus, who is the Lord, fulfills every demand of the Levitical code and loves every neighbor more than Himself, we shall be holy. It's as Paul wrote: when we are Christ's, we *are* holy. And when Jesus loved His enemies enough to let us kill Him, He made us perfectly holy.

**You Must Be/You Shall Be/
You Will Be/You *Are* Holy—
Especially in Loving All Your
Neighbors—
for You Are in Your Holy Lord,
Not in Your Iniquities.**

We have two choices this week for the **Hymn of the Day**. Enjoy singing them both.

Eighth Sunday after the Epiphany Year A

READINGS

Isaiah 49:8–16a
Psalm 115:(1–8) 9–18 (antiphon: v 1)
1 Corinthians 4:1–13
Matthew 6:24–34

HYMN OF THE DAY

LSB 819 "Sing Praise to God, the Highest Good"

Our Epiphany propers for eight Sundays now have been revealing something each week about the little toddler whom God's star of Bethlehem announced and the wise men worshiped. Next week, the last Sunday of the Epiphany season, will climax all these manifestations, these "shining upons," in a big, big way. But in truth, every Sunday of the season, and every Sunday of the entire church year, has been and will be revealing something far more powerful about Jesus than even "just" His glory in next Sunday's transfiguration. Back on Epiphany 3, 4, and 5, Paul in the Epistle readings made emphatic that the revelation of Christ par excellence is nothing other than the cross: "For I decided to know nothing among you except Jesus Christ and Him crucified" (1 Cor 2:2). "Nothing" is worth preaching if it's not the cross. Or, to put it positively, everything in God's Word (since it's all worth preaching!) is really about the cross.

We might think that goes without saying—but let's not think that. It *can't* go without saying! We might assume that everyone hearing all these propers for all these Sundays is keeping the cross of Christ clearly in mind as the foundation for everything that's being said. But that's a bad assumption.

On one of the streets where Claire and I often take our walks these days, there's a fairly large storefront church. Actually, it's a repurposed old-style movie theater. Above the marquee is a tall, simple cross. Unfortunately, the marquee projects over the sidewalk, so the cross is easily missed. (I didn't notice it for weeks.) From either direction, though, it's easy to read the changeable-letter messages on the marquee. Yesterday, one side read, "Be patient." On the other side, it said, "Throw a little kindness around today." The messages are usually along those lines. I assume this church is nondenominational, evangelical. I'm confident they believe that faith in Jesus' death and resurrection is how we're saved. And of course, patience and kindness are very good, biblical things. But what we can all read on the marquee doesn't at all make clear what we're likely to miss overhead.

This Sunday's last-for-now portion of the Sermon on the Mount includes Jesus' beautiful imagery of God caring for the birds of the air and the lilies of the field, assurance that He will provide for all our needs too. The cross isn't explicit. But it's all because of the cross. So this week, let's look forward to Sunday morning specifically by discovering where the cross is to be found in every proper.

The Cross Is Why We Can Trust We'll Receive the Kingdom and Every Other Good Thing Added to Us.

In our devotion-study for Epiphany 5, we briefly explained why Jesus' death on the cross really is the answer to every problem, the reason for every blessing. Again, briefly put, every good thing comes from God; apart from Him we'd have only death and whatever evils the devil would scheme up. But God's holiness means that nothing that isn't holy can be in any relationship with Him. So when Adam and Eve and we ourselves sinned, we separated ourselves from God, cut ourselves off from all God's blessings. That's where God's Son stepped in. Jesus took all those sins upon Himself and died for them. They're removed, forgiven. So now they no longer stand between us and God. We're reconciled to, back together with, God. He is again our dear Father, always embracing us tightly in His love. And that's true for the whole world; Jesus paid for the sins of the world; God is reconciled to all humankind. This is what the cross accomplished.

Now when the all-powerful, all-knowing, all-loving God (the God who can do everything, always knows what's really good, and wants to give us only what's best) is our loving Father again, we will always receive whatever is truly good for us. *Whatever* is truly good! Heaven, certainly—whenever it's the right time for us to be there. But also in the meantime, whatever is truly best for us to have right now.

So whatever problem we face, the answer is that God is with us, giving us whatever is really best (though we may not recognize it or understand it right now). And the reason: *because He's been reconciled to us by the cross.* Whatever blessing we receive, it's *because God has been reconciled to us by Jesus' death on the cross.* Therefore, whatever word we see in Scripture—any problem, any blessing—the message is *the cross.* It's a question of understanding clearly what the problem or blessing is and then realizing how the cross is the solution or source for each unique circumstance.

Take the Epiphany season **Gradual**:

Praise the LORD, all nations! Extol Him, all peoples! For great is His steadfast love toward us, and the faithfulness of the LORD endures

> *forever. Ascribe to the LORD the glory due His name; bring an offering, and come into His courts! (Ps 117:1–2a; 96:8)*

We praise, extol, God for His steadfast love and faithfulness. And not only is Jesus dying for us the greatest manifestation of that love, but without it we'd be cut off from all the blessings God's love desires to give. Only by the reconciliation of the cross do we have access to the "courts" of the Lord, so certainly it's our dearest reason to glorify Him and bring offerings.

Next, try the **Introit**:

> *Trust in Him at all times, O people; pour out your heart before Him; God is a refuge for us.*
>
> *For God alone my soul waits in silence; from Him comes my salvation. He only is my rock and my salvation, my fortress; I shall not be greatly shaken. Once God has spoken; twice have I heard this: that power belongs to God, and that to You, O Lord, belongs steadfast love. For You will render to a man according to his work.*
>
> *Glory be to the Father and to the Son and to the Holy Spirit; as it was in the beginning, is now, and will be forever. Amen.*
>
> *Trust in Him at all times, O people; pour out your heart before Him; God is a refuge for us. (Ps 62:1–2, 11–12; antiphon: Ps 62:8)*

Why can we trust God? If our sin still placed us under His wrath, He'd be no refuge or fortress for us; we'd only hope to flee from Him. Instead, with our sin forgiven by the cross, we can pour out to Him every concern of our hearts. We know He listens patiently and will answer wisely; by Jesus' reconciling death, He's our dear Father again. Power belongs to God, all right, but His power comforts us rather than terrifies because Jesus' death has appeased God's wrath. Imagine God rendering to me according to my work otherwise!

Now the **Collect** for this Sunday:

> *O Lord, mercifully hear our prayers and having set us free from the bonds of our sins deliver us from every evil; through Jesus Christ, Your Son, our Lord, who lives and reigns with You and the Holy Spirit, one God, now and forever. Amen.*

Jesus' cross is the reason God hears our prayers at all; if our sin still stood between us and God, there could be no communication. That's why we pray "through Jesus Christ" or "in Jesus' name." Freedom from our sins is, of course, the first blessing of the cross. And see where the Collect goes from there: forgiveness is, in turn, the basis for deliverance from *every* evil.

You've got the idea, I'm sure. So now with the lessons, beginning with the **Old Testament Reading**, Isaiah 49:8–16a.

Words like "salvation" (49:8) are, obviously, indications of the cross—even when we're being saved from hurts or threats or misfortunes in this life. In fact, anytime we're "helped" by the Lord (49:8) is likewise because He's reconciled to us by Jesus' death. So many wonderful ways He helps! He will keep us (49:8), free us (49:9), feed us (49:9), shade us (49:10), lead us (49:10). "Pity" (49:10), "comfort" (49:13), and "compassion" (49:13) are words from the cross.

And there's this one: "Behold, I have engraved you on the palms of My hands" (49:16). This is what some call a "handle" for the cross (a phrase that was perhaps not originally for the cross but can bring it to mind). We can't say whether Isaiah envisioned so vividly, but no doubt the Holy Spirit knew that we in the New Testament era might hear those words and picture the nail marks forever engraved in Jesus' hands.

Read the **Psalm** of the day, Psalm 115. It's all the cross, isn't it! God's glory is His steadfast love and faithfulness (115:1), which wouldn't desert us even when it cost Him His own life. Other "gods," whatever else we might trust, can do nothing for us (115:2–8), but we can trust the Lord to be our "help" and our "shield" (115:9–11)—a human shield, taking the bullet for us. We are blessed, enjoying "increase" (115:12–15), because we are no longer separated, cast down from, the Lord, even in death (115:16–18). That's reconciliation in the cross.

So much cross in the **Epistle**, 1 Corinthians 4:1–13! Paul, we remember, has established in 2:2 that it's nothing but.

Paul knows very well that he's sinful, but he's nevertheless confident that when the Lord judges him, he will be commended (4:1–5). That's because his sins are forgiven by Jesus' cross. Nothing we have (as, for example, Paul's stewardship of God's mysteries, 4:1) is something we can boast about. Everything we have we "received" (4:6–7), and that's always because our sins no longer separate us from God's blessings, thanks to Jesus dying for them.

And very important: apostles—and, in fact, all Christians—must endure sufferings. These are *our* crosses. They witness Jesus' sufferings to the world (4:8–13). But they also assure us that we are in Christ. We often won't understand, but somehow even as we go through pain, God is giving us what's best for us and for His whole Church. How do we know? Since Jesus' cross removed the sin that stood between us and God, nothing can separate us from the love of our Father.

Finally, that beautiful passage, Matthew 6:24–34, this Sunday's **Holy Gospel**.

What a comfort for day-to-day living! We really don't have to be anxious about anything. If He provides for the birds and the flowers, our heavenly Father will certainly give us everything we need—the kingdom of God and His righteousness and everything else He knows is good to add on to us (6:33). But these gifts are not earned by our seeking. Nor is this simply an ode to God's general generosity (some vague "Providence"). We have food and clothing, every single hour of life, and eternal life all because God is again our loving Father by the reconciling death of His Son.

"Nothing among you except Jesus Christ and Him crucified." This Sunday. Every day.

Where do you find the cross as you sing the **Hymn of the Day**, *LSB* 819? It's in every stanza!

The Transfiguration of Our Lord Year A

READINGS

Exodus 24:8–18
Psalm 2:6–12 (antiphon: v 6)
2 Peter 1:16–21
Matthew 17:1–9

HYMN OF THE DAY

LSB 413 "O Wondrous Type! O Vision Fair"

The Transfiguration of Our Lord is a fitting climax to the season of Epiphany, during which Jesus has been "shown forth," revealed, to be the King of the Jews and the Gentiles, God's beloved Son, the Lamb of God who takes away the sin of the world, history's greatest preacher, and the Blessèd One, who blesses us by fulfilling the Law for us and, ultimately, dying on the cross to reconcile us to God. Whoa! That's a lot! So, appropriately enough, the season ends this Sunday with a fireworks display that's way more than we can fully take in.

Jesus takes three of His disciples, Peter, James, and John, up a high mountain alone, and before their eyes, He's "transfigured" (that is, His appearance, His figure, is changed, transformed). He appears in His heavenly glory, and Moses and Elijah, great men of the Old Testament, are suddenly with Him. Then, as at Jesus' Baptism, the Father speaks from heaven. This was way more than Peter, James, and John could fully process. They were terrified.

The transfiguration is one of those events in the ministry of Jesus that's so significant all three synoptic Gospels (Matthew, Mark, and Luke) each give their unique perspectives. That's helpful, because there is indeed more to process than any one account could convey. Mark, as we'll note in Year B, focuses on the overwhelming visuals of Jesus' glory. Luke (Year C) is the only one to record the content of the conversation Jesus has with Moses and Elijah: His "departure," which will soon take place from Jerusalem. And this year, this week, we'll see Matthew's emphasis—and how the other propers develop it. I think we'll find it especially comforting.

Begin with the **Introit**:

Exalt the Lord our God, and worship at His holy mountain; for the Lord our God is holy!

The Lord reigns; let the peoples tremble! He sits enthroned upon the cherubim; let the earth quake! The Lord is great in Zion; He is exalted over all the peoples. Let them praise Your great and awesome name! Holy is He! The King in His might loves justice. You have established equity; You have executed justice and righteousness in Jacob. Exalt the Lord our God; worship at His footstool! Holy is He!

Glory be to the Father and to the Son and to the Holy Spirit; as it was in the beginning, is now, and will be forever. Amen.

Exalt the Lord our God, and worship at His holy mountain; for the Lord our God is holy! (Ps 99:1–5; antiphon: Ps 99:9)

Hearing the antiphon on this day, our minds immediately picture the Mount of Transfiguration. Like the disciples, the psalmist and "the peoples" are blown away. They "tremble"! "Let the earth quake!" It's not just that Yahweh is "awesome!" It's also that He's holy!—with another exclamation point! Because holy always puts the terror in unholy—and the more powerful the holy, the more terrifying! On the Mount of Transfiguration—like long ago on Mount Sinai—both God's holiness and power made it brilliantly obvious that we have neither.

But don't be blinded to this: "The King in His might loves justice." Remember from previous devotion-studies that God's justice is actually gracious to all who humbly depend on Him, that is, who know Him to be not just awesome but also gentle, loving, forgiving. That we'll see in the transfiguration too.

The **Collect** quite nicely summarizes the significance of the transfiguration, including Matthew's emphasis:

O God, in the glorious transfiguration of Your beloved Son You confirmed the mysteries of the faith by the testimony of Moses and Elijah. In the voice that came from the bright cloud You wonderfully foreshowed our adoption by grace. Mercifully make us co-heirs with the King in His glory and bring us to the fullness of our inheritance in heaven; through the same Jesus Christ, our Lord, who lives and reigns with You and the Holy Spirit, one God, now and forever. Amen.

"Glorious . . . beloved Son . . . confirmed"—how secure our faith in Jesus really is. (More on that later.) Moses and Elijah testifying to Him. The voice of the Father. A foreshowing of "our adoption . . . our inheritance in heaven," when we will shine with the very same glory we're seeing in our King, Jesus.

Amid all that glory, that power and holiness, we know we can't make demands of God. Still, we pray, we ask: "Mercifully . . ."

We pray and we trust that, even with all that glory, we still have a *merciful* God.

The connections of the **Old Testament Reading** to Jesus' transfiguration are quite apparent. Read Exodus 24:8–18.

Not surprisingly, the Old Testament Readings for Transfiguration all three years of the lectionary feature either Moses or Elijah. This year, Israel is at Mount Sinai, where God is establishing His covenant with them as His treasured possessions. God has just spoken the Ten Commandments in Exodus 20, and to confirm what's been said, He is going to give Moses the two tablets of stone (24:12). But first, He confirms His relationship with Israel by giving their leaders a glimpse: God standing above a sapphire pavement, clear as heaven (24:10). Awesome! "The appearance of the glory of the Lord was like a devouring fire on the top of the mountain" (24:17). Terrifying! Then, the remarkable thing: the leaders "saw the God of Israel. . . . And He did not lay His hand on [them]; they beheld God, and ate and drank" (24:10, 11). Holiness and power destroy the unholy. Unless . . .

"The blood of the covenant that the Lord has made with you" (24:8). The epiphany, the glimpse of God, does not destroy the leaders of Israel, because God has made them holy with the blood of His covenant. Blood washed away their unholiness. This, we know, is how Peter, James, John, and we will see the God of Israel!

The **Psalm**, too, is a kind of preview of the transfiguration: Psalm 2:6–12.

Again, we picture the mountain ("My holy hill"), and in verse 6, it is God the Father speaking. Then, in verse 7, the Son speaks, quoting what the Father says about Him: "You are My Son."

Next, the Psalm gives a warning we understand from the other propers: kings, rulers of the earth, though considered powerful among men, must serve the Lord with fear and trembling (2:10–11). "Kiss the Son" (2:12a) imagines them bowing before Him and kissing His feet. They must, for His anger can destroy even the powerful of the earth.

But as in the Introit, the Psalm concludes with a word of comfort: "Blessèd are all who take refuge in Him" (2:12b). The power of the Lord is overwhelming; it can wreak total destruction. But He is also the place of safety for those who bow before Him and trust His mercy.

As the Epiphany season has it, our recent Epistle lessons have followed Paul through 1 Corinthians. This week, though, as a festival day, the **Epistle** is chosen to reflect the celebration explicitly: 2 Peter 1:16–21.

Mark's Gospel is widely seen as written under the supervision of Peter, so in effect we have Peter's story of the transfiguration there. Here in Peter's second epistle, though, we have his theological commentary on it. The allusion is obvious: "We were eyewitnesses of His majesty. For when He received honor and glory from God the Father, and the voice was borne to Him by the Majestic Glory, 'This is My beloved Son, with whom I am well pleased,' we ourselves heard this very voice borne from heaven, for we were with Him on the holy mountain" (1:16b–18).

Peter uses this event to make a powerful point: "We have the prophetic word more fully confirmed" (1:19). The transfiguration confirms everything written in the Scriptures. Verses 20–21 are one of the two classic passages on the Bible's inspiration (along with 2 Timothy 3:16–17), asserting that the Scriptures are in every word and syllable reliable because they are inspired by the Holy Spirit. But the Bible is above all reliable because every word declares the Word Himself, Jesus Christ. From Genesis to Revelation, the whole Bible proclaims Christ, and now, Peter testifies, the very voice of God has affirmed this Jesus as His Son. If Jesus is the Son of God and every word of Scripture is about Jesus, every word of the Bible is true.

That day, however, the disciples had a more immediate need of confirmation. Read the **Holy Gospel**, Matthew 17:1–9.

The three Gospel accounts of this event do have their particular accents—Mark on the overwhelming sights of Jesus' glory, Luke on its direct succession to Jesus' Passion. And Matthew? All witnesses convey the terror the disciples felt. But interestingly, Mark notes the terror as the disciples see Jesus shining with Moses and Elijah (Mk 9:3–6). Luke says they were afraid as the cloud overshadowed them (Lk 9:34). Both true, certainly. Both terrifying! But see what Matthew cites as triggering fear (17:5–6): the voice of the Father! We've observed often that we sinners must tremble at the holiness and power of God. Facing "the Majestic Glory," as Peter called the Father in our Epistle lesson, would destroy us as long as we're still in our sin. Hearing the Father speak drove this home to the disciples: "They fell on their faces."

But then, "Jesus came and touched them, saying, 'Rise, and have no fear.' And when they lifted up their eyes, they saw no one but Jesus only" (17:7–8). What a sound for terrified ears! (And a sight for terrified eyes! And a caress for trembling flesh!) They fall down in terror, and the Son comes to touch *them*! They look up and see: it is their Jesus. The one they've heard and followed and lived with and eaten with for now almost three years. He's cared for them, been patient with their ignorance and foolishness, stilled storms to save them. Almighty, all-glorious God, but God who's become one of them to be with them. God, who now from the Mount of Transfiguration will go to the cross to reconcile them also to the heavenly Father—which, for every terrifying moment, can allay all our fears. *Our* Jesus. Matthew's accent:

**Though We Would Tremble—
Be Terrified!—
at the Voice of the Father,
the Presence of *Our* Jesus
Fully Confirms We Have Nothing
to Fear.**

Pray once more the **Gradual** for Epiphany, thankful that even Jesus' heavenly glory is shown forth in His love and faithfulness:

> *Praise the Lord, all nations! Extol Him, all peoples! For great is His steadfast love toward us, and the faithfulness of the Lord endures forever. Ascribe to the Lord the glory due His name; bring an offering, and come into His courts! (Ps 117:1–2a; 96:8)*

Close with the **Hymn of the Day**, "O Wondrous Type! O Vision Fair" (*LSB* 413).

Ash Wednesday Years A, B, C

READINGS

Joel 2:12–19
Psalm 51:1–13 (14–19) (antiphon: v 17)
2 Corinthians 5:20b–6:10
Matthew 6:1–6, 16–21

HYMN OF THE DAY

LSB 607 "From Depths of Woe I Cry to Thee"

This Wednesday, the pastor may step forward in the center of the chancel, face you, and begin the service:

Dear brothers and sisters of our Lord Jesus Christ,

> on this day the Church begins a holy season of prayerful and penitential reflection. Our attention is especially directed to the holy sufferings and death of our Lord Jesus Christ.
>
> From ancient times the season of Lent has been kept as a time of special devotion, self-denial, and humble repentance born of a faithful heart that dwells confidently on His Word and draws from it life and hope.
>
> Let us pray that our dear Father in heaven, for the sake of His beloved Son and in the power of His Holy Spirit, might richly bless this Lententide for us so that we may come to Easter with glad hearts and keep the feast in sincerity and truth. (*Lutheran Service Book: Altar Book* [St. Louis: CPH, 2006], 483)

The pastor may then invite you to come forward and receive ashes on your forehead, drawn in the shape of a cross, as he says: "Remember that you are dust, and to dust you shall return."

Ash Wednesday and the season of Lent begin with the pastor imploring, earnestly appealing to his people, to take up a journey with Jesus, repenting of their sins and trudging with Him to the cross. He begs them to this trek because he knows that at the cross they will receive forgiveness and renewal for living.

From the Mount of Transfiguration last Sunday, Jesus "set His face to go to Jerusalem" (Lk 9:51). He knew what awaited Him there. He would die to pay for the sins of the whole world; it would be finished, the journey completed once and for all.

We, however, are invited to return every year. Indeed, we *need* to return to the cross *daily*. That's how Martin Luther taught us to use our Baptism: "The Old Adam in us should by daily contrition and repentance be drowned and die with all sins and evil desires, and . . . a new man should daily emerge and arise to live before God in righteousness and purity forever" (Small Catechism, Baptism). So an annual Lenten return to the cross is a wholesome discipline.

The word *Lent* probably comes from an old Anglo-Saxon word for "spring season," a word meaning "long," as the time of year when the days become noticeably longer. The season lasts forty days—Ash Wednesday to Holy Saturday, Easter Eve—based on Jesus' forty days of temptation in the wilderness (the Holy Gospel for this coming Sunday). The mood of the season is, of course, penitential, with certain joyous elements such as Alleluias and the Hymn of Praise omitted from services.

It begins this Wednesday with the pastor imploring us to return to the cross.

Lenten midweek services generally follow readings and sermon texts that pastors themselves design as a series. But for Ash Wednesday only, there is a full set of assigned propers. The **Introit**, with verses from the penitential Psalm 51, makes a natural choice:

The sacrifices of God are a broken spirit; a broken and contrite heart, O God, You will not despise.

Have mercy on me, O God, according to Your steadfast love; according to Your abundant mercy blot out my transgressions. Wash me thoroughly from my iniquity, and cleanse me from my sin! For I know my transgressions, and my sin is ever before me. Create in me a clean heart, O God, and renew a right spirit within me. Cast me not away from Your presence, and take not Your Holy Spirit from me. Restore to me the joy of Your salvation, and uphold me with a willing spirit.

Glory be to the Father and to the Son and to the Holy Spirit; as it was in the beginning, is now, and will be forever. Amen.

The sacrifices of God are a broken spirit; a broken and contrite heart, O God, You will not despise. (Ps 51:1–3, 10–12; antiphon: Ps 51:17)

Psalm 51 is also the **Psalm** of the day, so perhaps reading it now in its entirety will be helpful as well. Notice the verses that have been selected as the Introit and, especially, as its antiphon.

David wrote Psalm 51 after repenting and receiving forgiveness for his horrific sins with Bathsheba and against Uriah (2 Samuel 11–12; see the superscription above the psalm). David, sitting on the throne and enjoying the pampered life as king, seems to have forgotten that he was dust and to dust he would return. Nathan snaps him out of that. Now David knows his transgressions, and his sin is ever before him (51:3).

But Nathan has also spoken the word of absolution: "The Lord also has put away your sin; you shall not die" (2 Sam 12:13). And David believes that "a broken and contrite heart, O God, You will not despise" (51:17). So David prays, "Wash me thoroughly from my iniquity, and cleanse me from my sin!" (51:2). And then the beautiful words we can all sing: "Create in me a clean heart, O God, and renew a right spirit within me. Cast me not away from Thy presence, and take not Thy Holy Spirit from me. Restore unto me the joy of Thy salvation; and uphold me with Thy free spirit" (51:10–12, our common Offertory, KJV). These words follow the sermon in our Divine Service, Setting Three, because the preaching we will just have heard should always have been a proclamation of Christ crucified; we have been brought back to the cross, where David's sins and ours were forgiven. Appropriate every Sunday, quite obviously, but particularly suited to this day and to the Lenten season, we return to the cross by returning to the Gospel and Sacraments because we constantly fall into sin—if not as heinous as David's, just as deadly—and we need continuous assurance of God's forgiveness.

Our **Collect**, therefore, largely mirrors David's penitential prayer:

Almighty and everlasting God, You despise nothing You have made and forgive the sins of all who are penitent. Create in us new and contrite hearts that lamenting our sins and acknowledging our wretchedness we may receive from You full pardon and forgiveness; through Jesus Christ, Your Son, our Lord, who lives and reigns with You and the Holy Spirit, one God, now and forever. Amen.

Lent, our Lutheran practice affirms, is anchored here—in the assurance of pardon and forgiveness through Jesus Christ. Sincere and earnest repentance is elicited by that gracious promise, rather than our self-denial or browbeating, giving the season its value.

Still, the readings for Ash Wednesday do propose holy living and discipline, even fasting, as the character of Lent. In that sense, the **Old Testament Reading**, Joel 2:12–19, may be the quintessential text for this day.

Joel, a prophet to Judah likely during the ninth century BC, has written vividly of a terrible plague of locusts (1:1–2:11). In ancient times, such an episode would devastate the land, bringing widespread starvation (see 1:16–18). The locusts were a judgment from God upon the people's sin (2:11).

"'Yet even now,' declares the Lord, 'return to Me with all your heart.'" So Joel, too, pleads, "Return to the Lord your God, for He is gracious and merciful, slow to anger, and abounding in steadfast love; and He relents over disaster" (2:12a, 13b).

The Lord Himself describes what that return will look like: "fasting, with weeping, and with mourning; and rend your hearts and not your garments" (2:12b–13a). So, again, the faithful prophet begs: "Blow the trumpet in Zion; consecrate a fast" (2:15). The fast will be a solemn assembly for which everyone, young and old, will drop all worldly pursuits and gather to the Lord for earnest prayer (2:17). Then what the locusts have destroyed the Lord will restore (2:18–19). For us, this depicts what Lent can and should be: a hard look at where we've become entangled in the things of the world and confession that we therefore deserve any punishment that comes (to dust we shall return!) but also faith in God's promise of forgiveness and a time to gather around Christ's Word and Sacraments. Come, cling to the cross, where all sins have been atoned for!

The apostle Paul repeats the same plea in the **Epistle**, 2 Corinthians 5:20b–6:10. "We implore you on behalf of Christ, be reconciled to God. . . . We appeal to you" (5:20; 6:1). It's just as your pastor will beg you on Wednesday. All has been accomplished! Christ has nailed your sins to His cross! "For our sake He made Him to be sin who knew no sin, so that in Him we might become the righteousness of God" (5:21). Please, do not "receive the grace of God in vain" (6:1b)! "*Now* is the favorable time; behold, *now* is the day of salvation" (6:2b)! Now! During this forty-day fast! Return to the cross!

Finally, in our **Holy Gospel**, our Lord gives crucial counsel so our Lenten fast would be truly a return to His cross, rather than vain self-serving. Read Matthew 6:1–6, 16–21.

Medieval practice of Lent badly distorted the ancient intent. Personal disciplines, including those Jesus cites here—almsgiving, prayer, literal fasting—were viewed as earning merit before God, that is, for one's own benefit. That's not really much different from doing the same things to be seen by men; it's still serving self, neither God nor others. Jesus' bottom line is that in Him, we have "treasures in heaven" (6:20), so that we need not impress others—or even God.

Our treasures in heaven are here for us already on earth in the places God chooses to give Himself: in the preaching of the Gospel, in our Baptism, and at the Lord's Table. In these, He gives us Jesus Christ crucified, the cross, for our eternal salvation. Lent should be nothing but eagerly returning to these means where God gives the cross to us, knowing that there He will forgive us and cleanse us. So with your pastor Wednesday,

**We Implore You
to Return to the Cross
during This Lenten Fast,
for There
the Lord Will Forgive Your Sin
and Create in You a Clean Heart.**

That journey is just beginning, but the **Gradual** for the season will keep the focus:

> *[O come, let us fix our eyes on] Jesus, the founder and perfecter of our faith, who for the joy that was set before Him endured the cross, despising the shame, and is seated at the right hand of the throne of God. (Heb 12:2)*

As you sing the **Hymn of the Day**, note all of Luther's phrases of confidence that God will answer repentance with forgiveness.

First Sunday in Lent Year A

READINGS

Genesis 3:1–21
Psalm 32:1–7 (antiphon: v7a)
Romans 5:12–19
Matthew 4:1–11

HYMN OF THE DAY

LSB 656, 657 "A Mighty Fortress Is Our God"

No doubt every one of us has some chapter in our personal histories that we'd like to rewrite. Something we'd like to do over. A great opportunity we blew. An investment we wish we'd made. A free throw we'd like to shoot again. Much worse: An unkind word we're sorry we spoke. A selfish advantage we should never have taken. A torched friendship we deeply regret torching.

As Christians, we always regret giving in to temptation—"little" sins we must surely have committed but we can't remember, awful sins we can't ever forget. And, of course, we'd give anything for the biggest do-over, rewriting all human history: the first bite of evil in the Garden of Eden. "O day of sadness when the breath of fear and darkness, doubt and death, its awful poison first displayed within the world so newly made" (*LSB* 561:2).

The First Sunday in Lent in all three years of the lectionary is keyed to the temptation of Christ—Matthew's, Mark's, and Luke's accounts in the Gospel lessons for Years A, B, and C, respectively. Most of the other propers—the Introit, the Collect, the Gradual, the Verse, and the Hymn of the Day—are identical for all three years, which means the particular accents among the three years become most apparent in the Old Testament Readings and the Epistles, both of which help highlight features that are unique in the various Gospel narratives.

This year's Lent 1 Old Testament Reading, closely paired with the Epistle, is that history of the first (tragically successful) temptation, which will be reprised in Matthew's telling of Jesus' temptation. Imagine if that history could be rewritten!

I remember an embarrassing moment when we'd packed the house at Dallas's world-famous Meyerson Symphony Center for a Lutheran hymn festival but had failed to put "A Mighty Fortress" on the program. So before the postlude, the officiant announced, "Just by memory, let's all sing one stanza of 'A Mighty Fortress Is Our God.'" The embarrassment was less over the programming omission than it was over the way that one stanza comes out. Sing just that first stanza of the **Hymn of the Day** for the First Sunday in Lent: your choice, *LSB* 656 or 657.

See what I mean? Don't worry; we'll sing the rest later. But this day does start out with the evil foe seemingly winning—"on earth he has no equal"—which is why the **Verse** is Ephesians 6:11: "Put on the whole armor of God, that you may be able to stand against the schemes of the devil."

Among the devil's schemes, as we'll be reminded in the Gospel lesson, is his clever (mis)use of God's own word. As you read the **Introit**, see if you recognize the verses Satan will quote to Jesus.

When he calls to Me, I will answer him; I will be with him in trouble; I will rescue him and honor him. With long life I will satisfy him and show him My salvation.

Because you have made the Lord *your dwelling place—the Most High, who is my refuge—no evil shall be allowed to befall you, no plague come near your tent. For He will command His angels concerning you to guard you in all your ways. On their hands they will bear you up, lest you strike your foot against a stone. You will tread on the lion and the adder; the young lion and the serpent you will trample underfoot.*

Glory be to the Father and to the Son and to the Holy Spirit; as it was in the beginning, is now, and will be forever. Amen.

When he calls to Me, I will answer him; I will be with him in trouble; I will rescue him and honor him. With long life I will satisfy him and show him My salvation. (Ps 91:9–13; antiphon: Ps 91:15–16)

Did you catch the devil's line? If not, I'll leave it to you to find when you read the Gospel lesson in a bit. But do realize that Satan would like to rewrite even the record of Holy Scripture to his own slant.

Rightly understood, Psalm 91 is a wonderful assurance that "for us" against the evil foe "fights the valiant One." (You know that's coming up to sing.) The Lord says, "I will be with [you] in trouble, . . . rescue [you] . . . no evil shall be allowed to befall you."

The **Collect** highlights an element of Jesus' temptation that we find quite significant for Year A's Lent 1 emphasis:

O Lord God, You led Your ancient people through the wilderness and brought them to the promised land. Guide the people of Your Church that following our Savior we may walk through the wilderness of this world toward the glory of the world to come; through Jesus Christ, Your Son, our Lord, who lives and reigns with You and the Holy Spirit, one God, now and forever. Amen.

The Collect describes Jesus' temptation in the wilderness as a recapitulation of ancient Israel's wilderness wanderings on the way to the Promised Land. The parallels are substantial: The Israelites were in the wilderness forty years; Jesus, forty days. For both, it was a time of testing. The wilderness was barren, requiring both Israel and Christ to depend on God for their provision. History seems to be repeating itself. But Israel often failed its test, while Jesus . . .

The **Old Testament Reading** is that sad day at what could be called the dawn of history—but might have been the sunset, Genesis 3:1–21.

Study this text carefully; there's always more to it. The essence of Satan's temptation is that God is holding out on Eve and Adam, that with all this beautiful creation, there's still something better He's not sharing. And our first parents falling for it has affected us every moment since. Most try to hide from God, and we may often get together with Him as a chore rather than as the joy it had been (3:8). We know disharmony in marriages (3:12, 16b), pain not only in childbirth (3:16a) but in accidents, illnesses, aging. We know hard labor for crops or paycheck (3:17–19a). We know death (3:19b). Sin, beginning with this one, is The Problem—always.

Several details to notice as you read: The devil, in the form of the serpent (see Rev 12:9), tempts by calling into question whether God can actually be trusted: "Did God actually say . . . ?" (3:1). Notice, too, the sequence of the temptation: it's about food, eating (3:1); it proposes that Eve and Adam won't really die (3:4); and it promises that they will become like God (3:5). (The devil likes to use half-truths. Adam and Eve, like God, *would* now know good and evil; before this, they only knew good. But, of course, God knew that for them, knowing evil would not be good.) Finally, note that when God speaks, He calls Adam, not Eve, to account (3:9). All that is history as it happened—and nothing any of us could do to rewrite it.

But God also gives a prophecy of history as it *will* happen. Read again 3:15, the first promise of the Gospel. God speaks to the serpent (3:14) and tells him that the offspring of the woman will bruise his head, even as he (the serpent) bruises the offspring's heel. The offspring of Eve is her great-great-grand-descendant Jesus, and the bruising is the cross. Satan certainly will bruise Jesus, even kill Him, but Jesus' death would crush Satan's head. This part of 3:15 is well known.

Perhaps not as well understood is this part of the verse: "I will put enmity between you and the woman, and between your offspring and her offspring." Enmity is separation, as between enemies. And see what God is saying: Satan and people (the woman, representing all people) will be separated. That's good news! Sin made us allies of the devil, enemies of God. But now enmity with the devil means reconciliation with God. The bruising (Jesus' cross) would reunite us with God. That would change history!

Pairing Genesis 3 with the Matthew **Gospel** of Jesus' temptation highlights precisely that. Read Matthew 4:1–11. It's more than just history repeating itself.

As for Israel, it's in the wilderness. And as with Eve and Adam, the devil comes tempting—very much the same way. "Did God really say . . . ?" becomes "*If* You are the Son of God . . ." Why, yes, at His Baptism just days before, God had truly said, "This is My beloved Son." But can God be trusted?

Last time, this approach worked with Eve. We'll start with eating—this time, stones into bread. Then, "you will not surely die" if you throw yourself down from the pinnacle of the temple. And the clincher: "Why, who rules all the kingdoms of the world but God?"

Satan knew that if history repeated itself, just once, the only Savior of the world could not save. He could not crush the serpent at the cross, because He would have to die for His own sin.

But no, no, and no. Jesus trusted His Father, relied on God's Word, desired only what God was giving Him. This was the Great Do-Over. This is why Jesus came—to do *for* man what man had failed to do. We call this Jesus' active obedience, His perfect keeping of the Law. And this He had to do before His passive obedience, being bruised on the cross, could crush the serpent's head.

We often, rightly, complain these days about "revisionist history"—looking back centuries and changing the record books to fit what today's political sensitivities think should have happened. But what Jesus did against Satan's temptations did indeed rewrite our histories. Because Jesus did keep the Law perfectly, God says that *we* who are baptized into Christ and His cross have kept the Law perfectly, that Adam and Eve and we have said no to all of those traps. *We* have the Great Do-Over.

Savor Paul's theological explanation of this in our **Epistle**, Romans 5:12–19. Adam plunged the whole human race into sin and therefore death (remember, it's Adam, not Eve, that God holds first of all responsible). We've all inherited it. But "as by the one man's disobedience the many were made sinners, so by the one man's obedience the many will be made righteous" (5:19). This is how our **Psalm** can say we are "blessed," Psalm 32:1–7, for we have our transgression forgiven, our sin covered, our history rewritten.

By Jesus Obeying Where We Had Given In to Satan's Temptation, Jesus Rewrote Our History.

So, in the Lenten **Gradual**:

> *[O come, let us fix our eyes on] Jesus, the founder and perfecter of our faith, who for the joy that was set before Him endured the cross, despising the shame, and is seated at the right hand of the throne of God. (Heb 12:2)*

We can't forget to sing the rest of "A Mighty Fortress Is Our God." With our new history, "the Kingdom ours remaineth."

Second Sunday in Lent Year A

READINGS

Genesis 12:1–9
Psalm 121 (antiphon: v 8)
Romans 4:1–8, 13–17
John 3:1–17

HYMN OF THE DAY

LSB 708 "Lord, Thee I Love with All My Heart"

The **Gradual** for the season of Lent boils a whole Bible-full of theology down to its essence:

> *[O come, let us fix our eyes on] Jesus, the founder and perfecter of our faith, who for the joy that was set before Him endured the cross, despising the shame, and is seated at the right hand of the throne of God. (Heb 12:2)*

It may be, though, that for most Christians, that same essence of theology is boiled down to the **Verse** for this Second Sunday in Lent: "For God so loved the world, that He gave His only Son, that whoever believes in Him should not perish but have eternal life."

Our Gospel lesson for this Sunday includes John 3:16. It, like Hebrews 12:2, really is a magnificent summary of the Christian faith. If we could know only one verse of Scripture—or share only one verse with a friend—it would be a wonderful choice. But Jesus didn't wrap "the Gospel in a nutshell" in a nutshell or in isolation. He spoke it as part of a very enlightening dialogue and with the assumption that His dialogue partner knew very well thousands of years of theology.

Our propers this day will culminate with Jesus speaking John 3:16 to Nicodemus, a teacher of the Jews. But our other propers, first, will help us understand the context in which Jesus spoke and thus give a fuller understanding of what our favorite passage means.

To begin to establish that context for us, the **Introit** looks back more than two thousand years before Christ:

He remembers His covenant forever, the word that He commanded, for a thousand generations.

Seek the Lord *and His strength; seek His presence continually! Remember the wondrous works that He has done, His miracles, and the judgments He uttered, O offspring of Abraham, His servant, children of Jacob, His chosen ones! He is the* Lord *our God; His judgments are in all the earth.*

Glory be to the Father and to the Son and to the Holy Spirit; as it was in the beginning, is now, and will be forever. Amen.

He remembers His covenant forever, the word that He commanded, for a thousand generations. (Ps 105:4–7; antiphon: Ps 105:8)

Psalm 105 in its entirety (along with Psalm 106) relates much of Israel's early story as a nation. It starts with God's covenant with Abraham. God's covenant is the thread that runs through the entire Old Testament—"for a thousand generations"—and ultimately reaches its fulfillment in Jesus Christ. It's tempting to think God worked quite differently in the Old Testament than He does in the New. For example, we might think that since Jesus hadn't come yet, God's Old Testament people were saved by their observing circumcision, the Sabbath, and the sacrificial system. There's a widespread theology called dispensationalism that does say God saved the generations after Abraham in a different way than He saves us now since the coming of Christ. (Actually, dispensationalists teach that God saved *seven* different ways during seven different time periods, or "dispensations," through history.) But in the Introit, we hear that God "remembers His covenant forever," that is, for "offspring of Abraham" far beyond just the Old Testament age; the covenant is with us too.

The **Collect** for this Sunday:

O God, You see that of ourselves we have no strength. By Your mighty power defend us from all adversities that may happen to the body and from all evil thoughts that may assault and hurt the soul; through Jesus Christ, Your Son, our Lord, who lives and reigns with You and the Holy Spirit, one God, now and forever. Amen.

"Of ourselves we have no strength." That admission is foundational to faith. If we think we have strength, then we won't see ourselves as completely dependent on God. Our faith will be at least partly in ourselves—false faith. We'll think that our covenant with God is some sort of "deal" we negotiated together—that we have something to offer in trade for His goodness. True faith is recognizing, "I'm helpless, Lord. I'm depending totally on You." That, we'll see in a few minutes, is the kind of covenant God made with Abraham and with us.

The **Old Testament Reading**, Genesis 12:1–9, is the actual narrative of God's first encounter with Abraham toward establishing that covenant.

The preceding chapter introduced us to Abram (his given name, which God would change to Abraham in Gen 17:5) and his family (11:26–32). Seemingly a parenthetical but, as we know, crucial detail is that Abram's wife Sarai is unable to have children. (God will change Sarai's name too, 17:15.) Chapter 11 gives no motivation, but it reads as if Abram is just along for the ride when Terah, the patriarch, moves the clan from Ur of the Chaldeans, a city in the lower Euphrates valley, near the Persian Gulf, to Haran, along the upper Euphrates, a journey of perhaps six hundred miles. Already, though, this is planned to be just a first stop on the way to Canaan (11:31).

In fact, the New Testament tells us that God had already spoken to Abram in Ur (Acts 7:2–4). And when Terah dies, Abram, Sarai, and Abram's nephew Lot proceed on to God's destination, another four hundred miles or more.

This is a remarkable story of faith. God's command is that Abram leave his home and go to a place he's never seen before. Ur was a major cultural center; in Canaan, Abram wouldn't know a soul and would live as a nomad. God promised to make of Abram a great nation (12:2), implying many descendants, but by age seventy-five (and Sarai sixty-five, 12:4, 17:17), he had not one. All Abram had to go on was God's word. And yet "Abram went" (12:4). It's especially noteworthy that God's word was able to create this faith in a man who was an idol worshiper (Josh 24:2). God chose to establish His covenant with a man who had been an unbeliever. That's always the way it is with faith; faith is never something we have of ourselves, but rather, God's word of promise creates it out of nothing.

The most important word of God's promise to Abram: "In you all the families of the earth shall be blessed" (12:3). This is one of the pivotal passages of the entire Old Testament! How could all the families of the earth be blessed in one nomad who did not even have an heir? Well, twenty-five long years later, as we know, God would give Abraham and Sarah one child, Isaac (21:1–3), and his line would continue twenty centuries more until the Savior of all families of the earth, Jesus, was born into it. "To your offspring," the nation of Israel, God told Abram, "I will give this land" (12:7). But we who are Abraham's offspring in a different way are blessed with a much greater inheritance.

The **Psalm** follows nicely after the story of Abram's travels. Our family often reads Psalm 121 before we leave on a trip, because it declares God's care whenever and wherever we go ("by day," "by night," "going out" and "coming in," 121:6, 8). But the psalm also expresses the faith by which we not only travel but also live every day: "My help comes from the LORD" (121:2). The Introit assured us that God "remembers His covenant forever, . . . for a thousand generations." Here the psalmist echoes, "The LORD will keep your going out and your coming in from this time forth and forevermore" (121:8).

It's the **Epistle**, Romans 4:1–8, 13–17, which makes most explicit the basis for God's covenant with Abraham and with us.

Did God work differently with Old Testament Abraham and his offspring "according to the flesh" (4:1), his biological descendants, the nation of Israel, than He does with us?

Was His covenant with them based on circumcision, Sabbaths, sacrifices? Those would each be kinds of works. "What does the Scripture say? 'Abraham *believed* God, and *it* was counted to him as righteousness.' . . . To the one who does not work but believes in Him who justifies the ungodly, his *faith* is counted as righteousness" (4:3, 5). "The promise to Abraham and his offspring . . . did not come through the law but through the righteousness of faith" (4:13). "It depends on faith, in order that the promise may rest on grace and be guaranteed to *all his offspring* . . . to the one who shares *the faith of Abraham*" (4:16).

Abraham was saved by faith in Christ. God's covenant was always that those who believed in Jesus—had faith in Him—were Abraham's offspring, heirs of eternal blessing. We are Abraham's offspring. We are saved by faith in Christ.

All this is necessary, first, if one is to understand fully *how* one *becomes* the true offspring of Abraham—and, therefore, to understand fully John 3:16. Nicodemus should have known all this, but Jesus teaches him in our **Holy Gospel**, John 3:1–17.

Nicodemus is a Pharisee, a ruler and teacher of Israel (3:1, 10)—who, we notice, at this point wants to protect that reputation by keeping his interest in Jesus a secret ("by night," 3:2). He knows Abraham's story as his own. He should understand God's covenant with Abraham—who receives the kingdom of God and how. Instead, he must learn.

One receives the kingdom by being "born again"; or the Greek ἄνωθεν can be equally well translated "from above," "born from above." It's a play on words to mean both, and both happen when "one is born of water and the Spirit" (3:5). We know this to be Baptism. Baptism is a miraculous means God uses to create faith. Faith that makes us "offspring of Abraham," that incorporates us into the covenant.

It would take Nicodemus some time more, but eventually he would realize that the One into whom we're born again—born from above, baptized—the One in whom Abraham believed, was the very One teaching him. If not before, Nicodemus had this faith by the time he saw "the Son of Man . . . lifted up," nailed to a cross (3:14; 19:30, 38–42). There he saw the covenant fulfilled, thousands of years of theology finished.

This is John 3:16. Our one short verse summarizes the covenant that ran through the entire Old Testament, for God was always working His love in the world, in every age bringing souls to eternal life, always by faith, by believing in the Son, who was lifted up on the cross. Born again, born from above, as Abraham's offspring, by Baptism into Jesus. No other way. Always this way.

God's Covenant with
All the Offspring of Abraham
Is the Covenant of Faith
in God's Son,
Which We Now Share
by Our Baptism.

Ponder this rich Gospel—and even our fellowship with Abraham—as you close with the **Hymn of the Day**, *LSB* 708.

Third Sunday in Lent Year A

READINGS

Exodus 17:1–7
Psalm 95:1–9 (antiphon: v 6)
Romans 5:1–8
John 4:5–26 (27–30, 39–42)

HYMN OF THE DAY

LSB 823, 824 "May God Bestow on Us His Grace"

In the design of the three-year lectionary, the Epistle lessons play interesting roles. The Gospel lesson directs the theme for the Sunday, and the Old Testament Reading is always selected to follow the lead of the Gospel. But depending on the time of the church year, the Epistle lessons serve now one, now another of two possible purposes.

Remember how we've explained this before. During the seasons of Epiphany, Easter, and Pentecost (not including their festivals), the Epistle lessons read semicontinuously through a particular Epistle book, like 1 Corinthians or Galatians. That's edifying because it gives us an appreciation of the overall message of that book. But since the Gospel lessons follow their own progression through, say, Matthew's Gospel, the Epistles then don't always coordinate with the Holy Gospels and the Old Testament Readings.

On the other hand, in Advent, Christmas, Lent, and on all festivals, the Epistles not only coordinate with the Gospels, *they often add the theological commentary or explanation* behind events in both the Holy Gospel and the Old Testament Reading. Two weeks ago, Paul, in the Epistle, explained the impact on us of Adam falling into temptation and Jesus overcoming the tempter. Last week, Paul explained that the Old Testament covenant with Abraham was all about faith so "whoever believes in [God's only Son] should not perish but have eternal life" (the Gospel, including Jn 3:16).

This is certainly another of those weeks. The Old Testament Reading and the Holy Gospel are lively stories, closely connected by an interest in water. But why Israel and a Samaritan woman at a well (and we) receive water—of two very different kinds—well, Paul explains that in our **Epistle**. So this week, just to see how this often works, let's begin there, and afterward we'll hear the other readings play out as living examples. Read Romans 5:1–8 (and peek at 9–11).

"Therefore" (5:1) always calls us back to something preceding, and, conveniently, last week's Epistle was from Romans 4. (Not, by the way, because it's a continuous reading in Romans, but because each followed the week's theme. Remember, this is the season of Lent.) In Romans 4, Paul explained at length that, like Abraham, "we have been justified by faith" (5:1; 4:3–5, 16). To be justified means to be declared not guilty, the best words accused criminals like ourselves could ever hear in court.

But to be declared not guilty doesn't just mean you don't go to jail (or hell!)—though it does mean that. It also means that the former accused returns to regular life, with all that's supposed to be, no stigma or strings attached. (It's not always that tidy, of course, in our world, but it is that clean with God!) In Paul's words, having been justified by faith, "we have peace with God through our Lord Jesus Christ" (5:1). That's life as it's supposed to be, the way God set it up in the beginning: at peace with God, where He is our dear Father and nothing separates us from Him. We have "access" to His grace (5:2) and can bring any request before Him and know He hears and answers in the most gracious way. Even when we suffer, we can rejoice, because we know God is *never* giving us anything but His best (5:3–5). That's what comes when we're at peace with God.

"For" (5:6). Now that always tells us that the reason is coming. And there's never an effect without a cause—always God's best because we're at peace with God. At peace with God because we've been justified. Justified by faith. But faith in what? This is the crux of it all. And it is the *crux*! "For while we were still weak, at the right time Christ died for the ungodly" (5:6).

A man might die for his wife, a woman for her child, a soldier for his buddy. But see what we were: "weak" (that's the weakest term, just for starters), "ungodly," "still sinners" (5:8), and, if you skip ahead to 5:10, "enemies" of God. There's the killer. We weren't pretty okay with God and messed up a little. We hated God. Would have killed Him if we could. Failing that, we at least hoped He'd play dead and never once bother us. And guys just don't die for folks who treat them like that.

But God did. Jesus did.

And this is how we have peace with God. The sin that made us enemies of God Jesus took upon Himself. When those sins died with Jesus, they no longer separated us from God. God was reconciled to us. He is at peace with us. And that's what counts. Now He is always giving us His best, everything that's truly good for us. Then God declares this in the Gospel—like these very words of Paul—and through it, the Holy Spirit creates faith in our hearts. We can approach Him with our prayers; we can trust Him even amid suffering. We hope in Him (5:5).

That's what's going on in our propers this week, and the **Holy Gospel** is an example of a life it changed: John 4:5–30, 39–42.

Jesus meets a woman who needs to know God is at peace with her. She's a Samaritan, which doesn't just make her an object of ethnic prejudice by the Jews, it also means she follows a heretical religion. The matter of worshiping "on this mountain," Mount Gerizim, rather than in Jerusalem (4:20) reflects the Samaritans' corrupted worship of Yahweh ever since the intermarriages of Israelites with foreigners brought here by Assyrian conquerors over seven centuries before (2 Ki 17:6, 24–34).

The fact that this woman comes to the well at the "sixth hour," noon, in the heat of the day, shows her isolation. The friendly chit-chat other women of the town would exchange at the well in the morning and evening might not be so friendly toward her (4:18). We don't know the circumstances of her five marriages plus, but Jesus' silent implication is that she's not innocent. Jesus knows that these broken relationships are manifestations of her broken relationship with God—what Paul talked about in the Epistle. She's "weak," but worse: ungodly, still a sinner, an enemy of God, as by nature we all are. She knows a lot about broken relationships. Not much about peace.

Quite apart from her own wisdom or strength, though, she *has* come to the right place. The well. Surprisingly often in Scripture, the well is the place to find marriage. Rebekah's routine trip to the well one day led to her marriage to Isaac (Gen 24:10–19). Jacob met his beloved Rachel at a well (Gen 29:1–12). Moses met Zipporah at the well (Ex 2:15–22). The writer of Proverbs (Prov 5:15–18) pictures the joy of marriage as "flowing water from your own well." (He also knows that "stolen water," not drawn from one's own well, "is sweet" to the adulteress, Prov 9:17.)

Sure enough, Jesus offers this woman living water (4:10). And if water is a symbol for marriage, Jesus' living water is the ideal symbol of her restored relationship, peace, with God. Christ's relationship with His Church is as bridegroom to bride (Eph 5:22–32). Jesus is proposing that kind of marriage to the Samaritan woman. Though she was an enemy of God, Jesus has committed His life to her. That meant even giving up His life for her. And she receives all the blessings of being united once more with God.

The **Old Testament Reading** is another example of God providing for people who were ungodly and enemies: Exodus 17:1–7.

Israel has only very recently left Egypt. They're on their way to the Promised Land; this is before they earned themselves a forty-year delay. Only weeks before, God worked ten plagues on the Egyptians and brought Israel through the Red Sea. Already He's giving them manna to eat every day. He's even sweetened a bitter spring for them to drink (15:22–27). But again they grumble. Again the problem is water. They think God is dumping them to die.

Natural reaction? "Fine! You don't like how I've been providing? You're on your own . . . and you will die."

Instead, while the Israelites were weak, ungodly, still very much sinners, enemies of God, God works another miracle. Moses, "strike the rock, and water shall come out of it, and the people will drink" (17:6). God doesn't wait until the people get their act together, get godly. "While we were still sinners . . ." (Notice, by the way, that the text doesn't actually say water came out. We just know it did, because God said it would.)

Nothing spiritual about this water. It's plain old H_2O. But just as surely as the Samaritan woman's "living water," this wet water was a result of Christ's dying. Recall, if our sin still stands between us and God, we get no good thing. It's Jesus' death on the cross, removing that sin, reconciling us to God, that gives us *every* good thing—spiritual, eternal, physical, temporal, living water, H_2O.

When We Were Enemies of God, Jesus' Death Reestablished Peace with Him for the Whole World, So That Now Christ Gives the World Living Water—and Water.

The rest of the propers remind us of the joy of being at peace with God. We "come into His presence with thanksgiving" (Ps 95:1–9) and find His dwelling place "lovely" (the **Psalm** and **Introit**) because Jesus' death has made God again "our God" and we "the people of His pasture" (Ps 95:7).

Blessèd are those whose strength is in You, in whose heart are the highways to Zion.

How lovely is Your dwelling place, O Lord of hosts! My soul longs, yes, faints for the courts of the Lord; my heart and flesh sing for joy to the living God. Even the sparrow finds a home, and the swallow a nest for herself, where she may lay her young, at Your altars, O Lord of hosts, my King and my God. Blessèd are those who dwell in Your house, ever singing Your praise!

Glory be to the Father and to the Son and to the Holy Spirit; as it was in the beginning, is now, and will be forever. Amen.

Blessèd are those whose strength is in You, in whose heart are the highways to Zion. (Ps 84:1–4; antiphon: Ps 84:5)

Finally, the **Collect** and the **Hymn of the Day** for this Sunday both pray that this same joy Christ extended to foreigners—the Samaritan woman and her new friends in Sychar—would reach those who are still "astray," still enemies of God, or still distant from His Good News.

O God, whose glory it is always to have mercy, be gracious to all who have gone astray from Your ways and bring them again with penitent hearts and steadfast faith to embrace and hold fast the unchangeable truth of Your Word; through Jesus Christ, Your Son, our Lord, who lives and reigns with You and the Holy Spirit, one God, now and forever. Amen.

So sing now Luther's mission hymn "May God Bestow on Us His Grace."

Fourth Sunday in Lent Year A

READINGS

Isaiah 42:14–21
Psalm 142 (antiphon: v 5)
Ephesians 5:8–14
John 9:1–41
or
John 9:1–7, 13–17, 34–39

HYMN OF THE DAY

LSB 571 "God Loved the World So That He Gave"

The propers for this Fourth Sunday in Lent develop—in an interesting way—one powerful cluster of images. As usual, they're derived from the Gospel reading, which, as we know, sets the theme for the day. But my guess is that an alert Sunday morning worshiper or a careful reader looking forward to Sunday morning will pick up that imagery long before she or he meets the Gospel lesson.

Let's see about that. Read each of the following, simply in the order you'll hear them on Sunday, and I'll hold any further comments until you've had a chance to look for yourself. No fair peeking ahead to the Gospel.

First, the **Introit**:

My eyes are ever toward the LORD, for He will pluck my feet out of the net.

One thing have I asked of the LORD, that will I seek after: that I may dwell in the house of the LORD all the days of my life, to gaze upon the beauty of the LORD and to inquire in His temple. For He will hide me in His shelter in the day of trouble; He will conceal me under the cover of His tent; He will lift me high upon a rock. And now my head shall be lifted up above my enemies all around me, and I will offer in His tent sacrifices with shouts of joy; I will sing and make melody to the LORD.

Glory be to the Father and to the Son and to the Holy Spirit; as it was in the beginning, is now, and will be forever. Amen.

My eyes are ever toward the Lord,
for He will pluck my feet out of the net. (Ps 27:4–6; antiphon: Ps 25:15)

Now, the **Old Testament Reading**, Isaiah 42:14–21.

Next, the **Psalm** of the day, Psalm 142.

The, the **Gradual** for Lent:

[O come, let us fix our eyes on] Jesus, the founder and perfecter of our faith, who for the joy that was set before Him endured the cross, despising the shame, and is seated at the right hand of the throne of God. (Heb 12:2)

Just a couple more. Read the **Epistle**, Ephesians 5:8–14.

And in case it's not clear already, the clincher, the **Verse**: "With You is the fountain of life; in Your light do we see light" (Ps 36:9).

Got it? How many references did you notice to eyes, seeing, and light and to blindness or darkness? Go back and look again, if you'd like. We'll come back to most of these later. See how the lectionary people think?

By now you won't be surprised at all to find that the **Holy Gospel** is John 9:1–41, Jesus giving sight to a blind man and calling Himself "the light of the world." This is a rather unique text, because Jesus directly uses the very real, earthly, physical situation as, in effect, the sermon illustration for a point that is not physical but spiritual. We've emphasized before that when biblical texts speak of physical things, we should honor them as that, not dismiss physical human needs as unimportant while skipping ahead to spiritual needs. (Last week, for example, God gave the Israelites real H_2O because they were really thirsty.) Jesus certainly honors this blind man's immediate need—He heals him—but then He does move on to talk about spiritual light/darkness, spiritual sight/blindness.

Read today's lengthy Gospel lesson.

The very real, earthly need: a man has been blind from birth. As absurd as the disciples' question (9:2) sounds (some especially wicked sin while he was still in the womb might have earned this?), they're actually working with a common assumption. In Eastern religions, it's known as karma: You do bad stuff, eventually what goes around comes around. You do good, and you get rewards. In some (incorrect) Christian teaching, your assurance that you're one of God's elect is in seeing that good, not bad, is happening to you. But so commonly, outside of any theological understanding, people assume that misfortunes are a result of some particular sin a person has committed—and that blessings are a result of some good deed.

Jesus dismisses this (9:3). It's absolutely true that all evil and suffering is a result of sin; there wouldn't be any if Adam, Eve, and all of us had never sinned. And some sinful activities (sinful sex, driving while intoxicated) do bring painful consequences. But most of the time, we don't know (and would be foolish to speculate) why sadnesses come. Always, we *do* know God is still giving us the best, because He is reconciled to us by the cross of Jesus. And this time, Jesus tells us what that best really is: "that the works of God might be displayed" in this blind man (9:3).

The work of God that will be displayed most obviously is Jesus opening his eyes to see. Jesus does always care about our physical ailments, pains, and prosperity. Our daily, earthly lives are important to Him! Never think otherwise!

But this miracle Jesus also interprets spiritually: "We must work the works of Him who sent Me while it is day; night is coming, when no one can work. As long as I am in the world, I am the light of the world" (9:4–5). The rest of the text, then, is about spiritual seeing.

The man who's now been healed is interrogated. This was a Sabbath (9:14), and the Pharisees are incensed that someone did the work of healing when God had forbidden Sabbath labor (Ex 20:8–11). But God uses this questioning to bring the man to spiritual light and sight. At first, he only knows his healer as "the man called Jesus" (9:11). Under the Pharisees' examination, he ups his estimate: "He is a prophet" (9:17). The Pharisees can't see it. Anyone who heals on the Sabbath is a sinner! But now the man's confession has become bolder yet: "If this man [Jesus] were not from God, He could do nothing" (9:33). Enough of this! The Pharisees are furious! They remain blind (9:40–41). They cast the man out of the synagogue, which really meant excommunication.

So Jesus seeks him out: "Do you believe in the Son of Man?" The former blind man answers, "And who is He, sir, that I may believe in Him?" Jesus said to him, "You have seen Him, and it is He who is speaking to you." Now the light has come on! "Lord, I believe," and he worshiped Him (9:35b–38). He has been given physical sight, but now also spiritual sight. The light of the world has shined on his eyes and into his heart. In the words of this week's **Collect**, Jesus provides for all our needs of *both* body and soul:

> *Almighty God, our heavenly Father, Your mercies are new every morning; and though we deserve only punishment, You receive us as Your children and provide for all our needs of body and soul. Grant that we may heartily acknowledge Your merciful goodness, give thanks for all Your benefits, and serve You in willing obedience; through Jesus Christ, Your Son, our Lord, who lives and reigns with You and the Holy Spirit, one God, now and forever. Amen.*

As we've seen, the other propers all reflect these images of light and darkness, sight and blindness. And seeing is always only by the light of the world, Jesus Christ.

The Old Testament Reading, again, has both those who see and those who don't. Following just a few verses after the First Servant Song (Is 42:1–9; see our devotion-study for the Baptism of Our Lord), we read that as a result of the Servant, Christ, coming, Yahweh will no longer hold His peace (42:14). Now He will accomplish His great works. In particular, "I will lead the blind . . . , I will guide them. I will turn the darkness before them into light" (42:16).

Unfortunately, those who were previously appointed to be the Lord's servants, Israel, will refuse to see: "Look, you blind, that you may see! Who is blind but My servant . . . ? Who is blind as My dedicated one, or blind as the servant of the Lord? He sees many things, but does not observe them" (42:18b–19a, 19c–20a). Already the Pharisees had their ancient forebears, blind when they refused to believe in the Lord's Messiah.

On the other hand, David in the Psalm recognizes the futility of looking anywhere else for help: "Look to the right and see: there is none who takes notice of me; no refuge remains to me; no one cares for my soul" (Ps 142:4). David sees clearly that the Lord is his refuge (142:5), "for You will deal bountifully with me" (142:7).

The Lord has dealt bountifully with us, and, Paul knows, the Christians in Ephesus have been enlightened to see that: "For at one time you were darkness, but now you are light in the Lord" (Eph 5:8a). Christ has redeemed the Ephesians by His death on the cross. Their Baptism and the preaching of the Gospel have thrown the switch, turned on the lights in their hearts, to believe this. Therefore, Paul's exhortation in the Epistle is that they "walk as children of light" (5:8b). Be what God has made you. Live as you now are. All good and true works can be pictured as "light." In the light, we do those things we're glad to have seen by others. We thank God in worship and prayer. We deal honestly in business. We express our affection purely. We love and care for others with quality time and material support. As children of light, we avoid "the unfruitful works of darkness" (5:11), those thoughts, words, and deeds that we'd like to keep hidden from sight: dishonest dealing, sexual sins, coveting, obscene language. Above all, as children of light, we live and speak in such a way that when others see us, they see the light of Christ, the one who loved them and gave Himself into death for them: "Awake, O sleeper, and arise from the dead, and Christ will shine on you" (5:14).

This truly is what children of light delight to do. "My eyes are ever toward the Lord," our Introit said. "One thing have I asked of the Lord, that will I seek after: that I may dwell in the house of the Lord all the days of my life, to gaze upon the beauty of the Lord and to inquire in His temple." All the new woman or man in us really wants is to gaze on the beauty of the Lord!

And so, as our Gradual invited us, "[Let us fix our eyes on] Jesus, the founder and perfecter of our faith, who for the joy that was set before Him endured the cross." When the Christ has shined His light upon us, that, above all, is what we see: Jesus enduring the cross! That darkest day was the Light for every eye to see.

**Jesus, the Light of the World,
Opens Our Eyes
to Be Fixed on, to Gaze upon, Him.**

As you sing the **Hymn of the Day**, "God Loved the World So That He Gave" (*LSB* 571), envision Jesus loving the man born blind, pray that "all . . . would in Him believe" by the Holy Spirit opening their eyes, and thank God that He has turned on the light in your heart to faith in Christ.

Fifth Sunday in Lent Year A

READINGS

Ezekiel 37:1–14
Psalm 130 (antiphon: v 7)
Romans 8:1–11
John 11:1–45 (46–53)
or John 11:17–27, 38–53

HYMN OF THE DAY

LSB 430 "My Song Is Love Unknown"

In serving my members through the years, I was surprised to discover that many folks—active Lutherans, some lifelong—had a very cloudy understanding of the resurrection of the body. They all knew that when we die we go to heaven (though, of course, reassuring of just how we get there was always part of the pastoral task too). But for more than I would have thought, "heaven" was just about that vague. A real grasp that when Christ returns, these, our physical bodies, will be raised, glorified, and reunited with our souls for eternity—that was often missing. We confess this every Sunday in the creeds: "I believe in the resurrection of the body"; "I look for the resurrection of the dead." I certainly taught it explicitly in confirmation and adult instruction classes. I spoke about it in sermons. But for many, a fuzzy, disembodied, clouds-and-harps sort of imagination lingered. And clearly, *that* prospect of eternity (while preferred to the alternative!) was far less comforting and thrilling than what God really has in store.

This Sunday should be an occasion to bone up on this. Not only do we have the resurrection of one particular body, Lazarus's, in the Gospel lesson, but each of the propers broaches the issue. What's more, the Gospel event, Jesus raising Lazarus, sets in motion the sequence that will very shortly be played out also in our churches: Holy Week, culminating in *The* Resurrection of *The* Body.

The matter of death and life-after confronts us from the very first words of the **Introit** for the Fifth Sunday in Lent:

> *Precious in the sight of the Lord is the death of His saints.*

I love the Lord, *because He has heard my voice and my pleas for mercy. Because He inclined His ear to me, therefore I will call on Him as long as I live. The snares of death encompassed me; the pangs of Sheol laid hold on me; I suffered distress and anguish. Then I called on the name of the* Lord: *"O* Lord, *I pray, deliver my soul!" For You have delivered my soul from death, my eyes from tears, my feet from stumbling.*

Glory be to the Father and to the Son and to the Holy Spirit; as it was in the beginning, is now, and will be forever. Amen.

Precious in the sight of the Lord *is the death of His saints. (Ps 116:1–4, 8; antiphon: Ps 116:15)*

Now, pray also the **Collect** for Sunday:

Almighty God, by Your great goodness mercifully look upon Your people that we may be governed and preserved evermore in body and soul; through Jesus Christ, Your Son, our Lord, who lives and reigns with You and the Holy Spirit, one God, now and forever. Amen.

In God's view, death is the ultimate tragedy, because it disrupts His perfect creation, the beautiful harmony and constant exchange of love that was never to end. So not one of us dies without God feeling anguish; our death is "precious" in His sight. (Look ahead to Jn 11:35 in our Gospel.) Immediately at the moment of death, God lovingly receives our souls into heaven, where we will be with Christ, which is far better than the trials of this earth (Phil 1:23). But God wants no more death. His earnest pursuit is to restore His perfect creation, to make all things again what He intended them to be.

What God intended people to be was "body and soul." Our Collect makes that point, just as the Collect did last Sunday. Body and soul is distinct for humans as the crown jewel of God's creation. Animals have only bodies. Angels have only spirits. We have both—and since that moment God became a man, He does too! People are *always*, for eternity, intended by God to be *body* and soul; the Collect prays we would be "preserved *evermore* in body and soul."

Death is the violent ripping apart of soul from body. It is the chief consequence of sin; it is the greatest undoing of God's creation. Therefore it's unthinkable that God would give His Son into death just to take our souls to heaven. No! What we'll celebrate in two weeks is Christ's body and soul reunited. That's what Easter is! Likewise, when Christ, body and soul, returns to earth on the Last Day, each precious saint will have his or her body, now glorified, joined again to the soul. (So will every unbeliever have body and soul reunited but with terribly different destinies.)

A small but important aside: in the Introit, the psalmist prayed, "O Lord, . . . deliver my *soul*!" and declares, "For You have delivered my *soul* from death." Actually, depending on the context, the Hebrew that we translate as *soul* can also be rendered as *life* and can really mean "self" or "being" (compare various other English versions). That is, it can mean the whole person, not just what we narrowly call the soul. In this case, the parallel construction—"You have delivered my soul from death, my eyes from tears, my feet from stumbling"—clearly indicates that the body is also included.

The **Old Testament Reading**, Ezekiel's vision of the dry bones, is a vivid (if initially rather eerie) picture of the resurrection. Read Ezekiel 37:1–14.

I'm always a little uncomfortable with those Halloween lawn decorations of plastic skeletons seeming to crawl out of graves. They make light of what will be a glorious moment. Besides, the biblical depiction is, at first, grotesque enough. God shows Ezekiel a valley, perhaps as one would imagine a great battlefield of unburied bodies. It's a vision. (Compare 37:1 with 8:3, the way an earlier vision for Ezekiel began.) Almost surely there was really no such scene, no such actual valley. But the vision—and soon enough, the point—was very clear to Ezekiel.

Ezekiel and many of God's people were in captivity in Babylon (some time after 586 BC). History tells us that a nation deported and scattered abroad simply does not revive, reassemble, return. Thus the dead, dry bones symbolized God's people. Judah was feeling hopeless: "Our bones are dried up, and our hope is lost; we are indeed cut off" (37:11). God's design, though, was for Judah to return home and become the birth family and birthplace of the Messiah. So He would make a miracle happen—and illustrate it with a miracle.

"Can these bones live?" Ezekiel answers rightly: I don't know, Lord, but You do. Whatever You say (37:3). They will, and God will do it through His word, actually His word He has Ezekiel speak (37:4–8a). But the crucial, final breath of life is missing (37:8b).

It's the Spirit that initiated this vision for Ezekiel (37:1), and the Hebrew plays with the idea that the Spirit is also working the miracle. The Hebrew word רוּחַ (*ruach*) can be translated "spirit," "wind," or "breath," and you see how the rest of the miracle is all about "breath"—or "spirit" and even "winds" (37:5, 6, 8, 9, 10). In the Nicene Creed, Third Article, when we confess the resurrection of the dead, we call the Holy Spirit "the Lord and giver of life." And when Peter writes about Jesus' resurrection, it can be translated that He was "made alive in the spirit" (1 Pet 3:18). Surely the Spirit is very much involved in the resurrection. See what happens: spirit (soul) is back together with body, and now we have life (37:9–10).

In this case, Ezekiel's vision, the first referent is no doubt Judah's "resurrection" as a nation. However, it just as surely teaches that God's Old Testament people were aware of the future, ultimate resurrection of the body.

For another picture of spiritual "resurrection" from near despair and hopelessness, read the **Psalm** of the day, Psalm 130. The psalmist cries out from "the depths," a suggestion of Sheol, the realm of the dead (130:1). But God forgives his sins (130:4), and where there is forgiveness of sins, there is also deliverance from sin's effects. The Lord "will redeem Israel" (130:8). It will rise again, as we will rise again on the Last Day.

One reason some of my own members misunderstood the resurrection is that they saw the body as frail, corrupted, inferior to the spirit. The ancient Greeks even saw the body as a prison from which the soul longed to escape. Read the **Epistle**, Romans 8:1–11.

Paul clarifies this "body bad, soul good" error. He says that "the flesh" *is* evil ("to set the mind on the flesh is death," 8:6a), and he contrasts the flesh to "the Spirit" ("to set the mind on the Spirit is life and peace," 8:6b). *But* Paul is using the word *flesh* (σάρξ, *sarx*, in the Greek) not to mean the physical body but rather as a synonym for the sinful nature, the fallen old Adam in us. Nothing good about that. We do long to be set free from that "flesh." And sin *is* going to kill our physical bodies (8:10). But "if the Spirit of Him who raised Jesus from the dead dwells in you, He who raised Christ Jesus from the dead will also give life to your *mortal bodies* through His Spirit who dwells in you" (8:11). Our actual physical bodies (not the old sinful "flesh") are not only worth saving but the physical body is also precisely what the Holy Spirit raised when He raised Jesus from the dead. "Soul good, body good." God made both, and both will live together for eternity—for Christians, in the joy of the Lord.

Finally, read the full-length **Holy Gospel**, John 11:1–53. So many details!

Jesus has actually delayed coming to help His friend, so when He arrives, Lazarus has been dead four days (11:17). Rabbinic tradition thought the soul hovered near the body for three days, so by any standard, he's dead!

The most revealing element of the text may be Jesus' dialogue with Martha (yes, that Martha who was too busy to listen in Lk 10:38–42). Read again 11:20–27. Martha believes very firmly in the resurrection of the body on the Last Day (11:24)—more definitely, certainly, than many among us—and she believes that even now Jesus can raise her brother (11:22). Does she understand *this*?: "Jesus said to her, 'I am the resurrection and the life. Whoever believes in Me, though he die, yet shall he live, and everyone who lives and believes in Me shall never die. Do you believe *this*?'" What is "this"? Martha gets it. "This" is rising again, never dying. But it can be summarized: "Yes, Lord; I believe that You are the Christ, the Son of God." Believing that Jesus is the Christ, the Savior, is knowing and believing all the rest. He is the resurrection and the life. If we have Him, we have the certainty of our bodies rising someday to reunite with our souls for endless joy. And we have real life now, because life as God intended is that we are constantly receiving His love, even though we'll die. We do, we are, because the death of the Resurrection and the Life has reconciled us to God.

Jesus Is the Resurrection and the Life, So That Whoever Believes in Him, Though He Die, Yet Shall He Live.

Jesus raising Lazarus, just two miles from Jerusalem, so near it can't escape notice, now forces the hand of Caiaphas and the Jewish leaders (11:47–53). He must die! The **Hymn of the Day** reminds us that we've nearly come to that Holy Week when this all plays out. "Mine the tomb Wherein He lay" (st 6), but with Him we will also rise.

Palm Sunday / Sunday of the Passion Year A

READINGS

John 12:12–19 (Processional)
Isaiah 50:4–9a
Psalm 118:19–29 (antiphon: v 26)
or Psalm 31:9–16 (antiphon: v 5)
Philippians 2:5–11
Matthew 26:1–27:66
or Matthew 27:11–66
or John 12:20–43

HYMNS OF THE DAY

LSB 442 "All Glory, Laud, and Honor" (Processional)
LSB 438 "A Lamb Goes Uncomplaining Forth"

"All glory, laud, and honor
To You, Redeemer, King,
To whom the lips of children
Made sweet hosannas ring.

A Lamb goes uncomplaining forth,
The guilt of sinners bearing . . .
To slaughter . . ."

So which is it? Will this Sunday be a glorious celebration with joyous throngs? Or will it be a death march to strains of mourning and lamenting? It's Palm Sunday, but it's also identified as Sunday of the Passion. So it's really both—but not two different occasions happening to share the same day. It's both, with one being the cause of the other.

This is certainly a Sunday with much to do. Palm Sunday, the day that Jesus rode triumphantly into Jerusalem, is a huge festival. It's a grand coronation: Jesus hailed by the crowds as the Son of David, the messianic King, the one who comes in the name of the Lord. All those shouts need to be heard! But it's also the beginning of the week that will take Jesus to the cross. Recent lectionaries have acknowledged a rather unholy irony about this Holy Week: if the actual narrative of Jesus' suffering and death were only read on Good Friday, someone could come to church every Sunday of the year but still miss it! Surely the cross is narrated briefly every week, but there's nothing like hearing the full plodding-step-by-plodding-step, nail-by-nail, blow-by-blow account. This Sunday will therefore address the Passion of Jesus too.

You, of course, will be in church *not only for Sunday* but also for Maundy Thursday, Good Friday, and, if your congregation offers,

Holy Saturday as well. (Right?) You'll even look forward to Thursday, Friday, Saturday by reading extra devotion-studies. So, here, we'll hold commentary on Jesus' Passion itself (Mt 26:1–27:66) for the following "bonus" Holy Week chapters. (Read ahead if you like.) This time we'll focus on how this day's two designations are inseparably related.

There is indeed an integral cause-effect relationship between Palm Sunday and the Sunday of the Passion. It's just not the usual, in which the first causes the second. On the contrary, the Passion of Christ is what causes Palm Sunday to be a glorious celebration.

The dual nature of the day is reflected in its having multiple-choice Gospel readings. The last three shown are intended to be either/or. But the first, John 12:12–19, may be read both/and with one of the others. It's offered as the **Palm Sunday Processional Gospel**.

Many congregations begin Palm Sunday services with a palm frond procession while reading these verses. In my last congregation (in Texas, where the weather was often quite nice by this time of year), we actually began with many worshipers lined up outside and those inside joining in as we entered. A wireless mike let everyone hear the entire reading.

It is the most festive time of the Jewish year. "The feast" (12:12) is Passover, celebrated by this time for almost fifteen centuries, ever since God brought Israel out of Egypt by killing the firstborn of the Egyptians and passing over the Israelite homes (Ex 12:1–14). There's even a special sense of anticipation this Passover, because the crowds had heard of Jesus recently raising Lazarus, just two miles from Jerusalem in Bethany (12:17–18). Jesus must be their long-promised king!

The palm branches express that; they were a popular symbol of Jewish patriotism. (Of the four Gospel writers, John is the one that specifies palms. John would also later envision palms waved by saints of every nation, Rev 7:9.) The words of the crowd, too, proclaim Jesus "the King of Israel." They shout from a coronation psalm that was part of the Passover liturgy: "Hosanna!" (Save us!) "Blessed is He who comes in the name of the Lord!" (12:13; Ps 118:25–26). And John affirms it with his quotation of the prophet Zechariah: "Your king is coming, sitting on a donkey's colt!" (12:15; Zech 9:9). Plenty of Palm Sunday pomp, all quite proper.

What the crowd almost surely doesn't understand is why they ought to be celebrating what they're celebrating. Jesus is the King, all right; He'll save them, most assuredly. But He'll save them and be their King by dying. It was the blood of the Passover lamb over the doorposts that saved Israel from death. And Jesus' kingly glory would be from the cross. "His disciples," even, "did not understand these things at first, but when Jesus was *glorified*, then they remembered" (12:16). John's Gospel frequently speaks of Jesus being glorified in the events just ahead (7:39; 13:31–32; 17:1; see especially 12:23, 28, 32–33. In fact, read the full alternate **Holy Gospel**, John 12:20–43). The glory, laud, and honor of Palm Sunday are because your King is coming to die.

The ones who did understand, though only from their self-serving perspective, were

Jesus' enemies (12:19). Jesus' popularity was dangerous. It's as Caiaphas told the Pharisees and the Jewish Council in last week's Gospel: "It is expedient for you that one man die for the people" (Jn 11:50 NASB).

Jesus knows He's entering Jerusalem to die. He knows it must be Jerusalem. Jerusalem is the Holy City, the city of the temple, the holy place, the most holy place. Holy Week is a mini-season in itself, so it has its own **Gradual**, and in it, the writer to the Hebrews explains:

> *[Christ] entered once for all into the holy places, by means of His own blood, thus securing an eternal redemption. Therefore He is the mediator of a new covenant, so that those who are called may receive the promised eternal inheritance. He sent redemption to His people; He has commanded His covenant forever. (Heb 9:12a, c, 15a; Ps 111:9a)*

The innermost sanctuary of the temple, the most holy place (the holy of holies), only the high priest could enter, and only once a year on the Day of Atonement (Leviticus 16). He entered with the blood of a sacrificed bull; to enter otherwise meant death. But with his action, God forgave the sins of the nation.

Palm Sunday is Jesus entering into the holy places to offer Himself as the sacrifice for all sins. Entering will mean His death. But it will atone for the sins of the whole world. This is Jesus' triumphal entry, and it very well expresses the theme for both Palm Sunday and the Sunday of the Passion.

Christ's Triumphal Entry Is into the Holy Places, by Means of His Blood, Thus Securing an Eternal Redemption.

Pause at this point to sing the processional **Hymn of the Day**, "All Glory, Laud, and Honor," and note particularly stanza 4.

The rest of the propers move progressively from glory, laud, and honor toward the solemn theme of our other hymn.

The **Introit** still speaks plenty of glory:

> *Blessèd is he who comes in the name of the Lord! We bless you from the house of the Lord.*
>
> *Lift up your heads, O gates! And be lifted up, O ancient doors, that the King of glory may come in. Who is this King of glory? The Lord, strong and mighty, the Lord, mighty in battle! Lift up your heads, O gates! And lift them up, O ancient doors, that the King of glory may come in. Who is this King of glory? The Lord of hosts, He is the King of glory!*
>
> *Blessèd is he who comes in the name of the Lord! We bless you from the house of the Lord. (Ps 24:7–10; antiphon: Ps 118:26)*

The antiphon we've already heard from the crowd in our Processional Gospel. The verses from Psalm 24, on the other hand, we perhaps associate more with Advent. (We pointed out way back in Advent 1 that we have two beloved hymns for that season based on these words.) Of course, this is fitting, since both Advent and Palm Sunday see Jesus coming, entering. The Lord is here repeatedly called the "King of glory." It's only this week, though, that we'll see most vividly what His glory is.

By now, the **Psalm** of the day, Psalm 118:19–29, is familiar, but it, too, makes the move toward the Lamb going forth. Besides the crowd's Palm Sunday chant, we all recognize verse 29, and who doesn't love verse 24? We see the triumphal entry in verse 19: "Open to me the gates of righteousness." But amidst all that triumph is the tragedy: "The stone that the builders rejected has become the cornerstone" (118:22, and cited six times in the New Testament!). The cross is coming. But even "this is the LORD's doing; it is marvelous in our eyes" (118:23). The greatest tragedy in history is to be God's great victory!

The **Old Testament Reading** clearly evokes Sunday of the Passion: Isaiah 50:4–9a. It's the Third Servant Song of Isaiah, and the Servant is suffering. We see Thursday and Friday coming: "I gave My back to those who strike, and My cheeks to those who pull out the beard; I hid not My face from disgrace and spitting" (50:6). But the Servant also sees Easter: "The Lord GOD helps Me; therefore I have not been disgraced; . . . I know that I shall not be put to shame. He who vindicates Me is near" (50:7a, b, d, 8a).

Paul makes the same point—suffering then glory—in what may be the most sublime synthesis of the whole Palm/Passion pairing: the **Epistle**, Philippians 2:5–11. Christ Jesus empties Himself, refrains for a time (His "state of humiliation") from fully and continually using all His divine powers. He allows Himself to be arrested, beaten, mocked, killed—even in the most agonizing and degrading way. But then God exalts Him. (Only then does Christ again use fully all those divine attributes—His "state of exaltation.") And, see, God did not exalt Him because the Son has always been all powerful, all glorious (though He has). God exalts Him because ("therefore," 2:9) He had humbled Himself to secure our eternal redemption. God's greatest glory is that He who has all power and glory cares enough, loves His creatures enough, to humble Himself. That's how Sunday of the Passion makes Palm Sunday.

In my congregations, we usually followed this sort of theme throughout the service and waited to *end* the service with a quiet reading, without comment, of the **Passion Gospel**, a way to begin our Holy Week meditations. Read, then, Matthew 26:1–27:66.

Finally, close your devotion and prepare for next week by praying the **Collect** and singing the Passion **Hymn of the Day**, "A Lamb Goes Uncomplaining Forth."

Almighty and everlasting God, You sent Your Son, our Savior Jesus Christ, to take upon Himself our flesh and to suffer death upon the cross. Mercifully grant that we may follow the example of His great humility and patience and be made partakers of His resurrection; through the same Jesus Christ, our Lord, who lives and reigns with You and the Holy Spirit, one God, now and forever. Amen.

Holy Week and Holy Thursday Year A

READINGS

Matthew 26:1–27:2 (Passion)

Exodus 24:3–11
Psalm 116:12–19 (antiphon: v 17)
Hebrews 9:11–22
Matthew 26:17–30

or

Exodus 12:1–14
Psalm 116:12–19 (antiphon: v 17)
1 Corinthians 11:23–32
John 13:1–17, 31b–35

HYMN OF THE DAY

LSB 617 "O Lord, We Praise Thee"

Each of us has a number of events in life so formative to who we are that we commemorate them: a ceremony at graduation, a dinner out to celebrate a new job, a housewarming after a move. Some we celebrate every year: our birthdays, our wedding days, our children's birthdays. Other events are so significant that entire civilizations mark them as historic: the demise of the Roman Empire, the discovery of America, V-E Day and V-J Day ending World War II. The Reformation belongs in that category. And the world has come to measure its time from the (slightly miscalculated) date of Jesus' birth. Very fitting! It's that important.

But in the really, really big picture, there are four important markers in time. The week God created the universe. The day Adam and Eve sinned. The Last Day when Christ will return. And those three only have value now because of the biggest of all: this week. Holy Week. The week the Son of God came to Jerusalem to die on the cross and rise from the grave to save the human race. Everything moved toward and now moves from that. Without Jesus reconciling the world to God, even God's sustaining the planet would have ceased way back in the fallen Eden—which means that Jesus had each of our personal commemorations in mind when He went to the cross, and each of our special days can be a little celebration of this week.

Holy Week is the one week of the church year that has appointed propers for all eight days. (The week even has an extra day, counting Palm Sunday. And if you're counting, there are actually propers for Easter Monday, Tuesday, and Wednesday as well; that's eleven straight days!) The Gospels for Monday, Tuesday, and Wednesday of this week are the synoptic Passion Gospels: Matthew 26:1–27:66; Mark 14:1–15:47; and Luke 22:1–23:56, respectively. This year, Year A, that Matthew Gospel was assigned also to Sunday of the Passion. As we explained in that chapter, though, we'll be studying that lesson in this devotion-study. I invite you to read the others too, and we'll discuss those next year and the following.

Of course, on Holy Thursday, the Passion stories serve to set the stage for Jesus' institution of the Lord's Supper and for His crucifixion on Good Friday. In our devotion-study, we'll follow the sequence of the Passion events—those leading up to the Last Supper, then the focus on the Sacrament, which will usually be the emphasis of the Thursday service, and finally the late-night events after the Upper Room. We'll use the first set of readings listed; next year we'll study the alternate set. (Feel free to read ahead, p 356, or at least to read those alternate lessons; they may be the ones your pastor chooses this year.)

By the way, the common name for Holy Thursday, Maundy Thursday, comes from the Latin *mandati* ("commandment"), based on Jesus' words in the alternate Gospel, "A new commandment I give to you, that you love one another: just as I have loved you" (Jn 13:34).

Let's begin with the first section of the Passion reading, Matthew 26:1–16.

Everyone but the disciples, it seems, knows Jesus' death is coming. Jesus knows, and He's telling the disciples for at least the sixth time (26:2; previously 12:40; 16:21; 17:9–12, 22–23; 20:18–19). The Jewish leaders know they have to make it happen (26:3–5). Mary of Bethany knows (26:12; see John 12:1–8). Very likely, Judas *doesn't* believe his betrayal (26:14–16) will actually lead to Jesus' death. He is, after all, one of the Twelve. Already the disciples are in denial!

Which brings us to Matthew 26:17–30, the appointed **Holy Gospel**.

Passover (26:17) would usually be a festive meal. It was an independence day, with a prescribed liturgy that recalled coming out of Egypt. But it was the *blood* of the lamb over the doorpost that saved the Israelite firstborn. And even the disciples are sensing that this night is unlike any other. They are "very sorrowful" when they learn one of them will betray Jesus (26:22). Still, there's no outrage when Judas is identified (26:25). In denial.

The deniers of what follows *aren't* the disciples. There's no protest when Jesus tells them the unleavened bread and wine are His body and blood. No demand for explanation. That's as it should be. The bread *is* the body of Christ. The wine *is* Jesus' blood, soon to be shed on the cross, to fulfill the ancient covenant (26:26–28). Really present. The deniers have come later, claiming that the elements only represent the body and blood of Jesus—as if He couldn't or wouldn't work the miracle He just spoke. But if we had only bread and wine in the Sacrament, it could only be us playacting out this night; it wouldn't be God acting. And we know nothing we do can secure forgiveness of sins. But that's precisely what Jesus says is happening: "This is My blood of the covenant, which is poured out for many for the forgiveness of sins."

"And when they had sung a hymn, they went out to the Mount of Olives" (26:30), leaving us what the **Collect** calls "this wondrous Sacrament":

O Lord, in this wondrous Sacrament You have left us a remembrance of Your passion. Grant that we may so receive the sacred mystery of Your body and blood that the fruits of Your redemption may continually be manifest in us; for You live and reign with the Father and the Holy Spirit, one God, now and forever. Amen.

Both the **Introit** and the **Psalm** for Maundy Thursday are cuttings of Psalm 116. Read the Introit and then Psalm 116:12–19.

Gracious is the Lord, and righteous; our God is merciful.

I love the Lord, because He has heard my voice and my pleas for mercy. Because He inclined His ear to me, therefore I will call on Him as long as I live. The snares of death encompassed me; the pangs of Sheol laid hold on me; I suffered distress and anguish. Then I called on the name of the Lord: "O Lord, I pray, deliver my soul!"

Gracious is the Lord, and righteous; our God is merciful. (Ps 116:1–4; antiphon: Ps 116:5)

Psalm 116 is an apt selection for this day, because Psalms 113–118 were the major hymns of the Passover liturgy. They're known as the "Egyptian Hallel," with the Hebrew *hallelu yah*, "Praise Yahweh," featured prominently (116:19). The deep appreciation for what the Lord has done exudes: "Gracious is the Lord, and righteous; our God is merciful. I love the Lord." He has "loosed my bonds" of sin (116:16); He has delivered us from "the snares of death" (116:3).

That's exactly what He does for us when we're blessed to "lift up the cup of salvation" (116:13). Notice how verses 13–14 are parallel to 17–18, the variable being "offer to You the sacrifice of thanksgiving." And turn in your *Lutheran Service Book* to pages 159–60 and see how these words are used in our Divine Service. Notice that the order is reversed? We render to the Lord the sacrifice of thanksgiving, but then we eagerly anticipate the cup of salvation. And what follows immediately? The Service of the Sacrament. There is no greater reason to give God thanks than that He has given us His very blood and body for forgiveness and deliverance from death!

Picture, though, this celebrative psalm being sung by Jesus as He and the disciples concluded their Passover meal that Maundy Thursday night. (Remember that they sang as they left the Upper Room, Mt 26:30.) "The snares of death" had a meaning for Jesus no one else grasped. "I suffered distress and anguish." He knew He would! And now He was on His way to Gethsemane: "Then I called on the name of the Lord: 'O Lord, I pray, deliver my soul!'" The cup of salvation is joy for us, but bitter for Jesus!

Key verses of the **Old Testament Reading**, Exodus 24:3–11, we heard and discussed for Transfiguration Day. Read it again, though, and picture the parallels to the scene as Jesus instituted Holy Communion. Twelve pillars (24:4), almost as if gathered around a table. The chief men of the people eating and drinking (24:11). Very significantly, the Lord "did not lay His hand" on them. Sinful men, fraught with failure, still privileged to be in the presence of the almighty God—because God by His impending death would declare them holy. Above all, "the blood of the covenant" (24:8). The blood it was that would wash away those sins. Finally, the words of bravado: "All the words that the LORD has spoken we will do." They said it twice (24:3, 7). Lord, we'll never deny You!

"Though they all fall away because of You, I will never fall away. . . . Even if I must die with You, I will not deny You!" Peter said it twice. "And all the disciples said the same." Read Matthew 26:30–75.

From here, it's almost nothing but one denial after another. "My soul is very sorrowful, even to death. . . . Could you not watch with Me one hour?" (26:38, 40).

"My Father, if it be possible, let this cup pass from Me." That would be denied too, but Jesus willingly denied Himself: "Not as I will, but as You will" (26:39).

Judas, the betrayer. Arrest. "Then all the disciples left Him and fled" (26:56).

The high priest. False witnesses. Caiaphas and Council knew Jesus had raised Lazarus from the dead (Jn 11:45–53; 12:17–19—our last two Sundays), but they simply wouldn't allow what they knew to be true. In denial.

The only one who wouldn't deny was our Lord: "The high priest said to Him, 'I adjure You by the living God, tell us if You are the Christ, the Son of God.' Jesus said to him, 'You have said so. But I tell you, from now on you will see the Son of Man seated at the right hand of Power and coming on the clouds of heaven'" (26:63–64).

So Caiaphas passes judgment on Jesus(!) when Caiaphas's one role, really, was as stand-in: Hebrews 9:11–22, the **Epistle**.

"When *Christ* appeared *as a high priest* of the good things that have come," the **Gradual** for Holy Week picks up there: He "entered once for all into the holy places, by means of His own blood, thus securing an eternal redemption. Therefore He is the mediator of a new covenant, so that those who are called may receive the promised eternal inheritance" (9:11a, 12a, c, 15a). For with the shedding of the blood of the covenant is forgiveness of sins (9:22).

Peter would deny—three times. All others deny. We deny. But

**AGAINST ALL DENIALS,
JESUS' BLOOD OF THE COVENANT
DELIVERS US FROM SIN AND DEATH.**

Look forward to the Sacrament Thursday with Luther's **Hymn of the Day**, *LSB* 617.

Then know what follows. One by one, the vessels, the candles, the paraments, the linens, all adornments may be stripped from the altar in your sanctuary. And you know what that symbolizes. *It marks all time:*

"When morning came, all the chief priests and the elders of the people took counsel against Jesus to put Him to death. And they bound Him and led Him away and delivered Him over to Pilate the governor" (Mt 27:1–2).

Good Friday Years A, B, C

READINGS

Isaiah 52:13–53:12
Psalm 22 (antiphon: v 1)
or Psalm 31 (antiphon: v 1)
Hebrews 4:14–16; 5:7–9
John 18:1–19:42
or John 19:17–30

Matthew 27:1–66
or Mark 15:1–47
or Luke 23:1–56

HYMN OF THE DAY

LSB 454 "Sing, My Tongue, the Glorious Battle"

"For I decided to know nothing among you except Jesus Christ and Him crucified," the apostle Paul told us (1 Cor 2:2). He wasn't oversimplifying, picking out one event, Jesus' death on the cross, and trying to suggest it was more important than it really is. Quite the opposite. He was making the point that Jesus dying for us, if we understand everything that involves, really is all we need to know. That the crucifixion (which can never be separated from the resurrection) is what makes every blessing—in fact, every *day*—happen. It truly is the day from which all history is marked.

And here we are. Once again, at the foot of the cross.

Cherish it.

Good Friday is worth two trips to church, if that's available to you. In places where several of our congregations are quite close together, they might (or might be encouraged to) join together to offer an afternoon Tre Ore ("three hour") service. This customarily consists of six half-hour devotions, usually shared by several pastors, noon to 3:00 p.m. (the hours of darkness as Jesus hung on the cross). Worshipers may enter or leave at the beginning of any half hour and stay for all six or fewer of the services.

Very common in our churches now is for the Good Friday evening service to be some form of Tenebrae (meaning "darkness"). Tenebrae services involve a progressive darkening of the sanctuary by extinguishing candles and dimming other lights. This visualizes, of course, the darkness that covered the land during the crucifixion, which in turn symbolizes the deathly effects of sin for which Jesus was dying. The order may follow the propers given here or other elements such as Jesus'

Seven Words from the Cross. At the very beginning of the service, I used to explain its meaning to the children—and prepare them for the *strepitus*, the slamming of the book, at the end (which we always made quite resounding!). When there is both an afternoon and an evening service, they're almost always quite different. This is a day for worship!

Every Good Friday sermon worth its homiletical salt will have a THEME. (That's out of consideration for the listeners; it's awfully tough to follow if the preacher doesn't have a point!) But to try to boil down the whole *day*, Good Friday, into one sentence—that might be presumptuous. Recognizing it's a tall order that an author really shouldn't presume, let's do this: key phrases from two precious passages of God's own Word, one from the Old Testament and one from the New, combined to summarize what happened on Jesus' cross:

WITH HIS STRIPES, IT IS FINISHED!

How about that? In the Lord's own profundity, a few words give us more than we'll ever be able to discuss or even fully comprehend. What is "it"? How is "it" finished? How can it be all that all history needs to know?

The Old Testament phrase of our THEME occurs already in the antiphon to the **Introit**:

> *He was wounded for our transgressions; He was crushed for our iniquities; upon Him was the chastisement that brought us peace, and with His stripes we are healed.*
>
> *O LORD, rebuke me not in Your anger, nor discipline me in Your wrath! For Your arrows have sunk into me, and Your hand has come down on me. There is no soundness in my flesh because of Your indignation; there is no health in my bones because of my sin. For my iniquities have gone over my head; like a heavy burden, they are too heavy for me. I confess my iniquity; I am sorry for my sin. Make haste to help me, O Lord, my salvation!*
>
> *He was wounded for our transgressions; He was crushed for our iniquities; upon Him was the chastisement that brought us peace, and with His stripes we are healed. (Ps 38:1–4, 18, 22; antiphon: Is 53:5)*

The antiphon is from Isaiah's Fourth Servant Song. The **Old Testament Reading** for Good Friday is the entire song, Isaiah 52:13–53:12. Read it now as well.

By this week in Year A, we've seen all four of these signal passages from Isaiah's prophetic pen (see Baptism of Our Lord, Epiphany 2, and Palm Sunday), and this one is the climax. Yahweh's servant, we know, is Christ Himself, sometimes speaking through the prophet, or, in this case, being described by Yahweh ("*My* servant").

What a vivid description of Jesus' Passion! Marred. Despised, rejected, sorrowful, grieving. Stricken, smitten, and afflicted. Wounded, crushed, chastised, beaten until the blood made those stripes down His back. Oppressed. A lamb led to the slaughter. Silent. Cut off from the living. Buried.

And for what? "By His knowledge shall the righteous one, My servant, make many to be accounted righteous, and He shall bear their iniquities. . . . He bore the sin of many, and makes intercession for the transgressors. . . . He has borne *our* griefs and carried *our* sorrows; . . . He was wounded for *our* transgressions; He was crushed for *our* iniquities; upon Him was the chastisement that brought us peace, *and with His stripes we are healed*" (53:11, 12, 4, 5). How clearly did the Old Testament prophet, seven hundred years before the fact, see this day in history!

And David, three centuries before Isaiah, in both of our **Psalms**, Psalms 22 and 31. "My God, my God!" Has David been reading the script (22:1)? "Into Your hand I commit my spirit." Did *Jesus* read the script (31:5)? Look back down to 22:31: "He has done it." Sound familiar? "It is finished!"

Good Friday, you see, was the day David and Isaiah and all the Old Testament saints looked forward to, ever since God told them way, way back that the offspring of Eve would crush the head of the serpent while Himself being fatally bruised. That's Genesis 3:15, almost as far back in history as you can get—the very day we all began to need someone to crush the devil for us. And now, with Jesus going to the cross, that waiting was over. That's part of what "it" was that those stripes finished.

All four Gospels have detailed accounts of Jesus' crucifixion (of course!—this being the day to which they were all headed from chapter 1, verse 1). John's record is the one appointed for primary attention in our Good Friday services, assuming you'll hear the others read on Sunday of the Passion, this past Sunday, each of the three years. Perhaps you also read the Matthew, Mark, and Luke Passion accounts on Monday, Tuesday, and Wednesday this week. If not, read again the synoptic version appropriate to the year you're on: Matthew 27:1–66 (Year A), Mark 15:1–47 (Year B), or Luke 23:1–56 (Year C).

Matthew has several unique features. Only he gives us the sad story of Judas being betrayed by those to whom he betrayed Jesus (27:3–10). He alone mentions Pilate's wife (27:19), Pilate washing his hands (27:24), and the crowd taking responsibility for Jesus' blood (27:25). Matthew quotes the revealing words of the mockers: "He trusts in God; let God deliver Him now, if He desires Him. For He said, 'I am the Son of God'" (27:43). And Matthew has the memorable details of the earthquake with saints rising (27:51b–53) and of the chief priests and Pharisees requesting a guard to prevent the disciples of "that impostor" stealing His body (27:62–66).

Mark adds that Simon of Cyrene, who carried Jesus' cross, was father of Rufus and Alexander (15:21; Rom 16:13), that it was the third hour (9:00 a.m.) when Jesus was crucified (15:25), that Joseph of Arimathea "took courage" to request Jesus' body (15:43), and that Pilate verified Jesus was really dead (15:44–45). Mark, with Matthew, reports Jesus' fourth word from the cross: "My God, My God, why have You forsaken Me?" (15:34; Mt 27:46).

Luke has numerous singular elements: specifics of the charges against Jesus (23:2, 5), the hearing before Herod (23:6–12), Jesus' words to the women on the way to Golgotha

(23:27–31). Most important, Luke records Jesus' beloved first, second, and seventh words: "Father, forgive them, for they know not what they do" (23:34); to the penitent thief, "Truly, I say to you, today you will be with Me in paradise" (23:43); "Father, into Your hands I commit My spirit!" (23:46).

Yet John's account is well chosen as the **Holy Gospel** for the day. The brief cutting, John 19:17–30, goes directly to Golgotha. The full version, John 18:1–19:42, takes us all the way back to betrayal and arrest in Gethsemane, the hearing before Annas (unique to John), and Peter's denials, and then includes the remarkable dialogues of Pilate with Jesus and the Jews (18:28–19:16): "My kingdom is not of this world" (18:36); "What is truth?" (18:38); "Behold the man!" (19:5); "We have no king but Caesar" (19:15).

Then at the cross, John reminds us that David had prophesied the soldiers casting lots for Jesus' clothes (19:24; Ps 22:18). John himself relates Jesus' love asking him to care for His mother (His third word from the cross): "Woman, behold, your son!" . . . "Behold, your mother!" (19:26–27). And again, just as David had prophesied, Jesus spoke His fifth word, "I thirst" (19:28; Ps 69:21; 22:15).

Above all, though, John's Gospel quotes the words that declare history remade: "It is finished" (19:30). What is finished? Jesus' suffering? Yes, that's part of it too.

But read the **Epistle**, Hebrews 4:14–16; 5:7–9. By Jesus' suffering, He was "made perfect" (5:9), not, of course, in the sense that something in Him had been wrong before, but in that now His mission was complete. Thus "He became the source of eternal salvation to all who obey Him" (5:9). "Let us then with confidence draw near to the throne of grace, that we may receive mercy and find grace to help in time of need" (4:16). The "it" that is finished by Jesus' stripes is *chiefly* our separation from God, the breach caused by every sin since the first, which had cut us off from God's throne of grace. That separation is finished! We draw near to God now with joy and confidence! The too-heavy burden of sin (Introit) is lifted. We are now God's family! The **Collect** for Good Friday:

Almighty God, graciously behold this Your family for whom our Lord Jesus Christ was willing to be betrayed and delivered into the hands of sinful men to suffer death upon the cross; through the same Jesus Christ, Your Son, our Lord, who lives and reigns with You and the Holy Spirit, one God, now and forever. Amen.

That is now where all history is headed forever. Again from the Holy Week **Gradual**:

[Christ] entered once for all into the holy places, by means of His own blood, thus securing an eternal redemption. Therefore He is the mediator of a new covenant, so that those who are called may receive the promised eternal inheritance. He sent redemption to His people; He has commanded His covenant forever. (Heb 9:12a, c, 15a; Ps 111:9a)

Sing the **Hymn of the Day** gloriously!

Holy Saturday and Vigil of Easter Years A, B, C

READINGS

Daniel 6:1–24
Psalm 16 (antiphon: v 10)
1 Peter 4:1–8
Matthew 27:57–66

Selected Readings

HYMN OF THE DAY

LSB 448 "O Darkest Woe"

"O darkest woe!
Ye tears, forth flow!
Has earth so sad a wonder?
God the Father's only Son
Now is buried yonder.

O sorrow dread!
Our God is dead . . ." (*LSB* 448:1, 2)

And so it truly was. Our God really had died, and from Friday afternoon until early on the third day, God lay lifeless in a tomb. Perhaps not a soul who heard Jesus' words "It is finished" on Friday understood what He meant. And so even the most faithful—the dear women, Joseph of Arimathea, Nicodemus—could think to do nothing but give Him a proper burial. The Twelve . . . the Eleven? Paralyzed even from doing that, awash, no doubt, in their self-recriminations over denials and desertions.

That was the first Holy Saturday. But, of course, we would never call it "Holy" and would never celebrate it if we didn't now understand that Jesus really had finished atoning for the sins of the world and had fully reconciled us to God, and that God had broadcast that for all to see and hear by raising His Son from the dead. So we come to Holy Saturday reverently, acknowledging Jesus' burial in a tomb we deserved, but also in hope. The liturgical color of the day is still black, as it was on Good Friday. The propers will reflect the reality of death. But by the end, we'll see what comes next.

It may even be that your congregation observes Holy Saturday evening with the Vigil of Easter. By the end of that service, you *will be* celebrating the resurrection. We'll talk about the Easter Vigil during the last portion of this devotion-study.

The event to be observed this day ("observed" is probably a better word in this case than "celebrated") is the burial of Jesus, the **Holy Gospel**. Read Matthew 27:57–66.

Joseph of Arimathea (a town we can't identify with certainty) was not only rich but also a "respected member" of the Sanhedrin, or Jewish Council (Mk 15:43). He had not consented to the council's action to condemn Jesus (Lk 23:51), but neither had he openly followed Jesus before (Jn 19:38). Now, though, he "took courage" and asked Pilate for Jesus' body (Mk 15:43), burying Him in a new tomb he'd prepared for himself. In doing so, he fulfilled Isaiah's prophecy: "His grave was assigned with wicked men, yet He was with a rich man in His death" (Is 53:9, NASB). John tells us that Nicodemus, whose conversation with Jesus John had previously recorded, assisted (Jn 19:39; 3:1–21). The mention of the two Marys sets the stage for chapter 28 and their blessed trip to the tomb.

While we perhaps don't *celebrate* Jesus' burial, it was significant enough to be explicitly mentioned in the Apostles' Creed: "crucified, died and was buried." Not only Isaiah but also Jesus Himself cited His burial: "Just as Jonah was three days and three nights in the belly of the great fish, so will the Son of Man be three days and three nights in the heart of the earth" (Mt 12:40; see also 26:12). For Paul, too, Jesus' burial is important (Acts 13:29; 1 Cor 15:4). Burial is the exclamation point that Jesus was really dead!

That was certainly crucial to Jesus' enemies. They go to Pilate to be sure He stays buried! They knew Jesus had promised to rise again on the third day (27:63). What if the disciples of "that impostor" steal His body and claim He's risen? Hence, the seal and the guards. See if He can "rise" now!

Despite the party line soon to be circulated by the Jews (Mt 28:11–15) and despite modern foolishness, the fact that Jesus was buried, sealed, guarded means that the next chapter is not only true but undeniable.

But this is still Holy Saturday, and no one seemed to know that next chapter was coming. The **Introit** describes how all of us would feel about ourselves if Saturday were the end of the story.

> *For my soul is full of troubles, and my life draws near to Sheol.*
>
> *O Lord, God of my salvation; I cry out day and night before You. You have put me in the depths of the pit, in the regions dark and deep. Your wrath lies heavy upon me, and You overwhelm me with all Your waves. I am shut in so that I cannot escape; my eye grows dim through sorrow. Every day I call upon You, O Lord; I spread out my hands to You.*
>
> *For my soul is full of troubles, and my life draws near to Sheol. (Ps 88:1, 6–7, 8c–9; antiphon: Ps 88:3)*

You may have noticed that during Holy Week, beginning with the Sunday of the Passion, the Introits have had no Gloria Patri. Adornments are stripped away. On this day, surely, Jesus' followers didn't feel like singing

"Glory be" to anyone. They themselves felt drawn near to Sheol, the realm of the dead, "the depths of the pit, in the regions dark and deep." "I am shut in so that I cannot escape." Sounds like hell!

But this is not that *first* Holy Saturday. Even in despair of death, "Every day I call upon You, O LORD." Still praying. There is hope. Our Saturday looks ahead.

Likewise, the **Collect** is still praying:

> *O God, creator of heaven and earth, grant that as the crucified body of Your dear Son was laid in the tomb and rested on this holy Sabbath, so we may await with Him the coming of the third day, and rise with Him to newness of life, who lives and reigns with You and the Holy Spirit, one God, now and forever. Amen.*

Prayer and hope from the depths. Daniel would have known what that was like on Saturday night. Look at the **Old Testament Reading**, Daniel 6:1–24.

Marvelous choice for one of the lessons this day, isn't it! Righteous Daniel, beloved by Darius, unjustly accused, condemned to die. And then in the den through what, to the king, seemed one very long night: "Sleep fled from him" (6:18).

Our mental picture of the lions' den—probably accurate—is of an opening above into a deep cavern below. (Daniel was eventually "taken up out of the den" and his accusers, cast to "the bottom," 6:23, 24.) Undoubtedly dark, perhaps devoid of any light at all. A long night indeed.

Darius could only hope: "O Daniel, servant of the living God, has your God, whom you serve continually, been able to deliver you from the lions?" (6:20). But for Daniel there was the *hope* that comes from *knowing* the *living* God. This is the faith of Holy Saturday.

It's the same faith David also wrote in centuries before its confirmation, our **Psalm** of the day, Psalm 16.

Not until verse 10 do we have any inkling that David is facing death. "The lines have fallen for me in pleasant places; indeed, I have a beautiful inheritance. . . . My heart is glad, and my whole being rejoices; my flesh also dwells secure" (16:6, 9). But verse 10 does actually explain it all: "For You will not abandon my soul to Sheol, or let Your holy one see corruption." David will die, but God's promise of resurrection sets him on "the path of life; in Your presence there is fullness of joy; at Your right hand are pleasures forevermore" (16:11).

In fact, verse 10 explains even more. On Pentecost, Peter preached that David knew he would die and his body "see corruption," but that he looked ahead and spoke instead of his descendant, the Christ. He, Jesus, would rise from the grave without His body decaying (Acts 2:25–36)—and that is what gave David such joy and eternal pleasures.

Knowing what follows Saturday lifts us from Sheol and lions' dens and fear of death to faith and hope and joy.

The one proper for Holy Saturday yet to be discussed is the **Epistle**, 1 Peter 4:1–8. Interestingly, it follows immediately after the Epistle appointed for this same day in the one-year lectionary and in older lectionaries,

1 Peter 3:17–22. Read them together as a unit: 1 Peter 3:17–4:8.

The obvious relevance to Holy Saturday is the reference to Jesus' descent into hell (3:19). As the Creed teaches, after Jesus "died and was buried," but before any living human knew that "He rose again from the dead," He first descended into hell. Sometime after sunset on Saturday (when, by Jewish reckoning, the third day began), Jesus was "made alive" (3:18), risen—though no one on earth knew, because the stone had not yet been rolled away from the tomb. At that point, then, the risen Christ went to hell, not to suffer, but to show His resurrection victory to Satan and the damned already there.

Peter goes on to explain how that resurrection victory changes our lives. Baptism now saves us by connecting us to Jesus' resurrection (3:21). And as people who have ourselves been raised to new life in Baptism, we put away the old sinful behaviors (4:3–4) and instead love one another earnestly (4:8).

People who understand Holy Saturday have become Easter people. Even our **Hymn of the Day** ends on that note. Sing "O Darkest Woe," and don't quit before stanza 7.

Now what of the Easter Vigil? It's actually a service of an entirely different character. While the Holy Saturday propers are themed by Jesus' burial and, nevertheless, the hope to follow (a Passion service, symbolized by the black paraments), the Vigil of Easter is actually a first Easter service. The ancient practice of the vigil was to meet through the night with the service climaxing at dawn, Easter sunrise. Therefore, ideally, the vigil would be a very early Sunday service. That may be worth a try. A Saturday service would then use the Holy Saturday appointments. Unfortunately, when the vigil is celebrated in our day, it may instead take place on Saturday night, with the Holy Saturday lessons being unused.

Our *Lutheran Service Book: Altar Book* offers a (dare we say?) dramatic service that incorporates ancient vigil tradition. The service begins in darkness, with a prayer that we may "share in the Feast of Light which has no end; through Jesus Christ, Your Son, our Lord, who *lives*." Then candles are lit, by which are read a series of lengthy Old Testament lessons interspersed with collects. The readings begin with creation (Gen 1:1–2:3) and then tell many stories of God's deliverances, such as the flood (Gen 7:1–5, 11–18; 8:6–18; 9:8–13), the Red Sea (Ex 14:10–15:1), dry bones (Ezek 37:1–14), and the fiery furnace (Dan 3:1–30). A significant early element of the vigil was the Baptism of those who had completed thorough instruction. Thus the *Altar Book* includes a special order for Holy Baptism. As the climax of the service, the pastor and congregation acclaim, "Alleluia! Christ is risen!" "He is risen indeed! Alleluia!" and all sanctuary lights are turned on for a brief sermon and Holy Communion.

Here ends the Passion and only begins our celebration of Easter! Taken together, the two services, Holy Saturday and the Vigil of Easter, whether both are observed in practice or one simply remembered, prepare our hearts to see how

From Darkest Woe
Emerges the First Light
of Christ's Resurrection.

The Resurrection of Our Lord Year A

READINGS

Acts 10:34–43
or Jeremiah 31:1–6
Psalm 16 (antiphon: v 10)
Colossians 3:1–4
Matthew 28:1–10

Exodus 14:10–15:1
Psalm 118:15–29 (antiphon: v 1)
1 Corinthians 15:1–11
John 20:1–18

HYMN OF THE DAY

LSB 458 "Christ Jesus Lay in Death's Strong Bands"

If ever we've been looking forward to Sunday morning, this is it! If ever you've prepared your heart to come into God's house, you were preparing for Easter—not only all this Holy Week, but every week. Every Sunday, in fact, is a celebration of this Sunday. Ever since the early Christians set aside the first day of the week to be the Lord's Day, they were recognizing that our reason for coming together is that our Redeemer lives.

Alleluia! Christ is risen!
He is risen indeed! Alleluia!

We know what we're getting Sunday. Jesus Christ, God's Son, suffered and died on the cross to take away our sins, which separated us from God. And God has accepted Christ's sacrifice as sufficient; He is fully reconciled to us. How do we know? Because on the third day, this day, He raised Jesus back to life. That's it! If Jesus is raised again, God is no longer angry with us; He is our loving Father again; we have every good thing He desires to give us right now and for eternity. That's Easter. That's this Sunday. We know that!

But there will be literally millions of Easter sermons this week, and each will seek to offer something that either we *don't* know or at least would be blessed to know, to understand, to trust, more deeply. And God's Word never disappoints! Even with what we know, the Holy Spirit will most surely give us something more.

Let's begin to prepare, then, with prayer, the first **Collect** (of two) for Easter Day:

> *Almighty God the Father, through Your only-begotten Son, Jesus Christ, You have overcome death and opened the gate of everlasting life to us. Grant*

that we, who celebrate with joy the day of our Lord's resurrection, may be raised from the death of sin by Your life-giving Spirit; through Jesus Christ, our Lord, who lives and reigns with You and the Holy Spirit, one God, now and forever. Amen.

Since the glorious event of this day is so familiar, let's work from what we know best. Perhaps that'll open up something that's less well known. In the first Collect, for example, we work from the recognition that our Lord has overcome death by His resurrection. Then we ask that we may also be raised. That, too, we know is going to happen. But might there be more there? In words that our other propers will give us,

YOU YOURSELVES KNOW WHAT GOD DID FOR JESUS, BUT DO YOU KNOW THAT YOU YOURSELVES HAVE DIED AND BEEN RAISED?!!

That is, died and raised *already*?

What we know best about Easter, of course, is the story of Jesus' resurrection. So even though it's the lesson we'll hear last on Sunday, let's start our study there. Let's actually look at all the propers in almost the *reverse* order you'll hear them. By the way, notice that there's a second set of readings listed. Officially, those are for Easter Sunrise, but your pastor may choose to substitute any of them for the primary readings. You might, therefore, want to read those ahead as well. Here, we'll discuss the first set, beginning with the **Holy Gospel**, Matthew 28:1–10.

You know what God did for Jesus!

The Sabbath (28:1) ended at sundown on Saturday; Sunday, the first day of the week, began at that time. Thus, by Jewish counting, sundown of "our Saturday" began Jesus' promised "third day" (Friday, Saturday, now "Sunday"). So at some moment after that, perhaps very shortly after, God raised His Son back to life; Jesus' body and soul were reunited in the tomb. Jesus began His "state of exaltation," so He brushed aside small inconveniences like graves and stones (and space and time). This is when Jesus "descended into hell," not to suffer any more, but to show Satan and the lost souls that He had conquered (1 Pet 3:18–19)! (Fully stated, Jesus' resurrection was really accomplished by all three Persons of the Trinity together: Acts 10:40; Jn 10:18; 1 Pet 3:18).

No one "on the outside" knew any of this, however, until the angel rolled away that stone (28:2). Eventually the guards returned to the city and reported the news (28:11–15). An early Jewish source confirms that the Jews were indeed circulating the story of the disciples stealing Jesus' body. That, though, only confirms that His tomb was really empty. Otherwise, Jesus' enemies would have had no need for a story; they could have discredited the early Christians simply by showing the evidence, the body itself.

The women, too, are afraid at first—angels will do that to us! But the angel's words are the greatest comfort: "risen, *as He said*" (28:6). And then the Lord Himself meets them. "And they came up and took hold of His feet and worshiped Him" (28:9). This was really Jesus! Their Jesus! Not a spirit, but a dear friend they could hug! (In John's account, Jn 20:17, Jesus tells Mary Magdalene not to "cling" to Him—not because He was a ghost, but because He had an assignment for her.) "Go and tell My brothers" (28:10).

Your dearest friend, closest loved one. Someone you see every day, build your world around. Who would that be? Imagine: Dead. Gone. Buried. Your world collapsing. Your purpose in life over. Now . . . you're hugging him again. Or her. For all of us, that's really Jesus. You know God raised Jesus from the dead.

> *Christ has risen from the dead. [God the Father] has crowned Him with glory and honor, He has given Him dominion over the works of His hands; He has put all things under His feet. (adapted from Mt 28:7; Heb 2:7; Ps 8:6)*

—the **Gradual** for this season of Easter.

The **First Reading** for Easter, as, for the most part, throughout the Easter season, is not from the Old Testament but from the book of Acts. Peter, too, begins with what his hearers know: Acts 10:34–43.

This is a short portion of the radically important encounter of Peter and a Roman centurion, Cornelius (10:1–11:18). A vision from God sent Peter to meet with this Gentile and his friends. Though non-Jews, they are well versed in recent goings-on. That's Peter's foundation: "*You yourselves know* what happened throughout all Judea . . . Jesus of Nazareth . . . they put . . . to death by hanging Him on a tree, but God raised Him on the third day" (10:37–40). They themselves know that.

That now becomes the basis for what they probably didn't know—and what Peter himself was just learning. The resurrection of Jesus means everyone is now welcome in God's kingdom. Finally Peter is able to look back at the Old Testament Scriptures and realize, "To Him [Christ] all the prophets bear witness that everyone who believes in Him receives forgiveness of sins through His name" (10:43). Of course, you yourselves know that now too.

What about what Paul tells us in the **Epistle**, Colossians 3:1–4?

You know God raised Jesus from the dead. That's Easter. But do you know that you yourselves have died and been raised? That's what Paul says: "You have died, and your life is hidden with Christ in God" (3:3). "If then you have been raised with Christ" (3:1)—and his argument clearly is that you have! How so? Do you know this? Look back to the previous chapter, Colossians 2:12: "Having been buried with [Christ] in *baptism*, . . . you were also raised with Him through faith in the powerful working of God, who raised Him from the dead."

Easter is the celebration of Baptism! Baptism is how we are "in Christ," or, as Paul puts it here, "hidden with Christ in God." Baptism is how we share in everything that Christ did: His righteous life and perfect obedience to God, His death to sin (and to the evils of this world), His resurrection. Baptism, in which we *have* died and *have been* raised, is how we *will be* raised with Christ (3:4), the answer to our prayer.

It's how the **Psalm**, which Peter says is about Christ (Acts 2:25–36), is also about us. Psalm 16: "For You will not abandon my soul to Sheol, or let Your holy one see corruption. You make known to me the path of life; in Your presence there is fullness of joy; at Your right hand are pleasures forevermore" (Ps 16:10–11). Baptized into Christ, we are as secure in God's deliverance as was Jesus.

This is where the rest of the propers go too. Do you find Baptism in the **Introit**?

I will sing to the Lord, *for He has triumphed gloriously; the horse and his rider He has thrown into the sea.*

The Lord *is my strength and my song, and He has become my salvation. Your right hand, O* Lord, *glorious in power, Your right hand, O* Lord, *shatters the enemy. You have led in Your steadfast love the people whom You have redeemed; You have guided them by Your strength to Your holy abode. You will bring them in and plant them on Your own mountain, the place, O* Lord, *which You have made for Your abode, the sanctuary, O Lord, which Your hands have established. The* Lord *will reign forever and ever.*

Glory be to the Father and to the Son and to the Holy Spirit; as it was in the beginning, is now, and will be forever. Amen.

I will sing to the Lord, *for He has triumphed gloriously; the horse and his rider He has thrown into the sea. (Ex 15:2a, 6, 13, 17–18; antiphon: Ex 15:1b)*

Israel is celebrating after just passing through the Red Sea. Paul interprets in 1 Corinthians 10:2: "[Our fathers] all were *baptized* into Moses in the cloud and in the sea."

And Baptism in the second **Collect**?

O God, for our redemption You gave Your only-begotten Son to the death of the cross and by His glorious resurrection delivered us from the power of the enemy. Grant that all our sin may be drowned through daily repentance and that day by day we may arise to live before You in righteousness and purity forever; through Jesus Christ, our Lord, who lives and reigns with You and the Holy Spirit, one God, now and forever. Amen.

"Drowned . . . daily repentance . . . arise to live before You in righteousness and purity forever"? You know the Small Catechism: "What does such *baptizing* with water indicate?" That's Easter! Having died and been raised—already!—that's our new, Easter life.

From what we know about Easter, well, we know that life is just beginning!

Finally, you know how many magnificent Easter hymns you'll be singing Sunday—hymns you know!—but for a starter, another of Luther's: the **Hymn of the Day**, *LSB* 458.

Second Sunday of Easter Year A

READINGS

Acts 5:29–42
Psalm 148 (antiphon: v 13)
1 Peter 1:3–9
John 20:19–31

HYMN OF THE DAY

LSB 470, 471 "O Sons and Daughters of the King"

Too good to be true, Thomas must have felt, but he came around when he saw the risen Christ. Since then, millions have been blessed when they didn't see Jesus and yet believed in His resurrection.

Meanwhile, that Gospel reading about Thomas is just too fitting not to use for the Second Sunday of Easter all three years of the lectionary. Jesus' appearance to Thomas takes place on this very Sunday, "eight days" after Easter by Jewish reckoning, meaning the following Sunday. It's a rare treat to have Scripture texts coincide with our church calendar in real time. So, sure enough, on this Sunday after Easter, Years A, B, and C of the three-year lectionary share not only John 20:19–31 but most of the other propers as well. The only variables are the First Reading and the Epistle (this year, from Acts 5 and 1 Peter 1).

That can be a challenge for a preacher—to declare something fresh each year. Truth is, the Second Sunday of Easter could be seen as a challenge that way anyway. How can we possibly say anything more after all that we celebrated *last* Sunday?

As always, God's Word provides. We certainly don't try to top last week; it's still the resurrection of Jesus that's making our day. And we will hear those oft-repeated words to Thomas. As the **Verse** summarizes, "Alleluia. We know that Christ being raised from the dead will never die again; death no longer has dominion over Him. Alleluia. Blessed are those who have not seen and yet have believed. Alleluia" (Rom 6:9; Jn 20:29b). But discovering all the ways we're blessed will always be a new adventure.

The **Introit** suggests that there's a lot more yet to find in Easter:

> *Like newborn infants, long for the pure spiritual milk, that by it you may grow up to salvation—if indeed you have tasted that the Lord is good.*
>
> *Oh give thanks to the* Lord*; call upon His name; make known His deeds among the peoples! Sing to Him, sing praises to Him; tell of all His wondrous works! Glory in His holy name; let the hearts of those who seek the* Lord *rejoice! Seek the* Lord *and His strength; seek His presence continually! Remember the wondrous works that He has done, His miracles, and the judgments He uttered. He remembers His covenant forever, the word that He commanded, for a thousand generations.*
>
> *Glory be to the Father and to the Son and to the Holy Spirit; as it was in the beginning, is now, and will be forever. Amen.*
>
> *Like newborn infants, long for the pure spiritual milk, that by it you may grow up to salvation—if indeed you have tasted that the Lord is good. (Ps 105:1–5, 8; antiphon: 1 Pet 2:2–3)*

When the antiphon of the Introit isn't from the Psalms, especially when it's from the New Testament, it should catch our attention. It's usually then a very explicit comment on a major festival or something in the life of our Lord. Peter is giving us that here; we've "tasted that the Lord is good"—specifically in raising Jesus from the dead.

And that's anything to us but old hat: "Like newborn infants, long for the pure spiritual milk, that by it you may grow up to salvation." We're just getting our first taste! There's so much more to drink in. So much growing up to do. We should "*seek* the Lord and His strength; *seek* His presence continually!" We've got so much to learn about our relationship with God that Easter creates. And as we learn, as we taste more and more, we have more to "make known," to "tell," because giving His Son into death and raising Him back to life are His greatest "deeds," His most "wondrous works." So much of what we have to learn about Easter is how to proclaim it, tell it.

We pray for that in the **Collect**:

> *Almighty God, grant that we who have celebrated the Lord's resurrection may by Your grace confess in our life and conversation that Jesus is Lord and God; through the same Jesus Christ, Your Son, who lives and reigns with You and the Holy Spirit, one God, now and forever. Amen.*

We haven't seen the risen Christ, but "we know" (Verse), we "have tasted" (Introit), we "have celebrated" (Collect) His resurrection—which not only qualifies but demands us to "confess" Jesus "in our life and conversation." Celebrating Easter cannot mean simply going home to a life of ham or lamb and Cadbury eggs. Easter people tell. Do we count that as a *blessing* to us who have not seen and yet have believed?

We mentioned last week that during the Easter season, the Old Testament Reading is replaced with a First Reading from Acts. That's because the resurrection of Jesus was the impetus for the apostles to get up and go with the Gospel. Knowing Jesus was alive drove them to be His "witnesses in Jerusalem and in all Judea and Samaria, and to the end of the earth" (Acts 1:8). The **First Reading** this week has them in that first stage of the mission, in Jerusalem, but in hot water. Read Acts 5:29–42.

In the days after Easter and Pentecost, the apostles were regularly in the temple, worshiping, preaching, and working miracles—always in the name of Jesus, who they insisted had risen. This, of course, was not popular with those immediately responsible for killing Jesus (especially when it was becoming so popular with so many others!). So Peter and John and the rest were repeatedly arrested and threatened. Once again, they now find themselves before the Jewish Council. When last warned, Peter had challenged the Jews: "Whether it is right in the sight of God to listen to you rather than to God, you must judge, for we cannot but speak of what we have seen and heard" (Acts 4:19–20). Now he closes the loop for them. In case you didn't get it when I let you be the judge, here's the way it is: "We must obey God rather than men" (5:29). He knows this could cost all the apostles their lives (5:33), but they must be witnesses of Jesus' death and resurrection (5:32, 30).

By God's grace, using the counsel of Gamaliel, they are spared—though not without serious pain (5:40). And see how the apostles evaluate this experience: "They left the presence of the council, rejoicing that they were counted worthy to suffer dishonor for the name" (5:41). The apostles saw the opportunity to declare Jesus, Good Friday and Easter—even when it meant danger and beating—as, yes, a blessing. And they went on doing it (5:42).

The **Psalm** is an exuberant hymn of praise that's right at home in the season of the Resurrection: Psalm 148.

Everyone gets into the act! Verses 1–5 have those "from the heavens" praising the Lord: angels, sun, moon, stars, the skies and waters above. In verses 7–13, it's those "from the earth" praising, climactically people: kings, rulers, men, women, children, young and old. As usual, when the Psalms call for praise, they give reasons, what God has done to bless. Here, the markers are the word "for" (148:5, 13). And notice this: the inanimate objects above, plus even the angels, praise God for His creating them (148:5–6). But human beings—we praise God for "He has raised up a horn for His people" (148:14). "Horn" is a common Old Testament image for strength that saves (1 Sam 2:1; Ps 18:2). We praise God not just because we're created but also because we're saved, redeemed. Easter crowns us (again!) as the jewel of all of God's creatures. Praise the Lord!

The **Epistle** begins a series of six consecutive Sundays through Peter's first letter. But it could not fit more aptly with the theme of this day. Read 1 Peter 1:3–9.

The book of 1 Peter is seen by many as a treatise on the baptismal life, the new life of the Christian, and, as we discovered last week, Easter is the celebration of Baptism. Peter blesses God for the resurrection of Jesus Christ because we have been born again into it (1:3). "Born again" (remember, we are "like newborn infants"; that's coming up in Peter's next chapter) is the language of Baptism (Jn 3:3–5).

Peter then talks about the blessings that we have being born again, baptized, into Jesus' resurrection: "an inheritance that is imperishable, undefiled, and unfading, kept in heaven for you" (1:4). Unfading blessings! So far surpassing all the things of this world to which we cling. That's our lifelong encouragement because "now for a little while, if necessary, you have been grieved by various trials" (1:6), as Peter, John, and all the apostles were by the Jews. Yet, consider it a blessing, because it results in the "genuineness of your faith—more precious than gold that perishes"—being "tested" and proven. This is the blessing that comes from confessing, telling, speaking Christ and His resurrection—a blessing of Easter that newborn infants might not recognize but will grow into.

Peter promises this to us "though you have not seen Him." For "though you do not now see Him, you believe in Him" (1:8).

Clearly, Peter had learned Jesus' lesson when He spoke to Thomas in our **Holy Gospel**, John 20:19–31.

So much more than Thomas is here—plenty for all three years of the three-year lectionary! Most of the apostles are getting their first taste of the joy of the risen Christ. His word, "Peace" (spoken three times, 20:19, 21, 26), is the much-needed absolution that they are forgiven for their desertions and denials; Jesus' death and resurrection has reconciled all of us to God.

What more beautiful confirmation of that restored relationship than this: the apostles will be privileged (blessed!) to be Jesus' sent ones (20:21–23). They will speak His resurrection, announce His forgiveness. They will confess Him, including before the Sanhedrin, when it could mean their deaths.

That will even include Thomas. His demand to see Jesus' wounds is completely out of line; the word spoken by Jesus' witnesses should always be sufficient. But Jesus is gracious to show Himself nevertheless. And now Thomas makes the clearest confession of Jesus' divinity anywhere in the Gospels: "My Lord and my God!" (20:28).

It's the apostles' witness spoken and then recorded for the centuries which has brought us, who have not seen, the unfading blessings of Easter. That includes the blessing of confessing Jesus in ease or in danger.

**We, Who Without Seeing
Have Nonetheless
Known, Tasted, Celebrated
the Lord's Resurrection,
Now Find
Unfading New Blessings
as We Confess Him.**

May we like newborn infants grow into that!

Conclude with the story of the Gospel reading set to music, the **Hymn of the Day**, "O Sons and Daughters of the King."

Third Sunday of Easter Year A

READINGS

Acts 2:14a, 36–41

Psalm 116:1–14 (antiphon: v 5)

1 Peter 1:17–25

Luke 24:13–35

HYMN OF THE DAY

LSB 483 "With High Delight Let Us Unite"

"Blessed are those who have not seen and yet have believed," the resurrected Christ said to Thomas and to all of us last week. Two thousand years later, we still haven't seen Jesus with our eyes, and yet the Easter celebration continues—as it will this week and for seven Sundays of the Easter season. For we do believe the words of the **Gradual** for this season:

> *Christ has risen from the dead. [God the Father] has crowned Him with glory and honor, He has given Him dominion over the works of His hands; He has put all things under His feet. (adapted from Mt 28:7; Heb 2:7; Ps 8:6)*

How good is that?!! If Christ has risen and has everything under His feet, it means that we have every good thing He graciously wishes to give us. It's as the beautiful Easter hymn "I Know That My Redeemer Lives" (*LSB* 461) declares: "He lives [thirty times it says that in the eight stanzas!] to" do just about every blessed thing we could imagine. To save. To bless me with His love. To plead for me above. To guide. To comfort. My mansion to prepare. To bring me safely there. Some of these blessings we haven't seen or don't always see with our eyes either, but Christ's Word promises they're real and they're ours.

This Third Sunday of Easter we pray that God would enable our hearts—if not our eyes—to be opened to whatever He would have us believe. We'll see examples of that in our propers, especially for the two disciples with Jesus on the road to Emmaus in our Gospel reading.

The **Introit**, the full Psalm 133, lifts up a blessing we wish we could alway see:

Behold, how good and pleasant it is when brothers dwell in unity!

It is like the precious oil on the head, running down on the beard, on the beard of Aaron, running down on the collar of his robes! It is like the dew of Hermon, which falls on the mountains of Zion! For there the Lord *has commanded the blessing, life forevermore.*

Glory be to the Father and to the Son and to the Holy Spirit; as it was in the beginning, is now, and will be forever. Amen.

Behold, how good and pleasant it is when brothers dwell in unity! (Ps 133; antiphon: Ps 133:1)

Everyone shares the sentiment! Brothers in unity; friends, family loving one another. We all wish every home, neighborhood, workplace, classroom, congregation could be like that! The imagery would perhaps be different nowadays, but for ancient Israel, the psalmist pushed all the right emotional buttons. Aaron, the first high priest, kneeling, bowing, Moses pouring olive oil over his head. He looks up toward heaven as that expensive anointing runs through his hair, down his cheeks, dripping from his beard onto his holy robes. Ecstasy! Divine honor! How good, how pleasant it is! Or in a land often so desperate for water, dew, collecting high on the slopes of Mount Hermon, funneling into rivulets that run down into the valleys. Oh, how good! How pleasant!

Far more often, our eyes see discord, jealousy, broken homes and relationships. But God's Word tells us this unity does exist, and we have a term for it: *the Church.* All those who believe in Jesus as their crucified and risen Savior have not only eternal life but also perfect love for and fellowship with all other believers. Sadly, that's often invisible, but we confess it to be true when we say, "I believe in . . . the holy Christian Church, the communion of saints." Our old sinful nature makes a shambles of brotherly unity, but the new heart the Holy Spirit creates when He brings us to faith really does love every brother and sister this sweetly.

The **Collect** for Easter 3:

O God, through the humiliation of Your Son You raised up the fallen world. Grant to Your faithful people, rescued from the peril of everlasting death, perpetual gladness and eternal joys; through Jesus Christ, our Lord, who lives and reigns with You and the Holy Spirit, one God, now and forever. Amen.

Lest we forget, there is no Easter without Good Friday. It was the humiliation of the cross that "raised up the fallen world" and "rescued" us from "everlasting death." And having rescued us, Christ really does live to give us every blessing already now. However, while we live in this fallen world, "perpetual gladness and eternal joys" are yet to be seen. For now, we cling to God's promise that we have what He knows to be best and that we will see the rest in God's perfect time.

Our **First Reading** is one of the more heart-opening-by-heart-rending moments in the entire Bible. Read Acts 2:14a, 36–41.

This, obviously, is a cutting from Peter's great Pentecost sermon. (We'll hear parts of it again on both Pentecost and Trinity Sundays.) As already observed, Pentecost and all of the apostolic preaching in Acts are declarations of Easter. God has made Jesus "both Lord and Christ" (2:36) by raising Him up (see 2:24, 31, 32). But, of course, the kicker is that it's that Lord and Christ "you crucified." Peter's audience are Jews who intend to be faithful. They're celebrating God's prescribed festival on the fiftieth day of firstfruits; many, as we know, have come from great distance (2:5, 9–11). Surely some had been in the Jerusalem mob seven weeks earlier. And now they're hearing that the very Christ for whom their nation had looked for millennia *they had killed!*

"Now when they heard this they were cut to the heart" (2:37). And their question, "Brothers, what shall we do?" was *not* expecting a doable answer. (Do this, this, and this, and all will be well.) What they meant was, "We're done for, then, aren't we!" They've done the worst—killed God's Son!—and they know it! Cut to the heart! By the preaching of the Word, the news of the risen Christ, the Holy Spirit has opened their hearts to see their deathly sin.

To their absolute surprise, God has a gracious answer: "Repent and be baptized every one of you in the name of Jesus Christ for the forgiveness of your sins, and you will receive the gift of the Holy Spirit" (2:38). The death of Christ that they caused has saved them too! No sin is too wicked. Every sin is forgiven! And once the word of the Law had cut them to the heart, the word of this Gospel opened their hearts to believe in God's forgiveness, and three thousand were baptized!

Do note the strong testimony to infant Baptism: "The promise is for you *and for your children* and for all who are far off, everyone whom the Lord our God calls" (2:39).

Appreciate, too, that these three thousand become the original core of the Church, those among whom the "good and pleasant . . . unity" of the brothers and sisters prevails.

The **Psalm** includes verses that sound almost like a poetic voicing of the Pentecost crowd after Peter's sermon. Read Psalm 116:1–14. Imagine especially verses 3--6 on the lips of Peter's hearers. "I suffered distress and anguish. Then I called on the name of the Lord: 'O Lord, I pray, deliver my soul!'" ("Brothers, what shall we do?") "Gracious is the Lord . . . ; our God is merciful. The Lord preserves the simple; when I was brought low, He saved me." ("Repent and be baptized every one of you in the name of Jesus Christ for the forgiveness of your sins.") We are *all* the Jerusalem crowd, guilty of killing Christ—and His death avails for us all.

Now fast-forward three decades or so from Pentecost and imagine Peter writing his first letter, including our **Epistle**, 1 Peter 1:17–25. Might he have had a gleam in his eye, a fatherly smile, envisioning some of his Pentecost converts now as he wrote?

In Peter's preaching, they had come face-to-face with the "Father who judges impartially according to each one's deeds" (1:17), and they had been rightly terrified, cut to the heart. But then their hearts had been opened "through the living and abiding word of God" that "remains forever" (1:23, 25). They had heard that they "were ransomed . . . , not with perishable things such as silver or gold, but with the precious blood of Christ, like that of a lamb without blemish or spot" (1:18–19). (And yes, these are the verses Luther had in mind as he wrote his explanation of the Second Article of the Apostles' Creed in the Small Catechism.) Then, as now, Peter had proclaimed that God raised Jesus from the dead (1:21). And by that word they had been "born again" (1:23), made believers with "faith and hope . . . in God" (1:21).

Now Peter would surely have smiled to picture his first dear congregation loving one another "earnestly from a pure heart," "a sincere brotherly love" (1:22). Maybe he would have recalled Psalm 133. That's a good and pleasant result of being raised to faith in the crucified and risen Christ.

Finally, this example of being blessed by *not* seeing until hearts have first been opened by the Word: the **Holy Gospel**, Luke 24:13–35.

We don't know the location of Emmaus; it was certainly a small town, perhaps to the northwest of Jerusalem on a hill looking back down a valley toward the city. It's definitely not the place the two disciples would have been heading had they believed the news of the day. They were leaving Jerusalem because the crazy story about Jesus being alive wasn't really worth investigating further. The mood probably matched the lengthening shadows.

As He'd be the following Sunday with Thomas, Jesus was gracious to seek them out. He was also gracious to keep their eyes from recognizing Him (24:16), because they learned so much more by listening than they could have by seeing. They can hardly believe this stranger didn't know about Jesus' crucifixion (24:18); it was no doubt all the talk. They had hoped He would redeem Israel (24:21), but those hopes had been dashed. The women's story of seeing Jesus alive amazed them (24:22), but they didn't believe.

So now Jesus takes over. "O foolish ones, and slow of heart to believe all that the prophets have spoken!" (24:25). It had to be this way! And with all the Old Testament Scriptures ("Moses and all the prophets"), He proves it (24:26–27).

Not until Jesus begins the actions that remind us of His Supper do they recognize Him (24:30–31). But even then, it wasn't the seeing that impressed: "Did not our hearts burn within us while He talked to us on the road, *while He opened to us the Scriptures*?" (24:32). As with Peter's hearers and readers, it's the Word that opened their hearts to know their Redeemer—who lives!

Recall all that the Word has opened to us in this coming Sunday's propers:

**THE WORD
OF THE RESURRECTED CHRIST
OPENS OUR HEARTS
TO THESE REALITIES:
THE KILLING EFFECTS OF OUR SIN,
THE CRUCIFIED AND RISEN REDEEMER,
AND THE ETERNAL JOYS AND UNITY
OF THOSE RAISED TO FAITH IN HIM.**

It's especially those eternal joys that the **Hymn of the Day** proclaims. Sing "With High Delight Let Us Unite" (*LSB* 483).

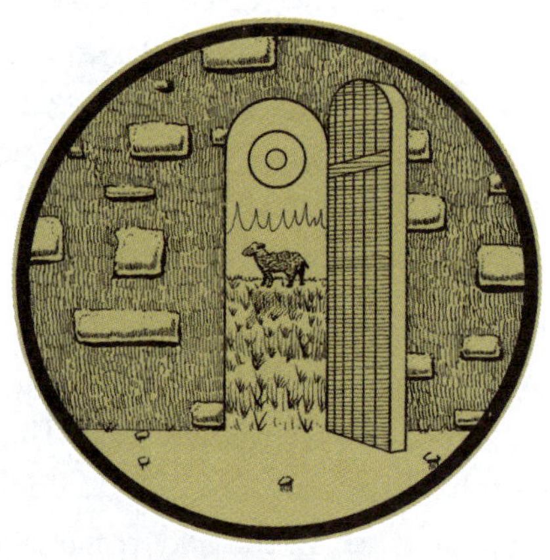

Fourth Sunday of Easter Year A

READINGS

Acts 2:42–47
Psalm 23 (antiphon: v 1)
1 Peter 2:19–25
John 10:1–10

HYMN OF THE DAY

LSB 709 "The King of Love My Shepherd Is"

The Fourth Sunday of Easter is unusual. It has an almost festival-like identity and even a popular name without being based on a major event in the life of our Lord or His Early Church or on a doctrine or even a landmark in church history. The highest holy days, of course, observe happenings like Jesus' birth, death, and resurrection and His giving the Holy Spirit to His first followers. The Church has added festivals like Trinity Sunday and Reformation Day to teach doctrine and remember God's working in more recent centuries. But the Fourth Sunday in Easter derives its identity as "Good Shepherd Sunday" from a metaphor Jesus uses for Himself in the traditional Gospel lesson for this day.

"I am the good shepherd," Jesus says in John 10:14. "I know My own and My own know Me, and I lay down My life for the sheep." There's no reason that has to be read the fourth week of the Easter season (or the third week, as it was in the past and still is in the one-year lectionary)—or during the Easter season at all. It would be welcome any time of year. But that, perhaps, is why Good Shepherd Sunday has come to be almost a feast of its own. The image of Jesus as our Good Shepherd, incarnating the beloved Twenty-Third Psalm ("The Lord is my shepherd"), carrying the little lamb on His shoulders—it's so comforting for so many life situations that we beg to spend a day on it.

The truth is, too, seeing Jesus as Good Shepherd *is* very fitting in the Easter season. The Good Shepherd laid down His life for the sheep that He might "take it up again" (Jn 10:17). And caring for His sheep is what "He lives" to do (*LSB* 461). Feeding, guiding, calming—that's what the risen Christ is always doing for us.

Interestingly, the thematic words of this Sunday are spoken as the antiphon to the Introit but not in this year's Gospel. That's because the three-year lectionary divides the Good Shepherd *chapter*, John 10, into three separate readings. Jesus actually tells us He is the Good Shepherd in the Year B cutting, John 10:11–18. In Year C, He goes on to talk about knowing His sheep—and those who are not His sheep (10:22–30). This year, Year A, Jesus begins the discourse by introducing the sheep-and-shepherd imagery, but it's not as straightforward as the middle verses of the chapter. Read this year's **Holy Gospel** for Good Shepherd Sunday, John 10:1–10.

Initially, the text seems direct enough—at least to us who've seen all the paintings and sung all the Shepherd hymns. Sheepfold, sheep, robbers, shepherd. The sheepfold has its obvious way in, the door. Whoever climbs in another way isn't the shepherd; he only comes to wreak havoc. The shepherd does it right—comes in through the door, calls the sheep by name, leads them in and out—and they follow him because they know his voice. Easy for us to see Jesus doing all that for us.

But Jesus' hearers didn't get it (10:6). So now we'd expect Jesus to explain, "I am the Good Shepherd." He doesn't. Not yet. Rather, Jesus says to them, "Truly, truly, I say to you, I am the *door* of the sheep" (10:7). Wait a minute. Rewind. Back to verse 1. Jesus is the door: "Truly, truly, I say to you, he who does not enter the sheepfold by *the door* but climbs in by another way, that man is a thief and a robber." And Jesus goes on to unpack the metaphor with Himself as door: "I am the door. If anyone enters by Me, he will be saved and will go in and out and find pasture" (10:9).

Jesus as door is itself a rich metaphor. The crucial thing to recognize is that when Jesus says "door," He's really referring to Himself as a door*way*. A door, as we might picture it, is often the heavy wooden thing on hinges. Its purpose—think about it—is to *close* an opening, to keep things from going out or in. But the term *door* can also mean "doorway," the opening that *allows* passage. That's Jesus. He is our way into pleasant pastures, not someone who stands in our way. Clearly, that's what Jesus means in verses 7–10.

What about in verses 1–5? We know that in verse 14 (and 11) Jesus will tell us He is the good shepherd. But is He also the shepherd in the earlier verses? Maybe. If so, then Jesus is changing His metaphor; first He's shepherd, then, when His hearers don't understand, He introduces a new idea, Plan B: He's the door. Possible, and everything verses 1–5 say about the shepherd *is* true of Jesus.

But here's another possibility: The shepherd in verses 1–5 is someone other than Jesus. And from verse 1 all the way to verse 10, Jesus is the door. Then from verse 11 on, Jesus says, in effect, "Not only am I the door, but I'm also the *good* shepherd, the best shepherd. Those shepherds in verses 1–5 were good too, because they led people in and out through Me, the door. But I'm the even better shepherd, the one who makes those shepherds good as well." How about that?

Who would those other "good" shepherds be, then? They receive their authority to be shepherds from Jesus. They speak with a voice their sheep recognize; they know their sheep by name, and the sheep know them. They only lead their sheep the way of Jesus (the door), and through the door they bring the sheep to blessed pasture. All the while, they protect the sheep from thieves and robbers. Who might that be?

Pastors. The word *pastor* means "shepherd," and shepherding has always been understood as the pastor's duty. (Not, primarily, organizing, administrating, coaching.) It may be that in this first portion of the Good Shepherd chapter, Jesus is telling us how He cares for us through faithful shepherds He places over us. And soon enough, the very next verse, He'll make clear that faithful pastors are only stand-ins for Himself, the *Good* Pastor, who lays down His life so that His undershepherds have salvation to proclaim.

With both possible interpretations in mind, we propose our THEME for the week:

JESUS IS THE WAY BY WHOM ALL GOOD SHEEP AND ALL GOOD SHEPHERDS GO IN AND OUT AND FIND PASTURE.

With the other propers, then, let's consider what Jesus' "way" of going in and out is.

What does the **Introit** tell about the way *the* Good Shepherd leads to pasture?

I am the good shepherd. I know My own and My own know Me, and I lay down My life for the sheep.

Oh come, let us sing to the LORD; let us make a joyful noise to the rock of our salvation! Let us come into His presence with thanksgiving; let us make a joyful noise to Him with songs of praise! For the LORD is a great God, and a great King above all gods. Oh come, let us worship and bow down; let us kneel before the LORD, our Maker! For He is our God, and we are the people of His pasture, and the sheep of His hand.

Glory be to the Father and to the Son and to the Holy Spirit; as it was in the beginning, is now, and will be forever. Amen.

I am the good shepherd. I know My own and My own know Me, and I lay down My life for the sheep. (Ps 95:1–3, 6–7a; antiphon: Jn 10:14, 15b)

Psalm 95, familiar as the Venite in our Matins liturgy, demonstrates how prominent the sheep-shepherd metaphor is throughout Scripture: "We are the people of His pasture, and the sheep of His hand." The psalmist finds that to be a delight! Being sheep of the Lord has him rejoicing! "Sing to the LORD; let us make a joyful noise to the rock of our salvation!" The Shepherd has saved him as a good shepherd would—by laying down His life on the cross. So the psalmist will make that joyful noise "with songs of praise!" He'll "worship and bow down." That's the way the Good Shepherd—and His faithful undershepherds—will lead us out and in: the way of joy and praise and worship.

As we'd expect, the appointed **Psalm** of the day for Good Shepherd Sunday all three years of the lectionary is Psalm 23.

“The Lord is my shepherd; I shall not want.” Christ, our Good Shepherd, and His faithful pastors lead us in a way of contentment. Picture the greens and the blues. The grass on a gently rolling hillside. The stream, clear and clean, but moving slowly—easy to step down and drink from (23:1). It’s even a way of opulence: a rich banquet table, the finest wines flowing freely (23:5). Christ is providing our every need—and in lavish supply.

But the way in and out to pasture also winds through the “valley of the shadow of death” (23:4a). Our Shepherd leads us in the way of trials and sufferings—and He’s caring for us no less. For He is with us (23:4b), He provides faithful shepherds to hold our hands, and He knows how this, too, will bring us to the blessed pastures forever (23:6).

Peter in the **Epistle** also reminds us of our Shepherd’s way of suffering: 1 Peter 2:19–25. “For to this you have been called, because Christ also suffered for you, leaving you an example, so that you might follow in His steps” (2:21). If we are Jesus’ sheep, we hear His voice and follow where He goes. And He went to the cross. Peter draws his language from Isaiah 53:4–9, where Jesus Himself is the lamb led to the slaughter. We don’t always wish to follow *that* way—“for you were straying like sheep.” But now we have “returned to the Shepherd and Overseer of [our] souls” (2:25).

The one proper that isn’t explicit about sheep and shepherd is the **First Reading**, Acts 2:42–47. See in it, though, the way our Good Shepherd and His undershepherds lead us to pasture. After Peter’s preaching on Pentecost of the resurrection (recall the Acts reading last week), the infant Church is “day by day” assembled for “the apostles’ teaching and fellowship, . . . the breaking of bread and the prayers” (2:42). From those first days until Christ returns, He will always shepherd His flock to heaven by His Word and Table, received and celebrated in worship with fellow believers. This is the chief service of His faithful pastors.

So our Good Shepherd and the good shepherds He provides lead us, His sheep, in and out to pasture by way of joy and praise and worship, by way of contentment and opulence but also sufferings, always by way of His Word and Sacrament in fellowship with His Church. It is our Shepherd’s way.

Lutheran Service Book has many hymns that use the shepherd-and-sheep imagery or even paraphrase Psalm 23 (especially 710 and 740, but also others such as 707, 711, 716, and 722). Among the most beautiful is the **Hymn of the Day**, “The King of Love My Shepherd Is” (*LSB* 709). Sing one or more of your favorites.

Then close by praying the **Collect** for Easter 4, Good Shepherd Sunday:

Almighty God, merciful Father, since You have wakened from death the Shepherd of Your sheep, grant us Your Holy Spirit that when we hear the voice of our Shepherd we may know Him who calls us each by name and follow where He leads; through the same Jesus Christ, Your Son, our Lord, who lives and reigns with You and the Holy Spirit, one God, now and forever. Amen.

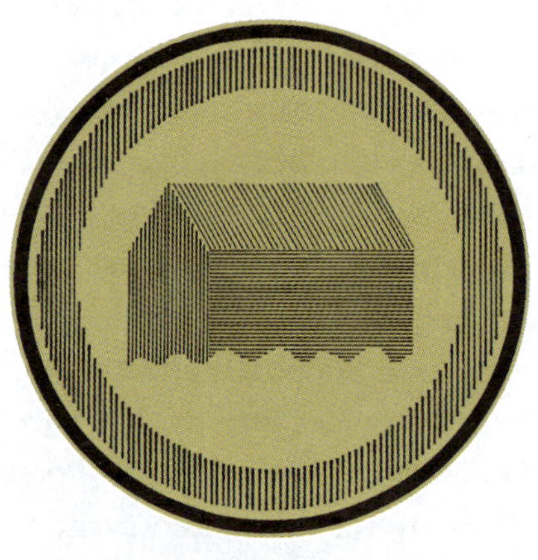

Fifth Sunday of Easter Year A

READINGS

Acts 6:1–9; 7:2a, 51–60
Psalm 146 (antiphon: v 2)
1 Peter 2:2–10
John 14:1–14

HYMN OF THE DAY

LSB 633 "At the Lamb's High Feast We Sing"

We continue this week to celebrate the Easter season and the resurrection of our Lord. The **Gradual**:

> *Christ has risen from the dead. [God the Father] has crowned Him with glory and honor, He has given Him dominion over the works of His hands; He has put all things under His feet. (adapted from Mt 28:7; Heb 2:7; Ps 8:6)*

However, the last three Sundays of Easter, beginning this week, do turn us toward the ascension of Jesus, His visible departure from our world. Just when the disciples are starting to settle into a new normal—Jesus risen again and visiting with them frequently if not every minute—life is going to change again. Radically.

The approach to Ascension, the preparation for this radical change, is reflected in the lectionary. All three years, the Gospel readings for Easter 5, 6, and 7 are drawn from Jesus' farewell discourse, John 14–17, which He spoke after supper the night before His death. This year, Year A, uses two readings from John 14, followed by the first third of John 17. Year B will take two Gospels from John 15, along with the middle portion of John 17. Then in Year C, we'll hear twice from John 16 and finish with the final section of John 17.

This year especially, the Fifth Sunday of Easter highlights world- and life-altering changes like the one the disciples were soon to experience. The **Collect** lays these before God—praying what we may only fear and fume about:

O God, You make the minds of Your faithful to be of one will. Grant that we may love what You have commanded and desire what You promise, that among the many changes of this world our hearts may be fixed where true joys are found; through Jesus Christ, Your Son, our Lord, who lives and reigns with You and the Holy Spirit, one God, now and forever. Amen.

"That among the many changes of this world our hearts may be fixed where true joys are found."

"Change and decay in all around I see," the hymn says (*LSB* 878:4). We know the feeling. Just as I'm writing this, I've received a pop-up saying there's an available update to the publishing platform I'm using. *(But I'm used to the version I've got!)* And—who knows?—maybe by the time you read this, you'll wonder what a pop-up was. *(Did you know TV used to be black-and-white? And come by broadcast over the "airwaves"? I didn't think so.)* Technology's only the illustration.

Values—the sanctity of human life from conception to natural death, marriage only between one man and one woman, male or female as one was born—these are real things. Till death us do part. Dad around as I'm growing up. These are real things. Knees that can get me a football scholarship. A job past the next round of layoffs. Retirement savings still there when we need them. Health to enjoy that retirement and all those trips we'd planned. These are real things. And they change—can change as suddenly as new technology. And often not for the better. If we're counting on things of this world—health, wealth, relationships, even life—we're eventually going to be disappointed. They change. They fail.

"That among the many changes of this world *our hearts may be fixed where true joys are found*." "O Thou who changest not, abide with me" (*LSB* 878:4). Amen!

Our **Introit** points us to those true joys:

Praise the LORD! Sing to the LORD a new song, His praise in the assembly of the godly!

I will extol You, O LORD, for You have drawn me up and have not let my foes rejoice over me. O LORD my God, I cried to You for help, and You have healed me. O LORD, You have brought up my soul from Sheol; You restored me to life from among those who go down to the pit. Sing praises to the LORD, O you His saints, and give thanks to His holy name. For His anger is but for a moment, and His favor is for a lifetime. Weeping may tarry for the night, but joy comes with the morning.

Glory be to the Father and to the Son and to the Holy Spirit; as it was in the beginning, is now, and will be forever. Amen.

Praise the LORD! Sing to the LORD a new song, His praise in the assembly of the godly! (Ps 30:1–5; antiphon: Ps 149:1)

The greatest change we all face, of course, is death. David knew this danger very presently—fleeing from Saul, going again and again into battle. He often felt he was on the verge of "the pit." But he was "brought up . . . from Sheol," the realm of the dead, because of a very different, a blessed, change—where true joys are found. That is, God's disposition toward him: "His anger is but for a moment, and His favor is for a lifetime. Weeping may tarry for the night, but joy comes with the morning." God's favor and our joy that results are forever. And they come because Jesus' death on the cross turned away God's anger by taking the sin that caused it.

Even God's never-ending favor, though, will not save us forever from temporal death. We don't know how soon that change might come. Read not only Acts 6:1–9; 7:2a, 51–60, our **First Reading**, but all of Acts 6–7.

Stephen, whom we remember as the first martyr, becomes prominent because of another major change for the Early Church. Call it "growing pains." The Church is still almost exclusively in Jerusalem, but it's grown from a dozen to thousands. Where once a few dear brothers and sisters could sit down and talk through any new question, now, with the larger body, ethnic factionalism has set in (Greek-speaking Jews, "Hellenists," vs. Aramaic-speaking Jews, "Hebrews"). The Church needs organization. Many a new congregation today would understand! The answer is in Christian love and caring, being guided by the Word, and in prayer (6:4, 6).

Stephen is among those chosen to manage the works of mercy, the distribution of food. But he also works miracles and speaks of Christ (6:8, 10). Some from "the synagogue of the Freedmen," former slaves from North Africa, Asia Minor, and perhaps elsewhere (6:9), drag him before the Jewish Council, the Sanhedrin, the same body that had framed Jesus. They even bring false charges similar to those raised against Christ (6:13–14; Mt 26:59–61). Stephen's lengthy defense reviews Israel's history from Abraham to Joseph and his brothers to Moses and finally to Joshua, David, and Solomon's temple. Along the way, he shows more and more pointedly how Israel had consistently rejected God's spokesmen—until finally they "betrayed and murdered" "the Righteous One" (7:52), who happens to be the temple made without hands (7:48).

Stephen's audience will tolerate no more. "But he, full of the Holy Spirit, *gazed into heaven* and saw the glory of God, and Jesus standing at the right hand of God" (7:55). That is, his heart—and, in this case, even his eyes—were, in the words of our Collect, "fixed where true joys are found." He died very much as his Lord had—forgiving his enemies (7:60; Lk 23:34) and commending his spirit to God (7:59; Lk 23:46)—the one "who changest not."

Stephen understood the wisdom of our **Psalm**—to trust the One who never changes. Read Psalm 146.

"Put not your trust in princes. . . . When his breath departs, he returns to the earth; on that very day his plans perish" (146:3–4). Not only princes or politicians but whole political systems, governments of law, bills of rights, can all seem so secure. But they do not guarantee our future. They can change.

On the other hand, "Blessed is he whose help is the God of Jacob, whose hope is in the LORD his God, who made heaven and earth, the sea, and all that is in them, who keeps faith forever" (146:5–6). Even as Stephen was "bowed down," falling on his knees under the pelting of the stones, he knew this Lord would lift him up (146:8).

The **Epistle** is the fourth of six weeks in Peter's first epistle: 1 Peter 2:2–10. Peter cites one of Holy Scripture's most solid descriptions of the One who never changes.

We "have tasted that the Lord is good" (2:3) in Jesus' resurrection. (Recall the Introit for Easter 2.) Jesus alive is the certainty, the security, that not even death can negate God's care for us. And see the symbol Peter uses for that certainty, that security (quoting Is 28:16 and Ps 118:22): "a stone, a cornerstone chosen and precious" (2:6). The cornerstone was the large, solid stone carefully placed to establish the square of a building. It was foundational literally, but even more, figuratively.

By dying ("rejected") and rising to defeat Satan and destroy sin, Jesus has "become the cornerstone" (2:7). With Christ the cornerstone of the Church, then, we are being built into "a spiritual house" (2:5). Even the mighty Jerusalem temple (or America's World Trade Center or Notre Dame Cathedral in Paris) is vulnerable to catastrophe and collapse. But this house, the Church, will never perish—and we are that Church. We "will not be put to shame" (2:6). That's certain!

Those who reject Christ will "stumble," will not endure (2:8). "But," because Christ is your cornerstone, "you are . . . a people for [God's] own possession" (2:9). There, in God's hands, true joys are found.

No changes known to man compare with God becoming incarnate, entering His creation, dying to redeem the world, rising from the grave, and then ceasing His visible presence. The disciples are in the midst of that in the **Holy Gospel**, John 14:1–14.

Their hearts are troubled; they sense the separation coming. They'd like to hold on to what they have. But Jesus offers better: "I go to prepare a place for you" (14:2)—where true joys are found.

To take them there, He must go first: "I am the way, and the truth, and the life. No one comes to the Father except through Me" (14:6). That meant Jesus Himself could not hold on even to His own life. He is the way to heaven by going to the cross the next day. To say He is the truth means that knowing Him is the necessary insight into *what is really what*: that the Father loves us, that He operates the universe for our good, that living according to His Commandments is also the true good. So, then, believing in Jesus is life that is true and eternal. Everything else we can give up, as long as we have Christ.

Everything that's of this world really will change, finally disappoint. Therefore,

**SINCE WE CAN REALLY HOLD ON TO NOTHING IN THIS WORLD—
EVEN LIFE—
GOD GRANT THAT OUR HEARTS BE FIXED ON JESUS, THE CORNERSTONE, THE WAY TO TRUE JOY AND TRUE LIFE.**

Anticipate the joy and life to be found at the Lord's Table this Sunday as you close with the **Hymn of the Day**, *LSB* 633.

Sixth Sunday of Easter Year A

READINGS

Acts 17:16–31

Psalm 66:8–20 (antiphon: v 8)

1 Peter 3:13–22

John 14:15–21

HYMN OF THE DAY

LSB 556 "Dear Christians, One and All, Rejoice"

For three years, Jesus had been there with them—teaching them, amazing them, even setting their daily agenda. It had been heady stuff! Most days huge multitudes had been gathering around, the disciples' egos swelling as they managed crowd control. Jesus' posse. They'd seen miracles up close. They'd also felt Jesus' love, very personally.

Now those days were numbered, though the disciples didn't know how small the number was. Jesus knew that the very next day He would be separated from them by death. He'd come back to life, but then forty days later He'd leave again, at least visibly. Would this tiny entourage, who'd so come to depend on Jesus even to know when to eat and sleep, be left almost like orphans?

Jesus is preparing His disciples for all this, and by giving us Jesus' words, our lectionary is doing the same for us. These last Sundays of the Easter season, our propers are equipping us for this age in which Jesus is not visibly among His people, the age in which we'll live until He returns. Our Gospel lessons are from Jesus' farewell discourse, John 14–17, spoken that night before He died on the cross. And in our Gospel lesson today, Jesus assures us that He does not leave us helpless.

How did Jesus prepare the disciples—how does He prepare us?—to live these days of His visible absence? Our propers for the Sixth Sunday of Easter, including that Gospel reading, assure us that God's Word teaches and guides and equips us for living with the very same power as Jesus in His visible presence. Through the Word, the Holy Spirit will be as present and active for us as if Jesus were still walking with us.

Centuries *before* anyone knew the Son of God in the flesh, His Word was already guiding and giving life. Pray this week's **Introit**:

> *Your word is a lamp to my feet and a light to my path.*
>
> *Forever, O Lord, Your word is firmly fixed in the heavens. Your faithfulness endures to all generations; You have established the earth, and it stands fast. By Your appointment they stand this day, for all things are Your servants. If Your law had not been my delight, I would have perished in my affliction. I will never forget Your precepts, for by them You have given me life.*
>
> *Glory be to the Father and to the Son and to the Holy Spirit; as it was in the beginning, is now, and will be forever. Amen.*
>
> *Your word is a lamp to my feet and a light to my path. (Ps 119:89–93; antiphon: Ps 119:105)*

The psalmist and his Old Testament readers only knew Christ through His Word, but what an intimate relationship the Word has created! Throughout Psalm 119, the author speaks to Yahweh as if he were an adoring fan gushing thanks for an autograph—or an adult son who's finally telling Dad all he's meant to him.

The Lord, through His Word, has given the psalmist direction in life: "a lamp to my feet and a light to my path." And it is the path that has "given me life." The Holy Scriptures, even hundreds of years before Jesus, revealed to believers the coming birth, death, and resurrection of the Messiah for their eternal salvation. The psalmist knows these full well; he piles on his praises because the One he so adores is his Redeemer.

Then, knowing the Lord as he does, and knowing he has life in the Lord, the psalmist delights to live according to God's "law," remembering His "precepts." When this dear Lord, Yahweh, gives a command, the psalmist trusts that following that command, holy living, will be a delightful path.

Notice how the **Collect** for this Sunday also speaks of God's Word:

> *O God, the giver of all that is good, by Your holy inspiration grant that we may think those things that are right and by Your merciful guiding accomplish them; through Jesus Christ, Your Son, our Lord, who lives and reigns with You and the Holy Spirit, one God, now and forever. Amen.*

God's "holy inspiration" here describes His moving us to think and act rightly. But, of course, "inspiration" is also the process by which the Holy Spirit moved the prophets and apostles to write the Bible (2 Tim 3:16). And the connection is inseparable: it is the Bible, the inspired Word, which informs us of what's right, and it's only the Gospel of Christ, given to us in Holy Scripture, that enables us to accomplish those things God would have us do. That's because the Gospel assures us Jesus has given us eternal life and every good already now; we need not, cannot, make our own lot any better than Christ has already, so instead we're free to serve God and neighbor. Thus, by the power of God's Word, Christians do accomplish true good works, do (imperfectly!) live holy lives.

Paul's very famous speech on Mars Hill is this week's **First Reading**: Acts 17:16–31.

This is Paul's second missionary journey. Athens is the intellectual capital of the Greek culture, though by now these philosophers may be living off the reputations of Socrates, Plato, and Aristotle four centuries earlier. (The current crop seems to produce very little that's actually useful, 17:21.) What's new this week is Paul's claim that a Jew named Jesus has risen from the dead (17:18). This strikes the philosophers as strange, because the dualism of Greek thinking wouldn't even desire a resurrection; the body was seen as an evil prison from which the immaterial spirit longed to escape. They invite Paul to explain.

The *Areopagus* (Ἄρειος πάγος) literally means the "Hill of Ares," the Greek god of war. (The Roman name for the same god was Mars, hence, Mars Hill.) No question, Paul's approach is clever. In Jewish synagogues, he would make the case that Jesus was the fulfillment of the Old Testament. But here, where the Hebrew texts would be unfamiliar, he appeals to the Athenians' own religion, their attempt to please so many gods, even one they might have overlooked.

Paul's point of contact is life itself. The God he proclaims "gives to all mankind life and breath and everything. And He made from one man every nation of mankind to live on all the face of the earth" (17:25–26). "In Him we live and move and have our being" (17:28). Everyone agrees life exists. And everyone must admit it came from somewhere, likely even Someone. However, natural man is entirely ignorant as to how *real* life, life in a relationship with the Creator God, comes about. The Athenians, like all people before and since, left to themselves, will guess we must win our way into God's favor by satisfying His desires or demands. Only when God reveals He is already pleased with us because of Christ's cross do we ever come to believe such an amazing reality. And God reveals that truth *in His Word*.

Sadly, most of the Areopagites were intrigued by Paul only until he spoke the most important words of his oration: "[God] has given assurance to all by raising [a man whom He has appointed] from the dead" (17:31). The resurrection of Jesus is the proof that God's Word of Christ is entirely reliable. (Rising again was surely the most difficult promise Jesus made; everything else is easy by comparison.) But to most of the Athenians, it was foolishness (see 17:32). Man can be so intelligent, but apart from God's Word, especially the word of Jesus' death and resurrection, he is clueless.

The **Psalm** identifies a particular situation in which we would be clueless if not for God's Word: testing. Read Psalm 66:8–20. David says God has just "laid a crushing burden on our backs" (66:11). Defeat by an enemy maybe? A plague of locusts? An illness, a lost job, a stock crash? If we're flying blind, we might well see any of these as evidence that God is absent, doesn't care, is too weak to help. But God's Word tells us that

Christ's death has reconciled us to God so that He's always caring for us in the perfect way. The Word may be the *only* evidence that says that! But the Word is always faithful, always true. Christ's resurrection attests to that. So David trusts, "You, O God, have *tested* us; You have tried us as silver is tried" (66:10). This, too, is for our good. Therefore, "I will come into Your house with burnt offerings; I will perform my vows to You, that which my lips uttered and my mouth promised when I was in trouble" (66:13–14). On the evidence of the Word alone.

Some testing Christians go through will be persecution by those who resent our different way of living. With the Word helping us understand testing, though, suffering can actually become opportunity for sharing the Word. Read the **Epistle**, 1 Peter 3:13–22.

If you suffer for good behavior (3:16), "have no fear . . . always being prepared to make a defense to anyone who asks you for a reason for the hope that is in you" (3:14–15). The natural reaction to suffering is to blame someone, to curse our fate, or to do whatever we can to escape it. You're asked, "Why don't you hate those who hurt you?" Or "Why not just give it up, go along, and get yourself off the hook?" And you, understanding suffering in the light of God's Word, answer, "Because 'Christ also suffered' and has set me on the path to life (3:18). You too."

It's true. You are on the path to life. And if ever you yourself should doubt, God has given you assurance: "Baptism . . . now saves you . . . through the resurrection of Jesus Christ." That's the very simple truth.

Finally, our **Gospel**, John 14:15–21.

Jesus will not leave us as orphans (14:18). Very soon, the disciples would see Jesus no more, but He would come back. And in the meantime, He would send the Holy Spirit. "Helper" (14:16) is one of several useful translations of *parakletos* (παράκλητος), literally "one called alongside." Jesus sends the Holy Spirit to stand with us in every life situation. In fact, His roles in caring for us are too many for any one English word. So other translations include "Advocate," "Counselor," "Comforter," "Intercessor," or just "Paraclete."

Most explicitly, Jesus calls the Holy Spirit "the Spirit of truth" (14:17). That reminds us that the Spirit's task above all is to reveal Jesus, who is the truth (and the way and the life; recall 14:6 last week). Likewise, it teaches us that the Spirit comes not directly out of thin air but rather by the Word and Sacraments—which means we need not wonder when or if He'll come to us. He does come whenever the Word is proclaimed.

That Word is chiefly the word of the crucified and risen Christ: "Because I live, you also will live," Jesus promises (14:19). Through that word, the Holy Spirit gives us life—and enables living life in keeping with Jesus' commandments (14:15, 21).

**God's Word
of Jesus and the Resurrection
Is the Truth
That Sets Us on the Path
of Life and Living.**

Close with Luther's powerful (and autobiographical) "Dear Christians, One and All, Rejoice" (*LSB* 556), the **Hymn of the Day**. See how stanzas 9 and 10 anticipate Ascension Day, next Thursday.

The Ascension of Our Lord Years A, B, C

READINGS

Acts 1:1–11
Psalm 47 (antiphon: v 5)
Ephesians 1:15–23
Luke 24:44–53

HYMN OF THE DAY

LSB 491 "Up through Endless Ranks of Angels"

It's an iconic scene: the eleven disciples, gazing into heaven; Jesus having just disappeared from sight, ascended and now hidden by a cloud. The text says nothing of their emotions, but in our mind's eye, it's written all over their faces. "Men of Galilee, why do you stand looking into heaven?" They're in wonder—and wondering. What now? Will we ever see Him again? We miss Him already.

That's the Ascension of Our Lord, and we understand that look on the disciples' faces, those questions in their hearts. We've said goodbye to loved ones—our parents as they dropped us off for freshman year; our kids as they drove away, "Just Married" written on the back window; our grandparents, or maybe someone much closer, as we left the graveside. And we sometimes wish we could see Jesus too, don't we? Especially when we're already sad about something else, maybe one of those goodbyes.

But the angels' question is actually rhetorical—"Men of Galilee, why do you stand looking into heaven?"—because they have the solution to the disciples' grief already in mind: "This Jesus, who was taken up from you into heaven, will come in the same way as you saw Him go into heaven" (Acts 1:11). Our Hymn of the Day for Ascension says that Jesus leaves the disciples "in *happy* tears." Properly understood, the ascension of Jesus is a joyous occasion. That's the point our propers for Ascension Day will make.

Ascension Day, like the Day of Pentecost ten days later, is rare among the major festivals because the occasion is most fully narrated not in the Gospel lesson but in the reading from Acts, the **First Reading**: Acts 1:1–11.

The book of Acts is universally seen as Luke's sequel to the Gospel that bears his name. So Luke writes (also to Theophilus, "lover of God"; compare Lk 1:1–4), "In the first book, . . . I have dealt with all that Jesus *began* to do and teach" (Acts 1:1). Jesus will henceforth accomplish much, much more through the apostles and the Church, by the power of the Holy Spirit through the Word and Sacraments.

The sequel, then, really begins when Jesus is taken up to heaven. For forty days, numerous times, He's shown the apostles and others that He's truly risen (1:3). (This, of course, is why Ascension Day is always celebrated on a Thursday, forty days after Easter by Jewish counting.) Then, on that fortieth day, Jesus leads the disciples out to near the town of Bethany, on the Mount of Olives, just east of Jerusalem (see 1:12; Lk 24:50). (This is a different event, by the way, from the day Jesus gave the so-called Great Commission, Mt 28:16–20, one of those other appearances; that one was on a mountain to the north in Galilee.) From the Mount of Olives, near Jerusalem, Jesus is visibly, physically, lifted up to heaven until the disciples can see Him no longer. "Behold" (ἰδοὺ) is a word always to get our attention, and this is a surprise: "Two men stood by [the disciples] in white robes" (1:10). The angels bring the disciples' thoughts back to earth and yet set their sights toward heaven. Jesus will return!

That's good news. But actually, already before ascending, Jesus had told the disciples they had much to anticipate. They were to wait in Jerusalem "for the promise of the Father . . . ; you will be baptized with the Holy Spirit not many days from now" (1:4, 5). We know that would be Pentecost. "You will receive power when the Holy Spirit has come upon you, and you will be My witnesses in Jerusalem and in all Judea and Samaria, and to the end of the earth" (1:8). Jesus' ascension really would be just the beginning of an even greater future, and the disciples would be in the middle of it.

As a result, all the rest of the propers for Ascension Day reflect anticipation and joy, even celebration. In particular, the **Introit**:

> *God has gone up with a shout, the LORD with the sound of a trumpet.*
>
> *The LORD says to my Lord: "Sit at My right hand, until I make Your enemies Your footstool." The LORD has sworn and will not change His mind, "You are a priest forever after the order of Melchizedek." The LORD is at Your right hand; He will shatter kings on the day of His wrath.*
>
> *Glory be to the Father and to the Son and to the Holy Spirit; as it was in the beginning, is now, and will be forever. Amen.*
>
> *God has gone up with a shout, the LORD with the sound of a trumpet. (Ps 110:1, 4–5; antiphon: Ps 47:5)*

The disciples surely weren't shouting and blowing trumpets as Jesus ascended, but the hosts of heaven probably were! They could see already what we on earth have to take on faith. Jesus' ascension back to heaven was His coronation, the visible proclamation that

He had triumphed over all His enemies, that Satan and his allies, using sin and death as their chief weapons, had been no match for David's Lord. Jesus' mission has been a total success. Jesus ascends to sit at the right hand of the Father, which is not a place but an exercise of power, as Paul will explain in our Epistle. And we anticipate the day when He will make that triumph visible to all—shattering kings, propping His feet up on all those who still oppose and harm us. Then we'll be shouting too!

The **Collect**, though more subdued, also reflects joyful anticipation:

Almighty God, as Your only-begotten Son, our Lord Jesus Christ, ascended into the heavens, so may we also ascend in heart and mind and continually dwell there with Him, who lives and reigns with You and the Holy Spirit, one God, now and forever. Amen.

Ascension Day certainly anticipates our own ascension; Jesus' human nature enters heaven as our forerunner. But the Collect is actually praying that we would also "ascend in *heart and mind*." That's in the meantime, already now, before the Last Day when our bodies will be raised to join Jesus in heaven. This happens by the Word and Sacrament. Christ is truly present in the preaching of His Word and His Holy Supper, and these means create and strengthen faith, whereby we know the joys of God's presence already here.

The **Psalm** of the day for Ascension, Psalm 47, includes verse 5, which we've heard previously as the antiphon to the Introit. Again we shout for joy!

"Clap your hands, all peoples! Shout to God with loud songs of joy!" (47:1). And with very good reason! The victory that David saw in Psalm 110 (the Introit)—the Lord making Christ's enemies *His* "footstool"—the psalmist now sees as *our* victory: "He subdued peoples under *us*, and nations under *our* feet" (47:3). Jesus' ascension into the clouds shows that He is "a great king over all the earth" (47:2). He "reigns over the nations"; He "sits on His holy throne" (47:8).

That last reference needs to be understood properly, because a king sitting on his mighty throne way up above the clouds might either be aloof from our needs down here or else terrifying if we are the ones he's dominating. In the **Epistle**, Ephesians 1:15–23, Paul does explain this. It's really the definitive commentary on the significance of the ascension and, specifically, Jesus sitting at the right hand of God.

The disciples would no longer see Jesus; the Ephesian Church and we today have never seen Jesus with our eyes. But Paul is confident when he prays to God that "the eyes of [our] *hearts*" would be "enlightened, that you may know what is the hope to which He has called you, what are the riches of His glorious inheritance in the saints" (1:18). Hope is trusting what is not seen, but it does not disappoint when it is based on God's promises (Rom 5:5; 8:24; Heb 11:1). God's promise here is that a rich, glorious inheritance awaits.

It is also the promise that Christ is working for us right now. The night before His death, Jesus told His disciples that it was to their advantage that He go away (Jn 16:7). We see that in Paul's words, for now God has "raised [Jesus] from the dead and seated Him at His right hand in the heavenly places" (1:20). We confess in the creeds that Jesus "sits at the right hand of God the Father Almighty." We misunderstand, though, if we think that places Jesus far away, as many Christians assume. In fact, it means that Jesus now exercises all "the immeasurable greatness of [God's] power . . . far above all rule and authority and power and dominion" (1:19, 21). During Jesus' time on earth, in His state of humiliation, the disciples caught only glimpses of Jesus' power. But now, risen and ascended, in His state of exaltation, Christ uses all His divine powers to the full. It's like saying Jesus is God's right hand or His "right-hand man," the one who wields all God's power. Most important, His power is "toward us who believe" (1:19). God has given Jesus "as head over all things *to the church*" (1:22). That is, He uses all that power for our benefit; He controls all things here on earth for the good of believers, His Church. In His ascension, Jesus is anything but distant or aloof. He "fills all in all" right here where we need Him (1:23).

Luke's other account of the ascension, in our **Holy Gospel**, Luke 24:44–53, is much less detailed than in our First Reading, anticipating the fuller treatment in Acts. But it does tell more about Jesus preparing the apostles for what would follow.

It's really not until this point that Jesus lets the apostles themselves experience the "eyes of their hearts" seeing, as Paul prays for us: "Then He opened their minds to understand the Scriptures" (24:45). The Old Testament ("the Law of Moses and the Prophets and the Psalms") had always testified that the Messiah would die and then rise from the dead (24:44, 46). It had also always taught that when the time was right the Church would witness to the end of the earth, "all nations" (24:47). In just ten more days, Pentecost, the time would be right for the apostles to be those witnesses (24:48–49). And what would they say? That all must repent and that in Jesus, crucified and risen, all sins are forgiven (24:46–47). This has been the word of the Church ever since—and will be until Christ returns.

This account of Jesus' ascension gives no hint of the disciples' melancholy. Luke writes, "They worshiped Him and returned to Jerusalem with great joy, and were continually in the temple blessing God" (24:52–53).

And why not? The ascension prefigures our ascensions at our resurrections. It sets Jesus at God's right hand, where He prays to the Father for us and rules all things on earth for our good. And it means He not only hasn't left but is always with us. The **Verse**: "Alleluia. We know that Christ being raised from the dead will never die again; death no longer has dominion over Him. Alleluia. Behold, I am with you always, to the end of the age. Alleluia" (Rom 6:9; Mt 28:20b).

Jesus' Ascension Is No Cause for Sadness, but Rather to Shout for Joy!

The **Hymn of the Day**, "Up through Endless Ranks of Angels" (*LSB* 491), is a new Ascension hymn set to a new, mighty tune.

Seventh Sunday of Easter Year A

READINGS

Acts 1:12–26

Psalm 68:1–10 (antiphon: v 32)

1 Peter 4:12–19; 5:6–11

John 17:1–11

HYMN OF THE DAY

LSB 539 "Christ Is the World's Redeemer"

After the celebration of the Ascension of Our Lord on Thursday, the Seventh (and final) Sunday of Easter three days later is, in a sense, a step backward. We said goodbye to Jesus, but in our Gospel lesson for Easter 7 He's still with us. We worked through the initial disappointment of seeing Jesus leave, but now Jesus' parting words, His last lengthy speaking before His crucifixion, revert to the gravity of separation and seem to weigh heavy with sadness: "I am no longer in the world, but they are in the world, and I am coming to You[,] Holy Father" (Jn 17:11).

The fact is, though, the Seventh Sunday of Easter very much takes the ascension into account. The Collect acknowledges that Jesus has ascended, and the First Reading does fit into the natural sequence; it happens in the days after Ascension and before Pentecost, which we'll observe a week from Sunday. And the weight of Jesus' words in this week's Gospel does still fit the mood of the Church as it adjusts to His visible absence.

Here, too, is a very practical consideration for Ascension and Easter 7. If a congregation does not have a service on Thursday, Ascension Day itself, it may wish to remember Jesus' ascension the Sunday following, that is, Easter 7. In that case, the pastor might substitute all the Ascension propers for the Easter 7 ones. But a wholesome compromise could be to use some of the Ascension propers, especially the First Reading, the actual ascension narrative, Acts 1:1–11, combined with others of the Easter 7 appointments, probably including the Easter 7 Gospel from John 17. A close comparison among all the propers reveals how very compatible, in some cases almost interchangeable, they are between the two days. (This blending is made easier in that the First Reading for Easter 7, Acts 1:12–26, is used in all three years of the lectionary. So it could be read one year and the Ascension lesson, Acts 1:1–11, the next.) There really is a close interaction between these two days.

Our THEME for this devotion-study will reflect that. For Ascension Day, we found that Jesus' ascension is truly no cause for sadness but rather cause to shout for joy. Now, for the Seventh Sunday of Easter, we'll see that those parting words of Jesus, heavy though they be, also ought not cause us sadness. Instead, the propers suggest what they should elicit from us.

The **Collect** for Easter 7 essentially picks up where Ascension Day left off and then looks forward to the following Sunday:

> *O King of glory, Lord of hosts, uplifted in triumph far above all heavens, leave us not without consolation but send us the Spirit of truth whom You promised from the Father; for You live and reign with Him and the Holy Spirit, one God, now and forever. Amen.*

Most weeks the Collect is addressed to God the Father, but on this occasion, we address the Son—and as "King of glory, Lord of hosts." That's because we're still marveling at His ascension, being "uplifted in triumph far above all heavens," which confirms His glory. But with Christ no longer visible, prayer takes on new importance. We ask Him not to leave us "without consolation," because the pain of separation is very real. We even ask Him to answer this prayer in a specific way, because we know what He Himself promised: "Send us the Spirit of truth whom You promised from the Father." So we confidently expect Jesus to turn our sadness to rejoicing as we move from His parting to Pentecost.

David is ready to lead our singing for joy in the antiphon to this Sunday's **Introit**:

> *I will sing of steadfast love and justice; to You, O LORD, I will make music.*
>
> *Make a joyful noise to the LORD, all the earth! Serve the LORD with gladness! Come into His presence with singing! Know that the LORD, He is God! It is He who made us, and we are His; we are His people, and the sheep of His pasture. Enter His gates with thanksgiving, and His courts with praise! Give thanks to Him; bless His name! For the LORD is good; His steadfast love endures forever, and His faithfulness to all generations.*
>
> *Glory be to the Father and to the Son and to the Holy Spirit; as it was in the beginning, is now, and will be forever. Amen.*
>
> *I will sing of steadfast love and justice; to You, O LORD, I will make music. (Ps 100:1–5; antiphon: Ps 101:1)*

An Introit built on Psalm 100 noises aloud that this is an occasion for rejoicing: "Make a joyful noise to the LORD, all the earth! Serve the LORD with gladness! Come into His presence with singing!" The psalmist knows that the Lord is infinitely above us, as high above us as the heavens are above the earth. After all, "the LORD, He is God." (I also like the way the King James Version humbles us: "It is He that hath made us, and not we ourselves.") But the psalmist can sing, make that joyful noise, because we're still invited into God's "presence," to "enter His gates." Jesus is parted from us, but we're not apart.

Like the two psalms in our Introit, the **Psalm** of the day is an exuberant song of praise: Psalm 68:1–10, with its antiphon, 68:32. "The righteous shall be glad; they shall exult before God; they shall be jubilant with joy! Sing to God, sing praises to His name; . . . exult before Him!" (68:3–4). Part of the reason for such rejoicing is God's victory seen in military images (68:1–2). But He's also concerned for "the fatherless" and "widows," for whom He is "father" and "protector," and for "the solitary" and "prisoners" and "the needy" (68:5–6, 10). He hasn't forgotten the lowest and the lowliest down here.

The **First Reading**, Acts 1:12–26, is a course-setting example of what Jesus' parting from the disciples caused in them.

The apostles aren't long paralyzed by Jesus' visible departure. They wait in Jerusalem as He told them to do (Acts 1:4), but they're not inactive. They're "devoting themselves to prayer" (1:14), readying for whatever is to come next. And in the meantime, there's important business: a replacement for Judas Iscariot (not to be confused with Judas the son of James, 1:13). Jesus' apostles know they are to "witness to His resurrection" (1:22), and that will require a full twelve. Peter begins to assume the leadership role Jesus intended for him, and his source is Holy Scripture; Psalm 109:8 says that another should fill Judas's office. The essential criterion is that the man must have accompanied Jesus and the Twelve throughout His ministry, most critically to be one who saw Jesus alive after His resurrection (1:21–22; see also 1 Cor 15:3–7). Two nominees are put forward. The company prays for Jesus to make the selection, and lots are cast. Matthias becomes the new twelfth apostle (1:23–26).

This is the last time the Bible reports the Church casting lots (although Christians could reverently choose to make some decisions this way). The congregation's use of prayer, though, should always be an example for us. With Jesus no longer standing before us to direct each action, we now pore over His Word and simultaneously pray that He would guide our understanding and reshape our thinking according to it. Prayer is the act of trust that God is directing all things—and all people, especially ourselves.

Did Matthias think he'd won the lottery? Did Peter and the rest know what they were getting into? Jesus had told them they would have to carry crosses (Mt 10:38; 16:24). The very day after our Gospel account, they would see how literally that could be true. And, as we've seen these last six weeks, suffering is a recurrent theme through 1 Peter, including in this **Epistle**: 1 Peter 4:12–19; 5:6–11.

Even if they—and we—know "the fiery trial" is coming ("do not be surprised," 4:12), this is a tall order: "If anyone suffers as a Christian, let him not be ashamed, but let him glorify God in that name" (4:16). Glorify God in suffering. Hmm. More naturally we'd "curse God and die" (Job 2:9)—curse Him for not being around when we need Him. That's our sinful nature's go-to assumption: that because we can't see Jesus' hand smoothing the way for us, He must be far away. But Peter says, on the contrary, that when we suffer as Christians, it's evidence of how close Christ is: "you share Christ's sufferings" (4:13). "If you are insulted for the name of Christ, you are blessed, because the Spirit of glory and of God rests upon you" (4:14).

Therefore, we can rejoice now, for we will "rejoice and be glad when His glory is revealed" (4:13). "At the proper time" He will "exalt you. . . . And after you have suffered a little while, the God of all grace, who has called you to His eternal glory in Christ, will Himself restore, confirm, strengthen, and establish you" (5:6, 10). In the meantime, we pray. "Entrust [your] souls to a faithful Creator, . . . casting all your anxieties on Him, because He cares for you" (4:19; 5:7).

Now that **Holy Gospel**, John 17:1–11.

It's significant that Jesus' last recorded discourse is a prayer. It's known as His High Priestly Prayer, because, as *the* Priest, He's interceding for His disciples (17:9)—and for us who would eventually come to believe in Him through their word (see 17:20). "Holy Father, keep them in Your name" (17:11).

In this first portion of the prayer (the rest will be the Gospel lessons for Easter 7 in Years B and C), Jesus' request is this: "Father, the hour has come; glorify Your Son that the Son may glorify You. . . . I glorified You on earth, having accomplished the work that You gave Me to do. And now, Father, glorify Me in Your own presence with the glory that I had with You before the world existed" (17:1, 4–5). How is that a prayer *for us*? Because Jesus will glorify the Father and the Father will glorify Him by His death on the cross. That's the hour that has come. And that gives us eternal life (17:2). Jesus is "no longer in the world" (17:11), but He's never stopped providing for our eternal joy. So,

Jesus' Parting Words Are No Cause for Sadness, but Rather for Rejoicing, Glorifying God, and Prayer.

We conclude the seven weeks of Easter with a final hearing of the **Gradual** for the season, with the **Verse** for Easter 7, and with the **Hymn of the Day**. God has glorified His Son in the resurrection:

> *Christ has risen from the dead. [God the Father] has crowned Him with glory and honor, He has given Him dominion over the works of His hands; He has put all things under His feet. (adapted from Mt 28:7; Heb 2:7; Ps 8:6)*

Christ does turn our sadness into rejoicing: "Alleluia. We know that Christ being raised from the dead will never die again; death no longer has dominion over Him. Alleluia. I will not leave you as orphans; I will come to you. Alleluia" (Rom 6:9; Jn 14:18). And the Hymn, *LSB* 539, puts an exclamation point "Amen!" on Jesus' mighty saving works from cross to empty tomb to heaven!

The Day of Pentecost Year A

READINGS

Numbers 11:24–30
Psalm 25:1–15 (antiphon: v 4)
Acts 2:1–21
John 7:37–39

HYMN OF THE DAY

LSB 497 "Come, Holy Ghost, God and Lord"

"When the day of Pentecost arrived . . ." (Acts 2:1)

When the day of Pentecost arrived, God worked one of the most dramatic miracles of all time—and three thousand less dramatic, but no less miraculous, other miracles. When the day of Pentecost arrived, Christ fulfilled His promise to clothe His faithful followers with power from on high—and the Church was born. And when the Day of Pentecost arrives, Christians celebrate one of our three greatest festivals of the year: the outpouring of the Holy Spirit.

Christmas and Easter—Christ becoming flesh to die for us, Jesus rising from the grave victorious—still need Pentecost. Even with Jesus having finished His saving work, no one would be saved unless she or he heard that news and believed it. And that could never happen without the Holy Spirit. It's the Holy Spirit who moves the proclaimer to speak; it's the Holy Spirit who comes in the word that's spoken; it's the Holy Spirit who works each miracle to awaken spiritually dead hearts to embrace the Gospel. So Christ giving His Church the Holy Spirit climaxes His ministry and begins the *rest of* history—just as Pentecost concludes the festival portion of the church year and begins the rest.

All that when the day of Pentecost arrived.

What about before the day of Pentecost arrived? In the Gospel lesson for this day, John comments that when Jesus spoke of the Holy Spirit to Jerusalem, "as yet the Spirit had not been given" (Jn 7:39). Was the Third Person of the Trinity waiting in the wings for all eternity—or at least for all human experience—until His grand entrance? What did that mean for people in the Old Testament—that "as yet the Spirit had not been given"? And what made the day of Pentecost the right time for Him? As we look forward to the Day of Pentecost in its propers—and its magnificent gifts!—let's keep those questions in mind.

As with Ascension Day, the primary telling of the Pentecost account is not in the Gospel lesson but in a reading from Acts. Actually, it's this week's **Second Reading**, Acts 2:1–21.

The day of Pentecost arrived, as the name implies, fifty days after the Israelite Feast of Firstfruits. (Pentecost was also known as the Feast of Weeks, seven weeks after Firstfruits: 7 weeks × 7 days per week = 49 days by our math, 50 by Jewish count.) This particular Pentecost also arrived fifty days after Jesus' resurrection (hence our date). Pentecost was one of three major festivals God had prescribed already for His Old Testament people (along with Passover in early spring and Feast of Booths, following the Day of Atonement, in the fall). At Firstfruits, Israelites were commanded to bring an offering from the first of each year's crops (Lev 23:10, 15–16). Only God knew the rich "firstfruits" He'd always been planning for this one Pentecost!

By the first century, the Jews were scattered widely around the Mediterranean and beyond, but the faithful still tried to visit Jerusalem at least once—perhaps staying several months to attend both Passover and Pentecost. This, of course, accounts for the many well-traveled visitors listed (2:5, 9–11).

On this day "all" were "together in one place" (2:1)—probably all the believers. Earlier (Acts 1:15), we learned that this company was now about one hundred and twenty souls—the Twelve plus others, both men and women. It appears that when the Holy Spirit came, all were gifted (2:4). It's important to notice, though, that when the public preaching began, only the apostles ("Peter, standing with the eleven," 2:14) are mentioned.

We all know the scene: a rushing wind, flames of fire over the believers' heads, and suddenly the ability to speak in languages they'd never known before. The fact is the great majority of those guests could already understand one another in Greek (which was almost universal for business dealings in the Roman Empire). But how much sweeter—and how much more attention-getting!—to hear of Christ in one's native language (2:8).

Peter's sermon continues well beyond this week's reading (more coming next Sunday; recall, too, hearing a portion on Easter 3). Here he only explains the day of Pentecost itself. He quotes the Old Testament prophet Joel (2:16). Beginning today, we are "in the last days," when the Holy Spirit shall be poured out "on all flesh"—men, women, young, old, servants or slaves as surely as anyone else. All will tell the Good News (2:17–18). *And* this day is preparation for *the* Last Day (singular), Judgment Day (2:19–20). What's happening today, Pentecost, Peter is saying, is preparation for that Last Day. For "it shall come to pass that everyone who calls upon the name of the Lord shall be saved" (2:21)—and how to do that is precisely what you're going to hear today!

Well, if the Spirit is given in these last days, beginning at Pentecost, what was He doing in former days? And how were people of the past to prepare for Judgment Day?

The Introit, the Psalm, and the Old Testament Reading all make clear that the Holy Spirit was very active in those days. First, the **Introit**:

> *Come, Holy Spirit, fill the hearts of the faithful, and kindle in them the fire of Your love. Alleluia.*
>
> *O Lord, how manifold are Your works! In wisdom have You made them all; the earth is full of Your creatures. These all look to You, to give them their food in due season. When You give it to them, they gather it up; when You open Your hand, they are filled with good things. When You send forth Your Spirit, they are created, and You renew the face of the ground.*
>
> *Glory be to the Father and to the Son and to the Holy Spirit; as it was in the beginning, is now, and will be forever. Amen.*
>
> *Come, Holy Spirit, fill the hearts of the faithful, and kindle in them the fire of Your love. Alleluia. (Ps 104:24, 27–28, 30; antiphon: Liturgical Text)*

The antiphon (which is also the Alleluia **Verse** for Pentecost) is a "Liturgical Text," meaning a composition of the Church rather than a quotation from Scripture. It's a prayer that the Holy Spirit would do for us the most important thing He did on Pentecost—not enable us to speak in foreign languages, but fill our hearts with faith in Christ and fervent love for one another.

The psalm, however, predates the Christian Pentecost. And yet the psalmist is well aware of the work of the Holy Spirit: "When You [Lord] send forth Your Spirit, they are created, and You renew the face of the ground." That is, the Spirit is involved in creation, in feeding God's creatures—really, in all God's "manifold" works. We're reminded of the Nicene Creed calling the Holy Spirit "the Lord and giver of life."

Likewise, still centuries before Pentecost, David, in the **Psalm** of the day, evidences the work of the Holy Spirit: Psalm 25:1–15. Jesus Himself affirms that the Old Testament authors like David were working under the inspiration of the Holy Spirit when they wrote (Mt 22:43–44). Then David both prays for and trusts in the Spirit's primary activity, to instruct people in God's saving truth: "Make me to know Your ways, O Lord; teach me Your paths. Lead me in Your truth and teach me, for You are the God of my salvation; . . . He instructs sinners in the way. He leads the humble in what is right, and teaches the humble His way. . . . Him will He instruct in the way that he should choose" (25:4–5, 8–9, 12). Leading God's people into all truth, Jesus says, is the work of the Spirit (Jn 14:26; 16:13).

The **Old Testament Reading** gives quite a remarkable example of the Spirit's work pre-Pentecost: Numbers 11:24–30.

At God's command (see 11:16–17), seventy leading men of Israel are chosen to share the burden of responsibility with Moses. In order to certify them before the people—and assure them that God was with them—the Holy Spirit enabled these seventy to prophesy. This was probably an ecstatic expression of worship that others could see, and it was not necessary for their leadership, because it did not continue (11:25). Joshua was properly concerned that men not use this gift to undermine Moses' authority (11:26–29a), but there is a different sense in which we wish "the LORD would put His Spirit on" all people (11:29b). That is, that the Holy Spirit would create faith in every heart. "No one can say 'Jesus is Lord' except in the Holy Spirit" (1 Cor 12:3). That was true of Old Testament believers as well. In every era, every believer in Christ has the Holy Spirit.

But as the Old Testament Reading showed, in an era past, there were limitations on the gift of the Spirit. That's what John sees in our **Holy Gospel**: John 7:37–39.

Now, it's the fall Feast of Booths (see 7:2). On the climactic day, water carried to the temple from the pool of Siloam was poured out in prayer, asking Yahweh to provide that essential commodity. And Jesus stands up and cries out that He is the answer to this prayer: "Whoever believes in Me, . . . 'Out of his heart will flow rivers of living water.'" He was promising "the Spirit, whom those who believed in Him were to receive, for as yet the Spirit had not been given" (7:38, 39a).

But John finishes His thought: "because Jesus was not yet glorified" (7:39b). The Spirit had been active from eternity—creating, sustaining, inspiring the Scriptures, bringing Old Testament saints to faith. But, as with the elders of Israel, He was not poured out fully—until Jesus was glorified. The hour for Jesus to be glorified came when He died, rose, ascended, and now sent the Spirit at Pentecost (Jn 12:16, 23; 13:31–32; 16:13–14; 17:1). Since then, these are the "last days" to which Joel and Peter referred. Faith in Jesus' death and resurrection is the preparation for *the* Last Day Joel and Peter offered. And that day of Pentecost, three thousand believed and were baptized (Acts 2:41), the firstfruits of the Church. But only the *first*fruits.

Now That Jesus Has Been Glorified, the Spirit Is Given without Limit,

with countless more fruits since and future!

Now the Spirit is for all. The **Gradual**:

> *I will pour out My Spirit on all flesh, and your sons and your daughters shall prophesy. With the heart one believes and is justified, and with the mouth one confesses and is saved. (Acts 2:17b; Rom 10:10)*

And the "right understanding" for which the **Collect** prays is chiefly to see that Jesus is glorified by the cross:

> *O God, on this day You once taught the hearts of Your faithful people by sending them the light of Your Holy Spirit. Grant us in our day by the same Spirit to have a right understanding in all things and evermore to rejoice in His holy consolation; through Jesus Christ, Your Son, our Lord, who lives and reigns with You and the Holy Spirit, one God, now and forever. Amen.*

Close with Luther's Pentecost hymn, the **Hymn of the Day**, *LSB* 497.

The Holy Trinity Year A

READINGS

Genesis 1:1–2:4a
Psalm 8 (antiphon: v 9)
Acts 2:14a, 22–36
Matthew 28:16–20

HYMN OF THE DAY

LSB 498, 499 "Come, Holy Ghost, Creator Blest"

Open your hymnal and count the number of references to the Holy Trinity you find in any of our Divine Services—between namings of the Father, Son, and Holy Spirit, triple *Alleluias* and triple *Holies* and triple *Amens*, and all such things. For example, I see at least sixteen in *LSB* Divine Service, Setting One. Plus the Gloria Patri for the Introit and the closing for the Collect of the Day and some of the Proper Prefaces. That is, it's quite a lot.

So you wonder, why a Trinity Sunday? Isn't every Sunday a Trinity Sunday? Popes in the eleventh and twelfth centuries agreed and discouraged having a single day for the Feast of the Holy Trinity. However, by the fourteenth century (quite late for major festivals), it was universally observed in the Western Church.

Surely every Sunday *is* a Trinity Sunday. From the Invocation "in the name of the Father and of the Son and of the Holy Spirit" that begins every service to the Trinitarian Benediction that concludes it, the Church makes clear that we worship only one God, but He is the One who is also three persons. Still, the Church has found it wholesome to set aside one Sunday each year to teach this doctrine of the Trinity. That makes this festival unique, because it's not based on an event in the life of Christ or His Church but rather on a specific teaching.

That also makes the design of the propers interesting, because not only is there no specific Bible account to define the day (as with Christmas or Easter or Pentecost), but there's no biblical passage at all that uses the words "Trinity" or "triune God" or "three in one" or even "persons" (in the sense we use that term for the three persons of the Trinity). Instead, the Bible teaches the doctrine of the Trinity *throughout*, and the propers draw upon various texts—adding also the unique language the Church has come to use to describe this mystery.

The doctrine of the Holy Trinity is nothing less than the *doctrine* of God. (The Lutherans even labeled it as such in Article I of the Augsburg Confession.) Who is the true God? And when teaching about God, one obvious element that recurs on every page of Scripture is that God is great, awesome, wondrous. Our **Gradual** (which will be used each Sunday until near the end of June):

> *Great is the Lord, and greatly to be praised, and His greatness is unsearchable. On Your wondrous works, I will meditate, and I will declare Your greatness. (Ps 145:3, 5b, 6b)*

Similarly, the **Verse**, quoting seraphim before God's throne (Is 6:3b): "Alleluia. Holy, holy, holy is the Lord of hosts; the whole earth is full of His glory! Alleluia." (Did you count this as one of your references to the Trinity when you saw it in the Sanctus?)

Isaiah, witnessing that scene, was blown away! "Our God is an awesome God," we may be pleased enough to say (or sing?), but when God is so great, so much greater than we ourselves, what kind of relationship can we have with Him? Our propers for Trinity Sunday, Year A, will explore this.

It's not only God's greatness that could be off-putting, either. It's also His complexity. Who can really understand Him? No one! So the Church has done its best to develop vocabulary for describing the triune God, as in the antiphon to the **Introit**:

> *Blessèd be the Holy Trinity and the undivided Unity. Let us give glory to Him because He has shown His mercy to us.*
>
> *I have set the Lord always before me; because He is at my right hand, I shall not be shaken. Therefore my heart is glad, and my whole being rejoices; my flesh also dwells secure. For You will not abandon my soul to Sheol, or let Your holy one see corruption. You make known to me the path of life; in Your presence there is fullness of joy; at Your right hand are pleasures forevermore.*
>
> *Glory be to the Father and to the Son and to the Holy Spirit; as it was in the beginning, is now, and will be forever. Amen.*
>
> *Blessèd be the Holy Trinity and the undivided Unity. Let us give glory to Him because He has shown His mercy to us. (Ps 16:8–11; antiphon: Liturgical Text)*

"The Holy Trinity and the undivided Unity." Like last week for Pentecost, this is a "Liturgical Text," not a citation from Scripture but written by Christians to summarize biblical teaching. One of the tasks for every preacher this Sunday is to devote a few moments in the sermon to explaining this Trinity in Unity. Most congregations will also spend the time once a year on Trinity Sunday to confess the Athanasian Creed (*LSB*, p 319)—the very detailed parsing of the doctrine of the Trinity. Nothing we can say will unravel all the secrets of God's inner relationship, but Scripture attests that He is only one ("undivided Unity," for example, Deut 6:4; 1 Cor 8:4), yet He is three ("Trinity," Is 48:16; Mt 3:16–17; and other passages in today's readings). This we confess to be true.

Understanding it, on the other hand, is way above our pay grade. And that would cause us to distrust Him, be suspicious of Him, wish to remain far from Him. Except the Introit calls us to "give glory to Him *because He has shown His mercy to us.*" Rather than wishing distance and distrusting such an incomprehensible being, we glorify Him. We do that because He reached out to us, showed us mercy—"[made] known to me the path of life," is "at my right hand" and lets me be at His. (Remember, that's Jesus' place, and in our Second Reading, Peter tells us this psalm is about Christ. How amazing that, being in Christ by our Baptism, we can say it too!) Maybe the sweetest way of all to say it: "In Your *presence* there is fullness of joy." Great and wondrous, incomprehensible, but the triune God invites us into His presence!

The **Collect**, too, is a prayer by God's people that recognizes the biblical teaching:

> *Almighty and everlasting God, You have given us grace to acknowledge the glory of the eternal Trinity by the confession of a true faith and to worship the Unity in the power of the Divine Majesty. Keep us steadfast in this faith and defend us from all adversities; for You, O Father, Son, and Holy Spirit, live and reign, one God, now and forever. Amen.*

This Collect is one of a kind for the church year in that it's addressed to the entire Holy Trinity: "Almighty and everlasting God, . . . You, O Father, Son, and Holy Spirit." We acknowledge God's glory, His "Divine Majesty," and we confess the Trinity in Unity. But as we saw in the Introit, we can do so only because He deigned to give us the insight ("You have given us grace to . . ."); we can't appreciate or reason this out ourselves.

The Trinity's gracious self-revelation is explicit in the New Testament, but He did show Himself from the very beginning in the **Old Testament Reading**, Genesis 1:1–2:4a.

The creation account could busy us for many Sundays on its own. For Trinity Sunday, though, consider not so much what's falling into place down here on these six days. Picture instead what's going on with God as He does the crafting. Perhaps even close your eyes on Sunday as you listen—and imagine.

The first hint that God is triune comes already in verse 2: "The *Spirit* of God was hovering over the face of the waters." Then follows that regal rhythm, "And God said . . ." (1:3, 6, 9, 11, 14, 20, 24), and "good" things happen. Doesn't that beg a question? *Who's listening?* If God were alone, He'd just create by thinking. But He speaks. Finally, in verse 26, we get the surprise answer: "Then God said, 'Let *Us* make man in *Our* image, after *Our* likeness.'" God has been the one listening—and speaking! From all eternity,

God has been carrying on delightful conversation, Father, Son, and Holy Spirit. God the Father has always been loving the Son, the Son receiving that love, the Holy Spirit going out from both. And when the Holy Trinity knew that it was just the right occasion, He created two new creatures to love, with billions more planned. He honors us with His own image!

The **Psalm** for Holy Trinity may be the most intriguing of all the propers: Psalm 8.

Here we have the most striking demonstration of Trinity Sunday's resolution: how majestic is the Lord's name in all the earth! Look at all He's made: the heavens, the moon and stars. What glory! By contrast, what am I? Why would God pay any mind to me? Yet, He has crowned us human beings, glorified us, made us rulers over everything He's created! Why, He's made us just a little lower than the angels!

What makes this most appealing is that Hebrews 2:6–8 says that Jesus is the "man" and the "son of man" made a little lower than the angels and then crowned with glory to rule. Of course, He is. And see what that means: it's Jesus who brings the majestic God into relationship with lowly man. His lowering Himself below the angels elevates us to heaven into fellowship with God. It's in Jesus humbling Himself, becoming human—and only in Jesus—that we know the Holy Trinity at all. But in Christ, we do know the eternal, unsearchable Trinity intimately. So we exclaim His glory!

The **Second Reading**, Acts 2:14a, 22–36, continues Peter's Pentecost sermon heard last Sunday; historically, Trinity Sunday was often seen as a continuation of Pentecost. See also what we wrote about Peter's sermon in the chapter for Easter 3-A (pp 124–25).

Two observations for this week. First, Peter expresses God's saving work as that of all three persons of the Trinity: Jesus died and was raised by the Father (2:32), and the Father promised the Holy Spirit, whom Jesus has now poured out (2:33). Second, if that's so and God is triune, then this very triune God has deigned to come to us. Jesus of Nazareth did "mighty works and wonders and signs . . . in your midst, as you yourselves know" (2:22). God "attested" to Him, that He is the very Lord David proclaimed (2:22, 34). So the triune God Himself made the sacrifice, death, to have us with Him.

Finally, in the **Holy Gospel**, Jesus confirms this "to the end of the age." Read Matthew 28:16–20. Fully appreciate now this Holy Trinity: the God who created the universe and rules all things so desires to love all people ("all nations") that He brings us into personal discipleship with Him in Holy Baptism. We have the name of the three equal persons of the one true God put upon us. We are His! And "behold," He says, "I am *with you* always, to the end of the age." So as the Introit antiphon invited,

**WE GLORIFY THE HOLY TRINITY
BECAUSE IN JESUS, THE SON,
HE DEIGNS TO GLORIFY US
WITH HIS PRESENCE.**

The **Hymn of the Day** reflects the history of this day as continuing Pentecost. Notice, though, that the final two stanzas have full references to the Trinity.

The Sundays after Pentecost: Proper 3 (May 24–28) Year A

READINGS

Isaiah 49:8–16a
Psalm 115:(1–8) 9–18 (antiphon: v 1)
Romans 1:8–17
Matthew 6:24–34

HYMN OF THE DAY

LSB 732 "All Depends on Our Possessing"

Trinity Sunday last week brought us into the second half of the church year, what we call "The Time of the Church." After "The Time of Christmas" and "The Time of Easter," which both focus on events in the life of our Lord, the remainder of the sacred calendar studies what Christ in the Holy Spirit continues to work in and through His people, to do what He kicked off with Peter's explosive Pentecost sermon. Thus this Time of the Church is also rightly named "The Season after Pentecost."

The Season after Pentecost is by far the longest of the church year. The length varies according to the moving date of Easter—an early Easter means a longer Pentecost season; a later Easter means a shorter one. Since Easter always has seven Sundays followed by the Day of Pentecost, Trinity Sunday may fall as early as May 17 or as late as June 20. Then follow the numbered Sundays after Pentecost—at least twenty-two, with a maximum of twenty-seven.

In our previous lectionary (in *Lutheran Worship*), the Second Sunday after Pentecost (the Sunday after Trinity) always used the same certain set of propers—whether that Second Sunday fell early, perhaps in May, or much later, well into June. Subsequent Sundays would use the propers for the Third, Fourth, and Fifth Sundays after Pentecost, and so on until the end of the church year—however many Sundays the calendar permitted. (With a late Easter, a number of Sundays toward the end would be omitted.)

Look at our current *Lutheran Service Book* lectionary, though. On *LSB* page xv, you'll see that each set of propers during this season is now tied to a seven-day period of calendar dates. They're no longer designated Pentecost 2 or 3 or 4 but rather as Proper 3, Proper 4, and so forth. Each set of propers will always be used during the week of the dates shown. Thus Proper 3 might in one year be the Second Sunday after Pentecost (that would happen with a very early Easter). But in another year (when Easter is later), it would simply be omitted. So for a shorter Pentecost season, the old system omitted Sundays near the end of the church year, but the current lectionary omits Sundays as needed on the front end.

Confused? I understand.

Here's the bottom line: for these Sundays after Pentecost, to know which devotion-study to read when you're looking forward to Sunday morning, check the date given in parentheses on the title column. If the coming Sunday falls within those dates, you're good to go. That part's simple, eh?

So if you're still with us, I'm assuming you had a very early Easter (sometime in late March), and this coming Sunday is somewhere between May 24 and 28. If that's not the case, you might want to skip ahead to Proper 4 or 5 or 6 or whichever shows the right date for this Sunday. Or just read on for additional enrichment; frankly, it could be quite a few years before Proper 3, Year A, actually comes up. Might as well get this while you're here.

The fact is, the propers for this Sunday are so valuable that most of them are in the lectionary twice. Most of them were also the appointments for Epiphany 8, this Year A. Do you get why? Because for Epiphany to have eight Sundays, Easter must be almost as late as it can be, and if it was, we skip this Proper 3. (Remember? Proper 3 requires a very *early* Easter. Now you're starting to catch on!) Unfortunately, most years, Easter isn't quite so early or quite so late; it's somewhere in between. Which means we'd miss this set of propers on both ends.

Pity.

The propers for this week are pastoral, encouraging, really offering the key to joyful living—and they demonstrate why the proper distinction between Law and Gospel, which Lutherans so appreciate, is truly essential to sustaining Christian faith. For Epiphany 8 (pp 66–69), we explored most of these same propers in one direction. This time we take a different look.

"Don't worry. Just don't worry. Don't worry!" We've all said it. We've all heard it said to us. It's (almost) always well intentioned. And how much does it help? If that's all we get, not much.

The problem is "Don't worry" by itself is all Law. It's a command, something we're supposed to do (not do). But in itself, it offers no hope. Whatever we were worried about hasn't gone anywhere. Still there. So what's *not* to worry about? That's the way the Law works. God gives the Law, and when it's truly God's Law, it's holy. But the Law always makes demands; it never gives power to obey and fulfill. That's "Don't worry" if left to itself.

Our propers, especially Jesus' own words in the Gospel lesson, tell us not to be anxious. But none of the propers stops there. Each one also delivers God's promise, God's assurance, God's comfort. That's Gospel. That's what's not to worry about.

Look first at the **Introit**:

> *Trust in Him at all times, O people; pour out your heart before Him; God is a refuge for us.*
>
> *For God alone my soul waits in silence; from Him comes my salvation. He only is my rock and my salvation, my fortress; I shall not be greatly shaken. Once God has spoken; twice have I heard this: that power belongs to God, and that to You, O Lord, belongs steadfast love. For You will render to a man according to his work.*
>
> *Glory be to the Father and to the Son and to the Holy Spirit; as it was in the beginning, is now, and will be forever. Amen.*
>
> *Trust in Him at all times, O people; pour out your heart before Him; God is a refuge for us. (Ps 62:1–2, 11–12; antiphon: Ps 62:8)*

See the imperative right away? "Trust in Him," the Lord. That may sound more sanctified than "Don't worry," but if that's all David gave us, we wouldn't know why God could be trusted or what He could be trusted to do for us. So David goes on: "God is a refuge for us. . . . My rock . . . my salvation, my fortress." Best part: "that power belongs to God, and that to You, O Lord, belongs steadfast love." God is powerful enough, mighty enough, to protect anyone from anything *and* He loves us constantly, unwaveringly. He'll use His power to save us. He gives reason to trust rather than to worry.

Similarly, the **Collect** for Proper 3:

> *Eternal God, You counsel us not to be anxious about earthly things. Keep alive in us a proper yearning for those heavenly treasures awaiting all who trust in Your mercy, that we may daily rejoice in Your salvation and serve You with constant devotion; through Jesus Christ, Your Son, our Lord, who lives and reigns with You and the Holy Spirit, one God, now and forever. Amen.*

God "counsels" us not to be anxious. That sounds much kinder, gentler. But a lot of bad counseling (sometime labeled "Christian counseling") only encourages one to look inside oneself and find peace, inner strength, or serenity (instead of anxiety). Not so here. The prayer recognizes that God has given us "salvation"—"through Jesus Christ."

God's counsel also does get to the very root of so many of our anxieties, earthly things: "'What shall we eat?' or 'What shall we drink?' or 'What shall we wear?'" Jesus hears the worrier say (Mt 6:31). All are real concerns. But "heavenly treasures" await "all who trust in [God's] mercy." If He provides those, surely He'll provide day to day.

And as long as God's counseling, here's that key to joyful living: "yearning for those heavenly treasures . . . we may daily rejoice in [His] salvation." Those treasures, our salvation, are not things for which we must fuss or fume. They have already been secured, they are already ours, by Jesus' death and resurrection for all people.

The **Old Testament Reading** puts no demands whatsoever on the one who feels anxious, "forsaken," "forgotten." It's pure, sweet Gospel: Isaiah 49:8–16a. Especially for those who are concerned with earthly needs, the Lord promises the most immediate relief: "To the prisoners, 'Come out.' . . . They shall feed along the ways; . . . neither scorching wind nor sun shall strike them, . . . and by springs of water [He] will guide them" (49:9–10). Can we be sure He'll really come through for us? "Can a woman forget her nursing child? . . . I will not forget you. Behold, I have engraved you on the palms of My hands" (49:15, 16). It's as David wrote in the Introit: to the Lord belongs steadfast love.

And it's as David wrote in the Introit: power belongs to God. Read the **Psalm** of the day, Psalm 115. Idols "do not" (repeated seven times, 115:4–7). Impotent. Helpless. But "our God . . . does all that He pleases" (115:3). And He pleases to be our "help" and our "shield" (repeated three times, 115:9–11) and to "bless" us (repeated four times, 115:12–13). That's why, rather than being anxious, we can "trust in the LORD!" (repeated three times, 115:9–11).

The **Epistle**, Romans 1:8–17, is the first of seventeen consecutive Sunday Epistles through Paul's letter to the Romans. (Recall that during this season, as through the Epiphany and Easter seasons, the Epistles are generally continuous readings through a book.) This passage includes the verse that many regard as Paul's theme for the letter: "I am not ashamed of the gospel, for it is the power of God for salvation to everyone who believes, to the Jew first and also to the Greek" (1:16). In Christ's cross we are saved! Paul is eager to preach this Gospel in Rome (1:15) and to share mutual encouragement with the Church there (1:11–12). He finds his joy in these "heavenly treasures" for which we prayed in the Collect. Interestingly, near the end of the book, Paul will also ask the Romans for material support for a mission to Spain (15:24). Those things matter too.

And they are well supplied: the **Holy Gospel**, Matthew 6:24–34. "Look at the birds of the air. . . . Consider the lilies of the field. . . . Will [God] not much more clothe you?" (6:26, 28, 30). Commanding not to be anxious is never enough. Christ offers the relief from anxiety. "Your heavenly Father knows that you need them all"—food, drink, clothing. He's way ahead of us and our worry. From all eternity, He's been planning to provide everything we need—heavenly and earthly—all by sending His Son to take away our sin so that it no longer separates us from Him. So that as our dear Father again, He could head off our reasons to worry. Before we ever knew we needed, He knew how He was providing. Everything.

THE LORD DOESN'T JUST PROHIBIT BEING ANXIOUS; HE PREEMPTS IT.

It's as the **Hymn of the Day** sings: "All depends on our possessing God's abundant grace and blessing." And in Christ Jesus, that we already surely have!

The Sundays after Pentecost: Proper 4 (May 29–June 4) Year A

READINGS

Deuteronomy 11:18–21, 26–28
Psalm 4 (antiphon: v 8)
Romans 3:21–28
Matthew 7:15–29

HYMN OF THE DAY

LSB 768 "To God the Holy Spirit Let Us Pray"

For these early Sundays after Pentecost, see the Proper 3 devotion-study (p 154) explaining why some Propers may be omitted in some years.

We're just getting in on the ground floor of the Time of the Church, the second half of the Christian year that began with Trinity Sunday and now will run all summer and through the fall. We'll be building on the foundation Christ and the Holy Spirit laid for the Church at Pentecost. At the same time, we're getting closure, in this week's Gospel lesson, on Jesus' Sermon on the Mount—the last installment, after having heard earlier portions during the Epiphany season.

It happens that that concluding section of Jesus' sermon is very interested in building and in foundations, what's beneath the ground floor. It's a familiar parable:

> Everyone then who hears these words of Mine and does them will be like a wise man who built his house on the rock. And the rain fell, and the floods came, and the winds blew and beat on that house, but it did not fall, because it had been founded on the rock. And everyone who hears these words of Mine and does not do them will be like a foolish man who built his house on the sand. And the rain fell, and the floods came, and the winds blew and beat against that house, and it fell, and great was the fall of it. (Mt 7:24–27)

Jesus' point seems simple enough. Being built on Jesus' words, we'll stand firm for eternity, as on a rock. Ignoring Jesus' words will be like building on sand, causing us, sooner or later, to be swept to our doom. Quite right. Like most of Jesus' parables, though, this may require more careful thought than first assumed. What, precisely, is the message of Jesus' words? What does He mean by *doing* them? And what's the "sand" that we might choose as an alternative to Jesus' words? Misunderstanding these will change entirely the point we take from the text.

As is always the case, the propers are designed to shed light on one another, to help us sort out their meanings. Start with this week's **Introit**:

How great are Your works, O Lord! Your thoughts are very deep!

The righteous flourish like the palm tree and grow like a cedar in Lebanon. They are planted in the house of the Lord; they flourish in the courts of our God. They still bear fruit in old age; they are ever full of sap and green, to declare that the Lord is upright; He is my rock, and there is no unrighteousness in Him.

Glory be to the Father and to the Son and to the Holy Spirit; as it was in the beginning, is now, and will be forever. Amen.

How great are Your works, O Lord! Your thoughts are very deep! (Ps 92:12–15; antiphon: Ps 92:5)

We always speak well of a deep thinker. At the same time, we appreciate when someone is able to keep it simple—especially to make deep thoughts, complex matters, easy to understand. Jesus accomplishes both in His parables.

The images—houses, foundations, standing, falling—are familiar and clear. And we've got the basic idea. Similarly, the psalm here is vivid in picturing stability, permanence, like those built on the Lord, who "is my rock": palm trees, cedar trees, planted and flourishing. Firmly rooted, they're not going anywhere. And "they still bear fruit in old age." This is how "the righteous" are. There's a blessed eternity in store. We can see it. We understand.

But Jesus' parables also tickle us into deeper thought, draw us in. And God's very deep thoughts are understood only when He reveals them in His Word. Jesus' words, to which He calls us in this Sunday's parable, aren't as shallow as, say, a to-do list that we can check off. That's our native thinking in our fallen condition. Want to stand firm for eternity? Do all the right things Jesus prescribes. Simple. Straightforward. Give me the list, and I'll get on it. That's not really where Jesus is going at all. We need to look more, deeply, into His words, the Word.

That's our prayer in the **Collect**:

Lord of all power and might, author and giver of all good things, instill in our hearts the love of Your name, impress on our minds the teachings of Your Word, and increase in our lives all that is holy and just; through Jesus Christ, Your Son, our Lord, who lives and reigns with You and the Holy Spirit, one God, now and forever. Amen.

If we're to understand Jesus' parable—more importantly, if we're to stand firm for eternity—we need God to "impress on our minds the teachings of [His] Word." That, of course, requires being *in* His Word. God doesn't just press Himself directly onto our gray matter. He only promises to work through the Word heard and read. This is certainly part of what Jesus had in mind for being built on the rock: "Everyone then who *hears* these words of Mine and does them will be like a wise man who built his house on the rock." It's wise to hear the words of Christ—actively, eagerly, often—and foolish not to.

Notice also in the Collect another reference to stability and permanence: "Lord of all power and might." The Lord is the rock because He is strong. No one pushes Him where He doesn't want to go, and no one dislodges those He holds on His shoulders.

One of my favorite passages about being in God's Word is the **Old Testament Reading**, Deuteronomy 11:18–21, 26–28 (along with its near parallel, Deut 6:6–9).

To begin with, I enjoy the imagery of "wearing" the Scriptures—"on your hand" (like a cheat sheet?) and "as frontlets between your eyes" (hard for you to read them there, but they tell everyone else what you're about; 11:18). Likewise, displaying God's Word "on the doorposts of your house and on your gates" (an *IXTHUS* fish on the front door, perhaps; 11:20).

But as a dad, I especially appreciate the encouragement to "teach them to your children, talking of them when you are sitting in your house, and when you are walking by the way, and when you lie down, and when you rise" (11:19). *My Devotions* before breakfast. Confirmation memory work driving to school. Jesus stories before bed and Jesus songs from the hallway as they drift off to sleep in their rooms. It's the sweetest investment God enables parents to make toward "the blessing, if you obey the commandments of the LORD your God" (11:27). An investment in standing firm on the rock: "that your days and the days of your children may be multiplied in the land that the LORD swore to your fathers to give them, as long as the heavens are above the earth" (11:21).

On the flip side, the Lord tells us about some of the sand on which we otherwise build: "other gods that you have not known" (11:28). Canaanite fertility gods. Or the office (that precludes Jesus time with the kids). Or the "toys" the paycheck buys (which are bad replacements for Jesus time, even when some of the toys are Fisher-Price). Or the dream retirement (for when you no longer have every day to share Jesus with the kids). Sand.

More sand in the **Psalm**, Psalm 4.

"How long will you love vain words and seek after lies?" (4:2). Quite a long time, apparently. A thousand years after David, Jesus noted that the scribes and Pharisees "love . . . respectful greetings in the market places, and being called Rabbi by men" (Mt 23:6, 7, NASB). In every age, compliments are nice, and receiving them graciously is godly. But the compliments we fish for by making ourselves look good will be no more substantial—and maybe no more sincere—than the false front we're putting up. And anyway, in the end, it's not the approval of men that will stand.

Rather, "trust in the LORD" (4:5). He's the rock. His kind words of promise are true, certain. "You alone, O LORD, make me dwell in safety." The night sky may be flashing with lightning, crashing with thunder, the rain pelting, the wind howling, but in the house built on the Lord's faithful words, we can "lie down and sleep" in peace (4:8).

Okay, then. "Everyone . . . who hears *these words* of Mine." What exactly do Jesus' words say that makes for a solid foundation? Read the **Epistle**, Romans 3:21–28.

Jesus' words are the very ones to which "the Law and the Prophets," the entire Old Testament, "bear witness" (3:21). Yes, they're rock solid—every word God has given from the beginning. And what is their message? "The righteousness of God through faith in Jesus Christ for all who believe" (3:22). That we are "justified by [God's] grace as a gift, through the redemption that is in Christ Jesus" (3:24). Jesus' blood shed on the cross has redeemed us, bought us back for God, by paying the price for our sins. Therefore God declares us "not guilty." That's what "justification" means—it's the courtroom act of being declared not guilty of our sin. And it *is God's* declaration, His announcement, for the sake of what Jesus did—not anything we do. It's simply "to be received by faith" (3:25), just believing He's done it all, that we do nothing.

"Then what becomes of our boasting?" (3:27). Sand. Claiming that we've done anything or could do anything to contribute even the tiniest credit toward our salvation? Sand. They're excluded. Our boasts and our works will all fall down—along with anyone who trusts in them. So we don't! "We hold that one is justified by faith apart from works of the law" (3:28).

By now, then, all these words of God have laid out for us Jesus' very deep thoughts in our **Holy Gospel**, Matthew 7:15–29.

"These words of Mine" are the Word of Christ. That certainly means the words spoken *by* Christ. But chiefly they are the Word *about* Christ. The Word of Christ is that Jesus has done everything for our salvation by His death on the cross; nothing remains for us to do. So we won't be interested in hearing from "prophets" who preach Jesus as the siding on the house rather than the foundation; they're false (7:15–20). They're sand. And we won't seek to enter the kingdom of heaven by the "mighty works" we've done in Jesus' name (7:21–23). Sand. In fact, since Christ has done it all for our salvation, the one who "hears these words of [Jesus] *and does them*" is actually everyone who just believes them. These words aren't a to-do list. Nothing as flimsy as our doing.

Rather, "When Jesus finished these sayings, the crowds were astonished at His teaching, for He was teaching them as one who had authority" (7:28–29)—solid!

**THE WORD OF CHRIST
IS THE ROCK ON WHICH WE'RE
BUILT—ALL SAND EXCLUDED!**

Pray, as you sing with Luther the **Hymn of the Day**, that God's Spirit would "teach us Jesus Christ," our Rock, "to know aright."

The Sundays after Pentecost: Proper 5 (June 5–11) Year A

READINGS

Hosea 5:15–6:6
Psalm 119:65–72
(antiphon: v 65)
Romans 4:13–25
Matthew 9:9–13

HYMN OF THE DAY

LSB 689 "Let Me Be Thine Forever"

For these early Sundays after Pentecost, see the Proper 3 devotion-study (p 154) explaining why some Propers may be omitted in some years.

The very last words we'll hear spoken this Sunday from the propers are these of Jesus in the Gospel lesson: "Go and learn what this means: 'I desire mercy, and not sacrifice.' For I came not to call the righteous, but sinners" (Mt 9:13).

This, presumably, could be our homework assignment for after church: "Go and learn . . ." But since we're looking *forward* to Sunday morning, we can work ahead instead. Proper 5 unpacks all this: mercy, sacrifices, who the righteous are, and how Jesus calls sinners—like us. In doing so, this day also delivers us into an important new stage of development in Jesus' ministry.

The Lord is calling in the **Introit**:

The Mighty One, God the Lord, speaks and summons the earth from the rising of the sun to its setting.

Hear, O My people, and I will speak; O Israel, I will testify against you. I am God, your God. Not for your sacrifices do I rebuke you; your burnt offerings are continually before Me. I will not accept a bull from your house or goats from your folds. For every beast of the forest is Mine, the cattle on a thousand hills.

Glory be to the Father and to the Son and to the Holy Spirit; as it was in the beginning, is now, and will be forever. Amen.

The Mighty One, God the Lord, *speaks and summons the earth from the rising of the sun to its setting. (Ps 50:7–10; antiphon: Ps 50:1)*

The Lord is calling—calling everyone "from the rising of the sun to its setting" a sinner: "I will testify against you." It's not that lots of "religion" isn't going on. "Your sacrifices" and "your burnt offerings are continually before Me," God says. He doesn't "rebuke" us for lack of those. But all these particular offerings and sacrifices aren't acceptable to Him. Why not? Well, because He's looking for something else. If He really needed a bull or goat, simply giving Him the goods would be sufficient. But He doesn't need them. "Every beast of the forest . . . , the cattle on a thousand hills" are all His. So when He commands those sacrifices, they're to be symbols or expressions of something else, something a lot more important to Him.

That's the question: Are we just giving the Lord "cattle"? At our best, we talk about how "things" don't really matter. The car is totaled in an accident, but nobody was hurt. It's okay. It was just a thing. But what if we only give God "things"? A check—but smaller than it might be because it comes with more doubt than trust. My name on the Board of Evangelism—but only half a heart actually to tell anybody about Jesus. A hotdish for the church supper—but with the hope that it outdoes Marlys's. God doesn't need any such things. He wants something different.

He wants us, and He wants us to follow Him. We pray this in the **Collect**:

Almighty and most merciful God, You sent Your Son, Jesus Christ, to seek and to save the lost. Graciously open our ears and our hearts to hear His call and to follow Him by faith that we may feast with Him forever in His kingdom; through the same Jesus Christ, our Lord, who lives and reigns with You and the Holy Spirit, one God, now and forever. Amen.

We're all sinners who can't offer God anything He needs. But He considers us ourselves to be precious! What mercy He has on us! "Almighty and *most* merciful God!" He sent Jesus to seek and to save us, lost though we were. That really defines what mercy is—God giving His own Son into death on the cross for people who were totally helpless and undeserving, giving us each a seat at the heavenly feast.

So now God's call to us isn't just to testify against us; it's to call us to follow Him. And that we do "by faith." We follow our Lord when we believe He is leading us to dine with Him in His kingdom.

In the **Old Testament Reading**, the Lord's call through His prophet is that sinners would repent: Hosea 5:15–6:6.

God's people have been guilty of the same sort of hypocrisy that He decried in the Introit—sacrifices and burnt offerings that were empty (6:6). "Your love," God says, "is like a morning cloud, like the dew that goes early away" (6:4). This is the sad state of affairs Hosea has been witnessing in Israel and Judah throughout his book.

God's people have been like the prostitute, Gomer, that God commanded Hosea to marry (Hos 1:2). They would profess their love for the Lord for a time, but it was as superficial as morning dew, not soaking deep. Like Gomer (2:5), they would then quickly run off to chase other affections. The Lord desires "*steadfast* love," love that is true and lasting (6:6).

Especially does He desire love that shows itself in caring for those in need. (The Septuagint, the early Greek translation of the Old Testament, renders "I desire steadfast love" as "I desire mercy.") This is where true religion, rather than hypocrisy and empty "things," becomes most evident. Those who love Yahweh will also demonstrate that love to the benefit of others. When mercy for the needy is absent, it shows that behind sacrifices and offerings is still a heart that loves only self. The Lord announces, "I will return again to My place, until they acknowledge their guilt and seek My face, and in their distress earnestly seek Me" (5:15). He will leave His people to the sufferings that their hypocrisies have earned.

Yet even now, Hosea trusts that God is acting in mercy to save these sinners. He calls out, "Come, let us return to the LORD; for He has torn us, *that He may heal us*" (6:1). Hosea believes that God is abandoning His people only in order that He may bring them to repentance and forgive them. Hosea's call is a declaration of faith: "He *will* bind us up. After two days He *will* revive us; on the third day He *will* raise us up. . . . His going out is *sure as the dawn*; He *will* come to us as the showers, as the spring rains that water the earth" (6:1–3). No fleeting dew, the Lord! (By the way, if "raise up on the third day" rings a bell, it's interesting to learn that ancient Jewish rabbis also took this to be a prophecy of resurrection!) God had taught Hosea all about His steadfast love; God had sent Hosea to go to Gomer yet again and love her again after her harlotries (3:1–5). God calls sinners to repent—and He *will* have mercy!

The poet of Palm 119, too, has experienced God's steadfast love and mercy for himself. Read the **Psalm**: 119:65–72.

"I went astray," he confesses (119:67a), but, like Hosea, he realizes, "It is good for me that I was afflicted" (119:71). God used affliction to teach. "Now I keep Your word" (119:67b). Since until heaven we each retain our sinful natures, we don't usually thrive if we *only* thrive. When all is well, the old Adam or Eve in us is much too inclined to smugness, to think we're prospering because *I'm really that good!* God knows when adversity is needed to humble us.

It's important to understand, though, that afflictions alone don't call the sinner to Christ. While they may knock away the props on which we're otherwise depending, it's God's promise of deliverance that creates and strengthens faith. This, too, the psalmist grasps. "Your law" in the Psalms (119:70, 72) refers to all the rich Gospel the Lord speaks in the Old Testament, along with what we speak of as His Law (which includes afflictions). The psalmist says, "I *believe* in Your commandments" (119:66). That's an expression of faith. The Lord desires "mercy, not sacrifice," right? Well, the psalmist gets it!

God's Word is so sweet and comforting that he desires it rather than "thousands of gold and silver pieces" (119:72). They're just things.

Sacrifice, as we've seen, can be empty, and until the Lord knocks away such hypocrisy, we won't realize we're the very sinners He calls. "For I came not to call the righteous, but sinners." Paul's entire book of Romans is dedicated to kicking down what really is the hypocrisy, the empty sacrifice, the prop we all lean on—and then giving sinners what they need instead. That's evident in our **Epistle**, Romans 4:13–25.

This Epistle lesson, we recognize, is a step in Paul's lengthy chain of logic explaining "the gospel" of which he's "not ashamed" (Rom 1:16), justification by grace through faith (3:24–25), which our lectionary will follow all summer. Even as we look forward to each Sunday with its theme, it'll be helpful also to follow Paul's progression of thought through Romans.

The antithesis to the Gospel of justification is works of the Law. These truly are what we all sinfully, naturally offer to God as the sacrifice we think He'll accept. Our obedience, our being good. The cattle on a thousand hills. Our things. Things we think make us righteous. He doesn't need them. He doesn't call that kind of righteousness.

To say He instead calls sinners means that He brings those who confess they have nothing to offer to believe He receives them anyway—for the sake of Jesus' death and resurrection. That's faith. And that makes one *truly* righteous—"the righteousness of faith" (4:13). "Faith was 'counted to [Abraham and to us] as righteousness'" (4:22).

All this Jesus teaches by action and then by word in the **Holy Gospel**, Matthew 9:9–13.

The nasty things we know tax collectors were reputed to be are all true. Not only were they collaborators with the Romans, but they were liars and cheaters and extortionists. The tax gig was almost a license to steal from your neighbor. We might want to sugarcoat it—"Matthew was probably better than most"—but the text gives no hint of that. He was a sinner, and Jesus called him. That call—"Matthew, you're precious to Me. I want you to follow Me"—created faith in his heart. No work of the Law, no sacrifice, to buy his way in. No righteousness on Matthew's part. Only the righteousness of Christ given to him. And now he dines with the Lord in His kingdom (9:10).

The Pharisees couldn't stomach it. Their problem was that they didn't know what this means: Jesus desires to have mercy on those who have nothing to offer, and that those who've received it will have mercy likewise.

**The Lord Calls
Not the "Righteous,"
Who Offer Sacrifices of the Law,
but Sinners,
Who Can Only Follow Him in Faith.**

We *have* learned what this means! And Matthew has too. This is the last report of Jesus calling one of the Twelve. The roster is set. Next week, He'll announce the starting lineup. From there, it's on with Jesus' ministry through Matthew's telling.

Now having been called by Christ as well, sing the prayer we can only sing after He has first made us His: "Let Me Be Thine Forever," the **Hymn of the Day** (*LSB* 689).

The Sundays after Pentecost: Proper 6 (June 12–18) Year A

READINGS

Exodus 19:2–8
Psalm 100 (antiphon: v 5)
Romans 5:6–15
Matthew 9:35–10:8 (9–20)

HYMN OF THE DAY

LSB 571 "God Loved the World So That He Gave"

For these early Sundays after Pentecost, *see the Proper 3 devotion-study (p 154)* *explaining why some Propers may be omitted in some years.*

Somebody knows something. And apparently it's something everyone should know: "Let the peoples praise You, O God; let all the peoples praise You!" (Ps 67:3).

There *is* reason to praise God! We know that, and we do wish everyone knew it. But let's see now: Just *how* do we know it? And how will others know? There's only one way they can find out—the same way we did. Unfortunately, what they think they know, what they think they've figured out or learned any other way, will be wrong, will give them a tragically false understanding of God and why we might (or might not) praise Him.

Proper 6 raises and answers these queries and encourages us to be part of the answer.

It's the **Introit** that gets us asking:

Let the peoples praise You, O God; let all the peoples praise You!

Let the nations be glad and sing for joy, for You judge the peoples with equity and guide the nations upon earth. Let the peoples praise You, O God; let all the peoples praise You! The earth has yielded its increase; God, our God, shall bless us. God shall bless us; let all the ends of the earth fear Him!

Glory be to the Father and to the Son and to the Holy Spirit; as it was in the beginning, is now, and will be forever. Amen.

Let the peoples praise You, O God; let all the peoples praise You! (Ps 67:4–7; antiphon: Ps 67:3)

What's obviously clear is that this something is for everyone: "the peoples . . . *all* the peoples . . . the nations . . . the peoples . . . the nations upon earth . . . the peoples . . . *all* the peoples . . . all the ends of the earth . . . the peoples . . . *all* the peoples." Pretty emphatic! It's just as clear that all the peoples are to praise, "praise You, O God."

What isn't so clear is that reason for praising Him. The psalmist tells us God "shall bless us." That's reason to praise Him—but not too specific. Other than that, the only thing resembling a reason is "for You judge the peoples with equity and guide the nations upon earth." Okay, we'll work with that. Guiding can be good, but only good if the destination is too, and we're left to guess where He'll guide us. Judging with equity certainly sounds fair enough, but from these verses alone, we'd have to assume what His standards for "fair" might be. And you know what we human beings will naturally assume. We'll jump to the logical conclusion that if we want to come out well in a fair, equitable judgment, we'll have to do enough to come out on God's "plus side"—be better than we are bad, more good than goofs. Of course, what kind of reason is that then to praise *God*? Wouldn't judgment like that just be God doing His job, giving us what He owes us? Wouldn't that be reason for praising *us*?

That's where our thinking would always go. Without more help, we couldn't yet know why we and all the peoples can praise God.

The **Old Testament Reading** gives us insights into the way God Himself answered our questions during the centuries before Christ. Read Exodus 19:2–8.

This is the prelude to God giving Israel the Ten Commandments. It's the third month after the exodus, and the Israelites have arrived at the spot God told Moses they were to come and worship Him, the same place God had spoken through the burning bush, Mount Sinai. Moses goes up to the Lord and then brings His words back to the people. This, the event of Mount Sinai, would be remembered as God's official act of taking Israel to be His people. They know what He's already done so recently to make that happen: "You yourselves have seen what I did to the Egyptians, and how I bore you on eagles' wings and brought you to Myself" (19:4). Ten plagues, including the death of the Egyptian firstborn—while passing over the Israelite homes and leaving their children unharmed. The miracle of the Red Sea, destroying the Egyptian army. Quail and manna in the wilderness. Water from a rock.

"Now therefore, if you will indeed obey My voice and keep My covenant, you shall be My treasured possession among all peoples, for all the earth is Mine; and you shall be to Me a kingdom of priests and a holy nation" (19:5–6a). For the rest of the Old Testament age, Israel could now always recall their reason for praising God! He had made them His! Why Israel, among all peoples of the earth? Surely it wasn't because they'd come out ahead on God's balance sheet. When you're being carried on eagles' wings, you're just dead weight; you're just riding along. Fact is, when God had sent Moses to lead Israel out of slavery, he'd first had to tell them who this God was (Ex 3:13). Israel had believed there were many gods, just as all the other nations did. They hadn't been God's faithful people.

There was no reason Yahweh, the Lord, should be taking Israel as His people. But here He was saying just that through His prophet Moses. "'Thus you [Moses] shall say to the house of Jacob. . . .' So Moses came and called the elders of the people and set before them all these words that the LORD had commanded him" (19:3, 7). God spoke through His prophet. And "all the people answered together and said, 'All that *the Lord has spoken* we will do'" (19:8). It was the voice of Moses they heard, but the people knew this was the Lord Himself speaking.

As for all the other nations, "all the peoples," the only way they could praise Yahweh in those Old Testament days was to see Him through Israel. Being "a kingdom of priests and a holy nation" meant that the tribes of Israel were set apart to be God's intermediaries to the world. That's what a priest was—the "go-between," God to people. Moses wouldn't go out on preaching trips to the Amalekites and Amorites, but Israel was to live as holy people modeling God's just and loving decrees so that the nations could see them and say, "What other nation has a God so near as Yahweh whenever they call on Him?" (See Deut 4:5–8.)

Likely it was in the very months that followed, while Israel remained at Sinai, that Moses recorded these words, along with Genesis, the rest of Exodus, and Leviticus. (Numbers and Deuteronomy would come in the years after.) And thus we, too, have God's Word through the prophet these millennia later. (See, by the way, how Peter applies these words of God to Israel also to us: 1 Pet 2:9.)

The poet of our **Psalm** of the day understands well God's act of taking Israel as His own. He also understands that this is by God's gracious work alone: Psalm 100.

"The LORD, He is God! It is He who made us, and we are His; we are His people, and the sheep of His pasture" (100:3). Yahweh is God; He's our Creator. We had nothing to do with our being here. But this almighty God who could make a universe has made us His—His precious lambs He feeds and nurtures.

The psalmist knows this because he's heard or read Moses. And now he himself becomes an inspired writer and proclaimer, and he calls all the peoples to proclaim the Lord's praises as well: "Make a joyful noise to the LORD, all the earth! . . . Enter His gates with thanksgiving, and His courts with praise!" (100:1, 4).

It's Paul, though, who puts perhaps most starkly why we could in no other way figure out our reason to praise God—that He has made us His apart from anything in us. Our **Epistle**, Romans 5:6–15.

Ask anyone on the street what he or she thinks of God. Some will say He doesn't exist. Some will say they don't know. Lots will say something pleasantly innocuous about Him being big or powerful or maybe Father of us all—whoever He may be. Not too many will say, "I'd like to punch 'im out!" But that's where Paul says we all were.

See how Paul works up to it: "We were still weak"—couldn't find it in ourselves to love Him (5:6a). We were "ungodly"—going our own way, not His (5:6b). "We were still sinners"—all right, actively (and innately, 5:12) disobeying Him (5:8). But much more than those, "*we were enemies*" (5:10). We hated God. Would have killed Him, erased Him from existence, if we could have.

But that's when Christ died for us! Christ died for us! When we were God's enemies, God reconciled us to Himself by *Himself* dying for our very hatred of Him! God's grace, a free gift, abounded to us—and to the "many" (5:15). That is, to all! No one could ever have grasped—even guessed—that someone would do this for His enemies! But the apostle tells us so, and, as with Moses and the Old Testament prophets, that is as certain as God Himself speaking. We read the Scriptures; we hear God.

Jesus, of course, is the very God that we hated, that we really did kill, but He never treated us as enemies. In our **Holy Gospel**, He provides for all people to know that He is reconciled to us: Matthew 9:35–10:20.

Jesus sees our weakness, our helplessness in sin: "harassed and helpless, like sheep without a shepherd." He knows our evil wanderings, and He knows we could never find our way back to Him. So He has compassion on us (9:36). First, He preaches the Gospel Himself (9:35). Then, He chooses twelve of His followers to be apostles and sends them out (ἀπόστολος, "sent ones") to proclaim the kingdom and to work miracles. Their mission is to be pure grace: "You received without paying; give without pay" (10:8). For while we were weak, ungodly, sinners, and enemies of God, Jesus paid the full price to have us as His own again.

The apostles would preach, and their words would be God's own words (10:20). Later, some—Matthew, John, Peter, like Paul—would also write, joining their inspired words to those of Moses and the other Old Testament prophets. So we pray in the **Collect** for this Sunday:

> *Almighty, eternal God, in the Word of Your apostles and prophets You have proclaimed to us Your saving will. Grant us faith to believe Your promises that we may receive eternal salvation; through Jesus Christ, our Lord, who lives and reigns with You and the Holy Spirit, one God, now and forever. Amen.*

And let's not forget to add that one more prayer Jesus encouraged in the Gospel reading, the **Verse** for this Proper 6 week: "Alleluia. The harvest is plentiful, but the laborers are few; therefore pray earnestly to the Lord of the harvest to send out laborers into His harvest. Alleluia" (Mt 9:37b–38). You know that you and I are each part of God's answer to this prayer.

By the Word of the Prophets and Apostles, We Believe—and Proclaim—What No One Could Grasp Any Other Way: That Christ's Death Makes God's Enemies His Again.

It's as "His Spirit in the Word declares" in the **Hymn of the Day**, *LSB* 571.

The Sundays after Pentecost: Proper 7 (June 19–25) Year A

READINGS

Jeremiah 20:7–13
Psalm 91:1–10 (11–16) (antiphon: v 1)
Romans 6:12–23
Matthew 10:5a, 21–33

HYMN OF THE DAY

LSB 659 "Lord of Our Life"

For these early Sundays after Pentecost, see the Proper 3 devotion-study (p 154) explaining why some Propers may be omitted in some years.

It had to be quite a thrill—and, as the centuries since have proven, a truly historic honor. Of all the thousands of people who'd followed Jesus, in last week's Gospel reading, He sent out Peter and Andrew, James and John, Philip, Bartholomew, and the rest as His apostles. They would heal the sick, raise the dead, drive out demons, be God's own spokesmen, so that eventually through their baptizing and teaching, Jesus would have disciples among all nations (Mt 10:1–4, 8, 20; 28:19–20). Millions, perhaps even billions, of disciples. Heady stuff!

What's more, like the entire Old Testament people of Israel, we Christians are all part of a whole "kingdom of priests and a holy nation" (Ex 19:6). We, too, are God's intermediaries to the world. He has set us, too, apart for this holy calling.

Can't wait to get at it! Turn us loose!

Except in this week's readings, we get the other side of the story. Jesus' prophets and apostles won't ride the wave of fame and triumph all the way to Christ's return. They'll be mocked, hated, killed. And therefore, so will we. Jesus is quite up front about this. So we might very well be scared to death. Or worse, scared into shutting up. Scared into keeping quiet about our faith, about knowing Jesus. Scared into blending in, letting our Christianity become invisible. Maybe even scared into denying Christ.

But our propers this week have one more lesson: that we don't *need* to be afraid, that we can confess Christ openly, boldly, because He will be there to deliver us.

That's certainly the encouragement we hear in the **Introit** this week:

> *For You have delivered my soul from death, yes, my feet from falling, that I may walk before God in the light of life.*
>
> *When I am afraid, I put my trust in You. In God, whose word I praise, in God I trust; I shall not be afraid. What can flesh do to me? In God, whose word I praise, in the LORD, whose word I praise, in God I trust; I shall not be afraid. What can man do to me?*
>
> *Glory be to the Father and to the Son and to the Holy Spirit; as it was in the beginning, is now, and will be forever. Amen.*
>
> *For You have delivered my soul from death, yes, my feet from falling, that I may walk before God in the light of life. (Ps 56:3–4, 10–11; antiphon: Ps 56:13)*

David knew from experience that God was with him in dangers—from lion and bear, in battle, fleeing from Saul. Time and again the Lord had saved him from death. "I shall not be afraid." And he was able boldly to acknowledge God as Savior: "God, whose word I praise." Three times he repeats this.

But David had been afraid. He even speaks of his fears still in the present tense: "When I *am* afraid, I put my trust in You." That's the key, isn't it! To be afraid—in a fallen world, where Satan and so many enemies threaten and where our own sinfulness causes us to doubt God's care—that's a way of life for us, it is to be admitted. But even as we are afraid, David invites us to trust, however haltingly, trembling, that God is with us.

The **Collect** is also a prayer for trust in the face of danger:

> *O God, because Your abiding presence always goes with us, keep us aware of Your daily mercies that we may live secure and content in Your eternal love; through Jesus Christ, Your Son, our Lord, who lives and reigns with You and the Holy Spirit, one God, now and forever. Amen.*

We recognize that since Jesus' death on the cross has reconciled us to the Father, God's "abiding presence always goes with us." But we pray that He would "keep us aware" of that. That is to say, we often forget; we frequently doubt that God will truly deliver us. Because the threats are real. The prayer "that we may live secure" underscores this; we install security systems, a university hires campus security, because powerful forces wish to make us *in*secure. We need God's assurance if our trust is to stand firm.

In the **Old Testament Reading**, the prophet Jeremiah is living out what Jesus' apostles and all Christians are told to expect. Read not only Jeremiah 20:7–13 but also the preceding verses, 1–6.

You remember, perhaps, what a tough lot in life Jeremiah had. God had called him when he was just a youth during the days of good King Josiah, but already then the Lord had alerted Jeremiah that His people would reject his message and persecute him. No wonder! The news Jeremiah would bring from the Lord would often be bad: "Whenever I speak, I cry out, I shout, 'Violence and destruction!'" (20:8). Jeremiah's ministry would continue through the evil reigns of Jehoiakim and Zedekiah, and he would have the almost constant duty of condemning Judah's wickedness. Not once, not twice, but three times the Babylonian army would carry off captives—culminating in the destruction of Jerusalem and the temple in 586 BC (1:1–19). Jeremiah has come to be known as "the weeping prophet" because he got to announce it all.

See what's happened to Jeremiah now: he's spent the night in the stocks (20:2). For being faithful. For saying what God has told him to say. So you picture him going home, his ankles a bit sore, and having some debriefing time with the Lord. "O Lord, You didn't tell me it was going to be this bad!" "You have deceived me, and I was deceived. . . . I have become a laughingstock all the day; everyone mocks me" (20:7a, c). This is what God's spokespeople can expect.

We should know. If we're delivering the hard words we ought, we will know. We'll be a laughingstock for telling our friends that moving in together before marriage is a sin. Folks will mock us if we say homosexual activity will earn God's punishment. We'll surely be pilloried for saying that Jesus Christ is the only way to heaven. So maybe we get scared and keep silent.

But Jeremiah couldn't. Not "speak any more in [God's] name"? "I cannot" (20:9). Jeremiah couldn't hold it in. Despite the pain and ridicule, he just had to say what God wanted him to say, because "the Lord is with me as a dread warrior; . . . He has delivered the life of the needy from the hand of evildoers" (20:11, 13)—as He will deliver us.

The writer of our **Psalm** shares this same trust. Read Psalm 91.

"I will say to the Lord, 'My refuge and my fortress, my God, in whom I trust.' For He will deliver you" (91:2–3). Yes, the dangers are still out there: arrows will fly; pestilence and destruction stalk; plagues, lions, snakes each could take our lives (91:5–6, 10, 13). Okay, make that piercing words and biting insults; they still hurt. But "you will not fear" (91:5)—even though you are very much afraid!—because "the Most High . . . is my refuge" (91:9).

But notice this: "*Because he holds fast to Me* in love, I will deliver him" (91:14). It is the one who clings to the Lord who will be delivered. Trust in the approval of friends, in acceptance by the world, in playing it safe and keeping quiet, and you'll have no refuge in the Lord.

The ultimate threat we may fear Paul identifies in our **Epistle**: Romans 6:12–23.

We've got it pretty good. We don't really fear arrows and armies and stocks and snakes. Truth be told, from day to day, we don't even fear dying. (Not that we like the idea, of course; we're just not convinced it's going to happen to us any time soon.) But when Paul tells us "the wages of sin is death" (6:23a), he's speaking of "death" as only the visible manifestation of what no living human has ever seen: death beyond the grave. We die physically because of sin, but sin doesn't release us when our bodies stop breathing. As "slaves of sin" (6:17), we would have lived in its grasp for eternity. That's hell. Of that we should be very much afraid.

So "thanks be to God" you "have been brought from death to life" (6:17, 13). The Lord has delivered our *souls* from death! We have "the free gift of God," eternal life in the death and resurrection of Christ Jesus, our Lord (6:23b). This above all else is why we need not fear. And this is why we not only *can* confess but *can't help* confessing Christ to the world. We, "having been set free from sin, have become slaves of righteousness" (6:18). The new men and women inside us can't *not* speak up for Him. The believer in Christ in each of us wouldn't have it any other way.

All of this is, as always, taught best by Jesus Himself. Read our **Holy Gospel**: Matthew 10:5a, 21–33.

With the immense honor of proclaiming Christ, either as an apostle or as a member of the priestly nation of all believers, comes the frightening reality: brother, father, children will turn on us. We will be hated by all (10:21–22).

We shouldn't expect otherwise. We're servants of Christ, and we should anticipate being treated the same way our Master was (10:25). Not only did His enemies call Jesus Beelzebul (the prince of demons, Mt 9:34), but they crucified Him. "How much more will they malign those of His household"!

That's not a "might"; it's a "will." Often it's still subtle. For almost the entire histories of the United States and Canada, Christianity has been protected. But even in those days, all unbelievers, including those who for social reasons claimed church membership, have hated the faith. That's the secret of the old sinful nature. And now, with societal favor a thing of the past, real persecution appears imminent. Tax pressures. Restrictions on free speech. Even prison. They're coming—as we should expect.

But "do not fear." Satan and the world can only kill the body—much as we do fear that (10:28). The truly fatal mistake would be to succumb to those fears and deny the One without whom we would be lost to hell: "Everyone who acknowledges Me before men, I also will acknowledge before My Father who is in heaven, but whoever denies Me before men, I also will deny before My Father who is in heaven" (10:32–33). Christ is the one we should fear—but Christ is the one who has delivered our souls from hell. And He knows our fears, for "even the hairs of your head are all numbered" (10:30). Therefore,

WE CAN ACKNOWLEDGE THE LORD BEFORE MEN WITHOUT FEAR (THOUGH WE MAY BE VERY MUCH AFRAID!) BECAUSE THE LORD HAS DELIVERED OUR SOULS FROM HELL.

As you close with the **Hymn of the Day**, "Lord of Our Life" (*LSB* 659), consider what the "hungry billows curling," the "foes their banners . . . unfurling," and the "fiery darts" they're "hurling" are in your life. Sure, you're afraid. But you can rest in the peace Christ has secured by dying and rising for you. And then confess Him bravely.

The Sundays after Pentecost: Proper 8 (June 26–July 2) Year A

READINGS

Jeremiah 28:5–9
Psalm 119:153–160
(antiphon: v 154)
Romans 7:1–13
Matthew 10:34–42

HYMN OF THE DAY

LSB 685 "Let Us Ever Walk with Jesus"

From this week's Holy Gospel and Old Testament Reading:

> Do not think that I have come to bring peace to the earth. I have not come to bring peace, but a sword. (Mt 10:34)

> As for the prophet who prophesies peace, when the word of that prophet comes to pass, then it will be known that the LORD has truly sent the prophet. (Jer 28:9)

No question, the instructions Jesus has been giving His apostles as He sends them out (Mt 10:5a, 16–33) have been tough. They will be opposed—even to the point of death. And we can't expect Jeremiah, "the weeping prophet," to give a message that's any easier to take. So get ready for another of that kind of Sunday.

The message we're always eager to hear is a word of peace. Calm. Quiet. Harmony. Everyone—family, neighbors, classmates, coworkers, political parties, countries—getting along. Sleeping easy at night from all the kind words and mutual admiration we heard today and anticipate tomorrow. A Canada Day or Independence Day that waves flags and thanks those who serve their country—from nice, safe posts here at home rather than overseas in harm's way.

Jesus alerts us not to count on any of that. But Jeremiah hints that Jesus will bring something better—though by a most difficult means.

The **Introit** for this Sunday doesn't seem to go in such an ominous direction:

> *I will sing of the steadfast love of the LORD, forever; with my mouth I will*

make known Your faithfulness to all generations.

Blessèd are the people who know the festal shout, who walk, O Lord, in the light of Your face, who exult in Your name all the day and in Your righteousness are exalted. For You are the glory of their strength; by Your favor our horn is exalted. For our shield belongs to the Lord, our king to the Holy One of Israel.

Glory be to the Father and to the Son and to the Holy Spirit; as it was in the beginning, is now, and will be forever. Amen.

I will sing of the steadfast love of the Lord, forever; with my mouth I will make known Your faithfulness to all generations. (Ps 89:15–18; antiphon: Ps 89:1)

Christians always have reason to "sing," to sound "the festal shout," to "exult." We know that Christ's suffering, death, and resurrection have earned for us eternal joy and God's care for us every day now. That's true every Sunday of the church year and every day of the week, whatever else we'll hear.

But the Introit does drop clues that our joy doesn't come easily. By God's favor "our horn is exalted." And "our shield belongs to the Lord." "Horn" is a common Old Testament image for strength; an animal, like a ram or a stag, uses his horns or antlers in battle—to stake out his territory or protect his herd. "Shield," of course, is also a military reference; an arrow or sword thrust must be aimed our way for us to need a shield. So the Lord will be defending us against danger. What's more, notice the repetition of "Your," speaking of the Lord: "Your face," "Your name," "Your righteousness," "Your favor." That's emphatic. It's a heads-up that God gives blessing and joy *His* way, not ours. We'd plan to sing about peace and prosperity; God's way to singing may be quite different.

It's as the **Gradual** (new, beginning with Proper 8 this week) reminds us:

Oh, the depth of the riches and wisdom and knowledge of God! How unsearchable are His judgments and how inscrutable His ways! For from Him and through Him and to Him are all things. To Him be glory forever. Amen. (Rom 11:33, 36)

The **Collect** for this Sunday includes a similar subtle reminder:

Almighty God, by the working of Your Holy Spirit, grant that we may gladly hear Your Word proclaimed among us and follow its directing; through Jesus Christ, Your Son, our Lord, who lives and reigns with You and the Holy Spirit, one God, now and forever. Amen.

While this prayer is universally appropriate (When would we *not* pray to "hear Your Word" gladly and "follow its directing"?), in this Sunday's context, the petition is more pointed. Not everything in God's Word are we by nature glad to hear and follow.

Like when Christ tells us He doesn't come to bring peace on earth but rather a sword. Only the Lord Himself can open our hearts to receive that teaching gladly.

And He does! The believer in us, the new woman or man, does receive even the hard words of God in joyful faith. Read Psalm 119:153–160, our **Psalm** for the week.

The psalmist isn't experiencing peace and quiet: "Look on my affliction and deliver me. . . . Many are my persecutors and my adversaries" (119:153a, 157a). Yet he doesn't "swerve from [the Lord's] testimonies" (119:157b). Instead, he trusts that "the sum of Your word is truth, and every one of Your righteous rules endures forever" (119:160). This is actually the faith of every believer. Though the old sinful nature complains and murmurs as soon as God allows adversity, the new person God created in each of us in our Baptism always says, "Yea, amen"—even as the arrows fly.

If any of God's faithful ones ever struggled to keep that peace of mind, it could have been Jeremiah. Consider the **Old Testament Reading**, Jeremiah 28:5–9. In fact, reading all of chapters 27 and 28 would be helpful.

Recall Jeremiah's personal history (perhaps turn back to pp 171–72). By the time of this week's prophecy, the Babylonians have already sacked Jerusalem twice, not only taking captives (like Daniel, Ezekiel, and King Jeconiah, or Jehoiachin), but also stripping the temple of many of its sacred objects. In chapter 27, Jeremiah counseled new King Zedekiah to accept God's punishment; these captives (and the vessels from the temple) would be held in Babylon for a long time (seventy years, it would turn out to be, 25:12; 29:10). The people should honor the Babylonian king, Nebuchadnezzar, whom God had placed over them (27:5–6, 11). Further rebellion would bring even greater disaster (27:8). Unfortunately, along comes Hananiah, who falsely prophesies that in two short years, all will be well—the captives and sacred vessels would all come home (28:1–4). In other words, Judah's sins must not really have been so bad after all; God just had to give them a little slap on the wrist.

This is just what people—Judah, each of us—would want to hear. Jeremiah *especially* would have wanted to believe this; surely after all the bad news he'd had to deliver and all the suffering it was earning him, he was ready for some calm and quiet! "Amen! May the Lord do so" (28:6).

It just wasn't true. And Jeremiah knew it (27:14–17). Prophets usually had the hard job of announcing "war, famine, and pestilence" (28:8), the bitter results of sin. They didn't want to say that; no one wanted to hear it. But in a fallen world, it always came true. It was even a safe bet.

But Hananiah was prophesying what everyone wanted to hear: peace. It's what he wanted to say too; it's the kind of prediction that will make a prophet or a pastor popular. But in a sinful world, it's not likely. "As for the prophet who prophesies peace, when the word of that prophet comes to pass [and not until that word comes to pass!], then it will be known that the Lord has truly sent the prophet" (28:9). The word everyone wants to hear is the word the prophet might very well be making up.

And so with Hananiah. God would confirm Jeremiah's word—Judah would serve its full sentence; yet a third Babylonian deportation would come, the worst of all—and Hananiah would die for lying in God's name (28:12–17).

It's not that a prophecy of peace would *never* come true. Read 28:9 again. Does Jeremiah have a double entendre in mind? We think so. The Lord would indeed send a Prophet, whose word of peace would come to pass. It would just come true in a way we'd never choose.

Read Sunday's **Holy Gospel**, Matthew 10:34–42. Is Jesus denying that He's the Prince—and Prophet—of Peace? Not really.

Jesus' coming does bring a sword. Following Him will divide families, even put members of a household at war with one another (10:34–36). Many of us know how painful this is. A Fourth of July family reunion that some won't attend because "we always wind up arguing about religion"—or a "scene" at the picnic that ruins the day for everybody. A loved one not speaking to you for years because you once made clear that living without Christ is a sure road to hell. Even divisions in the family that come with a faithful practice of closed Communion. Jesus disturbs that peace. "Whoever does not take his cross and follow Me is not worthy of Me" (10:38).

But Jesus does bring peace, a different peace, a peace that can only come in God's way. "Whoever finds his life will lose it, and whoever loses his life for My sake will find it" (10:39). Jesus brings peace that comes through loss of life. Taking our crosses follows Jesus taking His. Jesus' death on the cross, by paying for the sin that separated us from God, has restored our peace with Him. That automatically means war with the world, with those who oppose Christ, even within our families. So it isn't pitch-perfect harmony in the life we see. It's only a perfect unison of everything that matters, of everything that has real value, of everything that lasts, of God and man, both now and forever.

To have this peace, we must lose the life we thought we wanted so badly—the life of getting along, going along. But in our Baptism, we have already died this death and been joined to the peace of Christ. Sure,

**We're All Eager to Hear
a Word of Peace,
but the Prophet Whose Peace
Will Truly Come to Pass
Is the One Who Promises It
through Loss of Life.**

And that's Jesus, who lost His life for us. That's God's way to peace.

We look at the **Epistle**, Romans 7:1–13, last because it pictures so well the blessing of this losing life. See how many times Paul mentions death. We've died to the obligation of earning salvation by keeping the Law (7:6). Now we who have lost that life have found new life in Christ's death and resurrection (7:4). We serve God and bear His good fruit in the new, free way of the Spirit (7:4, 6). This is living out God's way of peace.

"Let Us," then, "Ever Walk with Jesus" (**Hymn of the Day**, *LSB* 685) by suffering with Him, bearing our crosses, gladly dying with Him, and mortifying sinful passion—so that we may live with Him on high.

The Sundays after Pentecost: Proper 9 (July 3–9) Year A

READINGS

Zechariah 9:9–12
Psalm 145:1–14 (antiphon: v 19)
Romans 7:14–25a
Matthew 11:25–30

HYMN OF THE DAY

LSB 699 "I Heard the Voice of Jesus Say"

A Canada Day or an Independence Day off. The lazy days of summer. No school. Vacation time. Sitting out on the deck or in the backyard or by the pool, sipping a cold lemonade. The life of leisure. We're surely all relaxed, well rested.

Or not.

Planning the vacation. Getting ahead at work so we're not too far behind when we get back. Summer job. Little League. Mowing the lawn. Detasseling corn. And, of course, this is the "down" season—before things get busy again in the fall.

I don't think it's just me. One of the biggest frustrations folks in my congregations always expressed was just being pooped. Tired. Too much to do, too little time to do it. It's a result of sin in the world—things don't always run as smoothly as we think they should; we get behind, we hurry to catch up; we feel the stress, it wears us down. An appointment for this, a text about that, a last-minute rush order from the boss. And then there's all the stuff we'd *planned* to do today. I get tired just writing about it.

There's physical fatigue and mental fatigue. And "weary" is also a powerful metaphor for the spiritual impact sin has on all of us.

Well, Jesus offers us just what I think every one of us often needs the most. Our **Verse** for this Sunday, drawn from the Gospel reading: "Alleluia. Come to Me, all who labor and are heavy laden, and I will give you rest" (Mt 11:28). To which I'll second, "Alleluia!"

As we look forward to this Sunday morning—and Jesus' words of rest—think about what makes you feel tired, weary, burdened. Our propers raise quite a few ideas.

Start with the **Introit**:

He who dwells in the shelter of the Most High will abide in the shadow of the Almighty.

I will say to the Lord, *"My refuge and my fortress, my God, in whom I trust." Because you have made the* Lord *your dwelling place—the Most High, who is my refuge—no evil shall be allowed to befall you, no plague come near your tent.*

Glory be to the Father and to the Son and to the Holy Spirit; as it was in the beginning, is now, and will be forever. Amen.

He who dwells in the shelter of the Most High will abide in the shadow of the Almighty. (Ps 91:2, 9–10; antiphon: Ps 91:1)

What is the psalmist picturing as an image of something that might make us weary? Look at the antiphon. In the ancient Near East, the burning sun was not a friend; it could "smite thee by day," to quote another familiar psalm (Ps 121:6, KJV). To be lost in the desert without sufficient water would be fatal. The Israelites understood well the curse on Adam: "By the sweat of your face you shall eat bread" (Gen 3:19). Building forms for the foundation of a truck-trailer factory, pouring concrete, hanging steel, in July—in Texas!—how much you'd welcome "the *shadow* of the Almighty"!

What about the **Collect**? It sees something quite different as wearisome:

Gracious God, our heavenly Father, Your mercy attends us all our days. Be our strength and support amid the wearisome changes of this world, and at life's end grant us Your promised rest and the full joys of Your salvation; through Jesus Christ, Your Son, our Lord, who lives and reigns with You and the Holy Spirit, one God, now and forever. Amen.

Who doesn't see change as wearisome—especially at the rate we see changes today. Sixteen major league baseball teams—and the Dodgers in Brooklyn (look it up—online!—it was true until 1958). Dial-up modems, desktops, laptops, iPhones. Cable, satellite, Netflix. Meeting, married, divorced, deceased. A baby daughter, a teenager, off to college, out of the house. A job, a promotion, a move, retirement, another move. Red hymnal, blue (green?), maroon. Thank You, gracious God, that "Your mercy attends us *all* our days"—whatever each one may hold!

Childhood, adulthood, aging, life's end. Or perhaps childhood, adulthood, life's end. Or even childhood, life's end. Whenever, however: a change we'll each face—perhaps even *before* it all becomes wearisome. "Gracious God, at life's end grant us Your promised rest."

We might identify two burdens from which the **Old Testament Reading** offers rest. Read Zechariah 9:9–12. (If it sounds familiar, you're undoubtedly recognizing the Palm Sunday event and perhaps also the

Gradual for the season of Advent. Christ is certainly the King coming to us.)

In the immediate context, Zechariah was assuring the people of Judah, recently returned from exile in Babylon, that their king would protect them from foreign enemies. What a burden God's people had suffered during seventy years of captivity! The Babylonian deportation had been characterized as a yoke, like an animal would wear while pulling a cart or a plow (Jer 27:2, 8, 11). God's people must have felt they'd spent a lifetime like beasts of burden.

Most of us have never lived under a foreign conqueror, but more and more, those who wish to subjugate the Church are right here at home. We Christians in North America are in a fight. Every means at our civic, legal, and political disposal needs desperately to be engaged if we are to maintain our freedom to speak God's Law and Gospel rightly in our own countries. Voting, campaigning, marching, speaking at school board meetings and local caucuses. We need to be doing all these things. But do we have the energy? When our plates are already so full? Are we too tired? "Rejoice greatly! Your king is coming to you!"—and He rules also the affairs of nations.

A second image of fatigue: the Lord says, "I will set your prisoners free from the waterless pit" (9:11). The prophet sees a cistern, dug out to collect precious rainwater but now dry. The kind of pit into which Joseph's brothers cast him before selling him into slavery (Gen 37:23–24). No way out. But left there to die, we'd try. Try climbing, try pulling ourselves up by our own bootstraps—the way, left to ourselves, we'd try to pull our souls up to heaven. Struggling, straining, stressing to do enough to earn God's favor. But always falling back. Until finally, the last ounce of strength spent, we'd collapse to the bottom in despair. That's a tired from which we need rest! "I will set your prisoners free from the waterless pit."

Now, there's plenty of exuberance in this Sunday's **Psalm**: Psalm 145:1–14, 19. The psalmist doesn't sound tired at all as he extols God's "mighty acts." But God's "awesome deeds" and "abundant goodness" are deliverances from the many consequences of our sin (notice we cry out to be saved, 145:19). And those effects of sin are the very things that make us tired—physically, emotionally, and spiritually.

So, the psalmist writes, "On Your wondrous works, I will meditate" (145:5). Isn't this among the first casualties when we feel hurried and hassled? We skip peaceful time with God's Word. The fact is God is doing "mighty deeds" for us every moment, but most are so quiet we'll miss them if we don't let His Word point them out. The Lord's "greatness" (145:3) is that He reconciled us sinners to Himself by dying for us—which lets us meditate on this: since God is reconciled to us, He is *always* working mightily for us. As we stress, wear ourselves out running and worrying, He is actually orchestrating every tiny action for us. Not ours to worry about. Ours to lie back and meditate on His Word—and so to rest in His care. "The LORD upholds all who are falling and raises up all who are bowed down" (145:14).

Can you sense the emotional and spiritual fatigue Paul is suffering as you read the **Epistle**, Romans 7:14–25a?

Paul, like all of us, *simul justus et peccator* ("simultaneously saint and sinner"), lives with a terrible burden: believer who truly wants to do God's will *and* old Adam who sins constantly. What frustration! The new man or woman inside us hates what the old sinful nature keeps doing. Years ago, I preached a sermon on this text I called "Tossing and Turning," imagining that I was lying awake at night, unable to fall asleep because I kept tossing back and forth between "the good I want" to do and the "evil . . . I keep on doing" (7:19). I picture Paul being very tired of this—probably really losing sleep.

One of the greatest delights of heaven will be being set free from the frustration of our own sin, "wretched man that I am!" (7:24). But already now, "Thanks be to God through Jesus Christ our Lord!" (7:25a). When the burden, the frustration, of our own sin keeps us awake, Jesus assures us that He has taken all those sins as far away as the east is from the west.

That's the rest Jesus gives us in the **Holy Gospel**, Matthew 11:25–30.

Yet one more source of fatigue, a big one: "Father, . . . You have hidden these things from the wise and understanding" (11:25). Jesus has just been working magnificent miracles in cities of Galilee, close to home, cities that should have known and welcomed Him. Instead, they rejected Him (11:20–24). They wouldn't stoop to think the local carpenter's son could teach them anything. Surely they were at least as wise and understanding as Him. They'd figure out the things of God for themselves, thank you very much!

That burden will break any of us! Leave it to me, an astrophysicist, to figure out the workings of the cosmos. Leave it to me, a social critic, to solve the world's injustices. Leave it to me, a regular guy, to figure out where I fit into the big picture and how God feels about me. Until I snap under the load of such responsibilities.

"Come to Me, all who labor and are heavy laden"—under the weight of having to be wise and understanding, fatigued by constant change, surviving by the sweat of our brows, under the burden of civic assaults and, much worse, of our own sins, and believing we have to climb our way to God. "Come to Me . . . and I will give you rest" (11:28).

"You will find rest for your souls. For My yoke is easy, and My burden is light" 11:29–30). Light because Jesus has already carried all our burdens to the cross, yoked Himself to our sins and taken them away, reconciled us to God so that He is doing all the hurrying, "worrying," for us.

So what makes you tired? Stop—right now—and think about that for a few minutes. Really take some time. Then meditate for a few minutes more on what it means that Jesus and His cross are, even now, carrying all those for you.

Christ Jesus Gives Us Rest by Carrying the Burdens That Make Us So Weary.

Look forward to Sunday morning resting in Christ by singing the **Hymn of the Day**, "I Heard the Voice of Jesus Say" (*LSB* 699).

The Sundays after Pentecost: Proper 10 (July 10–16) Year A

READINGS

Isaiah 55:10–13
Psalm 65:(1–8) 9–13 (antiphon: v 5)
Romans 8:12–17
Matthew 13:1–9, 18–23

HYMN OF THE DAY

LSB 577 "Almighty God, Your Word Is Cast"

Many of Jesus' best-known sayings are His parables. Up to one-third of our Lord's recorded teachings are in the form of parables; depending on one's definition, scholars count from thirty to seventy of them. Even two thousand years removed from their original settings, they deal in images we can recognize—farmers, weddings, family squabbles, good and bad investments, nobles, scoundrels—which makes them familiar and memorable. They always seem simple, but there always turns out to be more. So when we get to Matthew 13, a collection of seven parables about the kingdom of heaven, our ears perk up. Five of those parables we'll hear over the coming three Sundays, beginning today with the Parable of the Sower.

Pretend you're as new to Jesus' teachings as the crowd gathered on the lakeshore. Read just the first portion of Sunday's **Holy Gospel**, just Matthew 13:1–9.

What if you knew nothing else about Jesus? What would you guess He was talking about? I know, "To you it has [already!] been given to know the secrets of the kingdom of heaven, but to them it has not been given"—at this point, not even to the disciples (13:10–11). So pretend. All you've got is a man sowing seed that falls on four kinds of ground. The results for three out of four are bad. Hmm. Pretty lousy odds. A seed problem? A soil problem? A farmer problem? But some grows. And Jesus has invited you to think about it: "He who has ears, let him hear" (13:9).

Okay, when you come to church this Sunday, not only may you have heard this parable (and Jesus' explanation) many times before but the **Collect** will also be something of a spoiler. Fair enough. You've been alerted. Read on if you wish:

Blessed Lord, since You have caused all Holy Scriptures to be written for our learning, grant that we may so hear them, read, mark, learn, and inwardly digest them that we may embrace and ever hold fast the blessed hope of everlasting life; through Jesus Christ, Your Son, our Lord, who lives and reigns with You and the Holy Spirit, one God, now and forever. Amen.

This collect you might recognize not only as appointed for Proper 10 (and Proper 6, Year B) but also as the Collect for the Word often used in non-Communion services. Clearly its emphasis is the proper use of Holy Scripture. So there's the hint. Jesus' parable must have to do with God's Word.

Appreciate especially the phrase "that we may so hear [the Scriptures], read, mark, learn, and inwardly digest them." Nice rhythm, isn't it? We should hear the Word, be present when it's read and preached. Read it on our own too. But with more than a passive hearing or reading. We should mark it—not necessarily literally with a yellow highlighter, but noting mentally passages that have special relevance for us. And having done so, go back to those passages again and again to learn them, know them well, perhaps memorize them. Why? So that they become a part of us—inwardly digested—deep in our hearts to shape our thinking, speaking, and acting.

Using the Word like this is to God's purpose: "that we may embrace and ever hold fast the blessed hope of everlasting life." God gives every word of Scripture to bring us to know and firmly to cling to Jesus as our Savior for eternity.

Cat's out of the bag. Jesus' parable of the sower is about the working of His Word. But you knew that.

So, then, what's the **Introit** of the week got to do with this?

The Lord is merciful and gracious, slow to anger and abounding in steadfast love.

As for man, his days are like grass; he flourishes like a flower of the field; for the wind passes over it, and it is gone, and its place knows it no more. But the steadfast love of the Lord is from everlasting to everlasting on those who fear Him, and His righteousness to children's children, to those who keep His covenant and remember to do His commandments. The Lord has established His throne in the heavens, and His kingdom rules over all.

Glory be to the Father and to the Son and to the Holy Spirit; as it was in the beginning, is now, and will be forever. Amen.

The Lord is merciful and gracious, slow to anger and abounding in steadfast love. (Ps 103:15–19; antiphon: Ps 103:8)

There's the reference to keeping God's covenant and doing His commandments. That's the Word—and well worth noting. But it's a bit different from the parable's focus on the way the Word works.

Perhaps another hint, the **Verse**—unusual this week, because the Verse is most often drawn from the Gospel reading or at least from one of the other propers. This week it's not but is quite independently chosen to underscore Sunday's theme. Isaiah 40:8: "Alleluia. The grass withers, the flower fades, but the word of our God will stand forever. Alleluia."

So back to the Introit. See the connection? "As for man, his days are like grass; he flourishes like a flower of the field; for the wind passes over it, and it is gone, and its place knows it no more. But the steadfast love of the Lord is from everlasting to everlasting on those who fear Him." Things of men don't last; they fade like grass and flowers. What does last is the Word of our God—which forever delivers His love, for that is steadfast, everlasting too. Keep this in mind when we come back to Jesus' parable.

In the meantime, the **Old Testament Reading** pictures a sower as well. Read Isaiah 55:10–13.

Another good horticultural image for the Word of God. God's Word causes crops to grow, "giving seed to the sower and bread to the eater" (55:10). Three-fourths of the sower's seed in Jesus' parable seems to fall to no avail. But God's Word "*shall* accomplish that which I purpose, and *shall* succeed in the thing for which I sent it" (55:11). Remember the thorns in Jesus' parable? Here, "Instead of the thorn shall come up the cypress; instead of the brier shall come up the myrtle" (55:13).

You know by now that the hundred-, sixty-, or thirtyfold that some of the seed brings forth in Jesus' parable are those who hear the Word, believe, and are saved. But that's only one of four kinds of ground. How can Yahweh say through Isaiah that "My word . . . shall not return to Me empty"? (55:11). Doesn't seventy-five percent seem to do just that? God's purpose is that all believe His Word and be saved (1 Tim 2:4). But God's Word does always declare both the need for salvation (Law) and the certainty of salvation by Christ's cross and empty tomb (Gospel). It never fails to accomplish this—even among those who reject and are lost. Hence our Collect for the Word!

The **Psalm** for this Sunday provides yet another helpful insight to understanding the parable of the sower. Read Psalm 65.

Who makes the crop grow? "Praise is due to *You*, O God, in Zion. . . . *You* visit the earth and water it; *You* greatly enrich it; . . . *You* provide their grain, for so *You* have prepared it. *You* water its furrows abundantly, . . . blessing its growth. *You* crown the year with Your bounty" (65:1, 9–11). It's not the soil that produces a crop. Remember this, too, in a moment.

The **Epistle** has a precious lesson in itself, as Paul takes us through his progression of guilt and justification and faith and new life in Romans, but he also makes a valuable contribution to our overall theme for this Sunday. Read Romans 8:12–17.

Chapter 8 of Romans emphasizes particularly the working of the Holy Spirit. See what Paul says here: "By the Spirit you put to death the deeds of the body. . . . Led by the Spirit of God [you] are sons of God. . . . You did not receive the spirit of slavery to fall back into fear, but you have received the Spirit of adoption as sons, by whom we cry, 'Abba! Father!'" (8:13, 14, 15). The Holy Spirit has brought us to believe we are God's children, able to address Him affectionately ("Abba!" is like "Daddy!")—because of Jesus' death and resurrection.

But—and here's the connection to this week's other propers—*how* do we come to believe that? "The Spirit Himself bears witness with our spirit that we are children of God" (8:16). And the Spirit doesn't bear witness by whispering in our ear or appearing in dreams. He bears witness right here in the pages of Scripture—in Romans 8 and every other passage. The working of the Spirit is the working of the Word.

Which, of course, brings us back to Jesus' parable of the sower. Now read Jesus' explanation: Matthew 13:18–23.

We can probably all fill in examples of the four kinds of ground Jesus names. Those who hear but don't understand, from whom the devil snatches away the Word, may be those who, in the language of our Collect, never really "hear" or "read" the Word other than to let it bounce off the eardrums or pass under the eyes. Those represented by rocky ground receive the Word with joy but perhaps don't "mark" it so that they can return to it as their comfort and strength when the world attacks. And we need to "learn" the Word well, since we're all still vulnerable to the worry and temptations that come with materialism. No wonder the odds sound so poor—three crop failures out of four. But how sweet when the Word is "inwardly digested," really cherished as our own personal vocabulary. What a crop that bears!

So crucial to remember, though, what we harvested from the Introit and the Psalm. The best works of man are passing. That is, if we think Jesus is exhorting us to "become good soil," somehow to make ourselves proper hearers of the Word, the most we'll get from the parable is a resolution we'll try to keep—and soon enough abandon. As in our Psalm, it's Christ who brings the crop.

A most helpful insight with Jesus' parables of the kingdom is that they're all really about the One telling them. Jesus *is* the Kingdom. The one who "hears the word of the kingdom and does not understand" (13:19) is the person who doesn't understand that Jesus is God's kingdom come among us. Jesus takes concrete-hard paths and rocky soils and thorny ground, which every one of us is by nature, and somehow brings forth a hundredfold or sixty or thirty: us. The one who hears Jesus' parables and follows *Him* gets it! Understands. Because Jesus will do what it takes, the very thing it takes, to grow the crop. *He'll die for the crop.*

**Against All Odds,
the Seed Produces
an Abundant and Enduring Crop
Because
It Is the Word of the Kingdom.**

That is, the Word that proclaims Christ.

The **Hymn of the Day** is a delightful paraphrase of the Gospel lesson. Sing it, together as a family if you have opportunity.

The Sundays after Pentecost: Proper 11 (July 17–23) Year A

READINGS

Isaiah 44:6–8
Psalm 119:57–64
(antiphon: v 89)
Romans 8:18–27
Matthew 13:24–30, 36–43

HYMN OF THE DAY

LSB 772 "In Holy Conversation"

In one of the great sports movies of all time, *Hoosiers*, a veteran coach, played by Gene Hackman, takes over a high school basketball team in a small town in basketball-crazy 1950s Indiana. For the first few days of practice, he won't let his boys touch a basketball. In the early-season games, he won't let them shoot until they've made four passes—and they lose. Most of the town is screaming for his head. But all along, the old coach keeps insisting he knows what he's doing—he's coached championship teams at the college level—and eventually things start to click. You know how it ends: a last-second shot goes in, and the team from the little burg has beaten the big-city high school for the state title. Great film! If you haven't seen it, get it!

An eight-year-old wants an Oreo at five o'clock, but Mom knows dinner will be better if he waits. A fourteen-year-old is sure she can drive, but the state is probably right that she'll be safer at sixteen. You'd like to manage a project just three years out of school, but your boss believes you still need another couple of years of seasoning—in order for you to shine and your career to really take off.

"Lord, give me patience . . . and give it to me now!"

We're often shortsighted, especially in the things of God. We see only what we can see, and only over a very short horizon. God sees the invisible and the future, on into eternity—which means God's ways will often be different, and always wiser, than ours. Which also means we may become impatient with God and jump to conclusions He knows would be foolish. Like the veteran coach or Mom or the California DMV or the boss, He knows what's best for our and everyone's future. And *that* is what He—as God!—will do.

We do well to say with our **Gradual** for this portion of the Pentecost season:

Oh, the depth of the riches and wisdom and knowledge of God! How unsearchable are His judgments and how inscrutable His ways! For from Him and through Him and to Him are all things. To Him be glory forever. Amen. (Rom 11:33, 36)

Our other propers this week all develop this point, with the culmination being the second of Jesus' parables in Matthew 13, The Wheat and the Weeds (or Tares). As with all of Jesus' parables, it enlightens us above all to the One telling it, understanding how God's kingdom works in Christ Himself.

The **Introit** gets us started heading toward this THEME.

Give ear, O LORD, to my prayer; listen to my plea for grace.

Teach me Your way, O LORD, that I may walk in Your truth; unite my heart to fear Your name. I give thanks to You, O LORD my God, with my whole heart, and I will glorify Your name forever. For great is Your steadfast love toward me; You have delivered my soul from the depths of Sheol. O God, insolent men have risen up against me; a band of ruthless men seek my life, and they do not set You before them. But You, O LORD, are a God merciful and gracious, slow to anger and abounding in steadfast love and faithfulness.

Glory be to the Father and to the Son and to the Holy Spirit; as it was in the beginning, is now, and will be forever. Amen.

Give ear, O LORD, to my prayer; listen to my plea for grace. (Ps 86:11–15; antiphon: Ps 86:6)

Prayer will be a recurrent element in discussing God's patient big-picture view: "Give ear, O LORD, to my prayer." We always have much to pray about, including "thanks" for God's "great" and "steadfast love toward me." Especially, though, do we pray petitioning God for things we need, want, or think we need. Of course, our prayers should always be with the caveat "Thy will be done," for God may know better. Therefore, a very valuable prayer is "Teach me *Your* way, O LORD." Your way, O Lord, will always be best, and the believer in me really does want what You design to give—even if it's different or later than my limited view asks.

Particularly relevant for our theme and Jesus' parable of the weeds is the last verse of the psalmody: "You, O LORD, are a God merciful and gracious, slow to anger and abounding in steadfast love and faithfulness." We should all appreciate this deeply—God being gracious, slow to anger, with us. But when might we *resent* God's patient and unwavering love? Jesus' parable will make us think about that.

Speaking of prayer, the **Collect**:

> *O God, so rule and govern our hearts and minds by Your Holy Spirit that, ever mindful of Your final judgment, we may be stirred up to holiness of living here and dwell with You in perfect joy hereafter; through Jesus Christ, Your Son, our Lord, who lives and reigns with You and the Holy Spirit, one God, now and forever. Amen.*

God does "rule and govern our hearts and minds" because He rules and governs everything. He's God. And one thing He and He alone can govern is His "final judgment." He alone knows exactly when—and when best—that will be. This will be the destination of our Gospel lesson, Jesus' parable. In the meantime, since we don't know when God will judge all things, we may forget the "perfect joy hereafter" that awaits us, become impatient, and despair of living in "holiness" in the here and now.

The **Old Testament Reading** continues very much in the same vein: Isaiah 44:6–8.

God is God. "I am the first and I am the last; besides Me there is no god. . . . I know not any" (44:6b, 8f). Now, others—people, false, imaginary gods—may have ideas about how things ought to be done. But if so, "Let him declare and set it before Me. . . . Let them declare what is to come, and what will happen" (44:7). You want to run things? Then show us you know how they'll turn out. You don't! I do! "Have I not told you from of old and declared it?" (44:8b).

God does rule and govern all things, but this is crucial: "The Lord, the King of Israel" is also "his Redeemer" (44:6a). The One who runs everything—whether we always like it or not—runs everything according to His redeeming love, the love by which He sent His Son to buy us back from our sin. It's great news that the God who died for us is in total control. It couldn't be better than that!

Now read our **Psalm**: Psalm 119:57–64, including also verse 89 as the antiphon.

Again, we see the element of prayer ("I entreat Your favor with all my heart") and the request that God would be gracious to us, always do the best for us, in the way He operates His world: "Be gracious to me according to Your promise" (119:58).

Of course, the times we're most likely to take issue with God's management of affairs are when evil around us seems to get the better: "the cords of the wicked ensnare me" (119:61). This will be the conflict in Jesus' parable. We're living among tares, weeds! Why doesn't God get rid of them?

Without knowing the answer, the psalmist still has a response of faith. God's ways are ultimately always right (he praises God's "righteous rules," 119:62); God's love remains "steadfast" (119:64); and God's "word is firmly fixed in the heavens" (119:89). That last means God's promises are certain. All the gracious words God has written for us will come to pass, even when our view says He should be fired. And among those "fixed" words of God is His word that He has fixed that day of judgment. On that day, right will surely, finally, be served—to the never-ending benefit of God's holy people.

Two parts to Sunday's **Epistle**, Romans 8:18–27, both relevant to our theme:

First, Paul uses nature as a comforting illustration. All creation is "groaning" as in "pains of childbirth" to be set free from the curse of the fall (8:21–22; cf Gen 3:17–19). Floods, famine, earthquakes, wildfires—nature is entirely out of kilter. But God has subjected creation to futility (that is, it's going to end) "*in hope*" (8:20). God will call an end to this universe so that He can replace it with a *perfect* new heavens and earth. So much the more for us. Since sin has ruined our lives, God won't force us to live this way forever. He's fixed a day when our bodies will be raised in perfection. We see only death and natural disasters. God sees the bigger picture: "glory that is to be revealed to us," which infinitely exceeds "the sufferings of this present time" (8:18). Hard as it is for us, then, "we wait for it with patience" (8:25).

Then prayer. God invites us to pray, but, with our limited point of view, "we do not know what to pray for." So, "the Spirit Himself intercedes for us with groanings too deep for words" (8:26). God knows best; He sees from the eternal perspective. So God the Holy Spirit corrects our prayers to be truly "according to the will of God" (8:27).

Finally, to the parable, the **Holy Gospel**, Matthew 13:24–30, 36–43.

It seems as if Jesus explains every detail, but, in fact, He equips us to ponder the real significance of the parable. Remember that the parables above all else reveal the identity of the teller. "The kingdom of heaven" (13:24) is Christ, come in the flesh. To understand the parable is to grasp that this man sitting in the boat before us is the Messiah, the Savior sent from God.

A proper interpretation, then, must go beyond the obvious, that there will be a judgment someday—though that's true enough (13:41–43). It must consider how the judgment is a consummation of Jesus' ministry.

The key verses are 28–30. Upon seeing the weeds, the servants ask, "Do you want us to go and gather them?" This would be our prayer. We believers, as wheat, suffer much from living among unbelievers, weeds. How often we ask God to uproot them right now! But the master says, "No, lest in gathering the weeds you root up the wheat along with them. Let both grow together until the harvest." Our prayer is shortsighted. We feel pain; we see enemies. God, slow to anger, sees unbelieving yet precious souls for whom Jesus died—*just like we all were!* And God knows that among them are men and women, boys and girls, who by His gracious patience will become wheat, someday to be gathered into the barn and delivered from the fire.

There will be a righteous judgment. Unbelief will finally be punished for eternity. But not until God's righteous judgment receives into eternal glory every soul that Christ's Gospel will win. Christ Jesus by His cross has redeemed the whole world, and God wants no one to miss out on that.

Thank God He's God,
Because While Even Our Prayers
Are Often Shortsighted,
He in Christ
Is Patiently, Graciously
Moving All Things
to a Righteous Judgment.

"So let us pray securely"! (**Hymn of the Day**, "In Holy Conversation," *LSB* 772:3).

The Sundays after Pentecost: Proper 12 (July 24–30) Year A

READINGS

Deuteronomy 7:6–9
Psalm 125 (antiphon: v 2)
Romans 8:28–39
Matthew 13:44–52

HYMN OF THE DAY

LSB 713 "From God Can Nothing Move Me"

Ask many a biblical scholar, and he'll tell you: the parables of Jesus are among the trickiest of passages to interpret properly. Ask many a scholar, pastor, or faithful Christian, and he or she will tell you: few doctrines are more confusing, confused, and potentially troublesome than predestination. Proper 12, Year A, gives us both.

Truth be understood, both the parables of Jesus, including the three in our Gospel reading this week, and the doctrine of predestination, mentioned by Paul in our Epistle lesson, offer magnificent comfort in Christ Jesus. So, with nothing to fear, let's take on that mammoth, double task.

To do this, we'll reverse our usual order, looking at those two most challenging propers first, beginning with the **Holy Gospel**, Matthew 13:44–52.

The Parable of the Treasure, the Parable of the Pearl of Great Value, and the Parable of the Dragnet are the final three of seven Jesus speaks in Matthew 13—and the last of three consecutive Gospel lessons from the chapter. Not a bad time, then, for a little instruction in principles for interpreting parables.

There are, in common use, two general approaches to interpreting what we call parables. The first approach is to treat the parable as an "allegory." That means we would look at each detail in the story and try to figure out what that detail corresponds to in real life. If, for example, there's a treasure hidden in a field in the story, what real-life thing does that treasure represent? The man who finds the treasure, whom does he represent? In an allegorical interpretation, we'd ask that for *every detail* in the story.

The other common approach is to interpret the story by looking only for a *single point of comparison*. (In Latin, it's called the *tertium comparationis*.) That is, we won't interpret every detail but only consider the one big point to which all the details "add up." (Not to be any more confusing, but this approach is referred to as interpreting the parable *as* a "parable," *not as an allegory*.)

Our best guess is that *some* of what we call the parables of Jesus should be interpreted allegorically, while *others* should be interpreted only according to the single point of comparison. And yes, that's tricky. But now an example from our text:

The allegorical approach always carries some risk, because one is interpreting so many details, lots of moving parts. And the results can be bad. Try this: "The kingdom of heaven is like treasure hidden in a field" (13:44a). What does the treasure represent? Perhaps heaven—after all, heaven *is* a wonderful treasure! "Which a man found and covered up." Who's the man? Would that be each of us? Let's try that. Then what would the finding represent? Years ago, a popular bumper sticker read, "I Found It!"—to which we Lutherans responded, "He Found Me!" Do *we* find heaven? Hmm. And what about covering up the treasure? Do we try to keep our salvation a secret? That's a problem. Finally, "Then in his joy he goes and sells all that he has and buys that field" (13:44b). So now we're buying our way to heaven? With what? All the good works we can sell?

We know that can't be right! How do we know it's wrong? Another important principle in interpreting parables is that we never use them to be the basis of a doctrine, but instead, we always use the clearer passages of Scripture to interpret the less-clear passages. Parables are always more difficult passages, and we've got countless clear passages that say God in Christ Jesus does all the work of saving us. We don't find heaven! We don't buy heaven!—with our works or anything else! We also don't keep the good news of salvation a secret. Passages throughout the Bible that are clearer than the parables leave no doubt that this can't be a proper interpretation of the parable of the treasure.

However, the allegorical approach can give wonderful, faithful interpretations. Let's try again. "The kingdom of heaven is like treasure hidden in a field, which a man found." What if the man isn't you and me? Who else could he be? The Sunday School (and very proper!) answer: Jesus! And what does Jesus consider a priceless treasure? Each one of us! So now, Jesus finds us, covers us up by protecting us from anything that would snatch us away, and then what? He "sells all that he has and buys that field"—buys us for eternal salvation at the price of His own life. Jesus surely did give up all that He had, even to death on the cross—as every clear word of Scripture testifies. Simple. Clear. Done.

Except that there's that other approach—to interpret the parable *as* a parable, that is, according to a single point of comparison. Many Lutherans have preferred this approach because of its simplicity—fewer "moving parts," perhaps less subjectivity. Look back at the whole parable (13:44). And remember from our discussions for the last two Sundays that all of Jesus' parables above all point to the teller. Jesus is the kingdom of heaven, come in the flesh. Now, isn't it true that the kingdom, Jesus, is so precious that having Him is worth everything, even if it means giving up everything else? Certainly. That is the single point of comparison, and, according to this approach, that's all Jesus is intending to convey in this specific passage. He doesn't mean for us to worry about the particular details of the covering or the selling or the buying. We surely know from other passages of Scripture that Jesus does it all to give us the kingdom and that we do nothing, but, according to this approach, Jesus isn't intending to make those points here.

So which is the correct interpretation? "Oh, the depth of the riches and wisdom and knowledge of God!" (from the **Gradual**, Rom 11:33). "Alleluia. I will open My mouth in parables; I will utter what has been hidden since the foundation of the world. Alleluia" (the **Verse**, Mt 13:35b). Jesus' parables are deep indeed, deep enough, we think, to tickle us into considering both the second and third interpretations we've offered. Both are entirely consistent with the clearer, non-parable, passages of God's Word. And both declare Christ—so precious, worth everything; so loving, giving up everything to have us. Alleluia, indeed!

Many preachers interpret the subsequent parable of the pearl (13:45–46) to be exactly parallel to this one. That may well be so, though the slight twist, making the kingdom of heaven "like a merchant" rather than like "the treasure" (or, we would have expected, the pearl), could possibly mean the parable of the treasure is to be interpreted in the third way we've shown above, and the parable of the pearl is to be understood in the second way, with Jesus as the merchant. Intriguing.

Lastly, the parable of the dragnet (13:47–50) repeats part (but only part) of the message of last week's parable of the wheat and the weeds (13:24–30, 36–43). There will be a final separation of the faithful from the evil, which, too, is comforting for believers.

The **Epistle**, Romans 8:28–39, won't solve every mystery of predestination but does put it in the proper, comforting context.

False doctrines of predestination can be terrifying: double predestination, taught by John Calvin, says that from eternity, God in His sovereignty predestined some people to heaven and all the rest to hell. However, the two clearest texts on the subject, our Epistle and Ephesians 1:3–14, emphasize that predestination is only a matter of God's grace; they speak only of a single predestination to heaven. See what Paul says here: from the foundation of the world, God knew He would predestine those "to be conformed to the image of His Son" (8:29). These He *also* called, *also* justified, *also* glorified (8:30). Also, also, also. Predestination is just one of all these steps God takes to assure that we will one day be glorified. Like the man in Jesus' parable of the buried treasure, God leaves no stone unturned to bring us to heaven.

Paul goes on. In order to bring us to heaven, God, as in Jesus' parables, spares no expense: He "did not spare His own Son," but gave Him up to die (8:32, 34). And then He goes to every length to see that nothing "will be able to separate us from the love of God in Christ Jesus our Lord" (8:39). Look at the list (8:35–39). Shall this, or, or, or? No. Not this, nor, nor, nor is able to separate us from God. These words of absolute certainty are the very power by which even at this reading God is calling you to eternal salvation. How can we, from such a context, ever doubt that He has *also* predestined you?!!

See briefly how all of this is borne out by the other propers. The **Introit**:

> *Oh give thanks to the Lord; call upon His name; make known His deeds among the peoples!*
>
> *Sing to Him, sing praises to Him; tell of all His wondrous works! Glory in His holy name; let the hearts of those who seek the Lord rejoice! Seek the Lord and His strength; seek His presence continually! Remember the wondrous works that He has done, His miracles, and the judgments He uttered, O offspring of Abraham, His servant, children of Jacob, His chosen ones!*
>
> *Glory be to the Father and to the Son and to the Holy Spirit; as it was in the beginning, is now, and will be forever. Amen.*
>
> *Oh give thanks to the Lord; call upon His name; make known His deeds among the peoples! (Ps 105:2–6; antiphon: Ps 105:1)*

We "seek the Lord" because, as Jesus taught, having Him is of infinitely greater value than anything else. And we are "His chosen ones," predestined, called, justified, to be glorified.

The **Collect**:

> *Almighty and everlasting God, give us an increase of faith, hope, and love, that, receiving what You have promised, we may love what You have commanded; through Jesus Christ, Your Son, our Lord, who lives and reigns with You and the Holy Spirit, one God, now and forever. Amen.*

In any faithful interpretation of the parables, God acts first; we only receive what He has promised. But then we also treasure Him, so that we love what He has commanded.

The **Old Testament Reading**, Deuteronomy 7:6–9, could have been on Jesus' mind as He described the treasure, for Israel is called "His treasured possession, out of all the peoples" (7:6). As Paul later wrote, nothing could change God's "steadfast love" toward them (7:9). Likewise, while the "upright" and "evildoers" will finally be separated (the **Psalm**, 125:4–5), nothing can separate us from God's love in Christ, just as Mount Zion "cannot be moved" (125:1).

And so our Theme:

**Since the Foundation of the World,
God Has Spared No Expense,
Left No Stone Unturned,
Seeking and Buying Us
as His Treasured Possession
So That We Will Someday
Be Separated from Evil,
but Nothing Can Separate Us
from His Love in Christ Jesus.**

The **Hymn of the Day** paraphrases our Epistle, but notice also stanza 3, the treasure.

The Sundays after Pentecost: Proper 13 (July 31–August 6) Year A

READINGS

Isaiah 55:1–5
Psalm 136:1–9 (23–26) (antiphon: v 26)
Romans 9:1–5 (6–13)
Matthew 14:13–21

HYMN OF THE DAY

LSB 642 "O Living Bread from Heaven"

After three weeks of Gospel readings that gave us parables of Jesus—in which we're always asked to look beyond the immediate, tangible details of the story to discern heavenly or spiritual things—this week the Gospel takes us to something about as immediate and tangible as you can get: hunger and food, Jesus feeding the five thousand. Five thousand men plus women and children needed to eat, and Jesus gave them real, honest-to-goodness, edible, digestible, nourishing food.

At the same time, the **Verse** for Sunday says, "Man ate of the bread of the angels; He sent them food in abundance" (Ps 78:25). Psalm 78 is recounting Israel's wandering in the wilderness, when God gave them "food in abundance," manna that physically, healthfully kept the people alive for forty years. Real food. But by calling it also "the bread of the angels," the psalmist is surely suggesting that there was something heavenly going on too.

That's the way our propers this week play out. *Both* the physical and the spiritual are essential!—both to us and to God. Let's look at each of the propers and see how

The Lord Provides Real Earthly Food as an Expression of the Heavenly Covenant in Christ.

The **Introit** again refers to God's provision for Israel during its wilderness wandering:

> *Oh give thanks to the Lord; call upon His name; make known His deeds among the peoples!*
>
> *He spread a cloud for a covering, and fire to give light by night. They*

asked, and He brought quail, and gave them bread from heaven in abundance. He opened the rock, and water gushed out; it flowed through the desert like a river. For He remembered His holy promise, and Abraham, His servant. So He brought His people out with joy, His chosen ones with singing.

Glory be to the Father and to the Son and to the Holy Spirit; as it was in the beginning, is now, and will be forever. Amen.

Oh give thanks to the LORD; call upon His name; make known His deeds among the peoples! (Ps 105: 39–43; antiphon: Ps 105:1)

You recognize the pillar of cloud and the pillar of fire by which, by day and by night, God led His people through the desert (Ex 13:21–22). Then there was water from a rock (Ex 17:6) and food—quail and manna (Ex 16:1–36). Just as real as our eggs and toast in the morning, a salad with grilled chicken and vinaigrette dressing on the side at lunch, and spaghetti with meat sauce at dinner.

Notice, too, *why* God fed and cared for Israel: "For He remembered His holy promise, and Abraham, His servant." Abraham had been dead almost six centuries by the time of the Israelites' wanderings, but God's care for them was an extension of His covenant made with Abraham so long before. That covenant was to build of Abraham a great nation *and* to bless *all* nations through him (Gen 12:1–3). That last part of the promise was directly pointing to the Messiah, the only one in whom all people can be blessed. So feeding Israel, keeping this nation alive with real protein, carbs, and calories, was carrying out the promise to send Jesus, the eternal Savior of the world.

The **Collect** for this Sunday also makes explicit the connection between God's physical and spiritual blessings:

Heavenly Father, though we do not deserve Your goodness, still You provide for all our needs of body and soul. Grant us Your Holy Spirit that we may acknowledge Your gifts, give thanks for all Your benefits, and serve You in willing obedience; through Jesus Christ, Your Son, our Lord, who lives and reigns with You and the Holy Spirit, one God, now and forever. Amen.

God provides "*all* our needs"—of both "body and soul." The bodies that God created and which He will raise on the Last Day He values just as highly as He does the souls—and He provides for them just as certainly.

So then we pray that the Holy Spirit would enable us to receive all God's gifts faithfully—to "acknowledge Your gifts, give thanks for all Your benefits, and serve You in willing obedience." First, acknowledge God's blessings—simply realize that every good gift is from the Lord. Being as richly blessed as we are—and as easily as these blessings seem to come—we're prone to take them for granted. We can't buy the whole grocery store, but we can opt for a few selections on just about every aisle. And if we're too tired to cook (possibly because we've been so busy making money all day), we can often pick up what someone else has cooked for us. Easy to forget it's from God as surely as is manna on the ground in the morning. Second, may the Holy Spirit move us to thankfulness—rather than grumbling that manna and quail and ground beef aren't prime rib. Third, our prayer is that we serve God the Giver willingly and joyfully, especially by serving His children who have fewer of these blessings than we do. We who have been granted eternal riches have plenty to share in the meantime!

It is primarily heavenly blessings that Isaiah is illustrating as food and drink in our **Old Testament Reading**: Isaiah 55:1–5.

Everyone understands how much she or he needs bread and water—and how much we appreciate milk, wine, and "rich food" (55:2). The spiritual illustration works because the physical referents are so important to us all. The heavenly blessings are to be pictured as the very things we want the most. And God gives the heavenly blessings the way we'd all love to receive the earthly ones—of highest quality, in unlimited supply, and absolutely free. (By the way, Isaiah elsewhere gives perhaps as savory a sampling of the heavenly banquet as we find anywhere in Scripture, 25:6).

As with our Introit, too, Isaiah explains the basis for God's rich provision: "an everlasting covenant, My steadfast, sure love for David" (55:3). God's physical feeding of Israel in the desert was an action of His covenant with Abraham. Now, by Isaiah's day (seven centuries after Israel's arrival in the Promised Land), the same covenant is "updated," identified with David, the nation's greatest king. So once more, food is an expression of the covenant. And we undoubtedly remember that David is the ancestor by whom the Messiah would be named: "the Son of David."

The **Psalm** seats us right down at the banquet (or at least the dinner) table: Psalm 136:1–9, 23–26.

Verse 1 is likely best known among us by the King James Version: "O give thanks unto the Lord; for He is good: for His mercy endureth for ever." Not only do countless families return thanks after meals with these words, but the psalm is appointed also for Thanksgiving Day, our national banquet. The manifestations of God's goodness for which we give thanks (including in the intervening verses, 136:10–22) are, this time, virtually all physical, beginning with the creation of the universe (136:4–9) and climaxing with, again, food (136:25).

And yet again, the reason for every blessing points us beyond just time and space: quite emphatically(!), they're because "His steadfast love endures forever." It's the covenant again. God has committed Himself to us, and nothing will move Him from that.

That last point is driven home in the **Epistle**. Read Romans 9:1–13.

Paul almost weeps on the papyrus as he reflects on so many of his brother Israelites being eternally lost (9:2–3). Did God abandon them? fail them? Did His steadfast love grow cold after all? Not at all! The fact is, God's covenant with Israel was never based on biological descendancy (9:6–8). God's covenant was that He would save all people, whatever their ancestry, through faith in Christ Jesus. Every Israelite who believed in the coming or the arrived Messiah is saved. Every Gentile who believes in the Messiah is saved. Both of these are the *true* Israelites. Old Testament Israel's honored role in the covenant was simply to bear that promise (9:4–5). The covenant was carried out by earthly means, a nation of people eventually producing one Special Heir, but it has always, in fact, been heavenly.

Both matter—the earthly and the heavenly. In the **Holy Gospel**, finally then, earthly food is an expression of what the King from heaven will accomplish: Matthew 14:13–21.

"When Jesus heard this" (14:13) refers to the preceding verses, the death of Jesus' dear relative and friend, John the Baptist. Jesus would truly love some quiet time alone for prayer, down time for the very human (and divine) emotion of grief. But as always, He has compassion on and *makes time* for the crowds. Notice that He "healed their sick" (14:14)—physical healing, addressing earthly human needs.

Then the miraculous feeding. It's John who tells us about the boy with the bread and fish (Jn 6:9); Matthew only lets us know how little is available. It's enough. Jesus looking up to heaven and blessing the pittance (14:19) reminds the crowd of what we pray in our Collect (that we may acknowledge, thank, and serve the Giver). And as per usual, Jesus' gift is huge; all five thousand men plus women and children have not a snack or a mouthful but a feast, with each disciple collecting a basket full for tomorrow. Real physical sustenance.

We badly sell short the steadfast love of the Lord if ever we skip ahead to the heavenly and short-shrift the earthly—this or any example in Scripture of God providing what we need for this life (healing miracles, stilled storms, food in the desert). In fact, we miss the point!

The point—always!—is the cross of Jesus Christ. And the cross of Christ is the only source of *every* blessing! Forgiveness. Life in heaven. Bread and fish. Why? Because what Jesus did when He died on the cross is take away the sin that separated us from God. If our sin still stood between us and God, we'd be lost to hell, of course, but we'd also be cut off from every good gift (James 1:17). We'd get no manna or quail or ground beef or prime rib. No eggs or salad or spaghetti. No sunshine, no rain, no friends, no life on God's good earth *or* in His heaven. But we do. We get so much that we might forget—even as we're picking up twelve baskets left over.

You see? When we read about a dinner or eat one, God is preaching to us the death of His Son, Jesus, on the cross. Just one of the blessings of the cross—but it *is* a blessing of the cross. The cross and then dinner are fulfillment of God's heavenly covenant with us. And because of that covenant fulfilled in Jesus' cross, we know God is always with us, reconciled, to give us the very best—earthly, heavenly, now, forever.

Very appropriately, the **Hymn of the Day** is a Lord's Supper hymn, "O Living Bread from Heaven" (*LSB* 642). That Supper is a heavenly blessing right here on earth.

The Sundays after Pentecost: Proper 14 (August 7–13) Year A

READINGS

Job 38:4–18
Psalm 18:1–6 (7–16)
(antiphon: v 46)
Romans 10:5–17
Matthew 14:22–33

HYMN OF THE DAY

LSB 717 "Eternal Father, Strong to Save"

First, a little lesson in Greek. (Those of you who've been down this road already can just daydream for a minute—back to your first summer or fall at the seminary, or wherever and whenever you took yours. We'll invite you back in just a minute.) Something simple: a form of the verb "to be." It looks like this: εἰμι—or, in our alphabet, like this: *eimi*. It's pronounced like *I me*. Yep, like I'm talking about myself, "I" and "me." Say that: εἰμι (*I me*). That's actually convenient, because this is the first-person singular of "to be"—in others words, "I am." That's right—εἰμι means "I am." Got that? εἰμι means "I am." Notice, in Greek, for forms of the verb "to be," you can just give the verb ("am") and you don't actually have to say the pronoun. Everybody knows automatically that you mean "I am."

Then again, when you do say the pronoun with the form of "to be," it's emphatic; it's making a big deal: "*I* am!" Yeah, not just anybody, but "*I* am the one we're talking about!" In Greek, the word for "I" looks like this: ἐγώ (or, again, in roman letters, like this: *ego*). It's pronounced like "egg oh!" (Yes, like the toaster waffles.)

Put 'em together, and here's what you've got: ἐγώ εἰμι is an emphatic Greek statement that says, "I am!" It could also be translated "It is I." (Notice, still a form of the verb "to be" with "I.") Don't forget that. But for now, we're getting ahead of ourselves.

Okay, we're all back together now. Our Gospel lesson for this Sunday is the very famous story of Jesus walking on the Sea of Galilee—so famous, in fact, that people who don't know much about the Bible at all still know the expression "he can [or, probably can't] walk on water."

It's an amazing moment in history in its own right, of course, but anything so familiar we might still take for granted. Unless we know a little Greek!

We'll get there.

The **Introit** for this week:

> *I will bless the* Lord *at all times; His praise shall continually be in my mouth.*
>
> *I sought the* Lord*, and He answered me and delivered me from all my fears. Those who look to Him are radiant, and their faces shall never be ashamed. This poor man cried, and the* Lord *heard him and saved him out of all his troubles. The angel of the* Lord *encamps around those who fear Him, and delivers them. Oh, taste and see that the* Lord *is good! Blessèd is the man who takes refuge in Him!*
>
> *Glory be to the Father and to the Son and to the Holy Spirit; as it was in the beginning, is now, and will be forever. Amen.*
>
> *I will bless the* Lord *at all times; His praise shall continually be in my mouth. (Ps 34:4–8; antiphon: Ps 34:1)*

The most obvious connection between these words of the psalmist and the story of Jesus walking on water is the line "This poor man cried, and the Lord heard him and saved him out of all his troubles." Remember, Peter is going to get out of the boat and walk on the water too—until he panics and cries out, "Lord, save me!" Jesus will.

But here's something else to notice in the Introit: six times David uses the special covenant name for this God who answers his cries and delivers him: in English, "Lord," rendering the Hebrew *Yahweh*. Recall this one? Yahweh, Lord, is based on the Hebrew verb "to be." It was God's way of assuring His fearful people, like Moses (Ex 3:13–15), that I am always present, with you, wherever, whenever, in a personal, intimate relationship. Just a little Hebrew too.

The **Collect** for this Sunday is certainly appropriate with our Gospel reading:

> *Almighty and most merciful God, preserve us from all harm and danger that we, being ready in both body and soul, may cheerfully accomplish what You want done; through Jesus Christ, Your Son, our Lord, who lives and reigns with You and the Holy Spirit, one God, now and forever. Amen.*

The disciples were terrified that night out on the sea; they sensed imminent "harm and danger." But Jesus had big plans for them; they would soon "accomplish" great things that He wanted done. So He has in mind for us. Every day of life and safety He gives us He has good works prepared beforehand for us to do (Eph 2:10).

This week we also introduce a new **Gradual**, which will be used for each of the next seven Sundays. Whether in perils on the sea or anywhere else in life, it offers comfort:

> *Fear the Lord, you His saints, for those who fear Him lack nothing! Many are the afflictions of the righteous, but the Lord delivers him out of them all. (Ps 34:9, 19, alt)*

Again, the covenant name of God: Yahweh, the Lord. He Is the one who delivers.

The **Old Testament Reading** begins to introduce this week's seafaring imagery explicitly. It also develops the underlying message of the week. Read Job 38:4–18 (and notice from 38:1 that it is Yahweh, I am, speaking).

Job 38 is the beginning of the resolution to this very intriguing book. The Lord has permitted Satan to oppress Job; he's lost everything (Job 1–2). Then the bulk of the book (chapters 3–37) has been the dialogue between Job and his well-intentioned but theologically misguided friends trying to explain why God has allowed all this to happen. Job himself eventually cries out in protest against the way the Lord has been running things, until, finally, Yahweh appears in a storm cloud and puts an end to the foolishness.

The Lord's rhetoric is brilliant! Job, what do you really know? Did you create the world, design the landscape—dry land here, water there ("shut in the sea with doors . . . limits for it . . . and [say], 'Thus far shall you come, and no farther, and here shall your proud waves be stayed,'" 38:8, 10, 11)? Do you tell the day when to begin each morning? "Have you entered into the springs of the sea, or *walked in the recesses of the deep*?" (38:16). "Well," Yahweh says in effect, "I have!"

The message of the entire book, then, is that Job can cease worrying and speculating about things he can't understand; Yahweh, the Lord, is always graciously operating the entire enterprise to care for you in ways better than you can imagine. Your crying out to Him can be prayers for help, not complaints. He hears. He knows.

David, in our **Psalm** for the week, was able to look back and see how powerfully and graciously the Lord had heard and answered his calls for help: Psalm 18:1–16 and verse 46 as the antiphon. Note the superscription; for many years before becoming king, David had been pursued with murderous intent by King Saul, who feared that David would steal his throne. "In my distress I called upon the Lord; to my God I cried for help. . . . He heard my voice, and my cry to Him reached His ears" (18:6). We don't ever hear of David in danger of drowning, but he does illustrate his straits using images of water: "The torrents of destruction assailed me. . . . The channels of the sea were seen. . . . [The Lord] drew me out of many waters" (18:4, 15, 16).

David knew his deliverance was because "the Lord [Yahweh, I am] lives" (18:46). Or perhaps, to paraphrase, "I am is." If it sounds redundant, well, it, too, is emphatic. At no time, in no situation, is I am not there for David, for us. I am always Is. And since this is God's covenant name, the name He offered to "insiders only," He is always there *for us*. That's because He made us His people, insiders, if you will, by reconciling us and the whole world to Himself by the cross of David's Greater Son and then bringing us into His covenant by Baptism into Jesus' death. The almighty, all-present power of I AM Is delivers us because He also died.

The **Epistle** advances Paul's continuing discourse in Romans, now describing how one receives the gift of justification—that is, by faith which confesses Christ, created by hearing the word preached. Read Romans 10:5–17.

For this Sunday's THEME, two passages stand out. The confession "Jesus is Lord" (10:9) was an early Christian creed declaring that Jesus of Nazareth was none other than the same Lord believed upon by God's Old Testament people: Yahweh, I AM. Therefore, "everyone who calls on the name of the Lord will be saved" (10:13). That, as we've seen, will be critical to Peter very soon.

Time to read about Jesus walking on water: Matthew 14:22–33, the **Holy Gospel**.

Jesus has just fed the five thousand. At evening, He sends the disciples on ahead by water while He goes off alone to pray. But a voyage that should have been at most four miles (just skirting the north shore of the Sea of Galilee) was literally taking the disciples all night as the wind pushed them away from their nearby destination. Unlike another familiar sailors' story (Mt 8:23–27), the disciples this time feel no fear of drowning. Their terror is when in the witching hour of the night ("the fourth watch," 3:00–6:00 a.m.) they see a ghost! They think.

The real terror was the thought that "it"—*whatever* "it" might be—was anything or anyone other than Jesus. Whether one realizes or not, when the object of a person's focus is other than Christ, he or she should be afraid, very afraid.

But then Jesus' wonderful reply: "Take heart; it is I. Do not be afraid" (14:27). As comforting as that sounds, it's sweeter yet in Matthew's original. Time to use our Greek. Jesus says, "Take heart; ἐγώ εἰμι." Remember? "Take heart"; literally, "I am." Take heart! The one who's coming to you—quite remarkably this time!—is I AM, Yahweh. The God who brought you into His covenant, who made you His. The God who always Is—present for you, powerful for you. For you. Because soon enough I AM going to die for you. If IT IS I, you have nothing to fear. Ever. Whatever the circumstance. On the Sea of Galilee or on the freeway, in the hospital or in the sweatbox pressure cooker of a high-stress job or a high school class.

So then when Peter panics, his cry is spot-on: "Lord, save me" (14:30). Yahweh, I AM, Lord, I'm desperate! I'm dying here! You're the one who can save me! And He does. Always. Everywhere. However He knows best.

And the disciples get this: "Truly You are the Son of God" (14:33). You are I AM. A nice ring to it.

Who is that out there coming to us when things look dark and frightening? "It is I!" we hear the answer. Which really means I AM, ἐγώ εἰμι. And

**SINCE ἐγώ εἰμι ("IT IS I"),
OUR CRIES FOR HELP
ARE SURELY HEARD!**

Sing the **Hymn of the Day**, "Eternal Father, Strong to Save" (*LSB* 717), perhaps using the alternate (original) stanzas 2 and 3 from the United States Navy Hymn.

The Sundays after Pentecost: Proper 15 (August 14–20) Year A

READINGS

Isaiah 56:1, 6–8
Psalm 67 (antiphon: v 5)
Romans 11:1–2a, 13–15, 28–32
Matthew 15:21–28

HYMNS OF THE DAY

LSB 615 "When in the Hour of Deepest Need"
LSB 653 "In Christ There Is No East or West"

How does this grab you? "Jesus went away from there and withdrew to the district of Tyre and Sidon. And behold, a Canaanite woman from that region came out and was crying, 'Have mercy on me, O Lord, Son of David; my daughter is severely oppressed by a demon.' But He did not answer her a word" (Mt 15:21–23a). Why not, Lord? "I was sent only to the lost sheep of the house of Israel. . . . It is not right to take the children's bread and throw it to the dogs" (15:24, 26). Is that our Jesus?

You know it's going to get better, and indeed our Gospel reading will come to a magnificent conclusion of God's mercy and Jesus' love, along with a memorable example of faith by this woman, a foreigner. But, initially, it certainly does sound insensitive on Jesus' part, doesn't it! Turns out, the Teacher knows how to teach; this story and all the propers this week are highly instructive in *the way* God showers His lavish mercy on all people.

Picture what you already know about Jesus' encounter with the Canaanite woman as you read the **Introit**:

> *The Lord is the strength of His people; He is the saving refuge of His anointed.*
>
> *To You, O Lord, I call; my rock, be not deaf to me, lest, if You be silent to me, I become like those who go down to the pit. Hear the voice of my pleas for mercy, when I cry to You for help, when I lift up my hands toward Your most holy sanctuary. Blessèd be the Lord! For He has heard the voice of*

my pleas for mercy. The LORD *is my strength and my shield; in Him my heart trusts, and I am helped; my heart exults, and with my song I give thanks to Him.*

Glory be to the Father and to the Son and to the Holy Spirit; as it was in the beginning, is now, and will be forever. Amen.

The LORD *is the strength of His people; He is the saving refuge of his anointed. (Ps 28:1–2, 6–7; antiphon: Ps 28:8)*

David, the psalmist, a thousand years before the fact, almost seems to have written an inspired commentary on our Gospel lesson. His own descendant Son is surely the "strength," the "saving refuge," to whom any desperate mother (or father or child) should come. "Hear the voice of my pleas for mercy, when I cry to You for help," you can almost hear this Canaanite woman begging. Not a word, Lord? "Be not deaf to me, lest, if You be silent to me, I become like those who go down to the pit." And then the key: hear my pleas for mercy, "*when I lift up my hands toward Your most holy sanctuary.*" That is, when I cry to You where You promise to be found. In David's day that was still the tabernacle that centuries earlier had moved about through the wilderness. After his son Solomon's labors, it would be the temple. When Jesus arrived, He was the sanctuary to which the woman lifted up hands. And now for us? Back to that in a minute. She is seeking God's help the way God Himself designs to give it. And we can already guess how the Canaanite woman's story will resolve: "He *has heard* the voice of my pleas for mercy. The LORD is my strength and my shield; in Him my heart trusts, and I *am* helped."

The **Collect** for this Sunday now makes explicit something crucial that the Canaanite woman and David in the Introit understood:

Almighty and everlasting Father, You give Your children many blessings even though we are undeserving. In every trial and temptation grant us steadfast confidence in Your loving-kindness and mercy; through Jesus Christ, Your Son, our Lord, who lives and reigns with You and the Holy Spirit, one God, now and forever. Amen.

The woman and David both plead for "mercy." Mercy always implies that the recipient is undeserving. That certainly is our situation. And so we plead to God, "Give Your children many blessings even though we are undeserving." Recognizing that we are undeserving will always be crucial if we are to seek God's help the way He promises to give it.

Meanwhile, "every trial and temptation" should be a reminder of just how undeserving we are. And yet we can have "steadfast confidence" in God's "loving-kindness"—precisely because what we beg is indeed "mercy." It would take that kind of confidence for the Canaanite woman to remain persistent when Jesus seemed deaf toward her cry.

Finally, this is one case when we should especially appreciate those words we might overlook at the close of every collect: "through Jesus Christ." It really can never go without saying that, since we are undeserving, we only receive our Father's "many blessings" because Jesus by His death on the cross has reconciled us to God.

Two interesting ironies to note in the **Gradual** for this part of the Pentecost season:

> *Fear the Lord, you His saints, for those who fear Him lack nothing! Many are the afflictions of the righteous, but the Lord delivers him out of them all. (Ps 34:9, 19, alt)*

First, we all know from experience that God's people suffer many "afflictions." Yet we nevertheless "lack nothing!" God knows that, somehow, afflictions (perhaps even with Him seemingly insensitive to our prayers) followed by His deliverance truly is everything good for us. Second, we who just confessed we're undeserving are still called "saints." And rightly, for sainthood is not by our merit but by Christ making undeserving sinners holy.

It's of course our sin that makes us undeserving. But the woman in our Gospel lesson many would have considered undeserving of Jesus' attention for another reason. See how Isaiah addresses that in our **Old Testament Reading**, Isaiah 56:1, 6–8.

So much of the Old Testament is the narrative of God working through one family of people—Abraham's descendants, Jacob's twelve tribes, the Israelites. Clearly that was God's plan. But even in the Old Testament, we see frequent indications that "the foreigners who join themselves to the Lord . . . will be accepted" (56:6a, 7b). "These I will bring to My holy mountain, and make them joyful in My house of prayer," the place God promised to be found (56:7a)! "I will gather yet others," Gentiles, "besides those already gathered" (56:8b). The Canaanite woman knew that this is the way she fit in.

Don't miss this, though: "The Lord God . . . gathers the outcasts *of Israel*" (56:8a). Israel, too, has its outcasts. No one was "in" simply by genealogy, by birth into the family. Even for Israelites, there was still that problem of sin, and it would take more than natural birth to overcome that. In truth, every one of us is by nature an outcast.

See how badly that can be forgotten! Read the **Epistle**, along with some of the verses not included in the lectionary cutting: Romans 11:1–2a, 13–32.

By the time of Paul's writing, Isaiah's prophecy has come to fulfillment: Gentiles are now fully incorporated into the Gospel. Undeserving Canaanites, Greeks, Romans have joined undeserving Jews in the New Testament Church. But now a new problem: those new Gentile Christians are becoming "arrogant" (11:18), "wise in [their] own sight" (11:25). Most of the people of Israel, the Jews, have rejected Christ, and Gentiles have been "grafted" into "the olive tree" to replace them (11:17). But now Paul must warn the Gentiles that they were not chosen for salvation because they were more virtuous than the Jews. "You were at one time disobedient to God but now have received mercy" (11:30). So, too, the Jews are now disobedient. But God wants the Jews to realize that, and He wants you, Gentiles, to remember that! "For

God has consigned *all* to disobedience, that He may have *mercy* on *all*" (11:32). For just one purpose, God in His Law announces to everyone that we are all disobedient, sinful, undeserving: that we would eagerly receive the mercy He wishes so much to give.

That's exactly what the Canaanite woman was counting on when she came to Jesus in the **Holy Gospel**. Read the full story now: Matthew 15:21–28.

Tyre and Sidon were seaport cities of ancient Phoenicia, to the north of Israel. Their people were remnants of the pagan Canaanites God had commanded Israel to eradicate fifteen centuries earlier when they entered the Promised Land (because of their great wickedness, even child sacrifice). Obviously this troubled mom is no Israelite. That becomes the evident reason why Jesus seems to put her off—first, by His silence.

When have you felt that God was deaf to your cry, silent in answering your pleas? During a long period without a job? When rejected by the one school that had the only major you really wanted to study? After your husband didn't get well? When your girlfriend said it was over? Why no word, Lord?

But this woman is persistent. The disciples are losing patience: "Lord, give her what she wants and be done with her."

Instead, the really low blow: "I was sent to others, not to you. Helping you would be like taking food from the kids and feeding their pets instead." ("Dogs" here, 15:26, is probably an affectionate term for the family's beloved Fido, a different Greek word than, for example, for the perverts called "dogs" in Rev 22:15. Still, one sees where she stacks up in the priorities.) How is she to take that? How dare You degrade me, Jesus?!! I've got as much right to Your help as any Jew!

Not where she goes at all. She not only calls Jesus by a title that's messianic but also confesses him to be *Israel's* Messiah—the heir of David's line (15:22). And she's fine with that. "Yes, Lord, You didn't come first for me. I'm not deserving. But You're so good, so kind, so loving, and so powerful that even a crumb of Your mercy will be a feast for me. Do it Your way! Care first for Israel. But I know You have lots left—and I know You intend some of it for me!"

Do we presume, take offense, when God seems to handle things other than the way we just know must be best (and happens to favor us)? Or do we trust that His way, whatever that is, will be a feast for us? His way, the cross—that we would never design. The place He promises to be found: Word, Baptism, His Supper—not every miraculous healing or every answer we ask. And they are enough.

Even the Lord's Crumbs Satisfy All Who Plead God's Way of Mercy on Their Disobedience, Their Being Undeserving.

That's great comfort "when in the hour of deepest need we know not where to look for aid" (*LSB* 615), one of two **Hymns of the Day** for this Sunday. And who may join in singing that hymn? Everyone who's included in this week's **Psalm**, Psalm 67: "all nations . . . all the peoples . . . all the ends of the earth." "Let the peoples praise You, O God; let all the peoples praise You!" (67:5). For "in Christ there is no east or west" (*LSB* 653).

The Sundays after Pentecost: Proper 16 (August 21–27) Year A

READINGS

Isaiah 51:1–6
Psalm 138 (antiphon: v 8a)
Romans 11:33–12:8
Matthew 16:13–20

HYMN OF THE DAY

LSB 645 "Built on the Rock"

Many would say this is the climax of Matthew's Gospel. Located near the center of the book (in Shakespearean drama, the climax was always at the center, Act 3 of 5), this moment in Sunday's Gospel reading is the turning point of the story. From here, everything moves toward the resolution: Jesus' cross and resurrection. And that climactic moment occurs when Peter confesses, "You are the Christ, the Son of the living God" (Mt 16:16).

Just how important is that confession? Jesus immediately responds, "On this rock I will build My church" (16:18). The rock is about as universal a symbol as can be, isn't it! In every place, every era, "a rock" says "solid, permanent, lasting." If the confession "You, Jesus, are the Christ" is a rock, it means anything that's built on that will last, will be permanent. Anything built on something less . . .

See how the propers this week distinguish what's forever from what's for just now—in every case because Jesus is the Christ.

Begin with the **Introit**:

But we will bless the Lord from this time forth and forevermore. Praise the Lord!

As for Me, I have set My King on Zion, My holy hill. I will tell of the decree: The Lord said to Me, "You are My Son; today I have begotten You." Praise the Lord, all nations! Extol Him, all peoples! For great is His steadfast love toward us, and the faithfulness of the Lord endures forever. Praise the Lord!

Glory be to the Father and to the Son and to the Holy Spirit; as it was in the beginning, is now, and will be forever. Amen.

But we will bless the Lord *from this time forth and forevermore. Praise the* Lord*! (Ps 2:6–7; Ps 117; antiphon: Ps 115:18)*

Psalm 2:7, "The Lord said to Me, 'You are My Son; today I have begotten You,'" is quoted three times in the New Testament (Acts 13:33; Heb 1:5; 5:5), each time declaring emphatically that Jesus is the Son of God. In the psalm itself, it's actually the Christ, centuries before His incarnation, speaking through the psalmist, citing what God the Father says about Him. In other words, long before the Son became human, in fact, *reaching back to all eternity*, God the Father and God the Son have had this loving relationship—and the Father confesses it just as Peter will do in our Gospel lesson.

Now this eternal relationship has been extended to us: "Great is His steadfast love toward us, and the faithfulness of the Lord endures *forever.*" The result is that "we will bless the Lord *from this time forth and forevermore.*"

The **Collect** for this Sunday is very specific to the event of Peter's confession:

Almighty God, whom to know is everlasting life, grant us to know Your Son, Jesus, to be the way, the truth, and the life that we may boldly confess Him to be the Christ and steadfastly walk in the way that leads to life eternal; through the same Jesus Christ, our Lord, who lives and reigns with You and the Holy Spirit, one God, now and forever. Amen.

"That we may boldly confess Him to be the Christ." "That *we* may boldly confess Him to be the Christ." God gives us our moments too—and may we be ready to make the good confession before our high school friends, our bosses, our workout buddies at the gym.

We pray this for our own benefit too, because confessing Jesus as the Christ "leads to eternal life." In fact, knowing the Christ is the only way to know the "Almighty God, whom to know is everlasting life" (see Jn 14:6–7). Life that is lasting, permanent.

In our **Old Testament Reading**, Isaiah makes the direct contrast between what's lasting and what's passing: Isaiah 51:1–6.

Isaiah tells us to "look to" or "look at" three different visuals. "Look to Abraham your father and to Sarah who bore you" (51:2a). Great figures from Israel's history—the patriarch and his wife from whom came the whole nation. God's people often looked back with pride on their lineage from Abraham (for example, Jn 8:33–40). But when we look at Abraham, what does Isaiah wish us to see? "He was but one when I [the Lord] called him, that I might bless him and multiply him" (51:2b). Abraham and Sarah themselves were insignificant. Of their own flesh and blood, they would have produced no offspring; their legacy would have died out with their own generation. But the Lord blessed them and multiplied them.

The people of God would last forever by His doing.

Next, Isaiah has us "lift up your eyes to the heavens, and look at the earth beneath." What of those? "The heavens vanish like smoke, the earth will wear out like a garment, and they who dwell in it will die in like manner" (51:6). Things of this creation don't last!

But Isaiah also invites us to "look to the *rock* from which you were hewn" (51:1). And he is looking ahead to the same rock expressed as Peter's confession. "My righteousness draws near, My salvation has gone out" (51:5). Isaiah sees the day when the Christ, the righteous Savior, will come. Then "My salvation will be forever, and My righteousness will never be dismayed" (51:6c). Things of the Christ are lasting.

Read the **Psalm** for this day, Psalm 138. Here David does what Peter will do a thousand years later: confess Christ. "I give You thanks, O Lord, with my whole heart; before the gods I sing Your praise" (138:1). A confession of faith is always "before" someone. We believe in our hearts, but then we speak our confession so that others will hear. It may be among friends, as was Peter's confession or as we confess together with the Church in the creeds. It may be before "gods," who will always be enemies of the true God—whether they be pagan idols or colleagues we simply fear won't approve. A confession can't be hidden; we can't go on forever keeping our faith a secret. (Recall from the Epistle lesson two weeks ago Romans 10:9–10.) But we can always be confident of the eternal worth of confessing the true God: "The Lord will fulfill His purpose for me; Your steadfast love, O Lord, endures forever" (138:8). Again, forever.

Peter's confession in our Gospel reading will come after nearly three years of discipleship training. Peter and the boys will have heard Jesus teach, seen Him do miracles. And yet Jesus will say to Peter, "Flesh and blood has not revealed this to you"—that I am the Christ—"but My Father who is in heaven" (Mt 16:17). Why couldn't Peter have figured this out himself? Paul explains in our **Epistle**. Read Romans 11:33–12:8.

After his lengthy Romans discourse on God's way of salvation—by faith in Christ alone—Paul raises this doxology: "Oh, the depth of the riches and wisdom and knowledge of God! How unsearchable are His judgments and how inscrutable His ways! 'For who has known the mind of the Lord, or who has been His counselor?'" (11:33–34). We could never have deduced that God saves us completely apart from anything we do. It makes no sense in human economy. In the same way, it will make no sense that God's Anointed could be a poor, uneducated carpenter's son from Nazareth. "From *Him* and through *Him* and to *Him* are all things" (11:36)??? He *couldn't* be the Christ!

Paul also adds this to our theme: "not to think of [yourself] more highly than [you] ought to think," but only "according to the measure of faith that God has assigned" (12:3). Whatever is of *us* is invariably overrated; it will have no lasting value. The measure of faith God gives will have value to eternity. See how Paul outlines the various gifts God gives with faith in Christ (12:6–8).

The prophesying, serving, teaching, giving, and so on that God enables, He knows how to use for never-ending blessings.

And that which makes all these things last forever is what Peter confesses at this climactic moment, our **Holy Gospel**, Matthew 16:13–20.

Jesus knows His itinerary—where He's been, where He's going. So He has the disciples with Him out of the way for a rare quiet teaching moment. The first quiz question (16:13) reveals that the masses see Jesus as a very big deal—John the Baptist had drawn huge crowds; Elijah was the great Old Testament prophet expected to come again to usher in the Messiah (Mal 4:5); Jeremiah or another prophet back from the dead! All big deals. But not THE Big Deal.

So, gentlemen, after these three years, "Who do *you* say that I am?"

"Christ" (or, the Hebrew-based equivalent, "Messiah"), we do well to remember, isn't just another name for Jesus, though we often use it that way. "The Christ" is the Anointed One; it's the *office* God established for the One who will accomplish the whole work of mankind's salvation. From Genesis on, God's people believed there would come such a hero, and by now that had been thousands of years and more than seventy-five generations. You're saying, Peter, that this guy, leading around your ragtag bunch, is that One, that Only? No wonder Peter could never have gotten that on his own!

So when Jesus says He'll build His Church on "this rock," He's surely not staking all things on Peter! Even if Roman Catholics take these verses as the basis for the papacy—Peter, they say, being the first pope. If the Church were built on "flesh and blood" Peter, it—like any human building—would surely pass away. But "the gates of hell shall not prevail against" this Church (16:18).

No! It's as Paul says in our **Verse** (Eph 2:19b–20): Christ Jesus Himself is "the cornerstone." He is the One anointed by God to undo thousands of years of billions of people's sin. To fulfill every word of John the Baptist and Elijah and Jeremiah and all the rest of the prophets. In next Sunday's Gospel, even Peter will have to learn just how He's going to do that. Flesh and blood certainly couldn't reveal *that* to Peter.

But in the meantime, Jesus already gives us the means by which He'll make His work as the Christ lasting, eternal, for us: "the keys of the kingdom" (16:19). They are as certain, as eternal, also in heaven, as if Christ our Lord administered them to us in person. For

Jesus Is the Christ,
Revealed by the Father,
So That All Things of Him
Are on the Rock Which Is Forever,
While All Things Only of
Flesh and Blood
(Even of Abraham and Sarah,
Paul and Peter)
Will Vanish.

As you sing the **Hymn of the Day**, "Built on the Rock" (*LSB* 645), especially appreciate stanza 4, which proclaims those absolutely certain and eternal keys ("the font," "the altar," "the Scriptures") by which we receive "Christ yesterday, today, the same, And *evermore*, our Redeemer."

The Sundays after Pentecost: Proper 17 (August 28–September 3) Year A

READINGS

Jeremiah 15:15–21
Psalm 26 (antiphon: v 8)
Romans 12:9–21
Matthew 16:21–28

HYMN OF THE DAY

LSB 531 "Hail, Thou Once Despised Jesus"

So Jesus is the Christ. Simon Peter said so last week, and he was right on the money: "Blessed are you, Simon Bar-Jonah!" (Mt 16:17). Now what does that mean for Jesus? Perhaps more important in Peter's mind, what does that mean for us? We (I!) get it. So then what do I (we) get?

Flesh and blood would *certainly* not reveal *this* to Peter! He (we) will have to find out the hard way, beginning with this Sunday's propers—but then also by sometimes-painful experience for the rest of our lives.

Our **Introit** for this week begins with a beloved verse that's precisely where Peter thinks he's going:

> *Delight yourself in the* Lord, *and He will give you the desires of your heart.*
>
> *Commit your way to the* Lord; *trust in Him, and He will act. He will bring forth your righteousness as the light, and your justice as the noonday. Be still before the* Lord *and wait patiently for Him; fret not yourself over the one who prospers in his way, over the man who carries out evil devices!*
>
> *Glory be to the Father and to the Son and to the Holy Spirit; as it was in the beginning, is now, and will be forever. Amen.*
>
> *Delight yourself in the* Lord, *and He will give you the desires of your heart. (Ps 37:5–7; antiphon: Ps 37:4)*

"Delight yourself in the LORD, and He will give you the desires of your heart." Of course He will! We're on the Christ's team!

Psalm 37:4 is indeed a delightful verse (and the confirmation verse of many), but it can be easily misunderstood. It could be taken as a formula for manipulating God: if I just get my priorities right, put God first, delight in the Lord, He'll give me whatever I want. That misses the point. This verse isn't about us doing something; it's about God's gracious giving. The truth is, we can never manipulate God into giving us better than He already always gives us. The believer in every Christian, the new man or woman God creates in us in our Baptism (Titus 3:5), believes this firmly, so he or she is *always* delighting in the Lord. That is, the believer in us always wants whatever God wills to give; *whatever* God wills to give *is* the desire of our hearts, *is* our delight. Which means, of course, we always get it.

What we don't get from God is what the old sinful nature in us wants. And that may well have been what Peter was desiring even as he confessed Jesus to be the Christ. If He's the Christ and we're His closest followers, well then, surely there's a cushy government job with all kinds of perks for us!

The problem with that starts to appear already here in the Introit: "Be still before the LORD and wait patiently for Him; fret not yourself over the one who prospers in his way, over the man who carries out evil devices!" That sounds an awful lot like we won't always get what we want, at least not right away. Sounds as if evildoers will get some of those perks while we suffer!

The prophet Jeremiah certainly knew that by painful experience—even as he was delighting in the Lord. Consider the **Old Testament Reading**, Jeremiah 15:15–21.

Jeremiah is often known as the "weeping prophet," and this passage is an example of why. Jeremiah has made the Lord his delight: "Your words became to me a joy and the delight of my heart" (15:16). Jeremiah is saying all the right things, just as Peter did when he confessed Jesus to be the Christ.

Yet Jeremiah is being persecuted, for God's sake bearing "reproach" (15:15). He prophesies during the Babylonian exile, when many of God's people have been dragged away because of their sins, and wicked kings, faithless priests, lying prophets, and stubborn hearers just won't learn their lesson. He did not join in their idolatries, but "I sat alone" (15:17). So, "Why is my pain unceasing, my wound incurable, refusing to be healed? Will You be to me like a deceitful brook, like waters that fail?" (15:18). Has God, like one of those rivers of Judah that flows after a rain but then quickly dries up, proved unreliable to Jeremiah as he finds himself suffering?

God promises better: "I will make you to this people a fortified wall of bronze; they will fight against you, but they shall not prevail over you, for I am with you to save you and deliver you, declares the LORD. I will deliver you out of the hand of the wicked, and redeem you from the grasp of the ruthless" (15:20–21). For now, this promise will have to suffice for Jeremiah.

In the **Psalm**, David, too, is having to wait patiently for the Lord as he suffers: "Vindicate me, O LORD." Read Psalm 26.

David has "walked in [his] integrity, and . . . trusted in the LORD without wavering" (26:1). But the plea for vindication always means one is facing opposition, accusation, threats. David is surrounded by "hypocrites," "evildoers," "the wicked" (26:4–5), men who are out to get him: "bloodthirsty" (26:9). Clearly all is not easy for the Lord's faithful people.

Still, David can say, "O LORD, I love the habitation of Your house and the place where Your glory dwells" (26:8). David still delights to come into God's house. That's because the new man in David, the believer, does indeed trust without wavering that God will vindicate him. Even as he suffers, he believes that "my soul," "my life" (26:9), is safe in God's hands.

When Peter confessed Jesus to be the Christ, he was quite sure what that meant: God's kingdom had arrived (Mt 3:2; 4:17)! No doubt he had visions of how the kingdom would look and how he and the disciples would fit in. Would it be some kind of utopia? Read the **Epistle** for Sunday, Romans 12:9–21, and try to picture a world in which everything Paul commands actually happens.

With the Prince of Peace on His throne, will we "let love be genuine. Abhor what is evil; hold fast to what is good" (12:9)? Who could argue with that? (A Buddhist tale states that its chief teaching is "Do no evil. Do only good.") Who wouldn't endorse this: "Love one another with brotherly affection"? Even this one: "Outdo one another in showing honor" (12:10)—and all the rest? Go through the whole list of imperatives. Virtually everyone would commend such behaviors.

These are indeed marks of the kingdom of God. *But* Paul knew (as evidenced by everything preceding in Romans) and Peter had yet to realize what was still necessary to bring the kingdom to consummation. And that would still require Christ's people to "be patient in tribulation. . . . Bless those who persecute you. . . . Repay no one evil for evil, . . . but overcome evil with good" (12:12, 14, 17, 21).

Jesus is the Christ! Peter rightly confessed that He is now here! But what does being the Christ mean? What must the Christ do to bring in God's kingdom? And just what does that mean for us? That's what Jesus has to explain even to Peter in our **Holy Gospel**, Matthew 16:21–28.

What a turn of events! No sooner is Jesus announced to be the Christ than "*from that time*," immediately, "Jesus began to show His disciples that He must go to Jerusalem and suffer many things from the elders and chief priests and scribes, and be killed, and on the third day be raised" (16:21). No wonder Peter is shocked! This makes no sense! "Lord! This shall never happen to You" (16:22). Lord, didn't You hear what I just said? You're the Christ, the Son of God, the King! Now's when we parade into Jerusalem for Your coronation!

Part of Peter's horror at this is no doubt his sincere love for his Master; he hates the thought of Jesus suffering. (He doesn't seem to note the third day!) But Jesus' rebuke—that Peter's reaction is not helpful, but satanic—indicates Peter's other motivation: "You are not setting your mind on the things of God, but on the things of man" (16:23).

The believer in Peter (and in us), we remember, delights in all things of God—however contrary they may appear to our sensibilities. The new man trusts that God knows best and always gives us the best. But the old man in each of us has in mind the things of man. Like that cushy position sure to come when Jesus is crowned.

Of course, Peter was on to something. Because if being the Christ meant dying, then not only can you forget about the corner office upstairs in the Praetorium, but "if anyone would come after Me, let him deny himself and take up *his* cross and follow Me" (16:24). In fact, "whoever would save his life will lose it" (16:25a)! Peter knew exactly where this was going. Jesus going to the cross means we are going to suffer. Evil men will carry out their devices against us. We will be reproached, the pain unceasing, the wounds perhaps incurable. Bloodthirsty enemies will do their worst. And our call will be to overcome their evil with good.

These are our crosses. To suffer because we are Christians, followers of the Christ, and to delight that the sufferings are somehow God's perfect will for us. Whether the suffering is the real persecution pastors may soon face for upholding God's design for marriage and condemning the alternatives; whether it's doors closed to careers in journalism, the arts, or politics; whether it's a bombardment with sinful images in media that we can hardly avoid.

The only way Jesus could accomplish the saving work of the Christ was by going to His cross. And the only way we can follow Him is by carrying ours. But in going to the cross, Jesus did win for us eternal life. We may lose everything this world offers, even life itself, but He has redeemed our souls (16:25b–26). In Jesus' death and rising on the third day, the Kingdom has come, and one day we will see it. *Then* we will be vindicated (16:27–28).

The **Gradual** for this portion of the Pentecost season sums it up well:

> *Fear the Lord, you His saints, for those who fear Him lack nothing! Many are the afflictions of the righteous, but the Lord delivers him out of them all. (Ps 34:9, 19, alt)*

"Whoever would save his life will lose it, but whoever loses his life for My sake," for following Christ to the cross, "will find it."

**Being a Christian—
like Being the Christ—
Means Delighting Even That Life
Comes Only Following Crosses.**

Therefore, we pray this week's **Collect**:

> *Almighty God, Your Son willingly endured the agony and shame of the cross for our redemption. Grant us courage to take up our cross daily and follow Him wherever He leads; through the same Jesus Christ, our Lord, who lives and reigns with You and the Holy Spirit, one God, now and forever. Amen.*

Before singing the **Hymn of the Day**, "Hail, Thou Once Despised Jesus" (*LSB* 531), note all the references to Jesus' suffering *and* all those to His glory. They go together!

The Sundays after Pentecost: Proper 18 (September 4–10) Year A

READINGS

Ezekiel 33:7–9
Psalm 32:1–7 (antiphon: v 1)
Romans 13:1–10
Matthew 18:1–20

HYMN OF THE DAY

LSB 820 "My Soul, Now Praise Your Maker"

In our society today, it's considered just not nice not to "make nice." We're supposed to avoid confrontation. We're to affirm everyone and just about everything. The only thing sure to be criticized is criticizing, correcting, or condemning anyone else's opinions, behaviors, or lifestyle. Ironic what vehement confrontation and condemnation *that* will bring! It's almost sure to cost you your job in journalism, the entertainment industry, most circles of academia, even sports. (For an eye-opening discussion of this, read Anthony Esolen's excellent book *Out of the Ashes: Rebuilding American Culture* [Washington DC: Regnery Publishing, 2017]).

Sadly, the Church so often follows society, and we Christians are surely influenced by this secular doctrine: "just get along" (even COEXIST). Like everybody else, we don't want to make waves or be confrontational. We especially hate to confront sin, particularly if it's a member of our own congregation or our own family who's sinning. We'd much rather sweep it under the rug, cover it up. But in the Church, the stakes are so high (sin and the one and only way of salvation from it are matters of eternity!) that we must tell the truth, including uncomfortable truths.

Our propers this Sunday are clear about that. But they're also clear why, when the Church *does* address sin, as God commands, it's always to a blessed purpose!

While Our Way Is Not Only Sinful but Also to Cover Up Sin, God's Way Is to Confront Sin Directly So That He May Bless Us by *Christ* Covering Our Sin.

God would always have us confront sin so that people repent and receive His forgiveness in Christ. Understanding this is *so essential* to the health and vitality of our churches! Let's see how all our propers this coming Sunday will teach it.

The **Introit** this week will introduce the premise that God's ways are different from our ways:

How great are Your works, O LORD! Your thoughts are very deep!

It is good to give thanks to the LORD, to sing praises to Your name, O Most High; to declare Your steadfast love in the morning, and Your faithfulness by night, to the music of the lute and the harp, to the melody of the lyre. For You, O LORD, have made me glad by Your work; at the works of Your hands I sing for joy.

Glory be to the Father and to the Son and to the Holy Spirit; as it was in the beginning, is now, and will be forever. Amen.

How great are Your works, O LORD! Your thoughts are very deep! (Ps 92:1–4; antiphon: Ps 92:5)

God's "thoughts are very deep"—certainly deeper than ours. We don't initially sense the purpose in ruffling feathers. It just makes people mad, we figure. Leave well enough alone; that's a motto we like. It keeps the party polite, let's everybody have a good time. Saying "Stop right there!" when the gossip starts, saying "Count me out!" when the gang's headed off to buy using Jeff's fake ID, those aren't our thoughts. But they are God's. And "how great" they turn out to be! "You, O LORD, have made me glad by Your work; at the works of Your hands I sing for joy." God's ways may at first bring anger from the person being admonished, pain to the one doing the reproving. But His goal is always our joy. When there is repentance, there is forgiveness by the cross of Jesus Christ. That brings eternal gladness.

That's always God's highest good, which is where the **Collect** for this Sunday begins:

O God, from whom all good proceeds, grant to us, Your humble servants, Your holy inspiration, that we may set our minds on the things that are right and, by Your merciful guiding, accomplish them; through Jesus Christ, Your Son, our Lord, who lives and reigns with You and the Holy Spirit, one God, now and forever. Amen.

It's hard to trust that "*all* good proceeds" from God. Our sin always arises from the delusion that we can grab something better (more fun, more profitable, more endearing to those we'd like to please) than God is giving us. Surely making ourselves unpopular by confronting sin (including facing up to our own sin!) can't be good, we're convinced. No, only God can "grant to us . . . [His] holy inspiration, that we may set our minds on the things that are right"—rather than our way of going along, getting along, that we think is right. So we pray.

The **Old Testament Reading**, spoken by Yahweh to Ezekiel 2,700 years ago, is so clear and unequivocal for Christians and congregations today. Read Ezekiel 33:7–9, and then read it again slowly.

Can we look at ourselves and our congregations and pretend we've always obeyed God's clear command? Someone we know is living in open sin: a couple we know well is living together outside of marriage; another couple has divorced simply because they've decided marriage isn't for them; a close acquaintance is carrying on a homosexual relationship or has even entered into a same-sex marriage. Maybe they're members of your church. Maybe they're your own brothers or sisters or children. Have you, have we as a Church, said to them that if they remain in their sins rather than repenting, they "shall surely die" (33:8)—and that means die eternally in hell?

Oh, but who are we to judge? We, of course, are sinners too—no less guilty than the persons we confront. *But it's not a matter of us judging!* It's God's Word that confronts the sin: "Whenever you hear *a word from My mouth*, you shall give them warning *from Me*" (33:7). God's commandments tell us that sex outside of marriage, unscriptural divorce, and homosexuality are sins. (And those are just one commandment! God has given nine others.) We don't judge. We simply speak *God's* judgment.

Burying our heads in the sand won't make God's judgment go away. "If . . . you do not speak to warn the wicked to turn from his way, that wicked person shall die in his iniquity" (33:8a–b).

"That wicked person shall die in his iniquity, but his blood I will require at *your* hand" (33:8b–c).

Our way is sinful. That's true of all of us. And we compound our sinful ways by trying to cover up our or our neighbors' sins. That's our way too.

God's way is altogether different. He commands us so sternly to warn our sinning loved ones and fellow members of the Body of Christ solely because He wants them to repent and receive the forgiveness Jesus won for all on the cross. David appreciated this very personally, as is evident in our **Psalm**. Read Psalm 32:1–7.

You can guess the occasion of David's writing, eh? Yes, like Psalm 51, this he wrote after his terrible sin with Bathsheba and the lifesaving visit by Nathan. After committing adultery and murder (2 Samuel 11), David "kept silent" (Ps 32:3), tried to cover up his sin, for nine months. Fortunately, God did not keep silent, wouldn't let David go his deathly way: "Day and night Your hand was heavy upon me," so that David's "bones wasted away" (32:4, 3). Finally, God sent Nathan to confront David face-to-face: "You are the man!" (2 Sam 12:7).

At last, then, David confessed (2 Sam 12:13). "I acknowledged my sin to You, and I did not cover my iniquity." As we likewise speak in our liturgy, "I said, 'I will confess my transgressions to the Lord, and You forgave the iniquity of my sin'" (Ps 32:5). Had the Lord not stared David down with His Law, turned him from his evil way, the great king of Israel, the man after God's own heart, would now be spending forever in hell. That didn't happen, because God loved David enough to send Nathan, and Nathan loved God and the king enough to risk his own life for David's salvation.

Now David understood God's loving intention: "Blessed is the one whose transgression is forgiven, whose sin is covered" (32:1). God brought David to repentance so that He could cover David's sin in the blood of David's descendant, Christ Jesus. So David is blessed for all eternity.

See how the **Epistle** gives us yet another demonstration of God confronting sin: Romans 13:1–10. Paul says that civil governments—even wicked ones like the Roman Empire in his day—are "instituted by God" (13:1) to be "the servant of God, an avenger who carries out God's wrath on the wrongdoer," yet "for your good" (13:4). Through the centuries, secular authorities have executed punishment on crimes—actually a warning from God against those certain sins. Governments do this imperfectly, of course, but God's Commandments, "You shall not commit adultery, You shall not murder, You shall not steal, You shall not covet, . . . love your neighbor as yourself" (13:9), leave no doubt.

It's easy to see how that portion of the **Holy Gospel** perhaps most familiar (Mt 18:15–18) makes the point of our THEME for the week. But read the full lesson, Matthew 18:1–20, and consider how the entire context teaches God's way of both confronting sin and then covering it in Christ's forgiveness.

Hard to imagine a harsher warning against sin than to cut off your hand or foot or to tear out your eye rather than end up in "the hell of fire" (18:8–9). (In fact, obviously, hands, feet, and eyes are never the real cause of sin, so Jesus is using this as a vivid illustration, not literally commanding such drastic actions.) Everyone, even Jesus' own disciples, must repent ("turn") or they "will never enter the kingdom of heaven" (18:3). That means humbling ourselves to confess our sins (18:4) rather than covering them up.

But Jesus' *reason* for confronting sin is illustrated just as vividly (18:10–13): He is always going "in search of the one that went astray." "It is not the will of My Father who is in heaven that one [*even one!*] of these little ones should perish" (18:14).

Therefore, Christians and congregations *must* follow Jesus' instructions to go searching for the sinning brother or sister. "Go and tell him his fault" (18:15). "But, Pastor, we don't want to offend them. Won't that drive them away?" That's *our* thinking, *our* way.

God's way is to speak privately first, to protect the sinner's reputation. Then go as just two or three caring members (18:16; see also Deut 19:15). If necessary, then let "the church," the whole congregation, know so that each member may pray for and speak to the needy soul (18:17). And the goal is always to gain the brother (18:15), to have the opportunity to "loose on earth" by announcing forgiveness what God has "loosed in heaven" (18:18). That is God's way—the way that sent God's Son to the cross so that our sins need never be covered up but *are* covered!

"The poor and contrite spirit Finds His compassion nigh; . . . So far, since He has loved us, He puts our sins away" (**Hymn of the Day**, *LSB* 820, st 2). Sing it!

The Sundays after Pentecost: Proper 19 (September 11–17) Year A

READINGS

Genesis 50:15–21
Psalm 103:1–12
(antiphon: v 13)
Romans 14:1–12
Matthew 18:21–35

HYMN OF THE DAY

LSB 501 "Come Down, O Love Divine"

Forgive us our trespasses as we forgive those who trespass against us."

Praying this as often as we do, including again this Sunday, we could never forget those words. Is it possible, though, that we might ever forget to trust and practice the words we so easily speak? And if so, which are we more likely to forget—to forgive those who trespass against us *or* that God has forgiven us our trespasses?

Our propers this week include two magnificent stories about forgiving and being forgiven. One ends beautifully; the other, not well. And the difference is in remembering what the Lord has done for us.

Both of those two marvelous stories—in our Old Testament Reading and our Holy Gospel—describe desperates pleading for mercy. In our **Introit** this week, we ourselves are doing just that:

> *Deliver me from my enemies, O Lord! I have fled to You for refuge!*
>
> *Hear my prayer, O Lord; give ear to my pleas for mercy! In Your faithfulness answer me, in Your righteousness! Enter not into judgment with Your servant, for no one living is righteous before You.*
>
> *Glory be to the Father and to the Son and to the Holy Spirit; as it was in the beginning, is now, and will be forever. Amen.*
>
> *Deliver me from my enemies, O Lord! I have fled to You for refuge! (Ps 143:1–2; antiphon: Ps 143:9)*

So many enemies from which we need deliverance! Satan has so many henchmen out to get us! But in particular this week, we're reminded that we are our own worst enemies. "Enter not into judgment with Your servant, for no one living is righteous before You." When we stand before the judgment seat of God, our own sin would be our undoing—that is, except that God does "give ear to [our] pleas for mercy." In His faithfulness, He answers us and gives us Christ's own righteousness.

That's the confidence with which we pray the **Collect**:

O God, our refuge and strength, the author of all godliness, hear the devout prayers of Your Church, especially in times of persecution, and grant that what we ask in faith we may obtain; through Jesus Christ, our Lord, who lives and reigns with You and the Holy Spirit, one God, now and forever. Amen.

God always does "hear the devout prayers" of His people—especially our prayers for forgiveness—"*through Jesus Christ, our Lord.*" That, after all, is why Jesus came to earth and died on the cross—to forgive the sin that separated us from God, so that, having been reconciled, we always have certain access to His throne of grace. "Forgive us our trespasses"—and He does!

Now the first of our two stories, the **Old Testament Reading**, Genesis 50:15–21.

Do you remember the back story? It's roughly a third of the book of Genesis, beginning way back in chapter 29. Jacob has two wives (and adds a couple of maids besides)—one of them, Rachel, loved above the others. After Leah and the maids have ten sons, Rachel finally has one of her own, Joseph, who immediately becomes Dad's favorite. That sits so badly with the older brothers that they sell Joseph into slavery and lie to Jacob, who assumes Joseph has been killed by a wild animal (Genesis 37).

Yet God is with Joseph, and, after a time in prison, he interprets the pharaoh's dreams about a coming famine and is therefore named second-in-command of all Egypt (Genesis 41). With the Lord's insights, Joseph stores up grain during seven plenteous years and thus saves Egypt from starvation through the seven years of famine.

Then his brothers also come to Egypt to buy grain. Joseph tests them and finds they've changed; they're willing to become his slaves rather than abandon their still younger brother, Benjamin (Rachel's second son). At this, Joseph weeps, embraces them, and invites them to bring their father and all they have to Egypt, where he will provide the best of the land (Genesis 42–45). From here, the nation of Israel will flourish, a historic step toward giving the world the Messiah. This should be the happy ending to the story.

But now, seventeen years later, Jacob dies. And the brothers wonder: "Maybe the kid was just biding his time until the old man was gone. Now maybe he'll take his revenge." "So they sent a message to Joseph, saying, 'Your father gave this command before he died: "Say to Joseph, 'Please forgive the transgression of your brothers and their sin, because they did evil to you'""" (50:16–17). There's nothing in the reading that suggests Jacob gave such instruction; most likely, the brothers invented it to buy Joseph's leniency. And they plead, "Please forgive."

Joseph weeps! For all these years, they've still been living under this pall, this fear? He's been gracious to them, providing for them for so long, and they still think he was just waiting to drop the hammer! They still don't believe they've been forgiven! They fall down before him, the posture of desperation, and say, "Behold, we are your servants" (50:18).

Joseph remembers what God has done through all this. Forgiveness always originates in God forgiving first. "You meant evil against me, but God meant it for good, to bring it about that many people should be kept alive" (50:20). All *is* forgiven! "Thus he comforted them" (50:21). That's the happy ending! The way forgiveness is to be!

After a narrative that so well illustrates mercy and forgiveness, our **Psalm** uses poetic language to add the exclamation point. Savor Psalm 103:1–13.

We sin and we sin and we sin some more, but "the LORD is merciful and gracious, slow to anger and abounding in steadfast love" (103:8). He keeps forgiving, continues to hold back His wrath; His mercy remains steadfast forever. David knew what Joseph's brothers knew (and what we should know!): that our sins deserve God's eternal punishment. Yet "He does not deal with us according to our sins, nor repay us according to our iniquities" (103:10). All the punishment we deserve has been laid on the Messiah, the one to come from the line of Jacob and his family. And as Jesus stretched out His arms on the cross, picture this beautiful image: "As far as the east is from the west, so far does He remove our transgressions from us" (103:12). Stretch out your arms as far as you can, one to your left, one to your right. Point your fingers into the distance—in opposite directions. As those imaginary destinations reach infinitely farther from one another, so God has removed your sin forever farther from you.

Let us never forget that! "Bless the LORD, O my soul, and forget not all His benefits, who forgives all your iniquity" (103:2–3). If we forget, we're going to dwell on our brother's sins because we think we're better—or just to convince ourselves we're not so bad. We're going to demand our pound of flesh from him, because we fear we'll have to be paying up soon. On the other hand, remembering that God has forgiven us so infinitely enables us to let go of our brother's sin, to forgive and forgive and forgive.

The **Epistle** for Sunday addresses an entirely different matter, what we call "adiaphora," things neither commanded nor prohibited in Scripture. But Paul's reason for raising the issue is actually the very same reason that forgiving our brother is so vital. Read Romans 14:1–12.

God allows but never requires eating meat (14:1–2). Likewise, while Old Testament believers were commanded to worship on the Sabbath (our Saturday), God allows Christians to choose which day to set aside (14:5). We should not "pass judgment" on our brother (14:10) who chooses the Saturday evening service or who loves (or opts out on) ribs. (In 1 Corinthians 8, Paul explains further: Ancient butcher shops offered meat first as sacrifices to pagan gods, then sold it. Some Christians chose not to eat meat, fearing they would be endorsing idolatry.) Here's Paul's point: *making a point* of indifferent things can harm "the one who is weak in faith" (14:1). Someone of strong faith, who knows that pagan gods are just imagination, should be sensitive about eating meat if it causes a believer of weak faith to think worshiping idols is safe. The weaker brother might lose his faith as a result (1 Cor 8:9–11).

In the same way, one of the great destroyers of faith is refusal to forgive. Say someone has sinned against you. If you refuse to forgive him, he may assume that God doesn't forgive him either. He might be overcome with guilt, despair of God's mercy, be lost.

We dare not create barriers to another person's faith by judging him on matters where God allows flexibility—or by refusing to forgive. After all, "we will all stand before the judgment seat of God" to face judgment ourselves. "Each of us will give an account of himself to God" (14:10, 12)—as becomes vivid in our **Holy Gospel**, Matthew 18:21–35.

Peter's question elicits Jesus' powerful story, which we call the Parable of the Unforgiving Servant. Peter assumes that forgiveness has reasonable limits, and seven is one of those divine numbers that, in fact, goes well beyond the rabbinic guideline of three. He's forgotten, though, *how much* God has forgiven him.

Ten thousand talents the servant owes. Like Joseph's brothers, he falls on his knees, pleading, "Have patience with me, and I will pay you everything" (18:26). No way. Just *one talent* would take a common worker *twenty years* to earn. *Ten thousand* talents? Might as well be a gazillion dollars! That's right—beyond any real number, an imaginary one! This debt could never be repaid! This is Peter's debt, our debt: every impatient thought, unkind word, selfish action; our very condition of constant, nonstop rebellion. And yet, "Out of pity for him, the master of that servant released him and forgave him the debt" (18:27). Mark well: forgiving a debt means the master suffers loss; *he* forfeits an infinitely large asset. Precisely what the Master did when He gave up His infinitely precious Son to death!

Somehow the servant forgets. A hundred denarii might be paid off in three months. And the fellow servant pleads—yes, on his knees (18:28–29). But no mercy! And then, for the unforgiving servant, the jailers . . .

"Forgive us our trespasses *as we forgive those who trespass against us.*" "If you forgive others their trespasses, your heavenly Father will also forgive you" (Mt 6:14, the **Verse**).

**Our Master Always Has Mercy
When We Plead before Him,
but We Dare Not
Forget His Forgiveness
When our Brother Pleads with Us.**

And if we do forget? fail to forgive? Then let us remember: our Master *always* has mercy when we plead before Him—ten thousand talents' worth. We plead. And then we forgive. We do forgive. We must forgive.

Closing with the **Hymn of the Day** (*LSB* 501), ponder that "no soul can guess" or begin to fathom the full extent of "His grace."

The Sundays after Pentecost: Proper 20 (September 18–24) Year A

READINGS

Isaiah 55:6–9
Psalm 27:1–9 (antiphon: v 4a)
Philippians 1:12–14, 19–30
Matthew 20:1–16

HYMN OF THE DAY

LSB 555 "Salvation unto Us Has Come"

It makes perfect sense to us: if you want it, you have to earn it. It's the way everything in this world works. At your job, you've got to work to get paid. At the grocery store, you have to pay at checkout to take home your bagels. With people, you have to be friendly to make friends. Fair enough. Of course, if we *do* work hard, pay the price, go out of our way to smile, we expect *our* payoff. What's fair is fair. Makes perfect sense.

So it's no surprise that folks expect God to work that way too. Those who believe there's a God at all but don't believe what He reveals about Himself—that is, most of the human population apart from Christians—assume He pays off the good we do and punishes the bad that people (hopefully others) do. Grace—that God saves us by Jesus' death for us, without any of our doings—is nowhere on the radar screen. It's a complete reversal of everything expected.

We who look forward to Sunday morning every week should know very well about grace. God has revealed His grace in Christ Jesus to us Christians, and we Lutherans have articulated it with particular clarity: "Salvation unto us has come By God's *free grace* and favor" (our Hymn of the Day). *Our* problem may be to think that by trusting in grace alone we might just earn a little bonus above what grace alone gives. Sure, salvation is solely by grace, not by our works, so doesn't believing that make us a little better than the guy who doesn't believe it?

Turns out we're still of this world too! We expect much of the very same system!

Through our propers from His Word this Sunday, therefore, God will seek to reverse also our expectations—for His grace gives so much better than we could earn!

The antiphon, the opening and closing verse of this week's **Introit**, begins to show how God's way of grace reverses the very order of the world's economy.

I will offer to You the sacrifice of thanksgiving and call on the name of the Lord.

What shall I render to the Lord for all His benefits to me? I will lift up the cup of salvation and call on the name of the Lord. Precious in the sight of the Lord is the death of His saints. O Lord, I am Your servant; I am Your servant, the son of Your maidservant. You have loosed my bonds.

Glory be to the Father and to the Son and to the Holy Spirit; as it was in the beginning, is now, and will be forever. Amen.

I will offer to You the sacrifice of thanksgiving and call on the name of the Lord. (Ps 116:12–13, 15–16; antiphon: Ps 116:17)

Appreciate the two passages here, which may be familiar from liturgical use. "What shall I render to the Lord," we sing as an Offertory in Divine Service, Settings One and Two (*LSB*, pp 159, 176). And often on All Saints' Day, we hear quoted, "Precious in the sight of the Lord is the death of His saints."

But for this week's theme, the key phrase is "sacrifice of thanksgiving." "Sacrifice" and "thanksgiving" are often essentially an oxymoron. Sacrifices are made to earn something, appease or placate someone. That's the very opposite of giving thanks. The ancient pagans wouldn't sacrifice to Baal or Zeus out of gratitude; they'd sacrifice from fear or to gain the god's attention. Every world religion aside from Christianity offers worship in order to earn rewards or avoid punishment (for example, the Five Pillars of Islam or deeds that accumulate good karma).

The one true religion reverses these. First, by grace, His undeserved love and goodness, God gives us "His benefits," "the cup of salvation"; He holds us "precious," has "loosed my bonds." No strings attached, purchased by Jesus dying and rising. *Then* we sacrifice to Him—purely in thanks for His gifts.

Our relationship with God can be no other way, we confess in the **Collect**:

Lord God, heavenly Father, since we cannot stand before You relying on anything we have done, help us trust in Your abiding grace and live according to Your Word; through Jesus Christ, Your Son, our Lord, who lives and reigns with You and the Holy Spirit, one God, now and forever. Amen.

Anything we might do—and *everything* we could ever do—cannot earn us standing before God. Our sin would always stand between us and Him; the holy God cannot be in a relationship with anything or anyone tainted by sin. That's why Jesus acted out God's grace in atoning for our sins on the cross. We pray here in the Collect that we would always place our trust there and nowhere else, in God's "abiding grace."

The **Old Testament Reading** is another exposition of how God's way of relating to us is the very opposite of what the world expects. Read Isaiah 55:6–9.

We recognize, of course, that God's ways are not our ways, that they're higher than ours (55:8–9). Here, though, He's not speaking about His ways in general. He has in mind a certain specific way that's so different.

"Seek the LORD while He may be found" (55:6). That says to us that we're to do something in order to become close to God: seek Him. Makes sense. We expect that. But to whom is the Lord saying this? "Let the *wicked* forsake his way, and the *unrighteous* man his thoughts" (55:7a). The wicked, the unrighteous, won't, can't, seek God; *they're wicked*, going their own way, not caring about God at all. And our way would be to say, "If that's the way they want it, fine, let 'em. Forget about 'em." God's way reverses that. God's way is that they "return to the LORD, that He may have compassion . . . for He will abundantly pardon" (55:7b). Those who won't, can't, seek God, God will pardon. He does that by calling out through this very word and His every word of compassion, and by that Word making the wicked into righteous, already-now-believing seekers. He saves them, *then* they seek Him. Not really anything they do at all, but the produce of what He's done. God's way is to seek the wicked, do all that it takes for sinners to have a relationship with Him. Good thing, because while our way might well have been to "forget about 'em," we might easily forget that the wicked were . . . us!

The same order of things is evident in this week's **Psalm**. Notice how David writes about seeking in Psalm 27:1–9.

David knows what the Lord is doing and has done for him: "The LORD is my light and my salvation; whom shall I fear? The LORD is the stronghold of my life; of whom shall I be afraid?" (27:1). The Lord has saved David, protected him. The Lord has also enlightened David to know Him. ("The Holy Spirit has called me by the Gospel, enlightened me with His gifts"; Luther's explanation of the Third Article of the Apostles' Creed.) That, God saving and creating faith, comes first, before we do anything.

Then David asks one thing of the Lord: "That will I seek after: that I may dwell in the house of the LORD all the days of my life" (27:4). The Lord is pleased: "You have said, 'Seek My face.'" And David answers, "My heart says to You, 'Your face, LORD, do I seek'" (27:8). David is delighted to seek the Lord, because the Lord has already revealed to him what he will find: a God who was already gracious to him before he ever came looking.

After an entire summer in the book of Romans, our **Epistle** this Sunday begins four weeks in Philippians. Start with Philippians 1:12–14, 19–30. See how many examples Paul cites of God reversing our worldly expectations.

Paul writes his letter to the Philippians from confinement in Rome (1:7), probably the house arrest Luke describes in Acts 28:16–31. One might see this as a defeat for

God's mission. But Paul writes that this "has really served to advance the gospel" (1:12). The imperial guard, elite troops close to Caesar, have heard his message, and others have become bolder to preach by seeing Paul bearing up under adversity (1:13–14).

Paul realizes that his death is a real possibility, and one would expect him to be discouraged, even desperate. But he knows that he actually faces a win-win: being with Christ after death ("far better") or continuing to serve the Church on earth (1:21–24). Our best guess from history is that Paul was released this time and resumed his work, before being executed in Rome after a later imprisonment (2 Tim 4:6–8).

Finally, the Philippians themselves will soon suffer—surely a sign that their faith is futile. But no, as they endure bravely, it will only signal that their opponents will ultimately be destroyed (1:28–30).

Still, God's chief reversal of worldly expectations is the one with which we began: that everything we have is a gift of His grace, not earned, not our doing. That's the surprise of our **Holy Gospel**, Matthew 20:1–16.

This parable Jesus speaks to the loyal soldier, the faithful laborer, the disciple. Peter has rightly pointed out that he and the brethren have devoted everything to follow Jesus, and he's asking, "What's in it for us?" (Mt 19:27). Oh, there will be rich, eternal rewards (19:28–29), but also ponder this: "Many who are first will be last, and the last first" (19:30).

Thus the parable. Why do the all-day workers grumble (20:11)? A denarius was the standard wage for a day. Besides, they'd agreed to it. Yet, when Johnny-come-latelies receive a denarius, the all-day workers expect more. We understand. It's not fair. We look forward to Sunday morning, read ahead, come to church focused and attentive. They slip in during the third stanza of the opening hymn, swivel heads to follow every distraction, get up to use the restroom during the sermon. Probably put a fiver in the plate too. Okay, we're glad they're here, hearing the Word, receiving Christ's body and blood. But, Lord, you and I, we've got a little more goin' on between us, right?

The all-day workers grumble because they don't understand grace. "Alleluia," we'll say Sunday in the **Verse**. "By grace you have been saved through faith. And this is not your own doing; it is the gift of God. Alleluia" (Eph 2:8). Perhaps they received less than they expected, but did they—does anyone—ever receive less from God than deserved? "Do you begrudge my generosity?" (20:15). Generosity, grace—and nothing tops what grace gives. The eleventh-hour workers received more than they deserved, but haven't we also? A "job" for which *He* came seeking us, which "pays" not what our sins deserve. We *don't want* to be paid what we've earned—and the Master doesn't! He "pays" what Christ Jesus earned by His labors, and He surprises us in giving it to us by grace, free! Not what we expect; not what we've earned.

God's Ways (Grace, Not Our Doings) Reverse Everything We Expect in Seeking Him.

You won't find this expressed any better than in our **Hymn of the Day**, *LSB* 555.

The Sundays after Pentecost: Proper 21 (September 25–October 1) Year A

READINGS

Ezekiel 18:1–4, 25–32
Psalm 25:1–10 (antiphon: v 4)
Philippians 2:1–4 (5–13) 14–18
Matthew 21:23–27 (28–32)

HYMN OF THE DAY

LSB 655 "Lord, Keep Us Steadfast in Your Word"

Authority.

Is it a good word or a bad word?

Years ago, what some have called "The Greatest Generation," the generation that won World War II, revered (or at least respected) authority—presidents, commanding officers, drill sergeants, factory foremen, Dad as head of the household, pastors, teachers. "Policemen are our friends," they taught. But then came eras of sit-ins and campus unrest, Watergate and impeachments, charges of police brutality and racism. Politics of personality and character assassination, Supreme Court oversteps and Supreme Court nominations with more character assassinations. Distrust of authority.

The Fourth Commandment demands that we honor, serve, obey, even love and cherish "our parents and other authorities." But somehow "the authorities" has become an ominous term—or else one to lampoon.

Why do we often have such a problem with authority? It all goes back to the fall into sin, and it's really quite simple. Just as Eve and Adam wanted to be their own gods, we sinful people also want to be our own ultimate authorities. Anything that's in authority over us makes us at best Number Two, and that's always one spot too low. We always believe (foolishly!) that we can do a better job of looking out for Number One than anyone else can or will. After all, we're always convinced that the next guy is looking out for *him*self, that he'll always sell us out to put himself ahead. Distrust of all authorities. Even when the authority is God.

In our **Verse** for this coming Sunday, Jesus says, "All authority in heaven and on earth has been given to Me" (Mt 28:18b).

Anything Jesus has must be good, but we distrust Jesus' authority too. That truly is foolish, because, as our propers will remind us, Christ is always exercising His authority for our very best.

Begin your preparation for Sunday morning by praying the **Collect** for the week:

Almighty God, You exalted Your Son to the place of all honor and authority. Enlighten our minds by Your Holy Spirit that, confessing Jesus as Lord, we may be led into all truth; through the same Jesus Christ, our Lord, who lives and reigns with You and the Holy Spirit, one God, now and forever. Amen.

Jesus does indeed have all authority. He is Lord! But we pray in this petition that the Holy Spirit would enable us to recognize this—and to confess it joyfully rather than resent it. Our minds darkened by sin could never believe that the One who reigns over all things would use His authority for us rather than for Himself; that's absolutely contrary to our most basic sinful assumptions. Only when the Holy Spirit turns on the light in our hearts can we see how blessed it is to have Christ in charge of our lives.

Of course, confessing Christ's authority means accepting the lower place, humbling ourselves. While this offends every fiber of our sinful nature, it's both to our great benefit and delights the Lord. Sunday's **Introit**:

The LORD lifts up the humble; He casts the wicked to the ground.

Praise the LORD! For it is good to sing praises to our God; for it is pleasant, and a song of praise is fitting. The LORD builds up Jerusalem; He gathers the outcasts of Israel. He heals the brokenhearted and binds up their wounds. He determines the number of the stars; He gives to all of them their names. Great is our Lord, and abundant in power; His understanding is beyond measure.

Glory be to the Father and to the Son and to the Holy Spirit; as it was in the beginning, is now, and will be forever. Amen.

The LORD lifts up the humble; He casts the wicked to the ground. (Ps 147:1–5; antiphon: Ps 147:6)

See how the psalmist acknowledges God's authority: the Lord created every last star, knows precisely how many billions of trillions there are, and probably has more endearing names for each than Alpha Centauri A and B. "His understanding is beyond measure." But rather than flaunt His authority to keep us down, He "lifts up the humble"; He "builds up Jerusalem"; He "binds up . . . the brokenhearted." Those without any title or pretense the Lord lifts up. His "abundant power" is always turned toward the cause of the humble.

How unhelpful, then, ever to challenge the Lord's authority, as in the **Old Testament Reading**, Ezekiel 18:1–4, 25–32!

Ezekiel is in Babylon, prophesying to God's people there in exile. But they have a complaint. They're arguing that they're only in captivity because previous generations of Judah sinned: "The *fathers* have eaten sour grapes, and the *children's* teeth are set on edge" (18:2)—we, the children, are suffering for our fathers' sins. "The way of the Lord is not just" (18:25). God doesn't know what He's doing! We'd do a better job of running things. A direct challenge to God's authority.

God will have none of it. No, "*All* souls are Mine; the soul of the father as well as the soul of the son is Mine" (18:4a). I have authority over everyone, and "I *will* judge you, O house of Israel, every one according to his ways" (18:30). I know everything you *and* your fathers have done. And every one of you will be judged accordingly. "The soul who sins," the one who's truly guilty, is the one who "shall die" (18:4b). Still want to complain? Every father, every son, *every one of us* deserves death, for we all sin!

Challenging God's authority will always end badly. But that's never how God wants it to end. "Repent and turn from all your transgressions," the Lord pleads (18:30). Don't try Me! Humble yourself! Confess your sin! "When a wicked person turns away from the wickedness he has committed . . . he shall surely live; he shall not die" (18:27, 28).

That's always what God desires. "For I have no pleasure in the death of anyone, declares the Lord God." Obviously not, for the Lord Himself died in order that His sinful people might not! Here's what does please God: "Turn, and live" (18:32).

Now read the **Psalm** for this Sunday: Psalm 25:1–10. This is a psalm of David, a man who would become king.

David would be "the authority" in Israel. And yet he trusts in "my God" (25:2). He prays that the Lord would lead him and teach him; he knows that he needs the Lord to save him. In fact, King David will "wait all the day long" for the Lord and His timetable (25:5). Imagine a doctor (or even a clerk at city hall) sitting all day in her waiting room for whenever *the patient* (or applicant) decides to pop in. David sets aside his own agenda, humbles himself to accept the Lord's plans and schedule, because he trusts that God uses His far greater authority for David's best.

"Good and upright is the Lord. . . . He leads the humble in what is right, and teaches the humble His way. All the paths of the Lord are steadfast love and faithfulness" (25:8, 9–10a). God's good pleasure is to lead and teach the humble, those who make no claims to authority of their own.

In the **Epistle**, Paul makes the point of our Sunday's Theme with the example par excellence. Read Philippians 2:1–18.

Every congregation knows the Philippians' experience: someone has his or her ambition (to continue as chairman, to choose the carpet) and refuses to yield to the needs of others (for a new point of view or hypoallergenic tile floors). It's a power play, a grab for or challenge to authority. Paul says, "Do nothing from rivalry or conceit, but in humility count others more significant than yourselves. Let each of you look not only to his own interests, but also to the interests of others" (2:3–4).

The chief example, we know, is Christ Jesus, "who, though He was in the form of God, did not count equality with God a thing to be grasped, but made Himself nothing, taking the form of a servant, being born in the likeness of men. And being found in human form, He humbled Himself by becoming obedient to the point of death, even death on a cross" (2:6–8).

But Jesus isn't *just* the example. His humiliation has secured for us the perfect exaltation so that we *can't* improve our position by grabbing honor or authority for ourselves; He has already used His to give us better than we could ever grasp. God's "good pleasure" (2:13) is always to exalt those who humble themselves, just as He "highly exalted [Jesus] and bestowed on Him the name that is above every name" (2:9).

Tragically, the Jewish temple authorities didn't understand this. They could only see Jesus as a *threat* to *their* authority. Read the **Holy Gospel**, Matthew 21:23–32.

It's Tuesday of Holy Week. On Sunday, Jesus rode into Jerusalem on the donkey, and on Monday, he sent coins rolling everywhere on the temple floor, casting out the money-changers. After such a ruckus, the chief priests and elders ask a legitimate question: "By what authority are You doing these things, and who gave You this authority?" (21:23).

Except that Jesus has already answered this question countless times—not only with words, His authoritative preaching of God (Mt 7:28–29), but also by innumerable miracles (Jn 10:25). Why, only very recently Jesus had raised Lazarus from the dead—right in the nearby suburb, Bethany—and even these Jewish leaders know it (Jn 11:43–47). But they are convinced Jesus' actions will undermine their authority (Jn 11:48). And so they feel they must challenge Him.

Anyone challenging Jesus' authority will always find himself at an immediate disadvantage. Jesus knows His opponents cannot safely answer His question about John (also a question about authority—did John baptize on heavenly, divine authority or his own?).

On the other hand, had they come to Jesus truly asking Him to teach them, humbling themselves as pupils, His approach would have been entirely different. Thus it had been with the lowest, the humblest, of the community: "For John came to you in the way of righteousness, and you did not believe him, but the tax collectors and the prostitutes believed him" (21:32). And with tax collectors and prostitutes, Jesus humbled Himself to gather, to dine, and, finally, for them, to die.

That is always God's delight—when we bow to Christ's authority so that He, by Jesus' humiliating death, may lift us up.

God's Pleasure Is That We Humble Ourselves before Christ's Authority Rather Than Challenge It, Because He Exercises His Authority to Lift Up the Humble.

Martin Luther's German original of our **Hymn of the Day**, "Lord, Keep Us Steadfast in Your Word" (*LSB* 655), sang the famous denunciation of "murderous Pope and Turk." There's much history behind that, but the message remains clear: Lord, deliver us from anyone who would wrest from Christ His rightful authority over the kingdom. For You, Lord Jesus, are Lord of lords alone!

The Sundays after Pentecost: Proper 22 (October 2–8) Year A

READINGS

Isaiah 5:1–7
Psalm 80:7–19 (antiphon: v 7)
Philippians 3:4b–14
Matthew 21:33–46

HYMN OF THE DAY

LSB 544 "O Love, How Deep"

Perhaps nothing is as painful for any of us as love that's rejected. A serious girlfriend, even a fiancée, who decides she doesn't want to spend the rest of her life with you after all. A child you've raised, prayed for, assisted through college, who then renounces everything you stand for and vows never to come home again. A husband or wife who suddenly tells you he or she has found somebody else.

It's the deepest kind of hurt. You look back on the moments of intimacy, affection, the promises you each made. You think about the emotions, the endless hours, even the money you invested in your loved one—the perfect dinner date, the stake to set up that first apartment, the ring. You wonder what you could have, should have, done differently. Did you give everything you had to give?

That's what the heavenly Father and Jesus Christ, His Son, suffer in our propers for this Sunday: rejected love—except that They know They really did give it all. And how do They respond? Deep depression? Bitterness? Anger? We'd understand. But remarkably, They respond with more love.

The **Collect** for this Sunday morning actually summarizes what we'll read later in the Gospel lesson—and hints at where we'll fit into it. Begin looking forward to Sunday by praying:

Gracious God, You gave Your Son into the hands of sinful men who killed Him. Forgive us when we reject Your unfailing love, and grant us the fullness of Your salvation; through Jesus Christ, Your Son, our Lord, who lives and reigns with You and the Holy Spirit, one God, now and forever. Amen.

In the Gospel reading, Jesus will tell a parable that predicts His murder by the Jewish leaders just a few days hence. But we pray for forgiveness of the very same sin: rejecting God's unfailing love. Thank God that His love is indeed unfailing!

That's the refrain that opens and closes our **Introit** this week:

Oh give thanks to the LORD, for He is good; for His steadfast love endures forever!

The stone that the builders rejected has become the cornerstone. This is the LORD's doing; it is marvelous in our eyes. This is the day that the LORD has made; let us rejoice and be glad in it.

Glory be to the Father and to the Son and to the Holy Spirit; as it was in the beginning, is now, and will be forever. Amen.

Oh give thanks to the LORD, for He is good; for His steadfast love endures forever! (Ps 118:22–24; antiphon: Ps 118:1)

The Lord is indeed good, chiefly in that "His steadfast love endures forever!" God's love is foundational to everything! It's the reason He created the human race—to love us. It's the reason He created the world—to give His beloveds a beautiful place to live. And it's the reason we're still here—after our sin rejected His love. Not only is the Hebrew word חֶסֶד (*chesed*), which we translate "steadfast love" (or "loving kindness" or "mercy"), frequently said to "endure forever," but it often carries with it a connotation of forgiveness. That, of course, is why it continues to endure toward us sinners.

Jesus will quote verse 22 of Psalm 118 in our Gospel lesson, and it's tragic: "The stone that the builders rejected" will be Christ Himself. But from the tragedy somehow arises salvation: the rejected stone "has become the cornerstone." On Christ is built the Church—in which we each receive God's grace and eternal life. "This is the LORD's doing; it is marvelous in our eyes."

Which part of verse 22 is the Lord's doing? Which part is marvelous in our eyes? Christ becoming the cornerstone of the Church? Certainly. The rejection of Christ by the builders? No . . . and, well, yes. God never causes sin or rejection of His love. But in a way that's *literally* "marvelous" (that is, it makes us marvel; it's beyond our comprehension), God does use sinful rejection to accomplish His perfect will. In the face of rejection, God's love remains steadfast. That's how, even on a day we're recalling rejected love, we can chant, "This is the day that the LORD has made; let us rejoice and be glad in it."

The **Old Testament Reading** and the **Psalm** describe rejected love using closely related images, both of which Jesus was surely picturing as He spoke His upcoming parable. Read them together: Isaiah 5:1–7 and Psalm 80:7–19. It may be true for almost every era of history and every musical genre:

some of the most popular songs tell stories of brokenhearted love. Isaiah is singing a "love song" for his "beloved" (5:1a), and it goes badly. Isaiah's beloved is Yahweh, the Lord, and the song tells Yahweh's own love story by comparing His loved one to a vineyard: "My beloved had a vineyard on a very fertile hill" (5:1b).

The Lord courts His beloved, showering gifts upon her: clearing out the stones, selecting the choicest varietal vines, building a watchtower to ward off thieves and wild animals that might trample the grapes, even digging into the bedrock to hew a vat where the grapes could be crushed (5:2). No expense spared. Taking her to the most elegant restaurants, advancing six months' salary for the engagement diamond, building her dream house to start their married lives together.

It's just as in the Psalm, where Asaph sees God caring for the vine itself: "You brought a vine out of Egypt; You drove out the nations and planted it. You cleared the ground for it" (80:8–9a). You did everything You could to enable it to produce the finest grapes. "What more was there to do for My vineyard, that I have not done in it?" Yahweh asks in Isaiah's love song (5:4a). And He knows the answer: nothing! No expense has been spared!

Well, then, "When I looked for it to yield grapes, why did it yield wild grapes?" (5:4b). Grapes that could just as well have grown in the forest, no better than without the slightest cultivation and tending. Worthless for wine. Loved but without returning the affection. Cared for, receiving the lover's tender touches, gentle smiles, complete devotion, and then spurning it all. Giving back only a tight-lipped nod and a cold "Good day."

So "now I will tell you what I will do to My vineyard. I will remove its hedge, and it shall be devoured; I will break down its wall, and it shall be trampled down. I will make it a waste; it shall not be pruned or hoed, and briers and thorns shall grow up; I will also command the clouds that they rain no rain upon it" (5:5–6). You, O God, have "broken down its walls, so that all who pass along the way pluck its fruit. The boar from the forest ravages it, and all that move in the field feed on it" (80:12–13). Love scorned!

What does it all mean? "The vineyard of the Lord of hosts is the house of Israel, and the men of Judah are His pleasant planting" (5:7). Unfaithful lovers again and again—with the final rejection coming in our Gospel lesson.

And yet, in faith, the psalmist pleads, "Turn again, O God of hosts! . . . Have regard for this vine, . . . and for *the son* whom You made strong for Yourself" (80:14, 15). Israel itself was God's son (Hos 11:1), but from Israel one other Son was coming. Rejection answered with more love.

Few could ever have appreciated this as deeply as Paul, since he had so actively opposed Christ, persecuting the Church. Read his **Epistle**: Philippians 3:4b–14.

Paul had once tried his very best to establish his own righteousness by his Israelite heritage and his strict Pharisaic keeping of the Law (3:4b–6). Even persecuting the Church he chalked up to sincere, misguided zeal. But all that turned out to be "rubbish" (3:8). All that mattered, he learned, was that Christ had made him His own (3:12). That, Paul now also understood, happened because Christ, too, suffered the loss of all things when He went to the cross. Christ's love for Paul had spared nothing. Now, therefore, Paul was also willing to "press on" in his faith (3:12, 14), a new zeal that was properly directed.

Following immediately after last week's Gospel, the **Holy Gospel** for this Sunday again takes place on Tuesday of Holy Week. Read Matthew 21:33–46.

Jesus knows what's coming very soon, and He knows the Scriptures. He understands that the events of the next few days will play out the final stanza of Isaiah's tragic love song. So He frames His parable: "There was a master of a house who planted a vineyard and put a fence around it and dug a winepress in it and built a tower and leased it to tenants, and went into another country" (21:33). It is Isaiah's (and Asaph's) meticulously groomed vineyard. The master has given his tenants everything they need to produce the finest fruit.

How strangely they repay! Beat, killed, stoned those who came to get the master's share. Beat, killed, stoned some more (21:34–36). What to do? Put those wretches to a miserable death? We'd understand. Instead, "he sent his son" (21:37). Crazy! Insane! You know what's going to happen!

So did the Father. So did the Son. So why would they do it? No expense spared!

How many times had Israel and Judah rejected God's love for them? God who had brought them out of Egypt, made them His own, given them a land flowing with milk and honey, delivered them from the Philistines and Assyrians, led them home from Babylon. Wooed them with kind words and, yes, love songs. And they had worshiped the golden calf and the Baals, beaten, killed, and stoned God's prophets. Now made themselves and their keeping of the Law their idol.

Returned a tight-lipped nod and a cold "Good day" toward a Sunday in His house. Received rich gifts and offered Him a pittance. Jilted a lover and chased after another. Told our parents we're too busy this week. Rejected love.

You know what's going to happen! "The stone that the builders rejected . . ." (21:42). They're going to kill the Son!

And so, the Son comes—knowing and willing. Because He still loves the chief priests and Pharisees and all of us who've rejected His love. And He still wants them and us to repent and receive His love. That is—we are!—the fruit He wants His vineyard to produce. And His death at our hands has given the Kingdom to us to produce fruit (21:43). No expense spared!

Many of us know about rejected love. And God promises to be with us in our pain, because He understands—and because He responds with more love.

**Even If It's to Be Rejected,
the Lord Spares No Expense
in Enabling His Vineyard
to Produce the Fruit He Loves.**

As you sing the **Hymn of the Day**, "O Love, How Deep" (*LSB* 544), count how many times the hymnwriter tells us that God's love is still and always will be "for us."

The Sundays after Pentecost: Proper 23 (October 9–15) Year A

READINGS

Isaiah 25:6–9
Psalm 23 (antiphon: v 5a)
Philippians 4:4–13
Matthew 22:1–14

HYMN OF THE DAY

LSB 510 "A Multitude Comes from the East and the West"

In the spring of 2020, the initial days of the coronavirus pandemic, most of us all over the world were hunkered down at home in virtual isolation. We were looking to get out, to do just about anything with other people, but almost all major gatherings were canceled. You had to feel especially for families who lost loved ones and couldn't even attend their funerals, or for families who'd planned weddings and had to delay or scale down to perhaps only the couple and parents. The festivities, the food, the celebration, every detail so carefully drawn, had to be scrapped.

Then came the gradual reopening, and we were ready to party! I remember the first wedding in our circle of friends after the lockdown, and was it ever a welcome coming-out! The service of God's Word was beautiful, as were the flowers, the ladies' dresses, the gents' tuxes (well, I guess they were handsome). We caught up with dear folks we hadn't seen in months; everybody had a story to tell! And then there was the food. With Easter get-togethers scrubbed, restaurants closed, no opportunities to host, we hadn't had a feast like that since Christmas. Boy, did it taste good—particularly in that setting of celebration and fellowship! You wouldn't have dared miss it!

So frequently in Holy Scripture—including in our propers for this Sunday—God speaks of celebrations like this. Weddings. Feasts. Especially wedding feasts. He knows that whether we're coming out of a pandemic or just looking for a marvelous time, such images have a deep appeal to all of us. Who doesn't love a great party? Who doesn't appreciate an invitation like that?

Perhaps we'd be surprised.

But not by our **Introit** or the **Verse** for this week. Read them both, along with the **Collect** for Sunday. The Introit:

I will praise the Lord as long as I live; I will sing praises to my God while I have my being.

I will greatly rejoice in the Lord; my soul shall exult in my God, for He has clothed me with the garments of salvation; He has covered me with the robe of righteousness, as a bridegroom decks himself like a priest with a beautiful headdress, and as a bride adorns herself with her jewels.

Glory be to the Father and to the Son and to the Holy Spirit; as it was in the beginning, is now, and will be forever. Amen.

I will praise the Lord as long as I live; I will sing praises to my God while I have my being. (Is 61:10; antiphon: Ps 146:2)

The Verse:

Alleluia. The Spirit and the Bride say, "Come." Let the one who hears say, "Come." Let the one who is thirsty come; let the one who desires take the water of life without price. Alleluia. (Rev 22:17)

The Collect:

Almighty God, You invite us to trust in You for our salvation. Deal with us not in the severity of Your judgment but by the greatness of Your mercy; through Jesus Christ, Your Son, our Lord, who lives and reigns with You and the Holy Spirit, one God, now and forever. Amen.

Life in the Lord is always a celebration—a reason to "sing praises" "as long as I live," as long as "I have my being"! That's because He's taken away the filthy rags of our sins and "clothed me with the garments of salvation; He has covered me with the robe of righteousness," so that we're ready for a wedding!—"as a bridegroom decks himself like a priest with a beautiful headdress [and that's just the groom!], and as a bride adorns herself with her jewels." A gorgeous wedding!

"Come!" say the Bride and the Spirit! You're invited! "Come!" After all, it's free! "Let the one who desires take the water of life *without price*." The Host provides everything! Who wouldn't want to come? "Almighty God, You *invite* us to trust in You for our salvation." Who wouldn't jump at the invitation?

Well, apparently, *someone*, because the Collect goes on, "Deal with us not in the severity of Your judgment." That doesn't fit the party spirit! Not at all. But God's severe judgment comes when someone spurns His invitation. Who would do such a thing?

Why Wouldn't Everyone Want to Come to the Lord's Wedding Feast!?!

That's the question to be explored in the rest of the propers for Sunday. And notice our punctuation. Exclamation point. Question mark. Exclamation point.

First, the first exclamation point. Why, wouldn't *everyone* want to come to the Lord's wedding feast! It's rhetorical, right? Of course everyone wants to come to the feast! Right?

Surely no one would turn down an invitation to the feast Isaiah describes in the **Old Testament Reading**, Isaiah 25:6–9!

Why does God use this imagery of feasting, especially wedding feasts, so often in Scripture? Surely one reason is because the appeal is so universal; everyone loves good food and drink! And this is the best: "a feast of rich food, a feast of well-aged wine, of rich food full of marrow, of aged wine well refined" (25:6b). Let your mouth water even as you read those words out loud! When we say food is "rich," we usually mean it leaves us feeling a little too full—sauces of heavy cream, lavishly marbled Wagyu beef, the calorie count enough for three days. But worth it for an occasion. And the wine—Isaiah pictures the sort of vintage about which someone who knows (which I don't!) says, "Ahhh, a '43."

The "Lord of hosts" is hosting this "for all peoples" (25:6a).

I think a second reason God uses feasting images so often in Scripture is that it's something we really will be doing for eternity. When our bodies are raised, we'll certainly live physically, and dining may well be part of that. Isaiah's vision of course symbolizes God's gracious provision already now, especially in Holy Communion, but he also sees the end result: The Lord "will swallow up . . . the covering that is cast over all peoples, the veil that is spread over all nations. He will swallow up death forever" and "will wipe away tears from all faces" (25:7–8). The ultimate Debbie Downer, the pooper for every party, is that it's finally going to end badly, in death. The "covering," the "veil," the shroud, is the pall of certain death that hangs over all of us. But Christ has swallowed that up by His own death and resurrection. So we look forward to Isaiah's vision also being fulfilled literally in the new creation! Communing at a literal table of the Lord—that's where the food and wine will truly exceed anything we've tasted here. And in sinless bodies where metabolism is 100 percent efficient, we won't count calories. Just saaaaavor it!

Who wouldn't want to be there!

We all know Psalm 23, but this Sunday of the church year, the antiphon appointed for the **Psalm**, for special focus, is verse 5a.

The point of the beloved "Shepherd's Psalm," we realize, actually has nothing to do with sheep. The point is that by the Lord's loving care, we "shall not want" (23:1). If we were sheep, He'd give us precisely the green pastures and still waters we need. But we're people—and what we really want is "a table" filled with those rich foods and a "cup" of the finest drink that "overflows" (23:5). Notice, it's just as Isaiah said: the party never ends; it will last "forever" (23:6). Who doesn't want that!

Even writing from prison, even though he isn't feasting at all, Paul clearly rejoices in God's invitation. Read our **Epistle**, Philippians 4:4–13.

How can Paul "rejoice in the Lord always" (4:4), even in "hunger" and "need"

(4:12)? Even under these circumstances, Paul knows that he shall not want: "Do not be anxious about anything, but in everything by prayer and supplication with thanksgiving let your requests be made known to God" (4:6). The Lord will provide. Even if, for now, it doesn't appear to be "plenty," "abundance" (4:12), He does provide "whatever is true, whatever is honorable, whatever is just, whatever is pure, whatever is lovely, whatever is commendable" (4:8). That's plenty to think about! Wouldn't everyone want that!

But now there's the question mark. Why wouldn't everyone want to come to the Lord's wedding feast? In our **Holy Gospel**, many don't! Why? Read Matthew 22:1–14.

The king's wedding feast for his son is everything Isaiah promised: "oxen" and "fat calves" (22:4) indicate animals set aside just for this occasion. USDA Prime! And this is an invitation to the king's place!

Incredibly, no takers! Why not? It's not just a matter of coronavirus caution.

Some simply "paid no attention," going off to their farms and businesses (22:5). We all have to make a living. We all have other daily duties, social engagements, family needs too. But it's God who gives us our jobs, our friends, our families—for *this* life. He never books them to conflict with His invitation to the eternal banquet. We're the ones who sometimes choose today over forever. Foolishly! We put the "Save the Date" on our refrigerator but forget to RSVP.

Others the king invited "seized his servants, treated them shamefully, and killed them" (22:6). Who does such a thing? Those who hate the king so much that they would rather surely die (22:7) than sit down at his table to enjoy his free and opulent dinner. Those today who are resolved to silence the voice of the Church, to martyr Christ's people, to mock God for everyone to hear.

Finally, there's the one who does enter the wedding hall but without the proper garment. "'Friend, how did you get in here without a wedding garment?' And he was speechless" (22:12). Speechless because, according to the custom of the day, the host *gave* everyone their wedding clothes ("He has clothed me with the garments of salvation"). Remember? It's all free, without price! But some are willing to come to the Lord's wedding feast only on their own terms, rejecting His "robe of righteousness" and insisting on appearing in the rags of their own pathetic works. "Outer darkness" for this one too. "In that place there will be weeping and gnashing of teeth" (22:13).

No doubt, though, a third reason God uses the wedding feast imagery so often in Scripture is that He throws this banquet for Christ and His Bride, the Church (Eph 5:22–33). And this wedding Christ solemnized by dying on the cross—to seat us not only in the wedding hall but also next to Him at the head table, front and center—where the food is rich, the wine well aged. Endless and flowing. And free. That despite our deserving outer darkness.

That's the final exclamation point! Why wouldn't everyone want to come to the Lord's wedding feast!?! Oh, how much we do!

Close with the **Hymn of the Day**, looking forward to joining the multitude from east and west to sit at the feast of salvation.

The Sundays after Pentecost: Proper 24 (October 16–22) Year A

READINGS

Isaiah 45:1–7
Psalm 96:1–9 (10–13)
(antiphon: v 9a)
1 Thessalonians 1:1–10
Matthew 22:15–22

HYMN OF THE DAY

LSB 940 "Holy God, We Praise Thy Name"

Well-known Washington commentators Mark and Mollie Hemingway have written:

> It is undeniable that there is profound need to remain vigilant against the onslaught directed at the rights of believers and churches to practice their faith. . . . We should feel compelled, not just as Christians but by our vocation as citizens, to make the case that religious liberty is the very first freedom mentioned in the Bill of Rights for a reason. . . . We have arrived at a place where the media often put the phrase "religious liberty" in scare quotes as if it were some new or debatable idea. (*Concordia Pulpit Resources*, 30.1 [CPH, 2020]:10–11)

We've come a long way—unfortunately—since a so-called "separation of church and state" (yes, scare quotes) was asserted *for the protection of churches* and believers' rights to practice their religion. In so many specific ways that the Hemingways go on to elaborate, our religious freedom is more and more being threatened—or taken away!

When we do make the case for religious liberty, we're most often doing it in the public square—"out there" (hopefully, *not* scare quotes) in the world. There we're trying to persuade also unbelievers, so our arguments must appeal largely to rationale and evidence other than Scripture. But as Christians, we certainly want to be clear first on what God Himself teaches us in His Word about our place as citizens and about the relationship between God's authority and the authorities of this world, like governments.

Some of the most definitive instructions on church and state in all of Scripture—certainly the clearest by Jesus Himself—are found in this week's Gospel lesson. Jesus' words about rendering unto Caesar teach us much about the Christian's relationship with secular government. Along with the other propers for the week, they can be foundational for our understanding of this very pressing issue.

The big question, of course, is who is really in authority. Our **Introit** declares:

> *The Lord is your keeper; the Lord is your shade on your right hand.*
>
> *I lift up my eyes to the hills. From where does my help come? My help comes from the Lord, who made heaven and earth. He will not let your foot be moved; He who keeps you will not slumber. Behold, He who keeps Israel will neither slumber nor sleep. The Lord will keep you from all evil; He will keep your life. The Lord will keep your going out and your coming in from this time forth and forevermore.*
>
> *Glory be to the Father and to the Son and to the Holy Spirit; as it was in the beginning, is now, and will be forever. Amen.*
>
> *The Lord is your keeper; the Lord is your shade on your right hand. (Ps 121:1–4, 7–8; antiphon: Ps 121:5)*

David is emphatic! Yahweh, "the Lord," is the one in authority! David's key word to express this is "keeper" (or "keep" or "keeps")—seven times. What does that word teach about how the Lord exercises authority?

When David would "lift up [his] eyes to the hills," he saw pagan sites of worship there on the high places. He knew the pagan gods weren't his authorities. The Lord was. But that authority of Yahweh David explicitly calls "my help." We may think of "keeping" as something done selfishly—"I keep such and such for myself, and you can't have it"—and we often view authority that way. Government-imposed speed limits keep me from driving as fast as I'd like. The IRS keeps (withholds) the portion of "my" income (definitely scare quotes!) the law says it may before I get any of it. David instead understood that having the Lord keep him—always on duty for us, neither slumbering nor sleeping—was the safest and most loving care he could receive. The Lord keeps us, owns us, exercises authority over us in the kindest divine love.

The **Collect** for this Sunday underscores that point and adds an indication of the differing jurisdictions of authority:

> *O God, the protector of all who trust in You, have mercy on us that with You as our ruler and guide we may so pass through things temporal that we lose not the things eternal; through Jesus Christ, Your Son, our Lord, who lives and reigns with You and the Holy Spirit, one God, now and forever. Amen.*

God is "our ruler." That's an unmistakable authority word. But He is also "the protector of all who trust in" Him. Just as David knew, God rules over us to protect us.

And see the different areas of responsibility: "things temporal" and "things eternal." God sometimes delegates to others, like secular governments, authority over "things temporal," things in time, things of this world, through which we're just passing. But He always retains for Himself direct control over our eternity. Jesus will focus on this distinction in the Gospel reading.

The **Verse** summarizes well. (When the Verse isn't drawn from one of the assigned readings, it's especially chosen to point us to the theme for the week.)

Alleluia. You have been filled in Him, who is the head of all rule and authority. Alleluia. (Col 2:10)

Paul's context makes explicit that "Him" refers to Christ (Col 2:8–9). Jesus Himself, as God, holds all authority.

The **Old Testament Reading** describes a secular authority, Cyrus, ruler of the great Persian Empire, being used by Yahweh, the Higher Authority, for His purposes. Read Isaiah 45:1–7.

Cyrus came to power in 559 BC, about 150 years after Isaiah wrote. (This causes, as you might guess, those who reject predictive prophecy to assume that someone later wrote this portion of Isaiah. Take that one up with the Holy Spirit, and consider how many times Isaiah looked even farther ahead and foresaw Christ: Is 7:14; 9:6; 53:4–6 as just a few examples.) Cyrus is the king who in 539 BC conquered Babylon, the previous greatest empire of the day (see Daniel 5). Secular history records this as one of the great moments in ancient history.

However, through Isaiah, the Lord declares that everything Cyrus accomplished was by His design and power: "I am the Lord, who does all these things" (45:7). Cyrus was Yahweh's "anointed" (the same word we recognize as "messiah"!), whom He took by the hand and enabled to "subdue nations" (45:1). That included breaking down "the doors of bronze" and "bars of iron" of Babylon (45:2). Cyrus may have changed the world, conquered more of it than any previous emperor in history, but make no mistake: "Besides Me [Yahweh] there is no God" (45:5a), no other original authority.

And as we've seen, God exercised that authority for the blessing of His people: "for the sake of My servant Jacob, and Israel My chosen" (45:4a). Sure enough: among his next acts after conquering Babylon, Cyrus in 536 BC issued the decree that the Jews could return home from their Babylonian captivity. God used Cyrus, a secular authority who did not even believe in Him (45:4b, 5b) to return the lineage of David (Joseph, Mary) to the place where His true Messiah would come.

Read Psalm 96:1–13. See how according to the **Psalm**, too, there is only one final authority (96:5). While kings and courts, presidents and judges, may act out important legislation, it is still always the Lord who reigns and judges, and He always does so "with equity," "in righteousness" (96:10, 13).

The **Epistle** for Sunday, 1 Thessalonians 1:1–10, now teaches us about another kind of authority, still the Lord's, but carried out in a different way. Authorities like governments (also bosses, commanding officers, schoolteachers, and such) operate in what Lutherans call the "kingdom of the left." These all motivate by coercion—jail, firing (or giving raises), dressing down (or giving *A*'s). These are actually all forms of God's *Law*, which, obviously, God uses too.

But Paul is depicting here to the Thessalonians the beautiful, *Gospel*-motivated "kingdom of the right," the Church. Read it again and note how, once the "gospel came . . . in power and in the Holy Spirit" (1:5a), the Christians in Thessalonica willingly, eagerly, followed the example of the authorities God the Father and the Lord Jesus Christ placed over them: Paul, Silas, and Timothy (1:1, 5b–6). Paul here gives no hint of coercion; the motivation is purely that Jesus, by His death and resurrection, has delivered them from God's wrath (1:10).

Finally, read the **Holy Gospel**, Jesus' own words on authority: Matthew 22:15–22.

Just days before they will succeed, Jesus' enemies are looking for a way to destroy him. They hit on this: If Jesus okays paying taxes to Caesar, His huge Palm Sunday following will surely abandon Him; He's not the one to free us from Rome after all! But if He opposes paying taxes to this secular, even evil, government, they'll charge Him with treason before Pilate, the Roman governor. Either way, they think, they've got Him!

Rather, Jesus endorses God's authority fully, while teaching that God also delegates *certain realms* of His authority. Here's how.

God actually holds all authority over everything ("the things that are God's," 22:21). But God allows others to carry out some functions of that authority, establishing lesser authorities under Himself (see Rom 13:1). To begin, way back in the Garden of Eden, before the first sin, He delegated some authority to families (Gen 1:26–28). So families have duties to raise children, see that they're educated, feed them, set bedtimes, determine family budgets. Then families may delegate parts of their authority to others: for example, to schools to teach their children or to governments to protect their shores, to keep law and order, to collect the garbage ("the things that are Caesar's," Mt 22:21, which are always "things temporal"). Realize, governments are established by families, as delegation of God's own authority.

In this way,

**THE LORD, WHO IS ALWAYS
OUR KEEPER, PROTECTOR, AND RULER,
DOES SOME OF HIS KEEPING THROUGH
OTHER AUTHORITIES HE ANOINTS.**

Always for our good!

Final thought: never does God delegate to anyone the authority to establish what we are to believe or what's truly right or wrong ("things eternal"). He always keeps that for Himself. Thus if any "authority" (yup, scare quotes) commands us to sin or believe in anything other than Jesus Christ, our Savior, *on that subject* it is no authority (even if it still has God's authority to collect taxes). In such cases, "We must obey God rather than men" (Acts 5:29). That's the limit.

Close by reaffirming God's holy and everlasting reign over all other authorities: the **Hymn of the Day**, *LSB* 940.

The Sundays after Pentecost: Proper 25 (October 23–29) Year A

READINGS

Leviticus 19:1–2, 15–18
Psalm 1 (antiphon: v 1a)
1 Thessalonians 2:1–13
Matthew 22:34–46

HYMNS OF THE DAY

LSB 411 "I Want to Walk as a Child of the Light"
LSB 579 "The Law of God Is Good and Wise"

Many congregations observe the Festival of the Reformation during their regular service on the Sunday that falls between October 25 and October 31, inclusive. Therefore, the elements for Proper 25 detailed in the following devotion-study may in many years be omitted and the Reformation propers used in their place. When this is the case, refer to the devotion-study for Reformation Day (p 250) to look forward to this Sunday morning.

The Holy Gospel for Proper 25 has two distinct parts. In some respects they are quite independent of each other; they could well be two separate readings. Further, the other propers for the day are clearly connected to the first part of the Gospel lesson rather than to the second. However, reading both portions of the Gospel lesson together, along with the other propers for the day, will reveal how helpful that second portion of the lesson is to the first.

Let's begin, therefore, with the first part of the Gospel reading and continue with most of the other propers. Eventually, we'll consider the last portion of the Holy Gospel and see how that throws new light on everything we've previously read.

The **Holy Gospel** once again takes place during Holy Week as Jesus' enemies are seeking to trap Him in His words. Read the first portion, Matthew 22:34–40.

Each group of Jesus' opponents has taken its shot. The Sadducees have just failed, as had the chief priests and elders and the Pharisees and Herodians before them. Now the Pharisees come back "to test Him" (22:35) one more time. A "lawyer" was a scholar of the Old Testament scriptures, "the law," or Torah, plus the countless man-made laws added to God's Word over the centuries. With such a morass of legal literature, to identify one commandment as the greatest was a significant question.

Jesus names *two* commandments, since they are so closely related as to be virtually equal ("like") in value (22:39). To "love the Lord your God with all your heart and with all your soul and with all your mind" (22:37) was originally attached to the *Shema*, the great creed of the Old Testament faithful, "Hear, O Israel: The Lord our God, the Lord is one" (Deut 6:4–5). Nothing is more important than loving God above all things.

But one can never separate loving God from loving one's neighbor as oneself (22:39). When one loves God, he or she will most certainly also love those fellow souls God also created and loves. Conversely, if someone does not love his neighbor (whom he has seen), he most surely does not really love God (whom he has not seen; cf 1 Jn 4:20). This commandment to love the neighbor summarizes so many of the commands throughout Scripture, as the Old Testament Reading will illustrate.

In fact, these two commandments we use to summarize the entire Ten Commandments—which we understand as a summary of God's entire moral law. Picture the two tablets of stone (though we don't really know how many commandments were written on each). "Love God" sums up what we call the "First Table of the Law," Commandments One through Three by Lutheran counting. No other gods, God's name used only in holy ways, worship on the Lord's Day—these are all expressions of loving God. Then, "love our neighbor" summarizes the "Second Table of the Law," Commandments Four through Ten. We love our parents; we love others so that we don't harm them or break our marriage vows or steal from them, slander them, or desire sinfully what belongs to them. "On these two commandments," Jesus says, "depend all the Law and the Prophets" (22:40).

But consider: "the Law and the Prophets" was a shorthand way of speaking of all the Old Testament. And the Old Testament includes more than just commandments that *we* are to keep. What about those many things in the Old Testament that *God* did? More on that later.

For now, see how the other propers elaborate on God's commands to us to love Him and our neighbor. First, the **Introit**:

For the needy shall not always be forgotten, and the hope of the poor shall not perish forever.

I will give thanks to the Lord with my whole heart; I will recount all of Your wonderful deeds. I will be glad and exult in You; I will sing praise to Your name, O Most High. The Lord is a stronghold for the oppressed, a stronghold in times of trouble. And those who know Your name put their trust in You, for You, O Lord, have not forsaken those who seek You.

Glory be to the Father and to the Son and to the Holy Spirit; as it was

in the beginning, is now, and will be forever. Amen.

For the needy shall not always be forgotten, and the hope of the poor shall not perish forever. (Ps 9:1–2, 9–10; antiphon: Ps 9:18)

It's easy to see in the antiphon the moral obligation we have to love our "poor" and "needy" neighbors. We must not forget them or allow them to perish in their destitution. And, of course, "poor" and "needy" can take many forms—the previously successful entrepreneur who overextended this time and has fallen into bankruptcy, the divorced woman who very much needs a friend, the kid who's all alone on the playground.

Likewise, David loves the Lord with all his heart, his "whole heart." He will "give thanks to the Lord," "be glad and exult" in Him, "sing praise" to His name. Our worship and praise of God (the Third Commandment), whether on Sunday morning, with our families at home, or in conversations with friends that witness to His name (Second Commandment), are active keepings of the great (and First) commandment.

The **Old Testament Reading** is actually Jesus' text when He cites that "like" commandment. Read Leviticus 19:1–2, 15–18.

You "love your neighbor as yourself" (19:18b) when you're fair—in court (19:15) or in caring equally for each of your children, your students, your employees; not favoring one who's richer, smarter, or more cooperative. You love your neighbor when you speak kindly about her (19:16a), not blaming her to get yourself off the hook, not telling a story about her to grab the spotlight for yourself. You love your neighbor when you do stand up for the life of the unborn (19:16b). You love your neighbor when you don't hold a secret grudge against him (19:17–18a) but rather air your hurts with him privately so you can forgive each other. Obviously, the list goes on and on and on—through the book of Leviticus even (who'd have thought!) and from Genesis through Revelation.

Psalm 1, perhaps not surprisingly, focuses on Jesus' first commandment, love of God. Read the **Psalm**. Two ways of life the psalmist sees: "the wicked" and the man whose "delight is in the law of the Lord" (1:2). The man who loves the Lord is "blessed" (1:1), firmly planted, secure, now and for eternity. But wickedness, breaking this commandment, means being blown away (1:4).

Our **Epistle** brings both commandments together. Read 1 Thessalonians 2:1–13.

Paul came to the Thessalonians not in "flattery" to "please man" or in "pretext for greed" (2:4–5); he came "to please God," "to declare . . . the gospel of God," "approved by God" (2:4, 2, 4). Love God. But he did care about man, love his neighbor. He was "gentle among you, like a nursing mother taking care of her own children. . . . Like a father with his children, we exhorted each one of you and encouraged you" (2:7, 11–12a). "So, being affectionately desirous of you, we were ready to share with you not only the gospel of God but also our own selves, because you had become very dear to us" (2:8).

For our keeping of both commandments, we pray the **Collect** for this Sunday:

O God, You have commanded us to love You above all things and our neighbors as ourselves. Grant us the Spirit to think and do what is pleasing in Your sight, that our faith in You may never waver and our love for one another may not falter; through Jesus Christ, Your Son, our Lord, who lives and reigns with You and the Holy Spirit, one God, now and forever. Amen.

But who *can* keep these commandments?

Remember that "all the Law and the Prophets" depend on these two commandments—but also that the Law and the Prophets are more than just what *we* are to do with these commands. So there's the rest of the **Holy Gospel**. Read now Matthew 22:41–46.

"As long as you're here," Jesus goes on with the Pharisees, "*I've* got a couple of questions *for you*." The first one's easy. "Son of David" was a universally recognized title for the Christ. Fair enough; we all agree. But then, Jesus points out that, in Psalm 110, David quotes Yahweh, the Lord, God Himself, as saying to someone else, *who's also David's Lord*, "Sit at My right hand." Everyone agrees that that someone else is the Christ, David's son. But a king as great as David normally would never call a descendant his "Lord." The descendant (the "son") would normally call the ancestor (David) "lord," not the other way around. How this then?

This turnaround is possible only because David knew his descendant was also God Himself. He would truly be David's Son because He would be born of David's descendant Mary (and adopted by another of David's descendants, Joseph). But by the Holy Spirit working the miracle of the virgin birth in Mary, this Christ, David's Son, is also the Son of God. David was a great prophet (writing "in the Spirit," 22:43), but his Son, Christ, was Lord over even the great prophet.

The Pharisees didn't want to see that in Jesus. But for us, *that's* what all the Law and Prophets depend on. The entire Old Testament (and New) is about Christ (since He's God) fulfilling the demands of God's commandments as Adam, Eve, and all of us have failed to do—very soon now even taking the punishment for our failure upon the cross.

Christ is the one who loves God and neighbor perfectly—and then gives us His love to do the same (imperfectly). Look again at each of the propers and envision Christ as the one doing all the loving—with us then loving because of Christ's "wonderful deeds" for us (Introit), which we receive by "faith in You," that "our love for one another may not falter" (Collect). We *shall be* holy because Christ is holy (Old Testament Reading). We delight in the law of the Lord because Jesus did (Psalm). We are righteous in our conduct toward others because He was to us (Epistle).

On the Commandments to Love God and Love Neighbor Depend All the Law and the Prophets, but Keeping Them Depends on the One Who Is Lord of the Law and the Prophets.

Two **Hymn of the Day** options: note especially, *LSB* 579 teaches the demands of God's Commandments but stanza 6 directs us to the one and only who fulfills them for us.

The Sundays after Pentecost: Proper 26 (October 30–November 5) Year A

READINGS

Micah 3:5–12
Psalm 43 (antiphon: v 3)
1 Thessalonians 4:1–12
Matthew 23:1–12

HYMN OF THE DAY

LSB 585 "Lord Jesus Christ, with Us Abide"

Many congregations observe the Festival of the Reformation during their regular service on the Sunday that falls between October 25 and October 31, inclusive. Likewise, many observe the Feast of All Saints during the regular service on the Sunday between November 1 and 7 inclusive. Therefore, the elements for Proper 26 detailed in the following devotion-study may in many years be omitted and the Reformation or All Saints' propers used in their place. When either is the case, refer to the devotion-study for Reformation Day *(p 250)* *or All Saints' Day* *(p 254)* *to look forward to this Sunday morning.*

What, exactly, was the Pharisees' problem? And when does it become our problem?

Jesus concludes this Sunday's Gospel reading, the first part of His lengthy diatribe against the Pharisees, with this assessment: "Whoever exalts himself will be humbled, and whoever humbles himself will be exalted" (Mt 23:12). He speaks almost identical words two other times (Lk 14:11; 18:14), both also critiquing the Pharisees.

That fits. When we say "Pharisee," even of a contemporary person, it almost always brings to mind pride, conceit, exalting oneself. But exalting oneself over what or whom? And when do *we* do this?

The **Introit** implies the ultimate answer:

> *Praise the name of the Lord, for His name alone is exalted; His majesty is above earth and heaven.*
>
> *Praise the Lord! Sing to the Lord a new song, His praise in the assembly of the godly! Let Israel be glad in*

his Maker; let the children of Zion rejoice in their King! Let them praise His name with dancing, making melody to Him with tambourine and lyre! For the LORD *takes pleasure in His people; He adorns the humble with salvation.*

Glory be to the Father and to the Son and to the Holy Spirit; as it was in the beginning, is now, and will be forever. Amen.

Praise the name of the LORD, *for His name alone is exalted; His majesty is above earth and heaven. (Ps 149: 1–4; antiphon: Ps 148:13)*

Quite rightly, the Lord's name "*alone* is exalted." We are exalting ourselves any time we take something away from the Lord. To Him alone belongs all credit, honor, glory. To humble oneself means above all to exalt Him—to "praise the name of the LORD, . . . sing to the LORD a new song, . . . be glad in [our] Maker." And those who humble themselves the Lord does indeed exalt: "He adorns the humble with salvation."

The **Collect** for this Sunday, then, suggests what may be the chief expression of exalting ourselves above the Lord:

Merciful and gracious Lord, You cause Your Word to be proclaimed in every generation. Stir up our hearts and minds by Your Holy Spirit that we may receive this proclamation with humility and finally be exalted at the coming of Your Son, our Savior, Jesus Christ, who lives and reigns with You and the Holy Spirit, one God, now and forever. Amen.

"Lord, You cause Your Word to be proclaimed in every generation." God comes to us in His Word. That's how we know Him. That's how we have a relationship with Him. We don't see God; we don't even yet see His Son. But we are intimate with Him as He speaks to us in Holy Scripture. So it's in honoring God's Word that we exalt His name.

Luther reminds us as he writes about the First Petition of the Lord's Prayer, "Hallowed be Thy name": "God's name is kept holy when the *Word of God* is taught in its truth and purity, and we, as the children of God, also lead holy lives according to it." That's exalting God's name. We thus pray in the Collect "that we may receive this proclamation [of the Word] with *humility* and *finally be exalted* at the coming of Your Son, our Savior, Jesus Christ." He who humbles himself to receive God's Word will be exalted.

"But," Luther goes on to write, "anyone who teaches or lives contrary to God's Word profanes the name of God among us." Teaching or living contrary to God's Word is nothing other than exalting ourselves above His Word, determining that we know better than the Word tells us. That, of course, is exalting ourselves above God Himself.

Exalting God is done by humbly receiving His Word. We exalt ourselves when we disregard or dishonor His Word.

The four readings give examples of this—exalting self above God's Word or exalting

God by humbly receiving His Word—culminating with Jesus and those Pharisees. First, the **Old Testament Reading**, Micah 3:5–12.

Micah was a contemporary of Isaiah, both of them speaking to Judah in the latter portion of the 700s BC, but clearly not all prophets of the day were as faithful. The prophet's task was to proclaim God's Word, but too many "lead My people astray" (3:5), giving an encouraging word, "Peace!" when they get paid for it, but condemning those who don't grease their palms. They "practice divination for money" (3:11c). Likewise, the "heads" or "rulers" of Israel "give judgment for a bribe" (3:9, 11a), and the "priests teach for a price" (3:11b). Never mind what God says. What matters is how I profit. They were exalting themselves above God by exalting themselves above His Word.

Pastors, beware! Do you get to the hospital every day for three weeks while your best giver is rehabbing but figure a phone call is enough before a delinquent member goes into surgery? Do you soft-pedal preaching against abortion because an MD in your congregation is on the other side? Do you allow visitors and family members from other church bodies to commune because you're afraid turning them away will discourage growth of the congregation?

Micah says prophets like this "shall be disgraced, . . . put to shame" (3:7). Jerusalem, which follows them or is misled by them, "shall become a heap of ruins" (3:12). Whoever exalts himself above God's Word will be humbled!

"But as for me," Micah says, "I," when I speak only what Yahweh gives me to say, "am filled with power, with the Spirit of the Lord, and with justice and might, to declare to Jacob his transgression and to Israel his sin" (3:8). Some of it may be unpleasant; like all the true prophets, Micah suffered when he decried sin. But bowing to God's Word, he knew the Lord's power would bring His results—and eventually exalt him as well.

As you read the **Psalm**, especially note the antiphon, verse 3 of Psalm 43.

The psalmist is facing persecution from "an ungodly people" (43:1). He even feels as if God has rejected him (43:2). But see where he still looks for help: "Send out Your light and Your truth; let them lead me; let them bring me to Your holy hill and to Your dwelling!" God's "light," God's "truth," is His Holy Word. When he needs help the most, the psalmist doesn't look to his own cleverness or to other helpers he might find for himself (exalting himself)—the way we might hide our faith to avoid argument or be quiet about, say, Baptism or the Lord's Supper in order to fit into a larger Christian gang. The psalmist trusts that God's Word will lead him. He will be exalted to the holy hilltop! He "shall again praise" God (43:5).

The **Epistle** shows how one of the most common temptations known to man and woman is also an exalting of self over God's Word. Read 1 Thessalonians 4:1–12.

Paul is very explicit in addressing sexual immorality (even more so in the Greek; in 4:4, σκεῦος, translated as "body" in the ESV, can be much more explicitly sexual). To state the obvious: not only is the temptation to sexual thought and activity outside of marriage almost universal, but in our day, every imaginable (and unimaginable) sexual behavior is fully endorsed. This, we know, has had its influence on every one of us and on every Christian congregation.

Few sins are more selfish, self-exalting. They gratify one's desires while always hurting and degrading another person. They are a direct contradiction to "the will of God" for us: our "sanctification" (4:3), our new life of holiness in the Lord. So the Lord Jesus is clear in His "instructions" on the matter (4:2). "Therefore whoever disregards this, disregards not man but God," for we "have been taught by God to love one another" (4:8, 9). Whoever exalts himself above *this* word of God will surely be humbled: "The Lord is an avenger in all these things" (4:6).

So many ways to be a pharisee.

Including the original one. Read the **Holy Gospel**, Matthew 23:1–12.

The Pharisees were religious conservatives of first-century Israel. They actually had a noble heritage, having vigorously opposed the corruption of Jewish tradition after Greek occupation two centuries earlier. They took the sacred texts very seriously—they thought. "So practice and observe whatever they tell you," Jesus said, "but"—and this turned out to be a very big "but"—"not what they do. For they preach, but do not practice" (23:3).

The list of their hypocrisies was long (23:4–7)—and longer (read also the seven "woes" in 23:13–36). In particular, they loved the honor and praise of men, to be exalted in public opinion. And they were that—highly admired by the common people.

We do know the Pharisees' problem, don't we. Keeping the "right people" in the congregation happy does matter to us, doesn't it. So do numbers that show growth. We do want to be noticed for what we wear—even if it might tempt someone else's "sanctification." We do sometimes say one thing among our Lutheran friends and something different to be approved by others.

"They preach, but do not practice." Precisely what Luther warned: "Anyone who . . . lives contrary to God's Word profanes the name of God among us." The Pharisees claimed God's Word, but in fact exalted themselves above it. That was their real problem, because with it came the inevitable result, exalting themselves above the Giver of the Word: "You are not to be called rabbi, for you have one teacher. . . . Neither be called instructors, for you have one instructor, the Christ" (23:8, 10). By failing to humble themselves to God's Word, they rejected God Himself, Jesus. How tragic!

For it is at Jesus' coming that we will be finally exalted. Jesus is the one who humbled Himself even to death on the cross. That's the Word God has proclaimed in every generation. So by humbly receiving that Word which promises life in Christ, we receive Him. And receiving Him, we are exalted.

Those Who Exalt Themselves above God's Word Disregard Him and Will Be Put to Shame, but Those Who Are Humble to Receive and Practice His Truth Praise Him and Will Be Exalted.

"Restrain, O Lord, the human pride That seeks to thrust Your truth aside" (**Hymn of the Day**, "Lord Jesus Christ, with Us Abide," by Nicolaus Selnecker, *LSB* 585:5).

Reformation Day Years A, B, C

READINGS

Revelation 14:6–7
Psalm 46 (antiphon: v 7)
Romans 3:19–28
John 8:31–36
or Matthew 11:12–19

HYMNS OF THE DAY

LSB 656, 657 "A Mighty Fortress Is Our God"
LSB 555 "Salvation unto Us Has Come"

Five centuries ago, on October 31, 1517, the door of the Castle Church in Wittenberg, Germany, was massive and heavy and made of wood, able to receive nails and hammer blows and serve as the town bulletin board. Today, the same door of the great Gothic structure is still massive and even heavier and made of bronze. No one enters or exits that way anymore, and nails couldn't penetrate. But on the bronze surface are raised letters spelling out the Ninety-Five Theses, the call to debate that Luther posted that famous day over five hundred years ago.

The fact that the door has changed over the centuries is to be expected. The fact that the words haven't changed speaks volumes. The fact that those words are read by new generations even today is a testimony to the continuing power and grace of God.

My Lutheran heart always beats a little faster on Reformation Day. The one and only time I've lost my voice for preaching was a Reformation Sunday morning in my last congregation, and not being able to sing "A Mighty Fortress," along with having to whisper the sermon into the microphone, I count as mischief of the devil. But belted out or whispered, even after so many centuries, the Reformation *must* be proclaimed every year! The Reformation is, after all, the means by which God safely delivered to us today the unchanging Gospel that has given you and me and our children eternal life.

Most of our churches will, of course, celebrate Reformation Day on Sunday morning, the nearest Sunday on or before October 31. Perhaps your congregation also has a special Reformation festival or you're blessed to live in an area where several congregations get together for a festival service on Sunday afternoon or even the evening of the 31st. (I know; it's Halloween.) If your Reformation service is on Sunday morning, it's likely the Reformation Day propers will be substituted in whole or in part for the Pentecost season Proper 25 or 26 appointments. It's those Reformation Day propers we'll look at here. They're typified, I think, by that Wittenberg door and Reformation preaching five hundred years later.

Therefore, this week, let me give my THEME right up front, and, as we proceed, check back and see how each proper develops some aspect of it.

GOD, AS OUR REFUGE AND STRENGTH, ENABLES HIS REFORMERS TO SPEAK TO THE NEXT GENERATION THE ETERNAL GOSPEL THAT SETS US FREE: JUSTIFICATION BY GRACE THROUGH FAITH IN JESUS CHRIST.

The **Introit** begins with an antiphon long associated with the Reformation.

I will speak of Your testimonies before kings, [O Lord,] and shall not be put to shame.

I will bless the LORD at all times; His praise shall continually be in my mouth. My soul makes its boast in the LORD; let the humble hear and be glad. Come, O children, listen to me; I will teach you the fear of the LORD. The LORD redeems the life of His servants; none of those who take refuge in Him will be condemned.

Glory be to the Father and to the Son and to the Holy Spirit; as it was in the beginning, is now, and will be forever. Amen.

I will speak of Your testimonies before kings, [O Lord,] and shall not be put to shame. (Ps 34:1–2, 11, 22; antiphon: Ps 119:46)

The antiphon (Ps 119:46) might easily bring to mind two iconic Reformation scenes. On April 18, 1521, Luther stood before Emperor Charles V and representatives of the pope, his life on the line, and spoke his famous "Here I stand." Then in 1530, June 25, at Augsburg, the Lutheran princes made their confession, again before Charles. The title page of the Augsburg Confession bears those words: "I will also speak of your testimonies before kings, and shall not be put to shame." The Reformation went forward because the Gospel moved brave men to speak up—even when it was dangerous—and God did vindicate them. "Reformers" in our THEME is intentionally plural, and "enables" is intentionally present tense. When do we each have opportunity to reform perhaps one soul by speaking, even if it seems uncomfortable? God can make even a whispered voice a Wittenberg door.

Luther was accused by his enemies of dividing the Church, but that was never his intent. Pray the **Collect** for Reformation:

Almighty and gracious Lord, pour out Your Holy Spirit on Your faithful people. Keep us steadfast in Your grace and truth, protect and deliver us in times of temptation, defend us against all enemies, and grant to Your Church Your saving peace; through Jesus Christ, Your Son, our Lord, who lives and reigns with You and the Holy Spirit, one God, now and forever. Amen.

Luther considered himself a loyal son of the Church. He never sought danger or enemies. When he called for debate on the Ninety-Five Theses, he actually assumed that open discussion would be welcomed and that the truth would be embraced—including by the pope. But very quickly it became obvious that some were not willing to be persuaded by Holy Scripture and preferred to silence Luther. That's when it becomes necessary to remain steadfast against temptation to compromise. Keep posting the words on the door. And Lutherans continue to pray for peace in the Church, but only peace that is faithful to God's Word. What we speak must be the pure Gospel.

The **First Reading** also has an interesting Reformation history: Revelation 14:6–7.

At Luther's funeral in 1546, Johannes Bugenhagen, Luther's pastor, declared that "there is no doubt that he was the angel of whom it is written in Revelation 14" (*Luther's Works*, AE: Companion Volume, *Sixteenth-Century Biographies of Martin Luther*, ed. Christopher Boyd Brown, trans. Matthew Carver [CPH, 2018], 27). C. F. W. Walther also printed this verse on the masthead of *Der Lutheraner*, for many years The Lutheran Church—Missouri Synod's general periodical. Whether Revelation was really prophesying Luther or not, the more important point is that the angel flying overhead had "an eternal gospel to proclaim."

That most certainly *is* what the Reformation was about. Wooden doors become bronze, great churchmen pass the baton to others, empires become democracies, and buying indulgences morphs into checking the boxes on Christmas and Easter. But the Good News of how we're really saved, by faith in Jesus dying for our sins, never changes. It's eternal. The medieval church had badly obscured that Gospel behind purgatory and relics and prayers to the saints and all kinds of works-righteousness. This was the desperate need for reform. So the Reformation was all about getting God's Word straight, getting that Word out.

We probably don't need a history lesson to pick up the Reformation images in the **Psalm**. That's right, Psalm 46 was Luther's text for writing "A Mighty Fortress Is Our God." After Worms, Luther was an outlaw of the empire. His life truly was in danger. Yet God provided supportive princes who protected him. You probably know the story of Frederick the Wise arranging a friendly kidnapping and hiding Luther for almost a year in the castle Wartburg. That was a real stone-and-mortar "refuge and strength" (46:1)—still our God Himself as the protector.

Pause to sing that first **Hymn of the Day**, *LSB* 656 or 657.

Reformation has a **Gradual** of its own:

Great is the Lord and greatly to be praised in the city of our God! Walk about Zion, go around her, number her towers, consider well her ramparts, go through her citadels, that you may tell the next generation that this is God, our God forever and ever. (Ps 48:1a, 12–14a)

What an important inclusion in the propers! Like an ancient Israelite looking up at the mighty fortress walls of Jerusalem and considering the great things God has done for her throughout history, we must recall the events and teachings of the Reformation so that we can "tell the next generation" God's precious, eternal Gospel. Gazing at the inscription on the door. Preaching it year after year. Generation after generation. Your children. Your grandchildren. Their children.

If there's any one passage in Scripture that best summarizes what the Reformation posted for all to read, it's probably the **Epistle**, Romans 3:19–28.

It wasn't just the sixteenth-century Roman Church with Johann Tetzel hawking indulgences that was inclined to works-righ teousness. Every one of us personally suffers that natural inclination. Paul teaches the *first*-century Roman Church that "by works of the law no human being will be justified" (3:20). It's not about us.

It's all about Jesus. We are "justified by [God's] grace as a gift, through the redemption that is in Christ Jesus" (3:24). What Jesus did on the cross ("propitiation by His blood," 3:25) was to solve a dilemma between God's justice and God's love. God's justice must treat sin as it is (intolerable to His holiness), but His love wants to justify the sinner (declare him not guilty). When Jesus died as the Man for all people, all our sins were punished to the satisfaction of God's justice. Now, then, God can be at the same time "just and the justifier of the one who has faith in Jesus" (3:26). "Alleluia. Fear not, little flock, for it is your Father's good pleasure to give you the kingdom. Alleluia" (the **Verse**, Lk 12:32). Forgiveness of all our sins, right standing before God, that is, justification, by grace through faith in Jesus—that is the inscription on the Reformation door.

Celebrate justification by grace through faith with the first five stanzas of the second **Hymn of Day**, *LSB* 555.

The world certainly has changed since the Castle Church door was wood. But the best changes have been because the Reformation set free the eternal, unchanging Gospel to be preached. Read both **Gospel** lessons: John 8:31–36 and the less often used alternate, Matthew 11:12–19. How different would your world be if you thought you had to win God's favor by being "good enough"? Always trying, never sure, ultimately despairing. That's slavery. How different is your world since the Gospel brought you to know Jesus procured God's favor for you, as a gift, absolutely free? That's freedom! And by God's grace, through the miracle of the Reformation, millions are still reading the door.

So once more our THEME: God, as our refuge and strength, enables His reformers to speak to the next generation the eternal Gospel that sets us free: justification by grace through faith in Jesus Christ.

Finish looking forward to Reformation Day with the last five stanzas of "Salvation unto Us Has Come" (*LSB* 555).

All Saints' Day
Years A, B, C

READINGS

Revelation 7:(2–8) 9–17

Psalm 149 (antiphon: v 4)

1 John 3:1–3

Matthew 5:1–12

HYMN OF THE DAY

LSB 677 "For All the Saints"

Perhaps you choke up a bit as on All Saints' Day you sing "For All the Saints Who from Their Labors Rest." I do. Maybe the lump in your throat swells as the bell tolls and Pastor reads the names of the past year's faithful departed. Maybe tears well up in your eyes. You're not alone.

All Saints' Day has no doubt always had that effect, ever since its earliest observation around AD 360 in Syria as the Festival of All Martyrs. To this day, All Saints' recalls especially the Church's martyrs of those first three centuries (Luther D. Reed, *The Lutheran Liturgy* [Philadelphia: Muhlenberg Press, 1947], 510). Countless generations of Christians have surely wept and breathed a prayer of thanksgiving to God for those faithful brothers and sisters who advanced the Kingdom toward us by giving their lives to crosses, arenas, and flames.

But we probably choke up thinking of Mom or Dad or Grandma or My Darling. And that is most certainly All Saints' Day too. In fact, you might just as appropriately shed a tear for your spouse who's singing right next to you in church or for your infant who was baptized in July. They're saints for All Saints' as well. Only may all these tears—for the ancients, for our recently departed, for those with us in worship now—be tears of joy, because the same eternity with Christ is ours all.

Officially, All Saints' Day is November 1. (Remember, it was the Eve of All Hallows Day, October 31, that Luther chose to post his Ninety-Five Theses—a high-traffic day at church back then.) Since few of our congregations hold special services that day, however, many observe the festival on the nearest Sunday on or after November 1. As a practical matter, that generally means the Sunday after the Sunday on which Reformation is celebrated. As with Reformation, then, most or all of the All Saints' propers are usually substituted for those that would be Proper 26 or 27 of the Sundays after Pentecost. That's our assumption here.

The **Gradual**, though, is quite intentionally and quite comfortably the Gradual also for the last four Sundays of the Pentecost season with their emphasis on the end times. It summarizes this day quite fully:

> *These are the ones coming out of the great tribulation. They have washed their robes and made them white in the blood of the Lamb. Blessèd are those whose strength is in You, in whose heart are the highways to Zion. (Rev 7:14b; Ps 84:5)*

That isn't everything one wants to know about All Saints', but it's close. It tells who the saints are, what they must expect to go through in this world, and that they are yet blessed. More on each of those coming up.

A key verse of the Gradual is repeated as antiphon of the **Introit**. (It'll show up yet again in fuller context in the First Reading.)

> *These are the ones coming out of the great tribulation. They have washed their robes and made them white in the blood of the Lamb.*
>
> *In You, O Lord, do I take refuge; let me never be put to shame; in Your righteousness deliver me. For You are my rock and my fortress; and for Your name's sake You lead me and guide me. Into Your hand I commit my spirit; You have redeemed me, O Lord, faithful God.*
>
> *Glory be to the Father and to the Son and to the Holy Spirit; as it was in the beginning, is now, and will be forever. Amen.*
>
> *These are the ones coming out of the great tribulation. They have washed their robes and made them white in the blood of the Lamb. (Ps 31:1, 3, 5; antiphon: Rev 7:14b)*

Who are the saints? I think the three most common usages of the term are these: First, those exceptional Christians whom tradition or a very formal process of the Roman Catholic Church has granted the letters *St.* in front of their names: St. Paul, St. Peter, St. Teresa of Calcutta. Second, the "street usage": "She's a saint to put up with that!" Or third, Christians who've died and gone to heaven. There's something to each of those, I suppose.

But the biblical idea is different. The term *saint* comes from the Latin rendering of the Greek ἅγιος, *hagios*, or "holy ones." A saint is a "holy one." And who are the holy ones? "These are the ones . . . [who] have washed their robes and made them white in the blood of the Lamb." To be holy requires not just a lot of patience or the imprimatur of the Church. It requires being without sin, and neither Paul nor Mother Teresa nor any of us is that on our own. So being without sin requires having our sins taken away. That, we know, happens when they're washed away in the blood of Jesus' death on the cross, received by faith. A saint, a holy one, therefore, is one—anyone—who believes Jesus has died to save him or her.

To be a saint doesn't require martyrdom, but those early Christians who died for their faith weren't the exceptions either. All the saints sooner or later come out of "tribulation." That's the Christian's lot in life. To be wearing the white robe of Jesus means to share in Him, including His sufferings. All of us are, at least, to see ourselves in those early martyrs. We must expect this too.

But in the Lord we do have a "refuge," a "fortress." (Does follow nicely after Reformation Day, doesn't it!) Even if I should face the worst, into His hand I can confidently "commit my spirit." Saints do, after all, *come out of* the great tribulation. We are blessed.

Who are the saints, and with what are they blessed? Pray the **Collect**:

> *Almighty and everlasting God, You knit together Your faithful people of all times and places into one holy communion, the mystical body of Your Son, Jesus Christ. Grant us so to follow Your blessed saints in all virtuous and godly living that, together with them, we may come to the unspeakable joys You have prepared for those who love You; through Jesus Christ, our Lord, who lives and reigns with You and the Holy Spirit, one God, now and forever. Amen.*

"Faithful people of all times and places." St. Peter. St. Laurence, who was killed in Rome in AD 258 when he dispersed the treasures of the Church to the poor. Grandpa Helmreich. Rachel, Daniel, and Gabriel. All are "one holy communion, the mystical body of . . . Jesus Christ." These are the holy ones. And to each belongs "unspeakable joys."

The **First Reading**, Revelation 7:2–17, gives us a glimpse of the "unspeakable joys."

When we think of the book of Revelation as John's vision of heaven, this is really the passage we have in mind. John sees first the saints of the Old Testament age (144,000, a number of completeness: each of the twelve tribes of Israel times 12,000), then of the New Testament era (even more: "a great multitude that no one could number, from every nation, from all tribes and peoples and languages," 7:9). Most are not famous, but no one who has been washed in the blood of Christ will be missing. All the saints.

They have suffered that tribulation, but now, what joys! Serving God (7:15) is what Adam and Eve so perfectly delighted to do before sin turned all of us in on ourselves. Christ shelters His saints. They lack nothing (7:16). God wipes away every tear (7:17). Even that is part of the joy, because God bringing His saints through tribulation is sweeter than their never experiencing suffering at all. Compare the thrill of triumph, the embrace of reunion, the ecstasy of finally viewing from the summit to the tepid existence of a whole life spent on easy street.

The **Psalm** of the day, Psalm 149, pictures the same celebration of God's saints . . . but here on earth. Believers of Israel, the holy ones, "the godly" (149:1, 5, 9), "sing" and "rejoice" to be in the presence of their "Maker" and "King." They dance and make music. For He "takes pleasure" in them (149:1–4). But notice, they are yet in tribulation, still in the fight (149:6–9). For now.

Do also notice that the saints are called "*children* of Zion" (149:2). "And so we are," John tells us in our **Epistle**, 1 John 3:1–3.

This, too, is an important description of who the saints are. "Children" is a common way of seeing God's people throughout Scripture because young children are totally dependent; what they need and have they can only receive. So with God's saints. No one but God alone is holy on his or her own; yet the lowliest "child of God" is as holy as St. John ("pure" in the blood of the Lamb, as Christ, the Lamb Himself, is pure, 3:3). "Children of God" is also a divine term of endearment. Read this short text again and hear God's voice calling you His precious little one. This, God's children, is what we are already now, but when Christ returns, even this shall be enriched in greater glory (3:2).

Once again, however, we're reminded to expect persecution: "The world does not know us" because "it did not know" Christ (3:1). It will do to Jesus' saints as it did to Him.

Nevertheless, Jesus says so emphatically that His saints are blessed: the **Holy Gospel**, Matthew 5:1–12.

This same magnificent reading was the Holy Gospel for Epiphany 4, Year A, and we won't repeat what we wrote there (pp 50–53). This time, read each beatitude as a picture of someone we would surely call "saintly": meek, merciful, peacemaker. *Then*, read each again as describing you yourself as one of God's holy ones. *You* are poor in spirit . . . and blessed to possess the kingdom of heaven. *You* mourn . . . and yet are blessed with God's comfort. *You* are dot, dot, dot. Does the glass slipper fit? Yes, it does, because by your Baptism, you are in Christ—are in "the mystical body" of God's Son, our Collect acknowledged. You *are* holy because He has washed you in His blood. By faith, you are among the "blessèd."

You are "called sons [children] of God" (5:9)—and so you are. We may doubt that when we are "persecuted for righteousness' sake" (5:10). When the world does "revile you and persecute you and utter all kinds of evil against you falsely on [Jesus'] account" (5:11), you may wonder if God is still counting your sins against you so that you're anything but holy, if being in Christ does count for anything. But it's on Jesus' account that we're all saints, that we're blessed.

**BLESSED ARE ALL THE SAINTS,
FOR, BY OUR WASHING
IN THE BLOOD OF THE LAMB,
WE SHALL BE CALLED
CHILDREN OF GOD,
AND, DESPITE PERSECUTION,
SO WE ARE!**

As I'm writing this, it really is All Saints', and as we sang the **Hymn of the Day**, *LSB* 677, just a couple of hours ago in church, I was especially picturing my mom and dad, my father-in-law, a dear uncle, and a special friend. Sing it now yourself, and don't be at all embarrassed to shed a tear thinking of your certain beloved saint now living the unspeakable joys of the Lord in heaven!

The Sundays after Pentecost: Proper 27 (November 6–12) Year A

READINGS

Amos 5:18–24
Psalm 70 (antiphon: v 4)
1 Thessalonians 4:13–18
Matthew 25:1–13

HYMN OF THE DAY

LSB 516 "Wake, Awake, for Night Is Flying"

Many congregations observe the Feast of All Saints during their regular service on the Sunday that falls between November 1 and November 7 inclusive. Therefore, the elements for Proper 27 detailed in the following devotion-study may in some years be omitted and the All Saints' propers used in their place. When this is the case, refer to the devotion-study for All Saints' Day (p 254) to look forward to this Sunday morning.

The **Gradual** signals that we're almost done—with another church year, but, much more, with our millennia of sojourn in a fallen world:

> *These are the ones coming out of the great tribulation. They have washed their robes and made them white in the blood of the Lamb. Blessèd are those whose strength is in You, in whose heart are the highways to Zion. (Rev 7:14b; Ps 84:5)*

The Gradual, as we know, expresses the theme of the season, or, in this very lengthy season of Sundays after Pentecost, the theme of this last miniseason-within-a-season. This Sunday is the third-last of the church year, and the countdown is on. In these final Sundays, we look ahead to Christ's coming at the end of the world, to the judgment that will bring, and to the everlasting consummation thereafter. The tribulation will end, and the faithful will follow their Lord—marching or dashing or skipping—down the highway to the eternal Zion.

That will be soon—from God's point of view. We ourselves haven't a clue just when, which, of course, calls us to a crucial message of these last three Sundays: be awake, be alert for whenever our Lord returns!

But there's also the magnificent message of the destination. Read the **Introit** for this Sunday and see if you catch what it has to do with the Last Day. Then immediately read the **Collect**, and notice how it confirms that same connection.

Even the sparrow finds a home, and the swallow a nest for herself, where she may lay her young, at Your altars, O Lord of hosts, my King and my God.

How lovely is Your dwelling place, O Lord of hosts! Behold our shield, O God; look on the face of Your anointed! For a day in Your courts is better than a thousand elsewhere. I would rather be a doorkeeper in the house of my God than dwell in the tents of wickedness. For the Lord God is a sun and shield; the Lord bestows favor and honor. No good thing does He withhold from those who walk uprightly. O Lord of hosts, blessèd is the one who trusts in You!

Glory be to the Father and to the Son and to the Holy Spirit; as it was in the beginning, is now, and will be forever. Amen.

Even the sparrow finds a home, and the swallow a nest for herself, where she may lay her young, at Your altars, O Lord of hosts, my King and my God. (Ps 84:1, 9–12; antiphon: Ps 84:3)

Now also the Collect:

Lord God, heavenly Father, send forth Your Son to lead home His bride, the Church, that with all the company of the redeemed we may finally enter into His eternal wedding feast; through the same Jesus Christ, our Lord, who lives and reigns with You and the Holy Spirit, one God, now and forever. Amen.

Our life everlasting is often pictured in Scripture as the "eternal wedding feast" (recall our discussion for Proper 23), and we'll see that as the primary image for heaven again this week. But first, notice how both the Introit and the Collect describe it. "Even the sparrow finds a home." "Lord God, heavenly Father, send forth Your Son to lead home His bride, the Church."

One of the greatest blessings God can give any of us in this life is a home that's safe, happy, loving. Sadly, not everyone has had this experience, but those whom God has blessed in this way know what a delight it makes life. Waking up in the morning, going to bed at night in a place where conversation is affirming, encouraging, where you can be yourself, developing your talents, loved and forgiven in your failures, above all, centered in Christ Jesus and His love and forgiveness for each of us—even with its imperfections in this life, we'd be happy to see that go on and on. A home like that becomes the safe haven from which we venture out in confidence to face a much less pleasant world. But someday, when Christ returns, that home will be our whole world!

The eternal feasting won't just be the wedding *banquet*, but the home that the wedding creates, when Christ leads home His Bride, the Church, and carries us over the threshold of the home He's gone to prepare for us. And that home will be secure and loving also for those who haven't yet experienced it on earth. "How lovely is Your dwelling place, O LORD of hosts! . . . For a day in Your courts . . . in the house of my God . . . is better than a thousand elsewhere."

One last note here. Look back at the Gradual. In our previous hymnal, *Lutheran Worship*, the last lines, based on the NIV translation, read, "Blessed are those whose strength is in You, who have set their hearts on pilgrimage." That's helpful, too, depicting people who are wandering toward a sacred place, but the new ESV rendering, "in whose heart are the highways to Zion," makes much clearer to me the idea of heading *home*.

From here, the readings go on to focus on the urgency of being prepared for the day of Christ's return. Begin with the **Old Testament Reading**. God's people at the time were eager for "the day of the LORD," expecting Him to come and put down their rivals. But read the warning: Amos 5:18–24.

Amos prophesied in an era of prosperity for both Judah and Israel (under Kings Uzziah and Jeroboam II, respectively, 1:1). So God's people were feeling good about themselves and uppity toward their neighbors (1:3–2:3). They couldn't wait for the Lord to come and give those petty Syrians and Philistines and Edomites what they had coming. But Amos sobers them: "You think you want the Lord to come? Think again! Look in the mirror and see who's in for judgment when He shows up!" "Is not the day of the LORD darkness, and not light," when bear and serpent will bite *you*?! (5:18–20).

Why? Because Israel's own house was not in order, not at all ready for a divine visitor. "I hate, I despise your feasts. . . . Even though you offer Me your burnt offerings and grain offerings, I will not accept them" (5:21, 22). The problem is that these were "your" (Israel's) feasts, not the Lord's feasts. The *Lord's* feasts were always acts of faith, people moved by the knowledge that Yahweh was caring for them. And that faith would always result in "justice," serving others in need (5:24). Instead, Israel assumed it was prepared for the Lord's coming simply by going through motions—"solemn assemblies," "offerings," "songs" (5:21–23)—which were actually self-serving. How foolish!

The **Psalm** for Sunday is familiar because of its use in our Matins liturgy (*LSB*, p 219): Psalm 70. "Make haste, O God, to deliver me! O LORD, make haste to help me!" (70:1). By contrast to Amos's hearers, David is rightly eager for God to come. He knows the divine visitation will mean deliverance. The difference? David is properly prepared. He admits that he is "poor and needy," and he loves the Lord's "salvation" (70:5a, 4b). "O LORD, do not delay!" (70:5d).

In the **Epistle**, Paul is comforting those who fear Christ was too *late* in returning: 1 Thessalonians 4:13–18.

First-century Christians widely assumed that Jesus would return in their lifetimes (Acts 1:9–11). But by now some had already died, and, as yet, no second coming. Paul's assurance is that those loved ones—Mom, Grandpa, a baby daughter—who've died before Jesus' return aren't forgotten or left behind. They will be raised from their graves and join those still alive on that great day.

And what a great day! "The Lord Himself will descend from heaven with a cry of command, with the voice of an archangel, and with the sound of the trumpet of God" (4:16). And all believers, "the quick [the living] and the dead," will be caught up to the clouds to be with Christ in heaven forever (4:17). Such a sweet comfort for us and our loved ones also in the twenty-first century! (By the way, don't be misled by those who talk about this "rapture," from the Greek ἁρπάζω, to mean that believers will be caught up to heaven while the world keeps operating down below, à la the *Left Behind* books and movies of years ago. Christ's return will be the last day of earth as we know it.)

The **Holy Gospel** is (yes, cliché but) both thrilling and chilling: Matthew 25:1–13.

In ancient custom, once a bride and groom became engaged, they were committed; they were married (like Joseph and Mary, "his espoused wife," Lk 2:5, KJV). But they did not yet come together until the groom had built the house, established his business, whatever. Thus the time really was unspecified, as is made somewhat more dramatic in the parable.

As with most parables, it's not helpful to press every detail for a corresponding reality. (What do the lamps stand for? What does the oil represent? Why can't the wise share with the foolish?) The big point *is* the point: when the time comes, those who are prepared will be welcomed into the eternal wedding feast, and those who aren't will be shut out. "At the thrilling cry," "The bridegroom is coming!" those who have faith in Christ will be received into eternal joy. But feel the chill down your spine at this prospect: the door is shut, and the voice of the Savior speaks: "I do not know you" (25:12). Pause there. Stand outside the door for a long minute. This is how Jesus ends His parable.

Are you wise or foolish, prepared or ill-prepared? Both. How often we foolishly ignore God's warnings of sin! How often we take for granted God's grace and goodness with all its now-and-eternal benefits! And as Amos taught, none of *your* offerings to God can prepare you. But Christ has died for you, forgiven you all your sins. In your Baptism, He has made you His Bride, the Church. And in His Supper, He has already welcomed you into the heavenly wedding feast. *He* has prepared you. For whenever. For

AT A DAY WE DO NOT KNOW,
THE BRIDEGROOM WILL TAKE HOME
TO THE ETERNAL WEDDING FEAST
HIS BRIDE, THE CHURCH—
ALL WHO ARE WISE, PREPARED—
BUT THE FOOLISH, ILL-PREPARED,
WILL BE SHUT OUT
IN ETERNAL DARKNESS.
MAKE HASTE, O GOD!

The **Hymn of the Day** (*LSB* 516) is a true classic by Lutheran hymnist Philipp Nicolai, based on the Holy Gospel.

The Sundays after Pentecost: Proper 28 (November 13–19) Year A

READINGS

Zephaniah 1:7–16
Psalm 90:1–12 (antiphon: v 17)
1 Thessalonians 5:1–11
Matthew 25:14–30

HYMN OF THE DAY

LSB 508 "The Day Is Surely Drawing Near"

How do you feel about Judgment Day? Terrified? Nightmares? Excited? Eager anticipation?

It probably depends on how you feel about the Judge before whom you'll stand that day. Will He be angry, a demanding master you can't hope to satisfy? Or will He be smiling, gracious, reaching out to embrace you?

You're right.

That's right. You're right.

Either way.

This Sunday is the second-last of the church year, continuing to count down toward Christ's second coming and the end of the world. Which means Judgment Day is very much in view in our propers. And what we'll find is that standing before Christ on that day will feel exactly the way we'd probably expect. Either way. If we think Christ is a judge who'll be looking to make us pay with our eternal lives, He'll be just that to us. But if we trust that He's our loving Redeemer who's been looking forward to the perfect moment to welcome us into His kingdom, we'll see Him swing the gate open and take us by the hand.

This, of course, isn't saying that *we make* God whatever we want Him to be. It's rather a question of whether we *believe* Christ is who He says He is—and who He deeply wants to be toward us. To see our Lord Jesus in that way is where the propers for this Sunday should take us.

As you read the **Introit** for Sunday, ask yourself how David, the psalmist, sees God.

Hear my prayer, O Lord; give ear to my pleas for mercy! In Your faithfulness answer me, in Your righteousness!

Enter not into judgment with Your servant, for no one living is righteous before You. I remember the days of old; I meditate on all that You have done; I ponder the work of Your hands. I stretch out my hands to You; my soul thirsts for You like a parched land. Teach me to do Your will, for You are my God! Let Your good Spirit lead me on level ground! For Your name's sake, O Lord, preserve my life! In Your righteousness bring my soul out of trouble!

Glory be to the Father and to the Son and to the Holy Spirit; as it was in the beginning, is now, and will be forever. Amen.

Hear my prayer, O Lord; give ear to my pleas for mercy! In Your faithfulness answer me, in Your righteousness! (Ps 143:2, 5–6, 10–11; antiphon: Ps 143:1)

David has a wonderful reverence for and faith in the Lord, doesn't he! He comes as a supplicant, knowing he's in desperate need: "Give ear to my pleas for mercy! . . . Bring my soul out of trouble!" But he's confident God will hear his prayer. "I remember the days of old; I meditate on all that You have done; . . . for You are my God!" Such an intimate relationship: "My soul thirsts for You like a parched land."

It's not that David thinks he's worthy, "for no one living is righteous before You." He knows he's accountable to God; he's God's "servant," subject to "judgment." But he knows what God's judgment toward him will be. David sees God as merciful, as someone he can always approach for the good he needs. He *wants* to stand before God and await His judgment.

The **Collect** for this week likewise recognizes that God gives good things and implies that there will be a final accounting:

Almighty and ever-living God, You have given exceedingly great and precious promises to those who trust in You. Dispel from us the works of darkness and grant us to live in the light of Your Son, Jesus Christ, that our faith may never be found wanting; through the same Jesus Christ, our Lord, who lives and reigns with You and the Holy Spirit, one God, now and forever. Amen.

Already God has given us "exceedingly great and precious promises," which we know always come true. So what is our prayer at this time? "That our faith may never be found wanting." Here we can picture Judgment Day—or countless tiny crossroads of judgment in life. Daily we face challenges to our faith: Will we give in to this or that temptation? Will we despair of God's promises when we suffer illness or family crises or attacks from unbelievers? And finally, on the Last Day, will Christ find in our hearts saving faith that His death and resurrection has earned for us admission to the heavenly kingdom?

Like David in the Introit, we've come to the right place with our prayer. We pray to the "Almighty and ever-living God" because we believe He will preserve our faith in Jesus "through the same Jesus Christ, our Lord." Our prayer teaches us to see God like that . . . with, therefore, a joyful expectation of the Judgment.

But Zephaniah in the **Old Testament Reading** warns of a "day of the LORD" that will be "a day of wrath," "a day of distress and anguish, a day of ruin and devastation": Zephaniah 1:7–16.

"The day of the LORD" described often by Old Testament prophets refers also to days of temporal judgment against the ancient peoples (for example, a plague of locusts, Joel 1:4–15, or the destruction of Israel by Assyria after last Sunday's reading, Amos 5:18–27). But surely the ultimate "day of the Lord" is the Last Day. Those whose attitude toward the Lord mirrors that of Zephaniah's original audience should fear the day!

It's not just that they were imitating pagan dress ("foreign attire," 1:8) or practices ("everyone who leaps over the threshold," as idolatrous priests did in their temples, 1:9). They were "complacent" about God Himself, thinking "the LORD will not do good, nor will He do ill" (1:12). The Hebrew translated as "complacent" is a most interesting image. Take a bottle of wine, lay it down, and forget about it—not for a pleasing six months, a year or two or three, but far past its prime. Ten years, a hundred years. Ignored. Forgotten. It turns to vinegar; the sediment thickens; it becomes totally undrinkable. This is how God's people were regarding the Lord. Forget about Him. He does nothing, either good or ill. He's a nonfactor, no one with whom we have to be concerned. Complacent. Their lives, they thought, would go on quite without Yahweh.

Seeing the Lord that way, they would find "that day" to bring wailing (1:10). They would lose everything—their lives shattered (1:11), their goods "plundered," their houses "laid waste" (1:13). If the Lord is viewed as distant, unimportant, then finally seeing Him face-to-face is to be feared!

Moses, "the man of God," enjoyed a face-to-face friendship with Yahweh (see Ex 33:11; Deut 34:10), so in the one **Psalm** attributed to him, he expresses trust even as he knows God's fierce judgment: Psalm 90:1–12, 17.

"O God, our *help* in ages past, Our *hope* for years to come" is how hymnwriter Isaac Watts famously paraphrased 90:1 (*LSB* 733). Moses knows God as our pleasant "dwelling place." But he also knows "we are brought to an end by Your anger; . . . all our days pass away under Your wrath" (90:7, 9). We must face death: "You return man to dust" (90:3).

Yet even this could cause complacency. We are like grass that in the morning "flourishes" and in the evening "withers" (90:6). We may live seventy or eighty years (in the KJV, "threescore years and ten" or "by reason of strength . . . fourscore"), but "they are soon gone, and we fly away" (90:10). So what does our life matter? Isn't it all futile?

Faithful Moses has a totally different perspective: "So teach us to number our days that we may get a heart of wisdom" (90:12). Rather than thinking nothing matters (as Zephaniah's people did), make every day count! Use every opportunity, every gift of God! Receive His precious Word and blessed

Sacraments daily! Use our talents actively! And see what God will do with our labors: "Establish the work of our hands upon us; yes, establish the work of our hands!" (90:17). Though our lives on earth pass away, God will cause our works to have permanent value. Bringing my child to infant Baptism, telling one coworker about Jesus, a "mite" in the offering plate to help spread the Gospel—God will use these to give never-ending life to others. Whenever the final accounting takes place ("for a thousand years in Your sight are but as yesterday," 90:4), this is the judgment we look forward to hearing.

No, we can't know when the Judgment will come, but we can know the Judge. Read the **Epistle**, 1 Thessalonians 5:1–11.

Those taking for granted that "peace and security" will go on forever will be surprised, as by "a thief in the night," they will meet "sudden destruction" (5:2–3). They, again, see the Lord as distant, really of no account, another example of complacency.

But Paul says that we are "children of light, children of the day" (5:5), which most importantly means that we have the God who created light and day as our Father. And He "has not destined us for wrath, but to obtain salvation through our Lord Jesus Christ, who died for us" (5:9–10a). "Therefore encourage one another" (5:11) with the assurance that our Judge is He who gave His life on the cross out of love for us.

That's actually where Jesus' parable in our **Holy Gospel** begins—with Christ giving to us: Matthew 25:14–30.

While this parable seems to focus on the work of three servants, everything is precipitated by the master giving his servants gifts (25:14). Jesus' death and resurrection has secured for us everything truly good: forgiveness, eternal life, His Means of Grace, as well as abundant earthly blessings—including each day and resources (talents, opportunities, money) to make the most of those days. All these are because Jesus' cross, by atoning for our sin, has reconciled us to God.

The first two servants knew their master just this way—gracious and giving—and they joyfully went about using his gifts. The third servant's problem wasn't a lack of return on investment (an absence of good works). His failure to use the master's gift was because he thought entirely differently of the master: "I knew you to be a hard man . . . so I was afraid" (25:24–25). He played it safe by doing nothing, was satisfied with complacency, because he saw the master as eager to punish, rather than ready to forgive. He forgot how much the master loves to give. So that's the judgment he got: "outer darkness" (25:30). See Christ instead as loving Savior! To you "will more be given, and [you] will have an abundance" (25:29).

Whenever the Lord Returns, Those Who Have Known Him as the Generous Giver of All Good Will Be Given Abundantly More and Their Work Established Forever, but Those Who Have Seen Him as a Hard Master Will Lose Everything and Be Condemned for Their Complacency.

The **Hymn of the Day** (*LSB* 508) is a vivid picture of the Judgment. Be sure you don't despair before stanzas 5–7.

Day of Thanksgiving Years A, B, C

READINGS

Deuteronomy 8:1–10
Psalm 67 (antiphon: v 7)
Philippians 4:6–20
or 1 Timothy 2:1–4
Luke 17:11–19

HYMN OF THE DAY

LSB 785 "We Praise You, O God"

In the United States, with Thanksgiving Day being celebrated on the fourth Thursday of November, the holiday will fall during either the week before or after the Last Sunday of the Church Year, Proper 29. In Canada, where Thanksgiving is observed on the second Monday of October, it will occur the day after either Proper 22 or Proper 23. This devotion-study can be read those weeks.

Looking forward to *Thursday* morning this week (or maybe to Wednesday evening, or, in Canada, looking forward to Monday) makes you different. Not that everybody isn't looking forward to Thanksgiving. Just about everybody is. But the fact that you're reading this means you're looking forward to *church* on Thanksgiving. That makes you different.

Again, it's not that you're looking forward to being thankful on Thanksgiving. That's not so very different either. Most folks, when they're doing the turkey and cranberry sauce, know that they're supposed to be thankful. Quite a feast we see before us. Quite nice getting a long weekend to watch football. Quite pleasant having the fam over. We're thankful for these festive days of the year. Just about everybody is.

What makes you different is that you know *to whom* you're thankful. You're going to be in church for an extra service this week because you know that every good gift comes from our gracious God, Father, Son, and Holy Spirit. Thanksgiving isn't just a warm feeling that life is good. It's a devotion of life to the almighty Creator, Redeemer, and Sanctifier, who has given us so much more than turkey. Most people don't know that or don't do that.

The reality is, *we* wouldn't know that or do that either if even the giving of thanks weren't given to us. The awareness that *God* gives us all those good things, the devotion of thanks to Him—that's a gift of God too. We couldn't figure it out for ourselves or move ourselves to thank God truly. Our propers for a Day of Thanksgiving show us this—and, in doing so, give us all the more reason to give thanks to our holy God.

Begin your Thanksgiving worship already now by singing the very familiar **Hymn of the Day**, "We Praise You, O God" (*LSB* 785). It's a vastly improved version of an earlier (and still popular) Dutch war hymn, "We Gather Together to Ask the Lord's Blessing." Notice that the emphasis is on whom we're thanking: it addresses God, our Redeemer, Creator, directly ("You" or "Your") twelve times!

Why does Julia Cory, the hymnwriter, know that it's God we thank? Well, that *seems* natural enough. And perhaps for "nature" it is. Consider the **Introit**:

> *I will sing to the Lord as long as I live; I will sing praise to my God while I have being.*
>
> *O Lord, how manifold are Your works! In wisdom have You made them all; the earth is full of Your creatures. These all look to You, to give them their food in due season. When You give it to them, they gather it up; when You open Your hand, they are filled with good things. When You send forth Your Spirit, they are created, and You renew the face of the ground.*
>
> *Glory be to the Father and to the Son and to the Holy Spirit; as it was in the beginning, is now, and will be forever. Amen.*
>
> *I will sing to the Lord as long as I live; I will sing praise to my God while I have being. (Ps 104:24, 27–28, 30; antiphon: Ps 104:33)*

"The earth is full of Your creatures. These all look to You, to give them their food in due season." The preceding verses of Psalm 104 mention wild donkeys, birds, goats, and rock badgers receiving all they need. The Lord causes grass to grow for the cattle. "The young lions roar for their prey, seeking their food from God" (104:21). Okay, so animals don't have any faith (or even cognitive) awareness of the Triune God; we get that. But their God-given instincts drive them to forage or fress on the food He fixes.

Why don't all *humans* look to God and thank Him for His provision? Much bigger problem! Despite our "instincts," our natural knowledge of God, we higher creatures go to the ends of space to explain Him out of existence. We don't necessarily "sing to the Lord as long as [we] live; . . . sing praise to [our] God while [we] have being." And even we who acknowledge His existence often try to explain away or at least overlook Him opening His hand to fill us with "good things"—so that, of course, we can claim some of the credit. After all, I paid the MasterCard bill for the turkey and sweet potatoes.

Above all, most Thanksgiving Day celebrants don't realize that they receive dressing and pumpkin pie only because their sin has been forgiven. Remember, since God is holy, He can't be in any relationship with the unholy. If we still stood in our sin, it would separate us from any of God's goodnesses. *Thanks* be to God that He sent His Son to take that sin away from us, onto Himself, on the cross! And He took the sin of the *whole world*—even of those who dine in complete ignorance and unbelief. How many who gather around the table this week believe that their green bean casserole and soft, warm, buttery rolls are gifts of God specifically by Jesus' death on the cross? They are! And you know it!

That, you see, is something no one figures out on his or her own. That's why we pray in the **Collect**:

> *Almighty God, Your mercies are new every morning and You graciously provide for all our needs of body and soul. Grant us Your Holy Spirit that we may acknowledge Your goodness, give thanks for Your benefits, and serve You in willing obedience all our days; through Jesus Christ, our Lord, who lives and reigns with You and the Holy Spirit, one God, now and forever. Amen.*

The Introit noted that "when You send forth Your Spirit, they [God's creatures] are created." But, see, the Spirit has a role far beyond creating. It's by the Holy Spirit "that we may acknowledge [God's] goodness" and "give thanks for [His] benefits"—that is, have faith in our hearts. That forgiveness in Christ Jesus is the goodness that makes all others possible, so the Spirit's enlightening our hearts to believe in Jesus as Savior is how we're ever able truly to give thanks—"for all our needs of body and soul." We give thanks even for God enabling us to give thanks!

Moses helped Israel learn this in our **Old Testament Reading**, Deuteronomy 8:1–10.

Much as our Thanksgivings take place near the end of harvest season—a good time to take stock of how the year has gone—Moses addresses the Israelites near the end of their forty-year wandering. Look back. How has God done by us these years? Miraculously well! Manna every day. And now a good land before us—crops and fruit and minerals. A very good land! And Moses springs this on them: "Your clothing did not wear out on you and your foot did not swell these forty years" (8:4). As miraculous as manna—and I think they hadn't realized it! Just got up every day and had perfectly serviceable clothes to put on. Hadn't even noticed they should have needed a new simlah or mitpahath decades ago!

They would have taken it for granted unless the Lord had "humbled you and let you hunger . . . that He might make you know that man does not live by bread alone, but man lives by every word that comes from the mouth of the LORD" (8:3). We can't give thanks to God unless He opens our eyes to see all He's done for us.

The **Psalm** might seem to suggest that all people eagerly praise God: Psalm 67. But actually even here, in order "that Your way may be known on earth," God must "make His face to shine upon us" (67:2a, 1b).

Two **Epistle** options are offered for a Day of Thanksgiving. Brief words about each:

In Philippians 4:6–20, the oft-quoted phrase "the peace of God, which surpasses all understanding" (4:7) should not be overlooked. This peace means being reconciled to God by the atoning death of Jesus, and something so good, so free, so self-sacrificing we could never fathom without the Holy Spirit working faith. Paul also says he's learned "the secret" of facing both plenty and need. It's "through Him who strengthens me" (4:12, 13). Christ is the one we thank, a secret God has now revealed. And enabling us to give thanks is a gift God gives for our benefit; Paul encourages the Philippians' thank offering "not that *I* seek the gift, but I seek the fruit that increases to *your* credit" (4:17).

Then in 1 Timothy 2:1–4, Paul indicates that among the chief reasons for thanksgiving is the "peaceful and quiet life" that comes with stable government. Why? Because in that calm and stability the Gospel of Jesus Christ may go forth freely, that "all people [may] be saved and . . . come to the knowledge of the truth" (2:4). God's greatest desire is that all Thanksgiving revelers would know Him as God their Savior (2:3–4).

The classic Thanksgiving **Holy Gospel** is Jesus healing the ten lepers. Read Luke 17:11–19.

It's so tough to read this story—or preach on it—and not jump to the obvious: be thankful. But that would badly oversimplify the message. It's not just about the lepers being thankful or not.

Jesus told the lepers to follow God's procedure of Leviticus 13–14 to verify their healing. As they went, all ten were cleansed, and nine of them continued on their way.

Were the nine thankful? Sure! They were glad as could be that they were healed, had their lives extended, could do Thanksgiving this year with their families. They even went to church to celebrate! Unfortunately, they didn't fully recognize *who* it was to be thanked—which sent them running off to church in the wrong direction.

The Samaritan grasped that Thanksgiving worship was right here! Going to the priests was proper, but Jesus was the source of his healing and every good. Faith in Jesus as Savior had made him well (17:19). And faith in Christ is, as always, a gift of the Holy Spirit. Hence, he's thankful.

**IT IS YET ANOTHER GIFT OF GOD—
A WORKING OF THE HOLY SPIRIT—
THAT WE GIVE GOD THANKS
FOR ALL HIS GOODNESSES TO US.**

The Thanksgiving dinner table will be an excellent opportunity to do that. And you might consider as a most excellent table prayer to express that thanks the **Gradual** for Thanksgiving Day. Let us pray:

The eyes of all look to You, [O Lord,] and You give them their food in due season. You open Your hand and satisfy the desire of every living thing. Oh give thanks to the LORD, for He is good; His steadfast love endures forever. (Ps 145:15–16; 118:1)

Amen.

The Sundays after Pentecost: Proper 29 (November 20–26) Year A

READINGS

Ezekiel 34:11–16, 20–24
Psalm 95:1–7a (antiphon: v 7a)
1 Corinthians 15:20–28
Matthew 25:31–46

HYMN OF THE DAY

LSB 532 "The Head That Once Was Crowned with Thorns"

What's simply enough labeled Proper 29—seemingly just another number—is *not* just another Sunday. It's The Last Sunday of the Church Year. It looks forward to Jesus returning to earth in glory on what we call "the Last Day," "the end of the world," Jesus' "Second Advent," "the Parousia," "the last trumpet," "Gabriel blowing his horn." Heady stuff! Climactic stuff! And anything so big, so final, is potentially terrifying. Especially when, perhaps above all, we refer to this climactic moment in time as Judgment Day.

When, as they say, "There's no tomorrow," when the game clock counts down to triple zeros, when "This is it!" we're almost sure to ask ourselves the "What if?" question. What if I'm not ready? What if I come up short? And then to realize that we're facing the Judge—well, that conjures up images of being the accused, standing up in the courtroom to hear a verdict. What if the Judge slams down His gavel and says, "Guilty!"—forever and ever . . . and ever? Because this is the *final* judgment. For eternal punishment or innocence.

This could be a scary Sunday.

And there is some of that.

But for Christians, the prospect is decidedly different. For unlike a courtroom decision, which is always uncertain until the verdict is read, we know what the final judgment will be. And it's a decision to which we look forward!

Peter starts us there with the antiphon to our **Introit** for the Last Sunday:

> *In keeping with His promise we are looking forward to a new heaven and a new earth, the home of righteousness.*

O Lord, make me know my end and what is the measure of my days; let me know how fleeting I am! Behold, You have made my days a few handbreadths, and my lifetime is as nothing before You. And now, O Lord, for what do I wait? My hope is in You. Deliver me from all my transgressions. Do not make me the scorn of the fool! Hear my prayer, O Lord, and give ear to my cry; hold not Your peace at my tears! For I am a sojourner with You, a guest, like all my fathers.

Glory be to the Father and to the Son and to the Holy Spirit; as it was in the beginning, is now, and will be forever. Amen.

In keeping with His promise we are looking forward to a new heaven and a new earth, the home of righteousness. (Ps 39:4–5, 7–8, 12a; antiphon: 2 Peter 3:13, NIV)

"Looking forward to" something always means more to us than just thinking about the future; we always say it to express eager anticipation, the confidence that that future will be fun, exciting, or better. "I'm looking forward to it!" For Christians, looking ahead to the Last Day is to be like that—in the grandest way.

Just what the "new heaven" and "new earth" will be like isn't at all clear. Some see Holy Scripture as teaching that we'll be on a beautifully reworked, restored renewal of this very planet. But Peter, in the immediately preceding verse, says that the elements will melt with burning and intense heat. So the actual location may well be elsewhere. That's not really the main issue. The new heaven and earth will be a real place where our souls and resurrected bodies, reunited, will be with the Lord in unending and perfect joy. It will be "the home of righteousness," where Christ is and sin isn't.

And its joys will dwarf everything in this life. "My days" here on earth are "a few handbreadths," "fleeting." We cling to them so tenaciously. But what God has for us next will never end. Thus, facing up to "know my end" is not a fatalistic resignation, an admission of inevitable defeat. It's looking forward to something much better: "Now, O Lord, for what do I wait? My hope is in You." Being just a "sojourner" here "like all my fathers" were before me, having my days end as they did for every past generation, is okay because of the Lord's promise for the future.

We made the point last week that the reason we need not fear the Judgment is because we know the Judge. That's the basis for our prayer this week too, in the **Collect**:

Eternal God, merciful Father, You have appointed Your Son as judge of the living and the dead. Enable us to wait for the day of His return with our eyes fixed on the kingdom prepared for Your own from the foundation of the world; through Jesus Christ, our Lord, who lives and reigns with You and the Holy Spirit, one God, now and forever. Amen.

Our Judge is the Son of God, "the Alpha and the Omega, the first and the last, the beginning and the end," as He calls Himself in our **Verse** (Rev 22:13). In other words, He's the one who created everything and will reign for all eternity, which means whatever He says is also the first and the last word. Well, this is the Son who gave His life on the cross to save us—and who said, "It is finished!" That was the final word. That was the Judge's verdict, announced loud and clear for the whole world to hear. Everything necessary to exonerate us is complete! Now it's just a matter of waiting for the day when He returns to read the transcript for those who missed it. *We know.* And so we pray that God will enable us to look forward without fear or distraction, "our eyes fixed on the kingdom prepared for Your own from the foundation of the world."

The **Old Testament Reading** now introduces an illustration that Jesus will also use in our Gospel lesson: judging the sheep. Read Ezekiel 34:11–16, 20–24.

You may remember that Ezekiel prophesied from captivity in Babylon. And for most of his first thirty-three chapters, he speaks of bad to worse; the Babylonian army would come back to Jerusalem yet again and carry off most of those who remained. But after Ezekiel receives word from home that the city has indeed been captured, he begins to speak of restoration (33:21–22). The Lord "will search for My sheep . . . and will bring them into their own land" (34:11, 13).

That's the way Christ would have us view His second coming as well. See Ezekiel's description, and notice the details, because they're remarkably close to the way Jesus will speak of His return in the Gospel. Ezekiel sees the Lord, as a shepherd, gathering His people from all the countries where they have been scattered. It will be "a day of clouds and thick darkness" (34:12–13). And then He will judge between the sheep. He will separate the fat sheep from the lean sheep (34:20, 22). That would be a fearful judgment for Judah's wicked kings and priests who'd been growing fat by oppressing their people (34:21; see also 34:1–10). But it would be comfort for those poor souls they'd been victimizing.

From then on, "one shepherd" would care for them: "David" (34:23). The original David had lived four hundred years before Ezekiel, but this future David would fit the bill: the first David had been a shepherd and then became king; this David would be the Good Shepherd and is King of kings. In fact, by Ezekiel's time and on into the New Testament, God's people universally recognized "David" or "Son of David" as a name for the Messiah. They looked forward to the time when He would "feed them with good pasture, . . . seek the lost, . . . bring back the strayed, . . . bind up the injured, . . . strengthen the weak" (34:14, 16).

The **Psalm** reminds us that we, too, look forward to coming into the presence of our King and Shepherd—already every time we worship. You'll recognize Psalm 95:1–7a.

We always sing the Venite with joy (even a "joyful noise")—even though the one we're facing is the "great God" and "great King" who made everything. The reason we don't fear standing before Him is that He's also taken us as His people, "the sheep of His hand." To do that, this Good Shepherd laid down His life for the sheep (Jn 10:11).

The **Epistle** for this Last Sunday, 1 Corinthians 15:20–28, emphasizes two additional aspects of the Last Day: the resurrection of the body and the end of all evil.

Paul's great resurrection chapter begins with Jesus' own resurrection, the key to everything since He is "the firstfruits" (15:20). We, then, are the fruits to follow. "At His coming" is the general "resurrection of the dead" (15:23, 21)—the bodies of all who have died reunited with their souls. We look forward to living forever in heaven not just as spirits but in our very own human bodies, raised and glorified, as was Jesus'.

The Judgment will be separating "those who belong to Christ" (15:23) from "all His enemies" (15:25). Christ "delivers the kingdom," including especially all of us who are His, "to God the Father." But every enemy, including "every rule and every authority and power" that would oppose Christ—above all, death—He will destroy (15:24–26). We look forward to an eternity without evil!

And now, this *is* it!—the Bible's most vivid picturing of Christ's return, our **Holy Gospel**, Matthew 25:31–46.

It will be so much the way Ezekiel saw it: Christ the King, coming in glory on the clouds of heaven (cf 26:64), gathering before Him all the nations. "And He will separate people one from another as a shepherd separates the sheep from the goats" (25:31–32).

It won't be much of a trial. Before a word is spoken, the judgment: sheep on Jesus' right, goats on His left (25:33). This is crucial, because otherwise what follows could sound like a decision on the basis of our works. No, already the judgment is made based on what *God alone can see*: faith in Christ in the heart. Those who believed that Jesus' cross has given them heaven (that He truly "finished" it!) inherit the kingdom He's been preparing for us from the beginning (25:34). Those who did not believe: eternal fire (25:41). The verdict we've known all along.

What follows is simply the evidence that *we can all see*—to make evident even to objectors how proper God's invisible decision really is. Those who believed in Jesus weren't doing their acts of love to earn anything; they didn't even notice they were doing them (25:37–39). Unbelievers were clueless that every day they had opportunity to serve Christ (25:44)—and they hadn't cared. Notice, too, that what believers *failed to do* or did sinfully is never mentioned—all washed away in the blood of Christ. And whatever unbelievers *did do* is likewise never mentioned, because apart from faith in Christ, such acts are really always self-serving.

So there's no hidden agenda, no surprises. The Last Day will all be exactly as we can most certainly trust.

IN KEEPING WITH HIS PROMISE, WE LOOK FORWARD TO THE RESURRECTION OF THE DEAD, WHEN THE SHEPHERD-KING COMES TO JUDGE BETWEEN THE SHEEP AND THE GOATS FOR THE ETERNAL KINGDOM OR ETERNAL FIRE.

The **Hymn of the Day** (*LSB* 532) reminds us once more why we do look forward to it: Jesus' cross, our "everlasting theme."

Year B

First Sunday in Advent Year B

READINGS

Isaiah 64:1–9
Psalm 80:1–7 (antiphon: v 7)
1 Corinthians 1:3–9
Mark 11:1–10
or Mark 13:24–37

HYMN OF THE DAY

LSB 332 "Savior of the Nations, Come"

I'm beginning to feel it! I'm definitely getting in the mood. And I'm writing this right after Thanksgiving, so it's real. I'm starting to get excited about Christmas!

The First Sunday in Advent does that to us, doesn't it! It's a new church year; the Advent wreath will be out, and maybe some of the Christmas decor. And at home this week, it may be looking even more like Christmas. While the kids were with us on Friday, we cut and decorated our tree. I can't wait to celebrate Jesus' coming!

Since it is a new church year, let's review some of the things we've explained before. First, about this book. I hope it's helping you look forward to each Sunday morning. Doing a little reading ahead makes listening on Sunday more focused and perhaps raises some questions you'll hear answered in the pastor's message. Of course, these devotion-studies are never to suggest what he might preach; they're just to give you a sense of the context in which you'll get to hear him. We call them devotion-studies because we hope you'll be learning, but we also hope you'll find the reading devotional and use it as time to consider what God is doing, to pray, and to sing, even with your family if you like.

Now about the church year and the Sundays to which we're looking forward. This Sunday begins Year B of the three-year lectionary. Last year was spent largely in Matthew's Gospel (Year A). This year, the Gospel readings will be primarily from Mark. (Next year, Year C, Luke.) Since Mark is the shortest of the four Gospel books, we also get the largest sampling of John this year. Each Sunday, the Introit, the Collect, the Verse, the Psalm, the Hymn of the Day, and, especially, the Old Testament Reading pick up some cue from the Gospel lesson, and on festivals and during some seasons of the year (Advent, Christmas, Lent), so do the Epistles. The Gradual expresses the theme for the entire season (or a part of the long Pentecost season).

Looking forward to the First Sunday in Advent, we might find that's a good place to start, the **Gradual**:

Rejoice greatly, O daughter of Zion. Shout aloud, O daughter of Jerusalem. Behold, your king is coming to you; righteous and having salvation. Blessed is he who comes in the name of the Lord. From the house of the Lord we bless you. (Zech 9:9; Ps 118:26, alt)

We may not know what Mark's Gospel will have for us this First Sunday in Advent or that the Old Testament Reading will be from Isaiah, but we know what season it is! We know *advent* means "coming," and we're excited about our King coming to us! We're eager to shout aloud— or at least sing aloud!

So we'll shout it again! The **Introit**:

Behold, your king is coming to you; righteous and having salvation.

To You, O Lord, I lift up my soul. O my God, in You I trust; let me not be put to shame; let not my enemies exult over me. Indeed, none who wait for You shall be put to shame; they shall be ashamed who are wantonly treacherous.

Glory be to the Father and to the Son and to the Holy Spirit; as it was in the beginning, is now, and will be forever. Amen.

Behold, your king is coming to you; righteous and having salvation. (Ps 25:1–3; antiphon: Zech 9:9b, alt)

We're excited! And not just for the coziness of Christmas. We're excited because our King is coming with salvation. It's the same excitement we express as we open our Collect for Sunday: "Stir up Your power, O Lord, and come."

That's very much the same prayer with which Isaiah begins our **Old Testament Reading**, Isaiah 64:1–9.

Isaiah envisions that earthquaking day when the Lord came down on Mount Sinai. The prophet pictures God rending the skies and thundering, His power overwhelming the people with terror (Ex 20:18). And Isaiah knows exactly what he wants God's power display to do: "Make Your name known to Your adversaries, and that the nations might tremble at Your presence!" (Is 64:2b). Judah was threatened by foreign powers like Assyria, and Isaiah wanted God to destroy them. He knew that "You meet him who joyfully works righteousness, those who remember You in Your ways" (64:5a). Isaiah is on a roll. He's excited for the Lord to come. "Stir up Your power, O Lord, and come." Read Isaiah 64:1–5a again.

Suddenly something changes. "You meet him who joyfully works righteousness, those who remember You in Your ways." Then,

"Behold, You were angry, and *we* sinned; in *our* sins we have been a long time, and shall *we* be saved? *We* have all become like one who is unclean, and *all our righteous deeds* are like a polluted garment" (64:5b–6a). God delivers those who joyfully work righteousness, but we don't! Our righteousness is like dirty laundry!

Oops! Isaiah catches himself! Maybe we're not so eager for God to rend the heavens and come down after all! "We all fade like a leaf, and our iniquities, like the wind, take us away. There is no one who calls upon Your name, who rouses himself to take hold of You; for You have hidden Your face from us, and have made us melt in the hand of our iniquities" (64:6b–7). Perhaps, Lord, we'd be better off if You just stay in heaven and leave us to ourselves down here.

Or, better yet, Lord, You just handle things the way You know is best. "O LORD, You are our Father; we are the clay, and You are our potter; we are all the work of Your hand" (64:8). Perhaps, You, Lord, have a better plan.

And He does. He has a different way to come down—a way He can come down that won't burn us or boil us, a way for which we really can pray. The rest of the **Collect**:

Stir up Your power, O Lord, and come, that by Your protection we may be rescued from the threatening perils of our sins and saved by Your mighty deliverance; for You live and reign with the Father and the Holy Spirit, one God, now and forever. Amen.

God had a plan to come down all along, but not in a show of power. Not yet. He'd come in a way that would save us, but not from what we thought we feared. He wouldn't blast the Assyrians, but He would rescue us from the perils of *our* sin.

"Restore us, O God; let Your face shine, that we may be saved!" (Ps 80:3). The psalmist has the right idea. Read the **Psalm**, 80:1–7.

The Lord of hosts has every reason to "be angry with Your people's prayers" (80:4). But if the Lord first smiles on us, shows us His face shining with love instead of lightning, then He could "stir up [His] might and come to save us!" (80:2). He could come to restore us, make us righteous, then come in power.

That's exactly the way the Lord comes in the first **Holy Gospel** for Sunday. Read Mark 11:1–10.

We have a clearer understanding than did the Palm Sunday crowd as to why this is such an appropriate reading for Advent 1. Jesus' preaching and miracles have attracted wild popularity; He's being widely hailed as the long-promised Messiah. It's now Passover, and tens of thousands have come to Jerusalem for the feast. It seems the perfect time—many expect Jesus to be their national champion, and the duking it out ought to begin now while the mob is there to overpower the Roman garrison. They shout, "Hosanna!" Save us now! The kingdom of our father David is coming! (11:9–10).

It's rend the heavens and come down all over again.

But look more closely. Jesus has to borrow a donkey, no stable of steeds—to say nothing of putting armed riders on them.

And look ahead. The crowd had no idea that when the bloodshed did start, the only one bloodied would be King David's Son. And what they really didn't realize was that the way He would "hosanna" them was by giving up His life willingly, without a fight.

We know this is the way God intended to come all along. Not Mount Sinai-ish, making Assyrians or Romans or abortionists or evolutionists or radical Islamists tremble. Not to gratify our desire for a safer, saner society. Certainly not to put us or even the Christian Church on top of the heap. Rather that we "be rescued from the threatening perils of our sins." And that could happen only if God came in humility, humbling Himself to death, even death on a cross.

That's why the manger, not Jerusalem General and a private suite, is now coming in four weeks.

God coming to earth first in humility makes it possible for us to receive Him. Read the **Epistle**, 1 Corinthians 1:3–9

"Grace to you and peace from God our Father and the Lord Jesus Christ" (1:3). That might seem to us a throwaway because we may hear it as the first words of every sermon. But Paul is able to speak peace to the Corinthians only because God came to us in peace. Unrighteous as Isaiah knew we were, we could only have been destroyed if confronted by God's holiness. That's why the Israelites cowered before Sinai. If God had come in power, it would have been to wreak justice on our sin. But since Jesus took our sins upon Himself and gave us His righteousness, we are now at peace with God. The sin that offended God's holiness is gone; we've been reconciled. "God is faithful." We "were called into the fellowship of His Son, Jesus Christ our Lord" (1:9). We are in fellowship, at peace, able to be together.

That enables us then to look forward without fear to Christ's final advent—when He does come in power at the end of the world. "As you wait for the revealing of our Lord Jesus Christ, [He] will sustain you to the end, guiltless in the day of our Lord Jesus Christ" (1:7b–8).

And that day will come. This Sunday in worship, you may hear the other **Holy Gospel** option for Advent 1, Mark 13:24–37, which focuses there.

"In those days, . . . the sun will be darkened, and the moon will not give its light, and the stars will be falling from heaven, and the powers in the heavens will be shaken. And then they will see the Son of Man coming in clouds with great power and glory" (13:24–26). There's the show of power, but we're prepared for it because first came Jesus not gloriously but quietly, humbly, in peace.

This is why we're so excited as we begin the season of Advent, isn't it.

**YES, DO STIR UP YOUR POWER, O LORD, AND COME . . .
BUT ONLY BECAUSE
YOU FIRST CAME NOT IN POWER
BUT IN HUMILITY AND PEACE.**

Begin to get in the mood for Advent by singing the **Hymn of the Day** for Advent 1, "Savior of the Nations, Come" (*LSB* 332). There is no show of power here, but there is marveling that the Lord of heaven and earth "chose such a birth" (st 1).

Second Sunday in Advent Year B

READINGS

Isaiah 40:1–11
Psalm 85 (antiphon: v 9)
2 Peter 3:8–14
Mark 1:1–8

HYMN OF THE DAY

LSB 344 "On Jordan's Bank the Baptist's Cry"

A memorable image to me (and easily accessed by anyone these days) is a few moments of Charlton Heston playing John the Baptist in the old classic *The Greatest Story Ever Told*. Heston surely looks the camel's-hair-locusts-and-wild-honey part, and it wasn't quite this simple, but it seems as if his only line was one word repeated over and over: "Repent!" Preaching to the crowds, decrying the Pharisees and Sadducees, dunking Herod's arresting officers in the Jordan, and just before the executioner's blow, it's "Repent! Repent!"

Undoubtedly *repent* (with an exclamation point) was a very big word in John's sermonic vocabulary. But there was more to his preaching than that. In fact, "Repent!" was only the prerequisite—and absolutely vital—to his main message.

The Second and Third Sundays in Advent look forward to Jesus' coming through the ministry of John the Baptist. And the propers will definitely let us hear John's call to repentance. But they'll emphasize that his ultimate purpose was to prepare us for the saving work of Christ Jesus.

Let's begin with prayer, the **Collect** for the Second Sunday in Advent:

> *Stir up our hearts, O Lord, to make ready the way of Your only-begotten Son, that by His coming we may be enabled to serve You with pure minds; through the same Jesus Christ, our Lord, who lives and reigns with You and the Holy Spirit, one God, now and forever. Amen.*

Make ready the way of the Lord!

That's certainly John's mission. Read the **Holy Gospel**, Mark 1:1–8.

It's just the second Sunday of Year B, which means we've got almost a whole year ahead to spend in Mark's Gospel. So it's nice to see how he introduces it: "The beginning of the gospel of Jesus Christ, the Son of God" (1:1). It's about as nondescript as one could be, we might think. Except that Mark is the author who gives us the term *gospel* for the kind of literary piece we've come to call, well, a *Gospel*. Matthew, Luke, and John can all thank Mark for the label we've given their books. And it's significant because, of course, *gospel* (the Greek εὐαγγέλιον, *euangelion*) means "good news." The point here is that we shouldn't expect the very first episode, the ministry of John the Baptist, to be somehow other than good news. It shouldn't only tell us how sinful we are and that we've got to clean up our act. It has to be going somewhere further.

Mark lets the Old Testament prophets—Isaiah, with Malachi thrown in for good measure—background John for us. His marching orders are explicit: Prepare for the Messiah. He is to be the Christ's "messenger," going ahead of Him to "prepare Your way" (1:2b, quoting Mal 3:1). He is to "prepare the way of the Lord, make His paths straight" (1:3b, from Is 40:3).

Then we see how John does that: "Proclaiming a baptism of repentance for the forgiveness of sins" (1:4). John prepares the way of the Lord by calling us to prepare for Him. And we prepare by, yes, repenting. The Savior is coming. But we won't care to receive a Savior if we don't think we need to be saved. If we're comfortable, we won't want comfort. The last thing we'll want is someone who offers anything besides the status quo. What's more, we might even *love* our sins, so we'll hate that release from them! Prepare for the Lord! Repent!

That's how we'll be ready when the mightier One comes (1:7). But, see, that's a word of Gospel from John the Baptist. For He, the Messiah, "will baptize you with the Holy Spirit" (1:8). The Holy Spirit is the gift of God living in us, that one who unites us with God. This would be fulfilled dramatically for the Church on the day of Pentecost. It's also fulfilled for each of us, though, in our Baptism, when with water by the Word we receive the Holy Spirit.

So John, even as he's preaching repentance, is also a preacher of the Gospel of Christ. We'd love to hear more of what John actually said. Since Mark gives us very little more, however, we turn to the other propers to elaborate on this "gospel of Jesus Christ, the Son of God"—which, if John didn't make explicit, he knew was coming with the Christ. We'll start our theme for the Sunday and then add on to it as we study each new proper. To start,

**PREPARE THE WAY OF THE LORD
WITH REPENTANCE,
FOR HIS COMING IS . . .**

The **Introit**:

Restore us, O God; let Your face shine, that we may be saved!

Give ear, O Shepherd of Israel, You who lead Joseph like a flock! You

who are enthroned upon the cherubim, shine forth. You brought a vine out of Egypt; it took deep root and filled the land. Restore us, O God of hosts; let Your face shine, that we may be saved!

Glory be to the Father and to the Son and to the Holy Spirit; as it was in the beginning, is now, and will be forever. Amen.

Restore us, O God; let Your face shine, that we may be saved! (Ps 80:1, 8a, 9b, 7; antiphon: Ps 80:3)

We heard Psalm 80 as the appointed Psalm last week. And here it is again: "Restore us, O God." Prepare the way of the Lord with repentance, for His coming is *restoration.* Jesus' coming restores the relationship with God that we broke by our sin. God reaches across the great divide, comes to us by becoming one of us, and then removes the sin that created that divide by dying for it.

Jesus' coming also restores the very humanity we lost by sin. From creatures who were dear friends of God, naturally loving and caring of one another, we became self-serving enemies of God and, really, of everyone. Isolated. Defensive. Aggressive. But when Christ comes to redeem us, He restores what we were. Free. Connected. Loving.

Mark showed us a moment ago that the **Old Testament Reading**, Isaiah 40:1–11, includes the program for John's ministry. See how rich it is in Gospel!

This passage is truly one of the quintessential Advent lessons. It's the text of great musical settings such as *LSB* 347 ("Comfort, Comfort Ye My People") and an aria in Handel's *Messiah* ("Ev'ry Valley Shall Be Exalted"). It stakes a new and comforting direction in Isaiah's prophecy, just after he looks ahead to the tragedy of the Babylonian captivity (39:5–7). The comfort will be in the coming of the Messiah, the one a voice crying in the wilderness will announce (40:3). How many specific words of Gospel do you find in the reading?

Comfort for a people facing exile (40:1). Pardon, the assurance that the sin which put them in such a mess will no longer haunt them (40:2). Glory, the sight of the Lord revealed in His majesty, yet not terrifying His people because they have been pardoned (40:5). Nothing shall stand in the way of His coming—not mountain, not valley, not desert, not rough ground. He's coming through to save His people.

They feel helpless—like grass and flowers that wither and fade. But look and hear beyond that! Look up to the high mountain and hear the herald calling from there—the word of the Lord that lasts forever—*good news!* Yes, good news! (40:9). Our Hymn of the Day will call that "*glad tidings* of the King of kings!" (*LSB* 344:1). "Behold your God!" He's come! And He brings you His reward and recompense (40:10). It's not a reward you've earned, nor a recompense you deserve as payback for your sin. It's a reward credited to you that Christ earned on the cross—a payback to Satan and every enemy he's hurled against you.

Prepare the way of the Lord with repentance, for His coming is restoration, comfort, pardon, glory, good news, glad tidings, reward, and recompense.

The **Psalm** echoes our Introit and Old Testament Reading but adds new Gospel words to our picture of the Lord's coming. Read Psalm 85.

Suffering Israel is again restored, her iniquity covered. God's wrath, hot anger, was just. But His *steadfast love* means He won't be angry with His people forever (85:5–7a). He will grant them His *salvation* (85:7b). Our personal histories must appreciate this, right? We can't imagine it was just the Jordan crowds or Herod and the Jewish religious leaders John would have called out, eh? Advent is a time for each of us to confess our sins and realize we've each earned God's indignation. So then how deeply grateful we can be that His love never waivers. Despite our sin, He is at *peace* with us (85:8a), because He Himself came and made our sins His own and in exchange gave us His *righteousness* (85:11).

The Lord's coming is steadfast love, salvation, peace, and righteousness.

There's even Gospel in Peter's **Epistle**, 2 Peter 3:8–14, which describes the final destruction of earth.

Here's the climactic witness that John's preaching of judgment is true: when Christ returns on the Last Day, "the heavens will be set on fire and dissolved, and the heavenly bodies will melt as they burn!" (3:12). But even here, Peter makes clear that God's people need not be terrified. The Lord's return is not a threat to us but a *promise* (3:9). And the destruction of earth as we know it will usher in *new heavens and a new earth* (3:13). We who have received Christ's righteousness will have a magnificent eternal home.

So our propers today are loaded with Gospel that the Lord's coming will bring. Can we really see all this, though, in the ministry of John the Baptist with his call to repent?

Think again about the way Mark summarized John's mission: "John appeared, baptizing in the wilderness and proclaiming a baptism of repentance *for the forgiveness of sins*" (Mk 1:4). Quite rightly do we picture John preaching repentance. But repenting of our sins is always preparation to receive the Gospel, forgiveness. And it will be John who first most clearly declares how that forgiveness will come: "Behold, the Lamb of God, who takes away the sin of the world!" (Jn 1:29). The Lamb sacrificed on the cross—that's where John is always going as he prepares the way of Lord. Therefore, let us

Prepare the Way of the Lord with Repentance, for His Coming Is Restoration, Comfort, Pardon, Glory, Good News, Glad Tidings, Reward, Recompense, Steadfast Love, Salvation, Peace, Righteousness, Promise, New Heavens and Earth, Forgiveness.

Perhaps you're like me and you really know it's Advent when you sing this Sunday's **Hymn of the Day**, "On Jordan's Bank the Baptist's Cry" (*LSB* 344). It is "glad tidings from the King of kings" (st 1) John brings. Therefore, "Let us all our hearts prepare for Christ to come and enter there" (st 2).

Third Sunday in Advent Year B

READINGS

Isaiah 61:1–4, 8–11
Psalm 126 (antiphon: v 5)
1 Thessalonians 5:16–24
John 1:6–8, 19–28

HYMN OF THE DAY

LSB 345 "Hark! A Thrilling Voice Is Sounding"

The **Gradual** for Advent articulates the theme for the entire season, and it's certainly appropriate for all four Sundays. Especially, though, does it express the direction of Advent 3:

> *Rejoice greatly, O daughter of Zion. Shout aloud, O daughter of Jerusalem. Behold, your king is coming to you; righteous and having salvation. Blessed is he who comes in the name of the Lord. From the house of the Lord we bless you. (Zech 9:9; Ps 118:26, alt)*

Do you remember what you'll see up in the chancel as worship begins on the Third Sunday of Advent? The first three candles of the Advent wreath will be lighted, and the new one this week will be the rose-colored candle. As a break from the penitential purple or blue, the rose candle signals the Third Sunday of Advent as the Sunday of joy. "Rejoice greatly, O daughter of Zion." Joy, rejoicing will be prominent throughout our propers this day.

We know why we rejoice this week, of course. "Behold, your king is coming to you; righteous and having salvation." Advent is a season to take a long, hard look at ourselves and repent of the sins that made Christ's coming necessary. But the overarching point is that Christ *did* come—and came to save. He comes "having salvation."

Our **Introit** opens by praying that God would fulfill that promise to save us:

> *Show us Your steadfast love, O Lord,*
> *and grant us Your salvation.*

Let me hear what God the LORD will speak, for He will speak peace to His people, to His saints; but let them not turn back to folly. Surely His salvation is near to those who fear Him, that glory may dwell in our land. Yes, the LORD will give what is good, and our land will yield its increase. Righteousness will go before Him and make His footsteps a way.

Glory be to the Father and to the Son and to the Holy Spirit; as it was in the beginning, is now, and will be forever. Amen.

Show us Your steadfast love, O LORD, and grant us Your salvation. (Ps 85:8–9, 12–13; antiphon: Ps 85:7)

No sooner does the psalmist pray that God would grant us salvation, though, than he confidently declares his own answer to the prayer: "Surely His salvation is *near* to those who fear Him. . . . Yes, the LORD *will* give what is good, and our land *will* yield its increase. Righteousness *will* go before Him" (Ps 85:9, 12–13). The psalmist wrote this passage centuries before Jesus' birth, and he was able to prophesy with confidence because God always keeps His promises.

But now in this season of Advent, we hear these words with greater immediacy. Advent 3, like Advent 2 last week, is a "John the Baptist Sunday." Again in our Gospel reading, we'll hear of John's ministry. And once the forerunner of the Messiah appeared, God's people could speak of the Christ's arrival as an accomplished fact. When John the Baptist came on the scene, it meant that the mission of the Messiah was also now set in motion. He *will* come is henceforth He will come *soon*, "His salvation is near." "Alleluia. Behold, I send My messenger before Your face, who will prepare Your way before You. Alleluia" (the **Verse**, from a prophecy of Malachi, as we also heard quoted last Sunday by Mark). The forerunner is here; we can rejoice that the Lord Himself can't be far behind!

The **Collect** for this Sunday introduces another image of Christ's coming that we'll see later in the Gospel lesson:

Lord Jesus Christ, we implore You to hear our prayers and to lighten the darkness of our hearts by Your gracious visitation; for You live and reign with the Father and the Holy Spirit, one God, now and forever. Amen.

Christ's "gracious visitation," His coming to earth, was to "lighten the darkness of our hearts." The light-dark imagery is used often of Christ and Advent (e.g., Is 9:2; 60:1–3; Jn 8:12). It's easy to understand how it fits. Aside from Christ coming to us, we could only be in the dark about who God is and how He looks at us. But since Christ came, we see clearly that God loves us, is gracious toward us, and wants to be with us. We'll see how central this was to John's mission.

The **Old Testament Reading** this week gives exceptionally beautiful pictures of our rejoicing at the coming of the Messiah. Read Isaiah 61:1–4, 8–11.

The first few lines of this prophecy may be familiar from a sermon of Jesus. One Sabbath in the synagogue in Nazareth, Jesus uses this text from Isaiah as His preaching text: "The Spirit of the Lord God is upon Me, because the Lord has anointed Me to bring good news to the poor; He has sent Me to bind up the brokenhearted, to proclaim liberty to the captives, and the opening of the prison to those who are bound; to proclaim the year of the Lord's favor" (61:1–2a; cf Lk 4:16–19). Then Jesus shocks the local folks by applying the passage to Himself: "Today this Scripture has been fulfilled in your hearing" (Lk 4:21).

Eventually that sermon incites the crowd to push Jesus toward the cliff (Lk 4:22–30), but what magnificent reason the text gives us for rejoicing! "Good news to the poor." Most of us have everything we need and lots of things we want, but often there's a poverty of love in our families; we know what it means to be "brokenhearted" by divorce or our children's divorces, death of a spouse or death of a child, cold feelings at home or frigid relationships with our parents. All of us were "captives," prisoners of our sin, locked away in a holding cell awaiting final transfer to hell. But Christ brings God's love, embodied by brothers and sisters in His Church. He announces forgiveness that not only springs the prison door open but enables us to forgive and repair those broken relationships. We all mourn (61:2b), but He comforts by assuring us that He'll one day wipe every tear from our eyes.

Now see how Isaiah pictures the rejoicing all that raises. "The oil of gladness instead of mourning, the garment of praise instead of a faint spirit" (61:3b). "I will greatly rejoice in the Lord; my soul shall exult in my God, for He has clothed me with the garments of salvation; He has covered me with the robe of righteousness, as a bridegroom decks himself like a priest with a beautiful headdress, and as a bride adorns herself with her jewels" (61:10). Something about a candlelight wedding in December may be even more stunning than an afternoon in June. Whenever the Lord comes to save us from the effects of sin, we will rejoice, exult!

Our **Psalm**, a Song of Ascents (perhaps to be sung while ascending the steps of the temple), also declares how joy follows after sadness. Read Psalm 126.

This psalm celebrates the return of God's people from captivity in Babylon. Some of the Jews have been away from their homeland for seventy years. Many remember the glory of Solomon's temple. Could we really be going home, or was it a dream? No, it is real! "Then our mouth was filled with laughter, and our tongue with shouts of joy. . . . The Lord has done great things for us; we are glad" (126:2a, 3). Like Isaiah, the psalmist uses vivid imagery. Streams that had run dry flow again (126:4). Farmers who had planted in anxiety, fearing drought, reap "with shouts of joy," coming home "with shouts of joy" bringing in the sheaves (126:5–6). The Lord has preserved His people against all odds and always with a grand design—that His Messiah could now come to the intended land and nation.

It doesn't take Paul long in our **Epistle** lesson to get to the rose word for Advent 3. See 1 Thessalonians 5:16–24.

"Rejoice always" (which, by the way, is the shortest verse in the Bible in the original language, just two words or fourteen letters in Greek, compared with three Greek words of sixteen letters for Jn 11:35) is one of eight imperatives Paul gives as he nears the end of his letter (5:16–22). The other seven are actions that can be commanded and obeyed, but Paul knows you can't simply order someone to feel joyful. Instead, he's beginning his series by reminding readers of the context for all Christian living. For the Christian, "rejoicing always" isn't a feeling we're to have; it's faith that God is caring for us always, whatever the circumstances and however we feel. "Now may the God of peace Himself sanctify you completely, and may your whole spirit and soul and body be kept blameless at the coming of our Lord Jesus Christ" (5:23). Believing God would do that—make us completely holy and preserve us until we're called to heaven—would be rejoicing, always. But is that just a "may," which would really only be a "maybe"? Nonsense! "He who calls you is faithful; He will surely do it" (5:24).

That became a *fait accompli* as of the events of the **Holy Gospel**, John 1:6–8, 19–28.

The metaphor of light (1:6–8) will be extended when these verses are part of the Christmas Day Gospel. John the Evangelist introduces John the Baptist by calling him above all a witness to the light. But the Gospel writer is just as clear that John "was not the light." This will always be John's legacy; one of the most important men who ever lived (Mt 11:11) is great because of who he is not (Jn 3:26–30).

The question put to him, then, must be, "Who are you?" (1:19). Not the Christ (1:20). Neither, then, is he "the Prophet" promised by Moses (1:21b; Deut 18:15), who many didn't realize was also the Christ. And John isn't even Elijah—in the sense that those sent by the Pharisees are asking (1:21a). He's not the physical, literal Elijah some expected to return. (Remember, Old Testament prophet Elijah never died, 2 Ki 2:11, and he had been promised to return, Mal 4:5–6). Instead, he is the one "in the spirit and power of Elijah" who would prepare God's people for the Christ (Lk 1:17; Mt 17:9–13).

Okay, then, who are you? We heard it last week too: "The voice of one crying out in the wilderness, 'Make straight the way of the Lord.'" He is unworthy even to untie His sandals (Jn 1:23, 27). But this week, John adds, "Among you stands one you do not know" (1:26). He is here, already among you! Your salvation is that near! If that voice is here crying out, then the Christ, who comes to live among us, to die on the cross for our sins, and to rise again to give us eternal life, must be here! Rejoice!

**THOUGH JOHN THE BAPTIST
IS NOT THE LIGHT, THE CHRIST,
HIS CRYING IN THE WILDERNESS
DOES CAUSE US TO REJOICE,
BECAUSE IT MEANS
THAT LIGHT OF SALVATION IS NEAR.**

How thrilling! Christ is near! Sing that in the words and tune of our **Hymn of the Day**, "Hark! A Thrilling Voice Is Sounding" (*LSB* 345).

Fourth Sunday in Advent Year B

READINGS

2 Samuel 7:1–11, 16
Psalm 89:1–5 (19–29)
(antiphon: v 8)
Romans 16:25–27
Luke 1:26–38

HYMN OF THE DAY

LSB 357 "O Come,
O Come, Emmanuel"

The **Epistle** for the Fourth Sunday in Advent, Romans 16:25–27: "Now to Him who is able to strengthen you according to my gospel and the preaching of Jesus Christ, according to the revelation of the mystery that was kept secret for long ages but has now been disclosed and through the prophetic writings has been made known to all nations, according to the command of the eternal God, to bring about the obedience of faith—to the only wise God be glory forevermore through Jesus Christ! Amen."

It may not sound like "Merry Christmas!" but it's closer than we might think.

If you remember that as a kid waiting for Merry Christmas seemed to take f-o-r-e-v-e-r, well, it's a much longer haul Paul doth recall. The apostle looks back over "long ages," thousands of years, as God's people waited for "the revelation" of the Christ, the Savior. The "prophetic writings" gave a hint of who He would be and where He would be born. But crucial details remain a "mystery." And when He would come is a complete secret.

It's a mystery, a secret. But Paul concludes our Epistle, and, in fact, his whole letter to the Romans, with this: "*To the only wise God* be glory forevermore through Jesus Christ! Amen" (16:27). What's that saying? It's saying more than just that God is wise and God knows everything. Paul is telling us that through all those millennia, God in His wisdom was orchestrating the plan of salvation that Paul has been articulating so well throughout Romans. Or to express it seasonally, God has been moving everything toward Christmas.

Since this is our last Sunday looking forward to Christmas, let's look forward the way

God's Old Testament people did—when the waiting was truly a long time and so much about the big day was still a mystery.

The **Introit** on Sunday won't sound very Christmassy either, but we'll look more closely.

Shower, O heavens, from above, and let the clouds rain down righteousness; let the earth open, that salvation and righteousness may bear fruit.

The heavens declare the glory of God, and the sky above proclaims His handiwork. In them He has set a tent for the sun, which comes out like a bridegroom leaving his chamber, and, like a strong man, runs its course with joy. Its rising is from the end of the heavens, and its circuit to the end of them, and there is nothing hidden from its heat.

Glory be to the Father and to the Son and to the Holy Spirit; as it was in the beginning, is now, and will be forever. Amen.

Shower, O heavens, from above, and let the clouds rain down righteousness; let the earth open, that salvation and righteousness may bear fruit. (Ps 19:1, 4c, 5–6; antiphon: Is 45:8a, b)

Psalm 19 does seem a surprising choice as an Introit just before Christmas. The premise is that simply gazing into the sky, perhaps especially on a clear, starry night, seeing the immensity of the universe, one can't help but recognize a Creator: "The heavens declare the glory of God, and the sky above proclaims His handiwork." Very true! But Christmas isn't about a God way up there somewhere, or even about His creating power. It's about God coming right down here to be intimate with us—and as a tiny baby.

The connection? It's as Paul meant wrapping his letter by acknowledging God's wisdom. Look at the Big Dipper, Orion's Belt, and so much further, billions of light years of distance, and then consider that all this was for a single purpose. God created the universe as a beautiful, intriguing place for the crown of His creation, mankind—a place we could live as we enjoyed friendship with Him. And even as He was creating it, then us, He knew we would spoil it by sin and cut ourselves off from that loving relationship. So as He was creating, God designed not only the Milky Way but a plan of redemption that went through Nazareth to Bethlehem and up a little hill.

No doubt God's ancient people had a keener appreciation of this than we do. After all, they saw the stars more clearly. They probably spent more time imagining that the sun rising in the morning could be "like a bridegroom leaving his chamber, and, like a strong man, runs its course with joy." And surely they were more grateful than most of us when the heavens would "shower . . . from above, and let the clouds rain." That would then enable them to appreciate righteousness being like rain, "that salvation and righteousness may bear fruit."

So when believers in the Old Testament pictured distant stars, the rising sun, and life-giving rain, they would much more readily than we think of the Lord of creation leaving His dwelling in the sky and coming down to bring us the salvation and righteousness we need since, let's realize, He promises this very thing. From that first sin, God promises that the seed of the woman would crush the serpent's head (Gen 3:15). Eve already knows that means that the Lord Himself would come down and be born as a baby; she is just six or seven dozen generations of mothers too early (Gen 4:1). The when is always anybody's guess.

The promised blessing would come by a descendant of Abraham (Gen 12:3)—and through his son Isaac and his son Jacob. Then major new information is introduced. Of Jacob's twelve sons, the ruler would come from the line of his fourth son, Judah (Gen 49:10).

Another eight centuries or so pass. Israel demands a king. No matter that God gives what they ask from the tribe of Benjamin (1 Sam 10:17–23); he quickly proves to be only man's choice. The next king, after God's own heart (1 Sam 13:13–14), is from the tribe of Judah. And this one we know: King David.

Pick up there with the **Old Testament Reading**, 2 Samuel 7:1–11, 16.

David finally has peace; he's been victorious on all sides. He's able to sit back and look at the big picture. His idea is well intended. God's place of worship is still the tabernacle, the tent that served so efficiently when Israel was moving about in the wilderness but now seems indecorous since the nation has been settled for four hundred years. David wants to build a house for the Lord, the temple.

God's answer is surprising. David isn't the one to build the temple. (That will fall to his son, Solomon.) But the Lord will do David one better: "The LORD declares to you that the LORD will make you a house" (7:11). David aspires to build a house of cedar, gold, and precious stones for the Lord, but God builds David a family, a lineage, that will be "established forever" (7:16). David understands exactly what that means. If his line is to sit on the throne forever, it could only mean that his line will produce the everlasting King. From that time on, the Messiah will be known above all as the Son of David.

That's often celebrated in the Psalms and Prophets. Read the **Psalm** for this Sunday, Psalm 89:1–5, 8, 19–29.

"I have made a covenant with My chosen one; I have sworn to David My servant: 'I will establish your offspring forever, and build your throne for all generations'" (89:3–4). Israel will cling to this promise of a Davidic king: "I have found David, My servant; with My holy oil I have anointed him. . . . The enemy shall not outwit him; the wicked shall not humble him. . . . I will establish his offspring forever and his throne as the days of the heavens" (89:20, 22, 29).

But for yet another thousand years, the sons of David are sometimes good, often evil, sometimes strong, often weak. And for the last nearly six hundred of those years, they really sit on no thrones at all; they are exiles in Babylon or subjects of Persians, Greeks, and Romans.

Then in the days of Herod called Great, king of Judea (but definitely not in the line of David!), "the angel Gabriel is sent from God to a city of Galilee named Nazareth." You know what happens next. Read the **Holy Gospel**, Luke 1:26–38.

Finally, the time has come! The mystery has been disclosed. "You"—a particular woman in a particular place living right now—"will conceive in your womb and bear a son, and you shall call His name Jesus" (Lk 1:31).

It's explicit that Mary's fiancé, Joseph, is "of the house of David" (1:27). And her son will possess "the throne of His father David" (1:32). So just as it was promised to David, "of His kingdom there will be no end" (1:33).

But it's just as crucial that Mary is a virgin (1:27). One of those weak, evil kings of the house of David, Ahaz, had quite against his will received that blessed prophecy: "The virgin shall conceive and bear a son, and shall call His name Immanuel" (Is 7:14). I've always found this quite delightful: This young girl, perhaps as young as fourteen, suddenly finds herself at the center of the event that tops the creation of the starry hosts, that all God's people have awaited since the fall, and she accepts every bit of it without hesitation (Lk 1:38)—with only one question. Her momma had explained to her how things work, and, well, "How will this be, since I am a virgin?" (1:34). Not, "Will it be?" She believes. Just, "Since I'm in on this, anything special I should know?" Good girl.

Of course, the virgin birth is essential to the entire cosmic plan of saving the world. "The Holy Spirit will come upon you, and the power of the Most High will overshadow you; therefore the child to be born will be called holy—the Son of God" (1:35). Only the Son of God, therefore very God of very God Himself, will do. Likewise, only virgin-born and thus without original sin. Because only the sinless God-man could accomplish this. Read the **Collect**:

> *Stir up Your power, O Lord, and come and help us by Your might, that the sins which weigh us down may be quickly lifted by Your grace and mercy; for You live and reign with the Father and the Holy Spirit, one God, now and forever. Amen.*

Very God, sinless man will take the weight of our sins upon Himself, beginning at long, long last here and now.

God's Prophetic Mystery Is Now Revealed: David's Son, the Virgin's Son, God's Son Has Come Down to Lift from Us the Weight of Sin.

Sing the **Hymn of the Day**, "O Come, O Come, Emmanuel" (*LSB* 357), and the "Great O Antiphons."

A note for the Christmas season: Since the propers for Christmas Eve, Midnight, Dawn, and Christmas Day are the same for Years A, B, and C, you'll find the one devotion-study for all of them in Year A on page 18. You'll also find brief thoughts about the Festival of Holy Innocents (which your congregation might observe on December 28 or a day close to that) on page 26 as part of the devotion-study for Holy Innocents and New Year. The devotion-study for the First Sunday after Christmas, Year B, is on the next page.

First Sunday after Christmas Year B

READINGS

Isaiah 61:10–62:3
Psalm 111 (antiphon: v 9a, b)
Galatians 4:4–7
Luke 2:22–40

HYMN OF THE DAY

LSB 389 "Let All Together Praise Our God"

Holder Knabe im lockigen Haar." I'm not sure Father Mohr was right about that in his original German text of "Silent Night." There's maybe a little poetic license. There's certainly nothing in Scripture that tells us the dear boy had curly hair.

But He is a little boy, that Child of Mary. And when Mary and Joseph and the shepherds—and, this Sunday, Simeon and Anna in the temple—look down at Him, they see hair and a nose and fingers and toes, just as our parents saw us. They see a human baby that the labor and delivery nurse (didn't Mary wish!) could have laid on a scale and then measured for length. (It's never height for a baby, is it!) It was probably very cute, but that's only because all babies are cute. It's just a baby.

Still, as they look at that baby, He is so much more than they are seeing! There is no halo, no glow around His head as we might like to imagine. There is surely no radiant glory like the disciples would see at His transfiguration many years later. And yet they are seeing nothing less than the salvation of the world.

To us a child is born, to us a son is given; and the government shall be upon His shoulder. And His name shall be called Wonderful Counselor, Mighty God, Everlasting Father, Prince of Peace. Sing to the Lord a new song, for He has done marvelous things! (Is 9:6; Ps 98:1a)

That is the **Gradual** for Christmas. All that weight on the shoulders of a child, a baby!

It's remarkable that He could carry so much when what we see looks so little.

As we look forward to this Sunday and continue our Christmas celebration, let's look at that child, that baby, and see what else is there.

The **Collect** for this Sunday recognizes what's plainly before our eyes:

> *O God, our Maker and Redeemer, You wonderfully created us and in the incarnation of Your Son yet more wondrously restored our human nature. Grant that we may ever be alive in Him who made Himself to be like us; through Jesus Christ, our Lord, who lives and reigns with You and the Holy Spirit, one God, now and forever. Amen.*

"Him who made Himself" as human as we are. With diaper changes and crying to let Mom know we needed nourishment. (If we're not sure about the *lockigen Haar*, we're quite sure that the line in "Away in a Manger," beloved carol that it is, is wrong: "No crying He makes." Silly! It's no sin for babies to communicate in their language.) Before long, there'd be growth spurts and school and learning a trade.

But the doctrine of "the incarnation" of God's Son will ever remind us that the child we see growing is Himself God. That's the miracle of Christmas! God, who our eyes couldn't see, becomes incarnate and takes on our flesh and blood.

The **Introit** sees much more:

> *The Lord has bared His holy arm before the eyes of all the nations, and all the ends of the earth shall see the salvation of our God.*
>
> *Oh sing to the Lord a new song, for He has done marvelous things! His right hand and His holy arm have worked salvation for Him. The Lord has made known His salvation; He has revealed His righteousness in the sight of the nations. He has remembered His steadfast love and faithfulness to the house of Israel. All the ends of the earth have seen the salvation of our God. Make a joyful noise to the Lord, all the earth; break forth into joyous song and sing praises!*
>
> *Glory be to the Father and to the Son and to the Holy Spirit; as it was in the beginning, is now, and will be forever. Amen.*
>
> *The Lord has bared His holy arm before the eyes of all the nations, and all the ends of the earth shall see the salvation of our God. (Ps 98:1–4; antiphon: Is 52:10)*

In the antiphon, Isaiah sees the Lord as a tough guy, rolling up His sleeve. It may not be to fight but to scare off anyone who might dare take Him on. And what are the nations seeing when they see the Lord that way? "The salvation of our God."

Then there's the babe who can't bare His arm but needs to be borne *in* arms. It's the same Lord. As we see the little child, we're seeing "the salvation of our God." "Oh sing to the LORD a new song, for He has done marvelous things! His right hand and His holy arm have worked salvation for Him." And that salvation the world *has* seen: "The LORD has made known His salvation; He has revealed His righteousness in the sight of the nations. . . . All the ends of the earth have seen the salvation of our God."

Where have they seen it? Consider that one of these Christmas days, we'll probably sing Isaac Watts's paraphrase of Psalm 98: "Joy to the World." It's Christmas language, this Introit. The ends of the earth see the salvation of our God when He shows them His Son in the flesh.

Just two weeks ago (Advent 3), we saw much of the imagery of this Sunday's **Old Testament Reading**, Isaiah 61:10–62:3. It's worth seeing again.

Remember the bride and bridegroom decked out? They're wearing "the garments of salvation" and "the robe of righteousness" (61:10). Again, the text is inviting us to *see* salvation, to imagine what it looks like. Or this one: "[Zion's] righteousness goes forth as brightness, and her salvation as a burning torch. The nations shall see your righteousness" (62:1c–2a). That's what we see when we look at swaddling cloths in a dimly lit cattle shed. The adornments, the glory God gave up to lie in a manger, He gives to us. Because we see Him lying on a bed of straw, we "shall be a crown of beauty in the hand of the LORD, and a royal diadem in the hand of [our] God" (62:3).

Psalm 111, the appointed **Psalm** for this day, is the first of a series of "Hallel Psalms," featuring the words "Hallelujah," "Praise the LORD." (See also Ps 112:1; 113:1, 9; 115:18; 116:19; 117:1–2.) It's appropriate for any occasion, of course, but the verse chosen as the antiphon makes the connection for Christmas: "He sent redemption to His people; He has commanded His covenant forever" (111:9a, b). Redemption came down to us in the person of a baby.

As we discussed during Advent, though, God's Old Testament people, even the inspired prophets and poets, caught only glimpses of their salvation. The full revelation was waiting until a precise moment God had ordained from eternity. Read the **Epistle**, Galatians 4:4–7.

"When the fullness of time had come," God let mankind see His Son with human eyes—His and theirs. "Born of a woman," so truly one of us, He was able to keep the Law in our place so that we could become what He is, sons of God (4:4–5).

And that timing—amazing! The Christ couldn't come during a period of prosperity, when one of David's descendants was actually ruling on an earthly throne; Jesus' kingdom was of a different kind. He had to come at a time when Israel was suffering in subjection; otherwise, who'd want His deliverance. Christ came at a time when God's people were longing to hear a word—any word—from the Lord. Never since before the days of Moses had God been silent to His people for so long. Jesus even had to come during the reign of Rome for this grisly reason: He had to die by hanging on a tree (Deut 21:22–23;

Gal 3:13), not the swift death of a rope. He had to suffer the agonizing hours of hanging the Romans favored—crucifixion. Then there were the blessings that made the Roman era opportune: the Greek language, which was universal around the Mediterranean, and Roman roads and law enforcement, all of which would facilitate Paul and other missionaries spreading the Gospel throughout the empire.

The time was now right—also for the memorable events of the **Holy Gospel**, Luke 2:22–40.

"When the time came for their purification according to the Law of Moses, [Mary and Joseph] brought [Jesus] up to Jerusalem to present Him to the Lord" (2:22). Forty days after the birth of a firstborn son, Jewish families were commanded to present him, an expression of thanks that God had redeemed their firstborn from Egypt (Lev 12:6–8; Ex 13:2, 14–15).

This day was precisely the time Simeon and Anna had waited for. We don't know how the Holy Spirit had revealed to Simeon that "he would not see death before he had seen the Lord's Christ" nor how the Spirit pointed him to the temple and this little family that day (2:25–28). We don't know what prompted dear Anna to come looking "at that very hour" (2:38). But they have no doubts. And they know what they're seeing—far more than appeared. "Lord," Simeon rejoices, "my eyes have seen Your salvation that You have prepared in the presence of all peoples" (2:29–31). This child is "the redemption of Jerusalem" (2:38).

We delight to sing Simeon's song as we depart in peace from the Sacrament of the Altar. Joseph and Mary marvel at it too (2:33). But then Simeon speaks of that future from which we all wish to turn our eyes: "Behold, this child is appointed for the fall and rising of many in Israel, and for a sign that is opposed (and a sword will pierce through your [Mary's] own soul also)" (2:34–35). Simeon sees what's coming—even if it isn't literally with his eyes. The baby, curly haired or straight, the swaddling cloths, the manger—when our eyes see those, it's already time to look ahead to the cross.

The Time Has Fully Come That the Lord Has Revealed His Salvation for All to See.

Our eyes see "an infant small," "an earthborn form," "our human frame." Nevertheless, "*today* He opens heaven again," as the **Hymn of the Day**, "Let All Together Praise Our God" (*LSB* 389:1–4), says.

A note for the upcoming holy days: Since the propers for New Year's Eve and Day, for the Second Sunday after Christmas, and for the Epiphany of Our Lord are identical in Years A, B, and C, you'll find the devotion-studies for each of them in Year A, pages 26, 30, and 34. (Be aware that in some years, because of the calendar, there is no Second Sunday after Christmas. Also, your congregation may observe Epiphany on a Sunday near January 6 or have a separate service for this feast, whatever day of the week it falls.) In addition, you'll find brief thoughts about the Festival of Holy Innocents (which your congregation might observe on December 28 or a day close to that) on page 26 as part of the devotion-study for Holy Innocents and New Year. The devotion-study for the Baptism of Our Lord (the First Sunday after the Epiphany), Year B, appears on the next page.

The Baptism of Our Lord Year B

READINGS

Genesis 1:1–5
Psalm 29 (antiphon: v 3)
Romans 6:1–11
Mark 1:4–11

HYMN OF THE DAY

LSB 406, 407 "To Jordan Came the Christ, Our Lord"

First, here's a bit of an orientation. The First Sunday after the Epiphany is designated as the Baptism of Our Lord. In simplest scheduling, that would play out like this: On January 6, whatever day of the week that happens to fall, a congregation would have a service for the Epiphany of Our Lord, the coming of the wise men to worship the toddler Jesus. Then the Sunday immediately following would be the Baptism, and from there the Sundays after the Epiphany would continue—however many the church calendar provides that year.

Since in most years, though, January 6, Epiphany, does not fall on a Sunday, many congregations do not have a special service for it. In that case, the congregation might choose to use the propers for Epiphany Day on the Sunday closest before or after January 6. If it does use the Epiphany propers on the Sunday following January 6, the congregation would then either skip the Baptism of Our Lord or observe it one Sunday later (actually then the Second Sunday after the Epiphany) and omit one of the later Epiphany Sundays. The bottom line is that if you're looking forward to a Sunday morning that falls between January 7 and January 12, check and see what your congregation is planning to do. You'll want to read this devotion-study, the one for Epiphany that begins on page 34, or both.

Well, now, the coming of the wise men has begun the "epiphany," the showing forth, literally the "shining upon," of Jesus. The star has revealed that that little boy is the King of the Jews *and* Gentiles. We can picture the scene of the wise men in the **Gradual** for the season of Epiphany:

Praise the LORD, all nations! Extol Him, all peoples! For great is His steadfast love toward us, and the faithfulness of the LORD endures forever. Ascribe to the LORD the glory due His name; bring an offering, and come into His courts! (Ps 117:1–2a; 96:8)

For the rest of the Epiphany season, more will be shown forth about the adult Jesus. And that begins in a big way with His Baptism in the Jordan River. Though the event *du jour* of this Sunday is the same for all three years of the lectionary, we can highlight different emphases one year to the next. This year, let's see how the propers for Year B especially make this point:

**IN THE BAPTISM OF OUR LORD,
BY THE ANOINTING OF THE SPIRIT
IN <u>OUR</u> BAPTISM,
THE VOICE OF THE MIGHTY GOD
SPEAKS HIS PLEASURE ALSO OF US.**

The foundational event is Jesus' own Baptism. The Year B **Holy Gospel** for the Baptism of Our Lord takes us back to the ministry of John the Baptist. Read Mark 1:4–11.

You recall that John makes clear he is only the forerunner of the Messiah: "After me comes He who is mightier than I, the strap of whose sandals I am not worthy to stoop down and untie" (1:7). Now He comes. Mark does not record a conversation between Jesus and John (Matthew does, Mt 3:13–15); he gives no preliminary fanfare, only saying that Jesus "was baptized by John in the Jordan" (1:9).

But then, there's plenty of fanfare. As Jesus comes up out of the water (1:10), the heavens are "torn open." (Only Mark uses this dramatic language, from the Greek σχίζω, *schizo*, literally, "split in two," which gives us the word *schizophrenic*. Matthew and Luke use forms of the tamer word ἀνοίγω, *anoigo*, simply "open.") It's as if the Holy Spirit, in appearance as a dove, flies through a great rip in the sky. He does alight, gently it seems, above Jesus. Then, however, the big thunder comes. Through that tear in its very fabric, "a voice comes from heaven, 'You are My beloved Son; with You I am well pleased'" (1:11).

The actions of both the First and Third Persons of the Trinity upon God the Son are of enormous importance. The Spirit's anointing marks Jesus as the Christ—as kings and priests of Israel were always anointed, and, indeed, *Christ* and *Messiah* present the Greek and Hebrew renderings of "the Anointed One." Moreover, the Spirit's anointing was a special strengthening of the human Christ for the challenge immediately to follow—Jesus' temptation by Satan in the wilderness (Mk 1:12–13). The voice of the Father, then, identifies Jesus as His Son and places His approval on the saving mission Jesus is now to commence. What Jesus will do from here on—confront the devil, preach, heal, finally die, and rise—all are well pleasing to the Father and part of His plan to save us.

The other propers each develop some aspect of this singular event. The **Introit**:

Behold My servant, whom I uphold, My chosen, in whom My soul delights.

I will tell of the decree: The Lord said to me, "You are My Son; today I have begotten You. Ask of Me, and I will make the nations Your heritage, and the ends of the earth Your possession. You shall break them with a rod of iron and dash them in pieces like a potter's vessel." Now therefore, O kings, be wise; be warned, O rulers of the earth. Serve the Lord with fear, and rejoice with trembling, for His wrath is quickly kindled. Blessèd are all who take refuge in Him.

Glory be to the Father and to the Son and to the Holy Spirit; as it was in the beginning, is now, and will be forever. Amen.

Behold My servant, whom I uphold, My chosen, in whom My soul delights. (Ps 2:7–11, 12c; antiphon: Is 42:1a)

Centuries before God ripped the heavens and boomed down at the Jordan, He was already telling the world about His well-pleasing Son. Psalm 2:7 says, "You are My Son; today I have begotten You," and is quoted three times in the New Testament (Acts 13:33; Heb 1:5; 5:5). And Isaiah 42:1, "Behold My servant, whom I uphold, My chosen, in whom My soul delights" is likely the specific text the Father was intending to bring to mind at Jesus' Baptism.

From there, the Introit goes on to warn just how mighty is this God speaking from heaven—and therefore how highly to be respected is His Son: "'You [the Son] shall break [the nations] with a rod of iron and dash them in pieces like a potter's vessel.' Now therefore, O kings, be wise; be warned, O rulers of the earth. Serve the Lord with fear, and rejoice with trembling, for His wrath is quickly kindled." This is the mighty God who causes kings to cower.

Imagine, then, how His voice must have sounded. David gives us a good idea of that in the **Psalm** of the day, Psalm 29.

"The voice of the Lord is over the waters; the God of glory thunders, the Lord, over many waters" (29:3). Certainly over the River Jordan! Thunder! (as in Ex 19:16–19; Jn 12:28–29). The "voice of the Lord" is also "powerful," "full of majesty" (Ps 29:4), "breaks the cedars" (29:5), "flashes forth flames of fire" (29:7), "shakes the wilderness" (29:8), "strips the forest bare" (29:9b). And here's one more for you: "The voice of the Lord makes the deer give birth" (29:9a)

Yet to this mighty God of terrifying voice, David is able to pray, "May the Lord give strength to His people! May the Lord bless His people with peace!" (29:11).

It's the same way in the **Old Testament Reading**, Genesis 1:1–5. See what God's voice can do!

God simply speaks, "Let there be light," and it's created (1:3). So is almost everything else in the universe—created just by God's voice. But this voice that commands such power also gives strength to His people. Light, day, night, the earth, the sky, and all the rest of those things God creates just by speaking, He creates for His people. In fact, do you know which two things God made not simply by His voice? (Check Gen 2:7, 22.) For the two creatures for whom He did all His creating, God slowed down and did some special handiwork.

And don't overlook the waters. "The voice of the LORD is over the waters." "The Spirit of God was hovering over the face of [these] waters" too (1:2). "And God said . . ." (1:3).

Here's where all this matters the most to us. The voice of God speaks over the waters at creation, thunders over the waters in the psalm, booms from heaven over the Jordan waters at Jesus' Baptism, and, through the mouth of the pastor, speaks over the font at our Baptism. All this working of God comes to us in our Baptism. Read the **Epistle**, Romans 6:1–11.

"All of us who have been baptized into Christ Jesus were baptized into His death" (6:3). Jesus' Baptism put Him in our place; Jesus accepted Baptism when He had no need for forgiveness of sins in order to become the needy sinner we are. That meant that Jesus' righteous life became ours. And then Jesus' innocent death was as if He were being fully punished for our sins. "If we have been united with Him in a death like His, we shall certainly be united with Him in a resurrection like His" (6:5).

So at our Baptism, when we hear, "I baptize you in the name of the Father and of the Son and of the Holy Spirit," we're hearing, "You are now in Me, as at My Baptism anointed with the Holy Spirit and approved by My Father." Or to put it as it was spoken from above, "You are My beloved child; with *you* I am well pleased!"

This week, our **Hymn of the Day** merits special attention. That's because Luther so skillfully weaves the event of Jesus' Baptism with instruction about ours. "To Jordan came the Christ, our Lord, to do His Father's pleasure" (*LSB* 406:1, 407:2). Yes, but "the Father's Word was given *us* to treasure." "O hear and mark the message well, for God Himself has spoken. Let faith, not doubt, among *us* dwell and so receive the token" (st 2). "There stood the Son of God in love, His grace to *us* extending; the Holy Spirit like a dove upon the scene descending; the triune God assuring *us*, . . . that in *our* Baptism He will thus among *us* find a dwelling" (st 4).

It would be hard to summarize the point of this Sunday better than praying the **Collect** together:

Father in heaven, at the Baptism of Jesus in the Jordan River You proclaimed Him Your beloved Son and anointed Him with the Holy Spirit. Make all who are baptized in His name faithful in their calling as Your children and inheritors with Him of everlasting life; through the same Jesus Christ, our Lord, who lives and reigns with You and the Holy Spirit, one God, now and forever. Amen.

We heard the **Verse** for this Sunday at Jesus' Baptism: "Alleluia. You are My beloved Son; with You I am well pleased. Alleluia." But in our Baptism into Christ, the mighty God is just as surely speaking His pleasure upon us.

Second Sunday after the Epiphany Year B

READINGS

1 Samuel 3:1–10 (11–20)
Psalm 139:1–10 (antiphon: v 14)
1 Corinthians 6:12–20
John 1:43–51

HYMN OF THE DAY

LSB 402 "The Only Son from Heaven"

It's a big job being the beloved Son of God the Father (Mk 1:11) and the King of all nations (Mt 2:1–2). That's a lot of responsibility the Father has been well pleased to give Jesus—and it's a very large kingdom to administer. Much of what's "epiphanied" (revealed about Jesus during this Epiphany season) is such as this, His divine glory and power. It's as the **Gradual** for the season of Epiphany says in part: "Praise the LORD, all nations! Extol Him, all peoples! . . . Ascribe to the LORD the glory due His name." Or as this week's **Collect** prays,

> *Almighty and everlasting God, who governs all things in heaven and on earth, mercifully hear the prayers of Your people and grant us Your peace through all our days; through Jesus Christ, Your Son, our Lord, who lives and reigns with You and the Holy Spirit, one God, now and forever. Amen.*

God surely "governs all things in heaven and on earth" through Jesus Christ, His Son. That's a lot to manage.

And yet we ask that through this same Jesus Christ, God would "mercifully hear the prayers" of His people—us—and "grant *us* [His] peace." Little old us. Even little old me. For all His cosmic duties, we nevertheless pray that God would have time and interest and attention and mercy for each of us personally, individually.

In the propers for the Second Sunday after the Epiphany, we see sweet assurance that He does. The Lord is intimately aware of who we are—each of us—and what we need. The wondrous works by which He cares for a planet full of people are the same for you and me personally. And that invites us to be equally intimate in knowing and speaking of Him.

David composed the words of our **Introit** from this intimate rapport with God.

I have not hidden Your deliverance within my heart; I have spoken of Your faithfulness and Your salvation.

I waited patiently for the LORD; He inclined to me and heard my cry. He drew me up from the pit of destruction, out of the miry bog, and set my feet upon a rock, making my steps secure. He put a new song in my mouth, a song of praise to our God. Many will see and fear, and put their trust in the LORD. Blessèd is the man who makes the LORD his trust, who does not turn to the proud, to those who go astray after a lie! You have multiplied, O LORD my God, Your wondrous deeds and Your thoughts toward us; none can compare with You! I will proclaim and tell of them, yet they are more than can be told.

Glory be to the Father and to the Son and to the Holy Spirit; as it was in the beginning, is now, and will be forever. Amen.

I have not hidden Your deliverance within my heart; I have spoken of Your faithfulness and Your salvation. (Ps 40:1–5; antiphon: Ps 40:10a, b)

David understands God's immense governance: "You have multiplied, O LORD my God, Your wondrous deeds . . . ; none can compare with You! . . . They are more than can be told." But he knows that the Lord is "my God" and that His thoughts are "toward us." "I waited patiently for the LORD; He inclined to me and heard my cry. He drew me up from the pit of destruction, out of the miry bog, and set my feet upon a rock, making my steps secure." Therefore, David is delighted to proclaim God's works: "I have not hidden Your deliverance within my heart; I have spoken of Your faithfulness and Your salvation. . . . He put a new song in my mouth, a song of praise to our God."

It was likewise David who wrote our appointed **Psalm** for this Sunday. Read Psalm 139:1–10, 14.

Here the whole point of the psalm is how intimately God knows us. "O LORD, You have searched me and known me! You know when I sit down and when I rise up; You discern my thoughts from afar. You search out my path and my lying down and are acquainted with all my ways. Even before a word is on my tongue, behold, O LORD, You know it altogether" (139:1–4). There's nowhere we could "flee" from God's Spirit (139:7), but the point is, who'd want to? I'm thankful, Lord, that wherever I am, "there Your hand shall lead me, and Your right hand shall hold me" (139:10). God knows every individual and cares dearly for all of us.

And here again, that creates a relationship that is a most affectionate two-way street: "I praise You, for I am fearfully and wonderfully made. Wonderful are Your works; my soul knows it very well" (139:14). As he is known so intimately, David also knows God and how His works touch him personally, and he finds them, especially God creating him, to be wonderful.

Enjoy this psalm devotionally. Have you ever felt alone? You really never were, were you! Are you anxious about a new "adventure" in life—a new job, a new baby, a place you've just moved? God's Holy Spirit will be there with you, leading you by the hand through doors He opens one at a time. Are you experiencing sadness—separation from a child or a spouse, a dangerous or painful illness, a lost livelihood? The Lord is holding you. Perhaps you'll see His works work things out. If not, know that sometimes "such knowledge is too wonderful for me; it is high; I cannot attain it" (139:6). I can't see yet how He is still working a higher purpose for my future blessing.

In the **Old Testament Reading** for Epiphany 2, the Lord establishes one very personal relationship. See 1 Samuel 3:1–20.

You may remember the account of how Samuel came to serve in the tabernacle. (The "temple," 3:3, by the way, was actually still the tent sanctuary, probably with some more substantial buildings now around it. The first permanent temple, Solomon's, was still a century or so away.) Samuel is a child of special promise from God to his mother (1 Sam 1:1–20). These are spiritually impoverished days in Israel; the period of the judges was often very sinful anyway (Judg 21:25), and the sons of the current judge, Eli, are particularly corrupt (1 Sam 2:12, 17, 22). "They did not know the Lord" (2:12). No surprise that "the word of the Lord was rare in those days; there was no frequent vision" (3:1).

Young Samuel himself "did not yet know the Lord, and the word of the Lord had not yet been revealed to him" (3:7). That isn't to suggest Samuel hadn't yet been told about Yahweh and didn't yet believe in Him. Undoubtedly, his faithful parents and Eli had taught him. But God has not yet called Samuel to know or see Him as a prophet.

Now that changes. Not once, twice, but three times the Lord calls Samuel (3:4–8). Make that four! (3:10). Yahweh knows Samuel by name. And He "came and *stood*" (3:10) by him. This is the same Son of God who eleven centuries later would become Jesus of Nazareth—not yet in the flesh, but already appearing in a way that could be comfortable for Samuel.

The word is tragic (deserved!) for the house of Eli (3:11–14). But it is the beginning of an intimate lifelong conversation between Yahweh and His prophet. "The Lord was with" Samuel (3:19).

In this Sunday's **Epistle**, Paul demonstrates that the Christian's intimate relationship with God must be honored also in the most intimate human relationship. Read 1 Corinthians 6:12–20.

"The body is not meant for sexual immorality, but for the Lord, and the Lord for the body" (6:13). Greek philosophy understood a strict dualism, or separation, between soul and body. The soul was seen to be immortal and therefore valuable, while the body was considered disposable. Some of the new believers in Corinth are still inclined to think, then, that if they commit their souls to Christ by confessing Him in their hearts, whatever they do with their bodies doesn't matter—including giving themselves over to sexual sin such as prostitution.

Isn't this Satan's chief point of attack against the Church today? Christians either don't realize that sex outside of marriage is truly sin or else think it's a common enough sin that it can't really bother God much anymore. It can't really be wrong, right? As long as we're in love and planning to get married, there's no issue. I mean, everybody lives together before marriage nowadays, right?

God permits no such thing!

The reason is that God wants to enjoy an unadulterated intimacy with us! "He who is joined to the Lord becomes one spirit with Him. . . . Your body is a temple of the Holy Spirit within you, whom you have from God" (6:17, 19). God bought us to be His own at the price of Jesus' death on the cross (6:20a). This relationship is holy, perfect, for the Lord and two people He may join to each other in marriage.

What we do with our bodies, therefore, is an essential confession of what our spirits believe. "So glorify God in your body" (6:20b).

Jesus' epiphany continues to reveal the Son of God as He begins to gather a following. Read the **Holy Gospel**, John 1:43–51.

Jesus has briefly been in the south, not far from Jerusalem, near the Jordan where John the Baptist has been preaching. Now He returns home to the north, to Galilee. After the first tier of disciples (Peter, James, John, and Andrew), Philip is one of the most prominent (see Jn 6:5, 7; 12:20–22; 14:8–9). One of his chief acts is telling Nathanael (also named Bartholomew, Mt 10:3) about Jesus (Jn 1:45).

Even to a fellow Galilean (from Cana, 21:2), Nazareth isn't promising (1:46). But it turns out Nathanael is an easy sell: "Jesus saw Nathanael coming toward Him and said of him, 'Behold, an Israelite indeed, in whom there is no deceit!' Nathanael said to Him, 'How do You know me?' Jesus answered him, 'Before Philip called you, when you were under the fig tree, I saw you.' Nathanael answered Him, 'Rabbi, You are the Son of God! You are the King of Israel!'" (1:47–49).

It's an amazing confession of Christ on such short notice. Nathanael is wowed by Jesus knowing such a specific detail about him—as if Jesus has been looking in on his every move. But, Jesus says, "You will see greater things than these" (1:50). That's just the beginning. Jesus knows far more about us than that—our every need, our every sin, and the answer to all of them. Jesus will open heaven (1:51) to Nathanael, to me, to you—personally, individually—by His most wondrous work, giving His life.

The Lord Knowing Us So Intimately Brings Us to Know and Confess Him and to Begin to Know His Wondrous Works.

Sing the **Hymn of the Day**, "The Only Son from Heaven" (*LSB* 402). "O Lord, our hearts awaken to know and love You more."

Third Sunday after the Epiphany Year B

READINGS

Jonah 3:1–5, 10
Psalm 62 (antiphon: v 8)
1 Corinthians 7:29–31 (32–35)
Mark 1:14–20

HYMN OF THE DAY

LSB 839 "O Christ, Our True and Only Light"

It all comes together in Jesus.

That's true of the eternal big picture, of course. It's also true of the propers for the Third Sunday after the Epiphany.

Jesus is the intersection, the common denominator of one of the most beautiful truths in the entire psalter, the greatest fish story of all time, Paul's endorsement of celibacy, the greatest fish*ing* story of all time, and more for every person everywhere. That should make quite clear that turning to Him, following Jesus, is worth leaving everything else.

Begin with that beautiful truth from the Psalms. The **Introit** for Epiphany 3 is selected verses from Psalm 113.

From the rising of the sun to its setting, the name of the Lord is to be praised!

Praise the Lord! Praise, O servants of the Lord, praise the name of the Lord! Blessèd be the name of the Lord from this time forth and forevermore! The Lord is high above all nations, and His glory above the heavens! He raises the poor from the dust and lifts the needy from the ash heap, to make them sit with princes, with the princes of His people.

Glory be to the Father and to the Son and to the Holy Spirit; as it was in the beginning, is now, and will be forever. Amen.

From the rising of the sun to its setting, the name of the Lord is to be praised! (Ps 113:1–2, 4, 7–8; antiphon: Ps 113:3)

Picture the sun rising in the east, crossing the entire sky, and setting in the west. It countenances the whole earth as we see it, but we realize it actually shines on much more—beyond what we can see, beyond the horizons both east and west and then, really, beyond even this earth itself. All of this is the Lord's, and He intends that all nations under the sun would praise Him. He intends it not because it further honors Him but because to praise Him is to enjoy all the blessings He gives.

And that brings us to a most beautiful revelation about God's own nature: "The Lord is high above all nations, and His glory above the heavens! He raises the poor from the dust and lifts the needy from the ash heap, to make them sit with princes, with the princes of His people." Yes, God is infinitely above us, but this God who is so far above us delights to come down to us and lift us up to Him! Think about that! In our human experience, how many big shots truly care about or make time for the little guy? (And not for publicity shots or political capital or their own "feel-good" but solely for the sake of the one who can do them no good.) Even those who'd like to are usually just too busy. But this is our God! His greatest glory *isn't* that He's huge, powerful, oversees and runs everything. (To Him, after all, being almighty is nothing more than breathing!) God's greatest glory is that *while being all powerful, He's also all loving.* It's a combination of the two! He rules from the rising of the sun to its setting but also stoops down to pick us up off the ash heap. That's what's really amazing about God! And we are the ones who receive all the benefits! Mark down Psalm 113 in your playbook! It's a go-to again and again!

This is actually the same point being made in the **Psalm** of the day, Psalm 62, when David writes, "Once God has spoken; twice have I heard this: that power belongs to God, and that to You, O Lord, belongs steadfast love" (62:11–12a). Power *and* steadfast love.

The same magnificent truth prompts our prayer in the **Collect** for Sunday:

Almighty and everlasting God, mercifully look upon our infirmities and stretch forth the hand of Your majesty to heal and defend us; through Jesus Christ, Your Son, our Lord, who lives and reigns with You and the Holy Spirit, one God, now and forever. Amen.

God is almighty and everlasting, but He has assured us of His mercy, that He will indeed reach down to us, "stretch forth the hand of [His] majesty," and care for us. This, the almighty being merciful to us who are so beneath Him, is how we enjoy a relationship with God that is not slave and master but mutually loving.

The **Gradual** for the Epiphany season continues from the Psalms:

Praise the Lord, all nations! Extol Him, all peoples! For great is His steadfast love toward us, and the faithfulness of the Lord *endures forever. Ascribe to the* Lord *the glory due His name; bring an offering, and come into His courts! (Ps 117:1–2a; 96:8)*

Is this really for all nations, for all people everywhere? Jonah doesn't think so. At least he doesn't think God's steadfast love should apply to the Ninevites—those wicked people who are terrorizing Israel and the whole ancient Near East. Nineveh was the capital of Assyria, the dominant empire of the ninth through seventh centuries BC, and its cruelty over conquered peoples was infamous. So when God calls Jonah to go and preach at Nineveh, he runs, sails the other way (Jonah 1:1–3). Surprisingly, though, Jonah flee not because he's afraid. He flees because he foresees exactly what eventually happened.

Well, not the fish part (1:4–17). The part everybody knows best is actually just a sidelight to the real story, and Jonah probably didn't see *that* coming! But what Jonah did see happening is the **Old Testament Reading** for Sunday. Read Jonah 3:1–5, 10.

Jonah finally goes, preaches destruction, and—darn it!—these wicked people actually repent. Then, sure enough, God does what God always does—has mercy. When sinners think they're riding high, there's no hope for them. But as soon as they realize they're toast and put on sackcloth (and, yep, some ashes, 3:6), God relents. He reaches down and picks those poor souls up off the heap.

Jonah knows what will happen. He knows God is gracious and merciful and that the preaching of God's Word works miracles—even in the worst of the worst. That's precisely why he doesn't want to go (4:1–2). He wants his enemies to get what he figures they had coming. So now it is Jonah's turn to hear God's preaching and repent (4:4–11).

This Sunday's **Epistle** is a short cutting of Paul's lengthy counsel on marriage in 1 Corinthians 7. Read 7:29–35.

Much of chapter 7 is about abstaining from marriage, as Paul himself had. Then comes the seemingly odd extension of that in verse 29: "This is what I mean, brothers: the appointed time has grown very short. From now on, let those who have wives live as though they had none." Is Paul saying not only that we're better off not marrying but that even if we are married, we should set it aside? Certainly not, and a full reading of the chapter, including verse 35 ("I say this . . . not to lay any restraint upon you"), makes clear that marriage is the joyous gift God intends for *most* people. But Paul realizes that the time to be about the mission of the Church is always "very short"; we can't let ourselves be distracted from a single opportunity to witness to Christ. Paul probably also knows that persecution of the Church is coming soon. Being married would add to a husband the duty of protecting his wife when his own life would be in danger. It makes practical sense.

The broader principle, though, is this: "Let . . . those who deal with the world [live] as though they had no dealings with it. For the present form of this world is passing away" (7:29, 31). We should all, whether married or single, be willing to leave everything of this world for the things of the Lord (7:32).

(Those of us who are married should rejoice that being faithful husbands and wives *is* being about the holy work of the Lord!)

Peter was married, as undoubtedly were other apostles. But they certainly understood what it meant to leave all for the work of the Lord. The **Holy Gospel** for Epiphany 3 is Mark 1:14–20.

Jesus' epiphany goes public. The preparatory period of John the Baptist, including Jesus' Baptism, ends with John's arrest by Herod. Now Jesus begins to preach the kingdom, and the substance of His call is the same as Jonah's: "Repent." Jesus, though, makes explicit what Jonah recoiled to accept. Repentance is always God's invitation to receive His mercy: "Repent and believe in the gospel" (1:15). The imperative, "repent" (μετανοεῖτε, *metanoeite*), is not just a command to stop some particular sin or sins; it is an invitation to turn to a new direction. And the new direction is faith that God has mercy on those who confess themselves to be helpless—that is, believe in the Gospel.

The new direction of faith naturally, then, means following after, walking in the way of the leader in whom that faith is placed. Thus began the two-thousand-year-and-counting fishing expedition on which all disciples of Jesus have a net. "Follow Me," Jesus says to Peter and Andrew, James and John, "and I will make you become fishers of men" (1:17). "Follow Me." It's another imperative, but it likewise means, "Believe in the Gospel, which I am." And because they believe in Jesus, they do what is automatic: "They left their father Zebedee in the boat with the hired servants and followed Him" (1:20).

"Him." It all comes together in Jesus.

The beautiful truth that God, who is above all things, reaches down to us who are lying on the ash heap—all powerful *and* all loving—is the truth of Jesus. Jesus is God coming to live on the ash heap Himself. When the kingdom of God is suddenly at hand, it is Jesus reaching down from heaven to lift us up to heaven. And that is the cross—Jesus' death taking away the sin that so separated heaven from earth.

God's mercy on the Ninevites is Jesus. No wickedness is greater than His cross. Repentance is always met with the forgiveness Christ earned for all. That really does extend to every sinner of every nation from the rising of the sun to its setting.

And surely we can leave all the things of this world when we have Jesus. For when we have Jesus, we have all been caught up from this pile of dust and ashes to the kingdom of almighty, all-loving God.

God Calls All People Everywhere to Leave Our Sins and the Things of This World and Follow Jesus, Believing That He Will mercifully Lift Us from the Ash Heap.

Close your preparation for the Third Sunday after the Epiphany by singing the **Hymn of the Day**, "O Christ, Our True and Only Light" (*LSB* 839). Picture Jonah and Paul and Peter and yourself inviting to repentance and faith "those afar," "the souls now lost in error's maze," "those gone astray" (st 1, 2, 3).

Fourth Sunday after the Epiphany Year B

READINGS

Deuteronomy 18:15–20
Psalm 111 (antiphon: v 3)
1 Corinthians 8:1–13
Mark 1:21–28

HYMN OF THE DAY

LSB 842 "Son of God, Eternal Savior"

We're looking forward to Sunday morning, looking forward to entering God's house, and, well, are we expecting anything to happen? Anything extraordinary? Anything beyond feeling pretty good about doing the right thing, being where we know we ought to be? Anything beyond getting church checked off the list for another week?

This particular week in Capernaum, "immediately on the Sabbath [Jesus] entered the synagogue and was teaching. And they were astonished at His teaching" (Mk 1:21). There are big doings in that worship service! But, of course, Jesus is there. If you were coming into God's house when Jesus shows up, you'd always expect something pretty special!

But we're back in good old Orange, California, or Del Rio, Texas, or Fort Wayne, Indiana, coming into Immanuel or Cristo el Salvador or St. Paul's, probably looking for just another Sunday. And we begin the Service of the Word with the **Introit**:

Many are the sorrows of the wicked, but steadfast love surrounds the one who trusts in the LORD.

Blessèd is the one whose transgression is forgiven, whose sin is covered. Blessèd is the man against whom the LORD counts no iniquity, and in whose spirit there is no deceit. I acknowledged my sin to You, and I did not cover my iniquity; I said, "I will confess my transgressions to the LORD," and You forgave the iniquity of my sin. Therefore let everyone who is godly offer prayer to You at a time when You may be found; surely in the rush of great waters, they shall not reach him. You are a hiding place for me; You preserve me from trouble; You surround me with shouts of deliverance.

Glory be to the Father and to the Son and to the Holy Spirit; as it was in the beginning, is now, and will be forever. Amen.

Many are the sorrows of the wicked, but steadfast love surrounds the one who trusts in the Lord. (Ps 32:1–2, 5–7; antiphon: Ps 32:10)

Something's happening here! What it is may not be exactly clear just yet. But we'll come back to it.

In the meantime, let's look at all the other propers for the Fourth Sunday after the Epiphany. We pray the **Collect**:

Almighty God, You know we live in the midst of so many dangers that in our frailty we cannot stand upright. Grant strength and protection to support us in all dangers and carry us through all temptations; through Jesus Christ, Your Son, our Lord, who lives and reigns with You and the Holy Spirit, one God, now and forever. Amen.

"We live in the midst of so many dangers that in our frailty we cannot stand upright." Perhaps we don't remember how true that is. Most of us feel quite safe most of the time. Airbags, home security systems, the Second Amendment, the FDA, FAA, USDA, HMOs, PPOs. But every one of those is protecting against something dangerous. Freeway accidents and felons, airborne diseases and air disasters, viruses and cracked vertebrae. The dangers are out there. The reason we so often forget about them is that the Lord is constantly protecting us from nearly all of them. We forget that there's an enemy, Satan, who could and eagerly would bring any of these catastrophes upon us this very moment if not restrained by our gracious and infinitely more powerful God. So we pray!

One of the greatest dangers around us—one that Satan especially likes to exploit—is false speaking, untrue or deceptive words that lead away from the Lord. God's protection from this threat is His Word spoken truly. Look up the **Old Testament Reading** for Sunday, Deuteronomy 18:15–20.

This is one of the very prominent Old Testament prophecies of the Messiah; the Jews understood they are to look for "the prophet" like Moses (18:15; Jn 1:19–21; 6:14). But this prophecy conveys a quite specific aspect of the messianic office. Moses is warning the Israelites against seeking a word from any other source than Yahweh. The Canaanites, whose land they are about to enter, relied on fortune-telling, omens, mediums, and the like for information (Deut 18:9–14)—all means that even to this day invite Satan to speak. Israel is to hear only from the Lord, and He will speak through the spokesmen He Himself will designate. When God's prophet would speak, it would be Yahweh's own Word: "I will put My words in his mouth, and he shall speak to them all that I command him" (18:18). Anyone claiming to speak in the Lord's name without His authorization—or anyone speaking in the name of another god—is to be classed with those fortune-tellers and spiritists, a capital offense (18:20).

Truth versus error is that important! We pastors in teaching the Second Commandment always warn our confirmation students of the dangers of toying with Ouija boards, séances, and horoscopes—"satanic arts," as the catechism calls them ("witchcraft" in previous editions). But any false teachings in religious matters are dangerous. God gave every doctrine of Scripture, every word of the Bible, for the one purpose of saving souls for eternity. Anything that changes, omits, waters down, or misrepresents any word of Scripture, then, at least diminishes the resource the Holy Spirit uses to create and sustain saving faith. Not only non-Christian religions but errors regarding creation, sexuality, conversion and the work of the Holy Spirit (like decision theology and speaking in tongues), Baptism, the Lord's Supper, and every other teaching, even from well-meaning Christians or other denominations, endanger souls.

The true prophet, the one who speaks only the faithful Word of the Lord, "to him you shall listen" (18:15).

There's nothing more we need to know, as the psalmist understood! Read the **Psalm** for the week, Psalm 111.

There's no need to hear from anyone else, for the Lord is "holy and awesome" (111:9); He's the one operating everything that goes on in the universe. And more than that, He lets us in on whatever we need to know: "He has shown His people the power of His works" (111:6). He's not keeping from us any valuable secrets that could be helpful. Rather, His great works are "studied by all who delight in them" (111:2). "Wisdom" is fearing and loving the Lord and trusting Him to reveal everything we need to know (111:10).

In fact, *thinking* we know something while forgetting what God has taught us is anything but true knowledge. Read 1 Corinthians 8:1–13, the **Epistle**.

"We know that 'all of us possess knowledge,'" Paul says, but "this 'knowledge' puffs up" (8:1b). What knowledge is that? "That 'an idol has no real existence,' and that 'there is no God but one'" (8:4). That's absolutely true, but the Corinthians are forgetting something else God has taught: love. "Love builds up" (8:1c). Knowing that idols are no gods at all has made them arrogant. In ancient Greek cities like Corinth, meat sold in the butcher shops was first offered to the pagan gods. These Corinthian Christians were using their knowledge (that Zeus and company aren't real) to allow them to eat such meat. That's fine as far as that goes. But, Paul points out, some new Christians aren't as clear about this, and when they see their brothers in Christ eating this meat, they think it is in worship of idols. That could cause them to worship the idols, too, and perhaps be lost from the faith (8:7, 9–11).

We may do many things in Christian liberty that we must not do if it harms another person. We can drink an alcoholic beverage, but not in front of someone struggling with alcohol, or maybe even a friend who believes it's wrong to drink. A skirt another inch above the knee, but not if it might intentionally tempt someone to look too long. The Corinthians are right. There is but "one God, the Father, . . . and one Lord, Jesus Christ" (8:6).

So to the synagogue on the Sabbath came the Lord. Read the **Holy Gospel**, Mark 1:21–28.

"Immediately" (εὐθύς, *euthys*, in Greek) is a word Mark uses often, not only to move the story along quickly but to signal something important about to happen. Jesus' teaching is always important, and hearers recognized that: "He taught them as one who had authority, and not as the scribes" (1:22). Synagogue teaching always began with readings from God's Word, the Old Testament Law and Prophets. But the comments teachers would offer about the Scriptures were always dependent on earlier rabbis' commentaries. Jesus taught the Scriptures with His own authority ("*I* say to you . . ." Mt 5:18, 20, 22, 26, 28, 32, 34, 39, 44). He, after all, is the Prophet promised by Moses to speak God's words. And at the same time, He would speak *His* words, because they are one and the same. He is God!

"Immediately," more! (1:23). The unclean spirit, of course, knows exactly who Jesus is: "The Holy One of God" (1:24). Once again, absolutely true. But here, surely, is knowledge that puffs up. The spirit is a henchman of Satan, one of the fallen angels, and he speaks the truth only to try to claim a share of authority with Jesus, to have a voice in the assembly. Jesus will have none of that! He silences the unauthorized speaker and frees the poor oppressed victim. Now folks are *really* amazed! "A new teaching with authority! He commands even the unclean spirits, and they obey Him" (1:27).

Let us turn back to our churches this Sunday morning. Is there anything worth Mark's "immediately"? Again from the Introit: "I said, 'I will confess my transgressions to the LORD,' and You forgave the iniquity of my sin." Recognize it? It's from the Divine Service, Setting Three (*LSB*, p 184), just as we begin to confess our sins to God, our Father. And then what happens? "I, by virtue of my office, as a called and ordained servant of the Word . . . in the stead and by the command of my Lord Jesus Christ . . . forgive you all your sins in the name of the Father and of the Son and of the Holy Spirit." This Sunday, that will happen! Jesus comes here! And Satan's most dangerous threat, our sins, will be forgiven for the sake of Jesus' cross by the very speaking of Christ Himself through His authorized prophet, right here at Immanuel or Cristo el Salvador or St. Paul's. That's why we look forward to Sunday morning!

JESUS SPEAKS WITH THE AUTHORITY OF THE ONE HOLY AND AWESOME GOD AND LORD TO DELIVER US FROM SIN, SATAN, AND ALL DANGERS.

And He'll do that this Sunday in our churches with the very same power and authority through our pastors. That's happening!

And that's how "here on earth [His] will [is] done" (the **Hymn of the Day**, "Son of God, Eternal Savior," *LSB* 842:4).

Fifth Sunday after the Epiphany Year B

READINGS

Isaiah 40:21–31
Psalm 147:1–11 (antiphon: v 5)
1 Corinthians 9:16–27
Mark 1:29–39

HYMN OF THE DAY

LSB 398 "Hail to Lord's Anointed"

Why did Jesus come? What was His mission as the Messiah? Well, we know He came so that the world God so loved would not perish but we would instead have everlasting life. We know that it was to die on the cross for the sins of the world, for that is how we're saved from death and have eternal life. We know Jesus came to do the will of Him who sent Him (Jn 6:38). And we could say essentially the same thing in lots of other ways. But in the Gospel for the Fifth Sunday after the Epiphany, Jesus Himself says in so many simple words why He came.

Or are His words so simple?

One of the great blessings of the lectionary is that it brings together what the Church and her thoughtful scholars have seen as passages that elucidate one another. The various propers are all designed to address the same primary issue from different angles. That means one reading will help us understand another. Since it's the Gospel lesson that guides the choices of the others, it's usually the Gospel that brings the big point to clearest focus. But sometimes, like this week, the Gospel *raises* the big question, which can then perhaps be best *answered* from the other elements. So this week, let's begin looking forward to Sunday morning with the reading we'll actually hear last in worship, the **Holy Gospel**, Mark 1:29–39, set in Capernaum. Jesus' seemingly simple statement about His mission turns out to be more complex than we might have thought. But the other propers will then help us understand what Jesus means.

Of all the countless healings Jesus did during His earthly ministry, there's something special about this first one in the Gospel reading: it's for Simon Peter's mother-in-law (1:29–31). Yes, Peter was married. Jesus is very pleased to share His kindness and power with those close to home. And you've gotta love this part: No sooner is this woman healed than she gets up and begins to serve the guests! We all know how we feel after being laid out with flu, maybe fever delirium. It takes at least a couple of days to regain our energy. This, though, shows how thorough, how powerful, Jesus' miracle was (as well as making us admire what a dear and dedicated woman this was!).

Of course, the word gets out, and soon Jesus' dance card is overbooked. "At sundown" (1:32) indicates that the crowd waits until the Sabbath (1:21) had ended, but no longer. Many more are sick; perhaps just as many, it seems, are possessed by demons. (Recall last Sunday. Jesus casting out evil spirits is an especially significant motif in Mark's report. Recall from last week, too, that Jesus does not permit the evil spirits any share in His authority to speak, 1:34.) Again Jesus is pleased to care for all these poor and oppressed.

But in the morning, He slips away for quiet prayer. And when Peter arrives and tells Him, "Everyone is looking for You," Jesus speaks those words that seem so simply to describe His mission: "Let us go on to the next towns, that I may preach there also, for that is why I came out" (1:38).

"*That* is why I came out." That's about as straightforward as you can get. And to what does "that" refer? "That I may preach there also, for *that* is why I came out." To preach is why Jesus came, eh? Jesus' mission was to preach, eh? Sounds simple enough.

Except that would mean everything Jesus has been doing in the first part of the reading—healing and casting out demons—*isn't* His mission; He has to get away from all these folks wanting miracles because they are a distraction, a time-waster, from His real mission of preaching. Really? Oh, . . . and . . . wouldn't that mean *the cross* isn't why Jesus came?

Read the whole sentence again: "Let us go on to the next towns, that I may preach there also, for *that* is why I came out." Hmm. To what *does* "that" refer? What is the "that" which is the reason Jesus came?

The final verse of the Gospel is also the liturgical **Verse** for the day, and the Verse is always chosen with the Sunday's theme explicitly in view. So perhaps it helps clarify. What does Jesus do immediately after announcing His purpose? "And He went throughout all Galilee, *preaching* in their synagogues *and casting out demons*" (1:39). So maybe Jesus' mission is to preach *and* cast out demons?

Let's look further.

The **Introit**:

I will sing to the LORD, because He has dealt bountifully with me.

Consider and answer me, O LORD my God; light up my eyes, lest I sleep the sleep of death, lest my enemy say, "I have prevailed over him," lest my foes rejoice because I am shaken. But I have trusted in

Your steadfast love; my heart shall rejoice in Your salvation.

Glory be to the Father and to the Son and to the Holy Spirit; as it was in the beginning, is now, and will be forever. Amen.

I will sing to the Lord, because He has dealt bountifully with me. (Ps 13:3–5; antiphon: Ps 13:6)

Does this shed any light on the theme of the day and therefore on Jesus' words in the Gospel lesson? There's nothing much here about preaching or demons specifically (only "enemy" and "foes" in general). What David, the psalmist, does sing about is that the Lord has "dealt bountifully" with him, delivering him from "the sleep of death" by His "steadfast love." It sounds more like what Jesus does for Peter's mother-in-law and the sick in the city. David, the Messiah's great ancestor, seems to think that sort of thing matters quite a lot to the Lord.

Similarly, the **Collect** is intended to bring before our God in prayer the matters suggested by the readings of the day, to "collect" the major elements of the Sunday.

O Lord, keep Your family the Church continually in the true faith that, relying on the hope of Your heavenly grace, we may ever be defended by Your mighty power; through Jesus Christ, Your Son, our Lord, who lives and reigns with You and the Holy Spirit, one God, now and forever. Amen.

Certainly it's through preaching that Christ keeps His family, the Church, in the faith. No question, preaching matters, and it was surely *part* of Jesus' mission, which He continues today. But Jesus' "mighty power" is also demonstrated in the healings and exorcisms He performs throughout His earthly ministry, and we count on that today too. His power in words (the Word) brings us to faith and keeps us in faith, but His power in providential care also protects us from Satan's oppressions, from illness, and from constant dangers.

The **Old Testament Reading** is always closely keyed to the Gospel lesson. In fact, after the Gospel lesson sets the direction for the Sunday, the Old Testament Reading is the next proper selected to follow it. See how Isaiah 40:21–31 illuminates Jesus' words this week.

Here preaching is indeed prominent; the prophecy is God's self-revelation through the mouth of His prophet Isaiah, as also from previous spokesmen: "Do you not know? Do you not hear? Has it not been *told you* from the beginning?" (40:21). Yahweh even preaches for Himself: "To whom then will you compare Me, that I should be like him? says the Holy One" (40:25).

But *what* is being said is even more important than the medium of its delivery (the preaching). Yahweh is all powerful ("It is He who sits above the circle of the earth, and its inhabitants are like grasshoppers; . . . who brings princes to nothing, and makes the rulers of the earth as emptiness," 40:22a, 23), and He uses His power for the weak ("He gives power to the faint, and to him who has no might He increases strength," 40:29). "They who wait for the LORD shall renew their strength; they shall mount up with wings like eagles; they shall run and not be weary; they shall walk and not faint" (40:31). What Christ does for the sick and demon-possessed in Capernaum cannot be a mere distraction, a time-waster. It is central to what the Lord is about!

See the same point being made in the **Psalm** of the week, Psalm 147:1–11. "Great is our Lord, and abundant in power; His understanding is beyond measure. . . . He determines the number of the stars; He gives to all of them their names" (147:5, 4). And He uses this power for the needy: "He heals the brokenhearted and binds up their wounds" (147:3).

Now the **Epistle**, 1 Corinthians 9:16–27. Here, too, preaching is prominent: "If I preach the gospel, that gives me no ground for boasting. . . . Woe to me if I do not preach the gospel!" (9:16). Paul must preach! But in this reading, preaching is a given; it's assumed.

Probably more to the point of this reading is why Paul preaches *the way* he does (for free, rather than for pay, 9:18). He does this so that nothing will be a barrier to anyone hearing the Gospel, that *all* may be reached: "To the Jews I became as a Jew, in order to win Jews. . . . To those outside the law [Gentiles] I became as one outside the law. . . . To the weak I became weak, that I might win the weak. I have become *all* things to *all* people, that by all means I might save some" (9:20a, 21a, 22). Paul, a Jew, wants to see that all people, Jews and Gentiles, have the opportunity to hear of Christ and be saved.

It brings to mind lines from the **Gradual** we're hearing throughout the Epiphany season: "Praise the LORD, *all nations*! Extol Him, *all peoples*!" (Ps 117:1).

What does all this suggest for our understanding of Jesus' words about His mission, "*That* is why I came out"?

Jesus has been healing and casting out demons in Peter's hometown, where He's already well known, but then He declares that He must leave: "Let us go on to the next towns, that I may preach there also, for that is why I came out" (Mk 1:38). We've seen that His leaving can't be so that He's free to preach and do nothing else and avoid doing miracles. Healing and delivering from Satan's oppression are definitely the Lord's business. And His mission can't be just preaching *and casting out demons*, as we might guess from the Verse: "He went throughout all Galilee, preaching in their synagogues and casting out demons" (Mk 1:39). There's so much more going on in the other propers than that.

What else is in all these verses? "The *next* towns." "Throughout *all* Galilee." "Let us go on *to the next towns,* that I may preach *there* also, for *that* is why I came out." To serve all! Paul stressed this in the Epistle. Isaiah and the poet of Psalm 147 tell us this. Jesus came *for all*—those who need His preaching, His healing, His freedom from Satan, His cross!

THE REASON JESUS CAME IS TO SERVE ALL THE NEEDY WITH HIS MIGHTY WORDS AND WORKS.

As you sing the **Hymn of the Day**, "Hail to the Lord's Anointed" (*LSB* 398), appreciate especially the word *all* in stanza 5.

Sixth Sunday after the Epiphany Year B

READINGS

2 Kings 5:1–14
Psalm 30 (antiphon: v 2)
1 Corinthians 10:(19–30) 31–11:1
Mark 1:40–45

HYMN OF THE DAY

LSB 394 "Songs of Thankfulness and Praise

Can't stand prosperity.

That's a saying we use sometimes in sports. A football team is playing great defense for three quarters in a close game, until its offense puts it ahead with two touchdowns early in the fourth quarter. Suddenly, the defense gives up two quick scores right back to squander the lead. A pitcher posts six shutout innings in a scoreless game, until his teammates score two runs in the top of the seventh. He promptly gives up three runs in the bottom of the inning. A golfer takes a four-shot lead to the back nine of the final round of the Masters. Then he collapses with bogey, bogey, double bogey and loses the tournament. Can't stand prosperity. As soon as things start to go well, they fall apart.

Other examples are a lot more serious. The original, of course, is Eve and Adam. They have everything, but they can't (really it was a "wouldn't") stand prosperity; they want more. And the bad examples have been piling up ever since. Solomon, who has wisdom, wealth, and wives, forgets why he's been so blessed and begins to worship idols. David, in our Psalm this Sunday, confesses, "As for me, I said in my prosperity, 'I shall never be moved'" (Ps 30:6). Maybe it's that kind of arrogance that makes him vulnerable to temptation when he sees Bathsheba. And maybe we could confess the same: "As for *me* . . ."

True prosperity is always a gift of God. But as sinners, we don't always handle it well.

Our propers this week revolve around two accounts of men who suffered from leprosy, that disfiguring skin disease that terrorized people in Bible times. It's quite the opposite of prosperity. Both were healed, so they knew prosperity as well as adversity. How did they do with each? How are their examples instructive for us in receiving whatever God in His wisdom and His grace for Jesus' sake gives us?

How Do We Stand Prosperity or Adversity (Picture Leprosy) or Both?

The **Introit** for this coming Sunday, the Sixth Sunday after the Epiphany, is a wonderful demonstration of how God's people may indeed receive and use the prosperity He bestows:

Light dawns in the darkness for the upright; He is gracious, merciful, and righteous.

Praise the Lord! Blessèd is the man who fears the Lord, who greatly delights in His commandments! Wealth and riches are in his house, and his righteousness endures forever. He is not afraid of bad news; his heart is firm, trusting in the Lord. His heart is steady; he will not be afraid, until he looks in triumph on his adversaries. He has distributed freely; He has given to the poor; His righteousness endures forever; His horn is exalted in honor.

Glory be to the Father and to the Son and to the Holy Spirit; as it was in the beginning, is now, and will be forever. Amen.

Light dawns in the darkness for the upright; He is gracious, merciful, and righteous. (Ps 112:1, 3, 7–9; antiphon: Ps 112:4)

The psalmist is experiencing great prosperity: "Wealth and riches are in his house. . . . His horn is exalted in honor." But he is "upright; He is gracious, merciful, and righteous." Not being able to stand prosperity is often the result of overconfidence: "It's going so well, I can take it easy." Here the psalmist is confident, but not overconfident—and his confidence is not in himself: "He is not afraid of bad news; his heart is firm, trusting in the Lord." "His heart is steady; he will not be afraid" because he knows that the Lord, not he himself, is the one who's prospered him. Therefore, he "greatly delights in His commandments"—loves doing whatever God commands—and in gratitude to the Lord for the blessings received. "He has distributed freely; He has given to the poor."

Prosperity is a gift of God to be received with thanks, enjoyed, and used for others.

The **Psalm** of the day prepares us nicely for the two accounts of men with leprosy prosperity *and* adversity. Read Psalm 30.

David's early years were in almost constant danger—from jealous King Saul, from the Philistines (like Goliath!), and from other enemies. God was with him through it all: "You . . . have not let my foes rejoice over me. O Lord my God, I cried to You for help, and You have healed me" (30:1b–2).

But then David's throne is established, and times are easier. (This psalm "at the dedication" may have been on the occasion of dedicating the ground on which Solomon would later build the temple, 1 Chr

21:28–22:1, or it could have been at the dedication of David's own house, 2 Sam 5:11–12. Either way, it was a peaceful and prosperous time.) David didn't always handle that well: "As for me, I said in my prosperity, 'I shall never be moved.'" So God had to humble him: "You hid Your face; I was dismayed" (30:7b; e.g., 1 Chr 21:1–4, 7–14).

Yet David knows God continues to be gracious: "For His anger is but for a moment, and His favor is for a lifetime. Weeping may tarry for the night, but joy comes with the morning. . . . You have turned for me my mourning into dancing." "I cried to You for help, and You *have* healed me" (30:5, 11a, 2).

Naaman is one of the two men in our lessons this week in particular need of healing. Learn about him in the **Old Testament Reading**, 2 Kings 5:1–14.

The reading sets us up for a surprise. Naaman is riding high!—"a great man," highly honored by his boss, the king of Syria, a brave and victorious military officer. Oh, but did I mention one other minor detail? Naaman has that dreaded disease that made the baddest, most feared tough guy helpless, unfit for command, and doomed. "He was a leper" (5:1). There's big-time prosperity and now big-time adversity!

But his suffering is probably no more painful than that of the little girl Naaman had torn from her home and family in Israel to serve his wife. She obviously wasn't taken as an infant—when perhaps memories and separation wouldn't be so traumatic—because she is old enough to have learned her faith. And she's learned it well. So well that instead of hatred for her mistress and master, she cares (5:3). That's the reaction to adversity that should come from knowing the true God loves you.

So off Naaman goes with his horses and chariots carrying a letter from his king and 750 pounds of silver and 150 pounds of gold (5:5)!

Elisha isn't wowed. He doesn't even come out of his house. He just sends his servant, saying, "Go and wash in the Jordan seven times, and your flesh shall be restored" (5:10).

Here's what prosperity can do to you—even to a man suffering from leprosy. All that fame, all those achievements, all that money make the man arrogant. He who ought to be begging thinks the prophet in Israel owes him a little pomp and circumstance—at least face time: "Behold, I thought that he would surely come out to me and stand and call upon the name of the Lord his God, and wave his hand over the place and cure the leper" (5:11). He storms away!

Fortunately, there's a happy ending. Naaman's servants are the voice of reason (5:13–14). If Elisha had asked him to climb a mountain or defeat an army, he would have done it. Here's a great deal: do a tiny thing and be cleansed! Know, Naaman, that your healing isn't by anything you do or can do. "Know that there is a prophet in Israel" (5:8) because there is a God in Israel who humbles the mighty but lifts up the needy.

In the **Epistle**, Paul picks up again a kind of prosperity the Corinthians can't seem to stand. Read 1 Corinthians 10:19–11:1.

Paul is continuing his discussion of Christian freedom going back to chapter 8, the Epistle from two weeks ago. That passage begins, "Now concerning food offered to idols: we know that 'all of us possess knowledge.' This 'knowledge' puffs up" (8:1). It's surely a prosperity of knowledge to understand that idols simply aren't real. But in that prosperity of knowledge, the Corinthians have become arrogant, eating meat sacrificed to idols even when it might harm consciences of weaker Christians who didn't understand.

From such a position of prosperity, knowledge, one should instead avoid even some things one knows are "lawful" (10:23), because the Christian is not to seek "his own good, but the good of his neighbor" (10:24). At the same time, let us recognize that all prosperity we do enjoy is to God's credit: "So, whether you eat or drink, or whatever you do, do all to the glory of God" (10:31).

"If you will," the desperate man says to Jesus in the **Holy Gospel**. "I will; be clean," Jesus says. So sweet! Read Mark 1:40–45.

A leper is a most sympathetic figure in Scripture. Not only did the disease cause physical agony as the flesh rotted and extremities fell away but an infected person was excluded from fellowship with family and the temple. Many Israelites also saw leprosy as a sign that God was cursing the victim. Today's very popular "prosperity gospel" makes the same error, suggesting that if we are faithful, God will assuredly prosper us with material and earthly goods. (You get the implication: If we *don't* see ourselves being materially prosperous, it must mean we're somehow being unfaithful to God!) "Prosperity gospel" is no Gospel at all!

This man, though, is indeed prospered by God for the very same reason we receive every truly good thing: Jesus, who speaks these cleansing words, has reconciled the whole world to God by His death on the cross. Thus, while we have no guarantees as to just *how* God will bless us, we know that He *is* always giving us the very best—both for now and for eternity.

That does, however, call us to trust God's way of operating and blessing. And here, the man Jesus heals can't stand prosperity. "See that you say nothing to anyone," Jesus sternly charges him (1:44). "But he went out and began to talk freely about it, and to spread the news, so that Jesus could no longer openly enter a town" (1:45). Make no mistake; this talking was a sin. While we are to tell of Jesus' works at every opportunity, the time wasn't right yet. Popularity wasn't to get in the way of Jesus going to the cross. God's way is always gracious and wise.

So instead, we'll acknowledge we deserve only adversity and pray that God prosper us as His mercy knows best. Read the **Collect**:

O Lord, graciously hear the prayers of Your people that we who justly suffer the consequence of our sin may be mercifully delivered by Your goodness to the glory of Your name; through Jesus Christ, Your Son, our Lord, who lives and reigns with You and the Holy Spirit, one God, now and forever. Amen.

Sing "songs of thankfulness and praise" for all our prosperities since each manifests what "God in man made manifest," Jesus Christ, earned for us (**Hymn of the Day**, *LSB* 394:1).

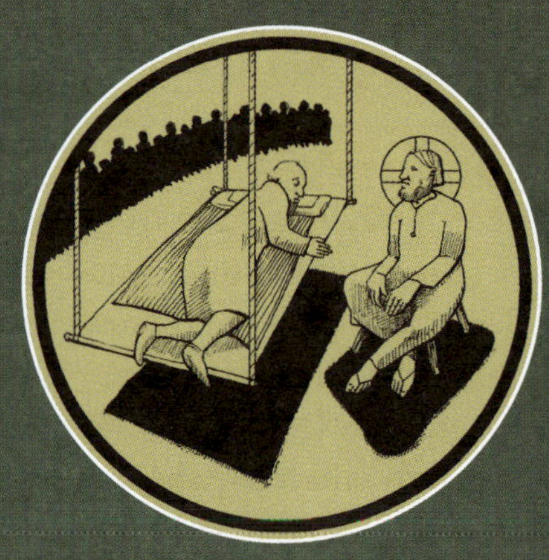

Seventh Sunday after the Epiphany Year B

READINGS

Isaiah 43:18–25
Psalm 41 (antiphon: v 4)
2 Corinthians 1:18–22
Mark 2:1–12

HYMNS OF THE DAY

LSB 820 "My Soul, Now Praise Your Maker"
LSB 834 "O God, O Lord of Heaven and Earth"

"Which is easier," Jesus asks the skeptics in this week's Gospel lesson, "to say to the paralytic, 'Your sins are forgiven,' or to say, 'Rise, take up your bed and walk'?" (Mk 2:9).

And the answer is . . . yes.

Jesus might also have asked, "Which is more difficult?" And the answer would still be yes.

It's nice that sometimes you don't have to choose.

The Gospel reading for this Sunday, the Seventh Sunday after the Epiphany, is the lovely account of friends so concerned for their paralyzed mate that they lower him through the roof to get him to Jesus. And, sure enough, Jesus does both—forgives his sins and heals his body. What's interesting is how each of those miracles is possible—how the answer is yes.

The **Introit** is explicit about God's both/and.

The Lord is merciful and gracious, slow to anger and abounding in steadfast love.

Bless the Lord, O my soul, and all that is within me, bless His holy name! Bless the Lord, O my soul, and forget not all His benefits, who forgives all your iniquity, who heals all your diseases, who redeems your life from the pit, who crowns you with steadfast love and mercy, who satisfies you with good so that your youth is renewed like the eagle's. He does not deal with us according to our sins, nor repay us according to our iniquities. For as high as the heavens are above the earth, so great is His steadfast love toward those who fear Him; as far as the east is from the west, so far does He remove our transgressions from us.

Glory be to the Father and to the Son and to the Holy Spirit; as it was in the beginning, is now, and will be forever. Amen.

The Lord is merciful and gracious, slow to anger and abounding in steadfast love. (Ps 103:1–5, 10–12; antiphon: Ps 103:8)

Psalm 103 is one of faith history's greatest hymns of praise. And like all proper expressions of praise, it doesn't simply call on *us* to Praise the Lord, PTL, PTL, repeat. It leads us to speak what *He* has done. Declaring God's mighty and gracious acts—that's true praise.

"Forget not all His benefits." And what are those benefits, God's mighty and gracious acts? He "forgives all your iniquity" *and* He "heals all your diseases." He cares about your physical "good so that your youth is renewed like the eagle's." How precious will renewed youth be to the paralytic in the Gospel lesson! And "He does not deal with us according to our sins, nor repay us according to our iniquities. For . . . as far as the east is from the west, so far does He remove our transgressions from us." I love that last metaphor!

Notice that it's actually forgiveness of sins that's mentioned first: "forgives . . . iniquity . . . heals . . . diseases." Is that in order of importance? Not exactly. Rather, it's a logical sequence. You'll see how.

As we pray the **Collect** for Sunday, we might consider how these twin adversities, sin and sickness, are related:

O God, the strength of all who put their trust in You, mercifully grant that by Your power we may be defended against all adversity; through Jesus Christ, Your Son, our Lord, who lives and reigns with You and the Holy Spirit, one God, now and forever. Amen.

"Defended against all adversity." We should understand that sin is our first adversity. It was sin in the Garden of Eden that made us slaves of Satan. It was sin that sentenced us to death. And, above all, it was sin that separated us from God. The perfect relationship Adam and Eve enjoyed with God was shattered. That's because God is holy, and holiness can't coexist with sin. It's not a matter of God being vengeful; it's just His nature. He can't be in relationship with sin or anything (anyone!) corrupted with it. If something wasn't done about this predicament, we and the whole human race would be cut off forever from every one of God's blessings. (That's what hell will be, of course!)

One immediate consequence of this is illness. Mankind's sin drove a wedge between God and the universe He'd created for us; the creation was cursed. That meant infection, aging, deterioration. The perfect health and well-being God bestowed on His creatures was lost. And it will only be restored when the relationship with God that enables His blessings is restored. So sickness, too, is a result of sin, and it needs the same ultimate solution.

The **Old Testament Reading** has God healing the broken creation and forgiving sins. Read Isaiah 43:18–25.

"Remember not the former things. . . . Behold, I am doing a new thing" (43:18a, 19a). The former things, the fallen creation, is being replaced with a renewed one. The Lord pictures this new creation with a very earthy blessing, water: "Water in the wilderness, rivers in the desert, to give drink to My chosen people" (43:20). Water is the most essential element of earthly, physical life. There is no physical health without it.

God's people would forfeit the blessings of restored health in the new creation because they have "burdened" the Lord with their "sins," "wearied" Him with their "iniquities" (43:24) . . . except that "I, I am He who blots out your transgressions for My own sake, and I will not remember your sins" (43:25). Blotting out sin reconciles God to His people and opens again the door for His blessings. Also notice that the Lord blots out transgression for His own sake. That is, He takes upon Himself the responsibility for dealing with our sin.

The **Psalm** for this Sunday foresees the Gospel narrative, the healing of the paralytic, in surprising detail. Recall what you know of that account as you read Psalm 41.

"Blessed is the one who considers the poor! In the day of trouble the LORD delivers him" (41:1). We're touched in the Gospel account by the love the four men have for their poor, helpless friend, and they have faith that the Lord Jesus can make him well.

"The LORD sustains him on his sickbed; in his illness You restore him to full health" (41:3). The enduring image of the account of the paralytic is his friends carrying him to Jesus on his sickbed and lowering him through an opening they make in the roof.

"As for me, I said, 'O LORD, be gracious to me; heal me, for I have sinned against You!'" (41:4). The petition of the friends is obvious: "Lord, please heal our friend." But Jesus also addresses his spiritual illness, sin.

"All who hate me whisper together about me; they imagine the worst for me" (41:7). When Jesus announces forgiveness to the poor man, His enemies accuse Him "in their hearts" (Mk 2:6), thinking He's blasphemed.

But, of course, Jesus has the last word, and the paralytic is healed: "The LORD protects him and keeps him alive; he is called blessed in the land" (41:2).

Appropriately, the verse selected as the antiphon, or theme verse, of the Psalm is 41:4. Again, "As for me, I said, 'O Lord, be gracious to me; heal me, for I have sinned against You!'" David knows that the Lord cares about both sickness and sin.

Or, as we might paraphrase Paul in our **Epistle**, 2 Corinthians 1:18–22, "Yes" and "Yes."

Paul has been wanting to visit the Corinthians again in person, but sometimes man's plans change. Often the best we can do is, "We'll see. Maybe yes, maybe no." But Paul says that God's plans never vacillate. "For the Son of God, Jesus Christ, . . . was not Yes and No, but in Him it is always Yes.

For all the promises of God find their Yes in Him" (1:19–20a).

What does that mean? God certainly says "no;" it's called His Law. There are many things "thou shalt not" do. But the Law is God's alien work. Saying "no" is only what God says so that soon enough He can say "yes." And soon enough is the moment a sinner repents and believes that Jesus has forgiven her sin by His death on the cross. In fact, Christ has already secured the Yes for the entire world, for His death has atoned for all sins, reconciled the whole world to God—even those who will never believe and are lost. This is always what God is really about. The Gospel is God's proper work. *In Christ*, God's word to us is always Yes.

So we know Jesus' answer to the paralytic and his friends is "Yes" and "Yes." But which will be easier? Consider this as you read the **Holy Gospel**, Mark 2:1–12.

The roof of the house probably consists of tiles with earth for insulation, so removing it involves light engineering and digging (cf Lk 5:19). While Jesus alone can see into hearts, in this case, the faith of the men is obvious for all to see—going to such lengths to reach Jesus. We don't learn whether their faith is temporarily disappointed when Jesus first speaks forgiveness rather than physical healing, because immediately Jesus knows the hearts of the scribes: "Who can forgive sins but God alone?" (2:7).

Jesus asks, "Which is easier, to say to the paralytic, 'Your sins are forgiven,' or to say, 'Rise, take up your bed and walk'?" Yes.

On the one hand, it's cheap and easy to say, "Your sins are forgiven," since no one can prove you wrong; there's nothing for anyone to see. It's much harder to say, "Get up and walk," because if you fail, it'll be evident to everyone.

On the other hand, for Jesus to heal a paralytic is a piece of cake, easy; He's omnipotent God. But forgiving this man's sins, that would take Jesus' death on the cross—the hardest thing ever done!—and not made easy by the fact that Jesus is God. As true man, bearing the punishment for every human sin, suffering separation from God and the torments of hell, was the greatest agony.

But let us not forget that physical healing, like water to drink, like every other physical and temporal blessing, *also* required Jesus suffering the due penalty of all sin. Remember, every blessing we receive is only because the world has been reconciled to God—that sin has been removed. For if not for forgiveness, we would all remain separated from all God's blessings—physical and spiritual.

So which is easier? Yes. But let's realize that the more pointed question is, "Which was harder?" Yes, both required the death of Jesus. And He said "yes!" to doing just that!

**Bless the Lord, O My Soul,
and Forget Not All His Benefits,
Who—Yes!—Forgives All Your Iniquity,
Who—Yes!—Also Heals All Your Diseases!**

The **Hymns of the Day**" (*LSB* 820 and 834) are a paraphrase of Psalm 103 (820) and a newer text by Martin Franzmann (834).

Eighth Sunday after the Epiphany Year B

READINGS

Hosea 2:14–20
Psalm 103:1–13 (antiphon: v 22)
2 Corinthians 2:12–3:6
Mark 2:(13–17) 18–22

HYMN OF THE DAY

LSB 819 "Sing Praise to God, the Highest Good"

There's something very sweet about a wedding between two Christian people who have found each other a little later in life. Perhaps they're in their thirties, maybe their forties, maybe older. Perhaps there's been sadness before—a divorce, a previous spouse lost to death, a getting-your-hopes-up-only-to-be-disappointed relationship. Or maybe they've just both been waiting, praying, hoping God would finally send the right person. It may really have been only a few short years, but for those years, it seemed like forever—and with many moments of near despair. But now it's happened, and in many ways, it's all the better for the wait.

The story of God and His people is like that. God always had just the right person in mind for just the right moment, but it did require waiting. And there were lots of sadnesses along the way, as we haven't always waited patiently, faithfully, trustingly. But when God's appointed wedding day came, when the Bridegroom appeared, it was indeed so very sweet! In fact,

THE CELEBRATION MIGHT BE EVEN SWEETER WHEN WE'VE HAD TO WAIT AWHILE FOR OUR BRIDEGROOM.

Our propers for the Eighth Sunday after the Epiphany describe the celebration of God's people in Christ, but they also remind us of some of the highs and lows of the waiting.

Already in the Old Testament, God gave His people an anticipation of what was coming, as in the **Introit** for Epiphany 8:

Let Your priests be clothed with righteousness, and let Your saints shout for joy.

For the Lord *has chosen Zion; He has desired it for His dwelling place: "This is My resting place forever; here I will dwell, for I have desired it. I will abundantly bless her provisions; I will satisfy her poor with bread. Her priests I will clothe with salvation, and her saints will shout for joy. There I will make a horn to sprout for David; I have a prepared a lamp for My anointed. His enemies I will clothe with shame, but on him his crown will shine."*

Glory be to the Father and to the Son and to the Holy Spirit; as it was in the beginning, is now, and will be forever. Amen.

Let Your priests be clothed with righteousness, and let Your saints shout for joy. (Ps 132:13–18; antiphon: Ps 132:9)

It's a celebration! Picture Israel's priests leading the procession up to the temple, the faithful following with shouts of joy. (Psalm 132 is one of the Songs of Ascents, or Songs of Degrees, Psalms 120–134, which may have been explicitly for such processions up the steps of the temple.) As was often the case, the celebration involves food: "I will abundantly bless her provisions," the Lord says. It's a most festive occasion.

We're celebrating God taking Israel as His own: "For the Lord has chosen Zion." This is the covenant God established with ancient Israel, binding Himself to her in what truly was a marriage. But, as always in the Old Testament, it was anticipating a consummation to come later: "I will make a horn to sprout for David; I have a prepared a lamp for My anointed." David had been a great king in his own right, but Israel knew he was the forerunner of his greater Son, the Messiah, the Anointed. "A lamp for My anointed" is like the Olympic flame being carried by one runner after another, never going out or being forgotten, until it finally lights the grand cauldron. God promises to keep the line of David alive through generations and centuries until His perfect point in time.

The **Collect**, of course, is our prayer from our point in time, so it looks back on Christ's coming. See, though, how it also looks back on our state when His saving work hadn't yet been revealed to us:

O Lord, mercifully hear our prayers and having set us free from the bonds of our sins deliver us from every evil; through Jesus Christ, Your Son, our Lord, who lives and reigns with You and the Holy Spirit, one God, now and forever. Amen.

"Having set us free from the bonds of our sins." Every one of us, at the moment of conception, was living as if Christ's salvation had not been accomplished. We were in the bonds of sin.

Perhaps you've observed—or experienced for yourself—that a couple that meets and marries later in life sometimes has a deeper appreciation of the gift of marriage than some who dated since high school. Not always, certainly. But knowing first what it's like not to have that love can make the one and only seem even more heaven sent.

Surely we all appreciate Christ, our Bridegroom, more deeply when we remember that we were truly hopeless sinners without a future before He came along for us. We all had that before, even if it was only until our Baptism at a few days after birth.

The marquee story of looking for love in our propers is the **Old Testament Reading**, Hosea 2:14–20. Check it out. Better yet, read all of Hosea 1–3. These chapters blend narrative and prophecy to tell of Hosea and his wife, Gomer, a prostitute, and their children.

God commands Hosea to marry this prostitute in order to illustrate Israel's harlotry against the Lord, joining herself to other gods (1:2). In particular, the blessings God has showered down on Israel have been attributed to the fertility god, Baal (2:8). The Lord will therefore teach Israel the painful lesson of being abandoned, which is symbolically expressed in the names He gives two of Hosea and Gomer's children: No Mercy (Lo-ruhamah) and Not My People (Lo-ammi)(1:6, 8–9).

But it gets worse. Gomer leaves her husband and children and returns to her former life (2:5), exactly as Israel continues to wander from the Lord. What to do?

The Lord answers Israel: "Behold, I will allure her, and bring her into the wilderness, and speak tenderly to her. And there I will give her her vineyards and make the Valley of Achor a door of hope. And there she shall answer as in the days of her youth, as at the time when she came out of the land of Egypt" (2:14–15). A tender word, a fresh start. "The wilderness" recalled the days when at Mount Sinai God spoke His vows to Israel (Ex 19:1–6). Immediately after the exodus from Egypt, it was Israel's honeymoon. Even the "Valley of Achor," the place of trouble, one of Israel's early infidelities against her husband (Josh 7:24–26), would now be transformed into "a door of hope" for the new relationship (Hosea 2:15a).

The older couple that comes to the altar after surviving the most heartrending sadness—divorce—is now reconciled, just as if she were the blushing bride of years ago the first time: "as in the days of her youth" (2:15b). "And there she shall answer," renew her vows: "You will call Me 'My Husband,' and no longer will you call Me 'My Baal.' For I will remove the names of the Baals from her mouth" (2:16–17a).

The Lord intends this new covenant (2:18) to last ("I will betroth you to Me forever," 2:19a), and He will provide everything for that to happen: "I will betroth you to Me in righteousness and in justice, in steadfast love and in mercy. I will betroth you to Me in faithfulness" (2:19b–20a). The past is forgiven. The Lord invites us to celebrate!

We discussed the **Psalm** for this Sunday, Psalm 103, as the Introit last week. Take a glance back. As you read it again, savor that when we've broken our marriage vows to the Lord, He is "slow to anger and abounding in steadfast love. . . . Nor will He keep His anger forever" (103:8b, 9b). That surely invites celebration: "Bless the LORD, all His works. . . . Bless the LORD, O my soul!" (103:22).

The **Epistle** is another comfort regarding God's time: 2 Corinthians 2:12–3:6.

Paul's coming to Troas (northwest coast of Asia Minor, present-day Turkey) is probably during his third missionary journey. He has to move on before he prefers (2:12–13). But already on his second journey, Troas is the city Paul has to leave abruptly when Christ by a vision calls him over to Macedonia (Acts 16:8–12). He makes it back later on that third trip (Acts 20:6), but waiting for the Lord's time is difficult. Fortunately, "Christ always leads us in triumphal procession, and through us spreads the fragrance of the knowledge of Him everywhere" (2 Cor 2:14). Christ's leading always achieves God's best—even when we have to wait.

For Paul, Christ's triumphal procession—on Christ's timetable—includes not only Macedonia but Corinth, in Greece. And that means souls won for the Savior: "You yourselves are our letter of recommendation, written on our hearts, to be known and read by all" (2 Cor 3:2). The Corinthian believers are among the firstfruits of the "new covenant" God has promised to His Old Testament people—a better covenant, not of Law but of Gospel (3:6). It was the covenant to come when the waiting would finally end, when David's lamp would reach its destination.

Now He's here! Read Sunday's **Holy Gospel**, Mark 2:13–22.

The Bridegroom has arrived! It's time for new wine in fresh wineskins (2:22).

That means gathering followers who never would have qualified in a covenant of the Law. Levi, better known to us as Matthew (Mt 9:9), may or may not have been the most blatant example of tax collectors' indiscretions; we're not told. But we know the reputation. And we see the sort of folks he called friends: "many tax collectors and sinners" (2:15). Even putting the best construction on everything, these people needed a "physician;" they were "sick" (2:17).

But now, finally, is their time. Not that they'd waited so patiently. Rather, it is the time that their Bridegroom is with them, and He speaks tenderly to them, allures them, gives them hope. He sets them free from the bonds of their sin. He has chosen Levi, his fellow tax collectors, and sinners like us to be His own, to be His Bride, the Church.

The consummation would come within three more short years when the Bridegroom would give Himself up for the Church, sacrificing Himself for her on the cross. And then each of our times would come when His Spirit would call us to faith in our Baptism and the preaching of His Word. He has betrothed us to Himself forever.

The Bridegroom says that when He is with us, we "cannot fast" (2:19). We must celebrate, and surely more sweetly than if this had come any other way or time!

Close by singing the **Hymn of the Day**, *LSB* 819, to God, who has made us His "chosen generation" (st 1).

The Transfiguration of Our Lord Year B

READINGS

2 Kings 2:1–12
or Exodus 34:29–35
Psalm 50:1–6 (antiphon: v2)
2 Corinthians 3:12–13 (14–18); 4:1–6
Mark 9:2–9

HYMN OF THE DAY

LSB 413 "O Wondrous Type! O Vision Fair"

High feasts of the church year create a different experience for worshipers than most Sundays. Coming into the sanctuary on Christmas Eve, we see the tree, wreath, and dimmed lights, and in our minds, we immediately picture the manger and angels and shepherds. Entering on Easter—the lilies, the white paraments, the altar redressed—causes us to visualize the open and empty tomb. The red on Pentecost creates flames of fire flash in our imaginations. We come into worship on feast days knowing what to expect, already seeing in our heads the story from the life of Christ or His Church that we're about to celebrate.

For the most regular worshipers, that'll be true this Sunday, the Transfiguration of Our Lord. Folks may not notice the paraments changed from green to festival white. But opening the bulletin and seeing "The Transfiguration of Our Lord" should ring a bell. Or, better, start the mental video. The feasts and festivals are especially visual.

The corresponding challenge of the festivals is that familiarity. The fabulous stories make them memorable; remembering them can cause us to fast-forward. That's even more likely if a festival event is presented multiple times in Scripture—perhaps in two, three, or all four of the Gospels. But then the subtle intrigue, not always anticipated by worshipers, is to identify what's *unique* about the way this Gospel writer or that describes the same event.

Jesus' transfiguration is narrated in Mark, Matthew, and Luke. Last year, in our devotion-study for Year A, we considered Matthew's emphasis that Jesus' presence after the terrifying light show comforts us. Next year, Year C, Luke will focus on the transfiguration leading directly to the cross. This year, Mark is particularly visual. The transfiguration will, of course, be visually powerful no matter who describes it, but Mark adds at least one detail that suggests he wants us to remember the image in our minds. That, then, will encourage us to look for visual cues in this year's other propers as well.

We'll begin with the transfiguration account itself, Mark 9:2–9, the **Holy Gospel**.

Most of the details of the transfiguration are common to all three Gospels. That doesn't make the event common at all! "After six days" is six days after Peter's great confession that Jesus is the Christ (Mk 8:27–9:1). That perhaps places the transfiguration still near Caesarea Philippi (8:27), well north of Galilee, which would in turn make Mount Hermon, yet farther north, a possible location, as many have guessed.

"Transfigured" (9:2) translates the Greek μετεμορφώθη, *metemorphothe,* which more directly gives us the word *metamorphosis*, a transformation or a complete change in appearance or character. That's what happens here! The disciples are suddenly seeing Jesus in His heavenly glory!

Elijah and Moses are two of the greatest figures of the Old Testament, but Peter misses the point of their appearance. "He did not know what to *say*" (9:6). Fine, Peter, but no one asked you a question. Hush! Instead, "Rabbi, it is good that we are here. Let us make three tents, one for You and one for Moses and one for Elijah" (9:5). Peter knows such high-level company marks Jesus as an A-lister. And "tents" could also be translated "tabernacles," like Israel's tent-church in the wilderness. (It's the same Greek root John uses for Jesus "dwelling" or "tabernacling" among us in Jn 1:14.) But this isn't a triumvirate; it is more like a private audience, and no question which *one* is host. Besides, Peter, this isn't the real show yet. That will be on another mountaintop.

Fortunately, the heavenly Father sets the record—and Peter—straight: "This [not those] is My beloved Son [not just prophet]; listen to *Him*." And, as an exclamation point, "suddenly, looking around, they no longer saw anyone with them but Jesus only" (9:8). Jesus alone is God's Son and the Savior.

Luke will develop this further next year, but we mustn't overlook that "coming down the mountain" (9:9) would now take Jesus quite straight away to the cross—and to His rising from the dead. That's why our church year so well places the Transfiguration of Our Lord as the last Sunday before Ash Wednesday and the beginning of Lent.

All of this is also in Matthew or Luke or both. But Mark also includes this: Jesus' "clothes became radiant, intensely white, as no one [actually "no launderer," γναφεύς, *gnapheus*] on earth could bleach them" (9:3). Matthew and Luke dazzle us enough, but Mark wants us to stop and visualize the scrubbing, the sunning, and, in our day, the harsh chemicals that just can't match what the disciples saw. What, after all, is white? Reflecting *all* light. Haven't we seen that? A brand new shirt? Fresh snow. White, not ivory or eggshell, paint. Apparently not this white! Mark wants us to picture all the "whites" we've ever seen and then realize that Jesus is otherworldly. Can you see Him?

Visual detail is a characteristic of Mark's writing. Look for other examples in this year's Gospels—examples like the cushion under Jesus' head (4:38) and the "very large" size of the stone sealing Jesus' tomb (16:4).

The **Introit** for Transfiguration Sunday, Year B, is the same as in Year A. So this year, let's just scope the visuals:

Exalt the LORD our God, and worship at His holy mountain; for the LORD our God is holy!

The LORD reigns; let the peoples tremble! He sits enthroned upon the cherubim; let the earth quake! The LORD is great in Zion; He is exalted over all the peoples. Let them praise Your great and awesome name! Holy is He! The King in His might loves justice. You have established equity; You have executed justice and righteousness in Jacob. Exalt the LORD our God; worship at His footstool! Holy is He!

Glory be to the Father and to the Son and to the Holy Spirit; as it was in the beginning, is now, and will be forever. Amen.

Exalt the LORD our God, and worship at His holy mountain; for the LORD our God is holy! (Ps 99:1–5; antiphon: Ps 99:9)

On top of mountains, like Mount Hermon, one can see for miles. Perhaps that's why God used so many as "His holy mountain." The Mount of Transfiguration is part of a long holy history: Mount Moriah (Gen 22:1–19), Mount Sinai (Ex 19:18–20:21), Mount Nebo (Deut 34:1–5), Mount Carmel (1 Ki 18:20–40), the "Sermon Mount" (Mt 5:1–7:29), Mount Calvary (Mk 15:22), the Mount of Olives (Acts 1:6–12). Can you see them? Can you see the stories that unfolded on each?

Can you see the Lord "enthroned upon the cherubim"? Like the mountains, this bids us to look up. But what Peter, James, and John see right in front of them is this heavenly glory brought to earth—in a person they certainly could see with their own eyes. Jesus transfigured is truly the glory of heaven.

Amazingly, it's also a glimpse of our future glory. The **Collect**:

O God, in the glorious transfiguration of Your beloved Son You confirmed the mysteries of the faith by the testimony of Moses and Elijah. In the voice that came from the bright cloud You wonderfully foreshowed our adoption by grace. Mercifully make us co-heirs with the King in His glory and bring us to the fullness of our inheritance in heaven; through the same Jesus Christ, our Lord, who lives and reigns with You and the Holy Spirit, one God, now and forever. Amen.

"You wonderfully foreshowed our adoption by grace. Mercifully make us co-heirs with the King in His glory and bring us to the fullness of our inheritance in heaven." You, me, all believers someday shining in garments of Jesus' own glorious white, whiter than our eyes have ever beheld. What we see in Jesus' transfiguration is what we'll eventually get.

God gave ancient Israel similar glimpses of their future glory. In the Psalm for this week, Psalm 50:1–6, we see the Lord as "the perfection of beauty" (50:2). In our two Old Testament Readings, 2 Kings 2:1–12 and Exodus 34:29–35, we see our future glory in Elijah and Moses.

Elijah was a likely choice to join Jesus on the mountain, not only because he'd had his own mountaintop experience on Mount Carmel but also because he was one of two men who never died. (Recall also Enoch, Gen 5:21–24.) What a sight Elisha saw when Elijah was taken up! (2 Ki 2:11–12). And that was crucial, because Elisha would receive the special gift of Elijah's prophetic spirit *if* he saw Elijah being taken up to heaven (2:9–10).

Next to Jesus, Moses was king of the hills. Numerous times, Moses ascended Mount Sinai to speak with the Lord, and when he returned to the people, his face glowed with God's glory (Ex 34:29). As usual, God's glory terrifies sinful people (34:30). But interestingly, Moses did not cover his face with the veil while he was speaking with the people but rather after he finished speaking (34:33–35).

Paul explains why in the **Epistle**, 2 Corinthians 3:12–4:6.

Moses, Paul says, does not want the Israelites to "gaze at the outcome of what was being brought to an end" (3:12), to fixate on the glory that was fading away. For Mount Sinai was not the final glory. As Moses' face had to fade, the glory of God's Law and the old covenant of Sinai had to give way to greater glory. The greater is "the glory of God in the face of Jesus Christ" (2 Cor 4:6). And even Jesus' transfiguration had to fade—Peter could not remain on that mountain forever—because the greatest glory is on Mount Calvary. There, Jesus suffers the greatest ignominy so that we can share in His transfiguration glory, so that "we all . . . are being transformed into the same image from one degree of glory to another" (3:18), and so that when we see the suffering of the cross now so soon, "we do not lose heart" (4:1).

Rather, we take heart at what our **Hymn of the Day**, *LSB* 413, expresses so well:

THE TRANSFIGURATION OF CHRIST
REVEALS TO US THE WONDROUS TYPE,
THE VISION FAIR, OF GLORY
THAT WE, THE CHURCH, WILL SHARE.

Close the Epiphany season by praying once more the **Gradual** that's been revealing this glory all along:

> *Praise the LORD, all nations! Extol Him, all peoples! For great is His steadfast love toward us, and the faithfulness of the LORD endures forever. Ascribe to the LORD the glory due His name; bring an offering, and come into His courts! (Ps 117:1–2a; 96:8)*

A note for next week: Ash Wednesday, the Wednesday immediately following Transfiguration Sunday, uses the same propers for Years A, B, and C. Therefore, you'll find the one devotion-study for Ash Wednesday in Year A on page 74. The devotion-study for next Sunday, the First Sunday in Lent, Year B, appears on the next page.

First Sunday in Lent Year B

READINGS:

Genesis 22:1–18
Psalm 25:1–10 (antiphon: v 14)
James 1:12–18
Mark 1:9–15

HYMN OF THE DAY:

LSB 656, 657 "A Mighty Fortress Is Our God"

On Wednesday, we began again the Lenten journey. We follow Jesus with the **Gradual** for the season of Lent.:

> *[O come, let us fix our eyes on] Jesus, the founder and perfecter of our faith, who for the joy that was set before Him endured the cross, despising the shame, and is seated at the right hand of the throne of God. (Heb 12:2)*

We follow Jesus to the cross, where He perfected, finished our faith, that which we believe. But Jesus is also the "founder" of our faith, the one who lays the foundation. And before Jesus' death on the cross could atone for our sins, a foundation had to be laid. Before taking the punishment for our failures to keep God's Law, Jesus first had to fulfill all the Law's demands for us. That's where this first Sunday of the Lenten journey will take us.

This year, Year B, the readings for Lent 1 will also confront us with an uneasy distinction—that between temptation and testing. While Jesus fulfills the Law *for us* by overcoming the devil's temptation, *we* are also both tempted by the devil and tested by God. We have to take one of these for ourselves. The other . . . well, that's the story of the First Sunday in Lent.

The Gospel lessons for Lent 1 in all three years of the lectionary describe the temptation of Christ. Matthew in Year A and Luke in Year C both give the well-known details: three temptations, beginning with stones into bread and then Satan's invitations for Jesus to jump from the pinnacle of the temple and to bow down and worship him. You might wish to read one or both of those this year: Matthew 4:1–11 and Luke 4:1–13. (And, of course, these are discussed in our devotion-studies for Years A and C.)

This year, though, Mark gives a very brief telling of the temptation, actually just two verses. That clues us in to examine more closely certain elements he does include—and to appreciate how the Old Testament Reading and the Epistle raise the matter of temptation or testing. Begin with the **Holy Gospel**, Mark 1:9–15.

With such a brief account of the temptation itself (1:12–13), our lectionary has added preceding and following events. It's quite helpful to see that the temptation of Christ follows immediately after His Baptism (1:9–11). The fact that Jesus is God's "beloved Son" will echo significantly words we'll actually hear earlier in the service in our Old Testament Reading (and which we'll note momentarily here). Jesus' Baptism also prepares Him for the temptation to come—just as our Baptism is the means by which we successfully struggle against temptation and the "Old Adam in us" who is always inclined to sin. (See Martin Luther's explanation in the Small Catechism of what baptizing with water indicates.)

"Immediately" (a word that Mark likes so much) after that, the Holy Spirit "drove" Jesus out into the wilderness (1:12). Here is the most intriguing detail of Mark's brief narrative. The Spirit "drove" Jesus out to be tempted. Matthew and Luke use much more tepid—in fact, passive—verbs: Jesus "was led" by the Spirit into the wilderness. Mark's word is a form of the Greek ἐκβάλλω, *ekballo.* Literally, that means to "throw out." (*Ek* is a prefix meaning "out," and *ballo* means "throw" or "cast," reminding us of throwing a ball.) Literally, the Spirit threw Jesus out into the wilderness to be tempted. Why such strong language?

Mark is driving home the absolute necessity of what's going to follow. There was no option for Jesus. Jesus could not simply go about for three years preaching, working miracles, and generally being God's beloved Son. Jesus could not even *just* go to the cross and suffer for the sins of the whole world—as if that could be a "just"! Certainly Jesus couldn't simply teach us what to do—as if the temptation of Christ were only a helpful lesson in how *we* can resist the devil. Rather, it was absolutely necessary that Jesus first keep the Law perfectly on our behalf. God's commandments have never been abolished; the bar has never been lowered. What God commands, God demands. And we have never kept, couldn't ever keep God's Law. From Adam and Eve's sin, passed down to us, we have been sinful since conception. If humankind were to be saved from the curse of the Law, humankind had to fulfill the Law, and no one among us could.

Thus God the Holy Spirit, by the Father's design and with full agreement from the Son, *ekballo*ed human Jesus into the wilderness, threw Him out there to be tempted.

Think overtime in a basketball game. Your starting point guard has just fouled out, and you have no choice but to go with a sub. So you throw him out there (*ekballo*) and tell him to break the press and run the offense . . . and he just has to come through.

In our case, the entire starting lineup has fouled out, and if anyone is going to be saved, it is absolutely necessary that Jesus get in the game for us.

Fulfilling the Law, perfect obedience, would be restoring what once was—back when man did live in perfect obedience to God. Mark makes this point with another detail not included in Matthew or Luke: "And He was with the wild animals" (1:13). This doesn't seem to indicate danger; animals weren't the threat Jesus was facing. Instead, it seems to picture man at peace with nature. For a very short time, Adam lived in harmony with all the animals (Gen 2:19–20). It was sin that had so disrupted creation's tranquility (Gen 3:17). But Isaiah prophesied that it would one day be restored (Is 11:6–9). That would happen when man was once again obedient to God. Jesus' words, "The time is fulfilled" (Mk 1:15), surely include this fulfilling of the Law.

That was accomplished in particular when Jesus was tempted by Satan ("in every respect . . . as we are," Heb 4:15) but fully obeyed God and His commands. This—Christ fulfilling the Law on our behalf, in our stead—is the message of the temptation of Christ.

Now the **Old Testament Reading** for Sunday begins, "After these things God tested Abraham." Read Genesis 22:1–18.

What a test! Knowing how it comes out, we still shudder! The King James Version even reads, "God did tempt Abraham," and how tempting it would be to ignore such a command! (We surely ignore much less testing commands of God all too often!) We know Abraham passed the test, but why would God ask this when He never intends human sacrifice? (Deut 12:31; Jer 7:31).

The **Epistle**, James 1:12–18, gives important clarification.

"Let no one say when he is tempted, 'I am being tempted by God,' for God cannot be tempted with evil, and He Himself tempts no one" (1:13). God's test is different, with a different purpose and different result: "Blessed is the man who remains steadfast under trial, for when he has stood the test he will receive the crown of life, which God has promised to those who love Him" (1:12). Testing can strengthen our faith. We pass only by trusting the Lord, as Abraham believed God would raise Isaac back to life (Heb 11:17–19). Then when we've survived, we can often look back and see all the more clearly how God was there for us as He was for Abraham. When a Christian passes one of God's tests, it can also be a witness to others; others see how God enables His people to bear up under suffering (Heb 12:1–3, 11–12).

But what if we fail the test? You can't *ekballo* a sub to take your SAT for you (at least not without committing a felony). No one can take your driver's test for you. Or your black belt qualifier. Or the exam for your real estate license. The test is testing you. Nobody else. That's the point.

But it is for every test we fail—just as for every time we give in to temptation—that Jesus has stepped in for us. Look back at Abraham's test, and see where Christ is: The son whom the father loved (Gen 22:2; Mk 1:11). The wood laid upon the son's back (Gen 22:6; Jn 19:17). The lamb for the sacrifice (Gen 22:7; Jn 1:29). The son back from the dead (Gen 22:13; Mk 16:6). This test is less about Abraham and much more about the heavenly Father and His Son indeed being our substitute. What Jesus did in His confrontation with the devil, God credits to us who are baptized into Christ.

In His Temptation, Jesus Passed the Test God Threw Him Out to Take for Us.

As you hear and speak and chant the other propers this Sunday, listen for reminders that Jesus was thrown into the fray in your place. The **Introit**:

When he calls to Me, I will answer him; I will be with him in trouble; I will rescue him and honor him. With long life I will satisfy him and show him My salvation.

Because you have made the Lord *your dwelling place—the Most High, who is my refuge—no evil shall be allowed to befall you, no plague come near your tent. For He will command His angels concerning you to guard you in all your ways. On their hands they will bear you up, lest you strike your foot against a stone. You will tread on the lion and the adder; the young lion and the serpent you will trample underfoot.*

Glory be to the Father and to the Son and to the Holy Spirit; as it was in the beginning, is now, and will be forever. Amen.

When he calls to Me, I will answer him; I will be with him in trouble; I will rescue him and honor him. With long life I will satisfy him and show him My salvation. (Ps 91:9–13; antiphon: Ps 91:15–15)

The **Psalm**: "Remember not the sins of *my* youth or *my* transgressions; according to *Your steadfast love* remember me, *for the sake of Your goodness*, O Lord!" (Ps 25:7). God sees not our disobedience but Jesus' goodness.

The **Collect**:

O Lord God, You led Your ancient people through the wilderness and brought them to the promised land. Guide the people of Your Church that following our Savior we may walk through the wilderness of this world toward the glory of the world to come; through Jesus Christ, Your Son, our Lord, who lives and reigns with You and the Holy Spirit, one God, now and forever. Amen.

You, Lord Jesus, went into the wilderness because I "walk through the wilderness of this world."

If you're surprised to find "A Mighty Fortress Is Our God" (*LSB* 656, 657) as the **Hymn of the Day** this week, remember that the real struggle of the Reformation was the very battle Jesus, "the valiant One" (656:2), fought for us this week against "the old evil foe" (656:1). Because Jesus passed the test that we all failed, "our victory has been won" (656:4)!

Second Sunday in Lent Year B

READINGS

Genesis 17:1–7, 15–16
Psalm 22:23–31 (antiphon: v 22)
Romans 5:1–11
Mark 8:27–38

HYMN OF THE DAY

LSB 708 "Lord, Thee I Love with All My Heart"

If a season of the church year is reflected by its **Gradual** and, conversely, the Word of God chosen as a Gradual should shape that season, the prime example is probably Lent. Let's hear this clearly every Lenten Sunday:

> *[O come, let us fix our eyes on] Jesus, the founder and perfecter of our faith, who for the joy that was set before Him endured the cross, despising the shame, and is seated at the right hand of the throne of God. (Heb 12:2)*

Though every season truly takes us to the cross, Lent does especially!

Each of the hymnals that most of us remember has included a section of hymns called "Trust." Several of the hymns that *Lutheran Service Book* places in the "Trust" section previous hymnals listed in another section headed "Cross and Comfort." They're very closely related—trust and the cross.

Now the "Cross and Comfort" section of previous hymnals wasn't actually referring to the cross on which Jesus died, at least not directly. These hymns are explicitly about the crosses *we* carry as Christians. But, of course, if not directly, that still connects them very intimately to the cross of Christ. In fact, that's what the propers for Lent 2, Year B, are about: trust, our crosses, and the cross of Jesus.

The **Holy Gospel** will ultimately get us there, but in a way Peter didn't see coming. We'll start with it. Read Mark 8:27–38.

Matthew relates this same telling moment in Jesus' ministry in two Gospel readings in Year A: Matthew 16:13–20 and 16:21–28. You might want to reread portions of our devotion-studies for those two Sundays, Propers 16 and 17 (pp 206 and 210), for further comments on the incident itself.

Essentially, this text teaches us four things.

First, Jesus is the Christ (Mk 8:27–29). People were saying Jesus was somebody very special, but Peter cuts through the preliminaries and gets to the point: "You are the Messiah, the Anointed One of God, whom His faithful people have been awaiting since the fall. You are the one to fulfill all of God's promises. You are the seed of the woman (Gen 3:15), the lion and scepter of Judah (Gen 49:9–10), King David's greater son (2 Sam 7:12), and more." God's Son. Our Savior. We call this Peter's Great Confession, and it surely is our confession as well. Jesus is the reason there is a *Christ*ian Church.

Second, and here's where the cheese begins to bind, if Jesus is the Christ, it means there will indeed be a cross for Him: "And He began to teach them that the Son of Man must suffer many things and be rejected by the elders and the chief priests and the scribes and be killed, and after three days rise again" (Mk 8:31). That shouldn't really be a surprise after hearing Jesus is the Christ, because the prophets had also described the Messiah as the one forsaken by God (Ps 22:1: "My God, My God, why have You forsaken Me?") and the Suffering Servant of Isaiah (Is 53:5: "He was pierced for our transgressions; He was crushed for our iniquities.").

Peter doesn't like this at all (Mk 8:32), because he knows this means, third, that Jesus' followers will also have to suffer crosses. Quite right: "If anyone would come after Me, let him deny himself and take up his cross and follow Me. For whoever would save his life will lose it" (8:34b–35a). If they kill the head, what will they do to the body?

There's the cross! The cross of Jesus. The cross we'll each bear. So where's the comfort part of "Cross and Comfort"? What can we trust when we're suffering our crosses?

That's the plea of the **Introit**:

Remember Your mercy, O LORD, and Your steadfast love, for they have been from of old.

You who fear the LORD, trust in the LORD! He is their help and their shield. The LORD has remembered us; He will bless us; He will bless the house of Israel; He will bless the house of Aaron; He will bless those who fear the LORD, both the small and the great. We will bless the LORD from this time forth and forevermore. Praise the LORD!

Glory be to the Father and to the Son and to the Holy Spirit; as it was in the beginning, is now, and will be forever. Amen.

Remember Your mercy, O LORD, and Your steadfast love, for they have been from of old. (Ps 115:11–13, 18; antiphon: Ps 25:6)

"Remember Your mercy, O LORD. . . . You who fear the LORD, trust in the LORD!" Sure, sure, trust is what we must do when we're carrying crosses. But how can we trust in the Lord when we're suffering?

Likewise, the **Collect**:

> *O God, You see that of ourselves we have no strength. By Your mighty power defend us from all adversities that may happen to the body and from all evil thoughts that may assault and hurt the soul; through Jesus Christ, Your Son, our Lord, who lives and reigns with You and the Holy Spirit, one God, now and forever. Amen.*

We're weak. We have all kinds of physical adversities and our own sinful thoughts to oppress us spiritually. We pray that You, O God, will defend us, but it's hard to trust that when we're hurting and struggling in our sins.

No doubt Abraham asked himself many times how he could trust God's promises. By the time of our **Old Testament Reading**, he'd been waiting almost a century for a son. Pick it up in Genesis 17:1–7, 15–16.

Abram is already seventy-five years old and Sarai sixty-five when God first promises them a son. Hard to believe even then. Now twenty-four more years have passed without a sign of progress.

Many couples know a feeling of deep sadness at being childless. It's probably not accurate to count such suffering (or other burdens like illnesses and lost jobs) among the "crosses" Jesus promises in our Gospel lesson, although some do. (It's probably more precise to say Christian crosses are those sufferings, such as persecutions, that are inflicted upon us *because we are Christians.*) Nevertheless, childlessness is most certainly a burden that can make our trust in God waver.

So God renews that promise to Abram. The name change is important; *Abram* means "exalted father"—ironic, perhaps bitterly so, given the long wait to be a daddy!—but the name *Abraham* means "father of a multitude" (17:5). Just when Abraham might be tempted to fold, God actually raises. Not only will you be a father but a father of many nations, and Sarah will be a mother of many peoples (17:15–16). Notice how emphatic God is about the many and diverse nations, peoples (17:4, 5, 6, 16).

Yet it's all still a promise. Abraham still has to trust something he can't yet see.

And then there's quite surely the most difficult moment to trust God *ever*. The appointed verses from the **Psalm** are Psalm 22:22–31, but recall verse 1, which you read earlier.

David wrote it, undoubtedly amid intense danger, but Jesus cited it. Where? From the cross (Mk 15:34). At that moment, when the Son of God really was forsaken by His Father, suffering damnation for the sins of the world, Jesus calls out this psalm, which is really a psalm of trust. "I will tell of Your name to my brothers; in the midst of the congregation I will praise You" (22:22).

How in the world?

Yes, how? Paul has the answer in our **Epistle**, Romans 5:1–11.

How can "suffering [produce] endurance, and endurance [produce] character, and character [produce] hope"? And how can we "rejoice" in that? (5:3–4). Because "we were reconciled to God by the death of His Son" (5:10).

Here's how it works. Like Peter, we think being followers of the Christ should bring us glory, prosperity, ease. So when we suffer—crosses of persecution, sadness of childlessness, pain of waiting—our natural reaction is to think God must have forsaken, forgotten us. But that simply can never be, "for while we were still weak, at the right time Christ died for the ungodly. . . . While we were still sinners, Christ died for us. . . . While we were enemies we were reconciled to God by the death of His Son" (5:6, 8b, 10a). "*Much more*, now that we are reconciled," we shall be saved by His life (5:10b)! And "*more than that*, we also rejoice in God through our Lord Jesus Christ, through whom we have now received reconciliation" (5:11). When we've been reconciled to God—by such love!—He can never leave us nor forsake us! He must always be with us! So instead of forgotten, we know that our crosses, Christ's sufferings that we share, are the very evidence that we are in Christ! Our crosses mean we share His cross! And in that, we are comforted! And we rejoice! And we trust.

All Peoples May Trust This: That God Remembers Us through Sufferings and Crosses.

See the double meaning? God remembers us through—that is, for the duration of—*our* sufferings and crosses. And He does it, remembers us, through—that is, by means of—*Christ's* cross and sufferings. It's the point Peter misses. He wants the Christ to avoid the cross. But it's the cross that reconciles us to God so that He is with us come whatever may. For now, that means sufferings and crosses. But eventually . . .

The Introit again: "The Lord *has* remembered us; He *will* bless us. . . . We *will* bless the Lord from this time forth and forevermore."

Again the Old Testament Reading: God *did* give Abraham and Sarah a son, Isaac, and through his descendant, Jesus Christ, all the families, nations, peoples of the earth *have* been blessed—and we will be for eternity.

That's how we can trust God *will* "defend us from all adversities that may happen to the body and from all evil thoughts that may assault and hurt the soul," as we ask in the Collect. It is, as always, "through Jesus Christ, Your Son, our Lord." His suffering. His reconciling death on the cross.

Psalm 22, which Jesus cries out from the cross, ends with this: "He has done it." It's just as He cried out from the cross to end His saving work: "It is finished." We're reconciled to our heavenly Father! He cannot forget us nor forsake us.

Oh, and the Gospel teaches *four* things. "For whoever would save his life will lose it, *but*," fourth, "whoever loses his life for My sake and the gospel's will save it" (Mk 8:35). There will be an end to our sufferings.

Our **Hymn of the Day**, "Lord, Thee I Love with All My Heart" (*LSB* 708), comes from the "Trust" section, but it could just as well be called "Cross and Comfort." "Give strength and patience unto me to bear my cross and follow Thee" (st 2). "Forsake me not! I trust Thy Word" (st 1).

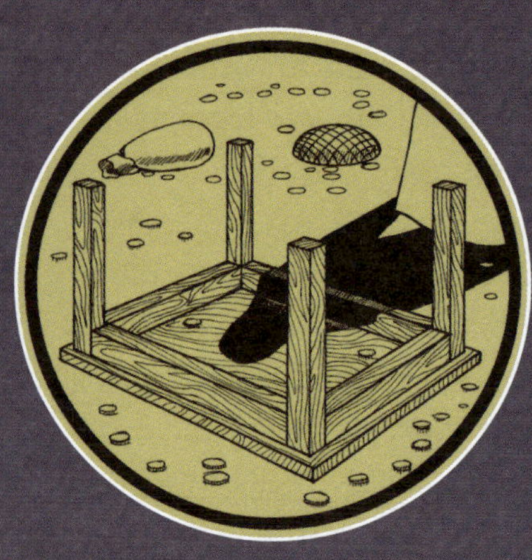

Third Sunday in Lent Year B

READINGS

Exodus 20:1–17
Psalm 19 (antiphon: v 8)
1 Corinthians 1:18–31
John 2:13–22 (23–25)

HYMN OF THE DAY

LSB 823, 824 "May God Bestow on Us His Grace"

Begin looking forward to Sunday morning with the **Gradual** for the season of Lent:

> *[O come, let us fix our eyes on] Jesus, the founder and perfecter of our faith, who for the joy that was set before Him endured the cross, despising the shame, and is seated at the right hand of the throne of God. (Heb 12:2)*

Lent fixes our eyes where they always belong: on Jesus enduring the cross.

How will our journey take us to the cross this week?

Before we arrive at Mount Calvary this Third Sunday in Lent, we'll first pitch our tents for a while before Mount Sinai. The Ten Commandments are surely one of the best—likely *the* best—known of all passages in Scripture. Lutheran kids, asked what they learned in the catechism, often recall, "The Ten Commandments and . . ." hopefully go on from there. The Decalogue is embraced by both Christianity (of all stripes) and Judaism. The Commandments remain the core of American civil religion; many a North American town used to have a plaque of them posted outside city hall. People who don't know *any* of them know the moniker for all of them. In fact, there's so much more to learn from the Ten Commandments than any of us ever will. This is the one week in the entire three-year lectionary that we hear them. Listen carefully on Sunday.

In the meantime, read not only the **Old Testament Reading** itself, Exodus 20:1–17, but the occasion, Exodus 19:1–20:21.

The scene excels even a Cecil B. DeMille epic, doesn't it! Israel has just come out of Egypt, through the Red Sea, and camps before the mountain. God tells Moses His sacred plans for Israel (19:5–6) and commands Israel to prepare for the ultimate summit. On the appointed day, Israel stands together at the foot of Sinai to hear what God has to say, and the fireworks erupt! (19:16–19). Thunder, lightning, earthquake, trumpet blast! Fire and smoke! If anyone gets too close, he's dead (19:21).

Did something get lost between the original and the first time we opened our catechisms and began to memorize, "Thou shalt have no other gods before Me"? Maybe even more by the hundredth time we recited, "You shall have no other gods"? I'm guessing we don't hear the thunder, feel the ground shake, every time we let God's name slip out irreverently, every time we sleep in instead of going to worship, every time we break curfew or the speed limit, every time we shout at our kids, every time we sneak a second glance at someone on the sidewalk, every time we fudge our income tax, every time we delight to bear bad news, every time we're jealous the other guy's house is bigger or her husband is more romantic. See the smoke! Hear the trumpet!

Feel the heat, see the flash as you listen this Sunday. What we did learn in confirmation class wasn't bad either. Sometime before Sunday, get out your catechism and read again each commandment with Martin Luther's explanation. Read slowly, devotionally, with each commandment confessing to God the ways you've ignored it or forgotten what Sinai was like.

Israel *is* feeling the heat! They tremble, retreat (20:18). They know they can't stand in the presence of God. God's holiness overwhelms them, and they know it will destroy them (20:19). That's always the way it is. God is holy. That is, everything about Him is pure and good, and anything conflicting with Him is evil, sinful. Therefore, God cannot tolerate sin, and anything sinful coming into His presence will be destroyed. The Commandments have just declared to Israel what holiness is—and have shown them how very unholy they are. This, above all, is what we learn from the Ten Commandments: God's holiness, our sinfulness, and that in sin we can't stand in the presence of the holy God.

But God's intention that day isn't to destroy Israel. Quite the opposite. It's an unimaginable act of grace that God would appear personally to this nation to establish a covenant. Remember, God has taken the Israelites to be His own special people (19:4). God even prologues the Commandments with this: "I am the Lord your God, who brought you out of the land of Egypt, out of the house of slavery" (20:2). (Judaism, by the way, counts that as the First of the "Ten Words," the literal translation of the Hebrew for the Decalogue.) God fully intended that His people *would* be able to stand in His presence, and *He* would make that possible, just as He had initiated the relationship in the first place.

We know how He would do that, of course, but we would never have come up with the idea. That's the subject of the **Epistle**, 1 Corinthians 1:18–31.

If we were to be holy and thus able to stand in God's presence, the almighty God would have to make it so. How would He do it? Another earthquake—maybe a bigger one yet? A meteor from some distant, uncorrupted corner of the universe? A worldwide flood? That had been done, and the survivors it left were still sinful. Okay, be realistic. Maybe a divinely insightful curriculum that would teach us how to keep all Ten Words perfectly. Or maybe wisdom that would teach us to love one another right now.

"Jews demand signs and Greeks seek wisdom" (1:22) just like those. But what do we preach? What was God's plan? Christ crucified. The word of the cross.

The word of the cross? Christ crucified?

That's foolishness! Dead guys can't save anybody. It's kind of a definition of death.

I was a debater in high school and college. You won by sounding smarter than the other guys, making the judges think you were wise. So I love the way Paul puts us (me!) in our places: "Where is the one who is wise? Where is the scribe? Where is the debater of this age? Has not God made foolish the wisdom of the world?" (1:20). If we think the wise idea would be for God to kick His power into overdrive (whatever that might mean) to make us holy, we're fools. If we think we can wisen up enough to love God and our neighbor and keep the First through Tenth Commandments and earn our standing before the holy God, we're fools.

But almighty God allowing Himself to be killed, holy God taking on Himself the sins of the world, begotten God letting Himself be cast from the presence of His Father—that relieves us of the sin that ruined our standing before God.

None of this made any sense to Jesus' Jewish naysayers. Surely Greeks would have preferred something fathomed by Socrates or Plato or Aristotle. Even Peter didn't get the wisdom of the cross last week. (Remember?) But this is "the power of God and the wisdom of God" (1:24). Christ crucified.

The temple (and before that, the tabernacle, given by God at Sinai immediately after the Commandments) symbolized God's presence with His people and showed His desire that they stand before Him. How were God's people entering His presence in Jesus' day? Read the **Holy Gospel**, John 2:13–25.

You know the Israelites weren't setting up tables to do business that day beneath Sinai! But it's come to this! They're not seeing the lightning, hearing the thunder anymore either! They've forgotten the holiness of God!

Jesus is consumed by this (2:17). And the temple officials are just as angry with Jesus' behavior. "What sign do You show us for doing these things?" (2:18). In other words, "You'd better have some kind of authorization from God Himself!"

So Jesus gives them a sign: "Destroy this temple, and in three days I will raise it up" (2:19). Now there's a foolish sign! We all agree! It was foolishness to the Jews: "It has taken forty-six years to build this temple, and will You raise it up in three days?" (2:20). And to the ears of faith, foolishness—the foolishness of the cross. For "He was speaking about the temple of His body" (2:21). (Notice, by the way, Jesus never says *He* will destroy the temple, as later charged in Mk 14:58. The Jews would destroy His body; He would raise it.) "When therefore He was raised from the dead, His disciples remembered that He had said this, and they believed" (2:22).

About forty years later, the Romans would destroy the Jerusalem temple. So much for it symbolizing God's presence. But that most foolish sign, the temple of Jesus' body destroyed and raised, the foolishness of the cross, has taken away our sins, made us holy. Therefore,

The Most Foolish of Signs Bids Us Stand in the Presence of the Holy God.

Look forward to hearing how the other propers for Sunday will make this point. Especially the **Psalm**, Psalm 19. Contrast David's joy in beholding the majesty of God to the terror Israel felt before God's holiness at Sinai. David knows the pure commandments of the Lord (19:8), but he also knows his Redeemer (19:14).

The antiphon to the **Introit** is the verse John cites for Jesus cleansing the temple:

For zeal for Your house has consumed me, and the reproaches of those who reproach You have fallen on me.

Deliver me from sinking in the mire; let me be delivered from my enemies and from the deep waters. Let not the flood sweep over me, or the deep swallow me up, or the pit close its mouth over me. Answer me, O Lord, for Your steadfast love is good; according to Your abundant mercy, turn to me.

Glory be to the Father and to the Son and to the Holy Spirit; as it was in the beginning, is now, and will be forever. Amen.

For zeal for Your house has consumed me, and the reproaches of those who reproach You have fallen on me. (Ps 69:14–16; antiphon: Ps 69:9)

Then the **Collect** recognizes that when God shows His power as at Mount Sinai, it is always for a gracious purpose rather than simply to terrify. His glory is always in having mercy.

O God, whose glory it is always to have mercy, be gracious to all who have gone astray from Your ways and bring them again with penitent hearts and steadfast faith to embrace and hold fast the unchangeable truth of Your Word; through Jesus Christ, Your Son, our Lord, who lives and reigns with You and the Holy Spirit, one God, now and forever. Amen.

Martin Luther's mission hymn "May God Bestow on Us His Grace (*LSB* 823, 824), our **Hymn of the Day**, conveys both Sinai ("Thou shalt judge the earth, O Lord. . . . Let solemn awe possess us," st 2, 3) and our delight at "the brightness of [God's] face" (st 1) when He looks at us through Jesus' cross.

Fourth Sunday in Lent Year B

READINGS

Numbers 21:4–9
Psalm 107:1–9 (antiphon: v 19)
Ephesians 2:1–10
John 3:14–21

HYMNS OF THE DAY

LSB 571 "God Loved the World So That He Gave" or
Lutheran Service Builder 972 "I Trust, O Christ, in You Alone"

We're beginning each of our devotion-studies this Lenten season with the theme for the season, the **Gradual**:

> *[O come, let us fix our eyes on] Jesus, the founder and perfecter of our faith, who for the joy that was set before Him endured the cross, despising the shame, and is seated at the right hand of the throne of God. (Heb 12:2)*

On this Fourth Sunday in Lent, our propers will quite literally invite us to "fix our eyes on Jesus" and His cross.

If last Sunday featured a blockbuster text, the Ten Commandments, this Sunday doubles that up. This week includes nothing less than John 3:16 and tacks on Ephesians 2:8–10 for good measure. "For God so loved the world . . ." "For by grace you have been saved through faith . . ." Need we say more?

We will.

In a very real sense, those texts teach us all we need to know. But just as we noted last week with the Ten Commandments, we often learn the vital teachings not simply by recitation of great words or by discussing rich theology but by story, by pictures, by images we can see (as we saw recently with the transfiguration). And God's immense love for us, grace and faith, play out vividly this week in a story that fixes our eyes on Jesus and His cross 1,400 years before Jesus' cross.

Read that account, Numbers 21:4–9, this Sunday's **Old Testament Reading**.

We know all about the Israelites grumbling. This time it's because they've waited out nearly all those forty years they were condemned to wander (their parents' fault!), and now a route through Edom could get them to the Promised Land post haste. Nope, can't go that way. Edom refuses to let them pass (Num 20:14–21), and Edom is a relative nation, descended from Jacob's brother, Esau, so God won't let Israel intrude. They're tired of waiting. Besides, they want a new menu—although the description of manna sounds quite delicious (Ex 16:31; Num 11:7–8). And it was free.

Impatient and wanting more. *(Long, reflective pause.)* Another way to say it could be undeserving, ungrateful. And now they're going to die (Num 21:6).

There is nowhere to hide; here they come, the serpents, slithering under the tent even as one slept. Scholars have felt this was a species of snake still identifiable in the Middle East. Its poison causes an intense, burning pain that could be called fiery, often before causing death. It gets God's message across: "We have sinned" (21:7).

Then God is His always-amazing self. He doesn't say, "You made your snake-infested bed; now lie in it." He doesn't even say, "Think about it for a while." Immediately He commands Moses to give the deliverance (21:8). That's grace. It's totally undeserved and purely from God's love for His sinful people.

It's ugly, no doubt. Don't envision finest craftsmanship in shining brass. This was a rush-job *snake*. We in the New Testament age have no difficulty seeing another image in that bronze serpent lifted up on the pole. But God's ancient people see that fixing their eyes on that grotesque figure saves them. That's faith. They believe the promise God speaks, and, believing, they look up. Realize that it isn't the *looking* that saved them; it is the believing. For when they believe, they of course look.

Here's an interesting footnote: Israel kept this bronze serpent for seven hundred years, and it became an idol for them. Good King Hezekiah had to destroy it (2 Ki 18:4). Faith, which is never anything more than receiving what God has done, can be perverted.

Now the **Holy Gospel** will include John 3:16, but, there's a story behind it. Read John 3:14–21.

In so many different ways, God gave His Old Testament people hints of how His Son would eventually come to save them. Many are those direct prophecies that He would, for example, be born in Bethlehem (Micah 5:2) of a virgin (Is 7:14) and suffer and die (Is 53:5) to break Satan's power and reconcile us to God (Gen 3:15). We sometimes call these rectilinear prophecies. But countless other Old Testament passages give pictures or images of Christ through ancient people or places or actions. The passover lamb (its blood spread over the door), the temple (the place God dwelt among His people), and David (God's anointed king) are of this type. In fact, we call them "types," and the New Testament realities they point to we call "antitypes."

Jesus tells us explicitly that the bronze serpent is a type of Him, the antitype, being lifted up on the cross: "As Moses lifted up the serpent in the wilderness, so must the Son of Man be lifted up" (Jn 3:14). In other words, God giving the bronze serpent was a picture of God loving the world so much that He gave His Son. And God inviting the Israelites to look to the bronze serpent and live is an image of believing in the only Son and not perishing but having eternal life. This is how we can understand John 3:16—and understand God's grace and faith.

You see, God loving the world isn't just a sweet, "Oh, yes, God is love," as in a big ol' softy. It's not just a sweet idea to stitch on throw pillows. It's certainly not a mantra to memorize and meme. The world is impatient, undeserving, wanting-more ingrates. We are creatures who've been given everything we have—life, food, home—and do nothing but grumble. The world poisoned itself with the first snakebite, and we all died.

And then God, loving the world, couldn't be just Pops telling his kids it's okay after all. No, John 3:16 is the Father's only Son being lifted up on an ugly, roughly cut pole to hang until He'd paid for every sin of that whole ungrateful world—that "loved the darkness rather than the light because their works were evil" (3:19), that didn't even want Him. But God *did* love the world that much.

That's grace.

And "whoever believes in Him"—that's faith. It's not a universalist throwaway that now everybody goes to heaven. But neither is it a burden placed on us to have some kind of revved up psyche or some intense experience that makes us weep with joy. It's pathetic wilderness wanderers who really only want their skin saved but who believe God will save them by that ugly thing up on the pole. Maybe they're too weak, too near death to lift their heads. But they believe that God has done what it took.

That's John 3:16.

We discover the same in the **Epistle**, Ephesians 2:1–10. Maybe you can recite verses 8–9 and even 10 before you read it.

Could you? "For by grace you have been saved through faith. And this is not your own doing; it is the gift of God, not a result of works, so that no one may boast. For we are His workmanship, created in Christ Jesus for good works, which God prepared beforehand, that we should walk in them."

Was grace as easy as that is to say? We "were by nature children of wrath" (2:3b), "indulging the desires of the flesh" (2:3a NASB). We wanted a new menu, just like Israel, something tastier, something racier. We were just as ungrateful, not at all lovable, and we might even think unforgivable.

But God is "rich in mercy." "Because of the great love with which He loved us," the John 3:16 love, the love that was His Son lifted up on a pole, God "raised us up with [Christ] and seated us with Him in the heavenly places" (Eph 2:4, 6). Look! Now we're the ones lifted up—but in glory!—because Christ was lifted up in shame! That's grace!

And faith? Remember, faith can be perverted. It can be made into something we do: believe *enough*, *decide* to believe in Jesus, *give* my heart to Christ. Well, we "were dead in [our] trespasses and sins" (2:1). When the snake bit, you were dead. And spiritual corpses don't decide, don't give, don't hold on tight enough. Those Israelites, face down in the sand, that burning sensation killing them, wouldn't claim they'd done a thing when Moses said, "Look and live." Faith knows that it can do nothing and believes that the One on the pole has done everything. That's Ephesians 2.

The Son of Man Lifted Up on the Cross, Pictured by the Serpent Lifted Up in the Wilderness, Is the Highest Act of Grace, That the Dead Who Look to Him in Faith Are Saved.

Listen for the cues to our Theme in the other propers Sunday. In the Psalm, the redeemed of the Lord "wandered in desert wastes" and were "hungry and thirsty" just as the Israelites were. But when they cried to the Lord in faith rather than in grumbling, He "delivered them from their distress" (Ps 107:4, 5, 6).

In the **Introit**, the psalmist longs to fix his eyes on Jesus, to "gaze upon the beauty of the Lord."

The Lord is my light and my salvation; whom shall I fear? The Lord is the stronghold of my life; of whom shall I be afraid?

Though an army encamp against me, my heart shall not fear; though war arise against me, yet I will be confident. One thing have I asked of the Lord, that will I seek after: that I may dwell in the house of the Lord all the days of my life, to gaze upon the beauty of the Lord and to inquire in His temple. For He will hide me in His shelter in the day of trouble; He will conceal me under the cover of His tent; He will lift me high upon a rock.

Glory be to the Father and to the Son and to the Holy Spirit; as it was in the beginning, is now, and will be forever. Amen.

The Lord is my light and my salvation; whom shall I fear? The Lord is the stronghold of my life; of whom shall I be afraid? (Ps 27:3–5; antiphon: Ps 27:1)

Yes, Jesus lifted up on the cross is "beauty" and means "He will lift me high" too.

That is surely only by grace, for "we deserve only punishment," as the **Collect** says:

Almighty God, our heavenly Father, Your mercies are new every morning; and though we deserve only punishment, You receive us as Your children and provide for all our needs of body and soul. Grant that we may heartily acknowledge Your merciful goodness, give thanks for all Your benefits, and serve You in willing obedience; through Jesus Christ, Your Son, our Lord, who lives and reigns with You and the Holy Spirit, one God, now and forever. Amen.

Only by grace received by faith that "You receive us as Your children."

Two **Hymns of the Day** are offered. Quite obviously by its title, *LSB* 571 paraphrases John 3:16. The second hymn, "I Trust, O Christ, in You Alone," is accessible in Lutheran Service Builder and in *Lutheran Worship* 357 and *The Lutheran Hymnal* 319.

Fifth Sunday in Lent Year B

READINGS

Jeremiah 31:31–34
Psalm 119:9–16 (antiphon: v 10)
Hebrews 5:1–10
Mark 10:(32–34) 35–45

HYMN OF THE DAY

LSB 430 "My Song Is Love Unknown"

Throughout the season of Lent, we know we can look forward to hearing the message of the **Gradual** each Sunday morning:

> *[O come, let us fix our eyes on] Jesus, the founder and perfecter of our faith, who for the joy that was set before Him endured the cross, despising the shame, and is seated at the right hand of the throne of God. (Heb 12:2)*

We know we're going to hear about the cross of Jesus.

Then, if we read ahead, we begin to get more specific ideas about how the suffering and death of Christ will be applied to our lives this week. We peruse the Old Testament Reading, the Epistle, the Gospel lesson, and maybe the other propers, and we begin to notice a hint here, an explicit reference there, and implications of the cross everywhere.

A most engaging aspect of the study may be the questions it raises. What does this verse mean? Who's he talking about here? What's this reading got to do with that one? You may not figure out all the answers, but that makes going to church on Sunday all the more interesting. Will the pastor talk about this? Will he answer my question in the sermon? Pastors are actually trained to read the lessons with that sort of thinking in mind: What questions might occur to my people as they hear these readings during the service? How can I handle those in my message?

The readings for Lent 5, Year B, are loaded with potential questions. Before we go on with our devotion-study, therefore, read all three of the primary lessons: Old Testament, Epistle,

Gospel. As you read each one, think about—or even jot down—any questions that come up for you. Then we'll resume here together and go through the readings one at a time. We can't guarantee we'll answer all of your questions, but we hope we can answer some. And Sunday's still coming. Your pastor will surely be delighted to tackle any he and we haven't covered. Okay? Go read.

All right. You've done your assignment. Now glance back at the **Old Testament Reading**, Jeremiah 31:31–34, to refresh your memory.

What questions did you have? When are "the days" that are coming (31:31)? What exactly is the "new covenant" (31:31)? Is it the same thing as the New Testament, these years since Jesus came? Is the new covenant a new deal, like a different way we get to heaven? Is this covenant just with the Jews? (31:31–32). What does "I will put My law within them, and I will write it on their hearts" (31:33) mean? How about this: "No longer shall each one teach his neighbor and each his brother, saying, 'Know the Lord,' for they shall all know Me" (31:34)? Is that talking about when we're in heaven? Because we'll certainly still tell people about the Lord until we get there, right? So the whole new covenant isn't until heaven?

That's a lot to cover! Here we go. "The days are coming" is a frequent prophetic phrase (especially in Jeremiah) that sometimes refers to the near future, sometimes to the end of the world, but often to the messianic age—the time that began with Jesus' first coming to earth and continues on for eternity. Here, we'll see definite indicators the Lord is speaking of the messianic age.

The new covenant must, obviously, replace an old one, and we know God placed lots of stipulations on His Old Testament people that help identify that old covenant: the Sabbath, the temple, sacrifices, feasts like the Passover, the priesthood descended from Aaron, and so on. God established many of these at Sinai, beginning when He announced the Ten Commandments, and all this was ratified with the "blood of the covenant" upon the people (Ex 24:3–8).

The reason we don't observe these covenant stipulations anymore is because Christ has initiated the new covenant. It was inaugurated with Jesus' death: "This . . . is the new covenant in My blood," He said the night before His death as He instituted His Supper (Lk 22:20). The old covenant is entirely fulfilled in Christ (Col 2:16–17).

But what, really, is the essence of the new covenant? The Lord is clear: "I will forgive their iniquity, and I will remember their sin no more" (Jer 31:34). Hmm. Didn't forgiveness happen in the Old Testament? Or were Old Testament people saved some other way? And the part about no one saying "Know the Lord" anymore "for they shall all know Me." We're living in the New Testament (messianic) age, but we still tell people about Jesus. And not everyone knows Him!

Here's the key: There have been markers in time by which we see the old and new covenants (Sinai with its laws through those ancient centuries, the cross and the sacraments ever since). But the covenants themselves are *not periods of time*. They are *actually*

Law and Gospel—old covenant Law, new covenant Gospel. God is outside of time, and from all eternity, He's seen everyone the same way. Everyone in every age since Adam and Eve has been conceived in sin and therefore under the old covenant, the Law. We were *all* obligated to keep the Law, and not just Israel and Judah, but we all broke that covenant (31:32). However, what Jesus did on a particular date on Calvary, God has also seen from all eternity. And the Gospel is equally for all people of all epochs. Adam, Eve, Abraham, the children of Israel, we today are all saved by the new covenant—the Gospel that Christ has fulfilled all the Law's demands for us.

Then all who are in the new covenant, that is, all who believe this Gospel of Christ, know the Lord; His Law is written in their hearts. We do, of course, speak the name of the Lord to fellow believers, but not as introducing a stranger. And we do most eagerly say "Know the Lord" to those who are not yet in the new covenant—those who do not yet know the Gospel of Christ. Yes, this new covenant will be forever in heaven, but it is also now in the messianic age in which we are already living. Does that answer your question(s)?

Ready for the **Epistle**? Review Hebrews 5:1–10. What questions did you note?

Who's Melchizedek (5:6)? Did Jesus really pray "with loud cries and tears" (5:7)? How could Jesus *learn* obedience and be *made* perfect (5:8–9)? He's already perfect, and He knows everything! How are those for starters?

Way back in Abraham's day, Melchizedek was a priest of God and king of Salem (which means "peace," from the Hebrew *shalom*, and which later became Jeru*salem*, Gen 14:18–20). Because we know nothing else about Melchizedek's background, Hebrews sees him as a type of Christ (Heb 7:1–10). (Some have speculated that he *was* Christ!) The point here is that Jesus, like Melchizedek, is a priest who isn't descended from Aaron (and Aaron's patriarch, Levi). That is, He's a priest of the new covenant.

The other point is that Christ did not take upon Himself this honor, for no priest—either Melchizedek or Aaron's sons—would ever do so (5:4–6). On the contrary, even Christ would take up the office of great High Priest only if called by God. That's because it meant a horrific task even the Son of God could not desire. We know Jesus suffered terribly on the cross, and we picture the agony of blood He sweated in Gethsemane. But since He is eternal God, perhaps we imagine that the anguish was only *so* bad. In reality, of all living humans, only He could know just *how* awful hell would be—and He knew it was coming down on Him. Yes, add to your mental painting of Jesus in Gethsemane loud cries and tears!

Likewise, the very human Jesus did learn from His sufferings and was made perfect. Just as He didn't use His omnipotence to save Himself from death, He only used His omniscience when it would serve His salvific purpose. The rest of the time, He relied on the very same source we have for knowing God's will: He studied the Scriptures. (Remember that back when He was twelve, He listened, asked, and increased in wisdom, Lk 2:46, 52.) Similarly, the fully human Jesus, perfect from His conception by the Holy Spirit, was made perfect, complete, by completing His saving sufferings. That finished His perfect obedience to the Father, just as it finished the task of redeeming us.

By now, we likely know the answer to this question in the **Holy Gospel**, Mark 10:32–45: What is the cup Jesus must drink (10:38)? If Jesus was to give us the cup of the blood of the new covenant, He would have to drink the cup of suffering the Father had for Him—after all those loud cries and tears.

The more difficult question might be, this: Why don't James and John and the other disciples get it? We'll find the answer to that if we think of those places our minds go when God's Word is being taught to us—places like honors I might gain for myself.

How very different is that from the psalmist's devotion to everything God will say to him in His Word: the **Psalm**, Psalm 119:9–16.

Last question: What's all this about? Perhaps this:

**IN THE NEW COVENANT,
NO ONE TAKES HONOR UPON HIMSELF,
BUT EVEN THE GREATEST
BECAME OUR SERVANT,
LEARNING OBEDIENCE FROM SUFFERING.**

As you chant the **Introit** Sunday, hear Jesus' voice pleading for mercy:

Vindicate me, O God, and defend my cause against an ungodly people, from the deceitful and unjust man deliver me!

I love the LORD, because He has heard my voice and my pleas for mercy. Because He inclined His ear to me, therefore I will call on Him as long as I live. The snares of death encompassed me; the pangs of Sheol laid hold on me; I suffered distress and anguish. Then I called on the name of the LORD: "O LORD, I pray, deliver my soul!" For You have delivered my soul from death, my eyes from tears, my feet from stumbling.

Glory be to the Father and to the Son and to the Holy Spirit; as it was in the beginning, is now, and will be forever. Amen.

Vindicate me, O God, and defend my cause against an ungodly people, from the deceitful and unjust man deliver me! (Ps 116:1–4, 8; antiphon: Ps 43:1)

Then as you ask God in the **Collect** to look down on us mercifully in His great goodness, think of Jesus' goodness in making Himself our servant:

Almighty God, by Your great goodness mercifully look upon Your people that we may be governed and preserved evermore in body and soul; through Jesus Christ, Your Son, our Lord, who lives and reigns with You and the Holy Spirit, one God, now and forever. Amen.

End with the **Hymn of the Day**, "My Song Is Love Unknown" (*LSB* 430). See how Jesus came not to be served but to serve.

Palm Sunday / Sunday of the Passion Year B

READINGS

John 12:12–19 (Processional)
Zechariah 9:9–12
Psalm 118:19–29 (antiphon: v 26)
or Psalm 31:9–16 (antiphon: v 5)
Philippians 2:5–11
Mark 14:1–15:47
or Mark 15:1–47
or John 12:20–43

HYMNS OF THE DAY

LSB 442 "All Glory, Laud, and Honor" (Processional)
LSB 438 "A Lamb Goes Uncomplaining Forth"

It's Palm Sunday!

"Rejoice greatly, O daughter of Zion! Shout aloud, O daughter of Jerusalem! Behold, your king is coming to you; righteous and having salvation is He, humble and mounted on a donkey, on a colt, the foal of a donkey" (Zech 9:9).

And "the large crowd that had come to the feast heard that Jesus was coming to Jerusalem. So they took branches of palm trees and went out to meet Him, crying out, 'Hosanna!'" (Jn 12:12–13). Read the **Introit**:

Blessèd is he who comes in the name of the LORD! We bless you from the house of the LORD.

Lift up your heads, O gates! And be lifted up, O ancient doors, that the King of glory may come in. Who is this King of glory? The LORD, strong and mighty, the LORD, mighty in battle! Lift up your heads, O gates! And lift them up, O ancient doors, that the King of glory may come in. Who is this King of glory? The LORD of hosts, He is the King of glory!

Blessèd is he who comes in the name of the LORD! We bless you from the house of the LORD. (Ps 24:7–10; antiphon: Ps 118:26)

It's Palm Sunday, or it will be when you arrive for worship. You know the story well. Your congregation may even act it out with a processional and palm fronds. Palm Sunday is a festive day in our congregations. Years ago, it was widely chosen to be Confirmation Day, with first Communion to follow on Maundy Thursday. In Jerusalem that year two millennia ago, the first day of the week, the week of Passover, it was far more festive. The Messiah was coming!

It was a great day! But we have to read on.

In our devotion-study for Palm Sunday last year (Year A), we talked about the dual character of Palm Sunday. Remember, it's also Sunday of the Passion. It's the first day of Holy Week, which takes us to the arrest, trial, suffering, and death of Jesus. From the festivities of Palm Sunday, we go forward to the cross—and even the appointed lessons for this day take us there. (If you like, look back at last year's devotion-study, p 98, for more on the why and how of this Palm Sunday/Sunday of the Passion pairing.) So we can't just shout "Hosanna!" today. We have to read on.

That might seem disappointing. Peter, you recall, six weeks ago, would have loved to camp out forever on the Mount of Transfiguration, never having to do this whole Lenten thing at all. And four weeks ago, he was quite ready to have Jesus be a Palm Sunday processional sort of Christ but would hear nothing of Jesus' next instruction about the cross. Palm Sunday with adoring crowds could be a nice place to stop and stay.

But if we read on, the story actually gets better—bitterly, agonizingly, but better.

From Palm Sunday, Read On to See How Jesus Brings Us to a Greater Glory by Humbling Himself to Death on a Cross.

We opened with the first verse of our **Old Testament Reading**, Zechariah 9:9–12, and indeed the King is coming mounted on a donkey. But now, read the rest of the lesson.

The king riding into Jerusalem conjures up just the images the Jews crave—of David returning after routing Philistines or Arameans. The crowds project where that might go with their present state of affairs. But read on: "I will cut off the chariot *from Ephraim* and the war horse *from Jerusalem*" (9:10a). The problem here? It's Jerusalem and Israel laying down their weapons—not Philistines or Arameans . . . or Romans. The Messiah will "speak peace to the nations" (9:10b). Yeah, what will that accomplish? The Romans aren't going to pull out because He asks them politely.

Well, in fact, this new Davidic king would rule—and rule a far greater empire than His famous ancestor. Greater by far even than the Jerusalem crowds could imagine: "From sea to sea, and . . . to the ends of the earth." But the bloodshed to accomplish that would be "the blood of [His] covenant with [Israel]" (9:10c, 11a). There's that new covenant language we heard last week. And we know whose blood it will be. It will be given to His disciples four days from now and shed for the sins of the world in five.

Next, the **Psalm** for Palm Sunday. We already heard verse 26a in the antiphon to our Introit: "Blessèd is he who comes in the name of the Lord!" But read Psalm 118:19–29.

The Palm Sunday procession's in there all right: "Open to me the gates of righteousness, that I may enter through them and give thanks to the LORD. This is the gate of the LORD; the righteous shall enter through it" (118:19–20).

But read on: "The stone that the builders rejected has become the cornerstone" (118:22). And soon we'll read still further about Jesus and His disciples singing a hymn as they left the Upper Room that Thursday night for the Garden of Gethsemane (Mk 14:26). That hymn was very possibly Psalm 118; it was a climactic element of the Passover liturgy. Jesus knows where the hymn is sending Him. The one the crowds are now blessing as coming in the name of the Lord will be rejected by His own people and killed. The palm branches and hosannas will be short-lived. But keep reading. The rejected one will become the cornerstone.

The **Palm Sunday Processional Gospel**, John 12:12–19, is, of course, the familiar story itself, but don't miss this: "His disciples did not understand these things at first, *but when Jesus was glorified, then* they remembered that these things had been written about Him and had been done to Him" (12:16). See that? The real glory isn't there yet. It is still coming.

For more on that, read the **alternate Gospel**, John 12:20–43.

The dust seems to save settled a bit. At least Jesus is off His donkey. Now it's time to get down to the real business of the week: "The hour has come for the Son of Man to be glorified" (12:23). All the hubbub, that isn't the glory. Here's how Jesus will truly be glorified: "'If [a grain of wheat] dies, it bears much fruit. . . . And I, when I am lifted up from the earth, will draw all people to Myself.' He said this to show by what kind of death He was going to die" (12:24b, 32–33).

This is not the kind of glory people want. Peter hadn't wanted it. And by now, "many even of the authorities believed in [Jesus], but for fear of the Pharisees they did not confess it, so that they would not be put out of the synagogue; for they loved the glory that comes from man more than the glory that comes from God" (12:42–43).

Jesus' glory will be the glory from God, and it will come by giving His life on the cross: "'Now is My soul troubled. And what shall I say? 'Father, save Me from this hour'? But for this purpose I have come to this hour. Father, glorify Your name.' Then a voice came from heaven: 'I have glorified it, and I will glorify it again'" (12:27–28).

The Father is bidding us to read the climactic events of Holy Week. Palm Sunday cannot be Jesus' greatest glory. We'll see that next Thursday, Friday, Saturday, and Sunday. But already this Sunday the lectionary has us read ahead, the **Passion Gospel**, Mark 14:1–15:47.

This is glory: A woman anointing Jesus with costly perfume. "She has anointed My body beforehand for burial," Jesus said (14:8).

This is glory: Jesus gathers one last time with His disciples and gives them "My blood of the covenant, which is poured out for many" (14:24).

This is glory: Jesus prays desperately in the Garden of Gethsemane, "Yet not what I will, but what You will" (14:36).

This is glory: Jesus not fighting, not fleeing arrest, but going willingly to "let the Scriptures be fulfilled" (14:49).

This is glory: "'Are You the Christ, the Son of the Blessed?' And Jesus said, 'I am, and you will see the Son of Man seated at the right hand of Power, and coming with the clouds of heaven'" (14:61–62).

This is glory: "Jesus made no further answer, so that Pilate was amazed" (15:5).

This is glory: The inscription of the charge against Him, "The King of the Jews" (15:26).

This is glory: "Save Yourself, and come down from the cross!" (15:30). And He did not.

This is glory: "My God, My God, why have You forsaken Me?" (15:34). He is the eternal Son of God forsaken by His Father so that we will never be.

This is glory: "When the centurion, who stood facing Him, saw that in this way He breathed His last, he said, 'Truly this man was the Son of God!'" (15:39).

Paul sums all this up in the **Epistle**, Philippians 2:5–11, with one word: "therefore" (διό, *dio*, in Greek). "*Therefore* God has highly exalted" Jesus (2:9). In other words, Jesus was exalted, glorified, *because* He read on past Palm Sunday and "humbled Himself by becoming obedient to the point of death, even death on a cross" (2:8). What we call Jesus' state of exaltation could only be possible *after* His state of humiliation (voluntarily not using fully all of His divine powers). For while the Son of God has always been all glorious, the human Christ is now exalted by the Father for completing the task God deems most glorious: redeeming us.

That means reading on from Palm Sunday to the cross not only brings us to Jesus' greater glory. It brings that greater glory also to us! By Jesus' cross, we "receive the promised eternal inheritance." The **Gradual** for Holy Week:

[Christ] entered once for all into the holy places, by means of His own blood, thus securing an eternal redemption. Therefore He is the mediator of a new covenant, so that those who are called may receive the promised eternal inheritance. He sent redemption to His people; He has commanded His covenant forever. (Heb 9:12a, c, 15a; Ps 111:9a)

We are made "partakers of His resurrection." The **Collect**:

Almighty and everlasting God, You sent Your Son, our Savior Jesus Christ, to take upon Himself our flesh and to suffer death upon the cross. Mercifully grant that we may follow the example of His great humility and patience and be made partakers of His resurrection; through the same Jesus Christ, our Lord, who lives and reigns with You and the Holy Spirit, one God, now and forever. Amen.

"Today I declare that I will restore to you double" (Zech 9:12).

"Save us, . . . O Lord!" (Ps 118:25). That is, in Hebrew, "Hosanna!" And He does.

Look forward to Palm Sunday morning by singing both **Hymns of the Day**, "All Glory, Laud, and Honor" and a "A Lamb Goes Uncomplaining Forth."

Holy Week and Holy Thursday Year B

READINGS

Mark 14:1–15:47 (Passion)

Exodus 24:3–11
Psalm 116:12–19 (antiphon: v 17)
1 Corinthians 10:16–17
Mark 14:12–26

or

Exodus 12:1–14
Psalm 116:12–19 (antiphon: v 17)
1 Corinthians 11:23–32
John 13:1–17, 31b–35

HYMN OF THE DAY

LSB 617 "O Lord, We Praise Thee"

That Was the Week That Was was a short-lived comedy series that ran on British and American TV in the early 1960s. It aired live and took a humorous look at the news of the past week. Although remembered as groundbreaking in television satire, neither the original British nor subsequent American version lasted beyond two seasons. The show would seem to have affirmed the premise of its theme song: "That was the week that was, it's over, let it go . . ."

Still, the title sounds as if it's attaching great weight and importance to a particular week in history.

The week before us now, Holy Week, is deadly serious. It is the most important week in human history. And while the events of Holy Week really did happen over a fixed period of days now long ago, this week can never be seen as over, just let it go. It's certainly the week that was, but it's more. This is the week that continues to give meaning to every week since.

**THIS IS THE WEEK THAT IS
THAT IS FIRST FOR US—
THE DAY, THE HOUR WHEN JESUS POURS
OUT HIS LOVE FOR US, HIS BODY.**

Holy Week is so important that the lectionary assigns readings for every day, the only week of the year like that. The Gospels for this Monday, Tuesday, and Wednesday are, respectively, the Passion accounts in the three Synoptic Gospels: Matthew 26:1–27:66; Mark 14:1–15:47; and Luke 22:1–23:56—or readings from John 12 and 13: 12:1–23; 12:23–50; 13:16–38. If you can, set aside time to read some or all of these. You might even wish to look at comments on these readings in our past and future devotion-studies: Holy Week, Year A (p 102), for Matthew; Sunday of the Passion, Year B (p 352), for Mark and John; and Sunday of the Passion, Year C, (p 582) for Luke. That's a lot to ask, but if at all possible, at least rehearse again the grand sweep of events and special services ahead by reading Mark's Passion account for Year B: Mark 14 and 15.

The **Introit** and more of the **Psalm** from which it's taken, Psalm 116:12–19, are the same for Holy Thursday in all three years. Comments on these are also offered in our devotion-study for this day in Year A (p 102). Read the Introit and Psalm prayerfully. Jesus likely prayed these very words during the liturgy of the Last Supper.

Gracious is the Lord, and righteous; our God is merciful.

I love the Lord, because He has heard my voice and my pleas for mercy. Because He inclined His ear to me, therefore I will call on Him as long as I live. The snares of death encompassed me; the pangs of Sheol laid hold on me; I suffered distress and anguish. Then I called on the name of the Lord: "O Lord, I pray, deliver my soul!"

Gracious is the Lord, and righteous; our God is merciful. (Ps 116:1–4; antiphon: Ps 116:5)

The setting of Jesus' Last Supper, the Passover, recalls the month, the week, and the night that, more than any other, was in the formation of the nation of Israel. And God wants to be sure the Israelites will never let it go. Read Exodus 12:1–14, one of the **Old Testament Reading** options for Holy Thursday.

The first Passover night can be seen as the birthday of the nation of Israel. Jacob's brood, just a handful of people, seventy-plus, had gone down to Egypt 430 years before, a squabbling ragtag band. They'd multiplied greatly but then been enslaved. By the time God sends Moses to lead them out, they don't even know who this Yahweh is that is promising to deliver them. It is really only the previous nine plagues against Egypt that make them begin to think of themselves as one unified and special people. But from here on, they will have a heritage: "This month shall be for you the beginning of months. It shall be the first month of the year for you" (12:2). Henceforth, first on their calendars *and* first in importance.

The doorposts are vertical; the lintel lay horizontally across the top (12:7). For all of us these years later, God couldn't have painted an easier picture to interpret. But this will also establish the very way of life for Israel: that blood is God's way of saving. Just three months later at Sinai, God commands a whole host of bloody sacrifices by which He forgives the Israelites their sins.

"That night," that very night (12:12), the Lord passes through the land of Egypt and kills the firstborn of every family of the Egyptians. But "the blood shall be a sign for you, on the houses where you are. And when I see the blood, I will pass over you, and no plague will befall you" (12:13). Thus that very night, the Passover event saves Israel from slavery; Pharaoh orders them to leave in haste.

From then on, that would be the day that was for Israel—and was always to continue to be: "This day shall be for you a memorial day, and you shall keep it as a feast to the LORD; throughout your generations, as a statute forever, you shall keep it as a feast" (12:14).

Now it is something like the 1,475th Passover. At various times, Israel has been more or less faithful in observing the memorial feast, but this night, among this small group, the Passover is most faithfully kept. Read the primary **Holy Gospel**, Mark 14:12–26.

The "first day of Unleavened Bread" actually begins a week in which no leaven is to be eaten or even found in the house (Ex 12:15–20). So there is much preparation involved (Mk 14:12). The house first had to be purged of any leaven, and then there is the meticulous ritual of preparing the meal—blood of the spotless lamb spewing out as its throat was cut, the bread kneaded and baked without yeast, the bitter herbs (Ex 12:8) symbolizing centuries of hardship in Egypt. Since, like so many Jews, Jesus and His disciples had traveled to Jerusalem for the feast, this has to be done in a house that welcomed Jesus as a guest. This clearly seems to be a case in which Jesus uses His omniscience to facilitate the arrangements (14:13–16). He knows that this night will begin the climactic events of His mission.

The disciples are still a step behind. They are sorrowful at the announcement that one of them will betray Jesus (14:18–19), but there seems to be no outrage; such shocking news doesn't end the party. (Mark has earlier told us that Judas will be the betrayer, 14:10–11, but that's not specified here.)

Then comes the moment *we've* all been waiting for—but one the disciples could not possibly have foreseen: "As they were eating, He took bread, and after blessing it broke it and gave it to them, and said, 'Take; this is My body.' And He took a cup, and when He had given thanks He gave it to them, and they all drank of it. And He said to them, 'This is My blood of the covenant, which is poured out for many'" (14:22–24). This is the week Jesus pours out His blood for us. And it will continue to be that week "until that day when" Jesus drinks of the cup again with us "new in the kingdom of God" (14:25).

The **Collect** for Holy Thursday:

O Lord, in this wondrous Sacrament You have left us a remembrance of Your passion. Grant that we may so receive the sacred mystery of Your body and blood that the fruits of Your redemption may continually be manifest in us; for You live and reign with the Father and the Holy Spirit, one God, now and forever. Amen.

One of our Post-Communion Collects names the two chief "fruits" of Christ's redemption in the Sacrament as "faith toward You," almighty God, and "fervent love toward one another" *(LSB*, pp 166, 183, 201, 212, 218). The first is faith—that is, believing that God does for us what He promises, especially in the Supper. Read the **Epistle** for Holy Thursday, 1 Corinthians 10:16–17.

The "cup of blessing," "the bread that we break," aren't they each "a participation" in the blood and body of Christ (10:16)? Paul's asking, but the question is rhetorical! "Yes!" Paul is saying. Putting it in the form of a question invites us to be just as emphatic. "Participation" translates the Greek κοινωνία, *koinonia*, that beautiful word that describes intimate sharing, fellowship. At the Lord's Table, we receive the true body and blood of Jesus.

A chief purpose of Christ giving Himself to us this way is to strengthen our faith. Jesus' words intend just that: "This is My body. . . . This is My blood." "When you receive these, you can be certain that everything I did on the cross I did for you, because My very body and blood, killed and shed on the cross, have come into your body!" What a tragedy when such certainty of forgiveness, life, and salvation is undermined by denying that Jesus' body and blood are truly present. O Lord, grant that that fruit of the Sacrament, faith in Your promise, would never be taken from us!

The second is love for one another. Paul says we who share the "one bread" are "one body" (10:17). Loving one another as one body becomes a reality because of the hour that *is*—when Jesus pours out His love for us. Read the **alternate Holy Gospel**, John 13:1–17, 31b–35:

"When Jesus knew that His hour had come to depart out of this world to the Father, having loved His own who were in the world, He loved them to the end" (13:1). Jesus' love for the disciples is, of course, more than doing the menial task of foot washing. "To the end" would be loving them to His death the next day. That's why Peter desperately needs to be washed.

Our love for one another, then, will also be so much more than a bath ritual here or there. "A new commandment I give to you, that you love one another: just as I have loved you" (13:34). This is the basis for our familiar name for Holy Thursday: Maundy Thursday (the Latin *mandatum*, "commandment"). Jesus' "hour" of loving us bids us fill every hour, day, week with acts of love for our neighbors' real needs of body and soul.

Such a week as this actually also offers a **Hymn of the Day** for each: Monday, "Lamb of God, Pure and Holy" (*LSB* 434); Tuesday, "Upon the Cross Extended" (*LSB* 453); Wednesday, "When I Survey the Wondrous Cross" (*LSB* 425, 426); and Thursday, Martin Luther's hymn for Holy Communion, "O Lord, We Praise Thee" (*LSB* 617). Sing them all! This is the week that is!

Many of our congregations will strip the altar, the entire chancel, as the service on Maundy Thursday concludes. The week that was will now become what it is—the week of our redemption! The day, the hour is here for Jesus to pour out His love for us, His Body, by pouring out His life.

A note for Good Friday and Holy Saturday: Since Good Friday and Holy Saturday use the same propers for Years A, B, and C, you'll find the devotion-studies for those days in Year A, pages 106 and 110. The devotion-study for Easter Sunday, Year B, appears on the next page.

The Resurrection of Our Lord Year B

READINGS

Isaiah 25:6–9
Psalm 16 (antiphon: v 10)
1 Corinthians 15:1–11
Mark 16:1–8

Exodus 15:1–11
Psalm 118:15–29 (antiphon: v 1)
1 Corinthians 5:6b–8
John 20:1–18

HYMN OF THE DAY

LSB 458 "Christ Jesus Lay in Death's Strong Bands"

He suffered and was buried. And the third day He rose again according to the Scriptures."

We know He did! That's what our faith is all about!

Alleluia! Christ is risen!

He is risen indeed! Alleluia!

I've got to admit, though, those words in the Nicene Creed used to bother me. "He rose again according to the Scriptures." I always used to think that was a pretty weak way to affirm the resurrection. As in, "Well, at least according to the Scriptures, He rose."

"According to my calculations, we should be arriving in about five hours and fifteen minutes." That means plan on six.

"The Giants are the team to beat in the National League this year according to all the preseason pundits." That means they'll probably finish third in the division.

"According to the forecast, it should be a beautiful weekend." Better bring an umbrella.

"According to" never sounds so certain, does it!

We look forward to this Sunday morning—of all Sunday mornings!—because we know we'll hear again the glorious announcement that Jesus really is risen! That gets us juiced, thrilled. We love Easter! And, boy, do we look forward to it every year because Jesus rose again on the third day.

The first Easter people, Mary Magdalene and the other women, Peter and John and the rest, didn't wake up that morning with the same anticipation. But they could have. If only they'd believed that Jesus would rise again according to the Scriptures. It had actually been right there in front of them the whole time, spelled out in the Law and the Prophets and the Psalms. And Jesus had taken pains to tell them that at every step of the way He was fulfilling the Scriptures—to the cross, yes, but also to rise again.

There's so much to look forward to in our propers this week. Notice that there are two full sets of readings; the first set listed is designated as Easter Day, the second as Easter Sunrise. Your pastor might in fact choose either, or mix and match, so you might wish to read them all ahead. For our purposes, let's just focus on how the lessons demonstrate that Christ rose according to the Scriptures and how that's really a good and certain thing, and how important it is for us!

Begin with the **Holy Gospel** for Easter Sunrise. Read John 20:1–18.

We know the whole story. The first witnesses are picking it up piece by piece. We know that it is not just Mary Magdalene who goes early to the tomb; several women come together. But apparently when Mary sees the stone rolled away, still at some distance, without going closer, she jumps to the conclusion that Jesus' body has been stolen. She leaves the other women (misses the angel's great news!) and runs back to tell the disciples the bad (20:1–2).

What Peter and John ("the other disciple") see is remarkable (20:6–7)! The neatly folded face cloth and the body linens laid in place aren't the work of hasty grave robbers or sadistic desecraters. How to explain them? John writes "saw and believed" (20:8). But it doesn't seem he fully caught on, because confusion continues to reign throughout that first day. And it's still John who explains why and tells on himself: "For as yet they did not understand the Scripture, that He must rise from the dead" (20:9). It should have all been clear now. It is going precisely according to the Scriptures.

Soon enough, Mary makes her way back to the tomb—apparently without crossing paths either with the other women or with Peter and John. "Woman, why are you weeping?" the angels and then Jesus ask her (20:13, 15). The question isn't asking for information; they know why she is weeping. The question challenges her. "You shouldn't be weeping. It's the third day. You should surely know He's alive. He told you what the Scriptures said."

And, indeed, the Old Testament is full of promises of the resurrection. Read the **Psalm** for Easter Day, Psalm 16.

"You will not abandon My soul to Sheol, or let Your holy one see corruption" (16:10). Peter later applies this prophecy of David explicitly to the Christ during his Pentecost sermon (Acts 2:31). The grave couldn't be the end for Jesus. "The lines have fallen for Me in pleasant places; indeed, I have a beautiful inheritance. . . . You make known to Me the path of life; in Your presence there is fullness of joy; at Your right hand are pleasures forevermore" (Ps 16:6, 11).

Likewise, read the **Psalm** for Easter Sunrise, Psalm 118:15–29.

"I shall not die, but I shall live" (118:17). Not die forever, that is. Oh, the Messiah will die: "The stone," the Christ, "the builders rejected." But He "has become the cornerstone" (118:22). "The Lord has disciplined me severely"—even to death on the cross—"but He has not given Me over to death," not abandoned Me to the grave (118:18). And all this, the downs and the ups, "this is the LORD's doing; it is marvelous in our eyes" (118:23). It's not marvelous as in "*Marvy!*" It's marvelous as in causing us to marvel that God's ways are so much higher and wiser than our own, including dying and then rising in order to save the world! It's all His doing, just as His inspired writers wrote.

No more beautiful words of the resurrection can be found even in the New Testament than the **Old Testament Reading** for Easter Day, Isaiah 25:6–9. Savor the imagery!

Delicious! But better yet, picture the pall draped over a casket ("the covering," "the veil . . . over all nations," 25:7) suddenly lifted to reveal the grave clothes so neatly arranged in Jesus' empty tomb. And then picture our loved ones standing with Jesus in their glorified bodies. "He will swallow up death forever; and the Lord GOD will wipe away tears from all faces" (25:8). On that day, the faithful will look back and say, "We have waited for Him" (25:9). We waited because You told us in Holy Scripture it would turn out like this!

Then there's this triumphal event that typified Christ breaking Satan's power of death: the **Old Testament Reading** for Easter Sunrise, Exodus 15:1–11.

It is Pharaoh and the Egyptian army the Israelites see bearing down at the Red Sea. But invisibly, Satan is "the enemy" who says, "I will pursue, I will overtake, I will divide the spoil, my desire shall have its fill of them. I will draw my sword; my hand shall destroy them" (15:9). Envision the devil and his minions salivating over the spoils as Jesus lay dead. However, Satan's fiercest weapon, death, could not win. The **Introit**:

I will sing to the LORD, for He has triumphed gloriously; the horse and his rider He has thrown into the sea.

The LORD is my strength and my song, and He has become my salvation. Your right hand, O LORD, glorious in power, Your right hand, O LORD, shatters the enemy. You have led in Your steadfast love the people whom You have redeemed; You have guided them by Your strength to Your holy abode. You will bring them in and plant them on Your own mountain, the place, O LORD, which You have made for Your abode, the sanctuary, O LORD, which Your hands have established. The LORD will reign forever and ever.

Glory be to the Father and to the Son and to the Holy Spirit; as it was in the beginning, is now, and will be forever. Amen.

I will sing to the LORD, for He has triumphed gloriously; the horse and his rider He has thrown into the sea. (Ex 15:2a, 6, 13, 17–18; antiphon: Ex 15:1b)

All these were Old Testament prophecies that foresaw the resurrection of Christ. Those Scriptures then became the basis for the New Testament writers' understanding of

Easter. Read the **Epistle** for Easter Sunrise, 1 Corinthians 5:6b–8.

Paul sees that it was all there in the Passover. The "old leaven," which was forbidden at Passover, symbolized sin that had to be removed. That's what the sacrifice of the Lamb, Christ, accomplished. And that gave rise (yes, pun intended) to the bread of the festival: Jesus risen from the dead. Christ rose according to the Scriptures. That's certain enough after all. But in case the language is still a bit uncomfortable for you, you might like the way the English Standard Version reads in the **Epistle** for Easter Day, 1 Corinthians 15:1–11. Read it first in whatever version you use.

Now here's the ESV rendering of 15:3–4: "For I delivered to you as of first importance what I also received: that Christ died for our sins *in accordance with the Scriptures*, that He was buried, that He was raised on the third day *in accordance with the Scriptures*." That's what the words of the Creed mean! Christ rising from the dead isn't, "Well, we hope the Bible got it right." Paul goes on to show just how certain the resurrection is—even explaining that Jesus appeared to five hundred witnesses at once (15:5–8)! But that fact that God had promised all along in Scripture that it would come out just this way is a precious assurance to us.

Since Jesus Rose Again in Accordance with the Scriptures, We Know God Will Fulfill All the Promises He's Made to Us in Scripture.

Go with the other women now to the tomb and hear what they hear by reading the **Holy Gospel** for Easter Day, Mark 16:1–8. "He has risen . . . just as He told you" (16:6, 7). And don't weep for Mary Magdalene. "Jesus said to her, 'Mary.' She turned and said to Him in Aramaic, 'Rabboni!' (which means Teacher)" (Jn 20:16). Yes *(emphasize "has" as you read)*,

> *Christ has risen from the dead. [God the Father] has crowned Him with glory and honor, He has given Him dominion over the works of His hands; He has put all things under His feet. (adapted from Mt 28:7; Heb 2:7; Ps 8:6)*

It's as the Scriptures always promised (the **Gradual** for Easter).

That means we can count on what God promises us. Read the **Collect** for Easter Sunrise:

> *Almighty God, through Your only-begotten Son, Jesus Christ, You overcame death and opened to us the gate of everlasting life. We humbly pray that we may live before You in righteousness and purity forever; through the same Jesus Christ, our Lord, who lives and reigns with You and the Holy Spirit, one God, now and forever. Amen.*

Luther's great Easter hymn, the **Hymn of the Day**, *LSB* 458, shows us what "Holy Scripture plainly saith"—in particular, in stanzas 5–7, what Paul taught so well in 1 Corinthians 5:6b–8. Compare those texts.

Second Sunday of Easter Year B

READINGS

Acts 4:32–35

Psalm 148 (antiphon: v 13)

1 John 1:1–2:2

John 20:19–31

HYMN OF THE DAY

LSB 470, 471 "O Sons and Daughters of the King"

Those who don't believe Jesus rose from the grave face a tall order. Not only do the biblical texts stand as the most reliable documentary evidence of the ancient world and claim hundreds of witnesses of the risen Christ (e.g., 1 Cor 15:3–8) but secular and non-Christian historians also testify to Jesus and the circumstances surrounding His resurrection. Then there's the undeniable historic fact that both the apostles and countless other early Christians were willing to die rather than deny that Jesus was alive. Obviously those early witnesses were fully convinced. And there's a lot more. Yes, Jesus is alive!

One of the theories by skeptics, though, is that all those witnesses hallucinated the postresurrection appearances of Jesus. They thought they saw Him, but it was their imagination. The biggest flaw in this theory (which was popular in the nineteenth century and has been making a recent comeback) is the universally-admitted fact that there were so many who claimed to see Jesus arisen from the dead (like the five hundred Paul mentions). Hallucinations are personal, individual events. But the witnesses of Jesus' resurrection would have had to experience a "mass ecstasy." That would probably have taken a miracle in itself!

Pretend, nevertheless, that hundreds of people *did* share such a mass ecstasy. Did all hallucinate the very same thing? And a good thing? A great thing! A thing they would all have wanted to imagine: their dear friend alive again! Think of the bond that would have formed among them. Think of how close they would have felt toward one another. "The world thinks we're crazy; they're all against us, but we 'know' what we saw, and at least we'll listen to one another when we want to talk on and on about it." Think of the fellowship that would create among those in the club!

Well, then, think of the fellowship it would create if the world were still against you, thought you were crazy, threatened your life, and the Savior you all saw really is alive. Not only would you be locked tight with one another but you'd also now enjoy fellowship with the risen Savior and the heavenly Father who sent Him.

That, of course, is what really happened for those early Christians, and our propers for the Second Sunday of Easter demonstrate it. We'll see Jesus really alive (even if not with our own eyes), be invited into fellowship with Him, and then sense the intimacy and eagerness that He creates among the fellow witnesses.

The **Holy Gospel** is two of Jesus' appearances after rising from the dead—with a famous sidebar story. Read John 20:19–31.

This reading is the Gospel for Easter 2 in all three years of the lectionary. The obvious reason is that the second portion actually took place on the Sunday after Easter. ("Eight days," 20:26, by Hebrew counting, remember, is one week by our calendars.) But using this lesson in all three years is a wise lectionary decision also because it simply has so much rich content.

This (20:19) is almost surely the first time the resurrected Christ has appeared to the body of the disciples at once. He's already shown Himself to the women (Jn 20:16; Mt 28:9) and Peter (1 Cor 15:5), and apparently the conversation with two on the road to Emmaus has just preceded (Lk 24:31–36). There's no mistaking that it's Jesus; there are the wounds (Jn 20:20). It's no hallucination!

But seeing Jesus alive might not be such cause for rejoicing if not for His words, "Peace be with you." After all, these men had deserted Jesus at His hour of greatest need. What if He'd come back just to exact His revenge? "Peace" (εἰρήνη, *eirene*) expresses the Hebrew concept of *shalom*, the condition of complete well-being that exists only when all is right between God and man. Since the fall, that's possible only if sins are forgiven. Jesus is telling His disciples that their sins *are* forgiven—and all that that entails.

Ultimately, this is the message of seeing Jesus alive. Jesus had taken the sins of the world upon Himself, offering Himself to the Father as the sacrifice, the payment. Jesus alive means that God the Father has accepted that sacrifice as sufficient for all human sin. God's righteous wrath has been satisfied; He is no longer angry with us. That means He receives us again as our dear Father, we as His dear children. We are reconciled, at peace.

Or to put it another way, our fellowship with God has been restored.

Those who have witnessed Him alive then makes witnesses—with a second word of "peace": "Peace be with you. As the Father has sent Me, even so I am sending you" (20:21). The disciples are now tasked with extending Jesus' peace to others, to bring them also into fellowship with God. There will be more on this when we revisit this reading in Year C.

The sidebar story, which often grabs top headline, is "Doubting Thomas." It's worth noticing that on this critical evening, Thomas isn't availing himself of fellowship that is so supportive. "Thomas," John writes quite simply, "was not with them" (20:24). He refuses to believe the witness of those who've seen Jesus (20:25).

How gracious, though, is Jesus! What Thomas sinfully demands, Jesus gives (20:26–27). And not grudgingly, but with the same, beautiful *shalom*, He says a third time, "Peace be with you." Jesus still extends that perfect fellowship of God to Thomas. Thomas gets to see, even touch.

"Blessed are those who have not seen and yet have believed." In fact, this and John's whole Gospel "are written so that you"—who have not seen—"may believe that Jesus is the Christ, the Son of God, and that by believing you may have life in His name" (20:29, 31). But understand what those two verses together mean. We who believe without seeing believe because we've heard and read the words of those who *did* see! We believe because the risen Christ *was* seen! Blessed are the witnesses who saw . . . and believed . . . and then witnessed to us who aren't privileged to see (yet)!

That created such a special bond of fellowship. A lovely example is the **First Reading** for this Sunday, Acts 4:32–35.

Those who had witnessed the resurrected Christ by seeing are now witnessing to Him by speaking, "giving their testimony to the resurrection of the Lord Jesus" (4:33). Throughout the book of Acts, it's the resurrection that spurs the Church forward. And the message of the resurrection is what Jesus had given the disciples: God is reconciled to you by the death and resurrection of Christ. Your fellowship with the heavenly Father is restored.

The fellowship the early Christians practiced with one another has sometimes been caricatured as a nascent form of communism. That's not accurate; communal property wasn't required—or even recommended—here or anywhere else in the Bible. The important word is that they "were of one heart and soul" (4:32). They held the same confession of faith in the crucified, risen, saving Christ. What they believed was the same for all. That did create such intimacy that they put the needs of fellow believers above their own.

Next, in the **Epistle**, the resurrected Christ is again witnessed, then witnessed to, resulting in fellowship with God and the Church. Read 1 John 1:1–2:2.

John is no doubt remembering the very experience of our Gospel lesson: "We have heard, . . . we have seen with our eyes, . . . we looked upon and have touched with our hands" (1:1). No hallucination! As if seeing with his eyes (using the common Greek word for sight) isn't convincing enough, John adds a form of the Greek θεάομαι, *theaomai*, which means to look on attentively, especially at something unusual. In English, we sometimes say "behold," with almost a play on words that emphasizes "hold." Yes, John and the boys touched the risen Christ.

Now they "testify to it and proclaim to you the eternal life," which the crucified and living Christ gives (1:2). The witnesses witness to what they've heard, seen, beheld, touched. Why? "We proclaim . . . to you, so that you too may have fellowship with us; and indeed our fellowship is with the Father and with His Son Jesus Christ" (1:3).

Witnessing the Resurrected Christ Brings Us into Fellowship with God and One Another.

Those early witnesses like John knew what they'd seen, and that it's shared with us today is their joy made "complete" (1:4).

Look for the witness of, the witness to, and the fellowship in the risen Christ in each of the other propers too. In the **Psalm**, Psalm 148, fellowship in the Lord (to be "near to Him," 148:14) is shared by people of all ages and social strata, men and women (148:11–12). All of them witness by praising the Lord.

In the **Introit**, the witness of the risen Lord is again sensory ("tasted"), witness to Him will "make known His deeds," and His people seek fellowship in "His presence."

Like newborn infants, long for the pure spiritual milk, that by it you may grow up to salvation—if indeed you have tasted that the Lord is good.

Oh give thanks to the Lord; call upon His name; make known His deeds among the peoples! Sing to Him, sing praises to Him; tell of all His wondrous works! Glory in His holy name; let the hearts of those who seek the Lord rejoice! Seek the Lord and His strength; seek His presence continually! Remember the wondrous works that He has done, His miracles, and the judgments He uttered. He remembers His covenant forever, the word that He commanded, for a thousand generations.

Glory be to the Father and to the Son and to the Holy Spirit; as it was in the beginning, is now, and will be forever. Amen.

Like newborn infants, long for the pure spiritual milk, that by it you may grow up to salvation—if indeed you have tasted that the Lord is good. (Ps 105:1–5, 8; antiphon: 1 Pet 2:2–3)

And in the **Collect**, we pray that "our life and conversation" would faithfully witness to Jesus as Lord and God so that future generations of Christians might share the fellowship we have with Christ and with believers of the past who witnessed Him to us:

Almighty God, grant that we who have celebrated the Lord's resurrection may by Your grace confess in our life and conversation that Jesus is Lord and God; through the same Jesus Christ, Your Son, who lives and reigns with You and the Holy Spirit, one God, now and forever. Amen.

The **Hymn of the Day**, "O Sons and Daughters of the King" (*LSB* 471), is the natural choice for the Second Sunday of Easter, including as it does a paraphrase of the Gospel reading.

Third Sunday of Easter Year B

READINGS

Acts 3:11–21
Psalm 4 (antiphon: v 7)
1 John 3:1–7
Luke 24:36–49

HYMN OF THE DAY

LSB 483 "With High Delight Let Us Unite"

I've decided I'm too old for roller coasters. I know the reason. You can't feel the exhilaration of flying almost to the sky until after what seems like a free fall into the depths. I know . . . that's the point. And if *I'm* retired from roller coasters, Coney Island and Cedar Point and Magic Mountain will always have another generation lining up to ride their rides. You can't deny the thrill. And it's easy enough to understand that the ecstasy is only heightened by the near-death experience first. That's the way it works. That's also often how it works in life.

The disciples of Jesus have been on a wild roller-coaster ride the last week or so. From the jubilant procession on Palm Sunday, they plunged almost to hell itself when they saw Jesus damned by His Father on the cross.

But now it's Easter!

> *Christ has risen from the dead. [God the Father] has crowned Him with glory and honor, He has given Him dominion over the works of His hands; He has put all things under His feet. (adapted from Mt 28:7; Heb 2:7; Ps 8:6)*

And since, as the **Gradual** says, Christ is risen, we're now riding high—infinitely higher than if Jesus had never taken the dive. No one could ascend to heaven if Christ hadn't first gone down to the depths of the earth. But now that He's risen, we rise with Him.

This is also what that good Lutheran concept of Law and Gospel is all about—the roller-coaster point. You can't know the joy of being saved from death and hell (Gospel) unless you know you were falling toward death and hell (Law). And the more deeply you know—even sometimes *feel*—that you were falling, the more fully you'll feel the joy of being saved.

This week, our propers continue the high delight of Easter while reminding us of the depths through which Christ passed. They also include some of the New Testament's sternest preaching of the Law with some of the sweetest preaching of the Gospel. That might just take us along on the same roller-coaster ride.

The first proper we'll hear on Sunday will be the **Introit**:

> *In Your presence there is fullness of joy; at Your right hand are pleasures forevermore.*
>
> *I will extol You, O Lord, for You have drawn me up and have not let my foes rejoice over me. O Lord my God, I cried to You for help, and You have healed me. O Lord, You have brought up my soul from Sheol; You restored me to life from among those who go down to the pit. Sing praises to the Lord, O you His saints, and give thanks to His holy name. For His anger is but for a moment, and His favor is for a lifetime. Weeping may tarry for the night, but joy comes with the morning.*
>
> *Glory be to the Father and to the Son and to the Holy Spirit; as it was in the beginning, is now, and will be forever. Amen.*
>
> *In Your presence there is fullness of joy; at Your right hand are pleasures forevermore. (Ps 30:1–5; antiphon: Ps 16:11b)*

Easter is "the fullness of joy." It's not a joy *ride*, not a day at Six Flags. In fact, David writes this antiphon (Ps 16:11b) immediately after a reference to death and burial. Remember that? Psalm 16 was appointed for Easter Day, and the preceding verse was explicitly about Jesus: "You will not abandon My soul to Sheol, or let Your holy one see corruption" (16:10). Sure enough, Christ was killed and laid in the tomb, but, "O Lord, You have brought up My soul from Sheol; You restored Me to life from among those who go down to the pit."

The "fullness of joy" David writes about is simply being "in Your [that is, the Lord's] presence." As we saw last week, being in God's presence is because Christ by His death paid for the sins that separated us from God. Then the resurrection shows that God has accepted that payment as sufficient; God is reconciled to us. That is always sufficient, because it means we have everything the Lord knows is truly good for us at this moment, even if we have to wait for other good things later. First there is the "weeping [that] may tarry for the night, but joy comes with the morning."

David puts it just as well in the appointed **Psalm** for this day, Psalm 4: "You have given me relief when I was in distress. . . . You have put more joy in my heart than they have when their grain and wine abound" (4:1b, 7). Distress is relieved, which multiplies the joy.

The **Collect** for this Sunday acknowledges the same dying to rise and prays for the same ascent from peril to joy:

> *O God, through the humiliation of Your Son You raised up the fallen world. Grant to Your faithful people, rescued from the peril of everlasting death, perpetual gladness and eternal joys; through Jesus Christ, our Lord, who lives and reigns with You and the Holy Spirit, one God, now and forever. Amen.*

Eternal joys are always a rescue from everlasting death, always because Christ died and then rose. They come no other way.

As usual during the Easter season, the **First Reading** is from Acts. We're dropped into the middle of a story here. It's just days after Pentecost, so only two months or so since Easter. Peter and John have just healed a lame man near a gate of the temple. Start there, with Acts 3:11–21.

Does anything grab you about Peter's sermon? This is one I've often discussed with my preaching students. Why? Because Peter is so direct! He makes clear that it's Jesus, not Peter and John, who worked the miracle. Then he lowers the boom: "Men of Israel, . . . the God of our fathers, glorified His servant Jesus, whom *you* delivered over and denied in the presence of Pilate, when he had decided to release Him. But *you* denied the Holy and Righteous One, and asked for a murderer to be granted to you, and *you* killed the Author of life, whom God raised from the dead" (3:12b, 13b–15a). This is Law preaching in its full sternness! There's no escape! *You* are guilty!

How does this fly when your pastor looks you (and the rest of the congregation) in the eye and tells you from the pulpit that *you* are responsible for the death of Christ and then gives you specific reasons why? For your (and other members') divorces that weren't because your spouses left or were unfaithful. For the unkind words you (and others) have been spreading about sisters in Christ. For your (and others') sexual activity before marriage. For the movies and TV shows you (and others) so casually absorb. For your (and others') failure to speak and act to save unborn lives. The roller coaster is plunging, and it *should* feel like a free fall.

"But what God foretold by the mouth of all the prophets, that His Christ would suffer, He thus fulfilled. Repent therefore, and turn again, that *your* sins may be blotted out, that times of refreshing may come from the presence of the Lord, and that He may send the Christ appointed for *you*" (3:18–19). And then a few verses after our reading, "God, having raised up His servant, sent Him to *you first*, to bless *you* by turning *every one of you* from your wickedness" (3:26). If you felt the coaster coming off the track . . . suddenly turning right side up! When the Law is fully stern, oh, how sweet is the Gospel! You're forgiven for *your* divorce, gossip, unholy dates, unholy thoughts, inactivity for life by Jesus' descent into the depths and His resurrection.

Can you ride the ride again? If you're still feeling a little queasy, maybe just get off now. Stop here. Really. Stop here with the assurance that every sin that came to your mind truly is gone, taken away, forgiven. It was nailed to Jesus' cross. But He is risen! *He is risen indeed! Alleluia!* And that means the Father has announced your forgiveness.

If you are up for another go-round, read the **Epistle**, 1 John 3:1–7.

Here's John's scary line: "No one who abides in Him keeps on sinning; no one who keeps on sinning has either seen Him or known Him" (3:6). But I do keep on sinning, every day, every moment. Does that mean I don't know the Savior?

Now John is actually referring to making "a practice of sinning" (3:4)—letting sin be our life rather than daily repenting. But that should be a warning. Stern Law. So then, every day, let us hear this: "See what kind of love the Father has given to us, that we should be called children of God; and so we are" (3:1a). Sinners, absolutely, inescapably guilty. And yet at the same moment, children of God. "And so we are."

Surely it was the disciples who most wanted to get off the ride. Fortunately, Jesus didn't ask them, because they would have missed the good part. Read the **Holy Gospel**, Luke 24:36–49.

The first portion of the reading (24:36–43) is probably the same appearance we witnessed last Sunday. It's Easter evening, and the Emmaus disciples are still panting from their seven-mile run (24:31–35). They add their excitement to the word that Peter has also seen Jesus. Curiously, though, when Jesus appears, they're still scared (24:37). So deep has been their pain, their despair. They are *sure* the coaster has come off the tracks!

So Jesus speaks that same comforting word John reported last week: "Peace." And since they are still troubled, He removes all doubt: Not spirit. Flesh and bones. The nail prints in His hands and feet. And He eats! It's our real Jesus, all right!

Verse 44 on likely takes place some days later, perhaps forty days, leading right into Jesus' ascension (compare 24:49–53 with Acts 1:8–12). Everything finally makes complete sense; salvation had to be by roller coaster: "The Christ should suffer and on the third day rise" (24:46). And it must be that way for each of us individually; the best rendering of the original text: "Repentance *for* forgiveness of sins should be proclaimed in His name to all nations" (24:47). Without repentance, without confessing that we really are diving toward hell, there is no forgiveness (Law). But repentance is always *for, toward the intended end of,* forgiveness (Gospel). And when we're at our lowest and feel our desperation most deeply, forgiveness can be an incredible, exhilarating lift.

Jesus' Resurrection from Death Raises Us from the Depths to the Fullness of Joy.

In the end, Jesus' Easter triumph is the triumph of the Gospel for us. From the depths of death He burst forth, and ours "shall be like victory." His love shall give us "all joy and full consolation." "With High Delight Let Us Unite!"—the **Hymn of the Day**, *LSB* 483.

Fourth Sunday of Easter Year B

READINGS

Acts 4:1–12
Psalm 23 (antiphon: v 6)
1 John 3:16–24
John 10:11–18

HYMN OF THE DAY

LSB 709 "The King of Love My Shepherd Is"

The joy of Easter is way too much to celebrate on just one Sunday or two or three. It takes all seven Sundays of the Easter season—and the rest of the year too. So this Fourth Sunday of Easter, we'll continue to alleluia! the resurrection of our Lord.

Easter 4, though, adds another festivity to our celebration. You'll see it in the **Collect**:

> *Almighty God, merciful Father, since You have wakened from death the Shepherd of Your sheep, grant us Your Holy Spirit that when we hear the voice of our Shepherd we may know Him who calls us each by name and follow where He leads; through the same Jesus Christ, Your Son, our Lord, who lives and reigns with You and the Holy Spirit, one God, now and forever. Amen.*

The risen Christ is also our Shepherd.

The shepherd is such an important figure in the Bible—from shepherd Abel in Genesis (4:2), to the Lamb who became the Shepherd in Revelation (7:17), and big names like Moses (Ex 3:1) and David (1 Sam 16:11–13) in between. But, of course, the Shepherd to whom all biblical shepherds point is Jesus (who, by the way, is the Lamb-Shepherd of Revelation 7). And Shepherd is such a descriptive image of Jesus, the Savior, that the Church has set aside each Fourth Sunday of Easter to celebrate His resurrection as Good Shepherd Sunday.

The two best-known shepherd texts head our propers this week: Psalm 23 and John 10:11–18. The **Psalm** plus two verses from

John 10 together form the **Introit** for Good Shepherd Sunday, Year B.

I am the good shepherd. I know My own and My own know Me, and I lay down My life for the sheep.

The Lord is my shepherd; I shall not want. He makes me lie down in green pastures. He leads me beside still waters. He restores my soul. He leads me in paths of righteousness for His name's sake. Even though I walk through the valley of the shadow of death, I will fear no evil, for You are with me; Your rod and Your staff, they comfort me. You prepare a table before me in the presence of my enemies; You anoint my head with oil; my cup overflows. Surely goodness and mercy shall follow me all the days of my life, and I shall dwell in the house of the Lord forever.

Glory be to the Father and to the Son and to the Holy Spirit; as it was in the beginning, is now, and will be forever. Amen.

I am the good shepherd. I know My own and My own know Me, and I lay down My life for the sheep. (Ps 23; antiphon: Jn 10:14, 15b)

All of Jesus' "I am" statements in John's Gospel (such as Jn 6:35; 8:12; 10:7; 11:25; 14:6; 15:5) are loaded, always bringing to mind God's announcement to Moses that He is the eternal I Am (Jn 8:58). But this one is especially rich because of the picture David has already painted of Yahweh as his shepherd. David knows all the things he has to do for his father's sheep—bring them to safe pasture, water them, defend them against the lion and bear. So David deeply appreciates what the Lord is always doing for him. David is almost constantly at war, a man wearing the heavy burden of the crown, a man who sins greatly and suffers tragic losses in his own family. How comforting, calming it must have been for him to know that the Lord is still protecting and providing so that he will never really be in want. It must allow his mind to wander back to quieter, peaceful days alone with the flocks on those shady hillsides beside the spring-fed pools.

During nearly every funeral I've conducted, we've read the Twenty-Third Psalm. It's comforting, calming during all those moments in life when we need that the most. When our lives are stressful and burdened, the Lord, our Shepherd, takes everything off our plate. He lets us be helpless sheep and takes upon Himself every duty, every task, every assignment, every deadline, every bill, every danger, every sin. He takes them all with the promise that we shall never come up wanting.

In fact, "my cup overflows." He's setting the table with more good things than I can possibly drink, eat, and enjoy, and He's already begun to serve it.

A fellow pastor pointed out a delightful insight to me years ago. In the initial verses of the psalm, in those green pastures, beside those still waters, David talks *about* his shepherd: *He* makes me lie down, *He* leads me,

He restores my soul for *His* name's sake. That's all very pleasant. But then the storyline turns more desperate: "I walk through the valley of the shadow of death." And notice then the way David writes: "*You* are with me; *Your* rod and *Your* staff, they comfort me. *You* prepare a table before me in the presence of my enemies; *You* anoint my head with oil." Notice that? Now David isn't talking *about* his shepherd anymore; he's talking *to* Him. David understands that when our times are most threatening, fearsome, the Lord is especially near to us. And then when Jesus comes along a thousand years later, the Lord is nearest of all; He stands right here with us in the flesh and speaks to us with His own voice: "I am the good shepherd."

There's one more thing to try with the Introit. Read the antiphon (the last verses from John 10) again, this time out loud.

Did you do it? Chances are your voice emphasized the words "shepherd," "know," and "lay down My life." Is that the way it came out? That's the natural reading. It emphasizes who Christ is and what He does and did.

But read it again. Again out loud. This time, instead, emphasize "I" and "good." What does that suggest?

Read the **Holy Gospel** from which the antiphon is taken, John 10:11–18. Do you see where this is going?

Jesus is the *good* shepherd, but He's not the only shepherd. Plenty of the guys out there tending sheep are just doing it for the money. It's "just a job." The hireling gets paid the same whether the flock has a hundred sheep or maybe loses one or two. It's certainly not worth risking his own life if a wolf comes prowling.

Jesus is illustrating those entrusted with the spiritual care of souls who, when push comes to shove, put themselves first. This can be as blatant as the media evangelist who profits while feeding his sheep clever catchlines that use Christ's name but aren't truly about Jesus' cross and forgiveness of sins He gives us. Or it can be any pastor who runs from his own cross, who avoids saying the unpopular thing or championing the controversial cause rather than risking criticism.

So here's how Jesus compares Himself: "*I* am the *good* shepherd." He's entirely different from those others. And what sets Him apart *is* the cross: "*I* lay down My life for the sheep" (10:15). For an ancient shepherd, this was a real possibility; he really might lose his life fending off a wolf or a lion or a bear. But he would only fight those fights because he cared for the sheep, because he knew each one as his own. If the Lord as my shepherd in idyllic pastures is a beautiful scene, this is even more beautiful: Jesus hanging on the cross thinking of me.

Then comes Easter. Good Shepherd Sunday is still Easter: "I lay down My life that I may take it up again" (10:17). That, too, sets Jesus apart from those hirelings.

Unlike the Many False Shepherds, the Good Shepherd Lays Down His Life and Takes It Up Again to Save His Sheep.

Want an example? That would be the **First Reading**, Acts 4:1–12.

This incident follows Peter's sermon from last week ("You killed the Author of life," Acts 3:15), which had been precipitated by Peter and John healing a lame man (3:1–10). The disciples are arrested for "proclaiming in Jesus the resurrection from the dead" (4:2). And you see by whom: the false shepherds, the hired hands, Annas and Caiaphas and the same priests who killed Jesus Himself.

These men were to be the trusted shepherds of Israel, but they care nothing for the sheep—only for preserving their places of honor in the temple. Therefore their teachings cannot save the sheep. "There is salvation in no one else, for there is no other name under heaven given among men by which we must be saved" . . . than "the name of Jesus Christ of Nazareth, whom you crucified, whom God raised from the dead" (4:12, 10). There is no Savior except our Good Shepherd, who laid down His life and took it up again.

The last reading to be examined shows what a difference this makes for the way we live our lives now. Read the **Epistle**, 1 John 3:16–24.

John no doubt recalls the words Jesus spoke in his hearing: "He laid down His life for us" (3:16). There's the Good Shepherd again. And by that, John says, "We know love, that He laid down His life for us, and we ought to lay down our lives for the brothers." That is, we ought to "love . . . in deed and in truth" (3:18).

See, we follow our shepherds, whomever they may be. The hired hands who don't know and care for the sheep love only themselves. That's why they cut and run when trouble brews. Following them, we, too, will really only care for ourselves. That's not loving the brothers in deed or truth. And it's not just that we'd be following their bad examples. False shepherds don't feed their flock the food that nourishes the heart, that enables it to love.

That food is the love of God in Christ Jesus. God's love for us, giving us eternal life by Jesus' death and resurrection, assures us that we don't need to fend for ourselves. He feeds, guides, leads us to pleasant pastures, gives us everything that's truly good. And when we have everything truly good given to us by our Good Shepherd, we can care for others, following Him in the path of love. We're able and eager to keep God's commandment: "That we believe in the name of His Son Jesus Christ and love one another" (3:23).

Good Shepherd Sunday is a special reason to celebrate the resurrection! Read the **Verse**:

Alleluia. We know that Christ being raised from the dead will never die again; death no longer has dominion over Him. Alleluia. I am the good shepherd. I know My own and my own know Me. Alleluia. (Rom 6:9; Jn 10:14)

We have quite a number of fine hymns based on Psalm 23 or John 10, probably one or more among each of our personal favorites. One of the very best musically is our **Hymn of the Day**, "The King of Love My Shepherd Is" (*LSB* 709). Enjoy singing it. Then peruse the hymnal for others. You'll probably sing a couple of them Sunday.

Fifth Sunday of Easter Year B

READINGS

Acts 8:26–40
Psalm 150 (antiphon: v 6)
1 John 4:1–11 (12–21)
John 15:1–8

HYMN OF THE DAY

LSB 633 "At the Lamb's High Feast We Sing"

Jesus spoke the first verse, the antiphon, of this Sunday's Introit to His disciples on the night before He died on the cross: "A little while, and you will see Me no longer; and again a little while, and you will see Me" (Jn 16:16). That first "little while" was the few hours until He would be crucified; He'd be dead and buried, and the disciples wouldn't see Him. And again the "little while" would be the time between Friday and Sunday when the disciples knew Jesus was dead and held no hope they'd ever see Him again. But alleluia! Christ is risen! *He is risen indeed! Alleluia!* And sure enough, the disciples did see Jesus.

So as we hear these words on the Fifth Sunday of Easter, the setting has changed. Christ isn't going to leave us in death, yet for a little while, we don't see Him. What happened, of course, is that a little while after He rose from the grave (forty days, to be precise) He ascended back to heaven. Now for a little while—here we can't be precise at all, or even guess *how little* a while—we no longer see Him. But we will! He's promised us He'll come back.

That's the little while we're living right now—the time between Jesus' ascension and His return to earth on the Last Day. And our church year prepares us for this. The last three Sundays of Easter—Easter 5 this week, then Easter 6 and Easter 7 the next two weeks—point us toward the ascension of Christ. It's the updated version of that first "little while." After that, we'll be ready for the long Pentecost season, living out the other "little while" that will be who-knows-how-long.

The important thing to understand is that during the first go-round, the disciples' "little while" from Good Friday to Easter was a time of deep mourning and, because of shaky faith, terrible uncertainty. Our "little while" of waiting to see Jesus again is entirely different. For us, this is an epoch of great joy!

Sense that in the words of our **Introit** for Easter 5:

> *A little while, and you will see Me no longer; and again a little while, and you will see Me.*
>
> *I will extol You, my God and King, and bless Your name forever and ever. Every day I will bless You and praise Your name forever and ever. The Lord is gracious and merciful, slow to anger and abounding in steadfast love. All Your works shall give thanks to You, O Lord, and all Your saints shall bless You! My mouth will speak the praise of the Lord, and let all flesh bless His holy name forever and ever.*
>
> *Glory be to the Father and to the Son and to the Holy Spirit; as it was in the beginning, is now, and will be forever. Amen.*
>
> *A little while, and you will see Me no longer; and again a little while, and you will see Me. (Ps 145:1–2, 8, 10, 21; antiphon: Jn 16:16)*

The disciples' Easter joy came when they saw the Lord. Since we don't see Jesus, we can "extol" Him, "bless" and "praise [His] name forever and ever" only if we remain connected to Him some other way. Or, as the **Collect** prays, "our hearts . . . be fixed where true joys are found"—on Jesus Christ:

> *O God, You make the minds of Your faithful to be of one will. Grant that we may love what You have commanded and desire what You promise, that among the many changes of this world our hearts may be fixed where true joys are found; through Jesus Christ, Your Son, our Lord, who lives and reigns with You and the Holy Spirit, one God, now and forever. Amen.*

In the **Holy Gospel**, Jesus gives us a memorable illustration of remaining connected to Him. Read John 15:1–8

Isn't that a helpful analogy! The word repeated again and again is "abide," and that suggests such a close and ongoing connection. What better way to see this than in Jesus being the vine and we the branches? Jesus is probably picturing a grape vine, cultivated for years, thick and woody, with climbing shoots or tendrils branching out from it. The biology, obviously, is that the vine provides the water and nutrients the branches need. A branch has no life, no productivity, no potential (except as fuel for the fire) if it's not connected to a vine. You see a branch lying on the ground, and you know from there it can only dry up. But shooting out from a vine, you anticipate ripe, plump Thompson Seedless or, maybe better yet, vino.

Jesus gives us what we need to live and flourish. He, the vine, possesses perfect righteousness, keeping God's Law spotlessly for mankind and being obedient to His Father even to die for all human sin. The perfect righteousness of Jesus' life and death is passed to us when we become connected to Him, become His branches, in the water of our Baptism. From then on, it's a constant flow of vital nutrients from Him to us in His Word and His very body and blood in His Holy Supper. That—His Word and Sacraments—is how Christ abides in us, and we abide in Him when we continue to believe He's doing precisely this for us.

There's more to the analogy. There's the purpose for which a vine is planted and for which a vine nourishes its branches: to bear fruit. "I am the vine; you are the branches. Whoever abides in Me and I in him, he it is that bears much fruit" (15:5a). Fruit is the point of it all. So, "My Father is the vinedresser. Every branch in Me that does not bear fruit He takes away, and every branch that does bear fruit He prunes, that it may bear more fruit" (15:1b–2).

"Apart from Me," Jesus says, "you can do nothing" (15:5b). No fruit. Ignoring the word of Christ's love and forgiveness, absenting from the nutrients of His Table, one loses faith. No fruit. The Father takes those branches away; they're "gathered, thrown into the fire, and burned" (15:6b).

On the other hand, branches need not despair when it may seem God is distant, when we suffer pain. The vinedresser may just be pruning. The shears might hurt, but He knows how to produce more fruit. And these fruits of faith glorify God and witness of Him to the world (15:8).

Remaining Connected to Christ—and Only When Remaining Connected to Christ—We Do Bear Much Fruit.

Again this week, we get a living example of how this all works in the **First Reading**, Acts 8:26–40.

Great story, isn't it! It's got sympathetic, dynamic characters; surprising plot twists; and a miracle finish. Philip (not Philip who's one of the Twelve, but Philip the deacon, Acts 6:1–6) goes off to the desert, where you don't expect to find a living soul, simply because an angel sent him. But, voilà! A man who just happens to need—and want!—a Bible study teacher is there.

Your heart goes out to this man. Being a big shot (8:27) doesn't satisfy a kind of loneliness. He's a God-fearer (that is, a foreigner who's come to believe in the God of Israel), but he's still disconnected from the body of the faithful, not only because he's a Gentile but because the Old Testament has something to say about eunuchs (Deut 23:1). This is probably his one dreamed-of visit to the temple, and from now on, he'll be distant again. He's bringing home the most precious souvenir he could collect: a scroll of Isaiah. He says, "How can I [understand it], unless someone guides me?" (8:31). It's a sad prospect to be isolated, disconnected from the body.

Then comes the other big surprise: Could God set the table better? The eunuch is reading Isaiah 53, perhaps the clearest ancient prophecy of Jesus' suffering and death. "And beginning with this Scripture [Philip] told him the good news about Jesus" (8:35).

(Perhaps Philip even takes him three chapters further in Isaiah to see what God had in fact always intended for both Gentiles and eunuchs in Is 56:3–8.)

This is how people become connected to Christ. Immediately, the man becomes one of Jesus' branches: "'See, here is water! What prevents me from being baptized?' And he commanded the chariot to stop, and they both went down into the water, Philip and the eunuch, and he baptized him" (Acts 8:36–38).

Suddenly, Philip is carried away by the Holy Spirit, but here's the fruit: the Ethiopian "went on his way rejoicing" (8:39). Joy is being connected to Christ. There's joy in the assurance we have. Because of our Baptism, Christ Jesus is always in us, with us, and caring for us. And we can guess there was more fruit from this story. Ethiopian Christians to this day see their church as the direct heir of the eunuch proclaiming Jesus once he got home.

Here's more fruit as a result of being connected to Christ: the **Epistle**, 1 John 4:1–21.

John begins the reading by warning us to "test the spirits to see whether they are from God" (4:1). A "spirit" in this case is anyone claiming to speak for God. During this "little while" between Jesus' ascension and His return, false prophets, even "the spirit of the antichrist," will be among us (4:1, 3). (The antichrist is someone or some institution that asserts himself or itself in Christ's place. Ask your pastor for lots more thoughts!) The determining criterion for true spirits is whether they are connected to Christ: "Every spirit that confesses that Jesus Christ has come in the flesh is from God" (4:2). Those who speak of Christ are "from God" (4:6), connected to Him; those who do not speak of Christ are only connected to the world (4:5).

The faithful word of Christ also connects us to God (4:15), and another fruit of His Word is love (4:7). It works this way: "God sent His only Son into the world, so that we might live through Him. In this is love, not that we have loved God but that He loved us and sent His Son to be the propitiation for our sins" (4:9–10). That's what connects us to Christ and to the Father. Jesus dying on the cross "propitiates" our sins. It pays for them so they no longer separate us from God. Now that God is reconciled to us, we receive all the blessings of His love. And since He's loving us with every good thing, we need not worry about "loving" ourselves or looking out for ourselves. "Beloved, if God so loved us, we ought to love one another" (4:11); we really will—though always imperfectly. Being branches of Christ, the vine, we really do produce the fruit of love.

Christ is arisen! Christ is making us His branches! Christ is enabling us to bear the fruit of joy and love! This is why the "little while" of waiting for His return is a time to praise the Lord. Do so with the **Psalm**, Psalm 150.

Our **Hymn of the Day**, "At the Lamb's High Feast We Sing," is placed in "The Lord's Supper" section of *LSB* (633), but it's certainly an Easter hymn, too, as it was classified previously in *Lutheran Worship*. After all, it's being connected to Christ by "His sacred blood for wine," "His body for the feast" (st 2) that gives us our "Easter triumph, Easter joy!" (st 7).

Sixth Sunday of Easter Year B

READINGS

Acts 10:34–48
Psalm 98 (antiphon: v 2)
1 John 5:1–8
John 15:9–17

HYMN OF THE DAY

LSB 556 "Dear Christians, One and All, Rejoice"

The first two appointed propers we'll hear this Sixth Sunday of Easter probably raise more questions than they answer—but in a good way. The Introit and Collect will very nicely begin to point us toward our THEME for Sunday, but only with hints.

Let's dive in. Read the **Introit** for Easter 6:

Come and hear, all you who fear God, and I will tell what He has done for my soul.

Shout for joy to God, all the earth; sing the glory of His name; give to Him glorious praise! Bless our God, O peoples; let the sound of His praise be heard, who has kept our soul among the living and has not let our feet slip. Blessèd be God, because He has not rejected my prayer or removed His steadfast love from me!

Glory be to the Father and to the Son and to the Holy Spirit; as it was in the beginning, is now, and will be forever. Amen.

Come and hear, all you who fear God, and I will tell what He has done for my soul. (Ps 66:1–2, 8–9, 20; antiphon: Ps 66:16)

The psalmist is clearly delighted: "Shout for joy to God, all the earth; sing the glory of His name; give to Him glorious praise!" He knows that God loves him with a "steadfast love." But *how* has God loved him? What has God done that gives the psalmist such joy? It's tantalizing the way he hooks us, isn't it! "Come and hear, all you who fear God, and I will tell what He has done for my soul." *Pause. Pause some more.* Well . . . *pause yet a little longer.* What *has He done* for your soul?

Read the **Collect**:

> *O God, the giver of all that is good, by Your holy inspiration grant that we may think those things that are right and by Your merciful guiding accomplish them; through Jesus Christ, Your Son, our Lord, who lives and reigns with You and the Holy Spirit, one God, now and forever. Amen.*

New question. "Grant that we may think those things that are right and by Your merciful guiding accomplish them." Fine. *What are those things* that are right that we should accomplish?

This is a good exercise for us as worshipers, isn't it. We want to be active listeners—hearing clues among the propers, seeking to sort them out, looking for answers as the rest of the service unfolds. What has God done for my soul, and what are the right things for me to be doing?

The **Psalm** appears only to amplify the questions without helping us find the answers. Read Psalm 98.

Again, the psalmist is certainly rejoicing: "Make a joyful noise to the Lord, all the earth; break forth into joyous song and sing praises! . . . With trumpets and the sound of the horn make a joyful noise before the King, the Lord! . . . Let the rivers clap their hands; let the hills sing for joy together" (98:4, 6, 8). And again, the psalmist knows the Lord's steadfast love: "He has remembered His steadfast love and faithfulness to the house of Israel" (98:3).

But how? Why? "Oh sing to the Lord a new song, for He has done marvelous things!" What marvelous things? "His right hand and His holy arm have worked salvation for Him" (98:1). Nice anthropomorphism, but what does it really mean? Likewise, "He comes to judge the earth. He will judge the world with righteousness, and the peoples with equity" (98:9). But what will God's people be doing when He judges righteously? What are those "right" things?

We'll get a bigger hint if we recall from the Christmas season that Psalm 98 is Isaac Watts's text for his hymn "Joy to the World" (*LSB* 387, set, by the way, to music adapted from George Handel's *Messiah*).

The truth is, we know the marvelous things God has done, don't we! We know what He has done for our souls. So as we get to the **First Reading** Sunday, we'll know what we're hoping to hear. And it's there in Acts 10:34–48.

The first portion of this reading is also appointed for Easter Day, Year A. It follows that remarkable vision by which God begins to show Peter that He welcomes Gentiles as well as Jews into His kingdom (10:9–16). On the basis of that vision, Peter has entered the home of the Roman centurion Cornelius and addresses the small company assembled there (10:17–24, 28).

Though they're Gentiles, Cornelius and his friends have read the Old Testament Scriptures and become believers in the true God. That allows Peter to sort out for them something else they know: "You yourselves know what happened throughout all Judea, beginning from Galilee after the baptism that John proclaimed" (10:37). In the words of Watts, paraphrasing Psalm 98, "The Lord is come!" (*LSB* 387:1).

"God anointed Jesus of Nazareth with the Holy Spirit and with power. He went about doing good and healing all who were oppressed by the devil, for God was with Him. . . . They put Him to death by hanging Him on a tree, but God raised Him on the third day" (10:38, 39b–40). You know that these are the marvelous things God has done! This is what He has done for your soul! "Everyone who believes in Him receives forgiveness of sins through His name" (10:43).

And, indeed, this is for everyone! "God shows no partiality, but in every nation anyone who fears Him and does what is right is acceptable to Him" (10:34b–35). Cornelius, you, I can all be certain that God has done this for *my* soul. Jesus put to death on a tree and raised the third day forgives *my* sins.

As evidence, the Holy Spirit enables these Gentiles to speak in tongues, just as the apostles had done at Pentecost (10:44–46). God does one more marvelous thing for their souls—as He has done for us. They are "baptized in the name of Jesus Christ" (10:48).

All this is why we shout for joy, make a joyful noise to the Lord, why Cornelius and his friends are "extolling God" (10:46).

Here's one more note in passing before we move on. Notice Peter's language: "Anyone who fears [God] and *does what is right* is acceptable to Him" (10:35). There's our Collect again: "Those things that are right." What those things are is still coming up. But for now, rest assured that "everyone who believes in [Jesus] receives forgiveness" (10:43)—not everyone who does the right things.

We knew it would come out like that, didn't we. Jesus coming, living, dying, rising for our forgiveness is the marvelous way God showed His steadfast love for our souls. Now in the **Holy Gospel**, Jesus goes a step further and explains how that leads to doing things that are right. Read John 15:9–17.

The night before Jesus finishes His marvelous things done for us, He summarizes them all: "As the Father has loved Me, so have I loved you. . . . Greater love has no one than this, that someone lays down his life for his friends" (15:9, 13). This will be the ultimate demonstration of *agape* (ἀγάπη), the kind of love that is always self-giving. It's not erotic, and it's more than brotherly.

Everyone loves love—even if it's one of those human forms that falls so far short of *agape*. (In counseling many couples before their marriages, I almost invariably surprise them by saying that love as God talks about it here isn't a feeling or an emotion; it's action—action that sacrifices oneself for another and action they'll promise each other even if feelings of love flicker.) On the other hand, Jesus' other key word in this reading isn't so universally appreciated: *commandment*. Unless we're giving the commands, we don't much like them. We like to be in charge.

But see how inextricably love and commandments are linked. "If you keep My commandments, you will abide in My love, just as I have kept My Father's commandments and abide in His love. . . . This is My commandment, that you love one another as I have loved you. . . . These things I command you, so that you will love one another" (15:10, 12, 17).

Loving one another encompasses all those right things that we pray we'll think and accomplish. Consider it this way: The Ten Commandments are all commands to love. The first three: love God. The last seven: love your neighbor. If that sounds too general, tick them off, one commandment at a time. Honor your parents. Help your neighbor with anything he needs for his body. Be faithful to your spouse—and wait for your spouse. Keep going. There's plenty to work on there. Perhaps even better is "Love one another as *I* have loved you." He's telling us to give up everything we own—all glory, almighty power, eternal ease—for the lowliest. Suffering insults without protest—for the sake of My attackers. Serving those who should be My slaves. Laying down My life for My friends. These are those things that are right for us to do. And amazingly, because Jesus first loved us in these ways, loving others like this is precisely what we rejoice to do: "These things I have spoken to you, that My joy may be in you, and that your joy may be full" (15:11).

John has a frank way of expressing this in our **Epistle**, 1 John 5:1–8.

"His commandments are not burdensome," John writes (5:3). Not at all. Loving God and others is no burden because Jesus Christ loved us first—took our entire burden upon Himself—"came by water and blood" (5:6), the very blood and water that poured from His side on the cross (Jn 19:34), the water and blood He now gives us with His Spirit in Baptism, Holy Communion, and the Word. Because we are loved, to love can't be a burden.

Because Jesus Loved Us with the Greatest Love, It's a Joy to Keep His Commandment to Love.

This is the second-to-last Sunday of the Easter season. In four days, we'll see our Lord ascend back to heaven. Do, then, enjoy every minute of the Easter **Gradual**:

> *Christ has risen from the dead. [God the Father] has crowned Him with glory and honor, He has given Him dominion over the works of His hands; He has put all things under His feet. (adapted from Mt 28:7; Heb 2:7; Ps 8:6)*

It's hard to imagine a more apt **Hymn of the Day** than Luther's autobiographical "Dear Christians, One and All, Rejoice" (*LSB* 556). We do rejoice in "holy rapture" because of "the wonders God has done" (st 1), including sending "His beloved Son" to save us from "Satan's chains" (st 2). The hymn even prepares us for Ascension Day (sts 9–10).

A note for Ascension Day: Since the Ascension of Our Lord, which falls on the Thursday after Easter 6, uses the same propers for Years A, B, and C, you'll find the one devotion-study for that festival in Year A, page 138. The devotion-study for the Seventh Sunday of Easter, Year B, appears on the next page.

Seventh Sunday of Easter Year B

READINGS

Acts 1:12–26
Psalm 1 (antiphon: v 6)
1 John 5:9–15
John 17:11b–19

HYMN OF THE DAY

LSB 539 "Christ Is the World's Redeemer"

The **Collect** for the Seventh Sunday of Easter recognizes its unique place in the church year:

> *O King of glory, Lord of hosts, uplifted in triumph far above all heavens, leave us not without consolation but send us the Spirit of truth whom You promised from the Father; for You live and reign with Him and the Holy Spirit, one God, now and forever. Amen.*

For one more Sunday, we're celebrating Easter, the season of our resurrected King of glory appearing to His disciples, giving them and us convincing evidence that He really is alive. But on Thursday, our Lord was "uplifted in triumph far above all heavens" in His ascension. So now we're actually with the disciples in that ten-day period anticipating that Jesus will "send us the Spirit of truth whom [He] promised from the Father." Next Sunday will be Pentecost, and we'll see that Christ did not "leave us . . . without consolation." The Holy Spirit is with us for what is now a much longer period of waiting—waiting for that day when our resurrected and ascended Lord will return to earth and all flesh will be raised.

It's just as the **Verse** says: "Alleluia. We know that Christ being raised from the dead will never die again; death no longer has dominion over Him. Alleluia. I will not leave you as orphans; I will come to you. Alleluia" (Rom 6:9; Jn 14:18). For this last Sunday, it's still Easter, but now we're also waiting for the Lord's return.

Another consideration for this Sunday is that since not all congregations have a separate Ascension Day service on Thursday, pastors will often observe Ascension Day as part of the Easter 7 Sunday service. That might mean transferring one or more of the Ascension propers to Sunday. Therefore, if your congregation doesn't have an Ascension Day service on Thursday, you might want to look forward to those propers by reading our devotion-study for Ascension on page 138. At the very least, it would be good preparation to read the account of Jesus ascending, Acts 1:1–11.

If your pastor chooses the Easter 7 **Introit**, picture the ascension as you hear it in worship on Sunday and as you read it now:

Hear, O LORD, when I cry aloud; be gracious to me and answer me!

The LORD is my light and my salvation; whom shall I fear? One thing have I asked of the LORD, that will I seek after: that I may dwell in the house of the LORD all the days of my life, to gaze upon the beauty of the LORD and to inquire in His temple. For He will hide me in His shelter in the day of trouble; He will conceal me under the cover of His tent; He will lift me high upon a rock. For my father and my mother have forsaken me, but the LORD will take me in. Wait for the LORD; be strong, and let your heart take courage; wait for the LORD!

Glory be to the Father and to the Son and to the Holy Spirit; as it was in the beginning, is now, and will be forever. Amen.

Hear, O LORD, when I cry aloud; be gracious to me and answer me! (Ps 27:1a, 4–5, 10, 14; antiphon: Ps 27:7)

Undoubtedly, as the disciples watch Jesus disappear into the clouds, they feel anxious. How would they go forward without their leader and Lord walking with them? Would He hear them now when they cried aloud to Him? Would He answer?

The ascension doesn't really take Jesus away from us at all. Even if "my father and my mother have forsaken me, . . . the LORD will take me in." The ascended Christ is now using His omnipresence (as well as His omniscience and omnipotence) fully and continually so that He most certainly is hearing us, answering us, and working all things on earth for our benefit.

Perhaps this line caught your ascension-tuned ears too: "He will lift me high upon a rock." Christ was lifted up to heaven in order to go and prepare a place for us, that where He is we may be also (Jn 14:3). Christ was lifted up in order to lift me high on the Last Day.

Since we can look forward to that and be assured Jesus is working for us in the meantime, we wait. "Wait for the LORD; be strong, and let your heart take courage; wait for the LORD!"

What do we do while we wait? Do we do what David, our poet, longed to do? "One thing have I asked of the LORD, that will

I seek after: that I may dwell in the house of the LORD all the days of my life, to gaze upon the beauty of the LORD and to inquire in His temple. For He will hide me in His shelter in the day of trouble; He will conceal me under the cover of His tent." Do we withdraw from the world? sit in church 24-7 and contemplate God's holiness? hide out? Knowing David, we're sure he was up to more than that. We'll come back to this.

What were the disciples up to as they waited. Well, to begin, they *were* in church every day (Lk 24:50–53). They were also devoting themselves to prayer with purpose. See about that in the **First Reading**, Acts 1:12–26.

The disciples, too, are under orders to wait (1:4), but they know Jesus will send them the Holy Spirit (1:5), and they know that will mean serious action (1:8). So from these several days of worship, study, listening to Holy Scripture, a plan! There's at least a first baby step: "Peter stood up among the brothers . . . and said, 'Brothers, the Scripture had to be fulfilled, which the Holy Spirit spoke beforehand by the mouth of David concerning Judas. . . . "Let another take his office." So one of the men who have accompanied us during all the time that the Lord Jesus went in and out among us, beginning from the baptism of John until the day when He was taken up from us—one of these men must become with us a witness to His resurrection'" (1:15a, 16a, 20b–22).

The apostles understand that Jesus' work is not over. And without knowing when or exactly how, they perceive that He will continue it through them. They sense that they are going to have a very active role in telling the world about Jesus. And they know it will take everyone doing what he (and, in other callings, she) will be slotted to do. Eleven apostles won't be enough. There will be work for twelve—every bit of it essential. "And they put forward two, Joseph . . . and Matthias. And they prayed. . . . And they cast lots for them, and the lot fell on Matthias, and he was numbered with the eleven apostles" (1:23a, c, 24a, 26). All was now ready for the Gospel to explode at Pentecost.

We grasp how critical this is, don't we. Everyone is about her or his business in getting out the word of Jesus' death and resurrection. It's truly the way of life. Read the **Epistle**, 1 John 5:9–15.

God has given His testimony concerning His Son. (Notice from the preceding verses, last week's Epistle, 5:6–8, that God's witnesses are the Spirit, water, blood, the Word, Baptism, and the Lord's Supper, which proclaim Jesus' death on the cross, Jn 19:34.) "And this is the testimony, that God gave us eternal life, and this life is in His Son. Whoever has the Son has life; whoever does not have the Son of God does not have life" (1 Jn 5:11–12). God wants everyone to have life in Christ. Therefore everyone's witness matters.

Even as we wait for Jesus' return, we already have eternal life. "Whoever has the Son has life"—present tense. "You who believe in the name of the Son of God . . . have eternal life" (5:13)—present tense. We're not in limbo, a state of suspended animation, or hiding out in the temple. We're living our eternal lives now; we're about God's business now. And He is just as actively working for us now: "This is the confidence that we have toward Him, that if we ask anything according to His will He hears us. And if we know that He hears us in whatever we ask, we know that we have the requests that we have asked of Him" (5:14–15).

It's such an encouragement to be active in God's business! We can pray to Jesus, and He hears us. And to that, from the **Holy Gospel**, add this: while we wait for Christ's return, He is praying for us. Read John 17:11b–19.

This is the middle of what we call Jesus' High Priestly Prayer. (Easter 7, Year A hears 17:1–11, Year C, 17:20–26). On the night before His crucifixion, Jesus prays for the disciples and for the whole Church. He's been doing the same ever since, constantly interceding with the Father on our behalf.

Jesus' chief petition to the Father is that He would "keep them in Your name" (17:11). Jesus' care for us never ceases, never pauses. "While I was with them, I kept them in Your name. . . . But now I am coming to You" (17:12a, 13a). So His care for us must continue. Even while visibly absent, Jesus is actively working for our blessing.

And He is indeed working through us. "I do not ask that You take them out of the world," Father. Rather, "as You sent Me into the world, so I have sent them into the world" (17:15a, 18). Peter, John, Matthias, Joseph (who wasn't chosen by the lot), you, me—Jesus hasn't given us the blessing we might most desire: to be taken out of this world to the perfect joys of heaven the moment pain strikes, the day everything seems to be coming undone. He's instead sent us into the world with the message that Good Friday and Easter have won eternal life for everyone.

So what was with David praying in the Introit to dwell in the house of the Lord all his days, to gaze upon the beauty of the Lord? Was he shirking his mission? Of course not. "I have given them Your word. . . . Sanctify them in the truth; Your word is truth" (17:14a, 17). The mission to the world always begins and is always sustained as we are sanctified by the Word. "Blessed is the man" who "meditates day and night" on the Word of the Lord (the **Psalm**, 1:1a, 2b). That man is actively about the work of the Lord!

We Wait Quite Actively for Our Ascended Lord's Return, Knowing That He Continues to Work For and through Us.

The **Hymn of the Day**, "Christ Is the World's Redeemer" (*LSB* 539), melds Easter, Ascension, and beyond: "At the hour appointed He rose triumphantly. And now, to heaven ascended, He sits upon the throne," "our trust and hope secure" (sts 3, 1).

Close your preparation for the final Sunday of Easter by meditating once more on the **Gradual** for the season:

> *Christ has risen from the dead. [God the Father] has crowned Him with glory and honor, He has given Him dominion over the works of His hands; He has put all things under His feet. (adapted from Mt 28:7; Heb 2:7; Ps 8:6)*

The Day of Pentecost Year B

READINGS

Ezekiel 37:1–14
Psalm 139:1–12 (13–16)
(antiphon: v 17)
Acts 2:1–21
John 15:26–27; 16:4b–15

HYMN OF THE DAY

LSB 497 "Come, Holy Ghost, God and Lord"

He comes with a purpose.

We know the day of Pentecost as the coming of the Holy Spirit. And it was quite a coming! The rushing wind, the flames of fire. The languages—the apostles of Jesus are suddenly able to speak the native tongues of "every nation under heaven." Three thousand people become new believers in one day! It's quite a coming for the Holy Spirit!

Rightly, Pentecost is one of the great festivals of the church year, and the story is amazing. But sometimes it's possible when the pageantry is so colorful to lose sight of the real purpose. The Holy Spirit comes, but what's He up to?

Our **Second Reading** for Sunday (but a good place to start) describes the confusing, chaotic, yet powerfully creative scene on the day of Pentecost. It doesn't, however, explain much of the point behind the Holy Spirit's dramatic unveiling. We'll work on that. First, though, read the account itself, Acts 2:1–21.

Pentecost, meaning "fiftieth," was the second of Old Testament Israel's three great annual festivals. It was fifty days after Passover, the first of the three. (The other was the Feast of Booths with the Day of Atonement in the fall.) By this time, the Jewish people are scattered throughout the Mediterranean world. They all hope to travel to Jerusalem at least once for the holy days. That might mean arriving for Passover and staying the next couple of months to celebrate Pentecost as well.

This particular Pentecost is also fifty days since Jesus' resurrection, and His apostles, fully restocked with the addition of Matthias, know what is coming soon (Acts 1:4–5, 8). The believers, "all together in one place" (2:1), by this time number 120 (1:15). Suddenly comes the sound of the wind, the tongues of fire, the miraculous ability to speak all those languages. It is explicitly the Holy Spirit who gives them the ability (2:4).

And it is impressive! The visitors in Jerusalem come from all over the Roman Empire and even beyond. Parthians, Medes, Elamites, and residents of Mesopotamia come from the east—Iran and Iraq today. Judeans are, of course, the home folks. Cappadocia, Pontus, the Roman province they call Asia, Phrygia, and Pamphylia are all in Asia Minor, present-day Turkey. Egypt and Libya are in North Africa. Then come visitors from Rome, the Greek island of Crete, and what is now Saudi Arabia. It may have been the sound like the rushing wind that brought the crowds running (2:6), but they stay in amazement at the languages that are being spoken (2:11–12). Well, there are the mockers too (2:13).

The best part of Peter's sermon will be in next Sunday's Second Reading. All we really hear this week is Peter's defense of what seems so perplexing. He dismisses the foolish charge of drunkenness (2:15)—as if alcohol could produce proficiency in Parthian. Rather, all this was as Joel had prophesied eight centuries before (Joel 2:28–32a): "God declares, that I will pour out My Spirit on all flesh" (Acts 2:17). This is what the apostles have been waiting for, the power from on high Jesus had promised, the Holy Spirit. That much is clear. "Even on My male servants and female servants in those days I will pour out My Spirit" (2:18).

Okay, but *why* the Spirit? His coming is quite the display, but what did He have to say? So far, we get precious little. The crowd hears the believers telling "the mighty works of God" (2:11). But what mighty works? Surely the point of all this isn't just that there is a Holy Spirit or that He's mighty—and mighty good with languages.

Unfortunately, that's essentially the takeaway some Christians today find in Pentecost. So-called "charismatic" or "pentecostal" groups see this day as primarily teaching us to expect similar gifts from the Holy Spirit, such as a gift of languages. Actually, charismatics who seek to "speak in tongues" aren't even looking for ordinary human languages as here in Acts; they imagine the Spirit will give them private prayer language that only those with another "gift," "interpretation," can understand. Such Christians perhaps intend to honor the Spirit. Of course, it doesn't really honor Him if it misses the point *He* intends.

Following all the talk of prophecy, visions, dreams, and wonders (2:17–20), it seems almost an afterthought when Peter quotes his last line from Joel: "And it shall come to pass that everyone who calls upon the name of the Lord shall be saved" (2:21).

So where will we hear what the Holy Spirit is really about? Perhaps the **Introit**:

Come, Holy Spirit, fill the hearts of the faithful, and kindle in them the fire of Your love. Alleluia.

O Lord, how manifold are Your works! In wisdom have You made them all; the earth is full of Your creatures. These all look to You, to give them their food in due season. When You give it to them, they gather it up; when You open Your hand, they are filled with good things. When You send forth your Spirit, they are created, and You renew the face of the ground.

Glory be to the Father and to the Son and to the Holy Spirit; as it was in the beginning, is now, and will be forever. Amen.

Come, Holy Spirit, fill the hearts of the faithful, and kindle in them the fire of Your love. Alleluia. (Ps 104:24, 27–28, 30; antiphon: Liturgical Text)

The antiphon certainly states what we pray would be a purpose for the Holy Spirit's coming: "Fill the hearts of the faithful, and kindle in them the fire of Your love." So with what will the Holy Spirit fill our hearts that leads to love?

Instead of an obvious answer, the Introit itself seems to shift from filling our hearts to filling our stomachs: "These all look to You, to give them their food in due season." But then here's an important advance: "When You send forth Your Spirit, they are created." Perhaps we don't often think of the Third Person of the Trinity active in First Article things—creating and sustaining. But we were reminded earlier this year that the Spirit certainly was there at creation (Gen 1:2, the Old Testament Reading for the Baptism of Our Lord). In fact, in the Nicene Creed, we refer to the Holy Spirit as the "giver of life." Is that also part of His Pentecost work?

The **Collect** makes direct reference to Pentecost and strongly hints at the Spirit's grand purpose that day:

O God, on this day You once taught the hearts of Your faithful people by sending them the light of Your Holy Spirit. Grant us in our day by the same Spirit to have a right understanding in all things and evermore to rejoice in His holy consolation; through Jesus Christ, Your Son, our Lord, who lives and reigns with You and the Holy Spirit, one God, now and forever. Amen.

By the Spirit on Pentecost, God "taught the hearts" of His people. Ah, now we're filling hearts—with teaching. Then we pray that "by the same Spirit" God would give *us* "a right understanding in all things." Again, teaching, learning all the right things.

The **Old Testament Reading** brings together these activities of the Spirit—giving life and teaching. Read Ezekiel 37:1–14.

It's strange all right, but remember that it's a vision that the Spirit lets Ezekiel see. The dry bones represent Israel, conquered by Assyria, captive in Babylonia, seemingly dead (37:11). But the nation will rise again. In the vision, it's by Ezekiel prophesying over the bones. The Lord tells him, "Prophesy to the breath; prophesy, son of man, and say to the breath, Thus says the Lord God: Come from the four winds, O breath, and breathe on these slain, that they may live" (37:9). It's helpful to know that the same Hebrew word, רוּחַ (*ruach*), can mean "breath," "wind," or "spirit." So it's the Holy Spirit at work as God breathes life back into His people.

But notice this too: As on the day of Pentecost, the high drama—dry bones miraculously standing on their feet as a great army—isn't really the main point. Rather, when all this happens, "You shall know that I am the LORD" (37:6, 13). And "I will put My Spirit within you, and you shall live, and I will place you in your own land. Then you shall know that I am the LORD" (37:14). The Spirit gives life, with the ultimate purpose that we are taught to know God rightly.

Read the **Psalm** with this same idea in mind, Psalm 139:1–17. This is one of our favorite texts to lift up the sanctity of human life against abortion (139:13–16). The Holy Spirit knows us that well (139:7)! And see the verse selected as the antiphon: "How precious to me are Your thoughts, O God! How vast is the sum of them!" (139:17). Above all, we wish to know God.

Finally, the **Holy Gospel** tells us what the Spirit teaches about God; what He fills our hearts with, which gives life; and the fire of His love. It teaches us why the Spirit came at Pentecost. Read John 15:26–27; 16:4b–15.

The next day Jesus will die on the cross, and there's so much the disciples don't yet understand about that. They cannot bear to know it all yet (16:12). But after Jesus dies, rises, and ascends back to heaven, He'll send the Holy Spirit. And "when the Spirit of truth comes, He will guide you into all the truth" (16:13). And that truth will be about the one who is the way, and the truth, and the life (14:6). "He," the Spirit, "will bear witness about Me," Jesus says (15:26). "He will glorify Me, for He will take what is Mine and declare it to you" (16:14). Not believing in Jesus is the world's chief sin; Jesus ascending to the Father proves that He is the one who makes us righteous; Jesus has defeated Satan, "the ruler of this world" (16:8–11). The Holy Spirit's message is all about Christ.

Pentecost isn't about high drama. It's not about exalting the Spirit Himself. It's the Spirit enabling Peter and the Church to declare the great work of God: the Son becoming flesh, dying on the cross, and rising again. That's what we need to be taught about God. It's how we have life. It's how we who call on His name are saved. What moves us to love is all Christ.

BEGINNING AT PENTECOST, THE HOLY SPIRIT, THE GIVER OF LIFE, GIVES US TO KNOW ALL THINGS ABOUT CHRIST.

We understand the **Gradual** then rightly.

I will pour out My Spirit on all flesh, and your sons and your daughters shall prophesy. With the heart one believes and is justified, and with the mouth one confesses and is saved. (Acts 2:17b; Rom 10:10)

By the outpouring of the Spirit, we believe in and confess Jesus!

Sing "Come, Holy Ghost, God and Lord" (**Hymn of the Day**, *LSB* 497). "Teach us to know our God aright. . . . Let none but Christ our master be" (st 2).

The Holy Trinity Year B

READINGS

Isaiah 6:1–8

Psalm 29 (antiphon: v 2)

Acts 2:14a, 22–36

John 3:1–17

HYMN OF THE DAY

LSB 498, 499 "Come, Holy Ghost, Creator Blest"

"Who in here," Lutheran teacher Miss Leslie asked her third and fourth graders one day, "understands the Holy Trinity?"

Several students raised their hands.

"Great!" she replied. "Hold that for a few seconds while I get the pastor. You can explain it to him."

Trinity Sundays have been happening in the Church each year since about the fourteenth century, but we still haven't come to *understand* the Holy Trinity, how the one and only true God can be triune—one God yet three persons. And we never will. But Trinity Sunday is a day on which we especially teach what Scripture teaches about the Trinity. We do so because every third or fourth grader, every pastor or teacher, every man, woman, or child who is truly a Christian *believes* this truth that we can't understand.

That means the Bible must tell us whatever we do need to know about the triune God. Scripture must somehow teach us to know Him whom we can't fully explain or grasp. That's what we'll find in our readings today, and the very comforting discovery is that we do come to know the Trinity in a beloved and very familiar Way (John 14:6).

The first propers we'll hear Sunday declare the Trinity explicitly. The **Introit**:

> *Blessèd be the Holy Trinity and the undivided Unity. Let us give glory to Him because He has shown His mercy to us.*
>
> *I have set the* Lord *always before me; because He is at my right hand, I shall not be shaken. Therefore my*

heart is glad, and my whole being rejoices; my flesh also dwells secure. For You will not abandon my soul to Sheol, or let Your holy one see corruption. You make known to me the path of life; in Your presence there is fullness of joy; at Your right hand are pleasures forevermore.

Glory be to the Father and to the Son and to the Holy Spirit; as it was in the beginning, is now, and will be forever. Amen.

Blessèd be the Holy Trinity and the undivided Unity. Let us give glory to Him because He has shown His mercy to us. (Ps 16:8–11; antiphon: Liturgical Text)

The antiphon to this Introit is another of those occasional "Liturgical Texts," meaning that it is a long-honored composition of the Church rather than a quotation from Scripture. On Trinity Sunday, that's especially significant, because there is no passage in God's Word that uses the words *Trinity, triune*, or *Three in One*. Surprising? There are plenty of references to God being one and only (e.g., Deut 6:4; Is 45:5; 1 Cor 8:4). The three persons are also clear (Mt 3:16–17; 28:19; and even in the Old Testament, Is 48:16). What's far more obvious is that the Father, Son, and Holy Spirit are mentioned individually countless times in the Bible. So early in Christian history, theologians formulated language that could summarize this doctrine in a unique and memorable way. This says it well: "Blessèd be the Holy Trinity and the undivided Unity." Unity: one God. Trinity: three. In the early centuries, they were called persons. (Never "three people," of course. That's how technical terms work; you choose the words, give them a certain definition, and then stick to them.)

Added on to every Introit is the "Gloria Patri" (Latin for "Glory to the Father"): "Glory be to the Father and to the Son and to the Holy Spirit; as it was in the beginning, is now, and will be forever." Again, this is especially noteworthy on Trinity Sunday. Since the body of the Introit is always from the Psalms (the Old Testament), the trinitarian Gloria is included to make this point: the God of the Old Testament—Elohim, Yahweh, Adonai—is one and the same God that we in the New Testament Church worship. As it was in the beginning, still today, and forever, He's the Holy Trinity.

The **Collect**, too, uses the Church's language to pray to the one God:

Almighty and everlasting God, You have given us grace to acknowledge the glory of the eternal Trinity by the confession of a true faith and to worship the Unity in the power of the Divine Majesty. Keep us steadfast in this faith and defend us from all adversities; for You, O Father, Son, and Holy Spirit, live and reign, one God, now and forever. Amen.

Not only does the Collect reaffirm the "Trinity" and the "Unity." See how it addresses God: "Almighty and everlasting God, You . . ." And who is the "You"? At the close, "You, O Father, Son, and Holy Spirit, live and reign, one God, now and forever." All other appointed Collects throughout the church year are addressed either to the Father (most of the time) or the Son (occasionally). This one addresses all three persons, which is to say they are equal and *together* they are the one "almighty and everlasting God."

The petition in this Collect is of paramount importance: "Keep us steadfast in this faith and defend us from all adversities." That directs us to the Athanasian Creed, which most of our congregations will confess aloud on Trinity Sunday (see *LSB*, p 319). "This faith" to which the Collect refers is the confession of the triune God, "the catholic [or universal Christian] faith; whoever does not keep it whole and undefiled," the Athanasian Creed says, "will without doubt perish eternally." Being *that* vital, this doctrine of the Trinity is a chief battleground where Satan will bring "adversities," such as so many historic and modern heresies. Among the ancient ones, the Manichaeans and Arians are worth further reading. Today, Judaism, Islam, the Jehovah's Witnesses, and Mormons all imagine gods other than the Trinity. Whether they call them God, Allah, or anything else, they are *not* God!

How do we know the one who *is* the true God? We have to admit there's a lot we *don't* know, certainly that we don't understand. Consider the **Gradual** for Trinity and for the first part of the season coming up:

> *Great is the LORD, and greatly to be praised, and His greatness is unsearchable. On Your wondrous works, I will meditate, and I will declare Your greatness. (Ps 145:3, 5b, 6b)*

God's greatness surely is "unsearchable." Look all we want; read and study all we can; think hard; be smart. We still can never understand how the Father is God (not a part of God or an aspect of God or one way of thinking about God), how the Son is God (not just a way God appeared for a while), and how the Holy Spirit is God (not just a way God works). They're distinct, yet they're all the one God. The pastor doesn't understand either.

But Isaiah's encounter with the Trinity in the **Old Testament Reading** is revealing. Read Isaiah 6:1–8.

"Holy, holy, holy is the LORD of hosts" (6:3). We might say it this way: Yahweh is holy (once), holy (twice), holy (three times). Or still more accurately: Holy is the First Person, Holy is the Second Person, Holy is the Third Person. The Trinity is revealed more transparently in the New Testament, but He's there throughout the Old too.

What's really remarkable about this incident, however, is how Isaiah "saw the Lord" (6:1). God the Father has no visible form; it seems that even in heaven we won't see Him. The Holy Spirit once appeared as a dove, but He also really has no form. So when Isaiah sees the Lord, he's seeing the Son, the one who later would become flesh. In verse 1, Isaiah says he saw the "Lord" (lowercase, the Hebrew Adonai). But in verse 5, it's the "LORD" (small caps, the Hebrew Yahweh), just as in verse 3. On many occasions in the Old Testament,

God the Son is called Yahweh (Lord), but there may be a distinction in Isaiah 6. Having seen the Son in verse 1, Isaiah is telling us in verse 5 that he's actually seen the Trinity. When we see Christ, we see everything there is to see about the Holy Trinity (see Jn 14:8–9).

This is why Isaiah, a man who is sinful, unclean, sees God without being undone. He sees the Trinity in the Son, the One who nearly eight hundred years later atones for Isaiah's sins and the sins of the world by dying on a cross (6:5–7). The Son's atoning death is also why the Lord (back to Adonai) can use any of us (6:8).

Christ is likewise the key to the **Psalm**, Psalm 29. The one God is powerful enough to thunder and smash cedar forests. But He also does "bless His people with peace" (29:11) because He, the Son, makes our peace with Him, the Father, becoming man, atoning for sin.

Acts 2:14a, 22–36, the **Second Reading** for Trinity Sunday, continues Peter's Pentecost sermon from last week. Read how he, too, sees the Holy Trinity through Christ.

The Pentecost crowd is largely devout Jews (Acts 2:5). They revere God and His workings. Peter's sermon, therefore, has one aim: to show that Jesus of Nazareth is the very Son of God who carries out the workings of the Father. Jesus was attested by God, and God worked through Him (2:22). Jesus was delivered up to be killed according to God's plan (2:23). But God raised Jesus (2:24); God did not abandon Jesus to corruption (2:27). (Notice how Peter explains that these words of David apply to Jesus: 2:29–31.) Bottom line: God, whom you worship, has declared this Jesus to be "Lord" (2:36). He is the One you are to worship. Since you devout Jews know you must worship no one but the Lord your God and that there is only one God, this Jesus (whom you crucified!) is that God. So here's the Three in One: "Being therefore exalted at the right hand of God, and having received from the *Father* the promise of the *Holy Spirit, He* has poured out this that you yourselves are seeing and hearing" (2:33). You're seeing the Trinity through the Son.

That's what Jesus brings Nicodemus to realize in the **Holy Gospel**, John 3:1–17.

Nicodemus is another faithful Jew who seeks to understand the works of God (3:2). What's more, he believes in the Trinity, for he doesn't protest Jesus bringing up the Holy Spirit (3:5, 8)—even though he doesn't get what Jesus means about being born again (3:3–4, 9). How does Jesus fit in?

No one sees the Father. You can't see the Spirit either (3:8). But there is One who has "descended from heaven." It's the "Son of Man," whom you can see and are seeing right now (3:13). He is most certainly God—with the Father and the Spirit—because "whoever believes *in Him*" has eternal life (3:15, 16). And He is the One who lets us see God by being "lifted up" to die (3:14), removing the sin that would keep us from seeing Him.

**The Son of God, Christ,
Enables Us to See the Holy Trinity.**

The **Hymn of the Day**, "Come Holy Ghost, Creator Blest" (*LSB* 498, 499), ends with two trinitarian stanzas, and it's the Son who bestows on us the Spirit's gifts.

The Sundays after Pentecost: Proper 3 (May 24–28) Year B

READINGS

Hosea 2:14–20
Psalm 103:1–13 (antiphon: v 22)
Acts 2:14a, 36–47
Mark 2:(13–17) 18–22

HYMN OF THE DAY

LSB 819 "Sing Praise to God, the Highest Good"

She couldn't say he'd been unkind to her. In fact, he'd been a sweet husband. He'd known her past and had still been proud to have her as his wife. He'd cared for her. They'd had children together. One day she wanted something different, so she up and left. Now it was pretty obvious life wasn't any better. It was much worse! She felt degraded, guilty, but, it seemed, there was no going back.

The reunion was festive; everybody was having a good time. There was lots of catching up from the old days, seeing who was there, wondering who was missing. Then someone started asking, "What about *him*? Yeah, remember *him*? We never treated him very well. We thought he was strange. You know what he's up to now? He's made it bigger than any of us!"

So this is what success was like. He'd made his decision long ago, decided this was the life he wanted. It meant giving up his friends, even double-crossing some of them. Now he ran with a whole new crowd, but run they did. He had money all right. He had gotten what he was shooting for, but not much else.

There's more to each of these stories in the lessons for Proper 3, Year B. But first, a procedural question: Are you supposed to be reading these this week?

The answer, if "supposed to" means reading what you'll hear in church this coming Sunday, is yes . . . *if* last Sunday was Holy Trinity and this coming Sunday will fall between May 24 and May 28, inclusive. If last Sunday was Trinity but this coming

Sunday's date is something later, your congregation will likely be using one of the subsequent propers—Proper 4 or Proper 5 or Proper 6 or Proper 7. Why? Well, it all depends on the date Easter occurred this year. But for a detailed explanation, turn back to the devotion-study for Proper 3, Year A, on page 154. Then, if you're in the right place here, come back and read on. Otherwise, skip ahead to the Sunday your congregation will be observing this week. (Unless, of course, our three hooks have you hooked. Then be my guest to read this devotion-study and the other.)

In any case, the Sundays after Pentecost, from Trinity Sunday on, constitute the lengthy nonfestival portion of the church year, sometimes known as the Time of the Church. With a few exceptions, such as Reformation and All Saints' Day, the paraments are green, like summer—though the season will reach well into autumn. The overarching theme for the season is God's working in the world through His people, the Church. Christ is at the heart, as He is in every season, and it's always the Holy Spirit who's using the proclamation of Christ to grow and preserve the Church, as we saw Him begin to do at Pentecost.

The **Gradual** for the first portion of this long season is the same one we heard on Trinity Sunday:

Great is the Lord, and greatly to be praised, and His greatness is unsearchable. On Your wondrous works, I will meditate, and I will declare Your greatness. (Ps 145:3, 5b, 6b)

The season of Pentecost will show us plenty of wondrous works of God to meditate on and declare.

Now back to those stories. Each is about relationships. So is our **Introit**:

Let your priests be clothed with righteousness, and let your saints shout for joy.

For the Lord has chosen Zion; He has desired it for His dwelling place: "This is My resting place forever; here I will dwell, for I have desired it. I will abundantly bless her provisions; I will satisfy her poor with bread. Her priests I will clothe with salvation, and her saints will shout for joy. There I will make a horn to sprout for David; I have a prepared a lamp for my anointed. His enemies I will clothe with shame, but on him his crown will shine."

Glory be to the Father and to the Son and to the Holy Spirit; as it was in the beginning, is now, and will be forever. Amen.

Let your priests be clothed with righteousness, and let your saints shout for joy. (Ps 132:13–18; antiphon: Ps 132:9)

"The Lord has chosen Zion; He has desired it for His dwelling place: 'This is My resting place forever.'" God establishes a special relationship with His people, Israel. His city, Jerusalem, with His temple, on Mount Zion, symbolizes His presence with them. God's priests carry out His righteous commands on behalf of the people. The line of David is promised an eternal kingdom—the Messiah. In the meantime, God provides abundant blessings, including crops that flourish. The psalmist hears shouts of joy!

You'd think the marriage was idyllic.

Instead, the **Collect** reminds us that God's people badly broke the relationship and need Him to restore it:

> *Merciful Father, You have given Your only Son as the sacrifice for sinners. Grant us grace to receive the fruits of His redeeming work with thanksgiving and daily follow in His way; through Jesus Christ, our Lord, who lives and reigns with You and the Holy Spirit, one God, now and forever. Amen.*

Friendships, families, marriages involving sinners will never be only still waters. We broke our relationship with God, and only Christ's redeeming sacrifice on the cross could mend it. But He did make the sacrifice, so we do have opportunity to live with Him again, follow Him, and receive the fruits.

How much did that mean to a woman who'd left her faithful husband? Read not only this week's **Old Testament Reading**, Hosea 2:14–20, but the whole back story as well, chapters 1–3.

Gomer—don't let the name put you off; she was apparently attractive enough—had been a prostitute. No doubt more willingly than Hosea, the Lord pities her, and He commands the prophet to take her as his wife. Now she has a husband, security, and soon, three children. She is loved.

Was it the drudgery of diapers? Was he a bit roughhewn, not too stylish, maybe not as dashing and romantic as a woman might dream? Did she need to see the world, spread her wings, find herself? Whatever the reason, walking the streets again was no life.

But one day, he is back. He comes for her, speaking tenderly to her, inviting her to come home (2:14). He tells her she is as beautiful as when she was a young girl, before she fell into any of this (2:15). "Call Me, 'My Husband'" (2:16). Could there ever be two sweeter words after all we've been through?

The words were really all God's. Oh, yes, there was a real Gomer and a real Hosea. And their marriage was the real thing. But it is God's love that not only delivers her from shame but plays out this whole story as an allegory for Israel. God brought Israel in "her youth" out of Egypt and had taken her as His own, but she prostituted herself with the Baals, Canaanite fertility gods (2:17). Again and again. For a time, she suffers the pain and humiliation of her adulteries. But then, just as God orders Hosea to buy Gomer back from prostitution, He redeems Israel. "And I will betroth you to Me forever. I will betroth you to Me in righteousness and in justice, in steadfast love and in mercy. I will betroth you to Me in faithfulness" (2:19–20). He offers forgiveness to a broken woman, a despairing people who don't deserve and perhaps couldn't have hoped for it.

Eight centuries later, it isn't balloons decorating a ballroom that suddenly go flat. Realizing how they treat God's Son lets all the air out of the mood. They don't just think He's strange. They kill Him. Remember the occasion of Peter's sermon in our **Second Reading**, Acts 2:14a, 36–47.

It's still the day of Pentecost. Jews from all over the Roman Empire are celebrating the feast—until Peter spoils the party: "God has made Him both Lord and Christ, this Jesus whom you crucified" (2:36).

"Now when they heard this they were cut to the heart, and said to Peter and the rest of the apostles, 'Brothers, what shall we do?'" (2:37). My God, what *can* we do? We've killed the Savior! We were so busy earning grades, impressing friends, so wrapped up in where we had to be, running busy schedules, being popular. He was right here with us, and we ignored Him, treated Him like trash.

But Peter said to them, "Repent and be baptized every one of you in the name of Jesus Christ for the forgiveness of your sins. . . . The promise is for you and for your children" (2:38, 39). The very death you caused has forgiven you, and forgiveness is yours in Baptism! God is calling you back to Himself!

Forgiven! Restored by God to Himself! Three thousand! And the relationships that spawned! "All who believed were together," devoted to the apostles' teaching and fellowship, "attending the temple together and breaking bread in their homes" (2:44, 42, 46).

We're only guessing how Levi chose his first career, but it wasn't an honorable one. Read how it went from here in the **Holy Gospel**, Mark 2:13–22.

A Jewish person didn't become a tax collector for the Romans in order to serve his fellow man. Tax collectors were not only collaborators with the hated conquerors; they maxed income by charging whatever excess they could finagle—from their own people. It did indeed cost you your friends; your only buds would be fellow cheats. The job's one redeeming quality: all the money you could make. We don't know if Levi, better known to us as Matthew (Mt 9:9), is feeling the emptiness, but when Jesus calls him, he goes.

What he follows Jesus into is a new relationship—"unshrunk cloth" (2:21), "new wine" for "fresh wineskins" (2:22). That is, a relationship was established when Jesus went to the cross that made us God's dear ones, not by obedience to an old covenant of law but by faith in what Christ has done for us. Jesus' forgiveness means God does not see us as tax-collecting swindlers trying to makes amends. He sees us as brand new, as beloved, as forever His beautiful betrothed.

Our Broken Relationship with God Restored by Christ's Forgiveness Is Truly as Good as New.

"Bless the Lord, O my soul" for this new relationship! (the **Psalm**). He "forgives all your iniquity. . . . He does not deal with us according to our sins, nor repay us according to our iniquities. . . . As far as the east is from the west, so far does He remove our transgressions from us" (Ps 103:1, 3, 10, 12).

The **Hymn of the Day** describes our new relationship with God. Because "our Savior saw our helplessness," we are "His flock," "His own, His chosen band" (sts 3, 4).

The Sundays after Pentecost: Proper 4 (May 29–June 4) Year B

READINGS

Deuteronomy 5:12–15
Psalm 81:1–10 (antiphon: v 13)
2 Corinthians 4:5–12
Mark 2:23–28 (3:1–6)

HYMN OF THE DAY

LSB 906 "O Day of Rest and Gladness"

For these early Sundays after Pentecost, see the Proper 3, Year A, devotion-study (p 154) explaining why some propers may be omitted in some years.

It's a gift of God that, like so many others, man manages to open and then rewrap in paper that just doesn't fit the occasion.

The Sabbath.

"Observe the Sabbath day, to keep it holy, as the LORD your God commanded you. Six days you shall labor and do all your work, but the seventh day is a Sabbath to the LORD your God. On it you shall not do any work" (Deut 5:12–14a).

Orthodox Jews today depend on technology like Shabbat elevators (which stop automatically at every floor) and Shabbat clocks (timers that can be set before the Sabbath to turn appliances on and off on the Sabbath) to avoid breaking the prohibition of work.

Along with other distinctive tenets, Seventh-day Adventists require observation of the Old Testament Sabbath—worship and refraining from work or secular entertainment on Saturday.

Blue laws in much of the United States and Canada are used to prohibit various businesses from operating on Sundays. The original intent was certainly to encourage religious piety, but some have argued that the laws hung around into recent years more because mom-and-pop stores didn't want the big-box competitors (with large staffing) to take away any more customers.

The Lord's command to Israel to observe a Sabbath day was, like all of God's commands, very good. Yet on countless occasions, the

Sabbath was the bone of contention between Jesus' opponents and our Lord. Proper 4, this Sunday after Pentecost, shows us what a blessing the Sabbath was made to be—and how in related ways, the Lord of the Sabbath continues to bless us in the post-Sabbath, New Testament age.

Without mentioning the Sabbath specifically, the **Introit** expresses its purpose:

> *For God alone my soul waits in silence; from Him comes my salvation.*
>
> *For God alone, O my soul, wait in silence, for my hope is from Him. He only is my rock and my salvation, my fortress; I shall not be shaken. On God rests my salvation and my glory; my mighty rock, my refuge is God. Trust in Him at all times, O people; pour out your heart before Him; God is a refuge for us.*
>
> *Glory be to the Father and to the Son and to the Holy Spirit; as it was in the beginning, is now, and will be forever. Amen.*
>
> *For God alone my soul waits in silence; from Him comes my salvation. (Ps 62:5–8; antiphon: Ps 62:1)*

Perhaps today more than ever, quiet is hard to come by. "Noise pollution" isn't just a challenge for areas around airports and along freeways; it's life as we know it. Traffic, a guy's bass booming through his rolled-down window, the party next door or in the apartment above, the vacuum cleaner, the phone ringing, the TV that for some reason gets so much louder on commercials. We actually buy ourselves a white noise machine to drown it all out.

We wish these words: "For God alone my soul waits in silence." Hence, the Sabbath. It's a day to shut out the noise and contemplate: "From Him comes my salvation. . . . My hope is from Him." It's a day to hear nothing but that "God alone . . . is my rock . . . my fortress; I shall not be shaken." Silent "trust in Him at all times." Or it's a day to "pour out your heart before Him" without any horns honking or brakes squealing to interrupt. God wants us to have this day.

David says it again in the **Gradual** for these first Sundays after Pentecost:

> *Great is the Lord, and greatly to be praised, and His greatness is unsearchable. On Your wondrous works, I will meditate, and I will declare Your greatness. (Ps 145:3, 5b, 6b)*

"On your wondrous works, I will meditate." Given the chance.

We truly long for that opportunity, don't we! That says something about how the new man or woman inside us feels about the Ten Commandments. Our **Old Testament Reading** this week is the Third of the Ten. Read Deuteronomy 5:12–15.

Deuteronomy 5 is the second—and less familiar—locus of the Commandments, after Exodus 20. (*Deuteronomy*, by the way, means "Second Law.") The only major difference between the two is here, regarding the Sabbath day. *Sabbath* comes from the Hebrew word for "rest," and God is clear in both Exodus and Deuteronomy that His people were to rest from ordinary work that day. They'd find no manna, and they weren't to cook (Ex 16:22–30). Gathering wood (Num 15:32–36) or kindling a fire (Ex 35:2–3) were capital offenses. It's easy to see how Sabbath-breaking became dreaded violations.

So, as we're tempted to ask with all of God's Law, was it given to be a burden, even fearful for us? Was it a trap to catch us, or God's heavy-handed plan to assert His authority and restrict our freedom? Unbelief always sees the Law that way.

A hint for proper understanding, though, comes in the reasons given with the Third Commandment itself. Here, Exodus and Deuteronomy are different. In Exodus, the Sabbath is designated as a day of rest because God rested from all His creating on the seventh day (Ex 20:11). That's a good reason. But another good one is here in Deuteronomy: Israel was to rest so "that your male servant and your female servant may rest as well as you. You shall remember that you were a slave in the land of Egypt" (Deut 5:14–15). Before the Lord brought the Israelites out of Egypt, they got no rest. Now they were to be sure those who served them would not be treated so badly. God's point is that everyone needs rest. It's the way He made us. So clearly God gave the Sabbath as a way to love—Him loving us in our needs, us caring for others in theirs.

The Sabbath, then, wasn't intended to be a burden. Sabbath rest, though, also wasn't meant to be no alarm, sacking out till noon, and then a big chair with chips and a beer at night. The **Psalm** tells us what should be going on. Read Psalm 81:1–10, 13.

When the Lord brought Israel out of Egypt, "I relieved your shoulder of the burden; your hands were freed from the basket" of slavery (81:6). Obviously, God didn't plan to create new burdens for His people. But this was to happen: "Hear, O My people, while I admonish you! O Israel, if you would but listen to Me!" (81:8). The Lord commanded that a day be set aside when His people would listen to Him. It's just what the silence was for! "Oh, that My people would listen to Me" (81:13).

And hearing the Lord is always good for us! Not only hearing when He warns us of our sin and its dangers but hearing that He delivers us, hearing His answers when we call out to Him in our distress (81:7). This is what we need—the comfort, the encouragement, the forgiveness God's Word speaks to us! "Open your mouth wide, and I will fill it" (81:10). The Lord's day is for Him to fill us!

Yes, it's surely for us to "sing aloud to God," "shout for joy," "raise a song," even "sound the tambourine, the sweet lyre," and "blow the trumpet," too, if we're thus talented (81:1, 2, 3). And talented or not, when we sing in worship, let's sing with gusto!

But chiefly, it's for us to be on the receiving end—to rest, listen, be filled by what God has to bring us. Even Paul, who did all the talking when he came to his congregations, knew it was really about God in action. Read the **Epistle**, 2 Corinthians 4:5–12.

"What we proclaim is not ourselves, but Jesus Christ as Lord" (4:5), Paul says. He knows he's just a clay jar "to show that the surpassing power belongs to God and not to us" (4:7). Paul even understands his sufferings as pointing to Christ and His death as that which gives us eternal life (4:8–11).

Paul is warning us not to come to the Lord's day for the sake of a personality, for an attractive preacher, or for any human accoutrements—great music, beautiful sanctuary, friends. He also advises us not to come looking for something that's actually about ourselves—an emotional mountaintop, meeting a specific need we're feeling.

It's the Word—and nothing else—that proclaims Christ and that shines "the light of the knowledge of the glory of God in the face of Jesus Christ" (4:6). It's the Word to which we listen, which fills us, in which we rest. (Remember Luther's explanation of the Third Commandment, *LSB*, p 321).

Man's rewrapping of the Sabbath—in the wrong paper—*and*, thankfully, the gift of God that the Sabbath truly is are both most fully seen in the **Holy Gospel** for this Lord's day, Mark 2:23–3:6.

How often Jesus' enemies take issue with His Sabbath-keeping! (See also Lk 13:10–14; 14:1–6; Jn 5:8–9, 16; 9:14–16.) Their objection is deeply rooted in a whole false theology. They believe that holiness before God is by man's own obedience to the Law. And yet they reduce the Law to an attainable standard—as if checking outward boxes like not working one a day a week qualifies as holiness while at the same time the heart is loveless. The Pharisees care nothing that these men are in need of food (Mk 2:23), that another man is suffering, probably incapacitated from earning a living by his withered hand (3:1). They think they're pleasing God by doing nothing to help. To them, refraining from Sabbath work is a burden God laid on Israel, which they are nobly bearing.

For Jesus to respond that He is lord of the Sabbath (2:28) doesn't mean He created the Sabbath so He's allowed to break it. It doesn't even mean He made the Sabbath so He can change the rules. It means that as creator of the Sabbath, He knows its true purpose: "The Sabbath was made for man, not man for the Sabbath" (2:27). It was always to be a day when God's people would rest in, listen to, be filled with the Lord of the Sabbath Himself. It was always a day when they would hear and be comforted by the assurance that He would fulfill the Law for them. His fulfilling all releases us from the obligations of the Sabbath (Col 2:16–17).

God Made the Sabbath
Not to Burden Man
but That in the Lord of the Sabbath,
We May Rest, Listen, and Be Filled.

Read the **Collect**:

Eternal God, Your Son Jesus Christ is our true Sabbath rest. Help us to keep each day holy by receiving His Word of comfort that we may find our rest in Him, who lives and reigns with You and the Holy Spirit, one God, now and forever. Amen.

Sing our **Hymn of the Day** to celebrate the new Lord's day, the first day of the week.

The Sundays after Pentecost: Proper 5 (June 5–11) Year B

READINGS

Genesis 3:8–15
Psalm 130 (antiphon: v 7)
2 Corinthians 4:13–5:1
Mark 3:20–35

HYMN OF THE DAY

LSB 668 "Rise! To Arms! With Prayer Employ You"

For these early Sundays after Pentecost, see the Proper 3, Year A, devotion-study (p 154) explaining why some propers may be omitted in some years.

Many—at least in the United States—who've never heard or read the Gospel lesson for Sunday are quite familiar with a paraphrase drawn from it: "A house divided against itself cannot stand." And Abraham Lincoln was right; America could not endure permanently half slave and half free. "I do not expect the Union to be dissolved—I do not expect the house to fall—but I do expect it will cease to be divided" (June 16, 1858).

Jesus' original context was entirely different—as were the referents in His metaphor. "If a house is divided against itself, that house will not be able to stand. And if Satan has risen up against himself and is divided, he cannot stand, but is coming to an end" (Mk 3:25–26). The bloody and tragic Civil War resolved the division of the house Lincoln was describing. If only it had been so easy with Satan's house!

In looking forward to this Sunday morning, let's consider first the two propers that most concretely develop the theme for the week and will indeed require us to confront Satan and his house: the Old Testament Reading and the Gospel.

The **Old Testament Reading** for Proper 5 is the immediate aftermath of the devil's greatest blow. Read Genesis 3:8–15 (and perhaps sneak a peek back at 3:1–7 as well).

Satan, the angel who conspired to seize God's throne, still desires nothing but to undo everything of God. And for now, he's succeeded. The crown jewels of God's creation, the reason for those six days of divine craftsmanship, the devil has now stolen away.

The Lord God comes "walking in the garden in the cool of the day" (3:8), presumably as He's done before. This should be the highlight of every day. Claire and I do our work, often she in one place, I in another, but we look forward to our walk—together—each evening. It's great exercise. We see a different neighborhood each day, but, above all, we talk about our day, about decisions we have to make, about whatever's exciting or anxious at the moment. Adam and Eve have the opportunity to walk and talk with, undoubtedly, the Son of God, the person in whom the Holy Trinity presents Himself to the human race. There is so much to learn. There are exciting discoveries. Nothing is anxious.

Until now. Now Adam and Eve hide themselves among the trees of the Garden of Eden. *God's* house is divided! And how painfully, fearfully! The best time of the day has become this: "I heard the sound of You in the garden, and I was afraid, because I was naked, and I hid myself" (3:10). The man is so terrified that he will climb over anybody in his haste to escape the Lord: "The woman whom You gave to be with me, she gave me fruit of the tree, and I ate" (3:12). Blame Eve! Blame God! God's house, His *family*, is divided.

Precisely according to plan, Satan sneers. God's house, the first marriage, is in shambles. A house divided against itself cannot stand. And Satan's house has grown by two—with the prospect of billions more.

For now.

In the **Holy Gospel**, too, it's not only Satan's house that's up for discussion. Read Mark 3:20–35.

God's house, the one in which Jesus Himself grew up, isn't exactly in order either, is it (3:20–21)! Jesus' mom and brothers are divided against Him—don't believe in Him, think He's crazy. They want to shut Him down.

At least they mean to be helpful. The scribes, experts in the Old Testament Law, call Jesus satanic (3:22). Beelzebul, literally "lord of the fly," is an obviously insulting title connecting Jesus to the ancient Canaanite Baals. And worse, they know Jesus is casting out demons, the work God does, but they say He's doing it by Satan. This is why Jesus cautions them against committing the unforgivable sin (3:28–30).

Here's a short note about that. Sin can never be forgiven if God Himself, the Holy Spirit, ceases to work in someone's heart, because forgiveness comes through repentance and faith, which only happen by the Spirit's work. When would God ever cease to work on someone? We can never know, and we are right always to assume He will continue to work even in the most hardened unbeliever. (Or, if *I'm* afraid I've committed this sin, *I can be certain I haven't*, because that fear itself is the Spirit working on me.) But if someone is convinced that Christ is the Savior and yet steadfastly insists on denying it, God may come to that point. The scribes are pushing this, and Jesus wants to save them.

Now see how Jesus responds to the charge that His work is satanic. Enter

Lincoln. The scribes say Jesus is casting out demons by Satan, but Jesus asks, "How can Satan cast out Satan? If a kingdom is divided against itself, that kingdom cannot stand. And if a house is divided against itself, that house will not be able to stand. And if Satan has risen up against himself and is divided, he cannot stand, but is coming to an end" (3:23–26). "So you see," Jesus tells them, "I'm obviously not satanic, because *Satan would never do this to himself.*" Satan's house *isn't* divided! We wish it were! If it were, he'd destroy himself. But he's no fool.

Do you see the difference between Jesus' statement and Abraham Lincoln's? Lincoln was saying that the Union *was* divided—northern states against southern states—and couldn't long survive that way. Jesus was proving He wasn't in Satan's house by a simple obvious assertion: Satan would never let that happen! God's house is divided—God's children from their Father, Christian husbands from their wives, Christian parents and siblings from one another—but not Satan's! He won't make eternity easy for us by dividing and falling.

God's people rebel against Him every day by sinning, and on that one terrible day in history, the whole human race seceded from union with God. But there has never been a successful escape *from within* Satan's prison house. He's too strong for that.

That will take someone from the outside. Someone stronger.

"No one can enter a strong man's house and plunder his goods, unless he first binds the strong man. Then indeed he may plunder his house" (3:27). The house of Satan, the "strong man," wasn't going to collapse from within, so Christ Jesus, a stronger man yet, broke in. And the first order of business was to engage the householder and tie him up. That hand-to-hand fighting was more violent than four years of war.

Back to the Old Testament Reading. We skipped the final and most important verse, didn't we. The Lord said to the serpent, "I will put enmity between you and the woman, and between your offspring and her offspring; He shall bruise your head, and you shall bruise His heel" (Gen 3:15). This was the battle, the stronger man entering the strong man's house, wasn't it. Eve's Descendant, Jesus, would suffer total body bruising at the hands of the devil; He would be brutally beaten and killed on the cross. But even in death, He would prove to be stronger. Jesus' resurrection would announce to Satan that Jesus had crushed his head. He would bound him, render him powerless. Then indeed Christ would plunder his house.

That's what the Lord is saying in the first part of Genesis 3:15: "I will put *enmity* between you [the serpent] and the woman." Before Christ broke in, we were in Satan's house, not just as his prisoners but as his willing allies. Now, though, enmity between us and Satan, worked when Christ bound him and set us free, means we are again in God's house! God's house is reunited!

"Looking about at those who sat around Him," Jesus said, to conclude our Gospel reading, "'Here are My mother and My brothers! For whoever does the will of God, he is My brother and sister and mother'" (Mk 3:34–35). God's house is reunited!

That's what we'll hear through the other propers this Sunday as well, as in the **Introit**:

> *Blessèd be the Lord! For He has heard the voice of my pleas for mercy.*
>
> *The Lord is my strength and my shield; in Him my heart trusts, and I am helped; my heart exults, and with my song I give thanks to Him. The Lord is the strength of His people; He is the saving refuge of His anointed. Oh, save Your people and bless Your heritage! Be their shepherd and carry them forever.*
>
> *Glory be to the Father and to the Son and to the Holy Spirit; as it was in the beginning, is now, and will be forever. Amen.*
>
> *Blessèd be the Lord! For He has heard the voice of my pleas for mercy. (Ps 28:7–9; antiphon: Ps 28:6)*

"The Lord is my strength and my shield. . . . The Lord is the strength of His people." A stronger man than Satan! "Blessèd be the Lord!" For He has saved His people from the devil's prison house!

"Alleluia. Unless the Lord builds the house, those who build it labor in vain. Alleluia" (the **Verse**, Ps 127:1a). Any house *we* build would be another cell in Satan's "big house." Christ has built God's house as our home for eternity, and, by His grace, a home to share with our families.

Read the **Psalm**, Psalm 130. The psalmist cries out from "the depths." "O Lord, hear my voice!" (130:2). He knows his sin has made him helpless in Satan's power. But with the Lord "is plentiful redemption. And He will redeem Israel from all his iniquities" (130:7–8). He will buy him back to be His own.

Even the **Epistle** picks up this accent of God's house reunited: "He who raised the Lord Jesus will raise us also with Jesus and bring us with you *into His presence*. . . . We have a building from God, *a house not made with hands*, eternal in the heavens" (2 Cor 4:14; 5:1).

The **Collect** summarizes the following:

> *Almighty and eternal God, Your Son Jesus triumphed over the prince of demons and freed us from bondage to sin. Help us to stand firm against every assault of Satan, and enable us always to do Your will; through Jesus Christ, our Lord, who lives and reigns with You and the Holy Spirit, one God, now and forever. Amen.*

The conflict in our propers is entirely different from what we might guess based on Lincoln's famous usage alone. But it resolves in a far more blessed way.

The House Divided Wasn't Satan's But God's— until the Strong Man Was Bound by the Stronger Christ.

Now that Christ has bound Satan, we Christians also "Rise! To Arms!" (**Hymn of the Day**, *LSB* 668). Against the devil's forces, we, too, will be victorious. For "the strong foes yield to Christ, our shield" (st 1).

The Sundays after Pentecost: Proper 6 (June 12–18) Year B

READINGS

Ezekiel 17:22–24
Psalm 1 (antiphon: v 6)
2 Corinthians 5:1–10 (11–17)
Mark 4:26–34

HYMN OF THE DAY

LSB 500 "Creator Spirit, by Whose Aid"

For these early Sundays after Pentecost, see the Proper 3, Year A, devotion-study (p 154) explaining why some propers may be omitted in some years.

The Gospel of Matthew is rich in parables of Jesus, including seven of them in chapter 13 alone. Luke has numerous parables in chapters 13–16 and 18–20. The Gospel of Mark, not so many. In fact, this Sunday's Gospel reading gives us one of our few samplings of Jesus' parables in the entire Year B lectionary. But these are two good ones—one of them totally unique to Mark (and among my personal favorites).

Rather than just lead by telling you what they are, let's see if you can guess. They won't come to mind with the ease of, say, the Parable of the Sower or the Prodigal Son, but you'll probably recognize them. Let's pretend you've come to church with only this information; guess the parables. See if you can figure them out from just the first two assigned propers you'll hear Sunday, the Introit and the Collect.

What's the primary motif you see developing in the **Introit**?

It is good to give thanks to the Lord, to sing praises to Your name, O Most High.

The righteous flourish like the palm tree and grow like a cedar in Lebanon. They are planted in the house of the Lord; they flourish in the courts of our God. They still bear fruit in old age; they are ever full of sap and green, to declare that the Lord is upright; He is my rock, and there is no unrighteousness in Him.

Glory be to the Father and to the Son and to the Holy Spirit; as it was in the beginning, is now, and will be forever. Amen.

It is good to give thanks to the Lord, to sing praises to Your name, O Most High. (Ps 92:12–15; antiphon: Ps 92:1)

The chief image is pretty clear, isn't it. "The righteous flourish like the palm tree and grow like a cedar in Lebanon. They are planted in the house of the Lord; they flourish in the courts of our God. They still bear fruit in old age; they are ever full of sap and green." Plants growing, flourishing.

It's a metaphor, of course. God cares only very minimally about trees and fruit. The psalmist is illustrating God's very great care for His people, "the righteous." Palm trees were a sign of life, vitality; palm trees in the desert meant an oasis; springs of water must be nearby. The cedars of Lebanon were the tall, stately trees Solomon bartered from the king of Tyre to use in building the temple. We appreciate the sweet smell of cedar wood today. God gives His people life, enables us to stand tall and strong against enemies of His kingdom, holds us as precious. And how comforting to hear, later in life, perhaps as we become confined to home or wheelchair, that we still "bear fruit in old age," that we are still useful to God and His Church by our prayers, by the wisdom we share with our families, by our *receiving* a congregation's love. Even then the Lord keeps us "full of sap and green" that we may "declare" that He is "upright." God enables His believers to grow and flourish. For that we "give thanks to the Lord" and "sing praises to [His] name."

Any parables coming to mind?

Okay, then, the **Collect**. What does it add to our imagery of growing?

Blessed Lord, since You have caused all Holy Scriptures to be written for our learning, grant that we may so hear them, read, mark, learn, and inwardly digest them that we may embrace and ever hold fast the blessed hope of everlasting life; through Jesus Christ, Your Son, our Lord, who lives and reigns with You and the Holy Spirit, one God, now and forever. Amen.

This prayer may be as familiar as the parables we're thinking of. It's essentially what in *The Lutheran Hymnal* was known as The Collect for the Word (*TLH*, p 14), and it continues to be an option as the closing collect in non-Communion services (*LSB Altar Book*, p 171, 211, 254; see also *Lutheran Worship*, p 156).

Here the focus is obviously on God's Word, Scripture, as the source of "our blessed hope of everlasting life." As we listen to it, study it, turn it over in our minds, make it truly a part of our personalities, it's what causes growth in God's people, right?

Got the parables yet?

Spoiler alert: If you want to play all the way to Sunday, don't turn the page.

The rest of you may have guessed, eh? Jesus will tell us the Parables of the Growing Seed and the Mustard Seed. We'll look at them in a minute. With those parables in mind, though, we'll see how God's people growing through His Word is reflected also in the other propers.

Read the **Psalm** for this week, Psalm 1.

The outcome of the righteous compared to the wicked will be so very obvious. The wicked will be blown away—not as we use the phrase since the inventions of gun powder, TNT, and nuclear weapons, but as chaff with a poof of the wind (1:4). Those who are not in the Lord, it turns out, simply have no weight, no real substance. It takes but a gentle breath of air to scatter them.

The righteous man, on the other hand—he's that pleasant planting of Yahweh firmly rooted "like a tree," well watered, "planted by streams." Healthy and productive, it "yields its fruit in its season, and its leaf does not wither" (1:3). It grows, prospers.

And what makes the difference, what separates the righteous man from the wicked, is God's Word. "His delight is in the law of the LORD, and on His law he meditates day and night" (1:2). Those who hear, read, mark, learn, and inwardly digest the words of the Lord trust in what's solid, live for what's real. They should depend on God's love for them in the cross and resurrection of Christ, reflect that love in their lives by actions that touch others for eternity.

The **Old Testament Reading** is Ezekiel 17:22–24, but it would be helpful to read all of chapter 17. It's a parable too.

Could you follow the story? In 597 BC, the Babylonian king, Nebuchadnezzar, like "a great eagle," besieges Jerusalem (a second time already) and carries off young King Jehoiachin, "the topmost twig," to Babylon (17:3–4, 12). Nebuchadnezzar installs Jehoiachin's uncle, Zedekiah (another of the "royal offspring" of the previous king, Josiah) as king of Judah, and he makes Zedekiah swear allegiance to him in the name of Zedekiah's God, Yahweh (17:5–6, 13–14).

After a few years, though, Zedekiah, "this vine," sends envoys to Egypt, the land of "abundant waters" (the Nile), conspiring with Pharaoh, the other "great eagle," to rebel against Nebuchadnezzar (17:7–8, 15).

It wouldn't work. Zedekiah is actually sinning against the Lord by breaking the oath taken in His name, and God would punish him. Nebuchadnezzar would come against Judah yet again, and Pharaoh would be no help. Nebuchadnezzar would capture Zedekiah, drag him off to Babylon, and he would die there. The "noble vine" would be pulled up by its roots and wither (17:9–10, 16–21).

Now, however, Ezekiel looks further into the future: "Thus says the Lord GOD: 'I Myself will take a sprig from the lofty top of the cedar and will set it out. I will break off from the topmost of its young twigs a tender one, and I Myself will plant it on a high and lofty mountain'" (17:22). This time, the lofty top of the cedar is Judah, the royal line of Jehoiachin, but six centuries later. Christ Jesus is the "sprig," the "topmost" of the tree's "young twigs a tender one." From Christ Jesus will grow a "noble cedar. And under it will dwell every kind of bird; in the shade of its branches birds of every sort will nest" (17:23). This cedar is the Church, the gathering of all believers in Christ, our place of shade and refuge. And this tree will forever grow and flourish.

But don't overlook the last note. How will this all happen? "I am the LORD; *I have spoken*, and I will do it" (17:24c). It's God's Word that uproots evil and prospers His Church.

Our **Epistle**, 2 Corinthians 5:1–17, following as it does Paul's progression of thought through this letter, really has a theme of its own. We live and witness courageously through the groanings of this life because Christ's death and resurrection has secured a new heavenly home for us.

We will notice, though, that these two verses are relevant to the overall theme of the Sunday: "We walk by faith, not by sight" (5:7). "We persuade others" (5:11).

Now read Jesus' parables, Mark 4:26–34, the **Holy Gospel**.

"The kingdom of God" is always, in one way or another, referring to God's work in Christ, bringing to earth God's eternal, heavenly enterprise. That is to say, in the Crucified One, God is accomplishing great things among and for us, His people, the Church. The Church, both parables tell us, grows.

The first parable (4:26–29) is most assuring. The kingdom of God grows entirely without us! The farmer plants the seed and goes about life without worry. Surely he does all the things farmers do, but what he does isn't important enough for Jesus to mention here. The farmer sleeps. He doesn't know how his field full of seeds will grow. But it does. And then he simply has the delight of harvesting. We Christians go about our vocations; Paul says, "we persuade." But, above all, "we walk by faith, not by sight." We coordinate clever outreach programs, share a friendly welcome to visitors, and speak Christ as clearly as we can. Sure. Fine. In some cases, even very good. But it's not what grows the Church. What does? "Blessed Lord, . . . You have caused all Holy Scriptures to be written for our learning."

And how much can the Word accomplish? "A grain of mustard seed . . . is the smallest of all the seeds on earth, yet when it is sown it grows up and becomes larger than all the garden plants and puts out large branches, so that the birds of the air can make nests in its shade" (4:31–32). Will the growth always be in numbers? Not necessarily. Our **Verse**: "Alleluia. Grow *in the grace and knowledge* of our Lord and Savior Jesus Christ. Alleluia" (2 Pet 3:18a). God knows who, how, how many.

**QUITE APART FROM US,
GOD'S WORD OF CHRIST
GROWS HIS KINGDOM.**

It's His wondrous work. Read the **Gradual**:

> *Great is the LORD, and greatly to be praised, and His greatness is unsearchable. On Your wondrous works, I will meditate, and I will declare Your greatness. (Ps 145:3, 5b, 6b)*

Come, Holy Spirit! Through the Word of Christ, "who for all humankind has died," "pour Your joys on humankind" (**Hymn of the Day**, *LSB* 500:4, 1).

The Sundays after Pentecost: Proper 7 (June 19–25) Year B

READINGS

Job 38:1–11
Psalm 124 (antiphon: v 8)
2 Corinthians 6:1–13
Mark 4:35–41

HYMN OF THE DAY

LSB 726 "Evening and Morning"

For these early Sundays after Pentecost, see the Proper 3, Year A, devotion-study (p 154) explaining why some propers may be omitted in some years.

Waves pounding Gulf and Atlantic shores are sure to come again this hurricane season. Winter storms will come on the Great Lakes. Towering breakers will hit the north shore of Oahu. Tsunamis will form in the Indian Ocean. They're all terrifying!

Gales whip up the Sea of Galilee.

Our propers for this week, Proper 7 of the Sundays after Pentecost, put us on stormy waters, and about them they ask two questions:

"Who shut in the sea with doors . . . and said, 'Thus far shall you come, and no farther, and here shall your proud waves be stayed'?" (Job 38:8, 11).

And, "Who then is this, that even wind and sea obey Him?" (Mk 4:41).

In neither case does the reading give an answer. But we know them. And the answers mean much, much more than safe passage on a cruise. For anyone who stays in the shallow end just as surely as for Galilean fishermen. We'll see how important this is as we work through each of the propers.

The storm at sea begins already with the **Introit** for Sunday:

Then they cried to the Lord in their trouble, and He delivered them from their distress.

He made the storm be still, and the waves of the sea were hushed. Then they were glad that the waters were quiet, and He brought them to their desired haven. Let them thank the Lord *for His steadfast love, for His wondrous works to the children of men! Let them extol Him in the congregation of the people, and praise Him in the assembly of the elders.*

Glory be to the Father and to the Son and to the Holy Spirit; as it was in the beginning, is now, and will be forever. Amen.

Then they cried to the Lord *in their trouble, and He delivered them from their distress. (Ps 107:29–32; antiphon: Ps 107:28)*

The preceding verses in Psalm 107 make clear that those who "cried to the Lord in their trouble" were specifically in danger on the sea (107:23–27). The Israelites were not by tradition a seafaring nation. Most of their sailing was confined to the tiny but turbulent Sea of Galilee. For a time, though, David and Solomon's close relationship with the king of Tyre enabled Israel to partner with the Phoenicians, the greatest of the ancient Mediterranean mariners. They sailed trading ships not only on the Mediterranean but even down the east coast of Africa (1 Ki 9:26–28; 10:11–12, 22). Thus they knew the hazards of the sea.

But the Lord "delivered them from their distress. He made the storm be still, and the waves of the sea were hushed. Then they were glad that the waters were quiet, and He brought them to their desired haven." If the disciples had known the answer to the question they'll soon be asking in the Gospel reading, they could have relied on this precedent of Scripture.

Since we do know the answer, we ask this of God in the **Collect**:

Almighty God, in Your mercy guide the course of this world so that Your Church may joyfully serve You in godly peace and quietness; through Jesus Christ, Your Son, our Lord, who lives and reigns with You and the Holy Spirit, one God, now and forever. Amen.

God is the almighty Creator. Therefore we ask Him to guide how everything in this world plays out. That includes the elements of nature—sea, wind, hurricanes, tidal waves. No such thing is too powerful for God to control, but no such thing is too insignificant even in the eternal picture for Him to care about for our wellbeing. He can silence the roar of the surf, order it to "godly peace and quietness," because He brings peace of a greater kind. Always through Jesus Christ, His Son, our Lord, who reigns over all creation just as the Father does.

This control over nature is another example of the greatness of the Lord we exalt in the **Gradual** for these weeks:

Great is the Lord, *and greatly to be praised, and His greatness is unsearchable. On Your wondrous works, I will meditate, and I will declare Your greatness. (Ps 145:3, 5b, 6b)*

The first of our two rhetorical questions is raised in the **Old Testament Reading**, Job 38:1–11.

Perhaps you remember that Job 38 begins with the Lord's climactic speech after so much human foolishness throughout the book. Back in chapters 1–2, Satan challenges the Lord for permission to torment Job. No one on earth has been privy to the agreement, so Job's friends accuse him of secret sin, which they assume must be the cause of his misery. Eventually, even faithful Job has lost patience with God, begging for a chance to look God in the eye and defend himself.

Sure thing! As the last vain speculation is being voiced, a storm cloud appears out of the north, and from the whirlwind the Lord speaks! Enough of this counsel "by words without knowledge" (38:2). Let's just see how much you really know, Job! Let's see who has the wisdom to guide the course of this world! Tell Me this, Job: "The foundation of the earth. . . . Who determined its measurements? . . . Who laid its cornerstone?" (38:4, 5, 6). Surely you know, Job!

And let's talk about the sea. "Who shut in the sea with doors when it burst out from the womb, when I made clouds its garment and thick darkness its swaddling band, and prescribed limits for it and set bars and doors, and said, 'Thus far shall you come, and no farther, and here shall your proud waves be stayed'?" (38:8–11). Who, Job?

We've all been to the beach. Growing up in Southern California, I spent a lot of time in a little over my head. That's a big ocean out there! And wave after wave after wave comes rolling in. But at some point—even at highest tide and stormiest surf—they stop. The last lace of foam runs up the sand and then falls back every time. And we know why. We know who laid the foundations of the earth, set the dimensions, declared just how far the oceans would reach. The Lord.

Only part of God's purpose was to humble Job. (And He did that!) God's greater message was that we needn't worry when the universe doesn't seem to be running well. When like Job we're sick and in pain, when we have lost children and our retirement savings, when another named storm bears down on Biloxi or Delray Beach, our gracious God somehow knows how He's operating everything for our greatest good.

That was David's trust in the **Psalm** for the week, Psalm 124.

I'm not sure David would ever have seen a storm at sea. Maybe. But I picture him watering his sheep one day down in a trickling rivulet. Even today in Israel, many riverbeds are entirely dry until . . . a sudden torrential rain. A rush of water, gushing through a narrow channel, would send David and his flock scrambling for higher ground. And then he would thank God for just enough warning. If the Lord had not been on Israel's side when enemies attacked, David writes, "the flood would have swept us away, the torrent would have gone over us; then over us would have gone the raging waters" (124:4–5).

But David knows the Lord *is* on our side against Goliaths on the battlefield, in catastrophic weather events, or *whenever* Satan attacks our bodies or souls. "Our help is in the name of the LORD, who made heaven and earth"—*because* He made heaven and earth (124:8).

Paul isn't writing about rough seas—literally—as he pens the **Epistle**, 2 Corinthians 6:1–13. He's exhorting the Christians in Corinth to receive the saving Gospel of Christ, for whom Paul is an ambassador, and hoping they in no way see him as a stumbling block to it. But as part of his credential for preaching, Paul cites many "afflictions, hardships, calamities" (6:4). Among these are indeed dangers on the sea—*three* shipwrecks (11:25–26), including the very famous one (Acts 27:9–44).

Now for the other question of the day, the one the disciples ask in the **Holy Gospel**. Read Mark 4:35–41.

The Sea of Galilee, really just a lake, sits down in a bowl surrounded by mountains so that the wind can indeed whip up sudden and violent storms. Jesus, though, is the picture of serenity. Mark's Gospel, as we've seen already this year, often adds striking details. Here it's the cushion (4:38a), and that really does enhance our sense of Jesus' peaceful rest under His Father's watch.

The disciples, meanwhile, are panicked. They're veteran sailors. They've been through storms before. This one must have been the Witch of November come stealin'. They wake Jesus: "Teacher, do You not *care* that we are perishing?" (4:38b).

"And He awoke and rebuked the wind and said to the sea, 'Peace! Be still!' And the wind ceased, and there was a great calm" (4:39). Wow! Think about that! When water—even in a glass or a bathtub—is agitated and the shaking or stirring stops, it takes time for the water level to stabilize, for calm to be restored, and the bigger the body of water, the longer it takes. On the Sea of Galilee, it took many minutes. Instead, at Jesus' words, there is suddenly, apparently instantly, a "great calm" (γαλήνη μεγάλη, *galene megale*).

"Who then is this, that even wind and sea obey Him?" (4:41). The answer should be as obvious as it became to Job. This is the Son of God, the same Creator who told the sea thus far, no farther. But here's why all these sailing stories are so important. They show that the Creator does indeed care (4:38b)—and cares in the biggest way. The power of the Creator would not save us but destroy us, unless He also removes the sin that earns us His condemnation. This Son of God is the one who brings us "godly peace and quietness" (remember our Collect)—that is, reconciles us to God. That would be not with a word to the waves but by a far more painful perishing. Deliverance from drowning or freeway accidents or viral infections or random terror come from the same cross as our eternal salvation in heaven. When we're back together with God, He will always give us everything He knows is best for us.

As He Delivers Sailors from the Sea, the Creator-Son Delivers Us from All Perils— Always by His Peace-Restoring Cross.

Sing the **Hymn of the Day** (*LSB* 726). "Though billows tower, and winds gain power, after the storm the fair sun shows its face. Joys e'er increasing and peace never ceasing" (st 3).

The Sundays after Pentecost: Proper 8 (June 26–July 2) Year B

READINGS

Lamentations 3:22–33
Psalm 30 (antiphon: v 10)
2 Corinthians 8:1–9, 13–15
Mark 5:21–43

HYMN OF THE DAY

LSB 755 "In the Very Midst of Life"

We all need a little help now and then. Yes, but what about when I need a lot of help right now? And what about when now looks absolutely hopeless?

That, of course, is really where we are all the time. Without God's complete and total care at every minute, we'd be helpless victims of Satan. But sometimes we're especially aware of that. Tragedy hits our country, my family, my own life, and I'm suddenly reminded how very much I need help!

Our propers for this Sunday give a variety of scenarios of people needing help. At first, the need seems rather mild, but then it becomes desperate and immediate. Let's work through each one and see how the Lord helps every time. And notice as we go how God treats our needs for help as very personal.

The **Introit** acknowledges God's help without initially appearing too urgent.

I lift up my eyes to the hills. From where does my help come? My help comes from the Lord, who made heaven and earth.

The Lord is your keeper; the Lord is your shade on your right hand. The sun shall not strike you by day, nor the moon by night. The Lord will keep you from all evil; He will keep your life. The Lord will keep your going out and your coming in from this time forth and forevermore.

Glory be to the Father and to the Son and to the Holy Spirit; as it was in the beginning, is now, and will be forever. Amen.

I lift up my eyes to the hills. From where does my help come? My help comes from the Lord, *who made heaven and earth. (Ps 121:5–8; antiphon: Ps 121:1–2)*

My family would often read Psalm 121 as we began vacation trips. We knew we needed the Lord to keep us, shade us, and watch over our goings and comings as we traveled. There were so many unseen hazards as we drove. But, of course, we were always excited, never anxious as we set out.

Psalm 121:1 is also famously quoted at a far more intense moment—by the Reverend Mother to Maria in the movie classic *The Sound of Music*. The von Trapps are about to flee over the Alps into Switzerland, with the Nazis in hot pursuit. The Mother Abbess recites the King James Version: "I will lift up mine eyes unto the hills, from whence cometh my help." There was a big problem, though. In the movie context and the KJV rendering, it sounds as if Maria's help in escaping will come from the hills. (Remember, Maria grew up on the nearby mountain and seems to draw her strength from the Alps' majestic mass and beauty.)

That's not what the psalmist had in mind at all! It may be that this "Song of Ascents" is encouraging God's people, as they ascend to worship at Zion, to look upward to the hills (or Mount Zion itself) as a reminder of *God's* strength. But here's even another take. It may be that the psalmist looks up at the hills around him and sees the high places where the Canaanites offered sacrifices to Baal and other idols. And he responds, in effect, "The pagans who worship on the hills look to those gods for help, but where does *my* help come from? Yahweh! Why, He made those very hills and everything else!"

If that was the psalmist's thinking, the situation was tense. Surrounded by idolaters, enemies also at war, he might have felt very much alone—as we might feel alone in a world where Christians are progressively more opposed. He would have been much more desperate for the Lord's help, and much more appreciative that "the Lord will keep [me] from all evil; He will keep [my] life." I'm not alone!

Here's a second scenario—and one that was desperate indeed: the **Old Testament Reading**, Lamentations 3:22–33.

The prophet Jeremiah wrote Lamentations as he saw Jerusalem overrun, torn down, burned by the Babylonian army. Priests, soldiers, maidens, little ones—dead or carried off to captivity. The capital of the nation that was to bring the Messiah into the world was destroyed. There was no human reason to think this people would continue. Abraham, Isaac, Jacob, Judah, Ruth, David, Solomon—the whole holy history was apparently at an end.

We live in a nation in ruins. Laws declare sin—homosexual behavior, same-sex marriage—to be honorable, and media ostracize expression to the contrary. Abortions have by any conservative count totaled *one hundred to two hundred times* more deaths in the United States than any pandemic. Distrust and unkindness between races. Free exercise of religion being rebranded as freedom of worship—to be kept inside church walls.

Will all that be healed by the time you read this? We pray, yes. God can work miracles. But our countries will never be without sin. And God may allow Christians to feel the lash of persecution as we speak out against these evils. "He does not *willingly* afflict from His heart or grieve the children of men" (3:33). But sometimes "it is good for a man," Jeremiah writes, "that he bear the yoke in his youth. . . . Let him give his cheek to the one who strikes, and let him be filled with insults" (3:27, 30). History shows that the Church becomes strong, committed, resilient in times of persecution.

When that happens, though, can anyone help me? Even then, "'The LORD is my portion,' says my soul, 'therefore I will hope in Him'" (3:24). It's very personal, isn't it. The nation is collapsing, but *I* can hope in Him. "The LORD is good to those who wait for Him. . . . Though He cause grief, He will have compassion according to the abundance of His steadfast love" (3:25a, 32). God would bring Judah back from Babylon, and He will be with me if persecution is ahead.

Next scenario. Read the **Epistle**, 2 Corinthians 8:1–9, 13–15.

Second Corinthians 8–9 is one of the clearest passages in all of Scripture on financial stewardship. Paul is encouraging the Corinthians to follow the example of the churches in Macedonia, to give a special offering to care for the saints in Jerusalem (8:4). The motivation is pure Gospel: "For you know the grace of our Lord Jesus Christ, that though He was rich, yet for your sake He became poor, so that you by His poverty might become rich" (8:9).

What's behind the text is a situation some of us have experienced. The believers in Jerusalem are hit hard by a famine (Acts 11:28) severe enough that Jewish historian Josephus also records it. For us, that may be months without a job. It could be losing our house or being overwhelmed by medical bills. Who can help me when I'm going through financial stresses?

Often God helps through His Church. The Macedonians are suffering "a severe test of affliction," yet they come to the aid of brothers and sisters in Christ they'd never even met. "Their abundance of joy and their extreme poverty have overflowed in a wealth of generosity. . . . For they gave according to their means, as I can testify, and beyond their means, of their own accord" (8:2, 3). This should be each of our congregations—and for the same reason: every one of us has eternal riches because Christ gave His everything, His very life, for us.

Two more cries for help come in the **Holy Gospel**, Mark 5:21–43—both extreme.

I have two daughters. My greatest scare was when Rachel, our first, was under two, and one night she was running a very high fever. Claire and I were new at this, and we didn't know infants' temperatures could be much higher than adults'. A phone call to Dr. Martinez and a little infant Tylenol in applesauce did the trick. But we were worried!

I stress for Jairus, too, especially when I think of Jesus sidetracking for another urgent care case. But to this woman, her condition was every bit as desperate. Twelve years! And all those doctors, her last denarius spent, and only getting worse. Who can help me now with my cancer diagnosis? with my advancing diabetes? with my kidney stones that lead to infection that leads to . . . ?

This woman's faith is that when no one else could help, Jesus not only could but does (5:28). And not only does Jesus heal her. "Perceiving in Himself that power had gone out from Him, [Jesus] immediately turned about in the crowd and said, 'Who touched My garments?' And His disciples said to Him, "You see the crowd pressing around You, and yet You say, 'Who touched Me?'" (5:30–31).

"But the woman . . . came in fear and trembling and fell down before Him and told Him the whole truth. And He said to her, 'Daughter, your faith has made you well; go in peace'" (5:33–34). This woman isn't just a patient chart for Jesus to sign off and move on. She is worth His time because He intends an eternal relationship with her.

By now, though, Jairus is beside himself. Hurry, Jesus! But the bad news comes: "Your daughter is dead. Why trouble the Teacher any further?" Who can help Jairus now?

Death is the final scenario for all of us. Except that it's not. Jesus comes privately to desperate Jairus and his wife. And He is able to raise their little girl because He Himself would overcome death. We're all subject to death because we're all sinful. But Jesus took the sin of the whole world upon Himself to the cross. He died because He now bore all sin. But when He rose, it was the Father announcing that Jesus' sacrifice was sufficient for you, for me. And, lo and behold, my sin has been lifted from me so that I'll join Jairus's daughter in rising someday.

It's true for every scenario:

WHO CAN HELP ME NOW?
EVEN NOW JESUS ANSWERS
YOUR PERSONAL CRY FOR HELP.

Enjoy the **Psalm**, Psalm 30, and see how it recapitulates many of Sunday's scenarios—the Lord's deliverance from enemies, illness, death, my own sin—and how God can use these to strengthen us. It's all in His wise and loving hands.

Read the **Gradual** for the next six weeks:

Oh, the depth of the riches and wisdom and knowledge of God! How unsearchable are His judgments and how inscrutable His ways! For from Him and through Him and to Him are all things. To Him be glory forever. Amen. (Rom 11:33, 36)

Martin Luther was no stranger to danger, poverty, illness, death, even national uproar. But his **Hymn of the Day**, "In the Very Midst of Life" (*LSB* 755), directs us well: "Thou only, Lord, Thou only!" Sing it.

Then close with prayer, the **Collect**:

Heavenly Father, during His earthly ministry Your Son Jesus healed the sick and raised the dead. By the healing medicine of the Word and Sacraments pour into our hearts such love toward You that we may live eternally; through the same Jesus Christ, our Lord, who lives and reigns with You and the Holy Spirit, one God, now and forever. Amen.

The Sundays after Pentecost: Proper 9 (July 3–9) Year B

READINGS

Ezekiel 2:1–5
Psalm 123 (antiphon: v 1)
2 Corinthians 12:1–10
Mark 6:1–13

HYMN OF THE DAY

LSB 839 "O Christ, Our True and Only Light"

The **Collect** for Proper 9:

O God, Your almighty power is made known chiefly in showing mercy. Grant us the fullness of Your grace that we may be called to repentance and made partakers of Your heavenly treasures; through Your Son, Jesus Christ, our Lord, who lives and reigns with You and the Holy Spirit, one God, now and forever. Amen.

God's power "made known chiefly in showing mercy." That's quite an assessment! When we know God shows His power in so many mighty ways, to assert that showing mercy is chief—well, that says an awful lot about His mercy.

Mercy is always giving someone something that isn't earned or deserved . . . or *not* giving something that *is* deserved . . . or both. It's a thumbs up rather than a thumbs down to a fallen gladiator, a pardon to a convicted criminal, a C- to a failing student who begs to pass. It doesn't always have to do with wrongdoing; sometimes it involves helplessness. It could be a meal and a place to spend the night for a homeless man, a shelter for a battered woman, a visit in the hospital.

God shows His almighty power chiefly in lavishing every good on sinners who are indeed guilty and deserve only eternal punishment. And the list of all those blessings—some we notice, some so familiar that we don't—is so long, so generous, and so costly that surely it is God's chief business.

Why does the acknowledgment of God's mercy then lead us to pray "that we may be called to repentance"? It's more than just God's mercies being so many that we can't notice or count them all, isn't it. It's that so many of His mercies are right there before us in plain view, and we take them eagerly as not mercy at all but as honors, as credits, as assets I've earned, as goodies I've got coming.

Our propers this week will give us a rich taste of God's mercy . . . and then severe warnings against receiving His mercy thanklessly. "Grant us the fullness of Your grace [O God] that we may be called to repentance and made partakers of Your heavenly treasures; through Your Son, Jesus Christ."

Sample God's mercies in the **Introit**:

Oh, taste and see that the Lord is good! Blessèd is the man who takes refuge in Him!

For the Lord has chosen Zion; He has desired it for His dwelling place: "This is My resting place forever; here I will dwell, for I have desired it. I will abundantly bless her provisions; I will satisfy her poor with bread. Her priests I will clothe with salvation, and her saints will shout for joy."

Glory be to the Father and to the Son and to the Holy Spirit; as it was in the beginning, is now, and will be forever. Amen.

Oh, taste and see that the Lord is good! Blessèd is the man who takes refuge in Him! (Ps 132:13–16; antiphon: Ps 34:8)

We often identify provision for the body as mercy ministry: "I will abundantly bless her provisions; I will satisfy her poor with bread. Her priests I will clothe with salvation." Clothing and shoes, food and drink, house and home—deaconesses in our church often work with the needy to provide mercy of these kinds. And such acts of charity are most certainly extensions of God's First Article mercy upon us.

The psalmist does also, though, use these very real earthly mercies as appetizers for spiritual mercies ("clothe with salvation"). And the metaphor works. We all love to "taste" delicious things; we're delighted that our salvation is somehow akin. So the tastiest mercy of the Introit is this: "The Lord has chosen Zion; He has desired it for His dwelling place." Zion, representing God's people Israel, wasn't a particularly majestic mountain, just as Abraham and his descendants weren't in themselves special, holy. They were just sinners. But God made a merciful, entirely undeserved choice to take them as His holy ones. That's how all the milk and honey came flowing their way. Undeserved. God's mercy. Remembering that, they would prosper in the land, the kingdom, the honored position the Lord had given them. Forgetting that, ah, we know how it often went.

The appointed **Psalm** demonstrates that humble reception of God's mercy. Read Psalm 123.

The psalmist knows to look above himself for all he needs: "Behold, as the eyes of servants look to the hand of their master, as the eyes of a maidservant to the hand of her mistress, so our eyes look to the Lord our God, till He has mercy upon us" (123:2). It's a rather quaint picture in our day of employment contracts and unions and climbing the corporate ladder, isn't it! We don't look up to our bosses—perhaps even on bended knee—and wait for them to be gracious to us. But that should be our posture before God. We beg, we pray, "Have mercy upon us, O Lord, have mercy upon us" (123:3a).

And we need His mercy! "For we have had more than enough of contempt . . . of the scorn of those who are at ease, . . . of the proud" (123:3b, 4b, c). Maybe that actually describes our workplaces—employers who don't value our labors. It certainly describes the way much of society views Christians today—scorning us as bigoted or simple-minded or hopelessly old fashioned. "Have mercy upon us, O Lord."

The **Old Testament Reading** begins to develop the Collect's call to repentance. It's God's tough job for Ezekiel: Ezekiel 2:1–5.

Ezekiel was among the captives carried off to Babylon. You'd think the exiles would have gotten God's message, but they haven't. Here's My assignment for you, Ezekiel: "Son of man, I send you to the people of Israel, to nations of rebels, who have rebelled against Me. They and their fathers have transgressed against Me to this very day. The descendants also are impudent and stubborn: I send you to them, and you shall say to them, 'Thus says the Lord God'" (2:3–4).

The reason Judah is in captivity is that they forgot God's mercy in choosing Zion, choosing them, to be His precious possession. The blessings of a Promised Land He'd given them to taste they no longer see as evidence that Yahweh is good. Some among them assume that because they have the "temple of the Lord," they have a claim on Him; they took His protection for granted (Jer 7:4). They are "stubborn," "impudent." They no longer see God's mercy as mercy; they are entitled, they think.

For the most part, God's people won't listen to Ezekiel. And you remember from the last time Ezekiel spoke to us, three weeks ago, that worse is coming. The Babylonians will return to Jerusalem and level the trusted temple. Then the rebellious people will "know that a prophet has been among them" (Ezek 2:5).

We, unfortunately, haven't heard the last of such stubborn impudence.

Paul realized the danger of conceit like that, of feeling entitled, forgetting God's mercy is mercy. Thankfully, God kept him humble. Read the **Epistle**, 2 Corinthians 12:1–10.

Paul isn't really boasting in the sense we mean. He reminds the Corinthians that he is a true apostle of Christ in order that they not discount his message. And Paul has colossal evidence; almost certainly he's the man who has the vision of heaven (12:3). Now there's a mercy of God! None of us—Paul the former persecutor especially—deserves to see heaven even in the end, let alone get a glimpse of it in the meantime!

But such special kindness of God could lead to conceit. So "a thorn was given me in the flesh, a messenger of Satan to harass me, to keep me from being too conceited" (12:7). We don't know what this "thorn" was; speculation has included recurring malaria, poor eyesight, enemies among the Jews, and lots more. But Paul receives it in the way God intends. He assumes the position of the servant looking up at his master asking for mercy: "Three times I pleaded with the Lord about this, that it should leave me" (12:8). And when God has other plans, Paul sees that even this thorn is a merciful gift of God: "My grace is sufficient for you, for My power is made perfect in weakness," the Lord tells him. And Paul responds, "Therefore I will boast all the more gladly of my weaknesses, so that the power of Christ may rest upon me. . . . For when I am weak, then I am strong" (12:9, 10).

It's a different story, sadly, with the people of Jesus' hometown, Nazareth. See the **Holy Gospel**, Mark 6:1–13.

While Jesus based much of His work out of Capernaum, He still on at least this occasion (which likely is the same event related in Luke 4:16–30) returned to His roots. We all understand how difficult it can be for the people who "knew you when" to respect someone in a new capacity. Nazareth had seen Jesus as an eight-year-old. Joseph and Mary had always been plain folks in town. Their other children (either together or Joseph's by a first wife) were surely ordinary (6:3a). Nothing Nazareth recalled about Jesus explained His amazing rise to fame. So "they took offense at Him" (6:3b).

How tragic! To have the Savior grow up among them was a unique mercy of God to these townspeople. And this day there is no mistaking that a prophet—and more—has been among them. But they, too, feel entitled. They think the local boy owes them the same bounty of miracles He'd done elsewhere (Lk 4:23). So with a few exceptions, "He could do no mighty work there." He has to refuse doing miracles.

Beginning with a brief foray (6:7–13), Jesus' apostles would bring God's mercy to us. And their word delivers the fulfillment of all God's merciful acts. We, like Israel and Judah, like Paul, like Nazareth, are sinful and undeserving. We've felt that a successful career was due to smarts and hard work, that a house in a pleasant neighborhood puts us a cut above those in other parts of town, that I earned an answer to prayer by being in church. Yet we have received mercy of both body and soul by Jesus' final rejection, the price for all mercy, His death on the cross. So let us heed: "If any place will not receive you and they will not listen to you," Jesus told the Twelve, "when you leave, shake off the dust that is on your feet as a testimony against them" (6:11).

In mercy, "the Lord has chosen Zion," and today that is His Church, you and me.

Since the Lord Has Chosen Us to Be His Zion, May We Not Be Another Nazareth, Stubborn Rebels When He Shows His Great Mercy.

Or, as our **Hymn of the Day** (*LSB* 839) puts it, when "Christ, our true and only light" (st 1) comes to us, may we "evermore such grace with wondering thanks adore" (st 5).

The Sundays after Pentecost: Proper 10 (July 10–16) Year B

READINGS

Amos 7:7–15
Psalm 85:(1–7) 8–13
(antiphon: v 7)
Ephesians 1:3–14
Mark 6:14–29

HYMN OF THE DAY

LSB 743 "Jesus, Priceless Treasure"

Dr. Peter Scaer, a professor at Concordia Theological Seminary in Fort Wayne, Indiana, has written, "Persecution is beginning to press down on us as has not happened in our lifetimes. Our culture is not simply post-Christian, but decidedly anti-Christian. For years, we have seen this in the holocaust of abortion, but now it is particularly pressing us via the sexual revolution and the LGBT agenda. . . .

"Many of our young people have bought into the ideology of the sexual revolution, abandoning basic teachings about marriage, as well as male and female. This may seem shocking to us, especially as America has for so long been at least nominally a Christian nation. What is arising among us, though, is a new kind of paganism. In this brave new world, God is set aside, as is natural law. The warnings of Jesus sound fresh to our ears: 'Brother will deliver brother over to death, and a father his child, and children will rise against parents and have them put to death' (Mt 10:21)" (Scaer, "Preaching in an Age of Persecution," *Concordia Pulpit Resources* 31, part 3 [May 30–August 29, 2021]: 13).

I'll be safely into retirement as a pastor *in time*, I think, but my pastor son has many years ahead, and our grandchildren, God willing, many years more. I don't think it's silly alarmism to anticipate them living a story like John the Baptist's. Not the John story of austere fashion and diet with, nevertheless, crowds of penitent hearers. Rather, the story of John in a lonely dungeon and then, one day, the steely sound of a guard with a key to his cell.

I really don't like to go there—for obvious reasons—but our propers for this week, Proper

10, read in the context of our current nations, leave me no choice. "If we wish to do our jobs as preachers," Pastor Scaer goes on, "we must both warn of the dangers and encourage our people to faithfulness. If we avoid the topic of suffering and persecution, our people will be left unprepared" (Scaer, 13).

Let's begin with prayer, the **Collect** for Sunday:

> *O Lord, You granted Your prophets strength to resist the temptations of the devil and courage to proclaim repentance. Give us pure hearts and minds to follow Your Son faithfully even into suffering and death; through the same Jesus Christ, our Lord, who lives and reigns with You and the Holy Spirit, one God, now and forever. Amen.*

This is what facing persecution is all about for the Christian, isn't it. It involves following Christ "even into suffering and death." Christians don't go looking for trouble; being persecuted isn't a medal we're out to earn. We simply follow Christ, and since the world hated Him, it will hate us too. Going where Christ goes, speaking God's truth and living out God's will as Jesus did, will always put us in conflict with a sinful world that belongs to Satan.

And Satan doesn't play nice. All social pleasantries and civility only whitewash the evil Heart that would sadistically torture and kill every child of God. We've been so blessed in Canada and the United States that laws—grounded in God's natural law—have limited what enemies can do to us. And the strong Christian influence in our countries for most of their histories has even implied ground rules, acceptable manners, for how they might oppose us. But that is changing. Openly ridiculing the Church and values her Scriptures teach is now fair game, not even considered impolite. And that rhetoric is leading—as loud voices always eventually do—to a re*thinking*, that is, changing peoples' core attitudes toward God and Christianity. As that happens, the gloves may come off and Satan's bare knuckles start cutting.

The Collect also reminds us how we run afoul of Christ's enemies: "O Lord, You granted Your prophets strength to resist the temptations of the devil and courage to proclaim repentance." God's people can avoid persecution by staying under the radar, by keeping quiet where God's Word calls out sin in the world. It's very tempting to do that! But prophets like Amos and John this week proclaimed their hearers' need to repent. It's the Lord who provides strength to do that. And so we pray.

David was already living full contact persecution as he wrote the words of our **Introit**:

> *For Your name's sake, O Lord, preserve my life! In Your righteousness bring my soul out of trouble!*
>
> *Hear my prayer, O Lord; give ear to my pleas for mercy! In Your faithfulness answer me, in Your righteousness! Enter not into judgment with Your servant, for no one living is righteous before You. Let me hear*

in the morning of Your steadfast love, for in You I trust.

Glory be to the Father and to the Son and to the Holy Spirit; as it was in the beginning, is now, and will be forever. Amen.

For Your name's sake, O Lord, preserve my life! In Your righteousness bring my soul out of trouble! (Ps 143:1–2, 8a; antiphon: Ps 143:11)

For perhaps ten years or more, David was constantly facing death at the hands of jealous King Saul. And even for most of his own reign, David's life was at risk as he fought the Lord's battles against foreign armies. His most famous victory was explicitly fighting for the honor of Yahweh against Goliath's blasphemies (1 Sam 17:45–47). David was bold to face every enemy for the Lord because he knew God would be with him: "Let me hear in the morning of Your steadfast love, for in You I trust."

So many of the psalms arose from David's life under persecution. So often he cries out for the Lord to preserve his life. A veteran pastor told me years ago that the older he got, the more he appreciated the Psalms. I've come to understand that. As years go by, every Christian, I suppose, may sense more personally the devil's deep-seated hatred for us who are in Christ. The Psalms, so often coming from that very perspective, then make us more deeply aware that when we're under attack, the Lord hears our pleas for mercy.

The **Old Testament Reading** is from one of those prophets who resisted the temptations of the devil and courageously proclaimed repentance. Hear him in Amos 7:7–15.

Amos is definitely not a guy who came looking for martyrdom. "I was no prophet, nor a prophet's son, but I was a herdsman and a dresser of sycamore figs." He is just minding his own business. "But the Lord took me from following the flock, and the Lord said to me, 'Go, prophesy.'" And not even at home in Judah. "Prophesy to My people Israel" (7:14–15).

That got Amos in trouble. God sends him to Bethel, a worship site (illegitimate!) in the Northern Kingdom, where a false priest, Amaziah, is especially displeased to hear him. Amaziah tattles to the king, Jeroboam II, and actually distorts Amos's message. (It was the "house of Jeroboam," Jeroboam's son, not Jeroboam himself, who would be assassinated, 7:9, 11.) More important, Amaziah seeks to keep Israel from hearing Amos's divine warning: the "plumb line" of God's Law, held up to Israel's spiritual condition, would show how out of plumb she was (7:7–8). Unless there was repentance, there would be judgment!

We don't know whether Amos paid for his prophecy with his life or actually suffered any more than just expulsion from the North. What we see is the contrast between a faithful prophet, who isn't in it for himself, and a priest, Amaziah, who is eager to say whatever the king wants to hear—with the intent, of course, of currying his favor. One form of suffering for the faith is forfeiting personal gain. Jobs are terminated, promotions are missed, elections are lost, careers are smeared for being honest with God's Word.

It's why the **Psalm** offers this choice: "The LORD will speak . . . peace to His people, to His saints; but let them not turn back to folly" (85:8). The Lord promises us peace, life with Him for eternity. It would be folly to give that up for anything a king, a career, the prince of this world might offer.

The **Epistle**, Ephesians 1:3–14, begins eight consecutive Sundays in Paul's letter to the Christians in Ephesus. The book as a whole will teach that by our Baptism ("sealed with the promised Holy Spirit," 1:13), Christ has united us to live together as one holy Church, His Bride.

For this week's focus on persecution, though, note two things. First, Paul is writing this letter from prison, probably in Rome. Paul was an expert in suffering for the Gospel of Christ! Second, Paul's discussion of predestination is—as this doctrine properly taught always is—a tremendous comfort for times we might suffer doubts or fears when facing persecution. "We have redemption through [Jesus'] blood, the forgiveness of our trespasses, according to the riches of His grace. . . . In Him we have obtained an inheritance, having been predestined" (1:7, 11a). Satan and death itself can't take that away from us!

The **Holy Gospel** is surely Scripture's second-most infamous persecution. The story tells itself, and it's a sordid one. Read Mark 6:14–29.

Everyone is appalled at Sixth Commandment sins when they go so far beyond divorce to wife stealing, incest, sexual exploitation of a minor, and drunken orgies. But how frightening that our society has legalized and normalized other direct assaults on marriage. The charges most likely to come against Christians in the near future, therefore, are not so different from the sort that lost John his head. We must declare, for example, that homosexual activity is sin. We must hold up marriage between a man and a woman as the only real marriage. And for speaking so, we *must* expect legal, illegal, subtle, violent attacks from the world.

We each share in the *most* infamous persecution of all. Once more, Dr. Scaer: "The church is the very body of Christ. As Christians, we are called to be Christ's disciples. And what does the life of the Christian look like? The life of Christ Himself. As Christ would have to be crucified, so we would have to suffer. Only through suffering do we reach glory, and only through the cross do we find our new life in Christ" (Scaer, 13).

Even in his prison cell, John has been living the new life in Christ. Now he is able to live it without fetters. In Christ's death and resurrection, the believer has new life.

That's true for every Christian who suffers or dies. That's Jesus' promise to us in the last Beatitude, our **Verse**—and THEME—for this week (Mt 5:10):

BLESSED ARE THOSE WHO ARE PERSECUTED FOR RIGHTEOUSNESS' SAKE, FOR THEIRS IS THE KINGDOM OF HEAVEN.

"Yea, whate'er I here must bear, Thou art still my purest pleasure, Jesus, priceless treasure!" (**Hymn of the Day**, *LSB* 743:6).

The Sundays after Pentecost: Proper 11 (July 17–23) Year B

READINGS

Jeremiah 23:1–6
Psalm 23 (antiphon: v 6)
Ephesians 2:11–22
Mark 6:30–44

HYMN OF THE DAY

LSB 644 "The Church's One Foundation"

Luther's Small Catechism teaches us to pray before meals:

> The eyes of all look to You, [O Lord,] and You give them their food at the proper time. You open Your hand and satisfy the desires of every living thing (Ps. 145:15–16). . . . Lord God, heavenly Father, bless us and these Your gifts which we receive from Your bountiful goodness, through Jesus Christ, our Lord. Amen. (SC, Daily Prayers)

Five thousand men plus women and children had special occasion to ask such a blessing in our Gospel for Proper 11. We'll certainly enjoy sitting down to pray and dine with them.

Interestingly, though, the propers for this day—and even the Gospel reading itself—are not so much about the feeding of the five thousand per se as they are about a larger role Jesus plays, for which the feeding is just one scene. The propers are really about Jesus as Shepherd. Yes, the Shepherd feeds His flock, but that's not until after He gathers and leads them. Even as we sit down on the green grass this week to eat, we bless the Lord for *all* His care in shepherding us!

The **Introit** opens with some of those words we pray at the table:

You open Your hand; You satisfy the desire of every living thing.

Sing to the Lord with thanksgiving; make melody to our God on the lyre! He covers the heavens with clouds; He prepares rain for the earth; He makes grass grow on the hills. He gives to the beasts their food, and to the young ravens that cry. His delight is not in the strength of the horse, nor His pleasure in the legs of a man, but the LORD takes pleasure in those who fear Him, in those who hope in His steadfast love.

Glory be to the Father and to the Son and to the Holy Spirit; as it was in the beginning, is now, and will be forever. Amen.

You open your hand; You satisfy the desire of every living thing. (Ps 147:7–11; antiphon: Ps 145:16)

We're thinking bread and fish. The psalmist is actually thinking grass and whatever young ravens like to eat. For all of the above, God provides the rain, which the ancients knew was so necessary. Obviously God cares about and provides for "every living thing." We should appreciate all of God's creatures too. But God's greater interest is in our wellbeing. "Beasts" and "ravens" are really the psalmist's way of making this point: If God so cares for the beasts of the field and the birds of the air, will He not much more provide for all our needs? Most surely! And His care will indeed be for *all* our needs.

That includes "all our needs of body and soul," our **Collect** for this Sunday adds,

Heavenly Father, though we do not deserve Your goodness, still You provide for all our needs of body and soul. Grant us Your Holy Spirit that we may acknowledge Your gifts, give thanks for all Your benefits, and serve You in willing obedience; through Jesus Christ, Your Son, our Lord, who lives and reigns with You and the Holy Spirit, one God, now and forever. Amen.

Body and soul always belong together, don't they. God made us that way, and even after death separates them, God will restore His original design in eternity; on the Last Day, at "the resurrection of the body," our bodies and souls will be reunited for "the life everlasting" (Apostles' Creed). So it only makes sense that God provides for both. That's never really a question or a trade-off—like, soul important, body not so. Like, since God is giving you heaven someday, who cares about what happens here on earth? Like, "Just get over it and quit your cryin'" when unemployment or loneliness or pain hits you now. Nonsense. God cares for all of our needs.

In the feeding of the five thousand, we'll of course hear about Christ providing for our needs of the body. But notice here in the Collect the request that God would grant us His Holy Spirit. The Spirit fills our spiritual needs, and He comes always through the Word and Sacraments. We'll keep that in mind through the propers too.

The important thing is to realize that God provides for both physical and spiritual needs for the same reason: the cross of Christ, which has reconciled the Father to us and to the whole world. So our focus is to be not on our particular needs but on the one who provides for them.

One of Scripture's most beloved ways of describing Him is as our Shepherd. Enjoy again our appointed **Psalm** for this week, the Twenty-Third.

We've commented on Psalm 23 in previous devotion-studies (e.g., for Easter 4, Year B, pp 372–74), and we will again in the future. This time, as we're studying the Psalm in the context of Proper 11, Year B, let's observe that the Psalm actually includes not one but two major metaphors. Here's the first: "The LORD is my shepherd." David sings from experience. His job shepherding the flock of his father, Jesse, was to see that they "not want" (23:1). For sheep, that meant leading and feeding them. Green grass wasn't just to lie down in; it was the menu—and the greener the better. Still waters weren't simply serene scenery; in an arid land, finding water was survival (23:2). Faithful shepherding also meant protecting the sheep. Everywhere was a "valley of the shadow of death" for any sheep wandering off by itself. It was essential that the "rod" and "staff" of the shepherd draw back any waywards, keep the flock together, and beat back any marauders (23:4).

This metaphor has as many applications as we have needs and fears in our lives. Am I harried, rushed, anxious about every deadline pressing at home, work, school, even for a church project? He lets me lie down at night and turn it all off by assuring me He's going to accomplish His perfect will even if I flop. Is my soul troubled with guilt for abusing some substance, for failure as a parent or spouse, for something I said that hurt a friend? He restores my peace with Him by declaring me righteous for the sake of Jesus' death for that very sin. Am I wandering from the faith? He reaches out with His Word—perhaps delivered by a pastor or a friend—to pull me back.

Then there's the second metaphor in the Psalm: "You prepare a table before me in the presence of my enemies; You anoint my head with oil; my cup overflows" (23:5). We're not eating grass anymore. Now it's a banquet—great food, drinks flowing, and the Lord honors us with the best seat; those who hate us can only watch and stew.

There are plenty of applications here too. Body and soul. Every meal we enjoy with our families is a table spread by our Lord. And the best banquet will be eternal, when we'll be seated with the Lord Himself and the finest wine really will overflow. Both are because our Shepherd laid down His life for us.

We all know what happens if sheep don't have a faithful shepherd. It's in the **Old Testament Reading**, Jeremiah 23:1–6.

One reason Jeremiah so often had to deliver bad news is that Judah's leaders—kings, priests, prophets—had been unfaithful shepherds. Bad moral examples, false teachings, and a movement that encouraged idolatry had allowed God's people to stray. These false shepherds had scattered the flock (23:1–2).

But "behold, the days are coming, declares the LORD, when I will raise up for David a righteous Branch," that is, a righteous descendant (23:5). He would be a king on David's throne and reign wisely. But He would also follow in His father David's first career as a shepherd. "I will gather the remnant of My flock out of all the countries where I have driven them, and I will bring them back to their fold" (23:3). That's the most basic job of all for the shepherd, isn't it! Gather the flock. Keep them near—to be led and fed. Then "they shall be fruitful and multiply" (23:3). In fact, since "this is the name by which He will be called: 'The Lord is our righteousness'" (23:6), He would make God's people righteous by forgiving their sin. They would be able to be in a relationship with the righteous God. Every hearer in Jeremiah's day knew this descendant of David, King, Shepherd, would be the Messiah, the Christ.

See if you pick up how the Christ has carried out that most basic shepherding task in the **Epistle**, Ephesians 2:11–22, even though Paul never uses the shepherd image.

What is Paul's point in this reading? That those "who were far off" from God for millennia, that is, Gentiles, and "those who were near" Him, Israel (2:17), are now "joined together" (2:21) "in one body" (2:16). And where's the shepherding? "In Christ Jesus you who once were far off have been brought near by the blood of Christ" (2:13). All sinners, Jews, Gentiles—equally guilty—have been equally and fully forgiven "through the cross" (2:16). And thus Christ "has broken down in His flesh the dividing wall of hostility" between them (2:14). Our Shepherd has gathered together all believers, scattered though they were, into one flock.

Finally, it's as Shepherd of this flock that Jesus will feed the crowd in the **Holy Gospel**, Mark 6:30–44.

Jesus' disciples rejoin Him after a successful but no doubt stressful first mission experience (6:7–13), and it's time for time off. No such thing. When Jesus sees a great crowd, "He had compassion on them, because they were like sheep without a shepherd" (6:34). Jesus is ever the Shepherd, and a shepherd leads: "He began to teach them many things" (6:34). Jesus leads them into the Word, which gives that gift of the Holy Spirit we'll pray for on Sunday in our Collect.

And now, the Shepherd feeds. It is "a desolate place" (see 6:31, 32, and 35!), reminiscent of the desolate wilderness in which Israel wandered forty years and in which Jesus was tempted for forty days. It was desolate for sheep without a shepherd, but now, Mark observes, there is "green grass" after all (6:39). When the Lord is my Shepherd, it's always green pastures beside still waters.

When Jesus was in His desolate wilderness, He refused to make bread; He wouldn't obey Satan by serving Himself. But now He's feeding His sheep, as God fed Israel manna. And, wow, does He feed them! Jesus Himself says the table blessing (6:41), and the rest, as they say, is history—history our Shepherd will make when He goes to the cross to earn us every blessing of body and soul. He continues to make history every time He sets His glorious Table—the Lord's Table.

**The Lord Is the Shepherd
Who by His Blood
Gathers Us, His Scattered Sheep,
to Lead Us and Feed Us
in His Green Pastures.**

Perhaps surprisingly, the **Hymn of the Day**, *LSB* 644, is most closely connected to the Epistle. But remember that the Church's sustenance is the feeding of our Shepherd, from whom she "partakes one holy food" (st 2).

The Sundays after Pentecost: Proper 12 (July 24–30) Year B

READINGS

Genesis 9:8–17
Psalm 136:1–9 (antiphon: v 26)
Ephesians 3:14–21
Mark 6:45–56

HYMN OF THE DAY

LSB 754 "Entrust Your Days and Burdens"

Along with feeding five thousand last week, Jesus walking on water in this Sunday's Gospel is surely one of our Lord's best-known miracles. This miracle is so well known that in popular thinking, "walking on water" is often the criterion by which the natural order almost seems to reach the divine. Basilisk lizards of Central America are nicknamed Jesus Christ lizards because on a pond or stream, their rapid slapping of the water with their feet actually enables them to run on its surface. A new football coach hired to turn around a losing program may caution for patience: "I can't walk on water." But if he wins, fans may start to think he can. When I arrived on campus as a seminary student, upperclassmen told us first-year guys you couldn't walk on water until your second year. It turned out that that was because, on sunny days in September and October, we didn't realize the lake froze for a few weeks in January or February, and you could take a shortcut to the dining hall.

Jesus walking out to the disciples on the Sea of Galilee is certainly a dramatic demonstration of His divinity. There's lots to say about that in our propers this week. But, as with the miraculous feeding last week, there's another detail in our Gospel reading, hinted also in the rest of Proper 12, that mustn't be overlooked. Perhaps you remember this from our discussion of Jesus' walk on the lake in Year A. This easily-missed detail is probably the most significant element of the story. We'll see about that again this year.

The **Introit** gets us thinking about the Lord's awesome power, which would enable one to do things like walk on water. But it also begins to suggest something more.

On the glorious splendor of Your majesty, and on Your wondrous works, I will meditate.

I will extol You, my God and King, and bless Your name forever and ever. Every day I will bless You and praise Your name forever and ever. Great is the L*ORD, and greatly to be praised, and His greatness is unsearchable. They shall speak of the might of Your awesome deeds, and I will declare Your greatness. They shall pour forth the fame of Your abundant goodness and shall sing aloud of Your righteousness.*

Glory be to the Father and to the Son and to the Holy Spirit; as it was in the beginning, is now, and will be forever. Amen.

On the glorious splendor of Your majesty, and on Your wondrous works, I will meditate. (Ps 145:1–3, 6–7; antiphon: Ps 145:5)

God's "majesty" is splendid. His works are "wondrous" and His deeds "awesome." "Great is the LORD, and greatly to be praised, and His greatness is unsearchable." That is to say, He has the power to control wind, water, and gravity.

But more than just applauding God's almighty power, the Introit makes the claim of singularity. Count how many times David, the psalmist, writes "You" or "Your." "Your majesty . . . Your wondrous works. . . . You, my God and King . . . bless Your name. . . . I will bless You . . . praise Your name. . . . Your awesome deeds . . . Your greatness. . . . Your abundant goodness . . . Your righteousness." Yours and no one else's. The Lord is unique. There's no one like Him. That means our help, our protection, all blessing is in Him. David knew pagan gods would fail those who trusted in them. Our own cleverness, hard work, sparkling personality, way with words will never be the source of our success or our deliverance from trouble. Only You, O Lord!

Notice this too. David speaks of God in the third person once in the Introit: "Great is the LORD," essentially to identify to whom he's speaking. The rest of the way, David's extensive use of "You," second person, indicates the personal, conversational relationship God invites us to have with Him. He is always accessible, near, eager to hear. Remembering that can be our greatest comfort when we're anxious or afraid.

This week's **Collect** likewise hails God's almighty power while also trusting His eagerness to hear from us and use that singular power on our behalf:

Almighty and most merciful God, the protector of all who trust in You, strengthen our faith and give us courage to believe that in Your love You will rescue us from all adversities; through Jesus Christ, Your Son, our Lord, who lives and reigns with You and the Holy Spirit, one God, now and forever. Amen.

It's never just God's power that comforts us. It's that He uses His power as "the protector of all who trust in" Him. (Note again: "*the* protector," not just one of many.) That fact is always a reminder of Christ crucified, because if Jesus had not reconciled God to us by His death, God would be our enemy and His power would be fearsome to us. Instead, because of the cross, God is always disposed to protect us.

Our prayer here is that God would give us "faith and . . . courage to *believe*" that He really does use His power to "rescue us from all adversities." We're always inclined to doubt or forget His promise to hear and help; we panic when crises come.

The **Old Testament Reading** has its obvious connection to the Gospel lesson, as well as a more subtle one. Read Genesis 9:8–17.

Noah and his family experience God's awesome but gracious control over all water—sending it, stopping it, saving from it. They are spared when the rest of the human race is destroyed; God continues the line of the Messiah through them—every bit the miracle to match Jesus walking on water.

This post-flood reading, though, is really about the covenant God makes with mankind. The Lord promises never again to destroy all flesh by water: "I establish My covenant with you, that never again shall all flesh be cut off by the waters of the flood, and never again shall there be a flood to destroy the earth" (9:11).

Why not? Simply because God in His love for man decrees it. Noah and his family have no bargaining chips—we of future generations no more so. God owes us nothing. But as in the Introit, see how the Lord invites us to trust Him, to know Him personally in His covenant. This time, as God is speaking, count His uses of "I," which He engages again and again with "you." Especially this one: "When I bring clouds over the earth and the bow is seen in the clouds, I will remember My covenant that is between Me and you and every living creature of all flesh" (9:14–15). God binds Himself to us; when the rainbow appears, *He* will remember the covenant, and He *must* do what He promises because He said He would. When God says, "I," you can count on it.

The **Psalm** has a unique way of expressing the certainty we have of any promise the Lord makes to us. Read Psalm 136:1–9, 26.

"Give thanks to the Lord, for He is good, for His steadfast love endures forever" (136:1). That's plenty familiar—especially in the King James Version: "His mercy endureth for ever." But the refrain quickly becomes *very* familiar, even if we've never prayed it before. Isn't that an interesting device the psalmist employs! By sheer weight of number, he assures us that God will never waver in His love for us. The Hebrew word we translate as "steadfast love," חֶסֶד, *chesed*, is loaded with both tenderness and permanence. It's intimate but also solid, secure. It's like knowing you can always run home to Mom and Dad (and brothers and sisters) after a bad day at school or three strikeouts in Little League; they'll always give you hugs and kind words. If the Lord says He still loves you, you're always okay!

Oh, and by the way, He rules over everything someone else might call a god or lord and over day, night, the stars and planets, all the heavens, *and the waters*. If *He* says He'll always love you . . .

The **Epistle** continues to track Paul's message to the Ephesians as the third of eight consecutive Sundays in the book. It does, though, pick up an aspect of the theme for this Sunday. Read Ephesians 3:14–21.

Paul is praying ("I bow my knees before the Father," 3:14) that the Holy Spirit would give us a fuller comprehension of "the breadth and length and height and depth" of "the love of Christ" that still always "surpasses knowledge" (3:18, 19). Add those dimensions to the psalmist's metric of time: "forever." God's love in Christ reaches infinitely in all directions, including into the future. So not only is there never a time when Christ's love will not hold us safe but there's no place He won't love us. "Now to Him . . . be glory" (3:20, 21). As we've seen from the beginning in the Introit, the Lord—and only the Lord—is the one deserving of glory, for He is the one who cares for us everywhere, every way, all the time. When He is with us, we need nothing more.

The fact that He can walk on water is really only one small reason for that. Consider Mark's take on this in the **Holy Gospel**, Mark 6:45–56.

Mark's account of Jesus walking on water is simpler than Matthew's in Year A of the lectionary (Mt 14:22–33). The obvious difference is that Mark makes no mention of Peter jumping out of the boat and walking on the water too. That's perhaps surprising since many scholars believe Peter was the primary source for Mark's writing from the time they were together in Rome.

Omitting Peter's splashing makes the story much less dramatic. We don't get a sense of being out there on the water ourselves. Mark even adds this comment: Jesus "meant to pass by them" (6:48c)—quite nonchalantly, it seems. The net effect is to downplay the walking on water. In Mark's telling, it isn't really the big deal. What is?

It's really a question of whom we look to when we're afraid. The disciples are terrified when they think they see a ghost. (Unlike two chapters before, the wind and waves aren't dangerous, just a nuisance, 6:48a). "But immediately [Jesus] spoke to them and said, 'Take heart; *it is I*. Do not be afraid'" (6:50). That's the detail we need! That's *all* we need! It's not the walking on water that's the assurance. It's simply that Jesus is the one who's here. That singularity again. You might remember the Greek lesson we gave for Proper 14, Year A. (Or look back at pp 198–201.) Jesus' words, "It is I," recall God's Old Testament covenant name, Yahweh, "I AM" (e.g., Ex 3:14). Looking to anyone or anything else when you're in trouble is seeing ghosts. But Jesus, the one who brings you back under God's care by His reconciling death on the cross, assures that "it is I" who is here with you now. And

When It Is I,
You Have Nothing to Fear.

Our **Hymn of the Day** (*LSB* 754) is a Paul Gerhardt work of great comfort. God, "while ruling the sky, the sea, the land," extends to you His "most loving hand" (st 1).

The Sundays after Pentecost: Proper 13 (July 31–August 6) Year B

READINGS

Exodus 16:2–15
Psalm 145:10–21
(antiphon: v 15)
Ephesians 4:1–16
John 6:22–35

HYMN OF THE DAY

LSB 918 "Guide Me, O Thou Great Redeemer"

Say the two short words "John six," and immediately you've got controversy.

Our Gospel lesson for Proper 13, Year B, is the first of three Sunday Gospels in the sixth chapter of John, a lengthy treatment of what's called Jesus' bread of life discourse. When He speaks them, Jesus' words raise confusion among and then the ire of His original Jewish audience. In the early centuries of the Church, pagan opponents latched onto the language of Jesus' discourse to charge the Christians with cannibalism: "Whoever feeds on My flesh and drinks My blood has eternal life" (Jn 6:54). Much later, Ulrich Zwingli, a Swiss reformer, defended his doctrine of the Lord's Supper against Martin Luther's by focusing on this chapter rather than on Jesus' Words of Institution. And even today among conservative Lutherans, there are sometimes sharp disagreement as to how directly Jesus' bread of life discourse refers to the Sacrament.

Ultimately, any proper interpretation of John 6 will point us where Scripture always does. If we get there, we're on solid ground.

Let's go right to it with the **Holy Gospel**, John 6:22–35, our first installment of Jesus as the bread of life.

"The next day" (6:22) reminds us that Jesus has just fed the five thousand. That's the trigger for the entire discussion. Our lectionary gave us Mark's account (Proper 11), but John reports the event as well (6:1–15). And John finishes his telling with this: "Perceiving then that they were about to come and take Him by force to make Him king, Jesus withdrew" (6:15). Jesus knows what the crowd wants: free lunch *every* day. That's not the kind of king He's come to be.

It is, though, why the crowd so eagerly hunts Him now. They have no idea what happened in last week's Gospel—how Jesus could have crossed the lake and arrived on the other side with His disciples without having embarked in their boat. (John relates Jesus walking on water, too, in 6:16–21.) It's in Capernaum that the people find Him. (Thus when naysayers disparage the Lord's Supper as cannibalistic, the term used is "Capernaitic eating.")

We've stressed before that Jesus' feeding the crowd was first of all His care for their physical hunger. Yet John wants to be sure we see the other dimension as well. He refers to the people eating the bread "after the Lord had given thanks" (6:23). In their accounts of the feeding, Matthew, Mark, and Luke all say Jesus "blessed" the loaves and fish (Mt 14:19; Mk 6:41; Lk 9:16), but John uses a form of the Greek word for "giving thanks," εὐχαριστέω, *eucharisteo* (in Jn 6:11 and here)—from which comes our word for the Lord's Supper, *Eucharist.*

Throughout the discourse, Jesus is one step ahead of the crowds. (No surprise!) They have their agenda; He has a higher one. They begin the conversation by asking how Jesus managed to make His way there (6:25). Jesus ignores that question and redirects: "Truly, truly, I say to you, you are seeking Me, not because you saw signs, but because you ate your fill of the loaves. Do not work for the food that perishes, but for the food that endures to eternal life, which the Son of Man will give to you" (6:26–27a). *Signs* (σημεῖα, *semeia*, in Greek) is a word John uses frequently for miracles that attest to Jesus as the Messiah (2:11, 23; 3:2; 4:54; 6:2; 7:31; 9:16; 10:41; 11:47; 12:18, 37; 20:30). The crowds have a skewed idea about that. They see, even eat, the miracles, but they're thinking too small. Bread and fish, real and nutritious as they are, are just two of the infinite examples of love this Son of Man has for them—love that is truly divine. Not the miracle but the miracle worker is the object they should be seeking. "For on Him God the Father has set His seal. . . . Believe in Him whom He has sent" (6:27b, 29).

That's Jesus' agenda.

The crowd goes back to its own. "Then what sign do You do, that we may see and believe You? What work do You perform? Our fathers ate the manna in the wilderness; as it is written, 'He gave them bread from heaven to eat'" (6:30–31). You see what they're doing, right? They're baiting Jesus. "We'd like to believe in You, Jesus, but, uh, well, we need to be sure. You know what Moses did. He gave our people manna. Awfully good stuff. Hint, hint."

Jesus, of course, has already given them a sign—why, just yesterday. A huge one. And lots more before. It's pretty obvious the crowd isn't looking for evidence to be sure Jesus is the right guy to believe. It's not really Jesus they care about. It's all about bread.

So Jesus ups the ante. "The bread of God is *He* who comes down from heaven and gives life to the world" (6:33). The true bread is a He. Chew on that one.

Instead, they choke. "Sir, give us this bread always" (6:34). They use the familiar vocative κύριε, *kyrie*, which is so often rightly translated "Lord," and we'd love to think they now get what Jesus means. But it's quickly clear that it's not Jesus Himself they're asking for always. "Sir" or "Lord" or whomever, what we want out of You is more of those tasty victuals You gave us yesterday.

So let's just say it flat out: "*I* am the bread of life; whoever comes to Me shall not hunger, and whoever believes in Me shall never thirst" (6:35). You had your appetizer. Delicious. Now I'm the main course.

The table is set. Jesus is ready to serve a proper banquet. But as the dialogue goes on the next two Sundays, will the crowds be interested in His menu?

Do we bring an agenda to Jesus . . . that isn't Jesus? Our need for groceries is very real. We really do need a place to live, appropriate clothing, yes, a car and some other things. Our jobs, our health, the welfare of our families are important––to us and to God. But what we really need is Jesus Himself. He takes care of all those needs as He knows best. But if His supplying doesn't seem to match up with our expectations, we always still have all we need. We have Him in our Baptism, in His Supper, in His words spoken to us. He gave Himself to us in the very worst of situations, when anyone else would hightail it and run, when He went to the cross. That means He'll give Himself to us in *every* moment, which, in turn, does mean that in every moment He'll give us whatever is really best—for dinner and for the eternal banquet.

It wasn't just the crowds in John 6—or just we—who have trouble trusting this. Read about Israel in the **Old Testament Reading**, Exodus 16:2–15.

The Israelites aren't nearly as subtle with their agenda for the Lord as the Capernaum crowd was, are they! "Would that we had died by the hand of the LORD in the land of Egypt, when we sat by the meat pots and ate bread to the full" (16:3). Their primary concern, too, is their stomachs.

Now, God is going to feed them; it's not as if He worked ten plagues in Egypt, parted the Red Sea, and brought them this far only to let them starve—or for God to be caught unprepared. What? They need food too? The Lord is going to provide. Of course. But without their grumbling, He uses food to teach them, test them, to walk in His Law (16:4). We'll do it God's way, precisely as He promises and prescribes (five days a week and twice on Friday, 16:4–5), and then you should get His point: "You shall know that it was the LORD who brought you out of the land of Egypt. . . . You shall know that I am the LORD your God" (16:6, 12). Again, it's not the food. It's the Lord.

Quail was a special treat. But then in the morning, "What is it?" (the Hebrew מָן, *man*). The simple answer: bread, evermore called manna. It's white in color and tastes like wafers with honey (16:31). Nice!

The richer answer, though: "It is the bread *that the LORD has given you to eat*" (16:15). Yet again, it's not really about the bread—or any physical or spiritual blessing. It's about the giver. Just as for the crowds following Jesus, the food is directing us to the Lord Himself. And for ancient Israel as for us today, the Lord is the one who gives us all things by restoring our broken relationship with God through God's greatest act of giving.

This, I think, gives us a most apt Theme for all the propers this day. Every blessing, bread, fish, manna—

What Is It?
It Is a Sign of the Christ.

Whatever else we'll see in John 6, He is the proper interpretation—as of all Scripture.

Read all the other propers for Sunday with that in mind. The **Introit**:

With upright heart He shepherded them and guided them with His skillful hand.

He commanded the skies above and opened the doors of heaven, and He rained down on them manna to eat and gave them the grain of heaven. Man ate of the bread of the angels; He sent them food in abundance.

Glory be to the Father and to the Son and to the Holy Spirit; as it was in the beginning, is now, and will be forever. Amen.

With upright heart He shepherded them and guided them with His skillful hand. (Ps 78:23–25; antiphon: Ps 78:2)

It is Christ's heart of love and creative skill that gave Israel manna, "the bread of the angels," and gives us "food in abundance." And, as always, it's because His cross reconciled us to God.

We prayed part of our appointed **Psalm** in the Introit two weeks ago. David has it entirely right: "The eyes of all look to You, [Lord,] and You give them their food in due season. You open Your hand; You satisfy the desire of every living thing" (Ps 145:15–16). Our eyes are to be on the Lord. He takes care of all the rest.

The **Epistle**, Ephesians 4:1–16, is Paul's urging to Christian unity among the believers in Ephesus—not a bad admonition when the subject of John 6 is afoot. Even when there is disagreement, let there be "humility and gentleness, with patience, bearing with one another in love, eager to maintain the unity of the Spirit in the bond of peace" (4:2–3). The key to that is sharing "one Lord" (4:5). He, Christ, is always the goal: "unity of the faith and . . . knowledge of the Son of God, . . . to grow up in every way into Him who is the head, into Christ" (4:13, 15).

The **Collect** brings all of this together. The Father's great gift was the Son. It is on Him that we feast, and we do so sumptuously whether His other gifts seem for a time to be much or little, because we always have Him abundantly in His Word and Sacraments.

Merciful Father, You gave Your Son Jesus as the heavenly bread of life. Grant us faith to feast on Him in Your Word and Sacraments that we may be nourished unto life everlasting; through the same Jesus Christ, our Lord, who lives and reigns with You and the Holy Spirit, one God, now and forever. Amen.

"Bread of heaven, feed me till I want no more" (the **Hymn of the Day**, "Guide Me, O Thou Great Redeemer," *LSB* 918:1).

The Sundays after Pentecost: Proper 14 (August 7–13) Year B

READINGS

1 Kings 19:1–8
Psalm 34:1–8 (antiphon: v 3)
Ephesians 4:17–5:2
John 6:35–51

HYMN OF THE DAY

LSB 534 "Lord, Enthroned in Heavenly Splendor"

The original stumbling block to hearing properly John 6, Jesus' discourse on the bread of life, wasn't the pagans' gross caricature of the early Christians as cannibals, eating the flesh and drinking the blood of their master. And it wasn't Ulrich Zwingli's obsession with proving from John 6 that Jesus couldn't mean His body and blood were really present in the Lord's Supper. The original aversion to Jesus' words—the problem that so offended His Jewish hearers live in Capernaum—was Jesus' insistence that man can in no way cooperate in coming to God. That's actually the universal bone of contention, not just with John 6 but with everything God says to us in Scripture.

We know that we're saved by grace alone, not by anything we do. We Lutherans confess that "I cannot by my own reason or strength believe in Jesus Christ, my Lord, or come to Him" (SC, Creed, Third Article).

So we've got to pause and think when Jesus begins our Gospel lesson for Proper 14 by saying, "I am the bread of life; whoever comes to Me shall not hunger" (Jn 6:35). Five times in the Gospel reading, in fact, Jesus talks about us coming to Him. How can we come to Jesus without it somehow becoming a work on our part? The propers for this Sunday, including the Gospel, the second installment in Jesus' bread of life discourse, will answer that question.

The **Old Testament Reading** is a good place to start because it gives an example of a guy who should have but wasn't coming to the Lord. Read 1 Kings 19:1–8.

Ahab's report (19:1) does not go well with Jezebel. Ahab, we remember, is the most wicked of all Israel's wicked kings. His wife

Jezebel, the daughter of the Canaanite king of Sidon, is much worse than spoiled. She is a zealous missionary of Baal, the ubiquitous (if one can be ubiquitous without really being anywhere at all) fertility god whose worship involves sacred prostitution and child sacrifice. The news is that Elijah, that pesky prophet of Yahweh, just fought a showdown with Baal's 450 prophets on Mount Carmel and showed up Baal but good. Fire rains from heaven! Oh, and all of your beloved prophets are dead.

"Then Jezebel sent a messenger to Elijah, saying, 'So may the gods do to me and more also, if I do not make your life as the life of one of them by this time tomorrow'" (19:2). Interesting move. Why fire a warning shot across the bow? Why not just send the soldiers to cut off his head right now? It seems Jezebel doesn't so much want Elijah dead as humiliated. If he were to run, it would show he wasn't so confident of Yahweh after all. It would discredit both Elijah and his God.

And she reads Elijah rightly. He flees!

Elijah travels south, past the populated borders of Judah to where no one can find him. He's not only scared, but he's despaired: "O Lord, take away my life, for I am no better than my fathers" (19:4). His whole prophetic career is a failure, he's convinced. "And he lay down and slept under a broom tree" (19:5).

"Come to Me, all who labor and are heavy laden," Jesus invites Elijah and us, "and I will give you rest" (Mt 11:28). But Elijah's *not* coming to the Lord with his burden when he needs rest. He's just asking Him to end it all.

This is a man who's tasted the Lord's goodness, and in dramatic ways. Without that, by nature, we could *never* come to God. See, many people don't come to God because they don't care to; they think all is fine without Him. You can't come to God if you're still being your own god. Other folks think they can come right up to God, kind of saunter over to Him, and strike up a deal. At least they hope they can. They want what God has to offer, and they figure a share of it is theirs because they surely fit into His "good enough" category. At least they hope they do.

And then there are people who feel the way Elijah does now. They realize they're failing; either they see how guilty they are of sin or how badly they're bombing life as students, as breadwinners, as parents, as fame fleets, as bodies wear out. But no one would just up and come to Christ on those credentials. Everything else we do is based on paying a price—in cash, in hard work, in giving affection to get some back. And neither guilt nor failure will buy us doughnuts. That's the whole problem. We've got no goodness to offer; we're sinners. We've got no résumés to impress; we've already proved we're flops in algebra or as dads. We can't come to God like that. People despair.

So the *Lord comes* to Elijah. "Behold, an angel touched him" (1 Ki 19:5). This is one of many cases in the Old Testament where "the angel of the Lord" (19:7) may very well be the Lord Himself, that is, the preincarnate Son of God in the role of "messenger" (same Hebrew word as "angel") of Yahweh. "Arise and eat." And again, "Arise and eat, for the journey is too great for you" (19:5, 7).

Twice the Lord comes to Elijah with bread and water. And Elijah "went in the strength of that food forty days and forty nights to Horeb, the mount of God" (19:8)—that is, to Mount Sinai, a place of refuge.

Elijah is in no condition to come to God. Surely he would never claim he'd brought himself to that life-giving bread. "If I invite a half-starved person to sit down to a well-set table and to help himself to anything he likes," C. F. W. Walther illustrates, "I do not expect him to tell me that he will take no orders from me." It's quite obvious that "Come, for everything is now ready" is no demand we're to meet but rather "the sweetest invitation" of the Gospel (Walther, *Law and Gospel: How to Read and Apply the Bible*, ed. Charles P. Schaum, trans. Christian C. Tiews [St. Louis: Concordia Publishing House, 2010], 287).

All of this is the point Jesus makes in the **Holy Gospel**. When we couldn't come to eat the bread of life, He came to us. Read John 6:35–51.

Coming to Jesus means believing in Him. Notice the parallel: "I am the bread of life; *whoever comes* to Me shall not hunger, and *whoever believes* in Me shall never thirst" (6:35). Faith, believing in Jesus, is trusting that He has done everything to save me, and that I've done nothing to help my cause. But many err by thinking, "I made a decision for Christ," or, "I asked Jesus into my life." Jesus will dismantle that thinking in these verses and then rebuild.

First, "You have seen Me and yet do not believe" (6:36). Not only has this crowd seen Jesus feed them miraculously from five loaves and two fish but Jesus has shown them many signs before. If these weren't convincing enough, we humans must, on our own, be unable to believe.

Next, "All that *the Father gives Me* will come to Me" (6:37). We can't come to Jesus ourselves. All who come are given to Him by the Father.

Then the bottom line: "*No one can* come to Me unless the Father who sent Me draws him" (6:44). This is really the stumbling block to Jesus' hearers for the rest of the John 6 dialogue. Wanting free lunches, the problem that surfaced last week, betrayed a sense of entitlement; the Messiah ought to give us something. Recoiling at the idea of eating and drinking Jesus' body and blood, which comes out next week, will show they'll only receive the Christ if He fits their tastes. Both are ways of insisting that I can somehow make my own arrangements with God. Jesus now says I can't.

But Jesus says, "I have come down from heaven. . . . I am the bread that came down from heaven. . . . I am the living bread that came down from heaven. If anyone eats of this bread, he will live forever" (6:38, 41, 51). That's so much better than our struggle to climb up to Him, which we can't do anyway. Jesus comes to us, and then the Father draws us to Him. For "it is written in the Prophets, 'And they will all be taught by God.' Everyone who has heard and learned from the Father comes to Me" (6:45). God brings us to Christ by that sweetest invitation of the Gospel—the Word that tells us He has come and redeemed us by His death on the cross, including especially that Word as it's spoken to us with water in Baptism (for many of us, at an age when we quite obviously couldn't come to Him ourselves). When we couldn't come to Christ, He came to us. That's the real controversy and the sweet solution of John 6.

Jesus Coming Down as Bread from Heaven Enables Us to Come to Him in Faith . . . and to Go On

as Elijah was able to go on.

The Introit and Gradual acknowledge our helplessness to come to Christ when they call us to fear the Lord. But they also express trust that He brings us His good. The **Introit**:

> *You open Your hand; You satisfy the desire of every living thing.*
>
> *Oh, taste and see that the Lord is good! Blessèd is the man who takes refuge in Him! Oh, fear the Lord, you His saints, for those who fear Him have no lack! The young lions suffer want and hunger; but those who seek the Lord lack no good thing.*
>
> *Glory be to the Father and to the Son and to the Holy Spirit; as it was in the beginning, is now, and will be forever. Amen.*
>
> *You open Your hand; You satisfy the desire of every living thing. (Ps 34:8–10; antiphon: Ps 145:16)*

The **Gradual** (new this week):

> *Fear the Lord, you His saints, for those who fear Him lack nothing! Many are the afflictions of the righteous, but the Lord delivers him out of them all. (Ps 34:9, 19 alt)*

He came to us! The **Collect** for Sunday:

> *Gracious Father, Your blessed Son came down from heaven to be the true bread that gives life to the world. Grant that Christ, the bread of life, may live in us and we in Him, who lives and reigns with You and the Holy Spirit, one God, now and forever. Amen.*

Finally, the **Psalm** and **Epistle** demonstrate that once Jesus has come to us, once we have been taught and believe in Him, we can go on with lives in Him.

Read Psalm 34:1–8. David tastes that the Lord is good (34:8). He seeks the Lord, cries out to the Lord in his troubles (34:4, 6), and the Lord hears.

Read Ephesians 4:17–5:2. Those who've not "learned Christ" (4:20) can't know Him, for their minds are in "futility" (4:17), "darkened in their understanding" (4:18). But when we have been "taught in Him" (4:21; "taught by God" in Jesus' citation), a "new self" has, in our Baptism, been "created after the likeness of God in true righteousness and holiness" (4:24).

Close by singing "Jesus, true and living bread, . . . life-imparting heav'nly manna" (**Hymn of the Day**, *LSB* 534:1, 4).

The Sundays after Pentecost: Proper 15 (August 14–20) Year B

READINGS

Proverbs 9:1–10
or Joshua 24:1–2a, 14–18
Psalm 34:12–22 (antiphon: v 11)
Ephesians 5:6–21
John 6:51–69

HYMN OF THE DAY

LSB 696 "O God, My Faithful God"

Why is the fear of the Lord the beginning of wisdom? The antiphon to the Introit tells us it's so, quoting Psalm 111:10. So does one of the two Old Testament Readings, in Proverbs 9:10. Then there's the Psalm for this day, Proper 15, in which David tells us he will teach the fear of the Lord to the man "who desires life" (Ps 34:12). Joshua, in our alternate Old Testament Reading, offers as his final counsel to Israel that they fear the Lord. And finally, the Gradual assures us that those who fear the Lord "lack nothing." There's something very wise about fearing the Lord.

All these Old Testament references to wisdom and fearing the Lord make an interesting pairing with the Gospel lesson since it's the climactic installment in Jesus' bread of life discourse from John 6. Jesus doesn't mention wisdom or fearing God there. Yet His teaching reveals what true wisdom is and how it's only possible when one has a healthy and holy fear of God. It turns out, that's what's been lacking all along among too many of Jesus' followers.

The **Holy Gospel** begins right where we left off last week, repeating the same verse that ended last Sunday's lesson. Read John 6:51–69.

It's such a beautiful invitation: "I am the living bread that came down from heaven. If anyone eats of this bread, he will live forever. And the bread that I will give for the life of the world is My flesh" (6:51). Eternal life!

As they've been throughout the dialogue, though, Jesus' hearers are slow on the uptake. While He's just offered the greatest gift—and He's *giving* it!—they lag behind, wondering about the logistics. "How can this man give us His flesh to eat?" (6:52).

So once again, Jesus has to move them forward. You were wondering about "eating" My flesh. How about "feeding on" My flesh? It's a significant move in the Greek. Jesus shifts from the ordinary word for eating, ἐσθίω, *esthio* (in 6:53 and earlier in the chapter) to the more graphic τρώγω, *trogo* (6:54, 56, 57, 58). *Trogo* implies the more physical actions of consuming—incising, masticating, swallowing. If they've got a problem with eating Jesus' flesh, now He's really given them something to chew on!

But is that what really causes the crowd offense? "This is a hard saying; who can listen to it?" (6:60). Jesus knows that the real problem is something different: "Do you take offense at this? Then what if you were to see the Son of Man ascending to where He was before?" (6:61–62). We might assume that feeding on someone's flesh is what makes the saying hard—and it ain't easy! But if that were the real issue, then seeing Jesus ascending to heaven should be no problem. There's nothing grotesque or unseemly about that. Instead, Jesus knows that seeing Him glorified would be even more problematic for these hearers. Why?

Because seeing Jesus ascend, just as if His flesh were indeed "true food" and His blood "true drink" (6:55), would prove how true this is: "Truly, truly, I say to you, unless you eat the flesh of the Son of Man and drink His blood, you have no life in you" (6:53). And "no one can come to Me unless it is granted him by the Father" (6:65). Jesus' claims assert that man can do nothing on his own to come to God and His Christ. That's always the great affront to man, because by sinful nature we always want to be in charge. If I must eat the flesh of this man Jesus in order to live, then I can't order off my own menu. And if I'm left standing on earth gawking to see this ordinary son of Joseph and Mary (6:42) lifted into heaven, then He must be infinitely above me, and I sure can't climb myself up to Him. That's why verse 65 ("no one can come to Me unless it is granted by the Father") is the kicker line: "After *this* many of His disciples turned back and no longer walked with Him" (6:66).

Errors about the Lord's Supper have the same root. Christian denominations that deny Jesus' body and blood are truly present in the Sacrament exalt human reason above God's Word: The human Jesus, people reason, can't be here in the bread and wine if He's up in heaven. That, of course, is exalting man himself, us, above God and the clear words of Christ when He gave us His Supper: "This is My body. . . . This is My blood" (Mt 26:26, 28).

Ulrich Zwingli, a Swiss reformer who debated this with Martin Luther, insisted that Holy Communion could not be rightly understood from those straightforward Words of Institution alone; instead, Zwingli argued, the Sacrament must be interpreted according to John 6. Zwingli focused on verse 63: "It is the Spirit who gives life; the flesh is no help at all." From this, he concluded that Jesus' body could not be present in the Sacrament because it would be worthless, of no avail.

In fact, "*the* flesh" in verse 63 means something entirely different from all Jesus' previous references to "*My* flesh" (6:51, 54,

55, 56) and "the flesh *of the Son of Man*" (6:53). "*The* flesh" (6:63) means *our* sinful fallen nature, and, right enough, that can avail nothing. Above all, it can't enable us to come to God and His Christ! On the other hand, *Jesus'* flesh avails everything! It's the very body and blood that was killed and shed on the cross for the life of the world! It's precisely what the Holy Spirit uses to give life!

When Luther and Zwingli met at the German city of Marburg in 1529, one of Zwingli's allies pleaded with Luther to stop clinging to Jesus' flesh and look rather to His divinity. Luther replied that he knew no God besides the one who became human—and that he wanted no other.

This reveals Zwingli's great error: thinking that fallen man can be with God without God veiling Himself in humble flesh. How very wrong! God's unveiled majesty would destroy sinful human beings. We can have no relationship with God at all except through His flesh, the God-man, Jesus Christ.

That was the great offense to Jesus' original hearers, and many left. "So Jesus said to the Twelve, 'Do you want to go away as well?' Simon Peter answered Him, 'Lord, to whom shall we go? You have the words of eternal life, and we have believed, and have come to know, that You are the Holy One of God'" (6:67–69). As with Peter's other great confession, his sinful flesh had been of no avail in figuring this out (Mt 16:16–17); no one can come to Christ unless it is granted him by the Father. But the Father has granted Peter and the Twelve to understand Jesus' words: "The words that I have spoken to you are spirit and life" (6:63c). And Jesus' words of eternal life are His words of Himself as the very human, flesh-and-blood Savior.

Is John 6 about Holy Communion? Even faithful Lutherans disagree. Certainly Jesus hasn't yet instituted the Sacrament—not until the night when He was betrayed. Certainly one can have eternal life without ever receiving the Sacrament, for only faith in Jesus is required for salvation. And certainly Zwingli was in error in insisting that John 6, rather than the very words Christ spoke when He gave us the Sacrament, should guide our doctrine of the Lord's Supper.

But by the time John wrote his Gospel late in the first century, Christians everywhere were celebrating Holy Communion as the climactic event of all of their worship services. Surely these early believers couldn't help but think of the Sacrament when they read of Jesus calling Himself the bread of life and speak of eating His flesh and drinking His blood. And surely Jesus, even before He instituted the Sacrament, knew His followers would later make that connection—especially when He intensified His language by using *trogo* toward the end of the discourse. So surely we are also blessed to remember when we hear John 6 that whoever feeds on Jesus' flesh and drinks Jesus' blood in Holy Communion has eternal life, and Jesus will raise him up on the Last Day.

What does all this have to do with the other propers focusing on the fear of the Lord as the beginning of wisdom? Fear of the Lord isn't terror that God will destroy us. Fear of the Lord is reverence that He is infinitely above us, that He made us, rules over us, and could rightly punish us when we disobey

Him. It's evident that the followers who left Jesus after the bread of life discourse were lacking that fear. They thought they could come to God on their own terms, apart from Jesus' words of life, apart from Him giving us His flesh.

Conversely, fearing God is the beginning of true wisdom because believing Jesus' words of eternal life gives us all that has true, eternal meaning. Read the propers with this in mind:

The Father Grants Us to Confess the One True Wisdom: The Spirit and Life Words of Flesh-and-Blood Jesus.

The **Introit**:

The fear of the LORD is the beginning of wisdom; all those who practice it have a good understanding. His praise endures forever!

Praise the LORD! I will give thanks to the LORD with my whole heart, in the company of the upright, in the congregation. Great are the works of the LORD, studied by all who delight in them. Full of splendor and majesty is His work, and His righteousness endures forever. He has caused His wondrous works to be remembered; the LORD is gracious and merciful. He provides food for those who fear Him; He remembers His covenant forever. He sent redemption to His people; He has commanded His covenant forever. Holy and awesome is His name!

Glory be to the Father and to the Son and to the Holy Spirit; as it was in the beginning, is now, and will be forever. Amen.

The fear of the LORD is the beginning of wisdom; all those who practice it have a good understanding. His praise endures forever! (Ps 111:1–5, 9; antiphon: Ps 111:10)

The **Gradual**:

Fear the LORD, you His saints, for those who fear Him lack nothing! Many are the afflictions of the righteous, but the LORD delivers him out of them all. (Ps 34:9, 19 alt)

The **Collect**:

Almighty God, whom to know is everlasting life, grant us to know Your Son, Jesus, to be the way, the truth, and the life, that we may steadfastly follow His steps in the way that leads to life eternal; through Jesus Christ, our Lord, who lives and reigns with You and the Holy Spirit, one God, now and forever. Amen.

Read both **Old Testament Readings**, the **Psalm**, the **Epistle**, and the **Hymn of the Day**. See how those who fear the Lord (or reverence Christ, Eph 5:21) are invited to live, walk, and, like Peter, speak (or sing) in true wisdom, having faith in their Redeemer—even eating His bread and drinking His wine.

The Sundays after Pentecost: Proper 16 (August 21–27) Year B

READINGS

Isaiah 29:11–19
Psalm 14 (antiphon: v 7a)
Ephesians 5:22–33
Mark 7:1–13

HYMN OF THE DAY

LSB 865 "Lord, Help Us Ever to Retain"

Which of the following properly reflect doctrines of God, and which are the wisdom of men?

- "Cleanliness is next to godliness."
- "What I really like about being in church is when I can think my own thoughts about God."
- "Let's face it: God's Word is exactly what we need to get to heaven, but it does kind of cramp your style in the meantime."
- "I can be anything I want to be."
- "The God I worship would never tell women to submit to men."
- "Don't tell me what Martin Luther says. I want to hear the Word of God."

In the Gospel lesson for Proper 16, Jesus quotes Isaiah to warn the Pharisees and scribes: "In vain do they worship Me, teaching as doctrines the commandments of men" (Mk 7:7). Obviously, the two are not to be confused—the teachings of God's Word and human inventions. One is always reliable; the other will often disappoint. One is eternal; the other can at best be helpful for a time. One is the truth; the other may be utterly false. Therefore, one must be subservient to and carefully judged by the other.

And now be honest: Would I rather hear one than the other?

That's the challenge that confronts us this Sunday—just as Jesus confronted the Jewish teachers. Read the **Holy Gospel**, Mark 7:1–13.

Cleanliness is at least a pretty good idea, even if not—as John Wesley, the founder of Methodism, asserted in a sermon in 1778—next to godliness. But the Pharisees' ceremonial washing really had nothing to do with proper hygiene. Literally "wash with the fist"

(7:3) meant they'd sprinkle a few drops of water on the palm of one hand and rub it around with the fist of the other. It didn't really disinfect from any germs they might have picked up at the market. What it did do in their minds, though, was purify them from any spiritual uncleanness that might have come from rubbing shoulders with the wrong kind of people or from unholy practices like buying and selling.

If rather trivial, it at least sounded well intentioned. In fact, however, it was one of hundreds of traditions the Jews added to the commands of God that really weren't for pious purpose. God's own commandments not only expressed perfect holiness already; they were already more than fallen humans could ever keep. God's commands always go to the heart, the motives behind actions, and our motives are always tainted with sin. So when the Pharisees and elders added prescriptions about particular (and picayune!) dos and don'ts, they were actually *lowering* the bar of God's Law, making the Law only a matter of outward actions, not reaching to the heart. "This people honors Me with their lips, but their heart is far from Me" (7:6).

The root problem is that they thought they could, should, and had to make themselves holy before God. They had missed God's promise to make them holy, to forgive all their failures to keep His Law. And now, in the presence of God's Son Himself, they reject the one who came to do this for them, criticizing His disciples for not following their lead (7:5).

Jesus cuts through their hypocrisy with an example showing where this false religiosity had led. The Fourth Commandment, honoring father and mother (7:10), is God's own Word (but notice that it was written down by a man, Moses). It surely demands caring for our parents in their old age. That takes loving time and patience—and often also dollars. But the Pharisees find a clever way to circumvent God's command: they declare their financial assets to be "Corban," dedicated to God, and thus unavailable for Mom and Dad. It's admirable, godly, they claim. Oh, and how convenient! It allows them to keep and spend their money as long as they live. It set aside God's doctrine of love for their own self-serving ingenuity. And in many other ways they substitute their own commandments for God's doctrines (7:13).

By the way, see what else the Pharisees wash: "cups and pots and copper vessels *and dining couches*" (7:4). That's significant, because the Greek words there translated as "wash" and "washing" are forms of βαπτίζω, *baptizo*, the basis for the English word *baptize*. And many Christians today whose name comes from that word tell us that to baptize must always mean to immerse, take completely under the water. Well, it's obvious the ancient Jews didn't take their couches down to the river to immerse them; they'd "baptize," wash them with a wet cloth or a sponge. So when we baptize a baby by sprinkling a little water on her forehead in the name of the Father and of the Son and of the Holy Spirit, it's a perfectly valid sacrament of Baptism. Let's not be adding human requirements!

Sure thing! We certainly want to rely on God's Word rather than our own ideas.

But don't we have to admit we'd sometimes rather follow our own thinking than what God has to say? Maybe there's some fun to be had that God says is a no-no—or maybe some profit? Consider the **Introit**:

O Lord, I love the habitation of Your house and the place where Your glory dwells.

Vindicate me, O Lord, for I have walked in my integrity, and I have trusted in the Lord without wavering. Prove me, O Lord, and try me; test my heart and my mind. I wash my hands in innocence and go around Your altar, O Lord, proclaiming thanksgiving aloud, and telling all Your wondrous deeds.

Glory be to the Father and to the Son and to the Holy Spirit; as it was in the beginning, is now, and will be forever. Amen.

O Lord, I love the habitation of Your house and the place where Your glory dwells. (Ps 26:1–2, 6–7; antiphon: Ps 26:8)

Why does David love going to church—apparently even more than spending a day lounging in pastures green admiring God's creation? It's because that's the place where God's glory dwells—and God's glory, above all else, is His loving and forgiving us. Yes, God is everywhere, and His creation does announce His glory. But far more glorious than His making a beautiful world is that He, the almighty Creator, would sacrifice Himself to save us who've sinned against Him. David could "wash [his] hands in innocence" not by some silly ceremony he'd invent but by what the Lord would do to forgive his sins, sending David's Son to die for them. And the place the Lord promises to give that forgiveness is in His house and "around Your altar." That's where we hear "all Your wondrous deeds": "I forgive you . . . I baptize you . . . My body and blood." That's where we should be blessed to hear only God's Word, never the commandments of men. That's where our own foolish ideas can be supplanted by the Word of Christ. It's where we love to be!

Unless we just don't get it. See the **Old Testament Reading**, Isaiah 29:11–19.

It was true of Judah seven centuries before Christ, but Isaiah's prophecy also pictures precisely what Jesus sees in the Pharisees and scribes. They bury God's book beneath such a stack of their own writings that it becomes sealed from them, as if they can no longer read at all (29:11–13). And by going their own way, apart from God's counsel, they turn everything upside down; they put themselves, rather than God, in charge, as if clay would talk back to the potter who was shaping it (29:16).

Is that the way we want things to go?

Thank God He flips everything over again. He humbles a forest of great cedars ("Lebanon") when it gets too proud (29:17), but He also makes the deaf hear and the blind see. And what do they hear and see? "The words of a book"—God's book, God's Word! "Fresh joy"! Reason to "exult" (29:18–19)!

Man is a "fool" when he prefers his way to God's. Read the **Psalm**, Psalm 14.

The end of those who turn aside from God's Word to their own devices is "great terror" (14:5). But those who "call upon the LORD" may "rejoice," "be glad," for salvation comes out of Zion for them (14:4, 7).

Still there's today's *really* big challenge, the **Epistle**. Wouldn't we like to bend it just a little to fit our thinking? Read those provocative words of Ephesians 5:22–33.

Really, Paul? In our day and age? Wives submit to husbands? This flies in the face of everything our society has come to stand for: being whatever, whomever I want to be, not only gender equality and gender interchangeability but gender *change*ability.

Perhaps so. But it's what God has always stood for, even before He created man and woman, and that, like all of God's Word, never changes. And like all of God's Word, it has the ultimate purpose of bringing us joy, reason to exult, so much to love, like rejoicing in, exulting over, loving the husband or wife God gives to so many of us, like being loved by Christ, as He has loved His Church from all eternity, as all of us are. He loved His Church so much that He died to make us holy, spotless, entirely apart from what we couldn't, don't have to do for ourselves. Ahhh, *vive la differénce*!

Jesus, who's God, submits to His Father. Every Christian submits to Jesus and receives eternal life. Submitting to her Christian husband, a wife receives his loving care. Man doesn't have a better idea.

It's ironic, perhaps, that this Sunday, when we're so strictly warned against relying on the words of men, that the **Hymn of the Day** is the one and only in *LSB* that mentions Martin Luther by name: *LSB* 865. It even focuses on the catechism he wrote. In fact, that's no contradiction, because Luther's Small Catechism is nothing more than a textbook teaching Holy Scripture. Its chief parts—the Ten Commandments ("Law to learn"), the Apostles' Creed ("faith" in the "Three in One"), the Lord's Prayer ("dear Father, when we pray"), Baptism ("whom You baptized"), Confession and the Keys ("absolve"), and Holy Communion ("the Sacrament")—comprise the primary doctrines of the Bible. Looking to Luther is always just to gain his insights into Christ and God's Word, the one source that's always sufficient for life and delight.

There's Plenty to Love and Rejoice Over in the Word of God without Teaching as Doctrines the Commandments of Men.

"Alleluia. Your words were found, and I ate them, and Your words became to me a joy and the delight of my heart. Alleluia," the **Verse**, Jeremiah 15:16a.

Therefore, the **Collect** for this Sunday:

> *Almighty and merciful God, defend Your Church from all false teaching and error that Your faithful people may confess You to be the only true God and rejoice in Your good gifts of life and salvation; through Jesus Christ, Your Son, our Lord, who lives and reigns with You and the Holy Spirit, one God, now and forever. Amen.*

The Sundays after Pentecost: Proper 17 (August 28–September 3) Year B

READINGS

Deuteronomy 4:1–2, 6–9
Psalm 119:129–136
(antiphon: v 132)
Ephesians 6:10–20
Mark 7:14–23

HYMN OF THE DAY

LSB 566 "By Grace I'm Saved"

Follow your heart.

It sounds like good advice. You're choosing a college or a career. You're wondering whether to take a personal relationship to the next level or even whether this is the person you should marry. You're weighing whether to re-sign for millions with the NBA team you've played for since they drafted you—or go the free agency route to a team you think gives you a better chance to win a ring . . . and more millions. Follow your heart.

It's common advice these days. But it may be advice that's defiled.

Say what?

"Heart," "common," and "defiled" are key words in the **Holy Gospel** for Proper 17. See where they'll lead us by reading Mark 7:14–23.

This Gospel reading continues where Jesus left off last week. The Pharisees and scribes complain, you may remember, about the disciples eating with "defiled" hands (Mk 7:2, 5). That, of course, was a trivial matter of ceremonial washing—a tradition created by the Jews, not commanded by God. Now, though, Jesus goes on to explain what truly defiles someone.

The word translated as "defile" (7:15a, 15b, 18, 20, 23) is from the Greek κοινόω, *koinoo*, which literally means "make common." (It's the same root as for Koine Greek, the version of Greek in which the New Testament was written and which was commonly spoken throughout the Mediterranean—as distinct from the earlier Classical Greek.) Now there's nothing necessarily bad about being common, nothing we would think of as being defiled, but read on.

Jesus says nothing external (like unclean hands) defiles a person. That would also include foods; there's nothing really wrong with a ham sandwich, even though Old Testament Israel was forbidden to touch pork. (A few years later, after Pentecost, God would make that clear to Peter in Acts 10, and by the time Mark wrote his Gospel, he was able to look back and notice, Heh! Jesus made that point back when He was on earth, 7:19.)

What defiles a person is deeper. It's inside. It may be as invisible as evil thoughts, coveting, deceit, envy, pride, foolishness. It may come out in ghastly scenes: sexual immorality, theft, murder, adultery, wickedness, sensuality, slander (7:21–22). They're all ugly.

And all of these come out of the heart. We conceive wickedness in our hearts before we do anything about it—or even form the conscious thoughts. *The heart is the problem.* And here's where common and defiled come together. Those evils that we easily recognize as defiled are the common, universal, inherent, inescapable nature of *every* heart. This wickedness is what every human heart now by nature has in common.

The Pharisees and scribes think they are setting themselves apart from the common, ordinary, beneath-them behavior of the masses. Jesus goes to the heart of the matter and declares to us that we're all defiled by the sin we all share in common—ever since the fall of our first parents. There's no getting around it.

Follow your heart?

What's our reason for pursuing this career or that? Might our heart be chasing the money or a title to impress? Will "the next level" of a relationship really mean sexual immorality? Jesus says our hearts love that. Will the heart move us to select a husband or a wife for that very sort of inclination? And . . . well, not many of us play in the NBA.

"From within, out of the heart of man, . . . all these evil things come, and they defile a person" (7:21, 23).

This is one of those weeks when the Gospel reading has virtually no Gospel. So after all that Law, the Holy Spirit probably has us ready for the **Introit**:

Wash me thoroughly from my iniquity, and cleanse me from my sin!

Purge me with hyssop, and I shall be clean; wash me, and I shall be whiter than snow. Create in me a clean heart, O God, and renew a right spirit within me. Cast me not away from Your presence, and take not Your Holy Spirit from me. Restore to me the joy of Your salvation, and uphold me with a willing spirit.

Glory be to the Father and to the Son and to the Holy Spirit; as it was in the beginning, is now, and will be forever. Amen.

Wash me thoroughly from my iniquity, and cleanse me from my sin! (Ps 51:7, 10–12; antiphon: Ps 51:2)

David, who wrote Psalm 51, knew just how thoroughly corrupt the heart is (sinful from the moment of conception, Ps 51:5) and on very recent experience recalled the depths to which that heart could plunge him (to two of the heart's favorites: adultery and murder, 2 Sam 11:1–12:12). But he'd also heard God's forgiveness (2 Sam 12:13), and he knew that that washing makes one "clean," no longer defiled, "whiter than snow." A thousand years before Christ, what Christ Jesus would do on the cross was already purging away David's sin. And see what he prays for now in those very familiar words of our Offertory: "Create in me a clean heart, O God." It's what we all need—a new, clean heart that God must create.

That's why we pray this **Collect**:

> *O God, the source of all that is just and good, nourish in us every virtue and bring to completion every good intent that we may grow in grace and bring forth the fruit of good works; through Jesus Christ, Your Son, our Lord, who lives and reigns with You and the Holy Spirit, one God, now and forever. Amen.*

The clean heart must be God's creation. God is the source of *all* that's good; *no* good thing comes out of our natural hearts. But something is now radically different! Did you catch it? Now we pray that God would "bring to completion every good intent." Once David's prayer is answered, the clean heart God gives us *does* intend good and really can "bring forth the fruit of good works." Christ dwells in the believer, the soul that trusts his or her sins are forgiven, and Christ in us does do good. That's a radical makeover!

The clean heart *wants* to do good works. That is to say, it has a whole new view of the Law. Read Deuteronomy 4:1–2, 6–9, the **Old Testament Reading**.

Deuteronomy (literally "Second Law") is Moses' reiteration of the Ten Commandments (Deut 5:6–21; cf Ex 20:1–17) and of the account of God leading Israel the past forty years, just as they are about to "go in and take possession of the land" God is giving them (4:1). The message is to "keep the commandments of the Lord your God" (4:2).

To the old sinful heart, any such command of God is repugnant, against everything the sinner wants to do. However, the believing heart, cleansed by forgiveness and with Christ indwelling, grasps that God's commandments are our "wisdom" and "understanding" and thoroughly "righteous" (4:6, 8). We truly believe that God's ways are the very best for us.

Well worth noting is that this passage indicates God's Old Testament approach to evangelism. In our New Testament age, since Christ's completed work and Pentecost, we are sent to all the world (especially our own neighborhoods) to tell of Jesus' saving death and resurrection. In the Old Testament, God prohibited His people from mingling with most nations (knowing how quickly they would be corrupted). But even then, God loved all people, and Israel's obedience to His commandments "in the sight of the peoples" (4:6) was to be the way the Gentiles would know this. God's commandments to love Him and their neighbor is such a cut above pagan thinking. Seeing Israel love causes some foreigners to recognize Israel as a "great nation," "wise and understanding" (4:6), whose God is near to them and always eager to answer whenever they call (4:7). The more faithfully Israel kept the Lord's commandments, the more likely others come to know the true God. That's true for our witness today as well!

None of this is ever to "depart from your heart" (4:9).

Psalm 119 is an exclamation of the clean heart's love for God's commandments. This week's **Psalm** is a portion of it: 119:129–136. The psalmist keeps God's testimonies because they are "wonderful" (119:129). In fact, "I long for" them (119:131). He wants to be redeemed from man's oppression specifically so that nothing will prevent him from keeping God's precepts (119:134), and his "eyes shed streams of tears" when "people do not keep Your law" (119:136).

That, of course, is Satan's evil design. Read the **Epistle**, Ephesians 6:10–20.

The old sinful heart is no target of the devil's flaming darts. The old sinful heart is his lounge and laboratory. But when Christ comes to dwell in the heart by faith, we must expect constant attacks. And here we are as defenseless as the natural heart was helpless. We can stand firm only when we stand in the armor of God. In our spiritual warfare, it becomes especially evident that God's commandments are the only wise, righteous, and safe course of action, for anything else is Satan's schemes. We cannot simply "follow our hearts," because that in itself is a lie the devil has sold us successfully. He would like nothing better than for us to play it the way we feel—with all the coveting, deceit, envy, pride, immorality, sensuality, wickedness.

Rather than following our sinful hearts, God offers the belt of truth, the Gospel of peace, the sword of the Spirit, which is the Word of God. The same Word that created our clean hearts by declaring us righteous (our breastplate) for the sake of Jesus' blood, that saved us (the helmet) by Jesus' death and resurrection, and that gave us faith (our shield) to the believe this will keep our clean hearts safe from the evil one.

"Follow your heart" is a devilish trap. But God has given us so much more that is better.

While Our Hearts Produce Only Evil, God Creates in Us Clean Hearts That Long for and Keep His Righteous Commandments.

For all the words Jesus spoke in the Gospel condemning our sinful hearts, He also spoke the words of the sixth beatitude that give us the **Verse** for the week: "Alleluia. Blessed are the pure in heart, for they shall see God. Alleluia" (Mt 5:8). There's much about which to say "alleluia!" when Christ creates in us a clean heart.

As you sing the **Hymn of the Day**, "By Grace I'm Saved" (*LSB* 566), appreciate especially the final stanza:

> By grace! On this I'll rest when dying;
> In Jesus' promise I rejoice;
> For *though I know my heart's condition*,
> I also know my Savior's voice.
> *My heart is glad*, all grief has flown
> Since I am saved by grace alone.

The Sundays after Pentecost: Proper 18 (September 4–10) Year B

READINGS

Isaiah 35:4–7a
Psalm 146 (antiphon: v 2)
James 2:1–10, 14–18
Mark 7:(24–30) 31–37

HYMN OF THE DAY

LSB 797 "Praise the Almighty"

Truth be told, most folks don't come to church on Sunday morning having read our devotion-study for the week. And truth be told, the divine service liturgy isn't designed with the expectation that they have. However, the service is designed with the intent that as the service proceeds, worshipers will begin to notice a theme developing—one big idea that makes this Sunday different from last week, different from next week. The changeable elements of the service, the propers, are connected, unified around that big idea.

So an active worshiper will be thinking as he or she listens, looking for the connections, even trying to guess where the service is going. We know that every week will be about Christ and Him crucified. But what *specific* need for the cross, what *specific* blessing from the cross will be in focus this Sunday?

This week, as we've done sometimes before, let's approach our devotion-study that way. Let's read (and, better yet, hear) each of the propers in the order they'll occur Sunday without much comment. Listen actively and see if you can pick up the commonalities. See if you can begin to guess where they're going. Afterward, we'll circle back to them together and identify the theme. Ready?

Besides the opening hymn (which may also give a clue to Sunday's theme), the first proper is the **Introit**. Congregations present it differently: chanted, spoken responsively, read by the pastor. For our exercise, why not read it out loud, alone or as a family?

The Lord is the strength of His people; He is the saving refuge of His anointed.

To You, O Lord, I call; my rock, be not deaf to me, lest, if You be silent to me, I become like those who go down to the pit. Hear the voice of my pleas for mercy, when I cry to You for help, when I lift up my hands toward Your most holy sanctuary. Blessèd be the Lord! For He has heard the voice of my pleas for mercy. The Lord is my strength and my shield; in Him my heart trusts, and I am helped; my heart exults, and with my song I give thanks to Him.

Glory be to the Father and to the Son and to the Holy Spirit; as it was in the beginning, is now, and will be forever. Amen.

The Lord is the strength of His people; He is the saving refuge of His anointed. (Ps 28:1–2, 6–7; antiphon: Ps 28:8)

Did any words or phrases stand out to you as significant? Make mental notes.

Next, the pastor or congregation will pray the **Collect**, a prayer that seeks to "collect" the major thoughts of the Sunday into a few short words. That means it's highly thematic for the day. Say it, too, so you can process through your ears as well as through your eyes.

O Lord, let Your merciful ears be open to the prayers of Your humble servants and grant that what they ask may be in accord with Your gracious will; through Jesus Christ, Your Son, our Lord, who lives and reigns with You and the Holy Spirit, one God, now and forever. Amen.

What did you notice here? Are there any words or ideas in the Collect that you also heard in the Introit? There could be connections forming already.

The first Scripture lesson during the Sundays after Pentecost is always the **Old Testament Reading**, this week Isaiah 35:4–7a. Again, say it aloud. Same questions: What stood out to you? Did anything in this reading ring familiar with the Introit and Collect? If so, look for more of the same in the propers that follow. By now you might be getting some definite ideas.

After the Old Testament Reading, congregations will typically speak or chant either the Gradual (more often) or the Psalm of the day (less common, unless the service is Matins, when it's very likely). The Gradual expresses the theme for the whole season (or, during these many Sundays after Pentecost, for a part of the season—this one for Propers 14–20). So the **Gradual** will be a bit more general, a little less specific to this Sunday. Read it with that in mind:

Fear the Lord, you His saints, for those who fear Him lack nothing! Many are the afflictions of the righteous, but the Lord delivers him out of them all. (Ps 34:9, 19, alt)

Now read aloud the **Psalm**, Psalm 146. Are you making connections?

Next, read the **Epistle**. This is interesting. As you may remember, during the Sundays after Pentecost—as well as certain other times of the year—the Epistle readings take us more or less straight through a particular letter. This week, for example, is our first of four Sundays in the book of James. Since the Epistles follow the progression of that book, they won't necessarily make the same thematic point as the rest of the service. But with remarkable frequency, there are some elements of the Epistle that support the Sunday's main idea. Is there anything you see as you read James 2:1–10, 14–18?

There's one more proper before the Gospel lesson: the **Verse**. The Verse is always brief, often taken from the Gospel reading, and always closely aligned with the overall theme. In fact, when, like this week, it's *not* from the Gospel, you *know* it's chosen for its close connection to the theme. "Alleluia. The LORD builds up Jerusalem; He gathers the outcasts of Israel. He heals the brokenhearted and binds up their wounds. Alleluia" (Ps 147:2–3). How does that align with your gleanings from the propers so far?

Finally, the Gospel reading is the proper by which all the others (except perhaps the Epistle and Gradual) are selected. So the theme of the day will usually become most evident here. Any ideas from the previous clues where the Gospel might go? Perhaps even a guess as to the events from Jesus' ministry the Gospel reading might report?

See that this week's **Holy Gospel** has a principal cutting, Mark 7:31–37, and then additional verses that might be read, 7:24–30. Read it all, but remember which one is primary.

So the propers this week have all been keyed by, first of all, Jesus healing the man born deaf and mute and, secondarily, His delivering from a demon the daughter of the Syrophoenician woman. Did you see anything like these coming? Let's go back and check the cues.

In the Introit, David wrote, "To You, O LORD, I call; my rock, be not *deaf* to me . . . *Hear* the voice of my pleas for mercy." Then the Collect prayed, "O Lord, let Your merciful *ears* be open to the prayers of Your humble servants." And in the Old Testament Reading, Isaiah prophesied, "Then the eyes of the blind shall be opened, and *the ears of the deaf* unstopped; then shall the lame man leap like a deer, and the tongue of the *mute* sing for joy" (Is 35:5–6a). Had any of that caught your ear?

But, of course, not all of the other propers mentioned ears or deafness or an inability to speak. You probably heard references to "the oppressed," "hungry," "prisoners," "blind," "sojourners," "the widow and the fatherless" (Ps 146:7–9), and "the poor man" (James 2:2, 3, 6). The Verse spoke of "the outcasts" and "the brokenhearted." The Gradual, as expected, was more general but summed up all of these: "*Many* are the afflictions of the righteous, but the LORD delivers him out of them all."

So the theme of the day includes more than just Jesus healing those who can't hear and speak. And the parenthetical verses of the Gospel reading (with the Syrophoenician woman) broaden the focus to other kinds of healings and deliverances.

But look still more closely. The Introit and the Collect don't really talk about *people* who are deaf, do they? "*O Lord*, . . . be not deaf to me." "O Lord, let *Your* merciful ears be open to the prayers of Your humble servants." And the answer comes: "Blessèd be the Lord! For He has heard the voice of my pleas for mercy . . . and I am helped." Surely the man born deaf and mute was healed of His deafness. But the real point of all this is that the *Lord's ears* are open to hear our cries and, always for the sake of His reconciling death on the cross, to deliver us from a whole host of very real sufferings.

Look once more at the two incidents in Mark. The Syrophoenician woman (from the region of Syria and Phoenicia, north of Israel, whose chief cities were Tyre and Sidon) begs Jesus to save her daughter from the demon, but He does indeed seem deaf to her. (Matthew's Gospel even says, "But He did not answer her a word," Mt 15:23.) When Jesus does answer, He says, "Let the children be fed first, for it is not right to take the children's bread and throw it to the dogs" (Mk 7:27).

We might take this as a great offense, that Jesus prioritizes one person above another. (Remember James's warning against partiality in the Epistle, James 2:1–9.) In fact, Jesus loves this woman and her daughter as He loves everyone, but it is true that God had an order by which He would carry out His loving plans: the Jew first and then the Gentile. We may think we know better than God how to love, but . . . how foolish!

This woman, rather, believes that Jesus' priorities are exactly proper—and the very best for her daughter: "Yes, Lord" (7:28). "Everything You've said about the children of Israel receiving first is proper. I know I don't have priority." But see why she could so humbly take a back seat: "Yet even the dogs under the table eat the children's crumbs." "Your love is so generous and Your power so great that all I need is a little scrap of it. I know You're *that* good!" And Jesus is not deaf to her plea for mercy.

The man can't cry out for Jesus' hearing. But his friends beg Jesus to lay His hand on him. And this, too, is a remarkable story. Jesus demonstrates His care for a man who can't hear by engaging other senses: touch (putting His fingers into the man's ears), taste (spitting and touching his tongue), and sight (looking up to heaven). The man could even recognize Jesus' sighing, usually heard by its very visual expression of face and the heaving of the upper body. In these ways, Jesus communicates to the man what He is doing for him. Jesus was not deaf—but instead very sensitive—to the needs of a man who couldn't hear.

The sermon we hear will no doubt explore a proper in much greater depth. Perhaps we could summarize the propers like this:

The Lord's Merciful Ears Are Open to His Afflicted—Including Those Who Themselves Can't Hear.

Conclude by singing the **Hymn of the Day**, "Praise the Almighty" (*LSB* 797). Compare it to the text it paraphrases, Psalm 146. It's as if someone planned it!

The Sundays after Pentecost: Proper 19 (September 11–17) Year B

READINGS

Isaiah 50:4–10
Psalm 116:1–9 (antiphon: v 5)
James 3:1–12
Mark 9:14–29

HYMN OF THE DAY

LSB 849 "Praise the One Who Breaks the Darkness"

It's the father's desperate plea in this week's Gospel reading. Is it ever ours too? "If You can do anything, have compassion on us and help us" (Mk 9:22). And is that a word of faith or of unbelief?

Well, Jesus' power to help never runs out, but what about His patience?

These may be the key questions in our propers for this Sunday, but they're only a few of many that are raised, particularly by the Gospel lesson. Let's begin with that reading. It'll put a lot of questions before us. Once we've worked through those, we'll see how the other propers affirm our answers.

Numerous questions are actually vocalized in Mark 9:14–29, but it probably sparks even more in our minds as we read it. There are some rather strange details! Read the **Holy Gospel**.

See what I mean? Does it get you wondering? Are there any questions that occur to you as you read? How about some of these?

- "And when they came to the disciples . . ." (9:14). When who came to the disciples, and from where?
- The scribes are arguing with the disciples (9:14). About what?
- When the crowd sees Jesus, they are greatly amazed (9:15). Why?
- "O faithless generation, how long am I to be with you? How long am I to bear with you?" (9:19). Who is this faithless generation?
- When the spirit saw Jesus, "immediately it convulsed the boy" (9:20). Why did it convulse at the sight of Jesus?
- How can the father wonder *if* Jesus can do anything (9:22)? "*If*," Jesus retorts (9:23)! Is Jesus losing patience with all this?

- "I believe; help my unbelief!" (9:24). So, is that faith, or is it unbelief?
- "Why could we not cast it out?" the disciples ask about the demon (9:28).
- "This kind" (9:29). What kind? Is there something extraordinary about this demon?
- What does Jesus mean about only prayer casting out this demon (9:29)?

Some of these questions have pretty clear answers. Others aren't as easy.

The setting is quite clear. Jesus and the inner circle (Peter, James, and John) are just coming down the mountain from His transfiguration (Mk 9:2–13). They rejoin the other disciples in the midst of their argument with the scribes.

What are they arguing about? We learn of the poor demon-possessed boy and the disciples' inability to free him. Earlier, Jesus had enabled the disciples to cast out demons, and they'd had good success (Mk 6:7, 13). But this failure surely gave Jesus' opponents, the scribes, occasion to mock and argue that Jesus must be a fraud. Likely, the disciples were getting the worst of the debate.

When Jesus arrives, though, the crowd is greatly amazed and rushes to Him. What's so amazing? Some have speculated that Jesus, so shortly after being transfigured, still exudes a glow, as Moses had when he descended from Mount Sinai in the Old Testament (Ex 34:29–30). That seems unlikely, though, since Jesus instructs Peter, James, and John to keep the transfiguration a secret until after His resurrection. Instead, the crowd is probably amazed simply at Jesus' perfect timing, arriving just at the crucial moment of the disciples-scribes argument.

Disciples, detractors, a demon, a dad. Doesn't anybody get it? How long has Jesus been answering all their questions? How many miracles, exorcisms, has He done for them in plain view? "O faithless generation"! Jesus had long been grieved by the unbelief of the scribes (Mk 3:5). He'd often upbraided His disciples for their lack of faith (Mk 4:40; 8:17). And the immediate cue to Jesus' exasperation comes from the father (9:17–19). All of us reveal our faithlessness, behaving as if we've never witnessed God's goodness to us. At this moment, though, Jesus may be especially rebuking His own disciples, the ones He'd equipped for just such situations.

The one who understands the most about Jesus—though eternally faithless—is the demon. Satan's henchmen all recognize Jesus as the Christ, the Holy One of God, and they know that His coming means their time is short. Their tiniest consolation, then, is to do, in that short time, whatever works pain and havoc in God's creation. That's why at the sight of Jesus, this spirit immediately lashes out with his evil.

We understand the father's desperation, but we can also understand Jesus having enough of this. Yes, He's exasperated: "'If You can do anything, have compassion on us and help us.' And Jesus said to him, '"If You can"! All things are possible for one who believes'" (9:22b–23). Christ has certainly proved His power to help by now! There should be no questioning it!

But our Lord continues to bear with His pitiful creatures, and the desperate father senses that. "Immediately the father of the child cried out and said, 'I believe; help my unbelief!'" (9:24). It's perhaps as strong a confession of faith as any of us might ever hope to utter! We are all part of an unbelieving generation; there's doubt, there's struggle, there's downright rejection of God in all of us—as long as the old sinful Adam or Eve remains. Let's admit it! Let's confess it! But it's a believer—no matter how weak the faith—that cries out, "Help me!" Jesus has brought the father to the point where he gets it! "I'm desperate, Lord. I'm struggling! But You're the one who can save us!"

And the smoldering wick, the bruised reed, Jesus will never snuff out, snap off (Is 42:3). The enslaved son is freed. The desperate father is comforted.

A question we might not think to ask of the text—but which we must answer—is *why* Jesus can help. We likely assume it's because of His omnipotence; all things are possible because Jesus has all power. In fact, it's more than that—as God's help for us always is. The truth is, our sin gave Satan and his demons the binding claim over us. We *all* would be his possessions. And God could not have us as His own as long as we were in our sin, because God cannot violate His own holiness.

So when Jesus casts out an unclean spirit or receives us as His own, it's always because for a time, He didn't exercise His omnipotence but allowed Himself to suffer Satan's worst. As always, Jesus can help us because of the cross. When He rose, we knew Satan's power was broken.

Jesus' debriefing with the disciples afterward (9:28–29) resolves the final questions. Why could the disciples not cast out this demon when they'd cast out others before? Matthew's Gospel inserts, "Because of your little faith" (Mt 17:20). In Mark, Jesus says, "This kind cannot be driven out by anything but prayer" (Mk 9:29).

There's no indication that this demon is more powerful than others, and that surely isn't the point. (It is important to acknowledge that the boy's suffering is from an evil spirit, even though in Matthew's Gospel, 17:15, the father says he has epilepsy or is a lunatic—from the Greek word σεληνιάζομαι, *seleniazomai*, literally "moonstruck.") Instead, Jesus is perhaps saying this kind *of suffering*—demon possession—cannot be relieved except by prayer. Jesus is teaching the disciples always to depend on Him; *that* is the point. Likely, after their earlier success as exorcists, the disciples forgot that they needed Jesus' power and perhaps tried to handle this one on their own. That's what Jesus means by their "little faith"; they aren't proceeding on faith at all but on their own. No avail! This is why Jesus directs them to prayer. Prayer, since it's asking God, thanking God, confessing to God, always places us under Him and never allows us to go it alone.

For all its difficult questions, Jesus' care for this demon-possessed boy and his father delivers an unmistakable message:

However Daunting the Affliction—
and However Exasperating
Our Struggles of Faith—
Jesus Can and Does Help Us.

As you read and then on Sunday hear the other propers, consider how often that message applies to the lives of God's people, including your own. First, the **Introit**:

Be strong, and let your heart take courage, all you who wait for the Lord!

But I trust in You, O Lord; *I say, "You are my God." My times are in Your hand; rescue me from the hand of my enemies and from my persecutors! Make Your face shine on Your servant; save me in Your steadfast love!*

Glory be to the Father and to the Son and to the Holy Spirit; as it was in the beginning, is now, and will be forever. Amen.

Be strong, and let your heart take courage, all you who wait for the Lord! *(Ps 31:14–16; antiphon: Ps 31:24)*

Even as the father struggles with unbelief, Jesus encourages him to take courage: "All things are possible for one who believes" (Mk9:23). Our times are in God's hands—however powerful our enemies and persecutors. And the father trusts in Him.

Whatever our needs, we pray the **Collect** with confidence:

Lord Jesus Christ, our support and defense in every need, continue to preserve Your Church in safety, govern her by Your goodness, and bless her with Your peace; for You live and reign with the Father and the Holy Spirit, one God, now and forever. Amen.

The **Gradual** assures us:

Fear the Lord, *you His saints, for those who fear Him lack nothing! Many are the afflictions of the righteous, but the* Lord *delivers him out of them all. (Ps 34:9, 19, alt)*

The **Old Testament Reading**, Isaiah 50:4–10, is one of the Servant Songs in Isaiah (the third), which means it's Christ Himself who's suffering (50:6). "But the Lord God helps" Him (50:7, 9), no matter who His adversary, who contends with Him, who declares Him guilty (50:8–9). As a result, He is able "to sustain with a word him who is weary" (50:4).

In the **Psalm**, Psalm 116:1–9, the psalmist is assured that the Lord has heard his pleas for mercy, even when the enemy is the most daunting of all: death and Sheol, the realm of the dead.

And it's a task that no human being can master, taming his own tongue. Even in this exasperating struggle of faith, Christ is our help, our forgiveness: **Epistle**, James 3:1–12.

What are your most daunting struggles, doubts, afflictions? Lord, can You help with these? He gives us His answer!

"Praise the One who breaks the darkness," "who drove out demons," who "died and rose victorious that we may know God by grace" (**Hymn of the Day**, *LSB* 849).

The Sundays after Pentecost: Proper 20 (September 18–24) Year B

READINGS

Jeremiah 11:18–20
Psalm 54 (antiphon: v 4)
James 3:13–4:10
Mark 9:30–37

HYMN OF THE DAY

LSB 851 "Lord of Glory, You Have Bought Us"

From our propers for this Sunday: "Delight yourself in the LORD, and He will give you the desires of your heart" (Ps 37:4).

"Let me see Your vengeance upon them, for to You have I committed my cause" (Jer 11:20).

"Humble yourselves before the Lord, and He will exalt you" (James 4:10).

"If anyone would be first, he must be last of all and servant of all" (Mk 9:35).

These are the words of the Lord.

Did they get you thinking? What does your heart desire? Which enemies would you like to see get theirs? How great would it feel to be exalted, number one? Proper 20 for these Sundays after Pentecost will give us the formula!

Hmm. That sure sounds like a minefield, doesn't it! Right you are! You noticed it immediately, didn't you!

But these are indeed the Word of the Lord. How are they to be understood properly? What's the potential misunderstanding?

They all sound like great ways to manipulate God and our futures, don't they. If I do this, God will do that. If I do what God instructs, He'll give me whatever I want. And I can imagine quite a few things I want!

We know that can't be right. So let's look more closely at God's Word for the week and see what is right.

We begin with the **Introit**, which already seems to dangle that carrot out before us:

> *Delight yourself in the LORD, and He will give you the desires of your heart.*

Commit your way to the Lord; *trust in Him, and He will act. He will bring forth your righteousness as the light, and your justice as the noonday. Be still before the* Lord *and wait patiently for Him; fret not yourself over the one who prospers in his way, over the man who carries out evil devices!*

Glory be to the Father and to the Son and to the Holy Spirit; as it was in the beginning, is now, and will be forever. Amen.

Delight yourself in the Lord, *and He will give you the desires of your heart. (Ps 37:5–7; antiphon: Ps 37:4)*

What does your heart desire? Younger skin? A sculpted body? A spouse with younger skin or a sculpted body? A lower handicap? Ability or accessibility? A retirement to Arizona? A two-seater convertible that combines Japanese engineering with the feel of a British roadster? And all you have to do to get it is delight yourself in the Lord.

That's overlooking an important premise in the Psalm. For if someone delights in the Lord, what does she desire? Answer: the Lord. To delight in the Lord means one's heart desires the Lord. In other words, delighting in the Lord won't get you the girl or guy of your dreams or a better golf game or a sports car, but it does mean you absolutely do already have what you really want.

Oh.

Disappointing? Well, yes, of course, to our old sinful desires—which want anything but the Lord and what He wants to give us. Remember a few weeks back when Jesus told us what comes out of our hearts (Mk 7:21–22)?

But the Lord *is* our delight and our desire. We just can't manipulate Him into making that true. He does it—initially against our kicking and screaming. "*He* will bring forth your righteousness as the light, and your justice as the noonday." To replace hearts that desire everything else, He brings forth in us righteous hearts by bringing forth His righteousness in the flesh. When David (and all the Scriptures) speaks of our righteousness, he's always speaking directly or indirectly of Christ. (That's what Martin Luther finally discovered in studying Romans 1:17.) Christ, the only human who is righteous in Himself, gives us His righteousness when He takes our place in sin—in His life and in His death.

We are totally passive in receiving the desires of our hearts: "Be still before the Lord and wait patiently for Him." There's no manipulating God; no striving to make ourselves delight in Him. There's no stressing, fuming, fretting—even when we think we see others getting those things we sinfully desire: "Fret not yourself over the one who prospers in his way, over the man who carries out evil devices!"

When we understand this—that our desires truly are the Lord and His gifts and that we're entirely passive even in that—we'll then see how those other difficult passages are also rightly applied. Next, the **Holy Gospel**, Mark 9:30–37.

This isn't the first time Jesus has intimated His suffering, death, and resurrection (8:31–32a; 9:9, 12), and Jesus' language is crystal clear. The reason the disciples don't understand what He's saying (9:32) is that they can't understand those key words that follow: "If anyone would be first, he must be last of all and servant of all" (9:35).

To the disciples, being first means being what they would argue is the greatest (9:34). They're fretting quite a bit about who among them deserves the greatest accolades. We understand. We all have our images of what it means to be great, to be first—and our hearts desire it. Most or most successful kids and grandkids. Bragging rights about the places we vacation. Corner office. Magna—better yet, summa—cum laude. Stanford.

The disciples don't grasp that being delivered into the hands of men, being killed, and after three days rising again can be the metric for greatness, that serving is the way to be first. We, of course, are more savvy. We know the story—that Jesus' dying on the cross was His greatness. So we're willing to play the game. Make yourself last, be a servant to all, including receiving children in Jesus' name (9:37), and we can be first! "He will give you the desires of your heart."

Except that, obviously, desiring bragging rights isn't delighting in the Lord. It's delighting in something the Lord isn't promising. Making ourselves last in order to get isn't really serving; it's self-serving. It's the desire of that old sinful heart again.

And once again, *we* can't really serve as Jesus describes anyway. We can't receive a child *in Jesus' name* unless we first have His name. And Jesus' name can only be *given* to us; we're just passive recipients. To give us His name, Jesus had to suffer, die, and rise again. And then the Father, Son, and Holy Spirit put His name on us in our Baptism, when we were baptized into His death. That's the same moment He gave us entirely new hearts that delight in Him. It would by definition be futile trying to make ourselves last, trying to serve, in order to become first. There's no use fretting about it. Instead, we serve children, fellow disciples, all people because the Lord has already given us what we truly desire: Himself unto death on the cross.

Now look at both the **Old Testament Reading**, Jeremiah 11:18–20, and the **Psalm**, Psalm 54.

Check Jeremiah's immediate context with a peek back to 11:9–10. God's people conspire to serve other gods. And the Lord reveals to Jeremiah that the conspiracy is also against him, the prophet to whom they should be listening for God's Word (11:18). No wonder Jeremiah prays to the Lord those tough words: "Let me see Your vengeance upon them, for to You have I committed my cause" (11:20b).

David is in the same boat. Notice the superscription of the Psalm: "When the Ziphites went and told Saul, 'Is not David hiding among us?'" It was a conspiracy to turn David over to murderous King Saul. "Ruthless men seek my life" (Ps 54:3). David prays that God would "put an end to them" (54:5).

We all know that "'Vengeance is Mine,' says the Lord" (Deut 32:35; Rom 12:19; Heb 10:30), so we won't take revenge ourselves. (Or will we?) But since I've committed my cause to God, doesn't He owe a little comeuppance to the guy who stole my girlfriend, the antique dealer who practically swindled me on the value of Grandma's heirloom, the member who slandered me to my congregation? If I'm faithful, don't You owe me that much?

Is that really what we want? Or don't we already have everything that's really valuable? The Lord "judges righteously," "tests the heart and the mind" (Jer 11:20a), and He knows we also deserve only His vengeance. But we have been given the Lord's own righteousness in Christ. So not only are we forgiven of our desire to get even, but, yes, our new hearts realize we can leave righteous judgment to God. There's no need to fret, for we have Him. He's with us as He was with Jeremiah and David. "God is my helper" (Ps 54:4).

We might pervert one more of those passages into a *quid pro quo*—we do for God, God gives to us. Look for it as the last verse of the **Epistle**, James 3:13–4:10.

James presents such a contrast! The desires of our sinful hearts (jealousy, selfish ambition, 3:14) produce quarrels, fighting, murder (4:1–2). "But the wisdom from above is first pure, then peaceable, gentle, open to reason, full of mercy and good fruits, impartial and sincere" (3:17). Therefore, James gives us a series of imperatives that are indeed wise (4:7–9): submit to God, resist the devil, draw near to God, cleanse your hands, purify your hearts, be wretched and mourn (that is, set aside the laughter of worldliness). These are all good things to do.

They culminate with this: "Humble yourselves before the Lord, and He will exalt you" (4:10). Once more, does that mean we do all these fine things in order to receive the attendant blessings from God?

We certainly are to do them! And as believers, we do do them, but only after we have been given all we truly desire. James says that God yearns over "the spirit that He has made to dwell in us" (4:5). He's placed it in us; we're passive. And that spirit is the Spirit of the one who is pure, peaceable, gentle, reasonable, merciful, good, impartial, sincere. That's Christ. God has given Christ to dwell in us, and He is exactly and only what that spirit, our new heart, desires. Why fret about what we don't have (4:2)? And why try to strike a deal with God for more? We have Christ! And that means complete forgiveness, perfect access to God's care in every moment, final vindication, and life eternal.

**You Need Not Fret,
for the Lord Has Already Given You
Your New Heart's
Desire and Delight: Himself.**

As you pray the **Collect** and sing the **Hymn of the Day** (*LSB* 851), remember the Gospel reading and how the Lord of glory was perfectly strong when He was weak, made Himself last, died to serve all. May God give us the childlike faith to realize that in Him, we have all we could ever desire.

O God, whose strength is made perfect in weakness, grant us humility and childlike faith that we may please You in both will and deed; through Jesus Christ, Your Son, our Lord, who lives and reigns with You and the Holy Spirit, one God, now and forever. Amen.

The Sundays after Pentecost: Proper 21 (September 25–October 1) Year B

READINGS

Numbers 11:4–6, 10–16, 24–29
Psalm 104:27–35 (antiphon: v 24)
James 5:(1–12) 13–20
Mark 9:38–50

HYMN OF THE DAY

LSB 505 "Triune God, Be Thou Our Stay"

Word association: Praise service. Where do you go next? Outreach. Seekers. Drums. Loud. Screens. Praise. Noise. Praise. Chaos. Praise. Outreach. Millennials. Boomers. Repeat. Repeat. Repeat. Praise.

What's *your* gut reaction to that phrase, "praise service"? Love it? Hate it? Not many people are neutral.

Our **Introit** for this week invites us all to a praise service. It and the other elements of Proper 21 are definitely *not* going to resolve issues—or feelings—we have about praise services as the term is used among us. But they will give us God's Word about praise and about our service to one another.

Your name, O Lord, endures forever, Your renown, O Lord, throughout all ages.

Praise the Lord! Praise the name of the Lord, give praise, O servants of the Lord, who stand in the house of the Lord, in the courts of the house of our God! Praise the Lord, for the Lord is good; sing to His name, for it is pleasant! Your name, O Lord, endures forever, Your renown, O Lord, throughout all ages. For the Lord will vindicate His people and have compassion on His servants.

Glory be to the Father and to the Son and to the Holy Spirit; as it was in the beginning, is now, and will be forever. Amen.

Your name, O Lord, endures forever, Your renown, O Lord, throughout all ages. (Ps 135:1–3, 13–14; antiphon: Ps 135:13)

This Introit calls us to a quick study of what praise is and isn't. Praise, of course, isn't defined by the type of music and instruments—if any—being used to accompany it. (Some of our congregations will surely *speak* this Introit Sunday; likely none of them will use the same instruments ancient Israel employed in worship.) More important, and perhaps less obvious, praise isn't determined by the emotions or intensity of emotions of those praising God. Emotions can be very wholesome—God made us emotional creatures—but worship that's more emotional isn't necessarily higher praise. If it were, it would mean our feelings determined praise.

The problem is, by nature, we bring nothing to the table to offer God except our sin. That means our emotions are more likely to be self-stroking than worshiping God. The only things that turn us from inward to Godward are those He does. (Every Lutheran will recognize that as another expression of justification by grace through faith, apart from any works of ours.) So true praise will always be declaring what God has done for us. Check the psalms or the hymns of praise in the New Testament. They're all based on—and usually explicitly announce—something about God and what He has done for the psalmist or for the Church. "Your name, O LORD, endures forever." "The LORD is good." "The LORD will vindicate His people and have compassion on His servants."

As a matter of fact, the highest praise is simply to believe what God says He is doing for us, because that's giving all honor to Him. Praise, then, can actually happen when God is talking in His Word and we're saying or singing nothing at all, just listening.

Recognizing that praise is always based on what God has done for us. Pray the **Collect** for this Sunday:

Everlasting Father, source of every blessing, mercifully direct and govern us by Your Holy Spirit that we may complete the works You have prepared for us to do; through Jesus Christ, Your Son, our Lord, who lives and reigns with You and the Holy Spirit, one God, now and forever. Amen.

God the Father is the source of *every* blessing. Praising Him in a worship service, therefore, will always begin by hearing what *specific* blessing or blessings the Word of God is declaring that day. This Collect gives an interesting hint to Sunday's particular blessing: "That we may complete the works You have prepared for us to do." We may not think of works God gives us to do as blessings—first, because blessings are gifts, not things we earn by working, and, second, because we might just think of work as a bad thing, no blessing at all! In fact, being about God's business is an honor He bestows, a gracious blessing, not a job our résumés win us. And, of course, nothing God gives us to do can be bad.

We'll look for the works God has for us to do this week as we read on, and we'll see how they result from the nature and doings of God that invited praise in the Introit: The mention of God's name ("Your name, O Lord"); God's name always brings with it God Himself. And that God will "vindicate His people," honor them when someone else has challenged them.

Read the **Old Testament Reading**, Numbers 11:4–6, 10–16, 24–29.

We've heard it before; we'll hear it again: Israel in the wilderness grumbling about God's provision. It's just too much for Moses! "All this people . . . all this people . . . all this people . . . all this people"! (11:11, 12, 13, 14). "If You don't lift this burden, Lord," Moses pleads, "just kill me now!"

So God gives Moses a lift by putting His Spirit on seventy elders of Israel to share his load. Not only is God drafting a cadre of lieutenants to assist Moses but, by dramatic visual evidence, coming down in a cloud, He is again certifying that Moses is His man, unquestionably the leader. (Notice that the seventy prophesied, but only this once, 11:25. This is a great and godly event, but it is not to be the norm. Moses is the one and only God has called as His ongoing spokesman.)

But then we have Eldad and Medad (11:26). Why they hadn't come to the tabernacle, we don't know. Homesick, perhaps? Or perhaps disobeying. And yet they prophesy too—just not in the appointed assembly.

Joshua fears a praise service breaking out: "My lord Moses, stop them" (11:28). Joshua isn't concerned particularly about prophesying in the camp becoming disorderly—whatever precisely that prophesying is. (We don't know, but for folks to notice, it must have been more like a lead singer on mic than quiet meditation.) What alarms Joshua is that the authority of and respect for Moses may be undermined. It's a legitimate concern—also for the Church today. The focus of worship is never to be on any individual worshiper (in this case, Eldad and Medad having personal spiritual experiences) but on the Word of God to be proclaimed. And in each congregation, God has called one man to be the legitimate proclaimer. Anything that moves the attention of hearers away from lectern, pulpit, font, and altar, or suggests that someone other than the called pastor belongs in those places, distracts from God's design for His Word.

But Moses knows no such offense is being given here (11:29). Rather, by all this, God vindicates him as the proper leader. And Moses knows that "all the Lord's people" have callings of their own—the vocations on which Martin Luther wrote so well. One of the seventy (not the Moses). Husband. Wife. Father. Mother. Son. Daughter. Citizen. Student. Bank teller. Brick craftsman. Engineer. They are all vital and equally holy works God has for Christians to perform. And those vocations are each a blessing for which we praise God! We don't deserve to be so honored, but the Lord is good!

Closely parallel to the Numbers reading is the **Holy Gospel**. Read Mark 9:38–50.

A man casting out demons in Jesus' name. Is it a reason to praise the Lord? The Twelve echo Joshua: "We tried to stop him, because he was not following us" (9:38). Jesus corrects them: "No one who does a mighty work in My name will be able soon afterward to speak evil of Me" (9:39). This man isn't one of the entourage, but he is working (mightily!) in Jesus' name. To be of lasting value, anything must be in Jesus' name, for Jesus' name means He Himself is present.

Jesus here is very instructive for us: "The one who is not against us is for us" (9:40). Or, in Luke's parallel, "The one who is not against you is for you" (Lk 9:50). We are to be charitable toward other Christians who disagree with us on certain issues (Organ or guitar? *LSB* or contemporary Christian music?). This is especially true on matters of adiaphora (things neither commanded nor prohibited in Scripture). But even for other Christians who err on scriptural matters, while we must speak clearly and strongly against their errors, we praise God wherever their teachings and actions are faithful to His Word. Other Christians are not against us; they are brothers and sisters. That's their relationship *to us.*

On the other hand, simply "not against" is not at all sufficient in relation *to Christ.* In Matthew 12:30 (and also Lk 11:23), Jesus says, "Whoever is not with Me is against Me." In one's relationship to Christ, there can be no halfway. Christ Jesus is the only salvation for the world. With Him—trusting in His life, death, and resurrection—we have eternal life. Without faith in Him, one will be forever His enemy, lost forever.

Thus the disciples need not fear Jesus being dishonored by the man's exorcisms. He is with Jesus, doing mighty works in His name. But neither should they worry about their own positions as the soon-to-be first pastors of the Church being diminished. Jesus vindicates them too: "Have salt in yourselves" (Mk 9:50b). Praise the Lord that they are called to be the salt of the earth, doing the mighty work of proclaiming Him and do so with a spirit of service toward all others in their vocations: "Be at peace with one another" (9:50c).

Praise the Lord That He Has Blessed You—and All His People—with Mighty Works to Do in His Name.

Several last examples of works of God for which we praise Him. The **Psalm**, Psalm 104:27–35, is far less exuberant than the Introit—a more meditative worship perhaps (104:34)—but we praise the Lord just as surely (104:35) for food (104:27–28) and for life (104:29–30a). In the **Epistle**, James 5:(1–12) 13–20, we are encouraged to "sing praise" (5:13), especially because God promises to hear our prayers. The new **Gradual** we begin reading this week reminds us that we are entering that portion of the season known as Michaelmas (St. Michael and All Angels, September 29). Protection by God's angels is reason for all within us to praise His name!

> *He will command His angels concerning you to guard you in all your ways. Bless the* Lord, *O my soul, and all that is within me, bless His holy name! (Ps 91:11; 103:1)*

And the greatest of all God's works for us is upholding our faith in Christ the crucified against the devil's wiles. Sing the **Hymn of the Day**, "Triune God, Be Thou Our Stay" (*LSB* 505). Praise the Lord!

The Sundays after Pentecost: Proper 22 (October 2–8) Year B

READINGS

Genesis 2:18–25
Psalm 128 (antiphon: v 1)
Hebrews 2:1–13 (14–18)
Mark 10:2–16

HYMN OF THE DAY

LSB 863 "Our Father, by Whose Name"

Family is the basic building block of society—marriage, parenting, children. By God's design, the first block was laid in the Garden of Eden, and the same building has been going up, block by block, generation by generation, ever since. Some will advertise "a new kind of family," but God's blueprint has never been replaced, can never be improved. In fact, bucklings, even collapses, of society can invariably be traced to deviation from that blueprint.

Some weeks, the theme among the propers is so obvious. Proper 22 is one of those weeks. God's design for marriage, parenting, children, the family will be front and center throughout the service, beginning with the **Introit**:

Unless the Lord *builds the house, those who build it labor in vain.*

Behold, children are a heritage from the Lord, *the fruit of the womb a reward. Like arrows in the hand of a warrior are the children of one's youth. Blessèd is the man who fills his quiver with them! He shall not be put to shame when he speaks with his enemies in the gate.*

Glory be to the Father and to the Son and to the Holy Spirit; as it was in the beginning, is now, and will be forever. Amen.

Unless the Lord *builds the house, those who build it labor in vain. (Ps 127:3–5; antiphon: Ps 127:1a)*

"The house" could refer to anything man might try to build: a city, a career, financial security. But here the psalmist envisions especially a house that is a home. "Children are a heritage from the LORD, . . . a reward." What a blessing of God for a couple to be given children! "Blessèd is the man who fills his quiver with them!"—and in ancient times, a full quiver was at least five arrows.

How different, sadly, is the attitude of many today. In North America, Europe, much of Asia, and South America, the birth ates are less than "replacement." In many nations, it is far fewer than two children per woman. Children are often viewed as an economic drain, what with the cost of college, another car, wedding expenses. (Long gone in many places are the agrarian days when children were free farmhands!) And freedom to travel, easy nights out, a woman's career outside the home, and even providing *for our children* a certain level of material things are often valued more highly than children themselves. And Christians, too, have been significantly influenced by this thinking.

The psalmist's view should be ours. Is there a price on holding newborn Rachel? on hearing teenage Daniel say he's proud of Dad? on seeing Gabriel grow into a woman who leads other children to Christ? It's well worth it! Is it an inconvenience to tell Jesus stories to the kids at night instead of clubbing? to sing them to sleep with hymns instead of catching the first quarter of the game? to drive to Grandma and Grandpa's for vacation instead of flying to Cancun? Nonsense!

And we should certainly understand what the psalmist did about the role of children in God's saving plan. Even before the first sin, the Father planned for His Son to come into our world as a child. Old Testament Israelites actually saw every child as, at least symbolically, a tiny fulfillment of that plan. And for those families in the line of Judah and David, each baby boy was even seen as, just maybe, the Messiah. Every time we hold a baby, every child we raise, we should think back to the Christ Child, our Savior. We're encouraged to see that in at least some circles in our Church, young couples may be appreciating this, welcoming a quiverful or more!

This, then, behooves us to remember the Introit's initial admonition: All the hard work and expense to raise children will be in vain unless the Lord is allowed to build the family. That can be part of our prayer this week in the **Collect**:

Merciful Father, Your patience and loving-kindness toward us have no end. Grant that by Your Holy Spirit we may always think and do those things that are pleasing in Your sight; through Jesus Christ, Your Son, our Lord, who lives and reigns with You and the Holy Spirit, one God, now and forever. Amen.

God's relationship with us is always as in a family; God is our "merciful Father." And "patience and loving-kindness" are certainly family words. Raising children and being a child with sinful parents aren't easy tasks. They require the cooperation and patient forgiveness that God has extended to us in His Son's death and resurrection for our rebellions. So faithful parenting and children being obedient to the Fourth Commandment—doing "those things that are pleasing in [God's] sight" family-wise—mean hearing and receiving God's Word and Sacraments constantly. Every Sunday worship—Dad, Mom, kids—and Bible study, family devotions at home, prayers before meals and bed, love and conversation that reflect those big and little visits with God are the cement that forms the building block.

It all began, of course, when God created the first marriage. Read the **Old Testament Reading**, Genesis 2:18–25.

Five-and-a-half days of creation all led up to this. The cosmos was created to be the mansion for mankind. And God has already handmade Adam from the dust of the ground—a more personal crafting than just speaking to a whole galaxy or phylum at once, as He's done with everything else. But the building is no house yet. It isn't yet good, and God never intends to leave it at that (2:18). He lets Adam discover this for himself; He introduces Adam to every this, this, and this, let him name them lion and tiger and bear, so that Adam realizes the obvious: none is "a helper fit for him" (2:20).

The rest is the beginning of history. Our translations generally say that from the rib God "made" a woman (2:22). More literally in Hebrew, He "built" the rib into a woman. When the Lord builds the house, the labor is blessèd.

Adam notices! "This at last is bone of my bones and flesh of my flesh" (2:23). At last! She's not like any of those others! She's the "Oh, my!" And for *this one* he delights to choose the name *Woman*! The connection we see in English—*Wo-man* "taken out of Man"—is sweeter yet in Hebrew. Say this out loud: man is *ish* and woman is *ishshah*. So, as Dean Wenthe, longtime president of Concordia Theological Seminary, Fort Wayne, Indiana, relished, noting, "The difference between man and woman is *'Ah!'*"

God's Word pronounces them the first husband and wife: "A man shall leave his father and his mother and hold fast to his wife, and they shall become one flesh" (2:24). One man. One woman. One block. No fissures or cracks. And no alternative models for marriage. This is as it "shall" be.

The last verse is hugely important: "And the man and his wife were both naked and were not ashamed" (2:25). Adam and Eve have nothing *inside* to hide. He is an open book to her, she to him. No wandering lusts, no selfish thoughts. The perfect oneness. We each know how that's changed since the fall. But here's where Christ's cross is the restoration of the Garden of Eden marriage. It forgives those sins, including the secret ones, that come between husband and wife, that, if unforgiven, could split a marriage apart. Then we forgive as He does.

Try to read the first two verses of the **Psalm**, Psalm 128, as if you didn't already know where all the propers are taking us.

So everyone who fears the Lord will be blessed (128:1–2). Well, just what blessing might the Lord be giving? Kids! "Your children will be like olive shoots around your table. Behold, *thus* shall the man be blessed who fears the Lord" (128:3b–4).

The **Epistle** explains how God procured our salvation: by subjecting Christ to humiliation, tasting death for everyone. See how that was a family matter in Hebrews 2:1–18.

Christ and we whom He sanctifies have "one source," God the Father. With Jesus, we are children of this Father. "That is why He is not ashamed to call [us] brothers" (2:11). And that's why "He Himself likewise partook of" our flesh and blood, "made like His brothers in every respect," to make propitiation for our sins (2:14, 17).

Christ, the Son of the Father, procures salvation for all God's children by His cross. And the children ordinarily receive this salvation by means of human families. Read the **Holy Gospel**, Mark 10:2–16.

Marriage, children, even divorce aren't the Pharisees' interests here. They test Jesus, hoping He might alienate either the rabbinic conservatives or the liberals on this issue (10:2). But Jesus shows them that divorce is always outside God's design. Moses' permission to divorce (Deut 24:1–4) had simply been a procedure by which a woman rejected by her hardhearted husband could remarry and thus have a new provider (Mk 10:5). Such sinfulness never fit the blueprint in Eden (10:6–8, quoting from the Old Testament Reading). Jesus gives the bottom line: "What therefore God has joined together, let not man separate" (10:9).

Every time we hear those words in a wedding service, we recognize the warning: Don't divorce! Divorce always involves sin somewhere (10:11–12), although there are complexities; the person securing the legal divorce may not be the one really committing the sin of divorce, especially if the other spouse has committed adultery, deserted, been abusive, and so on.

But perhaps we don't always catch the rich Gospel in those same words: "God has joined together." Every marriage—even those formed by less than wise and holy choices—God makes holy. And what God joins, God enables to thrive by His means, the Word and Sacraments. What an invitation to strong marriages, and what a comfort to struggling ones! In the forgiveness and eternal assurances of our Baptism, of the Lord's Supper, of preaching and absolution, God gives us what we need to be faithful.

And it's in faithful marriage that God performs His *primary* work of evangelism. God's ordinary way of bringing new souls into His kingdom is for children to be brought to Jesus and receive the blessings of faith as soon as possible. "Let the children come to Me; do not hinder them" (10:14b). Father and mother bringing an infant child to Baptism—what greater joy, what greater blessing than to know God has used us to bring a new heir into His kingdom! "For to such belongs the kingdom of God" (10:14c). This is God's design, building His house family block by family block.

When the Lord Builds the House, He Builds His Kingdom.

"Our Father, by whose name all fatherhood is known, . . . bless Thou all parents." "O Christ, Thyself a child within an earthly home, . . . our children bless in every place." "That every home . . . may be the dwelling place of peace" (**Hymn of the Day**, *LSB* 863).

The Sundays after Pentecost: Proper 23 (October 9–15) Year B

READINGS

Amos 5:6–7, 10–15
Psalm 90:12–17 (antiphon: v 1)
Hebrews 3:12–19
Mark 10:17–22

HYMN OF THE DAY

LSB 694 "Thee Will I Love, My Strength, My Tower"

Money, we know, is *not* the root of all evil. Possessions are not poison; they're gifts of God. But they're not the greatest gifts. If you think they are—now you're flirting with evil of all kinds. And a heart that loves earthly wealth is in grave danger of losing the greater gifts. On the other hand, when we realize that God has indeed given us far greater gifts than money, we're set free to use our earthly treasure in ways that can have eternal value.

Did the rich young man in this Sunday's Gospel reading learn that lesson?

We pray that *we* will as we study and then in worship hear proclaimed God's Word for Proper 23.

Wealth, its proper use, and the something greater are already explicit in the **Introit**:

Praise the LORD! Blessèd is the man who fears the LORD, who greatly delights in His commandments!

Wealth and riches are in his house, and his righteousness endures forever. Light dawns in the darkness for the upright; He is gracious, merciful, and righteous. It is well with the man who deals generously and lends; who conducts his affairs with justice. For the righteous will never be moved; he will be remembered forever.

Glory be to the Father and to the Son and to the Holy Spirit; as it was in the beginning, is now, and will be forever. Amen.

Praise the LORD! Blessèd is the man who fears the LORD, who greatly delights in His commandments! (Ps 112:3–6; antiphon: Ps 112:1)

Wealth and riches, the psalmist says, the Lord gives to the "blessèd" man, the one "who fears the LORD, who greatly delights in His commandments!" That tells us, of course, that wealth is a blessing of God. But the "blessèd" man isn't blessed simply in that he receives the blessing of wealth; that's not the big blessing. He's also not blessed with wealth because he fears the Lord and obeys His commands; being good won't get us more stuff. The "blessèd" man is already "blessèd" *before* he *either* keeps God commandments *or* receives wealth. The "blessèd" man is the man God has blessed to know Him, to fear Him, to delight in His commandments. God blesses us with faith in Christ Jesus as our Savior. Then we fear God and delight to do what He commands.

The blessing of faith and salvation is eternal: "For the righteous will never be moved; he will be remembered forever."

What follows that blessing is all kinds of other blessings. When that includes wealth, it is a blessing indeed! And the man who knows the Lord as Savior, who knows all his blessings are gifts of God, knows what to do with those material things: he "deals generously and lends"; he "conducts his affairs with justice." In fact, the believer in us "delights" to share his or her earthly blessings generously with those in need to see that they are treated justly.

The **Old Testament Reading** warns especially against sins regarding that last element. Those who love earthly wealth are likely to pervert justice toward the poor to get it. Read Amos 5:6–7, 10–15.

Amos prophesied during one of the last flourishing periods of Israel's monarchies—particularly for the Northern Kingdom. Jeroboam II's reign (793–753 BC) was a time of economic prosperity and relative military security: "You have built houses of hewn stone, . . . you have planted pleasant vineyards" (5:11). But we understand the temptations of prosperity. The prophet must frequently decry injustices of the rich upon the poor: "O you who turn justice to wormwood and cast down righteousness to the earth! . . . They abhor him who speaks the truth. . . . You trample on the poor and you exact taxes of grain from him, . . . you who afflict the righteous, who take a bribe, and turn aside the needy in the gate" (5:7, 10b, 11a, 12b).

Getting rich by taxing the crops of the poor. Turning away when seeing needs. Lying in court to cover their tracks. The profits of injustice—as with all earthly wealth—would be fleeting: "You have built houses of hewn stone, but you shall not dwell in them; you have planted pleasant vineyards, but you shall not drink their wine" (Amos 5:11).

Instead, the Lord calls Israel to "hate evil, and love good, and establish justice in the gate" (5:15). Since none of our possessions are really our own but all are from God, justice means seeing that all have a goodly share in them. The believer delights to follow this commandment.

Riches aren't mentioned explicitly in the **Epistle**, Hebrews 3:12–19, but see if you can infer how relevant they are there.

"Today," the writer trumpets (3:13, 15, and also earlier in 3:7). Be warned right now! Don't let your hearts "be hardened by the deceitfulness of sin" (3:13). What kind of sin? "The rebellion" (3:15) refers to Israel's quarreling with Moses over water in the wilderness ("Massah and Meribah," Ps 95:7–11; Ex 17:1–7).

Water is seldom our problem, but water bills, electric bills, medical bills, mortgage payments, car payments, credit-card payments . . . It's all money. The Israelites' complaint was just grumbling to the boss that they deserved a raise.

Tevye, in *Fiddler on the Roof*, was pretty sure all would be better if he were just a little bit rich. Not too much. Beware! Lest "the deceitfulness of riches choke the word, and it proves unfruitful" (Mt 13:22). When it comes to the deceitfulness of sin, earthly treasure is right at the top of temptations.

And how foolish if we ever give in to it because we have infinitely greater treasure: "For we have come to share in Christ" (Heb 3:14).

To share in Christ is Jesus' invitation in the **Holy Gospel**, but there's going to be that money thing. Read Mark 10:17–22.

"Good Teacher, what must I do to inherit eternal life?" (10:17). Matthew's Gospel tells us that this man is young (Mt 19:20), and we discover soon enough that he is rich (Mk 10:22), so unless he is quite the boy wonder entrepreneur, he probably knows about inheritances. Yet his question contradicts this; an inheritance is simply bestowed due to one's place in the family (probably the way he'd picked up Dad's fortune), but he thinks he must (and can) do something to gain God's inheritance.

This is why Jesus questions the young man calling Him "good" (10:18). He wants the young man to learn what *good* really is: "What's your basis for calling Me good? How do you think it works?" The young man doesn't realize that Jesus is good because He is the only good one, God Himself; he thinks *good* is by some work he must do. And he assumes it must be more than keeping the commandments, for he thinks he's already kept them (10:19–20).

This is what we might call a "Law moment," an occasion when Jesus must speak Law, not Gospel, because the young man is unaware of his sin. Often that's not comfortable for us; we'd rather speak Good News than warn someone of sin and its consequences. But this exchange teaches some important things about Law preaching.

First, the Law does need to be pointed, cutting, even stern. "Go, sell all that you have and give to the poor, and you will have treasure in heaven; and come, follow Me" (10:21b). Jesus knows He is making *the* most painful demand on this man; the young man doesn't yet realize that it is money he loves more than he loves God, certainly more than he loves justice for the poor. If the Law is to bring repentance, it must make clear to us that we can't get by with business as usual, that we're hopelessly sinful.

Second, when it's a Law moment, speaking the Law is the most loving thing we can do for someone. "Jesus, looking at him, loved him" (10:21a). He loves him with those tough Law words. Jesus dearly wants this young man to have eternal treasure, and that can only come by following Jesus rather than clinging to his earthly wealth. When we truly love our friends, we want them to have eternal treasure too. So we won't be shy about warning them of their sin.

Third, speaking the Law in love when it's a Law moment is the right thing to do even if we don't see the result for which we pray: "Disheartened by the saying, [the young man] went away sorrowful, for he had great possessions" (10:22). We may fear that rebuking sin will "turn her away." Perhaps. But we trust Jesus' perfect wisdom—even if speaking the Law seems to end sadly.

This was "today" for the rich young man, and he went away sorrowful. But was that really the end? Pray the **Collect**:

> *Lord Jesus Christ, whose grace always precedes and follows us, help us to forsake all trust in earthly gain and to find in You our heavenly treasure; for You live and reign with the Father and the Holy Spirit, one God, now and forever. Amen.*

We ask the Lord to preserve us from becoming possessed by our possessions. Jesus' atoning death gives us heavenly treasure. When we follow Jesus to the cross, we have wealth that reveals what a pitiful pittance is the second home in Aspen, season tickets to the Packers, the shoes we have to have to go with the dress.

And the Collect also reminds us that there was perhaps hope for Jesus' rich young man: Jesus' "grace always precedes *and follows* us." The young man walks away, but Jesus' grace pursues him. We hear nothing more about this young man explicitly, but it's thought by some that he may appear again in Mark's Gospel. Guess where. As the "young man" following Jesus in the Garden of Gethsemane who, when frightened, ran away leaving his linen cloth behind (Mk 14:51–52). And that young man is widely seen as the author of the Gospel recording his own cameo role. Was the rich young man who went away sad this John Mark, who became a missionary with Paul and Barnabas, later a companion of Peter in Rome, and eventually penned the second Gospel? Speaking the Law—Jesus, us—always prepares the sinner for the Gospel. And God knows the eternal results our faithful speaking will bring, even if we never see them in our lifetimes.

In heaven, we'll surely see how God has let us take part in saving souls. Some may even be from our generosity with earthly possessions. This is why Moses in the **Psalm** encourages us to "number our days" (90:12), for each one may be the "today" we bring someone else to Christ. And something as small as a gift to a homeless shelter may be a "work of our hands" that God will "establish" for eternal value (90:17).

Today Jesus' Love Calls You to Leave Earthly Wealth to Those in Need and Follow the Heavenly Treasure of Christ and His Commandments.

May it be Thee, Lord, not our earthly things, that we love (**Hymn of the Day**).

The Sundays after Pentecost: Proper 24 (October 16–22) Year B

READINGS

Ecclesiastes 5:10–20
Psalm 119:9–16 (antiphon: v 14)
Hebrews 4:1–13 (14–16)
Mark 10:23–31

HYMN OF THE DAY

LSB 690 "Hope of the World"

When your eyes get as old as mine, it's nearly impossible to coax a thread through the eye of a needle.

But in our Gospel reading for Proper 24, it gets a lot harder than that: "It is easier for a camel to go through the eye of a needle than for a rich person to enter the kingdom of God" (Mk 10:25). If it's hard *threading* a needle, it's even harder getting a camel through! That surely means it's impossible for a rich person to enter the kingdom of God.

Why is that so difficult? Obviously, the money doesn't help. Money can be a very seductive temptation. But that's not the greatest difficulty. In fact, Jesus goes on to tell us that it's so very hard—impossible!—*for us* to enter the kingdom of God, whether we've got a lot of money or a little. What is it that's so hard? And who then can be saved?

The propers this Sunday give us hope—even if we're rich.

The **Introit** will begin to describe God's way of doing the impossible:

The Lord is near to the brokenhearted and saves the crushed in spirit.

I will bless the Lord at all times; His praise shall continually be in my mouth. My soul makes its boast in the Lord; let the humble hear and be glad. Oh, magnify the Lord with me, and let us exalt His name together! I sought the Lord, and He answered me and delivered me from all my fears. When the righteous cry for help, the Lord hears and delivers them out of all their troubles.

Glory be to the Father and to the Son and to the Holy Spirit; as it was in the beginning, is now, and will be forever. Amen.

The Lord *is near to the brokenhearted and saves the crushed in spirit. (Ps 34:1–4, 17; antiphon: Ps 34:18)*

Have you ever had your heart broken? Was it by a girl who said she didn't want to see you anymore? Was it by a husband who left? Most often, I think, we speak of feeling brokenhearted in regard to romantic relationships. Of course, we might also feel brokenhearted at the loss of a child, when career dreams are shattered, when a home loaded with memories burns down. It's so comforting that the Lord is near us in those moments!

But elsewhere, David elaborates on what it can also mean to be brokenhearted: "The sacrifices of God are a broken spirit; a broken and contrite heart, O God, You will not despise" (Ps 51:17). A broken heart may also be one that is contrite, sorry for sins (and in the Introit, "crushed in spirit" can also be translated "contrite in spirit"). Every one of us by nature has a heart that *must* be broken before we can receive God's salvation, must be broken of its pride and foolish self-reliance. The sinful heart in each of us believes it is sufficient without God, and, like a wild stallion roped off the range, it must be broken of its resistance. Once a heart is broken in this way, the Lord is surely eager to be near with the forgiveness that comes from Jesus' cross.

Certainly riches are one thing that we may sinfully rely on. How hard it is to break that!

Therefore, we pray in the **Collect**:

O God, Your divine wisdom sets in order all things in heaven and on earth. Put away from us all things hurtful and give us those things that are beneficial for us; through Jesus Christ, Your Son, our Lord, who lives and reigns with You and the Holy Spirit, one God, now and forever. Amen.

God in His divine wisdom always knows what's best for us—including the right provision of material possessions. How much is beneficial? How much can we handle before our hearts pervert God's good gift to our own hurt? By this prayer, we're expressing our trust that whatever God gives is just right, even if it's Ventnor Avenue rather than Park Place (or Baltic rather than Ventnor) and an old Pontiac rather than a new Nissan.

Park Place won't satisfy anyway. The **Old Testament Reading**, Ecclesiastes 5:10–20.

Everyone says money can't buy happiness, but most people wish they had the money to find out for sure. Solomon did. Perhaps the richest man who ever lived (2 Chr 1:12), Solomon, now late in life, looks back and sees that money is just another of so many vanities: "He who loves money will not be satisfied with money, nor he who loves wealth with his income" (Eccl 5:10). Picture Solomon sitting on his throne, ivory overlaid with gold, countless elegantly-attired attendants before him, consuming ten fat oxen, twenty pasture-fed cattle, a hundred sheep, besides deer, gazelles, roebucks, and fattened fowl every day (1 Ki 10:4–5, 18; 4:22–23). "When goods increase, they increase who eat them, and what advantage has their owner?" (Eccl 5:11).

Wealth, Solomon knows, is of no eternal value: "As he came from his mother's womb he shall go again, naked as he came, and shall take nothing for his toil that he may carry away in his hand" (5:15). But Solomon has also discovered that money can create stress in this life: "Sweet is the sleep of a laborer, whether he eats little or much, but the full stomach of the rich will not let him sleep. . . . Moreover, all his days he eats in darkness in much vexation and sickness and anger" (5:12, 17).

A sidebar story in the musical *My Fair Lady* features Eliza Doolittle's father—and actually resonates the theme of the entire show. Alfred P. Doolittle has spent his whole life avoiding becoming respectable, always bumming just enough coins for today's drinks and girls. But in an entirely unforeseen twist, he finds himself the recipient of a large fortune—and miserable. His former lifestyle is forever lost to respectability and responsibility. When Eliza asks him why he doesn't just give the money back, he tells her that's the tragedy of it all: he doesn't have the courage to give it up. How hard for one who has money not to set his heart on it! You can't give it up; the heart has to be broken.

The **Epistle** doesn't mention money. But riches can indeed be one of the pitfalls against which it warns. Read Hebrews 4:1–16.

"While the promise of entering His rest still stands, let us fear lest any of you should seem to have failed to reach it. . . . 'Today, if you hear His voice, do not harden your hearts.' . . . So that no one may fall by the same sort of disobedience" (4:1, 7, 11). It is so hard for the rich to enter the kingdom of God because money can so easily become the temptation that hardens one's heart. And when the heart is hard, there's no hope—unless someone breaks it.

"How difficult it will be for those who have wealth to enter the kingdom of God!" Read the **Holy Gospel**, Mark 10:23–31.

This reading, you may notice, continues last week's story of the rich young man. After he goes away sad, Jesus debriefs with His disciples. They're amazed (10:24a) that the rich aren't fast-tracked into the kingdom; Jewish piety of the day assumes that riches are a stamp of God's special approval.

Quite the opposite; money can be a stumbling block. That should be a serious warning to us, because . . . we're rich. Anyone who can go into a restaurant and order all you can eat and then do it again tomorrow is rich. Any husband and wife who have two separate closets, maybe even two separate bathrooms to get ready for the day, and whose biggest complaint is that the hot water ran out during one of their showers, are rich.

But see what Jesus says next: "Children, how difficult it is to enter the kingdom of God!" (10:24b). Period. Not just for the rich. Difficult for anybody! (Some later manuscripts insert "difficult for those who trust in riches," and that's who Jesus has been talking about *mostly*, but the more likely reading is that He didn't specify this time.) See, money isn't the real problem. We're the problem. "Then who can be saved?" (10:26). You? Me?

"With man," Jesus said, "it is impossible, but not with God. For all things are possible with God" (10:27). It's impossible *for anyone* to be saved by man. For anyone to be saved, it takes a miracle! In fact, it took miracle*s*. It took the miracle of God becoming man, the miracle of God dying, the miracle of Christ rising from the dead.

And then it still took one more miracle. Those hearts of ours still had to be broken—broken of idolizing money or my job, my fantasy league, even that romance that broke my heart the other way. Me. Breaking our hearts took a miracle too. Luther reminds us of this as he explains the Third Article of the Creed: "I believe that I cannot by my own reason or strength believe in Jesus Christ, my Lord, or come to Him." Even when Jesus has redeemed me by His death on the cross, I couldn't believe it, because my heart couldn't give up those things that I was making hurtful to me. Giving them up would hurt, and my sinful nature couldn't tolerate that.

But God has worked the miracle. "The Holy Spirit has called me by the Gospel, enlightened me with His gifts" (SC, Creed, Third Article). The Holy Spirit has broken our hearts, using "the word of God [that] is living and active, sharper than any two-edged sword, . . . discerning the thoughts and intentions of the heart" (Heb 4:12). And once the heart is broken of clinging to things that are hurtful, the Holy Spirit turns on in our hearts the light of faith—the faith to believe that Jesus is infinitely more precious as Savior than anything we lost. "With man it is impossible, but not with God. For all things are possible with God."

God Does the Impossible by Breaking Our Hearts of What Hurts.

In its place, He gives us greater wealth: "Truly," Jesus says to you, "there is no one who has left house or brothers or sisters or mother or father or children or lands, for My sake and for the gospel, who will not receive a hundredfold now in this time, houses and brothers and sisters and mothers and children and lands, with persecutions, and in the age to come eternal life" (Mk 10:29–30). Eternal life. But *even "now in this time,"* with persecution, also a hundredfold houses, family, land. Not, of course, that God's people will all become rich in earthly property. But knowing that our Ventnor or Baltic or our old beat-up Pontiac is a gift of God's love makes it a hundred times more precious to the new man or woman inside us than the Park Place we grab for ourselves—just ask Solomon!

"I have stored up Your word in my heart. . . . In the way of Your testimonies I delight as much as in all riches" (Ps 119:11, 14). Enjoy the full appointed **Psalm**, 119:9–16.

Then sing the **Hymn of the Day**, "Hope of the World" (*LSB* 690).

A note for Reformation and All Saints' Day: Many congregations will observe these festivals on the consecutive Sundays closest to October 31 and November 1. Since they use the same propers for Years A, B, and C, you'll find the devotion-studies for these days in Year A, pages 250 and 254. The devotion-studies for Propers 25 and 26, Year B, appear on the following pages.

The Sundays after Pentecost: Proper 25 (October 23–29) Year B

READINGS

Jeremiah 31:7–9
Psalm 126 (antiphon: v 5)
Hebrews 7:23–28
Mark 10:46–52

HYMN OF THE DAY

LSB 713 "From God Can Nothing Move Me"

We all love this about Bartimaeus: "A blind beggar, the son of Timaeus, was sitting by the roadside. And when he heard that it was Jesus of Nazareth [coming with a great crowd of people], he began to cry out and say, 'Jesus, Son of David, have mercy on me!' And many rebuked him, telling him to be silent. But he cried out all the more, 'Son of David, have mercy on me!'" (Mk 10:46–48). Eager. Persistent. He won't take no for an answer.

But is that any more endearing than this self-portrait of David? "O Lord, my heart is not lifted up; my eyes are not raised too high; I do not occupy myself with things too great and too marvelous for me. But I have calmed and quieted my soul, like a weaned child with its mother" (Ps 131:1–2). He's anything but boisterous, insistent. The warrior-king is calm and quiet like a child in arms.

We appreciate both: assertive confidence crying out to the Savior and quiet faith resting in the Lord.

The healing of the blind man Bartimaeus, the Gospel lesson for Proper 25, sets the direction for this Sunday, so we'll see recurrent mention of blindness, eyes, and sight. But perhaps even more significant is this role of faith and how it expresses itself.

The **Introit** expresses faith both exuberantly and quietly. It brings together two closely connected psalms to demonstrate this contrast: Psalm 130 for the antiphon and Psalm 131 for the body.

> *Out of the depths I cry to You, O Lord! O Lord, hear my voice! Let Your ears be attentive to the voice of my pleas for mercy!*

O Lord, my heart is not lifted up; my eyes are not raised too high; I do not occupy myself with things too great and too marvelous for me. But I have calmed and quieted my soul, like a weaned child with its mother; like a weaned child is my soul within me. O Israel, hope in the Lord from this time forth and forevermore.

Glory be to the Father and to the Son and to the Holy Spirit; as it was in the beginning, is now, and will be forever. Amen.

Out of the depths I cry to You, O Lord! O Lord, hear my voice! Let Your ears be attentive to the voice of my pleas for mercy! (Ps 131; antiphon: Ps 130:1–2)

Psalm 130 is the great confessional psalm of one who is desperate for deliverance from his sin. Exclamation points didn't exist in ancient Hebrew, but the modern translators have made the right call by inserting them! This is an emphatic cry for mercy! In no way is that presumptuous before God; He loves when we plead, even demand of Him what He's promised to give! And He has always promised to be attentive to our pleas for mercy for Jesus' sake—that is, for the sake of Jesus' death on the cross that reconciled us to our Father. The psalmist is exuding faith that God will do as He's said.

On the other hand, in Psalm 131, David is calm, passive. "O Lord, my heart is not lifted up"—and neither is his voice. "My eyes are not raised too high; I do not occupy myself with things too great and too marvelous for me." Lord, I leave it all in Your hands, to Your wisdom. It's beyond me. David's eyes work just fine, but he knows they can't see the future or all the ramifications of his own best planning. He is entirely at peace with whatever God might do. He doesn't even tell God just what it is he might want. That's faith too.

The **Collect** is always a prayer we ask in faith for Jesus' sake—whether it's spoken aloud by the pastor with hundreds of worshipers or prayed silently in the heart by one soul. For this Sunday, read the following:

O God, the helper of all who call on You, have mercy on us and give us eyes of faith to see Your Son that we may follow Him on the way that leads to eternal life; through the same Jesus Christ, Your Son, our Lord, who lives and reigns with You and the Holy Spirit, one God, now and forever. Amen.

We're taking God at His word; we call on Him ("have mercy on us") because He's told us He helps all who petition Him in Jesus' name (e.g., Ps 50:15; Jn 16:23). It's an act of faith. And faith can be seen as eyes ("eyes of faith") because it means "seeing" in our hearts what can't be seen with our literal eyes. So often we observe tragedies, catastrophes, injustices that would make us doubt God really is merciful and Jesus really is our Savior. So often we don't see with our eyes results of our cries to God. A loved one still dies. We still don't have a job after months of looking. We still haven't found God's life partner for us after years of waiting. We pray in this Collect that the eyes of faith still see that all our pleas are answered in God's Son. For when Christ has reconciled us to God by His death and resurrection, God is surely always giving us the best—whether our physical eyes see that or not.

"Give us eyes of faith to see Your Son that we may follow Him on the way that leads to eternal life." That's the happy ending of Bartimaeus's story as well; he follows Jesus on the way. By eyes of faith as well as physical eyes that work.

In this week's **Old Testament Reading**, the Lord invites Israel to beseech Him with great exuberance—à la Bartimaeus. But it takes eyes of faith to see His answer to their pleas for mercy. Read Jeremiah 31:7–9.

"Sing aloud with gladness for Jacob, and raise shouts; . . . proclaim, give praise, and say, 'O LORD, save Your people, the remnant of Israel'" (31:7). Jeremiah wrote during the period of the Babylonian captivity; much of the tribe of Judah, the former Southern Kingdom, was suffering far from home. And Jeremiah delivers God's promise of restoration to them; after seventy years, Judah will return from exile (29:10–14). (The **Psalm** for this week, Psalm 126, echoes this.) Judah has reason to petition the Lord with loud singing, gladness, shouts, and praise.

But, in fact, this particular prophecy describes the restoration not of Judah but of the Northern Kingdom, Israel. (Ephraim, 31:9, was the chief tribe of the North and was often named as shorthand for it.) The Northern Kingdom had been carried off by the Assyrians more than a century earlier. Jeremiah says the Lord will "gather them from the farthest parts of the earth, . . . a great company, they shall return here" (31:8). However, that would never actually happen! The Northern Kingdom never returned.

Did God fail to keep His promise? Eyes seeing only geopolitical history would conclude so. Eyes of faith see that in every nation, in every century, there is a "remnant," "among them the blind and the lame, the pregnant woman and she who is in labor, together" (31:8b), a very great company, who will come to know Israel's Savior. And even "with weeping" in this sinful world, "they shall not stumble" (31:9). (See again also Psalm 126:5–6.) By faith, we see that we are among that remnant, not restored to a tract of land in the Middle East but restored to a now and forever relationship with God.

The **Epistle** reiterates why we can have such confidence. Read Hebrews 7:23–28.

The role of God's priests in the Old Testament was to serve as intermediaries between the Lord and His people, to offer sacrifices and pray on behalf of sinful man. Because of sin, the Israelites could not approach God directly.

Hebrews makes the point, though, that Christ is now and forevermore our High Priest, replacing those of ancient Israel (7:23–24). And He is what the mediation of the priesthood was always all about. He is "holy, innocent, unstained, separated from sinners, and exalted above the heavens" (7:26). Yet He is the one by whom sinners are able to approach God because He made the "once for all" sacrifice "when He offered up Himself" (7:27). Jesus' cross atoned for the sins that separated us from God. Therefore, in His name, we are always able to cry out to God for help. We are able to "draw near to God through Him, since He always lives to make intercession" for us (7:25). Our faith for God's answers to our pleas is forever in Jesus and His reconciling death.

Jesus was on His final approach to the cross when Bartimaeus cried out to Him. Read the **Holy Gospel**, Mark 10:46–52.

This, Bartimaeus knew, was no time to stand on ceremony or worry about decorum. This was the moment to shout—no matter what anyone said! From everything he'd heard, Bartimaeus believes this Jesus of Nazareth is the Son of David, the Messiah, which meant He can open blind eyes. And he believes Jesus will be willing. Faith had to shout and shout again: "Have mercy on me!"

"Go your way," Jesus said to him. "Your faith has made you well" (10:52a). Which means precisely what? That Bartimaeus's persistent, boisterous faith won the day? Oh, let us learn to be as bold in faith before God with our needs as he was!

That's not how the eyes of faith see it.

Faith claims for itself no credit, no personal victory in "your faith has made you well." Bartimaeus's faith made him well, sure enough, but only in the sense that faith is believing he was helpless and Jesus would have mercy. Bartimaeus's faith, so insistent and shouted out, was actually eyes not raised too high, not occupying himself with things too great and marvelous, calm and quiet like a child with its mother, just like David's. His faith was trusting that Jesus truly desired to have mercy, when Bartimaeus could do nothing. Sense how quiet and submissive he suddenly becomes when Jesus calls him: "Rabbi, let me recover my sight" (10:51). Behind the impassioned cry is a quiet faith.

Bartimaeus believes Jesus will do whatever is best for him. That is what Jesus' mercy is—whatever is best for us. For Bartimaeus, it is indeed recovery of his sight, and Jesus invites us likewise to cry out to Him for whatever we think would be best. Perhaps it's healing for someone in our family too. Perhaps it is a job or a godly husband or wife. God hears our cries. But He will give us what's best. As faith believes He will.

Jesus Does Have Mercy on Those with Eyes of Quiet Faith to Cry Out to Him.

"And immediately [Bartimaeus] recovered his sight and followed [Jesus] on the way" (10:52b).

"Alleluia. [Let us fix our eyes on] Jesus, the founder and perfecter of our faith. Alleluia" (the **Verse**, Heb 12:2a).

"From God can nothing move me. . . . In His good time He changes all sorrow into joy" (**Hymn of the Day**, *LSB* 713:1, 3).

A note for Reformation and All Saints' Day: Many congregations will observe these festivals on the consecutive Sundays closest to October 31 and November 1. Since they use the same propers for Years A, B, and C, you'll find the devotion-studies for these days in Year A, pages 250 and 254. The devotion-study for Proper 26, Year B, appears on the next page.

The Sundays after Pentecost: Proper 26 (October 30–November 5) Year B

READINGS

Deuteronomy 6:1–9
Psalm 119:1–8 (antiphon: v 5)
Hebrews 9:11–14 (15–22)
Mark 12:28–37

HYMN OF THE DAY

LSB 852 "O God of Mercy, God of Might"

What part of your life does the Lord occupy? What place does God hold in your life?

He holds first place, of course. And that's not just the "wished for" answer or the "supposed to" answer. When the Holy Spirit created faith in your heart in Christ Jesus as Savior, He also created a new man or woman who really does give God first place. That's true of every Christian, even though our faith is weak.

But until heaven, there also remains in every Christian the old sinful nature, and that old man or woman is constantly battling for territory. So the fact that God holds first place in our lives doesn't quite answer the other question: What *part* of your life does the Lord occupy?

Here it's always a struggle. We are tempted to compartmentalize God. He certainly runs Sunday morning for us—though not without plenty of sinful distractions even there. He undoubtedly occupies my what's-going-to-happen-to-me-when-I-die department. That means I might wisely also give Him a portion of my life for prayers before bed and perhaps evening devotions. Hopefully we also give Him the I-sure-want-my-kids-to-go-to-heaven-too part of life, so we pray before meals and bring them to church and Sunday School. Surely there's a big God part of our lives.

But is there also a which-movie-shall-we-watch-tonight part of life where we forget about Him entirely? Do we go about preparing a report for the boss or studying for an algebra exam or doing our taxes without giving our Lord much thought? Do we allow God to occupy the conversation-with-friends-when-talking-about-others part of our lives? Are there aspects of life where we perhaps don't want God to intrude?

The propers for this Sunday allow no such compromise; God demands our all. *And* He delivers *all.*

The psalmists in our **Introit** understand this all-in mentality:

> *I will give thanks to the Lord with my whole heart; I will recount all of Your wonderful deeds.*
>
> *I will sing of the steadfast love of the Lord, forever; with my mouth I will make known Your faithfulness to all generations. For I said, "Steadfast love will be built up forever; in the heavens You will establish Your faithfulness." You have said, "I have made a covenant with My chosen one; I have sworn to David My servant: 'I will establish your offspring forever, and build your throne for all generations.'"*
>
> *Glory be to the Father and to the Son and to the Holy Spirit; as it was in the beginning, is now, and will be forever. Amen.*
>
> *I will give thanks to the Lord with my whole heart; I will recount all of Your wonderful deeds. (Ps 89:1–4; antiphon: Ps 9:1)*

Notice how many all-inclusives we hear: "my whole heart," "all of Your wonderful deeds," "forever," "all generations"—most of those twice. David, in Psalm 9, is wholly committed to thanking the Lord, for he knows God's gracious acts on his behalf go on and on and on. And Ethan the Ezrahite (a very wise man indeed, 1 Ki 4:31) writes in Psalm 89 that singing of God's steadfast love can't be a now-and-then thing but is to be forever, for every future generation.

It's always that way; the psalmists' total commitments are results of the Lord going all in for David and all people first: "I have made a covenant with My chosen one; I have sworn to David My servant: 'I will establish your offspring forever, and build your throne for all generations.'" Since 2 Samuel 7:11b–13, 16, Israel had known that the line of the Messiah went through David; the Son of David would be the Christ. David was the geodetic benchmark that the Lord had committed Himself to redeem the whole world. In God's covenant with David, His people could always know His steadfast love and wonderful deeds.

Of course, long before David, God had already committed to send the Messiah. So He likewise already demanded to occupy every part of His people's lives. Read the **Old Testament Reading**, Deuteronomy 6:1–9.

This reading is another portion of Moses' final teachings to the new generation of Israelites, shortly before his death and their entrance into the Promised Land. It follows almost immediately after his reiteration of the Ten Commandments (5:6–21). Interestingly, Moses is able to summarize "the statutes and the rules" of the Lord with a singular: "Now this is the commandment" (6:1). The Ten Commandments and the many particulars

God gives will be summed up in what follows. It is that big of a deal.

"Hear, O Israel: The Lord our God, the Lord is one. You shall love the Lord your God with all your heart and with all your soul and with all your might" (6:4–5). In the Gospel reading, Jesus quotes this as the most important commandment. For Old Testament Israel (and in Judaism today), it's known as the *Shema*, from the Hebrew for "hear," and it has always been the core confession of the Old Testament.

The verses are cited (including by Jesus) as a *commandment*. But notice that the command that we are to obey, "Love the Lord your God . . ." (the essence of the first three of the Ten Commandments) cannot be separated from the preceding *confession of faith*: "The Lord our God, the Lord is one." That first portion of the "commandment" declares who God is; it doesn't command us to do anything. And that's really not surprising. Our obedience to God always begins with God. (More on what that confession, "the Lord is one," means when Jesus speaks in the Gospel reading.)

God makes it very clear how central the *Shema* is to be to the lives of His people. It is to be their whole life! "You shall love the Lord your God with *all* your heart and with *all* your soul and with *all* your might." There is nothing we are to believe that is not expressing love for the Lord. There is nothing we are to do that is not moved by love for the Lord. No word spoken, no emotion felt, no impulse that isn't loving God.

"You shall teach [these words] diligently to your children, *and* shall talk of them when you sit in your house, *and* when you walk by the way, *and* when you lie down, *and* when you rise. You shall bind them as a sign on your hand, *and* they shall be as frontlets between your eyes. You shall write them on the doorposts of your house *and* on your gates" (6:7–9). Is the Lord every word you speak to your children—not just during family devotions but also when you're just being yourself around the house? *And* does the Lord occupy the part of your life that goes to the grocery store? *And* the part that goes to a ball game? *And* to lunch with your coworkers? *And* on a date? That's the command.

And, yes, it is still for us in the New Testament. Jesus even inserts another "all." Read the **Holy Gospel**, Mark 12:28–37.

"With all your heart and with all your soul *and with all your mind* and with all your strength" (12:30). *And* Jesus adds the *all* important: "You shall love your neighbor as yourself" (12:31; cf Lev 19:18).

It's pretty clear, isn't it!

**The Lord Our God Is for . . .
All . . . All . . . All . . . All . . .
and . . . and . . . and . . . and.**

The Lord is to occupy every part of our lives.

Remember, though, the *Shema* isn't just what *we* are to do (*all* the time *and* in every phase of our lives). It's also about who the Lord Himself is. And Jesus retains that word of God for us too. "The Lord our God, the Lord is one" (12:29).

That part of the *Shema* has often been misunderstood. It doesn't mean that the one Lord isn't also triune, three persons. Quite the opposite is born out, rather, in the latter verses of the Gospel reading. It seems to be an entirely new subject when Jesus asks, "How can the scribes say that the Christ is the son of David?" (12:35). The assumption is that the son comes after the father, and, therefore, the father must be the master (the lord) and the son must be the subject, the lesser. But in Psalm 110, David writes that Yahweh ("the LORD") spoke, and the one to whom He spoke David called "my Lord" (that is, David's master). The Jews all agreed that this one to whom Yahweh speaks is the Christ. And, of course, they were correct that the Christ would be the son of David. So how could the Christ be both David's son and David's master?

The answer is that the Lord our God, the one Lord, is Father, Son, and Holy Spirit and that the Son became a human being, a descendant of David. So He is David's son but also David's eternal Lord, God Himself.

This—who the one Lord really is—is crucial to understanding the greatest "commandment." Why? Apart from this understanding, we could never love the Lord our God with *any part* of our lives. The scribe who came to Jesus was beginning to get this. Knowing who God is and loving Him and neighbor is more than all sacrifices (Mk 12:32–33), because apart from faith that this God becomes man to save us, sacrifices could only be efforts to save ourselves, not loving Him at all. But with this understanding, he was "not far from the kingdom of God" (12:34).

In fact, entrance into the kingdom was standing right in front of him. So teaches the **Epistle**, Hebrews 9:11–22.

Jesus is the one who is more than all burnt offerings and sacrifices. He is truly the Lord's all. As our High Priest, "He entered once *for all* into the holy places, not by means of the blood of goats and calves but by means of His own blood, thus securing an eternal redemption" (9:12). *And* "the blood of Christ . . . [does] purify our conscience from dead works to serve the living God" (9:14).

Read the **Collect**.

> *Lord Jesus Christ, our great High Priest, cleanse us by the power of Your redeeming blood that in purity and peace we may worship and adore Your holy name; for You live and reign with the Father and the Holy Spirit, one God, now and forever. Amen.*

"*Blessed* are those who keep His testimonies, who seek Him with their whole heart" (v 2 of the **Psalm**, 119:1–8).

Sing the **Hymn of the Day**, "O God of Mercy, God of Might" (*LSB* 852), appreciating that "for all" He died. For that matter, appreciate all the "alls" in stanzas 4 and 6.

Finally, a new **Gradual** begins our countdown to the end of the church year:

> *These are the ones coming out of the great tribulation. They have washed their robes and made them white in the blood of the Lamb. Blessèd are those whose strength is in You, in whose heart are the highways to Zion. (Rev 7:14b; Ps 84:5)*

The Sundays after Pentecost: Proper 27 (November 6–12) Year B

READINGS

1 Kings 17:8–16
Psalm 146 (antiphon: v 9a)
Hebrews 9:24–28
Mark 12:38–44

HYMN OF THE DAY

LSB 738 "Lord of All Hopefulness"

You probably know this familiar story:

> [Jesus] sat down opposite the treasury and watched the people putting money into the offering box. Many rich people put in large sums. And a poor widow came and put in two small copper coins, which make a penny. And He called His disciples to Him and said to them, "Truly, I say to you, this poor widow has put in more than all those who are contributing to the offering box. For they all contributed out of their abundance, but she out of her poverty has put in everything she had, all she had to live on." (Mk 12:41–44)

You know the story of the widow and her mites, but you don't know her whole story.

We do know enough about this woman to admire her deeply. We also know enough to see how relevant her story is to what many of our congregations are doing this time of year: encouraging pledges, a portion of our income, to support the work of the Church in the twelve months ahead. Maybe you've gotten your pledge in or have received the annual mailing that Pledge Sunday is coming up. You might even hear or preach a sermon this Sunday on this very text for that very purpose, as I did in my parishes. God bless your hearing or preaching, your prayerful deliberations, and your congregation in moving forward in the work of Christ's kingdom! The widow's story really is an inspiration to us in our use of God's financial blessings.

Our propers this week, though, will help us steer clear of two potential misuses of this splendid Gospel text. First, it's tempting to use this widow simply as an example for us to follow in our financial giving—an impressive(!) example of proportional giving. Give like the widow did until it hurts. Second, we might see the story simply as moving us to emulate her faith. That—because it's about faith—sounds a lot more pious and a lot less crass than just "Give!" But it's a misunderstanding of the text too.

We're helped to avoid both of those errors by not knowing the widow's whole story.

The **Introit** also helps send us in a better direction:

> *Let them thank the* Lord *for His steadfast love, for His wondrous works to the children of men!*
>
> *Oh give thanks to the* Lord, *for He is good, for His steadfast love endures forever! Let the redeemed of the* Lord *say so, whom He has redeemed from trouble. He raises up the needy out of affliction and makes their families like flocks. The upright see it and are glad, and all wickedness shuts its mouth.*
>
> *Glory be to the Father and to the Son and to the Holy Spirit; as it was in the beginning, is now, and will be forever. Amen.*
>
> *Let them thank the* Lord *for His steadfast love, for His wondrous works to the children of men! (Ps 107:1–2, 41–42; antiphon: Ps 107:8)*

Already this psalmody shifts our attention away from the widow or any widow or anybody else to the one on whom it belongs, the Lord. "Thank the Lord for *His* steadfast love, for *His* wondrous works." "His steadfast love endures forever!" We do indeed see the widow here: "He raises up the needy out of affliction and makes their families like flocks." In Bible times, a widow was among the most pitiable of the needy; piled on the sadness of losing her husband, she had very limited opportunity to make a living. It was all the worse if she had a family to feed. So the psalmist sees the widow sympathetically—but as the recipient of the Lord's gracious providing.

What a magnificent promise in those beloved words: "Oh give thanks to the Lord, for He is good, for His steadfast love endures forever!" Forever, whatever the circumstances and adversities, God's love for us never wavers.

As to the widow herself (or anyone else in need), it's not easy to "give thanks to the Lord," to believe "He is good," when you're starving—or alone. It must be terribly difficult to think about the offering plate! This is where faith comes in. And this, obviously, is where we sit in awe of the faith of the widow with her mites. We hope that God will grant us each such faith!

As a matter of fact, in the **Collect**, we pray that our faith would stand whatever tests might come:

> *Almighty and ever-living God, You have given exceedingly great and precious promises to those who trust in You. Grant us so firmly to believe in Your Son Jesus that our*

faith may never be found wanting; through the same Jesus Christ, our Lord, who lives and reigns with You and the Holy Spirit, one God, now and forever. Amen.

We pray that our faith in the almighty and ever-living God and His Son, Jesus Christ, "may never be found wanting"—particularly when we pass through days of trouble and uncertainty. We truly desire a faith like the widow in the temple.

But our faith is often wanting—at least lacking the strength to trust implicitly when we're pressed. We probably wouldn't give our last mite if it came down to that! Even as we pray for stronger faith, let's confess to God that ours isn't what it should be.

What is never found wanting is God's supply for all our needs. He gives us "exceedingly great and precious promises" for the sake of His Son—promises of His care every day in this life and of perfect joy with Him in eternity. Again the emphasis isn't on us and our faith but on our God.

Now to our lections. The **Old Testament Reading** complements the Gospel with a visit to a different widow in similar desperation. Read 1 Kings 17:8–16.

Elijah has prophesied a drought against wicked King Ahab that will last over three years. First, he hid by a brook, and God sent ravens to feed him. But now the brook has dried up.

Zarephath, near Sidon, is to the north of Israel, Canaanite country, very pagan. Their Baal was supposed to specialize in fertility—rain to make crops grow—and he was failing miserably. For a widow (and a Gentile widow at that!) to be Elijah's provider reminds him that these are lean times! Our mental picture of this woman is pathetic—"gathering a couple of sticks" (17:12; not a pile of logs, mind you). Asking her for a drink was asking quite a lot already. But asking her to feed him too? We discover that she has a son, and they're down to their last meal.

She's never seen the man before in her life. And Yahweh is "your God" (17:12), not hers. But He has a promise for her anyway: "The LORD, the God of Israel" (17:14), says she'll have food until all this mess is over. Somehow she believes and bakes up her last mite, uh, morsel. (Had God's command, 17:9, come to her earlier in some way? Perhaps by an angel? Or was this word of Elijah the command God meant? We don't know.) Then, as always, God is faithful to His promise.

See how we might misuse this widow's story, just as we might with the widow in the temple. Follow her example of giving; give to the Lord first, and He'll provide for you. You give, you get back. Firstfruits giving *is* good biblical stewardship. We are to give to the Lord first, not wait till the end of the week or the month and see what's left over. But we don't manipulate God. And our giving doesn't buy God's favor. No.

Neither is the focus here to have faith like she did. Yes, she showed remarkable faith. But she didn't look to her faith, listen to her faith, believe in her faith. She believed God's promise. And we can't trust in her faith. Her faith does nothing for us. By comparison, our faith will probably always be found wanting.

The focus is on God's promises and the certainty that He keeps them. What *He will do* for us is what we can trust.

See how the **Psalm**, which is about God's care for "the widow and the fatherless" and so many others in need, bears that out. Read Psalm 146. The key verse is 146:6, where *the Lord* is the one "who keeps faith forever," who is always faithful to us.

Everything God does for us is because of Christ's sacrifice of Himself on the cross. Our **Epistle** is Hebrews 9:24–28.

A priest entering God's presence, the holy places of the temple, without being purified would surely die—thus Jesus when He bore the filth of our sins to the cross. But now He stands there "in the presence of God on our behalf" (9:24). That is, He constantly stands before God, pleading that God would care for us. That makes it absolutely sure that we will always receive God's very best. And this, too, is absolutely certain: Christ "will appear a second time . . . to save those who are eagerly waiting for Him" (9:28).

So what don't we know about the widow in the **Holy Gospel**? Read Mark 12:38–44.

We don't know what happened to this poor widow *after* she gave all she had to live on. We'd like to think we know; we'd like to think Jesus and the disciples somehow provided for her future care. That's very possibly so. But maybe she starved. The Holy Spirit inspired Mark *not* to tell us.

And that's helpful, because in the first place, if we heard about a happy ending, we'd be tempted to make that first mistake: Give like she did, and surely God will give back to you. Or in the second place, the second mistake: Have faith like hers. We'd still be inclined to think that if we have strong enough faith, God will make things work out in a way we all like.

It's better not to know. You see, everything we do—including giving offerings to the Lord—we do in the face of uncertainty. We don't know how things will come out. We don't know if, after making a pledge to the congregation's mission, we might lose our job. We don't know whether we might have unexpected bills. It's better not to think God guarantees financial security. He doesn't.

It's better to know that what He promises is certain. Because He's been reconciled to us by Jesus entering the holy places in death, He is our loving Father who will never leave us wanting. We won't always believe that; our faith won't usually be like either of the two widows. *Our faith* will often be *found* wanting. But *God's care*—whatever it might be—will never *leave* us wanting.

Even in Greatest Need and Uncertainty, Faith in the Lord Will Never Be Left Wanting.

God always knows what's best for us. And for the sake of Christ's reconciling death, He always somehow gives it to us, even if our weak faith doesn't believe it, even if we starve. For "you know the grace of our Lord Jesus Christ, that though He was rich, yet for your sake He became poor, so that you by His poverty might become rich. Alleluia" (the **Verse**, 2 Cor 8:9).

Close with the **Hymn of the Day**, "Lord of All Hopefulness" (*LSB* 738).

The Sundays after Pentecost: Proper 28 (November 13–19) Year B

READINGS

Daniel 12:1–3
Psalm 16
(antiphon: v 11b, c)
Hebrews 10:11–25
Mark 13:1–13

HYMN OF THE DAY

LSB 508 "The Day Is Surely Drawing Near"

This will be the unmistakable refrain for Proper 28: "The one who endures to the end will be saved" (Mk 13:13b). It's the climactic word of this week's Gospel lesson. It'll be the Verse of the day. We'll even hear it twice as the antiphon to the Introit.

Proper 28 is the second-to-last Sunday of the church year, which means our focus is clearly directed toward the end of all things earthly. Jesus will alert us to sufferings ahead. Things we hold dear won't last. The last days will be a time of trouble such as never before. But the one who endures to the end of all that will be saved.

That then begs the question, Who *is* the one who will endure to the end? And that's the big question God's Word will answer for us this week.

Let's begin our devotion-study with the **Holy Gospel**, Mark 13:1–13.

Along with the big question "Who will endure to the end?" comes a related question: Who and what *won't* endure to the end? Jesus has some answers that surprise—and no doubt frighten—the disciples.

This is Holy Week; Jesus will die on the cross in just a few days. But the disciples don't know that. What they know is that this is Passover, the high point of the year for Jews. And given all the excitement of Palm Sunday and the crowds following Jesus, they sense that this Passover is a special one. To be here in Jerusalem, with Jesus at the height of His popularity, and now *in the temple*—to the disciples, it's just about like being in heaven: "Look, Teacher, what wonderful stones and what wonderful buildings!" (13:1). Ah, to linger here forever!

Herod's temple was a magnificent structure—an engineering marvel just that such stones, some nearly the size of a small house, could be moved into position. But this temple wouldn't endure. In AD 70, the Roman army under Titus would destroy it—by similarly amazing engineering of destruction.

This is a terrifying prospect to the disciples, and they ask Jesus when it will take place and what sign will presage it. Matthew's Gospel adds their words: "And what will be the sign of Your coming and of the end of the age?" (Mt 24:3). The disciples grasp that the destruction of Jerusalem would prefigure Jesus' return at the end of the world.

This world itself will not endure, and the signs Jesus gives of the end are also of things doomed to pass away. "Jesus answered them, 'See that no one leads you astray'" (Mk 13:4–5). Many false teachers will arise—not only in those years before AD 70 but ever since. Muhammad, Joseph Smith, and Charles Taze Russell (the founder of Jehovah's Witnesses) have led many astray. But their teachings will not endure. When Christ returns, their false doctrines and all those who have followed them will be exposed as lies and liars or victims, and all will be swept away.

Wars and rumors of wars, nation rising against nation and kingdom against kingdom, earthquakes, famines (13:7–8) are all signs that this world is passing away. It's very important to note that Jesus gave us signs that occur in *every* era. Already during the disciples' lifetimes, all these signs were accomplished, and they continue on our planet today. In just the last few decades, some have cited wars in the Middle East (as well as earthquakes and the rest) as indications that Christ will be returning in the next few years. Maybe so! But always maybe so.

World War I was called the war to end all wars. Then came World War II. Seemingly, wars will never end. But they will end. Nations and kingdoms like the Roman Empire, the British Empire, and the United States of America rise up and rise against other nations. But they don't endure. In fact, they're reminders that Christ will someday bring an end to this world.

Likewise, from the time of the apostles and continuing today, enemies of Christ "will deliver [His people] over to councils, and you will be beaten in synagogues, and you will stand before governors and kings for My sake, to bear witness before them" (13:9). The power of government in our own day can seem overwhelming. We're frustrated with evil policies on abortion, policies that go against biblical marriage, and policies that intend to limit religious liberty. Persecution of Christians all over the world is very real and is increasing in our own countries. We each have just one vote and hardly a voice, so we can feel helpless. "Our country has lost its mind!" we might say, and we think that's just the way it's always going to be. It's not always going to be that way. The governments of this world won't endure—and persecutions won't either. Until Christ returns, they will. But that will be the end, and they won't endure that. They won't endure Christ's coming.

That's comforting. But it's also very distressing that some of our closest relationships also won't endure: "Brother will deliver brother over to death, and the father his child, and children will rise against parents and have them put to death. And you will be hated by all for My name's sake" (13:12–13a). This, too, has been happening in every generation and will continue until Christ returns. Surely we want to think of the love of our families enduring forever. But those who confess Christ will always be hated by many who find Him to be an affront to their sin. That even crumbles families.

Talk of the end and the collapse of institutions and relationships we cherish is always going to be unsettling, perhaps frightening. Will *we* endure to the end? Will we be among those who are saved?

The assurance comes in looking to what else will endure. You sense the anxiety in Peter, Andrew, James, and John's voices as they ask about the end (13:3–4). But immediately, "Jesus began to say to them" (13:5). Suddenly there is reason for hope. When Jesus speaks, there is comfort, there is certainty. And having Him as our Teacher means all will be well.

That's because Jesus with His saving work endures. Read the **Epistle**, Hebrews 10:11–25.

In recent Epistles, Hebrews has been enlightening us to see Jesus as the end and fulfillment of the Old Testament priesthood. For nearly 1,500 years, the Levitical priests offered one sacrifice after another ("repeatedly") for the people. But these were never enough, for they could not themselves take away sin (10:11). The priesthood and the sacrificial system couldn't endure because they couldn't provide any eternal benefits.

But Christ "offered for all time a single sacrifice for sins" (10:12), His own blood on the cross. And "by [that] single offering He has perfected for all time those who are being sanctified" (10:14). For all time! Christ and His sacrifice endure to the end! The sacrifices of the Old Testament priests are no longer necessary, for "where there is forgiveness . . ., there is no longer any offering for sin" (10:18). Now "we have confidence to enter the holy places by the blood of Jesus" (10:19). We can be certain of entering heaven!

The One Who Endures to the End in the Once-for-All-Time Sacrifice of Christ Will Be Saved.

We will be the ones who endure and are saved!

We are simply "waiting" with Christ "until His enemies should be made a footstool for His feet" (10:13) on the Final Day. And we wait with confidence as we "see the Day drawing near" (10:25), "for He who promised is faithful" (10:23). Christ's promise will endure!

Listen Sunday for elements in the other propers that develop this theme of enduring in Christ's sacrifice. For example, read the **Old Testament Reading**, Daniel 12:1–3.

Daniel is one of the Old Testament books most interested in the end times—especially in its last six chapters. The last days, which Daniel prophesies to begin with the *first* arrival of the Messiah, "shall be a time of trouble," very severe. But the sufferings will not endure, for God's people "shall be delivered" (12:1). Then will come the resurrection, either to enduring life or enduring contempt (12:2). Those who will be saved are those who are "wise," and their glory will be "like the brightness of the sky . . . forever and ever" (12:3). They are wise because the "knowledge" in which they trusted shall endure ("shall increase;" see 12:4).

The **Psalm** prays that God would "preserve me" that I endure (16:1), and surely He will. The earth will quake and be destroyed, but "because He is at my right hand, I shall not be shaken" (16:8). He "will not abandon my soul to Sheol" (16:10, as He did not abandon Christ to the grave, Acts 2:25–31).

The **Introit** includes the words from Mark 13:

The one who endures to the end will be saved.

Let Mount Zion be glad! Let the daughters of Judah rejoice because of Your judgments! Walk about Zion, go around her, number her towers, consider well her ramparts, go through her citadels, that you may tell the next generation that this is God, our God forever and ever. He will guide us forever.

Glory be to the Father and to the Son and to the Holy Spirit; as it was in the beginning, is now, and will be forever. Amen.

The one who endures to the end will be saved. (Ps 48:11–14; antiphon: Mk 13:13b)

We who endure will be glad to see an enduring home. Jerusalem, the old Zion, would be razed. But walk about and admire the heavenly Jerusalem that we'll enter when Christ returns!

The **Collect** looks ahead to the Last Day:

O Lord, by Your bountiful goodness release us from the bonds of our sins, which by reason of our weakness we have brought upon ourselves, that we may stand firm until the day of our Lord Jesus Christ, who lives and reigns with You and the Holy Spirit, one God, now and forever. Amen.

Since Christ's for-all-time sacrifice has delivered us from our sins, we will stand firm until the end, the return of our Lord.

And "the day *is* surely drawing near"—whether God has set it to be today, tomorrow, or another thousand years. "Flames on flames shall ravage earth," but since "my Savior paid the debt I owe, . . . within the Book of Life I know my name has now been written." Sing the **Hymn of the Day**, *LSB* 508.

A note for Thanksgiving Day: In the United States, with Thanksgiving being celebrated on the fourth Thursday of November, the holiday will fall either the week before or after next Sunday, Proper 29, the Last Sunday of the Church Year. In Canada, where Thanksgiving is observed on the second Monday of October, it will occur the day after either Proper 22 or Proper 23. Since a Day of Thanksgiving uses the same propers for Years A, B, and C, you'll find the devotion-study for Thanksgiving in Year A, page 266. The devotion-study for Proper 29, Year B, appears on the next page.

The Sundays after Pentecost: Proper 29 (November 20–26) Year B

READINGS
Isaiah 51:4–6
Psalm 93 (antiphon: v 2)
Jude 20–25
Mark 13:24–37
or
Daniel 7:9–10, 13–14
Psalm 93 (antiphon: v 2)
Revelation 1:4b–8
John 18:33–37

HYMN OF THE DAY
LSB 336 "Lo! He Comes with Clouds Descending"

The Last Sunday of the Church Year, Proper 29, brings us face to face with the culmination of it all—of everything God has been doing in the world since we first needed a Savior. This is the Sunday that our eschatology, the study of the last things, gets down to the eschaton, the Last Day.

It'll be a day like no other, more going on than our mortal senses have ever been able to process. The end of the world, the second coming of Christ, the resurrection of all flesh, and the final judgment will all happen on this one day!

One Sunday of the church year—and even these last several Sundays of the church year—can't begin to describe everything the end times and the Last Day entail. But the Introit and Collect give us a helpful framework for thinking about what's coming.

The **Introit**:

We are looking forward to a new heaven and a new earth, the home of righteousness.

O Lord, make me know my end and what is the measure of my days; let me know how fleeting I am! Behold, You have made my days a few handbreadths, and my lifetime is as nothing before You. And now, O Lord, for what do I wait? My hope is in You. Deliver me from all my transgressions. Do not make me the scorn of the fool! Hear my prayer, O Lord, and give ear to my cry; hold not Your peace at my tears!

Glory be to the Father and to the Son and to the Holy Spirit; as it was in the beginning, is now, and will be forever. Amen.

We are looking forward to a new heaven and a new earth, the home of righteousness. (Ps 39:4–5a, 7–8, 12a; antiphon: 2 Pet 3:13b NIV)

The **Collect**:

Lord Jesus Christ, so govern our hearts and minds by Your Holy Spirit that, ever mindful of Your glorious return, we may persevere in both faith and holiness of living; for You live and reign with the Father and the Holy Spirit, one God, now and forever. Amen.

David asks a very good question for the Last Sunday of the Church Year and the Last Day: "And now, O Lord, for what do I wait?" Christ's return, the end of time—what's that going to mean? There's a very helpful question for us to explore in the propers this week:

As We Look Forward to the Last Day, What Are We Waiting For?

The Collect suggests two ways we might take this Theme. Looking forward to Christ's "glorious return," we pray that "we may persevere in both faith and holiness of living." Faith and holy living. What are we waiting for as we look ahead to the Last Day? What does Judgment Day hold for me? What comes after this world? We pray for answers in God's Word that will enable us to wait in *faith* rather than in fear and anxiety.

On the other hand, our Theme can be spoken rhetorically. As we look forward to the Last Day, what are we waiting for? As in, "Let's get on with it! No time to waste!" This is where our Collect prays that we would persevere in *holy living.* Christ is coming back! The world is going to end! Maybe today! There's no time to lose in living whatever God wants us to do right now! What are we waiting for?

The Introit starts to develop both aspects. As we look forward to the Last Day, what are we waiting for? "We are looking forward to a new heaven and a new earth, the home of righteousness." The present earth and the heavens overhead are all we know, and hearing they're going to be destroyed (2 Pet 3:10–12) may terrify us. But this creation we see is hopelessly corrupted by our sin. Peter knows that our new home, free of sin, nothing there but righteousness, will be infinitely more joyous than we can now imagine.

Then David prays that the Lord would let him know how soon comes his end; his days are "fleeting," "a few handbreadths;" his "lifetime is as nothing." What are we waiting for? Christ may be coming any day! Let us live each day in His holy purpose for us!

Proper 29, Year B, offers two sets of lections, and you may hear either. In recent years, the Last Sunday of the Church Year has come to be widely observed as Christ the King Sunday. The second set of lessons follows that new tradition. Its **Old Testament Reading** is Daniel 7:9–10, 13–14.

What are we waiting to see happen on the Last Day? Daniel saw the Ancient of Days, the heavenly Father, on His throne. Before Him, "the court sat in judgment, and the books were opened" (7:10). What we'll see—and what Jesus' enemies will also see (Mk 14:61–62)—is Christ coming on the clouds and receiving the everlasting kingdom (Dan 7:13–14). That will be terrifying to His foes! But to us who are in Christ, there is no greater comfort than knowing "His dominion is an everlasting dominion, which shall not pass away" (7:14).

We will delight to see Christ as King. Read the **Psalm** of the day, Psalm 93.

"The LORD reigns" (93:1). We've seen Him stripped, bloodied, crucified. But on the Last Day, we will see Him "robed in majesty; . . . Your throne is established from of old" (93:1, 2). That's what we're waiting for in faith.

And in that anticipation, we agree: "Your decrees are very trustworthy; holiness befits Your house, O LORD, forevermore" (93:5). In our short wait, holy living is only fitting.

The **Epistle** for Christ the King Sunday is Revelation 1:4b–8.

Verse 7 is one of the most vivid pictures of what we're awaiting: "Behold, He is coming with the clouds, and every eye will see Him, even those who pierced Him, and all tribes of the earth will wail on account of Him." There's no time to lose! The moment to repent is now! All of us ("*all* tribes") will be suddenly, deeply aware of our sins. Seeing the King in His holiness, we will all see clearly how unholy our lives have been. Each of us pierced Jesus.

But not everyone will be terrified. The Greek κόψονται, *kopsontai* ("wail"), does not indicate horror. For some will say, "Even so. Amen." We with faith that this pierced Jesus has redeemed us will even then be able to echo the waiting prayer of the Church: "Amen. Come, Lord Jesus!" (Rev 22:20).

In my parishes, I was surprised to find that some active, lifelong Christians didn't know we're waiting for the resurrection of our bodies. "Every *eye* will see Him." On the Last Day, everyone will be raised. We won't be disembodied spirits floating around in heaven for eternity. In our flesh, we will see God (Job 19:25–27).

In the **Holy Gospel** for Christ the King Sunday, Jesus demonstrates His eminence over earthly kingdoms. Read John 18:33–37.

We are surely waiting—perhaps quite impatiently—for Christ's heavenly kingdom to supplant the corrupt rule of this world. And what of Pilate? Man, what are you waiting for? Before you stands the eternal truth and your only salvation, and are you going to put Him off with your skepticism or sacrifice Him to get ahead in this doomed world?

The other set of lessons begins with the **Old Testament Reading**, Isaiah 51:4–6.

Not only governments but human civilizations are corrupt, often ignoring the helpless and persecuting the right. As we look forward to the Last Day, we're waiting for the Lord to correct that. And He will: "I will set My justice for a light to the peoples. My righteousness draws near, My salvation has gone out, and My arms will judge the peoples; . . . for My arm they wait" (51:4–5).

Judgment Day, as fearful as that sounds, really is the day we've been waiting for. Christ will bring just and righteous judgment in which the faithful are vindicated and evil is banished. Many of those who are scorned in this life will reign with Him in eternity. We look forward to a new world in which good is honored and there is no sin.

We're able to look forward to that because the Lord's salvation has also gone out! We need that! We have also been unjust. We must repent! Now! What are we waiting for? But the cross of Christ has saved us from our sin, saved us to rejoice in the Last Day. And it has saved us to care for the poor, the helpless, those who are persecuted. Caring for them is caring for our Savior (Mt 25:34–40).

"The heavens vanish like smoke, the earth will wear out like a garment, and they who dwell in it will die in like manner; but My salvation will be forever, and My righteousness will never be dismayed" (Is 51:6).

The **Epistle** for this set is Jude 20–25.

Jude's brief letter is all about "the last time" (see v 18; see also vv 4, 6, 8, 12–15). Jude has two concerns. The first is that we would persevere in faith, "building yourselves up in your most holy faith" (v 20). That happens as we are "waiting for the mercy of our Lord Jesus Christ that leads to eternal life" (v 21). We wait for the Last Day, trusting that Christ "is able to keep you from stumbling and to present you blameless before the presence of His glory with great joy . . . now and forever" (vv 24, 25).

Jude's other concern is that those not yet believing will be rescued from the final judgment. Feel his urgency: "Save others by *snatching* them out of the fire" (v 23). Those who don't know Christ need to hear from us! What are we waiting for?

The final reading of the church year is the **Holy Gospel**, Mark 13:24–37.

If we're waiting with trepidation for the sun darkened, the moon not giving light, stars falling, powers in the heavens shaken (13:24–25), Jesus reiterates why we can wait in eager faith: He will "gather His elect" (13:27)—that resurrection of the body and, for all believers in Christ, the life everlasting. Jesus has prepared us for this! By our Baptism into His death, He has elected us. Wherever we're buried, whatever our condition at death, Christ will raise us to live with Him in perfect vitality and joy.

And as if the fig tree has put out its leaves, so "these things"—those wars, rumors of wars, and such that we heard about last week—*are* all taking place (13:28–30). Like the doorkeeper, we must keep awake, for the master may come at any time (13:32–37). Yet the **Gradual** for these final Sundays sums up where this is all going. By the blood of Christ, we look forward to the end!

These are the ones coming out of the great tribulation. They have washed their robes and made them white in the blood of the Lamb. Blessèd are those whose strength is in You, in whose heart are the highways to Zion. (Rev 7:14b; Ps 84:5)

Conclude with the **Hymn of the Day**, *LSB* 336, a versification of the Epistle from Revelation 1.

Year C

First Sunday in Advent Year C

READINGS

Jeremiah 33:14–16
Psalm 25:1–10 (antiphon: v 6)
1 Thessalonians 3:9–13
Luke 19:28–40
or Luke 21:25–36

HYMN OF THE DAY

LSB 332 "Savior of the Nations, Come"

Advent! "Behold, your king is coming to you!" And everything that means!

It means a new church year, a new series of propers and readings, Year C, with its Gospel lessons drawn primarily from Luke. It means fifty-two more Sundays (plus festivals!) we can look forward to with these devotion-studies—at home on our own, with a Bible study group, with our families, in preparation to preach. If you've been with us for the whole ride, all the way since Advent 1, Year A, you're starting your last lap on the three-year lectionary. But maybe you just hopped on a few months ago, some random week in the middle of Year B. No matter. Year A's coming around again, and three years from now, you'll be right back here. (If you haven't done so already, you might want to read "Read This First: How to Use This Book" on p xi to see how this system works.) God knew—way back on day four when He created the sun and moon—that we'd thrive with the pulse of days and months and seasons and years, including new ones coming, old ones not really gone, a comfortable rhythm coming around again and again. So that's all coming this first Sunday of the "coming" ("advent") season.

Oh, and Christmas is coming.

"Behold, your king is coming to you." We're going to hear those words all four Sundays of the Advent season in the **Gradual**. (Remember that the Gradual expresses the theme for the season.)

Rejoice greatly, O daughter of Zion. Shout aloud, O daughter of Jerusalem. Behold, your king is coming to you; righteous and having salvation. Blessed is He who comes in the name of the Lord. From the house of the Lord we bless you. (Zech 9:9; Ps 118:26, alt)

And lest we should miss it, we'll hear that same verse from Zechariah twice more this week as the antiphon to the **Introit**:

Behold, your king is coming to you; righteous and having salvation.

Who in the skies can be compared to the Lord? Who among the heavenly beings is like the Lord? Righteousness and justice are the foundation of Your throne; steadfast love and faithfulness go before You. Blessed are the people who know the festal shout, who walk, O Lord, in the light of Your face, who exult in Your name all the day and in Your righteousness are exalted. For our shield belongs to the Lord, our king to the Holy One of Israel.

Glory be to the Father and to the Son and to the Holy Spirit; as it was in the beginning, is now, and will be forever. Amen.

Behold, your king is coming to you; righteous and having salvation. (Ps 89:6, 14–16, 18; antiphon: Zech 9:9b, alt)

We get the point. But to say that our King, the Messiah, Christ, *is coming* has multiple dimensions.

"*Is coming*," of course, points to the future. Not here yet. Gotta wait. Coming. But "*is* coming" also means a present reality. Something already is. Now.

It's like back when these looking forward to Sunday mornings were conversations, before they became written devotion-studies. Todd would say, "We're coming to you live on a Monday afternoon." But he'd also quickly add, "Our beloved, on-demand listeners, feel free to use the *Issues, Etc.* comment line . . ." Plenty of folks, we knew, would hear a recording of the show some day later in the week—or even years later. But "we're coming" also means happening right now. "We *are* coming." Live.

Advent has multiple dimensions.

"Behold, your king is coming to you" in Bethlehem. No one has to tell us that Advent means Christmas is coming. But everything does—from the parcels to the paraments to the partridge in a pear tree. And that's good. It creates eagerness, even as we have to wait. Getting ready for the birth of our Savior—in lots of ways—is not only a delight, but it's also a perfectly holy Christian lifestyle. We know we don't want to get all wrapped up in wrapping, but being a grinch doesn't honor baby Jesus either. Humming "Silent Night, Holt Night" beats "Bah! Humbug!" any day, even if it's at an office party. Feel free to enjoy Advent—a "festal shout," a little exulting and being "exalted"—as preparation for Christmas!

But our King is also coming again. You'll notice in a moment that one of the two options for this Sunday's Gospel reading, the one from Luke 21, sounds an awful lot like what you may have heard last Sunday from Mark (13:24–37). That's no accident.

The end of the church year focused on Christ's coming at the end of the world; Advent is also very much aware of Christ's coming at the end of the world. That's why Advent is also observed as a penitential season. We confess that we couldn't survive standing before Christ when He comes again in His glory. We repent of the sins that made His first coming, in poverty, necessary. But we celebrate that because of His first coming, His second coming will save us. That makes Advent different from the end of the church year. Those last Sundays focus on Christ coming to judge. With Advent, "Behold, your king is coming to you; righteous *and having salvation*."

And Advent is about something coming right now too. Present. Coming to us live. A "third coming" of Christ, if you will—in between His birth and His return. Since Bethlehem, before the Parousia, He comes to us on Advent 1 and Advent 2 and Advent 3 and on all the Sundays after and on every day Monday through Saturday as we hear His Word and receive His Holy Sacraments. That's advent, too, even when it isn't Advent.

For Old Testament believers, the emphasis was decidedly on the Messiah's first coming, the one we celebrate as Christmas (though they knew of the other comings as well). Advent is very much an Old Testament season. It's part of that rhythm God created and that the church year maintains. This time of year, we ourselves are always transported back to those centuries before Christ, then to be brought forward into the New Testament of His arrival, His saving work, and His return, only to be reassured next year by the past we've come to treasure. For this reason, the Advent Sundays always especially feature the **Old Testament Reading**. Read Jeremiah 33:14–16.

"The days *are coming* . . . when I *will* . . . I *will* . . . Judah *will* . . . and Jerusalem *will* dwell securely." It's all future tense. And the Old Testament believers' futures were entirely in the coming of a "righteous Branch to spring up for David" (33:15). Since Adam and Eve and God's first promise of a Seed to crush their deceiver (Gen 3:15), since Abraham, since Judah, God's faithful had looked for the Messiah. Since the days of David's mighty kingdom, they knew the Messiah would come from his line (2 Sam 7:11b–13).

What they didn't know was when He would come. So they waited. Read today's **Psalm**, Psalm 25:1–10. "For You I wait all the day long" (25:5). "Indeed, none who wait for You shall be put to shame" (25:3).

But by Jeremiah's time, David's family tree was just a stump (cf Is 11:1). In 587 BC, the Babylonians sacked Jerusalem and carried Judah off to captivity. Yet they had the promise of a branch. A Davidic king was still coming to them. Without having any idea how many, they counted the days till Christmas. We're right there with them. This month, we're Old Testament believers counting down the days to Christmas.

Our unknown, of course, is when the second coming of Christ will be. So we wait—in what should be a state of constant preparedness. Read again Jesus' warning of Judgment Day in the **Holy Gospel** that parallels last Sunday's in Mark: Luke 21:25–36.

No one escapes Christ the King coming to us (21:35). His glory will be overwhelming (21:27). People will faint with fear (21:26). If we let our hearts be weighed down with the sins of this world and the cares of this life, that Last Day will come like a trap (21:34).

But on this first day of Advent, we remember that Christ's second coming will be "righteous and having salvation." "Now when these things begin to take place, straighten up and raise your heads, because your *redemption* is drawing near" (21:28). "Know that the *summer* is already near" (21:30). As it begins to turn cold, that's Gospel.

It's as Paul, too, sees Christ's second coming in the **Epistle**, 1 Thessalonians 3:9–13.

Paul had been fearful for the Church he'd planted in Thessalonica. But now that he has received word they were continuing in the faith, he knows that "the coming of our Lord Jesus with all His saints" (3:13) will be a day of rejoicing. "What thanksgiving can we return to God for you, for all the joy that we feel for your sake before our God?" (3:9).

So the waiting is looking forward. The **Collect**:

> *Stir up Your power, O Lord, and come, that by Your protection we may be rescued from the threatening perils of our sins and saved by Your mighty deliverance; for You live and reign with the Father and the Holy Spirit, one God, now and forever. Amen.*

Yet for all the waiting—for Christ's first coming and the days until our celebration of it, for Christ's second coming in who knows how many days—there's still that "coming to you live" already now coming of Advent.

We sense *that* one in—and it's made possible by—Christ's coming in the other **Holy Gospel**: Luke 19:28–40.

"Blessed is the King who comes in the name of the Lord!" (19:38a). Present tense. Yes, it's Jesus' coming on Palm Sunday and neither at Christmas nor the end of the world. (See our devotion-studies for Advent 1, Years A and B, for more.) But Palm Sunday emphatically signals the "now" of Advent, especially in Luke's Gospel. Only Luke is explicit that "the King" is coming. And see how Luke (only) continues the crowd's accolades: "Peace in heaven and glory in the highest!" (19:38b).

When this season ends, on Christmas Eve, we'll hear those beloved words, "Glory to God in the highest, and on earth peace" (2:14). *Now*, as the season begins, Jesus comes to secure that peace the (only) way true peace is ever secured: by entering Jerusalem and removing the sin that destroyed our peace with God and all people by dying on the cross—the same peace we hear each time we leave the communion rail and each time our Divine Service of Word and Sacrament ends: ". . . and give you peace." When our King comes to the cross, all is finished. Today signals that.

The Waiting Is Over; Your King Is Coming Now!

Treasure the ancient Advent classic, the **Hymn of the Day**, "Savior of the Nations, Come" (*LSB* 332). "Glory to the Son, our king, . . . *now and* through eternity" (st 8).

Second Sunday in Advent Year C

READINGS

Malachi 3:1–7b
Psalm 66:1–12 (antiphon: v 12b)
Philippians 1:2–11
Luke 3:1–14 (15–20)

HYMN OF THE DAY

LSB 344 "On Jordan's Bank the Baptist's Cry"

In the opening scene of the classic (that means it's old but we still like the songs) musical *Godspell*, John the Baptist sings, "Prepare ye the way of the Lord" (Is 40:3 KJV). He sings it again and again. Except for a couple of "Ev'rybody nows," those are all the lyrics. Seven words. Ten notes. The original soundtrack recording includes two minutes, one second of that. In the movie, with a few more repeats, it runs 2:36. While it actually works, it certainly has John sounding like a broken record (though this was the day of 8-tracks and cassettes).

"Prepare the way of the Lord" (in modern translations, down to six words) is very clearly also the refrain for Advent 2, as John preaches at the Jordan. There is, however, much more variation.

We can see that in the propers for this Sunday. "Prepare" here is obviously an imperative, a command that we make ready the Lord's coming. We know how stridently the Baptist calls us to repent of our sins. But there's more to preparing than what we do. There's also the Lord preparing us. John and our propers for the day declare that too.

The **Verse**, which is always intended to encapsulate the theme of the day, introduces that added texture: "Alleluia. Prepare the way of the Lord, make His paths straight; all flesh shall see the salvation of God. Alleluia" (Lk 3:4b, 6; quoting Is 40:3, 5). Preparing includes us getting anything crooked out of the way. But it also involves "the salvation of God"—*God* saving.

The **Introit** has a particularly vivid way of expressing this salvation of God as it prepares us for the Lord's coming:

The voice of one crying in the wilderness: "Prepare the way of the Lord, make His paths straight."

Hear, O My people, while I admonish you! O Israel, if you would but listen to Me! I am the Lord *your God, who brought you up out of the land of Egypt. Open your mouth wide, and I will fill it. But My people did not listen to My voice; Israel would not submit to Me. Oh, that My people would listen to Me, that Israel would walk in My ways!*

Glory be to the Father and to the Son and to the Holy Spirit; as it was in the beginning, is now, and will be forever. Amen.

The voice of one crying in the wilderness: "Prepare the way of the Lord, make His paths straight." (Ps 81:8, 10–11, 13; antiphon: Lk 3:4b)

First, there's the familiar call to repentance: "Hear, O My people, while I admonish you!" But then how tragic that they won't listen!—because see what they're passing up: "Open your mouth wide, and I will fill it." The salvation of God is like a feast to gorge the starving man; it's like the most delectable morsel for the connoisseur. It's mac and cheese for the eight-year-old; it's truffles for the mature palate. It's beans and franks for folksy down-home people; it's escargot for the adventuresome. It's *always God* filling us. Preparing for the Lord's coming is receiving the delicacies He has prepared.

John the Baptist is ever the face of Advent 2 (and 3), the one calling us to prepare the way for Christ not only in the Gospel readings but also in the Old Testament. See him in this Sunday's **Old Testament Reading**, Malachi 3:1–7b.

The New Testament is emphatic that "My [that is, Yahweh of hosts'] messenger" who "will prepare the way before Me" (again, before Yahweh) is John the Baptist (Mt 11:10; Mk 1:2; Lk 1:76; 7:27). This is John's mission.

But then the text is a bit more tricky: "And the Lord whom you seek will suddenly come to His temple; and the messenger of the covenant in whom you delight, behold, he is coming, *says the* Lord *of hosts*" (Mal 3:1b, c). We naturally assume that the Lord whom we seek is Christ, and that is correct. But it is interesting that it is "the Lord" speaking who then speaks of "the Lord" in the third person. This is a case when Yahweh speaks *as* the Holy Trinity and then speaks *about* one person of the Trinity, God the Son. (Notice that the text indicates the coming one as "Lord," Adonai, rather than "Lord," Yahweh.) Christ is eternally with the Father and the Holy Spirit, speaking as one voice. But in His incarnation, He will alone come to His people in the flesh.

And "the messenger of the covenant" is coming. Is this the same messenger mentioned earlier in the verse, John? No, this time the messenger is Christ the Lord Himself. He is the one who brings Yahweh's covenant to us; that is, by His life, death, and resurrection, He will establish and fulfill God's plan to remove our sin and make us His again.

Okay, then, who are each "his" and "he" (or "His" and "He") in the next two verses (3:2–3)? Are they the messenger John or the messenger of the covenant Christ? John, we know, is the fiery preacher of repentance (Lk 3:9) who would purify God's people by turning fathers back to their children and disobedient back to righteousness (Lk 1:17). Who can endure John's message without standing condemned? On the other hand, John himself connects Jesus to fire (Lk 3:16–17), and Jesus' fire will surely burn up the wicked. But Jesus will also separate out the righteous, just as a refiner's fire separates and purifies silver and gold from dross.

So Malachi is describing Christ . . . and John. It really makes sense; John's mission and Christ's are that closely related. In fact, Matthew's Gospel uses identical language to summarize their message: "Repent, for the kingdom of heaven is at hand" (Mt 3:2 by John; Mt 4:17 by Jesus).

The Lord, in the person of Christ and by the preaching of John, "will draw near to you for judgment . . . will be a swift witness against" every kind of evil (Mal 3:5). Preparing for His coming must mean repenting of sorcery (yes, there are some out there practicing that, but if that's not you, then) sexual sins, lying and cheating, heartlessness toward those in need.

Preparing the way of the Lord, though, is also what the Lord and John do to us. They refine us, purify us. It's Christ who separates out the dross when He dies for it. Yes, we will pass through the fire, but "you, O children of Jacob, are not consumed" (3:6). For the Lord remains faithful to us; that never changes.

Now read the **Holy Gospel**, in which we hear John's call for us: Luke 3:1–20.

The opening verses (3:1–2) may sound like something better buried in a footnote of someone's dissertation, but they're actually quite significant. The names and places—some we all recognize—are Luke's exclamation point that the eternal God is breaking into human history. This really happened! John comes because God becomes man!

Luke also shows that John is the fulfillment of Isaiah's prophecy (3:4–6; see Is 40:3–4). By now, most of this is familiar. But notice the meaningful shift. We hear again that we are to prepare, make straight (3:4). Then, though, a shift from the imperative to the indicative: not that we are to prepare and straighten, but that all these things "shall" (3:5–6). Valleys, mountains, rough places, even crooked things "shall" be changed. We're not doing all that. But they shall all happen. God is doing them. "And all flesh *shall* see *the salvation of God*." John proclaims "a baptism of repentance" (3:3); we are most certainly to repent, prepare, make straight. But that baptism of repentance brings "the forgiveness of sins" Christ will earn on the cross. Forgiveness is God preparing us to meet Him when He comes.

The subsequent verses picture what true repentance looks like (3:7–14). Crowds can come out to see John because it's the pop thing to do (Matthew specifies the Pharisees and Sadducees, Mt 3:7), but real repentance is demonstrated by "fruits" (Lk 3:8–9). "What then shall we do?" What are those fruits? Some of the good works John prescribes are among those demanded by

Malachi: tunics and food for the needy, honesty and contentment in business and with advantages we're given. For each of us, it's a matter of our own vocations. How can we love our neighbor and honor God in whatever place He's placed us?

A summary of John's message grasps the point of the propers: "So with many other *exhortations* he preached *good news* to the people" (3:18). John exhorts us to prepare for Christ's coming by repenting and bearing its fruit. But that's made possible with the Good News that God prepares us by His very coming to us. He comes to fill our open mouths with all the good gifts of salvation. Advent 2 calls us to

Prepare the Way of the Lord by Receiving What He Brings So That We Bear the Fruits of Repentance.

The remaining propers each pick up elements of this Theme.

Read the **Psalm**, Psalm 66:1–12. You recognize the language of refining: "You, O God, . . . have tried us as silver is tried. . . . We went through fire and through water" (66:10, 12b). Like Malachi and John, the psalmist knows that sin must be burned away. But the Psalm exudes joy: "Shout for joy to God, all the earth. . . . How awesome are Your deeds!" (66:1, 3). That's because after "we went through fire . . . You have brought us out to a place of abundance" (66:12). The fire did not consume us. God was only preparing us by purging away our impurities.

The **Epistle** seconds this idea that being prepared by God is a joy. Read Philippians 1:2–11. Paul's Advent viewpoint is for the second coming of Christ: "He who began a good work in you will bring it to completion *at the day of Jesus Christ*" (1:6). "So that you may approve what is excellent, and so be pure and blameless *for the day of Christ*" (1:10). In the meantime, it is Paul's prayer "that your love may abound more and more," that we may be "filled with the fruit of righteousness that comes through Jesus Christ" (1:9, 11). Paul, too, expects our repentance to bear fruit—love for God and neighbor. And that is a joyful thing (1:4)! It's the joy of being in "partnership in the gospel" with our fellow believers under the Lord Himself (1:5)!

Our Theme is here in the **Collect**:

> *Stir up our hearts, O Lord, to make ready the way of Your only-begotten Son, that by His coming we may be enabled to serve You with pure minds; through the same Jesus Christ, our Lord, who lives and reigns with You and the Holy Spirit, one God, now and forever. Amen.*

It's God who prepares us, enables us to make ready the way of Christ, by stirring up our hearts. It's God who enables us to bear the fruit of repentance, to "serve [Him] with pure minds," and He does it "by His coming"—ultimately to die to make us pure. In Advent, we prepare for Christ's coming, and it's Christ's coming that prepares us.

On Jordan's bank the Baptist's cry, "Prepare ye, the way of the Lord," brings us those "glad tidings of the King of kings!" (st 1). Sing the **Hymn of the Day** (*LSB* 344).

Third Sunday in Advent Year C

READINGS

Zephaniah 3:14–20
Psalm 85 (antiphon: v 2)
Philippians 4:4–7
Luke 7:18–28 (29–35)

HYMN OF THE DAY

LSB 345 "Hark! A Thrilling Voice Is Sounding"

The Third Sunday in Advent has traditionally been called *Gaudete* Sunday, from the Latin of the first word of the Introit: "Rejoice." "Rejoice in the Lord always; again I will say, Rejoice." It's Rejoice Sunday. This week's candle on the Advent wreath is rose, not the penitential purple or blue. Not only the Introit but also the Epistle includes Paul's encouragement to the Philippians to rejoice in the Lord always—and even to do it again. The Old Testament Reading and the Psalm rejoice too. And we hear again the Gradual for the whole Advent season that begins, "Rejoice greatly, O daughter of Zion. Shout aloud, O daughter of Jerusalem. Behold, your king is coming to you." There's a whole lot of rejoicing going on.

But then there's the Gospel lesson—which is supposed to set the tone for the day. And it's John the Baptist in prison facing a real crisis of faith. We don't see him rejoicing. In fact, if I made a pastoral call on him at this point, I'd probably be downright insensitive to start off with, "Heh, it's *Gaudete*. Rejoice!"

Well, Jesus doesn't tell him, "Put on a happy face, John. Rejoice!" But He does give John and us reason to rejoice on what looks like anything but a day for it. The rest of the propers, too, reveal the Lord's deep sensitivity to our most difficult moments.

Look more closely at the **Introit**:

Rejoice in the Lord always; again I will say, Rejoice.

Blessed is he whose help is the God of Jacob, whose hope is in the Lord his God, who made heaven and earth,

the sea, and all that is in them, who keeps faith forever; who executes justice for the oppressed, who gives food to the hungry. The LORD *sets the prisoners free; the* LORD *opens the eyes of the blind. The* LORD *lifts up those who are bowed down; the* LORD *loves the righteous.*

Glory be to the Father and to the Son and to the Holy Spirit; as it was in the beginning, is now, and will be forever. Amen.

Rejoice in the Lord always; again I will say, Rejoice. (Ps 146:5–8; antiphon: Phil 4:4)

Rejoicing in the Lord isn't all fun and games. You've got people who are oppressed, people who are hungry, imprisoned, blind. Go up to a homeless man in a neighborhood in Southern California and tell him, "Rejoice, friend! The weather's gorgeous!" Visit a parishioner who's serving time for embezzlement and tell her, "You'll be outta here in seventeen more months. Rejoice!" Sit down with an elderly loved one whose glaucoma means he'll never be able to read again and say . . . well, no, you know better than to say that. And the psalmist understands.

So he offers real comfort instead—in the Lord. Sometimes, of course, the Lord brings immediate justice, food, freedom, sight. But He always "keeps faith forever." That's not the same as we might or might not say about ourselves: that we hang in there, don't give up, even keep trusting. It means He never stops or even interrupts providing the very best for us whether we're seeing it or not. He never breaks faith with us. We can trust that especially when we can't see it. It's true entirely apart from our evidence. It's true because He says so.

The Old Testament Reading also invites us to rejoice, but notice the sufferings of this present time that the Lord, by His prophet, acknowledges as well: Zephaniah 3:14–20.

"Sing aloud, O daughter of Zion; shout, O Israel! Rejoice and exult with all your heart" (3:14). What's more, *the Lord* "will rejoice *over you* with gladness; . . . *He* will exult over you with loud singing" (3:17)!

He says this to people "who mourn . . . suffer reproach," who are "lame . . . outcast," who live in "shame" (3:18, 19). Rejoice, you who grieve that age and frailty mean you'll probably never make it back to church—even for Christmas Eve—until the congregation gathers one last time just for you, you who are still able to get around but only in a wheelchair, you who feel you haven't a friend, you whose sins have become known to everyone. Rejoice?

A key to this passage is the verb tenses. Verses 14 and 15c describe things that are present or already accomplished: "sing," "rejoice," "has taken away," "has cleared away," "is." Then 15d talks about what is yet to come. The Lord will surely make all things right in the future. That's certainly comforting when we suffer today. But it's better than that. The real reason rejoicing, singing aloud, shouting, exulting can already be now is what has already been accomplished. The Lord has already "taken away the judgments against you; . . . cleared away your enemies" (3:15).

God allows Zephaniah, over six hundred years BC, to see from His perspective. To God, we celebrate at Advent what is already accomplished from all eternity: Christ has come, and by His death on the cross, our guilty verdict has been taken away; our enemies—Satan, sin, and all the damage they do to us—have been swept from the field. That's why this is also always a present reality: "The Lord . . . is in your midst" (3:15). When Christ took away our sins, which separated us from God, He reconciled us to God. So now (oh, yes, already now!) the Lord is always with us. And if the almighty, all-knowing, all-loving Lord is with us, we are always, even now, receiving only His best. That's reason to rejoice always!

In the **Psalm**, this same reconciliation is expressed in the word *peace*. Read Psalm 85. Israel has been sinful, provoking God's "indignation" (85:4). Yet the Lord "will speak peace to His people, to His saints. . . . Surely His salvation is near to those who fear Him" (85:8, 9). The Lord will forgive them because in Christ's cross, He is reconciled to them. That's how even as they suffer the consequences of their sin, "Your people may rejoice in You" (85:6).

The **Epistle**, of course, is where the *Gaudete* idea got started: Philippians 4:4–7.

We've recognized how Paul's exhortation to rejoice in the Lord always can be badly misused—like as the opening line to someone in prison. But what a rich encouragement it is in the proper context. And the context may be surprising. Remember where Paul wrote his letter to the Philippians? From prison (see 1:7, 12–14). And he wasn't sure he was going to get out alive (1:19–24). Paul surely wasn't jumping up and down with delight each day in his cell.

But he's not just trying to talk himself and the Philippians into smiling when they feel low. And he's no superhuman who always feels happy or can simply turn on pleasant emotions. He's writing about more than emotions.

Feel however you feel, Paul might say. Nevertheless, rejoice in the Lord—always—because He "is at hand" (4:5). He is coming again soon, and He's with us already. By that reconciling death of Christ, we have "the peace of God" (4:7). And that's not a peaceful, easy feeling. It's the certainty He is caring for us every moment, because with sins removed, nothing stands between us and His gracious giving.

That's why Paul is able to add another remarkable note: "In everything by prayer and supplication *with thanksgiving* let your requests be made known to God" (4:6b). Spill to God in prayer whatever you need or whatever troubles you. But here's the amazing thing: as you ask, says thanks for it at the same sitting. Why? Because even before you ask, He already knows how He's going to give it—or something better. There's no need to wait and see before thanking God. His goodness toward you is already a sure thing, even if we aren't seeing it, even if we *never* see it. That's why we need not "be anxious about anything" (4:6a). That's reason to rejoice always—even on the worst days.

If anyone would understand all this about rejoicing, it would be Christ. Not only did He create humankind—our bodies, minds, hearts, emotions—but He lived our bad days Himself—including one worse than we'll ever experience, which we call good. So it's no surprise that when John the Baptist needs pastoral care, Jesus has the perfect word. Read the **Holy Gospel**, Luke 7:18–35.

John hears "all these things" Jesus has been doing (7:18)—most immediately, healing a centurion's servant (7:1–10) and raising a dead young man in Nain (7:11–17). So why does this trigger his question? "Are You the one who is to come, or shall we look for another?" (7:19).

Some have suggested that John sent his disciples to Jesus not because he himself had questions, but instead to direct his disciples to the Master. After all, John had already proclaimed Jesus "the Lamb of God, who takes away the sin of the world" (Jn 1:29). He'd heard the voice of the Father and seen the Holy Spirit as a dove endorsing Jesus at His Baptism (Lk 3:21–22). How could John have questions? The same way perhaps nearly all faithful believers in Christ sometimes struggle and question when times are hard.

Frankly, what John was observing didn't make sense. He'd preached Jesus; why was Jesus leaving him in prison?

We all cling to a theology of glory, the idea that what we see as good must be good. So surely God will establish His glory the way and when we expect it, and God's people will prosper in this world. That wasn't happening for John, as so often it doesn't happen for us. And when it doesn't, we often wonder if God isn't God after all, can't really or doesn't care to get us out of prison.

Jesus doesn't say He'll get John out of prison either. And He doesn't tell him to smile anyway. He points John's disciples to the miracles He's been doing (7:21–23), which are precisely those promised of the Messiah by God's Old Testament prophets (Is 35:5–6; 61:1). They answer John's question. And not just by checking messianic prophetic boxes. They demonstrate that Jesus is God: the one who really does care for the blind, deaf, ill, downtrodden, homeless, imprisoned, aged, infirmed, lonely, guilty. It's just that His caring doesn't always look the way we expect. He answers our sufferings by the ultimate evil: His innocent death on the cross. "Blessed is the one who is not offended by" that, *His* way of caring for us (7:23). Joyful is the one who believes God really is caring for us that way, His way, even when we don't see it.

Yes, We Can Rejoice in the Lord Always—
Even at a Time like This!

Even in dark times. The **Collect**:

> *Lord Jesus Christ, we implore You to hear our prayers and to lighten the darkness of our hearts by Your gracious visitation; for You live and reign with the Father and the Holy Spirit, one God, now and forever. Amen.*

If you know the tune for the **Hymn of the Day** (*LSB* 345), which was a different tune in *The Lutheran Hymnal* (*TLH* 60), try singing that again. If that minor key doesn't sound much like *Gaudete*, recall what rejoicing really is.

Fourth Sunday in Advent Year C

READINGS

Micah 5:2–5a
Psalm 80:1–7 (antiphon: v 7)
Hebrews 10:5–10
Luke 1:39–45 (46–56)

HYMN OF THE DAY

LSB 357 "O Come, O Come, Emmanuel"

What is it about Christmas?

Well, that's about as open-ended as a question could be, so you're bound to get as many different answers as people you might ask on a street corner. Christ the Savior is born, we'd all say to start. But then you'll get things about "the spirit of Christmas," "the real meaning of Christmas," "giving rather than receiving," "peace on earth, goodwill toward men." And even today, in our very secular world, most folks—at least in North America—see some backdrop of a baby in a manger. Plenty of people are clueless or unbelieving as to what the baby really means, but most know He's the history (or the myth) behind it all.

Something about that baby in that manger scene is what it is about Christmas.

The Fourth Sunday in Advent has us very close to the manger. And we know who that baby is and why He came. But even our unbelieving neighbors have a sense—however cloudy—of the core "it" about Christmas when they happen to see a manger scene. Even they get that that helpless little baby in poor and humble surroundings represents the lowly, the weak. And everybody loves an underdog—the 1969 Mets, the 1980 US Olympic hockey team, David against Goliath. Giving, peace, real meaning—*they all reflect that* and care for someone who's down.

That *is* what it is about Christmas. But the world has it so confused. Our propers for this last Sunday before Christmas make it clear.

For three Sundays, Advent has trained us to wait, but this week, we get to feel the excitement of being just days away from Christmas, first with the antiphon to the **Introit**:

My soul magnifies the Lord, and my spirit rejoices in God my Savior.

My mouth derides my enemies, because I rejoice in Your salvation. There is none holy like the LORD; *there is none besides You; there is no rock like our God. The barren has borne seven, but she who has many children is forlorn. The* LORD *kills and brings to life; He brings down to Sheol and raises up. The* LORD *makes poor and makes rich; He brings low and He exalts.*

Glory be to the Father and to the Son and to the Holy Spirit; as it was in the beginning, is now, and will be forever. Amen.

My soul magnifies the Lord, and my spirit rejoices in God my Savior. (1 Sam 2:1b, 2, 5b–7; antiphon: Lk 1:46b–47)

That's Mary magnifying the Lord, as we'll hear in the full Magnificat in the Gospel. She rejoices because, poor and low as she is, she is now pregnant with her and the world's Savior.

This Introit gives an interesting pairing. First Samuel 2:1–10 is the song of Hannah, sometimes referred to as the Old Testament Magnificat because it's very similar to Mary's canticle. Hannah, living almost eleven centuries before Mary, was, one may remember, married to a faithful man named Elkanah but had no children. Besides the sadness that might bring any woman, in ancient Israel, childlessness was seen as a curse, as if God was specifically withholding from her the opportunity to participate in Israel's messianic future. To make matters worse, Elkanah had another wife, Peninnah, who had children and taunted Hannah as a result. Eventually, though, God answered Hannah's prayer for a son whom she would dedicate to the Lord, the boy and later great judge of Israel, Samuel. And God added to Hannah five more children (1 Sam 1:1–2:21).

Like Mary, Hannah exults as one who was downtrodden and then lifted up by the Lord: "The barren has borne seven, but she who has many children is forlorn. . . . The Lord makes poor and makes rich; He brings low and He exalts." Our focus at Christmas is on the helpless baby, but rejoicing around the manger are lots of other down-and-outers.

The **Collect** also signals that we've reached the end of Advent, because it's one more of those Collects for the season (for Advent 1, 2, and 4) that begins, "Stir up":

Stir up Your power, O Lord, and come and help us by Your might, that the sins which weigh us down may be quickly lifted by Your grace and mercy; for You live and reign with the Father and the Holy Spirit, one God, now and forever. Amen.

More than being lowborn or bearing no children, what makes everyone down and out, brings us low, are "the sins which weigh us down." We're all crushed low, smashed down under the weight of our sin. No one can stand up tall and proud before God.

Our prayer is that the Lord by His coming would change that, stir the pot, so that we who are the dregs might rise to the top, be "quickly lifted."

By the way, in the Psalm this week, we actually discover from whence cometh those "stir up" collects. Read Psalm 80:1–7. There it is: "Stir up Your might and come to save us!" (80:2). God's people have been weighed down by their sin; the Lord is angry with them (80:4), has "fed them with the bread of tears" (80:5). But see how God will stir things up: "Let Your face shine, that we may be saved!" (80:3, 7). God's shining face is figurative, of course, but it also appeared quite literally, when God became incarnate, born of Mary, and lived among us.

We certainly know Christmas is near when we hear this week's **Old Testament Reading**: Micah 5:2–5a.

This is one we've been waiting for. Sunday School Christmas programs, the beloved hymn—nothing says Christmas quite like the "little town of Bethlehem." Such a vivid prophecy! The "ruler" to come from Bethlehem will be the one who's been around from "ancient of days" (5:2). We see a woman in labor giving birth (5:3). He "shall be great to the ends of the earth" (5:4)—revealed to Micah seven hundred years before the fact. No wonder when the time does come and wise men from the east show up so that Herod asks the chief priests and scribes where the Christ is to be born, they don't hesitate (Mt 2:1–6). It couldn't be clearer, including the part about "little." Micah is referring to the fact that when Israel entered the Promised Land, a seemingly endless list names the cities given to the tribe of Judah—at least 116 cities (Josh 15:20–63). But Bethlehem isn't listed. It's too small, insignificant, didn't count—"you, O Bethlehem Ephrathah, who are too little to be among the clans of Judah" (Micah 5:2).

But this is interesting. When the wise men come asking about Jesus, and the chief priests and scribes give Herod their answer, they say it this way: "You, O Bethlehem, in the land of Judah, are *by no means least* among the rulers of Judah" (Mt 2:6). Notice that? Bethlehem isn't insignificant any more! By no means! Because "from you shall come forth for Me one who is to be ruler in Israel" (Micah 5:2). The one who "shall be great" (5:4).

That's exactly as it is with us. We may be young and anonymous. We may not have the family we've dreamed of. We're all laid low by sin. But when we're baptized into the one who is great, we are not insignificant. We count.

As do the elderly and the unborn—who, among all the lowly and downtrodden, should be the chief recipients of our care. We see them with Mary in the **Holy Gospel**, Luke 1:39–56.

Almost no sooner than the archangel Gabriel's visit (Lk 1:26–38), Mary goes to see the one person on the planet who could understand her situation, her relative (perhaps a cousin, but much older) Elizabeth. Like Hannah, Elizabeth had known the "reproach" people piled on a childless woman (1:25), but now she is also pregnant, also at the word of the angel (1:5–25). Her son will be John the Baptist.

Elizabeth knows that she, too, would be entirely anonymous to history—"Why is this granted to me?" (1:43)—but all these centuries later, she is remembered because "the mother of my Lord [has] come to me" (1:43) And most remarkably, "when the sound of your greeting came to my ears, the baby in my womb leaped for joy" (1:44). The unborn John was already a child of faith, joyful that his (also unborn) Savior was present. No one more helpless, lowly than the unborn. Yet two thousand years' worth of readers of Luke's Gospel took at simple face value that the child in the womb was human, a human soul—until only the most recent decades!

Now the magnificent Magnificat! "My soul magnifies the Lord, and my spirit rejoices in God my Savior, for He has looked on the humble estate [in the KJV, "the low estate"] of His servant. For behold, from now on all generations will call me blessed. . . . He has . . . exalted those of humble estate; He has filled the hungry with good things" (1:46–48, 52–53). "For He who is mighty has done great things for me" (1:49).

Hannah, Elizabeth, Mary, the little town of Bethlehem, sinful Israel, we who are weighed down by our sin—all of low degree, down and out, but exalted, lifted up. That's what it is about Christmas. Except Christmas can't be that at all unless we return to the poor, lowly, helpless One that everyone knows is somehow behind Christmas, the One we know really is what it is about Christmas: the baby in the manger scene.

The **Epistle**, Hebrews 10:5–10, gets to the point: "When Christ came into the world, He said, . . . 'a *body* have You prepared for Me.' . . . We have been sanctified through the *offering* of the *body* of Jesus Christ once for all" (10:5, 10). We who are lowly are lifted up because God, who was exalted above the heavens, humbled Himself, came down, took upon Himself a human body, and made Himself the very lowest of us. It only *began* in the animals' feeding trough.

Go back to our prophecy from Micah. It ends with the most important element of all: "And He [this great ruler] shall be their peace" (Micah 5:5a). We've pointed out again and again what God's "peace" means. It is always a summation of what Jesus accomplished when He became the lowest of the low—when the body that was born of Mary in Bethlehem was murdered on the cross, reconciling us to God by atoning for our sins. That's what it is about Christmas.

God Makes Himself Lowly to Exalt Those of Low Estate.

And now, you *know* it's Christmas—the **Verse**: "Alleluia. Behold, the virgin shall conceive and bear a son, and they shall call His name Immanuel. Alleluia." Sing that. It's the **Hymn of the Day**, "O Come, O Come, Emmanuel" (*LSB* 357).

A note for the Christmas season: Since the propers for Christmas Eve, Midnight, Dawn, and Christmas Day are the same for Years A, B, and C, you'll find the one devotion-study for all of them in Year A on page 18. You'll also find brief thoughts about the Festival of Holy Innocents (which your congregation might observe on December 28 or a day close to that) on page 26 as part of the devotion-study for Holy Innocents and New Year. The devotion-study for the First Sunday after Christmas, Year C, is on the next page.

First Sunday after Christmas Year C

READINGS

Exodus 13:1–3a, 11–15
Psalm 111 (antiphon: v 9a, b)
Colossians 3:12–17
Luke 2:22–40

HYMN OF THE DAY

LSB 389 "Let All Together Praise Our God"

"And she gave birth to her firstborn son and wrapped Him in swaddling cloths and laid Him in a manger." (Lk 2:7)

> "He leaves His heav'nly Father's throne,
> Is born an infant small,
> And in a manger, poor and lone,
> Lies in a humble stall."

(**Hymn of the Day,** *LSB* 389:2)

So tiny, so helpless. Like all babies, He's just sort of along for the ride. A great big world is happening all around Him, but He just lies there or gets picked up and cuddled or goes wherever Mom and Dad take Him. Oh, He makes His personal needs known, all right, but most of what's going on out there just isn't on His radar screen yet.

Of course, this particular baby is also the Creator and Sustainer of the universe. So even when He's not using His omniscience or His almighty power, the very continuance of the cosmos and the eternal future of the human race depend on Him. Therefore, in the Gospel reading for the First Sunday after Christmas, even as the babe is entirely passive, just going for an outing wherever Joseph and Mary take Him, that outing will be an essential step in His work of redeeming us. They're not going shopping, but there's a purchase to be made.

"When the time came for their purification according to the Law of Moses, [Mary and Joseph] brought [Jesus] up to Jerusalem to present Him to the Lord (as it is written in the Law of the Lord, 'Every male who first opens the womb shall be called holy to the Lord')" (Lk 2:22–23).

Little Jesus is on His first trip to the temple. Joseph and Mary are keeping a law of God spelled out in the **Old Testament Reading**. Read Exodus 13:1–3a, 11–15.

This was a long time before Christmas (over 1,400 years), but it was looking ahead. Already the firstborn was special. Israel was on its way out of Egypt because God had slain the firstborn sons of all the Egyptians but had passed over the Israelite homes. Israel's firstborn had been spared.

Therefore, God commanded Israel to consecrate, set apart to the Lord, every firstborn male, "both of man and of beast" (13:2). Consecrating an animal to the Lord could be by sacrificing it, giving it up by breaking its neck. But the owner could instead redeem the animal by sacrificing another animal in its place, a lamb (13:13a). To "redeem" means to buy back or to ransom. The firstborn donkey was owed to God, but the Israelite could buy it back for his own use by paying the ransom price.

The firstborn son, of course, was not to be sacrificed. Every firstborn son was to be redeemed (13:13b). His parents would pay the price by offering a different sacrifice as a substitute.

All this was to recall what God had done for the Israelites when they were in slavery in Egypt: "When in time to come your son asks you, 'What does this mean?' you shall say to him, 'By a strong hand the Lord brought us out of Egypt, from the house of slavery'" (13:14). The Old Testament often speaks of God's act of bringing Israel out of Egypt as redeeming them (Ex 6:6; 15:13; Deut 7:8; 1 Chr 17:21; Neh 1:10; Ps 77:15; 78:42; 106:10; Is 63:9). God had purchased Israel from slavery (Ex 15:16; Ps 74:2). But where was the redemption price? Not the Egyptian sons; their deaths paid no one anything. And the Israelite sons had been spared. God's people had been redeemed, but they were to look ahead to see the One who was the payment to redeem them.

In the meantime, generation after generation, faithful Israelites carried out the redemption of their own firstborn sons. Hence, the **Holy Gospel**, Luke 2:22–40.

Baby Jesus' visit to the temple actually fulfills two commands of God. Besides the redemption of the firstborn (2:23), there was also the matter of Mary's purification (2:22). Forty days after giving birth, the mother was to present the sacrifice—for those who could afford it, a lamb and either a pair of pigeons or turtledoves; for those who could not, two birds (Lev 12:1–8). Luke only mentions the sacrifice this poor family could afford.

Perhaps more interesting, though, is that the Old Testament gives that lesser option in regard to the woman's purification but appears not to give it for the matter of redeeming the firstborn. We can infer from other contexts that the less costly sacrifice was acceptable for a variety of sacrifices (Lev 5:7; 14:21–22, 30–32). And Luke's text gives every confidence that Joseph and Mary were being obedient (2:39). But for redeeming the firstborn, the Law only specifies a lamb (Ex 13:13). Is this a reminder to us? This firstborn son in Mary's arms must be redeemed; there can be no breaking of the Law if He is to fulfill it for us. But no lamb is required, because the child is already the Lamb of God who will take away the sin of the world.

At this point, only a handful of people could understand that, but one of them was Simeon. We don't know how long he had been "waiting for the consolation of Israel" (Lk 2:25)—we picture him as elderly, though the text doesn't tell us that—and we don't know how the Holy Spirit had revealed that he would see the Christ in his lifetime (2:26). But somehow, the Spirit revealed to him that this was the moment (2:27). The Church has been singing his song, the Nunc Dimittis, almost ever since: "Lord, now You are letting Your servant depart in peace . . ." (2:29–32).

Simeon understood what baby Jesus' visit to the temple meant.

The Firstborn to Be Redeemed Is Appointed the Redemption of His People.

And doubtless even before His parents, Simeon understood how Jesus would be the Redeemer. "Behold, this child is appointed for the fall and rising of many in Israel, and for a sign that is opposed (and a sword will pierce through your [Mary's] own soul also), so that thoughts from many hearts may be revealed" (2:34–35). By no means would everyone embrace the man this baby would become. Many, most, would reject Him. But His rejection, His cross, would be the ransom price that paid for Israel's exodus from Egypt and evermore also be the redemption to lighten the Gentiles.

Anna (who was indeed elderly, 2:36–37a) is a beautiful example of how we, too, receive Christ's redemption. There's no indication that she had any special revelation of Jesus' identity, as Simeon was given. Rather, she was at the right place *all the time* (2:37b) to hear the word of proclamation when Simeon spoke it. A stanza that could be added to *LSB* 855, "For All the Faithful Women," prays,

Like Anna, who in patience
Would tarry day and night
Where she would see her Savior
When He appeared to sight,
Oh, may we also linger
Where we may see You, Lord,
Still come as our redemption
In Sacrament and Word.

And may we have the same joy as Anna did "to speak of Him to all who were waiting for the redemption of Jerusalem" (2:38).

Enjoy looking forward to this Sunday by noting all the other Christmas gifts there to be opened.

The **Psalm**, Psalm 111. The psalmist, too, understood the reason we "praise the Lord!" (111:1) at Christmas: "He sent redemption to His people" (111:9).

The **Introit:**

The Lord has bared His holy arm before the eyes of all the nations, and all the ends of the earth shall see the salvation of our God.

Oh sing to the Lord a new song, for He has done marvelous things! His right hand and His holy arm have worked salvation for Him. The Lord has made known His salvation; He has revealed His righteousness in the sight of the nations. He has remembered His steadfast love and

faithfulness to the house of Israel. All the ends of the earth have seen the salvation of our God. Make a joyful noise to the LORD, all the earth; break forth into joyous song and sing praises!

Glory be to the Father and to the Son and to the Holy Spirit; as it was in the beginning, is now, and will be forever. Amen.

The LORD has bared His holy arm before the eyes of all the nations, and all the ends of the earth shall see the salvation of our God. (Ps 98:1–4; antiphon: Is 52:10)

We finally see the "strong hand" by which the Lord redeemed Israel from Egypt: "The LORD has bared His holy arm before the eyes of all the nations," even if the arm, hands, feet, fingers, and toes are tiny.

Remember that the "new song" Psalm 98 calls for Isaac Watts answered by writing "Joy to the World" (with music by George Frideric Handel from the oratorio *Messiah*).

The **Collect**:

O God, our Maker and Redeemer, You wonderfully created us and in the incarnation of Your Son yet more wondrously restored our human nature. Grant that we may ever be alive in Him who made Himself to be like us; through Jesus Christ, our Lord, who lives and reigns with You and the Holy Spirit, one God, now and forever. Amen.

Creating us from dust (and a six-day creation of the universe)—wonderful, amazing. God becoming incarnate, one of us, yet more wondrous. "Grant that we may ever be alive in Him who made Himself to be like us"—what the **Epistle**, Colossians 3:12–17, calls putting on "compassionate hearts," letting "the peace of Christ rule in your hearts" (3:12, 15).

Finally, the **Gradual** for the season of Christmas:

To us a child is born, to us a son is given; and the government shall be upon His shoulder. And His name shall be called Wonderful Counselor, Mighty God, Everlasting Father, Prince of Peace. Sing to the LORD a new song, for He has done marvelous things! (Is 9:6; Ps 98:1a)

We could certainly drum, pipe, leap, dance to hear this prophecy of Isaiah for twelve straight days and then some, couldn't we!

A note for the upcoming holy days: Since the propers for New Year's Eve and Day, for the Second Sunday after Christmas, and for the Epiphany of Our Lord are identical in Years A, B, and C, you'll find the devotion-studies for each of them in Year A, pages 26, 30, and 34. (Be aware that in some years, because of the calendar, there is no Second Sunday after Christmas. Also, your congregation may observe Epiphany on a Sunday near January 6 or have a separate service for this feast on January 6, whatever day of the week it falls.) In addition, you'll find brief thoughts about the Festival of Holy Innocents (which your congregation might observe on December 28 or a day close to that) on page 26 as part of the devotion-study for Holy Innocents and New Year. The devotion-study for the Baptism of Our Lord (the First Sunday after the Epiphany), Year C, appears on the next page.

The Baptism of Our Lord Year C

READINGS

Isaiah 43:1–7
Psalm 29 (antiphon: v 3)
Romans 6:1–11
Luke 3:15–22

HYMN OF THE DAY

LSB 406, 407 "To Jordan Came the Christ, Our Lord"

Depending on when you're reading this in anticipation of Sunday morning, it may still be one of the Twelve Days of Christmas, up to January 5. If so, first of all, Merry Christmas again! Next, you've got a scheduling decision to consider. January 6, of course, is the day of Epiphany, and many congregations will have a special service, whatever day of the week January 6 happens to fall. If yours does, a blessed celebration to you! And you can prep to hear about the coming of the wise men with the devotion-study on page 34?. It's the great epiphany ("revealing," literally "shining upon") that Jesus is not only King of the Jews but the Savior of all people. If you have church on January 6, the Sunday following is sure to be observed as the Baptism of Our Lord, the First Sunday *after* the Epiphany. And this is the place to look forward to that Sunday morning.

On the other hand, if your congregation doesn't have worship on January 6, you may be using the Epiphany propers on the Sunday closest to it. Just to be safe, you might want to read both studies—this one and the one for the Epiphany of Our Lord. You won't be disappointed.

Assuming you're staying here for now, begin by reading closely (better yet, singing—but still pay close attention to the words) the **Hymn of the Day**, "To Jordan Came the Christ, Our Lord," by Martin Luther—either tune: *LSB* 406 or 407.

What did you notice? This Sunday, obviously, observes Jesus going to the Jordan River and being baptized by John. Luther narrates the story in great detail. "The Father's voice from heav'n came down, which we do well to ponder: 'This man is My beloved Son, in whom My heart has pleasure.' . . . The Holy

Spirit like a dove upon the scene descending" (sts 3, 4). But this is more than good storytelling.

Luther wrote this hymn to be catechetical, to teach one of the chief parts of his catechism, the Sacrament of Holy Baptism (as he also wrote hymns on the Ten Commandments, the Creed, and the others: *LSB* 581; 607; 617; 766; 954). In other words, Luther used the historical event of Jesus' Baptism to teach what our Baptism means for us. Look again: "The Father's Word was given *us* to treasure. This heav'nly washing now shall be a cleansing from transgression and by His blood and agony release from death's oppression. A new life now awaits *us*" (st 1). See how thoroughly the subsequent stanzas unfold the doctrine of Baptism.

Ponder especially this—or, as Luther puts it, "O hear and mark the message well" (st 2): "Our Lord here with His Word endows pure water, freely flowing. God's Holy Spirit here avows *our kinship*. . . . That in our Baptism [God] will thus among us find *a dwelling*" (sts 2, 4). This gets to the very heart of what happens in Jesus' Baptism. Baptism means we have kinship with Christ; God dwells in us. That happens because when Jesus was baptized, He put Himself in our place, became us, so that when we are baptized, we are put in His place, receive what is His.

Behold, This Epiphany: In Baptism, the Son of God Exchanges Places with All God's Sons and Daughters.

Among the three synoptics, Luke's Gospel has the leanest account of Jesus' Baptism. Most of the **Holy Gospel**, in fact, includes what we just heard on Advent 2. But that additional context is helpful. Read Luke 3:15–22.

Luke seems to treat Jesus' Baptism (3:21–22) almost as assumed: "Now when all the people were baptized, and when Jesus also had been baptized . . ." But that's not a bad assumption. It emphasizes that Jesus *had to be* baptized. Matthew makes the same point when John balks at baptizing Jesus and the Lord replies that "it is fitting for us to fulfill all righteousness" (Mt 3:15). Why? Because Jesus could only redeem what He took on. God's Law ("all righteousness") was an obligation for man, and when we failed so miserably to keep it, the Son had to take our place under it in order to fulfill it for us. The blessed—and necessary!—exchange!

Luke's brief account includes that most vivid scene of the Trinity—the Son standing before us, the Holy Spirit as a dove, and the Father's all-important words, "You are My beloved Son; with You I am well pleased" (Lk 3:22). And the earlier context adds this significant prefiguring: John promises, "*He* will baptize *you* with the Holy Spirit and with fire" (3:16). For now, Jesus was being baptized, putting Himself in our place. But soon enough, He would put us in His place by baptizing us.

As we examine the other propers for the Baptism of Our Lord, let's focus on this amazing exchange. Let's read what each proper says about Christ and marvel that it's also now describing us!

The **Collect**:

Father in heaven, at the Baptism of Jesus in the Jordan River You proclaimed Him Your beloved Son and anointed Him with the Holy Spirit. Make all who are baptized in His name faithful in their calling as Your children and inheritors with Him of everlasting life; through the same Jesus Christ, our Lord, who lives and reigns with You and the Holy Spirit, one God, now and forever. Amen.

Far more than most Sundays, this collect also narrates the Gospel event of the day. We anticipate the words from God the Father about His beloved Son that will come in the reading from Luke. And then we hear where we fit in: "Make all who are baptized in His name faithful in their calling as Your children and inheritors with Him of everlasting life." When we are baptized into Christ's name, we become God's children, just as He is God's Son. We are heirs of everything that belongs to Him!

The **Introit**:

Behold My Servant, whom I uphold, My chosen, in whom My soul delights.

I will tell of the decree: The LORD said to Me, "You are My Son; today I have begotten You. Ask of Me, and I will make the nations Your heritage, and the ends of the earth Your possession. You shall break them with a rod of iron and dash them in pieces like a potter's vessel." Now therefore, O kings, be wise; be warned, O rulers of the earth. Serve the LORD with fear, and rejoice with trembling, for His wrath is quickly kindled. Blessèd are all who take refuge in Him.

Glory be to the Father and to the Son and to the Holy Spirit; as it was in the beginning, is now, and will be forever. Amen.

Behold My Servant, whom I uphold, My chosen, in whom My soul delights. (Ps 2:7–11, 12c; antiphon: Is 42:1a)

The antiphon may well be the passage God the Father is recalling as He speaks from heaven. It's the opening line from the first of Isaiah's four Servant Songs, and that makes it especially relevant here. Each Servant Song (Is 42:1–9; 49:1–13; 50:4–11; 52:13–53:12) is voiced by Isaiah, but each is actually speaking the words of Yahweh about or sometimes by the Son of God, seven centuries before His incarnation. See the exchange. The voice of the prophet actually becomes the voice of Christ. When the prophet speaks, it is Christ's voice being heard. Just as when pastors today proclaim the Word of God from Holy Scripture, it is actually Christ speaking to us.

Then the words of Psalm 2:7–8: "You are My Son; today I have begotten You. Ask of Me, and I will make the nations Your heritage, and the ends of the earth Your possession." Again we hear a prequel of the Father's announcement at Jesus' Baptism. And again, we contemplate the exchange: If Jesus' Baptism puts Him in our place and our Baptism puts us in His, we are the meek (and yet mighty!) who inherit the earth.

The **Old Testament Reading**, too, makes this identification—that what Christ is He gives to us in Baptism: Isaiah 43:1–7.

With Jesus at the Jordan in our minds, we can't miss these images: "When you pass through the waters, I will be with you" (43:2). "I have called you by name, you are Mine" (43:1). "You are precious in My eyes, and honored, and I love you" (43:4). "My Son." "Beloved Son." "Well pleased."

But the exciting thing is that all this is now Israel, God's people. God makes an "exchange for you. . . . Peoples in exchange for your life" (43:3, 4). The trade is pictured as being for Egypt and Cush and Seba, but that's not the real swap. No foreign nation held the place of God's name and honor and love that had to be given up for us to inherit. Christ is the beloved Son who alone possessed and could give us His sonship with the Father.

He gives it to "sons from afar" and "daughters from the ends of the earth"—from "east" and "west" and "north" and "south"—"everyone who is called by My name" (43:5, 6, 7). Called by God's name: "In the name of the Father and of the Son and of the Holy Spirit"—that is Baptism.

See if you can guess why Psalm 29 is the **Psalm** for the Baptism of Our Lord in all three years. "The voice of the LORD is over the waters" (29:3a). "The God of glory thunders, the LORD, over many waters" (29:3b). And yet the Lord will "bless His people with peace!" (29:11).

By now, we know why—and that's the **Epistle**, Romans 6:1–11.

Along with Baptism, what other word group stands out? Died. Death. Buried. Dead. Crucified. Paul's text is perhaps the clearest passage in all of Scripture as to how we identify with and are in the place of Christ in our Baptism. And the key idea is death.

When Christ was baptized, He put Himself in our place. That meant taking on everything our sin had made us—above all, subject to death. And Jesus knew full well that His would be an evil death, because it would bear even the eternal sufferings of hell. Jesus' Baptism in the Jordan was into our death and damnation.

But now *we* have also been baptized into death, His crucifixion: "We were buried therefore with Him by baptism into death" (6:4). That means we can expect to suffer the revenge of Satan and the world. But we have also received the life that has been His from eternity. In His Baptism, He united with us in a death like ours. Now, though, "if," in Baptism, "we have been united with Him in a death like His, we shall certainly be united with Him in a resurrection like His" (6:5).

It's quite the epiphany to see that, by blessed exchange, what God says about His Son is now also true of us! The **Gradual**:

> *Praise the LORD, all nations! Extol Him, all peoples! For great is His steadfast love toward us, and the faithfulness of the LORD endures forever. Ascribe to the LORD the glory due His name; bring an offering, and come into His courts! (Ps 117:1–2a; 96:8)*

There are more epiphanies in the Sundays to come.

Second Sunday after the Epiphany Year C

READINGS

Isaiah 62:1–5
Psalm 128 (antiphon: v 5)
1 Corinthians 12:1–11
John 2:1–11

HYMN OF THE DAY

LSB 402 "The Only Son from Heaven"

An epiphany is a revealing, a manifestation of something that might have previously been hidden or invisible. So far during this Epiphany season, the star and the coming of the wise men have revealed that the little toddler Jesus is King, not only of the Jews but of the Gentiles as well. And Jesus' Baptism in the Jordan has revealed that this man from Nazareth is God's beloved Son who has taken our place under the Law so that He might give us His place as children of God. Now we're looking for further epiphanies.

If you don't already know where this Second Sunday after the Epiphany, Year C, is going, resist the urge to look ahead to the Gospel reading that tells all. You'll figure it out before long; guessing it might even be an epiphany for you. But not the big one.

Start with the **Collect**. Does it give much of a hint?

Almighty and everlasting God, who governs all things in heaven and on earth, mercifully hear the prayers of Your people and grant us Your peace through all our days; through Jesus Christ, Your Son, our Lord, who lives and reigns with You and the Holy Spirit, one God, now and forever. Amen.

Great prayer! No greater gift really than God's peace! But pretty generic, eh? There's no specific occasion or need spelled out.

This is a very ancient collect. Our version is from the Latin that goes back to at least the 700s, perhaps as early as the 400s. Somehow, it's always been paired with the Gospel lesson for today. But it's not much of a hint as to what that Gospel lesson is, is it?

Do hang on to two elements that are, admittedly, rather broad but are probably the connection to the Gospel story: God "governs *all things* in heaven and on earth," and we ask that He would "mercifully *hear* the prayers of [His] people."

The **Introit** will doubtless direct our thinking a bit more:

[The Lord] brought me to the banqueting house, and His banner over me was love.

Your steadfast love, O LORD, extends to the heavens, Your faithfulness to the clouds. Your righteousness is like the mountains of God; Your judgments are like the great deep; man and beast You save, O LORD. How precious is Your steadfast love, O God! The children of mankind take refuge in the shadow of Your wings. They feast on the abundance of Your house, and You give them drink from the river of Your delights. For with You is the fountain of life; in Your light do we see light.

Glory be to the Father and to the Son and to the Holy Spirit; as it was in the beginning, is now, and will be forever. Amen.

[The Lord] brought me to the banqueting house, and His banner over me was love. (Ps 36:5–9; antiphon: Song 2:4)

Notice the source of the antiphon: Song of Solomon. Recall, perhaps, the plot line of the Song. It's a poetic description of the steadfast and loving marriage between Solomon and his bride. She has been brought to a banqueting house for a *wedding* banquet. Ah, now we're getting somewhere.

The designers of the liturgy have inserted that the one bringing her is the Lord. The text actually only says "he," and the only antecedents are Solomon and "the king" and "my beloved." But the insertion is very appropriate. Song of Solomon has long been understood as a picture of the relationship of Christ and His Bride, the Church.

The psalm that the antiphon accompanies continues the thought. "His banner over me was love." And "Your steadfast love, O LORD, extends to the heavens, Your faithfulness to the clouds. . . . How precious is Your steadfast love, O God!" When Claire and I would tell our Rachel, Daniel, and Gabriel how much we loved them, we'd sometimes extend both arms out as farrrrrrr as we could, with the fingers pointing even farther—no limit. If we look to the skies, we can see no limit, just as, God tells us, His love for us has no limit. It's true of your love for your kids, of your love for your spouse, and of Christ's love for His Bride.

Then back to the banquet: "They feast on the abundance of Your house, and You give them drink from the river of Your delights." The wedding feast is abundant!

Ideas about the Gospel lesson?

If we're still processing, the **Old Testament Reading** is also very specifically about marriage. Read Isaiah 62:1–5.

Isaiah wrote the last portion of his book of the Bible with a view toward tragic times ahead. The Northern Kingdom had now been destroyed, and Isaiah sees on the horizon a similar fate for Judah: captivity in Babylon. But he writes of the restoration of God's people after their hardships, and the final chapters have especially rich imagery. Beginning in 61:10, he gives us a collage of wedding pictures: "As a bridegroom decks himself like a priest with a beautiful headdress, and as a bride adorns herself with her jewels." The weeping of exile will be over; it will be time again for celebration!

Isaiah continues in our reading, "You shall no more be termed Forsaken, and your land shall no more be termed Desolate, but you shall be called My Delight Is in Her, and your land Married; for the Lord delights in you, and your land shall be married. For as a young man marries a young woman, so shall your sons marry you, and as the bridegroom rejoices over the bride, so shall your God rejoice over you" (62:4–5). Think about things that *delight*, things that brighten the eye. A man of God, standing before the Lord's altar, turns to see a godly woman dressed in white coming down the aisle, symbolizing purity and anticipation of the miracles God will soon work for them together. See the delight in his eye! See the delight in God's eye as He sees the Bride He has chosen to be His!

The **Psalm** follows quite, shall we say, naturally. Read Psalm 128.

As if marriage itself weren't delightful enough, the psalmist takes the next step: "Your wife will be like a fruitful vine within your house; your children will be like olive shoots around your table" (128:3). "Blessed" indeed (128:1, 2, 4, 5) are those God-given gifts with children! See the delight in the eyes of a believing couple when they gaze at their newborn or toddling or teenage child—or at their child who is herself or himself now marrying! And surely every Christian grandparent will say "Amen!" to the blessing of seeing "your children's children!" (128:6).

Very much in keeping with the other propers of the day, the Psalm sees also this blessing of marriage with children as a banquet. "You shall eat" (128:2). "Your children will be like olive shoots around your table" (128:3). "May you see the prosperity of Jerusalem all the days of your life!" (128:5). No blessing of God is a pittance. We may not live in worldly prosperity—often far from it. But when we dine at the Lord's Table, it will always be as the Introit declared: feasting on abundance.

Have you had your epiphany yet as to the Gospel lesson for the day? We're close, but first, here's a brief interlude, the **Epistle**: 1 Corinthians 12:1–11.

The Epiphany season is one of those portions of the church year when the Epistles proceed more or less continuously through a book, rather than being freely chosen to amplify the Gospel lesson. But Epiphany is unique in this way: it splits the book of 1 Corinthians among Years A (chs 1–4), B (chs 6–10), and C (chs 12–15). We dive in midstream with Paul's discussion "concerning spiritual gifts" (12:1). There's nothing about marriage or banqueting here; it's worth reading on its own merits—and following along in the coming Sundays.

Here's one important Epiphany season concept, though. "No one can say 'Jesus is Lord' except in the Holy Spirit'" (12:3). In discussing spiritual gifts, Paul is emphatic that the Spirit never wants to be the show. He always points us to believe in and confess Christ. The entire Epiphany season is epiphanies about Christ.

Including the epiphany that occurs at the wedding in Cana. There. We said it. The **Holy Gospel**, John 2:1–11.

A wedding is, on the one hand, an ordinary, very human occasion, and, on the other hand, a very big deal. In a small town in Galilee (Cana was perhaps a few miles north of Nazareth), this was likely the social event of the year, and perhaps for Mary also a family gathering. (She seems to be personally interested.) Running out of wine was likewise a very human faux pas, yet an extremely painful embarrassment. The wedding feast was to go on for days; this would end the festivities. Mary's hint to Jesus, "They have no wine" (2:3), may have been small stuff in Jesus' big picture, but she knew the couple might be deeply hurt.

Jesus certainly has the big picture in mind. "My hour has not yet come" (2:4) is neither rude nor a promise that an hour or two from now He'd fix the wine situation. This is His first reference to "the hour" when He would accomplish the salvation of the world (see Jn 7:30; 8:20; 12:23, 27; 13:1; 17:1; also Mt 26:45; Mk 14:35, 41; Lk 22:53). There would be an hour when Jesus would be glorified, the same hour when evil would seem to have its day. Nothing can interfere with Jesus going to the cross.

And yet Jesus' words are not a rebuke to Mary or indifference toward her request. Mary gets that (2:5). Remember the Collect, so long associated with the wedding of Cana: "Mercifully hear the prayers of Your people." He does. And very soon, the couple has their wine. The very, very good wine (2:10). And plenty(!) of it—120 to 180 gallons! (2:6). What may seem small still matters to our Lord. Again, the Collect: "God, who governs *all* things." And cares about all things that beset His children.

Always, though, in the context of and in keeping with the eternal big picture that He always knows best. This first "sign" (σημεῖον, *semeion*; see also Jn 2:23; 3:2; 4:54; 6:2, 14; 7:31; 9:16; 11:47; 12:18, 37; 20:30–31) is identified as a first epiphany for Jesus' disciples; they believe in Him. Now that His hour has come, it means even more to us. For very regularly—including this Sunday—we are able to come to the wedding banquet that He has prepared. We see for ourselves what happened at Cana:

**JESUS' FIRST SIGN
IS AN ABUNDANT EPIPHANY
FOR THOSE HE DELIGHTS TO BRING
TO HIS WEDDING BANQUET.**

And at the Lord's Table, the feasting is always in abundance.

Here's the epiphany that makes all epiphanies: "The only Son from heaven . . . in human form appears" (st 1). Sing the **Hymn of the Day** (*LSB* 402).

Third Sunday after the Epiphany Year C

READINGS

Nehemiah 8:1–3, 5–6, 8–10
Psalm 19:(1–6) 7–14
(antiphon: v 14)
1 Corinthians 12:12–31a
Luke 4:16–30

HYMN OF THE DAY

LSB 839 "O Christ, Our True and Only Light"

It must have been quite the epiphany, an eye-opening revelation, for the folks in Nazareth to see what the local kid had become. "The eyes of all in the synagogue were fixed on Him. . . . And all spoke well of Him and marveled at the gracious words that were coming from His mouth. And they said, 'Is not this Joseph's son?'" (Lk 4:20b, 22).

Sadly, some epiphanies—even of Christ—are taken with offense. In fact, Jesus' gracious words will always meet rejection, contention, and jealousy from some. But others will hear them as liberating, freeing, healing. That power of Jesus' words is remarkable! When He speaks, reality is radically changed for those who hear—one way or the other. When Jesus speaks, it is always God's moment of action.

The Third Sunday after the Epiphany gives us the same words of Jesus that the people of Nazareth rejected. As you read them now and hear them Sunday, God is acting again. May they be the epiphany He intends for us!

Already the **Introit** gives us many of the particulars we'll see recurring throughout the propers on our way to Nazareth:

> *You will arise and have pity on Zion; it is the time to favor her; the appointed time has come.*
>
> *Let this be recorded for a generation to come, so that a people yet to be created may praise the Lord: that He looked down from His holy height; from heaven the Lord looked at the earth, to hear the groans of the prisoners, to set free those who were doomed to die, that they may declare*

in Zion the name of the Lord, and in Jerusalem His praise, when peoples gather together, and kingdoms, to worship the Lord.

Glory be to the Father and to the Son and to the Holy Spirit; as it was in the beginning, is now, and will be forever. Amen.

You will arise and have pity on Zion; it is the time to favor her; the appointed time has come. (Ps 102:18–22; antiphon: Ps 102:13)

"It is the time to favor [Zion]." Jesus will begin His sermon in the Gospel lesson with this: "Today this Scripture has been fulfilled in your hearing" (Lk 4:21). Of the essence of Jesus' message will be time. "The appointed time has come." We don't actually know what time this is, the date of Psalm 102's writing. It is not explicitly ascribed to David, as are 101 and 103 (though he may have written it), so it could be well outside his lifetime. But not knowing the date turns out to be helpful, because "the time," then, is whenever this promise of God is delivered to us. The Word is active whenever it's proclaimed. "Let this be recorded for a generation to come." It will be just as powerful whenever it's read in the future.

Not knowing the date of the psalm, we also don't know the specific sufferings Zion is groaning over. God's people are described as "prisoners," "doomed to die." Again, that is very broad. At times, God's people were captives of foreign nations. In every era, some innocent people are imprisoned falsely. All of us are captives, prisoners, of our sin and doomed to all its effects—mortality, illness, broken relationships, shortages, ultimately deserving eternity in the prison of hell. From all of these, Zion will be "set free." Jesus will speak to this in Nazareth.

And for all of these, the psalm promises God's "favor." That, too, is widely inclusive, but it's also very specific. It includes every good gift of God, whatever need, whenever. But it is specifically the result of sinful man and holy God being reconciled. And that will be the "Today" of which Jesus will speak in His Nazareth sermon.

One more note from the Introit. God's time to favor Zion will be "when [and whenever] peoples *gather together*" to hear that message "recorded" for their generation. If the appointed time is whenever the Word is proclaimed, then it is the time *for those who are there* where it is proclaimed.

Now pray this Sunday's **Collect**:

Almighty and everlasting God, mercifully look upon our infirmities and stretch forth the hand of Your majesty to heal and defend us; through Jesus Christ, Your Son, our Lord, who lives and reigns with You and the Holy Spirit, one God, now and forever. Amen.

As in the Introit, the petitions that God "look upon our infirmities" and "heal and defend us" collect many possibilities. We are all oppressed by illnesses, weaknesses, threats far too many to name. Yet relief for all will come when God "stretch[es] forth the hand of [His] majesty." When did He do that?

The **Old Testament Reading** this week is the only occasion in the lectionary for the book of Nehemiah. Read Nehemiah 8:1–10.

The events of Nehemiah take place in the fifth century BC, about a hundred years after Judah's return from Babylon in 538. The temple has been rebuilt (completed in 516), but the spiritual life of the people not so much. Nehemiah, who had served as a trusted official of the king of Persia, has now come to Jerusalem as governor and, with the high priest, Ezra, is seeking to revive the nation.

So "all the people gathered as one man . . . . Both men and women and all who could understand what they heard" (8:1, 2). And Ezra the priest stood on a platform built for the event, "opened the book in the sight of all the people" (8:5), and from early morning until midday read the Law of Moses (the Torah, the first five books of the Old Testament) while the people stood and listened.

Imagine! This was not our print or electronic age when everyone has a Bible on her coffee table and phone. This may have been the one opportunity in their lives to hear the words on which their entire national heritage—to say nothing of their eternal salvation—was based. "The ears of all the people were attentive" (8:3). Oh, that we with our easy-access Bibles should be so eager! To help matters, a number of the Levites stood among the people explaining the text as Ezra read it—either simply translation, since by this time many in Judah did not speak Hebrew, or commentary, mini sermons on the texts (8:7–8).

The reading of God's Word had His desired effect. "The people wept" (8:9), no doubt when they heard the commandments they had broken, the sacrifices they had failed to offer, the holy days they had not kept. And surely also the punishments God had threatened. It suddenly made perfect sense why the nation was in shambles. It was all as God had warned. If they'd only listened!

But the Torah is also rich in Good News. Repentance is always met with forgiveness. "Do not mourn or weep. . . . Eat the fat and drink sweet wine, . . . for this day is holy to our Lord. And do not be grieved, for the joy of the LORD is your strength" (8:9, 10). This day, the Lord restores you!

Watch how strikingly this previews the Gospel lesson: gathering, standing, opening the book, reading, interpreting. And this day!

The **Psalm** of this day, Psalm 19, may be called a "Torah Psalm." It begins (19:1–6) by asserting that the very "heavens declare the glory of God," that all creation voices the Creator. Indeed they do! But to *know* this God (not just know that He's out there somewhere) takes the Word of God (the Torah, "law of the LORD," 19:7a, and parallel terms in 19:7b–8). The most lively voice that speaks Him is "the words of my mouth" when they speak what His Scriptures teach. Especially is the *spoken* Word powerful, active.

As we observed last week, the Epistles for Epiphany follow their own progression of thought. However, this Sunday's **Epistle** has important points of contact with the Gospel. Read 1 Corinthians 12:12–31a.

Recall from last week that this is part of Paul's discussion of spiritual gifts.

Unfortunately, spiritual gifts—given by God to edify the Church—have become a bone of contention. That is, jealousies have arisen over who has what and why mine is more important than yours. This should never be, Paul says—just as there should be no jealousies between Jews and Gentiles. "For in one Spirit we were all baptized into one body" (12:13). And then Paul develops that marvelous metaphor—that the Church's many members are like a foot, a hand, an ear, an eye, each indispensable to the others. "If one member suffers, all suffer together; if one member is honored, all rejoice together" (12:26). Therefore, let no member of the Body of Christ be jealous when another is gifted by God for a particular calling (12:28–30).

Tragically, that proved to be the problem in Nazareth, when one of their own arose as especially gifted: the **Holy Gospel**, Luke 4:16–30.

This text is notable as the only detailed report in Scripture of Jesus' formal, liturgical sermons (that is, during the worship service). He did them often, of course, since going to the synagogue on the Sabbath "was His custom" (4:16). Jesus went to church! That is, He with all God's faithful people gathered to hear the Word where the Word would be.

In the synagogue, the Word would be from the Torah, the Prophets, and the Psalms—according to a prescribed lectionary. So Jesus fully intends to preach on the passage expected this Sabbath. He stands, opens the book (the scroll), and reads from Isaiah 61. This text is all recognized as spoken by the Messiah (the "Me"); it's called by some "a Fifth Servant Song." The Messiah has been sent "to proclaim good news to the poor," "liberty to the captives," and "sight to the blind." He will "set at liberty those who are oppressed." As the sum of all, He will "proclaim the year of the Lord's favor" (4:18, 19).

By synagogue practice, the reader would sit when he began his exposition of the text (4:20a). We can sense the anticipation (4:20b). And then the moment: "Today" (4:21)! Everything Isaiah wrote, everything I just read, is fulfilled *as you hear it*. And the point is clear: it's all fulfilled in Me. The Messiah is here, and I am He!

It's not a welcome epiphany to the people of Nazareth. Jesus senses it, and He doesn't shy from bringing it out into the open (4:23–27). Now they're jealous—of Capernaum, of the Gentiles, above all, that this son of the local carpenter is hijacking their dreams of what the Messiah should do!

But His arrival today does liberate all held captive, oppressed by any of those imprisonments, "infirmities," grave consequences of sin. That's because He restores us to "the Lord's favor"—another of those blessed terms that is Jesus' reconciling death on the cross. And He delivers it whenever He speaks it.

Jesus Preaching to His Gathered People Is a Liberating Epiphany of the Lord's Favor . . . Today!

Like "Today" again this Sunday for all who are there to hear. "In the stead and by the command of my Lord Jesus Christ, I . . ."

"O Christ, our true and only light, enlighten" (st 1) us to this, Your epiphany, as we sing the **Hymn of the Day**, *LSB* 839.

Fourth Sunday after the Epiphany Year C

READINGS

Jeremiah 1:4–10 (17–19)
Psalm 71:1–6 (7–11)
(antiphon: v 12)
1 Corinthians 12:31b–13:13
Luke 4:31–44

HYMN OF THE DAY

LSB 842 "Son of God, Eternal Savior"

January 22, 1973, and June 24, 2022, are two days that changed the course of history in the United States—and changed life itself for millions of Americans. In 1973, the US Supreme Court's decision in the case of *Roe v. Wade* suddenly legalized abortion in every state by declaring that a constitutional right to privacy guaranteed that a woman could have an abortion at any point before fetal viability. The court justified this ruling by saying that it did not know when human life began and that unborn children were therefore not people in a legal sense, thus, not protected by the law. Over the next nearly fifty years, an estimated 43 million—perhaps up to 65 million—abortions were performed in the United States.

That changed in 2022, when a very differently constituted Supreme Court, in its decision on *Dobbs v. Jackson Women's Health Organization*, overturned *Roe*. Abortion, the Supreme Court now ruled, was *not* a constitutional right.

The landmark ruling on *Dobbs* changed the law of the land. But it did not change things *back*. One of the complaints by those who dissented from the majority on *Dobbs* was that two generations of American women had grown up with the understanding that the choice to get an abortion was their right; to take it away from them was like changing the rules in the middle of the game. That, of course, was a totally inane argument. Almost a century of Americans lived with laws that gave African Americans no rights as people, and we all agree that reversing that wickedness was crucial to the very soul of our country.

But that argument demonstrates how, to a great extent, the damage of *Roe* had been done.

Fifty years of legalized abortions have caused many sensitivities to be seared against seeing and feeling the horrors of death to infants. So it's not as if *Dobbs* brought America to its senses, to decry abortion, to view abortion again from a pre-*Roe* perspective. Many of those who grew up with *Roe have* come to think that since abortion was legal, it must be moral and right.

Dobbs did not outlaw abortion, did not end abortion. Rather, it returned the issue to the states, many of which were quick to halt or restrict abortions. Other states, though, were just as immediate in enacting laws to allow them. All this virtually assures that abortion will be a battle that continues to be fought, which means we Christians *must* continue to speak up in defense of the unborn.

Faithful congregations will surely want to continue to observe the annual Sanctity of Human Life Sunday, whether around the January 22 date or around June 24. The propers for the Fourth Sunday after the Epiphany, Year C, are particularly appropriate for that. In fact, pastors who plan carefully may even want to rearrange one or two Sundays of the Epiphany sequence to use these propers a bit earlier, on the Sunday closest to January 22. It may be another epiphany to us to discover how specifically these propers address the matter of the sanctity of human life.

That's certainly evident in the **Introit**:

Arise, O Lord; O God, lift up Your hand; forget not the afflicted.

The Lord is king forever and ever; the nations perish from His land. O Lord, You hear the desire of the afflicted; You will strengthen their heart; You will incline Your ear to do justice to the fatherless and the oppressed, so that man who is of the earth may strike terror no more.

Glory be to the Father and to the Son and to the Holy Spirit; as it was in the beginning, is now, and will be forever. Amen.

Arise, O Lord; O God, lift up Your hand; forget not the afflicted. (Ps 10:16–18; antiphon: Ps 10:12)

"Forget not the afflicted." How easy it is to forget those who can't yet speak for themselves, whose own faces aren't yet visible, whose tiny hands we can't yet see reaching up begging for help. God does not forget! He lifts up *His* hand! "You hear the desire of the afflicted." "The Lord is king forever and ever; the nations perish from His land." May He be merciful to nations who approve and even celebrate evil!

Think of the unborn as you read this line again: "You will incline Your ear to do justice to the fatherless and the oppressed, so that man who is of the earth may strike terror no more." Who is more oppressed than unborn infants being killed? So often, they don't have fathers willing to speak up for them; in fact, abortion has become an easy way for fathers to abdicate their responsibilities and leave women and children helpless—except perhaps with a one-time cash payment for a clinic "procedure." "Strike terror." Terror is fear that invades places we ought to feel safe.

The United States does not guarantee homeland security in the womb; all the terrorist attacks we've suffered, including 9/11, do not match the deadly toll of *two days* of abortions in the last years before *Dobbs* (or one day in the 1980s and 1990s). And even in our most blessed land, we can't always depend on courts or congresses or legislatures to deliver justice. But "You [O LORD] will incline Your ear to do justice"—not so much in the sense we usually think, justice as punishment, but as justice that is protection for the oppressed. Whatever the legal climate, the hope of the unborn is our God!

We pray to Him in the **Collect**:

> *Almighty God, You know we live in the midst of so many dangers that in our frailty we cannot stand upright. Grant strength and protection to support us in all dangers and carry us through all temptations; through Jesus Christ, Your Son, our Lord, who lives and reigns with You and the Holy Spirit, one God, now and forever. Amen.*

Surely this prayer is one we all bring to the Lord for ourselves; we are all frail and in danger. But what bitter truth that those who are most frail, who can literally not stand upright, and are in the place that should be safest, the womb, are in gravest danger! We must speak this prayer for them as well!

We also pray that God would "carry us through all temptations" to be part of the abortion problem—temptation to sex outside of marriage, temptation to what might seem the easy way out of an unwanted pregnancy, temptation to condemn those who need our forgiveness, temptation to be silent rather than speak for the unborn. We all find ourselves guilty, but we pray to a God whose love and mercy "through Jesus Christ our Lord" are without limit.

As you read the **Psalm** of the day, imagine it being prayed by a child in the womb. Read Psalm 71:1–12.

"In You, O LORD, do I take refuge. . . . Rescue me. . . . Rescue me, O my God, from the hand of the wicked, from the grasp of the unjust and cruel man. . . . Upon You I have leaned *from before my birth*; You are He who took me *from my mother's womb*." (71:1, 2, 4, 6). The abortion issue should be resolved by this question: Is the unborn a person, human? For us who believe God's Word, it is *no question*.

Note, too, the psalmist's prayer for end of life issues: "Do not cast me off in the time of old age; forsake me not when my strength is spent" (71:9). The elderly, weak, sick continue to be fully human, under God's care, to be encouraged with their value to Him, not misled to euthanasia or assisted suicide. "O my God, make haste to help me!" (71:12).

One of the most decisive passages in the entire Bible on life in the womb is the **Old Testament Reading**, Jeremiah 1:4–10, 17–19.

"Before you were born I consecrated you." Already while in the womb, Jeremiah was a person with a God-ordained purpose. In fact, God had huge plans for Jeremiah, "a prophet to the nations" (1:5).

Jeremiah is understandably overwhelmed at the idea (1:6), but God says, "You *shall* go

. . . you *shall* speak" (1:7). When God calls us to speak, we must. And God promised, "I am with you to deliver you. . . . Behold, I have put My words in your mouth" (1:8, 9).

Sometimes what God gives us to say will be painful Law: "See," He said to Jeremiah, "I have set you this day over nations and over kingdoms, to pluck up and to break down, to destroy and to overthrow" (1:10a). When we tell friends, coworkers, family—usually in settings of ordinary conversation—that abortion is sinful, some will hear it as unloving or just ignorant. We still must speak the words God gives at the opportunities He gives.

Above all, though, God's Word, including on life issues, is His word of love—"to build up and to plant" (1:10b). For those who have had abortions, caused a pregnancy outside of marriage, been unforgiving, or been silent, God's love in the cross of Jesus Christ washes clean, rebuilds.

That must be the what and the way we speak, as Paul does in the **Epistle**. Read 1 Corinthians 12:31b–13:13.

"If I speak in the tongues of men and of angels, but have not love, I am a noisy gong or a clanging cymbal" (13:1). If our voice to protect life is not loving, no one will listen. Love "does not insist on its own way" (13:5) simply to win an argument. Love "does not rejoice at wrongdoing" (13:6a); rather, it actively opposes it. But love most surely "rejoices with the truth" (13:6b). In fact, there is joy before the angels of God over one abortionist or committer of abortion who repents (cf Lk 15:10). And love "bears all things" (13:7)—especially helping bear the burdens of women in crisis pregnancies.

Is the task too great? Are the forces who push for abortion too powerful? Read the **Holy Gospel**, Luke 4:31–44.

After almost fifty years of toil, a historic victory from the highest power in the land did not fix the abortion crisis in the US. So our wholesome and God-pleasing efforts to reshape laws and public opinion must continue. But the opponent is too mighty for just that; it's Satan himself. And God has given us only one weapon that can engage him: His Word. It is powerful enough. Those who heard Jesus "were astonished at His teaching, for His word possessed authority" (4:32). "He commands the unclean spirits, and they come out!" (4:36).

For further thoughts on the incidents in 4:38–44, see the devotion-study for Epiphany 5, Year B (p 312), on the parallel account in Mark. But here, this: Jesus says, "I *must* preach the good news of the kingdom of God" (4:43), and we must speak too. We must speak God's Law against abortion. But ultimately, our speaking, like Christ's, is Good News, because by His love in going to the cross and rising, God's kingdom has overpowered Satan and his evils.

JESUS' WORD IS A POWERFUL EPIPHANY FOR THOSE WHO ALSO MUST SPEAK GOD'S POWERFUL LOVE FOR THE OPPRESSED AND ENDANGERED—ESPECIALLY THE UNBORN.

"Son of God, eternal Savior, *source of life* and truth and grace, Word made flesh, [Your] birth among us hallows *all* our human race" (st 1)! (**Hymn of the Day**).

Fifth Sunday after the Epiphany Year C

READINGS

Isaiah 6:1–8 (9–13)
Psalm 138 (antiphon: v 5)
1 Corinthians 14:12b–20
Luke 5:1–11

HYMN OF THE DAY

LSB 398 "Hail to the Lord's Anointed"

What's with Peter's fear?

Jesus, in the Gospel reading for the Fifth Sunday after the Epiphany, has just worked an impressive miracle; He's filled fish nets to bursting in a way Peter knows shouldn't have worked. Jesus has blessed Peter and his fishing partners with perhaps many weeks' or a month's worth of income. What a day! But then Peter pleads for Jesus to depart from him. Why not ride this Jesus for all He's worth—maybe a few more record catches? Or, a bit more sanctified, praise Him with thanksgiving? What's Peter afraid of?

The prophet Isaiah has a very similar experience in the Old Testament Reading. And Isaiah, too, if he'd had his way, would have missed out on the Lord's opportunity of an eternity.

This week, let's look at those two lessons, Old Testament and Gospel, side by side, step by step. God didn't give Isaiah or Peter what they thought they wanted; He had much better ahead for them. We'll see how the Lord allayed the fears of the prophet and the apostle and brought them to trust Him more fully. Then the other propers will amplify that God is using what terrified Peter and Isaiah to help us.

Both the Old Testament Reading and the Gospel lesson may be broken down into four steps. The **Old Testament Reading** is Isaiah 6:1–8 (9–13), but read just the first plot step, being sure to stop after verse 4.

King Uzziah had ruled for fifty-two years, the second-longest reign for any king of Judah. But his death called God's people to humility; this mighty (and good) king's pride, usurping the priests' role to burn incense in the temple, resulted in his last years being lived in isolation as a leper (2 Chr 26:1–5, 16–23). Now here was Isaiah amid the smoke of the same temple suddenly seeing the Lord high above him on a throne. The seraphim—especially honored angels! The earthquake! And their voice that caused it: "Holy, holy, holy is the LORD of hosts; the whole earth is full of His glory!" (6:3). That's the big thing! That Yahweh is holy, holy, holy! Yes, the one Lord is three holy persons—each one perfectly pure, without sin, set apart from anything that is sinful. This is the first step in the story: 1. God's man witnesses a show of His power and holiness. Awesome!

What Peter witnesses in the **Holy Gospel**, Luke 5:1–11, may lack the rocking and the sound effects, but it's powerful nonetheless. Read the first step in this story, 5:1–7.

In their Gospels, Matthew and Mark introduce Simon Peter, Andrew (his brother), and two other brothers, James and John, more formally (Mt 4:18–22; Mk 1:16–20); they were fishermen on the Sea of Galilee, here called the lake of Gennesaret. We love the picture of Jesus teaching from the boat (Lk 5:3). Calm. Gentle. And practical. Not only did it give Jesus room to gesticulate (as preachers will do!) but, if you've ever tried projecting your voice over the water, it works!

In this text, though, the focus is on what happens next. The pros know you do your fishing at night. And some nights, you strike out. Maybe it's more out of respect for this marvelous teacher than from expectation of a catch that Peter agrees to try again (5:4–5). We know Jesus, so we know the result! More fish than the two boats can handle (5:6–7)! God's man, Peter, like Isaiah, witnesses a show of God's power and holiness.

Back to Isaiah. This time, just 6:5.

Second plot step: *2. God's man expresses terror at God's power and holiness because of his sin.* "Woe is me! For I am lost; for I am a man of unclean lips, and I dwell in the midst of a people of unclean lips; for my eyes have seen the King, the LORD of hosts!" (6:5). It's the universal reaction when sinful human beings see God's holiness—even when it's just God's holiness reflected in a holy angel. Zechariah and Mary at the appearance of Gabriel (Lk 1:8–12, 26–29), the shepherds before the Christmas angel (Lk 2:8–9), Manoah and his wife in the Old Testament (Judg 13:19–22), and many others—all are stricken with fear, terrified when they see the Lord or His angel. Why? Because humans see the terrifying contrast between God's holiness and power and their own sin. And that's a proper reaction. Holy God cannot tolerate evil in His presence. If we were to stand before God in our sin, His almighty power would destroy us.

This was Peter's fear! Read Luke 5:8–10a.

With the exception of His transfiguration, Jesus, throughout His ministry, veiled the glory of His power and holiness. Yet at this moment, Peter realized what he was seeing. This miracle revealed Jesus as the almighty, holy Son of God. And Peter rightly understood that he as a sinful man could not survive in the presence of holy God. No sin—a little unclean or unkind word *à la* Isaiah, an impure thought about an attractive actress or coveting the dress another member can afford to wear to church, being out on the lake fishing on a Sunday morning instead of being in church—no sin just slides by. Every *one* condemns us to hell. In his sin, God's man Peter expresses terror at the power and holiness of God.

But until the day of grace is ended, God comes to sinful human beings to save them rather than destroy them. The third step in both of our stories: *3. God relieves His man's fear of His power and holiness.* First for Isaiah. Read 6:6–7.

If it was sins of the lips that terrified Isaiah at this moment, that's how God would symbolize his deliverance from all sin. This text is a vision. We don't know how God enabled Isaiah to "see" it, so we don't know whether Isaiah experienced any actual pain. But the message was unmistakable: "Behold, this has touched your lips; your guilt is taken away, and your sin atoned for" (6:7). Isaiah no longer had anything to fear; the sin for which there could only be "woe" ("lost," 6:5) was atoned. And some pain, real or only envisioned, was surely fitting, because atonement always comes with payment, sacrifice, reparations for sin. No prophet in the Old Testament would, soon enough, write as vividly about that as Isaiah.

Meanwhile, few texts are as vivid in picturing how that atonement is delivered to us: "This has touched your lips." For us, it's no mere vision; it's the very real presence of our Lord's own body and blood. And with it, we have the assurance again and again that our sin has been atoned for.

For Peter, this third step takes only these few words: "Jesus said to Simon, 'Do not be afraid'" (Lk 5:10b). Jesus relieves Peter's fear with the very same words Gabriel had spoken to Zechariah and Mary (Lk 1:13, 30), the Christmas angel spoke to the shepherds (Lk 2:10), the same words He would speak after His resurrection (Mt 28:10). "Do not be afraid" and "Fear not" are not encouragements to be brave; they are absolution. They are announcing that the sin that would have demanded God's power and holiness destroy us has been forgiven. Jesus is telling Peter—the angels were telling Isaiah and Zechariah and Mary and the shepherds—that Jesus will go to the cross to reconcile them to God.

So now God's power and holiness will not condemn Peter; they are not to be feared. Jesus' holiness and the power He wields to protect us is given to us. When they are *for us*—that is to say, when God is *with us*—it is great Good News.

Finally, the fourth step: *4. God affirms that He will use His power and holiness to aid, not destroy, His man by calling him to His mission.* Read Isaiah 6:8.

Isaiah would never have thought he of the unclean lips could be God's spokesman. But God's call confirms for Isaiah that his lips really are purified, his sins forgiven. That means God will be with him. Now Isaiah is an eager volunteer. How rich we are for it!—rich as in Isaiah 1:18; 7:14; 9:6; 11:1–9; 40:1–8; 52:13–53:12; 55:10–11; 60:1–6.

Of course, Jesus had a place in His mission for Peter too. Read Luke 5:10b–11.

Jesus' power and holiness wouldn't destroy Peter. Catching men comes with its own hazards. Talk about Jesus at the Super Bowl party? when visiting a coworker at the hospital? Maybe that scares us to death. Eventually it would literally cost Peter his life.

But when Christ calls us to His mission, it's still His mission.

Perhaps all this is another epiphany for us this Epiphany season,

An Epiphany for Us Sinful People with Unclean Lips: We Need Not Fear God's Holiness and Power or Christ's Call to Catch Men, for Christ Has Atoned for Our Sin.

Even if we only "speak five words . . . in order to instruct others" (1 Cor 14:19), Christ will use it to catch men, "in building up the church" (14:12)—the **Epistle**, 1 Corinthians 14:12b–20.

"Though the LORD is high, He regards the lowly. . . . Though I walk in the midst of trouble, You preserve my life" (Ps 138:6–7). God's power is for us! Even the most powerful of this world, "all the kings of the earth shall give You thanks, O LORD, for they have heard the words of Your mouth" (138:4)—heard the words of the Lord's mouth through our mouths (the **Psalm**, Psalm 138).

Therefore, unlike Peter, we do *not* want God to depart from us. The **Introit**:

O God, be not far from me; O my God, make haste to help me!

My mouth will tell of Your righteous acts, of Your deeds of salvation all the day, for their number is past my knowledge. With the mighty deeds of the Lord GOD I will come; I will remind them of Your righteousness, Yours alone. O God, from my youth You have taught me, and I still proclaim Your wondrous deeds. So even to old age and gray hairs, O God, do not forsake me, until I proclaim Your might to another generation, Your power to all those to come.

Glory be to the Father and to the Son and to the Holy Spirit; as it was in the beginning, is now, and will be forever. Amen.

O God, be not far from me; O my God, make haste to help me! (Ps 71:15–18; antiphon: Ps 71:12)

By God's help, we will not fear His holiness, but our mouths will tell of His righteous acts; we will not fear Christ's power but will proclaim His mighty deeds.

For by God's grace in Christ, His mighty power now defends us. The **Collect**:

O Lord, keep Your family the Church continually in the true faith that, relying on the hope of Your heavenly grace, we may ever be defended by Your mighty power; through Jesus Christ, Your Son, our Lord, who lives and reigns with You and the Holy Spirit, one God, now and forever. Amen.

The **Hymn of the Day**, *LSB* 398, hails the Lord's anointed as great, greater than David, powerful enough to be victorious over every foe, yet not fearsome, but helping the poor, needy, weak. His name to us is Love.

Sixth Sunday after the Epiphany Year C

READINGS

Jeremiah 17:5–8
Psalm 1 (antiphon: v 2)
1 Corinthians 15:(1–11) 12–20
Luke 6:17–26

HYMN OF THE DAY

LSB 394 "Songs of Thankfulness and Praise"

Every Sunday of the Epiphany season is an eye-opener. *Epiphany*, as we've learned, means, after all, a "revealing" of something that might otherwise have been hidden. This Epiphany 6 Sunday, Jesus will do that revealing by His teaching; the propers are keyed to the first portion of Luke's account of the Sermon on the Mount, Jesus teaching the Beatitudes. There will be plenty to learn. The key word is "blessèd" (our word, *beatitude*, comes from the Latin word for "blessed"), and blessedness will appear prominently in the other propers as well.

What may be the greater epiphany, though, isn't explicit in Jesus' teaching. It's behind it. In fact, it's behind everything Jesus teaches and does. It's behind every blessing God gives us.

From time to time in these weekly devotion-studies, we're just selling out to make that "behind-every-teaching" absolutely transparent, lest we should ever forget. (Read, for example, if you'd like, the devotion-study for Epiphany 8, Year A, on p 66.) And we're going to do that again this week. Behind every blessed thing is the cross of Jesus. No good thing ever comes to anyone except that God has been reconciled to the world by His Son's atoning sacrifice. So again in this devotion-study, as we hear each *blessèd*, we'll remind ourselves that it's from the cross.

Having thus revealed what otherwise we might have kept hidden for a while, here's our Theme:

**The Greatest Epiphany
Is Always to Learn
That the Lord's Cross Is Why
You Are Blessed with Every Fruit
Rather Than Cursed with All Woes.**

Begin with the **Introit**. Imagine sitting at the Teacher's feet as you speak the antiphon and hear His answer:

I will praise You with an upright heart, when I learn Your just and righteous decrees.

Blessèd are those whose way is blameless, who walk in the law of the LORD! Blessèd are those who keep His testimonies, who seek Him with their whole heart. You have commanded Your precepts to be kept diligently. Oh that my ways may be steadfast in keeping Your statutes!

Glory be to the Father and to the Son and to the Holy Spirit; as it was in the beginning, is now, and will be forever. Amen.

I will praise You with an upright heart, when I learn Your just and righteous decrees. (Ps 119:1–2, 4–5; antiphon: Ps 119:7)

Psalm 119 is chief of the Torah Psalms; *Torah*, remember, is the Hebrew word for the five Books of Moses (Genesis to Deuteronomy) and is usually translated "law." The Torah Psalms always voice the joy of the diligent student who has been listening to a master or poring over beloved scrolls. He truly loves what he is hearing or reading: "I will praise You with an upright heart, when I learn Your just and righteous decrees."

"*Blessèd* are those whose way is blameless, who walk in the law of the LORD! *Blessèd* are those who keep His testimonies, who seek Him with their whole heart." A student of the Torah is blessèd. Is that because he has lived blamelessly, walked properly, kept God's Law wholly?

Decrees, testimonies, precepts, statutes—all are synonyms for *law*. But they don't mean "Law" as we use the phrase "Law and Gospel." They really mean "instruction," which includes both Law and Gospel, as the Pentateuch is indeed rich with Gospel as well as stern with Law. A student of the Torah is truly delighting to learn how Yahweh would have him walk and live, because he knows what the Lord has done—and will do—for him. Old Testament believers didn't have all the details, but they knew that the Lord would suffer terrible bruising from the adversary while ultimately crushing his head (Gen 3:15). We know that happened on the cross of Calvary. A student of the Torah isn't blessed because he has been blameless according to the Law; he hasn't been. He is blessed because the Messiah would die for him. And now, as a result, he loves following in the teaching of the One who blessed him.

The **Collect** for this Sunday leaves no room for our blessedness being of our own:

O Lord, graciously hear the prayers of Your people that we who justly suffer the consequence of our sin may be mercifully delivered by Your goodness to the glory of Your name; through Jesus Christ, Your Son, our Lord, who lives and reigns with You and the Holy Spirit, one God, now and forever. Amen.

All we merit is to "suffer the consequence of our sin"—quite "justly." Yet we pray with confidence that we will be "mercifully delivered." What is our confidence? "Through Jesus Christ." Our prayers are always through Christ (even when we don't say it), because it was Jesus' death on the cross that removed the sin separating us from the Father. God's "goodness" to us is always for the sake of Christ's reconciling sacrifice.

In this week's **Old Testament Reading**, the prophet Jeremiah introduces the alternative to being blessed. Read Jeremiah 17:5–8.

In what is essentially a psalm (and noticeably like our Psalm 1 coming next), Jeremiah sets up a tight parallel between "blessed" and "cursed." The cursed man "is like a shrub in the desert," living in "the parched places of the wilderness," "an uninhabited salt land" (17:6), surely doomed to wither and die. The man who is blessed "is like a tree"—not just a shrub—who is "planted by water, . . . by the stream." With his limitless source of hydration, the hot sun only causes him to flourish: "leaves remain green" and, that which identifies him as blessed, the tree, which is this man, "does not cease to bear *fruit*" (17:8).

The reason one man is cursed and the other blessed is also parallel: "Cursed is the man who trusts in man." "Blessed is the man who trusts in the Lord." Everyone trusts someone or something. And the Lord shows clearly that the issue isn't how well or how firmly someone trusts; "trusts" is the same for both. (Many Christians erroneously think they'll receive certain blessings if their faith is "strong enough.") The difference is in whom we trust. "The man who trusts in man" above all trusts in his own man, himself. But man's strength will surely fail—if not before, certainly when it comes time to face eternity. "The man who trusts in the Lord" depends on everything Yahweh has and does.

And what is that? Almighty, all-loving God stoops to do what His man and His woman need in order to receive any blessing: they need to be made His people again. And He does that by taking away the sin that made them instead children of the devil. He goes to the cross. Blessed is the man who trusts in the Lord's own tree.

See how similar the **Psalm** is.

Psalm 1 is another Torah Psalm ("his delight is in the law [*Torah*] of the Lord," 1:2a), and this student is just as enraptured to learn ("on His law [again, *Torah*] he meditates day and night," 1:2b). Like Jeremiah's man, this one, too, is "blessed"—"like a tree planted by streams of water" (1:1, 3a). He, too, is contrasted to the dry, hapless plant, "like chaff that the wind drives away" (1:4).

As in Jeremiah's metaphor, the blessing is "fruit in its season" (1:3b). Not only is fruit the sign that the tree is healthy; fruit is the very thing that is good about this kind of tree. Fruit represents every blessing God gives. The psalmist is proclaiming an endless produce of all divine goodness.

The Psalm concludes by leaving the illustration and describing the contrast as it really is: "wicked" or "righteous" (1:5, 6). The fact is, "None is righteous, no, not one" (Rom 3:10), which, of course, brings us again to the cross. By nature, we are the wicked who deserve only to "perish." But instead, we are blessed with God's good fruits because He declares us to be righteous by faith in the death and resurrection of the Righteous One.

These "blessèds" in the Old Testament already hang from the cross. But by the time Paul writes the **Epistle**, Christ's cross is in plain view. Read 1 Corinthians 15:1–20.

The great resurrection chapter (also in the lectionary at Easter) is built on this premise: "I delivered to you *as of first importance* what I also received: that Christ died for our sins in accordance with the Scriptures" (15:3), that likewise He was buried, raised, and appeared to many. That's of first importance. "If Christ has not been raised, . . . your faith is in vain. . . . Your faith is futile and you are still in your sins. . . . Those also who have fallen asleep in Christ have perished. . . . We are of all people most to be pitied" (15:14, 17, 18, 19). It's that bad. And, of course, that means if Christ had not first died, if Christ had not died and risen, we would be cursed.

"But in fact Christ" did die for our sins and "has been raised from the dead, the *firstfruits* of those who have fallen asleep" (15:20). The tree of the cross has born its fruit, beginning with Christ Himself and now continuing with all of us who believe.

Matthew's telling of the Sermon on the Mount and the Beatitudes is heard more frequently than Luke's. See if you notice differences as you read the **Holy Gospel**, Luke 6:17–26.

Jesus "came down with them and stood on a level place, with a great crowd" (6:17). Apparently, Jesus has been up nearer the summit and comes down to do His teaching where crowds could gather—a "level place" still on the mountainside (see Mt 5:1).

Jesus is the Teacher of Torah *par excellence*. He is the bestower of every blessèd the psalmists or Jeremiah proclaims. And Luke's report actually makes that clear in ways Matthew is sometimes misunderstood. Matthew 5:3, 6, "Blessed are the poor *in spirit*. . . . Blessed are those who hunger and thirst *for righteousness*," are often misunderstood to mean that we are to do something (humble ourselves, pursue righteousness) in order to gain the blessings. Luke shortens Jesus' phrasing: "Blessed are you who are poor. . . . Blessed are you who are hungry now" (6:20, 21). Being poor and being hungry are obviously not things we do but rather circumstances forced upon us. On the other hand, unlike Matthew, Luke records the woes Jesus spoke. And being "rich" or "full" or one of those who "laugh" (6:24, 25) are not sins meriting "woe." Luke is clarifying that blessings and woes are not *because* of these descriptions; they are in spite of them. *Even though* you are poor or hungry, you are blessed. *Even though* you are rich, full, laugh now, you (for entirely different reasons) will suffer woes.

The reason for blessings, entirely apart from our works, is the cross, Jesus reconciling the whole world to God. The reason for woes is not pleasant circumstances now but lack of faith in Jesus' cross, thinking instead that one has earned those pleasantries himself.

Sing the **Hymn of the Day**, *LSB* 394. Christ's "great epiphany" (st 4) to our eyes will certainly be His appearing on the Last Day. But His greatest epiphany of faith is the cross. It's why God was made manifest in man.

Seventh Sunday after the Epiphany Year C

READINGS

Genesis 45:3–15
Psalm 103:1–13 (antiphon: v 8)
1 Corinthians 15:21–26, 30–42
Luke 6:27–38

HYMN OF THE DAY

LSB 820 "My Soul, Now Praise Your Maker"
or *LSB* 834 "O God, O Lord of Heaven and Earth"

Often we don't know what's ahead until we get there.

That's true most Sundays as we walk into church (unless, of course, we've been tipped off by *Looking Forward* to Sunday morning). We perhaps get clues from the bulletin, we sing the opening hymn, and we worship through one proper after another, looking for connections among them, until, most likely, the sermon brings the theme of the day together for us. During this Epiphany season, that may well mean a new discovery, an epiphany, about Christ we hadn't seen before.

It's surely also true that in life's fuller context, we usually don't know what awaits us. And this week, our propers make that very point; God promises an epiphany to us that won't be fully revealed until an unspecified time ahead. What epiphany is that?

No hints this week. Let's just find out by reading the propers as we would if showing up cold on a Sunday morning. We'll see as we go, and when we get to the end, we'll put the pieces together.

That means starting with the **Introit**:

> *Be still before the* Lord *and wait patiently for Him; fret not yourself over the one who prospers in his way.*
>
> *Fret not yourself because of evildoers; be not envious of wrongdoers! For they will soon fade like the grass and wither like the green herb. Trust in the* Lord*, and do good; dwell in the land and befriend faithfulness. Delight yourself in the* Lord*, and He will give you the desires of your heart.*

Commit your way to the Lord*; trust in Him, and He will act.*

Glory be to the Father and to the Son and to the Holy Spirit; as it was in the beginning, is now, and will be forever. Amen.

Be still before the Lord *and wait patiently for Him; fret not yourself over the one who prospers in his way. (Ps 37:1–5; antiphon: Ps 37:7a, b)*

What do you see? "Fret not" over "evildoers" or "wrongdoers" when they seem to prosper in their evil ways. Don't envy them. Instead, "trust in the Lord;" "trust in Him." "Wait patiently for Him," for "He will act." Evildoers will "fade" and "wither" like grass. But—and here's a verse that may be quite familiar—"Delight yourself in the Lord, and He will give you the desires of your heart."

Kids get off the hook by blaming their brothers. Girls get guys by offering too much. Applicants get jobs by lying in interviews. Companies grow sales with outlandish promises. Candidates win office by inventing dirt on their opponents. Integrity, faith don't seem to pay. "Trust in the Lord, and do good."

Next, the **Collect**:

O God, the strength of all who put their trust in You, mercifully grant that by Your power we may be defended against all adversity; through Jesus Christ, Your Son, our Lord, who lives and reigns with You and the Holy Spirit, one God, now and forever. Amen.

There's that idea again to "trust in You," O God. And notice, there's also again the idea that evil will happen around us and to us: we will face "adversity." So our prayer is that God would use His power to defend against those adversities all who put their trust in Him.

As you listen to the **Old Testament Reading** on Sunday morning, you'll have to recall the backstory. Read Genesis 45:3–15.

Do you remember how this all came about? Joseph was the eleventh of twelve brothers. Their father, Jacob, favored Joseph above the others because Jacob had four wives and Joseph was finally the first son of his most favored wife, Rachel. (It's the family of the Messiah, but they're dyyyyysfunctional!) That led to such bitter jealousy that the ten older brothers sold Joseph into slavery in Egypt and told their poor father that he had been killed by a wild animal. In Egypt, Joseph was a faithful slave, even being honored by his master—only to be falsely imprisoned. But eventually, God enabled Joseph to interpret dreams that foretold a terrible famine. Pharaoh was so grateful and impressed that he appointed Joseph second-in-command of all Egypt and entrusted him with guiding them through the crisis. Does any of this resonate with the Introit and Collect?

So now Joseph's brothers have come down to Egypt desperate to buy food. Unbeknownst to them, they are buying it from Joseph. (This was more than twenty years later, and they didn't recognize him.) Joseph tests them to see if they are as cold-hearted as before, but now he sees they are different men. They're even willing to become slaves in order to spare their youngest brother, the twelfth, Benjamin, the only other son of Rachel (and Jacob's new favorite). At this, Joseph can't restrain himself. He weeps with joy and reveals himself to them.

The brothers are understandably "dismayed at his presence" (45:3). Joseph certainly has the power to execute them. But instead, Joseph says to them, "Do not be distressed or angry with yourselves because you sold me here, for God sent me before you to preserve life" (45:5). It may take twenty years, but in the words of the Introit, God "will act." "It was not you who sent me here, but God" (45:8).

It's probably God's mercy *on us* that we usually don't get such golden opportunities for "sweet" revenge on the girl who stole our boyfriend, on the guy who smooth-talked his way into the job we worked so hard to earn, on the company that teased us out of our hard-earned savings. Seeing God's hand in all this, Joseph instead saw his brothers as God saw them: "I will provide for you" (45:11).

Evildoers prospering? Fret not. Trust in the Lord. Wait patiently for Him. And do good. Provide for them.

Okay. We're definitely picking up some of the leads in our propers. How does the **Psalm** fit in? Read Psalm 103:1–13.

It's one of the truly great psalms of praise! It teaches that our "PTL" (in fact, some translations, including NIV, go with "Praise the LORD!") isn't just our emotional hype. Praising or blessing God is always best done by recounting "all His benefits"—like when He "forgives all your iniquity" and "redeems your life from the pit" (103:2, 3, 4).

"The LORD works righteousness and justice for all who are oppressed" (103:6). So we don't have to dole out our own brand of "righteousness," maybe? Like Joseph didn't.

What about this part? "The LORD is merciful and gracious, slow to anger and abounding in steadfast love" (103:8). You suppose Joseph in prison thought the Lord might be a little slow and a little too loving with his brothers and his false accuser? Except then there's this: "He does not deal with us according to our sins, nor repay us according to our iniquities" (103:10). Oh. Maybe slow is a better idea than I thought. Evildoers. Waiting patiently for Him. He will act. "As far as the east is from the west, so far does He remove our transgressions from us" (103:12). Wrongdoers. We are the wrongdoers too. But "the LORD is merciful and gracious" with us. Take all the time You need, Lord!

Which He did, waiting nineteen centuries after Joseph until Jacob's heir took our iniquity to His cross. There's no revenge for us to take. God poured it all out on His Son.

We knew that had to be coming!

It always does!

Now the **Epistle**, 1 Corinthians 15:21–26, 30–42.

Sound like Easter? Indeed! Epiphany 6, 7, and 8, Year C, have us in Paul's great resurrection chapter. Especially valuable in this section is Paul's explanation of "how" the dead are raised. "With what kind of body do they come?" (15:35). He answers that each kind of flesh always remains of its own kind (15:39). In other words, we humans will be raised in real, human flesh, the kind already familiar to us now. Our very own bodies, the ones we occupy today, will be our bodies in the resurrection. Of course, they will then be in heavenly glory, which will far surpass the glory these same bodies enjoy now (15:40).

Is there anything here about evildoers, God's mercy to us, our doing good to them, trusting God to act in His perfect time?

"In Christ shall all be made alive. . . . Christ the firstfruits, then at His coming those who belong to Christ. Then comes the end, when He delivers the kingdom to God the Father after destroying every rule and every authority and power. For He must reign until He has put all His enemies under His feet. The last enemy to be destroyed is death" (15:22b, 23b–26). To take the last first: God may be slow as we count slowness, but the day will come when every enemy will be destroyed. We may think evildoers are prospering, but in God's time, when Christ returns on the Last Day, wrong will be punished. Whatever the wicked think they have gained, they'll see it dashed away. But remember, God is indeed slow in bringing this about, because He wants no one to be lost—including each sinner like ourselves.

Rather, He wants all people to see the other epiphany of the Last Day: "Made alive . . . those who belong to Christ." This is why revenge is never Christian thinking. We have a future of incomparable glory! And it is eternal: "What is raised is imperishable" (15:42). Paul could carry on despite "danger every hour" (15:30), being wronged in countless ways—thrown into the arena with wild beasts (15:32), flogged, held in prison, finally murdered—because of what he knew God had awaiting him.

By the time Pastor invites you to rise for the **Holy Gospel**, Luke 6:27–38, you'll have a good idea about what awaits.

Continuing Jesus' Sermon on the Mount: "Love your enemies, do good to those who hate you" (6:27). There's so many situations in life that applies to (6:28–30), like your brother who's now grown, lives across the country, and is still angling for the better part of the will by reminding Mom how devoted he was. God bless you, brother! The woman whose litter has now come to loneliness. Befriend her. It's the Golden Rule: "As you wish that others would do to you, do so to them" (6:31).

And you follow it because you have been the other woman, the real hater, and "your Father is merciful" to you (6:36). He gave His Son so that "you will not be condemned," so "you will be forgiven" (6:37). And ahead is "good measure, pressed down, shaken together, running over" (6:38).

One more proper, the **Hymn of the Day**, can be sung as the sermon hymn. Both options fit the day nicely, but if you sing *LSB* 820, based on Psalm 103, appreciate that He gives "mercies more than you dare claim" and "rights the wronged at last" (st 1).

Like our Theme of the day, we won't fully see that until the Last Day, but

**Love and Do Good to Your Enemies as Your Father Has Been Merciful to You.
For You Can Trust
He Has an Epiphany Awaiting You:
He Will Right Every Wrong
with Great, Imperishable Reward.**

Eighth Sunday after the Epiphany Year C

READINGS

Jeremiah 7:1–7 (8–15)
Psalm 92 (antiphon: v 4)
1 Corinthians 15:42–52 (53–58)
Luke 6:39–49

HYMN OF THE DAY

LSB 819 "Sing Praise to God, the Highest Good"

Mr. Adkisson of Fort Park High School would often say—and he did have a habit of repeating himself—"Destructions are instructions not followed." In the years since, I've come to appreciate why he said that over and over. No doubt he'd repeated over and over the instructions for many an algebra assignment, only to receive back homework that entirely missed the point.

Every teacher, coach, boss, pastor surely understands. You can tell your player not to leave his feet on the head fake, and his man can still take it to the hoop for a layup when he pulls it back down. You can ask your assistant to prepare the data in bar graphs, and you may still be forced to improv in front of the board when the PowerPoint flashes incomprehensible tables of raw numbers. Your confirmation kids can all nod when you show from Scripture that sex is only to be within marriage, but a few years down the line, you still have occasion for Confession and Absolution on this very matter.

It's not that they didn't hear your words.

In the **Verse** for this Eighth Sunday after the Epiphany, Jesus says, "Everyone who comes to Me and hears My words *and does them*, I will show you what he is like" (Lk 6:47). And you know the "like" is going to be a good thing.

These past three Sundays of the Epiphany season, Jesus has been holding forth in the Sermon on the Mount. His words have been an epiphany to many. But some of Jesus' hearers will have a very different, a painful epiphany in store: that we are not just to marvel at Jesus' instruction but follow it. Not just to hear His words but act on them.

Our first instruction from the Lord will be the **Introit**:

> *Trust in Him at all times, O people; pour out your heart before Him; God is a refuge for us.*
>
> *For God alone my soul waits in silence; from Him comes my salvation. He only is my rock and my salvation, my fortress; I shall not be greatly shaken. Once God has spoken; twice have I heard this: that power belongs to God, and that to You, O Lord, belongs steadfast love. For You will render to a man according to his work.*
>
> *Glory be to the Father and to the Son and to the Holy Spirit; as it was in the beginning, is now, and will be forever. Amen.*
>
> *Trust in Him at all times, O people; pour out your heart before Him; God is a refuge for us. (Ps 62:1–2; 11–12; antiphon: Ps 62:8)*

"Once God has spoken; twice have I heard this"—which is a Hebraic way of saying that God actually repeated Himself too. So we wouldn't miss it. We *have* heard. We've heard that God is powerful and God is steadfast, unchanging in His love for us.

What's the "doing" then—"for You will render to a man according to his work"? The doing is this: "Trust in Him at all times, O people"—among other things, but this is first, foremost, and essential to anything else we might do. This is important! When we think about being doers of the Word, it's easy—obviously—to think about things *we do*. And all sorts of good works are certainly part of doing Jesus' words. But chief of all we are to "do" is simply believe in what *He* has done. Another crowd will ask Jesus, "What must we do, to be doing the works of God?" And Jesus will answer them, "This is the work of God, that you *believe* in Him whom He has sent" (Jn 6:28, 29). "Trust in Him at all times."

Trust that "from Him comes my salvation. He only is my rock and my salvation, my fortress." "Rock" is an image used very frequently in the Psalms (over twenty times) to picture God as our protector. Here in the Introit, it anticipates Jesus also using it in the Gospel lesson. The comparison is easy to see: strong, immovable, reliable. Gibraltar. El Capitan. Trusting in my rock, "I shall not be greatly shaken."

Being doers of Jesus' words surely includes prayer. Ideally, prayer is speaking back to God the words He has given us. The historic Collects thus reflect the promises God has made us—as in the **Collect** for this Sunday:

> *O Lord, mercifully hear our prayers and having set us free from the bonds of our sins deliver us from every evil; through Jesus Christ, Your Son, our Lord, who lives and reigns with You and the Holy Spirit, one God, now and forever. Amen.*

We need to be exhorted both to hear and to do what Jesus says. But among God's promises to us is that He will *always* "mercifully *hear*" the prayers we bring before Him through Jesus Christ. And He will *always do* what He promises—forgive our sins and deliver us from evil.

The **Old Testament Reading** begins by pointing us emphatically to "the word," "this word," to "hear the word of the LORD." Notice that in Jeremiah 7:1–15.

Apparently the exhortation to hear the word was necessary. Jeremiah is to address "men of Judah who enter these gates to worship the LORD" (7:2). They were coming into the temple, but it couldn't be assumed that they were truly there to hear what Yahweh had to say. They had bought into "deceptive words" that the temple was a kind of good luck charm, that as long as the temple was standing and they were putting in their appearances, Yahweh was obligated to bless His people. Their mantra: "This is the temple of the LORD, the temple of the LORD, the temple of the LORD" (7:4).

That didn't impress the Lord one bit if they weren't heeding His word spoken there. In fact, if Judah continued on her present path, the great house of God would be destroyed, just as Shiloh, the place of the tabernacle, had been brought to ruin centuries before (7:12–14). For "when I spoke to you persistently you did not listen, and when I called you, you did not answer." They heard with their ears, but they did not do what God commanded them to do.

Do "amend your ways and your deeds" (7:3). *Do* "execute justice one with another" (7:5). "*Do not* oppress the sojourner, the fatherless, or the widow, or shed innocent blood in this place" (7:6a). "*Do no*t go after other gods" (7:6b). *Do not* "steal, murder, commit adultery, swear falsely, make offerings to Baal" (7:9). Otherwise, instruction not followed would lead to destruction of the house in which they were trusting.

In contrast to the "worship" Jeremiah was seeing, the **Psalm** bears the superscription, "A Song for the Sabbath." The Sabbath was for true worship—hearing and doing God's Word. Read Psalm 92.

The psalmist knows that doing the Lord's words is "to give thanks, . . . sing praises, . . . declare [His] steadfast love . . . and faithfulness" (92:1, 2). He will do this because "You, O LORD, have made me glad by Your work" (92:4).

Some of the work God does for us is visible to everyone; much more will become visible in the end. But most we know only through His Word. "Your thoughts are very deep!" (92:5); most of what God is doing for us would escape us. "The fool," reading only the worldly signs rather than hearing God's words, thinks he is flourishing (92:6–7a) when he is actually "doomed to destruction," "downfall" (92:7b, 11). At the same time, God's Word assures us that we are firmly "planted in the house of the LORD" (92:13) and, once again, that "He is my rock" (92:15).

Apart from God's words, we can't grasp this, because, above all, we by our own thinking could never fathom that Jesus dead on a cross is the ultimate exercise of God's power and that because that death has reconciled us to God, God truly is working our good when all seems in collapse. But that's what He teaches us in His Word.

The **Epistle** is the last installment in our Epiphany season walk through the final chapters of 1 Corinthians, once more from Paul's great resurrection chapter. Read 1 Corinthians 15:42–58. It's the ultimate application of Jesus' words in the Gospel.

This body—with this earth, this life—occupied and corrupted by the first Adam, we know so well, and we cling to it. It is "natural" (15:44), and it's natural to us. But Paul describes it in words like "perishable," "dishonor," "weakness," "dust," "mortal" (15:42, 43, 47, 54). That is to say, it's subject to death. Our origin as dust, in particular, contrasts to all the biblical images of the rock; a handful of it blows clean away in the breeze.

But Paul tells us this "mystery": when the trumpet sounds and the last Adam (15:45), the man of heaven (15:48), returns, we will be raised and changed into "imperishable" bodies, given "immortality" (15:50, 53). Death will be "swallowed up in victory" (15:54). Nothing will move us; imperishable, immortal are not subject to destruction.

That's the promise we hear in the Word. And Paul then exhorts us to do so: "Therefore, my beloved brothers, be steadfast, immovable, always abounding in the work of the Lord, knowing that in the Lord your labor is not in vain" (15:58).

Now the final installment of Luke's recording of the Sermon on the Mount: the **Holy Gospel**, Luke 6:39–49.

First we are to be hearers: "A disciple is not above his teacher, but everyone when he is fully trained will be like his teacher" (6:40). Unless we carefully hear, study, learn Jesus' words, we will be just blind leading the blind (6:39).

Then we are to be doers. "No good tree bears bad fruit, nor again does a bad tree bear good fruit" (6:43). Many hear the Good News that Jesus, by His life, death, and resurrection, has earned for them eternal life and never believe it. But the Holy Spirit brings others to faith by the very same words, and when that happens, a new person is created. The new person is "good," and a good person does produce good (6:45).

All those hearing the Sermon on the Mount heard this. So, then, "Why do you call Me 'Lord, Lord' ["The temple of the Lord, the temple of the Lord"?], and not do what I tell you?" (6:46). You can tell your safeties not to bite on the fake, and the receiver will still be long gone when it turns out to be a flea-flicker.

"Everyone who comes to Me and hears My words and does them . . . is like a man building a house, who dug deep and laid the foundation on the rock. And when a flood arose, the stream broke against that house and could not shake it. . . . But the one who hears and does not do them is like a man who built a house on the ground without a foundation. When the stream broke against it, immediately it fell, and the ruin of that house was great" (6:47, 48, 49).

To Some It Will Be an Epiphany That Hearing and Doing Jesus' Words Is Being Built on the Rock.

Thank the Lord that for all doers—all believers—"He is their refuge and their rock" (**Hymn of the Day**, *LSB* 819: 4).

The Transfiguration of Our Lord Year C

READINGS

Deuteronomy 34:1–12
Psalm 99 (antiphon: v 9)
Hebrews 3:1–6
Luke 9:28–36

HYMN OF THE DAY

LSB 413 "O Wondrous Type! O Vision Fair"

It doesn't get any better than this!

Surely Peter felt that way on the Mount of Transfiguration. This was Christmas, the last day of school, and the Fourth of July rolled into one. This was the family trip to Hawaii you'd been saving for for a decade. This was the cruise for your fortieth anniversary. To Peter, this was the climax, where, he was quite certain, it had all been heading and where it all should stay forevermore.

The transfiguration does climax an exciting season of the church year. Each week, beginning with the star and the wise men, we've seen something revealed about Jesus—baptized as the Second Person of the Trinity, His first miracle, more miracles, preaching like no other preacher in history. But the transfiguration pulls out all the stops—Jesus as even Peter and James and John had never seen Him. No wonder Peter was convinced this was the top of the world!

But "It doesn't get any better than this" is almost no one's last words. And "it" almost never stays the same. Either it *does* get better or, well, there's the almost-always alternative.

How about with the transfiguration?

As usual with high festivals, all the propers this Sunday cluster around the day's great event. So if you're not familiar with the transfiguration story, read through it right now: Luke 9:28–36. We'll come back to it later.

Then read the **Introit**:

Blessèd are those who dwell in Your house, ever singing Your praise!

How lovely is Your dwelling place, O Lord *of hosts! My soul longs, yes, faints for the courts of the LORD; my heart and flesh sing for joy to the living God. Behold our shield, O God; look on the face of Your anointed! For the LORD God is a sun and shield; the LORD bestows favor and honor. No good thing does He withhold from those who walk uprightly.*

Glory be to the Father and to the Son and to the Holy Spirit; as it was in the beginning, is now, and will be forever. Amen.

Blessèd are those who dwell in Your house, ever singing Your praise! (Ps 84:1–2, 9, 11; antiphon: Ps 84:4)

The transfiguration took place outdoors on a high, secluded mountain somewhere in Galilee, nowhere near God's temple in Jerusalem. But it's easy to understand how Peter and the others could feel as the psalmist did—that they were in the "house," the "dwelling place," of the Lord. Who needed a temple now? They were looking on the "face of [God's] anointed." Yes, they saw Jesus' face every day—and Peter had just declared Him to be the Anointed One, the Christ, a week earlier (Lk 9:20). But at this moment, they were for the first time seeing Him in His heavenly glory: "For the LORD God is a sun"—and today Jesus looked the part.

We can certainly understand Peter wanting to stay on the mountaintop like this forever: "My soul longs, yes, faints for the courts of the LORD; my heart and flesh sing for joy to the living God." We'd all love every Sunday morning to feel just like this. It doesn't get any better than this!

The **Collect** recalls additional details to come in the transfiguration narrative:

O God, in the glorious transfiguration of Your beloved Son You confirmed the mysteries of the faith by the testimony of Moses and Elijah. In the voice that came from the bright cloud You wonderfully foreshowed our adoption by grace. Mercifully make us co-heirs with the King in His glory and bring us to the fullness of our inheritance in heaven; through the same Jesus Christ, our Lord, who lives and reigns with You and the Holy Spirit, one God, now and forever. Amen.

As if Jesus' glorious appearance wasn't enough, the disciples had to be wowed by the presence of Moses and Elijah, two of the Old Testament's greatest figures. They were the living testimony that the faith Israel had long held—of the Torah (recorded by Moses) and the Prophets (epitomized by Elijah)—was in complete agreement with the mission of this Jesus. And then there was the voice of God speaking from the heavenly cloud. Peter likely hadn't been around the first time the Father had spoken upon His beloved Son—at Jesus' Baptism. (John may have been, and perhaps James too.) But now Peter would never forget it (2 Pet 1:16–18).

A quick side note of interest this week: the **Verse**. Most weeks, we don't mention the Verse separately, because it's generally from the Gospel reading. So when it's selected from elsewhere in Scripture, it bears attention. For Transfiguration, the Verse is Psalm 45:2a: "Alleluia. You are the most handsome of the sons of men; grace is poured upon Your lips. Alleluia." "Most handsome" underscores the singularity of the transfiguration event. While hearers were often taken with the "grace" pouring from Jesus' lips, at no other time during His state of humiliation is His appearance flattered. Isaiah rather pictures Him as having "no form or majesty that we should look at Him, and no beauty that we should desire Him" (Is 53:2).

The **Psalm** hearkens more to Sinai or Mount Zion than specifically to the transfiguration. But see how God works in such an intentional, unified way through history! Read Psalm 99, picturing Moses (99:6) at the holy mountain (99:9), God speaking from the cloud (99:7), and His people in awe: "The Lord reigns! . . . Holy is He! . . . Holy is He! . . . Our God is holy!" (99:1, 3, 5, 9).

The **Old Testament Reading** not only helps explain Moses' presence at the transfiguration, but it also encourages Israel that it *could* get better than what they had. Read Deuteronomy 34:1–12.

Moses had led Israel for forty years—out of Egypt, through the wilderness, to the edge of the Promised Land—despite rebellions and murmurings and apostasies. But in one of those last testings, he himself had broken faith with the Lord (Num 20:2–12), and God had declared that Moses would not enter Canaan. Instead, like the three disciples on their mountain, Moses, on Mount Nebo, receives a glimpse of the glory ahead.

The circumstances of Moses' departure probably prefigure his reappearing over fourteen centuries later. Moses dies without the usual scourge of aging (34:7). The Lord Himself buries him, and the place of his burial is unknown (34:6). Especially intriguing is that Moses is the author of Deuteronomy. Did he write about his own death? Very possibly. The Holy Spirit enabled countless prophets, including Moses, to see the future. Why not this time? On the other hand, nothing in Scripture rules out Joshua or another writer completing the history, and some wholesome evidence might suggest that is the case.

What is significant is the author's hint of someone greater coming: "There has not arisen a prophet *since* in Israel *like Moses*, . . . none like him for all the signs and the wonders that the Lord sent him to do" (34:10, 11). Earlier in Deuteronomy, Moses had promised, "The Lord your God will raise up for you a prophet *like me* from among you . . . —*it is to Him you shall listen*" (18:15). Moses would not be the final, greatest word. Nor would Joshua, the prophet God raised up immediately after Moses, because that Prophet had not come yet when Deuteronomy was first being read. Not until the transfiguration, when the Father would say of Jesus, "Listen to Him!" (Lk 9:35).

By the way, the backstory on the other transfiguration witness, Elijah, is read this day in Year B: 2 Kings 2:1–12. Elijah's departure almost begged for him to appear again.

Yet it did get better than either Moses or Elijah. Read the **Epistle**, Hebrews 3:1–6.

One could make a case for Moses being the second-most significant man in the Bible.

Second-most. As they were ascending the Mount of Transfiguration, Peter, James, and John might have still voted him first! But the author of Hebrews leaves no doubt. Moses: very great!—"faithful in all God's house" . . . "as a servant" (3:2, 5). Jesus: "counted worthy of more glory than Moses—as much more glory as the builder of a house has more honor than the house itself. . . . As a son" (3:3, 6). In the final analysis, Moses' service to God was "to testify to the things that were to be spoken later" (3:5), which brings him to the transfiguration.

So our THEME at this point could well be that Jesus' transfiguration is a climactic epiphany of His all-surpassing glory—blazing, blinding glory, glory greater than that of great Moses and Elijah, the glory of being God's Son. But, then, wouldn't Peter be right? Hold on to this forever! If it can't get any better than this, isn't the alternative all downhill from here? Read the **Holy Gospel**, Luke 9:28–36.

The transfiguration is a prime example of the various Gospels blessing us with different perspectives. Look back if you wish at elements we found to be unique in Matthew and Mark's accounts (devotion-studies on pp 70 and 328). What about Luke?

In all three Synoptic Gospels, we get quite the scene—Jesus' radiance (here "dazzling white"), Moses and Elijah talking with Jesus, the Father's voice. In all three, Peter wants to set up camp and hold on to the moment. And in all three, we're left with one unmistakable conclusion: Jesus stands alone atop *any* mountain (9:36). The race can *only* be for second.

But only Luke sends us back to the conversation that preceded ("after these sayings," 9:28). And only Luke gives us the content of Jesus' present conversation with Moses and Elijah. Both conversations were about "His departure, which He was about to accomplish at Jerusalem" (9:31), for Jesus had previously been telling His disciples that He "must suffer many things and be rejected by the elders and chief priests and scribes, and be killed, and on the third day be raised" (9:22). This, too, is the epiphany of the transfiguration—that the one who possesses surpassing glory would humble Himself to save us. This is how God answers our petition in the Collect: "Mercifully make us co-heirs with the King in His glory and bring us to the fullness of our inheritance in heaven."

In Shakespearean drama, the climax was never the end of the play but the third act of five, not the end, but the point from which the plot descended to resolution. The transfiguration is a climax but not the end, and it will seem to go badly downhill from here. Yet it will, in fact, get better than this!

**JESUS' TRANSFIGURATION
IS A CLIMACTIC EPIPHANY NOT ONLY OF
HIS ALL-SURPASSING GLORY
BUT ALSO OF
HIS DEPARTURE THAT BRINGS US GLORY.**

See the "wondrous type," the "vision fair" once more in the **Hymn of the Day**, *LSB* 413.

A note for next week: Ash Wednesday, the Wednesday immediately following Transfiguration Sunday, uses the same propers for Years A, B, and C. Therefore, you'll find the one devotion-study for Ash Wednesday in Year A on page 74. The devotion-study for next Sunday, the First Sunday in Lent, Year C, appears on the next page.

First Sunday in Lent Year C

READINGS

Deuteronomy 26:1–11
Psalm 91:1–13 (antiphon: v 1)
Romans 10:8b–13
Luke 4:1–13

HYMN OF THE DAY

LSB 656, 657 "A Mighty Fortress Is Our God"

Lent, the great penitential season, calls us to take a long, hard, sober, and contrite look at ourselves. Not so much, "Have I been faithful?"—because the final answer is no—but more, "*In what ways* have I failed to love God and my neighbor?" Not so much, "Am I being obedient to God's commandments?"—because the jury is no longer out on that question—but more, "*Which* temptations continue to trap me time and again?" Penitence means looking in the mirror and confessing that what we see doesn't look good.

The purple paraments, the hymns in minor keys, the stripped-down liturgy (no Alleluias, no Hymn of Praise), even, as one may choose, giving up something to suggest austerity, discipline, pruning anything that may distract us from God and seduce us into sin. The **Gradual** for the season exhorts us to "*fix* our eyes on Jesus"—don't glance, don't blink. Focus.

> *[O come, let us fix our eyes on] Jesus, the founder and perfecter of our faith, who for the joy that was set before Him endured the cross, despising the shame, and is seated at the right hand of the throne of God. (Heb 12:2)*

In looking so carefully, though, let's not *over*look that we are to fix our eyes *on Jesus*. The hard look at ourselves should not mean we look to fix anything ourselves. That's not Lent. And penitence doesn't mean "making up for." All the fixing, all the making up for will be done by Christ.

That's an important distinction to keep in mind on this First Sunday in Lent when the propers derive from the temptation of Christ in the Gospel lesson. We ought to gird ourselves for our own struggles against Satan and confess how badly we've succumbed to temptation. But the real focus is on Christ's victory over the devil in our place.

This week, let's begin right there: the **Holy Gospel**, Luke 4:1–13.

Jesus' forty days in the wilderness (4:1–2) give the season of Lent its shape (forty days, not including Sundays, from Ash Wednesday to Holy Saturday). The original referent is Israel's forty years of wandering in the wilderness on its way to the Promised Land. It was a time of testing for Israel—including hunger.

All three of the devil's temptations begin with "if" (4:3, 7, 9). It's a conditional calling something into question. The first one is particularly pointed. Jesus has just come from His Baptism in the Jordan where God the Father proclaimed Jesus His beloved Son (3:21–22). Now here comes Satan raising doubt: "*If* You are the Son of God, command this stone to become bread" (4:3).

God's curriculum for the Israelites during their time in the wilderness was that they learn He would take care of them, especially feeding them every day with manna. But if Jesus was God's Son, then surely He had every right—and certainly the power—to fend for Himself. "Surely," the devil was smiling, nodding, "the Father would want His Son to exercise His privilege."

No! Jesus knew Israel's lesson perfectly. "Man shall not live by bread alone" (4:4), the Lord had taught Israel through Moses (Deut 8:3). Food wasn't the real issue; God, not bread, is man's life. Israel, Jesus were not to take matters out of His hands into their own. They were simply to receive whatever, whenever God provided them, passively.

Second, the devil offers Jesus "all the kingdoms of the world . . . and their glory, for it has been delivered to me, and I give it to whom I will" (4:5, 6). That wasn't the sham we might think. Our sin did deliver the whole world into Satan's lap; the *world is* his. And hadn't Jesus come to redeem the world? Jesus was going to make the supreme sacrifice to accomplish that anyway, bowing His head to Satan's torture and murder. Why not one little bow down now instead?

No! "You shall worship the Lord your God, . . . only" (4:8). And that's not a matter of bowing head, shoulders, knees. It's bowing to God's plans, designs, ways, schedules. It's trusting that the Lord your God will accomplish His perfect will—even redeeming a world—*for* you and that you just receive it, entirely passively.

Finally, the devil takes Jesus to the pinnacle of the temple in Jerusalem. "If You are the Son of God, throw Yourself down from here," and he uses the Introit and Psalm to justify it (4:9–11). *Now, Jesus, wouldn't that be the ultimate trust in Your Father's care?—and such a powerful witness in front of so many people here at the temple!*

No! Trusting God means believing *everything* He says to us in Scripture, not just a few passages we take out of context to tell us what we want to hear. "You shall not put the Lord your God to the test," He'd also taught Israel (4:12; Deut 6:16). Playing to the crowd wasn't God's plan for Jesus' mission; He'd die abandoned by almost everyone. Jesus would take His assignment exactly as the Father delivered it. And we don't make decisions by picking and choosing even from His Word. We receive, as is, the entire counsel He gives us in Scripture, entirely passively.

None of this is to imply that we aren't active in living out our faith and struggling—very actively!—against temptation. But if we think Jesus' battle with Satan was primarily to show us how *we* can resist temptation, an example for us to follow, we miss the point, and *we're* trying to do the fixing.

It's probably significant that Luke reports this temple temptation, the one temptation in Jerusalem, last. (Matthew presents it second rather than third, Mt 4:5–10.) Luke also adds that, from this scene in Jerusalem, the devil left Jesus only "until an opportune time" (4:13). Luke wants us to anticipate the battle being rejoined *in the same place*. In Luke's Gospel, everything points to Jesus' final visit to Jerusalem.

That, the cross, is, of course, where all of Lent leads. "Jesus, . . . for the joy that was set before Him endured the cross, despising the shame." This we call Jesus' "passive obedience"; He passively (entirely!) allowed Himself to be killed.

But Lent 1 reminds us that before Jesus could be the all-sufficient sacrifice on the cross, He first had to obey God's Law perfectly on behalf of mankind. God's Law was never abrogated; it had to be kept. And since it was given to man, it had to be kept by man. Since we failed, the man Christ stepped in. This is what Jesus was doing in resisting the devil's temptation. We call it Christ's "active obedience"—His active doing of what God's Law demanded. Ironic, isn't it, that Jesus' active obedience was by passively trusting His Father in all things!

This is the point of Jesus facing the devil. Christ has obeyed God, turned away temptation, for us. Jesus has fully accomplished our salvation; all we do now is receive—entirely passively—what He has done.

Jesus' Active Obedience in Resisting the Devil's Temptations Rescues Us Who Can Only Receive Passively from the Lord Our God.

See how our other propers likewise fix our eyes on what the Lord has done for us and encourage us simply to receive.

Read Psalm 91, which gives us both the **Psalm** and the **Introit**:

When he calls to Me, I will answer him; I will be with him in trouble; I will rescue him and honor him. With long life I will satisfy him and show him My salvation.

Because you have made the Lord your dwelling place—the Most High, who is my refuge—no evil shall be allowed to befall you, no plague come near your tent. For He will command His angels concerning you to guard you in all your ways. On their hands they will bear you up, lest you strike your foot against a stone. You will tread on the lion and the adder; the young lion and the serpent you will trample underfoot.

Glory be to the Father and to the Son and to the Holy Spirit; as it was in the beginning, is now, and will be forever. Amen.

When he calls to Me, I will answer him; I will be with him in trouble; I will rescue him and honor him. With long life I will satisfy him and show him My salvation. (Ps 91:9–13; antiphon: Ps 91:15–16)

How sweet it is to "abide in the shadow of the Almighty," to say, "My refuge and my fortress, my God, in whom I trust" (91:1, 2). A mighty fortress is our God! And then, assuming we haven't put the Lord to the test by leaping, how sweet to know His angels will be there should we fall (91:11–12). "You will only look with your eyes and see" what God is doing (91:8). Entirely passive.

Remember Jesus telling the devil you shall worship only "the Lord your God"? Count the number of times the **Old Testament Reading**, Deuteronomy 26:1–11, uses that precious term.

That means He will always be the active giver, His people passive receivers. This reading commands the Israelites, once they've entered their new home, to bring the Lord its firstfruit offerings. But it is the land "that the LORD your God is giving you" (26:1, 2a), at "the place that the Lord your God will choose" (26:2b), that He "swore . . . to give us" (26:3) when our father was just a wanderer and we were "few in number" (26:5). He "brought us out of Egypt with a mighty hand" (26:8) to "a land flowing with milk and honey. . . . Which You, O Lord, have given" (26:9, 10).

Most important, of course, we receive eternal salvation entirely passively. As you read the **Epistle**, Romans 10:8b–13, do you recognize a common error among Christians?

Many Christians will say that two things have to happen to be saved: first, believe, then confess Jesus as Lord. That makes confessing Christ a requirement of our action. In fact, faith, believing, is a gift we receive passively, and confessing Jesus is not a separate act but an oral expression of the very same gift. (Notice in verses 11 and 13 that believing and speaking *each* result in salvation.)

They're received passively because Christ's active obedience in the face of Satan's temptations has done all that's required of us. Luther knew very well in the **Hymn of the Day**, "With might of ours can *naught* be done." "The old evil foe" is too powerful for us. "But for us fights the valiant One!" (*LSB* 656:2).

So we follow Him passively. The **Collect**:

O Lord God, You led Your ancient people through the wilderness and brought them to the promised land. Guide the people of Your Church that following our Savior we may walk through the wilderness of this world toward the glory of the world to come; through Jesus Christ, Your Son, our Lord, who lives and reigns with You and the Holy Spirit, one God, now and forever. Amen.

Second Sunday in Lent Year C

READINGS

Jeremiah 26:8–15
Psalm 4 (antiphon: v 8)
Philippians 3:17–4:1
Luke 13:31–35

HYMN OF THE DAY

LSB 708 "Lord, Thee I Love with All My Heart"

She had cried at his Baptism. It was a joyous occasion—grandparents, siblings, cousins all seated in the front two pews, family pictures afterward, lunch and a whole afternoon together. Their son had been made a member of God's heavenly kingdom. She cried for joy.

But something that was not quite joy had also brought a tear to her eye. It was a line from the hymn they sang: "Oh, blest the parents who give heed unto their children's foremost need and weary not of care or cost. *May none to them and heaven be lost!*" (*LSB* 862:3).

She was quite sure she and her husband had never grown weary of doing or paying whatever their kids had needed. Well, actually, she'd been plenty weary plenty of times, but that was weary of a different kind. They especially never tired of bringing him to church, helping him with confirmation work, encouraging him to choose a faithful Lutheran bride.

Now it wasn't a few tears welling up. Now sometimes she couldn't stop crying. Perhaps no emotion could be more intense than a Christian mother aching for her son who'd given up his faith.

"O Jerusalem, Jerusalem! . . . How often would I have gathered your children together as a hen gathers her brood under her wings, and you were not willing!" (Lk 13:34).

Other than in prayer in the Garden of Gethsemane, we never see Jesus as intensely emotional as He is in this week's Gospel reading. A mother would understand. So might a father. Jesus wants no one to be lost, and He's going to do everything possible to see that no one is. When there is rejection, He will ache.

The propers this week reflect this intense emotion. That's because the pain is so deep when someone we love might be lost to heaven. And because of God's love, His longing to save every soul is so very, very intense.

That's evident right away in the **Introit**:

> *For zeal for Your house has consumed me, and the reproaches of those who reproach You have fallen on me.*
>
> *O God, why do You cast us off forever? Why does Your anger smoke against the sheep of Your pasture? Remember Your congregation, which You have purchased of old, which You have redeemed to be the tribe of Your heritage! Remember Mount Zion, where You have dwelt. Direct Your steps to the perpetual ruins; the enemy has destroyed everything in the sanctuary!*
>
> *Glory be to the Father and to the Son and to the Holy Spirit; as it was in the beginning, is now, and will be forever. Amen.*
>
> *For zeal for Your house has consumed me, and the reproaches of those who reproach You have fallen on me. (Ps 74:1–3; antiphon: Ps 69:9)*

The antiphon may ring familiar from a different moment of Jesus' intense emotions, a different emotion. John quotes Psalm 69 to explain Jesus' zeal in cleansing the temple (Jn 2:17). The temple was the place God was most intimately with His people, where His love for them came down to earth. To desecrate God's house, as the merchants and moneychangers were doing, was to trample on that love, to scorn that relationship. Jesus couldn't stand it!

The psalmist writes of a time the house of the Lord has been desolated: "Perpetual ruins; the enemy has destroyed everything in the sanctuary!" And he pleads, "O God, why do You cast us off forever?" Yet he knows that God will not cast off those who repent: "Remember Your congregation, which You have purchased of old. . . . Remember Mount Zion [the site of the temple], where You have dwelt." The psalmist knows the Lord will always receive back His penitents.

The **Old Testament Reading** calls God's people to repent—to save both them and His house. Read Jeremiah 26:8–15.

"This house shall be like Shiloh, and this city shall be desolate, without inhabitant" (26:9). Shiloh was the location where the tabernacle had been settled when Israel first entered the Promised Land (Josh 18:1, about eight hundred years before Jeremiah) and had remained the site of God's house for several centuries, through most of the period of the judges. But then the wicked sons of Eli, the high priest, had disdained the Lord's holy things, and God had allowed Shiloh and the tabernacle to be overrun (1 Sam 2:12–17, 22; 4:1–11). In the centuries since, Shiloh had become proverbial as a symbol of abandonment and disgrace (Ps 78:54–64; Jer 7:12).

The priests, the prophets, and the people were furious at Jeremiah for threatening such disaster on the present temple (26:8). It wasn't just seen as disloyal, unpatriotic, or discouraging; prophesying was seen as *making* the event happen, not simply predicting it. They heard Jeremiah as calling down a curse that itself might bring the ruin. One can almost feel the rumbling music and the drumbeat crescendo of the movie soundtrack as the mob assembled around Jeremiah. The prophet knows he's on trial for his life.

His purpose, though, was *not* Jerusalem's destruction. "The Lord" has indeed "sent me to prophesy against this house and this city," but only so that you will "mend your ways and your deeds, and obey the voice of the Lord your God." If you do, "the Lord will relent of the disaster that He has pronounced against you" (26:12, 13). This is always God's intent in speaking hard words of rebuke or condemnation. He desires earnestly, desperately that His people would repent and He could lift His sentence. Jeremiah is in earnest too. In fact, he's willing to die in order to deliver this message (26:14–15). Saving Jerusalem, the temple, and God's people would be worth his death.

In this case, Jeremiah is spared. The officials and even the crowd are moved by God's warning (26:16–24). Sadly, in the years ahead, there would be more sin, a refusal to repent, the destruction of the temple, and, likely, Jeremiah stoned by his own people.

In the **Psalm**, David is angry, even trembles, over sin he sees. Read Psalm 4.

Surely it's in frustration that David asks, "How long will you love vain words and seek after lies?" (4:2). He's intensely distressed at what's going on around him. He's probably exhorting *himself,* "Be angry, and do not sin" (4:4). *When you're this upset, David—and rightfully so—channel that emotion in a holy way.*

Rather than *sinful* anger at evil in the world, we call the sinner to repentance. We know it's for his or her blessing. "There are many who say, 'Who will show us some good?'" (4:6), and we have an answer. When there is repentance, much good follows. "You have put more joy in my heart than they have when their grain and wine abound" (4:7). That is, a sinner who has been corrected and humbled and then repents often knows greater joy than one who continues merrily on in prosperity (grain and wine abounding) and never realizes his dangerous predicament. It's the sinner who's been brought to repentance and then assured of forgiveness for the sake of Jesus' death and resurrection who can truly say, "In peace I will both lie down and sleep; for You alone, O Lord, make me dwell in safety" (4:8).

Paul's letter to the Philippians exudes great joy, but he, too, weeps for those who have fallen away. Read the **Epistle**, Philippians 3:17–4:1.

Paul is very much aware of the threats to faith and of the need to persevere. Shortly before our lesson, he wrote, "Not that I have already obtained this or am already perfect. . . . I press on toward the goal for the prize of the upward call of God in Christ Jesus" (3:12, 14). In particular, Paul is alert to the threat of "those who mutilate the flesh" (3:2)—those who demanded that Christians be circumcised and keep the Old Testament law in order to be saved—Judaizers. They claimed to be followers of Christ; perhaps at first, some had been. But now they have become "enemies of the cross of Christ" because they made Jesus' death insufficient for salvation. See how intensely this hurts Paul: "I . . . tell you even with tears" (3:18).

It's a stern preaching of the Law! "Their end is destruction" (3:19). But it's meant to preserve in faith those who hear. "Our citizenship is in heaven." Therefore, against all the ways the world would mislead, "we await a Savior, the Lord Jesus Christ, who will" one day take us there in glorious bodies like His (3:20, 21). And for this, Paul is just as urgent: "Therefore, my brothers, whom I love and *long for*, my joy and crown, stand firm thus in the Lord, my beloved" (4:1).

Yet no one feels this longing for His loved ones as intensely as the Lord Jesus Himself: the **Holy Gospel**, Luke 13:31–35.

From Luke 9:51 on, Jesus has been traveling to Jerusalem where He knows He will meet His death. In fact, Herod would have had to wait in line to do the deed; the Pharisees (as well as the chief priests) were far more bent on destroying Jesus. Almost surely this "helpful" warning from the Pharisees was to frighten Jesus off, to discredit Him if He ran.

It's quite irrelevant to Jesus. Nothing would deter Him; He *would* go all the way to finish His course. The "third day" (13:32) may even refer to His resurrection. "I *must* go" (13:33a). This is that Greek word δεῖ, *dei*, which indicates a necessity even Jesus must follow. Why? Because even God Himself is bound by His own love, His own commitment to redeem us. That would take Jesus' death, and by God's design, for this Prophet, too, it would have to be in Jerusalem (13:33b).

By God's gracious choice, Jerusalem had always been the apple of His eye (Zech 2:7–8)—the place of His kings, of the temple, and, soon now, of His saving the world. Such honor! And in deepest fervor, He wished for that to be accomplished to her glory, not infamy. "O Jerusalem, Jerusalem! . . . How often . . ." The Father, the Son longed for it—as a mother would understand. But "you were not" (Lk 13:34).

The place would be desolate, like Shiloh: "Your house is forsaken" (13:35a). Still, Jesus would come. There would be those who would say, "Blessed is He who comes in the name of the Lord!" (13:35b; 19:35–38), and some of those would cling to Him in faith. To Jesus, they were worth it, even though it meant His death.

The Lord's Prophet
So Longs to Bless Zion
Rather Than Forsake Shiloh
That He Will Go All the Way
to Death.

Pray the **Collect** as the brood with "no strength" defended against all assaults on our faith by the mother hen:

O God, You see that of ourselves we have no strength. By Your mighty power defend us from all adversities that may happen to the body and from all evil thoughts that may assault and hurt the soul; through Jesus Christ, Your Son, our Lord, who lives and reigns with You and the Holy Spirit, one God, now and forever. Amen.

The **Hymn of the Day**, "Lord, Thee I Love with All My Heart" (*LSB* 708), is also intensely emotional.

Third Sunday in Lent Year C

READINGS

Ezekiel 33:7–20
Psalm 85 (antiphon: v 8)
1 Corinthians 10:1–13
Luke 13:1–9

HYMN OF THE DAY

LSB 823, 824 "May God Bestow on Us His Grace"

If you were to enter into your computer all the words of our propers for Lent 3, Year C, and then ask it to produce a word cluster diagram, one word that we use seldom in conversation would jump out as surprisingly prominent. Five times our propers use the word *perish*—along with another cluster of synonyms like *die*, *death*, *destroy*, *fall*, and *fell*. It's a grim graphic indeed!

We've observed before that the Verse is usually quite near to an overall theme for the Sunday and that it most often comes from the Gospel lesson so that when it comes from elsewhere in Scripture, it especially shouts for attention. That's certainly the case this week, with our **Verse** not coming from any of the other propers: "[The Lord] is patient toward you, not wishing that any should perish, but that all should reach repentance" (2 Pet 3:9b, c). There's "perish." But there's also the deliverance of all the propers—and, far more important, our deliverance!—from their otherwise grim reaping. As we hear all those perishes and dies and falls this week, listen also for the Lord's patience and pleasure in our salvation. That calls us to another prominent cluster in the diagram: "Repent!" "Turn!"

Let no one take this lightly! It's first of all a warning from the Lord! The **Introit**:

> *For the Lord knows the way of the righteous, but the way of the wicked will perish.*
>
> *For You are not a God who delights in wickedness; evil may not dwell with You. The boastful shall not stand before Your eyes; You hate all*

evildoers. You destroy those who speak lies; the Lord abhors the bloodthirsty and deceitful man. But I, through the abundance of Your steadfast love, will enter Your house. I will bow down toward Your holy temple in the fear of You. Lead me, O Lord, in Your righteousness because of my enemies; make Your way straight before me.

Glory be to the Father and to the Son and to the Holy Spirit; as it was in the beginning, is now, and will be forever. Amen.

For the Lord knows the way of the righteous, but the way of the wicked will perish. (Ps 5:4–8; antiphon: Ps 1:6)

We know that perishing is never good. Sometimes we use *perish* as a euphemism to soften the blow of death: "They perished at sea." But it's not a soft landing. When our texts speak of perishing, it's not as tidy as simply dying. Yes, death is what we see—and it may come at a ripe old age and appear quite peaceful. What we won't see is the eternal torment that the psalmist knows is in store. To perish in the sense that our propers mean is to lose forever all that one has by God's gracious creating and sustaining. Every blessing one has ever had will expire—including God's protection from the horrific imaginations of the evil one.

And "the wicked will perish." "Evil may not dwell with" the Lord. "The boastful shall not stand before [His] eyes." This is a certainty! For God "hates," "abhors," will "destroy" evildoers. Hard words! But God's Word.

These, though, are also God's words, inspired by the Holy Spirit for the psalmist to speak with equal certainty: "But I, through the abundance of Your steadfast love, will enter Your house." God's "steadfast love," from the Hebrew חֶסֶד, *chesed*, is how we who are by nature evil do not perish. God's love for us does not waver, is not shaken when we sin. He never ceases to want us back. Rather, He constantly calls us to repent, and when there is sorrow for our sin and faith in Christ, the Lord's Savior, He knows us as "the righteous."

Because God truly desires that sinners repent, He sends men to speak His warning. Our **Old Testament Reading** is Ezekiel 33:7–20.

"If I say, . . . and you do not speak" (33:8). The Lord speaks, and we don't. It happens all the time. *God*, in Holy Scripture, *says*, "I hate divorce" (e.g., Mal 2:16). Then our friends, our family members, our church members divorce, and we say nothing. Or *we* get unscriptural divorces, and the Christians on whom we should rely for a sobering word from the Lord don't warn us. "Let the marriage bed be undefiled," *God says* (Heb 13:4). Then our children or our sorority sisters are having sex before marriage, and we and maybe even their pastor say nothing. Or he does sound the warning, and we won't support him, because surely, we think, in this day and age, God must be a little flexible on such things. *God says* that when "women [exchange] natural relations for those that are contrary to nature" and "men [commit] shameless acts with men," they receive "the due penalty" (Rom 1:26, 27). Then same-sex marriage and transgenderism become accepted in our society, and we go quietly along so that our own kids never learn what's right and wrong. It won't turn out well. God's Word on this does not change. "That wicked person shall die in his iniquity, but his blood I will require at your hand" (Ez 33:8b). By saying nothing, we're only allowing those sinners for whom Christ died to perish. And we ourselves are guilty.

This, we see, is a vital warning even for us who are believers: "The righteousness of the righteous shall not deliver him when he transgresses. . . . If he trusts in his righteousness and does injustice, . . . he shall die" (33:12, 13).

On the other hand, you may be a faithful watchman, speaking God's warning firmly and lovingly. It won't make you popular, but "if you warn the wicked to turn from his way, . . ." and "he turns from his sin and does what is just and right, . . . he shall surely live; he shall not die" (33:9, 14, 15). This is what you want.

Much more, it's what God wants: "As I live, declares the Lord GOD, I have no pleasure in the death of the wicked, but that the wicked turn from his way and live; turn back, turn back from your evil ways, for why will you die, O house of Israel?" (33:11).

All God's spokesmen have this task of warning. In the **Epistle**, Paul reports "examples for us, that we might not desire evil" (1 Cor 10:6) as Israel did. Read 1 Corinthians 10:1–13.

No nation in history experienced God's presence as dramatically as the Israelites God brought out of Egypt (10:1–4)—witness the pillar of cloud (Ex 13:21), parting of the Red Sea (Ex 14:21), manna (Ex 16:13–15), and water from a rock (Ex 17:6). It was Christ Himself traveling with them every step of the way (10:4b). Yet most of them "were overthrown [perished!] in the wilderness" (10:5). Idolatry (Ex 32:1–6), sexual immorality (Num 25:1–9), testing the Lord (Num 21:4–6), grumbling (Num 16:41–49) led to their destruction. But the problem now isn't *their* sin. This was "written down for *our* instruction" (10:11). "Let anyone who thinks that he stands take heed lest he fall" (10:12).

On our own, we will fall for the same temptations. So do not struggle alone! "God is faithful"—that is, patient, steadfast—"and He will not let you be tempted beyond your ability, but with the temptation He will also provide the way of escape" (10:13). This very warning from God's Word, a timely rebuke from a brother or sister in Christ, or perhaps a holy alternative to sin—these are the ways of escape God is providing to deliver us from temptation. But when we do fall, our Lord remains faithful, steadfast; He provides another escape: we, too, are baptized, partake of the spiritual food and drink—which is the crucified Christ (10:2–4). The cross of Jesus shows that God wishes no one to perish. His desire is always that we repent and be saved.

God's desire is always our repentance. But *unless you repent* . . . Read the **Holy Gospel**, Luke 13:1–9.

Those must have been particularly heinous sinners—those Galileans, those folks on whom the tower fell. Pilate, the Roman governor, the same Pontius Pilate who would soon condemn Jesus, was not only cruel, but he was capricious, suddenly heavy-handed for no apparent reason. A tower falls on these, not on others, for no apparent reason. So the reason must have been some great wickedness known only to God. We sometimes think that way too. They must have had it coming.

But, no! That's not it at all. You *equally* have it coming! "Unless *you* repent, you will all likewise perish" (13:3). Repeat: "Unless you repent, you will all likewise *perish*" (13:5). And, no, you don't have to go digging in your secret soul for some unconfessed sin long ago. This is just the way you (all!) are. By nature, we're wicked to the core! Hard words! But Jesus' words. Fight it? Protest? Make a case for your defense? Forget it. Unless you repent, you will perish.

So, Jesus pleads, give it up. And see the patience of His steadfast love. That's the point of the parable (13:6–9). The time to cut us down, fruitless as by nature we are, was long past. But, "Sir, let it alone this year also, until I dig around it and put on manure" (13:8). Let me do *everything possible*, yes, even a little longer. Let me break my back to save this tree . . . *even if I perish.*

God's hard words—words like *perish*—calling us to repent are always intended to save us because Christ has forgiven our sins by His death and resurrection. This is about as clear as Law and Gospel can get!

"Then if [the tree] should bear fruit next year, well and good; *but if not*, you can cut it down" (13:9). Let it never be! Turn! Repent!

It's exactly as Peter said in the Verse:

The Lord Is Patient Toward You, Not Wishing That Any Should Perish but That All Should Reach Repentance.

We've saved a beautiful expression of this: the **Psalm**, Psalm 85. Appreciate especially the chiasm in verses 10–11:

A [God's] steadfast love [*chesed*] and
B faithfulness [He produces in us] meet;
C [His] righteousness and
C′ peace [Christ brings] kiss each other.
B′ Faithfulness [He produces in us] springs up from the ground, and
A′ [His] righteousness looks down from the sky.

We sinners are able to come in repentance to God who cannot tolerate sin because His righteousness has been kissed by the peace with God Jesus won on the cross.

We pray that all are brought to penitence, for the threats of God's Word are unchangeable, but so is His mercy. The **Collect**:

> *O God, whose glory it is always to have mercy, be gracious to all who have gone astray from Your ways and bring them again with penitent hearts and steadfast faith to embrace and hold fast the unchangeable truth of Your Word; through Jesus Christ, Your Son, our Lord, who lives and reigns with You and the Holy Spirit, one God, now and forever. Amen.*

It is God's "gracious will and pleasure" that all "His saving health may know"—Luther's mission hymn and the **Hymn of the Day**, *LSB* 823 and 824.

Fourth Sunday in Lent Year C

READINGS

Isaiah 12:1–6
Psalm 32 (antiphon: v 11)
2 Corinthians 5:16–21
Luke 15:1–3, 11–32

HYMNS OF THE DAY

LSB 571 "God Loved the World So That He Gave"
or LSB 972 "I Trust, O Christ, in You Alone"

Occasionally I'll hear a pastor say, "I don't use illustrations in my sermons." That always makes me chuckle. To begin with, it's almost surely not true. Everybody—in conversations as well as in sermons—uses analogies, descriptions, quotations, statistics—all of which make excellent sermon illustrations. What the pastor is probably thinking is that "illustrations" only means stories, and if he's convinced "I'm not a very good storyteller," then not using them is probably a good call.

A little more troublesome is when the pastor says he doesn't use illustrations because "all they remember is the illustration, not the point."

Take that one up with Jesus.

I really doubt any of us would prefer a world in which Jesus had never told the parable (sermon illustration, story even) of the Prodigal Son. All of us remember that story. Some folks, of course, do miss the point. But perhaps few words ever spoken more powerfully drive home and make memorable that God steadfastly loves and forgives sinners. In fact, the better we remember the last part of the parable, the more likely we are to remember the rest of the point.

Admittedly, Jesus is a brilliant storyteller! As well as we know the parable of the prodigal son, it's so rich that we probably notice something new each time we encounter it. Read it again, the **Holy Gospel** for the Fourth Sunday in Lent, Luke 15:1–3, 11–32.

The setting is important (15:1–3): Jesus addressing Pharisees and scribes, who resented Him associating with notorious sinners. Then intervening before our parable are two other parables, the Lost Sheep (15:4–7) and the Lost

Coin (15:8–10). Both make the point that heaven rejoices when a lost sinner repents and is won back. The naysayers should have gotten the message. But in case their hearts were still hard, Jesus says, essentially, "Let's make this personal. We're not really talking about a sheep or coin. Think about your son."

"Father, give me the share of property that is coming to me" (15:12). The younger son puts Dad in a tough situation. The older son would traditionally inherit the family real estate; couldn't break that up. "So, Pop, somehow, on short notice, with no time to do any long-term financial planning, give me cash. Oh, and in case you didn't get the hint, old man, what I'm really saying is I'd rather have you dead now than having to wait."

Incredibly, Dad does it.

But it doesn't last long. "Reckless living" (15:13) perhaps did include the prostitutes the older son later charges (15:30). And when the next recession hits, the kid is flat busted. Flippin' burgers is honorable, gainful employment; nowadays, so is feeding pigs. Not back then (15:15). God's people were forbidden to touch pigs, eat pigs, so this is not only a social but a spiritual disgrace. "Get your face out of that slop bucket, boy. Pigs gotta eat!"

"He was longing . . ." (15:16).

"*Good morning! What am I doing here?* My father's servants have plenty. Eating crow is at least eating! I will arise and go to my father, and I will say to him, 'Father, I have sinned against heaven and before you. I am no longer worthy to be called your son. Treat me as one of your hired servants'" (15:18–19).

The Law has done its work. The boy now understands what we all should grasp: that we've sinned against God, wished He were out of the picture so we could do whatever we wanted, and that living on our own surely leaves us eternally destitute and hopeless. The Law has done its work . . . but the Law has done all that it *can* do.

"But while he was still a long way off, his father saw him" (15:20b). He just happened to look up at the right moment? Probably not the picture. See instead the father going out every day, looking to the north or south or east or west, whichever direction his son had headed out, hoping, praying that he'd come back—and that this might be the day. This parable of the prodigal son is rightly often called the Waiting Father.

He was longing!

And today his prayers are answered! He "felt compassion, and ran and embraced [his son] and kissed him" (15:20c).

So the boy starts his spiel, just as he's rehearsed: ". . . sinned. . . . I am no longer worthy . . ." (15:21). But notice that the father cuts him off (15:22). He won't hear another word. The confession, "I have sinned; I'm unworthy"—that much is good and proper and ought to be spoken. It's the contrition the Law is supposed to bring. But that's all the Law can bring. As long as we're still living under the Law, all we can imagine is the son's would-be next line: "Treat me as one of your hired servants." "I'll try somehow to pay it off, earn my way back into your good graces." No can do. Never can. The father knows it, and that's not the way he wants it anyway. You, dear son, say no more. The work of the Law is done. From here, only the Gospel can close the deal.

And that's for the father to say: "Bring quickly the best robe"—no doubt one the patriarch himself would wear for festive occasions—"and put it on him, and put a ring on his hand"—a symbol of the family name, maybe even the father's signet—"and shoes on his feet. And bring the fattened calf"—not just *a* fattened calf, any one, but *"the"* calf we've been preparing, praying for just this occasion!—"and kill it, and let us eat and celebrate. For this my son was dead, and is alive again; he was lost, and is found" (15:22–24). Pure, sweet Gospel! Joy in heaven over one sinner who repents!

What an illustration of our heavenly Father's patient, waiting, forgiving love for us!

And then there's the last part of the parable we might *not* remember. The older son hears the good news and refuses to join the party. Here we see not only Jesus' genius as a sermon illustrator but perhaps His real intent in portraying the depth of the Father's love. To this stubborn, recalcitrant son, *too*, "his father *came out* and entreated" (15:28).

Turns out, for all these years, the older son has felt he's been slaving away under a master: "Look, these many years I have served you, and I never disobeyed your command, yet you never gave me a young goat, that I might celebrate with my friends" (15:29). That means he's never understood his relationship with his father: "Son, you are always with me, and *all that is mine is yours*" (15:31). "You're not an employee, an assistant manager. You're my son. I'm your dad. A young goat, a dozen young goats, a whole herd of fattened calves—they've been yours for the feasting all along."

Israel, the Jews, Pharisees, scribes—this is how God has *always* loved you! He still does! He doesn't want you to live by a religion of works, slaving for Him. He deeply desires that you're on board with Him and His love, for you, for all! "It was fitting to celebrate and be glad, for this your brother was dead, and is alive; he was lost, and is found" (15:32). The Greek is actually stronger: ἔδει, from *dei*, more literally translates, "It was *necessary*." God's patient, waiting, forgiving love for us *prodigals necessitates* us *older sons* to love and forgive every other prodigal.

Do you see Jesus' genius? In one and the same illustration, *we* are prodigals, wandering sinners who are welcomed back, *and* if we forget we're prodigals, *we* will quickly become older sons who refuse to forgive—which sin makes us prodigals again. We never escape the role of sinner, but we are never beyond the forgiveness of God's love.

See just how far this illustration reaches in application. Do you recognize the **Introit**?

Have mercy on me, O God, according to Your steadfast love; according to Your abundant mercy blot out my transgressions.

Wash me thoroughly from my iniquity, and cleanse me from my sin! For I know my transgressions, and my sin is ever before me. Against You, You only, have I sinned and done what is evil in Your sight, so that You may be justified in Your words and blameless in Your judgment. Behold, I was brought forth in iniquity, and in sin did my mother conceive me. Behold, You delight in truth in the inward being, and You teach me wisdom in the secret heart.

Glory be to the Father and to the Son and to the Holy Spirit; as it was in the beginning, is now, and will be forever. Amen.

Have mercy on me, O God, according to Your steadfast love; according to Your abundant mercy blot out my transgressions. (Ps 51:2–6; antiphon: Ps 51:1)

Psalm 51 is the great penitential psalm of one of Scripture's greatest prodigals. King David squandered his sacred trust as anointed ruler of God's people in his sins of adultery and murder (2 Samuel 11). Yet the Lord put away his sin (2 Sam 12:13) so that David could extol God's "mercy," "abundant mercy" that will blot out transgressions.

Likewise,the **Collect**:

Almighty God, our heavenly Father, Your mercies are new every morning; and though we deserve only punishment, You receive us as Your children and provide for all our needs of body and soul. Grant that we may heartily acknowledge Your merciful goodness, give thanks for all Your benefits, and serve You in willing obedience; through Jesus Christ, Your Son, our Lord, who lives and reigns with You and the Holy Spirit, one God, now and forever. Amen.

By our Father's mercies, we who deserve only punishment are received as children. May we willingly obey Him by receiving others.

Especially does the **Psalm** track with the prodigal, the father, and the older son. Read Psalm 32. In silent impenitence, the prodigal wasted away (32:3–4). But when he said, "I will confess my transgression to [my father]," he forgave the iniquity of his son's sin (32:5). Meanwhile, like a horse or a mule, the older son stubbornly resents (32:9) when it is fitting, necessary to be glad and rejoice (32:11).

The **Old Testament Reading**, Isaiah 12:1–6. Though God was angry with us, His anger is turned away. That compels us to "let this be made known in all the earth" (12:5).

Paul summarizes *"all this"* in 2 Corinthians 5:16–21, our **Epistle**, as reconciliation, "that is, in Christ God was reconciling the world to Himself, not counting their trespasses against them" (5:19). Father reconciled to prodigal, goes out to older son, declares that all that is His is yours, all this, because the cross of Jesus Christ has reconciled us to Him.

All this, "and entrusting to us the message of reconciliation. Therefore, we are ambassadors for Christ, God making His appeal through us" (5:19–20).

The Father's Abundant Mercy on Us in Christ Necessitates Us Also Being Ambassadors of Reconciliation.

The two options this week for the **Hymn of the Day**: *LSB* 571 or 972. The latter is only available digitally.

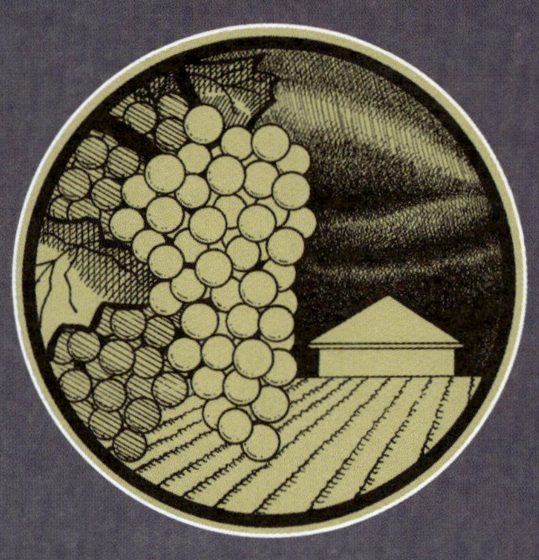

Fifth Sunday in Lent Year C

READINGS

Isaiah 43:16–21
Psalm 126 (antiphon: v 3)
Philippians 3:(4b–7) 8–14
Luke 20:9–20

HYMN OF THE DAY

LSB 430 "My Song Is Love Unknown"

I've always tipped my hat to my grandma, more and more so the older I've gotten. Grandma received "the upward call of God in Christ Jesus" at age 88, but right up to her last days on earth, she liked new things. "They do everything so much better these days," she often used to say. She may have been a bit overly optimistic. (Ask *your* grandma about refrigerators that used to last the whole life of a marriage—which, of course, meant fifty or sixty years.) But she was a delightful alternative to the stereotypical curmudgeon who rags on everything new and is always pining for the good old days. For many of us, especially as we get older, the one constant is resistance to change. Grandma always felt that something new and good was coming. What a great way to live! Behind it, ultimately, was a beautiful faith that, because of Christ Jesus, God would always take good care of her.

Our propers for the Fifth Sunday in Lent tell us that God is doing something new, and it's very good. It richly blesses us. Certainly, though, it's to be embraced, lest by clinging to the old, we miss out entirely.

The first proper we'll hear Sunday will be the **Introit**—select verses from Psalm 3:

Salvation belongs to the Lord; Your blessing be on Your people!

But You, O Lord, are a shield about me, my glory, and the lifter of my head. I cried aloud to the Lord, and He answered me from His holy hill. I lay down and slept; I woke again, for the Lord sustained me. I will not be afraid of many thousands of people who have set themselves against me all around.

Glory be to the Father and to the Son and to the Holy Spirit; as it was in the beginning, is now, and will be forever. Amen.

Salvation belongs to the Lord; Your blessing be on Your people! (Ps 3: 3–6; antiphon: Ps 3:8)

Focus on the antiphon: "Salvation belongs to the Lord; Your blessing be on Your people!" Sounds like a nice, general statement that Yahweh saves. But it's really emphasizing *to whom* salvation belongs and *to whom* the owner gives it. "Salvation belongs to the Lord" means it doesn't belong to anyone who'd wish to seize it for themselves. And the Lord *gives it* to *His* people, whoever His people truly are. In our Gospel lesson, Jesus will deliver a deadly-serious warning to some who thought salvation belonged to them, not to the Lord. They clung to an old idea about who would be God's people. They were rejecting the new thing the Lord was doing.

The **Collect**, this Sunday as every Sunday, is a prayer of God's new people, "Your people":

Almighty God, by Your great goodness mercifully look upon Your people that we may be governed and preserved evermore in body and soul; through Jesus Christ, Your Son, our Lord, who lives and reigns with You and the Holy Spirit, one God, now and forever. Amen.

Since salvation belongs to the Lord, those people who are truly His recognize that all blessings are by His "great goodness," never by our claim or right. In fact, we pray that we would live under Him ("governed" by Him, not free agents) and depend on Him ("preserved" by His goodness, admitting we are never self-sufficient).

Now the **Old Testament Reading** will make explicit Sunday's language of "old things" and "a new thing": Isaiah 43:16–21.

"Remember not the former things, nor consider the things of old. Behold, I am doing a new thing" (43:18–19a). Isaiah doesn't tell us what those old and new things are, but we get the clear message that the new will be amazing. In former times, God worked miracles as magnificent as parting the Red Sea ("a path in the mighty waters," 43:16) and extinguishing Pharaoh's army ("chariot and horse, army and warrior," 43:17). By doing so (as well as by ten plagues, the giving of the Law at Mount Sinai, and driving out the Canaanite nations), God took a people, Israel, to be His. In the future, though, what He does will be so impressive that even "the wild beasts will honor [Him], the jackals and the ostriches" (43:20). The implication: if the Lord's new thing wows brute beasts, how will any thinking, eyes-to-see, ears-to-hear human being "not perceive it"? (43:19b). It'll be sad to discover.

Nevertheless, He will always form for Himself a "chosen people" who will "declare My praise" (43:20, 21). Who will they be?

At various times in Israel's history, it appeared unlikely that God's people would endure. Read this week's **Psalm**, Psalm 126.

The dating of this psalm is uncertain, but one scenario "when the LORD restored the fortunes of Zion" (126:1a) is vivid. Picture the joy of those who returned from captivity in Babylon. Dragged away in chains from their homeland, Jerusalem in ruins, marched over eight hundred miles to a land of unknown speech and scenery, they could never have imagined this. This sort of thing just didn't happen. The ancient empires had subjugated countless tribes and kingdoms, deported them to slavery, and that was the end. Never heard from again, their histories never written, perhaps only a few artifacts to prove they ever existed.

But not the people of Yahweh. It would only have been the youngest of those taken captive who were still able to make the return trip when Cyrus of Persia released the Jews in 538 BC. But now here they were, viewing rubble, sure enough, but home. "We were like those who dream. Then our mouth was filled with laughter, and our tongue with shouts of joy. . . . The LORD has done great things for us; we are glad" (126:1b–2a, 3).

Remember not the former things—the grief, the desperation of Zion. The Lord was giving His people a fresh start. But let it be clear that this new thing was purely by God's grace. There was a reason He had sent His people into captivity. Salvation belongs to the Lord.

Notice the agrarian image (126:6) that will recur in the Gospel. The blessing of restoration should naturally produce fruit.

Paul had an especially personal sense of the value of God's new thing versus old. Read the **Epistle**: Philippians 3:4b–14.

The fact is, God's people, all the way back to Adam and Eve, were saved by God's new thing. But in the Old Testament, the Lord commanded Israel to live out its faith in some very specific ways, the ceremonial law, and, with few exceptions, it was only those born into the family of Israel who ever learned that law. That was an old thing. Never did one's keeping of the law save; salvation belongs to the Lord. But many an Israelite lost that understanding. Paul knew very well that many of his countrymen thought salvation did belong to those who kept the law.

When it came to those old things, few could top Paul (3:4b–6). He was indeed born into the proper family, Israel; his tribe, Benjamin, had even produced Israel's first king, his own namesake, Saul. He was circumcised as required. "A Hebrew of Hebrews" means he was exemplary in his behavior—and he was of the strictest sect; the Pharisees were the "conservatives" when it came to interpreting the demands of the Torah. So zealous was he that he pursued to the death folks like Stephen, who followed that "flaming liberal," Jesus of Nazareth—whose new ways threatened the "old-time religion." Bottom line, if righteousness before God had been based on keeping the law, Paul was "blameless."

But Paul had since come to realize that "a righteousness of my own that comes from the law" was indeed a misunderstanding of old things. The new thing—which had actually been the Lord's salvation from the beginning—was righteousness, "which comes through faith in Christ" (3:9). The rest, Paul now knew, was by comparison rubbish (3:8). (The Greek word here, σκύβαλα, *skubala*, potentially reeks of the outhouse.) God's new thing—ask Paul, ask Isaiah—is powered by Christ's suffering, death, and resurrection (3:10). Just as salvation had always been, but now He had arrived to accomplish it—and for all to see. It's how we, too, "attain the resurrection from the dead" (3:11).

So, Paul reminds us, "I press on to make it my own" that I not lose the prize—lose the prize by clinging to old things. For it doesn't work that way. "*Christ Jesus* has made me *His own*" (3:12); salvation belongs to the Lord. "Forgetting what lies behind, . . . I press on [to what lies ahead] . . . the upward call of God in Christ Jesus" (3:13, 14).

Grandma knew the new thing coming would be good.

If only everyone did. Read the **Holy Gospel** for Lent 5: Luke 20:9–20.

This was idolatry, that false understanding of the old things, with Israel itself as the idol. This was salvation belongs not to the Lord, but to me.

This is Holy Week, and the chief priests and scribes have been pressing their opposition (20:1–2). The direction of Jesus' parable couldn't be more clear. For two thousand years, God has furnished Israel with His lush "vineyard"—to enjoy, to cultivate, to eat and drink from. It's not too much to expect a share of the fruit—faith, worship, living as God's people. The vineyard belongs to the Lord. But Israel refuses. The Israelites have come to believe it all belongs to them—they of birth in Abraham's line, they of circumcision, they of keeping the law. Old things.

By the time they've beaten, wounded, and cast out centuries of "servants," all those Old Testament prophets, we know what will happen next. Jesus' original audience had to be screaming, "Don't do it, man! Don't send your son! They're going to kill him!" The owner would be insane to do this. But God is insanely in love with His people. It is only the Son's death that can save them or anyone, and—divine brilliance!—He will work Jesus' death by this act of love for Israel, giving it even one more, though fruitless, chance.

In just a few days, it will come to pass. Then what? The owner of the vineyard "will come and destroy those tenants and give the vineyard to others" (20:16). Bloody tragedy. But it will bring a new thing, a good thing: "'The stone that the builders rejected has become the cornerstone" (20:17; Ps 118:22). A new building. God would form for Himself a new chosen people, His Church—all people of all families who believe that salvation is from the Lord Jesus Christ. People who will give Him His fruit. Therefore,

**LEST WE, TOO,
LOSE THE LORD'S SALVATION,
WE FORGET WHAT LIES BEHIND,
BECAUSE IN HIS SON,
GOD IS DOING A NEW THING:
GIVING THE VINEYARD TO
A NEW CHOSEN PEOPLE.**

We know we're nearing the climax of Lent when the **Hymn of the Day** is "My Song Is Love Unknown" (*LSB* 430). See how closely it reflects the Gospel reading.

Palm Sunday / Sunday of the Passion Year C

READINGS
John 12:12–19 (Processional)
Deuteronomy 32:36–39
Psalm 118:19–29 (antiphon: v 26)
or Psalm 31:9–16 (antiphon: v 5)
Philippians 2:5–11
Luke 22:1–23:56
or Luke 23:1–56
or John 12:20–43

HYMNS OF THE DAY
LSB 442 "All Glory, Laud, and Honor" (Processional)
LSB 438 "A Lamb Goes Uncomplaining Forth"

> "So they took branches of palm trees and went out to meet Him, crying out, 'Hosanna! Blessed is He who comes in the name of the Lord, even the King of Israel!'" (Jn 12:13)
>
> "There was also an inscription over Him, 'This is the King of the Jews.'" (Lk 23:38)
>
> "And he said, 'Jesus, remember me when You come into Your kingdom.'" (Lk 23:42)

Palm Sunday takes us from the adulation and crowds of the triumphal entry to the desolation of the cross as the Sunday of the Passion. It introduces us to Holy Week, which did indeed begin with adoring crowds but by Friday would see Jesus left to a few executioners, mockers, and thieves—a span of days that accounts for almost 30 percent of the four Gospels.

It's a lot to cover in one week—and a great deal to introduce in one Sunday morning. It makes this day one of the most intense of the church year. And that's appropriate, because these are the events by which all human history even continues and by which it will reach its fulfillment. (The wider Church has long celebrated this day of the triumphal entry as the Sunday of the Passion, with Lutherans rejoining the custom in recent decades. For more on the reasons, you might visit the devotion-study for Palm Sunday, Year A, on p 98.)

With so much to cover, there are quite a number of options among the readings and hymns. Fortunately, many of the propers are the same in all three years of the lectionary. Therefore, in this devotion-study, we'll spend most of our energy on one particular issue that is especially prominent in Luke's Passion narrative (Year C) and track where it also occurs in several of the other propers. You may also read the Palm Sunday devotion-studies for Years A and B (pp 98 and 352), where propers omitted or touched lightly here receive more attention.

Did you notice the common motif among the three passages with which we began? Certainly the Palm Sunday crowds saw Jesus' arrival in Jerusalem as a coronation. John quotes them as proclaiming Him "King of Israel." So does Luke (Lk 19:38). But interestingly, as the palm fronds become thatch in the hot sun and the mood changes 180 degrees, a new mob shouting an entirely different chorus, Luke and his witnesses continue to describe Jesus as King. When He doesn't look much like a king at all. Palm Sunday asks, and the Sunday of the Passion—especially Year C—presses us to answer,

Is This Really the King You Want?

Rejoin the procession, John 12:12–19, the **Palm Sunday Processional Gospel**.

"Hosanna! Blessed is He who comes in the name of the Lord" (12:13) quotes Psalm 118, a psalm that was likely used in coronations. "Hosanna" entreats the new king, "Save, we pray!" And for Israel, the king was never to be simply man's choice (as the people had once demanded Saul, 1 Sam 12:13), but always, in the line of David, as coming "in the name of the Lord."

Significantly, though, the people add "even the King of Israel!" That isn't in the psalm. Instead, it expresses their jubilant interpretation of what's happening today. The Greek καί, most often translated "and" but here "even," is likely emphatic that "this man coming in the name of the Lord is *indeed* King of Israel!"

For good measure, John explains the event by citing Zechariah: "Fear not, daughter of Zion; behold, your king is coming, sitting on a donkey's colt!" (12:15; Zech 9:9).

What didn't the disciples understand about this (Jn 12:16)? Not the crowds or the accolades. They were used to those by now. Not the pronouncement that Jesus was King; one of them had confessed that long before (1:49). What they didn't understand was the *kind of* king their Jesus was. "When Jesus was glorified, then they remembered" (12:16). Surely the disciples thought Jesus was being glorified right now. But John (himself one of those disciples who didn't get it at first), by the time he was inspired to write his Gospel, had grasped that Jesus' glory was the end of Holy Week, not the beginning (12:23–24; 13:31–32; 17:1). Jesus would be glorified by dying for the sins of the world. That's not the kind of king the disciples were expecting.

The **Introit** carries out its function as the entrance psalm quite literally on the Sunday of the entrance procession of the King. See, though, if you notice a subtle indication that all is not pomp.

> *Blessèd is he who comes in the name of the* Lord*! We bless you from the house of the* Lord*.*
>
> *Lift up your heads, O gates! And be lifted up, O ancient doors, that the*

King of glory may come in. Who is this King of glory? The Lord, strong and mighty, the Lord, mighty in battle! Lift up your heads, O gates! And lift them up, O ancient doors, that the King of glory may come in. Who is this King of glory? The Lord of hosts, He is the King of glory!

Blessèd is he who comes in the name of the Lord! We bless you from the house of the Lord. (Ps 24:7–10; antiphon: Ps 118:26)

Psalm 24 is strongly associated with Advent; it's the text for two Advent hymns (*LSB* 339 and 340, 341). That's no coincidence, since the triumphal entry is often also heard on the First Sunday of Advent. Could the psalm be any more definite that the Lord is coming as King?! And a king mighty in battle at that—the kind the crowds and the disciples wanted.

But what's out of the ordinary about this Introit? No Gloria Patri. Why? Throughout Lent, the most exuberant elements of the liturgy, Alleluias and the Hymns of Praise, have been omitted to mark the solemnity of the penitential season. Now during Holy Week, even the last Gloria is also stripped away. Very soon, this King of glory is going to the cross. Not the king folks expected!

Same with the **Collect**:

Almighty and everlasting God, You sent Your Son, our Savior Jesus Christ, to take upon Himself our flesh and to suffer death upon the cross. Mercifully grant that we may follow the example of His great humility and patience and be made partakers of His resurrection; through the same Jesus Christ, our Lord, who lives and reigns with You and the Holy Spirit, one God, now and forever. Amen.

Our flesh and death on a cross. Not very regal, it would appear. And here's the real rub: if that's the kind of king we're getting, it means we're asking to "*follow* the example of His great humility and patience." How are we on that? Is being "partakers of His resurrection" worth that to us? It's easy for us to say now, but what if it meant our own suffering and death?

Ancient Israel so often desired gods other than the Lord, its King. See the **Old Testament Reading**, Deuteronomy 32:36–39. The Lord asks rhetorically, "Where are [those other] gods? . . . Let them rise up and help you." Yet those who acknowledge "there is no god beside Me," when "their power is gone," on them He will "have compassion."

In contrast to the coronation festivities of Psalm 118, the other **Psalm** selection, Psalm 31:9–16, lets us see King David at his most desperate. It is fittingly a prayer of Christ Himself during Holy Week; picture Jesus in the Garden of Gethsemane: "distress . . . sorrow . . . sighing . . . strength fails . . . bones waste away . . . as they plot to take my life" (31:9, 10, 13). Can this kind of king save ("Hosanna") us?

Only this kind of king can save! Paul's great "therefore" in the **Epistle** means that Christ reigns exalted, glorious, only because He first humbled Himself to death. Read

Philippians 2:5–11. Christ Jesus is exactly the King we want!

Luke wishes to leave no doubt. His Passion account not only emphasizes Jesus' kingship, but it also emphasizes what *His kind of* kingship promises us. This, before you read the **Passion Gospel**, cues to Luke's kingly motif.

The full Passion history includes the events of Holy Thursday and Good Friday, beginning with the Last Supper. As He institutes the Sacrament, Jesus tells the disciples that He "will not drink of the fruit of the vine until the kingdom of God comes" (22:18). Then immediately after, a dispute arises in which the disciples confirm the kind of king they want: "The kings of the Gentiles exercise lordship over them" (22:25). Jesus, instead, is a king who serves. Still, "in My kingdom" the disciples will "sit on thrones judging the twelve tribes of Israel" (22:30).

In their own council, the Jewish leaders trumped up religious charges against Jesus: blasphemy, claiming to be the Son of God. But before Pilate, they needed a charge that would violate Roman law: He claims to be a king (23:2–3). It was for that, then, that Herod and his soldiers mocked Jesus, putting the clothing of a king on Him (23:11). And, finally, it was for that charge that Pilate turned Jesus over to be crucified.

Of the four Gospels, Luke is the most pointed that the charge printed over Jesus' head claims His kingship: ὁ βασιλεὺς τῶν Ἰουδαίων οὗτος, literally, "The King of the Jews this one" (23:38), even if, no, He doesn't look like the kind of king who could save anyone (23:37).

But all of this is only prelude to the most touching moment of Luke's Passion narrative—and the most powerful witness to Jesus as King: "One of the criminals who were hanged railed at Him, saying, 'Are You not the Christ? Save Yourself and us!' But the other rebuked him, saying, 'Do you not fear God, since you are under the same sentence of condemnation? And we indeed justly, for we are receiving the due reward of our deeds; but this man has done nothing wrong.' And he said, 'Jesus, remember me when You come into Your kingdom'" (23:39–42). Jesus really was the King he wanted.

Read Jesus' answer slowly and devotionally in the account of the Passion, Luke 22–23.

Then sing both **Hymns of the Day**, a perfect pairing. First, with "all glory, laud, and honor," Jesus, "You are [indeed] the King of Israel" (*LSB* 442:1). But "my joy beyond all measure" is that You left kingly Your throne and went uncomplaining forth as a Lamb to bear the guilt of sinners (*LSB* 438:4, 1).

Finally, meditate on Christ's true triumphal entry and prepare to enter Holy Week by the **Gradual** for this brief "season":

[Christ] entered once for all into the holy places, by means of His own blood, thus securing an eternal redemption. Therefore He is the mediator of a new covenant, so that those who are called may receive the promised eternal inheritance. He sent redemption to His people; He has commanded His covenant forever. (Heb 9:12a, c, 15a; Ps 111:9a)

Holy Week and Holy Thursday Year C

READINGS

Luke 22:1–23:56 (Passion)

Jeremiah 31:31–34
Psalm 116:12–19 (antiphon: v 17)
Hebrews 10:15–25
Luke 22:7–20

or

Exodus 12:1–14
Psalm 116:12–19 (antiphon: v 17)
1 Corinthians 11:23–32
John 13:1–17, 31b–35

HYMN OF THE DAY

LSB 617 "O Lord, We Praise Thee"

This is the week it happens. Two Sundays ago (Lent 5), the Lord promised through Isaiah that He would do a new thing (Is 43:19). He would replace the old ways of living out the faith. The old designation of one family, Israel, as God's people would give way to a new understanding of the family of God, the Church. The Lord would open the way to a new heaven and new earth. And it would all happen because Christ Jesus would once for all accomplish the Lord's salvation. It happened this week when

> *[Christ] entered once for all into the holy places, by means of His own blood, thus securing an eternal redemption. Therefore He is the mediator of a new covenant, so that those who are called may receive the promised eternal inheritance. He sent redemption to His people; He has commanded His covenant forever. (Heb 9:12a, c, 15a; Ps 111:9a)*

—the **Gradual** for Holy Week. It happens this week!

**This Holy Week,
Christ Mediates the New Covenant
That Makes Us His People Forever.**

To mark the week when God inaugurated the rest of history, the Church has appointed propers for each day—the only such week of the year. In this devotion-study, we simply make those propers for Holy Monday, Tuesday, and Wednesday available to you. Then we'll comment on selected propers for Holy Thursday (for the others, see Years A and B on pp 102 and 356), with separate devotion-studies for Good Friday and Holy Saturday. All of this, of course, will help prepare us to celebrate the queen of all festivals, the Resurrection of Our Lord. God's blessings on your meditations!

Monday in Holy Week

The **Introit**:

Be gracious to me, O LORD, for I am in distress; my eye is wasted from grief; my soul and my body also.

For my life is spent with sorrow, and my years with sighing; my strength fails because of my iniquity, and my bones waste away. Because of all my adversaries I have become a reproach, especially to my neighbors, and an object of dread to my acquaintances; those who see me in the street flee from me. For I hear the whispering of many—terror on every side!—as they scheme together against me, as they plot to take my life. But I trust in You, O LORD; I say, "You are my God." My times are in Your hand; rescue me from the hand of my enemies and from my persecutors!

Be gracious to me, O LORD, for I am in distress; my eye is wasted from grief; my soul and my body also. (Ps 31:10–11, 13–15; antiphon: Ps 31:9)

The **Collect**:

Almighty God, grant that in the midst of our failures and weaknesses we may be restored through the passion and intercession of Your only-begotten Son, who lives and reigns with You and the Holy Spirit, one God, now and forever. Amen.

The **Lessons**: Isaiah 50:5–10; Psalm 36:5–10 (antiphon: v 9); Hebrews 9:11–15; Matthew 26:1–27:66 *or* John 12:1–23

The **Hymn of the Day**: *LSB* 434 "Lamb of God, Pure and Holy"

Tuesday in Holy Week

The **Introit**:

Why are you cast down, O my soul, and why are you in turmoil within me? Hope in God; for I shall again praise Him, my salvation and my God.

My tears have been my food day and night, while they say to me continually, "Where is your God?" I say to God, my rock: "Why have You forgotten me? Why do I go mourning because of the oppression of the enemy?" As with a deadly wound in my bones, my adversaries taunt me, while they say to me continually, "Where is your God?"

Why are you cast down, O my soul, and why are you in turmoil within me? Hope in God; for I shall again praise Him, my salvation and my God. (Ps 42:3, 9–10; antiphon: Ps 42:5–6a)

The **Collect**:

Almighty and everlasting God, grant us by Your grace so to pass through this holy time of our Lord's passion that we may obtain the forgiveness of our sins; through Jesus Christ, Your Son, our Lord, who lives and reigns with You and the Holy Spirit, one God, now and forever. Amen.

The **Lessons**: Isaiah 49:1–7; Psalm 71:1–14 (antiphon: v 12); 1 Corinthians 1:18–25 (26–31); Mark 14:1–15:47 *or* John 12:23–50

The **Hymn of the Day**: *LSB* 453 "Upon the Cross Extended"

Wednesday in Holy Week

The **Introit**:

In God I trust; I shall not be afraid. What can man do to me?

Be gracious to me, O God, for man tramples on me; all day long an attacker oppresses me; my enemies trample on me all day long, for many attack me proudly. When I am afraid, I put my trust in You. In God, whose word I praise, in God I trust; I shall not be afraid.

In God I trust; I shall not be afraid. What can man do to me? (Ps 56:1–4a; antiphon: Ps 56:11)

The **Collect**:

Merciful and everlasting God, You did not spare Your only Son but delivered Him up for us all to bear our sins on the cross. Grant that our hearts may be so fixed with steadfast faith in Him that we fear not the power of sin, death, and the devil; through the same Jesus Christ, our Lord, who lives and reigns with You and the Holy Spirit, one God, now and forever. Amen.

The **Lessons**: Isaiah 62:11–63:7; Psalm 70 (antiphon: v 5); Romans 5:6–11; Luke 22:1–23:56 *or* John 13:16–38

The **Hymn of the Day**: *LSB* 425, 426 "When I Survey the Wondrous Cross"

Holy Thursday

Worship on Holy Thursday takes us to the Upper Room, where Jesus celebrated one last Passover with His disciples. The Passover liturgy they used almost surely included the **Psalm** for this day, Psalm 116:12–19, which also provides the text for the Holy Thursday **Introit**:

Gracious is the LORD, and righteous; our God is merciful.

I love the LORD, because He has heard my voice and my pleas for mercy. Because He inclined His ear to me, therefore I will call on Him as long as I live. The snares of death encompassed me; the pangs of Sheol laid hold on me; I suffered distress and anguish. Then I called on the name of the LORD: "O LORD, I pray, deliver my soul!"

Gracious is the LORD, and righteous; our God is merciful. (Ps 116:1–4; antiphon: Ps 116:5)

Of the three Gospels that record Jesus' institution of the Lord's Supper, Luke alone explicitly identifies the covenant as new. So fittingly, Year C especially brings the new covenant to the fore, beginning with the **Old Testament Reading**, Jeremiah 31:31–34.

The chief feature of the new covenant is forgiveness of sins (31:34c). Surely God had always been forgiving sins; the whole sacrificial system of the Old Testament was mediating, delivering forgiveness. But now there would be a new intimacy in the way God would do that. No more lambs or bulls as visual aids to teach the people God's ways (31:34a). In the new covenant, they will receive forgiveness directly; that is, they will all know God personally (31:34b), His Law written on their hearts: "I will be their God, and they shall be My people" (31:33). Thus, the new covenant means we are God's people in a new way by receiving His forgiveness apart from the old sacrificial system.

That is possible because it is given to us by a new mediator—God Himself. Read the **Epistle**, Hebrews 10:15–25.

In the new covenant, "we have confidence to enter the holy places by the blood of Jesus, by the new and living way that He opened for us through the curtain, that is, through His flesh . . . [He is] a great priest" (10:19–20, 21). We have a new, open relationship with God because Jesus' death on the cross would rend the curtain of separation caused by our sin, the separation symbolized by the temple curtain of the old covenant (Lk 23:44–46).

In addition to Matthew, Mark, and Luke, Paul reports the words of Jesus' institution of the Supper: 1 Corinthians 11:23–32, the **alternate Epistle**. Paul, too, is explicit about the new covenant (11:25). Of great importance is his reminder that this intimate relationship as God's people at the Sacrament is to be taken most seriously (11:27–32). Hence our practice of close(d) Communion.

It all happens now as Jesus begins His finish: the **Holy Gospel**, Luke 22:7–20.

Holy Communion is the most intimate expression of the unity Christ initiates with and among His people: "I have earnestly desired to eat this Passover with you before I suffer" (22:15). That's because it's truly sharing Christ's very body and "the new covenant in [His] blood" (22:19, 20).

O Lord, in this wondrous Sacrament You have left us a remembrance of Your passion. Grant that we may so receive the sacred mystery of Your body and blood that the fruits of Your redemption may continually be manifest in us; for You live and reign with the Father and the Holy Spirit, one God, now and forever. Amen.

—the **Collect** for Holy Thursday.

One last joyous celebration of the new covenant before Jesus, like the altars in many of our churches, will be stripped for His work of establishing it. Sing the **Hymn of the Day**, Luther's hymn for Holy Communion, "O Lord, We Praise Thee" (*LSB* 617).

A note for Good Friday and Holy Saturday: Since Good Friday and Holy Saturday use the same propers for Years A, B, and C, you'll find the devotion-studies for those days in Year A, pages 106 and 110. The devotion-study for Easter Sunday, Year C, appears on the next page.

The Resurrection of Our Lord Year C

READINGS

Isaiah 65:17–25
Psalm 16 (antiphon: v 10)
1 Corinthians 15:19–26
Luke 24:1–12

Job 19:23–27
Psalm 118:15–29 (antiphon: v 1)
1 Corinthians 15:51–57
John 20:1–18

HYMN OF THE DAY

LSB 463 "Christ the Lord Is Risen Today; Alleluia"

Paul lays it right out there: "If Christ has not been raised, your faith is futile and you are still in your sins. . . . We are of all people most to be pitied" (1 Cor 15:17, 19). If Jesus' body is still in a tomb somewhere, He is a fraud, a corpse, and no help to us. Then we are pathetic, the saddest cases, as we daily pray to Him who can't hear, depend on Him who has no awareness of our life situations, count on Him whose promise to open heaven to us was a lie or at least failed miserably. If not for Easter, we've got nothing!

"But in fact Christ has been raised from the dead" (1 Cor 15:20).

Alleluia! Christ is risen!
He is risen indeed! Alleluia!

What had to happen for us to have anything good has happened! Say it again:

Alleluia! Christ is risen!
He is risen indeed! Alleluia!

Happy (looking forward to) Easter morning!

We know Easter is the biggest day of the Christian year. The alleluias, the lilies, the egg casseroles, and maybe even trumpets and timpani remind us of that. It's the day that moves all history forward, because without Jesus' death and resurrection, our sin would still separate us from God and His blessings. Easter had to happen! And it did! We pull out all the stops to celebrate!

For thousands of years, of course, all those millennia after Adam and Eve sinned, this that must happen hadn't yet happened. To God, though, since He exists outside of time, Jesus' death and resurrection already was and has always been an accomplished reality. Throughout the Old Testament, then, He gave His people "as if" glimpses of the cross and resurrection by triumphs that happened for them in their time. One that the Church has long seen as picturing Easter begins our propers. The **Introit**:

I will sing to the Lord, for He has triumphed gloriously; the horse and his rider He has thrown into the sea.

The Lord is my strength and my song, and He has become my salvation. Your right hand, O Lord, glorious in power, Your right hand, O Lord, shatters the enemy. You have led in Your steadfast love the people whom You have redeemed; You have guided them by Your strength to Your holy abode. You will bring them in and plant them on Your own mountain, the place, O Lord, which You have made for Your abode, the sanctuary, O Lord, which Your hands have established. The Lord will reign forever and ever.

Glory be to the Father and to the Son and to the Holy Spirit; as it was in the beginning, is now, and will be forever. Amen.

I will sing to the Lord, for He has triumphed gloriously; the horse and his rider He has thrown into the sea. (Ex 15:2a, 6, 13, 17–18; antiphon: Ex 15:1b)

Israel sang to the Lord as it came through the Red Sea. Slavery in Egypt had been like being dead and buried. And then, trapped against the sea with Pharaoh's army bearing down on it, it appeared that the wilderness would be its grave (see Ex 14:10–11). But now, death—the Egyptian horse and rider—had been drowned, and Israel had passed through to new life.

Not only was this a picture of the resurrection, emerging from the grave, but it happened because God viewed Jesus' resurrection as having happened. It was as true for ancient Israel as for us in the New Testament: if Christ has not been raised, the Israelites would still have been in the sin that separated it from God—worse than slavery in Egypt, still enslaved by their sin to death and hell. Christ's death and resurrection was a "must happen" for Israel.

And today, we celebrate precisely that! This year, we hear Luke's account of the resurrection, the **Holy Gospel**, Luke 24:1–12. Also read the **Holy Gospel** for Easter Sunrise, John 20:1–18.

"The first day of the week" reminds us how carefully God has laid out His plans from the beginning. Even before God said "Let there be light" (Gen 1:3), He intended Easter to be the first day of the new creation, the "eighth day" when eternity renews the fallen work of that first week.

Luke's narrative (like John's) tells of two angels bearing the great good news (Lk 24:4; Jn 20:12). (Matthew and Mark report only one, probably since only one did the stone-rolling and the actual speaking.) And Luke includes those words of the angels that most emphasize that all this was sure to be just so: "'Why do you seek the living among the dead? He is not here, but has risen. Remember how He told you, while He was still in Galilee, that the Son of Man must be delivered into the hands of sinful men and be crucified and on the third day rise.' And they remembered His words" (Lk 24:5b–8). Of course! Silly us! Just like He said! It had to happen just this way!

"The Son of Man *must*"—crucified and rise. The cross and Easter *must* happen. (John uses the same "must," Jn 20:9.)

To say Jesus must die and rise is true in two different senses. Not only must He have died and risen in the sense that it was essential for us—we needed it to happen—as Paul made clear in 1 Corinthians 15. But also—and primarily—Good Friday and Easter was a must from God's perspective, that is, in the sense that it was certain, inevitable. It was a must in that there was no way it wouldn't happen. That's the sense in which the angels were speaking: "The Son of Man must be delivered into the hands of sinful men and be crucified and on the third day rise." God willed it; Jesus promised it; it had to happen.

That sense just makes sense; whatever God intends must happen. But why was Jesus' death and resurrection necessary, "a must," for our sakes? This gets to the very heart of the Gospel. God created man to be His friends, to be in an endless relationship with Him—meaning to be the recipients of His love. But since God is holy, He cannot be in a relationship with anything or anyone that isn't; His holiness destroys anything that is sinful. So when we sinned, we cut ourselves off from God, and our sin would always have been the chasm that separated us from any of His good gifts. Any of His good gifts. Earthly or eternal. Life itself and certainly life everlasting. We can't stop sinning; we can't make up for sins of the past. We can't restore our relationship with God.

That's why we have the cross. All our sins were expunged from our accounts and transferred to Christ's. He became the one and only sinner, and for it, He was cut off from all God's gifts: "My God, My God, why have You forsaken Me?" (Mt 27:46). Would that pay the price *for us*? Jesus had promised that it would (Jn 5:21, 24–26; 12:24, 32–33). So at Easter, the Father rendered His answer: "Yes!" By raising His Son, God was saying, "Jesus' self-sacrifice has covered the checks He wrote for humankind." We are reconciled to God. And if we are back together with God, we now have all those good gifts He gives. All those good gifts. Earthly and eternal. Life and life everlasting. For our sakes, all that must be. And Easter says it is. What must happen has happened!

What now? Well,

SINCE WHAT MUST HAPPEN—
JESUS' DEATH AND RESURRECTION—
HAS HAPPENED,
WHAT GOD PROMISES SHALL HAPPEN
SHALL HAPPEN!

And the rest of our propers are loaded with "shalls"!

Read the **Old Testament Reading** for Easter Sunrise: Job 19:23–27.

"I know that my Redeemer lives, and at the last He will stand upon the earth. And after my skin has been thus destroyed, yet in my flesh *I shall see God*, whom I *shall* see for myself, and my eyes *shall* behold, and not another" (19:25–27).

Next, read the **Psalm** appointed for Easter Sunrise: Psalm 118:15–29.

"*I shall not die*, but *I shall live*, and recount the deeds of the LORD. . . . Open to me the gates of righteousness. . . . *The righteous shall enter* through it" (118:17, 19a, 20b).

The **Epistle** for Easter Sunrise: 1 Corinthians 15:51–57.

"Behold! I tell you a mystery. We shall not all sleep, but *we shall all be changed*, in a moment, in the twinkling of an eye, at the last trumpet. . . . For this perishable body must put on the imperishable, and this mortal body must put on immortality" (15:51–52a, 53).

And now for Easter Day: the **Old Testament Reading**, Isaiah 65:17–25. There are far too many "shalls" to quote here. Read it all and get the idea. But here are a few samples:

"Behold, I create new heavens and a new earth, and the former things *shall not be remembered*. . . . *They shall build* houses and inhabit them; *they shall plant* vineyards and eat their fruit. . . . Like the days of a tree *shall the days of My people be*, and *My chosen shall long enjoy* the work of their hands. . . . For *they shall be the offspring of the blessed* of the LORD" (65:17, 21, 22c–d, 23b).

Read also the **Psalm** for Easter Day, cited in Acts 2 by Peter about Christ: Psalm 16.

"I have set the LORD always before me; because He is at my right hand, *I shall not be shaken*. . . . For You will not abandon my soul to Sheol, or let Your holy one see corruption. You make known to me the path of life; in Your presence there is fullness of joy; at Your right hand are pleasures forevermore" (16:8, 10–11; see Acts 2:22–32).

Finally, back to the **Epistle** for Easter Day, 1 Corinthians 15:19–26, in which Paul declared what a must Christ's resurrection is for us. It also has a "shall": "In Christ shall all be made alive" (15:22).

That is the ultimate "shall" that shall happen because Christ has done what in God's eternal design is the "must happen." Because Christ has been made alive, so shall we. Therefore, we pray with certainty this **Collect** for Easter Day:

Almighty God the Father, through Your only-begotten Son, Jesus Christ, You have overcome death and opened the gate of everlasting life to us. Grant that we, who celebrate with joy the day of our Lord's resurrection, may be raised from the death of sin by Your life-giving Spirit; through Jesus Christ, our Lord, who lives and reigns with You and the Holy Spirit, one God, now and forever. Amen.

The **Hymn of the Day** for Easter Evening is one of many describing the "must" for the "shall." Because Christ the Lord is risen, God and sinners are reconciled (*LSB* 463:3).

Our celebration will continue for seven Sundays. The **Gradual** for this Easter season:

Christ has risen from the dead. [God the Father] has crowned Him with glory and honor, He has given Him dominion over the works of His hands; He has put all things under His feet. (adapted from Mt 28:7; Heb 2:7; Ps 8:6)

Second Sunday of Easter Year C

READINGS

Acts 5:12–20 (21–32)
Psalm 148 (antiphon: v 13)
Revelation 1:4–18
John 20:19–31

HYMN OF THE DAY

LSB 470, 471 "O Sons and Daughters of the King"

The **Gradual** for the season of Easter:

> *Christ has risen from the dead. [God the Father] has crowned Him with glory and honor, He has given Him dominion over the works of His hands; He has put all things under His feet. (adapted from Mt 28:7; Heb 2:7; Ps 8:6)*

"Alleluia. We know that Christ being raised from the dead will never die again; death no longer has dominion over Him. Alleluia" (Rom 6:9; the Verse for Easter 2).

Alleluia! Christ is risen!

He is risen indeed! Alleluia!

And we'll have lots more of all this for seven Sundays. For an obvious reason—the resurrection of Jesus Christ!—many things are the same week to week, year to year during Easter.

That's true in a unique way for this Second Sunday of Easter. Easter 2 is the one Sunday occurring every year (never skipped because of calendar anomalies) that uses the same primary Gospel reading all three years of the three-year lectionary. When using Year A, B, or C, we'll always hear John 20:19–31. It's designed that way because the second half of the lesson, Jesus showing Himself to Thomas, takes place precisely on the Sunday after Easter. The opportunity was just too good to pass up.

The fact is, of all the Easter 2 propers, *only* the First Readings and the Epistles vary among Year A, B, and C. That means, of course, that there's great overlap in the direction the Sunday takes, whichever year you're in. (And you can read more about most of the propers in our devotion-studies for Years A and B, pp 118 and 364.) But it also provokes intriguing investigation as to how the Sunday's theme is affected by those two propers, which *do* vary, perhaps the way choosing blue napkins for one dinner party and pastel yellow for another will cause guests to notice different colors in the dining room wallpaper. (Claire tells me that's so, and I believe her. I'm better with colors in a necktie—though Claire chooses most of those for me too.)

See how the first two propers we'll hear Sunday, which are the same for all three years of the lectionary, raise questions—which will then be answered differently according to the propers that change among Year A, B, and C. Starting with the **Introit**:

> *Like newborn infants, long for the pure spiritual milk, that by it you may grow up to salvation—if indeed you have tasted that the Lord is good.*
>
> *Oh give thanks to the LORD; call upon His name; make known His deeds among the peoples! Sing to Him, sing praises to Him; tell of all His wondrous works! Glory in His holy name; let the hearts of those who seek the LORD rejoice! Seek the LORD and His strength; seek His presence continually! Remember the wondrous works that He has done, His miracles, and the judgments He uttered. He remembers His covenant forever, the word that He commanded, for a thousand generations.*
>
> *Glory be to the Father and to the Son and to the Holy Spirit; as it was in the beginning, is now, and will be forever. Amen.*
>
> *Like newborn infants, long for the pure spiritual milk, that by it you may grow up to salvation—if indeed you have tasted that the Lord is good. (Ps 105:1–5, 8; antiphon: 1 Pet 2:2–3)*

One previous year, we focused on "newborn infants" and "pure spiritual milk," another on "His presence" and "[making] known His deeds." But in any case, Peter and the psalmist beg us to ask, "What is it that tastes good about the Lord?" "What are His deeds we're to make known? What are His wondrous works?" They all come down to the resurrection, but this year, we'll see different reasons to "give thanks to the LORD" and "sing praises to Him."

Same with the **Collect**:

> *Almighty God, grant that we who have celebrated the Lord's resurrection may by Your grace confess in our life and conversation that Jesus is Lord and God; through the same Jesus Christ, Your Son, who lives and reigns with You and the Holy Spirit, one God, now and forever. Amen.*

We have indeed "celebrated the Lord's resurrection." We do that joyously, thankfully, every year. What aspects especially *this* year?

For this devotion-study, let me invite you to read all four of the lectionary passages before we make any comments. Read straight through Acts 5:12–32; Psalm 148; Revelation 1:4–18; and John 20:19–31. Remember that the Acts and Revelation readings are the only elements that are unique to Year C. See if you notice anything that "brings out the blue" in the Psalm, the Gospel, and the other propers.

Now back to the **First Reading**, Acts 5:12–32.

You may recall that throughout the Easter season, we have First Readings from Acts rather than Old Testament Readings. That's because it was the resurrection of Jesus that drove the apostles to action, beginning at Pentecost (Acts 2). You saw that here. The once-terrified disciples, now sure that Jesus is alive, with them, and the conqueror of all things like mere death, are suddenly fearless. Their message of Christ risen is particularly galling to this high priest (still either Annas or Caiaphas, Acts 4:5–6; Jn 18:12–14, 24), not only because he had orchestrated Jesus' death but also because he and his cronies were Sadducees who denied bodily resurrection (Acts 5:17; 23:8).

In Acts 4, Peter and John had been imprisoned for preaching the resurrection and sternly warned to do so no more, but that hadn't deterred them (Acts 4:1–3, 18–21). This time, prison is even less a deterrent (5:19–21)! It's as Paul would later write: "I am suffering, bound with chains as a criminal. But the word of God is not bound!" (2 Tim 2:9). And clearly prison, even threat of death, would not stop the apostles in the future: "We must obey God rather than men" (Acts 5:29). They knew "the God of our fathers raised Jesus, whom you killed by hanging Him on a tree. God exalted Him at His right hand as Leader and Savior, to give repentance to Israel and forgiveness of sins. And we are witnesses to these things" (5:30–32).

So does anything in this lesson ring a bell with the others?

It's easy enough to catch the key phrase in Psalm 148: "Praise the Lord!" If Easter is for alleluias, this **Psalm** fits, because "Praise the Lord" is simply the combining of Hebrew words *hallelu* ("praise") and *Yah*, short for *Yahweh* ("the Lord").

Praise, though, is never to be just an outpouring of our emotions. God, not our innards, is always to be the source and object of praise. Properly, then, praise declares something about God or what He has done. Most of this psalm lists those who will praise the Lord, but search again for the two passages that declare what the praise is all about. They're the "fors," the reasons. Praise the Lord "*for* He commanded and they were created. And He established them forever and ever; He gave a decree, and it shall not pass away" (148:5b–6). And "let them praise the name of the Lord, *for* His name alone is exalted; His majesty is above earth and heaven. He has raised up a horn for His people" (148:13–14a). That is to say, first, the order God decreed will last forever; not even death can cancel His designs. Second, the Lord has raised up for us a horn, a source of strength (as a rhino's horn or the horns of a bull are their power, their weapons). "Horn" is an image often used this way in the Old Testament, and it finally points to our strength, Christ Jesus. He is that now that He's conquered death. We praise the

Lord because to us who always face death, He has opened the way to life.

Now the other proper unique to this year, the **Epistle**, Revelation 1:4–18.

As with the Easter readings through Acts, the Epistles for this Easter season, Year C, will progress through Revelation. That's fitting, too, because it's the resurrected Christ revealing these visions to John, beginning with this startling face to face on "the Lord's day," a Sunday (1:10). John is in exile on the island of Patmos (1:9), now an old man nearing the end of his apostolic ministry. The symbolism, as throughout Revelation, is a bit bizarre: "seven spirits" (1:4, actually the one Holy Spirit who's credited with giving seven gifts, Is 11:2), "seven golden lampstands" (1:12, representing the seven congregations to whom John is to write, 1:11), "seven stars" (1:16, the seven ἄγγελοι, *angeloi*, "angels" or "messengers," probably actually the pastors of the seven congregations; see 1:20).

But the comfort of the vision for John was seeing "the first and the last," "the Alpha and the Omega," who has become "the firstborn of the dead" (1:17, 8, 5a). For if Jesus has Himself come through death to be *first*born, it means He "has freed us" also to be born after death (1:5b). We are locked away in exile but soon to be free. "I died, and behold I am alive forevermore, and I have the keys of Death and Hades" (1:18). Anything you also noticed in Acts and John's Gospel?

To the **Holy Gospel**, then, John 20:19–31.

The first half of the text is still the evening of Easter Day. Where are the disciples? Probably still in the room in which they'd eaten the Passover, but with "the doors being locked . . . for fear of the Jews" (20:19). No matter for Jesus, the one who would send His angel to unlock prison doors, who Himself holds the keys not only to the Upper Room but even to death and hell, which means all those locks are now broken. Don't worry about any of that anymore! "Peace be with you!" (20:19, 21, 26).

In fact, I'm *giving you* the keys to hell and to lock and unlock the doors of heaven. "As the Father has sent Me, even so I am sending you. . . . If you forgive the sins of any, they are forgiven them; if you withhold forgiveness from any, it is withheld." (20:21, 23). Yes, we call it the Office of the Keys.

And you, Thomas, you've locked yourself into stubborn unbelief. "Put your finger here, and see My hands; and put out your hand, and place it in My side. Do not disbelieve, but believe." Thomas answered Jesus, "My Lord and my God!" (20:27, 28).

To that, our **Verse** adds a *third* Alleluia!: "Alleluia. We know that Christ being raised from the dead will never die again; death no longer has dominion over Him. Alleluia. Blessed are those who have not seen and yet have believed. Alleluia." By believing, you have life in His name (20:29, 31).

Easter 2, Year C!

ALLELUIA! PRAISE THE LORD!
FOR CHRIST HAS UNLOCKED THE DOOR
FROM UNBELIEF, DEATH, AND HELL
TO FAITH, LIFE, AND HEAVEN!

Not only does the **Hymn of the Day** tell the story of Easter 2 but you'll find unbelief to faith, death to life, and hell to heaven.

Third Sunday of Easter Year C

READINGS

Acts 9:1–22
Psalm 30 (antiphon: vv 11a, 12b)
Revelation 5:(1–7) 8–14
John 21:1–14 (15–19)

HYMN OF THE DAY

LSB 483 "With High Delight Let Us Unite"

There are two staples we're using throughout Easter. The **Gradual**, of course, is the same every Sunday of the season:

> *Christ has risen from the dead. [God the Father] has crowned Him with glory and honor, He has given Him dominion over the works of His hands; He has put all things under His feet. (adapted from Mt 28:7; Heb 2:7; Ps 8:6)*

The **Verse** also has the same opening line for each Sunday. But then, as we pointed out last week, it adds another Bible verse (which changes each Sunday) and a third Alleluia. This week: "Alleluia. We know that Christ being raised from the dead will never die again; death no longer has dominion over Him. Alleluia. Did not our hearts burn within us while He talked to us on the road, while He opened to us the Scriptures? Alleluia" (Rom 6:9; Lk 24:32, which actually is drawn from the Gospel for Easter 3, Year A, not from our propers for Year C. Sorry about that!).

There are joyful reminders that we're still celebrating the resurrection of our Lord!

Now the **Introit** will begin to focus our attention on this Sunday's particular result of Christ rising from the dead:

> *All Your works shall give thanks to You, O Lord, and all Your saints shall bless You!*
>
> *One generation shall commend Your works to another, and shall declare Your mighty acts. On the glorious splendor of Your majesty, and on Your wondrous works, I will meditate. They*

shall speak of the might of Your awesome deeds, and I will declare Your greatness. They shall pour forth the fame of Your abundant goodness and shall sing aloud of Your righteousness. The Lord *is good to all, and His mercy is over all that He has made.*

Glory be to the Father and to the Son and to the Holy Spirit; as it was in the beginning, is now, and will be forever. Amen.

All Your works shall give thanks to You, O Lord, *and all Your saints shall bless You! (Ps 145:4–7, 9; antiphon: Ps 145:10)*

Once again this week, the "work," the "mighty act," the "awesome deed" of the Lord, which we most celebrate, is Jesus rising from the grave. But this Introit especially emphasizes that we will *share* that "abundant goodness" of God with others: "One generation shall commend Your works to another," "shall declare Your mighty acts," and "shall sing aloud of Your righteousness." We'll teach our children and grandchildren "I Know That My Redeemer Lives"—or, from the old *A Child's Garden of Song*, "Jesus died our souls to save, but He did not stay in the grave. Oh, happy Easter morning!"

"They shall speak of the might of Your awesome deeds, and I will declare Your greatness." You'll be ready to tell a friend in the break room why you still come to work smiling when you know the branch might be closed: "Jesus is still alive."

"They shall pour forth the fame of Your abundant goodness." If the whole world hears of fame made in Hollywood and Yankee Stadium, it should know how abundantly good God is—giving His Son to die and rise to save every nation! This will be a major element in this Sunday's propers.

The **Collect** for Easter 3:

O God, through the humiliation of Your Son You raised up the fallen world. Grant to Your faithful people, rescued from the peril of everlasting death, perpetual gladness and eternal joys; through Jesus Christ, our Lord, who lives and reigns with You and the Holy Spirit, one God, now and forever. Amen.

I like the word "perpetual." It doesn't just mean "never-ending," though it does mean that. It also means "uninterrupted, continual." By Jesus' suffering and death ("humiliation")—never to be forgotten even though we're now into Easter!—we share in Jesus' resurrection; we're "raised up" with Him and the fallen world. Because, then, we've been rescued from everlasting death, we truly can be glad, joyful, perpetually. It's not just that we'll have joy forever in heaven, though we will. Knowing what eternity holds for us does offer gladness at every moment already now. Can this downturn or this bad day really change the big picture? No! Do we often forget that? Yes. That's why we pray this collect. O God, grant that we would remember *perpetually* that Christ has secured a perfect forever and is perpetually living for us now.

How will remembering that affect our eagerness to share God's abundant goodness with the world?

David had learned by experience that the Lord really was with him always, even when he felt he was passing through death itself. Read the appointed **Psalm**, Psalm 30.

David truly had faced death often—fighting Goliath, fleeing from Saul ("there is but a step between me and death," 1 Sam 20:3), constantly facing enemy armies. He surely felt he was on the doorstep of Sheol, the realm of the dead (Ps 30:3). Worse, he himself earned God's anger. David had flooded his bed with tears (Ps 6:6).

But God had seen him through, and after the fact, he was able to look back and see how infinitesimally brief his agony had been: "[The Lord's] anger is but for a moment, and His favor is for a lifetime. Weeping may tarry for the night, but joy comes with the morning" (30:5). We grieve over our sins, at the terrors of life, but Easter morning dawns.

This shaped David's outlook and did indeed move him to tell the world, "You [O Lord] have turned for me my mourning into dancing; . . . that my glory may sing Your praise and not be silent. O Lord my God, I will give thanks to You forever!" (30:11a, 12).

The other famous Saul had his memorable experience with a surprising similarity to David's—and to similar affect. The **First Reading**, Acts 9:1–22.

In the two thousand years since Easter and Pentecost, this may be history's most significant event. Saul had overseen the murder of the first Christian martyr. (Coat-checking for the killers wasn't passive; it was more like supervising—hearty approval while keeping oneself above the bloody mess, Acts 7:58–8:1a.) Now Saul wanted more blood.

Saul was certain that "the Way" (9:2, a name used prominently for the Church in the book of Acts: 19:9, 23; 22:4; 24:14, 22; see also Jn 14:6; Acts 18:25–26) was the wrong way. Jesus, he was sure, was a blasphemer and a fraud. But suddenly, clearly, *Saul* was wrong (9:3–5).

David wrote figuratively of "the night" of weeping followed immediately by morning; Saul had to sweat this out for three days (9:9). Blind, helpless, he only knew he'd been terribly in error in what he'd thought was his life's service to God—yet Jesus had something for him to do (9:6). Blind eyes still sob.

This was only Jesus' small preview to Saul of "how much he must suffer for the sake of My name" (9:16). Yet Saul would have joy with the (third) morning: "Brother Saul, the Lord Jesus who appeared to you on the road by which you came has sent me so that you may regain your sight and be filled with the Holy Spirit"—by Baptism into the death and resurrection of Jesus (9:17, 18).

Just as "immediately" as the scales fell from his eyes, Saul began to proclaim Jesus in the synagogues (9:20). Since our Lord Himself, perhaps no one—by his preaching and writing—has been a more powerful "instrument of [Jesus] to carry My name before the Gentiles and kings and the children of Israel" (9:15).

Recall that during the Easter season, Year C, the **Epistle** each Sunday is from John's Revelation. Read Revelation 5:1–14.

We understand why David and Saul would weep. Why John now too (5:4)? No one, it seemed, was able to open and reveal the content of the scrolls (5:3), so it seems to John that God's plans—whatever they may be—are being thwarted. We know this kind of weeping—when what seems to us the obvious will of God isn't happening.

But one of the heavenly elders comforts John, comforts us: "Weep no more; behold, the Lion of the tribe of Judah, the Root of David, has conquered, so that He can open the scroll and its seven seals" (5:5). Then appears the Lamb "standing, as though it had been slain" (5:6). He still shows the scars of fatal wounds, but He's very much alive and well. Not only have God's plans not been derailed, but soon, they'll be detailed—as the Lion, the Lamb, opens the seals of the scroll.

That's cause for a new song. The heavenly choir sings, "Worthy are You to take the scroll and to open its seals, for You were slain, and by Your blood You ransomed people for God from every tribe and language and people and nation" (5:9). Soon the whole heavenly host is joining in (5:11–14). With such news, voices simply can't be still!

That may be the reason the Holy Spirit inspired John to record this week's **Holy Gospel**, John 21:1–19. Read that now.

Once you've done that, read the last two verses of last Sunday's Gospel, John 20:30–31. Now doesn't that sound like an ideal way to end the Gospel of John? So why another chapter? The disciples, even Thomas, are now fully convinced that Jesus is alive, and we've been exhorted to believe even without seeing (20:29). It brings to mind the previous great catch of fish. At that time, the disciples were told their future fishing would be for men (Lk 5:1–10). Time to commence. And why does John report the number (21:11a)? The ancients believed there were 153 kinds of fish in the world. Was the Lord delivering not only a miraculous catch but a message? You will catch men of "every tribe and language and people and nation." And notice, unlike with that first great haul, this time, "the net was not torn (21:11b; see Lk 5:6). Not one of those we're to catch for the Lord will be lost.

It's a huge assignment, but it's one Jesus' Easter people welcome! Especially Peter. Because for him, it wasn't a matter of duty; it was a privilege that came only because Jesus welcomed him back into the discipleship. Three denials (Jn 13:36–38), now three commissionings (21:15, 16, 17)—which were nothing less than three absolutions. Peter, too, had had his moment to weep—bitterly! (Lk 22:54–62). And for him and the disciples, as for Saul, the "but a moment" had been a three-day ordeal. But now he was one of us—a sinner who'd mourned and wept but was ready to spend his life sharing the risen Christ.

Christ Raised from the Dead Means That We Who Wept Bitterly for a Moment Now for a Lifetime Perpetually Declare to Every Land His Abundant Goodness.

"With high delight let us unite" to send His Good News "to every land, every nation" (**Hymn of the Day**, *LSB* 483:1, 3).

Fourth Sunday of Easter Year C

READINGS

Acts 20:17–35
Psalm 23 (antiphon: v 4)
Revelation 7:9–17
John 10:22–30

HYMN OF THE DAY

LSB 709 "The King of Love My Shepherd Is"

In my last congregation, I was blessed to serve for a while with a wonderful associate pastor. For five years, we had a delightful team ministry, and he was dearly loved by our people. When he announced he was leaving, it was very emotional for all of us—for me, because he's a great friend; for our members, because he'd been a faithful, loving, and skillful shepherd. We all knew we'd miss him very much.

The following Sunday happened to be the Fourth Sunday of Easter, Good Shepherd Sunday. It struck me as one of those things only God could have scheduled. We all felt deeply saddened to be separated from one of our shepherds. But then along came the Psalm of the day, "The LORD is my shepherd" (Ps 23:1), and Jesus' words, "I am the good shepherd" (Jn 10:14). So my sermon THEME that day (and, yes, I really do always put my THEME in small caps) was WE'VE LOST A SHEPHERD, BUT WE STILL HAVE THE REAL SHEPHERD: THE LORD. The truth is, nothing life deals us can separate us from our Shepherd.

That, perhaps, is the special focus of Good Shepherd Sunday in Year C.

**NO THING AND NO ONE ELSE—
EVEN DEATH—
CAN SEPARATE THE SHEEP
FROM THEIR GOOD SHEPHERD.**

For all three years of the three-year lectionary, the **Psalm** is the beloved "Shepherd Psalm" of David. Read Psalm 23.

"I shall not want." It's such a simple statement, which makes it so comprehensive. I shall not be lacking . . . anything. No modifiers.

No limiters. This is what it means to have the Lord with us. For He is all powerful, all knowing, all loving. He *can* give us anything, *knows* what's best for us, always *desires* to give it, including the green grass or groceries His sheep need to eat, the still or bottled waters the sheep drink. Always on the schedules and in the quantities, price ranges, and brand names the Shepherd knows best, the blessings of a flock of friends, loved ones, fellow members of the Body of Christ. Christ Himself, who really is everything we might want; He always "overflows" (23:5), even at the most frightening moments. It's getting late. Before the sun sets on the distant horizon, it drops below the hills just to your west, because the path to a night's safety in the sheepfold takes you through this narrow ravine. The darker the shadows grow, the more dangerous the threats. Rocks and pits. Predators you can't see watching you. Still, "even though I walk through the valley of the shadow of death, I will fear no evil, for You are with me; Your rod and Your staff, they comfort me" (23:4). You, my Shepherd, are with me—and You carry a big stick!

That's Good Friday and Easter. My Good Shepherd is with me because He passed through the valley of the shadow of death, and by doing so, He took the sin that would have forever separated me from God. Removing sin has reconciled me to God. And He *passed through* the valley of death to emerge risen and alive to be with me. That means "goodness and mercy shall [surely!] follow me all the days of my life, and I shall dwell in the house of the LORD forever" (23:6).

No thing, no foe can undo this. Read the **Holy Gospel**, John 10:22–30.

This is the third installment of Good Shepherd Sunday Gospels from John 10, and the progression is interesting. While Jesus as Good Shepherd (10:11, 14) is behind the entire chapter, the Year A reading, verses 1–10, perhaps also suggests other lesser but still faithful shepherds, faithful pastors who lead the sheep safely through the door, which is Jesus too. Then Year B, verses 11–18, poses the alternative of false shepherds, hirelings who leave the sheep to wolves. Now in Year C, Jesus is confronted by enemies who insinuate He is that false kind of shepherd, not good at all. (See how this progression yields different THEMES in the devotion-studies for Years A and B, pp 126 and 372.)

The Feast of Dedication (10:22) actually commemorated the rededication of the temple in 164 BC, after it had been desecrated by Syrian Greeks who were then defeated by the Jews. Judaism celebrates it today as Hanukkah.

Jesus had never in fact kept His adversaries "in suspense" (10:24). He'd been so frank, in fact, that some of the Jews had already tried to stone Him (8:56–59). Countless miracles testified to His identity as well (10:25). And now recently, calling Himself the Good Shepherd (another of His many "I am" statements; see also 6:35; 8:12; 10:7; 11:25; 14:6; 15:5) was a claim to be the Lord in David's psalm: "Yahweh is my shepherd."

So Jesus turns the tables. *It's not that I'm a false shepherd. The problem is that you aren't the Good Shepherd's sheep* (10:26). Those who are "My sheep hear My voice, and I know them, and they follow Me. I give them eternal life" (10:27–28a).

Those who belong to the Good Shepherd have the same kind of intimate, knowing relationship with Him that David pictured so beautifully. "Honey, I'm home." "Time to eat." "Grace, mercy, and peace from God our Father and from our Lord and Savior Jesus Christ." The voice means something good is coming. The voice means love. The voice means "with me."

It wasn't too late for these critics to recognize this very voice and receive eternal life themselves. But if they refused, Jesus would not let them steal away those sheep who were listening: "They will never perish, and no one will snatch them out of My hand. My Father, who has given them to Me, is greater than all, and no one is able to snatch them out of the Father's hand" (10:28b–29). Here were real false shepherds, immediate threats to the sheep. But the Good Shepherd would never allow them to snatch away the sheep for whom He'd laid down His life.

Isn't this one of the sweetest assurances that comes with being sheep of this Shepherd! Satan marshals his forces—cults and false religions, anti-Christian media and academics, immoral entertainment, unbelieving friends, even doctrinal errors among Christians—all to pull us, our children, our fellow church members away from Christ. But no one is able to snatch us out of God's hand!

Only one, really, can separate us from our Shepherd. So we pray the **Collect**:

> *Almighty God, merciful Father, since You have wakened from death the Shepherd of Your sheep, grant us Your Holy Spirit that when we hear the voice of our Shepherd we may know Him who calls us each by name and follow where He leads; through the same Jesus Christ, Your Son, our Lord, who lives and reigns with You and the Holy Spirit, one God, now and forever. Amen.*

Even the Shepherd's death couldn't separate us from Him. No thing, no one *else* can. We pray that the Holy Spirit would protect us from ourselves. And He will—by His Means of Grace: the voice of the Shepherd continuing to call us by name in preaching, in the Sacrament of the Altar, in our study of His Word.

The rest of the propers affirm that confidence. The **Introit**:

> *I am the good shepherd. I know My own and My own know Me, and I lay down My life for the sheep.*
>
> *He chose David His servant and took him from the sheepfolds; from following the nursing ewes He brought him to shepherd Jacob His people, Israel His inheritance. With upright heart he shepherded them and guided them with his skillful hand. But we Your people, the sheep of Your pasture, will give thanks to You forever; from generation to generation we will recount Your praise.*
>
> *Glory be to the Father and to the Son and to the Holy Spirit; as it was*

in the beginning, is now, and will be forever. Amen.

I am the good shepherd. I know My own and My own know Me, and I lay down My life for the sheep. (Ps 78:70–72; 79:13; antiphon: Jn 10:14, 15b)

Psalms 78 and 79, "of Asaph," a Levite, were likely composed near the time of David. Israel would often reprise the story of God raising David from literal shepherding to become shepherd-king of Israel because it was more than history; it was prophecy. David was a prefiguring of the Messiah who would shepherd God's people with perfect skill, which meant that even when David was long gone, future generations would still give thanks for God providing their real Shepherd—"forever."

The Lord is always our comfort when we lose a beloved shepherd: the **First Reading**, Acts 20:17–35.

Paul knew that the elders (20:17) of the Church in Ephesus (that is, the pastors or, in 20:28, "overseers," ἐπισκόπους, *episkopous*, as the New Testament often uses the terms) would never see his face again (20:25). He also knew that after His departure, false teachers, "wolves," would attack the "flock" (20:28, 29). But better than His own personal presence, He was able to "commend [them] to God and to the word of His grace, which is able to build you up and to give you the inheritance among all those who are sanctified" (20:32). The Good Shepherd is still always with us wherever His Word is.

Someday we'll enjoy His nearer presence. Read the **Epistle**, Revelation 7:9–17.

Just as Jesus' death couldn't separate us from our Good Shepherd, neither can our own. Death will only mean we are delivered from the tribulations Satan tries to use to seduce us into despairing of Christ's care (7:14). As surely as the Lord is our Shepherd now, "the Lamb in the midst of the throne will be [our] shepherd, and He will guide [us] to springs of living water, . . . and God will wipe away every tear from [our] eyes," and we will live forever in "His presence" (7:17).

The day after I preached that sermon for Good Shepherd Sunday, I got a call from a member of a congregation two thousand miles away in the Pacific Northwest. His congregation had just lost its pastor, too, and he, a layman, was suddenly being asked to preach the coming Sunday. He'd seen my sermon on the internet and asked if he could use it. "Sure," I said, but I asked him about a vacancy pastor. He told me they were an independent Lutheran congregation and didn't have a way to get one. So I suggested an LCMS pastor I knew to be just a few miles away. It turned out, that pastor, who later became a buddy of mine on the seminary faculty, guided that congregation in the process of acquiring a pastor and eventually into our Synod. The congregation lost a shepherd, but nothing snatched them out of the Good Shepherd's hand.

His "goodness faileth never," the **Hymn of the Day**, "The King of Love My Shepherd Is" (*LSB* 709), says. It's one of several wonderful hymn paraphrases of Psalm 23.

Fifth Sunday of Easter Year C

READINGS

Acts 11:1–18
Psalm 148 (antiphon: v 13)
Revelation 21:1–17
John 16:12–22
or John 13:31–35

HYMN OF THE DAY

LSB 633 "At the Lamb's High Feast We Sing"

A few weeks ago, for the Fifth Sunday in Lent, I told you how much I admired my grandma, in that even as an elderly woman, she always appreciated new things. That was a great attitude—especially since the Lord declared through Isaiah that He Himself was doing "a new thing." Then, on Holy Thursday, we heard Christ institute the new covenant in His blood, and we continue to partake of that each week. But it's with Easter, the completion of Christ's saving work, that God begins to reveal more fully what He's always been planning, promising, and putting in place. So the propers for this Fifth Sunday of Easter will let us see where God's new thing ultimately leads, how it fully plays out.

Resistance to change or reticence about new things isn't always being a curmudgeon. Sometimes change really is more than we can handle. You've probably heard of life-change points, officially the "Social Readjustment Rating Scale." Research (which I suppose will sooner or later be considered old and discredited . . .) suggests that if in a period of one year a person earns too many points for changes in life—new experiences like death of a spouse, being fired, moving to a new city, even good ones like taking a new job, getting married, having a baby—the probability is high for a health breakdown. Change can be troubling.

That makes our **Collect** this week a precious prayer, since God *is* shaking things up!

O God, You make the minds of Your faithful to be of one will. Grant that we may love what You have commanded and desire what You promise, that among the many changes of this world our hearts may be fixed where true joys are found; through Jesus Christ, Your Son, our Lord, who lives and reigns with You and the Holy Spirit, one God, now and forever. Amen.

"Among the many changes of this world." There it is. Not only our own life change points but changes in laws, social mores, technology. Nothing seems stable.

And then God calls us to change too. "O God, You make the minds of Your faithful to be of one will." Indeed He does. And He commands us to love that. He commands us to love being joined together as Church, His faithful, with, for example, folks who once didn't speak our language or live in our neighborhood or even in our country. They didn't go to our schools or work at our jobs. Maybe we once didn't have to think about that—except to welcome a missionary speaker now and then and give offerings to support others doing the job. God has changed that, and we're to love it and desire that He keep His promise that people who are new to us will be our brothers and sisters in the faith.

We pray this because it's not easy or, in our sinfulness, natural for us. We can only do it if God turns our hearts away from ease and comfort and familiarity and fixes them "where true joys are found." Our later propers will remind us where that is.

In the meantime, there's plenty of joy over God's new thing in the **Introit**:

Oh sing to the LORD a new song, for He has done marvelous things! His right hand and His holy arm have worked salvation for Him.

The LORD has made known His salvation; He has revealed His righteousness in the sight of the nations. He has remembered His steadfast love and faithfulness to the house of Israel. All the ends of the earth have seen the salvation of our God. Make a joyful noise to the LORD, all the earth; break forth into joyous song and sing praises! Sing praises to the LORD with the lyre, with the lyre and the sound of melody! With trumpets and the sound of the horn make a joyful noise before the King, the LORD!

Glory be to the Father and to the Son and to the Holy Spirit; as it was in the beginning, is now, and will be forever. Amen.

Oh sing to the LORD a new song, for He has done marvelous things! His right hand and His holy arm have worked salvation for Him. (Ps 98:2–6; antiphon: Ps 98:1)

Do you happen to recognize Psalm 98? We chant it at Christmas, and we sing it as the basis for "Joy to the World." God began to do His new (and "marvelous"!) thing when Christ was born—much to the world's joyous noises and songs—but it comes to fulfillment ever since He died and rose again.

And now that the Lord's salvation has been "worked," accomplished, finished, it has also been "made known" fully, "revealed." To whom? This is new: "in the sight of the nations." When Old Testament Israel (and the psalmist) spoke of "the nations," גּוֹיִם, *goyim*, it always meant the *other* nations, the Gentiles. God had always intended to save people of every tribe and nation, but that wasn't widely announced, and it certainly wasn't clear to all Israelites. But as of this new thing, "*all the ends of the earth* have seen the salvation of our God." All nations get to share in the "joyous song" and "praises."

That's emphatically the emphasis of the **Psalm** for this Sunday, Psalm 148.

You may recall the Psalm even more easily, because it was also the Psalm three weeks ago. At that time, we focused on the object, the reason we "Alleluia," "Praise the LORD!"—that is, His raising up for us a horn of strength, the Messiah (148:14a).

This time, look at the subjects, the ones doing the praising. Everybody is! "All angels," "all His hosts," "all you shining stars," "all deeps," "all hills," "all cedars," "all livestock," "all rulers," "all peoples" (148:2, 3, 7, 9, 10, 11). We get the idea. The mighty works of the Lord are for everyone—even every thing. Here's the summary: "He has raised up a horn for His people, praise for all His saints" (148:14a, b). God's saints, His holy ones, the Church, are to come from among "all peoples." That was new in the New Testament age. That was a change.

This change first comes to a test in the **First Reading**, Acts 11:1–18.

Acts 10 (also worth reading as you look forward to this Sunday morning) gives more detail behind the hubbub, news "that the Gentiles also had received the word of God" (11:1). This is not well received. That Peter "went to uncircumcised men and ate with them" (11:3) did not violate a specific Old Testament command, but Peter no doubt agreed that it should not, in the past, have been done (10:28), because God had indeed commanded Israel to destroy, not pity, the nations they conquered (Deut 7:16). So now he must explain to his critics why he had gone to the home of Cornelius, a Gentile and a centurion in the Roman army, anyway.

Certainly God *had* prohibited Israelites from eating the animals Peter saw in his vision (Acts 11:5–8; Deut 14:3–20). From Acts 10, we see that Peter didn't at first grasp the real significance of the message. For the moment, he simply complied with the Spirit's instruction to accompany the servants of Cornelius to the centurion's home (Acts 11:11–12). Only upon arriving, seeing the assembly of eager, faithful Gentiles, and hearing their side of the story (10:27–33) was he able to say, "Truly I understand" (10:34). Now Peter got the point: the Lord's words, "What God has made clean, do not call common" (11:9), truly applied to people, the Gentiles, not food. They were to be full members of the Church, "making no distinction" from Jews (11:12).

For Jewish Christians, the idea of being one with Gentiles was radically new, a total makeover of their worldview. But God validated it by visibly giving Cornelius's gathering the Pentecost gifts (11:15–16). And in fact, Peter now explained, it wasn't a new idea to God, because Jews themselves had received the Holy Spirit on the same terms: "*When we believed* in the Lord Jesus Christ" (11:17). It wasn't about being Jew or Gentile after all; it was all a matter of faith in Jesus. He is where true joys are found! Jesus is where the hearts of all believers are fixed, and all who believe in Him are God's people, made to be of one will! The marvelous new thing God has done is remake the Church to include all nations by revealing Him to all!

That wasn't easy for Jews—even Jewish Christians—to accept. It took "the first church convention" (the Jerusalem Council, Acts 15:1–29), Paul's letter to the Galatians, and more to settle it. But there will not be resistance to this change when God makes *all things* new, when there are no more changes of *this* world: the **Epistle**, Revelation 21:1–7.

We'll all embrace the "new heaven" and the "new earth," the "new Jerusalem," because they'll not only replace the first earth but the tears and death, mourning and crying and pain of "the former things" (21:4). We'll like this new thing!

Think about how many of those "former things" have to do with separation—so many life change points: separation from a spouse, from an old home, from a job, from children, from comfortable routine. All separations result from the cataclysmic change from Eden to a fallen world. The new Jerusalem reverses that, and it happens because Jesus' death on the cross healed our separation from God. Remember the picture of heaven in last week's Revelation reading: every nation and tribe and people and language.

Jesus saw all this new revelation coming. But He knew His disciples would first have to face an even more radical change. Read the **Holy Gospel**, John 16:12–22.

Jews and Gentiles made to be one in the Church, a new Jerusalem free of sadness and separation—the Holy Spirit would guide the disciples into these truths in good time (16:13). That's His job. But that was more than the disciples could bear for now (16:12), because the very next day, their universe would change. They would "weep and lament, but the world [would] rejoice" when Jesus died. Yet in a little while more, their "sorrow [would] turn into joy" at His resurrection (16:20). Then "I will see you again, and your hearts will rejoice, and no one will take your joy from you" (16:22)—even though another little while, Ascension, is coming soon.

This is how God's people are able to embrace joyfully the "new commandment" Jesus gave us that night—that we love one another, all people, as He has loved us. That makes a good final reading for Easter 5: the **alternate Holy Gospel**, John 13:31–35. Then

ALL REJOICE
IN THE MARVELOUS NEW THING
GOD HAS REVEALED—
THAT ALL WHO BELIEVE
IN THE LORD JESUS
ARE ONE FOR THE JERUSALEM TO COME.

All who believe are "newborn souls" sharing "Easter joy!"—**Hymn of the Day**, "At the Lamb's High Feast We Sing" (*LSB* 633:7).

Sixth Sunday of Easter Year C

READINGS

Acts 16:9–15
Psalm 67 (antiphon: v 3)
Revelation 21:9–14, 21–27
John 16:23–33
or John 5:1–9

HYMN OF THE DAY

LSB 556 "Dear Christians, One and All, Rejoice"

Who you gonna call?

The pop answer is pretty silly, so we won't go into that. But if you've seen any of the movies or the T-shirts, if you've played the video games or maybe can even sing the key lines of the song, you know whom some might call. And for what needs.

In the real world, we need to be saved from dangers that may not be as splashy or slimy on the big screen but are much more (eternal-)life threatening. This is serious. And knowing whom to call makes all the difference in heaven.

Alleluia! Christ is risen!

He is risen indeed! Alleluia!

This will be our focus for the Sixth Sunday of Easter, beginning with the **Introit**:

Cast your burden on the Lord, and He will sustain you; He will never permit the righteous to be moved.

My heart is in anguish within me; the terrors of death have fallen upon me. But I call to God, and the Lord will save me. Evening and morning and at noon I utter my complaint and moan, and He hears my voice. He redeems my soul in safety from the battle that I wage, for many are arrayed against me.

Glory be to the Father and to the Son and to the Holy Spirit; as it was in the beginning, is now, and will be forever. Amen.

Cast your burden on the Lord, and He will sustain you; He will never permit the righteous to be moved. (Ps 55:4, 16–18; antiphon: Ps 55:22)

Again, David is facing the "terrors of death. . . . For many are arrayed against me." The "battle" he was waging was probably literal, as in swords and shields, but those arrayed against him were always also Satan's hosts. Every evil we face in life has the invisible forces of darkness behind it.

Yet David is confident: "I call to God, and the Lord will save me." "He will never permit the righteous to be moved." David knows whom to call. The devil and all his terrifying, unseen demons are no match for the Lord. Calling out, complaining, moaning to God is holy communication. He never tires of hearing us—"evening and morning and at noon." He will save us.

The **Collect** adds a vital element about whom we call in a way we might overlook:

O God, the giver of all that is good, by Your holy inspiration grant that we may think those things that are right and by Your merciful guiding accomplish them; through Jesus Christ, Your Son, our Lord, who lives and reigns with You and the Holy Spirit, one God, now and forever. Amen.

God, we know, is the one who gives us everything good. And when a collect is addressed to "God," it usually intends God the Father. We call Him, for example, "the fountain and source of all goodness" (*LSB*, pp 166, 183, 201, 212, 218). But in one form or another, our prayers also generally conclude with something like "through Jesus Christ, Your Son, our Lord." This is never to be just prattling. This Sunday, Jesus will teach us much about that in the Gospel. When we call on God for help, He answers always in the name of, for the sake of Jesus.

This week's **Psalm** makes a point much like last week's. It declares *who* may call whom. Read Psalm 67.

As always with a psalm of praise, we look for the reason for praising. Here it's God's "saving power" (67:2) and that He will "judge the peoples with equity" (67:4). That is, He'll save those who call on Him, *and* He'll do that equally for all peoples. With that, this Psalm, like Psalm 148 last week, really takes off. The psalmist prays that God's saving power "may be known on earth, . . . among all nations. Let the peoples praise You, O God; . . . all the peoples . . . the nations. . . . The peoples; . . . all the peoples. . . . All the ends of the earth" (67:2, 3, 4, 5, 7). All have reason to praise because all have One they may call to save them. As we saw last week, God's invitation is to everyone because it's purely by His grace, what He does in the saving work of Christ's death and resurrection, not because of anything in any of us.

The **First Reading** gives a historic example of this: Acts 16:9–15.

Paul is on his second missionary journey, along with Silas and Timothy (new to the entourage in 16:1–3). They've revisited many of the churches Paul and Barnabas had established on their first trip, but where will they go next? The Holy Spirit seems to be closing doors (16:6–7). Then He opens a big one. In Troas (16:8), a city on the west coast of Asia Minor, present-day Turkey (a city, by the way, often associated with the much more ancient city of Troy), Paul has a vision: a man of Macedonia calling out for help (16:9). From Troas, a short voyage across the Aegean Sea would bring one to Macedonia, just north of Greece. In other words, for the first time in the recorded mission of the Gospel, Europe. Christians of English, Irish, German, French, Dutch, Scandinavian, Polish, Italian, Slavic, Spanish ethnic backgrounds take note: from its origins in Asia and Africa, the message even reaches you. "That [God's] saving power [may be known] among all nations."

Verse 10 is historic for another reason too. All evidence points to Luke as the author of Acts (as well as, of course, the author of the Gospel of Luke, Lk 1:1–4; Acts 1:1). The first fifteen-plus chapters of Acts are written in the third person—by someone about others: "he" or "she" or "them." But in Acts 16:10, for the first time, the author speaks of "we": "Immediately *we* sought to go on into Macedonia." The clear implication is that Luke joins the expedition, perhaps even meets Paul for the first time, in Troas. From here on, Luke will be a faithful partner, even to the end (e.g., 2 Tim 4:11a).

A Roman colony (16:12) means Philippi had special status in the empire; its free residents held the same privilege of citizenship as those in Rome itself, and many in Philippi were pensioned soldiers. Paul knew the help for which Macedonia, Philippi, and Europe were calling: that he "preach the gospel" (16:10). They were calling for the right One; yes, calls are heard only "through Jesus Christ."

Paul finds Sabbath worshipers by the riverside; apparently the Jewish community was too small to have a synagogue. And Lydia, a "worshiper of God" (16:14), a technical term for a Gentile who had come to follow the God of Israel (Acts 18:7; see also 8:27; 10:1–2), believes Paul's message. Not only is she baptized but "her household" (16:15) is too. While this is not the strongest of the many arguments for infant Baptism, it is a reasonable one, since ancient households were much larger than our nuclear families (likely including children), since there were multiple such cases (also 10:44–48; 11:14–17; 16:31–34; 18:8; 1 Cor 1:16), and since all the cases seem simply to assume that everyone in the house was to be baptized. It would be odd to think that would exclude a whole segment of the human race—small children—from those emphatic "all peoples," "all nations."

Certainly God does not exclude them from heaven. See if you detect the way John's vision identifies all the residents of heaven in the **Epistle**, Revelation 21:9–14, 21–27.

Last week, we saw the new Jerusalem coming down before John's eyes. Now from the mountaintop, we telescope in for a tighter look. The angel wants to show us "the Bride, the wife of the Lamb" (21:9). Zoom in on the twelve gates of the city. See "the names of the twelve tribes of the sons of Israel" inscribed (21:12). Judah and Simeon and Reuben and the rest. They represent all Old Testament believers. That is, the Bride, the wife of the Lamb, will include all those who in the Old

Testament age believed in the promised Messiah. Now focus on the city's twelve foundations. See on them "the twelve names of the twelve apostles of the Lamb" (21:14). Peter, John, Matthew, and the others would preach Christ and write about Christ, and future generations would read their writings and preach their writings. They represent all New Testament believers in Christ. They're the Bride of the Lamb too. All believers in Christ from every age—and they'll come from "the nations" (21:24, 26), all peoples.

Then we have the most vivid picture of heaven in Scripture. We don't know whether the gold and giant pearls will be literal, but the image certainly works. Beautiful! Lustrous! Elegance beyond anything we've ever seen. And the best part: "No temple in the city, for its temple is the Lord God the Almighty and the Lamb" (21:22). The temple was the place that mediated God's presence, the place to which Israel would call out to Him. Forevermore, we'll see Christ face to face. In heaven, of course, we'll call to God only in praise, never trouble—there won't be any—but when we do call, it will be directly through the Mediator Himself, the Lamb.

That's actually how it's been ever since Jesus' words in the **Holy Gospel**, John 16:23–33, came to fulfillment.

"That day" (16:23a) came with Jesus' death, resurrection, and (to be celebrated next Thursday) ascension. Jesus would no longer be visibly present to ask anything. But we know whom to call. We're able to ask the Father for anything in the name of, for the sake of, through Jesus (16:23b). We call the Father, and He hears us. Why in the name of Jesus? Because it's Jesus' death on the cross that has reconciled us to God. As long as we were in our sin, it would have separated us from God. Our calls to God would never be heard. (Review what Luther wrote in his explanation of the Fifth Petition of the Lord's Prayer.) But with sin removed by Jesus' atoning sacrifice, we call to Him "and you will receive, that your joy may be full" (16:24b).

Until heaven, we'll have plenty of need for that. "In the world you will have tribulation," Jesus says. "But take heart; I have overcome the world" (16:33).

All Peoples, All Nations Who Call to God in the Name of Jesus, the Lamb, He Saves from This World for the Heavenly One.

Here's a very brief note on the **alternate Holy Gospel**, John 5:1–9. It's a kind and gracious miracle of Jesus. But notice what seems to be an odd question: "Do you want to be healed?" (5:6). Later, Jesus speaks a surprisingly stern warning of the Law: "Sin no more, that nothing worse may happen to you" (5:14). Did Jesus perceive that the sick man had lived in unbelief, *refusing* to call out to God for help, for all those previous years?

The **Hymn of the Day**, "Dear Christians, One and All, Rejoice" (*LSB* 556), is autobiographical of Luther. Think how often he called out to the Lord and was saved!

A note for Ascension Day: Since the Ascension of Our Lord, which falls on the Thursday after Easter 6, uses the same propers for Years A, B, and C, you'll find the one devotion-study for that festival in Year A, page 138. The devotion-study for the Seventh Sunday of Easter, Year C, appears on the next page.

Seventh Sunday of Easter Year C

READINGS

Acts 1:12–26
Psalm 133 (antiphon: v 1)
Revelation 22:1–6 (7–11) 12–20
John 17:20–26

HYMN OF THE DAY

LSB 539 "Christ Is the World's Redeemer"

Taken together, the Gradual and Collect tell us right where we sit on this Seventh Sunday of Easter.

The **Gradual** reminds us that for one more week, it's still the Easter season:

> *Christ has risen from the dead. [God the Father] has crowned Him with glory and honor, He has given Him dominion over the works of His hands; He has put all things under His feet. (adapted from Mt 28:7; Heb 2:7; Ps 8:6)*

But then the **Collect**:

> *O King of glory, Lord of hosts, uplifted in triumph far above all heavens, leave us not without consolation but send us the Spirit of truth whom You promised from the Father; for You live and reign with Him and the Holy Spirit, one God, now and forever. Amen.*

It's still Easter, but as of Thursday this week, Ascension Day, Christ, our King of glory, has been "uplifted in triumph far above all heavens." That's our unusual position on the final Sunday of Easter. In the original chronology, Christ is no longer visibly present with His disciples. And yet in the Gospel reading, He's still there—in fact, He's still preparing for His crucifixion, the first and very brief time when He wouldn't be with them visibly.

That creates an interesting liturgical anomaly. If congregations don't have a special Ascension Day Thursday service, they may use all the Ascension propers this Sunday in place of those for Easter 7. Or they may mix some of the Ascension Day elements with those for the Sunday. (To consider how that might be done, we offer our devotion-study for Easter 7, Year A, on p 142. Or to prepare for Sunday using the Ascension propers, the Ascension devotion-study in Year A, on p 138.)

In any case, Easter 7 brings us to the end of a season and, in the bigger picture, brings world history to the end of an era—the three-year era of our Lord's earthly ministry. But the propers for this week assure us that lots more is coming.

**The End of a Season—
Even of an Era—
Anticipates
an Even More Exciting Future.**

That'll be the Theme of our devotion-study as we look forward to a Sunday that has us very much looking forward.

On September 8, 2022, the world saw the end of an era that, while less important than Jesus' ministry, was much longer: the reign of Queen Elizabeth II of the United Kingdom. Her seventy years on the throne (since February 6, 1952) made her the longest-reigning English monarch and perhaps the longest-reigning woman anywhere. She was the only sovereign most of her subjects had ever known. Decades of printings of *The Lutheran Hymnal* included the quaint insertion in the General Prayer, "For Use in the British Empire," for "Her Majesty the Queen of the British Commonwealth of Nations" (*TLH,* p 23). More recently, *Lutheran Service Book* knew to hedge its bets with prayers that God would "direct and defend our *president/queen/king*" (*LSB*, p 289).

The moment Queen Elizabeth died, the chants of the people and even the national anthem became "God Save the King." A new era, the reign of her son, Charles III, began. How would that affect the lives of commonwealth citizens around the world? Would it lead to the demise of the monarchy? Simply doing the math, Charles ascending to the throne at age 73 meant the new era would not have the same stability of duration as his mother's.

Jesus' coronation as King of glory above all heavens no doubt left the disciples with some anxiety. "Leave us not without consolation." We know how often we wish we could see Jesus standing with us to bail us out. But there's also anticipation that comes with the new era: "Send us the Spirit of truth whom You promised from the Father." The disciples didn't know God's schedule, but we know next Sunday is Pentecost!

What the disciples did know from Jesus' last instructions was that they were to "stay in the city [Jerusalem] until you are clothed with power from on high" (Lk 24:49, from the Gospel for Ascension Day). That was loaded with anticipation. And that's what the disciples are doing in the **First Reading** for Easter 7, Acts 1:12–26.

The not-so-little gathering of 120 (1:15) is in the same (obviously larger than we picture) Upper Room where Jesus and the apostles had celebrated the Last Supper (1:13a; Lk 22:12), but they're not just calling the roll (Acts 1:13b). It seems instead that the pot is bubbling, eager to boil over. They're praying for whatever Jesus has next (1:14). And then Peter stands up, takes charge (1:15).

He's been doing a lot of thinking these forty days since Easter, going over in his head Bible passages from those familiar (probably memorized) psalms that no doubt meant very little to him a couple months earlier. Now that Jesus has died, risen, and "opened their minds to understand the Scriptures" (Lk 24:45)—how everything added up to Him and His Passion—Peter proposes the next step. Judas's betrayal of Jesus was exactly as David said it would happen (1:16; Ps 41:9), and it has consequences (Acts 1:18–20a; Ps 69:25), but now Scripture tells us to go forward: "Let another take his office" (Acts 1:20b; Ps 109:8).

And Peter knows this office isn't ceremonial, a palace figurehead. Jesus has a daunting but exciting job ahead for the apostles. They will be His "witnesses in Jerusalem and in all Judea and Samaria, and to the end of the earth" (Acts 1:8). They'll need the full complement of twelve. Someone "must become with us a witness to His resurrection" (1:22b).

That means this one must himself be an eyewitness of Jesus, to "have accompanied us during all the time that the Lord Jesus went in and out among us, beginning from the baptism of John until the day when He was taken up from us" (1:21–22a). Blessed are we who have not seen and yet have believed (Jn 20:29), but we believe only because of—we stake our eternal salvation only on—the testimony of those who did indeed see Jesus.

Joseph and Matthias fit the bill. Casting lots was common for learning God's will in the Old Testament (Lev 16:8; Josh 14:1–2; Prov 16:33), but just this once more in the New Testament. It's Matthias who's "numbered with the eleven *apostles*" (Acts 1:26), the Greek literally meaning the "sent ones." The stoplight is about to turn bright green!

The **Holy Gospel**, John 17:20–26, steps back in time to the night before Jesus died. But it, too, is brimming with anticipation.

This is the final installment in Jesus' "High Priestly Prayer" (17:1–19 were heard on Easter 7, Years A and B). It anticipates what Jesus is doing for us since His ascension—praying for the Church. It looks ahead to the era when not just a dozen or so on Holy Thursday dinner but we and billions of others "will believe in Me through their word" (17:20). Jesus "will continue to make [the Father's name] known" (17:26), but He'll do it through the preaching and writing of the apostles, as Peter anticipated—and then through the speaking and writing of us who've believed through the apostolic word. Pentecost is coming!

Jesus' prayer also anticipates the whole Church being one, just as Jesus and the Father are one (17:21–23). For now, there will be—and must be—divisions in the visible Church when even sincere Christians err on particular truths of Scripture. But even now, there is an invisible oneness among all believers in Christ. For we are constantly forgiving one another for errors we don't recognize, and we know that all believers are brothers and sisters, headed for an eternity together "with Me," Jesus says, "where I am" (17:24). This oneness will surely be a most exciting feature of heaven!

The **Psalm** is a lovely poetic expression of this. Read Psalm 133.

"Behold!" Read it again, slowly, and picture it. "How good and pleasant it is when brothers dwell in unity!" (133:1). Olive oil poured over the head was for the anointing of kings and priests, like the original high priest, Aaron. If that's not you today, perhaps think how good it feels to stand under a warm shower, with clean water drenching you head to toe. How good when we agree, support, work together, pray for one another.

It's as Jesus described: "Pleasant it *is*," right now. Jesus' death has reconciled God to man and man to man. And "the Lord has commanded the blessing, life *forevermore*" (133:3). We look forward to perfect oneness.

That certainly brings us to the **Epistle**, the last chapter of the Bible, Revelation 22:1–20.

John's final words look even beyond the era of life in this world. And the future is thrilling! No evil (22:3a, 11, 15), no dangers of night (22:5), no false teachings (22:18–19). The season is always Easter (22:1–2), for we will see the very face of the risen Christ (22:4), the loving Savior who has washed our robes in His own blood so that we "may have the right to the tree of life and . . . may enter the city by the gates" (22:14).

"Alleluia. We know that Christ being raised from the dead will never die again; death no longer has dominion over Him. Alleluia. I will not leave you as orphans; I will come to you. Alleluia" (**Verse** for Easter 7). Indeed! "He who testifies to these things says, 'Surely I am coming soon.' Amen. Come, Lord Jesus!" (Rev 22:20).

The sequence of Easter 7 is capsulized in the **Introit**—once more anticipating a king coming to the throne:

Hear my cry, O God, listen to my prayer; for You have been my refuge, a strong tower against the enemy. For You, O God, have heard my vows; You have given me the heritage of those who fear Your name. Prolong the life of the king; may his years endure to all generations! May he be enthroned forever before God; appoint steadfast love and faithfulness to watch over him! So will I ever sing praises to Your name, as I perform my vows day after day.

Glory be to the Father and to the Son and to the Holy Spirit; as it was in the beginning, is now, and will be forever. Amen.

Hear my cry, O God, listen to my prayer. (Ps 61:3, 5–8; antiphon: Ps 61:1)

With end of the era of Jesus' visible presence, even the end of the apostolic era, I "cry, O God," for I no longer see the one who has "been my refuge . . . against the enemy." But long live the King! May Christ "be enthroned forever before God!" I know my future, that I will "ever sing praises to Your name."

The **Hymn of the Day** (*LSB* 539) finishes nobly: "Christ the cross ascended. . . . Rose triumphantly. . . . And now, to heaven ascended." "Amen! So let it be" (sts 2, 3, 4).

The Day of Pentecost Year C

READINGS

Genesis 11:1–9
Psalm 143 (antiphon: v 10)
Acts 2:1–21
John 14:23–31

HYMN OF THE DAY

LSB 497 "Come, Holy Ghost, God and Lord"

Fifty-three days before Pentecost, by Hebrew counting, Jesus had promised His disciples "the Helper, the Holy Spirit, whom the Father will send in My name" (Jn 14:26).

Now that was happening! The Day of Pentecost! The sound like a mighty rushing wind. The tongues as of fire. Crowds rushing to see and hear. The languages of every nation under heaven. And "Peter, standing with the eleven, lifted up his voice" and began to preach (Acts 2:14).

There was Peter boldly taking his stand, with eleven partners alongside—encouraging, nodding, showing their support. But we know he couldn't have done it without the help, the support, the counsel, the comfort of the Holy Spirit—the Helper whom the Father would send in Jesus' name. The bold Pentecost sermon is the work of the Holy Spirit, which means the three thousand converts are the work of the Holy Spirit, which means the Church is the work of the Holy Spirit.

Some Helper!

And much more than a Helper.

A παράκλητος. *The Parakletos.*

When Jesus promised to send the disciples the Holy Spirit, He promised, quite literally, "one called to stand alongside" them. From the Greek word *kaleo*, "call," with the prefixed preposition *para*, which in this usage means "beside" or "to the side of."

We all know how precious it is to have someone stand beside us—literally or figuratively. Your spouse at a function where you don't know another soul in the room. Your wingman when you're a scared freshman during orientation week—or when you're flying an F-35 in combat. Your dad any time.

Or Pee Wee Reese, a good southern boy, white, from Kentucky going over and standing by his Dodger teammate, Jackie Robinson, the first African American player in Major League Baseball, when fans and other players were shouting the nastiest things at Robinson.

The Holy Spirit is sent, called by God the Father and God the Son to stand beside us every moment—during this period between Jesus' visible time on earth, which ended with His ascension, which we observed last Thursday, and His visible return, when we'll see Him face to face forever after. Think of how many ways in how many life situations that's a blessing to us!

That does, though, create a problem, a good problem. The *Parakletos* does so many things for us that it's hard to sum Him up in just one English word. How best to translate παράκλητος, the one called to stand beside us?

Several major English translations, like our English Standard Version, the New American Standard Bible, and the New King James, render παράκλητος as "Helper." It's a very helpful translation, because "helper" is broad enough to cover just about any good thing anyone does for anyone else. But broad can also be generic. There are so many specific things the Holy Spirit does as He stands by us. It would be nice to identify some.

So other Bible versions, including the King James Version (KJV) and The Living Bible, translate παράκλητος as "Comforter." How often we need God's comfort, His consolation, like that very night as Jesus spoke to the disciples: "Because I have said these things unto you, sorrow hath filled your heart. Nevertheless I tell you the truth; It is expedient for you that I go away: for if I go not away, the Comforter (παράκλητος) will not come unto you; but if I depart, I will send Him unto you" (Jn 16:6–7 KJV).

But the Greek παράκλητος has other dimensions too, and the one called to our side does other blessed things for us. Jesus tells us that "the Holy Spirit, whom the Father will send in My name, will teach you all things and will remind you of everything I have said to you." So the New International Version and also the Revised Standard Version call Him the "Counselor."

A very prominent connotation of the Greek and a very important activity of the Holy Spirit is to be our "Advocate." The Spirit doesn't just stand there next to us; He speaks up in our defense. The same word, παράκλητος, is used of Jesus in 1 John 2:1: "If anyone does sin, we have an advocate with the Father, Jesus Christ the righteous." The New Revised Standard Version and others go this way.

Closely related to *Advocate* is *Intercessor.* Paul writes that "the Spirit helps us in our weakness. For we do not know what to pray for as we ought, but the Spirit Himself intercedes for us with groanings too deep for words. And He who searches hearts knows what is the mind of the Spirit, because the Spirit intercedes for the saints according to the will of God" (Rom 8:26–27).

A rather loose paraphrase, but pleasant, is the rendering of παράκλητος as "Friend."

Finally, there's the option the New Jerusalem Bible takes. Since the *Parakletos* obviously does way more than any one English word can convey, don't translate it at all, just trans*literate* it: Paraclete. When you see that word (as in *LSB* 500:4), you may not know what it means, but it's a signal to learn *all* this.

Language was much simpler back when "the whole earth had one language and the same words" (Gen 11:1): the **Old Testament Reading**, Genesis 11:1–9.

Over perhaps a century following the flood, the descendants of Noah moved from Ararat to "a plain in the land of Shinar" (11:2), in Mesopotamia ("between the rivers," the Tigris and Euphrates), present-day Iraq. (Peleg was born approximately 101 years after the flood, 11:10–16, and "the earth was divided," likely this incident, in his days, 10:25). The city the people began to build would have been at least near the site of ancient Babylon (Dan 1:1–2).

Already they have a sense of history; scattering into small clans, each would be forgotten by future generations. By staying together, building a great city and tower, they would "make a name for [them]selves" (Gen 11:4), be long remembered. It turns out that they are—but in infamy. They were acting as "children of man" (11:5), sinfully, as contrasted to the children of God they were created to be (5:1). God had commanded them to fill the earth (9:1, 7), but their pride demands a different course. The problem is they don't realize they need the Lord to stand by them.

Man, of course, proposes, but God disposes. He must have laughed at their vain plotting (Ps 2:1, 4). Yet it is always our good He has in mind. If the people begin to believe all things earthly are possible for them (Gen 11:6), they will entirely forget how helpless they are in the truly important, eternal matters, how much they need God's plan to send a Savior. So by confusing their languages, God forces the people to live independently of one another (11:7–8)—and discover they do need someone to come alongside them.

Foolish self-sufficiency comes at the price of divisions, rivalries and hatred, loneliness. We see it in families, among nations. For thousands of years it divided most people on earth from the blessings of God's people.

That makes the Day of Pentecost so striking! It's our **Second Reading**, Acts 2:1–21.

You know the story well, and more details of the event are discussed in the devotion-studies for Years A and B (pp 146 and 388). This time, just focus on Peter standing before the crowd. Yes, the other eleven apostles are standing with him. But unseen, standing by him, is the *Parakletos*.

Just fifty-three days before, Peter had been afraid even to say he knew Jesus. Now, in the same city, some of the same crowd, all of the same powerful enemies, he will preach that this same Jesus "you crucified and killed by the hands of lawless men" (2:23; you'll hear this and the rest of Peter's sermon next Sunday). No way Peter does this without the *Parakletos*, the Comforter.

Peter explains to the crowd that the wondrous things they're seeing and hearing are the fulfillment of the prophecy of Joel 2:28–32 (2:16–21). No way Peter understands that if not for the *Parakletos*, the Counselor.

Visitors to Jerusalem from all those nations are hearing the Gospel in their own languages (Acts 2:8–11). That doesn't happen unless the *Parakletos*, the Intercessor, "gave [the apostles] utterance" (2:4).

It demonstrates a shortcoming of the otherwise, uh, helpful translation, "Helper." The Holy Spirit doesn't just help. The proclamation "that everyone who calls upon the name of the Lord shall be saved"—and the believing of it (2:21)—are the Holy Spirit's work, not ours. It was Peter's voice they heard, but the words were the Holy Spirit's.

Now read the **Holy Gospel** from whence all this comes: John 14:23–31.

We've seen the *Parakletos* as Counselor (14:26). He's also Comforter with the peace, the reconciliation of God and man, Jesus won on the cross (14:27). And He's Advocate, defending us against our own accusing consciences when Satan tries to claim us (14:30). But above all, He's just plain Paraclete, bringing the Father and the Son to "come to [us] and make [their] home with [us]" (14:23), to stand by us, as He does for everyone He calls into the Holy Christian Church.

No Matter How We Understand the Language, the *Parakletos* Brings Together Christ's Church.

Find the *Parakletos* as Intercessor, Advocate, Comforter, and Counselor also in the **Psalm** (Psalm 143) and the **Introit**:

Come, Holy Spirit, fill the hearts of the faithful, and kindle in them the fire of Your love. Alleluia.

O Lord, how manifold are Your works! In wisdom have You made them all; the earth is full of Your creatures. These all look to You, to give them their food in due season. When You give it to them, they gather it up; when You open Your hand, they are filled with good things. When You send forth Your Spirit, they are created, and You renew the face of the ground.

Glory be to the Father and to the Son and to the Holy Spirit; as it was in the beginning, is now, and will be forever. Amen.

Come, Holy Spirit, fill the hearts of the faithful, and kindle in them the fire of Your love. Alleluia. (Ps 104:24, 27–28, 30 antiphon: Liturgical Text)

The **Collect**:

O God, on this day You once taught the hearts of Your faithful people by sending them the light of Your Holy Spirit. Grant us in our day by the same Spirit to have a right understanding in all things and evermore to rejoice in His holy consolation; through Jesus Christ, Your Son, our Lord, who lives and reigns with You and the Holy Spirit, one God, now and forever. Amen.

Finally, which activities of the Paraclete does Luther cite in the **Hymn of the Day**, "Come, Holy Ghost, God and Lord" (*LSB* 497)? At least "guide" and "teach" and "comfort" (st 2, 3). Others?

The Holy Trinity Year C

READINGS

Proverbs 8:1–4, 22–31
Psalm 8 (antiphon: v 9)
Acts 2:14a, 22–36
John 8:48–59

HYMN OF THE DAY

LSB 498, 499 "Come, Holy Ghost, Creator Blest"

The Feast of the Holy Trinity is like the triune God Himself—much more than can be addressed in one Sunday or one devotion-study. Since the one true God is infinitely above us, since the reality of the Trinity is a mystery we can never understand, so also Trinity Sunday has an assignment it can't possibly fulfill: to bring all things trinitarian to clarity in perhaps sixty to ninety minutes. And yet God has revealed Himself to us as in one way being so down to earth that we *can* meaningfully and joyfully adore Him this festival Sunday.

Trinity Sunday is actually quite a new observation—as feasts of the church year go. In the early medieval period, scattered localities of the Western Church began to hold celebrations of the Trinity. However, two different popes, in the eleventh and twelfth centuries, discouraged such festivals because, after all, every Lord's Day that Christians come together must always only be a *Trinity* Sunday. By around AD 1300, though, Pope John XXII officially declared the feast day and set it to be held on the Sunday after Pentecost. So Trinity Sunday is only around over seven hundred years old.

Trinity is different from other major festivals in that it is based on a doctrine; the others observe chief events in the life and work of Jesus—events surrounding His birth, death, resurrection, ascension, and sending the Holy Spirit. Therefore, this Sunday is definitely an occasion to review the doctrine of the Trinity. Hence the custom of reciting on Trinity Sunday the Athanasian Creed.

Page 319 in *Lutheran Service Book* offers an excellent brief history and summary with the text of the Athanasian Creed. Not only is it informative, but the red ink and resulting split of the Creed onto two pages gives it a less ominous look than the solid gray of previous hymnals. Don't be put off. The Creed is long, but it's the best go the Church has ever made at explaining the unexplainable. It takes the language of Scripture and then adopts further phrasing, and technical terms that the Church has ever since agreed to use, where no adequate words otherwise exist. A teaching so complex and so essential to salvation takes some time. It's worth it!

"Whoever desires to be saved must, above all, hold the catholic faith." *Catholic*, of course, doesn't mean Roman. It means universal. Every true believer in Christ Jesus is a member of the universal, invisible Holy Christian, Holy Catholic, Church.

"And the catholic faith is this, that we worship one God in Trinity and Trinity in Unity, neither confusing the persons nor dividing the substance. For the Father is one person, the Son is another, and the Holy Spirit is another. But the Godhead of the Father and of the Son and of the Holy Spirit is one: the glory equal, the majesty coeternal . . ."

"Trinity" and "person" are two of those technical terms the Church has come to use; the Bible itself doesn't use either. But the Bible is very clear there is one and only one God (e.g., Deut 6:4; 1 Cor 8:4), yet He is three (Is 48:16; Mt 3:16–17; 28:19). The three persons are equal, have all existed from eternity, but are distinct—not just three different activities of God or three different ways to think about God or three "parts" of God. There's nothing else quite like this. But it's absolutely true, and "whoever desires to be saved must" believe it. Judaism, Islam, Hinduism, Buddhism, Mormonism, and Jehovah's Witness all deny this one true God and do not lead to salvation.

How can God demand that something so complicated, that all other world religions have wrong, that *none* of us can understand would be necessary for salvation? Surely we all have confusions about the Trinity. Well, it's not *understanding* that's necessary for salvation. God actually teaches us what we need to know about Him in a way any child can tell and even know personally. That—more than explaining the Trinity—is really what the propers for Trinity Sunday are about.

Begin with the **Introit**:

Blessèd be the Holy Trinity and the undivided Unity. Let us give glory to Him because He has shown His mercy to us.

I have set the Lord *always before me; because He is at my right hand, I shall not be shaken. Therefore my heart is glad, and my whole being rejoices; my flesh also dwells secure. For You will not abandon my soul to Sheol, or let Your holy one see corruption. You make known to me the path of life; in Your presence there is fullness of joy; at Your right hand are pleasures forevermore.*

Glory be to the Father and to the Son and to the Holy Spirit; as it was in the beginning, is now, and will be forever. Amen.

Blessèd be the Holy Trinity and the undivided Unity. Let us give glory to Him because He has shown His mercy to us. (Ps 16:8–11; antiphon: Liturgical Text)

The first sentence of the antiphon echoes the Athanasian formulation. (It's a "Liturgical Text"—that is, not quoted from Scripture but from traditional language of the Church.) But notice also the second sentence. God already deserves glory in that He's so infinitely above us. But here we give Him glory not for being overwhelming, awesome, incomprehensible, but "because He has shown His mercy to us." He's above all things, but He also cares about what's going on down here with us. "You make known to me the path of life." The way of salvation isn't complicated or unknowable. He *has* made it known to us—in one of those "persons." You already know.

Peter will be explicit about Him in the Second Reading, when he'll quote these very words of David from Psalm 16. But here's another detail to glean. David writes that "at *Your* right hand are pleasures forevermore." Being with God in heaven will certainly be pleasant. But a few verses earlier, he also wrote, "He is at *my* right hand." It's not just that someday we'll ascend to heaven. The awesome God who's so far above us also comes to be by me, "at *my* right hand"!

The **Collect** prays the same double truth about the Trinity:

Almighty and everlasting God, You have given us grace to acknowledge the glory of the eternal Trinity by the confession of a true faith and to worship the Unity in the power of the Divine Majesty. Keep us steadfast in this faith and defend us from all adversities; for You, O Father, Son, and Holy Spirit, live and reign, one God, now and forever. Amen.

Just once a year, the Collect is addressed to all three persons of the triune God: "You, O Father, Son, and Holy Spirit, live and reign, one God."

On the one hand, we "acknowledge the glory of" this mysterious "eternal Trinity." He is "the Divine Majesty" who so transcends us. But on the other hand, without understanding, we believe in this God; He is our "faith." That's because He's revealed Himself as the God who comes to be here with us in our world, our lives.

God is above us above all because He—as Trinity—created us. The **Old Testament Reading**, Proverbs 8:1–4, 22–31.

The Lord did quite the job on mountains, hills, fields, the deep, the sky. But who was the "master workman" beside Him (8:30) while creating? This is a poetic description of the Son of God as "wisdom" (8:1). He has been with the Father and Spirit from eternity. And He is the Trinity's self-revelation to His creation "rejoicing in His inhabited world and delighting in the children of man" (8:31). He's above us but delighting in us.

The appointed Psalm for Holy Trinity is Psalm 8. How remarkable that the Lord is "majestic," "above the heavens," but is praised by "babies and infants" (8:1, 2). So infinitely above us: "What is man that You are mindful of him, and the son of man that You care for him?" (8:4). But He does care! "You have made him a little lower than the heavenly beings and crowned him with glory and honor" (8:5). Hebrews interprets this quite provocatively (Heb 2:5–17). There's more about that in the devotion-study for Year A (p 153).

What was hinted often in the Old Testament becomes clear after Jesus' resurrection. Read the rest of Peter's Pentecost sermon we began last week, the **Second Reading** for Trinity, Acts 2:14a, 22–36.

The eternal triune God has revealed Himself to us by becoming a man, Jesus of Nazareth (2:22). Here's the proof, Peter says: you all know and respect David, not only as your great king but as a prophet of God. He told you (in the words we heard in the Introit) that God would not let His Holy One rot in the grave (2:25–27). But you all know David died and is still buried (2:29), so he wasn't talking about himself. He was talking about the Christ (2:31). I'm here to tell you that Jesus, whom you crucified, is that Christ, for "this Jesus God raised up, and of that we all are witnesses" (2:32).

It's how we know the Holy Trinity: "Having received from the *Father* the promise of the *Holy Spirit*, He [the *Son*] has poured out this that you yourselves are seeing and hearing" (2:33). We know the Trinity because the Son, who sits at the right hand of the Father (2:34), wasn't above coming down to His sinful creation to die for us (2:36).

Hear Him in the **Holy Gospel**, John 8:48–59.

The last section of the Athanasian Creed begins, "But it is also necessary for everlasting salvation that one faithfully believe the incarnation of our Lord Jesus Christ." For Jesus is none other than the great I Am (8:58) who revealed Himself to Moses in the burning bush (Ex 3:14) and to God's people as Yahweh, in the Old Testament. Now, He has revealed God to us as triune God in flesh, crucified and risen, saving His lost creation, with us here so that we do know Him (8:55).

As the One True God Is Both One God and Three Persons, So He Is Also Both Creator in Majesty above the Heavens and Active with His Creations, Us, Very Personally Down Here.

Two more propers express this both/and. The **Verse**, words of a seraph before God's throne (Is 6:3b): "Alleluia. Holy, holy, holy is the Lord of hosts; the whole earth is full of His glory! Alleluia." Isaiah was overwhelmed by his vision of the one thrice-holy God.

But then our **Gradual** for the first six weeks of this new season:

> *The word is near you, in your mouth and in your heart, the word of faith that we proclaim. For with the heart one believes and is justified, and with the mouth one confesses and is saved. (Rom 10:8b, 10)*

The triune God is so very far above us, surely beyond our understanding. But in the Word that came near to us and was made flesh, God revealed how present He ever is for us.

Trinity continues the day of Pentecost, thus the **Hymn of the Day**. See how well the trinitarian references in stanzas 6 and 7 fit.

The Sundays after Pentecost: Proper 3 (May 24–28) Year C

READINGS

Genesis 50:15–21
Psalm 112:1–9 (antiphon: v 1)
Acts 2:14a, 36–47
Luke 6:(20–26) 27–42

HYMN OF THE DAY

LSB 696 "O God, My Faithful God"

There's something we should mention right up front: the propers for this devotion-study likely won't be used in our churches until May 27, 2046. Yes, they're for the week after Trinity Sunday, but your congregation almost surely won't be using them unless it happens to be 2046 or 2073 or 2103 or . . . Say what?

The really short explanation is that the three-year lectionary often skips one or more sets of propers for these early Sundays after Pentecost, depending on how late or early Easter falls. Easter, as you know, can occur anywhere from March 22 until April 25 (see *LSB*, p xxiii). Whatever that date, there are always seven Sundays in the Easter season, followed by Pentecost Sunday and Holy Trinity. After that, we check the date on the calendar and start up with whichever Sunday after Pentecost the lectionary prescribes (indicated here in parentheses). To have the Sunday after Holy Trinity Sunday fall between May 24 and 28 requires a really early Easter, March 22–26 (and only one-third of such years will be Year C in the lectionary). For a more detailed explanation of how this works, look back at the devotion-study for Proper 3, Year A, on page 154.

Anyway, chances are, to look forward to the propers your congregation will be using this Sunday morning, you'll want to skip ahead to the devotion-study for Proper 4, 5, 6, or 7. Check the date. Of course, this present devotion-study may still be fine reading for personal enrichment. After all, any lessons from God's Word are enriching. It's also true that all of these readings are also used on other, more-likely-to-happen Sundays the lectionary designers didn't want you to miss.

But this will be a unique combination with a unique theme. Let's proceed.

Parents create a certain culture in the home. Some families are warm, affirming, constantly supportive, and complimentary to one another. Others families are less expressive, sometimes even cold, sometimes contentious, often trying to one-up one another. If Dad is openly affectionate to Mom, conspicuously adores her, holds her up before the kids and in public as "the absolute greatest," sons learn to treat their wives the same way, and daughters look for men who'll treat them likewise. If Mom is patient when children mess up, is an eager listening ear when they get home after a tough day at school, kids become open, confident, able to face new challenges. If oldest sister treats her younger brother as, in her two-year-old language, "both can same," he'll be a good big bro when younger siblings come along. Home becomes a delightful haven of love and forgiveness and kindness. And it's all something you learn by the way you're treated from the top down.

On top of it all, of course, is the Lord. He has created a culture, a way His people treat one another, that begins with the way He treats us. That's an excellent way for our propers to begin the Pentecost season, all these Sundays after Pentecost that will run to the end of the church year in November. The festival portion of the church year, now just completed, followed Jesus' birth, ministry, death, resurrection, and ascension—when He finished His work of creating a new world culture. Now that He's also sent His Holy Spirit to get us moving, we'll progress through the rest of the liturgical year (by far the longest season) hearing how this new culture He's created plays out in His family, the Church.

In the **Introit**, the Lord promises to teach us this way of His, the culture He wishes to instill in us:

> *Who is the man who fears the Lord? Him will He instruct in the way that he should choose.*
>
> *Good and upright is the Lord; therefore He instructs sinners in the way. He leads the humble in what is right, and teaches the humble His way. All the paths of the Lord are steadfast love and faithfulness, for those who keep His covenant and His testimonies. For Your name's sake, O Lord, pardon my guilt, for it is great.*
>
> *Glory be to the Father and to the Son and to the Holy Spirit; as it was in the beginning, is now, and will be forever. Amen.*
>
> *Who is the man who fears the Lord? Him will He instruct in the way that he should choose. (Ps 25:8–11; antiphon: Ps 25:12)*

It's "the way" that we should choose, "the way" we should learn. But first of all, it's "His way," the Lord's way of doing things. "Good and upright is the Lord." "All the paths of the Lord are steadfast love and faithfulness." He teaches us this way because it's the way He is, the way He treats us. Good. Upright.

Loving. Faithful. "Therefore," for that reason, because that's the way He is, "He instructs sinners in the way." See how this can't originally be our way. The Lord instructs sinners. By nature, we're not good, upright, loving, or faithful. So God's way, His culture for us, must begin with Him forgiving: "For Your name's sake, O Lord, pardon my guilt, for it is great."

That core value of God's way, His forgiving us, is also central to the **Collect**, as it will be to two of the other propers.

Almighty God, in Your mercy so guide the course of this world that we may forgive as we have been forgiven and joyfully serve You in godly peace and quietness; through Jesus Christ, Your Son, our Lord, who lives and reigns with You and the Holy Spirit, one God, now and forever. Amen.

It is God who creates the culture; He "guide[s] the course of this world." And He does it chiefly by forgiving. As children growing up in His family, we learn to "forgive as we have been forgiven." Then what a happy home that makes! We "joyfully serve [Him]"—and one another!—"in godly peace and quietness."

That's certainly what we want for the Church, isn't it! We come on Sunday mornings, to Tuesday meetings, to Saturday work days as sinful people who perhaps said something, did something thoughtless to the woman in the next pew, to the guy who's weeding the flower bed right next to the sidewalk I'm edging. We want them to pardon our guilt as we forgive those who trespass against us. We want to kneel side by side at the communion rail, even just open up a cold one together at break, knowing there's no silent smoldering between us. God's culture is that we speak forgiveness one to the other. God's way is that He's already spoken His forgiveness in the opening moments of the Divine Service and again with Christ's body and blood.

Think how desperately Joseph's brothers needed to hear God's way in the **Old Testament Reading**, Genesis 50:15–21.

Recall that Joseph had forgiven his brothers their terrible sin against him (Gen 37:28) way back when he first revealed himself to them as second ruler of Egypt (45:1–11). And Jacob, their father, lived seventeen more years (47:28). For seventeen years, the brothers had lived in a culture of anxiety: *What'll he do to us when Dad's gone?* Best guess is they concoct the story of Jacob telling Joseph to forgive them (50:16–17).

No wonder Joseph weeps! *Guys, all this time you've been thinking I still held a grudge? What a lousy seventeen years you've made for yourselves!* They'd missed understanding God's way: "Do not fear. . . . You meant evil against me, but God meant it for good, . . . that many people should be kept alive" (50:19, 20). "'I will provide for you and your little ones.' Thus he comforted them and spoke kindly to them" (50:21). God does good, despite our evil. "So we will truly on our part, also heartily forgive and readily do good to those who sin against us" (Luther's explanation of the Fifth Petition of the Lord's Prayer).

The same crisis appears in the **Second Reading**, Acts 2:14a, 36–47, for those who'd just heard Peter's Pentecost sermon.

You heard the same sermon the last two Sundays. You remember the point: God proved that Jesus is the Christ by raising Him from the dead—"Jesus whom you crucified" (2:36). The crowd was "cut to the heart"! "Brothers, what shall we do???!!!" (2:37, additional marks are mine but realistic!!!).

They couldn't imagine, but Peter tells them God's way: "Repent and be baptized every one of you in the name of Jesus Christ for the forgiveness of your sins" (2:38). And this is for the whole family: "for you and for your children and for all who are far off" (2:39). The greatest of evils they had done God turned to good. Their murder of Jesus God used to save them and the whole world! It was a total life-changer for three thousand souls that first day alone (2:41)!

Then here's the culture that results from God's way: "And they devoted themselves to the apostles' teaching and fellowship, to the breaking of bread and the prayers. . . . And all who believed were together and had all things in common. . . . Distributing the proceeds to all, as any had need. And day by day, attending the temple together and breaking bread in their homes, . . . with glad and generous hearts, . . . having favor with all the people" (2:42, 44, 45–46, 47).

They were a model of what the **Psalm** also describes. Read Psalm 112:1–9.

Those who fear the Lord are blessed (112:1), even, in this case (and unlike the early Jerusalem Church), with wealth and riches (112:3). Then they are "gracious, merciful, and righteous"; they deal "generously"; they've "distributed freely; . . . given to the poor" (112:4, 5, 9). And again, it reflects the way the Lord has treated them. The entire psalm is predicated in this: "Praise the LORD!" (112:1). Everything that follows is because the Lord has blessed His people so.

That's where the **Holy Gospel**, Luke 6:20–42, picks up: God blessing His people.

Luke's report of Jesus' Beatitudes (6:20–23) helps correct the common misinterpretation of Matthew 5:1–12, that we are blessed as a result of *our* doing—making ourselves poor *in spirit* (Mt 5:3), hungering *for righteousness* (Mt 5:6), and so on. Obviously we earn no blessing by being simply "poor" or "hungry" (Lk 6:20, 21). God creates the culture. He blesses purely because He is merciful (6:36), despite the poverty, hunger, sadness we experience in this world.

The Father creates the culture, and you, His children, learn to "love your enemies, do good to those who hate you" (6:27). It's the way of God's Golden Rule: "As you wish that others would do to you, do so to them" (6:31). In God's family, the Church, He's taught you to "be merciful, even as your Father is merciful" (6:36).

GOD'S WAY IS THAT HE FORGIVES, LOVES, IS MERCIFUL, AND DOES GOOD TO US SUCH THAT WE DO SO FOR OTHERS.

The **Hymn of the Day**, "O God, My Faithful God" (*LSB* 696), expresses this so precisely. God is the "true fountain . . . all perfect gifts bestowing." So we pray, "Help me, as You have taught, to love" (sts 1, 4).

The Sundays after Pentecost: Proper 4 (May 29–June 4) Year C

READINGS

1 Kings 8:22–24, 27–29, 41–43
Psalm 96:1–9 (antiphon: v 2)
Galatians 1:1–12
Luke 7:1–10

HYMN OF THE DAY

LSB 755 "In the Very Midst of Life"

For these early Sundays after Pentecost, see the Proper 3, Year A, devotion-study (p 154) explaining why some Propers may be omitted in some years.

The "Great Green Beyond" of the church year began as soon as we completed the festival portion of the year with the Feast of the Holy Trinity. Now through November, the remainder of the liturgical calendar, our propers will take up topics suggested by (in this Year C) Luke's Gospel that teach how the Church lives as a result of the birth, life, death, resurrection, and ascension of Jesus. We call these Sundays after Pentecost the Pentecost season since Christ is always with us through the Holy Spirit given on that day. And, yes, with a couple of exceptions, the paraments for the next six months or so will be green.

This week, the **Holy Gospel**, while being a tight, memorable story, brings together a number of important concepts, each of which is developed in one or more of the other propers. For a change, let's go there first, and with a special assignment. As you read Luke 7:1–10, pick out four or five key words or ideas that catch your attention. There are no right or wrong answers, but I will identify some that recur throughout the propers. (I read ahead.)

Okay, got your key ideas?

It's a familiar story, and one we love. It begins with a desperate cry for help. A centurion sends leaders of the Jews in Capernaum to go to Jesus and tell Him about his dear servant. "They pleaded with Him earnestly" (7:4a). So fundamental to the life of the Church is prayer to God when we're in need—which, of course, is every minute of every day. Crying out to

God is part of the conversation that makes the Church a family, just as earthly families ask one another for help and support.

I picked *crying out to God* as one of the key ideas in this reading.

The next part of the account is very interesting. The Jewish elders tell Jesus, "He is worthy to have You do this for him, for he loves our nation, and he is the one who built us our synagogue" (7:4b–5). There's a surprise, eh? The centurion is a Roman soldier, and we know what the Jews generally thought of their Roman occupiers. The disgust was usually mutual. But this Roman officer was more than fair and decent to these defeated subjects. To say "he loves our nation" is actually an indication that he was one of those rare Gentiles who had come to believe in the God of Israel as also *his* Savior (remember also Acts 10:1–2).

And how remarkable that he showed it by helping build their synagogue! This synagogue in Capernaum is famous in our own time as a major archaeological dig. We don't know if it was money, labor by his soldiers, or some other assistance the centurion had rendered, but it was obviously appreciated. The Jews say such kindnesses proves he is worthy of Jesus' help—or even *make* him worthy.

But see the centurion's understanding: "When [Jesus] was not far from the house, the centurion sent friends, saying to Him, 'Lord, do not trouble Yourself, for I am not worthy to have You come under my roof. Therefore I did not presume to come to You'" (7:6b–7a). "I am *not* worthy." The most admirable and sincere good works never make us worthy before holy, almighty God.

Did you note *worthiness or unworthiness to come to Jesus* as a key idea?

It didn't matter if the centurion knew whether Jesus came to his house: "Say the word, and let my servant be healed" (7:7). *That's all it'll take, just a word from You. I understand how it works, Lord. I've got a hundred soldiers under me, and if I give a command, it's done. They do it. And I'm under authority myself. If the chiliarch tells me to take my troops and attack, there's no question. I do it. You, meanwhile, outrank us all—even illness. Just say it, and my servant's disease has to obey. A word from You is all it takes.*

God works by His Word—to create the world, to pronounce us forgiven, to empower water, bread, and wine to give us heaven, to heal a servant. I think *God's word* doing the work is a key concept of this text.

"When Jesus heard these things, He marveled at [the centurion], and turning to the crowd that followed Him, said, 'I tell you, not even in Israel have I found such faith'" (7:9). This is an amazing story about faith, isn't it! Just say the word. We all know how difficult it is to believe God's promises we can't see. Will He really give me the dear Lutheran wife or husband for whom I'm keeping my standards high—or make my life fulfilling if He has other plans? Will He keep our children firm in faith so that they "will not depart from it" (Prov 22:6)? Will He sustain His Church and her pastors in the persecutions that lie ahead?

Faith is certainly key in this story.

And where did Jesus find such faith that caused Him to marvel? "Not even in Israel." It's very significant to this text that the man of great faith and the recipient of Jesus' miracle is a Gentile. Jesus invites everyone, of all backgrounds and back stories, to cry out to Him for help. And He will answer.

All nations, too, is a key concept of this text and will be prominent in other propers.

So by my count, we've got *crying out*, *unworthiness*, *word*, *faith*, and *all nations*. Are there other key ideas you noticed?

Well, then, how are these ideas from the Gospel reading developed in the other propers? The **Introit**:

> *Teach me Your way, O Lord, that I may walk in Your truth; unite my heart to fear Your name.*
>
> *Incline Your ear, O Lord, and answer me, for I am poor and needy. Preserve my life, for I am godly; save Your servant, who trusts in You—You are my God. Be gracious to me, O Lord, for to You do I cry all the day. Gladden the soul of Your servant, for to You, O Lord, do I lift up my soul. For great is Your steadfast love toward me; You have delivered my soul from the depths of Sheol.*
>
> *Glory be to the Father and to the Son and to the Holy Spirit; as it was in the beginning, is now, and will be forever. Amen.*
>
> *Teach me Your way, O Lord, that I may walk in Your truth; unite my heart to fear Your name. (Ps 86:1–4, 13; antiphon: Ps 86:11)*

What truth will the Lord teach us this time, especially so that we may cry out to Him, ask Him anything: "Incline Your ear, O Lord. . . . Preserve. . . . Save. . . . Be gracious. . . . Gladden." And for each petition, David has a reason God should answer. But see that the reasons always rest in Him, not us; in fact, they demonstrate our unworthiness: "For I am poor and needy . . . for to You do I cry all the day. . . . For to You, O Lord, do I lift up my soul. For great is Your steadfast love toward me; You have delivered my soul from the depths of Sheol." Even with this one: "For I am godly. . . . Your servant, who trusts in You—You are my God." "Godly" isn't a matter of good and godly works; godly is trusting. It's faith. It's recognizing I'm helpless, and my only prayer is that You, O Lord, are gracious, as He was to the centurion.

The **Collect**:

> *O God, by Your almighty Word You set in order all things in heaven and on earth. Put away from us all things hurtful, and give us those things that are beneficial for us; through Jesus Christ, Your Son, our Lord, who lives and reigns with You and the Holy Spirit, one God, now and forever. Amen.*

God works through His Word, even to set in order "all things in heaven and on earth." Surely we are unworthy to approach one so high above us. And yet we do. We, like the centurion, cry out to Him for deliverance from "all things hurtful," and we implore Him to give us "those things that are beneficial." Through the atoning death of Jesus Christ, He answers.

The **Old Testament Reading** is King Solomon's prayer dedicating the temple. Read 1 Kings 8:22–24, 27–29, 41–43.

How unworthy we are before You, O Lord! "Behold, heaven and the highest heaven cannot contain You; how much less this house that I have built!" (8:27). "*Yet* have regard to the prayer of Your servant and to his plea, O LORD my God, listening to [my] cry" (8:28). Our confidence that You will regard us is in Your Word. We "walk before you" (8:23) in faith because "You *spoke* with Your mouth" a promise to covenant with us, "and with Your hand have fulfilled it this day" (8:24).

"Likewise, when a foreigner . . . prays toward this house, hear in heaven Your dwelling place and do according to all for which the foreigner calls to You, in order that all the peoples of the earth may know Your name" (8:41, 42–43).

Roman centurions came much later in history, but the poet of Psalm 96:1–9 would have included them. Read the **Psalm**.

"All the earth." "The nations." "All the peoples." We've heard this before—and the centurion likely had too. The prayer book of Israel, the psalter, is replete with invitations to the Gentiles to join in worshiping Yahweh, to "sing to the LORD." They were indeed unworthy, because the Lord is "above all;" He "made the heavens" (96:4, 5). But *no one*, Jew, Gentile, could stroll up to the Creator with a claim. None of us could "come into His courts" (96:8)—except that here in His Word, He says we may, for the sake of Christ.

Has Christ, by His atoning cross and resurrection, really done all that's necessary, or must we add something to make ourselves worthy? That's the issue of Paul's letter to the Galatians. Read the first installment, the **Epistle**, Galatians 1:1–12.

"I am astonished," Paul writes, "that you are so quickly deserting Him who called you in the grace of Christ and are turning to a different gospel" (1:6). "False brothers" (2:4) were telling the Galatians that, while Christ was good and helpful, they also needed to be circumcised and keep the Old Testament ceremonial law. That was no Gospel at all! Paul calls it "man's gospel" (1:11). Throughout his letter, he'll make his emphatic response: Christ is sufficient! By faith in Him, not any works of man, we unworthies are centurions whose cries Jesus answers.

The word is near you, in your mouth and in your heart, the word of faith that we proclaim. For with the heart one believes and is justified, and with the mouth one confesses and is saved. (Rom 10.8b, 10)

—the **Gradual** for most of these same weeks.

THOUGH GOD IS SO HIGH ABOVE US THAT NO ONE ON EARTH IS WORTHY TO COME TO HIM, BY HIS WORD, HE ANSWERS THE CRIES OF FAITH FROM THOSE OF ALL NATIONS.

The **Hymn of the Day** (*LSB* 755), which is by Luther, is a three-stanza cry out to the Lord, confessing our faith that He will save us.

The Sundays after Pentecost: Proper 5 (June 5–11) Year C

READINGS

1 Kings 17:17–24
Psalm 30 (antiphon: v 5b)
Galatians 1:11–24
Luke 7:11–17

HYMN OF THE DAY

LSB 615 "When in the Hour of Deepest Need"

For these early Sundays after Pentecost, see the Proper 3, Year A, devotion-study (p 154) explaining why some Propers may be omitted in some years.

It's the Showstopper. The big one. The ultimate defeat.

It's always the top headlines. The assassination of a young president. The passing of an elderly queen or a beloved Hollywood matron. The sudden death of Walt Disney. The murder of dozens or hundreds or even three thousand in the latest terrorist attack. It's hundreds of thousands killed in a tsunami or twenty-two in a Category 4 hurricane. It's a plane crash or another school shooting. It's war.

Death dominates. In a sense, it dominates *all* of our lives. No one is immune. Wise and witty Ben Franklin told us that, but we didn't need anyone to tell us that. We do make jokes about it, but you really can't. It's no joke. Everyone in the parlor knows that when those days actually come.

And the day will come for each of us.

What's missing from every headline—and only rarely appears in a sidebar story—is that the ultimate defeat has been defeated. Behind every death notice, "life" is going on, and it can be real life for everyone. Jesus demonstrates that in the Gospel reading for Proper 5—a precursor to His accomplishing it. Death, the propers will remind us, is not finally the big story.

But it is stories. The **Introit** hints at both the Gospel and Old Testament stories:

Turn to me and be gracious to me;
give Your strength to Your servant,

and save the son of Your maidservant.

On the day I called, You answered me; my strength of soul You increased. Though I walk in the midst of trouble, You preserve my life; You stretch out Your hand against the wrath of my enemies, and Your right hand delivers me. The LORD will fulfill His purpose for me; Your steadfast love, O LORD, endures forever. Do not forsake the work of Your hands.

Glory be to the Father and to the Son and to the Holy Spirit; as it was in the beginning, is now, and will be forever. Amen.

Turn to me and be gracious to me; give Your strength to Your servant, and save the son of Your maidservant. (Ps 138:3, 7–8; antiphon: Ps 86:16)

"Save the son of Your maidservant" forms a nice Hebrew parallel—and as generic as could be, since every man has a mom. But in this usage, the antiphon is hinting that both the Old Testament and Gospel readings will be about saving particular sons of particular mothers—both widows. Stay tuned.

Their stories will stare down death—as do these verses from Psalm 138. "Though I walk in the midst of trouble, You preserve my life." As a warrior and then a warrior-king, David was never far from death. He knew, quite crassly, "the sword devours now one and now another" (2 Sam 11:25). Death was inevitable—maybe now, but surely later. And it is the greatest terror the world can threaten; self-preservation is every species's most basic instinct. But God, David knew, would preserve his life. Even with death a certainty, God's deliverance from death was more certain. With the Lord, life would go on.

"The LORD will fulfill His purpose for me." David's time—perhaps to die by the sword—might be soon, but it would not be before God accomplished for and through David all the good He had planned. Our lives on earth, and those of our loved ones, may be short, may be long. Death never thwarts God's gracious designs. And surely God's purpose for all His children includes a life evermore free from death.

A key word in our **Collect** is "comfort."

O Lord, Father of all mercy and God of all comfort, You always go before and follow after us. Grant that we may rejoice in Your gracious presence and continually be given to all good works; through Jesus Christ, Your Son, our Lord, who lives and reigns with You and the Holy Spirit, one God, now and forever. Amen.

Comfort is sweet and needed at so many moments in our lives, but especially when we face death—either our own or that of someone we love. It's what everyone tries to offer at the funeral or the funeral home. It's always difficult knowing what to say, and just meaning well is worth something. But some attempts are shallow; some really get to the heart.

Here's one from the God of all comfort: "You always go before and follow after us." Ponder that! In Christ Jesus, God has gone before us into death. He's lost loved ones before. And He's passed before us all from death to life. But He also follows after us. What we leave behind, He continues to watch over. He leads loved ones who go ahead of us by the hand to heaven. He'll love and shelter loved ones who'll miss us when we're with the Lord better than we did.

Sandy was just thirty-eight when she died unexpectedly, leaving a husband and young children. In her funeral sermon, Pastor was able to assure, "Glen, God *already knows* how He will care for you and the kids." God hasn't been caught by surprise. He doesn't have to reshuffle the deck and figure out how to win the next hand. He already knows. "The Lord will fulfill His purpose" for us. He has been there. He will be there. "Grant that we may rejoice in Your gracious presence."

It really did turn around that way for David—mourning into rejoicing, even dancing. Read the **Psalm**, Psalm 30.

We know all about David's cries for help (30:2, 8, 9): "What profit is there in my death?" Now he gives thanks. "O Lord, You have brought up my soul from Sheol; You restored me to life from among those who go down to the pit" (30:3). "Weeping may tarry for the night, but joy comes with the morning" (30:5). "You have turned for me my mourning into dancing; . . . that my glory may sing Your praise and not be silent. O Lord my God, I will give thanks to You forever!" (30:11, 12).

Now for our first "son of Your maidservant": the **Old Testament Reading**, 1 Kings 17:17–24. Do you remember the setup?

This is during the three-year drought the Lord inflicted upon Israel and wicked King Ahab. Elijah is in hiding, first by a brook, fed by ravens, but now with a widow and her son in the Canaanite town of Zarephath. Elijah has been miraculously providing for them (17:1–16).

But now the widow's son dies. "After all you've done for us, and my boy and I have trusted you, O man of God, is the real reason you came here to kill my son? I know I'm sinful, but did you have to punish me like this?" Even Elijah wonders, "O Lord my God, have You brought calamity even upon the widow with whom I sojourn, by killing her son?" (17:20). Death often brings questions. Why did God let this happen? Why *my* family? Am I being punished for some particular sin? What's my reason for living now?

Death, we know, became inevitable because of sin—Adam's sin, Eve's sin, my sin. We don't get every other answer. But we do have God's emphatic, "I have overcome death! I will fulfill My purpose for you!" And here's just one piece of proof: "The Lord listened to the voice of Elijah. And the life of the child came into him again" (17:22). That's just one piece of evidence that all of God's promises to overcome death and restore life are true. "Now I know," the widow said, "that the word of the Lord in your mouth is truth" (17:24).

“The word is near you, in your mouth and in your heart,” the **Gradual** tells us. That is, it’s God’s truth *for us.*

The Gradual goes on with “the word of faith that we proclaim. For with the heart one believes and is justified, and with the mouth one confesses and is saved.” That’s the point of the letter that gives us the **Epistle** again this week. Read Galatians 1:11–24.

This is the second of six consecutive Epistles from Galatians. It’s a different kind of death to life story. Paul had “persecuted the church of God violently and tried to destroy it” (1:13). He’d been responsible for the murder of Stephen and unnamed other believers. But now he was preaching the way that leads to eternal life—and fear of him was turned to glorifying God (1:23–24).

Paul’s point here is that the Gospel he’s now preaching was given to him not by man but by Christ Himself (1:12). God “had set me apart before I was born” and then “called me by His grace” (1:15). After that, rather than seeking instruction from other men, he went away to Arabia for a period of time (1:16–17). To do what? Scripture implies that during this period, he was tutored one on one, face to face by the risen Christ. (Compare 1 Cor 7:10, “not I, but the Lord,” with Gal 7:12, 25.) So Paul’s preaching was God’s saving truth, not “man’s gospel” (1:11).

That makes an eternal difference: man will always invent a system by which we earn our salvation. It makes sense; you want it, you have to earn it. But God’s Gospel is Christ doing it all—obeying the Law for us, dying to take our punishment for failing. We then receive Christ’s work and are justified, simply by faith, trusting that Jesus has saved us. That’s the way of eternal life.

Sunday’s other proof of eternal life is the other story of saving a maidservant’s son, the **Holy Gospel**, Luke 7:11–17.

It’s a vivid scene, and Luke describes it skillfully. Two large processions meet head on. A “great crowd” (7:11) is following Jesus as they approach Nain, a town of Galilee. But coming out of the city is also a “considerable crowd,” a funeral procession. The young man being carried to his burial is “the only son of his mother.” Then Luke tugs at our heartstrings: “And she was a widow” (7:12). Not only has she wept through this before, but now her son’s death is virtually hers. No social safety net. No one to provide for her now.

The town gate funnels the crowds into a single point of confrontation. Death would seem the irresistible force. But Jesus “came up and touched the bier, and the bearers stood still” (7:14a). He stops death in its tracks. And then He pushes back: “Young man, I say to you, arise” (7:14b). And Jesus gave him to His maidservant.

“They glorified God!” (7:16).

This was not death’s last stand. In fact, its best was yet to come. But its fate was sealed. In fact, even the resurrection in Zarephath signaled that death was no match for the Lord.

The Lord Has Turned Our Mourning into Praise, Overcoming Death to Restore Life.

“When in the hour of deepest need. . . . We cry for rescue.” The Lord will hear, and we will “ever praise” (**Hymn of the Day,** *LSB* 615:1, 2, 6).

The Sundays after Pentecost: Proper 6 (June 12–18) Year C

READINGS

2 Samuel 11:26–12:10, 13–14
Psalm 32:1–7 (antiphon: v 5)
Galatians 2:15–21; 3:10–14
Luke 7:36–8:3

HYMN OF THE DAY

LSB 915 "Today Your Mercy Calls Us"

For these early Sundays after Pentecost, see the Proper 3, Year A, devotion-study (p ?154 explaining why some Propers may be omitted in some years.

Cause and effect. It's a principle that's probably as old as human thought. ("If I take a bite of that fruit, what will it cause to happen?") This action causes that result.

Besides that first really big error, cause and effect is also subject to *logical* errors. Like if a dog barks just before sunrise, it doesn't mean he *caused* the sun to rise. It's just a coincidence.

On the other hand, when the sun does come up—quite apart from any canine vocalization—the sun does cause that side of the earth to become warmer over the next number of hours. That's a legitimate cause and effect.

Sometimes cause and effect errors aren't matters of coincidence. Sometimes the cause is mistaken for the effect, or vice versa. For example, when that sun starts shining longer and more directly on the Northern Hemisphere, schools in North America have traditionally taken off; it's hot, difficult to keep school buildings comfortable for learning. The warm sunshine is the cause; summer vacation is the effect. Obviously it would be an error for kids to think that getting out for the summer causes the weather to get hot.

And here's a real one for you. I once asked my confirmation students why we worship on Sundays. (We were going to learn about how each Sunday celebrated the Lord's resurrection and also how the early Church wanted to set aside the first day of the week for the most important activity.) The answer I got? Because that's the day people are off from work. Ouch!

They'd flipped cause and effect—and put the Church in the position of begging for a bone. Of course, the Church's early decision to worship on Sunday eventually caused Western civilization to honor it as the Lord's Day, free for worship.

Every proper on this Sunday after Pentecost is explicitly about forgiveness. There's more than enough to say about that any week. But Proper 6 especially raises the question of whether forgiveness is a cause or an effect. Confusing it isn't just a logical error; it determines whether our religion is truly *Christ*ian.

The **Collect** introduces the question:

> *Almighty and everlasting God, increase in us Your gifts of faith, hope, and love that we may receive the forgiveness You have promised and love what You have commanded; through Jesus Christ, Your Son, our Lord, who lives and reigns with You and the Holy Spirit, one God, now and forever. Amen.*

God has promised us forgiveness. That could be the entire message for the week. But check again what we're praying: "Increase in us Your gifts of faith, hope, and love that we may receive the forgiveness You have promised." See the cause-effect question? It sure sounds as if our faith, hope, and love are the necessary causes of God forgiving us. If we're faithful enough, hopeful, loving enough, it'll cause God to keep His promise and forgive.

The Latin original of this collect, dating back to AD 538 or earlier, and also a version used on other Sundays in *LSB*, does not specify that what God has promised is forgiveness. For this Sunday, "forgiveness" has been inserted to follow the theme. No problem there. But the original, ancient version did ask for that increase of faith, hope, and love "that we may *deserve* to obtain" what God promises. Big problem. That certainly makes *us* the cause and forgiveness just the effect. Needless to say, the reformers dropped those words, giving us the versions we use. Saying that anything in us causes God to forgive us undoes everything Scripture teaches about justification by faith in Christ alone, apart from our works!

But what *does* this mean? Let's come back to it once we've gleaned insights from the other propers.

The **Introit** begins to clarify after first raising a different cause-effect issue.

> *To You, O Lord, I lift up my soul. O my God, in You I trust; let me not be put to shame; let not my enemies exult over me.*
>
> *Turn to me and be gracious to me, for I am lonely and afflicted. The troubles of my heart are enlarged; bring me out of my distresses. Consider my affliction and my trouble, and forgive all my sins. Oh, guard my soul, and deliver me! Let me not be put to shame, for I take refuge in You.*
>
> *Glory be to the Father and to the Son and to the Holy Spirit; as it was*

in the beginning, is now, and will be forever. Amen.

To You, O Lord, I lift up my soul. O my God, in You I trust; let me not be put to shame; let not my enemies exult over me. (Ps 25:16–18, 20; antiphon: Ps 25:1–2)

Again, the proper asks God to "forgive all my sins." But look at the needs David cites first: "Let me not be put to *shame*; let not my *enemies* exult over me. . . . I am *lonely* and *afflicted. . . . Troubles. . . . Distresses.*" There's nothing explicit about sin. So is forgiveness of sin an unrelated concern, just a coincidence? Or is there some kind of cause-effect here?

Perhaps like this: David is ashamed of some sin he knows needs forgiveness. So his shame is caused by sin. And David is being pursued by enemies because God is using them as instruments to punish him for some sin. And David is lonely because . . . Wait a minute! Yes, it's possible that sinful behavior can drive away friends, spouses, children, and leave us lonely. But being lonely isn't always a result of some evil we've done. Perhaps a spouse died, kids moved far away, college is a tough adjustment. There's no sin in any that!

Here's the deal: these troubles *can* be caused by our sins—and David's got a lollapalooza coming up in a moment. But not necessarily. Most of our sufferings aren't direct effects caused by a particular sin. It's hugely important to understand that! God's not blasting us every time sadness strikes.

Yet all shame, stresses, afflictions *are* caused by sin. They're all effects of that really big first sinful cause. Trouble making friends freshman year isn't God's judgment because I cut some classes. But every freshman is a sinner like Eve. And Eve's sin, Adam's sin, my sin has made a mess of God's perfect creation. So not everyone we meet is a bud.

That means God's forgiveness *is* the cause of His care for all my needs. Christ's cross removing the sin that would have separated me—and Eve and Adam and everyone—from God makes Him my dear Father again when I'm lonely, ashamed, stressed.

Now read the **Old Testament Reading** and the **Psalm**: 2 Samuel 11:26–12:10, 13–14; Psalm 32:1–7. This psalm is David's own commentary on the event.

Jesus' death on the cross has for all time secured forgiveness for all people. But God knows we would eagerly ignore that forgiveness to remain in our sin. For nine months, David lived in his sin of adultery and murder. But the Lord would not leave him there. He nagged at David: "When I kept silent, my bones wasted away through my groaning all day long. For day and night Your hand was heavy upon me" (Ps 32:3–4). Then on the opportune day, the Lord sent Nathan with his brilliant subterfuge. David never saw the ambush till it hit like an Ammonite war club: "You are the man!" There was no denying it now. "I have sinned against the Lord" (2 Sam 12:7, 13a). God's Law is the cause; the effect is repentance. "I acknowledged my sin to You; . . . I said, 'I will confess my transgressions to the Lord'"(Ps 32:5).

"The Lord also has put away your sin; you shall not die" (2 Sam 12:13b). Repentance is not the cause of forgiveness;

forgiveness is an effect solely of Jesus' death for all sins. But forgiveness is then the cause of this: "Blessed is the one whose transgression is forgiven, whose sin is covered" (Ps 32:1)—David's expression of faith. Being forgiven by God through Nathan raised up faith in the penitent to believe that he was blessed. Cause: forgiveness; effect: faith.

Our series of readings through Galatians is all about proper cause and effect. Read this week's **Epistle**, Galatians 2:15–21; 3:10–14.

How can we be justified, declared not guilty, forgiven by God? To the faith, hope, and love we asked about in the Collect, Judaizers in Galatia would add circumcision.

That, Paul argues, would simply not be the Christian religion: "If justification were through the law, then Christ died for no purpose" (2:21). "Christ redeemed us from the curse of the law" (3:13). Christ alone is the cause of our forgiveness. And since "we know that a person is not justified by works of the law but through faith in Jesus Christ, so we also have believed" (2:16). We believe because we have something certain we *can* believe. We could never be sure our own works are sufficient, but if all the work of justifying, forgiving, is left up to Christ—that's something we can believe! Forgiveness, then, is the cause of faith.

It is also the cause of love demonstrated in the **Holy Gospel**, Luke 7:36–8:3.

Cause and effect—which is which? The sinful woman performs a beautiful act of love for Jesus. And when Jesus' host, Simon the Pharisee, thinks ill, Jesus tells Simon, "Her sins, which are many, are forgiven—*for she loved much*" (7:47). There it is again, just as in the Collect. It sounds as if love is the cause of forgiveness, that the woman is forgiven because she loved. Can it be?

Why did she show such love? Why did Simon show no love at all, not even the basic niceties of a host? The woman knew her sin, and she had obviously heard about Jesus, that He received sinners and befriended them. Simon, well, he needed a parable. When a master forgives two debtors, which one will love him more? "The one, I suppose, for whom he canceled the larger debt" (7:43). This woman knew she'd been forgiven. That's why she (and others, 8:1–3) loved so profusely. Simon didn't believe he'd been forgiven at all; he was sure he had no sins to forgive. Forgiveness is the cause. Love is the effect—whether much or none. "Her sins are forgiven, and she knows it—we can all see her faith!—*for* all of us can see how much she loved!"

It's the answer to the Collect question. See how the prayer goes on: "Increase in us Your gifts of faith, hope, and love that we may *receive the forgiveness* You have promised *and love* what You have commanded." Faith, hope, love don't cause forgiveness, but we pray that receiving that forgiveness would cause us, great sinners that we are, to love much. Cause and effect:

**Christ's Forgiveness
Raises Up Faith and Love
in Sinners Made Penitent
by God's Law.**

Our **Hymn of the Day**, "Today Your Mercy Calls Us" (*LSB* 915), is surely a hymn for David, for the sinful woman, for us.

The Sundays after Pentecost: Proper 7 (June 19–25) Year C

READINGS

Isaiah 65:1–9
Psalm 3 (antiphon: v 8)
Galatians 3:23–4:7
Luke 8:26–39

HYMN OF THE DAY

LSB 825 "Rise, Shine, You People"

For these early Sundays after Pentecost, see the Proper 3, Year A, devotion-study (p 154) explaining why some Propers may be omitted in some years.

This poor soul was the homeless man living under a freeway overpass. He was the prisoner of war in Southeast Asia stripped naked and crammed into a bamboo cage so small he could barely sit up. He was the hiker who'd lost his way in the desert, his canteen now empty. And worse.

This man was living in that "dark place" of depression. He was the user—actually the used—enslaved by his addiction. He was the victim buried alive in a horror movie. But this was real.

This was a real man in the **Holy Gospel** for Proper 7, this Sunday after Pentecost. But his plight really was worse than all of these agonies. He had a whole legion of them.

"Then [Jesus and His disciples] sailed to the country of the Gerasenes, which is opposite Galilee. When Jesus had stepped out on land, there met Him a man from the city who had demons." Read his story: Luke 8:26–39.

"The country of the Gerasenes" (8:26), the area around the city of Gerasa, is southeast of the Sea of Galilee, across the Jordan. ("The Gergesenes" or "Gadarenes," see Mt 8:28, represent other towns in the same broad area.) It's unclean, Gentile territory. Everything we see is unclean, pathetic. "For a long time" (8:27) this pitiful man has gone about naked, living among the tombs or in the desert. But not forever. At one time, he may have been someone's husband, father, certainly someone's son. Now, even chained and shackled, he was a terror to everyone and of superhuman strength (8:29) but a slave to the evil spirit—in fact to *many* evil spirits (8:30); a Roman legion was three thousand to six thousand soldiers. Mark adds that he went about cutting himself with stones and crying out (Mk 5:5). Matthew makes it even worse: apparently there were actually *two* poor prisoners (Mt 8:28)!

Jesus' arrival only intensifies the torture: "What have You to do with me, Jesus, Son of the Most High God? I beg You, do not torment me" (Lk 8:28). The demons know their eternal fate. The evil angels and their master, Satan, will be consigned to endless suffering in "the abyss" (8:31). "But, please, we beg You, not yet!"

Jesus gives the command; the demons *must* come out (8:29). But for this little while more—perhaps a couple thousand years?—they plead for the mercy God still gives even them. They move about on earth, still allowed a limited freedom to wreak whatever havoc on God's creation He permits. With Jesus' incarnation, Satan and his henchmen know they cannot win. But they console themselves with any little victories they can yet notch—that is, any damage they can do to undo any of God's perfect architectures.

That even includes unclean animals, the pigs. Jesus does have mercy; He lets the demons enter the nearby herd. *But if they are God's pigs, and if He'll let us, well, at least let's destroy them* (8:32–33)*! That's* pathetic!

Any time we follow Satan and his demons, though, we digress. Back to the real story.

The townspeople, hearing the report, hurry to the scene. "They came to Jesus and found the man from whom the demons had gone, sitting at the feet of Jesus, clothed and in his right mind" (8:35b). Can this be the same man? Picture Mary, the sister of Martha, sitting at Jesus' feet, quietly learning the one thing needful. Picture children being brought by their parents to sit on Jesus' lap and receive His blessing. Picture Stephen, his face like the face of an angel, gazing into heaven and seeing Jesus standing at the right hand of God (Acts 6:15; 7:55). Can this be the same homeless, naked, tormented man?

Picture a man with a family, friends, conversing, laughing. The same man?

The locals know it is. And that seizes them with great fear (8:35c–37a)! They've badly confused Law and Gospel. Sure, this Jesus clearly has the mighty power of God, and that can be a terrifying thing for us sinners to be around. But He's just shown how He intends to use His power: to conquer Satan and set us free from the devil's slavery. Jesus has performed dynamite Gospel, and all they can see in it is Law. So they "asked Him to depart from them" (8:37). That's pitiful.

The former demoniac, he never wants to be parted from Jesus. But Jesus has a more immediate assignment for him: "Return to your home, and declare how much *God* has done for you." And faithfully, "he went away, proclaiming throughout the whole city how much *Jesus*"—that's right, almighty God—"had done for him" (8:38, 39).

We're not going to top that story—in our lives or in the rest of the propers for the week. But even if our troubles are less dramatic, we have much to declare, just as much, really, that the Lord is doing for us, delivering us from the same enemies. So our **Introit**:

Be to me a rock of refuge, to which I may continually come; You have given the command to save me, for You are my rock and my fortress.

You who have made me see many troubles and calamities will revive me again; from the depths of the earth You will bring me up again. You will increase my greatness and comfort me again. I will also praise You with the harp for Your faithfulness, O my God; I will sing praises to You with the lyre, O Holy One of Israel. My lips will shout for joy, when I sing praises to You; my soul also, which You have redeemed. And my tongue will talk of Your righteous help all the day long, for they have been put to shame and disappointed who sought to do me hurt.

Glory be to the Father and to the Son and to the Holy Spirit; as it was in the beginning, is now, and will be forever. Amen.

Be to me a rock of refuge, to which I may continually come; You have given the command to save me, for You are my rock and my fortress. (Ps 71:20–24; antiphon: Ps 71:3)

"Rock" and "fortress" are, of course, wonderful symbols of the Lord's protection. And we need it as surely as the man in the Gospel reading. Satan and his many demons are behind our "many troubles and calamities" too. But the Lord has "given the command to save me," and my enemies must obey His command as the legion of demons did.

In his own way, the psalmist understands what the demoniac went through: "From the depths of the earth You will bring me up again." Both of them were as if buried alive. But we know their deliverer was literally dead and buried. Where does that lead? *Everything* they were, every ugly scene—under the bridge, in the bamboo cage, the sharp stones and bloody gashes—was Christ.

But now the psalmist can also do exactly what Jesus sent his Gerasene friend to do: "My lips will shout for joy, when I sing praises to You. . . . And my tongue will talk of Your righteous help all the day long"—how much You, Lord, have done for me!

That's our other psalmist of the week, David, as well. Read the **Psalm**, Psalm 3.

"O Lord, how many are my foes!" They, too, are legion! "Many are rising against me; many are saying of my soul, 'There is no salvation for him in God'" (3:1–2). Yet, "I will not be afraid of many thousands of people who have set themselves against me all around" (3:6). A whole army, whether Philistines or the invisible forces of Satan behind them, do not frighten David. "For the Lord sustained me. . . . Salvation belongs to the Lord; Your blessing be on Your people!" (3:5, 8).

Last week, we made the point that all of our troubles are about sin. That's still true this week. The **Collect** for Sunday:

O God, You have prepared for those who love You such good things as surpass our understanding. Cast out all sins and evil desires from us, and pour into our hearts Your Holy Spirit to guide us into all blessedness; through Jesus Christ, Your Son, our Lord, who lives and reigns with You and the Holy Spirit, one God, now and forever. Amen.

Though not as Hollywood as casting out demons, for God to "cast out all sin" is what we need most. Sin is Satan's claim over us; if we had no sin, we would be impervious to his threats. So it's Christ's death on the cross that delivers us. And see what follows: after casting out sin and evil desires, "pour into our hearts Your Holy Spirit to guide us into all blessedness." It brings to mind the exorcism in Luther's baptismal rite: "Depart, you unclean spirit, and make room for the Holy Spirit" (*LSB Agenda*, p 2). Set free from sin and Satan, we're now occupied with better things.

The **Old Testament Reading** picks up some of the images of the Gospel. See if you notice them as you read Isaiah 65:1–9.

The Lord is chastising His people for being inattentive. He calls to them, reaches out to them, but they continue to be "a rebellious people" (65:2). They show themselves to be as unclean as the Gerasene demoniac. They "sit in tombs." They "eat pig's flesh" (65:4). And like the demons possessing that hapless man, they want nothing to do with "the Most High God." What an irony. They say, "Keep to yourself, do not come near me, for *I am too holy for you*" (65:5). Is that not an odd claim?! But this is exactly as it was with the demons. Confirmed in evil as they are, they *like* evil, prefer it to anything good. How gracious that God nonetheless comes near to us, makes His room in us, that we do sit at His feet, "dwell there" (65:9)!

Galatians 3:23–4:7, the fourth **Epistle** of six straight through Paul's letter, again has a remarkable connection to this week's theme.

As we've seen, Galatians is Paul's manifesto that we are justified by faith in Christ alone, apart from any works, such as circumcision. What is the effect if we believe we must keep the Law in order to be saved? Well, "before faith came, we were held captive under the law, imprisoned" (3:23). In the Old Testament, the ceremonial law served a holy purpose: "our guardian until Christ came" (3:24). But now to think works of the Law are needed for salvation would mean we are "enslaved to the elementary principles of the world" (4:3; the Greek might even mean "the elemental *spirits* of the world"). But by that beautiful Christmas message (4:4–5), "you are no longer a slave" like the desperate demoniac, but set free, "a son" (4:7). You don't cry out for God to leave you to your satanic misery; the Spirit in your heart cries out, "Abba! Father!" You

**Declare with Joy
How Many Sins, Troubles,
and, Yes, Satanic Foes
Christ Has Cast Out Before You.**

Christ "sends the powers of evil reeling." Therefore, "Rise, shine, you people! . . . Tell the story!" (**Hymn of the Day**, *LSB* 825:1, 3).

The Sundays after Pentecost: Proper 8 (June 26–July 2) Year C

READINGS

1 Kings 19:9b–21
Psalm 16 (antiphon: v 11)
Galatians 5:1, 13–25
Luke 9:51–62

HYMN OF THE DAY

LSB 688 "'Come, Follow Me,' the Savior Spake"

Powerful people have always attracted followers. In ancient civilizations, the leader was often the most powerful warrior. We still frequently refer to a dictator or a rebel chieftain as the local "strong man." Often now, of course, the power is a product of political maneuvering, and that's true for democracies as well as totalitarian states—and wielded by five-foot, four-inch women as likely as by nine-foot Goliaths.

Using power to earn followers isn't in itself a sinister thing. Jesus attracted huge crowds by His miracles. The apostles often authenticated the Gospel and gathered a following by shows of power. (I've always liked Acts 13:4–12.) Likewise, according to fairly reliable histories, some of the early Christian missionaries to Europe won over the, yes, local strong men and gained wholes tribes of converts by working impressive "miracles."

But to gain and retain the kind of following Jesus desires takes more than power. Nearly all the adoring multitude abandoned Jesus when He seemed to be exposed as a weakling on the cross. And it had to be the substance of the Gospel, not miracles, that sustained the Church after the initial wows wore off.

Proper 8 is keyed by the Gospel and Old Testament Reading accounts of the Lord calling followers. We'll hear about power, as we'd expect, but since the Lord desires us to become a different kind of people, it won't be only power that leads us to follow Him.

To begin, pray the **Collect** for Sunday:

Lord of all power and might, author and giver of all good things, graft into our hearts the love of Your name and nourish us with all goodness that we may love and serve our neighbor; through Jesus Christ, Your Son, our Lord, who lives and reigns with You and the Holy Spirit, one God, now and forever. Amen.

It's natural for people to follow powerful leaders. Followers always hope they might just get a little of whatever the leader has.

The Lord we follow does have "all power and might." All earthly powers—physical strength or military might, political position or authority to command illness or evil spirits or forces of nature—come from Him. And we haven't seen the tiniest fraction of God's power if we haven't seen Him create a world in six days or send Satan falling like lightning from heaven. A leader that powerful could surely give His followers "all good things," and our God does.

But the Lord is making for Himself followers who aren't in it just for what they and we can get. We pray that we would "love [His] name" and "love and serve our neighbor." God is forming followers who love. For that to happen, He must "graft" that love "into our hearts"—that is, take of His love and implant it in us. So we follow a powerful God, and that brings us very good things. But the good things come not just from His power; they also come from His love.

In the **Old Testament Reading**, God teaches the prophet Elijah not to follow only power. Read 1 Kings 19:9b–21.

This reading is the sequel to one of the greatest displays of power anywhere in Scripture: Elijah's duel with the prophets of Baal on Mount Carmel (18:20–46). In all, 450 false prophets make public fools of themselves; the lone prophet of Yahweh prays, and the Lord sends fire from heaven; the crowd shouts "The Lord, He is God; the Lord, He is God"; the idolatrous prophets are slain; God sends a gully washer after three years of drought. The false religion is dead. The whole nation is faithful to Yahweh.

Except that that very day, Queen Jezebel, Ahab's wife, vows to kill Elijah in revenge for her beloved prophets, and Elijah flees. Now he's far away hiding in a cave. He's sure the people of Israel remain as unfaithful to the covenant as ever, that "I, even I only, am left, and they seek my life, to take it away" (19:10). The power wow has worn off very quickly.

So the Lord comes to speak with Elijah. Not the way he expected. "A great and strong wind [that] tore the mountains and broke in pieces the rocks"? He's got that power. He does do that sort of thing (Jonah 1:4; Acts 2:2). But He wasn't in this wind. Earthquake? He rocks mountains any time He chooses (Ex 19:16–18). But He's not in this earthquake. A fire! Ask the prophets of Baal about that one. Never mind. Too late. Anyway, "the Lord was not in the fire" (1 Ki 19:11b–12a). None of the power plays we'd expect—and that Elijah might wish Yahweh to use on Ahab and Jezebel right now. But "after the fire the sound of a low whisper" (19:12b)—or the King James Version, "a still small voice."

We're enamored with power. But if God only appeared to us as earthquakes and fire from heaven, we couldn't follow Him. Notice Elijah didn't leave the safety of the cave until all the fireworks were over (19:13, not 19:11a). We'd be terrified of God's power too, unless He had first come to us quietly, gently, even weakly—like in a manger and on a cross.

God had a plan for Elijah to follow; He's never *out* of power. Hazael as king of Syria would be a painful scourge of discipline on wicked Israel (2 Ki 8:7–13). Jehu would become king of Israel by exterminating the entire house of Ahab and Jezebel (2 Ki 9:1–10:25). And Elisha would carry on Elijah's work (including, actually, the succession of the two kings).

But the best word to Elijah was itself still and small, more like a low whisper than a great wind. You think, Elijah, that you're the only believer in Yahweh left. "Yet I will leave seven thousand in Israel, all the knees that have not bowed to Baal" (19:18). Percentage-wise, that's very tiny among the several million Israelites (much less than 1 percent). Not powerfully impressive but not insignificant. God works just fine that way.

The real point is that when almost all the people had deserted Yahweh, He continued to love them. He never wavered from His commitment to be their God. That's how Elijah could continue to follow the Lord and why Elisha could follow in Elijah's footsteps (19:19–21). The Lord is always almighty, but it's His unshakable love that prevents Him from destroying us, enables us to follow Him.

David chants this in the **Psalm**. Read Psalm 16.

David deeply appreciates that the Lord is a powerful stronghold: "In You I take refuge" (16:1). But "the Lord is my chosen portion. . . . I bless the Lord." "You will not abandon my soul to Sheol, or let Your holy one see corruption" (16:5, 7, 10). The Lord's love for David is unswerving, not even interrupted by death. (You may recall from our devotion-study for Trinity Sunday, pp 622–25, that Peter on Pentecost cites this passage as explicitly about Jesus—the Holy One God did not allow to see corruption in the grave. Christ crucified and risen is why God's love for us never ceases!) Therefore, David follows: "I have set the Lord always before me. . . . You make known to me the *path* of life" (16:8, 11).

In the **Epistle**, Paul calls following our Lord on the path of life being "led by the Spirit." Read Galatians 5:1, 13–25.

Remember that this is the fifth of six consecutive Epistles through Paul's incomparable treatise on justification by faith, apart from works. Paul is now reaching the end of his argument. Since we are free from the obligation to keep the Law for our salvation, we should freely, all the more, desire to fulfill the whole Law in this: "You shall love your neighbor as yourself" (5:14). Our motivation is now purely God's love, which has saved us by Christ's doing. (By no means coercion, as God's power could force us!) "If you are led by the Spirit, you are not under the law" (5:18). God's love moves us to follow Him in loving. We "walk by the Spirit," avoiding all those fleshly works Paul lists (5:19–21). Instead, we live in "love, joy, peace," and the rest (5:22–23). This is the kind of people God makes of His followers—people who don't follow power just for what it might give them.

See the resolve of Jesus' love we're called to follow in the **Holy Gospel**, Luke 9:51–62.

"When the days drew near for [Jesus] to be taken up, He set His face to go to Jerusalem" (9:51). Here is God's unwavering, unshakable, unswerving, uninterrupted love approaching its climax. Jesus will go to the cross to redeem the world, and nothing will dissuade Him. This is the love the disciples were to follow—and emulate.

James and John forget. They think Jesus builds His following by wielding His almighty power. They would fix "the Samaritan problem" with more fire from heaven. But Jesus rebukes them. Just as He will die for the chief priests and Pharisees, for Pilate, for Judas and Peter who kill Him, so He will die for the Samaritans who reject Him explicitly because He has set His face to save them (9:53).

So who else will follow Jesus? (9:57–62). No delays. "Okay, it's true. Dad hasn't died yet. But just give me a few years until he does. I'll be right there with you." No excuses. "You're right. I didn't really mean just a kiss goodbye. But one of these days, I'll be ready." Above all, there is no following the power for what it might get you—"The Son of Man has nowhere to lay His head." "Follow Me" because of My unassailable love for you (9:58).

The **Introit** (which, of course, is actually the first proper we'll hear Sunday) gives a name to this reason we follow Christ.

Show us Your steadfast love, O Lord, and grant us Your salvation.

Let me hear what God the Lord will speak, for He will speak peace to His people, to His saints; but let them not turn back to folly. Surely His salvation is near to those who fear Him, that glory may dwell in our land. Steadfast love and faithfulness meet; righteousness and peace kiss each other. Righteousness will go before Him and make His footsteps a way.

Glory be to the Father and to the Son and to the Holy Spirit; as it was in the beginning, is now, and will be forever. Amen.

Show us Your steadfast love, O Lord, and grant us Your salvation. (Ps 85:8–10, 13; antiphon: Ps 85:7)

Steadfast love. This is that magnificent Hebrew concept of *chesed*—that unflinching, unfaltering, unfailing love that sets its face to our salvation. Even if only 1 percent are faithful, even if they're Samaritans. It's what "God the Lord will speak," the low whisper we should hear, "peace," rather than only the thunderings of power we might wish. That "will go before Him and make His footsteps a way" for us to follow.

The Lord's Steadfast Love, Rather Than His Overwhelming Power, Enables Us to Follow and Love Steadfastly.

"'Come, Follow Me,' the Savior Spake"—our **Hymn of the Day** (*LSB* 688).

"How beautiful are the feet" of those who do. Our new **Gradual** for the next six weeks will tell us.

The Sundays after Pentecost: Proper 9 (July 3–9) Year C

READINGS

Isaiah 66:10–14
Psalm 66:1–7 (antiphon: vv 8–9)
Galatians 6:1–10, 14–18
Luke 10:1–20

HYMN OF THE DAY

LSB 533 "Jesus Has Come and Brings Pleasure"

This is the time of year when many congregations are receiving eager seminary graduates and their families for ordination into the office of the ministry and installation into the graduates' first calls. Claire and I still remember the thrill of arriving very late one night to find that the dear people of Messiah Lutheran Church in Midland, Michigan, had carefully received our few furnishings and had already made the parsonage into a lovely home—including setting up the bed for tired travelers to crash. Then there were the knocks on the door and new friends to tour us around town the next day, followed on Sunday by hundreds of names and faces, almost none of whom we knew but the owners of which all recognized us. And the best was ahead—years of proclaiming Christ, giving and receiving His Sacraments, caring for God's people, and all the loving relationships that fosters.

The most pleasant part of teaching at one of our seminaries now is picturing each student, his wife, and their kids having the same joy we had in parish ministry and life in a congregation of God's people. That means the heaviest burden of teaching at one of our seminaries is knowing we must prepare these men and their families the very best we can so they can equip the people of God for eternity.

While taking us through the Gospel of Luke, the lectionary well accommodates this season by giving us a Sunday that focuses on the pastor's call into ministry and on the blessed relationship between a pastor and his congregation. The Gospel reading is Jesus sending out the seventy-two, the first class of pastors beyond the apostles themselves. The propers will be especially clear that the ministry and that relationship are always for the purpose of Christ's kingdom in heaven. With that in view, it should be a joyous relationship indeed!

Let's begin with the **Introit** and discover its connection to the day's theme.

The heavens declare the glory of God, and the sky above proclaims His handiwork.

Day to day pours out speech, and night to night reveals knowledge. Their measuring line goes out through all the earth, and their words to the end of the world. In them He has set a tent for the sun, which comes out like a bridegroom leaving his chamber, and, like a strong man, runs its course with joy. Its rising is from the end of the heavens, and its circuit to the end of them, and there is nothing hidden from its heat.

Glory be to the Father and to the Son and to the Holy Spirit; as it was in the beginning, is now, and will be forever. Amen.

The heavens declare the glory of God, and the sky above proclaims His handiwork. (Ps 19:2, 4–6; antiphon: Ps 19:1)

Psalm 19 is one of the definitive passages in Scripture on what's called the natural knowledge of God—that is, that all people have an awareness of the existence of God simply by observing the universe. People try to deny that, of course, but to look at "the heavens," the order of orbits and planets and stars, the immensity of the galaxies and the tiniest of particles, continually pushes one to the realization that somebody really smart, really powerful made it all. "The sky above proclaims His handiwork." Not only is "nothing hidden from [the sun's] heat," but no one can hide from this nagging reality. The psalmist even characterizes nature's revelation of God as if it were language: "Day to day pours out speech."

But natural revelation of God is always incomplete. By looking at the creation, we couldn't tell that God is triune—hence Judaism and Islam on the "one" hand and Hinduism, Mormonism, and animism on the "poly" (many gods) hand. From creation alone, we wouldn't know God is gracious to us; hurricanes and earthquakes might make us think the opposite. Above all, we could never guess that when we offend against this almighty Creator, He takes our punishment upon Himself; that's contrary to the *quid pro quo* way everything in the universe operates.

So, we need language, words, to declare who this God really is and how He sees us. That's where the office of the ministry, the office of preaching, comes in. Read this verse again: "Their measuring line goes out through all the earth, and their words to the end of the world."

Now read the **Gradual**:

How beautiful are the feet of those who preach the good news, who publish peace and bring good news of salvation. Their voice has gone out to all the earth, and their words to the ends of the world. (Rom 10:15b, 18b; Is 52:7b, alt)

Did you see the connection? The second verse of the Gradual is Paul's citation of Psalm 19:4, the verse we repeated from the Introit. But in his new context, Romans 10, Paul rephrases; in place of "their measuring line goes out," he writes, "Their voice has gone out." Whose voice? It's not "the heavens" and the "sky" proclaiming, as in Psalm 19. Now it's "those who preach the good news, who publish peace and bring good news of salvation"—preachers, human pastors. It's now pastors who are called to take the Good News "to all the earth," "to the ends of the world."

What a beautiful calling! "How beautiful are the feet of those who preach." The calling is beautiful (even if most pastors' feet aren't!) because the office publishes, publicly announces, "peace." Remember how often we've discussed this most beautiful Gospel word. *Peace* (the last word in the Divine Service!) sums up all the blessings Christ has earned for us. By removing the sin that made us God's enemies, Jesus' death and resurrection has set us at peace with Him again, and being reconciled to God is how we receive anything and everything good. Peace is that condition of total well-being—a perfect summary of the mission of the holy ministry.

So here's where it all began: the **Holy Gospel**, Luke 10:1–20.

Earlier, Jesus had sent out the Twelve on a similar mission (9:1–6). These seventy-two (or, from other early manuscripts, seventy, recalling Num 11:16–17, 25) come from the broader group of "disciples" who have also been following Jesus faithfully. There's always a need for more pastors (10:2). Pray for them!

Like new sem grads today, the seventy-two receive sobering instructions. They aren't doing it for the money or a cushy life (10:3–4). Some faithful pastors will be rejected—even, we say in shame, by Lutheran Christian congregations. Woe to those congregations (10:10–15)! "The one who rejects you," Christ says, "rejects Me, and the one who rejects Me rejects Him who sent Me" (10:16b).

But what a joy when faithful pastors are received by faithful people! The congregation provides generously for the man and his family (10:7–8). And he brings them nothing less than Christ Himself (10:1). "The one who hears you hears Me" (10:16a). "*I* forgive you all your sins," Christ says through the pastor. "*I* baptize you!" "This is *My* body!" Jesus Himself says! The words have Jesus' own power (10:17–18). And it's all Christ's word of "Peace!" Peace is really the whole message of the ministry—the first word (10:5) and the word that lasts (10:6).

So it's your pastor who brings you the Word that brings you heaven: the **Old Testament Reading**, Isaiah 66:10–14.

In the Old Testament, "Jerusalem" was the home folks, the "regulars on Sunday." Jerusalem didn't mean us. Isaiah looks ahead, though, to the new Jerusalem that will "rejoice *with* Jerusalem" (66:10). For "I will extend peace," the great gift of the Gospel, "to her [Jerusalem] like a river, *and* the glory of *the nations* like an overflowing stream" (66:12). "You [Gentiles] shall be comforted *in* Jerusalem" (66:13). The office of preaching is the means by which new believers come to faith *and those every Sunday regulars are moved to tell their neighbors about it.*

It's all Christians, not just those in the public ministry who "shout," "sing," "praise," "say" the message of Christ: **Psalm** 66:1–9. "Shout for joy to God, *all* the earth" (66:1). "Bless our God, O *peoples*; let the sound of His praise be heard" (66:8).

That is to say, the life of a pastor and his congregation is always to be a sharing in the burdens and good things of God. Read the **Epistle**, Galatians 6:1–10, 14–18.

Every Christian is to carry every other Christian's burdens (6:2). But especially does a congregation support its pastor and a pastor suffer for the sake of his people. In particular, he has the often difficult task of restoring the member caught in transgression (6:1).

Look at other instructions Paul has for pastor and people. Pastor: "If anyone thinks he is something, when he is nothing, he deceives himself" (6:3). You *serve*, Pastor.

People: "One who is taught the word must share all good things with the one who teaches" (6:6). Generous, sacrificial giving.

Pastor and people: "Let us do good to everyone, and especially to those who are of the household of faith" (6:10). It's mutual.

Pastor: "Far be it from me to boast except in the cross of our Lord Jesus Christ" (6:14).

People: "From now on let no one cause [Pastor] trouble, for I bear on my body the marks of Jesus" (6:17).

Bottom line: God has created the office of the ministry to be this blessing to His dear children: "Peace and mercy be upon them" (6:16)—for pastor, for people, the peace of God that is and will be eternity with Christ.

One more reference to the Gospel reading: "The seventy-two returned with joy" that they were given such a powerful calling. But Jesus cautions you, Pastor, not to be overjoyed with the heady things of ministry, but in the great blessing you share with every one of your dear people: "Rejoice that your names are written in heaven" (Lk 10:17a, 20b).

You Who Are Appointed to Be Public Preachers of God's Peace and All of You Who Receive It, Rejoice above All in This: That Your Name Is Counted in the New Jerusalem.

So we pray that the Lord of the harvest would send forth laborers into His harvest. The **Collect**:

Almighty God, You have built Your Church on the foundation of the apostles and prophets with Christ Jesus Himself as the cornerstone. Continue to send Your messengers to preserve Your people in true peace that, by the preaching of Your Word, Your Church may be kept free from all harm and danger; through Jesus Christ, Your Son, our Lord, who lives and reigns with You and the Holy Spirit, one God, now and forever. Amen.

Sing the **Hymn of the Day**, *LSB* 533. May each pastor and congregation share the pleasures Jesus brings through them!

The Sundays after Pentecost: Proper 10 (July 10–16) Year C

READINGS

Leviticus (18:1–5) 19:9–18
Psalm 41 (antiphon: v 1)
Colossians 1:1–14
Luke 10:25–37

HYMN OF THE DAY

LSB 845 "Where Charity and Love Prevail"

Everybody (almost) knows the story of the Good Samaritan. Most people (at least many) think they know what it means.

Jesus' parable of the Good Samaritan is the Gospel lesson for Proper 10. The story itself really is quite familiar, and, as with many of Jesus' parables, the interpretation seems pretty straightforward. However, as with many of Jesus' parables, the meaning may be less obvious than we think.

This week, let's start with the parable, propose two potential understandings, and then see if the other propers might help us think through how we interpret it. Read the **Holy Gospel**, Luke 10:25–37.

The setup for the parable is important. "A lawyer" (10:25) was different from an attorney today. He didn't represent clients in legal cases; he was an expert in the Old Testament scriptures (the *Torah*, or "law"). Like so many of the credentialed Jewish leaders, he wants to check out this guy from Nazareth. Jesus answers his question with a question (10:26), as He often does. (Jesus is always actually the Teacher.)

The lawyer's answer (10:27) quotes Deuteronomy 6:5 (the verse following the *Shema*, the core confession of the Old Testament) and Leviticus 19:18 (which we'll hear later). It's a good answer; it resolves the lawyer's original question: "What shall I *do* to inherit eternal life?" Jesus commends it: "You have answered correctly; *do* this, and you will live" (10:28).

Of course, if we plan to get to heaven by what we do, we've got to be right about everything. So the lawyer, "desiring to justify himself, said to Jesus, 'And who is my neighbor?'" (10:29). He can't settle for Jesus dismissing his question so easily (in fact, making him supply his own response). He's an expert; he has to justify his question as being beyond the level of a good Jewish confirmation kid. Perhaps, too, he senses what Jesus is implying. If he's to inherit eternal life by his works, the requirement of the Law must be something he can attain. Surely we don't have to (can't!) love *everyone*. Besides, it should make for an impressively-tangled legal debate—with lots of good legalese ("The party of the first part . . .").

Instead, He tells the parable (10:30–35). The Jericho Road really was known to be dangerous—remote, rocky, rife with bandits. Poor victim! Priests and Levites should have been expected to do the loving thing. (Levites, of the priestly tribe of Levi but not in the line of Aaron, were temple assistants.) But, heaven forbid, if the man should die while they were lending aid, they'd be ceremonially unclean for a week (Lev 21:10–11; Num 19:11–13). And what if the robbers were still lurking?

Then along comes the Samaritan. We know that history. After destroying the Northern Kingdom of Israel in 722 BC, Assyria repopulated the land with other conquered peoples from its vast empire. These new arrivals intermarried with the few remaining Israelites and adopted a corrupted worship of Yahweh (2 Ki 17:1–6, 24–33, 41). The Jews, therefore, had nothing to do with them. Yet the Samaritan "had compassion" (Lk 10:33) on the wounded man, probably a Jew.

What does the parable mean?

Jesus Himself explicates the obvious meaning: "'Which of these three, do you think, proved to be a neighbor to the man who fell among the robbers?' [The lawyer] said, 'The one who showed him mercy.' And Jesus said to him, 'You go, and do likewise'" (10:36–37). The point is self-evident, even to the lawyer. If a hated Samaritan is loving to a Jew, well, then, if I'm to earn eternal life by doing the Law, I do indeed have to love everyone. The parable makes clear that we're commanded to love every neighbor.

That's an inescapable interpretation of the parable. The injured man is our neighbor; we are to love him as the Samaritan did, not as the priest and Levite failed to do. *Jesus said* go and do that.

Everybody (almost), including many who don't know much about Jesus, know this interpretation of the Good Samaritan. The world calls one who stops to help a stranded motorist on the freeway a Good Samaritan. And we have Good Samaritan laws protecting people who give aid to others who are believed to be injured, ill, or otherwise incapacitated.

As Christians, we know we can't ignore the homeless, the poor, the sick, the lonely. We certainly can't decide whether to love based on someone's race or ethnicity. And such examples only begin to touch on the opportunities and duty to love our neighbor.

But is that what Jesus is really getting at in *this* story? Remember, it's a parable—actually, probably, what we technically call an allegory. (Listen to my *Issues, Etc.* discussion of the difference.) So the key is knowing who each of the main figures represents. And by no means does everyone agree that the Samaritan is supposed to stand for us. There's a wonderful alternative, right? Who cared for those who were dying (in fact, *dead* in their trespasses and sins, Eph 2:1)? Who paid for their healing, whatever the cost? Jesus is the Good Samaritan, right? And we're the poor man lying in the road. It fits perfectly. Jesus, at the cost of His own life, has rescued us from death. To the lawyers, Pharisees, and priests, He from rural Galilee was just as surprising a savior as the Samaritan. It's a stunning picture of the Gospel of Christ!

But is it what Jesus means in *this* story? What about His command to the Christian ethic, "You go, and do likewise"?

The other propers of the day have been chosen to accompany the Good Samaritan story for a reason. What light do they shed on interpreting the parable?

Look at the **Introit**:

Give thanks to the LORD, for He is good, for His steadfast love endures forever.

It is He who remembered us in our low estate, for His steadfast love endures forever; and rescued us from our foes, for His steadfast love endures forever; He who gives food to all flesh, for His steadfast love endures forever. Give thanks to the God of heaven, for His steadfast love endures forever.

Glory be to the Father and to the Son and to the Holy Spirit; as it was in the beginning, is now, and will be forever. Amen.

Give thanks to the LORD, for He is good, for His steadfast love endures forever. (Ps 136:23–26; antiphon: Ps 136:1)

Every verse of Psalm 136 (beginning with our common after-table prayer, usually from the King James Version) gives a new element and then follows, "For His steadfast love endures forever" (KJV: "For His mercy endureth for ever"). We can envision the man in the ditch in Jesus' parable in "low estate," needing to be "rescued" from his "foes." And it's the Lord who renders aid. Here, the Lord's steadfast love makes Him the Good Samaritan.

What about in the **Collect**?

Lord Jesus Christ, in Your deep compassion You rescue us from whatever may hurt us. Teach us to love You above all things and to love our neighbors as ourselves; for You live and reign with the Father and the Holy Spirit, one God, now and forever. Amen.

The Samaritan "had compassion" (Lk 10:35) on the half-dead man, and our prayer here acknowledges that Jesus has "deep compassion" to "rescue us from whatever may hurt us." But we also pray that He would teach us to do likewise, "to love our neighbors as ourselves," to be Good Samaritans too.

Now the **Psalm** for the day, Psalm 41.

David begins with a clear statement on our role in loving our neighbor: "Blessed is the one who considers the poor!" (41:1). For most of the psalm, though, the Lord is delivering, protecting him who is in need. We even see ourselves as the man lying on the road: "All who hate me whisper together about me. . . . They say, 'A deadly thing is poured out on him; he will not rise again from where he lies'" (41:7, 8). Except the Lord will "raise me up" (41:10).

The Psalms teach us this: the Lord's people and His Anointed One often share the same role, greater or lesser. David speaks of himself as the sufferer, but we well recognize this as pointing to the Messiah: "Even my close friend in whom I trusted, who ate my bread, has lifted his heel against me" (41:9; Jn 13:18). Can we similarly "merge" the two understandings of the Good Samaritan?

The **Old Testament Reading** includes one of the texts the lawyer knew so well. Read Leviticus 18:1–5; 19:9–18.

There are many practical ways for the Israelites to "love your neighbor as yourself" (19:18)—and most of them have application for us. We are to care for the poor, not steal, not lie, be ethical in our business and legal dealings. We are to care for those with disabilities, protect all human life, such as from abortion, the way the Good Samaritan did!

But is that really what *Leviticus* is all about? Even in the Old Testament, God prescribed for Israel such lengthy civil and ceremonial laws not for them to gain eternal life by *doing* them. (Do these, and they *would* live, 18:5, but they couldn't.) Rather, these laws were to act out before them and give them daily reminders of *God's* holiness—what *He* was about: "I am the LORD" (18:2, 4, 5; 19:10, 12, 14, 16, 18). Other nations would learn how different Yahweh was from their gods by viewing Israel (18:1–4). *Yahweh* cared about the poor, the disabled, the hurting, the threatened. The nations would see that *Yahweh* loved. And one day, the world would see how perfectly the Lord loves when He came and fulfilled every jot and tittle of every Law, finally loving all of His neighbors by His death.

That's the book of Leviticus—a helpful guide book as to how we Samaritans are to be good *and* a foreshadowing of the real Good Samaritan—rolled into one scroll.

The **Epistle** begins a new series of four Sundays in Colossians. Does it corroborate this dual understanding? Read 1:1–14.

Like all of Paul's letters, Colossians is about Christ, the "beloved Son, in whom we have redemption, the forgiveness of sins" (1:13–14). But Paul always addressed the new life of love the Christian is to live. See the relationship between them: "We heard of your faith in Christ Jesus *and of the love* that you have for all the saints, *because of* the hope laid up for you in heaven" (1:4–5).

So the Good Samaritan is Christ . . . and you. And Christ, the Good Samaritan, loves you. And you, the good Samaritan, love your neighbor. Merge them:

THE GOOD SAMARITAN
(THAT IS, CHRIST/YOU)
SHOWS LOVE TO
THE POOR, THE HELPLESS
(THAT IS, YOU/YOUR NEIGHBOR).

"Where charity and love prevail, there God is ever found. . . . *And* let us love each other well in Christian holiness" (**Hymn of the Day**, *LSB* 845:1, 3).

The Sundays after Pentecost: Proper 11 (July 17–23) Year C

READINGS

Genesis 18:1–10a (10b–14)
Psalm 27:(1–6) 7–14
(antiphon: v 4)
Colossians 1:21–29
Luke 10:38–42

HYMN OF THE DAY

LSB 536 "One Thing's Needful"

One of the great blessings of the three-year lectionary (in fact, even an advantage over the also very helpful one-year lectionary) is that it takes us straight through long sections of books of the Bible, beginning with the Synoptic Gospels. One week after another, we hear what the Holy Spirit inspired Luke or Matthew or Mark to write next. We get a sense of the continuing story.

The parable of the Good Samaritan, last Sunday's Gospel reading, is one of the most well-known texts in Scripture. When we reach its resolution, Jesus' words, "Go, and do likewise" (Lk10:37), we feel closure, the end of something significant. Our minds want to close the book, reflect a bit, and then open it again when we're ready for Jesus to introduce the next memorable teaching, the Lord's Prayer (11:1ff).

Instead, Luke follows the Good Samaritan dialogue with what seems to be a filler, a totally different setting, a brief story seemingly detached from the two great lessons before and after. It's Jesus' visit with Mary and Martha. It's fairly well known too, mostly because we can easily remember their two names. But its message seems to be mostly common sense. We could probably skip it.

Except that the lectionary has us read it just as the Holy Spirit moved Luke to report it—immediately after the great parable—as this week's Gospel lesson. Perceptively, we think, the much later chapter divisions (the work of English archbishop Stephen Langton around 1227) make the story of Mary and Martha the epilogue to the Good Samaritan. Luke 10 *doesn't* end when we'd expect. We get one more brief note.

It makes us think. We recall that the parable may not be as simple as it first appears—*whichever* interpretation one may endorse. Remember how we eventually understood it in our devotion-study? Is it possible that Luke gives us the story of Mary and Martha as an addendum to the Good Samaritan story? Could Mary and Martha be a real-life playing out of what was previously just a parable?

The story of Mary and Martha itself raises two questions we'll explore. First, was Martha being bad, doing the wrong thing? Second, Mary, Jesus says, has chosen the "one thing necessary" (Lk 10:42), perhaps more familiarly, the "one thing needful" (KJV). But He doesn't really tell us what it is. So what is it? Faith in Christ? God's Word? Christ Himself? Let's look for indications of answers to both questions, beginning with the other propers for the week.

The **Introit** comes from the oft-cited (very long!) Psalm 119.

> *Your word is a lamp to my feet and a light to my path.*
>
> *The Lord is my portion; I promise to keep Your words. I entreat Your favor with all my heart; be gracious to me according to Your promise. When I think on my ways, I turn my feet to Your testimonies; I hasten and do not delay to keep Your commandments. The earth, O Lord, is full of Your steadfast love; teach me Your statutes!*
>
> *Glory be to the Father and to the Son and to the Holy Spirit; as it was in the beginning, is now, and will be forever. Amen.*
>
> *Your word is a lamp to my feet and a light to my path. (Ps 119:57–60, 64; antiphon: Ps 119:105)*

We've frequently discussed how Psalm 119 pictures the delight of the faithful poring over God's Word. The psalmist sees himself reading as he walks along the road, all the light he needs emanating from the beloved scroll; he's oblivious to the fact that the sun set hours ago. "I turn my feet to Your testimonies; I hasten and do not delay to keep Your commandments." He's on the move, but hearing these verses, it's easy to imagine Mary sitting at the feet of the Incarnate Word. "The earth, O Lord, is full of Your steadfast love; teach me Your statutes!"

Both would tell us the Word is necessary, needful. But both would also surely say, "The Lord is my portion." The Lord is Himself the possession I must hold on to always, walking or sitting.

The **Gradual** for this second part of the Pentecost season also reminds us that the Word is our focus these Sundays:

> *How beautiful are the feet of those who preach the good news, who publish peace and bring good news of salvation. Their voice has gone out to all the earth, and their words to the ends of the world. (Rom 10:15b, 18b; Is 52:7b, alt)*

Mary, it turns out, will later anoint those beautiful feet of Jesus and wipe them with her hair. (Jn 11:1–2; 12:1–3). The Good News of peace and salvation He preaches is precious to her! So is He!

The **Collect** for this Sunday is explicitly for the Mary-Martha Gospel. What does it suggest about the one thing—and about the two women?

> *O Lord, grant us the Spirit to hear Your Word and know the one thing needful that by Your Word and Spirit we may live according to Your will; through Jesus Christ, Your Son, our Lord, who lives and reigns with You and the Holy Spirit, one God, now and forever. Amen.*

Once again, the Word is obviously prominent. But we pray that by the Spirit, we would hear the Word "*and know* the one thing needful." The Collect distinguishes between the two. Presumably the Word is the means the Spirit uses to reveal the one necessary thing.

Hearing the Word, as Mary did, is a gift of the Spirit, and to listen is certainly to "live according to [the Lord's] will." But is there a place also for Martha's serving in living His will?

The **Old Testament Reading** suggests an answer. Read Genesis 18:1–14.

The initial connection to the Gospel lesson is readily apparent: the Lord comes to visit, and the host/hostess provides hospitality. This is one of actually many occasions when the Son of God, before (in this case, two millennia before) taking on human flesh, makes a physical appearance (Ex 3:1–6; Josh 5:13–6:2; Judg 13:2–24; 1 Sam 3:1–10, to list just a few others). This time, He appears as if He were an ordinary human. We learn later that the other two "men" were angels (Gen 19:1).

Abraham immediately recognizes his guests. ("The Lord" had spoken to him many times before, 12:1, 7; 13:14; 15:1; 17:1, though we don't usually know in what mode.) And consider the feast he puts out! A choice calf for just three guests . . . and bread baked from "*three seahs* of fine flour" (18:6)! Okay, I give. What's a "seah"? By different ancient criteria, one seah was about seven, nine, or eleven quarts! This was twenty-one to thirty-three quarts of flour! Five to eight gallons of flour! How much bread could even the Lord and two angels eat and Sarah bake? Perhaps this was Abraham's exuberant instruction, knowing the identity of his diners, which Sarah toned down to be more realistic. The point? Abraham, his wife, and staff were quite the Marthas! And the Lord approved: "Do as you have said" (18:5).

But the point *of the visit* was the Lord's announcement. The waiting was nearly over. The son the Lord had promised elderly Abraham and Sarah, now almost a quarter century earlier, was coming within the year. For all the baking and the butchering we might ever do, whatever the Lord is up to is always still the real story.

The **Psalm** is actually explicit about "one thing." Read Psalm 27.

"One thing have I asked of the Lord, that will I seek after: that I may dwell in the house of the Lord all the days of my life, to gaze upon the beauty of the Lord and to inquire in His temple" (27:4). Mary got to do exactly what David asked—to gaze into Jesus' eyes, inquire of Him. "Teach me Your way, O Lord" (27:11). The temple—or Jesus' feet—is where we hear His Word. But notice, the Lord Himself is the real reason David asks for his "one thing," to be in God's house: "Your face, Lord, do I seek" (27:8).

And what about Martha? David realizes that to "wait for the Lord" (27:14) is better than to wait *on* the Lord.

The **Epistle** is the second of four through Colossians. Read Colossians 1:21–29.

Paul's letter to the Church in Colossae was largely to combat a heresy that saw Jesus as less than He is—fully God, our complete Savior. Paul's response could well be the Gospel reading. First, Jesus has done the full and finished job of saving us: "He has now reconciled [you] in His body of flesh by His death, in order to present you holy and blameless and above reproach before Him" (1:22). He alone is needful for our salvation. Second, we are protected from being led astray into false teaching by thorough study and understanding of God's Word: "The word of God fully known. . . . [Christ] we proclaim, warning everyone and teaching everyone with all wisdom, that we may present everyone mature in Christ" (1:25, 28). That's necessary as well.

But can we be precise about just "one thing"? And about Martha? And the Good Samaritan! The **Holy Gospel**, Luke 10:38–42.

From elsewhere (Jn 11:1–2; 12:1–3), we know that Martha (with brother Lazarus and sister Mary) lived in Bethany, less than two miles from Jerusalem. It seems Martha is the official lady of the house; though this is Luke's first time to name Mary (10:39), it's not impossible she was already one of the women in Jesus' traveling party (8:1–3), perhaps the reason Jesus now visits their home.

The scene is vivid: Mary listening, Martha fretting. But we've seen with Abraham that such serving is *not* wrong. This isn't a lesson against busyness or even worry. Jesus doesn't rebuke Martha gently until she tries to interrupt Mary's better choice. But neither is this just an exhortation to be diligent in listening to God's Word. That would still be just a good "moral of the story" *for us* like Jesus' "Go, and do likewise" if not properly understood. Are you getting a sense of how Mary and Martha put into real life action the parable of the Good Samaritan? Martha was to be a good Samaritan, loving her neighbor with hospitality. Mary was the poor man lying on the road, with *the* Good Samaritan serving her. There is to be a merging of the two. It's a matter of serving versus being served. Both are proper, but what's needed, the one thing really, is for the Lord to serve us. The reason the Word is so crucial (but *pen*ultimate) is because the Word is *how* God serves us, setting before us, as our feast, Christ!

There's Nothing Wrong with Serving the Lord, But the One Thing Needful Is God Serving Us with the Word of Christ.

The **Hymn of the Day**, *LSB* 536, is obviously an explication of this. The "highest, noblest treasure, Jesus" (st 3), is ours when God serves us with the Gospel that declares Him.

The Sundays after Pentecost: Proper 12 (July 24–30) Year C

READINGS

Genesis 18:(17–19) 20–33
Psalm 138 (antiphon: v 3)
Colossians 2:6–15 (16–19)
Luke 11:1–13

HYMN OF THE DAY

LSB 766 "Our Father, Who from Heaven Above"

"Lord, teach us to pray." (Lk 11:1)

It's a profound request, probably deeper than the disciples realized. Prayer is such a basic part of Christian life—like breathing and eating—that we likely never asked anyone to teach us. Or, if we did, we were so small we don't remember. Our parents folded our hands for us; we heard them pray; we got used to saying a prayer before meals. We pray many times every Sunday in church. We talk to God in the dark at night, silently, or maybe aloud with our spouses or children. We think quick "Help me, Lord" prayers at random stressful times during the day. We even studied the Lord's Prayer in the catechism. But chances are, we never asked anyone to teach us, even then.

What would you *like* the Lord to teach you about prayer? We may not have a ready answer for that either. We'd all like to be more active in prayer, but perhaps we don't know enough about what we don't know to ask how.

We might like to learn to craft just the right words for each different occasion in life. (We can buy prayer books for that at cph.org.) We definitely might want the Lord to teach us a way to make prayer happen regularly in our busy routines. (You don't need CPH to find hundreds of self-help books on that, all of which claim to be the Lord's teaching.) Sinfully, we'd love to learn some magic formula for prayer that guarantees the answer *I* want. (If anyone is teaching that, he's not the Lord of heaven!)

Although Jesus does give us perfect words for every occasion, that's not His primary curriculum objective in teaching the Lord's Prayer in today's Gospel. What He teaches us is actually simpler and indeed more profound.

For what Jesus wants to teach us, we couldn't do better than this: begin by praying the Lord's Prayer.

Then let's continue learning from our Lord about prayer with the **Introit**:

Call upon Me in the day of trouble; I will deliver you, and you shall glorify Me.

With my whole heart I cry; answer me, O LORD! I will keep Your statutes. I call to You; save me, that I may observe Your testimonies. I rise before dawn and cry for help; I hope in Your words. My eyes are awake before the watches of the night, that I may meditate on Your promise. Hear my voice according to Your steadfast love; O LORD, according to Your justice give me life.

Glory be to the Father and to the Son and to the Holy Spirit; as it was in the beginning, is now, and will be forever. Amen.

Call upon Me in the day of trouble; I will deliver you, and you shall glorify Me. (Ps 119:145–149; antiphon: Ps 50:15)

Pairing Psalm 50:15 as antiphon with verses from Psalm 119 is itself excellent teaching by the designers of the Introit. It shows from whence proper prayer comes. It begins with the Lord. He invites. He bids us approach Him and promises to answer: "Call upon Me in the day of trouble; I will deliver you." Then and only then do we pray: "With my whole heart I cry; answer me, O LORD!" Once the Lord has struck up the conversation, we go on to ask whatever: "Save me." "Help." "Give me life." We know that the Lord hears us always "according to Your steadfast love; O LORD, according to Your justice." That gives rise—"before dawn," no less!—to an active routine of daily prayer: "My eyes are awake before the watches of the night, that I may meditate on Your promise."

In the **Collect** this Sunday, we join the disciples in asking to be taught to pray:

O Lord, let Your merciful ears be attentive to the prayers of Your servants, and by Your Word and Spirit teach us how to pray that our petitions may be pleasing before You; through Jesus Christ, Your Son, our Lord, who lives and reigns with You and the Holy Spirit, one God, now and forever. Amen.

An old soldiers' expression: "There are no atheists in foxholes." When the bullets are flying, when the troops are scared to death, everybody's praying. The question is whether you know God hears, or as a last resort you're just throwing it up: "God, if You're out there, . . ." As Christians, we pray, "Lord, let Your merciful ears be attentive to the prayers of Your servants." We know who's there, and *He's told us* His ears are merciful, tuned in to listen. As with the Introit, a Christian collect gets the order right: the Lord has assured us He's eager to hear. Then we ask of Him.

This week, we ask, we pray, specifically about prayer: "By Your Word and Spirit teach us how to pray." The request acknowledges that prayer must begin with God. We *wouldn't* know otherwise. The "right" words to use aren't only in a prayer book—even from CPH—but it is true that prayer at its best speaks back to what God has said to us in *His* Word, in the Scriptures. We're free to ask God for anything, always with the proviso, "Thy will be done," which is always the best! But when we pray the words God has spoken, ask for things He's promised in His Word to give us, we know "our petitions [are] pleasing before [Him]."

The most important thing God in His Word teaches us about prayer He teaches in nearly all of our collects. Do you know? Probably. But maybe it's one of those things we learned without thinking much about it. In case that's so, we'll be sure to let our Lord teach it from the Gospel reading in a minute.

Speaking of prayer books, the Psalter was the prayer book of Old Testament Israel—and also God's Word. Read the **Psalm**, Psalm 138.

Praying the Psalms has always been a precious part of the prayer life of Christians. Luther prayed them daily, and he felt that each psalm could be understood as expressing one or more specific petitions of the Lord's Prayer. For example, Psalm 138 expresses the Second Petition, "Thy kingdom come": "All the kings of the earth shall give You thanks, O Lord" (138:4). Thus our own hymnals have always made extensive use of the Psalms, not only in offering them in a section of their own but so often quoted in our liturgies.

Like Luther, we learn from David to converse with God intimately: "Though the Lord is high, He regards the lowly" (138:6). The Creator is infinitely above us, but we're not just sending up interstellar probes and hoping for the best. He has descended to be with us personally in the person of David's Descendant. We speak back His own record of hearing us: "On the day I called, You answered me" (138:3).

See how Abraham pushes this to full advantage in the **Old Testament Reading**, Genesis 18:17–33.

The nerve of Abraham! Got a lotta gall! Chutzpah! No shame! And the Lord loves it!

This is the sequel to last week's reading. The Lord, in appearance as a man with two angels, has given Abraham the great good news that his long-awaited son will soon be on the way. But the next item on the agenda frightens Abraham for the sake of his nephew Lot, who now lives in Sodom (Gen 13:1–13).

Abraham knows that he has no claim on God. His lengthy negotiation is really no negotiation at all. He isn't making deals with God; he has nothing to offer. He is "but dust and ashes" (18:27). He's just begging.

Yet he has "undertaken to speak to the Lord" (18:31)—and *not* "but this *once*" (18:32). Abraham shows no shame in pressing "the Judge of all the earth" (18:25) because God has initiated intimacy with him: "The Lord said, 'Shall I hide from Abraham what I am about to do, seeing that Abraham shall surely become a great and mighty nation?'" (18:17–18). It's God who called Abraham, brought him to this land, promised to make him ancestor of the Savior. "I have chosen him," God says (18:19). "*Then* Abraham drew near and said, 'Will you indeed sweep away the righteous with the wicked?'" (18:23). *Therefore*, as we say in our liturgy, "We are bold to pray" (*LSB*, pp 241, 251, 257).

The **Epistle**, Colossians 2:6–19, continues Paul's topic in that book, but it also teaches us crucial truths about prayer.

The Colossian heresy Paul is answering apparently included "philosophy and empty deceit, according to human tradition, according to the elemental spirits of the world," such as "questions of food and drink, or with regard to a festival or a new moon or a Sabbath. . . . Asceticism and worship of angels, going on in detail about visions" (2:8, 16, 18). The core problem in all of that was demeaning Christ and His sufficiency for our salvation. But, Paul replies, "In [Christ] the whole fullness of deity dwells bodily" (2:9). And Christ has "forgiven us all our trespasses, by canceling the record of debt that stood against us with its legal demands. This He set aside, nailing it to the cross" (2:13–15).

God isn't distant, some vague being somewhere up there. He came to live with us! Christ is the fullness of God in person.

That in-person intimacy is what invited the disciples to ask their question, "Lord, teach us to pray." The **Holy Gospel**, Luke 11:1–13.

Immediately we notice that Luke's reporting of the Lord's Prayer (11:2–4) is not the familiar version we know. Not only does Matthew (Mt 6:9–13, in a different context, the Sermon on the Mount, and without the disciples asking) give a more complete text, but, very likely, the early Church addended the final doxology from its use of the prayer in worship. Luke's difference teaches us that the prayer is not intended to be a formula for the perfect prayer; instead, it focuses us on the truly vital core teaching of prayer.

First, Jesus teaches us that in prayer, we may approach God as Father (see also 11:11–13). In the Old Testament, God is surprisingly rarely called Father. The Jews spoke of father Abraham, but Abraham himself probably never spoke of God that way. Now, Jesus says (through Luther), "With these words God tenderly invites us to believe that He is our true Father and that we are His true children, so that with all boldness and confidence we may ask Him as dear children ask their dear Father" (Small Catechism, Lord's Prayer).

Second, by a petition (11:4a) Luke includes, Jesus teaches us why we have access to the Father: forgiveness of sins. Our sins would stand like a prison wall between us and God. But Christ "canceling [our] debt . . . nailing it to the cross" has restored His dear Father-child intimacy with us. Like Abraham, we can speak to God with "impudence" (11:8), also translated "shamelessness," for Christ's sake. That is, as all those collects teach us, "through Jesus Christ, Your Son, our Lord."

That's how Jesus teaches us to pray.

THOUGH WE ARE BUT DUST AND ASHES, THE LORD'S INTIMACY WITH US INVITES US TO PRAY TO GOD SHAMELESSLY AS FATHER.

Close by singing the Lord's Prayer with Luther in the **Hymn of the Day**, *LSB* 766.

The Sundays after Pentecost: Proper 13 (July 31–August 6) Year C

READINGS

Ecclesiastes 1:2, 12–14; 2:18–26
Psalm 100 (antiphon: v 3)
Colossians 3:1–11
Luke 12:13–21

HYMN OF THE DAY:

LSB 782 "Gracious God, You Send Great Blessings"

The *least* important divide in the propers this Sunday is what seems so urgent to a man in the Gospel reading: the division of an inheritance he asks Jesus to arbitrate with his brother. Jesus dismisses that as not worth His or their trouble. But the man's request triggers Jesus' teaching on other divides that do truly matter. As a result, the propers for this Sunday after Pentecost are riddled with so many divides of some or much importance: rich or poor, wisdom or foolishness, God or what we may make our god, enjoyment from the hand of God or vanity, earthly goods versus heavenly treasure, things below or things above, physical life versus soul, God or self. Taken together, they divide eternal life from eternal death.

No surprise: The resolution will be Christ.

"Hear this, . . . low and high, rich and poor": the **Introit**.

Hear this, all peoples! Give ear, all inhabitants of the world, both low and high, rich and poor together!

Truly no man can ransom another, or give to God the price of his life, for the ransom of their life is costly and can never suffice. This is the path of those who have foolish confidence; yet after them people approve of their boasts. Like sheep they are appointed for Sheol; death shall be their shepherd. But God will ransom my soul from the power of Sheol, for He will receive me.

Glory be to the Father and to the Son and to the Holy Spirit; as it was in the beginning, is now, and will be forever. Amen.

Hear this, all peoples! Give ear, all inhabitants of the world, both low and high, rich and poor together! (Ps 49:7–8, 13–14a, 15; antiphon: Ps 49:1–2)

Rich or poor (and low estate versus high society) are often such a conspicuous division between people. We see it in dress and addresses, experiences and opportunities, jobs and leisure activities. But the wise psalmist calls for both, "all peoples," to listen together. Both will die. Equally surely. Nobody accumulates enough wealth to ransom her life.

A rich fool deludes himself into thinking so ("foolish confidence") and "people approve of their boasts"—they believe that if they, too, just had that much money, their worries would be over too. The rich are often seen as experts, become influencers, opinion makers, because folks assume someone successful must be wise. But it can be money, prosperity itself that causes delusion. And it doesn't alleviate worry; it only brings new kinds.

Meanwhile, the destitute man or woman frets and strains over lacks. Poverty can be just as entrapping for Sheol; we can worship an idol we want as much as one we have. Dior or dirt poor—not as different as they appear.

"But God will ransom my soul from the power of Sheol." Low and high together. For He pays in a far richer currency.

"Rich" or "poor," it's crucial to recognize that we are all richly blessed—and how(!). Pray the **Collect**:

O Lord, grant us wisdom to recognize the treasures You have stored up for us in heaven, that we may never despair but always rejoice and be thankful for the riches of Your grace; through Jesus Christ, Your Son, our Lord, who lives and reigns with You and the Holy Spirit, one God, now and forever. Amen.

Worshipers praying this prayer in your congregation Sunday will vary widely on socioeconomic scales—much more so if we consider worshipers in congregations around the world. But God-given wisdom sees that we each possess unimaginable treasure! "Stored up for us in heaven" is an eternity of loving interaction with our Lord Jesus and all Christians, perfect joy, perfect health, perfect vitality and busyness. It could be no other way, since all riches are gifts of God's grace, and He always gives more than we could imagine.

It's interesting that we use the same language of "treasure" for heavenly blessings and for earthly wealth. Here on earth, our treasure is of different kinds: life and whatever God knows we need to support it for however long He knows we should be on earth before heaven. It's always more than we sinners deserve, often much more than we realize we have. But it makes sense that we use the same language; both come from the same source. And both are to be received in the same way: "always rejoice and be thankful." This divide also is not as broad as we might think.

It's a fitting time to read Psalm 100, a wonderful **Psalm** of thanksgiving—and more.

"Enter His gates with thanksgiving! . . . Give thanks to Him!" (100:4a, c). The psalmist doesn't use "treasure" language; he certainly has in mind all God's blessings—earthly and heavenly. But he gives us a reminder that is very apropos to our theme this day. The psalmist is emphatic about the one *to whom* we give thanks. "Serve the LORD with gladness! . . . Know that the LORD, He is God!" (100:2a, 3a).

What are the alternatives? Whom else might we serve? Whom else might we make our god? Well, among many other fill-in-the-blanks, the psalmist could surely exhort us, "Don't serve your possessions! Don't think that money is god!" Our sin would be easier to see if we invested every penny of our savings in gold, melted it down, and out came a calf. But if we're complaining in our hearts each month when we pay the bills, we're not serving the Lord with gladness. If we think we need to fudge on our income tax to store up enough for retirement, we're trusting money, not the Lord. Understand, as well, worshiping possessions is always worshiping ourselves—our cleverness to gain them and the pleasure we get from them. But the psalmist writes, "It is [He] who made us, and we are His" (100:3b). "*The LORD* is good; *His* steadfast love endures forever" (100:5a).

Yet the wisest man who ever lived struggled to justify how anything could have enduring value. Consider the **Old Testament Reading**, Ecclesiastes 1:2, 12–14; 2:18–26.

Can it really be all that bad, Solomon? (1:1–2). With such wisdom (1 Ki 3:3–14), fame (1 Ki 4:29–34; 10:1–10), and wealth (1 Ki 10:14–25), you'd think Solomon would be happy. But, like all sinners, he fell into temptation, and his riches gave him virtually unlimited opportunity (1 Ki 11:1–4).

So now in his later years, what does he have? The same man who wrote, "The fear of the LORD is the beginning of wisdom" (Prov 9:10) now discovers that wisdom *apart from the Lord* sees only the breakdowns and contradictions of a fallen world—much as so many modern, atheistic philosophers reach pessimistic conclusions. Such "wisdom" is vanity (empty, worthless) and "unhappy business" (Ecc 1:13).

In particular, all material wealth Solomon has toiled to accumulate is vanity, "seeing that I must leave it to the man who will come after me, and who knows whether he will be wise or a fool" (2:18–19). In Solomon's case, his son Rehoboam was indeed a fool; though it was God's judgment on Solomon's own sin, Rehoboam's folly led to the dismantling of his father's great empire in just one generation (1 Ki 12:1–20).

Solomon's near despair is in reflecting only on the things of this world, which will surely pass away. Here, however, is a kernel of wisdom: "A person . . . should eat and drink and find enjoyment in his toil. *This also*, I saw, *is from the hand of God*, for apart from Him who can eat or who can have enjoyment? For to the one who pleases Him God has given wisdom and knowledge and joy" (2:24–26). The divide between earthly goods and heavenly treasure, recall, is not evil versus good. In fact, that both are from the Lord is very important, because it frees us from vain toiling for the earthly. The Lord will provide.

Eventually, Solomon returns to a hopeful view. Check Ecclesiastes 12:1, 7, 11, 13–14. Then see how Paul describes this perspective in the **Epistle**, Colossians 3:1–11.

"If then you have been raised with Christ, seek the things that are above, where Christ is, seated at the right hand of God. Set your minds on things that are above, not on things that are on earth" (3:1–2). There's a divide! Things above or things on earth.

By things on earth, Paul doesn't mean *all* things earthly. We've seen how God blesses us down here on earth, and these blessings are to be enjoyed. Paul doesn't call us to asceticism, abstaining from life as physical beings (remember last week's Epistle, Col 2:18). Rather, Paul is condemning as "earthly" the list of sins that typify the fallen world (3:5–9). He gives special attention to covetousness, "which is idolatry" (3:5). "Know that the Lord," not our possessions, "He is God!"

We abstain from these earthly things because we have already been raised with Christ. In Baptism, "you have died" (3:3), been joined to Jesus in His death, and then come out of the water. Therefore you are a "new self" (3:10), a new and holy person to live here on earth and who will again be raised with Christ to join Him above forever. There, we know, are the true riches that we seek. And chief among those riches is the true wealth: "Christ is all, and in all" (3:11).

That is why asking Jesus to divide an earthly inheritance was so trivial: the **Holy Gospel**, Luke 12:13–21.

The treasure Himself is walking among the crowd. It's no time to focus on things below. "Take care, and be on your guard against all covetousness," idolatry, Paul called it, "for one's life does not consist in the abundance of his possessions" (12:15).

So the parable. The crop has been plentiful. I've got it made, enough for many years. "I will say to my soul, 'Soul, . . . relax, eat, drink, be merry'" (12:19). What makes this foolishness different from Solomon's wisdom? Solomon encouraged us to eat, drink, and enjoy because the feast came from the hand of God. This man—count the "I's" and the "mys." "I will," "I will," "I will." "My barns," "my grain," "my goods." No thanks to God.

Then hear the bitter irony: "I will say to my soul, 'Soul, . . . relax.'" "Fool! This night your soul is required of you" (12:20). Vanity, vanity. Whose will those goods be?

Here's the great divide: "So is the one who lays up treasure for himself and is not rich toward God" (12:21). When our possessions become our god, we are our own god and doomed to final and eternal failure. Rich toward God is the one who has the treasure God gives and gave. By His death, He has ransomed our souls from death, seated us with Him above, and, with the same nail-scarred hands that earned us heaven, delivers the goods we enjoy here.

Let Us Give Thanks That Even All Earthly Goods Are from God So That We Seek the Things Above, Rather than the Foolish Vanities of This World, and Are Rich in Soul Toward God through Christ.

By the **Hymn of the Day**, *LSB* 782, thank God He is the one who sends us all blessings, all our days, all of them great.

The Sundays after Pentecost: Proper 14 (August 7–13) Year C

READINGS

Genesis 15:1–6
Psalm 33:12–22 (antiphon: v 20)
Hebrews 11:1–16
Luke 12:22–34 (35–40)

HYMN OF THE DAY

LSB 666 "O Little Flock, Fear Not the Foe"

During the dog days of summer (technically these days in late July, early August when the Dog Star, Sirius, is aligned with the sun), not only does life in general slow down in the heat, but the church year, too, may seem to drag just a bit. Attendance is often (inexplicably and inexcusably!) down, and the very lengthy Pentecost season is only approaching the halfway mark. Sunday morning might give a sense of sameness.

So the designers of the lectionary, in their wisdom, have divided the season into shorter segments, indicated by the Graduals. The Graduals, you remember, mark the season, generally one Gradual for all the Sundays of a season. Over the Pentecost season, though, we have five different Graduals, each for multiple weeks. And this week, the sameness of the dog days is livened up with a new one. That signals subtle progress in the long season. For the next seven weeks, we'll have a new subtheme, still, of course, following topics in the life of the Church through Luke's Gospel. Look forward to this Sunday morning with a renewed sense of anticipation!

Let's do our part to perk things up a little as well. The propers for this Sunday may not at first seem to be as tightly themed as usual. For example, the Gospel and the Old Testament Reading may not appear to have much in common; the Epistle, in fact, seems more closely connected to the Old Testament Reading. That, then, gives us fewer clues as to how all the other propers fit in. So let's send you exploring on your own, looking for the theme. Read through all the propers without any comment here. Write down major ideas you see, and look for key words and concepts that start to recur. See if you get an idea about how they add up. I'll be back later to collect some thoughts. (This is another of those weeks when it's no fair turning the page and seeing the conclusion I reached!)

Take the propers in something like the order you'll probably hear them Sunday, beginning with the **Introit**:

Sing to the LORD with thanksgiving; make melody to our God on the lyre!

He covers the heavens with clouds; He prepares rain for the earth; He makes grass grow on the hills. He gives to the beasts their food, and to the young ravens that cry. His delight is not in the strength of the horse, nor His pleasure in the legs of a man, but the LORD takes pleasure in those who fear Him, in those who hope in His steadfast love.

Glory be to the Father and to the Son and to the Holy Spirit; as it was in the beginning, is now, and will be forever. Amen.

Sing to the LORD with thanksgiving; make melody to our God on the lyre! (Ps 147:8–11; antiphon: Ps 147:7)

Continue with the **Collect**:

Almighty and merciful God, it is by Your grace that we live as Your people who offer acceptable service. Grant that we may walk by faith, and not by sight, in the way that leads to eternal life; through Jesus Christ, Your Son, our Lord, who lives and reigns with You and the Holy Spirit, one God, now and forever. Amen.

Okay, next look up the **Old Testament Reading**, Genesis 15:1–6.

Now read that new **Gradual** we'll hear for the coming seven weeks.

Fear the LORD, you His saints, for those who fear Him lack nothing! Many are the afflictions of the righteous, but the LORD delivers him out of them all. (Ps 34:9, 19, alt)

The rest of the readings now: the **Psalm**, Psalm 33:12–22.

Read the **Epistle**, also beginning a new sequence of four Sundays through the latter chapters of Hebrews, 11:1–16.

Finally, the **Holy Gospel** for Proper 14, Luke 12:22–40. (We'll save the Hymn of the Day until the end.)

Got your notes? Did several words or ideas step forward for you? In my reading, I identified three foundational ideas, with two more that elaborated on those. You'll see what I saw as we go along.

The Introit seems to be a fairly general call to "sing to the LORD with thanksgiving." The Lord provides rain and grass and food for animals, which is important for people also when their livelihood is farming and grazing. But His promise to provide isn't to the strong ("the strength of the horse").

Rather, it's to "those who fear Him, . . . who hope in His steadfast love."

That's a significant pairing—fear of the Lord and hope in Him. Fearing God can be misunderstood to mean, well, what fearing usually means: being afraid. But we're not afraid of God when we also have hope in His love. When by faith we know God loves us, we respect and honor Him. We know He could righteously condemn us because we're sinful, but we're not scared of Him. God doesn't want our fear of Him to be detached from faith in Him. As Luther taught us, "We should fear, love, *and* trust in God above all things" (Small Catechism, First Commandment).

The Collect, too, sounds rather general. It's always wholesome to be reminded that we live only by God's grace, His undeserved kindness earned by Jesus' death on the cross. The petition, however, is more specific: "Grant that we may walk by faith, and not by sight." We each see such a tiny corner of God's big picture. So often we don't see how He's taking care of us or where He has our future headed. Faith follows wherever He leads, trusting that His hand is always guiding us "in the way that leads to eternal life."

The Old Testament Reading is obviously a case in point. Already by Genesis 15, Abram has been following the Lord's leading, almost blindly, from Ur of the Chaldeans to Haran in upper Mesopotamia to Canaan. The promise of a son in Abram and Sarai's old age in now perhaps ten years older (Gen 16:3). No progress. These are times it's difficult to walk by faith without seeing any results. Abram may very well be afraid that God's promise will come to naught. So the Lord comes again with encouragement: "Fear not, Abram, I am your shield; your reward shall be very great" (15:1).

A shield can be protection from more than swords, spears, and arrows. It can "extinguish all the flaming darts of the evil one" (Eph 6:16)—that is, any threats to our faith that Satan may fire, like to fear that God has forgotten us, abandoned us. He never will. In God's perfect time, Abraham (by then) would see at least the first of that galaxy of descendants, the brightest of which, the Alpha Canis Majoris (yes, that's Sirius, the Dog Star, brightest in the night sky), would be the Christ.

Then one of the great verses of the Old Testament: Abram "believed the LORD, and He counted it to him as righteousness" (Gen 15:6). Paul quotes this three times to demonstrate that we are justified by faith in the promised Messiah (Rom 4:3, 20–22; Gal 3:6; see also James 2:23).

The Gradual may be for seven Sundays, not just this one, but it certainly struck me as on point: "Fear the LORD, you His saints, for those who fear Him lack nothing!" Where have we heard before about the Lord providing for those who fear Him?

Can you find fear of the Lord in the Psalm? Yep, it's in there (Ps 33:18). And again it's paired with "hope in His steadfast love." Fear and faith.

What else? The image of Abram under the night sky, the Lord picturing for him all those descendants: "The LORD looks down from heaven; He sees all the children of man" (33:13). The Lord is "our shield," just as He was for Abram (33:20). And once again, He provides not for the strong (33:16–17; even have the mighty horse again) but for us who "trust in His holy name" (33:21) and have faith in His promises.

The Epistle we recognize as referring to the Old Testament Reading with Abraham and Sarah. Hebrews 11, in fact, elaborates on faith being counted as righteousness (Gen 15:6): "Now faith is the assurance of things hoped for, the conviction of things not seen. For by it the people of old received their commendation" (Heb 11:1–2).

This chapter is sometimes called the "Faith Hall of Fame." (It continues beyond our reading with lots more examples.) It's a mistake, though, to think it's really about those all-time great players. Faith is credited to us as righteousness, but it isn't actually anything to our credit at all. It simply receives the commendation God has for us. God commends us, declares us righteous, for the sake of Jesus' perfect righteousness and righteous suffering in our place. Then faith receives *God's* action. Did you see how prominent the word "promise," or "promised," is in this reading? (11:9 twice, 11:11, 13.) Faith is never trusting in itself; it's always clinging to a promise. And the Christian faith is always clinging to the promise of the promised descendant of Abraham (11:12).

Ah, since you're asking (I know you are), a brief mention of Noah's "reverent fear" (11:7). What better example of fear that God's warning of punishment is real and proper, yet of faith, than to build the ark?

What most of us today probably fear most often is a lack of the ordinary provisions Jesus cites in the Gospel reading: "Your life, what you will eat, . . . your body, what you will put on" (Lk 12:22). Waiting for test results from the doctor. Wondering if we'll have enough for retirement. Watching our weight grow and our wardrobe seem to shrink. Jesus doesn't just give us a command, "Don't worry!" He assures us that "your Father knows that you need" the things of the body and earthly life (12:30)—and that He does a pretty impressive job of taking care of creatures who mean a lot less to Him.

Jesus' word of comfort here is also the **Verse**: "Fear not, little flock, for it is your Father's good pleasure to give you the kingdom" (12:32). It was your Father's good pleasure to give you His Son, and by His death, He has given you the Kingdom. How will He not add "these things" to you (12:31)?

By now, you've figured out the words I see as thematic: "fear" (the Lord, and nothing else!), "faith," and "promise"; then those three are made concrete with "shield" and "provide." Proper 14 teaches us to

FEAR NOT, EXCEPT TO FEAR THE LORD AND RECEIVE BY FAITH ALL HIS PROMISES TO SHIELD AND PROVIDE.

This week's **Hymn of the Day**, "O Little Flock, Fear Not the Foe," has an interesting side story. Our previous hymnals never had a hymn number as high as 666. But when *LSB* would indeed reach that, a decision was made. Since some today, misunderstanding Revelation 13:18, fear 666 as "the number of the beast," that number was given to a hymn that says we're not one bit afraid of Satan. Christ shields His little flock.

The Sundays after Pentecost: Proper 15 (August 14–20) Year C

READINGS

Jeremiah 23:16–29
Psalm 119:81–88
(antiphon: v 81)
Hebrews 11:17–31 (32–40); 12:1–3
Luke 12:49–53 (54–56)

HYMN OF THE DAY

LSB 655 "Lord, Keep Us Steadfast in Your Word"

We've all heard and discussed this fact before: more Christians have died for their faith in the twentieth and twenty-first centuries than in the first nineteen centuries of the Church's history combined. It's true. Christians have been martyred by Communist regimes in China, the former Soviet Union, and other Communist countries. Christians in the Middle East and Africa are constantly in danger from Islamic radicals and in India from Hindu nationalists. In various places, gang and tribal violence are ever-present threats.

Nevertheless, as of this writing (and this could change!), the persecution that touches Christians most often in North America isn't death by martyrdom. The persecution that most often assaults us is the perversion of God's Word. That includes pressure not to teach the full counsel of God—for example, by laws that criminalize as "hate speech" preaching against homosexual sins, fining pastors or worse. It also includes the incessant barrages against Christian faith and biblical morality in movies, on TV, and in music. Our faith and faithfulness are under attack, sometimes in ways that lead naive believers to become willing followers on the path to eternal death.

The most dangerous of those latter are the persecutors, the perverters of God's Word who are closest to us. That includes forces within the Church. Whole Christian denominations have signed on to the worldly agendas on sexuality, human life, and justice. In some cases, denominations that *were* Christian have de facto defected from clear teaching of the nature of the triune God Himself. And it can include our own family and friends whose disapproval can tempt us to give up the Word.

Proper 15 is a Sunday to acknowledge the grave threats against God's Church both from outside and in and to pray He will deliver.

The **Introit** invites us to do that:

Cast your burden on the LORD, and He will sustain you; He will never permit the righteous to be moved.

Give ear to my prayer, O God, and hide not Yourself from my plea for mercy! For it is not an enemy who taunts me—then I could bear it; it is not an adversary who deals insolently with me—then I could hide from him. But it is you, a man, my equal, my companion, my familiar friend. We used to take sweet counsel together; within God's house we walked in the throng. But I call to God, and the LORD will save me.

Glory be to the Father and to the Son and to the Holy Spirit; as it was in the beginning, is now, and will be forever. Amen.

Cast your burden on the LORD, and He will sustain you; He will never permit the righteous to be moved. (Ps 55:1, 12–14, 16; antiphon: Ps 55:22)

This time it's not Philistines attacking David. "It is not an enemy who taunts me"; he's defeated blaspheming giants before (1 Sam 17:26, 41–49). "It is not an adversary who deals insolently with me"; he spent years running and hiding from Saul. He turns to and addresses this adversary personally: "It is you, a man, my equal, my companion, my familiar friend. We used to take sweet counsel together; within God's house we walked in the throng." They used to go to church together! We don't know when David wrote Psalm 55, but it fits the occasion of his son Absalom's rebellion. Ahithophel, David's trusted counselor, turned traitor against him (2 Sam 15:12), and his aid to Absalom could have been David's undoing (2 Sam 16:20–23).

These are the attacks that hurt the most. The more intimate we've been, the more piercing the pain. And it is in the Christian congregation that betrayal is most devastating. (Denominational or synodical politics may be second most.) In the Church, we not only share our most private thoughts and emotions; we also share the one and same Savior and the promise of eternity together. How can we backbite, gossip, maneuver against one another? Brothers and sisters, this ought not be! Instead, let us "call to God" together "and the LORD will save me"—and you!

As usual, the **Collect** for this Sunday well *collects* the thoughts of the day:

Merciful Lord, cleanse and defend Your Church by the sacrifice of Christ. United with Him in Holy Baptism, give us grace to receive with thanksgiving the fruits of His redeeming work and daily follow in His way; through the same Jesus Christ, Your Son, our Lord, who lives and reigns with You and the Holy Spirit, one God, now and forever. Amen.

This prayer asks the Lord to protect His Church from all dangers external and arising within the visible pale. "Defend" refers primarily to protection against outside threats. But "cleanse" means purifying the visible Church from false teachings, false teachers, and hypocrites within the Church's membership. All are real perils. All are the work of Satan seeking to destroy God's kingdom.

Therefore, all are answered "by the sacrifice of Christ." At the cross, Satan did his worst; he killed God. And it wasn't enough. It couldn't destroy God's Church because her Lord lives again to guard and keep her. And Christ's sacrifice is the way the visible Church is cleansed as erring believers and even false teachers, if they repent, are forgiven.

Being "united with [Christ] in Holy Baptism" places us in Jesus' protection. In the Gospel, however, Jesus will also remind us that it makes us sharers in His suffering. We are persecuted because we are baptized into Christ.

The Collect has provided us much of the language that I see as theming this Sunday's propers. It is a day for prayer:

**LORD,
CLEANSE AND DEFEND YOUR CHURCH,
AS EVEN THOSE IN IT AND CLOSE TO US
PERVERT YOUR WORD
AND PERSECUTE YOUR PEOPLE.**

The **Gradual** assures us He will:

Fear the LORD, you His saints, for those who fear Him lack nothing! Many are the afflictions of the righteous, but the LORD delivers him out of them all. (Ps 34:9, 19, alt)

The other propers give numerous further instances of persecution, especially threats to pervert God's Word. The **Old Testament Reading**, Jeremiah 23:16–29, gives a particularly vivid one.

Jeremiah must have hated being such a killjoy. A whole cadre of professional prophets (they were making a lucrative career of it) was telling the people, "It shall be well with you"; . . . "No disaster shall come upon you" (23:17). And then Jeremiah has to go and spoil it for everybody: "Behold, the storm of the LORD! Wrath has gone forth, a whirling tempest; it will burst upon the head of the wicked. The anger of the LORD will not turn back until He has executed and accomplished the intents of His heart" (23:19–20a).

But Jeremiah did *have to* say it. The most immediate perversion of God's Word is simply failing to speak the Law (instead speaking a pseudo-Gospel) when sinners need to be warned. How often the Church—its pastors and people—fall into this! Not wanting to offend, to hurt feelings, to drive people away, we go along silently with immorality or with false doctrine another church body is allowing. That's not loving to those who need the warning. These prophets were speaking lies and their own dreams, not God's (23:25–28). If "they would have proclaimed My words to My people, . . . they would have turned them from their evil way" (23:22). They would have saved them. "In the latter days you will understand it clearly" (23:20b).

God's Word isn't easy listening. "Is not My word like fire, declares the LORD, and like a hammer that breaks the rock in pieces?" (23:29). Lord, cleanse Your Church by giving us the courage to speak Your Law when love requires us to speak it!

The author of the **Psalm** loves every word of God, and he depends on it for comfort in persecution. Read Psalm 119:81–88.

As the psalmist "longs for [God's] salvation," he hopes in His "word," "promise," "statutes," "law," "commandments," "precepts," "testimonies." The Word of God is his place of refuge. How dangerous, then, when he is persecuted by means of perverting the Word. "When will You judge those who persecute me? The insolent have dug pitfalls for me; they do not live according to Your law. . . . They persecute me *with falsehood*" (119:84b–85, 86b). Telling lies about us is damaging enough; telling lies about God, misrepresenting what His Word teaches, is worse even than sticks and stones. Since our salvation is in the Word God proclaims about Christ, any twisting of it imperils souls for eternity. Lord, defend us!

The **Epistle**, Hebrews 11:17–12:3, continues the great history of faith, but this time with a long list of persecutions of the saints.

God tested Abraham (11:17), but surely Abraham was *tempted* to choose his son Isaac over faithfulness to God. Likewise, Moses was tempted by the "fleeting pleasures" of Egypt (11:25).

Then there were so many frontal assaults against the Church. Moses was nearly murdered by "the king's edict" to kill all Hebrew baby boys (11:23). The whole Israelite nation faced death at the Red Sea (11:29). Daniel and his friends were thrown to lions and into a fiery furnace (11:33–34). "Some were tortured. . . . Others suffered mocking and flogging, and even chains and imprisonment. They were stoned, they were sawn in two, they were killed with the sword. They went about in skins of sheep and goats, destitute, afflicted, mistreated" (11:35, 36–37).

How were they all able to do it? By "looking to Jesus, the founder and perfecter of our faith, who for the joy that was set before Him endured the cross, despising the shame, and is seated at the right hand of the throne of God" (12:2).

It's in Christ, who endured the cross, that we'll also find ourselves enduring persecution. That's the **Holy Gospel**, Luke 12:49–56.

Christ and His Word bring that "fire" Jeremiah described, "division" (12:49, 51). The "baptism" with which Jesus is to be baptized (12:50) is the cross (Mk 10:35–39; 14:36), and the cross always brings division. On the one hand, it is the sweetest Gospel in which we have eternal life. But on the other hand, it also shows how badly in need we are; if God's Son had to die, we must be desperately sinful. Therefore, some will always reject it—and hate it.

We have been baptized into that same Baptism of Christ; we share His cross. So we will be divided from those who reject it. We may have to choose between the Lord and those closest to us, son or daughter (Lk 12:52–53), friends. We will be attacked by those who hate the cross. Sometimes the attacks will be overt. So we pray.

"Lord, keep us steadfast in Your Word!" "Defend Your holy Church that we may sing Your praise eternally" (**Hymn of the Day**, *LSB* 655:1, 2).

The Sundays after Pentecost: Proper 16 (August 21–27) Year C

READINGS

Isaiah 66:18–23
Psalm 50:1–15 (antiphon: v 23)
Hebrews 12:4–24 (25–29)
Luke 13:22–30

HYMN OF THE DAY

LSB 510 "A Multitude Comes from the East and the West"

It's a paradox, the **Collect** and the **Verse** for Proper 16:

> *O Lord, You have called us to enter Your kingdom through the narrow door. Guide us by Your Word and Spirit, and lead us now and always into the feast of Your Son, Jesus Christ, who lives and reigns with You and the Holy Spirit, one God, now and forever. Amen.*

And then "Alleluia. People will come from east and west, and from north and south, and recline at table in the kingdom of God. Alleluia" (Lk 13:29). The door into the kingdom of God is narrow. And yet people will enter its heavenly feast from far and wide.

Think of entering God's kingdom, perhaps, like a kitchen funnel. You want to pour sugar, let's say, or maybe some liquid into a very small-mouthed container. The funnel takes a goodly, wide dump or splash and guides it precisely into the receiver. The only problem will come if whatever you're pouring is too big and too hard to fit through that hole.

Both the narrow door and the east, west, north, south come from Jesus' words in the Gospel lesson. Together, they picture for us God's wide-open, embracing arms and warn us against being too big on ourselves, too hardheaded.

All of these elements are already hinted in the **Introit**, which includes the entirety of the shortest psalm, 117:

> *Splendor and majesty are before Him; we will bless the* Lord *from this*

time forth and forevermore. Praise the L*ORD!*

Praise the L*ORD, all nations! Extol Him, all peoples! For great is His steadfast love toward us, and the faithfulness of the* L*ORD endures forever. Praise the* L*ORD!*

Glory be to the Father and to the Son and to the Holy Spirit; as it was in the beginning, is now, and will be forever. Amen.

Splendor and majesty are before Him; we will bless the L*ORD from this time forth and forevermore. Praise the* L*ORD! (Ps 117; antiphon: Ps 96:6a; 115:18)*

"Praise the LORD, all nations! Extol Him, all peoples!" North, south, east, west. The Lord's "steadfast love" and "faithfulness" reaches out to everyone, wide and far.

"Splendor and majesty," though, carry a caution. They're more than just general praise words. They're qualities that inspire awe, even fear. You don't just saunter up to His Majesty and maybe go out with him for pizza. You don't approach unless he summons you. And royal protocol never just leaves a gaping gate agape. Rather, that's where the Lord's steadfast love (which, forgive me, in New Testament Greek would be *agape*) opens the door.

Even in the Old Testament, when one people, Israel, was the instrument of God's workings, He planned to save all nations. That's emphatic in the **Old Testament Reading**, Isaiah 66:18–23.

Isaiah's last chapter looks to the future: "The time is coming to gather all nations and tongues" (66:18). You've got to enjoy this image: the nations would come "on horses and in chariots and in litters and on mules and on dromedaries, to My holy mountain" (66:20b). (Visualize that procession when you sing the Hymn of the Day later.)

This prophecy is especially significant because it not only sees all nations *coming* to Yahweh, but it also sees the Lord *sending* His people to gather them: "I will send survivors to the nations . . . far away, that have not heard My fame or seen My glory. And they shall declare My glory among the nations. And they shall bring all your brothers from all the nations" (66:19–20a). This would be new. In the Old Testament, a handful of foreigners saw and heard about Israel and were drawn in to the Lord. But Isaiah envisions our day when missionaries go out to Tarshish and Tubal and down our own streets.

This verse in particular would be news to Israel—even shocking: "Some of them [these foreigners] also I will take for priests and for Levites, says the LORD" (66:21). Service in the temple was even more selective than being of the one chosen nation—just the tribe of Levi to assist and a tiny part of that tribe, the direct line of Aaron, as priests. All nations, then just Israel, then only the Levites, finally funneled down to the priestly line. It was a powerful lesson to Israel that no one could approach the Lord presumptuously. In fact, to enter the holy precincts without God's call would bring certain death. Surely Gentiles couldn't presume to enter and handle the holy things of God!

The **Psalm** cutting this week ends with a familiar and very comforting invitation, but first it lays down some firm ground rules. Read Psalm 50:1–15, 23.

Cut the niceties. I'm not here for chit chat, the Lord says through the psalmist. You know who I am, and when I talk, you listen: "The Mighty One, God the Lord, speaks and summons the earth from the rising of the sun to its setting" (50:1). You can hear the sonic boom—from east to west! And you can be sure, north to south too!

"Our God comes; He does not keep silence; before Him is a devouring fire, around Him a mighty tempest" (50:3). Got your attention?

"Hear, O My people, and I will speak; O Israel, I will testify against you. I am God, your God" (50:7). And here's what I've got to say. You think you're doing Me some great favor with your sacrifices. You think you're going to come to Me with a bull or a goat and I'm going to say, "Thanks, I needed that. What can I ever do to repay you?" Mighty big of you! Way too big of you! Get real. The cattle on every hill are already Mine. Every bird too. If I were hungry—which I never am—I wouldn't ask *you* to feed Me. How dare you presume that this relationship depends on you!

But *(hear the volume come down and the tone of voice soften)* "offer to God a sacrifice of thanksgiving" (50:14). That's right, *thanks*giving. I love to hear that from you. I even love when you give Me bulls or goats or tithes of whatever else you earn, when they're for thanks. See, I love giving you everything you need and so much more than you could really want. It's what delights Me. I am God, your God. And then when you recognize that everything you have came from Me and you just enjoy being My children, ah, I love that too!

So here's how we'll do things *(very gentle voice)*: "Call upon Me in the day of trouble; I will deliver you, and you shall glorify Me" (50:15). "The one who offers thanksgiving as his sacrifice glorifies Me; to one who orders his way rightly I will show the salvation of God!" (50:23). "Gather to Me My faithful ones" (50:5). All of you, from the rising of the sun to its setting. How does that sound?

The **Epistle**, Hebrews 12:4–29, remembers a time God actually spoke aloud the very sort of message we just heard through the psalmist.

We might sometimes think we'd like a God who could be a buddy, a pal. No rules. No one looking down on us. That would be foolish. If we were blessed with loving human fathers, they weren't like that. Kind. Patient. Probably even fun to hang out with. But they also disciplined us, and eventually, if not at first, we appreciated that (12:9).

God's relationship with us is Father-child, and that means He disciplines us too. Our dads did the best they could, but God's discipline is always wise, appropriate to the situation, always results in our good so "that we may share His holiness" (12:10).

Here's why that's so important: "Strive . . . for the holiness *without which no one will see the Lord*" (12:14b). In this respect, it's still as it was with the priests and Levites of Old Testament Israel: No one can presume to enter into God's presence without being holy. And no one can be holy except by "the grace of God" (12:15).

God's holy and wholesome discipline was perhaps most evident in the incident the text recalls next: when He thundered the Ten Commandments on Mount Sinai (12:18–20). God had Moses set a barrier around the mountain, for anyone touching it was to be put to death (Ex 19:12–13, 20–24). No one may approach God on his own terms.

"But you have come" not to Sinai but "to Mount Zion and to the city of the living God, the heavenly Jerusalem" (Heb 12:22). We're among the "firstborn who are enrolled in heaven," not by natural birth into a certain nation or tribe or priestly line but in "Jesus, the mediator of a new covenant, and [His] sprinkled blood" (12:23, 24). By the blood of Christ, we are holy to enter God's presence, even though the door is rightly described as "narrow." Read the **Holy Gospel**, Luke 13:22–30.

Jesus "journeying toward Jerusalem" (13:22) is, of course, on His way to the cross. "And someone said to Him, 'Lord, will those who are saved be few?'" (13:23). Jesus doesn't give a direct answer. The number isn't the important thing. What counts is each individual. I'm talking to *you*, Jesus means to say: "[You!] strive to enter through the narrow door" (13:24a). Nevertheless, "narrow door" clearly implies that *most* will not be saved. "Many, I tell you, will seek to enter and will not be able. When once the master of the house has risen and shut the door" (13:24b–25a).

The "many" who find the door shut won't be those who knew nothing or cared nothing about eternal matters. These will be the ones who presumed they were in: "Lord, open to us. . . . We ate and drank in Your presence, and You taught in our streets" (13:25b, 26). Priests and Levites, who thank God their birth set them apart from Gentile sinners. People who presume their sacrifices do God a favor. People who figure, "I'm better than most, probably good enough." People who pal around with God thinking He'll "wink, wink" at my sins. People who have no intention of coming to the Word and Sacrament, but "My father built this church and darn you if you think I'm not going to be buried through it!" People too big on themselves or too hardheaded to come through the very wide funnel. But Jesus will say, "I tell you, I do not know where you come from. Depart from Me, all you workers of evil!" (13:27).

Yet "people will come from east and west, and from north and south" and recline at that heavenly table (13:29). Jesus knows them and where they are going. In His steadfast love, He will guide them by His Word and Spirit. He will send for them from all the nations and take some of them for His priestly service. When they call, He will deliver them for the sake of the mediator, Jesus, and His sprinkled blood.

Those Who Presume Entrance into the Kingdom Will Find the Door Shut, but God Will Gather People from All Nations Far and Wide into That Narrow Door.

Envision that train of believers from all nations streaming to the feast of salvation with the **Hymn of the Day**, *LSB* 510.

The Sundays after Pentecost: Proper 17 (August 28– September 3) Year C

READINGS

Proverbs 25:2–10
Psalm 131 (antiphon: v 2)
Hebrews 13:1–17
Luke 14:1–14

HYMN OF THE DAY

LSB 842 "Son of God, Eternal Savior"

The **Verse** for Proper 17: "Alleluia. Everyone who exalts himself will be humbled, and he who humbles himself will be exalted. Alleluia" (Lk 14:11).

First we played with all the cool kids and avoided the misfits—or else we *tried* to play with the cool kids and were jealous when they wouldn't play with us.

Next we embellished our résumés and fibbed in job interviews to make ourselves sound more employable.

When we started finding ourselves at awkward cocktail parties or standing around at wedding receptions or high school reunions, the trick was to one-up the story she just told.

And where are we now? Wishing our Christmas letters could tell about travel as exotic as theirs? Pretending the Mercedes instead of the Buick is for the advanced safety features? Comparing pectoral crosses with the other pastors lining up for the processional?

I don't think we can do better for our Theme this week than Jesus' words from the Gospel lesson. We'll just repeat them right up front. (I'll explain the funny numbers shortly.)

Everyone who Exalts (E1-) Himself Will Be Humbled (H1-), and He Who Humbles (H2+) Himself Will Be Exalted (E2+).

However, while the exalting part may be obvious, one could fumble what Jesus means about humbling ourselves. We'll see.

In the meantime, we'll hear the **Introit** introduce humbling and exalting:

> *It is God who executes judgment, putting down one and lifting up another.*

We give thanks to You, O God; we give thanks, for Your name is near. We recount Your wondrous deeds. At the set time that I appoint I will judge with equity. For not from the east or from the west and not from the wilderness comes lifting up. But I will declare it forever; I will sing praises to the God of Jacob.

Glory be to the Father and to the Son and to the Holy Spirit; as it was in the beginning, is now, and will be forever. Amen.

It is God who executes judgment, putting down one and lifting up another. (Ps 75:1–2, 6, 9; antiphon: Ps 75:7)

Look again at our THEME, the Verse. Notice there are two exaltings going on and two humblings. First, someone exalts (himself), and someone else humbles him. This is a negative situation. Call those E1- and H1-. Second, someone humbles (again, himself), and someone else exalts him. This is a positive thing. Call these H2+ and E2+. The psalmist makes clear who does H1- and E2+. "It is God who executes judgment, putting down one and lifting up another." "At the set time that I appoint," God says, "I will judge." It can't be anyone else doing it: "Not from the east or from the west and not from the wilderness comes lifting up."

The psalmist doesn't say who does E1- and H2+. The clear implication, of course, is that we ought not exalt ourselves (E1-). Doing that would be all those examples we gave at the beginning. Instead, "We give thanks to You, O God; we give thanks, for Your name is near. We recount Your wondrous deeds. . . . I will sing praises to the God of Jacob." Rather than exalting ourselves, we acknowledge that everything we have God has given us. In fact, that He has exalted us (E2+).

Now as to who does the H2+, humbling himself, we have a guess, certainly, and we may be right . . . or slightly, but seriously, wrong. (By the way, last week's east, west, north, south doesn't help us here. Same directions; totally different happenings.)

The **Collect** prays for H2+ and that we would not fall into E1-. In actual words:

O Lord of grace and mercy, teach us by Your Holy Spirit to follow the example of Your Son in true humility, that we may withstand the temptations of the devil and with pure hearts and minds avoid ungodly pride; through the same Jesus Christ, our Lord, who lives and reigns with You and the Holy Spirit, one God, now and forever. Amen.

"Follow the example of Your Son in true humility." This is asking God to teach us to humble ourselves. Christ demonstrated the perfect humility, humbling Himself even to death on the cross. And we know the blessed result: "Therefore God has highly *exalted* Him and bestowed on Him the name that is above every name, so that at the name of Jesus every knee should bow" (see Phil 2:5–11). At the same time, we pray "that we may withstand the temptations of the devil and with pure hearts and minds avoid ungodly pride." Among Satan's chief temptations, his first temptation, Eve and Adam, in fact, is to exalt ourselves, "ungodly pride."

How do we follow Christ's example to humble ourselves? (Yes, that's H2+.) "By Your Holy Spirit . . . through the same Jesus Christ." That's more than just seeing Jesus' perfect example. "*Through* Jesus" means by virtue of His cross and resurrection, which reconciled us to God and brought the Holy Spirit to live in us. Being clear about that will help us see through the misunderstanding we'll talk about with this H2+ thing.

The **Old Testament Reading** offers two embarrassing examples of exalting oneself (E1-), one of which Jesus will cite in the Gospel coming up. Read Proverbs 25:2–10.

Has this happened to you—perhaps inadvertently? You thought the banquet was entirely open seating, and you wanted a good view of the after-dinner speaker. So you found a very nice table right up front. You didn't see the reserved sign. And then the guy in the penguin suit, trying to be as discreet as possible, came and whispered, "Major donors here." Problem is, the table was right up front in plain view of all, and by now, the only seating is wayyyyy in the back. Ouch. So much *more* painful if you took that table *in order* to schmooze with the big moneys! "Do not put yourself forward in the king's presence or stand in the place of the great, for it is better to be told, 'Come up here,' than to be put lower in the presence of a noble" (25:6–7a).

Or have you done this? Church meeting. Surprise item comes up during the trustees report. Aha! You once read an article on this in *Popular Mechanics*. You proudly volunteer your expert opinion and state your conclusion on what simply must be done. Amen. Then three guys who do this for a living politely point out your six crucial flaws. Slink home. "What your eyes have seen do not hastily bring into court, for what will you do in the end, when your neighbor puts you to shame?" (25:7b–8). Classic E1-s. Easy to spot.

Can you, though, envision any pitfalls in applying this E2+?: "It is better to be told, 'Come up here.'" Think of the H2+ question again.

The **Psalm** wonderfully expresses David's humility, not falling into a trap: Psalm 131.

This is a brief psalm worth reading often, even memorizing. At least remember the image. If it doesn't seem to be describing a mighty king, David would probably say so be it. "O Lord, my heart is not lifted up; my eyes are not raised too high; I do not occupy myself with things too great and too marvelous for me" (131:1). I may be a king, but some things are just above my pay grade. And that's okay. "I have calmed and quieted my soul, like a weaned child with its mother" (131:2) because the Lord has those great and marvelous things in His purview.

Trust in the Lord is true humility. I don't have to know everything, be the expert. I don't have to run every show, be in the spotlight. I don't need the accoutrements of wealth, to hang with the right people, to wow my friends. And that's not because I don't have knowledge and talents and gifts.

It's because the Lord is my hope (131:3), my sure confidence that all will be well.

The **Epistle**, our fourth and final week in Hebrews, is a valuable lesson in humility. Read Hebrews 13:1–17.

So often talking big or acting big (E1-) is hiding insecurities. Behind humility is often confidence—if the confidence is well placed. The writer of Hebrews speaks confidently while still being humble: "So we can confidently say." Say what? "The Lord is my helper" (13:6). Our confidence, and therefore the source of humility, is Christ: "I will never leave you nor forsake you. . . . Jesus Christ is the same yesterday and today and forever" (13:5, 8). His ultimate act of humility moves us to humble ourselves (H2+): Jesus "suffered outside the gate in order to sanctify the people through His own blood. Therefore let us go to Him outside the camp and bear the reproach He endured" (13:12–13).

Christ is why we don't have to impress. We have Him, so we can "be content with what [we] have," even "share what [we] have" (13:5, 16). Christ is why we don't have to be in charge. He is, so we can "obey [our] leaders and submit to them" (13:17). That is of great benefit to us, because the leaders this verse is talking about are pastors Christ gives us who "are keeping watch over [our] souls." They warn us of sin and comfort us with Christ so that we won't be lost from God's kingdom but will enjoy His final E2+.

Are we having fun yet with the *E*s and *H*s? Then you can't wait for the last reading, the **Holy Gospel**, Luke 14:1–14.

We have no problem identifying the Pharisees as E1-s, right? They're always exalting themselves. And those who "chose the places of honor" for themselves (14:7)—Jesus essentially quotes the E1- of Proverbs 25 to them (14:8–9). If on the Last Day one exalts himself to stand before God on his own merits, he will be humbled in endless suffering. Eternal H1-.

But back to the other side of the Proverbs scenario Jesus cites, the E2+: "When you are invited, go and sit in the lowest place, so that when your host comes he may say to you, 'Friend, move up higher.' Then you will be honored in the presence of all who sit at table with you" (14:10). Or now this that Jesus adds: "When you give a feast, invite the poor, the crippled, the lame, the blind, and you will be blessed, because they cannot repay you. You will be repaid at the resurrection of the just" (14:13–14). Another E2+. But do you see a potential trap? The H2+ question?

Trying to gain God's exalting (E2+) by being humble isn't humbling oneself at all. It's a clever way of exalting (E1-): "Umm, I'm so humble!" That earns no honor from God.

Truly humbling "ourselves" (H2+) can't be anything we do—any more than the man with dropsy did something to get Jesus to exalt him (14:2–4). Those God exalts (E2+) are those who know they can do nothing at all to earn God's favor, who simply trust that Jesus humbling Himself to death on the cross has exalted us. Yes, we can then be less desirous to talk big. But that's because Christ has already earned us God's E2+++.

Since Christ has hallowed our human race, "may we for others live" (**Hymn of the Day**, "Son of God, Eternal Savior," *LSB* 842:2).

The Sundays after Pentecost: Proper 18 (September 4–10) Year C

READINGS

Deuteronomy 30:15–20
Psalm 1 (antiphon: v 6)
Philemon 1–21
Luke 14:25–35

HYMN OF THE DAY

LSB 853 "How Clear Is Our Vocation, Lord"

Even when there were twelve disciples—the familiar Peter and Andrew, James and John, et al that we know so well—there was also always another group of Jesus' followers called "disciples." Then when Jesus sends out the apostles after His resurrection, He commissions them to go and "make disciples of all nations" (Mt 28:19). And by the book of Acts, Luke uses the term "disciples" as the equivalent of "Christians" (Acts 6:1–2, 7; 9:1–2; and many more). When a person becomes a believer in Jesus, he or she becomes a disciple of Christ.

That's worth pondering. Being a Christian isn't just an item on our résumés or even just a stamp on our eternal passports. It's not Sunday only, and it's not something we can hide under a bushel when it's inconvenient. Being a Christian is discipleship, and that's often tough, never easy, but certainly the joy of being in God's kingdom.

Proper 18 of these Sundays after Pentecost includes Jesus' alert in the Gospel reading that following Him requires counting the cost of discipleship. Therefore, this week, let's

**Take a Long—
Sometimes Hard, Sometimes
Delightful, Always Blessed—
Look at Discipleship.**

The **Introit** gives a very good overview:

Make me understand the way of Your precepts, and I will meditate on Your wondrous works.

My soul melts away for sorrow; strengthen me according to Your word! Put false ways far from me

and graciously teach me Your law! I have chosen the way of faithfulness; I set Your just decrees before me. I cling to Your testimonies, O Lord; let me not be put to shame! I will run in the way of Your commandments when You enlarge my heart!

Glory be to the Father and to the Son and to the Holy Spirit; as it was in the beginning, is now, and will be forever. Amen.

Make me understand the way of Your precepts, and I will meditate on Your wondrous works. (Ps 119: 28–32; antiphon: Ps 119:27)

"Make me understand," the psalmist prays. I want to take a good, long look, really grasp what's going on here.

"The way of Your precepts." There's a place in discipleship for learners sitting in a circle around their teacher. (In fact, we'll picture that in a minute in the Psalm.) But being a disciple of Jesus is in particular following Him, and that means being on the move. Especially in Luke's Gospel, we so often see Jesus traveling, with His disciples (the Twelve and the larger group) in tow. Discipleship is a "way," a journey, following the leader along a road. "Make me understand the way of Your precepts. . . . Put *false ways* far from me and graciously teach me Your law! I have chosen the way of faithfulness; I set Your just decrees before me." The "way" means discipleship is active—doing, living out the Christian life, on Monday in a college class, Tuesday when a coworker has a question or the boss has a questionable idea, Thursday in the stands at the junior varsity football game, Friday on a date.

But notice that Christ teaches us that way of life in His Word—His "precepts," "law," "just decrees," "testimonies," "commandments." So discipleship also involves serious study—it's contemplative; we'll "meditate on Your wondrous works" Wednesday evening in confirmation parents' prep, Sunday at Bible class.

This way of discipleship will be joyous: "I will run in the way of Your commandments when You enlarge my heart" Saturday night looking forward to Sunday morning. But it will often also be painful: "My soul melts away for sorrow; strengthen me according to Your word! . . . Let me not be put to shame" Saturday night when you realize there won't be another date because you lived your discipleship on Friday. The way Jesus leads His disciples won't be easy!

We know, in fact, that it is the way of the cross. The **Collect**:

O merciful Lord, You did not spare Your only Son but delivered Him up for us all. Grant us courage and strength to take up the cross and follow Him, who lives and reigns with You and the Holy Spirit, one God, now and forever. Amen.

We Christians truly delight to be Jesus' disciples, to "follow Him." We're asking for it, praying for it. But we must ask our Lord to "grant us courage and strength" to do it, because following Jesus means going where

He went. Being disciples means we must also "take up the cross." No one wants to do that; our Lord Himself prayed that, if there were some other option, the Father would take that cup from Him. Yet we know God is being "merciful" when He enables, even when He allows us to follow Jesus to the cross. For if God did not spare His own Son but delivered Him up for us all, "how will He not also with Him graciously give us all things?" (Rom 8:32).

Always, the **Psalm** tells us, the disciple of the Lord is blessed. Read Psalm 1.

Discipleship in the Lord is entirely incompatible with "the way of the wicked" (1:6), the "false ways" in the Introit. One cannot sit at the feet of the Master and also hang around the outer circles of sin. It won't work; too soon one will be drawn into evil. First, it's just a casual *walking* on the fringes of "the counsel of the wicked." But before long, it's stop and *stand* and listen "in the way of sinners." And inevitably, that leads to plopping right down to *sit* "in the seat of scoffers" (1:1) now as a disciple of sin. In the judgment, that person won't be able to sit, stand, or walk but will be blown away "like chaff" (1:4–6). The Lord's discipleship means constantly confessing and repenting of sin, not courting it.

But "blessèd" instead is this man: "His delight is in the law of the Lord, and on His law he meditates day and night" (1:2). He is the disciple who sits enraptured, soaking up every word the Lord speaks. And he will not be moved from that spot. "He is like a tree planted" right there in that place. The rich teaching he receives will be like "streams of water" so that the tree "yields its fruit in its season, and its leaf does not wither" (1:3). There's stability, security, certainty in being a disciple of the Lord.

The **Old Testament Reading** makes this distinction between discipleship and evil even more concrete. Read Deuteronomy 30:15–20.

The whole book of Deuteronomy, really, is taking a long look at what it means to be God's people. Moses is nearing death after leading Israel in the wilderness for forty years. The younger generation is about to enter the Promised Land, and he is preparing them for what's ahead. So here it is: "See, I have set before you today life and good, death and evil" (30:15).

Life and good looks like this: "You obey the commandments of the Lord your God." You love Him, you walk in His ways—discipleship—and the Lord will bless you in your new land (30:16). You have no other gods before the Lord—not the milk or honey or remodeled kitchen your new job will buy. You don't take the Lord's name in vain but pray to Him as a first resort and praise Him in ordinary conversation. You remember His holy day by gladly hearing and (with your very best intentional effort to focus) learning His Word. You love your neighbor as yourself by seeing that she has enough of the milk and honey too, that he is invited and welcomed to hear the Word with you on Sunday, that you choose life for the unborn and the elderly (30:19) as well as for yourself. "I have set before you life and . . . blessing." Take a good look.

"But if your heart turns away, and you will not hear, but are drawn away to worship other gods and serve them, I declare to you today, that you shall surely perish. . . . Death . . . and curse" (30:17–18a, 19). Take a long look at that as well.

The **Epistle** is the one appearance in the lectionary of Paul's letter to Philemon, and it includes almost the entire brief book. Read verses 1–21. Do you know the story?

After some opening pleasantries, Paul, in verse 6, gives a hint as to his agenda: "I pray that the sharing of your faith may become effective for the full knowledge of every good thing that is in us for the sake of Christ." That is, I want you to know the full ramifications of what it means to be a disciple of Jesus. You're a believer, so here's what that entails. I want you to do something you might not have wanted to do and something you have a legal right *not* to do. But it's what a disciple *does* want to do.

Onesimus (v 10) had been a slave of Philemon in Colossae, but he'd run away, probably robbing his master as he left (v 18). Somehow he'd met Paul where Paul was now imprisoned (v 1), probably Rome, and, like Philemon himself, become a Christian through Paul's word (vv 10, 19b). Onesimus, whose name means "useful," had become a useful, trusted helper to Paul, much more so than he'd been to Philemon as a mere slave (v 11). Nevertheless, Paul was sending him back to his former master, obeying the Fourth Commandment (vv 12–13).

By legal right, Philemon could punish Onesimus severely, even execute him, but Paul asks that he receive him back now as a brother in Christ. Paul could order him to do so, but instead, he asks, and he knows Philemon will agree (vv 8–9, 14–17, 21). Why? Not simply because Paul promises to make good his theft (v 18) but because of the implication Philemon couldn't miss: "If he has wronged you at all, or owes you anything, charge that to my account." God has charged everything Onesimus, Philemon, Paul, and we owe Him to Christ's account.

Therefore, as we count the cost of discipleship in the **Holy Gospel**, we know the real cost has been paid. Read Luke 14:25–35.

"He who has ears to hear, let him hear" (14:35). Take a long "look"—or listen. You cannot be My disciple if you love father, mother, wife, children, brothers, sisters, even your own life more than Me (14:26). You can't be My disciple if you won't bear your own cross and come after Me (14:27). You can't be My disciple if you're not going to remain salty, keep on seasoning the world by living and speaking Christ (14:34).

Know what you're getting into. You wouldn't start building a new house without knowing what the payments were going to be. You wouldn't accept a new job without being comfortable that you were qualified (14:28–32). If you aren't willing to live that holy life under the Sixth Commandment or the Fifth or the Fourth or the First and Third and all the others, "renounce all," you "cannot be My disciple," Jesus says (14:33).

But Christ did bear His cross. He has made you His disciple by faith—as surely as Peter. And you know what you're getting into: a hard road, but an eternally blessed one.

How clear this is. We are called to live according to Christ's Word, and He will not let us fall (**Hymn of the Day**, *LSB* 853).

The Sundays after Pentecost: Proper 19 (September 11–17) Year C

READINGS

Ezekiel 34:11–24
Psalm 119:169–176
(antiphon: v 176)
1 Timothy 1:(5–11) 12–17
Luke 15:1–10

HYMN OF THE DAY

LSB 609 "Jesus Sinners Doth Receive"

It is truly difficult—and we all must confess this—to understand fully someone whose life situation is different from our own. Right-handers are oblivious to the fact that many punch ladles discriminate against left-handers. A six-foot-four guest in a home wonders to himself why an otherwise careful housekeeper leaves a thick layer of dust atop her refrigerator. Reason: at five-foot-four, she's never seen the top of her refrigerator and had no idea anyone else could. Most Americans think Californians are strange for putting "the" in front of freeway numbers: "the 405." (Ask me. I'll tell you why.)

Those who've never struggled with addiction can't fully sympathize with someone who has. A driver who's never gotten a speeding ticket doesn't know how lingering the pain of one who killed a pedestrian decades ago while driving under the influence may be. A Christian blessed to be baptized as an infant and active in church all her life may not be able to relate to the experience of a fellow believer who spent his first thirty years as a hardened skeptic.

Not fully understanding—that's understandable. But blind spots, naivete, cluelessness can be a problem, can cause us to be insensitive. *And* it's an easy temptation to think that some blessing or advantage I have might be because I've worked harder, I'm smarter, I've been more faithful. Then I become judgmental; I'm being a good Pharisee, like the Pharisees and scribes in this Sunday's **Holy Gospel**. As long as they could see only from their "advantaged" perspective, they couldn't countenance Jesus' actions . . . or understand His teaching. See if we do. Read Luke 15:1–10.

Everything that follows is predicated by the setting: "Now the tax collectors and sinners were all drawing near to hear [Jesus]. And the Pharisees and the scribes grumbled, saying, 'This man receives sinners and eats with them'" (15:1–2). We know the rep of tax collectors—collaborators with the hated Romans. "Sinners" were those whose iniquities were public information—prostitutes, the town drunks—whereas the Pharisees and scribes were of sterling reputation, had never walked in those other shoes. *Why would Jesus?* they grumbled.

The Pharisees and scribes had no idea how it felt to be stared at, pointed to, whispered about at the synagogue—so that they probably wouldn't go at all. They'd never experienced the troubling duplicity of making a good living but knowing at the end of each day they'd cheated their brother Israelites by being in bed with the pagans. They hadn't felt the guilt of *literally* going to bed with whichever Israelite or Roman offered the night's wages. The Pharisees and scribes were quite sure they were indeed more faithful than these—and that that's why God had blessed them with their position of honor.

Jesus' parables pull back the veil of heaven to show the Pharisees and scribes how they should view these sinners.

Frankly, if we were shepherds, we might *not* go hunting for the one. It's not so much that leaving the ninety-nine puts them in greater danger; the shepherd cares about them too, probably makes provision. We just might not feel like making the effort. We've still got 99 percent of our inventory that we hardly miss the one. Most of the folks on my street probably go to church somewhere. Good enough. Can't win 'em all. But Shepherd Jesus does go. His point, clearly, is that every single lost sheep does matter. So much that when He finds it—her, him—He picks up the sheep, "rejoicing." And the rejoicing has to be shared with friends (15:5–6)!

This, now, is no parable. This is the real thing: "Just so, I tell you, there will be more joy in heaven over one sinner who repents than over ninety-nine righteous persons who need no repentance" (15:7).

Just to be sure His hearers get the point, Jesus doubles up. Losing a δραχμή, a drachma (15:8), would have been a big deal to an ordinary woman. It was worth about a day's labor. So she searches "diligently." That's crucial to both of Jesus' stories. Pursuing over cliffs and ravines or sweeping a dirt floor, the shepherd or the woman burns plenty of calories to find the one. The one lost is precious to the Lord, worth every ounce of energy.

That's quite evident, because the woman does call a party to rejoice with not only her friends and even her casual acquaintances but also the rest of the block (15:9)—a pretty wild overstatement in Jesus' parable. But again, we see what's really going on in heaven: "Just so, I tell you, there is joy before the angels of God over one sinner who repents" (15:10).

See, we really might not go looking for the one, but Jesus words His two parables in such a way that leaves no option: "What man of you . . . does not . . . ?" "What woman . . . does not . . . ?" (15:4, 8). The Pharisees and scribes have no wiggle room. It simply *should* be obvious we'd all go seeking.

So, Jesus is saying, we're not just to be tolerant of those lost souls. I won't just *receive* sinners and eat with them. We're to go *seeking* them high and low and not cease until we've found every one. Who among us wouldn't do just that? It's the joy of heaven!

The **Old Testament Reading**, Ezekiel 34:11–24, is almost like a third parable. It's the same message, but the Lord is explicitly the seeker.

Ezekiel prophesies from Babylon where he's among the captives from Judah. The destruction of Jerusalem was like "a day of clouds and thick darkness" (34:12). God's sheep are scattered, far from home. But the Lord, "I, I Myself will search for My sheep. . . . And I will bring them out from the peoples and gather them from the countries, and will bring them into their own land" (34:11, 13). There, back home, the Lord will feed them, guide them to good grazing land, make them lie down in safety (34:14–15).

Then the text introduces new characters: "The fat and the strong I will destroy. . . . Behold, I judge between sheep and sheep" (34:16, 17). The fat and strong sheep have been trampling down the pasture, muddying the water for the rest (34:18–19). They've been muscling in on the weak and lean sheep, even preying on them (34:20–22). Who are these fat and strong sheep? The context (34:2–10) makes clear that these are the people who should have been the shepherds of Judah; they're the leaders—in Ezekiel's day, the priests, prophets, kings. By Jesus' day, "Woe to you scribes and Pharisees!" You who should shepherd God's people Israel instead prey on them and make yourselves fat!

That's why the Lord will set a new shepherd over them, "My servant David" (34:23). Since God's promise to King David centuries before (2 Sam 7:12), every Israelite recognized all subsequent references to him as meaning the Messiah. Jesus is shepherding tax collectors and sinners according to plan.

But Jesus isn't seeking to shepherd *only* those "tax collectors and sinners." Whom did He seek in the **Epistle**, 1 Timothy 1:5–17?

Paul, a Pharisee of Pharisees (Acts 23:6), was, by his own assessment, *the* sinner: "Christ Jesus came into the world to save sinners, of whom I am the foremost" (1 Tim 1:15). Paul was a lost one!—all the trappings of holiness, yet "a blasphemer, persecutor, and insolent opponent" (1:13). And Christ came into the world seeking him.

The Pharisees and scribes who criticized Jesus couldn't understand His graciousness with sinners because they couldn't see themselves in the sinners' place. And they couldn't understand Jesus' call for them to embrace the lost if they couldn't see that *they were the lost!* Each Pharisee was the one, very lost, just like Saul, but also the one Jesus was seeking to save right then as He told the parables.

We can't go eagerly seeking the lost souls on our street if we don't realize we are the lost sheep, the lost coin Jesus searched diligently to find! We may never understand the struggles of addiction, but we should understand being slaves of sin, unable to stop, at one time not even wanting to, because we all were! We may not know the guilt of some sin on a police record, but we're each every bit as guilty. We may have been believers in church all our lives, but by nature, we were enemies of God. There are no "righteous persons who need no repentance" (Lk 15:7). Being "lost" may have a grand, dramatic story behind it. But it's each of our stories.

And Jesus understands all of our lostnesses because He walked in the shoes of sinners. On the cross, God declared Him "the foremost" sinner—in fact, the only sinner—so that "the grace of our Lord overflowed" for us (1:14). That's how we're also appointed "to His service" to seek the lost (1:12).

Look at the rest of the propers and read them with the understanding that you are the tax collector, sinner, and Pharisee Christ came and found.

Begin with the **Introit**:

You have turned for me my mourning into dancing; O Lord my God, I will give thanks to You forever!

O Lord my God, I cried to You for help, and You have healed me. O Lord, You have brought up my soul from Sheol; You restored me to life from among those who go down to the pit. Sing praises to the Lord, O you His saints, and give thanks to His holy name. For His anger is but for a moment, and His favor is for a lifetime. Weeping may tarry for the night, but joy comes with the morning.

Glory be to the Father and to the Son and to the Holy Spirit; as it was in the beginning, is now, and will be forever. Amen.

You have turned for me my mourning into dancing; O Lord my God, I will give thanks to You forever! *(Ps 30:2–5; antiphon: Ps 30:11a, 12b)*

"Joy comes with the morning"—joy in heaven because *I* who was lost to Sheol have been found. My thanksgiving forever will surely be by seeking others lost as I was.

Now read the **Psalm**, 119:169–176.

"I have gone astray like a lost sheep; seek Your servant." Then "my lips will pour forth praise. . . . My tongue will sing of Your word" (119:176a, 171a, 172a) to other sheep.

The **Collect** summarizes everything:

Lord Jesus, You are the Good Shepherd, without whom nothing is secure. Rescue and preserve us that we may not be lost forever but follow You, rejoicing in the way that leads to eternal life; for You live and reign with the Father and the Holy Spirit, one God, now and forever. Amen.

Good Shepherd, we need You to rescue us by Your cross so that we may no more be lost! Enable us to follow You in seeking others and to rejoice with You when each one is found!

What Joy(!) It Is That Christ Seeks and Rescues the Lost—of Whom We Are Foremost!

Our **Hymn of the Day**, "Jesus Sinners Doth Receive" (*LSB* 609), couldn't be more appropriate. "Also *I* have been forgiven" (st 7).

The Sundays after Pentecost: Proper 20 (September 18–24) Year C

READINGS

Amos 8:4–7
Psalm 113 (antiphon: v 3)
1 Timothy 2:1–15
Luke 16:1–15

HYMN OF THE DAY

LSB 557 "Seek Where You May to Find a Way"

We can thank God every day that His Word makes the essentials of our salvation extremely clear and simple. Jesus, by His death on the cross and His resurrection, has paid for all of our sins, has reconciled us to God so that everyone who believes this has eternal life, entirely apart from anything we do. As the **Verse** this week says, "Alleluia. For there is one God, and there is one mediator between God and men, the man Christ Jesus, who gave Himself as a ransom for all. Alleluia" (1 Tim 2:5–6a). Alleluia indeed! We're thankful the message of our salvation is so simple, so clear! Anyone can understand the John 3:16s and Ephesians 2:8–9s of the Bible. In fact, so much of the Bible is clear, simple, like all those Bible accounts we tell our children every night before bed.

That's good, because there are a few passages of Scripture that are reeeeeally tough to understand—passages that Bible commentators through history struggle to explain. One of those, perhaps the very top of the list, is the Gospel lesson for Proper 20, Year C, Jesus' parable of the Dishonest Manager.

Before we go any further, read Luke 16:1–15 to see if it throws you for a loop.

Any questions? Like, how can the master (who we correctly figure must represent God) commend the dishonest manager (16:8a)? Or this: "The sons of this world are more shrewd in dealing with their own generation than the sons of light" (16:8b). Is Jesus saying we ought to act more like the world? Or, "I tell you, make friends for yourselves by means of unrighteous wealth, so that when it fails they may receive you into the eternal dwellings" (16:9). Are we supposed to bribe folks to be our friends? And again, "When [wealth] fails they may receive you into the eternal dwellings." What does *that* mean? That friends we've bribed will somehow get us into heaven?

We know something's wrong with all this, but what *does* Jesus mean? This is a hard text!

Let's hold those questions for a while. There are no guarantees on the answers when we do come back to them, but first, let's look at some clearer passages, all the other propers for this week.

The **Introit**:

> *Your testimonies are righteous forever; give me understanding that I may live.*
>
> *Righteous are You, O Lord, and right are Your just decrees. You have appointed Your testimonies in righteousness and in all faithfulness. My zeal consumes me, because my foes forget Your words. Your promise is well tried, and Your servant loves it. Your righteousness is righteous forever, and Your law is true.*
>
> *Glory be to the Father and to the Son and to the Holy Spirit; as it was in the beginning, is now, and will be forever. Amen.*
>
> *Your testimonies are righteous forever; give me understanding that I may live. (Ps 119:137–140, 142; antiphon: Ps 119:144)*

On texts like the Gospel lesson, we join the psalmist to pray, "Give me understanding!" But we're thankful that understanding the toughest passages isn't necessary "that I may live." If we don't fully get everything in Scripture, we still know this: "Your promise is well tried, and Your servant loves it." The clear promise of God to be gracious to us will stand up to every test, every trial, even though we don't always know what's going on. We may be even more confused with life than with any difficult parable, but God will always come through for us. We know this because His love for us was tried to the fullest extent when it came down to His own life or us, and He chose us.

The **Collect** anticipates where Jesus' parable will eventually take us:

> *O Lord, keep Your Church in Your perpetual mercy; and because without You we cannot but fall, preserve us from all things hurtful, and lead us to all things profitable to our salvation; through Jesus Christ, Your Son, our Lord, who lives and reigns with You and the Holy Spirit, one God, now and forever. Amen.*

"Profitable" delivers us into the realm of business, where the manager in Jesus' parable works. Profits are a good thing, but some are "profitable to our salvation," while other profits we might chase as our god. When money replaces the true God, "we cannot but fall," because money will surely fail us. On the other hand, the Lord's mercy is "perpetual"; He is always, unfailingly generous.

That's the kind of master the Lord is. Read the appointed **Psalm**, Psalm 113.

Psalm 113 declares perhaps the ultimate reason to praise the Lord. True, He is "seated on high, . . . looks far down on the heavens and the earth" (113:5b, 6). And true, being high and almighty makes Him unlike any other. But His chief glory is that He who is so great and high above us "raises the poor from the dust and lifts the needy from the ash heap" (113:7). The One who could be way too proud and important and busy for us (the way all other "gods" are) cares enough about little old us "to make [us] sit with princes," to give "the barren woman a home, making her the joyous mother of children" (113:8a, 9a).

This will be crucial to Jesus' parable. It is God's greatest glory to be generous.

Such a generous God, therefore, cannot tolerate selfish dishonesty, as decried in the **Old Testament Reading**, Amos 8:4–7.

Amos wrote at a time (early eighth century BC under King Jeroboam II) when the "haves" in Israel had quite a lot. But they were trampling on the needy (8:4). They weren't allowed to do business on the Sabbath, so they couldn't wait for that inconvenience to be past, again to "deal deceitfully with false balances" and mix in plenty of chaff with the wheat they were selling, even to sell poor Israelites as slaves (8:5–6). The Lord swears, "Surely I will never forget any of their deeds" (8:7).

Obviously what the master endorses in the parable can't be the manager's dishonesty.

Unlike the Gospel reading, the **Epistle** is quite clear, on a couple of points. Read 1 Timothy 2:1–15.

As an aside to today's theme, skip to the last half of the reading. While it also means much more, this passage is *very* clear on one thing: Paul writes, "I do not permit a woman to teach or to exercise authority over a man" (2:12). God, through the apostle, is clear that He calls only men to be pastors (see also, among other places, 1 Cor 14:34–36). That's not because women are less capable of the various pastoral skills. It's simply God's wise and perfect design. Just as importantly, He gives only women the opportunity to be mothers. How important is that? It was "through childbearing" that the Savior of all the world came to us (2:15). And it's still the province of mothers to bring into the world every child, precious because God "desires all people to be saved" (2:4).

Now crucial to this week's theme is that other clear passage, cited earlier: "There is one God, and there is one mediator between God and men, the man Christ Jesus, who gave Himself as a ransom for all" (2:5–6a). The real problem Jesus will be addressing in the Gospel is having the wrong God. Money can become that. But the one true God is the one who became a man in order to reconcile us to Himself. And it was a matter of business: a full price paid, Jesus' death on the cross. No other God gives so generously!

Perhaps reread the **Holy Gospel**, Luke 16:1–15.

The manager was dishonest before he was fired, dishonest after he was fired. What could possibly be commendable? Not dishonesty, but shrewdness (16:8a). Here's what he finally (shrewdly!) realized: "My money has failed me, and my alternatives, digging and begging, are dim. But one thing I've seen: my master is generous. It's his character; it's what he loves to be. These debtors don't know yet that I've been fired. They'll assume he's the one who's discounted their debts. They'll further revere his generosity. So when my master sees in the debtors' own handwriting that they think he was generous, well, he'll never go back on that. He'll honor the lesser amounts, and those debtors will ever after be good to me. It's win, win, win. Sort of."

"Well played," the master commends. "You trusted in my generosity! At long last!"

And so it is Jesus would have of us all—trust in the generous God rather than the one that surely fails.

This is where "the sons of this world are more shrewd . . . than the sons of light" (16:8b). Unbelievers serve just one god, while believers often try to have it both ways—God and money. But "no servant can serve two masters" (16:13).

Instead, the shrewd believer worships his God by using money to bring others to Him. "Make friends for yourselves by means of unrighteous wealth, so that when it fails they may receive you into the eternal dwellings" (16:9).

(For a wonderful sermon that developed all of the above on this text before I ever thought of it, I thank Pastor Jared Melius, Mount Zion Lutheran Church, Denver.)

At this point, Luke alerts us that the Pharisees have been overhearing, and that raises one more important consideration: "The Pharisees, who were lovers of money, heard all these things, and they ridiculed [Jesus]. And He said to them, 'You are those who justify yourselves before men, but God knows your hearts'" (16:14–15a). God knows your hearts. Jesus knows who your God is. And if you love money, if that is your god, you will surely scoff, because none of this is any way to run a business. Generosity doesn't serve your god, doesn't make money.

But if your heart clings to the true God, the generous God, this entire passage has another message. It began, "He [Jesus] *also* said." "Also" connects it to the previous verses, which happen to be the parable of the Prodigal Son (15:11–32). And it should be ear catching that Jesus uses the same word for the action of both that son and this dishonest manager, διασκορπίζω, *diaskorpizo*: There was a son who squandered. . . . There was a manager who squandered. . . .

We have all squandered our Father's wealth. But remember how the father in that other parable "handled" his squanderer when his money failed him! He ran to him, embraced him, kissed him, put a robe and ring on him, and threw a party! When God, not money, is our God, we're not just dishonest managers to Him. We're His sons—prodigal but received back.

**Rather Than Trust the God
That Will Fail You, Money,
Use It in Faith
That the One True God
Is Eternally Generous—
If Even to a Manager,
Then Certainly to You, a Son.**

The **Hymn of the Day**, *LSB* 557, calls us to "seek Him alone," Christ, "not wealth nor pride nor fortune's tide" (sts 3, 4)

The Sundays after Pentecost: Proper 21 (September 25–October 1) Year C

READINGS

Amos 6:1–7
Psalm 146 (antiphon: v 2)
1 Timothy 3:1–13
or 1 Timothy 6:6–19
Luke 16:19–31

HYMN OF THE DAY

LSB 708 "Lord, Thee I Love with All My Heart"

For all the times I watched the 1964 Disney classic *Mary Poppins* as a kid and then with my kids, it wasn't until I saw *Saving Mr. Banks*, made almost fifty years later, that I realized the point of the film. Yes, *Mary Poppins* had a message—besides a lot of fun, fantasy, and Supercalifragilisticexpialidocious. *Saving Mr. Banks* is biographical, mostly, of P. L. Travers, the author of the original Mary Poppins series, and a bit about Walt Disney. We learn that she was dead set against a movie based on her books. She didn't want any animation, didn't want Dick Van Dyke, and definitely didn't want any made-up words. Finally, Walt figured out her real hesitation. George Banks, the father in the Mary Poppins series, was a tribute to Travers's own father, and she was being protective of his memory—the demons he'd suffered and his tragic death.

Listen sometime to the first line of the *Mary Poppins* overture. It actually tells you all you need to know. George Banks's problem is a social—dare we even say spiritual?—myopia. A man with an elegant home and servants, he walks every day to his job at a London bank without being able to see the poor "bird woman" who needs just a tuppence from him. Just as he's not able to see the needs of his wife and children.

Both movies have a happy ending; they're stories of redemption—because Mr. Banks finally learns to see past the tip of his own nose. Well, entirely seriously now, we look for that in our propers this week too.

Depending on Our Point of View, the Lord Offers Comfort for Need, Warning for Me-opia, and the Means to a Blessed End.

Yes, I made up a word as well, but it's a short one. *Me-opia* we'll define as thinking it's all about me.

That may be our last light comment for a while, because the **Holy Gospel** this Sunday is deadly sobering. Read Luke 16:19–31.

Unlike George Banks, this rich man is not at all a sympathetic character. The finest clothing. "Feasted sumptuously every day." And the worst possible case of me-opia. To him, it's all about him. Lazarus was right there at his gate; the rich man couldn't possibly miss seeing him day after day. In fact, Lazarus "was laid" at his gate, meaning that he was an invalid and someone had brought him there expressly because this was a place he would surely receive charity. He didn't get any at all, unless the dogs count (16:19–21).

Rich or poor, everyone dies (16:22). Jesus doesn't say so here, but we know Lazarus was received into heaven not because he was poor and suffered but because he had faith in the Savior. And the rich man was in hell not because he was rich or uncaring but because of unbelief. Those are the two possibilities for everyone. However, it quickly becomes evident that the rich man's me-opia was his unbelief in (in)action.

By faith, the torments of this world are transformed into endless bliss for Lazarus. "Abraham's side" would have been a sweet image to Jesus' Jewish hearers. They revered Abraham, saw him as their father. Fellowship with him for eternity would be as good as it gets. We'll chat with Abraham too—and with Paul and Luther and our dear Christian loved ones—and our Lord. And every pain and privation of this life will be forgotten.

There's no redemption, though, for the rich man. This is Scripture's most vivid view of the agonies of hell. A drop of water to cool the tongue! If *that's* considered relief! There's no escape, no further chance. This is *forever.* We don't know whether hell (and heaven) will be like this; it's a story Jesus is telling to illustrate His point. But we get the idea.

One aspect will almost surely be different: it's difficult to imagine a conversation between heaven and hell. In heaven, nothing will cause sadness, and it seems viewing such anguish would. For Jesus' story, however, the interaction serves an essential purpose.

Abraham isn't vindictive, just matter of fact: "Child, remember . . ." (16:25). But Abraham does imply that all those "good things" the rich man enjoyed in life were gifts of God ("received"), which means they were not really his, only entrusted to him to use kindly, not me-opically. "You remember Lazarus, right outside your gate, and all his 'bad things.' Put two and two together. He's now comforted, and you are in anguish."

Now the last straw: "Then I beg you, father, to send [Lazarus] to my father's house—for I have five brothers—so that he may warn them, lest they also come into this place of torment" (16:27–28). Ever wonder why God doesn't do something like that for everybody? A couple of resurrections, maybe a few other miracles right out there in plain sight where the whole world could see. It would shut up the critics and bring everyone over to God's side. After all, He doesn't want anyone to be lost. Sounds like a solid idea, but God, in His wisdom, fully desiring to save every soul, knows a better way. "Moses and the Prophets" (16:29) was a term for the entire Old Testament. It conveys the full warning of God against me-opia, His command to care for those around us in need, and His forgiveness in the Messiah, His escape from the fires of hell. "If they [brothers or any other sinners] do not hear Moses and the Prophets, neither will they be convinced if someone should rise from the dead" (16:31). So true, as proved just a short time later when a real-life Lazarus was raised (Jn 11:43–53; 12:9–11) . . . and then the One who is better (Mt 28:5–6, 11–15).

Depending on the point of view—looking from heaven, from hell, or from this side of eternity—Jesus' story is comforting or terrifying and certainly eye-opening, a warning against me-opia. Along with Moses and the Prophets, this word of Jesus and the New Testament is now His means to a happy ending.

Let's look at each proper from one of these perspectives. Take the **Introit** from the point view of Lazarus:

Let Your steadfast love comfort me according to Your promise to Your servant.

Your hands have made and fashioned me; give me understanding that I may learn Your commandments. Those who fear You shall see me and rejoice, because I have hoped in Your word. I know, O Lord, that Your just decrees are righteous, and that in faithfulness You have afflicted me. Let Your mercy come to me, that I may live; for Your law is my delight.

Glory be to the Father and to the Son and to the Holy Spirit; as it was in the beginning, is now, and will be forever. Amen.

Let Your steadfast love comfort me according to Your promise to Your servant. (Ps 119:73–75, 77; antiphon: Ps 119:76)

What do you suppose faithful Lazarus was thinking as he suffered on earth? Why is God putting me through this?! We often know that feeling. But now from his heavenly point of view, he could say with the psalmist, "I know, O Lord, that Your just decrees are righteous, and that in faithfulness You have afflicted me." Everything You allowed, Lord, was for my good. So here on earth, we pray, "give me understanding"—if not of each particular "why," at least to understand that, because Christ has reconciled us to You by His cross, You are always giving me the best even when I don't see it. The "comfort" is in the Lord's "steadfast love" and "promise." Then, when I do suffer, "those who fear [the Lord] shall see me and rejoice, because I have hoped in [His] word" to bear up as an even more powerful witness.

The **Collect** we pray from the perspective of saints still living on earth:

O God, You are the strength of all who trust in You, and without Your aid we can do no good thing. Grant us the help of Your grace that we may please You in both will and deed; through Jesus Christ, Your Son, our Lord, who lives and reigns with You and the Holy Spirit, one God, now and forever. Amen.

As long as we live this side of heaven, God always gives His "strength" and "aid" the same way it was available to the rich man's brothers: the Word and Sacraments, the Means of Grace. So we ask God to "grant us the help of Your grace." It's in God's Word, heard, preached, read, and our Baptism and the Lord's Supper that we're comforted with forgiveness and the assurance of a blessed end.

We begin a new **Gradual** this week, for this part of the Pentecost season known as Michaelmas, for St. Michael and all angels:

He will command His angels concerning you to guard you in all your ways. Bless the Lord, *O my soul, and all that is within me, bless His holy name! (Ps 91:11; 103:1)*

From the viewpoint of needy Lazarus, what greater comfort than to know the holy angels are watching over us and will someday carry our souls to heaven? (Lk 16:22).

The point of view shifts radically in the **Old Testament Reading**. Read Amos 6:1–7 from the perspective of me-opia.

"Woe to those who are at ease, . . . who lie on beds of ivory . . . and eat lambs from the flock, . . . who sing idle songs, . . . who drink wine in bowls and anoint themselves with the finest oils" (6:1, 4, 5, 6). The problem isn't that they're rich. (Recall from last week the situation in Amos's day.) The sin is that they "are not grieved over the ruin of Joseph!" (6:6c). They suffer severe me-opia—"you who put far away the day of disaster" (6:3). But it is coming: "They shall now be the first of those who go into exile" (6:7).

Me-opic, too, are those who "trust in princes." They'll join the rich man when "breath departs" (Ps 146:4). Read the entire **Psalm**. It changes perspective in verse 5: "Blessèd is he whose help is the God of Jacob, . . . who executes justice for the oppressed, who gives food to the hungry. . . . He upholds the widow and the fatherless" (146:5, 7, 9).

Read the **Epistle**, 1 Timothy 3:1–13; 6:6–19.

This week's warning against me-opia is as pressing for pastors like Timothy as for anyone (3:2–3, 6). The reading from chapter 6 is especially direct. You can't help but see Jesus' rich man: "We brought nothing into the world, and we cannot take anything out. . . . Those who desire to be rich fall into temptation, . . . into ruin and destruction. For the love of money is a root of all kinds of evils . . . many pangs" (6:7, 9, 10).

"But as for you, O man of God"—180-degree turn in point of view—"take hold of the eternal life to which you were called" (6:11, 12). Christ Jesus, by His death and resurrection, has secured for you a blessed end, "which He will display at the proper time" (6:15). Meanwhile, therefore, "godliness with contentment is great gain. . . . Be generous and ready to share. . . . Take hold of that which is truly life" (6:6, 18, 19).

What a final comfort the **Hymn of the Day** (*LSB* 708) is for every Lazarus! "Lord, let at last Thine angels come" (st 3).

The Sundays after Pentecost: Proper 22 (October 2–8) Year C

READINGS

Habakkuk 1:1–4; 2:1–4
Psalm 62 (antiphon: v 1)
2 Timothy 1:1–14
Luke 17:1–10

HYMN OF THE DAY

LSB 587 "I Know My Faith Is Founded"

One of the great blessings of Holy Scripture is that God inspired human authors to write it in the styles human beings communicate. He didn't use some heavenly language, perhaps a language of angels (1 Cor 13:1), which "cannot be told, which man may not utter" (2 Cor 12:4). He moved the human writers to write as people ordinarily write and speak—so that we're able to understand them. The Scriptures proceed in orderly ways where one thought leads to another (albeit in countless creative arrangements—stories, questions and answers, logical arguments) so that we can follow the progression of thought. They make sense. They don't jump around.

Usually.

But, of course, we also know that sometimes human beings *do* have one thought, finish it quickly, and then quickly move on to another. A conversation *can* shift from one subject to another without much connection. That works too. The folks chatting together just have to pick up the new drift and be satisfied to leave the previous one, maybe for more later. Literature can go that way as well. For example, whole sections of the book of Proverbs are essentially one-liners, each intended to stand on its own.

So, then, the various readings selected to be used in our Sunday services—six, eight, twelve, twenty verses long—usually each have one main idea. And the human beings who designed our lectionaries have usually followed that logic to select readings that go together. After recognizing the one main idea in the Gospel lesson, they've chosen other lessons and propers that further develop that same idea.

Usually.

But since ordinary conversation sometimes shifts quickly, and since human authors may decide to put various short pieces together as stand-alones, sometimes one reading may have several ideas. So what did the human designers of the lectionaries do when the Gospel lesson has multiple, independent ideas?

That seems to be the case this week. The Gospel reading has, probably, three equally important but separate ideas. The Holy Spirit inspired Luke to bring them together, but without apparent connection. How did the designers of the three-year lectionary then select the other propers? We'll talk about that.

Read the **Holy Gospel**, Luke 17:1–10.

How would you divide these ten verses into paragraphs? The earliest Greek manuscripts had no divisions (even between words!), but human editors have since made such decisions. The ESV divides the reading into three sections: verses 1–4, 5–6, and 7–10. Other versions have just two sections (verses 1–4 and 5–10), and still others have four (beginning new paragraphs with verses 1, 3, 5, and 7). That they differ so much shows the challenge of sensing any connections among the verses.

If we go with the ESV divisions, the three ideas are 1) sinning and forgiving, 2) a request for greater faith, and 3) what servants deserve.

The first section (17:1–4) presents material that also appears in a different context in Matthew 18. It may well be, therefore, that Luke isn't reporting chronologically, but, like all good authors (and under the directing of the Holy Spirit), has his purpose for relating Jesus' words here. These sayings are vital! Causing a fellow believer to fall into sin can become a stumbling block to his or her salvation! Better we were dead than to cause that! Instead, we warn our fellow believers against sin, and when they repent, we forgive them. Forgiving others is the heartbeat of the Church. By speaking forgiveness, we assure a fellow Christian that God Himself has forgiven her—and we restore our relationships with one another. On the other hand, refusing to forgive could be another stumbling block to faith, causing the sinner to fear that God *hasn't* forgiven him.

This idea is so important that the designers of the lectionary have chosen 17:3b to be the **Verse** of the day: "Alleluia. If your brother sins, rebuke him, and if he repents, forgive him. Alleluia." The Verse, as you know, often expresses the theme for the whole Sunday.

The week, however, sinning and forgiving isn't prominent among the other propers. That's because the Gospel lesson moves on to other also important thoughts. The lectionary designers knew these other major ideas also merit development in the other propers.

"Increase our faith!" (17:5). A fine request. But what do we do with Jesus' answer? "If you had faith like a grain of mustard seed, you could say to this mulberry tree, 'Be uprooted and planted in the sea,' and it would obey you" (17:6). Do we take that as a yes? a no? Or is Jesus redefining what we've asked?

If a mustard seed of faith can do such great things, maybe size or strength of faith doesn't matter. Maybe increasing our faith is to be something else. Now on this, the other propers of the day have much to say.

The final section of the Gospel reading (17:7–10) is an illustration of our unworthiness before God. It isn't a suggestion that bosses or parents or congregations take advantage of their employees or children or pastors. It isn't teaching that pastors shouldn't thank their members for faithful service to the Church. (It also isn't telling us to feel uncomfortable when others extend appreciation to us!) But as Christians, we owe everything to God. He owes us nothing. We don't get in good with God and have something on Him when we do this or that good work. We're supposed to be doing good works every moment, without break, without fail. And we fail. "We are unworthy servants." We have never done more than, and have never done as much as, "what was our duty" (17:10).

That never prevents God from giving us good things. He constantly does—daily bread of all kinds here and eternal life in heaven. Always by grace. Always because of Jesus' atoning death on the cross. Always more than we deserve.

We'll see this idea recur in a couple of our other propers, including in the **Introit**:

I hope for Your salvation, O LORD, and I do Your commandments.

I rejoice at Your word like one who finds great spoil. Seven times a day I praise You for Your just and righteous decrees. Great peace have those who love Your law; nothing can make them stumble. My soul keeps Your testimonies; I love them exceedingly.

Glory be to the Father and to the Son and to the Holy Spirit; as it was in the beginning, is now, and will be forever. Amen.

I hope for Your salvation, O LORD, and I do Your commandments. (Ps 119:162, 164–165, 167; antiphon: Ps 119:166)

Everything we do as Christians is in response to what God does for us: "I hope *for Your* salvation. . . . I rejoice *at Your* word. . . . I praise You *for Your* just and righteous decrees." We originate nothing good. We are unworthy servants receiving more than we deserve, like "great peace."

Our prayer for increased faith is also granted only by grace. Pray the **Collect**:

O God, our refuge and strength, the author of all godliness, by Your grace hear the prayers of Your Church. Grant that those things which we ask in faith we may receive through Your bountiful mercy; through Jesus Christ, Your Son, our Lord, who lives and reigns with You and the Holy Spirit, one God, now and forever. Amen.

Our prayer *for* faith "we ask *in* faith," but faith *in what*? That we receive "through [God's] bountiful mercy." Faith isn't ever the primary focus; what matters is the one in whom we have faith. God strengthens faith not by doing something *in* us but by continually doing things *for* us. His constant doing results in us believing more and more.

In Habakkuk 1:1–4; 2:1–4, the **Old Testament Reading**, the prophet is struggling to believe God will indeed do justly.

God's people are acting wickedly all around. God seems to do nothing (1:1–4). But Habakkuk is even more perplexed that God will use the Chaldeans (Babylonians) to punish the evil, because they will surely swallow up the righteous as well (1:6, 13). No one seems to be getting what he deserves!

Yet, like a watchman, Habakkuk will wait to see what God will do (2:1). In effect, he's begging, "Lord, it looks so bad! Increase my faith!" And the Lord assures him, "The vision awaits its appointed time; it hastens to the end—it will not lie. If it seems slow, wait for it; it will surely come; it will not delay" (2:3). The Lord will act, and justice will be done, but done God's way. Evil will be punished, and the righteous will be saved. Not because anyone is righteous in himself, "but the righteous shall live by his faith" (2:4b). Those who trust the Lord will survive the onslaught—if not in the invasion, then in the eternal victory. The Lord would increase Habakkuk's faith by acting faithfully Himself—to save His people of faith.

This magnificent verse (2:4) became the theme for Paul's letter to the Romans (Rom 1:17) and, in that context, the passage that increased (or even rekindled) Luther's faith.

Habakkuk might actually have learned his faith lesson from the **Psalm**, because God had taught David the same. Read Psalm 62. "For God alone my soul waits in silence; from Him comes my salvation. He only is my rock and my salvation, my fortress; I shall not be greatly shaken" (62:1–2). The Lord had taught David to wait in faith not by strengthening David but by being David's strength. "Power belongs to God" (62:11).

What of the **Epistle**, 2 Timothy 1:1–14?

Paul knows that Timothy has had "sincere faith" ever since his mother and grandmother taught him God's Word (1:5). But he prays that Timothy's faith would be increased now as he has been ordained, Paul's hands laid on him: "Fan into flame the gift of God" (1:6). That will happen as Timothy is reminded that God has "saved us and called us to a holy calling . . . in Christ Jesus, . . . who abolished death and brought life and immortality to light through the gospel" (1:9, 10). This is what faith always ultimately means. God has kept His promise to send the Savior, Christ the crucified. Faith, not how much, clings to that, to Him. That's enough.

Finally, of the three ideas raised by the Gospel lesson, increased faith is primary also in the **Hymn of the Day**, "I Know My Faith Is Founded" (*LSB* 587).

What a blessing God speaks in ways we can understand! This Sunday, His inspired Word and the lectionary, carefully designed by humans, will especially teach us that

Our Prayer for Increased Faith God Answers Chiefly by Assuring Us That He Himself Is Faithful.

But the Word in the propers will also remind us that God gives us, always unworthy servants, so much more than we deserve.

And don't forget that we are to warn our brothers and sisters in Christ when they sin and then eagerly forgive when they repent.

Fair enough.

The Sundays after Pentecost: Proper 23 (October 9–15) Year C

READINGS

Ruth 1:1–19a
Psalm 111 (antiphon: v 10)
2 Timothy 2:1–13
Luke 17:11–19

HYMN OF THE DAY

LSB 846 "Your Hand, O Lord, in Days of Old"

We've proposed many times that one purpose of looking forward to Sunday morning by reading ahead is to be more active listeners when we're finally in the pew and the propers are unfolding before us. Having an idea about the direction the service as a whole will go helps us pick up threads we might have missed, connections we might not have made. And seeing those pieces fit together progressively through the service enables us to see in clearer focus the one big point when it's ultimately revealed, usually in the Gospel lesson, always in the person and work of Christ.

An active listening question is "Where is this headed?" You're putting one and one and two together and guessing the sum. Admittedly, reading these devotion-studies changes the game on Sunday morning because you know ahead how it all adds up. So sometimes we try to create the inquiring experience here.

Like this week. Last week, we trisected the Gospel reading right up front because its three distinct points diffused (and potentially could have *con*fused) the theme of the day. This week, the Gospel lesson will give a simple, singular message. So let's wait not just to discover what that message is but even what the Gospel reading itself is. (If you can avoid glancing to the left and seeing the reference, that's ideal. If you've already seen it, perhaps at least you don't know what those verses are about. And if you're already ahead of me, ah, that's fine too.) For enrichment reading on this methodology, you might check out King Nebuchadnezzar in Daniel 2:1–13. Among us, however, no one will be torn limb from limb.

Here are a couple of clues as to our Gospel reading. First, this lesson occurs in all three years of the three-year lectionary. That's very rare. Second, this lesson actually occurs *twice* this year, Year C. That's very, very rare. After this Sunday, it'll still show up again in the few weeks this church year has remaining. Count 'em up—that's four hearings every three-year cycle, which makes the text quite familiar.

Now, what hints can we find in the **Introit**?

Great is the Lord and greatly to be praised in the city of our God!

My soul makes its boast in the Lord; let the humble hear and be glad. Oh, magnify the Lord with me, and let us exalt His name together! I sought the Lord, and He answered me and delivered me from all my fears. When the righteous cry for help, the Lord hears and delivers them out of all their troubles.

Glory be to the Father and to the Son and to the Holy Spirit; as it was in the beginning, is now, and will be forever. Amen.

Great is the Lord and greatly to be praised in the city of our God! (Ps 34:2–4, 17; antiphon: Ps 48:1a)

The Lord is "greatly to be praised." Not only is that always true, but it sounds pretty generic in the Psalms, appropriate for *any* Sunday morning. If that's all you've got to go on in guessing the Gospel reading, good luck. But do remember it. You'll see why.

"I sought the Lord, and He answered me. . . . When the righteous cry for help, the Lord hears." Again, this could apply to countless Sundays. But visualize seeking the Lord, knowing His reputation for kindness and looking for Him. And also crying for help, shouting out to Him, begging.

"He answered me and delivered me from all my fears. . . . The Lord hears and delivers them." Deliverance is a great Gospel concept, and it can include just about any way God saves us from just about any harm. But "deliver" can be used more properly, more specifically, for *certain aspects* of the Good News. The Gospel lesson will focus on those.

The same could be said for a key word in the **Collect** for Sunday:

Almighty God, You show mercy to Your people in all their troubles. Grant us always to recognize Your goodness, give thanks for Your compassion, and praise Your holy name; through Jesus Christ, Your Son, our Lord, who lives and reigns with You and the Holy Spirit, one God, now and forever. Amen.

Mercy can mean any expression of compassion for the undeserving. That certainly describes all of God's goodness toward us. As sinners, we deserve nothing but punishment, eternally. The Church, though, has come to use the term *mercy* especially for acts that care for the physical needs of people. This prayer acknowledges that God is merciful "in *all* . . . troubles." We underappreciate God's love if we think Christ's death and resurrection only brings spiritual, eternal blessings. The Gospel reading touches all the bases—heavenly and especially earthly.

"Grant us always to recognize Your goodness." That's a big hint toward the Gospel reading. We're always being blessed by God's mercy, but do we always recognize the blessings—and recognize whom they're flowing from? If we do, we'll "give thanks" and we'll "praise [God's] holy name." If we take our blessings for granted, not so much.

There's great joy in recognizing that our blessings come from God. If we forget that, we'll think our blessings are uncertain—maybe we just got lucky this time, or maybe they'll keep coming only if I'm as diligent as I was this go 'round. But when we remember that every good gift comes from God, we can relax and trust Him, because God never changes. He's always merciful.

The **Verse** for Sunday isn't from the Gospel reading (as it often is), but it gives a big new hint: "Alleluia. Now even more the report about [Jesus] went abroad, and great crowds gathered to hear Him and to be healed of their infirmities. Alleluia" (Lk 5:15). Again we see mercy: healing from infirmities. But notice also that news about Jesus was spreading "abroad"—beyond Israel.

Ready to solve the puzzle? You can still buy the **Old Testament Reading**, Ruth 1:1–19a.

"The days when the judges ruled" (1:1) were the generations after Joshua (the entrance into Canaan) until the first king of Israel, Saul (ca 1300–1000 BC). Moab was a near neighbor of Judah and related through Abraham's nephew Lot a thousand years earlier (Gen 19:30–38). The book of Ruth was likely written around the time of David's ascendance to the throne, so Bethlehem would have already caught the ear of the first readers; it was the new king's hometown. The journey from Bethlehem to Moab, traveling around the Dead Sea, was perhaps fifty miles—just a few days' walk, but a distance few ancients ever traveled from their homes. Elimelech and family wouldn't be getting home for Thanksgiving!

Ten years later, Naomi probably felt she had little for which to give thanks (1:3–5). But bereft of husband and sons, going home was all she had left to do (1:6). To say "the Lord had visited His people" is a sweet reminder that He never forgets us (Ex 4:31; Jer 29:10; Lk 1:68; 7:16). But Ruth and Orpah? Bethlehem wasn't their home. Their prospects for remarriage as foreigners in Judah weren't promising. Both loved their mother-in-law, but humanly speaking, Moab was the reasonable option.

"Go, return each of you to her mother's house. . . . Turn back, my daughters. . . . Turn back, my daughters" (1:8, 11, 12). It made sense—humanly speaking. But isn't this a sad outcome? "See, your sister-in-law has gone back to her people and to her gods" (1:15). For all the "practical" considerations, turning back can never be wise if it means turning from the one true and saving God.

We don't know how eternity came out for Orpah. Her faith may have survived the temptations to idolatry; we may see her in heaven. But we know the rest of Ruth's story. Since this is the only occurrence of Ruth in the lectionary, read the rest of the short book. Not only was she loyal to Naomi; she became the great-grandmother of David and an ancestor of Jesus (4:13–17; Mt 1:1–16).

Clues to the Gospel lesson? Foreigner. Turning back. The one true God.

Recollect a few others we've seen as you read the **Psalm**, Psalm 111: praise (111:1a), thanks (111:1b), mercy (111:4), God's wisdom compared to human practicality (111:10).

In the **Epistle**, Paul uses an illustration that is also most apropos to the Gospel. Read 2 Timothy 2:1–13.

"No soldier gets entangled in civilian pursuits, since his aim is to please the one who enlisted him" (2:4). He is single-minded. He has no other agenda. He doesn't go off pursuing anything else. His attention is entirely on his commanding officer.

"Remember Jesus Christ, risen from the dead, the offspring of David" (2:8). He is the one who "enlisted" us. Let nothing distract us from Him! "If we have died with Him, we will also live *with Him*; if we endure, we will also reign *with Him*; if we deny Him, *He* also will deny us; if we are faithless, *He* remains faithful" (2:11–13).

Have you guessed the **Holy Gospel**? Praise and thanks. Crying out. Mercy. Deliverance. A foreigner. Turning back. The wisdom of recognizing the one God, not being distracted by other pursuits. Look up Luke 17:11–19.

Jesus healing the ten lepers—Proper 23, Year C, and every year on Thanksgiving.

The report of Jesus' mercy, His care in particular for the needs of sick men like these, has spread abroad. The law requires them to keep their distance (17:12), but that doesn't prevent them from crying out at the top of their lungs (17:13). Remarkably, Jesus never says they'll be healed; it's just assumed: "Go and show yourselves to the priests" (17:14). But the lepers know what that means; the law also specified that the priests were to certify cleansing from leprosy (Lev 14:1–32). They believe, and, sure enough, they're healed.

One of them turned back, falling at Jesus' feet, praising and thanking Him. "Now he was a Samaritan" (17:16), the foreigner. What about the other nine? You can hardly blame them, right? They were doing exactly what the law prescribed and what Jesus told them to do. Unlike Paul's good soldier, unlike Ruth, they didn't recognize the one who enlisted them; they pursued another agenda. Before Levitical priests, before them was the Great High Priest.

"Your faith has made you well" (17:19), just as viably translated, "saved you" (the Greek σέσωκεν from σῴζω, *sozo*). Indeed, the Samaritan was saved! Now clearly he had faith in the Messiah and thus eternal life. *But* to be saved also means to be *delivered* from *all* the effects of sin, in this text, primarily from leprosy—Jesus' *mercy*. That, too, comes only by Jesus' cross removing sin that separated us from all God's blessings, reconciling us to God, so that He delivers us as well from earthly need. It comes from the God who died. And it's worth thanks and praise!

The One Place All People Everywhere Are to Turn for Deliverance and with Praise Is the God Who Is in Christ Jesus.

Lepers praise evermore our great deliverer—the **Hymn of the Day**, "Your Hand, O Lord, in Days of Old" (*LSB* 846).

The Sundays after Pentecost: Proper 24 (October 16–22) Year C

READINGS

Genesis 32:22–30
Psalm 121 (antiphon: vv 1–2)
2 Timothy 3:14–4:5
Luke 18:1–8

HYMN OF THE DAY

LSB 734 "I Trust, O Lord, Your Holy Name"

The last word of the last reading we'll hear this Sunday asks a question—and seemingly not a very optimistic one—that Jesus leaves unanswered: "Nevertheless, when the Son of Man comes, will He find faith on earth?" (Lk 18:8b). Our Lord asks it, so it's a good question, obviously. But is Jesus asking rhetorically, with a favorable answer assured? "Why, yes, of course He'll find faith on earth." Or is at an actual open-ended question with an answer yet to be determined?

Jesus' question comes in the context of a parable He tells in the Gospel lesson, and that context will help us understand it. The Church has also given it to us in the context of Proper 24, and that will be helpful too. When Jesus returns, will He still find faith on earth?

Begin our thinking with the **Introit**:

Remember Your congregation, which You have purchased of old, which You have redeemed to be the tribe of Your heritage!

Remember this, O Lord, how the enemy scoffs, and a foolish people reviles Your name. Do not deliver the soul of Your dove to the wild beasts; do not forget the life of Your poor forever. Let not the downtrodden turn back in shame; let the poor and needy praise Your name. Have regard for the covenant; arise, O God, defend Your cause.

Glory be to the Father and to the Son and to the Holy Spirit; as it was in the beginning, is now, and will be forever. Amen.

Remember Your congregation, which You have purchased of old, which You have redeemed to be the tribe of Your heritage! (Ps 74:18–19, 21, 20a, 22a; antiphon: Ps 74:2a)

If nothing else, Jesus' question implies that remaining faithful isn't easy. "The enemy scoffs, and a foolish people reviles [the Lord's] name." Foreign armies praised their gods as they sacked Jerusalem—Babylonians (Dan 5:1–4), later Romans, much later Muslims. For the longest time in Europe and North America, open scoffing was a no-no; public pressure required most unbelievers to keep quiet. No more. "Nones" (no religious affiliation) are a substantial, growing, and very comfortable segment of the population. In academia, including some "Christian" seminaries, it's not just that many deny God and biblical tenets; those who do confess Him and His Word are barred from teaching it. In today's entertainment, Christians are so often portrayed as buffoons or bigots. We're doves being thrown to wild beasts; we're the downtrodden. It's hard to remain faithful against such opposition.

So the psalmist prays, "Remember Your congregation, which You have purchased of old, which You have redeemed to be the tribe of Your heritage! Remember this, O Lord, how the enemy scoffs." God "remembering" is a rich Old Testament saying that He always fulfills His promises (Gen 8:1; 19:29; Ex 2:24; 1 Sam 1:19; Ps 105:8, 42; 106:45). He has "purchased," "redeemed" us by the blood of Christ, so He never forgets us, though it may seem that way when we're under fire.

Attacks on our faith and God's promise to remember move us to pray. The **Collect**:

O Lord, almighty and everlasting God, You have commanded us to pray and have promised to hear us. Mercifully grant that Your Holy Spirit may direct and govern our hearts in all things that we may persevere with steadfast faith in the confession of Your name; through Jesus Christ, Your Son, our Lord, who lives and reigns with You and the Holy Spirit, one God, now and forever. Amen.

If we are indeed to "persevere with steadfast faith" until Christ returns, it can only be by God's doing. We can never create our own faith, decide to have it, or keep it alive. It's a miracle worked by the Holy Spirit and sustained by the means He's promised to use: Word and Sacrament. So prayer is essential to our enduring; we *ask* God that His "Holy Spirit may direct and govern our hearts."

And as Christians, we're never asking our lucky stars that the slots just might pay off. "O Lord, almighty and everlasting God, You have commanded us to pray and have promised to hear us." We pray because God—who has the power to do anything—has told us in His Word that He's going to use it for our good—for Jesus' sake. (Notice our Collects generally begin by citing something about God that gives confidence to come to Him.)

The **Old Testament Reading** is a strange story—but a powerful teaching about enduring in faith. Read Genesis 32:22–30.

We're nearing the climax of the lengthy Jacob and Esau saga (25:19–33:17). Jacob, the younger twin, has well earned his name ("one who supplants" or even "deceiver") by tricking Esau out of his older-son blessing. He had to flee, but over twenty years, he's married (four wives, two of them here called "female servants"—32:22; see 30:1–13), and God has blessed him with wealth, eleven sons (one more coming), and at least one daughter.

Now God has sent him home, but he's terrified to learn that Esau, the tough guy hunter of the pair, is coming to meet him with four hundred armed men. What might have been a sleepless night anyway is suddenly very eventful. The narrative tells us only what Jacob knows—as he realizes it. He has no idea at first who this wrestler is (32:24), but after struggling to a draw all night, with one touch, he dislocates Jacob's hip (32:25). Clearly he's been allowing Jacob to fight on, and he doesn't need Jacob to let him go (32:26a). Now Jacob gets it; the man *wants* him to hold on. So "I will not let You go unless You bless me" (32:26b). This is the Lord! (32:30)—no doubt the Son of God two millennia before the world would see Him face to face.

A significant blessing is simply the new name (32:28). *Israel* means "he who strives with God" or "God strives." This is what the Lord has wanted Jacob to learn all along—to cling to God, even strive with God, trusting Him rather than getting ahead (supplanting) by his own devices (deceiving). Jacob hasn't beaten God, but he has "prevailed" upon Him by demanding that God do what He has promised (32:9–12).

The Lord wants us to prevail upon Him by asking, even demanding, that He keep His Word. Our prayers can be wrestling with God. They should always be recalling—at very best, speaking back to Him—what He has said. For it's by His Word that we prevail against the temptation to let go of faith.

The **Psalm** teaches the same lesson poetically. Read Psalm 121.

"I lift up my eyes to the hills. From where does my help come?" (121:1). The psalmist knows it's not from his own "jacobing"—or from pagan gods worshiped on the hilltops. "My help comes from the Lord, who made heaven and earth" (121:2). Whatever dangers to life or faith, He will "neither slumber nor sleep" on the job but will "keep" me "from this time forth and forevermore" (121:4, 8).

Paul knew that after his departure, many would not endure in faith. Read the **Epistle**, 2 Timothy 3:14–4:5.

Paul writes what is very likely his last letter from prison in Rome. His martyrdom, he knows, will be soon (see 4:6). And he anticipates the time when "people will not endure sound teaching, but having itching ears they will accumulate for themselves teachers to suit their own passions, and will turn away from listening to the truth and wander off into myths" (4:3–4). Meanwhile, "all who desire to live a godly life in Christ Jesus will be persecuted" (3:12). When the Lord returns, will He find faith on earth?

Paul's encouragement to Timothy and us, so that we *are* able to continue in faith, is to "continue in what you have learned and have firmly believed"—that is, "the sacred writings" (3:14, 15). Timothy had learned them from his mother and grandmother (1:5); perhaps we were similarly blessed. These Scriptures (you know these verses!) are "breathed out [inspired] by God and profitable for teaching, for reproof, for correction, and for training in righteousness, that the man of God may be competent, equipped for every good work" (3:16–17).

"Preach the word" (the motto of Concordia Theological Seminary, Fort Wayne, by the way!) is Timothy's task (4:2) because the Word and the Word made visible, the Sacraments, are God's means, "which are able to make you wise for salvation through faith in Christ Jesus" (3:15). God will use these to sustain your faith until Christ returns!

Therefore, even as we "endure suffering" (4:5), we have Jesus' parable "to the effect that [we] ought always to pray and not lose heart." Read it in the **Holy Gospel**, Luke 18:1–8.

The encouragements in the propers to pray all arise from this parable. The woman, a widow who had very little standing in court, perhaps no one to advocate for her, is persistent in pursuing justice herself. The judge is wicked—doesn't fear God or care about people. But because she presses him, he gives in. That's entirely self-serving. We get *a* point: we ought to be persistent in prayer too.

But *the* point of the parable isn't really the comparison of the woman's praying to our praying. The real comparison is between the unrighteous judge and our heavenly Father. If this creep, Jesus says, eventually gives justice, "will not God give justice to His elect? . . . I tell you, He will give justice to them speedily" (18:7a, 8a). The point of the parable is the eagerness of the Father to answer our prayers! We don't have to wear God down by our persistence! He's going to give us the very best—speedily! In other words, we pray, we wrestle with and cling to God, because He has promised to answer us.

So how does that lead to Jesus' question? It's the wonderful interplay among Word, faith, and prayer. God tells us in His Word that Jesus, by His death and resurrection, has made us children of our gracious Father again. He wants to hear us. That creates faith. And then we live in His love by asking, even demanding His answers. That interplay is the preventative to losing heart, losing faith.

So That Our Faith May Endure until the Son of Man Comes Again, God, in His Inspired Scripture, Invites Us to Wrestle with Him in Prayer and Promises to Answer Us Speedily.

Does that answer Jesus' question?

In many churches, the **Hymn of the Day** will actually be the last proper in the service; we'll sing it as the sermon hymn *after* hearing Jesus' question in the Gospel. "I Trust, O Lord, Your Holy Name" (*LSB* 734) is a prayer that amidst "woes and fear" the Lord would keep our faith firmly grounded in His Word. The last line of the hymn is the final word that answers Jesus' question: Yes, He will find faith: "we depart victorious" (sts 2, 5).

A note for Reformation and All Saints' Day: Many congregations will observe these festivals on the consecutive Sundays closest to October 31 and November 1. Since they use the same propers for Years A, B, and C, you'll find the devotion-studies for these days in Year A, pages 250 and 254. Alternatively, the devotion-studies for Propers 25 and 26, Year C, appear on the following pages.

The Sundays after Pentecost: Proper 25 (October 23–29) Year C

READINGS

Genesis 4:1–15
Psalm 5 (antiphon: v 11a)
2 Timothy 4:6–8, 16–18
Luke 18:9–17

HYMN OF THE DAY

LSB 745 "In God, My Faithful God"

What a setup! Proper 25 for these Sundays after Pentecost pairs an Old Testament Reading of Cain and Abel with the Gospel lesson of the Pharisee and the publican. How obvious can you get? It's easier to tell the good guys from the bad guys than in a Tom Mix (way before John Wayne) Western.

Of course, you know how it is. You can only use a trope so many times before it becomes trite. The audience knows what's coming. At some point, you've gotta start mixing up the black hats and the white hats. Today's films invariably feature more complicated characters—flawed heroes, sympathetic villains. Frankly, that's a lot more like real life.

And Cain and Abel were real. Is there perhaps more going on with them than the bad guy-good guy setup we think we see?

The Pharisee and the tax collector—we've got 'em pegged because we know how the story comes out. But as Jesus told that parable, His original audience surely had the two hats reversed. Do we, even knowing how the movie ends, fall into a misread of our own—which actually is the very same mistake recast?

One last preview: most congregations will celebrate the Festival of the Reformation the Sunday on or before October 31. If that happens to be this week, they may well use the Reformation Day propers (see p 250) instead of Proper 25. However, this Gospel lesson also makes an excellent Reformation text, especially if there will also be a separate afternoon or evening Reformation service.

Hit Play. The **Introit**:

> *When I am afraid, I put my trust in You.*

In God, whose word I praise, in the Lord*, whose word I praise, in God I trust; I shall not be afraid. What can man do to me? I must perform my vows to You, O God; I will render thank offerings to You. For You have delivered my soul from death, yes, my feet from falling, that I may walk before God in the light of life.*

Glory be to the Father and to the Son and to the Holy Spirit; as it was in the beginning, is now, and will be forever. Amen.

When I am afraid, I put my trust in You. (Ps 56:10–13; antiphon: Ps 56:3)

"When I am afraid, I put my trust in You. . . . In God I trust; I shall *not* be afraid." For every fear, God is our refuge. Trust in anything or anyone else—particularly ourselves—is dangerous. But in the Lord, we really need not be afraid.

And yet we are so very often. Not just because our faith is weak, but because there's so much out there that really does threaten us. Is there a specific fear that our propers this week will address?

The **Collect** names one:

Almighty and everlasting God, You are always more ready to hear than we to pray and always ready to give more than we either desire or deserve. Pour down on us the abundance of Your mercy; forgive us those things of which our conscience is afraid; and give us those good things for which we are not worthy to ask except by the merits and mediation of Jesus Christ, Your Son, our Lord, who lives and reigns with You and the Holy Spirit, one God, now and forever. Amen.

"Forgive us those things of which our conscience is afraid." Actually, that's not one fear but a longer list than we could ever count. Where do we begin? When we confess, "I, a poor, miserable sinner . . . ," "we have sinned against You in thought, word, and deed, by what we have done and by what we have left undone," what pops into our heads? Or maybe it's not suddenly "popping" into your head at all. Maybe it's constantly on your mind—something to do with putting God second or third, something toward your parents, your spouse, your kids, a business practice you know isn't quite right, a word you know you need to go back and take back in person, jealousy that keeps nagging. To think that just that one sin—to say nothing of all your others—earns you eternity in hell, that's to be afraid, terrified!

We deserve no quarter. "We are not worthy to ask" forgiveness. Our plea is only on "the abundance of [God's] mercy." But God is "always more ready to hear than we to pray and always ready to give more than we either desire or deserve." We are forgiven. Our consciences can be at peace "by the merits and mediation of Jesus Christ." Jesus' perfect life and His innocent death are our merit before God. They have mediated our rift from God, reconciled us to Him. Be not afraid!

The **Psalm** this Sunday could almost be viewed as a movie trailer for the Old Testament Reading and the Gospel. Read Psalm 5.

Flash these clips of Cain and Abel, the Pharisee and the tax collector. "O Lord, . . . in the morning I prepare a sacrifice for You and watch" (5:3). Abel brings his sacrifice without fanfare, just trusting God will receive it. "The Lord abhors the bloodthirsty and deceitful man" (5:6)—like one who lures his brother into the field and kills him.

"The boastful shall not stand before Your eyes" (5:5), but the Pharisee is proud to stand in the temple and state his claims before the Lord. Meanwhile, the tax collector "will bow down toward Your holy temple in the fear of You" (5:7). The Pharisee will "flatter with [the] tongue" (5:9), while the tax collector will plead, "Give ear to my words, O Lord; consider my groaning. Give attention to the sound of my cry" (5:1–2). Nevertheless, at the end of the day, it's the tax collector who will hear, "Let all who take refuge in You rejoice; let them ever sing for joy" (5:11). For the Lord blesses this man as "righteous" (5:12).

You can always tell 'em by their hats. Or not. The **Old Testament Reading**, Genesis 4:1–15.

So quickly we see the horror of Adam and Eve's first sin! Their own son is a murderer . . . of his brother!

A TV miniseries in the 1980s followed the parallel lives of William Kane, a highborn New York financier, and Abel Rosnovski, a poor immigrant who through diligence and hard work also becomes wealthy. At first, Abel is naive but simon-pure. Then, when the Depression causes a terrible tragedy, he blames his banker, Kane, and relentlessly schemes to destroy Kane. He doesn't realize that Kane had actually done all he could to extend Abel's credit and prevent the loss. It's not quite the good guy-bad guy we expect.

Biblical Abel gets the reputation of good guy because the Lord "had regard" for his offering (4:4). He gave the Lord his best, "the firstborn of his flock and of their fat portions." Yes, and if we see that white hat and think it makes him a good guy, we're falling for 1930s Westerns and ignoring real life. Abel was as much the heir of his parents' sin as was Cain, as are we. His sacrifice was acceptable to God not because it was good but because the good he gave was by faith (Heb 11:4). And faith is never a good of mine; it's believing that I'm evil and that God is good to me. It's God's gift, to me, which receives His other gifts to me, a sinner.

Then there's Cain. There's no indication his offering was any worse (Gen 4:3). But perhaps he thought it would cause God to see him as good. That's the opposite of faith. (In fact, it's Pharisaic.) And Cain's unbelief is evident in his jealousy and vengeance. Black hat! But God loves him too. That's why He speaks to Cain, brings the full weight of the Law down on him (4:11–12). And what's the effect? Cain is broken, desperate, pleading (4:13–14). Most important is this: "From Your face I shall be hidden" (4:14). Wanting to see the Lord's face—that's penitence. And the Lord answers his cry for mercy (4:15b). We don't know, but we might see Cain in heaven, where he will be a very good man.

If so, it will be for the same reason we're there—for the sake of the child Eve thought she had born. "She conceived and bore Cain, saying, 'I have gotten a man with the help of the LORD'" (4:1). Luther, though, understood the Hebrew this way: "I have gotten a man, the LORD." Perhaps actually a preferable translation. Get the difference? Eve believed God's promise (3:15) that her seed would be the Savior. But it was seventy-six or so generations early (Lk 3:23–38).

Paul, as he wrote the **Epistle**, knew he would soon be departing for heaven—and he knew he wasn't going there as a good guy. Read 2 Timothy 4:6–8, 16–18.

Paul's second imprisonment in Rome will soon end in his death. But he has "fought the good fight" (4:7). We'd surely call him one of the good guys. No thanks to all those who "deserted" him (4:16) like Demas (see 4:10)—to say nothing of Alexander the coppersmith who "did [him] great harm" (4:14).

But Paul never forgot that he himself was really a "rescue" (4:18). The evil deeds the Lord would save him from were above all his own (1 Tim 1:15). He would receive "the crown of righteousness" as just one of those many "who have loved [Jesus'] appearing" (ἐπιφάνεια, *epiphaneia*, 4:8)—His appearing on the Last Day (2 Thess 2:8) because they had loved His appearing to live, die, and rise in His incarnation (2 Tim 1:10).

By now we see the problem of good guy-bad guy, don't we. The **Holy Gospel**: Luke 18:9–17.

The first time I remember hearing this Bible account, I took the bait. I had the guy who fasted twice a week as hero—as Jesus' original hearers would have. To me, he sounded like the classic white hat. But he "trusted in [himself] that [he was] righteous, and treated others with contempt" (18:9).

We know now that the tax collector was the man who "went down to his house justified" (18:14)—a marvelous text for a Reformation Day sermon. His conscience was rightly afraid, as the Collect reminded us it should be. He bows low, "God, be merciful to me!" and calls himself, literally, "*the* sinner" (τῷ ἁμαρτωλῷ, *to hamartolo*, 18:13).

But by knowing his outcome, haven't we deep down come to think of him as the good guy in the story? Do you see the error? That somehow pretends his penitence is a virtue, when it's really only recognition that "I'm evil!" He wouldn't stand for calling him good! There are no good guys in any of our propers—not even the little children whom we see as so innocent (18:15)—except the son Eve just couldn't wait to have who would take all of our bad on Himself on the cross and send us home justified. That doesn't make us the good guys in the story, but it does make a very good story!

**THIS FILM ISN'T GOOD GUYS-BAD GUYS.
IT'S A SINNER
WHO KNOWS HIS ONLY PLEA
IS GOD'S MERCY IN CHRIST JESUS
OR ONE WHO TRUSTS HIMSELF.**

"My sins fill me with care, yet I will not despair" (**Hymn of the Day**, *LSB* 745:2).

A note for Reformation and All Saints' Day: Many congregations will observe these festivals on the consecutive Sundays closest to October 31 and November 1. Since they use the same propers for Years A, B, and C, you'll find the devotion-studies for these days in Year A, pages 250 and 254. Alternatively, the devotion-study for Proper 26, Year C, appears on the next page.

The Sundays after Pentecost: Proper 26 (October 30–November 5) Year C

READINGS

Isaiah 1:10–18
Psalm 130 (antiphon: vv 3–4)
2 Thessalonians 1:1–5 (6–10) 11–12
Luke 19:1–10

HYMN OF THE DAY

LSB 728 "How Firm a Foundation"

As long as it remains true that children are short, Zacchaeus will always be the memorable and beloved figure of Proper 26, Year C (or of whatever this Sunday morphs into in future three-year lectionaries)—especially as long as adults remember his song they learned as kids. Every VBS and Sunday School student under five or four feet feels an attraction to that "wee little man," even if he was a rich (probably filthy rich) tax collector. And we all grin to see him up there, leaning out, peering down from a branch of that sycamore tree.

Which angle do you see him from in your mind's eye? Are you down on the ground looking up at him, or are you up there with him on the next branch, looking down at the crowd below?

That could make a difference.

Our propers this week should help us get a wholesome viewpoint for seeing Zacchaeus. Picture him as you read the **Introit**:

The one who offers thanksgiving as his sacrifice glorifies Me; to one who orders his way rightly I will show the salvation of God!

The Mighty One, God the Lord, *speaks and summons the earth from the rising of the sun to its setting. Out of Zion, the perfection of beauty, God shines forth. Offer to God a sacrifice of thanksgiving, and perform your vows to the Most High, and call upon Me in the day of trouble; I will deliver you, and you shall glorify Me.*

Glory be to the Father and to the Son and to the Holy Spirit; as it was in the beginning, is now, and will be forever. Amen.

The one who offers thanksgiving as his sacrifice glorifies Me; to one who orders his way rightly I will show the salvation of God! (Ps 50:1–2, 14–15; antiphon: Ps 50:23)

Zacchaeus, quite obviously, has heard a lot about Jesus. He's curious, maybe more than curious. And now Jesus is coming to his town, Jericho. But there's that problem. He's short. He's also resourceful, though, so (sing it with me), "He climbed up in a sycamore tree." "And when the Savior passed that way, He looked up in the tree," and *"The Mighty One, God the LORD, speaks and summons the earth"*—including that diminutive tax collector. "Zacchaeus, you come down from there. For I'm going to your house today."

The psalmist, of course, has a wider view, the whole earth, "from the rising of the sun to its setting." But today, this particular day, the Lord Jesus is focused just on Zacchaeus. He speaks and summons him down for the moment of his life.

It's easy to see where the **Collect** fits in:

O Lord, stir up the hearts of Your faithful people to welcome and joyfully receive Your Son, our Savior, Jesus Christ, that He may find in us a fit dwelling place; who lives and reigns with You and the Holy Spirit, one God, now and forever. Amen.

Zacchaeus probably had a sizable household staff, so it wasn't a matter of phoning his wife with the dreaded, "Honey, I'm bringing a few folks home with me." But welcoming Jesus into our homes is more than putting together an impromptu dinner party. Being a "fit dwelling place" for Jesus is joyfully receiving Him in faith, believing that He has saved us, and that's a miracle worked by the Holy Spirit. We pray that God would ever renew our eagerness to have Jesus in our lives—and even literally in our homes.

There's more to the Zacchaeus story, however. Read the whole thing, the **Holy Gospel**, Luke 19:1–10.

We give Zacchaeus a mulligan, write him a pass, because he was "small in stature" (19:3), kind of cute, we think. But if we'd really known him, we wouldn't. He wasn't a nice man. The only reason a Jew would betray his people and collaborate with the Romans was money. That was his life. He was an ἀρχιτελώνης, *architelones*, not just a rookie publican exploring career possibilities but a "*chief* tax collector" (19:2)—hardened, good at what he did, promoted for doing exactly what the enemy expected.

Nevertheless, it appears God's Law has done its job. Perhaps he's finally truly been smitten by the Seventh Commandment (actually the Eighth by Hebrew numeration) that he'd memorized in Torah classes as a boy. Or maybe it's the pain of rejection by family and friends that's weighing heavily on him. In any case, it seems he knows he needs something beyond himself and his cash. And people are saying—some of them grumbling—that this Jesus has a soft spot for his kind (15:1–2), even has one of them in His entourage (5:27–32).

So when the big moment arrived, "he hurried and came down and received [Jesus] joyfully" (19:6). Luke matches Jesus' language to show how ready Zacchaeus was to comply: "Hurry and come down!" . . . "hurried and came down" (19:5, 6).

What follows could seem to read as continuing action, without interruption, right there under the sycamore tree, as Jesus and Zacchaeus take their first steps toward his house: more grumbling ("to be the guest of a man who is a sinner," 19:7), Zacchaeus stops and speaks ("Behold, Lord, . . ." 19:8), and Jesus answers ("Today, . . ." 19:9). More likely, though, these ensuing conversations take place after Jesus and Zacchaeus have entered his house (he "received Him joyfully," 19:6; "He has gone in," εἰσῆλθεν, *eiselthen*, aorist, 19:7). It's probably even after dinner that Zacchaeus stands up to speak.

And see what he says: "Behold, Lord, the half of my goods I give to the poor. And if I have defrauded anyone of anything, I restore it fourfold" (19:8). Recall the Introit: "Offer to God a sacrifice of thanksgiving, and perform your vows to the Most High." Zacchaeus vows a huge offering of his wealth and restitution for anyone he's cheated.

Why, then, is Isaiah 1:10–18 chosen as the **Old Testament Reading** to accompany this? Read it.

Isn't the word of the Lord here rejecting exactly what Zacchaeus vowed? "I have had enough of burnt offerings; . . . I do not delight in the blood of bulls, or of lambs, or of goats. . . . Bring no more vain offerings; incense is an abomination to Me. . . . I am weary of bearing them" (1:11, 13, 14).

Look back at the Gospel reading and consider the viewpoint from which you're looking. After hosting Jesus for dinner, Zacchaeus vows his offerings. Then Jesus responds, "Today salvation has come to this house, since he also is a son of Abraham" (Lk 19:9). What is the sequence here? If we're too fancied of Zacchaeus, too attracted to or distracted by his being wee (perhaps looking up at him in the tree and focusing on him), if we hear the story and the song as being *about Zacchaeus*, we might think his bank-busting offering brings the story to its climax. Maybe we even think that his vow is the reason "salvation has come to this house."

A better point of view, actually, might be from up in that sycamore with Zacchaeus, looking down. From there, we see Jesus. The real reason salvation came to Zacchaeus's house that day is because that day "the Son of Man came to seek and to save the lost" (19:10). See Jesus looking up at you, pointing, calling. From eternity, Jesus had been seeking Zacchaeus. Nothing started with Zacchaeus, his climbing, his hosting, his promising. He climbed the tree because he'd heard what *Jesus* was doing. He hosted Jesus for dinner because *Jesus* invited Himself. And he made his vow because *Jesus* had valued him, dined with him, not holding his sins against him.

So what of Zacchaeus's vow and offering? Well, they're as the Introit taught us from the beginning: "The one who offers thanksgiving as his sacrifice glorifies Me." The offering in which God delights is a *thank*offering. Our offerings and sacrifices do indeed glorify God—when they thank Him for what He's done. "Call upon Me in the day of trouble;

I will deliver you, and you shall glorify Me." When we're in trouble—guilt of our sin, loneliness and rejection (whether by our doing or entirely innocently), danger, stress, financial need—what Jesus did on the cross to reconcile us to God, long before we ever cried out, makes certain that He will deliver us. *Then* we glorify Him by giving thanks.

This is always the way it is. Remember the Collect: "O Lord, stir up the hearts of Your faithful people to welcome and joyfully receive Your Son." The Lord Himself must move us, stir us up to receive Him. "I believe that I cannot by my own reason or strength believe in Jesus Christ, my Lord, or come to Him" (Small Catechism, Third Article). The Holy Spirit calls me by the Gospel, just as He did through Jesus' call to Zacchaeus. *Then* we become "a fit dwelling place" for Christ and set before Him the very best fare we can offer.

All those offerings the Lord found so wearisome in the Old Testament Reading were like sacrifices from Sodom and Gomorrah (Is 1:10)—given to buy their gods' favor while living in evil and unbelief. God takes no delight in sinful people trying to impress Him. Rather, *He* calls His people to a holy convocation: "'Come now, let us reason together, says the LORD" (1:18a). *He* calls us to repent: "cease to do evil," "seek justice" (1:16, 17). And *He* promises, "though your sins are like scarlet, they shall be as white as snow; though they are red like crimson, they shall become like wool" (1:18b)—for the sake of the shed red blood of the Lord Himself. *That then* becomes the power by which we "remove the evil of [our] deeds from before [God's] eyes" and "learn to do good"—like Zacchaeus's good to the poor, "the fatherless," and the widow (1:16, 17).

The **Psalm** for this day also reminds us of the proper perspective for seeing Zacchaeus or ourselves in relation to Jesus: Psalm 130.

"Out of the depths I cry to You, O LORD! O Lord, hear my voice!" (130:1–2a). Spiritually speaking, we can't climb any trees to see Jesus. We're in the pits and can't get out. All we can do is "wait for the LORD" (130:5). "But with You there is forgiveness, . . . with the LORD there is steadfast love, and with Him is plentiful redemption. And He will redeem Israel from all his iniquities" (130:4, 7–8).

Finally, the **Epistle** reminds us that every member of the Church is thanks to God's doing—as is even the fulfilling of our vows: 2 Thessalonians 1:1–12.

"We ought always to *give thanks to God for you*, brothers, as is right" (1:3). "To this end we always pray for you, that *our God . . . may fulfill every resolve* for good . . . so that the name of our Lord Jesus may be glorified in you, and you in Him" (1:11, 12).

So the proper point of view on the beloved Zacchaeus story? From the **Verse**: "Alleluia. . . . For the Son of Man came to seek and to save the lost. Alleluia."

OFFERINGS AND VOWS THAT DELIGHT THE LORD ARE ALWAYS THANKS FOR HIS SEEKING AND SAVING US FROM THE DEPTHS OF OUR SIN.

Appreciate the way the **Hymn of the Day**, "How Firm a Foundation" (*LSB* 728), expresses this in stanzas 2–5. Even as we sing, it's actually the Lord speaking.

The Sundays after Pentecost: Proper 27 (November 6–12) Year C

READINGS

Exodus 3:1–15
Psalm 148 (antiphon: v 13)
2 Thessalonians 2:1–8, 13–17
Luke 20:27–40

HYMN OF THE DAY

LSB 713 "From God Can Nothing Move Me"

"Two things I take for granted,
Three things I oft ignore:
The Lord is God,
That death must come,
And I AM to live."
(not quite Proverbs 6:16–19; 30:15–31)

If not Proverbial, they may at least be true. In Western society, however that's being reinterpreted these days, there remains a long enough history of Christianity that "God" to most people still brings up at least some vague images of the God of the Bible. In our fallen world, a much, much longer history has deceived us into thinking death is natural, part of a circle of life; we've come to live with it. That, of course, then also means we've lost a clear understanding of what life really is—and of how we have it. But we think we know all this. We don't see much need to examine any of it. We take it for granted, pay it no mind.

In the biblical world, these were seen as livelier issues. They weren't taken as given. Moses, Israelite psalmists, Paul living and mixing with pagans had to address them. Even Jesus, speaking to monotheistic Jews, had to teach what they should have known.

Our propers this week look at these unquestioned questions—who the true God is, what about death and life! That's as basic as we can get.

The **Introit** introduces all of them:

You who fear the Lord, *trust in the* Lord*! He is their help and their shield.*

Why should the nations say, "Where is their God?" Our God is in the heavens; He does all that He pleases. Their idols are silver and gold, the work of human hands. Those who make them become like them; so do all who trust in them. The dead do not praise the Lord, nor do any who go down into silence. But we will bless the Lord from this time forth and forevermore. Praise the Lord!

Glory be to the Father and to the Son and to the Holy Spirit; as it was in the beginning, is now, and will be forever. Amen.

You who fear the Lord, trust in the Lord! He is their help and their shield. (Ps 115:2–4, 8, 17–18; antiphon: Ps 115:11)

The psalmist recognizes that actually very few people worship the Lord as the one true God. Other nations question, "Where is" this God of Israel? They have their idols (Baal of the Canaanites, Dagon of the Philistines, Bel of the Babylonians), but they "are silver and gold, the work of human hands"; they're dead, can't do a thing. So "you who [*do*] fear the Lord, trust in the Lord!" He's the God who's alive! "He does all that He pleases."

And it's in our God or god that we have life or death. "Those who make [those idols] become like them"—as dead as they are. In the Gospel lesson, Jesus will respond to testing by the Sadducees, and He may have this verse in mind: "The dead do not praise the Lord." Instead, our living God gives us life: "We will bless the Lord from this time forth and forevermore. Praise the Lord!"

The first two words of the **Collect** show how central this is to all this week's propers:

Living God, Your almighty power is made known chiefly in showing mercy and pity. Grant us the fullness of Your grace to lay hold of Your promises and live forever in Your presence; through Jesus Christ, Your Son, our Lord, who lives and reigns with You and the Holy Spirit, one God, now and forever. Amen.

We've noted that the Collects follow a carefully prescribed form. Many elements are rather predictable. But this is the only Collect in the three-year cycle that begins with the address "Living God." It seems so obvious and so minimal. It's like when someone is congratulated on "another" birthday and wisecracks, "It beats the alternative." It hardly seems necessary to acknowledge being alive.

But we've seen that living is what sets the Lord apart from all false gods. And God living is the only basis on which *we* have life. We think it goes without saying, but it never ought. Another birthday—or anything at all once we've reached the alternative—is not a given, except to say that it's given by the living God. "Grant us the fullness of Your grace to lay hold of Your promises and *live forever* in Your presence." How often, as each Collect winds down, have we mumbled without thinking, "through Jesus Christ, Your Son, our Lord, who lives . . ."? In Him, and only in Him, is life!

Jesus will build His case with the Sadducees in the **Old Testament Reading**, Exodus 3:1–15.

Fifteen hundred years of mankind's story turn when God calls Moses. Moses, you remember, has fled both the luxuries and the troubles of Egypt—a murder rap, even—quite content, it seems, to live out his days tending sheep, not a scratch in the human record. To his alarm, initially, God has in mind for him greater fame than any pharaoh (from Tut to Thutmose III—probably the one he actually faced).

Horeb is the same "mountain of God" (3:1), Sinai, Israel will come to after the Exodus (3:12). And that's the message: God has "seen the affliction" of His people in Egypt and will deliver them (3:7). He will bring them to "a good and broad land, a land flowing with milk and honey" (3:8), the same land of the Canaanites in which Abraham had sojourned six hundred years before and which God had promised to his descendants.

Understandably, Moses is scared to face Pharaoh (3:11). But that's not the only problem. "If I come to the people of Israel and say to them, 'The God of your fathers has sent me to you,' and they ask me, 'What is His name?' what shall I say?" (3:13). Egypt and the nations had many gods, and Israel was not at all clear that there was truly only one—even less clear that that one was theirs, the God of Abraham, Isaac, and Jacob (3:6).

Our era of Christendom is over. True, when the president signs off, "God bless America," we know who that should mean, and lots of our neighbors—churchgoing or not—have some idea too. But many in North America now picture "God" as the ones they learned in the Qur'an (of Islam) or the Vedas (of Hinduism) or the sutras (of the Buddha). Many others really think It is more like a Force that might be with us.

We and Israel need to know which God is the living God. "I AM" is derived from the four Hebrew consonants יהוה (YHWH), which we render Yahweh and present in Scripture as "LORD" (3:14–15). God chooses to reveal Himself to us, to converse with us by name. He's not an impersonal force (which would better describe Buddhism) or a god of our invention. And then, "I AM" shouts "Alive!" The Lord cannot be limited to "then not now" or His reach to "here not there." He's not just a sun god like the Egyptian Ra or a god of weather and fertility like Baal or one of the countless deities of Hinduism. He doesn't perish from memory when their nations do. Wher*ever*, when*ever* we need Him, He is.

Above all, unlike any other god (such as the Allah of Islam), "I AM" became a living human being. Here in the burning bush, it's the Son of God prior to His incarnation. But God's whole reason for selecting a nation, Israel, and bringing it to the Promised Land was so that through it in that place, He would live and die to make us alive.

Read the **Psalm**, Psalm 148. See all the activity, how much is going on in praising Yahweh! How alive He is! "His name alone is exalted" (148:13). He's the only God. And He is always active for those "who are near to Him" (148:14).

Now the **Epistle**, 2 Thessalonians 2:1–8, 13–17.

Paul's ascription of "our *Lord* Jesus Christ" (2:1, 14, 16) sails right by us unnoticed. But early believers knew the signal: this Jesus is, now in Greek, κύριος, *kyrios*. That is, Yahweh Himself (see 1 Cor 12:3).

In this text, the chief challenge to that is "the man of lawlessness" (2 Thess 2:3), often called "the antichrist" (1 Jn 2:18–22). He's not just a very wicked person, he "opposes and exalts himself against every so-called god or object of worship, so that he takes his seat in the temple of God, proclaiming himself to be God" (2 Thess 2:4). In other words, a religious leader who puts himself in God's place. The papacy of the Roman Catholic Church has claimed for itself the authority to declare doctrine beyond what God's Word says, and the Roman Catholic Church in its Council of Trent (1545–63) has officially condemned those who say that we are justified by faith apart from our works. Therefore, our Lutheran Confessions are not shy about naming the papacy as this "man of lawlessness," the antichrist (see Smalcald Articles, Part II, Article IV; The Power and Primacy of the Pope, 39–40). There is just one Lord.

We give thanks that in our Lord Jesus, we have life. He has made us "the firstfruits to be saved," to "obtain [His own] glory," to receive "eternal comfort and good hope through grace" (2:13, 14, 16).

Without knowing Him as the Lord God, we could never understand death or life. Read the **Holy Gospel**, Luke 20:27–40.

It will be Sadducees Annas and Caiaphas who orchestrate Jesus' execution (Jn 18:12–14; Acts 5:17). Obviously, in denying the resurrection (Lk 20:27), they misunderstand life. But behind that is also a glorification of death. See the test they put to Jesus, based on levirate marriage (20:28; Deut 25:5–6). The man dies; his six brothers die; the woman dies. It sounds very much like the bitter refrain in Genesis 5: "And he [Adam, Seth, Enosh, . . . Methuselah] died." It seems natural enough to us. That's life. No, it's not! The Sadducees had bought the idea that life in a physical body was evil; death provided a desirable escape. So the resurrection of the body would be evil. They rejected it—and shockingly, many Christians think eternity in heaven will be lived without bodies.

Completely wrong! There won't be marriage in heaven (Lk 20:34–35), but Jesus' point (20:37–38) is that Abraham, Isaac, and Jacob aren't just disembodied spirits. Soul separated from its body is the very definition of death! It would never have happened if not for sin. Life as the living God created it is always lived body and soul together. The patriarchs of Israel are awaiting that—the resurrections of their bodies—for our bodies God created as good, never to be discarded.

The living God was standing before these Sadducees. Soon they would kill Him. But even though from eternity He had no body, this God would not now shed His body. He would take it up again. His death will restore the day when we "cannot die anymore, . . . being sons [and daughters] of the resurrection" (20:36). If I am to live, it must be in I am, "for all live to Him" (20:38). And I am.

In the Lord, the God of the Living, We Have Life Forever.

As you sing the **Hymn of the Day** (*LSB* 713), consider the many references to death and to life in Christ—here and in heaven.

The Sundays after Pentecost: Proper 28 (November 13–19) Year C

READINGS

Malachi 4:1–6
Psalm 98 (antiphon: v 9b)
2 Thessalonians 3:(1–5) 6–13
Luke 21:5–28 (29–36)

HYMN OF THE DAY

LSB 508 "The Day Is Surely Drawing Near"

"The day is surely drawing near
When Jesus, God's anointed,
In all His power shall appear
As judge whom God appointed."
(*LSB* 508:1)

Proper 28, the second-to-last Sunday of the church year, reminds us that the end of the world is drawing near. "Near" in God's scheme of things may, of course, be quite different from what we think near would be. But the end is indeed coming, as the church calendar annually alerts us. Is that a thrilling thought, or an uneasy one, perhaps even terrifying?

In the **Verse** for this Sunday, taken from the Gospel lesson, Jesus tells us how God would have us anticipate His second coming: "Alleluia. Straighten up and raise your heads, because your redemption is drawing near. Alleluia" (Lk 21:28b). God's every intent is that the Last Day would be triumphant for us and the anticipation of it entirely comforting, truly thrilling. Our *redemption* is drawing near!

The lectionary brings out the triumph of that day when it assigns Psalm 98 to be the **Psalm** for this Sunday. See if it rings a bell (that's a hint)—perhaps in a surprising way.

Remember? Psalm 98 is also appointed for Christmas Day. It's the text for Isaac Watts's hymn "Joy to the World"—and as we hear it on this next-to-last Sunday of the church year, it certainly delivers a joyful exclamation point! "Make a joyful noise to the Lord, all the earth; break forth into joyous song and sing praises! . . . With trumpets and the sound of the horn make a joyful noise before the King, the Lord!" (98:4, 6). What we see at Christmas in its (His!) infancy, we now will see brought to consummation: "Oh sing to the

Lord a new song, for He has done marvelous things! His right hand and His holy arm have worked salvation for Him. The Lord has made known His salvation" (98:1–2). On the Last Day, "all the ends of the earth [will] have seen the salvation of our God" (98:3). The Lord wants us to chant this psalm with joyful anticipation of Christ's return.

But the lectionary also gives us an interesting twist. On Christmas Day, the antiphon designated for the Psalm is verse 2: "The Lord has made known His salvation; He has revealed His righteousness in the sight of the nations." For this Sunday, Proper 28, that's changed; the antiphon is verse 9b: "He will judge the world with righteousness, and the peoples with equity." The antiphon is intended to indicate the theme or focus of the Psalm, at least liturgically speaking. So why the switch?

Well, the Last Day is, after all, Judgment Day. Jesus shall appear as the Judge God appointed. Along with all that joy, the Psalm also reminds us that judgment is coming. Every one of us, no exceptions—yes, really you, yes, really me—will stand before Christ, the Judge, and hear an eternal assignment: perfect joy with our Savior in heaven, or endless and unspeakable sufferings in hell. Does that raise the stakes—and perhaps the anxiety—a bit? Sure. But in no way does it diminish God's intent that we look forward to the day. What we rejoiced to hear in the Verse and most of the Psalm is still true. It's a matter of understanding how raising our heads in excitement to see our redemption harmonizes with Christ judging the world with righteousness. The truth is, you *can*

Raise Your Heads, Because the Righteous Judgment of Your Redemption Is Near.

Redemption and righteous judgment really are melody and countermelody in the same song. The harmony will, as always, come in Christ Himself.

We'll begin to see that immediately in the **Introit**. It's quite rare for the Introit to draw from the Gospel reading, but here it is in the antiphon—Jesus' own words:

Heaven and earth will pass away,
but My words will not pass away.

I lift up my eyes to the hills. From where does my help come? My help comes from the Lord, who made heaven and earth. The Lord is your keeper; the Lord is your shade on your right hand. The Lord will keep you from all evil; He will keep your life. The Lord will keep your going out and your coming in from this time forth and forevermore.

Glory be to the Father and to the Son and to the Holy Spirit; as it was in the beginning, is now, and will be forever. Amen.

Heaven and earth will pass away,
but My words will not pass away.
(Ps 121:1–2, 5, 7–8; antiphon: Lk 21:33)

What reassurance!—and, therefore, reason for eager anticipation! It is most certain that creation as we see it will end, even be consumed with a roar and intense heat (2 Pet 3:10, 12). But Jesus' words "will not pass away," will continue to be reliable. We're wired to think stability, certainty is in the cosmos—the sun rising every day in the east, the moon repeating its twenty-eight-day cycle seemingly forever. It won't be forever. Or maybe we think stability is *terra firma*, solid ground, the hills, mountains, continents. But when we lift up our eyes to the hills ("Raise your heads!"), it isn't to find help in Mother Earth. "My help comes from" the one "who *made* heaven and earth." His words will remain when all else has melted. "The LORD will keep your going out and your coming in from this time forth and *forevermore*."

The **Collect** expresses why it's so thrilling that Christ's words will never pass away:

> *O Lord, almighty and ever-living God, You have given exceedingly great and precious promises to those who trust in You. Rule and govern our hearts and minds by Your Holy Spirit that we may live and abide forever in Your Son, who lives and reigns with You and the Holy Spirit, one God, now and forever. Amen.*

Christ's words offer "exceedingly great and precious promises," and the greatest and most precious of these all look beyond the Last Day. Week after week, we might mumble right through each "forevermore" and "ever-living" and "live and abide forever" and "now and forever" in our liturgy, but during these Sundays when we reflect on the end, we appreciate them. Christ's promise that "your redemption is drawing near" is not only sure; He will continue to fulfill it for eternity.

What about righteous judgment? Read the **Old Testament Reading**, Malachi 4:1–6.

What makes judgment righteous? It's when there is a clear distinction between those who are evil and those who are in the right, when the wicked are punished so that the righteous are vindicated, so that the righteous no longer suffer oppression at the hands of evildoers. In other words, such judgment is good news for the righteous.

See the distinction, which is this last word of the Old Testament: For "evildoers," for "the wicked," the "great and awesome day of the LORD" (4:5) will burn "like an oven," "ablaze," leaving them as "stubble" (4:1), "ashes under the soles of your feet" (4:3) in "utter destruction" (4:6).

"*But* for you who fear My name, the sun of righteousness shall rise with healing in its wings. You shall go out leaping like calves from the stall" (4:2). Freedom! Youthful delight! Kicking up your heels without a care in the world. That's also the great and awesome day of the Lord, Judgment Day.

And God's intention is that we be prepared for it. That's why He sends "Elijah" (4:5). Since Elijah had never died (2 Ki 2:11), Jews held that he would someday return from heaven quite literally. Rather, in fact, he was God's symbol for the man who truly would prepare the way for the Messiah. That turned out to be John the Baptist, who called Israel to repent as proper preparation for Christ's first coming (Lk 1:13–17; Mt 17:9–13).

So righteous judgment will be the thrill of redemption for those who are prepared, and being prepared means having one's head up and alert whenever that day arrives. Read the **Epistle**, 2 Thessalonians 3:1–13.

In both of his letters to the Thessalonians, Paul addresses misunderstandings about the Last Day—it's too long in coming; it's already come. The result here is that some in the Thessalonian Church are no longer staying on the alert for that day. They're "walking in idleness" (3:6), "not busy at work, but busybodies" (3:11). This wasn't just a matter of mooching their neighbor's bread (3:10) or sticking their noses into others' business. Idleness exemplified living "not in accord with the tradition [that is, the teachings of the faith] that you received from us" (3:6). They'd become complacent spiritually.

Drive through a rural countryside and see the cows—always head down, oblivious to anything but the grass they're munching. Millennia of domestication have dulled their instincts to watch for predators. But scan the tree line at dusk: one, then two, three, four deer, head up, poised, measuring your slightest move. Especially at this time of year, their survival depends on it.

Paul warns, "Keep away from any brother who is walking in idleness" (4:6). "Depart, please, from the tents of these wicked men," lest when Christ returns, it be for you, as in one terrifying Old Testament account (Num 16:12–14, 25–33).

"Straighten up and raise your heads, because your redemption is drawing near." Read the **Holy Gospel**, Luke 21:5–36.

Jerusalem and the magnificent temple that the Jews so admired would be "thrown down" by Roman armies in 70 AD (21:6, 20–24). The world will seem to come apart (21:10–11). Christians will be persecuted (21:12–17). Then, finally, even the cosmos will indeed come crashing down (21:25–26), and "all who dwell on the face of the whole earth" (21:35) "will see the Son of Man coming in a cloud with power and great glory" (21:27). For most, that day will come "suddenly like a trap" (21:34).

And how is that judgment righteous? It will be righteous because it will deliver God's people from their persecutors and even from a universe corrupted by sin. "Do not be terrified" (21:9), for "not a hair of your head will perish" (21:18).

But how do we know *we* will be singing a joyous new song, since most of mankind will be swept away to eternal destruction? We will be "the ones coming out of the great tribulation [who] have washed their robes and made them white in the blood of the Lamb" (**Gradual**). This discourse was Jesus' last teaching before embarking on His Passion. The blood of the Lamb shed on the cross would atone for every sin that causes us to fear, and in our Baptism, they have been washed away. While the world lives in dissipation, we are prepared for Christ's coming by feeding on His body and holy blood.

Sing the **Hymn of the Day** with no fear, for "my Savior paid the debt I owe." "Come, mighty judge, and set us free." "Do not delay" (*LSB* 508:5, 7).

The Sundays after Pentecost: Proper 29 (November 20–26) Year C

READINGS

Malachi 3:13–18
Psalm 46 (antiphon: v 7)
Colossians 1:13–20
Luke 23:27–43

HYMN OF THE DAY

LSB 534 "Lord, Enthroned in Heavenly Splendor"

By the time we get to the last four pages of a book of this length, we normally expect it to be wrapping up—the storylines resolving, all the loose ends tying up into one neat little bow. Or, with nonfiction, the major arguments having been made, the primary conclusions are being stated with finality.

Likewise, on the Last Sunday of the Church Year, we might expect our propers to bring the whole, magnificent biblical story to a tidy conclusion with Christ's final coming in judgment—end of the world, a Happily ever after.

But as you've seen, this is the book that doesn't end. Perhaps you happened to purchase it a few days before the First Sunday in Advent, Year A, and began reading page 2. But that's a 1-in-156 long shot. Way more likely is that you began reading during some random week in Lent, Year B, or Epiphany, Year C, or maybe just a couple months ago with these very Year C Sundays after Pentecost. Any of that would mean that next week you're going to turn back to the front and read Advent 1, Year A, as just another week. Even if you have read all the way through—a couple of times—there's still going to be an Advent 1 coming up next week, and you'll still be looking forward to Sunday morning.

Similarly, Proper 29, even as the last Sunday of the church calendar, isn't the end. Yes, we'll picture Christ's second coming, the Last Day. But our propers remind us that *until* Jesus returns (which *could* be before next Sunday!) the storylines of a sinful, fallen world will *not* be resolved. And when He does return, and when they are resolved, it's still not the end of the story. Then a happily-ever-after.

The **Introit** for this final Sunday of the church year lets us imagine the scene at Christ's return:

Let all the earth fear the Lord; *let all the inhabitants of the world stand in awe of Him!*

Come, bless the Lord, *all you servants of the* Lord, *who stand by night in the house of the* Lord! *Lift up your hands to the holy place and bless the* Lord! *May the* Lord *bless you from Zion, He who made heaven and earth!*

Glory be to the Father and to the Son and to the Holy Spirit; as it was in the beginning, is now, and will be forever. Amen.

Let all the earth fear the Lord; *let all the inhabitants of the world stand in awe of Him! (Ps 134; antiphon: Ps 33:8)*

When the "Lord, enthroned in heavenly splendor" (**Hymn of the Day**, *LSB* 534:1), returns with His angels hailing Him glorified (sts 2, 4), "all the inhabitants of the world" will be gathered before Him. Every grave will be opened, and all people who've ever lived will "stand in awe of Him"—all awestruck indeed, most of them horrified that the one they'd rejected or ignored is nothing less than "He who made heaven and earth." A few—we who have believed in Christ—will rejoice at His awesome appearance. This day will be the fulfillment in plain sight of everything we've hoped for.

But for now and perhaps for the rest of our lives, we still walk by faith, not by sight. The **Gradual** we've been hearing each of the last Sundays of the church year reminds us of the troubles we Christians will face up to the very end:

These are the ones coming out of the great tribulation. They have washed their robes and made them white in the blood of the Lamb. Blessèd are those whose strength is in You, in whose heart are the highways to Zion. (Rev 7:14b; Ps 84:5)

As long as the Last Sunday of the Church Year isn't the *last* Sunday, we, God's saints, will suffer tribulation—maybe even more intense as the Last Day approaches. Until the Last Day, the world will be just not right.

And that may cause us to wonder, to ask, whether the story truly is headed toward a just resolution. Hear what Malachi's original audience was saying in the **Old Testament Reading**, Malachi 3:13–18.

Appropriately enough, these last two Sundays, we've read the last book of the Old Testament. God's people have been back from the Babylonian captivity for more than a century, and the temple has been rebuilt. But complaints swirl—"hard" words against the Lord (3:13). God's people observe that "evildoers not only prosper but they put God to the test and they escape," flaunt their evil and get away with it (3:15b). "It is vain to serve God," His people say. "What is the profit of our keeping His charge or of walking as in mourning [in humble repentance] before the Lord of hosts?" (3:14). Why not just join with the wicked? "We call the arrogant blessed" (3:15a).

So it will often appear. We see the yachts tied up at Balboa during the week and sadly suspect many of them are out to sea on Sunday mornings. The back page of Section A shows gorgeous beach houses listed at "12" or "8" or "7" (million, that is), and we wonder if tithes are going to God's kingdom. Then maybe there's just a tinge of jealousy?

Meanwhile, some of the same prominent names who peddle influence for money seek to silence faithful Christians for "hate speech" when we warn against sins like homosexuality or abortion. Until the Last Day, it will often seem it's evil ones who get ahead.

But there will be "the day when I make up My treasured possession, and I will spare them as a man spares his son who serves him" (3:17). On the Last Day, it will be clear for everyone to see the punishment of the wicked and the joy of those who have served God in righteousness (3:18). We'll see that God has been paying attention to every slight we've suffered and has noted them with our names in His eternal book (3:16).

Other turmoil, too, can make it difficult to wait in trust. Read the **Psalm**, the mighty Psalm 46.

When Luther was inspired by this psalm to write "A Mighty Fortress," he was seeking God's refuge from satanic and human foes. But the psalmist also describes terrors of the earth giving way, mountains trembling, the seas roaring (46:2–3). For some 230,000 people in fourteen countries, the tsunami in the Indian Ocean on December 26, 2004, was the last day. During the Sylmar, California, earthquake of 1971, a cousin of mine ran out of the house, asking, "Is this the end of the world?" And so many other effects of sin—wars, terrorism, school shootings, urban violence, personal crises like divorce, a lost job, illness—can cause us to fear the happy ending will never come.

"Be still, and know that I am God." Such calming words! Remember, this is the God who loved us enough to die for us! No matter how badly out of hand things seem, "I *will be* exalted among the nations, I *will be* exalted in the earth!" (46:10). God is God now, and when Christ returns, we'll see that.

How will we see God exalted? Read the **Epistle** for this last Sunday: Colossians 1:13–20.

Even on the Last Day, God the Father will be invisible to us. But on that day, above us and before us will stand His beloved Son, the very "image of the invisible God" (1:15). Can we imagine that? A man, still a real human being with a face and touch and physical presence. And yet the One who created "all things . . . in heaven and on earth, visible and invisible," is over all other "thrones" and "dominions" and "rulers" and "authorities" because He created them too (1:16). In this man—with a body of height and weight—*"all the fullness of God was pleased to dwell"* (1:19). And this: "In Him all things hold together" (1:17). That is to say, the entire universe exists and continues to operate only by the power and will of this man we'll see standing before us. If He for a moment ceases to sustain creation, then the stars, planets, atoms spin off in chaos until they disappear into oblivion. That's this man we'll see standing before us. God.

"In Him all things hold together" teaches us something else too. On Judgment Day, everyone must pass through Christ. Those who in life knew Him in name only, or who knew Him only as an inconvenience, or who didn't know Him at all, will now face Him entirely unprepared, dressed quite unsuitably for the occasion in the emperor's old clothes of their sins—and hear that He never knew them. But we who believed in Jesus as Savior will see Him standing before us as a familiar friend and brother. In Him, "we have redemption, the forgiveness of sins" (1:14). Despite our sins, He has reconciled us to Himself, "making peace" by the great act, which climaxed earth's entire story: "by the blood of His cross" (1:20). We will be those wearing robes washed and white in the blood of the Lamb. Therefore, He will take us by the hand and lead us through, transfer us into His eternal kingdom (1:13).

All this is why Luke 23:27–43 is so fitting—if surprising—as the **Holy Gospel** for the Last Sunday of the Church Year.

Recall perhaps our discussion last year about Proper 29 as Christ the King Sunday (Year B, pp 501–2). On the Last Day, it will be evident to all that Christ is King of kings! But remember, this last Sunday isn't only about the Last Day. Christ is already King. He just reigns in a way we might easily mistake; He reigns from the cross.

The destruction of Jerusalem by Roman armies in AD 70, which Jesus refers to here (23:28–31), will be a foreshadowing of Judgment Day. On that day, too, punishment will be so terrifying that men will do anything to hide: "Mountains, 'Fall on us,' . . . hills, 'Cover us'" (23:30; see Rev 6:14–17).

But in the meantime, evil will seem to triumph. The Christ is being led out to die. The rulers scoff at Him (Lk 23:35). The soldiers mock Him: "Save Yourself!" (23:36–37). Even Luke hints that Pilate's inscription is an insult: "*This* is the King of the Jews" (23:38). This bloody mess!

Nevertheless, it is here at the cross that happily ever after begins. Here is the "Father, forgive them" (23:34) that prepares us for the Last Day. And here may be Scripture's most beautiful depiction—in real time for real sinners like ourselves—of the benediction that will begin our forever: "Today you will be with Me in paradise" (23:43).

**No Matter What Seems to the Contrary,
from the Prospering of Evil
to the Earth Itself Giving Way,
Our King,
by the Forgiveness of His Cross,
Assures Us of Paradise.**

We close this church year by praying for precisely that. The **Collect**:

> *Lord Jesus Christ, You reign among us by the preaching of Your cross. Forgive Your people their offenses that we, being governed by Your bountiful goodness, may enter at last into Your eternal paradise; for You live and reign with the Father and the Holy Spirit, one God, now and forever.*

Amen. Come, Lord Jesus.

Scripture Index

Psalm	Day
Ps 19	Lent 3 B
Ps 19:(1–6) 7–14	Epiphany 3 C
Ps 22	Good Friday ABC
Ps 22:23–31	Lent 2 B
Ps 23	Easter 4 ABC; Proper 11 B; Proper 23 A
Ps 24	Advent 4 A
Ps 25:1–10	Advent 1 C; Lent 1 B; Proper 21 A
Ps 25:1–15	Pentecost Day A
Ps 26	Proper 17 A
Ps 27:(1–6) 7–14	Proper 11 C
Ps 27:1–9	Proper 20 A
Ps 27:1–9 (10–14)	Epiphany 3 A
Ps 29	Baptism of Our Lord ABC; Holy Trinity B
Ps 30	Epiphany 6 B; Easter 3 C; Proper 5 C; Proper 8 B
Ps 31	Good Friday ABC
Ps 31:9–16	Passion Sunday ABC
Ps 32	Lent 4 C
Ps 32:1–7	Lent 1 A; Proper 6 C; Proper 18 A
Ps 33:12–22	Proper 14 C
Ps 34:1–8	Proper 14 B
Ps 34:12–22	Proper 15 B
Ps 36:5–12	Holy Monday ABC;
Ps 40:1–11	Epiphany 2 A
Ps 41	Epiphany 7 B; Proper 10 C
Ps 43	Pentecost Evening/Monday ABC; Proper 26 A
Ps 46	Last Sunday (Proper 29) C; Reformation Day
Ps 47	Ascension ABC
Ps 50:1–6	Transfiguration B
Ps 50:1–15	Proper 16 C
Ps 51:1–13 (14–19)	Ash Wednesday ABC
Ps 54	Proper 20 B
Ps 61	Easter Wednesday ABC
Ps 62	Epiphany 3 B; Proper 22 C
Ps 65:(1–8) 9–13	Proper 10 A
Ps 66:1–7	Proper 9 C
Ps 66:1–12	Advent 2 C
Ps 66:8–20	Easter 6 A
Ps 67	Easter 6 C; Proper 15 A; Thanksgiving
Ps 68:1–10	Easter 7 A
Ps 70	Holy Wednesday ABC; Proper 27 A
Ps 71:1–6 (7–11)	Epiphany 4 C
Ps 71:1–14	Holy Tuesday ABC
Ps 72:1–7	Advent 2 A
Ps 72:1–11 (12–15)	Epiphany ABC
Ps 80:1–7	Advent 1 B; Advent 4 C
Ps 80:7–19	Proper 22 A
Ps 81:1–10	Proper 4 B
Ps 84	Purification/Presentation
Ps 85	Advent 2 B; Advent 3 C; Lent 3 C
Ps 85:(1–7) 8–13	Proper 10 B
Ps 89:1–5 (19–29)	Advent 4 B
Ps 90:1–12	Proper 28 A
Ps 90:12–17	Proper 23 B
Ps 91	St. Michael and All Angels
Ps 91:1–10 (11–16)	Proper 7 A
Ps 91:1–13	Lent 1 C
Ps 92	Epiphany 8 C
Ps 93	Last Sunday (Proper 29) B
Ps 95:1–7a	Last Sunday (Proper 29) A
Ps 95:1–9	Lent 3 A
Ps 96	Christmas Midnight ABC
Ps 96:1–9	Proper 4 C
Ps 96:1–9 (10–13)	Proper 24 A
Ps 98	Christmas Dawn ABC; Easter 6 B; Proper 28 C
Ps 99	Transfiguration C
Ps 100	Proper 6 A; Proper 13 C
Ps 103:1–12	Proper 19 A
Ps 103:1–13	Epiphany 7 C; Epiphany 8 B; Proper 3 B
Ps 104:27–35	Proper 21 B
Ps 107:1–9	Lent 4 B
Ps 110:1–4	Christmas Eve ABC
Ps 111	Christmas 1 ABC; Epiphany 4 B; Proper 23 C
Ps 112:1–9	Epiphany 5 A; Proper 3 C
Ps 113	Pentecost Eve ABC; Proper 20 C
Ps 115:(1–8) 9–18	Epiphany 8 A; Proper 3 A
Ps 116:1–9	Proper 19 B
Ps 116:1–14	Easter 3 A
Ps 116:12–19	Holy Thursday ABC
Ps 118:15–29	Easter Sunrise ABC
Ps 118:19–29	Passion Sunday ABC
Ps 119:1–8	Epiphany 6 A; Proper 26 B
Ps 119:9–16	Lent 5 B; Proper 24 B
Ps 119:33–40	Epiphany 7 A
Ps 119:57–64	Proper 11 A
Ps 119:65–72	Proper 5 A
Ps 119:81–88	Proper 15 C
Ps 119:97–104	Christmas 2 ABC
Ps 119:129–136	Proper 17 B
Ps 119:153–160	Proper 8 A
Ps 119:169–176	Proper 19 C
Ps 121	Lent 2 A; Proper 24 C
Ps 122	Advent 1 A
Ps 123	Proper 9 B
Ps 124	Proper 7 B

Ps 125 ... Proper 12 A

Ps 126 ... Advent 3 B; Lent 5 C; Proper 25 B

Ps 128 ... Epiphany 2 C; Proper 22 B

Ps 130 ... Lent 5 A; Proper 5 B; Proper 26 C

Ps 131 ... Proper 17 C

Ps 133 ... Easter 7 C

Ps 136:1–9 ... Proper 12 B

Ps 136:1–9 (23–26) ... Proper 13 A

Ps 138 ... Epiphany 5 C; Proper 12 C; Proper 16 A

Ps 139:1–10 ... Epiphany 2 B

Ps 139:1–12 (13–16) ... Pentecost Day B

Ps 142 ... Lent 4 A

Ps 143 ... Pentecost Day C

Ps 145:1–14 ... Proper 9 A

Ps 145:10–21 ... Proper 13 B

Ps 146 ... Advent 3 A; Easter 5 A; Proper 18 B; Proper 21 C; Proper 27 B

Ps 147:1–11 ... Epiphany 5 B

Ps 148 ... Easter 2 ABC; Easter 5 C; Proper 27 C

Ps 149 ... All Saints' Day

Ps 150 ... Easter 5 B

Prov 8:1–4, 22–31 ... Holy Trinity C

Prov 9:1–10 ... Proper 15 B

Prov 25:2–10 ... Proper 17 C

Eccl 1:2, 12–14; 2:18–26 ... Proper 13 C

Eccl 5:10–20 ... Proper 24 B

Is 1:10–18 ... Proper 26 C

Is 2:1–5 ... Advent 1 A

Is 5:1–7 ... Proper 22 A

Is 6:1–8 ... Holy Trinity B

Is 6:1–8 (9–13) ... Epiphany 5 C

Is 7:10–14 ... Christmas Eve ABC; Annunciation

Is 7:10–17 ... Advent 4 A

Is 9:1–4 ... Epiphany 3 A

Is 9:2–7 ... Christmas Midnight ABC

Is 11:1–10 ... Advent 2 A

Is 12:1–6 ... Lent 4 C

Is 25:6–9 ... Easter B; Proper 23 A

Is 29:11–19 ... Proper 16 B

Is 35:1–10 ... Advent 3 A

Is 35:4–7a ... Proper 18 B

Is 40:1–11 ... Advent 2 B

Is 40:21–31 ... Epiphany 5 B

Is 42:1–9 ... Epiphany 1 A

Is 42:14–21 ... Lent 4 A

Is 43:1–7 ... Baptism of Our Lord (Epiphany 1) C

Is 43:16–21 ... Lent 5 C

Is 43:18–25 ... Epiphany 7 B

Is 44:6–8 ... Proper 11 A

Is 45:1–7 ... Proper 24 A

Is 49:1–7 ... Epiphany 2 A; Holy Tuesday ABC

Is 49:8–16a ... Epiphany 8 A; Proper 3 A

Is 50:4–9a ... Passion Sunday A

Is 50:4–10 ... Proper 19 B; Holy Monday ABC

Is 51:1–6 ... Proper 16 A

Is 51:4–6 ... Last Sunday (Proper 29) B

Is 52:7–10 ... Christmas Day ABC

Is 52:13–53:12 ... Good Friday ABC

Is 55:1–5 ... Proper 13 A

Is 55:6–9 ... Proper 20 A

Is 55:10–13 ... Proper 10 A

Is 56:1, 6–8 ... Proper 15 A

Is 58:3–9a ... Epiphany 5 A

Is 60:1–6 ... Epiphany ABC

Is 61:1–4, 8–11 ... Advent 3 B

Is 61:10–62:3 ... Christmas 1 B

Is 62:1–5 ... Epiphany 2 C

Is 62:10–12 ... Christmas Dawn ABC

Is 62:11–63:7 ... Holy Wednesday ABC

Is 63:7–14 ... Christmas 1 A

Is 64:1–9 ... Advent 1 B

Is 65:1–9 ... Proper 7 C

Is 65:17–25 ... Easter Day C

Is 66:10–14 ... Proper 9 C

Is 66:18–23 ... Proper 16 C

Jer 1:4–10 (17–19) ... Epiphany 4 C

Jer 7:1–7 (8–15) ... Epiphany 8 C

Jer 11:18–20 ... Proper 20 B

Jer 15:15–21 ... Proper 17 A

Jer 17:5–8 ... Epiphany 6 C

Jer 20:7–13 ... Proper 7 A

Jer 23:1–6 ... Proper 11 B

Jer 23:16–29 ... Proper 15 C

Jer 26:8–15 ... Lent 2 C

Jer 28:5–9 ... Proper 8 A

Jer 31:1–6 ... Easter Day A

Jer 31:7–9 ... Proper 25 B

Jer 31:31–34 ... Lent 5 B; Holy Thursday C

Jer 33:14–16 ... Advent 1 C

Lam 3:22–33 ... Proper 8 B

Ezek 2:1–5 ... Proper 9 B

Ezek 17:22–24 ... Proper 6 B

Ezek 18:1–4, 25–32 ... Proper 21 A

Ezek 33:7–9 ... Proper 18 A

1 Cor 1:3–9 … Advent 1 B
1 Cor 1:10–18 … Epiphany 3 A
1 Cor 1:18–25 (26–31) … Holy Tuesday ABC
1 Cor 1:18–31 … Epiphany 4 A; Lent 3 B
1 Cor 2:1–12 (13–16) … Epiphany 5 A
1 Cor 3:1–9 … Epiphany 6 A
1 Cor 3:10–23 … Epiphany 7 A
1 Cor 4:1–13 … Epiphany 8 A
1 Cor 5:6b–8 … Easter Sunrise B; Easter Evening/Monday ABC
1 Cor 6:12–20 … Epiphany 2 B
1 Cor 7:29–31 (32–35) … Epiphany 3 B
1 Cor 8:1–13 … Epiphany 4 B
1 Cor 9:16–27 … Epiphany 5 B
1 Cor 10:1–13 … Lent 3 C
1 Cor 10:16–17 … Holy Thursday B
1 Cor 10:(19–30) 31–11:1 … Epiphany 6 B
1 Cor 11:23–32 … Holy Thursday ABC
1 Cor 12:1–11 … Epiphany 2 C
1 Cor 12:12–31a … Epiphany 3 C
1 Cor 12:31b–13:13 … Epiphany 4 C
1 Cor 14:12b–20 … Epiphany 5 C
1 Cor 15:1–11 … Easter Sunrise A; Easter Day B
1 Cor 15:(1–11) 12–20 … Epiphany 6 C
1 Cor 15:19–26 … Easter Day C
1 Cor 15:20–28 … Last Sunday (Proper 29) A
1 Cor 15:21–26, 30–42 … Epiphany 7 C
1 Cor 15:42–52 (53–58) … Epiphany 8 C
1 Cor 15:51–57 … Easter Sunrise C
2 Cor 1:18–22 … Epiphany 7 B
2 Cor 2:12–3:6 … Epiphany 8 B
2 Cor 3:12–13 (14–18); 4:1–6 … Transfiguration B
2 Cor 4:5–12 … Proper 4 B
2 Cor 4:13–5:1 … Proper 5 B
2 Cor 5:1–10 (11–17) … Proper 6 B
2 Cor 5:16–21 … Lent 4 C
2 Cor 5:20b–6:10 … Ash Wednesday ABC
2 Cor 6:1–13 … Proper 7 B
2 Cor 8:1–9, 13–15 … Proper 8 B
2 Cor 12:1–10 … Proper 9 B
Gal 1:1–12 … Proper 4 C
Gal 1:11–24 … Proper 5 C
Gal 2:15–21; 3:10–14 … Proper 6 C
Gal 3:23–29 … Circumcision and Name of Jesus
Gal 3:23–4:7 … Proper 7 C
Gal 4:4–7 … Christmas 1 AB
Gal 5:1, 13–25 … Proper 8 C
Gal 6:1–10, 14–18 … Proper 9 C
Eph 1:3–14 … Christmas 2 ABC; Proper 10 B
Eph 2:1–10 … Lent 4 B
Eph 2:11–22 … Proper 11 B
Eph 3:1–12 … Epiphany ABC
Eph 3:14–21 … Proper 12 B
Eph 4:1–16 … Proper 13 B
Eph 4:17–5:2 … Proper 14 B
Eph 5:6–21 … Proper 15 B
Eph 5:8–14 … Lent 4 A
Eph 5:22–33 … Proper 16 B
Eph 6:10–20 … Proper 17 B
Phil 1:2–11 … Advent 2 C
Phil 1:12–14, 19–30 … Proper 20 A
Phil 2:1–4 (5–13) 14–18 … Proper 21 A
Phil 2:5–11 … Passion Sunday ABC
Phil 3:4b–14 … Proper 22 A
Phil 3:(4b–7) 8–14 … Lent 5 C
Phil 3:17–4:1 … Lent 2 C
Phil 4:4–7 … Advent 3 C
Phil 4:4–13 … Proper 23 A
Col 1:1–14 … Proper 10 C
Col 1:13–20 … Last Sunday (Proper 29) C
Col 1:21–29 … Proper 11 C
Col 2:6–15 (16–19) … Proper 12 C
Col 3:1–4 … Easter Day A
Col 3:1–7 … Easter Wednesday ABC
Col 3:1–11 … Proper 13 C
Col 3:12–17 … Christmas 1 C
1 Thess 1:1–10 … Proper 24 A
1 Thess 2:1–13 … Proper 25 A
1 Thess 3:9–13 … Advent 1 C
1 Thess 4:1–12 … Proper 26 A
1 Thess 4:13–18 … Proper 27 A
1 Thess 5:1–11 … Proper 28 A
1 Thess 5:16–24 … Advent 3 B
2 Thess 1:1–5 (6–10) 11–12 … Proper 26 C
2 Thess 2:1–8, 13–17 … Proper 27 C
2 Thess 3:(1–5) 6–13 … Proper 28 C
1 Tim 1:(5–11) 12–17 … Proper 19 C
1 Tim 2:1–15 … Proper 20 C
1 Tim 3:1–13 … Proper 21 C
1 Tim 6:6–19 … Proper 21 C
2 Tim 1:1–14 … Proper 22 C
2 Tim 2:1–13 … Proper 23 C
2 Tim 3:14–4:5 … Proper 24 C
2 Tim 4:6–8, 16–18 … Proper 25 C

Notes

ISBN 978-0-7586-6569-0
9 780758 665690
RELIGION / Christian Living / Devotional
124587